PIERS PLOWMAN

British Camp Reservoir, Malvern Hills, Worcestershire. Photograph by Glenys Burrows.

Medieval Institute Publications is a program of
The Medieval Institute, College of Arts and Sciences

 WESTERN MICHIGAN UNIVERSITY

WILLIAM LANGLAND

Piers Plowman

A Parallel-Text Edition
of the A, B, C and Z Versions

VOLUME II, Part 2.
COMMENTARY, BIBLIOGRAPHY and INDEXICAL GLOSSARY

By

A. V. C. SCHMIDT

Revised Edition

MEDIEVAL INSTITUTE PUBLICATIONS
Western Michigan University
Kalamazoo

Library of Congress Control Number: 95126458

ISBN 978-1-58044-160-5

P 5 4 3 2 1

'Alterum hoc volumen'

CONTENTS

C. COMMENTARY

The COMMENTARY is keyed to **C**; passus- and line-numbers for the other versions are given in brackets only when the relevant **Z/A/B** text is not immediately parallel. Comment on these versions is incorporated in the main sequence when no more than two short notes in succession appear. But when they are substantial and include separately-numbered notes *within* main entries, the initial note is indented. Works cited in abbreviated form are given their full references in the Bibliography. Biblical citations in Latin are from the *Biblia Vulgata,* ed. Colunga and Turrado; those in English are from the Douay-Rheims translation of the Vulgate. Citations from other Latin works are translated, but the original is given where the exact wording is important.

Prologue

The PROLOGUE consists in its original form of a waking 'prelude', 1–13, followed by a vision of human society placed in a mid-position between the spiritual poles of salvation and damnation: (i) [*a*] 14–164, (i) [*b*] 219–32. In the longer versions is added (ii) the exemplary *Fable of the Parliament of Rats and Mice* (B 146–210=C 165–218). Finally, Conscience's attack on idolatry is inserted at C 95–124 between the lines on clerics who take up secular work and those on the Pope and cardinals. Lines 1–13 form an outer 'frame' for the first two dreams (traditionally called the *Visio*). They are deliberately echoed in the opening of the third dream (10.2 // **AB**, but not in **Z**, which has concluded), the 'framing' effect being completed briefly in 9.293–6. The last 80 lines of Passus IX thus resemble a coda, and in all three versions could be read as the conclusion to an independent work. But as the mention of Dowel at 9.350 raises the prospect that this topic will be discussed in a third Vision, they effectively provide a preparation for / transition to it. The process of revision begins in 4 with *forth*] *wyde* suggesting a purposeful not an aimless journey and altering the line from a Type Ic to Type Ia. Though the May-morning opening goes back to the *Roman de la Rose*, **L** (unlike Chaucer and the *Purity*-poet) claims no direct knowledge of *RR*. And where Chaucer's dream-vision poems are verbally indebted to contemporary French masters, *PP* echoes earlier English alliterative pieces such as *The Simonie* (*c.* 1340), *Somer Sonday* (*SS, c.* 1327–50) and *Wynnere and Wastoure* (*WW, c.* 1352, though dated later by Salter 1978:30–65 [1988:180–198]). On the extent of **L**'s knowledge of earlier alliterative works see Hussey 1965 and Salter 1967.

1–13 PRELUDE to the First Vision. **1** A fusion of *SS* 1 'Opon a somer soneday se I þe sonne', which uses a Type Ib line (Robbins 1959:38), and *Parlement of the Thre Ages* [*PTA*] 2 'And the sesone of somere when softe bene the wedres' (which however is more likely to be echoing *PP*). *somer*: late spring or early summer, depending on whether *May* at 6 is 'May Day' or 'a day in May'. **L**'s 'summer' is usually 'the warm season' (see e.g. 15.295ff). **2** *shep*: 'sheep' (see the *Textual Notes* [*TN* hereafter])

because dressed in the coarse woollen garment characteristic of hermits (cf. *russet* 10.1 and *Wollewaerd* 20.1). On its possible Biblical resonance of 'exiled humanity as lost sheep' cf. Dyas 2001. **3** *vnholy of werkes*: hinting that the persona's 'countenaunce of clothing' is that of a 'wolf in sheep's clothing'; but this is ironic, because he is not *disgised* (B 24), though resembling many 'false hermits' (*gyrovagi*) who were. *Pe*'s rendering 'without holy works to his credit' and (after Mills 1969:186) 'but not, because of that, necessarily a man of sinful works', is lexically possible but unlikely. For the force of *un-* with evaluative epithets is negatively critical, not neutral (cf. *vnblessed, vnbuxum, vnrihtfole, vnsittynge, vntidy* in the *Indexical Glossary* [*IG* hereafter]), and Will is later seen as a (representative) sinner (6.2 and //). A diatribe against 'unholy hermits' is added in C 9.187–218. **4** The persona's journey superficially resembles a knight's on a quest 'wondyrs to seke', as in the *Alliterative Morte Arthure* [*AMA*] 2514, more than a lover's leisurely walk, as in *Romaunt of the Rose* [*Rom*]105. But he is more an observer, attempting to learn through listening, as is apt for one who will dispute like a clerk (10.20), so the 'mode' envisaged evokes a wandering scholar as well as a wandering hermit. The **ZAB** wording recalls *SS* 31: 'So wyde I walkede þat I wax wery of þe wey'. **5** Things marvellous and things rare or little known are linked in the mind through 'Platonic' wordplay, that which presupposes a real and necessary relationship between words (even when etymologically unconnected) and what they signify (see Jolivet 1962:93–9 and Schmidt 1987:90). **C** takes up much of the sense of **AB** 5–6 (*sellies = ferly, selkouthe // fairie*), but places the 'seeing' before the mention of the Malvern Hills, now become the site of Will's 'sleeping'. 5a appears in **Z** with a different b-half following: either a scribal echo of **C** introduced in the exemplar or, as here preferred, a draft form of a line that **AB** dropped but **C** recalled (and rewrote). **Z** also contains the *ferly* line (= **AB** 6), a redundancy such as might be expected in a draft (see *Intro.* III, *Z Version*, i; and cf. **Z** Pr 35, where **C** restores one line from a two-line draft on minstrels dropped in **AB**). **6** *Maluerne hulles*: a specificity rare in the dream-vision genre (cf. *The Crowned King* [in *PP Tradition*, ed. Barr] l. 20). The opening location of the *second* Vision (which in **C** now follows the new 'autobiographical prelude' to Passus V) will not seem necessarily at variance with 9.295 (which finds the dreamer on the hills again), if the 'cross' of 5.106 where he falls asleep is taken as located outside the building (Vision Seven in Passus XXI will occur *inside* a church). But since the Malvern Hills lack general symbolic significance, their mention may be just an 'authenticating' fictive detail, like Cornhill at 5.1, or included because corresponding to the writer's place of origin as known to his first audience. 'Malvern' may also be a 'cultural' flourish like the references to Western localities *WW* 8–9 and *Richard the Redeless* [*RRe*] 2. For as maintained by Kane 1965[2], the relationship between the author and the dream-vision persona involves a measure of historically accurate detail nonetheless meant to be ironically understood, the narrator being a poetic construct rather than an autobiographical self-portrait (Mills 1969; Burrow 1993, 6–27). Attempts have been made (e.g. by Bright 1928) to determine the actual site of the tower and field, and evidence for possible local connections is examined in Kaske 1968; but if **L** had wished this, he could have named the *kirke* at 5.105. **9** The Langlandian dream may be understood, in terms of the dominant medieval classification, as a *somnium*, open to both truth and falsehood and evoking a domain located between the mundane and the divine. See Kruger 1992, citing Macrobius: '[it] conceals with strange shape and veils with ambiguity the true meaning of the information being offered' (*Commentary on the Dream of Scipio*, I iii 10, tr. Stahl). On the number of the dreams in **A**, **B** and **C** see Frank 1951[1] and on their structural arrangement Weldon 1987[1]. **13** *slepynge*: on the figurative significance of sleep see Johnson 1994.

(i *a*) 14–21 More important than geographical 'facts' are the symbolic orientations (on which see Davlin 1993); heaven as a tower and hell as a ditch are illustrated in Nolan 1977: fig. 22. Despite resemblances in the imagined scene and locale, the influence of the staging of morality plays like *The Castle of Perseverance* seems excluded by their later date (early C15th). **14** *Estward*: towards the sun, the earthly paradise and the holy city, all associated (Ps 26:1, Jn 23:5, Js 1:17) with God as the source of heavenly light (Ps 42:3 links light, truth and God's holy hill = *toft* in // **ZAB**; and see also Ps 15:1). When these locations re-appear in Passus XX, the east will again be the place of Truth. **15** *tour*: a traditional symbol of divine strength (Ps 60:4; Prov 18:10). *Treuthe*: the strength of truth being familiar from I Esd 4:41 and the previous verse in Esd. also speaking of the 'God of Truth'; cf. the phrase *turris alethiae* in the Archpoet's *Confessio*, which goes back to the *Ecloga Theoduli* (Raby 1965:226). While collocating the tower with truth, **C** asymmetrically opposes *tour* and *dale* where **AB** have *tour: dongeon; toft: dale*, retaining

obliquity in *Treuthe: Deth*. A reflex of **ZAB**'s mysterious description, *as Y trowed...as Y leue* 15–17 offset **C**'s new certainty in the assigning of names. Though *Treuthe* is at once proclaimed the tower's occupant (something postponed till the half-line B 1.12b // **ZA** that is 15b's source), this is still in part a 'nature-name' (the first in the poem), concealing as well as revealing, and designed to provoke thought. The word (on which see Davlin 1989: 29n8, 32n18; Green 1999:8–31) here signifies both *fidelitas* 'faithfulness', the nominal of the OT epithet for the Lord of the Covenant, *fortis et fidelis* (Deut 7:9; I Cor 1:9), and *veritas* 'truth(fulness)', the familiar NT term (Jn 1:14, 18:37, and esp. 14:6, quoted at 10.258 //, and 8:32, source of Chaucer's *Trouthe*). Though the Bible does not directly name God *Veritas* but *Deus veritatis* 'the God of truth' (Ps 30:67), Christ calls himself *via et veritas* in Jn 14:6 (quoted at 10.258 //), while Apoc 19:11 says of the one seated on the white horse [i.e. Christ] that he is *Fidelis, et Verax, et cum iustitia iudicat et pugnat*. The name here betokens God as object of both *ratio* 'the intellect' (i.e. of *belief* in / that) and of *voluntas* 'the rational will' (object of *faith* as trust, 'known' at a distance and only partially revealed). But the 'asymmetric' antithesis with Death (rather than Falsehood) implicitly associates Truth with Life, the **C** revision incorporating at an early stage the fruits of Life's 'case' against Death as a case for *treuthe* specifically as 'justice'. See esp. B 18.390=C 20.431 and 294=325, where the Devil calls Christ 'Truth' in recognising his divine strength, and C 14.212 //, which links God with *treuthe* as *fidelitas* at the end of the Trajan section. **AB 15** *dungeoun*: apt for a castle keep; the devil's prison is a 'pinfold' at B 5.624 (no //) and 16.264 // 18.281. **16** *Westward*: where the sun sets and earth becomes dark. **17** *dale*: aptly death's abode because now in night, but also recalling Ps 22:4, which is quoted at B 7.116 // **A** (though Vg has *medio* for *valle*) and Is 9:2 (with *regione* for *medio*). **18** *wones*: hell, to judge from its occupants. Though the vowel in *wo-* is sounded |ʊ| not |ɔ| its visual form 'Platonically' suggests the *wo* of this place (cf. 20.208, 209). **19** is of uncertain scansion: *fair* or *ful* or both carry stress, giving different (authentic) metrical patterns. **21b** A formula (cf. *Sir Gawain and the Green Knight* [*SGGK*] 530; *AMA* 2187), repeated at 21.23 but taken as raising the serious issue of *why* the world should 'require' men to wander by Dyas (2002), who shrewdly relates it to the traditional notion of man's 'exile' from his 'native land' following the Fall and sees Will as taught to re-interpret wandering in terms of 'life-pilgrimage' (on which see Dyas 2001).

Z 16b–17 seem original, and in 17b the caesura should probably come after *there*. They are replaced in **A** by the dungeon-image (mentioned at Z 100) but partly evoke its idea of darkness. **16** Anticipation of A 3.180 (// **ZB**) would explain the b-half's revision in **A**; but the hesitancy of *as me thouȝte* has more the tone of **C** (11, 15, 17) and, if scribal, the lines could arguably be attempting to fill out an imperfectly written exemplar. **22–35** are virtually unrevised from **Z** to **C**. **26** *continance of clothyng*: the misleading appearance resulting from the garb adopted, whereas **Z** 25 seems to distinguish deceptive dress from deceptive looks and behaviour (MED s.v. *contenaunce* n., but sense 3a, not sense 3c). **C** makes the b-half refer to fashion rather than concealment. **28** *harde*: illustrating **C**'s propensity for rhetorical *repetitio* of key-ideas (cf. 23); the change blurs the suggestion in **ZAB** *streyte* of living by a rule. **29** *a good ende*: strengthening **ZAB**'s terse a-half with an idea that will become important in **C** (see 2.35, 3.339, 10.60), and is a pointer to its late date. **30** Anchorites lived enclosed in anchor-holds (Warren 1985), hermits more freely (Clay 1914; Darwin 1944), whether in solitary places, like those of the early Church (17.6ff), or as wanderers like the 'pilgrim-hermit' Patience (B 13.29–30). The Dreamer is first presented as resembling a suspicious example of the latter type; but it is the 'static' hermits living by roadsides who are actually criticised in 9.188ff. **33** *cheuede*: possibly punning on *cheuesaunce*, a dubious term associated with *chaffare, cheuen* at 6.252 (cf. B 5.245). **36–46 36–7** abolish any distinction between good and bad minstrels (on *japeres* see Schmidt 1987:5–11). The 'sinless' minstrels of AB 34 recall the *joculatores* in Thomas of Chobham's *Summa Confessorum* (ed. Broomfield 1968:291–2) 'who sing the deeds (*gesta*) of princes and the lives of saints, and make entertainments (*solatia*) for men in their sickness and trouble, and do not pour out scurrilous trash (*turpitudines*)': cf. 7.106 *geste*; B 7.85 *solas*; Pr 37 *foule fantasyes*. On 'good' minstrels, see further Du Boulay 1991:32–4 and Southworth 1989:57–100. While **Z** 35 could arguably be an echo of **C** incorporated by the first copyist of the **Z** draft, 36 seems authentic in its contrastive echo of 31b and its annominative cross-caesural pararhyme, resembling such lines as 13.92 (see Schmidt 1987:68–71). **C** may therefore be reverting here to an *original* comprehensive hostility to the minstrel-class and so have preserved one **Z** line while dropping the other (**Z** 36) in rewriting B 36ff. **AB 35** *Iudas children*: a general term of obloquy (like *Caymes kynde* at B 9.128), not implying that the apostle was a minstrel, though (as the type of treachery through false words and 'fair countenance') aptly linked with minstrels who use disguise and tell lying tales (see B 16.149, 154–5). His name is collocated elsewhere with alliterating *Iew, Iesu, iape* and *iangle* as at 1.63, where he himself is the victim of the devil's *iape,* while B 9.91, which compares the minstrel's *patron* to Judas, reveals the thematic depth of the association. **39** The changes from *dar not* **A** through *wol nat* **B** to *myhte* **C** show **L**'s final moral posture as altogether more definite. **40** This first macaro-

nic line alludes to Eph 5:3–5; but *turpiloquium* is found in the Old Latin translation of the Bible, the *Vetus Latina* (*VL*), for the *turpem sermonem* of Col 3:8 in the Vulgate (Vg), a text closely related in thought and wording ('*turpi*tudo...stulti*loquium*...scurrilitas...non habet haereditatem in regno Christi et Dei'), and in patristic citations of that verse (Alf*Q* 33). Craun's discussion of the motif (1997:157–86), citing various manuals, argues that **L**'s use of the quotation 'invokes..both a Pauline verbal sin and a monitory pastoral discourse directed against it'. The phrase in 40b renders an idea from Hugh of St Cher's gloss on Jn 8:34 (*peccati* = *diaboli*: for the devil as personifying or embodying sin, cf. 20.388). If 39 alludes to I Thess 3:10 (*Sk*), the phrase *Qui*....would be admonishing *himself* not to speak obloquy; but the precise contextual sense of *turpiloquium* makes this unlikely. **Z 37** *as*: if 'in the manner of', then implying for *bidder* the sense 'one who prays' (MED *s.v.* n (b)); but since elsewhere that term is a synonym for 'one who begs alms', *as* is more simply 'like' (= 'and'). **45** *Robardus knaues*: a variant on *roberdesmen* found in statutes of Edward III and Richard II, and perhaps derived from the homophonic association of *robber* with the name Robert exploited later with Robert the robber at B 5.462 // (*knaues*, echoing 40, is another **C** *repetitio* like that at 28). **47–65** are little altered from **A** to **C** save for omission of B 50–2. But **A**'s revision of **Z** 43–52 inverts *friars-hermits-pilgrims* to *pilgrims-hermits-friars* and elaborates on the friars' special 'threat' to the church (anticipating the poem's climax in XXII/XX). Since the texts from **A** onwards emphasise less the friars' preaching than their activities as confessors, **Z**'s *lack* of this theme points to its priority. **47** *palmers*: strictly pilgrims to Jerusalem, who wore a palm-frond badge; here virtually = *pilgrimes* (on whom see Jusserand 1899:338–403, Sumption 1975, Finucane 1977, Adair 1978, Dyas 2001). The implication 'professional' pilgrims (*Bn*) is unsupported, for though the one such encountered 'in pilgrim's wise' (7.160) has never seen a 'palmer' seeking Truth (7.179), Piers on his last appearance is dressed like a 'palmer' (15.34), while Patience wears 'pilgrim's clothes' in // **B**. Holy Land sites, including Jerusalem, are mentioned directly only at 7.170–1 and Z 5.70 (omitted **ABC**); so perhaps *palmers* implied simply 'pilgrim-travellers abroad' (cf. Chaucer's *GP*13). **48** *seynt Iame*: the reputed burial-place of St James the Apostle at Compostela Cathedral in NW Spain (Galicia, specified in // **Z**, an anticipation of Z 5.163 removed in revision to **A**). It was the most popular foreign shrine for English pilgrims, who reached it by sea, enjoying special protection following the marriage of Edward I to Eleanor of Castile in 1254. *Rome*: site of the shrines of SS Peter and Paul and the many 'martired amonges Romaynes' (17.282). The Rome pilgrimage is mentioned again at 4.123, 7.166, 9.323, 16.38, 17.282. **B 50–2** seem otiose (see *TN*) and, though anticipating the 'professional' saint-seeker of B 5.530, they are cut with no loss. **51** *hokede staues*: as illustrated in Jusserand 1899:139. **52** *Walsyngham*: site of a shrine of the Virgin Mary in N Norfolk, popular since the C12th and second only to Canterbury as an English place of pilgrimage (Adair 1978:114–200). At Z 5.102 it is where Greed will go to do penance, and the reference to the latter's 'wife' there may have prompted **A**'s revision here to the more critical *wenches* (though presumably *wyues* Z 48, like *suster* at B 5.642, is heavily sarcastic). **54** *copes*: 'long clothes', unsuitable for manual work, such as the Dreamer wears at 5.41 (and cf. 8.185, 9.210). **55** *made*: removing the echo of Pr 2 in // **AB** *shopen*.

   Z 53–8 describe bishops and religious in an ironic tone like that of the passage on the Pope's plenitude of power at 9.324–31 // (no **Z**); they are replaced in **A** by fuller criticism of friars. The lines intimate a gap between theory and common experience, though the scepticism implied in 56 is absent from later versions. The criticism of religious rectors at 57–8 is cut, though they are attacked for neglecting their churches (C 5.163–7). Here the charge is that the orders grow richer by drawing off the income while leaving the incumbent too little to live on, and so leading him to desert his pastoral duties (as described in 81–2 //). **Z**'s mild treatment of bishops is sharpened up in **A**, but the lines on religious are dropped. **53** *Bischopes blessed*: perhaps deleted here by **A** to avoid repetition at A 8.13. **58** *aprope*: the earliest use in this sense (MED s.v. *appropren* v 1(b)).

56–65 56 *freris*: the attack on their *confessional practices* (62–5) as the source of the Church's coming catastrophe, new in **A**, is unlikely to have been omitted by **Z** if that text were a scribal compilation. The friars' *preaching* is criticised for diluting the hard ethical (and especially penitential) demands of the bare Gospel text and authoritative commentaries on it (59b *doctours*). The repeated *shryuars* and the forceful language mark the change from hope of reform in **AB** to desire for some drastic action (more probably removal of their licences to hear confessions than their wholesale dissolution). *the foure ordres*: the Dominicans, Franciscans, Augustinians and Carmelites. The last, the White Friars, who were by no means a small order in C14th England (Lawrence 1994:92–8), get no further mention. The Dominicans (Order of Preachers or Black Friars) are alluded to at 22.252, and perhaps in the person of the Gluttonous Doctor, if he is modelled on Friar William Jordan (see at 15.30ff). The Austins (Augustinians) or friar-hermits appear at 17.15, a mildly satirical revision of non-satiric B 15.289. Though the mendicants are criticised collectively here and in 22, the Franciscans (Friars Minor or Grey Friars) are singled out (10.9ff //) for abandoning the ideal of poverty so warmly endorsed in XVI (see esp. 353–5, asserting that the charity

St Francis embodied is rare in his order now). The claim that **L** is writing from the position of reformers within the Franciscan order and even using a coded Franciscan discourse is overstated by Clopper 1997. **60** Mendicants in the universities had been a major force in the theological Faculties since the 13th c., and in the late 14th c. were conspicuous as defenders of orthodoxy against such radical seculars as Wyclif; most would have been trained at Oxford (Courtenay 1987:56–87). Franciscan 'masters' appear at 10.19 and a (possible) Dominican doctor at 15.30. **62** *charite*: metonymic for the friars ideally conceived (cf. 16.353–5), the sense of the line being 'since those whose special vocation was evangelical charity have become peddlers of cheap absolution'. **64** *choppe*: accrediting *charite* with a 'righteous violence' later found associated with *verray charite* in 19.273–4, lines that also link Holy Church and charity. **L**'s critique forms part of an English tradition of satirising the orders' mutual hostility that stretches from *WW* (156ff) to *Pierce the Ploughman Crede [PPCr]*. See Du Boulay 1991:80–6, 134–6; Szittya 1986:247–87. **65** *meschief*: related by Gwynn (1943) to the controversy (1356–60) between the friars and Abp. Fitzralph of Armagh. The new allusion in **A** may not be a direct reflex of this dispute, since **Z** notably lacks heavy anti-fraternal animus, though it must date from after 1362 (see on 5.116 below).

   Z 59–85 contain the material afterwards expanded (with omission of 64, 70–3) in different order, the pardoner coming last (59–60 interrupt a passage on the clergy and are understandably moved in **A** to the end of the Pr). A 65–97 look like authorial tightening of a loosely-organised draft rather than **Z** being jumbled recollection by a scribe. The heavy irony of Z 70–3 is like that of 53–8 and seems unsophisticated when compared with the more pointed attack on judges and jurors at B 7.44–6. **63** *annueles...togyderus*: a two-year arrangement to say commemorative masses that would provide a handsome supplement (the generalised *symonye* at A 83 replaces two specific forms of it). *annueles* here predates the first-cited MED ref. in *PPCr* 414. **69/70** illustrate true 'rich' rhyme with polysemantic wordplay (cf. Pr 122/3, B 7.36/7).

66–80 The *pardoner* was empowered by the Pope to grant indulgences for the remission of temporal punishments due for sin (such as those of 69) after formal forgiveness of sins in confession, in return for payment towards the work of the Church; but he would need the diocesan's authorisation to preach in church for this purpose. Pardoners could not give absolution, since they were usually only in minor orders, nor were they licensed to give formal instruction 'like a priest'. Their sermons aimed to stimulate and intensify feelings that would arouse a desire to make confession and only after this make the penitents eligible to receive an indulgence. On pardoners see further 2.229–32, B 5.639–42; and on indulgences in this period, Swanson 1989:291–3, Lunt 1962: chs 9–12. **71** *kyssen*: as a sign of reverence towards the Pope understood as the successor of St Peter, from whom they have come (cf. the very different tone at 20.474). **72** *bounched...blered*: perhaps envisaging a sharp tap on the head that brings water to the eyes (*not* 'religious' tears, on which see 6.1–2). *bulles*: again illustrating **C**'s favoured *repetitio*. **Z 75** *bille*: a cognate derivate of *bulle* (MED s.v. *bille* n. 1(b)); *breuet* **AB**: differing in sense but with its referent either the same or else the bishop's (supposed) licence. *Bn* aptly notes how the *Visio*'s climax, a dispute over the validity of pardons, is here foreshadowed. Whether this pardoner's groundless pretension to absolve suggests that he is an unlicensed or even false pardoner with a forged bull (see Swanson 1989:248), the 'power' of his indulgence could hardly be less spiritual (cf. Haukin's sardonic complaint about *bulles* at B 13.244–55 below, slightly toned down in // C 15.218–26). **73** *rageman*: short for 'ragmanroll', a long parchment document with its ends cut into strips forming a tattered fringe, on which hung the leaden seals of the Pope and bishops authorising the pardoner (cf. B 13.247 and MED s.v. *rageman* n. 2(a)). Use of this word metonymically for the devil at 18.122 invests its appearance here with dubious overtones. *rynges and broches*: cf. Chaucer *CT* VI 908. **76** *yblessed...eres*: 'holy [as when he was blessed at his consecration] and worthy of his office / worthy to keep his ears [because he made good use of them]' (Johnston 1959). **78** *by*: 'in accordance with [*sc.* the intentions of]' (*Bn, Pe*; MED s.v. *bi* prep. 8b (a) 'with the permission of'; the sense 'against' [*Sk* IV i:13–14], is not illustrated in MED and seems out of place. The line need not be ironic, since the pardoner could have obtained the seal by bribing an official and be using it without the bishop's knowledge (see also Kellogg & Haselmayer 1951:267), a situation where the latter certainly needed to 'use his ears'. And such a situation is described in a Wycliffite text of the 1380s (Matthew 1880:154) cited by Fletcher 1990:136 as illustrating a simony-topos of the time. This pardoner evidently colludes with the parson (for a payment), and the poor are the dupes of both; but '*ignorancia non excusat episopos* nec ydiotes preestes' (B 11.315–6). **81–94 81–4** explain **A**'s added criticism of collusion. **Z 61–4**, on priests' attempts to augment their incomes, imply but do not state that they desert their parishes to hold chantry-posts. **Z 65** appears the basis of **A 84–5**, the wordplay on *houide / houuis* resembling that in **Z** 64, which is expanded into **A** 80–3, with omission of the *to / therto* pun. The relationship between **A** and **Z** here is hard to see except as that of one authorial version developing out of another. **81** *persones*: the rectors of parishes, who received the great tithe (on grain) and sometimes employed a vicar. The latter was allowed the lesser tithe (on hay, wool etc) and might in turn devolve his duties to

an unbeneficed clerk whom he paid a small salary (Swanson 1989:214–5); cf. also 13.100ff on the position of priests lacking sufficient financial support. 'Simony' here is the purchase or sale of a chantry-office (an abuse not explicitly mentioned in *PP* but known to have taken place) rather than its taking-on, as **Z** specifies with *annueles* and *trentales* (chantries were increasing at this time and were not confined to London). Will later may be envisaged (5.44ff) as doing part-time a job like that of a chantry-priest, who had not only to say his agreed mass(es) but 'to recite daily the office of the dead' (Cook 1947:14 and Kreider 1979), or of a clerk supported by a parish fraternity (Hill in Du Boulay & Barron 1971:242–55; Barron 1985:13–37). **82** *pe pestelence tyme*: the Great Plague in 1348–9, which killed a third of the population and perhaps half the clergy, leaving many parishes unable to support a priest from their drastically reduced tithes and leading to the admission of poorly qualified candidates to replace them. Three further attacks in 1361–2 (of fresh memory at the time of Z Pr 62), 1369 and 1375–6 (see 5.115, 11.60 and B 13.249 respectively) helped to keep the original allusion topical. (On the general character and impact of the plague, see Keen 1973:169–74; Ziegler 1971, Shrewsbury 1975, Bean in Williman 1982:23–39). **85–9** elaborate on criticism first made in **A**, introducing the theme (dominant in Vision Three) of the split between learning and holiness, and anticipating that of Vision Five, with its diatribe against worldly clergy as corrupting Christian society. **85** *Bisshopes*: the 'curial' bishops who were given their sees for serving the king, or whose secular duties kept them from their dioceses (Swanson 1989:80–1). The puns suspected by *Bn* on *cure* (with *curial*) and *crownynge* (their service to the crown supplanting the religious work their vocation calls for) are possible, but *curial* itself is uninstanced before the late 15th c. *Bachelers*: university graduates in theology (cf. // **A**) who had lectured on the Bible and Peter Lombard's *Sentences. maystres; doctours*: interchangeable terms for holders of the highest degree in theology or canon law. Working as civil servants or in the king's courts (A 95), they were rewarded with canonries, and some with bishoprics (hence the appropriateness of bishops at the head of the list). **BC** have shifted the emphasis from clerics already holding offices to those with 'heigh clergie' which they use to the neglect of their spiritual obligations. **A 92** *Archidekenes*: the bishop's deputies who held courts in one of the divisions of the diocese; trained probably in canon law, they could end working in a royal law-court (see A 95). *denis*: here probably not the heads of cathedral chapters but rural deans responsible for a subdivision of the archdeaconry. **87** *with*: if taken with *Holy Chirche* making the latter an entity distinct from the clergy (and especially the hierarchy); but more naturally, forming a phrase *charged with* as at 22.237. The bishops and theologians are entrusted with the responsibility of governing and guiding the Church in order to 'cultivate' charity in the community (the figure echoes B 19.336–7). **89 BC** shift the stress from deserting the parish to neglecting the parishioners, who would especially need their confessors during the penitential season. **91** *Cheker*: the department of state that handled crown finances under the Treasurer, including both the treasury and the court of accounts; here specifically the Court of Exchequer dealing with revenue cases. *Chancerye*: the office of the Chancellor of England, keeper of the Great Seal, and effectively the King's first minister; here perhaps with special reference to the Court of Chancery, which issued writs for action at common law (Alford, *Glossary of Legal Diction* [AlfG]). *Bn* suspects an allusion to William of Wykeham, Bishop of Winchester, Chancellor from 1367–71; but both he and Bp. Brantingham the treasurer had been forced to resign in 1371 after the Commons demanded that churchmen be removed from government. The lines are not in **A**, so if **B** added them in allusion to Wykeham's prosecution in 1376, they will have lost their topicality by 1378–9. Although Simon of Sudbury, Abp. of Canterbury, became Chancellor in 1380 (which is conceivably not too late for a final version of **B** Pr), understanding **L**'s critiques of clerical abuses gains little from searching for particular targets. Both offices were largely staffed with clerics, who have the characteristic anonymity of civil servants (cf. Z 3.3, unchanged through **ABC**). **92** *wardus*: legal minors incapable of conducting their own affairs, here metonymically = 'guardianship-cases' (*Bn*); revenues from the estates of a deceased tenant-in-chief reverted to the crown during his heir's minority. *wardemotis*: meetings of citizens in city or borough wards, at which the Exchequer clerks claimed royal dues; the characteristic play on two senses of 'ward' is lost if *wardus* = 'city-wards' (*Sk*). *wayues*; *strayues*: lost property that reverted to the crown; though it included strayed animals, *strayues* may signify the property of 'aliens' (foreigners) dying without legitimate heirs (*Sk*; on these AF law terms see AlfG). **93–4** tighten up **B**'s somewhat repetitive lines, changing a rare Type IIb (95) to a Type Ia. **93** *seneschals*: the stewards of great lords (as opposed to the king), virtually their deputies in a manor's administrative and legal affairs (H. S. Bennett 1937:157–61). **94** *stewardus*: effectively synonymous with *seneschal* (AlfG s.vv.) **95–124 C** adds here (a) 95–106 (finished) and (b) 107–24, a re-writing of B 10.277–80 perhaps not in final form when copied into the archetype (see *TN*). The object of attack is not clerical venality in general but specifically prelates' encouragement of superstitious religiosity in order to raise money. It follows lines on the clergy's secular employment 'abruptly' (*Pe*) but not arbitrarily, the subject being their neglect of the laity's spiritual needs in encouraging thank-offerings for miracles supposedly

performed at shrines. The tone here is akin to that of near-contemporary Wycliffite criticism (Hudson, *Selections* 1978:87); but the point is moral rather than doctrinal, attacking less image-veneration as such (cf. B 18.429=C 20.474–5, with a significant revision at 475a) than clerics' cynical exploitation of pious and gullible laypeople. In the analogy of the OT exemplum, Ely (Heli) = the prelates, his sons Ophni and Phinees = the priests, to whom the bishops are as 'fathers', the priests in turn being 'fathers' to the laity (120–22). The slight incoherence here, perhaps due to the text's unrevised state, may have partly prompted the scribes of mss I and F to substitute respectively *peres* 'lords' and *prelatus* for archetypal *men*. Defects of metre and thought might render the passage suspect as a scribal intrusion (see *TN* and *Intro*. III *Z Version* § 6); but the phrasing, if unpolished, is authentic, as in the play on *wrother* and *raper* in the Type II line 117 and the use of *soffraunce* in the counterpointed Type III line 124 in connexion with *coueitise*, which anticipates 3.206–07. **95** *Conscience*: appearing earlier than in **ZAB** and already having for **L**'s 'audience' (*Intro*. V § 7) the significance accorded him in B XX as a spiritual leader in the Church (his earlier 'social' identity as 'knight', retained in 3.145, is not made explicit at this juncture). Though he is identified by his name and action of 'accusing', whether Conscience is to be interpreted in precise scholastic terms has been much debated (by Hort 1938, Jenkins 1969, Carruthers 1973, Harwood 1992:91–138 and passim). **L**'s view seems closest to the Thomistic conception of conscience (Morgan 1987[1]) as the application of the rules of reason to a particular moral act, such as refusal to marry or to kiss Meed (and for Aquinas, conscience crucially *can* err in practical reasoning about an act, as will be seen in XXII when Conscience admits Friar Flatterer into Unity). What is here understood may perhaps be the disposition (*habitus*) responsible for this act, rather than the act itself, though in each of his three major appearances in **B** Conscience indeed carries out a definite and significant moral decision (cf. further 3.155–6, 20.242–5 //, B 13.180–83). However, **L** nowhere cites or alludes to any specific theoretical account of Conscience, a personification whose polysemous common name, long treated as equivalent to native *inwit* (MED s.vv. 2 (a) and 4, citing *Ancrene Wisse* [AW]), should be interpreted in the light of his own words. The equation of Latin *consciencia* with English 'Conscience' at 16.189–91, 199a is compatible with the Thomistic account, but coming from an older, less technical tradition should not be forced to yield a stricter sense than **L**'s definition requires. **97** *boxes*: for the offerings made at shrines. **98** *vntrewe*: i.e. 'false', by analogy with such 'sacrifices' in the OT, and unacceptable to God less because of the sin of the person offering (e.g. Cain) than because the 'miraculous' images are untrustworthy or 'lacking in (objective) validity'. **99** *wax*:

the votive-candles lit there (*Pe*) or, if *hangeth* is taken literally, waxen images of limbs for which a miraculous cure had been obtained or was being sought (Radford 1949:164–8, Finucane 1977:95–7, Swanson 1989:233–4). **103** *for...coueytise*: 'because of your love of greed / your covetous desire'. The thought 'al þe world be wors' (104) anticipates 'al euel spredeth' at 16.244, giving **L**'s severest criticism of the clergy prominence by placing it near the poem's beginning. **104** *as Holy Writ telleth*: see I Kgs (= I Sam) 4:11, 18. The example of Eli's sons as representatives of priestly greed and incontinence is common in homiletic writing (Wenzel 1999:137–52). **107** *Fines his brother*: 'that of his brother Phinees'. **108** *Archa Dei losten*: the Ark of the Covenant, made of precious wood and plated with gold, and originally housing the stone Tablets of the Law. The most sacred emblem of the ancient Hebrew people and believed to represent the Divine Presence, it may here be taken as an allegorical figure of the Church, which risked the danger of being spiritually 'lost' through greed to the enemies of God as the Ark was to the Philistines. **109** *synne*: the covetous impiety of stealing from the sacrificial meats. **119** *maumettes*: such images as the Virgin and Child venerated at Walsingham (Adair 1978:119–20).

125–218 are substantially added in **B** and revised in **C**, only the short passage on lawyers having already appeared in A 84–9, which rewrote by expanding Z 65 into 84–5. **125–7** Coming now after the minatory Ophni-Phineas passage, this warning to priests adds their liturgical and devotional to their pastoral shortcomings and gains solemnity from the use of direct address (to fit in with 96ff), *constorie* and *acorse* taking on added irony from the allusion to Mt 25:31. *is... / Lest*: i.e. lest at the Last Day. *Con(si)story*: (a) the bishop's court for cases involving clergy (as at 3.34), presided over by the chancellor or the commissary (cf. 16.362 // below); (b) the Pope's solemn council of cardinals (alluded to at 134 below); but here (c) figurative for the *tribunal Christi* (II Cor 5:10) at Doomsday, with the Apostles as Christ's council of judges (Mt 19.28). It is a sign of the poem's structural cohesion that the eschatological note struck here will be echoed at the end with the appearance of Death and Antichrist. **128–38 128** *I parsceyued*: if given to Will as in **B** so as to fit with *fonde* 56 and *say* 231, this is free from the awkwardness found by *Pe*. But his (and *R–K*'s) ascription of 128–138 to Conscience is at variance with the context, and the abrupt change of speaker here posited at 138 may be explained by the need to avoid the ambivalent tone of B 111. The notion of the 'power of the keys' given to St Peter (and, in standard medieval acceptance, to his successors the popes) is based on Mt 16:19 (cited at 9.326*a* // and alluded to at 15.226 and 21.183–91). As *Bn* notes, the idea that Christians should see the 'cardinal virtues' (first so called by Ambrose) as forms of *love* goes back

to Augustine. Thus **L** can correctly affirm Christian rule as 'the exercise of power in a spirit of love'; otherwise, to make virtues of natural reason the 'hinges' of heaven's gates would be incongruous (the derivation of 'cardinal' from Lat *cardo* 'hinge' occurs in the Proem to the *Disticha Catonis* [*DC*], as noted by Baer 2001). The later allegory of Truth's 'court' makes the specifically Christian virtues of humility and love central (see esp. the manorgates 'hanging' on alms-deeds at 7.241). But here love appears a 'dimension' or a 'spirit' manifest in a proper exercise of the cardinal virtues, which are shown as capable of *im*proper exercise (in the spirit of covetousness) later at 21.458 ff. **130** Since Mt 16:19 does not explicitly describe Christ bequeathing the power of the keys 'with love', the true source may be Jn 13:13–16, with its lesson of Christian rule as a service of love. But the cardinal virtues may be emphasised because of the dominance of political and social concerns in this vision: they are *most vertuous* not, obviously, as higher than the theological virtues, but in their special function of fostering right order in secular governance. Their nature will be more fully explored in 21.275–320, where they are allegorically depicted as needing love to grow in their midst so as to protect them against vices (311–13). **132** *cardinales*: the *-s* pl. ending is imitated from French usage (cf. 7.82, B 11.316 and see Mustanoja, *Middle English Syntax* [*MES*] 277). **134–8** *Bn* sees in *court* 134 a specific allusion to the election of the anti-pope Clement VI in Sept 1378 by the French cardinals opposed to Urban VI (see also Bennett 1943:56). But this fits ill with the refusal at 136 to *impugne* 'find fault with', i.e. challenge the basis of their right [of election] (MED s.v. 2(b), with play on sense 2(a)); so the more probable referent is the general authority of the holiness and learning ideally to be found in a cardinal. **134** *caught han*: suggesting that actual cardinals do not deserve their name (as 'ideally' apprehended) because, while the Church as an organisation 'turns' on them as its structural hinges, their own lives do not 'turn' upon the spirit of the virtues (*Bn*). **135–6** The slight syntactical ambiguity (depending on whether or not the lines are run on) is well met by the rendering 'mak[e] a pope who will have the power that Peter had' (*Bn*). They have the right of election / the capacity (through it) to confer *plenitudo potestatis*. This 'power' of granting or withholding forgiveness of sins was held (on the basis of Jn 20:23) to be shared by the Apostles and their successors the bishops. But in 'high' papal theory it became associated with the Pope's prerogative of immediate jurisdiction in all parts of the Church and supreme spiritual authority over all, from peasant to Emperor. **138** The substituted line exhorts the post-1381 Dreamer (and the 'public' he represents) against disturbing the peace of the Christian community by disputation. *Contreplede*: a term perhaps introduced by **L** from Law French (Alf*G* s.v.). First used by Imaginatyf at B 12.98, it recurs in the new C 8.53 (echoing this line), where Piers defends the authority of Conscience 'counterpleaded' by the friars at B 20.385 (cf. also Piers's subtly-inflected advice to challenge *maystres and grete menne* at 8.87). This new view of Conscience's direct relationship with Will, further developed in 5.89ff, results from progressively absorbing the Dreamer's rôle as quester into Conscience's in the concluding passūs of **B**. The truth of 137 is *affirmed* by claiming that to *deny* it would cause harm. The addition may thus be (to modify *Bn*) a response to the papal wars of 1379 more than a pointed allusion to the Great Schism itself in Sept 1378 (at the time of the **C** revision, an event six or seven years past). But *Bn* is not wholly convincing in finding heavy reliance on the thought-sequence of II Pet 1:5–11; and any residual criticism of the cardinals in the Dreamer's words in **C** is counteracted by Conscience's interjection at 138 (while it is true that the referent of *hit* remains indeterminate). The provocative B 111 replaced implies both capacity and constraint, as do 217–8 below (see Simpson 1990:13–21).

139–64 139 *Knyghthede*: a distinct social order including the nobility and distinguished from the labouring, mercantile and clerical members of society by its responsibility for governing and protecting the realm; the earliest recorded use in this sense (see MED s.v. *knighthod* n. 2(c)). **L**'s main statements on the character and the duties of knights occur at 1.101–5, 8.23–53 and 17.287ff, which may be compared with the view of Gower in *CA* (on knighthood see Barber 1970, Bumke 1982; for the martial ideology of the medieval aristocracy, Keen 1984). **140** *tho men* (*Communes* **B**): the change of stress perhaps induced by awareness of the radical overtones of *communes* after 1381, when the peasant rebels sought an alliance between the king and what they called the 'true commons' against other lords secular and ecclesiastical. Or it may be no more than a recognition of the king's *de facto* dependence on the knightly estate for enforcing the authority he has directly from God. An extreme view that the C Pr revision presents 'the triumph of absolutism' is given by Baldwin 1981[1]:7–23. But the continuing (and increased) importance of Conscience (who is given the **B** Angel's lines at 151–7) demands a nuanced understanding of **L**'s robust stand for order (see further on B 145). **141–7** *Kynde Wit*: the 'natural reason' (Quirk 1953:182) that acquires knowledge through the data of experience; prior to formal reasoning, but also the *basis* of *clergie* 'understanding acquired through instruction' (see 14.34 and cf. A 12.41–6). This power seems more generally concerned with man's practical relations to the world than specifically with 'the moral aspect of human actions' (*Bn*), for the link with Conscience is not yet found in **B**. KYNDE WIT has been more exactly correlated with the scholastic *vis cogitativa*, a power of the 'sensible soul'

that provides material for use by the 'rational soul' and is especially concerned to apprehend what is of benefit to man (Harwood 1976); but most commentators agree with *Bn*. Thus Baldwin too finds KW equivalent to *ratio naturalis* as described by Aquinas, 'which teaches [man] the Law' (1981[1]:22). Morgan (1987[1]) sees it as the natural understanding of the first principles of both the speculative and the practical intellect which serves as the *source* of the knowledge Conscience then applies to a particular act (Conscience acknowledges KW's 'teaching' at 3.436). And for White (1988:3–40) KW is both a (natural) faculty and the (natural) knowledge it has access to (especially regarding the pursuit of the good and doing well), though its meaning changes through the poem and between versions and is developed greatly in **B** and **C**. But like long-naturalised 'Conscience' (see 95 above), and unlike *Liberum Arbitrium* later, 'Kynde Wit' does not seem to be a technical term. Though found first in **L** (and elsewhere only in Trevisa), it comes from the common language and so is presumably meant to be intelligible from its first appearance at Z Pr 142 (MED s.v *kinde* adj. 1(e) cites Trevisa using the phrase to render Lat. *sensus*, and it correlates closely with this term at 16.187–8). The expression's meaning in different contexts should not be determined by a specific scholastic theory; but Morgan's study helpfully elucidates the relations between Kind Wit, Conscience and Reason. **143** *Comune*: 'the people, community' more than 'the Commons in parliament' [= burgesses and knights of the shire]. **B 120** *tilie; trauaille*: the first of many 'alliterating matched pairs', comparable to the 'copulative' alliterative phrases found in OE prose, which 'participate in a kind of mutual semantic assimilation' (Ryan 1969:267; these formula-like pairs are listed on pp. 272–3). **B 122** *knowe his owene*: 'recognise their true rights and duties' (*Bn*). **149** *Lewte*: the moral and spiritual dimension or pervading spirit of human law, which is meant to reflect divine justice (cf. B 11.153–55). The word is etymologically linked (< OF *lealte* < Lat. *legalitatem*) with ideas of the abstract essence of law; near-synonyms like 'fairness', 'equity', 'fidelity' and 'integrity' bring out various aspects of its meaning (see AlfG 84, 159); and a native equivalent is *treuthe* (cf. *SGGK* 2366). LEWTE has been seen both generally as 'virtuousness of life', forming a 'triad' with *law* and *love* (Kean 1964, 1969), and even as corresponding specifically to the theological virtue Hope (Clutterbuck 1977). But perhaps the clearest gloss is **L**'s synonym *rihtfulnesse, rihtwisnesse* (21.83/89), emblematised by *gold* (which echoes the spiritual 'treasure' of *treuthe* praised at 1.81). This association, already present in its collocation with the king's *rightful ruylynge* at 150, supports Donaldson's gloss 'exact justice' (1949:66n). But its religious resonance aligns it with the *pietas* that clothes bare law (*nudum ius*) at 152ff below. Lewte is fleetingly again a personified character at 2.20 (as Holy Church's *lemman*), at 4.156 in close association with Love, and more extensively at 12.24–42, where his advice to Will is endorsed by Scripture. Here the term has been taken to imply 'the King's law-abiding subjects' by Kane (982:40), though perhaps this is only as part of its reference, not of its sense. **B 123–7** The *lunatik* could be an ironic persona of Will (cf. later his 'madness' at B 15.1–10). He could likewise stand for the 'unenlightened speaker' of what 'might have been spoken by a clerk' (*clergially*), addressing the King with the *thou* form of clerks 'careless of the pretensions of the world' (Burnley 1990:33, 36, 38), a touch echoed in **C**'s omission of *sire* 125. At 147 **C**'s replacement of the lean lunatic by KW makes for greater clarity. **151–7 151** *Conscience*: replacing, as befits the importance of his rôle in **C**, **B**'s lofty *angel* 131 (the low goliard who answers the latter being omitted). He is perhaps to be thought of here as a judge administering equity according to the dictates of 'conscience', in the light of later 4.186 (where it is however Reason who is envisaged as future 'Chancellor'). For increasingly the actual Chancellor's rôle in the Chancery Court was to correct law in individual cases where it was defective on account of its universality (J. H. Baker 1971:42; cf. also Baldwin 1981¹:22–3). **B 128** *on heiȝ an aungel*: perhaps recalling the one represented in a pageant at Cheap the day before Richard II's coronation on 16 July 1377 (Walsingham, *Historia Anglicana* 1, 331–2; Wickham 1980:54–5). But **B**'s collocation of angel and 'goliard' may have been suggested by the 'angels' who come to dissuade Golias from marriage in Walter Map's *Golias de conjuge non ducenda* (ed. Wright 1841:78), a work **L** seems to have known (see on 22.193–8 below). **152–7** The Latin Leonine hexameter and pentameter verses appear, added to the text of a 1315 sermon by Henry Harclay, Chancellor of Oxford, in Lambeth MS 61, f. 147v (*Bn*); whatever the source, the wordplay on *metere* 'measure / reap' will have appealed to **L**. Their use in an address to the king may allude to the sermon for the newly crowned Richard and for the peace of the realm preached by Thomas Brinton, Bishop of Rochester, on 17 July 1377 (ed. Devlin 1934: no.44; see also idem, xx, xxvii); but the sentiments have a general validity as well as a special aptness at the commencement of a reign. *Sum rex...metas*: '"I am King, I am Ruler;" one day you may be neither. You who control the lord Christ's lofty laws, The better to perform what you must do, Be pitiful as you are just; for naked law You must dispense in piety of heart. Sow such grain as you desire to reap. But strip law bare, the judgement you receive Will follow the naked letter of [God's] law. If you sow mercy, mercy you will harvest'. The verses oppose 'bare' justice to law administered with a sense of what is owed to God by his earthly deputy the king; 156 alludes to Mt 7:1–2, quoted at B 12.89*a,* and the thought echoes Js 2:13.

The sense of *pietas* here is close to that of ME *pite*, as in Gower's praise of Richard II for his 'justice medled with pite' in *CA* viii 2989–92 (*Bn*) and involves the religious awareness that should inform human law. Modern 'mercy', associated with but distinguished from 'pity' in Middle English, captures the sense, both terms being used interchangeably at 21.92–3 for one of the royal gifts the Three Kings bring Christ under the sign of myrrh. In Richard II's coronation oath was added (after the promise to maintain the laws) the phrase *iuste et racionabiliter* (McKisack 1959:399), the sense of the second adverb ('spiritually') coming close to *pietate* 155.

B 139–45 139 *gloton*: playing on the ultimate derivation of OF *goliardeis* from *gula* 'gluttony'. **141–2** 'As the name "king" is said to come from "rule", He who does not maintain the law with zeal Is but a king in name, and not in truth'. Though 'clothed' law is 'proper' law, the goliard's insistence complements rather than contradicts the angel's speech, highlighting the need to avoid arbitrary rule by linking the reality of kingly authority (*res*) with zealous maintenance of the nation's laws (*iura*). There is nothing Lollard-like about the sentiments (cf. *Bn*) and the ironic use of a speaker whose name is associated with gluttony is of a piece with the earlier recourse to a *lunatik* (this goliard is not especially loquacious). The Latin couplet has been related (*Sk, Bn*) to proverbial verses like those in Wright, ed. *Political Poems* (1859:278) stating that the king must rule himself rightly to be a true king, and to the fanciful derivation of *rex* from *recte agendo* (AlfQ 34). While this appears in a source **L** knew (Isidore's *Etymologies* 9.3), his own text speaks not of self-rule or right action but of kingship as nullified by neglect of law; so the lines in this form may be his own. **145** versifies the *Lex Regia*, the Roman law maxim *Quod principi placuit legis habet vigorem* (Justinian, *Institutes* 1.2.6; AlfQ 34) and appears in this form in Richard of Wetheringsette's C13th *Summa* as part of a 'vers of Latyn' (Wenzel, in Alford, *Companion to* PP [AlfC] 1988²:161). The commons' view of royal authority is extreme, and despite the invitation to interpret (*Bn* finding beneath the maxim a notion that power derives from the people), it seems that if *comune* here = the *lewed men* of 129, they do not know what they are saying. Fortescue, whose *De Laudibus Legum Angliae* IX *Bn* cites, *contrasts* the type of rule the maxim expresses ('regal') with that of the English monarchs ('political'), who cannot change the law without the people's consent (the type of rule both angel and goliard presuppose). The case for **L**'s shift from a 'political' to a 'regal' theory of government in revising to **C** is somewhat overstated by Baldwin 1981¹:12–17.

158–64 correspond to **B 212–17**, giving the King a neat exit before the mice enter and illustrating **C**'s increased concern for smooth transitions. The 'court' is a court of

Commentary

King's Bench for actions *coram rege* 'before the king' in criminal and other matters, where plaintiffs could bring a writ of *capias* against the accused (cf. 4.164, which cites the writ's opening words). **159** *houed...houes*: characteristic homophonic wordplay (cf. 61, 1.35–6). **160** *Seriantz...Barre*: senior barristers (*servientes ad legem*), who wore a coif of white silk covering the head and tied under the chin, and pleaded at a railed area in front of the judge's seat (cf. 3.447–48 and AlfG s.v. *sergeaunt* II, *barre*). **162** *for...Lord*: 'for pure charity's sake' (i.e. without payment). **164** *mum*: a non-committal sound through closed lips; the idea is personified in *Mum and the Sothsegger* [*MS*] 146 (*c*. 1410).

(ii) 165–218 The FABLE of the RATS, MICE and CAT, a traditional exemplum found in French and Latin, is used with a different purpose (urging action) by Brinton in a sermon (no. 69 in Devlin) before Congregation of 18 May 1376 (Owst 1925:270–9). It is depicted on a misericord in Great Malvern Priory Church (where the mice are hanging, not belling the cat). In the usual view, the fable's moral is the futility of attempting to curb royal power (Bennett 1943[2]), but any precise topical reference implied by 217–18 remains uncertain. If the *conseyl* of 167 alludes to the Good Parliament of 1376 (see Keen 1973: 261–64; Holmes 1975), the *cat* will be John of Gaunt, the most powerful man in England during Edward III's last years and Richard II's minority. The *rats* and *mice* then represent respectively the Lords and the Commons, the *rat of renown* 176 Sir Peter de la Mare, the Commons' speaker, and the *mouse* 196 a spokesman of the author's opinions. (By contrast, Orsten 1961 sees the mouse as a Gaunt-inspired 'mediator', whose argument for autocracy is *ironically* presented, and the events described as those of 1376 seen from the standpoint of 1377, when much of the Good Parliament's work had been undone). The *kitten* is usually identified as the young Richard, nine years old when his father the Black Prince died in 1376. Whichever interpretation is accepted here, there is no need for over-precision about the bell and the collar (180–4), presumably standing for constitutional restraints of some kind that might warn the commons of the King's threatening intentions. The popular animal fable, largely unaltered ten years after the event, is perhaps best regarded as a general allegory on the problems of balancing power within the body politic. **174** The small revision uses internal rhyme to enhance the near-formulaic antithesis of 'wit and will' found in an early alliterative piece of that name (and again collocated at 5.185, 6.167). **B 160** *Cite of Londoun*: stressing the independence of the capital, with its wealth, pride and political privileges. **C** generalises the location but, by specifying *segges* as knights rather than merchants and seeing them as a threat to the speaker, may evoke the liveried retain-

ers of great lords such as John of Gaunt. **178** *Bn* notes the parallel with *Purity* 1638 (translating Dan 5:16); but the indebtedness, if any, is more probably to **L** (cf. Schmidt 1984:155–6). **184** *oure comune profyt*: a phrase with elevated moral and political overtones (cf. Chaucer's *Parlement of Foules* [*PF*] 47, 75, using it without *oure*), but here and at 201 denoting perhaps no more than the shared advantage of the rats and mice. **B 163–64** are omitted by **C** as perhaps allegorically over-literal (163) and because used later (164a) at B 8.26, which is retained in // **C** (cf. B 181 //, a line virtually repeated at B 17.247, which is also retained as // **C** 19.213). **B 189–92** The concreteness enlivens the allegory, but it is uncertain whether the rabbits and deer are great nobles or rich merchants. **190** *thise*: a sg. with intrusive -*e*; perhaps influenced by the pl. sense of *route*, though ms X conversely also uses *this* as a plural (see *IG* s.v., and on the pleonastic use of *this*, *MES* 138). **191–92** already hint that even a bad ruler is better than none. **204–05a** *kitoun*: implying that if the young Richard [only ten when he was crowned in July 1377] ruled in place of his uncle, life would be even worse. **205a** 'Woe to thee, O land, when thy king is a child' (Eccl 10:16), a text the chronicler Adam of Usk applied to Richard in 1382 when the king, though now married, was still under the guidance of a council. At the probable date of the **C** revision, little in the fable will have required changing. **217–18** imply a hidden (and dangerous meaning), and the drop in tone seems deliberate. *deuyne*: later used (9.305) of the prophet Daniel's interpretation of Nebuchadnezzar's dream (see Schmidt 2000:5–6).

(b) 219–32 219 The added line, with *ʒut* perhaps taken from B 211, illustrates **C**'s tightening of transitions (as in its deliberate echo of Pr 20). **220** *bondemen of thorpes*: perhaps serfs who had become free through spending a year and a day in a borough-town (see Du Boulay 1991:48). The phrase, revising unspecific **B**, takes up an expression used at A 2.45, from a passage omitted in **B**. **226** *Dew...Emme*: 'God save you, Lady Emma!' The song quoted may originally have been about Emma, Canute's queen, who survived trial by ordeal for a (false) charge of unchastity. But so edifying a tale fits ill with those who 'do their deeds ill', and this reference may be (by way of ironic application) to the 'wise woman' Dame Emma of Shoreditch (see on B 13.339). **230–31** *Oseye*: Alsace (Auxois). *Gascoyne*: ceded to England under the Treaty of Brétigny (see 3.241ff), and regained by France in 1372. *Reule*: La Reôle, a French wine-exporting town on the Garonne; *La Rochelle*: a fortified town on the Atlantic coast in Charente, and a major centre for the export of Bordeaux wines; cf. Chaucer, *Canterbury Tales* [*CT*] VI 571. **B 230** *Ryn*: the Rhineland, source of fine white wines ('Rhenish'), the change in **C** suggesting that they were scarce or little known.

Passus I (Z Pr 94–145, I)

Title. The term *passus* used as the heading for each of the poem's numbered divisions is a common Latin name for a section in a narrative or treatise (e.g. in a 1356 sermon of Richard Fitzralph noted by Dolan 1985:5–7), whence its use here (such poems as *The Wars of Alexander* may imitate the practice in *PP*). The familiar English form *pas* is found in *William of Palerne* [*WPal*] 61 and *The Destruction of Troy* 663 (see MED s.v. *pas* n.(1), (4b)). The **ABC** versions of PASSUS I, all of similar length, run closely parallel. It is occupied almost entirely by a single long speech of HOLY CHURCH, which may be divided into (i) 1–80 and (ii) 81–203, broken respectively by the Dreamer's questions at 11, 41–3, 55–6, 70–1, 79–80 and his *dotede* comment at 136–7. The main revision of **Z** in **A** is the more logical dividing of I from Pr after the vision of the Field of Folk. The sternly 'eschatological' tone of Z Pr 98–100 (its last line referring back to the dungeon of 16–17) is softened, the people now being described as in confusion (*þe mase*), as later they will *blostren* (7.158) like helpless beasts without guidance.

(i) 1–11 (Z Pr 94–100) 1 *montaigne*: God's 'holy mountain' in the OT is Mt Sion, becoming a symbol in the psalms (14:1) of heaven, and in prophetic writing (Is 2:2–3, 11:9) of the Messianic community of the last days, and thence inspiring the Gospel image of the Church as a city on a mountain (Mt 5:14). **3** *lady*: a personification of the Christian Church (see 72) as a woman, deriving from the image of the Lamb's Bride in Apoc 19:8, whose white linen robe is made of *iustificationes* 'saving acts' of the Saints (cf. also Apoc 7:13–14). As the 'Church Triumphant' she is conceptually distinct from the 'Church Militant' on earth (= 'Unity' in 21.330) and the 'Church Suffering' in Purgatory, though substantively one with it because the justified living and dead are united in 'mystic sweet communion with Jesus Christ their Lord'. This idea of spiritual continuity explains both **L**'s later seeing the *early* church as striving to separate itself from the World in the search for 'holiness' and also his having HOLY CHURCH (HC) speak of receiving Will in baptism (72 below). **L**'s personage may here owe something to such authoritative instructresses as Philosophy in Boethius's *Consolation of Philosophy*, 'descended from the sovereign seat' (Chaucer's *Boece* Pr 3, 9), Nature in Alan of Lille's *De Planctu Naturae* (*DPN*) coming from the *palatium* of the *impassibilis mundi* (*PL* 210:432), and Reason in the *Roman de la Rose* 'comen doun / Out of hir tour' (*Rom* 4615ff) and Deguileville's *Pèlerinage de Vie Humaine* (l. 1333. = *Pilgrimage* [Eng. trans.] ed. Henry 8/310). But the Bible, which offers the deepest dimension of the image, would by itself have sufficed as a model. Medieval iconography commonly contrasts the image of *Ecclesia*

with that of *Synagoga* or Judaism (a blindfolded woman); but at 2.9 below HC's opposite is to be her eschatological adversary *Babylon*, 'the mother of fornication' (Apoc 17:50), = unbelief or false belief (a richly-attired harlot). **5** *Wille / Sone*: the name not being indicated in **B** until 5.61 (confirmed at B 8.26 //), and **C** perhaps relying on readers' familiarity with **B** in exploiting its allegorical sense. He is by baptism a 'son' of Mother Church, a relationship reflected in her *thou* to Will and his *ye* to her. *slepestou*: that the 'sleep' implies 'spiritual torpor' (Robertson-Huppé [*R–H*] 37–8) is denied by *Bn*; but no other interlocutor sees Will as asleep *within* a dream, so a symbolic meaning would be apt here. **6** *mase*: either vain activity or a 'gret perplexite' like Amant's in *Rom* 4624, which anticipates Will's in Pr 8, worn out with wandering (see MED s.v. (b), (c)). While perhaps suggesting the labyrinth of existence, it is unlikely to allude to the mazes sometimes inscribed in cathedral floors as symbolic 'routes of pilgrimage' to the 'Jerusalem' placed at their centre (Santarcangeli 1974:215–20, 296–98, MED s.v. (d), with 'maze' here being the 'concrete' rather than the 'literal' [*Pe*] sense). **9** In its **A** form re-writes Z 99–100, keeping its vocalic alliteration and an echo of *dale* in its *tale. halde...tale*: 'make no account of' / ?'never talk about' (evoking the Pauline contrast of those whose 'conversation' is in heaven with those who 'mind earthly things' (Phil 3:20). Two distinct notions of 'heaven [here] on earth' will recur at B 10.299, 14.141=C 5.152, 16.9. **12–40 12b** redundantly repeats Pr 15, but in // **ZAB** is new information; a symptom of the didactic explicitness expressed in **C** through *repetitio*. **15** *fyue wittes*: the physical or outer senses, whose use should be moderate (cf. *sobre* 15.257 //); their 'right uses' will be personified as the 'sons' of Inwit at 10.145ff. **16** *worschipe...þerwith*: perhaps echoing Deut 6:5 (Mt 22:37). **17** *elementis*: presumably impiying all four, earth, air, water and fire (see on 10.129–31, 20.245). **B 17** *erþe*: cf. Gen 1:29. **19** brings out as revised the concept of the *mean* as definitive of the virtues ('tempering' or giving proportion to each) by its use of the nominal form *mesure* (not introduced until 35 // in **B**) and stress on the need for it even in times of plenty (a theme introduced in **B** only at 6.257 //). **20–1** *comaunded*: the stress on the first syllable identical with *comune* hints at a 'Platonic' affinity between the divine will and the needs of human beings as a whole. *cortesye*: on this notion of God's kindness as a gratuitous gift, not a payment for desert, cf. at 14.215–16. *in comune*; *nidefol*: all men having a right to the necessary natural goods, which are provided by God's earth, not by human skill (contrast money at 42). In this idea ('rehearsed' by Need at 22.6–19) *Bn* discerns the medieval affirmation of *communis usus*, which is quite distinct from the denial of private ownership rejected at 22.277–80. To these three Ecclus 29:27 adds housing, which **L** does not see as abso-

481

lutely necessary (wandering hermits do without it). **24** *tyme*: in place of **ZAB** *resoun*, by warning against lechery (cf. 10.291) rather than the danger to man's work (B 26 //, suggested by Ecclus 19:1), tightens the link to the Lot exemplum. **25–32** *Loot*: a familiar homiletic proof (cf. *CT* VI 485–7) that gluttony can lead to lechery and the further evil of wicked offspring, revealing **L**'s deep conviction (like the *Purity*-poet's) that sexual acts should only be performed in a way pleasing to God (cf. 10.215–304, especially 288–96). **25** *likerous drynke*: 'delicious drink that arouses desire'; translating Prov 20:1 ('Luxuriosa res vinum') and recurring at 10.178 in connexion with Herod and Lot, figures likewise linked at *CT* VI 485–91 by Chaucer (who uses the phrase ibid. 549). **30a** '[Come], let us make him drunk with wine, and let us lie with him, that we may preserve seed of our father' (Gen 19:32). The association of drink misused with wrongful sexual acts perhaps recalls Eph 5:18, since Lot's drunkenness potentially 'contains' *luxuria*. **C** blames *man* for his misuse of two *wyttes*, while **ZAB** sees it as a means whereby the devil corrupts man. **32b** removes a phrase (*do the bettre*) that will have acquired 'Langlandian' meanings by the time of the revision. **33** *Mesure is medecyne*: a paradox, since temperate use of natural goods will make physic unnecessary (19 has adumbrated the perils of *excess*: the medicines necessitated by *gluttony* are specified at Z 7.274–8; cf. 8.290–6, and on the historical background to **L**'s use of medical imagery see Gasse 2004). **L**'s *mesure* as a rational norm of moderate sufficiency, a 'law' governing even that need which 'has no law' (20.22–3), is close to Platonic *sophrosyne* 'temperance' (rendered *sobrietas* at I Tim 2:9). But it also recalls the Aristotelian conception of *all* virtue as a mean between extremes of excess and defect (*Nicomachean Ethics* II 6–9). This, though not directly in question, will emerge later in **L**'s presentation of the deadly sins and the virtue of poverty, where *sobrete* is described as *good leche in siknesse* (B 14.315). Finally, it shows influence from the Biblical teaching on God's creation of everything 'in measure [*mensura*], number and weight' (Wisd. 11:21). **35–6** The **C** form of the verb (*Leef*), which punningly brings out how men choose to believe what they like (*lef* 35), appears in **Z** too and may be the original in all versions. The homophones **L** 'Platonically' exploits ('whom we like we tend to trust') are, as often, etymologically unconnected. **37** *bigyle*: replacing **ZAB** *bytraye* and having the demonic overtones acquired in B 18.340–61. The devil, appearing to bring up the rear, in fact 'animates' the World instrumentally through the *mundi rectores* of Eph 6:12 (hence *wolde*). 'World' and 'flesh 'have the standard NT senses 'worldliness' and 'corrupt bodily desires' (as at B 16.48; 19.312, B 11.399). The evil triad re-appear as enemies of charity at 10.44 and 18.29ff. **39** **L**'s 'dualistic' anthropology, with its Platonic strain coming through Augustine

and Gregory the Great (Straw 1988:107–27), finds the spiritual soul threatened not only by outward foes (devil, world) but by the wayward body it must vigilantly govern. *seeth*: see *TN* on this crux. *herte*: the locus of the soul as life-principle (*anima*) under the rule of a rational moral sense (*inwit*); see 10.175 //. B 9.60–6 expand on the danger to *inwit* from drink.

41–53 41 is either a Type I line with muted key-stave and trisyllabic dip before the last lift or, preferably, a T-type line. **42** *moneye*: a man-made value, not one of the *bona naturae*, hence not self-evidently for 'common' use (cf. on 20–1). *Gospel*: Mt 22:16–21. **44–53 C** tightens the link between Will's question (perhaps originally prompted by doubts about royal taxation) and the scriptural answer, which in context concerns payment of tribute to Rome. **44** is either of Type Ia scanning on |g| with rhetorical stresses on *God* and *sayde* or Type IIb on |g| and |s| with 'cognative' third stave, but not an anomalous *aa / bb* type with its third lift on *se* (**ABC** may be T-Type). **46** *God*: startlingly underlining the authoritativeness of Christ's utterance on this important subject; paralleled at 3.74 and 12.140. **48a, 49a** 'Render [therefore to Caesar the things that are Caesar's]; and to God the things that are God's' (Mt 22:21). **C** turns from the image and inscription to the coin itself, arguing that the proper use of money, like other earthly transactions, falls to Reason and Kynde Wit, and should be determined by necessity and by thrift, the virtue of *mesure*.

Z Pr 145 A summarising conclusion echoing Z Pr 104, omitted in **A** after re-division of Pr / I at Z Pr 93=A Pr 109, and echoed at Z 1.121a, which A 1.172 revises. From here until VI, passus-divisions correspond in **ZA**; but Z II is preceded by similar summarising lines with a 'draft' feel (*Intro*. III, *Z*, i) and A VI opens with Z V 155–66.

54–67 55 Revision in **C** to the rare Type IIb omits the *dongeon*. **56** *bymene*: showing that Will grasped HC's explanation of the tower's symbolic meaning at 12. **59** *Wrong*: personifying all that is 'twisted aside' (*Wrynglawe* 4.32 reflects **L**'s awareness of the word's etymology). This second 'nature-name' obliquely denotes the Devil through his leading feature, comparably to the use of 'Truth' for God (for it is by his 'oppositeness' to truth that he is opposed to love at 65). *þat...his name*: on this use of 'that followed by a possessive' see *MES* 202–3. **60** *Fader of falshede*: the devil being from the beginning a murderer, a liar and the father of lies (Jn 8:44). **61–2** *Adam...Caym*: see Gen 3:1–7 (describing the serpent's temptation) and 4:1–17, where Satan is to be inferred as the source of Cain's anger from the enigmatic vs 7's crucial opposition between *agere bene...male* 'doing well and ill' and personification of sin. **62–3** *Caym; Iudas*: the first murderer and the archetypal traitor, exemplifying enmity to God (cf. 10.215–31 and 18.166ff, esp. 174–15). Like Cain, Judas is one 'by whom the scandal comes' (Mt

18:7): followers of Wrong will 'ban' the day as these did. **63** See Lk 22:3 and Jn 13:7 (on the Temptation), Mt 26:15 (on the silver). **64** *hellerne*: the tree on which Judas was traditionally supposed to have hanged himself, which has hollow branches. But the (possibly original) **ZC** spelling allows a grim 'Platonic' pun, making hell's lord responsible for suicide as well as treachery and murder. **C**'s addition of *hey* makes the event more clearly a counter-type to Christ's 'hanging' at 169. **66–7** give clearer sense than **ZAB**: inordinate desire for worldly wealth (*coveitise*) is the devil's instrument to undo mankind. The added 67 anticipates 190 (=B 196).

68–80 70 *hey name*: that of God, or of Christ (Phil 2:9). **72–5** will be recalled by Will as a comfort at 12.54–5 // when frightened by Scripture's 'Many are called, few are chosen'. This link is made possible because of her earlier rôle as authoritative interpreter of scripture ('this textes' 200), baptism entailing loyal commitment to Church and Bible alike. HC's rebuke for failure to recognise her recalls Nature's in *DPN* (*PL* 210:442). **73** *fre man*: drawing on the Biblical notion of Christ's 'saving death' as freeing man from sin through sacramental grace, which will be interpreted (metaphorically) at 21.39–40 in terms of a legal and social liberation. A more directly 'political' motive for the revision may be to affirm that the baptized need no other freedom and should not rebel against the authority of the Church they are pledged to obey (cf. on Pr 138). The line is probably not of T-type structure since *fré man* could be the quasi-compound (see MED s.v. *freman* n.). **74** *borewes*: the godparents, on whose duties see B 9.75–9. **75** *Leue*: the command to belief in the Church being perhaps a 'loyalist' response to the growth of the Wycliffite heresy (condemned at the Council of Blackfriars in 1382). The line is fuller now in content than // B 78. **77** retains the polysemous wordplay of **ZAB** and could be T-type in structure. **78** *kyndly*: perhaps qualifying both verbs, though more closely the post-caesural *bileue*. Believing 'properly, in the right way' is explored in Harwood 1992:11ff.

(ii) 81–203 The sermon-like character of HC's reply to Will is brought out by Wenzel (in Alf*C* 165–7), specifically with reference to // B 85–209. On the place of the speech in the structure of the poem as a whole see Kaske 1974, and for sensitive analysis of its linguistic texture Davlin 1989:25–46. For the influence of sermons on *PP* see Owst 1961:548–75, Spearing 1972:107–34, Wenzel in Alf*C* 155–172, Fletcher 2001:61–84.

81–124 81 *tresor(es)*: Will having denied interest at 79 in *tresor of erthe* (cf. 66), HC can affirm the worth of spiritual treasure. *tried*: 'assayed', like gold or silver. *treuthe*: divine wisdom as 'an infinite treasure to men' and 'more precious than any wealth' (Wisd 7:14; Prov 3:15). **82** *Deus caritas*: 'God is charity' (I Jn 4:8). Crucial

to **L**'s elaboration of the relationship between knowledge and love is the preceding clause in Jn 'He that loveth not knoweth not God'. HC links cognitive *veritas* with affective *caritas* through a value (*fidelitas, sapientia*) that offers a second Biblically authorised 'nature-name' for God. **83** *druerie*: playing on senses 3(a) and (b) 'love token'; 'treasure' (MED s.v.). *dere*: 'excellent / precious' and 'beloved' (MED s.v. adj. (1) 1–3, 4); cf. the collocation at 13.17. **84–5** perhaps derive from Cato's *Distichs* i. 3 (Galloway 1987:9–13). The revised 84b, echoing B 5.287, underlines the dual intellectual and moral senses of *trewe*, supports association of *treuthe* with *sapientia* and anticipates 10.78b (for the 'hand = action, tongue = speech' collocation, see also 6.109 and 19.257). **86** alludes to Jn 10:34, quoting Ps 81:6 ('I have said: you are gods'). The b-half improves on the **ZAB** filler-phrase, claiming the power of physical and spiritual healing as a mark of the perfected Christian. This recalls Ac 3:6, which contrasts 'healing' with 'silver and gold' (a passage recalled in 15.220–23a, quoting Mk 16:18). **87** The source is (loosely) Lk 6:40; despite possible allusions to mystical 'deification' (cf. Vasta 1965[2]) a doctrine with wider import for ordinary Christians seems intended here, to be graphically illustrated in the image of Piers at 21.8. **Z 39** is somewhat otiose, since it has just been stated that Truth is valued by all men. **92** *transgressores*: more probably 'wrongdoers', as in Js 2:8–9, than 'trespassers' in the narrower legal sense of those who commit breaches of the law short of felony, misprision or treason (see Alf*G* s.v.). **93** *Treuthe*: clearly now with the sense '[ideal earthly] justice' (rather than heavenly justice at doomsday); for the close scriptural connection of justice with wisdom, see Wisd 1:1, 5:6, 8:7. *termyned*; *trespas*: legal terms denoting the hearing to the end and the judging of a case in court (Alf*G*). **94–100 C**'s focus on the duty of earthly justices to act without respect of persons (those who fail to are 'reproved by the law as transgressors' [Js 2:9]) may echo the breakdown of authority and morale among the seignorial class during the Peasants' Revolt, when they were paralysed into inaction (Harding, Tuck in Hilton & Aston 1984). The sixfold *repetitio* of *trewe* is notable. **95** *lordene loue*: on this form of the genitive pl. surviving from the weak OE ending *-ena* see *MES* 73. **97** *puyr ordre*: 'essential character' (but with *profession... appostata* perhaps playing on the religious sense), giving a second stave semantically richer than **AB**'s metrical filler (absent from **Z**, which is like *A*-**m** a Type III line); cf. on 86. **98** *poynt*: perhaps alluding to Js 2:10 'Whosoever shall keep the whole law, but offend in one *point* is become guilty of all' (*Pe*); but **L**'s stress is on truth as the *main* knightly quality (cf. *SGGK*, esp. 625–6). *appostata*: 'one who violates the code of an order (by quitting it without dispensation)' (MED s.v. 2), rather than 'violator of a code of ethics or morals' (MED s.v. 3, citing only this case from the 14th c.). **L** underscores less the 'religious character of the order of knighthood' (*Bn*) than the *parallel* between a religious vow and a knightly oath. **99** shows that **L** does not confuse knighthood with 'religion' but thinks of each 'order' as having a distinct sphere of action, though all must obey Truth in their different ways. *faste*: i.e. as a regular mortification, like monks. *forbere the serk*: and replace it with a penitential garment (see 6.6). **100** *leue*: the understood object in **C** being *treuthe*. **101–24 101** *Dauid*: a 'chivalricisation' of the warrior-king probably going back to I Par (= I Chr) 12:18 (*Bn*), where David creates thirty 'captains of the band'. To see him as having 'dubbed knights' flows naturally from the medieval conception of a king found in 21.29, 133–36, which affirms Christ's actions as *filius Dauid*, first knight, then king. But **L** cannot have been unaware of the romance tradition of tracing chivalry back to the Lord's warriors in the OT, such as those at 19.25 included amongst the 'Nine Worthies' of contemporary literature and iconography (e.g. *PTA* 451, *AMA* 3408–45; Keen 1984:265n64), and David himself, from whom the Grail knight Galahad was held to descend. See further Keen 1984:118–23 and (on the dubbing ceremony) 64–82. **102** *swere...swerd*: the chime of (etymologically unrelated) homophones hints at a 'Platonic' affinity between the associated virtues of fidelity and fortitude. **103** *God*: **C** is more straightforward theologically than **ZAB** *Christ* in not conflating the Son's post-Resurrection kingship (21.42) with his dominion as co-eternal Word before the creation of the angels. **104–5** *creatures*: (orders of) created being. *tene*: the 'number' of completed creation and that of the original orders of angels in apocryphal texts like II Enoch 29:3–4 (Russell 1984:94n). Lucifer may be envisaged here as head of a tenth order (?the highest), which fell with him, mankind's creation being meant to replace it and restore heaven's 'even number' (cf. 22.270). But Gregory the Great sees this order as a group drawn from the other nine, who fell with Lucifer (Hom. 34:6–11; cit. Russell 1984:94n, 237). The traditional *nine* orders as fixed by pseudo-Dionysius in the *Celestial Hierarchies*, proceeding downwards in choirs of three, were seraphim, cherubim and thrones; dominions, virtues and powers; principalities, archangels and angels. **L** names only the first two and last two and (as is clear from 107, B 108 // **ZA**) uses 'archangel' in a non-specific sense for all the higher orders above angels. His sequence need not imply the cherubim's priority in the hierarchy, since it echoes the standard phrase in the Preface to the Mass and the *Te Deum*. A depiction of seraphs leading the ranks of medieval society appears in the 'Orders of Angels' window in the church of All Saints, North St, York. *swiche...anoper*: 'seven like them and one other'. **B 109** *by*: 'by means of' (= *thorw* **ZA**); knowledge and obedience (reason and will) are ordained together from the beginning. **B 110 (Z 56, A 108)** Cf. B

77: man's submission to the Church parallels the angels' to God; but the clergy's authority over the laity depends on their own obedience to God. **C**'s deletion of B 107–10 removes the echo, with some loss; but *appostata* 98 has already made the point.

A 110–11 (Z 58–9, B *112–13) *louelokest of lyght*: 'most radiantly beautiful' (*reliquis angelis eminentiorem*), as argued by Gregory the Great in *Moralia* 32:23. Light is a common Biblical symbol of divine glory (Ex 14:20, Ps 103:2; I Jn 1:5) and an apt image of truth (cf. Pss 35:10, 42:3; II Cor 4:6). Lucifer's name therefore signifies his original status as 'bearer' of the divine light / truth, losing which he falls into darkness / falsehood and *fendes liknesse*, though still able to transform himself deceitfully into an angel of light (II Cor 11:14).

107 *Goddes knyghtes*: cf. on 13.125 (applied to priests). **108–10** tighten the link between Lucifer's fall and his 'dubbing', to make his rebellion seem like that of a feudal knight against his liege lord. **109** *lothly*: chiming with *luther*, with outer form echoing inner will; the same term is used of Lucifer at 21.56. *luther wille*: 'treacherous intentions'; the conjectured sense is close to that in 3.317, used of royal feudatories. **B 114–18** The fiends are damned eternally, by contrast with man, and hell's occupants are unnumbered (cf. 20.374–5 //; 22.270 //). The whole passage shows influence from Is 14:4–15 as figuratively interpreted in patristic tradition (e.g. compare 114 with vv. 11, 15), **C**'s removal of these lines here silencing the echoes later in the B // to C 20.345, 22.270. *mo thousandes...forme*: as depicted by Bosch in the left panels of his Last Judgement triptych at the Akademie, Vienna and in the Haywain triptych at the Prado, Madrid; cf. also *Purity* 220–28. **110a** 'I shall set my foot in the north, and I shall be like the Most High', a *VL* abbreviation (Hill 2000:155) of Is 14:13–14, which has 'sedebo...in lateribus *aquilonis...similis ero Altissimo*'. **L**'s substitution of *pedem* for *sedem* echoes Isaiah's *solium*, and *sedebo* and may show the influence of Augustine's gloss on *pes superbiae* 'the foot of pride' (Ps 35:12; and cf. vs 13) as 'self-love' (A. L. Kellogg 1958:386). It is cited by Augustine in his comment on Pss 1:4, 47:2 (*Enarrationes in Psalmos*, *PL* 36:69, 534) and found also in Alan of Lille (*PL* 210:706), as noted by *R–H* 1951:44. **L** may have come on it there or through a commentary on Avianus's *Fables*, a work alluded to at B 12.256 (Risse 1966). **112** *lefte syde*: the north (see *TN*) if one is facing *the sonne syde* (113), the eastern direction which is that of heaven (132) and of Jerusalem, and to which churches were oriented. The 'left' was in popular tradition the weak or bad side (MED s.v. *lift* adj. 2; for *luft* as noun see B 4.62), where the 'goats' (= the unjust) will stand at the Last Judgement, to be sent thence to hell (Mt 25:41; see the Ravenna mosaic illustrated in Russell 1984:24). Lucifer is to be thought of as leaping towards God's throne from his station in the north

(112) and then falling out of heaven from there upon the northern part of the earth. The north is associated with hell in Job 26:6–7 and is the source of coming evils in Jer 1:14. The idea is related to the patristic notion of 'cold' as a symbol of malice, and hence of hell as a place of intense cold. **L**'s account may owe something to Gregory's *Moralia* 32:23 (see further Kellogg 1949:413–14 and Hill 1969), while Bonaventure's Commentary on Eccl 11:3 also places hell in the north. In 20.166–7, more benignly, it is the direction from which Righteousness, the eldest (but severest) Daughter of God, approaches. **113** *sonne syde...roweth*: theoretically the east, but in fact the south, to which the sun moves as it climbs (as at Pr 14, 9.294). **114–24 C** elaborates the directional symbolism, where **B** described the fall of the angels. HC's remark about northerners is superficially of a piece with the Norfolk references in Z 5.98, B 5.235 and familiar passages in Chaucer (*CT* X 42–3) and Trevisa (Sisam *C14 V&P*) illustrating conventional southern prejudice; but the provoking digression at 122–4 hardly improves on its source. **116** *þe sonne regneth*: doubtless with a pun intended, since this is where the Son of God (who is *sol iustitiae* 'sun of justice') sits in glory, waiting to do judgement. **118–19** A parallel for this image is found by Hill (2000:156–7) in the C12th exegete Rupert of Deutz's *Commentaria* VIII:44 (*CCCM* 9:469). By a 'condign' punishment, Lucifer becomes king of the north (but not in heaven). **ZA 61/113** *hobeled*: an image possibly influenced by the folkloric notion that devils are lame and by patristic allegorisations of the 'feet of the soul' as 'love of God and neighbour', with 'lameness' being interpreted as 'sinfulness' (Hill 2000:158–60). **120** *helle...is*: cf. the parallel in Marlowe, *Dr Faustus* III 76 and Milton's *Paradise Lost* IV 75. *ybounde*: since the Harrowing of Hell; see 20.446, 21.57. **121a** 'The Lord said to my Lord: Sit thou at my right hand' (from the 'Messianic' Ps 109:1, alluded to at Heb 10:12–13). God speaks from a position in the west *facing* east, with the south on his right, where Christ (= *dominus meus*) sits as Lord (vs 3, 'from the womb before the day-star [*ante luciferum*] I begot thee,' has piquantly ironic aptness in this context). The south front as well as the west could sometimes be the location of cathedral tympana (as at Chartres) depicting Christ on doomsday. Once again, *dextris* has associations with the position of the just (see on 112), and with supreme authority conferred by God (Mk 14:62, Heb 1:3). **123–4** A piece of timeless popular lore used parabolically: suffering the 'cold' of earthly life will be worth it for the 'warmth' of heaven (cf. the use of similar imagery at 19.172–74).

    B 120–3 120 is to be read in the light of B 153a, which echoes it (*Bn*). **121** *but fellen*: an example of 'non-expression of the subject pronoun' of Type 1 (*MES* 140). *nyne dayes*: corresponding to the nine cosmic spheres and the nine orders of angels, from which he progressively

receded (Russell 1984:237n38). But the number of days could be distantly influenced by a tradition concerning the fall of the Titans found in Hesiod (*Sk*), which Milton may echo in *PL* VI 871, if he is not recalling **L** (see on C 120 above). **122–23** alliterate on *g* and *s*, the first a T-type, the second Type III with 'echoic' cognative counterpoint (see on *Intro* IV § 46 and Schmidt 1987:65). **125–35 125** *Holy Wryt*: 'early patristic tradition', rather than 'the Bible', a common sense of this phrase (MED s.v. *Holi Writ* n. (b)), as at 15.158, 19.288, A 10.94. The story of Lucifer's fall is based on Is 14:12 taken with Lk 10:18; but the scriptural origin of belief in demonic occupation of the elements is Eph 6:12 (other possible sources that develop the idea are Augustine, *Sunday Sermons* I 95 and Alan of Lille, *Anticlaudianus* IV 271ff [*Bn*]). These texts encouraged a view of natural disturbances as due to diabolic influence; but **L** commonly ascribes them to divine intervention for a moral purpose (e.g. 5.116–22), stressing the goodness of nature and its subjection to God (20.245–57). **Z 65** A line dropped in **A** and recalling Z 50, doubtless so as to underscore the parallel between fallen angels and false knights. *apostata*: taken up again in C 98, but in relation to knighthood (and so unlikely to be a scribal echo of **C**). *pelour*: either 'accuser' as at 20.39 or a spelling-variant for more common *pilour* 'robber', both apt names for the devil as enemy of mankind. **A 119** is substantially repeated at A 12.97 and **A 120b** echoed at A 12.98. **127** *Lucifer lowest*: since he fell from the 'highest' position (106), his sin being 'heaviest' and his condign punishment to end in the earth's centre: 'his fall was into a depth proportional to the height to which he aspired against his Maker' (Gregory, *Moralia* 34:21). **128** *ther*: the adv. partly filling in for the non-expressed subject relative *þat* ZAB (*MES* 205). **129–32** in effect translate the Latin of the Athanasian Creed quoted in Truth's pardon at 9.286–7 // (*Bn* aptly cites Jn 5:29 as the scriptural basis of this notion, as it is of the credal phrase). The references to the devil at B 7.114 // recall the present lines but are omitted in **C**. **131b** repeats 129b, showing **C** revising to a more explicitly formulaic mode. **132** re-stresses the directional symbolism of Pr 14, with assonantal wordplay on the eternity of heavenly bliss (*heuene; euere*). *Estward*: the direction from which just judgement arises (Is 41:2) and divine power is manifested (Apoc 7:2). **133** Whereas **ZAB** speak of God's 'enthronement' of the blessed, relying on Christ's promise at Apoc 3:21 (fulfilled at Apoc 20:4), **C**'s revision to make *truth* the throne of God anticipates the later view of the *heart* as the seat of Truth in Piers's allegory (7.254). The notion may be derived from texts about God judging with 'justice and truth' (Ps 95:13) and his throne as established on 'justice and judgement' (Ps 96:2), concepts close to **L**'s understanding of 'Truth' (cf. Ps 145:7 on how God 'keepeth truth for ever...executeth judgement for them that suffer wrong'). Both ideas come together suggestively in Is 16:5, on God as the merciful judge who 'shall sit upon [the throne] in truth...rendering that which is just'. **B 131** is a line already twice revised, but finally omitted in **C**. **135** The construction is elliptical: 'That there is no treasure better (than Truth).' **C** economically recalls *caritas* 82 and links *true* love with truth from the outset, obviating any possibility of misunderstanding *veritas* as sufficient. This replaces B 134–5 (Z 72–3, A 123–4), a summary recapitulating the opening of HC's homily on Truth (B 85 //).

136–44 form a transition from 'untruth' through 'truth and true love' to 'love' itself. **136** *kynde knowyng*: 'natural, instinctive knowledge or understanding.' It has been read as a vernacular equivalent to one or other scholastic or non-scholastic technical term: *synderesis* (Hort 1938:72–81), *ratio naturalis* (Erzgräber 1957:45), *sapientia* (Davlin 1981) and the *notitia intuitiva* of Ockham (Harwood 1992:9, who summarises its various non-technical senses; see id. 1983:246, and Strong 2003). But as with *kynde wit* (Pr 141–7 above) and *inwit* (6.420, 10.144 etc), a technical sense should not be insisted upon irrespective of context or even in any particular context. For the phrase does not translate any of the Latin names given to the soul or its acts at 16.199*a* (the power that 'knows' is *Mens* or 'Thouhte'). Nor is it personified as a character, and it may not have had the specificity of its congener Kynde Wit, the meaning being subtly inflected according to how, when and by whom it is used (see the helpful analysis in White 1988:41–59). Here Will disclaims direct knowledge of truth and asks to be instructed; at 7.182 Piers, having been 'instructed' by his whole way of life, will claim *kynde knowyng*. **137** The sense is: 'How truth grows up / originates, and whether it comes from / is beyond my capacities' (**C**); 'Through what power in a bodily organ it originates' (**ZAB**). The revision rules out regarding 'the faculty that knows Truth' as a corporeal power. **138–39*a*** HC seems to imply that if Will had bothered, he would have learned *how* Truth is known, by *ratio naturalis* or through the exercise of charity: '"kynde knowyng" pertains to love' (*R–H* 1951:46)). **139*a*** 'Alas, what a useless life I led in my youth'; a proverbial verse found in John Rylands Library Latin MS 394, which also contains part of the Latin at B 10.260*a* (Pantin 1930:81:114), and quoted again by Sloth at 7.54*a*. **140–2** make *kynde knowynge* a natural power (or *habitus* 'disposition' of a power) that teaches interiorly (the heart being the home of *Anima* at 10.175) what is part of divine positive law (Deut 6.5). It is here close to *synderesis*, the intuitive knowledge of the first principles of moral conduct to which the Commandments give formal expression. In action, this is *conscience*, as specified at 7.206–9, which repeat the two points made here: to love God above everything and to die rather than commit mortal sin. **142*a***

'Better it is to die than to live false' (cf. Usk, *TL* I vii. 61); new in **C** and repeated at 6.290*a*, 17.40*a*. This is not, *pace SkPe*, based on Tob 3:6 *Expedit enim mihi* mori magis quam vivere 'For it is better for me to die than to live' (which does not refer to sin), but on some proverbial utterance about death as preferable to an evil life, such as *Melius est mori quam vivere moleste* (Walther 38183, cited Alf*Q* 36), modified to yield an alliterating verse-line in Latin. Readiness to lose one's (earthly) life rather than commit a sin that 'kills' the soul ('the wages of sin is death' [Rom 6:23]) was standard doctrine, as in Piers's repetition of HC's teaching at VII 208–9. Here perfect obedience to the will of God, not formal profession of belief, is affirmed as the best evidence of 'treuth' (cf. Mt 7:21–4). **A 133–4** The tighter, more logical order indicates revision of Z 82–4. **B 147** is omitted in **C** with loss of an effective 'rich' rhyme. **A 137–8** The quasi-minstrel character of Will here is eliminated in the later versions' graduated critique of the minstrel class as a whole.

145–69 offer a direct treatment of love as exemplified in the life and death of Christ. Love of God having been described as 'truth' in living, Truth-as-God is now made to vouch for the healing efficacy of love.

145–53 145 *triacle*: a word derived from Lat *tyriaca* (< Gk *theriakon*) and denoting a supposed antidote to snake-bite made from the powdered body of a dead snake (a notion figuratively expounded at 20.153–59). The idea of a virtue as a *triacle* against sin is anticipated in *Ayenbite of Inwit* 144/28. **146** *souerayne salue*: foreshadowing 22.373, where the phrase refers to contrition (understood as sorrow for sin that arises from love of God). **147–53** The first instance of L's *stylus altus*, introduced in the **B** revision and to be used later in describing the Passion (7.122ff, 20.8ff). **B 149** *seene*: leaving no visible trace of the wound of sin, an idea spelled out in B 14.95–6 on the effect of Satisfaction in Penance. *spice*: quite possibly 'species [of remedy]' (*Sk*) rather than 'spice' (see MED s.v. n (2)), since *triacle* was not made from plants (a confusion eliminated in **C**); but a possible link with the 'plant' image is noted by *Pe*. *R–H* 46 relate the *triacle* to the *unctio* of I Jn 2:27, which Bede (*PL* 93:96) glosses as *Dei charitas*, an interpretation supported by **C**'s substitution of *salue* for *spice*. But the lines may allude to patristic allegorisation of the brazen serpent the sight of which healed those bitten by snakes in the wilderness (Num 21:8–9) as Christ, who 'became a serpent to provide a *tyriaca* against the devil's poison' (Hugh of St Victor, cited by Smith 1966:21–34). **B 150–1** develop from A 136, the added Moses reference being subsequently omitted in **C**, perhaps to underscore the uniqueness of the NT revelation of divine love as *agape* (though *Bn,* citing Mk 12:29–31, brings out L's sense of the continuity of Christian with Mosaic and pre-Mosaic teaching). **147** One of the poem's best-known lines, in this 'definitional' form giving due prominence to the idea even more strikingly than in **B** (the rich complex of imagery here is fully explored by Smith and by Kean 1965:349–63). Love is to be seen as both the chief theological virtue (I Cor 13:13) and the 'virtue' in the *plonte* (on the grounds for reading this in all versions, see *TN*). **148** Typical word-play (of the *lucus a non lucendo* type) on *heuene* and *heuy*, with // **B** ironically echoing B 120 (the 'gravity' of Lucifer's sin of *self*-love). Here the heavenly virtue paradoxically becomes 'light' only *after* taking on the weight that enables it to act in the material domain as Creator-become-Creature. **149** *yȝoten*: see MED s.v. *yeten* v. 3, 7b(b). The revision (see *TN* on the issues here) is from an image of *eating* to one of being *embodied*: earth = flesh, as in the allegory of 10.130; and cf. Gregory, *Sunday Sermons*1.121 ('The King of heaven has taken into himself the flesh of our earth' [*Bn*]), both fitting the metaphor of love as a plant. The latter image is evidently to be associated with the great Messianic prophecy of Isaiah 53:2: 'he shall grow up as a tender plant, and as a root out of a thirsty ground', with perhaps an allusion to 'the leaves of the tree [of life]...for the healing of the nations' (Apoc 22:2). But Adams 1991:12–13 plausibly traces the phrase *plantam pacis* to the Septuagint reading of Ezech 34:29 as given in *VL* versions (where Vg has *germen nominatum* 'bud of renown'); this appears in, e.g., Augustine's Sermon 47 on Ezechiel in *Sermones de vetere testamento* (*CC* 41:601). Heffernan 1984 relates the imagery to two well-known Latin hymns *Rorate celi* and *Crux fidelis* associated respectively with Christmas and Passiontide. **152** The figure of the divine word as a piercing needle may derive ultimately from Heb 4:12 ('For the word of God is...more *piercing* than any two-edged sword...and is a discerner of the thoughts and intents of the heart'), with some echo of *wisdom* (equated in patristic thought with the Divine Word) as 'subtile...more active than all active things' (Wisd 7:22–4). The 'armour' and 'walls' symbolise the resistance of the human will armed with pride (a chivalric metaphor that will undergo characteristically paradoxical transformation in 20.21–4 and its climax 80–7). *Bn* finds an allusion to the Resurrection in B 158 (the 'armour' that of the soldiers outside Christ's 'high-walled' tomb) and to the Ascension in B 156. But the passage seems to be overwhelmingly about the Incarnation (*lyhter* in context = 'easier to handle' / 'more cheerful'), only prospectively concerned with the Passion (see above), and not at all with the events of Easter and after. When Christ breaks through Hell's gates he is seen by his adversaries not as healing Love but as conquering Truth (20.325, 362–65).

154–60 Another transitional passage between the lyrically heightened accounts of Christ's incarnation and the crucifixion. 'Love' is an intermediary between God and his people, as at 20.184, and is an oblique nature-name for 'Jesus the mediator' of Heb 12:24 who is also 'God the judge of all' of vs. 23 (cf. further 18.202 on the Second Person of the Trinity as *mene*). But its reference is equivocal, since it also signifies the specific virtue to be found in man's heart. As *Bn* finely has it, 'Christ' who 'delivers judgement and assesses the fine...is the perfect king who clothes *nudum ius* with *pietas*'. **155** *mayre*: the choice of image perhaps reflecting the growing political influence of the Lord Mayor of London in the late 14th century. **157** *mercement*: a payment for pardon made to the king when a transgressor had been put 'in mercy' as a result of his offence (AlfG s.v.); the analogy is with the debt to God that man incurs through sin. The implicit play on 'mercy' and 'amercement' is later made explicit when Piers urges the knight to treat his tenants with mercy (8.37); Christ's justice is to be made the model for that of earthly lords. Mary (denoted by the nature-name Mercy at 7.287) herself becomes man's *mene* or mediatrix for grace at 9.347. **158–60** HC resumes the lesson begun at 140 and elaborates the oracular B 165 // into the triad of nature, heart and divine power (this last 'appropriated' to the First Person of the Trinity as at 18.34). The sense is roughly: God's power (*myhte* 158) operates in and through the heart, the seat of love, making it thus possible for man to 'know' God by virtue of the (created) nature he receives from (uncreated) Nature and the (recreated) nature he now sacramentally shares with God by adoption, following the Word's becoming incarnate. The syntactic balance of 161b and 163b reveals how God's creative and redemptive action are to be seen as continuous. On the relation of these lines to I Jn 4:7 see Davlin 1981:12. **159** *hed; heye welle*: 'chief source / origin', 'deep spring'; with perhaps some punning allusion to the contrast and complementarity of the intellectual and the affective. In order to 'know' God, man's 'heart' (in the Biblical sense of 'deepest spiritual self') must *be* his 'head'.

161–82a 162–63 echo I Jn 4:14, as *Bn* notes. **165–66** Two constructions are run together: Christ's beseeching God *for* mercy on those who crucify him, and *as* Mercy to have pity (cf. again the *pietas* of Pr 155 and comment on 154–57 above). This scene adumbrates the account at 20.89–94 of divine *pitee* shown in healing the blind Longinus without his asking: the allusion in pl. *hem* of 169b (Lk 23:34) is to all the executioners, but primarily to him. On the Passion theme in *PP*, see Bennett 1982:85–112 and Schmidt 1983[2]. **170–1** The injunction to the rich is to follow God's twofold 'examples' of power and mercy: their 'might' in the law courts is only a faint image of God's, so if *he* is humble, they should be all the more so. **171** *mote*: 'argue in court' (as at A 4.118), rather than 'cite, summon to court' (*Bn*), a sense not illustrated in MED s.v. **Z 100** 'Though you have charge of the laws, administer them [towards the poor] in a spirit of love'.

Despite being omitted in **A**, the line seems authentic in its use of the rare Type IIa and in its sense. Thus *loue-lawes*, a phrase used with a different sense at 17.130, here = *ius + pietas*, the key-ideas added in B Pr 135 and closely linked with the ultimate source of B Pr 137–38, which is that of Z 1.101//. **173a** 'For with the same measure that you shall mete withal, it shall be measured to you again' (Lk 6:38), repeated at 11.235a, B 11.226a (the first half of the vs is quoted at 195 // below). **174–8** HC sees simple obedience to the Commandments as insufficient for justification (*meryte* 178) without kindness arising from a love based on humility (cf. *meke* 171). **177** contains a favourite polysemantic pun (see Schmidt 1987:134–8): *good* (wealth) must be used *goodliche* (generously) in recognition of the 'metaphysical' affinity obtaining between the material and spiritual, which both derive from God. **179–82** Formal religion not finding expression in active charity counts as worth no more than a formal chastity untested by temptation. **179** *Malkyn*: diminutive of Mary or Matilda, the type-name of a homely lower-class girl (Cassidy 1948:52–3; Fletcher 1986:19–20). Chaucer's *Malkyns maydenhede* (*CT* II 30), perhaps ironically alluding to this line, implies a wanton rather than an ugly girl no one desires. *wham*: the sole instance in *PP* of the prepositionless oblique form of *who* (making the referent Malkyn), a small indication that **C** is later than **B**. **180** *gentele*: an alliteratively convenient epithet (as with Job at 11.21, 13.14; John at 21.266). **181** *feet*: both 'feet' and 'deed' (see *TN*). **182** *ded...nayl*: the earliest instance of this proverbial expression after *WPal* 628. *ded, dedes*: illustrating the contrastive *annominatio* seen at 148. **182a** '[For even as the body without the spirit is dead: so also] faith without works is dead' (Js 2:26, also 2:20); the basis for Dowel as good works that justify (all of Js 2:14–26 is relevant). **183–203 A** revises **Z**'s order, **B** retains **A**, and **C** revises anew, removing the repeat of the 'motto' line B 188/194 to produce a tighter argument, generally echoing I Cor 13:1–3. **184** *laumpe*: an image derived from traditional commentaries on Mt 25:13. These include Chrysostom (Homily 78 on St Matthew), Augustine (Sermo 93:5) and the *Summa* of Frère Lorens, whose source might have been *Castitas sine charitate, lampas sine oleo* from St Bernard's Epistle 42 (*PL* 182:817), a text **L** probably knew (Schmidt 1983[1]:108–10; see also *Fasciculus Morum* [*FM*] III.8, cit. Wenzel in Alf*C* 166n). **191** *yhasped*: an image seemingly of the cleric being fastened by lock and chain to greed and shut up inside a treasure chest. **193** *luther ensaumple*: contrasted with Christ's *ensaumple* at 167; the first of many attacks on covetous clerics. **195** 'Give, and it shall be given to you' (Lk 6:38), in context preceding the second half of the verse quoted at 173a. 195b completes the Gospel injunction from Js 1:5 ('God who giveth to all men'), possibly suggested

by the verbal echo of Lk 6.38 in the last phrase of that verse (*et dabitur ei*). **196** *lok of loue...grace*: elliptical for 'love is the lock which (when opened by acts of charity) unlocks also God's grace (for the giver)'. The image is resumed at 7.250–52 // and seems indirectly indebted to Js 2:13, a passage directly recalled at 19.215–52 //. The possible sense 'river-barrier' for *lok* (Davlin 2001:76 citing MED s.v. n.(2), 2(a)), yields a different figure that compares interestingly with *Pearl* 607–8. **197** *acombred*: taking up the image of sin at 190, and ultimately derived from that of one's 'iniquities...as a heavy burden' (Ps 37:5). **198–9** are progressively revised, save that 199 remains unaltered in **AB**. **198** *leche of lyf*: looking back to the medicinal imagery of 145 but also, insofar as 'love' personified = Christ, forward to his rôle as healer of mankind at 19.95 (and cf. 20.403–4). **199** *graffe*: echoing the *plonte* of 147 and foreshadowing the tree of charity in 18.11–15. *way*: making plain the sense of *gate* in // **ZAB**, so as to suggest that the relevant source is not Mt 7:13–14 (*Pe*), which speaks of the *narrow* way, but OT texts about the *direct* way and *right* path of truth that is also the way of love (Pss 25:12, 26:11) and Christ's reference to himself as sole 'way' to God (Jn 14:6). **200** *this textes*: what she has been saying generally, or specifically the texts about *tresore* at 48–9, 82–3. **201** concludes the sermon whose theme was enunciated at 135, though the force of directly restating B 135 at B 207 is lessened in consequence of that line's revision in **C**. **202–03** *Loue hit*; *loue is*: making explicit what may be overlooked in **ZAB**, that as the inner meaning of truth, love should have (and be) the last word. The literal sense of HC's valediction is '*Love* Truth; I cannot remain to teach you what *love* is [because only experience can do that].' *Lette*: the word used in HC's second farewell in A 2.31 (*om* **BC**).

Passus II

PASSUS II divides into: (i) a tableau-like opening in which Will sees LADY MEDE and HOLY CHURCH explains who she is (1–52), followed by a dramatic sequence in five movements: (ii) the enfeoffment of Mede by SIMONY and CIVIL (53–115); (iii) THEOLOGY's demand for the King to decide if her marriage is lawful (116–154); (iv) the journey of the parties to London (155–99); (v) the KING's intervention (200–16); and (vi) the villains' desertion of Mede (217–52). This ends part one of Mede's 'Trial' (the second 'act' of Vision One), which the next passus completes.

(i) 1–7 form a *transition* between the discourse of HC and the 'Trial' of Mede. **2** *for...heuene*: 'for the love of Mary in heaven'; on this 'split group genitive', see *MES* 78–9; and on the uninflected form of *Marie* as showing the influence of Latin genitives, ibid. p. 72. **3** *barn; rode*:

the juxtaposition of 'crib and cross', Christ's Incarnation and Passion, anticipates the startling image of the bloody babe at 19.86–90 //, B 17.123 (no //). **4** *craft*: continuing the stress in B 1.139 // (revised **C**) on a power or capacity through which to know truth and (now) falsehood. The answer to Will's request is a 'vision', since he is instructed to look; and this enables 'falsehood,' an abstract idea, to become visible as a personification, *Fals*. **5** *left*: bodily goods are assigned to the left, spiritual to the right in St Bernard's exegesis of Ps 90:7 (Vasta 1965:77; and cf. Prov 3:16, though this refers to wisdom). The left is contextually the *north*, since Will is looking east (*Bn*); for the north as source of evil and destruction, cf. Jer 4:6, 6:1, Ezech 4:4 and see on 1.112 above). *he* (*a* **Z**): a pronoun pl. in **Z** (so *they* 10) but clearly sg. in **ABC**, causing surprise; but a plurality of 'false' persons appear because 'their name is legion'. **6** *Fauel*: an OF name (< Lat. *fabella*), here first used in English (see MED s.v.); perhaps derived from the *Roman de Fauvel* (see Yunck 1963:221–6). In **ZA** it is almost a synonym for False (though for *hise* the immediate antecedent may be meant) but the two are better seen as distinct, Favel being the 'enchanting' flatterer (see 43 below). *Lyare*: the antithesis of Sothnesse (24), but given a much more active rôle (see 225ff). **7** The repetition of the b-half at 19.22a describes the just. **Z 10** is superfluous, even if 10a did not echo Z 2a (and recur at Z 6.29 //) or 10b repeat 8b; but the repetition at Z 31 may explain the deletions here from **A**.

8–18 The description of the 'woman' is continuously revised, **B** stressing the jewels (perhaps recalling Dame Richesse in *RR* 1053–1108 = *Rom* 1032–1128 [*Bn*]), **C** her wealth, with fivefold rhetorical *repetitio* of *riche*. **11a** A rhetorical device perhaps suggested by Apoc 17:4–5 (*inaurata auro*). **11b** hints at what **A** alone actually suggests (*perreiȝe* 12), an allusion to Alice Perrers, Edward III's mistress (see Huppé 1939:44–52, Bennett 1943[1] and for a recent interesting but tendentious account Trigg 1998:5–29); ZA 18/14 lends support. **15** In rejecting details of clothing, **C** loses the symbolism of scarlet, a colour suggesting the whore of Babylon in Apoc 17:4–5. The emphatic rhyme at 14/15 is a device anticipated in the assonance of A 6.81/2. **Z 19** *worthely*: repeating Z 2.12, which is revised at A 2.8. **B 13–16** *double manere*: the light (male) and dark (female) sapphires (Evans and Serjeantson 1933:101). *Orientals*: either the *margaritis* 'pearls' of Apoc 17:4 (cf. the adj. in Chaucer *LGW* Pr F 221) or sapphires (MED s.v.). *ewages...destroye*: referring to the supposed 'virtue' of the diamond, though here the gem intended is the beryl or the sea-coloured sapphire (see MED s.v., *AMA* 212–15 and *Rom* 1086–90 on gems that protect against 'venim'). *engreyned*: dyed fast in scarlet 'grain' (cochineal dye: cf. *coccino* in Apoc 17:4). **A 14** *quen queyntere*: 'queen more elegantly dressed' / 'harlot more cunning' (see MED s.vv. *quene* n. (2), 1 (b),

queinte adj. 1(f), (c): a masterly line, but dropped perhaps because no longer topical. **B 16** *reed gold*: the reddish tinge being imparted by copper used as a hardening alloy (cf. *Sir Orfeo*150). **16** revises **B** to stress the attractiveness of riches to Will. The woman indeed suggests cupidity (*Bn*; cf. 1.66 above), but the imagery more directly evokes the Pride of Life and by association Lust, as indicated by *raueschede*, a word with negative overtones used metaphorically in connexion with Fortune and excessive learning (11.168, 294) as well as literally of rape (4.47). **17** 'Whose wife she might be' (*?or* 'be about to become'). A woman's status depended on her husband's, hence the form of the enquiry. The revised line may still allude, if obliquely, to Alice Perrers, who in 1376 married William of Windsor, the king's deputy in Ireland.

19–52 *Holy Church's account of Mede* provides a moral frame within which to view the following action. **19** *Mede*: signifying both 'reward' in the neutral sense and 'dishonest reward' (e.g. payment for wrongdoing). *þe mayde*: MEDE (as plain 'reward') is technically a virgin and could remain chaste if she married Leute (see on Pr 149) but will become a harlot if she marries False, because her (married) name will then signify 'bribery'. HC implies that the neutral sense has been compromised in the real world and that Mede can now only be regarded as corrupt: she represents metonymically *tresor of erthe* contaminated by wrongful desire. Her clothing marks her as antithetical to the Bride of Christ and as HC's rival for man's loyalty. *Pe* points to the disintegrating effect of the new mercantile capitalist values upon traditional feudal society and the problems they raised for the older social morality, referring to Tawney 1926:14–55; but there is little direct treatment of economic issues as in *WW*. Discussions of Mede include Mitchell 1956:174–93; Yunck 1963; Benson 1980; Morgan 1987[1]; Simpson 1990:43–9; Eaton 1991; Carlson 1991; Burrow 1993[1]:34–50 and especially 2005:116, citing Noonan 1984:275 in support of his argument that Mede represents not *pecunia* 'money' (= coin) but *munera* 'bribery' (i.e. 'goods or money offered as improper inducements'). **21** *han to kepe*: taken unconvincingly in *MES* 531 in the sense 'be obliged to'; rather, the lords 'have the laws in their control', to watch over and admininster. **22** *kynges court*: the court of King's Bench, which heard cases concerning the Crown and trespasses against the King's peace. *comune court*: the court of Common Pleas, hearing most civil actions between subjects (see Alf*G* s.v. *court*, and Harding 1973). **23** *palays*: at Avignon, the seat of the papacy from 1309 until 1378, when Urban VI decided to remain in Rome; from June 1379 the seat of the anti-popes throughout the Great Schism. It was regularly attacked by satirists as a centre of luxurious living and clerical venality. **24** *Sothnesse*: the principle of truth(fulness) and esp. veridicity (so at 19.283); a 'nature-name' for God at B 18.282 and (in the form *Sothfastnesse*) for the Son at B 16.186. In the light of 31, the divine referent seems contextually more apt here than the transient personification of 2.200, A 4.138, Z 4.50 (see further on Z 45). *bastard*: illicitly begotten, *sc.* by the devil upon an unnamed mother (see Alf*G* 14 s.v. on the term's legal significance). *Bn* aptly notes antipathy to bastards voiced at 5.65, 71; 9.168 ff; but his doubts about Fals being Mede's father in **B** are unwarranted. However, since the Fals she is to marry is the devil's 'son', Wrong's 'incarnation' on earth (B 41) and hence her (half)-brother, the proposed union is incestuous, as *Bn* allows (see further Tavormina 1995:7n19). **C** clarifies the relation between Fauel and Fals, making the former Mede's father (25) and the one who persuades her to marry Fals (43). **A 20 / Z 24** *to wroþerhele manye*: 'to the harm / misfortune of many'. The first element of *wroþerhele* signifies 'anger' (hence = 'evil'), but **L** seems to have supposed an etymological link with *writhe* 'twist' (see 6.66 and cf. *croked* at 29 below). This archaic word (not found after 1400) returns once at 15.301 //. **26 C** revises to stress how the devil tells truth to pervert truth. **B**, as *Bn* notes, may allude to his lying temptation of Eve, a theme fully developed in 20.326, 376–81 //; but the direct reference is to Lucifer's fall to earth caused by his 'first' lie (B 1.118 and 18.310–12; B 26b is distantly recalled by the new lines on liars in C 20.350–58, esp. 353b). **27** *is manered*: 'takes her (moral) character' (for the phrase, cf. B 15.415). *of kynde*: 'about natural relationships' (in both human beings and plants); on *kynde* in *PP* see the wide-ranging discussion in White 1988 and Zeeman 2000. **27a** 'Like father, like daughter [son **B**]'. The **B** wording is identical with the opening phrase of the Athanasian Creed's 7th clause (Alf*Q* 36), giving an effect of mordant irony here; but **C** revises away from the credal to the proverbial form (Whiting F 80). The primary source, which *Pe* aptly cites, is Ezech 16:44 *sicut mater, ita et filia eius,* where unfaithful Jerusalem is denounced as *meretrix* (in **L** it is Mede's *father* who is evil). **28–9** 'virtually translate' Mt 7:16 (Tavormina 1995:11) except its first clause 'a fructibus eorum *cognoscetis eos*', where the 'fruits' are their works (the italicised words are apparently rendered at 47a). Also important is Mt 7:18: '*Non potest* arbor bona *malos fructus facere*,' where the good tree corresponds by implication to HC here. (The separateness of the purified apocalyptic Church personified in HC is later to be brought out in the application of this tree-image to the humanly flawed Church Militant, and specifically to its clergy, at 16.246–53). **29a** '[The] good tree brings forth good fruit' (Mt 7:17); the verse's wider context has relevance, notably the warning against false prophets in vs. 15, a notion linked with the 'falsehood' theme here. **30** *a bettere*: i.e. Christ, the 'father' of the Church which became the 'mother' of his 'children', all Christians (cf. 18.205–7). **31–3 (B 29–31)** This striking

figure provides the 'true' theological pattern of which the Mede-Fals relationship is an evil inversion. **B** less audaciously makes God the Father also the parent of HC, who is to marry Mercy (= the Spouse Christ). *BnSk* take 'mercy' B 31 as HC's dowry, while Tavormina 1995:12n26 understands *marie wiþ myselue* as 'with which to marry myself'. But the reading here preferred (which *Bn* notes) seems likelier on grounds of sense, and is supported by its other appearance at A 10.154, where the phrasal verb with reflexive means 'be married to' (MED s.v. *marien* v. 2 (c) cites both instances). **31** *Filius Dei*: 'the Son of God', a common NT phrase but perhaps with specific allusion to Mt 27:54 // Jn 19:34, where the moment of Christ's death is 'conterminous with the "birth" of HC' (Alf*Q* 36). **32** *neuere...lauhede*: a tradition recorded in the widely read *Vita Christi* (II xvii:45) of the C14th Carthusian Ludolf of Saxony (*Pe*); the ultimate Scriptural source may be the 'woe' addressed to the worldly prosperous who 'laugh' in Lk 6:25. The connection of lying with laughing may echo Gen 18:15, where Sarah denies that she laughed, a link that would have been closer still had **L**'s original verb-forms been *leiȝede...leyhede* (cf. the *liȝere / liȝen* pun in A 25). **33** *ducchesse*: i.e. 'sovereign duchess', a phrase avoiding possible confusion with the Marian title 'Queen of Heaven'. **33–5 C** distinguishes sharply between the heavenly and earthly church but stresses, in the first of many such passages of wordplay, that faithful believers will receive both earthly sufficiency and final grace. **B**'s radical contrast between the values of 'mercy' and 'meed' is formulaically reiterated at B 11.133=C 13.142. *good...good*: on this favourite wordplay of **L**'s see Schmidt 1987:34–8. **B 34** 'Whoever loves bribery / accepts Mede in marriage': allegorically, gives himself to her so that they become as one. **37** *here loue*: either a possessive genitive ('her love [of him]') or, more probably, an objective genitive 'his love of her'. *trewe charite / Caritatis*: **B**'s Latin is inflected (genitive), as elsewhere in macaronic staves (e.g. ablative after *with* at 7.116). That it denotes something more specific or technical than 'charity' (Alf*Q* 36–7) seems doubtful, as **C**'s translation with added adjective spells out its standard theological meaning. **38** *That...hevene*: in the context 'charity' (cf. I Cor 13:13, Col 3:14), though it is truth that Ps 14:2–3 commends in answer to the question in vs. 1. **39** *Dauyd*: King David (d. *c.* 970 BC), traditionally the author of the entire Book of Psalms (on the importance of the psalms in *PP* see Wurtele 2003, and on their general significance in the period Kuczynski 1995). *the doumbe*: an unparalleled usage; the Psalter, being a book, is without vocal speech and therefore *cannot* lie, though it is 'spiritually eloquent' (but at 20.240 the character Book ['the Bible'] is made to speak). **39a** 'Lord, who shall dwell in thy tabernacle? [...He that works justice...that speaks truth in his heart]' (Ps 14:1). In the Latin of the answer *Qui...operatur iustitiam*; *Qui loquitur veritatem*, the two nouns correspond to the dual senses of ME *trewthe* (see on Pr 15). **B 37** A possible T-type line, closer to the Latin source (*Bn*). **40a** 'He that hath not...taken bribes against the innocent' (Ps 14:5); indirectly indicating a negative action (refraining from bribes) where // B 37 (translating Ps 14:2–3) affirms a positive, if general one. **41–2** *Mede ymaried*: on the episode see esp. Tavormina 1995:1–47 and Fowler 2003, ch. 2. **B 40** *mansed sherewe*: applied to Mede at B 4.160, just as **C** makes its *Fikel-tonge* the attribute of another character, Fauel (25 above). *Bn* finds an allusion to Ps 5:11, quoted in Rom 3:13; the seminal Ps 14.3b is more likely (cf. C 26a, which inverts Ps 14:3a). **43** *Fauel*: Mede's father (25), who has planned her marriage to one with the attributes of the Antichrist (see on 21.220 below), being begotten of the devil as Christ is of God. The passage is recalled at the end of the poem, where Fauel's distinctive quality is embodied in a friar, B 42b being repeated at B 20.379, but the echo at C 22.379 is less direct because of the revision in 43b. **44** retains **B**'s revision, removing the pregnant pun on *Liʒeris* and *liʒen* that in **ZA** brought together verbal and sexual 'fickleness'. *this lady*: sarcastic politeness; the echo at 53 bringing out the 'bastard' character of Mede's position and claim (24 above). **45** (pre)-echoes B 11.410 / C 13.221. **46** *tomorwe*: a purely internal passage of time, events continuing without break at 54 // after HC's departure. The *division of this first dream*, introduced in **B**, serves to shift the viewpoint from the perspective of the Tower to that of the Field. **49–50** warn against premature, hence possibly ineffectual criticism. HC's reference to an ideal time when justice will prevail cautiously anticipates Leute's own sentiments at 12.39. **52** *consience*: 'conscience' in **C**, 'guilty conscience' (*Bn*) in **B**. The line, ending with the name the speech began with (which could be capitalised), conceivably warns against making gain out of criticising others' faults. **ZA 35a / 31a** HC's near-repetition of A 1.183 is cut in **B** doubtless as otiose.

(ii) 53–4 are transitional lines introducing a (strictly unnecessary) reference to Will's sleeping state that is perhaps the germ of the 'inner-dream' device developed first in B 11.5–6 (*aslepe...metels*). **53** *lyggynge aslepe*: this unusual reference to being asleep *within* the dream (absent from **ZA**) divides the vision of HC from that of MEDE and effects a shift from a world of supernal reality to one of sordid actuality.

55–66 56b–57 shift the focus of B 55 // from the parties to the parts of the country (north / south, east / west) or, possibly, of society (rich / poor), **C**'s change taking account of the B 56 repetition (added to **ZA** and not wholly apt here) of B Pr 18 (B 56b is re-used in a transitional line inserted as C Pr 219b). **A 38–9** are echoed in *Death and Liffe* 55–6: 'There was neither hill nor holte nor haunt

there beside / But itt was plaunted fful of people, the plaine and the roughe'. **58** *knyghtes*: generally exempted from criticism by **L** and treated sympathetically when driven to pecuniary extremes (see 6.250). **A 43** *of cuntres*: suggesting perhaps local landowners not actually of knightly rank. **59** *sysores*: jurors of the assise, whose function at this time was more to give true testimony about the facts as known to them and the character of the accused than to evaluate the sworn evidence of witnesses (whence their susceptibility to financial pressure). *sompnores*: those who summoned defendants to trial in the church courts for offences against morality as well as marital, testamentary and personal property cases. They were notorious for taking bribes or exercising blackmail. *shyryues*: the king's chief administrative officers in the shires (see Baldwin 1981[1]:28–9). **60** *Bydels*; *bailifs*: manorial officials, the one summoning tenants to the manor court, the other representing the lord's interests there. *brokeres*: dealers in business or trade. **61** *Vorgoers*: purveyors who commandeered or bought up in advance goods, materials and labour for the king or, earlier, for a great lord, an activity forbidden in 1362 (Baldwin 1981[1]:43). *vitalers*: especially suspected at this period of dishonest practices in retailing (cf. 3.79–89). *voketes...Arches*: barristers practising in the Archbishop of Canterbury's provincial court at St Mary 'le Bow' (so called from the arches supporting the steeple; on the Court of Arches see Woodcock 1952:6–14). Like all lawyers, they were suspected of taking *munera super innocentem* (Ps 14:5). The passage will be echoed at 22.136–9. **62** recalls the rodent assembly at Pr 165. **63** *Simonye*: personifying the sin (named after Simon Magus in Ac 8:18–24) of buying and selling spiritual benefits (e.g. absolution), church offices, benefices or, in an extended sense, 'any divine gift intended for the common good (such as justice, knowledge, health)' (AlfG 145, citing 9.55). *BnPe*'s view of him as specifically a canon lawyer in collusion with his colleague (a civil lawyer) fits but does not impose itself, given the wide reference of the name. Salter 1967 [1988]:158–69 argues for **L**'s indebtedness to the early C14th poem *The Simonie*, preserved in the Auchinleck MS (ed. Embree & Urquhart, also Wright 1839, Robbins 1959). *Syuile*: Civil Law, the form of the *ius gentium* operative in England, mainly in the conciliar or prerogative courts, 'supplementary jurisdictions [of the crown] intended to provide remedies where the common law could not' (Baker 1971:50). Their law and procedure, deriving from Roman jurisprudence, resembled the Canon Law of the consistory (episcopal) courts and all subordinate tribunals of the universal papal jurisdiction, canon lawyers having first to undergo a training in civil law at the universities and civilians to be examined in canon law (Boyle 1964:136–8, 141–7). If *Simonye* here personifies '(corrupt) Canon law(yers)' it is because Mede's case involves marriage, a question for the church courts. Gilbert (1981:57) identifies *Syuile* as 'both canon and civil law' and finds a 'near identity of Civil and Simony' (see further Barratt 1982). Tavormina's interpretation of these two figures as 'metaphorical equivalents to the local priest' (1995:13n) presses the allegory too closely. *contrees*: juries drawn from the inhabitants of a judicial district (MED s.v. 6b). **66** *brokor*: Fauel arranges Mede's marriage; the arranged marriage is a practice in society that is criticised at 16.104–9 //, as *Bn* notes, because often done *for coueytise of catel* on the part of the bride's father (see Tavormina 1995:17–18). **B 66** *enjoyned*: 'joined in wedlock'; the earliest recorded use in this sense (cf. 2.150 below).

  Z 40–57 / A 35–47 A omits Z 40–2 as partly redundant (Z 40 re-appears at 119). In Z 40–1 the comma after *fayle* could be omitted to make *sette* prolatively dependent on *fayle*. In Z 42 Civil's rôle is to *sese* 'take legal possession of' (MED s.v. *seisen* v. 1a) the lands that Fauel (her father) and Fals (her husband-to-be) are jointly to enfeoff her with (44), a jointure in lieu of a dowry. The A revision, dispensing with Z's use of Civil, simplifies the procedure but with some loss of clarity, *chartres* 35 not *londus* becoming the antecedent of *halden* and the sense elliptical: 'charters [of entitlement to those lands that are to be granted].' Z 45 disrupts the continuity and may have been cut so as to defer till A 150 (= Z 159) the introduction of a figure who remains a cipher (for the multiple referents of SOTHNESSE see on 24). This passage of rhetorical *amplificatio* that slows the action is reminiscent of *WW* 138–96; revised in A with omission of Z 47, it is omitted in **B**. **47** *lesewe*: see MED s.v. *leswe* n. (c). **56 (A 47)** *meble*: the earliest uses cited in MED s.v. *moeble* n. are from **L**, but OED (s.v. *moble* a. and sb.) records several from the earlier C14th. **A 48 (Z 57)** *þe fyn is arered*: 'the fine is levied'. The *fyn* was a final agreement concerning property (rights) or the vesting of lands in a feoffee based on an agreed legal fiction of a supposed dispute between the parties requiring a material settlement (see AlfG 59 s.v. *fyn*).

67–108 69 *chartre*: a deed conveying landed property; in the allegory the 'territories' of the capital sins. Possible sources are pseudo-Grosseteste's poem on the marriage of the devil's daughters (Meyer 1900:54–72) and the early C14th *Roman de Fauvel* Bk II (Cornelius 1932). *Bn* considers A's simple allegory slightly obscured in **BC**; however, the sins named in, e.g. 85–7, are not 'miscellaneous' but aptly specify 'locations' within particular symbolic regions such as the *chastel* of 89. The outline sketch of the Deadly Sins here will be elaborated dramatically in VI–VII and analytically in 16.43–96 (e.g. Gluttony at 97 is a summary foretaste of 6.349–432, 16.71–8). **70** *Gyle*: personifying a chief quality of the devil (see 20.377ff). **75–6** *vp lyking of*: 'at the will / pleasure of'. *Mede / mede*: the rich rhyme bringing out the relation between 'desire'

and 'bribery'; the explicit moral warning has dramatically ironic force coming from the vicious speaker (in **C** Simony). **76** *this*: i.e. the enactments of the charter (Tavormina 1995:24). *laste mede*: presumably alluding to the Last Judgement, though 79ff adhere to **B**'s pattern and do not recur to this theme. **78a** 'Let it be known to all present and to come', the standard opening of a charter of conveyance (AlfG 140). The device parodies the literary 'charter of Christ' of which Woolf (in Hussey 1969:57) cites a version from *c.* 1350 (and see further Spalding 1914:28–30, Keen 2002:27–49). **L** may also have had in mind the satirical form of the devil's *lettre* (83; cf. 107 below) such as the *Epistola Luciferi* of 1352 (Russell 1984:87–9), an ME version of which is discussed by Raymo in Pearsall and Waldron 1969:233–48. **80–1** Mede's allegorical marriage recalls the mercenary union criticised at 16.109; for the phrasing cf. 11.13, 18.13. **A 59 (Z 67)** *for...riche*: 'at all times, in all circumstances' (cf. B 102 // below); an ironic echo of the marriage service. Suggestions of the marriage ceremony (the reading of the *dotalium*) are found in this scene by Tavormina (1995:23). **84** *Pruyde...dispice*: the opposition between these two is developed at 16.57–9. **85; 87** For the phrasing cf. 16.361, 9.334. **88** *Enuye and Yre*: closely linked for **L**, the first having its broader sense of 'hostile ill-will' or *invidia* (MED s.v. 1(a)) as well as its narrower modern sense (ib. 3). The absence from **ZA** of a separate figure of Wrath after Envy in the Sins' confessions later may reflect an earlier view of 'Envy' as covering both sins, who appear effectively as a 'joint-sin' at Z 5.91 and the 'gloss' on this at 94. **90** *Coueytise*: generally 'greed', specifically 'desire for (obtaining) possessions' (cf. *auaryce* 91). *consenteth*: cited by MED as the only example of the sense '(agree to) concede something' (s.v. 2b(b)). **91** *vsurye*: lending money or goods at (exorbitant) interest (*usura*), which was not permitted to Christians, though loans (*mutua*) with agreed 'compensation' for any loss arising to the lender were (Gilchrist 1969:64–5, 68). See AlfG 162–3 s.v. for valuable refs. and for the distinction between bodily (or literal) and spiritual (or metaphorical) usury (on which cf. also on B 7.80–1a below). *auaryce*: though sometimes 'greed' generally, here specifically 'miserliness', greed *in* possession rather than *to* possess (= *coueytise*); see MED s.v. (a) and (b) and esp. *CT* X 744–5. **Z 71** *cheuysawnses*: 'trading in money or goods for profit, esp. by devious means, to circumvent the law (e.g. against usury)' (AlfG 27). In the context and in the light of 6.252 // B 5.245, illicit lending at interest would seem to be involved. **92** *bargaynes*: compacts or 'deals' setting out what each party is to give or take. *brocages*: business transactions, esp. by a third party (AlfG 13, 20), as in arranged marriages for profit (16.107–9); Fauel is a *brokor* 66. **93** *lordschip*: 'estate (belonging to a lord)', but with a hint that lechery is especially a vice of the higher classes (cf. 3.57, 22.90); see MED s.v. 4 (a) and cf. 5(c). **95** *woldes*: first recorded here and elsewhere only in Gower *CA* 6.924 (MED s.v. n. 2 misses this instance). **96** is recalled at 22.197; with the build-up to *wille* in a sequence of three lines alliterating on |w|, an ironic self-directed pun may be suspected. **97** resembles 6.360 below. *grete othes*: regularly thought of as a sin accompanying drunkenness (see on B 10.50); examples are at 22.226. **100** *before noone*: spelling out **B**'s *er ful tyme*; the fasting rule allowed only one meal, to be taken at midday, the normal time for the main meal being the evening (H. S. Bennett 1937:236). **A** 65 is new, a Type 3 line scanning on *d* and reminiscent of Z III 163, but is replaced with expanded 89–92 in **B**. The linking of gluttony with lust in **A** recalls the Lot exemplum, as that with sloth anticipates B 14.76. **B 98** *breden*: either from *breden* 'live, dwell' (MED v. (3), 3(c), with apt quotation from *WPal* 1782) or from *breden* 'spread out, distend' (MED v. (2), 3) as maintained by Kane 2000:45, though the exact sense required 'grow stout [*sc.* from eating abundant town-refuse]' is not instanced). The sense 'breed' (s.v. v. (3) 3 (a)) does not impose itself, despite *bedden*, since the issue concerns gluttony as leading to sloth, not lechery; but polysemantic wordplay cannot be ruled out, even if a pun on two phonemically distinct verbs would be less effective. **103–04** *wanhope*: final impenitence, produced by 'despair of the mercy of God' (*CT* X 692) results from 'believing' in False and is the converse of belief in Truth, which will bring the grace of a good end (see on 35 above). The lines spell out that for persistent sinners the prospect of salvation through a long period in purgatory, though possible, is remote. **C** lessens the strict charter-like quality of B 102 //, with its legal phrases referring to permanent possession (*habendum et tenendum*) in fee-simple (Woolf 1969:57, AlfG 69–70) and also echoing the marriage service (Tavormina 1995:2). **104–05** Echoic end-chime replaces the full rhyme of **B 100–01** ending the list of sins. **105** *This lyf*: 'during this life'; like *fastyng dayes*100, an absolute time-phrase without preposition. **108** *appurtinaunces*: an accurate legal term for 'something annexed to another thing more worthy as principal, and which passes in possession with it, as a right of way or other easement' (AlfG 8). In context richly ironic, since those who go to hell will have no use for (purgatorial) 'easements' or rights of way (cf. Christ's hope-giving promise cited in Woolf 57). **B 105 (Z 76, A 69)** *one yeris ende*: 'the date fixed for the repayment of a loan [here = one's life] or the fulfilment of an obligation [= to serve God]' (AlfG 170 s.v. *yere*); cf. Piers's words to the knight at B 6.43–4. The sinner's soul is repaid to Satan rather than to God (contrast Piers's bequest at 8.96–7). **B 107** *wo*: removing the possible ambiguity of // **ZA** 78 (71), where 'Wrong' may have as referent both the Devil and his earthly surrogate, the human evil-doer who witnesses

the deed at 108 and will appear before the king at 4.46. **109–15 109** *Wrong*: see at 1.59. **110 (B 109)** *Peres*: a popular ME name (<AN), the commonest English form of 'Peter'; see also 6.366. *Paulines*: with B 178 below the only contemporary reference. Identification of these 'Paulines' with the Crutched Friars, one of the minor orders suppressed in 1370, whose house lay just within the City wall (Chettle 1949), is uncertain though possible, notwithstanding that pardoners were rarely friars (*Bn*). **C** *queste*: the jury of a church court (MED s.v. n.1); *Bn*'s suggestion 'a collection of alms or donations' is not illustrated in MED. **B** *doctrine*: i.e. metonymically their order, lit. 'the teachings of the [Order of Paulines]' (see MED s.v. *doctrine* n.2 (a)). AlfG 111–12 takes it as 'general instruction of knowledge in any field, including the law' and *Paulynes* as referring to suitors and witnesses in the consistory court, since the word's every occurrence [*sc.* in L] 'is in a legal context, pointing towards the ecclesiastical court of St Paul's. B 178 (*Paulynes pryuees*) would support AlfG (see idem 111–12, 120–1), as would *queste* here. Du Boulay 1991:98–9 likewise takes *Paulynes* as 'the ecclesiastical lawyers who worked in St Paul's.' **A** *doctor*: i.e. learned member of the Paulines. *Bn*'s conjecture of an allusion to St Paul's and its neighbourhood is confirmed by **Z** *of Sent Poules chirche*, which fits with the present 'Piers' being a pardoner, yet not a friar (the revisions could allude ironically to a suppresssed order whose *former* members found employment on the margins of the Church in such rôles as the pardoner's). There is no lexical evidence for the term as referring to the cathedral or its court; OED cites 'Paulyns' for the crutched Friars from 1483 (s.v. *Pauline* a. and sb.) while Gregory's *Chronicle* (*c.* 1475) uses 'The ordyr of Powlys' (MED s.v. *Poule* n. 2(b)). **111** *Bette*: a man's name, recurring at B 5.32, with evident punning intent, here the assonance with *bedel* perhaps motivating the choice. Banbury in N Oxon. (Buckinghamshire in **ZAB**), like Rutland in B 111 (which kept its name 'Soke' until modern times), seems chosen for alliterative convenience, though gibes at particular regions occur (e.g. Norfolk at Z 5.98, B 5.235). **112** *Raynald*: 'Reginald'. *reue*: a manorial official elected by the peasants (Bennett 1937:166–78) and one who, besides being open to venality, would have a tendency to amass debts (11.301–2). *redyng-kynges*: here and at 6.371 found only in **L**; possibly a form of *rod-knight*, 'king' being a reversed-spelling variant of *knight* (MED s.v.). *Pe*'s suggestion that *redyng* may be from 'reeding', or 'redding' (i.e. dyeing red), or 'riding', the man being a master thatcher, a dyer or a lackey (with an ironic use of 'king') is little better supported. **113** *Munde*: a stock name for a miller (here a type of dishonesty), used again at B 10.44, where he seems a type of foolish ignorance. **114** *date...deuel*: a parody of the formula for dating a deed ('in the year of Our Lord', as at B 13.269), suggesting

Wrong's diabolic character, the document having been issued 'under the devil's aegis' (Tavormina 1995:22). **A 78** *signes*: the marks appended to official documents by the public notaries, who dealt with ecclesiastical matters like papal provisions to, and exchanges of, benefices (whence the reference at C 185–6; see Gilbert 1981:58–9, Alf*G*). The phrase is re-used at C 156.

(iii) 116–54 116 *Teologie*: THEOLOGY, whom *Bn* rightly sees as taking over HC's rôle, is presumably here the Church's systematised (especially moral) teaching as applied in actual life, aimed at promoting the reign of truth and charity. Dame Study later contrasts this with the discipline's more problematic 'speculative' aspects in B 10.182–99. **117** *Symonye*: his replacement of Cyuyle **B** is logical, since arranging an illicit marriage could be regarded as coming under this sin (Alf*G* s.v.) and he has already taken the initiative at 74 above. **B 117** *wrape wip*: 'with which to anger'. **120–26** Theology's view of Fikeltonge (?Fauel) as Mede's grandfather (*belsyre*) and Fals as her father (so HC at B 25) contradicts HC in **C**, who makes Fauel Mede's father (25) and Fals her intended (42). The discrepancy between these two authorities could be intended to highlight Mede's ambiguous character; or *Fals* at 121 may be an authorial oversight for *Fauel*. The only way to avoid seeing the proposed union as one of father and daughter (though still incestuous) is to regard the suitor Fals as a distinct character, the (bastard) son and representative of the same evil principle as the father (2.42 // B 41). But in Theology's view, Mede is not a bastard (as HC accused her at 24) but legitimate offspring (on the word *moilere* see Bradley 1906–7:163–4; Alf*G* 102), because her *mother* was 'an honest woman deceived into making an alliance with Fals' (*Bn*), whence the daughter is canonically *mulierata* 'of legitimate birth'. Mede is thus given a dual ancestry, good and bad (*Amendes*, though possibly neutral in its sense 'compensation', is here viewed positively) and God is thought of as having pledged to reward Amends (= 'satisfaction for sin') by allying himself with her through marriage, so countering the influence of Fals. The interpretation of 124 depends on *treuthe* in its three other occurences with *plihten* (3.469, 8.33, 10.274) having the sense 'make a promise', so if thus taken here (as by *Pe*) *Treuthe* (1) will refer *non*-univocally to both God and his representatives (as Fals does both to the Devil and his). **C**'s explicitness, however, arguably blurs **ZAB**'s suggestion that Mede ought in an ideal world to be the daughter of Amends and therefore noble, while in the *actual* world (as what follows shows) she has a greater propensity for evil than for good (i.e. rewards tend to be given for the wrong reason or to the wrong people). Theology's equivocal perspective on Mede may be due to his being *in via*, in contrast to HC's eschatological standpoint (*in patria*); but seen in purely social terms, it helps account for Mede's plausible posture before the King of an aristocratic lady worthy to be his 'kinswoman', like an heiress to one of the tenancies-in-chief (Baldwin 1981[1]:27, 33). In this passage the word-play on *treuthe* and *so* (124–25) amplifies that on *gyue* (126) in **ZAB** (see further Tavormina 1995:25–30, who finds in Theology's opposition to the marriage with Fals traces of objection on grounds of 'disparagement' and known enmity to Mede's lord). **127–8** The main attack is on Symonye himself, in **ZAB** on his crony Cyuyle, the corrupt ecclesiastical lawyer whose practices foster wrongful legal decisions that harm the Church. **129–30** *tixt*: in **C** not Scripture but the words of Lawrence the deacon (*Levita Laurentius* in the Magnificat antiphon at Vespers for his feast day, 10 August), who was believed to have been martyred by roasting on a gridiron at Rome in 258 for refusing to give up the riches of the Christian community and for referring to the poor as the 'treasure' of the Church (*Legenda Aurea* [*LA*] CXVII). Lawrence is cited again at 17.65–8, which echoes this passage in using *mede* in its 'true' sense of a just heavenly reward for a life of 'truth' on earth and *largenesse* in its honourable sense, by contrast with the suspect adverb at 138. *trewe doom*: the referent may be 'the reliable judgement' (of tradition) that what is described really happened thus. **132–3** His words echo the antiphon at Lauds (or *LA* 492): 'I thank you Lord that I have deserved to enter your gates' (on Lawrence and the liturgy see further Tavormina 1987). **B 123 (Z 94, A 87)** '[For] the labourer is worthy' (Lk 10:7, echoing Deut 24:14); the quoted words continue *mercede sua* 'his hire to have' (123b //). This 'text's' context concerns the right of apostolic preachers to food and shelter for preaching the gospel; but the wider reference here is to 'all who labour honestly with body or mind / do works of virtue' (anticipating the words of the pardon at 9.286). **Z 99** *nysotes*: a noun used as an adjective (*MES* 642–3), here in apposition with another preceding, with French pl. ending and even closer to French practice than B 11.316. **Z 100** *sowsest yow*: the lack of concord between sg. verb and pl. reflexive may be due to the attack being on Cyuyle both individually and in his complicity with Symonye and the notaries. *Seynte Marye rentus*: rents due for payment on Annunciation Day, 25 March ('Lady Day', the start of the New Year under the old scheme of reckoning the calendar); omitted as perhaps overspecific. **133–34** The rhyme-repetition of *diserue* 'earn by service' points up **L**'s singular quasi-Platonic notion of earthly institutions and practices as having their true ('authentic, original') archetype in heaven; cf. Schmidt 1987:117, and Simpson 1986[2] for a full discussion of this unnamed 'figure of thought' (which could perhaps be thought of as a form of 'transsumptio'). **136** *no man*: because those who live a life of 'truth' are one with 'Truth' and can be called by his name, just as followers of Christ are 'Christians'. Whether or not *treuthe* is capitalised here (balancing Fals 137), its (univocal) reference is to man, not to 'Truth (as God)'. **140** echoes 1.189, where destroyers of charity are also enemies of truth. **B 126 (Z 98, A 90)** *shenden*: licensed *s / sh* alliteration on 'metrical allophones' (*Intro.* IV § 46). **142** *Holy Writ*: presumably Jn 8:44, cited in note to 1.60 above. **144** *by3ete*: 'begotten', a puzzling expression if this is a simple adjective, since to have been born a bastard, Fals would have first to have been begotten. To make sense, *by3ete* must be given the meaning 'lawfully begotten' (so *Pe*), for which there is no lexical support, and treated as a nominal (as at B 41 above). The context implies that Fals = the Antichrist, the *false fende* who makes *fals sprynge* in 22.64, 55. **B 131 (Z 103, A 95)** *Belsabubbes*: the 'prince of the devils' in Mk 3:22–6; not mentioned by name later in the Harrowing of Hell sequence in Passus 20. **145** *moylore*: contradicting HC's assertion at 24 above that Mede is a bastard and so presumably a fit match for Fals. *a mayden of gode*: 'a lady richly left'; 'a girl of good family' (*Pe*). **ABC** suggest that 'maiden' merely = unmarried, as at 2.19 // (MED s.v. 1(a)), revising **Z**'s '(literally) a virgin' (ib. 2(a)). Theology's view in all versions does not square with Conscience's assertion of Mede's promiscuity at 3.164ff//, a discrepancy perhaps meant to signal the difference between theory and experience (cf. on 120–6). **148** *Londone*: implying, if literally meant, a hearing at the Arches in Cheapside (see on 61). They are intercepted by the king's officers (2.210, 3.1–2) and brought to the King's own prerogative court at Westminster (at this time a separate city); but at 174 Westminster is in any case their destination. This may be because Mede is envisaged as a royal ward, or the terms may be used without exactitude. The reference to journeying, however, is a reminder that the dream has occurred *opeland* (cf. 5.44 later) on the Malvern Hills, and the party are perhaps to be imagined as coming up to the capital from the west. **150** *iuroures othes*: testifying to their proclaimed character; see on 59 and cf. Z Pr 70. **151** *witty*: 'wise', a traditional attribute of God (cf. *witig god* in *Beowulf* 685). **152** *Conscience... consayl*: a member of 'Truth's privy council'; but the allegory does not insist on his function purely as the individual conscience, since he has already appeared both as spokesman of divine judgement (Pr 118–27) and (first in **C**) as a member of the king's Privy Council (Pr 158). **154** *soure*: a favourite transferred epithet describing the unpleasant consequences (= 'aftertaste') of a life of sin; cf. 15.49–51*a*, B 10.359 (see Schmidt 1987:91–2).

(iv) 155–74 155–6 The canon lawyer (Syuyle) is prepared to wait for his fee; the corrupt church official (Symonye) wants payment in advance for services to be rendered. The allegory allows that there may be a right use of the former, while the latter is always bad. **157** *floreynes*: gold coins imprinted with fleurs-de-lys on the obverse. The rare English florin, a gold piece with half and quarter, was first issued by Edward III in 1344 with the value of 6s (see *Sk* IV 51, illustration in Poole I:292, pl. 34b–d). Italian florins (named from the city of Florence) were coined in 1282 and circulated widely, as were Flemish. Legal charges are high (*plus ça change...*), having to be paid in gold, not in silver shillings (see also 3.194, 7.227, where the cost of bribing false witnesses is again reckoned in florins). **161** *amaystrye*: presumably overcome her (real or feigned) scruples about marrying False by lying about his character. **B 148** *maken...wille*: a phrase with sexual overtones, as suggested by 22.197. **164** *comen*: with unexpressed subject (i.e. False-Witness, the notaries etc) understood (*MES* 142, 5c). **167** *mery tonge*: repeating with variation 161b, in **C**'s characteristic way. Pleasant persuasiveness is needed to make Mede go happily (*with a goode wille*). **170** shows Mede subject to the desire which she tempts others with: greedy in herself and the cause of greed in others. **171–74** The party is swelled by supporters from the surrounding country drawn from classes especially prone to venality.

175–89 undergo continuous revision, not always in the direction of perfect clarity. **Z 143** *Symonye*: making a clear distinction between Symonye the master of summoners (who were church officials) and Cyuyle the (Canon) lawyer; **ABC** erase it. **Z 148** is either a scribal echo or an earlier form of a line dropped in **A** and revived for use as **B 174**. Though **C** omits these groups, it distinguishes between Mede's mount (a royal official) and the lawyers' (churchmen and church officials). The traditional 'riding' trope is found in Nicole Bozon's *Char d'Orguel* and in *The Simonie* 326, but derives ultimately from patristic commentary on Ex 15:1–4 and Cant 1:8 (Kellogg 1958). It recurs in 4.16–23 and, most strikingly, in 19.49ff (also B 17.108). **B 163** // *foles*: perhaps punning on 'fools', worldly wisemen who follow Wrong and are fools in God's eyes (contrast B 7.125, 22.61–2). **177** revises 'allophonic' *s / sh* alliteration to uniform *sh*. **178** *saunbure*: a word for a comfortable saddle or litter made of fine material, found only here (see MED s.v. *samburi* n., a blend of OF *sambüe* 'lady's saddle' and ML *saumarius* 'packhorse'). *syse to syse*: the twice-yearly progresses of the sheriff, when he could levy fines at the assize of bread and ale (*Bn*). **180** *righte faste by*: 'close on either side of'. **182** *prouisores*: those who held a 'provision' from the Pope to be appointed to a benefice when a vacancy occurred. Although strictly controlled by the Statute of Provisors of 1351 (confirmed and supplemented by *Praemunire* 1353), the system continued to function (McKisack 1959:272–85), even the stringent second Statute of 1390 remaining 'a dead letter' (idem, 282, and see further Pantin 1955:47–75, 82–9, Gee and Hardy 1921:112–25 for texts of the re-issued statutes, Swanson 1989:70–2 and refs. in Alf*G* 128). *serue*: i.e as mounts, but with a pun on 'serve as secretaries / assistants'. **184** *rectores*:

those who held as a benefice a church and the whole or best part of its endowment income (AlfG 128). The Latin form, as at 187, 191, characterises the learned speaker. *deuoutours*: an alteration from the usual form *auoutrie* (as at B 12.74), perhaps for metrical convenience, with a sardonic pun on *devout*. On the noun used as adj. see *MES* 642–3, and cf. on Z 148 below. **185** *permuten*: first found here and 'suggest[ing] a first-hand knowledge of the canonical pronouncements on the subject, e.g. Gregory IX, *Decret.* III 19' (AlfG 114). Exchanging benefices was considered simony if it involved a cash-adjustment (see on A 78). **186** *pore prouisores*: provisors *in forma pauperum*, who were granted precedence over other candidates for a benefice in the gift of a named *patron*, as opposed to those *in forma speciali*, who were granted a named *benefice* (Swanson 1989:70). *appeles*: metonymic for '[those who make] accusations alleging another's crime' or, more probably, 'supplications for mercy (AlfG 7) as at 244. The Court of Arches (see on 61) heard appeals from lower church courts of the province. **187** *Somnours*: apparitors, officers who summoned to a church court for offences against (mainly sexual) morality; see Woodcock 1952:45–9. *sodenes*: sub-deans (deputies of the dean), or rural deans acting locally for the bishop in testamentary, moral and other matters (*Bn*). The *south-* form (**AB**) shows *-th* standing for Norman French *-tz* (= *soutz* < Lat *subtus* 'under' [*Sk*]); see also 16.277. *supersedeas*: named from its first word, the Latin perhaps being used here as a false plural ('supersedeases'). The writ stayed or put an end to legal proceedings against persons accused of offences lying under its jurisdiction (here sexual misdemeanours). As it fell to the summoner to bring the accused to court, he might be dissuaded from doing so for a suitable payment (cf. *CT* I 653–7). The writ 'was meant to protect individual rights...but...was subject to abuses such as bribery' (AlfG 150; see also 4.190, 9.263). Mention of these writs, new in **C**, marks **L**'s increased awareness of and animosity towards abuses of the law. **188** *lyppeth... rydeth*: the satiric aptness of this image to the sin of *lecherye* is obvious in the light of the 'mounting' imagery at B 7.90 and the use of *ryden* at 13.154, B 11.337 (MED s.v. *riden* v. 9 'copulate'). **189** The danger of 'false friends' to the testator's soul is stated at B 12.257. Why the *secatours* should be mounts for summoners is not clear, but the three groups are linked again at 16.277.

B 174–9 174 (Z 148) *Erchedeknes*: primarily ecclesiastical judges who went on parish visitations and imposed fines for offences against sexual morality and church discipline (*Bn*). *officials*: officers presiding in a consistory court, e.g. as a bishop's chancellor; in **Z** perhaps in apposition with *Erchdekenus*, through being seen as a pl. adjectival form like *deuoutours* 184 (for an earlier reference see *The Simonie* 192). *registrers*: clerks of the church courts in charge of records, citations and receipts

(AlfG 129), who were always public notaries (Woodcock 1952:38). **175–77** The matters named fell to the archdeacon and gave opportunity for bribery, e.g. to overlook charges of adultery. The practice of *derne usurie* or *occulta usura* was the lending of money (at exorbitant rates of interest) under colour of a trading transaction. An example would be the lender's purchase of goods from the borrower at an excessive price, the excess being a secret interest-bearing loan to the seller (on usury see Gilchrist 1969:108). **176** *diuorses*: not as today the dissolution of a valid marriage but rather a canonical annulment or declaration that the marriage was invalid from the outset (see Du Boulay 1991:97f). The modern sense existed (MED s.v *divorce* n. 1 (1402)) but is not, *pace* MED, that of either of **L**'s two uses (see also 22.139 and AlfG 48, *The Simonie* 199–203, Helmholz 1974:74 and Tavormina 1995:29n60). **177** The suggestion could be that profits from church fines helped defray the costs of bishops' visitations of their dioceses (there is an advance in precision from **Z**→ **A**→ **B**, but **C** omits bishops, having mentioned *prelates* at 182). **178 (A 139)** *Paulynes...consistorie*: taken as 'having to do with the consistory court of St Paul's Cathedral' by AlfG 120. However, while *Poules* as 'the ecclesiastical court of St Paul's' seems proven, no instance of *Paulines* itself supports this sense; so a reference to ex-members of the Pauline Friars remains a possibility (see on 110). *pryuees*: 'parties to suits in legal actions' (*Bn*); on the use of a French pl. ending with *s* in post-positional adjs. see *MES* 277, and cf. on 184. **190–99 190** *commissarie*: the bishop's adminstrative legate exercising jurisdiction (particularly) in far-flung parts of his diocese. The supposition is that a living (*vitailes*) is to be got from fining those summoned for sexual sins. This is the first clear case in **C** of alliteration on |f| and |v| with a Latin macaronic stave (cf. 61 above). *cart*: the motif of allegorical animals drawing carts is traditional, as *Bn* notes, citing Bozon's *Char d'Orguel* and a C12th illustration of Greed's chariot (Katzenellenbogen 1989, fig. 60); **L**'s is individual in making the 'beasts' not personified vices but social types. **191** *fornicatores*: a technical term covering both fornicators and adulterers (AlfG 62). Taking *mede* for overlooking such cases among the clergy is criticised in *The Simonie* 49–52. **192** *lang cart*: the four-wheeled *longa caretta* used for military and other transport. Allegorically, these deceiving characters are 'contained within' Liar, who appears as a separate type-figure at 225. **193** *fobbes* / *fobberes*: found only in **L** (see MED s.vv.), the back-formed verb surviving in the phrase 'fob off'. **196** *no...telle*: a variant on the alliterative formula (also found in *SGGK* 719 and in *ZA* 6.76/82, from where it has been deleted in // **B**, perhaps to avoid repetition). *tayl*: both 'number' and 'tail', stretching out behind them (cf. the pun at B 12.245). **197** revises and strengthens **ZAB**'s tag-like b-half. **198** *forgóere*: here, by contrast with 61 above, stressed on the second syllable. Gyle, the principle of diabolic deceitfulness (see on 70) becomes 'embodied' in one of the type-figures of Mede's *route* at 62. **199a** anticipates 7.177a, where the repentant folk of the field seek a guide to Truth.

(v) 200–16 200 *Sothnesse*: evidently the same quality named at 24, defined by 'clear-sightedness' (*Bn*), the ability to recognise Guile. His 'horse' vividly realises an abstract idea, a virtue especially appropriate to that *veritas* which 'prevails' in the long run (III Esd 4:41) and so requires patience. This substitution of a symbolic mount for **B**'s *palfrey* foreshadows an important development (later in **B**) of the major figure Patience, whose companion Conscience becomes (13.180–82). **Z 160** *fiched*: the earliest use in this (and perhaps any) sense, not cited in MED s.v. *fichen* v.(1). **202** *Conscience*: here 'perhaps conceived of as the chancellor, "the keeper of the king's conscience..."' (*Bn*). The rôle also fits well enough in the earlier versions, though in **C** he has already been introduced as the authoritative speaker of the words on the king's duties given to the angel in **B** (see on Pr 151–57).

Z 163–70 give an accurate (if redundant) summary of 'the action of Passus II up to this point' (*R–B*) that bears the marks of an authorial draft (see *TN*) rather than a scribal interpolation, the purpose of which would be inexplicable. **L** generally avoids passages of summary, an exception being 15.5–24 //, an occasion to recapitulate an important completed sequence and furnish a transition between dreams. **164, 168** *al togyderes*: 'the whole business'. **165/6** *lache / Mede*: the collocation occurs at C 3.390, though in sense 4 (a) of MED *lacchen* v. (1), which is distinct from the present one (id. 3 (a)). **166** *hym lette*: sense uncertain, but either 'and how he [Fauel / Falsenesse treated as one] conducted himself' (MED s.v. *leten* v. 17b) or, 'how to prevent him'; 'he was prevented' (*R–B*) does not seem a possible translation. **167** virtually repeats 117, **169a** repeats 86. **170** recalls Z 1.43; but the play on *tene* in 169 is characteristic of **L** (cf. 7.38, 8.36, 11.128).

207–16 207 *maynteyneth*: aids and abets them through money, protection or influence; alluding to the 'maintenance' of retainers by great lords (see Alf*G* 94–5). Baldwin 1981[1]:26–7 plausibly sees here the specific abuse of 'maintenance-at-law' (paying administrative officials fees and liveries for furthering the lord's interests) and in Mede herself 'a life-like example' of using bribes to sustain and increase her power. Z 177 supports this reading, which for **ABC** sits awkwardly with Mede's being the *object* of False's designs. But if at one level she signifies a 'corrupt great lady' (like Alice Perrers), such a reading seems right. The King's threat implies that maintenance is itself a crime potentially as grave as those of the actual criminal types 'maintained'. **208** *maynprise*: 'take in hand' literally, i.e. stand as personal surety or

maynpernour (= Lat. *manucaptor*) for a prisoner to be released on bail, who will be produced when required. See further 4.107, the figurative use at 18.281 and Alf*G* 93–4. **209b** This instance of internal rhyme has the effect of a performative utterance (here a 'doom') and marks a decisive moment. **Z 177** *For...Mede*: 'in spite of any request for clemency made by Mede [i.e. supported by the offer of money]'. **A**'s removal of this line (with its characteristic asseveration) makes sense, as the King has not yet met Mede, and the general point is made at Z 179. **210** *constable*: here 'an officer of the king's peace' (Alf*G* 35), a subordinate (*Bn*) of the Lord High Constable, who dealt with offences in or near the king's court. **211** *tyrauntes*: 'vicious rogues, villains' (again used at 22.60 of the 'fals fende Auntecrist'); it comes nearest to the Chaucerian political sense (*Legend of Good Women* F 374) at B 15.419. *tresor*: the first appearance since HC's last use of the word at 1.201 in answer to Will's question at 1.43, highlighting the fundamental antithesis between Truth and Falsehood in the widest sense being allegorically enacted. **216** *pylorye*: a device in which the offender stood with head secured; a standard punishment for breaching regulations of the purity and weight / quantity of bread and ale (see Benson 2004:228–36). Liar is here briefly associated with the peccant tradesmen to be mentioned at 3.80–3 for whom Mede will intercede with the mayor. **A 165–66 (Z 183–84)** A clear case of a revised **A** line omitted in **B** (perhaps as too mild after the preceding threats of death and imprisonment). The use of A 166 at C 248 is a unique instance of whole-line restoration, suggesting that **Z** lines might also have been re-used (see Z 189 // C 3.78).

(vi) 217–52 217 *Drede*: a fleeting personification of 'fear of earthly punishment', parallel to Wit's *drede of* [God's] *vengeaunce* at B 9.96. Dread is more positively viewed at A 10.80–4 as 'the beginning of goodness' (**L**'s figure, who appears briefly in *MS* 1262, may have suggested to Skelton the hapless hero of *The Bouge of Court*). *dene* (so **Z**; *doom* **AB**; see *TN*): a possible reference to the 'crying of names' of those summoned at the door of the royal council chamber (*Bn*, citing Baldwin 1913). **Z 188–9** (omitted in **A**), which anticipate B 207, lack **B**'s *And* 207, thus seeming to render the *dene* the King's angry series of commands. **C** makes 218a a parenthetical explanation of *dene* (otiose if **L** had retained *doom* in **C**). **219–20** *feres...fere...freres*: the wordplay hinting 'Platonically' at an affinity of the friars with False's cronies. *freres*: here first since Pr 58–65 singled out as exemplars of deceit, preparatory to their assuming that rôle in Vision Eight for sinners seeking 'easy penance' (22.285 will sharply recall 2.220). **222** *marchauntes*: found suspect later in Greed's confession and in the Pardon Scene, where they are guilty of swearing falsely to the quality of their wares (9.25–6) as Guile does here (with *shewen* 223 cf. *mostre* 6.260).

230 *cloutes*: less probably 'a child's small clothes' (*Bn*) than 'patched clothes' (MED s.v. 6 (a)), which Liar is put in to make him look like one of the common people (cf. Piers at B 6.59). **231** *senten hym*: i.e. as a pardoner, in appropriately humble attire (see on Pr 66ff). **232** *And*: elliptical for 'Where he / And there he' (see *MES* 142, 5(b)). **233–36** The *leches* and *spysours* (dealers in 'med'cinable gums') are naturally linked, as both seek Liar's services after noting his success as a fraudulent pardoner (the implications of *poundmele* 232). Physicians receive for their dishonest treatments brief criticisms at 8.290–6, digesting a longer attack in Z 7.255–78. **235** *aspye*: i.e. look carefully over (with the aim of carrying out some deception). The deliberate echo of *spysours* 'Platonically' intimates real affinities between the referents of homophonous lexemes. **237** *mynstrals*: this first reference since Pr 35–40 sitting better with the **C** and also **Z** forms of those lines than with the more positive **AB** view, which distinguishes these minstrels from 'japers' (see Schmidt 1987:5–11). *mesagers*: popularly associated with rumour and tell-tales (Chaucer's *Hous of Fame* [*HF*] 2128–129, and on the connection with 'meed', *PF* 228, cited *Bn*). But they are more favourably treated in **C**, which adds a long passage on them (13.32–91). **238** *half ȝere...dayes*: the exact length of Edward III's French campaign of 1359–60, from landing in France to signing the Treaty of Brétigny, 'a period when rumour was rampant' (*Bn*). **239** *freres*: the ones who ultimately succeed in getting Liar to join them, where his companion False already waits (220). **241** scans *abb / ab* as Type Ie on vowels with 'double counterpoint' on *l* (see Schmidt 1987:62–7). **242** ironically anticipates the Mendicants' claim about Dowel at 10.18–19. **243–48** break up the description of the rogues' dispersal, but enable Conscience to achieve the prominence he had by the end of **B**. Though clearly an addition in **C**, with Conscience's 'accusation' here echoing Pr 95 (also new), these lines conclude with one originally in **A** and before that in **Z** (see *TN* and on A 165–66 above). They represent Conscience's delayed response to Sothnesse's intelligence at 202 and explain why the canon lawyers are not frightened away with the rest of the villains but seek the intervention of the sovereign religious authority in the matter of Mede's marriage (against pending adverse judgement from the secular one). This evokes Conscience's warning against the danger that corrupt clerks pose to state and church, which reaches its climax in the solemn rhyme of 246–47 (cf. 75–6), followed by recovered A 166; and it may indirectly echo the hostility shown towards lawyers in the 1381 Rising. **Z 214b–15** The presence of Fauel before the council is incompatible with Z 3.1 and will accordingly have been removed in revision to **A** (*R–B*).

Passus III

PASSUS THREE is the thematic centre of gravity of the First Vision. Nearly twice its length in **A** and half as long again as in **B**, it is the longest passus in **C** (double those that precede and follow) and falls into three main parts. First a *prelude* (1–67) shows LADY MEDE at her work of corruption and making her insincere confession to a friar. There follow (i) an authorial digression on civic evils (68–126), and Mede's defiant offer to the mayor. The climax is her allegorical 'Trial' before the King (127–499), in five sections: (ii) a preliminary dialogue (129–54); three long speeches giving (iii) Conscience's 'case' for rejecting Mede as bride (155–214), (iv) her response (220–82) of similar length, and (v) Conscience's crushing dismissal of this (285–482), prompted by the King's finding in favour of Mede; as a conclusion (vi), her angry rejoinder and Conscience's sarcastic dismissal of her desperate appeal to scriptural authority (483–99). Despite the encounter's practical purpose (if Mede may not marry False, can she marry Conscience?) and its impassioned tone (reflecting the antipathy between the two principles of truth and falsehood the antagonists embody), the handling owes less to legal than to scholastic debate. This is evident in Conscience's recourse to a formal *distinctio* (285–406) between the concepts of *mede* and *mercede* (amusingly broken by the king's request for clarification at 340–2) and his confutation of Mede's 'text' by proving it incomplete and quoted out of context.

PRELUDE **1–37** describe the reception of Lady Mede alone at Westminster. Although she is arrested (2.252) and suspected of crimes (3.8), the respectfulness shown when she is brought for interview ironically underlines her power and influence. **2** *bedeles*: minor civic officials, often ceremonial. *baylifs*: lesser officers of justice under the sheriff. **3** *clerke*: perhaps the clerk of the King's Council, if the meeting is meant to resemble a blend of a law-court and that body (*Pe*). Kennedy (2003:178) sees the setting as one of a 'nascent Court of Chancery', but an over-precise interpretation of the allegory is probably misplaced. *name*: either official or personal (cf. *CT* I 284). **5–9** The King will 'assay' Mede as 'a ward in Chancery who has got into bad company' (*Bn*). The problem she anticipates is his refusal to let her 'wed at her will' (19) someone the King might disapprove of. **7** *wys men*: later identified as Reason and Conscience. **C**'s replacement of *my wit and my wil* suggests a more cautious assumption about the King's own understanding and inclination. **11** *boure* (*chambre* **AB**): an antechamber where Mede waits for audience. **13** *That*: on non-expression of the antecedent see *MES* 190. *wendeth to* (*wonyeþ at* **ZAB**) *Westmynstre*: the **C** revision, echoing 2.174, stresses the suitors' venality as much as that of the judges 'residing' and the lawyers practising there. 'Westminster', so called from its nearness to the Benedictine Abbey, is metonymic for the royal law-courts held in the great Norman Hall of the palace, which was extended by Richard II about ten years after the date of the C-Text (Baker 1971:29; Harvey 1944:59, with ills. and plan). The scene is directly recapitulated at 22.131–3, where Couetyse overcomes 'the wit and wisdom of Westminster Hall'. **14** *the iustices somme*: 'a number of the judges' (MED s.v. *som* adj. 2 (a); cf. *monye* **Z**). Judges are ill spoken-of throughout *PP* (2.150, 3.192, 22.134, B 7.44, Z Pr 70). **15** *Boskede*; *buyrde*: words from the standard alliterative lexicon (cf. *WPal* 1862–3) that **L** normally avoids, evoking ironically a courtly milieu appropriate for one like Mede. **16** *as they couthe*: 'as they well knew how to'. *clerkes*: if sg. and referring to the person at 3, this softens the insistence in **B** // that corrupt Law and Church go hand in hand. **21** *mercyede*: a very rare word perhaps punning on a sense 'bribe, reward'; MED s.v. *mercien* v. (1) aptly illustrates from Audelay (*Poems* 36/718: *Pay mercyn hem with mone and med preuely*), recalling this line. **22** *Of here*: 'for their'. **23** *Coupes*: alluding indirectly to the *poculum aureum* held by the Whore of Babylon in Apoc 17:4 (and see on 2.9–16). *clene*: 'pure', 'unalloyed' (cf. 4.91), but contextually ironic, since in Apoc 'full of uncleanness'. For this cup as a symbol of greed, cf. *De Mundi Cupiditate* 7–18 (Map, 167): 'Calix quem Babylon in manu bajulat est *avaritia* quae passim pullulat.' **24** *rubees*: the red, most precious 'oriental' variety that Mede herself wears at 2.13. *ʒeftes*: revision replacing the pararhyming wordplay on *manye / meynee* of **B** // with tartly euphemistic semantic punning (='bribes'; see *IG* for other examples). **25** *here mayne*: 'their retinue', but hers also, in the sense that Mede buys support by bribing servants and masters alike. *motoun of gold*: the *mouton d'or*, a gold coin stamped with the image of the Lamb of God, worth five silver shillings. **29b** A rare example of three-stage revision from **Z** → **C**. **32** *prouendres*: here the stipend of a canon-prebendary, but perhaps punning on the sense 'food for horses' (with a glance at the animal-allegory in 2.183ff). **33** *benefices*: 'bought' not directly but by such means as 'permutation' (see 2.185). *pluralite*: here with negative overtones (by contrast with its positive use at A 11.200). **34** *consistorie*: the court for hearing more serious and (for canon lawyers) lucrative cases, e.g. involving divorce or separation, usually before the bishop's legal officer (2.190–1; 16.362). Mede promises advancement to poorly qualified clerks if they can pay bribes for the privilege of being called to plead (cf. 'A satyre on the consistory courts' in Wright: 1839:155–9 and Alan of Lille: 'Modo non queritur quid sit in mentis armario, sed quid sit in aerario. Qui sunt qui assistunt palatiis regum? pecuniosi. Qui sunt qui excluduntur ab aula? litterati. Jam honoratur familia cresi, contemnitur familia

Christi' (*PL* 210:181); and see Swanson 1989:160–66; Wunderli 1981, Brundage 1987:409–10). **37** *clokke*: found only here. If the **Z** reading shows confusion of *e* for *o*, the word is the same and the sense 'limp, hobble'. **38–67** describe *Mede's confession*. **38** *confessour*: apart from the king's confessors (who were often themselves friars), the three who actually appear (cf. B 11.70, 22.372) are all friars, and all venal. Criticism of the corruption of mendicant confessors in the period is common, *CT* I 218–32, III 2089ff being only the best known examples. **43** *Consience*: an abstract idea, not inevitably to be regarded as personified at this point in **AB** but in **C** more convincingly so, since he has already appeared at Pr 95. **46** A possible T-type line, with the caudal *l* alliteration supplementing the allophonic alliteration on *sh / s* (cf. B Pr 34). **47** *noble*: an English coin (so named because made of gold), with half and quarter, introduced in 1344 and worth £1/3 (see Poole I:292–3, pl. 34 e–g). This most valuable single unit of specie is mentioned usually in contexts of illicit or morally dubious payment (see *IG*). **49** The re-use here of B 42 has the effect of repetition-with-variation, amplifying and focussing the thought; but removal of explicit *brocour / baud* (after running together B 41, 46) leaves ironic *bedman* to carry the full weight of the critique. **51** *ful heye*: with pun on the dimensions of the window and its cost. **52** *gable*: the triangular-topped end wall of the nave or of the aisle of the friary church. The Austin Friars' church in London had been rebuilt with large Curvilinear aisle-windows by Humfrey de Bohun in 1354, perhaps a decade before **A**; but this description may allude to the London Greyfriars church near Newgate, since the only religious order **L** ever names is the Franciscans (10.9). In the last quarter of the 14th c. a gable-window would be in the new Perpendicular style that extended the size and glass-area of the window-space. The passage seems echoed in *CT* III 2099–2106 and is imitated in *PPCr* 118–29, 162, 175–9. **53–4** promise daily commemoration of Mede's benefaction. *For Mede*: perhaps with a pun (*Pe*), obscured by modern capitalisation. *ordre*: a grander recognition than *house* **B**, because going beyond the confines of the building contributed to. Mede will be enrolled a member of his community by letters of fraternity entitling her to special privileges and benefits, and treated as an honorary nun, though the 'sin' she seeks 'release' from is lechery (cf. later 12.4–10 and 22.365–8). **57** *lordes...ladies*: that *luxuria* 'lust of the flesh' was a vice peculiarly incident to the higher classes is a point repeated at 16.90–3, 22.312. When the sin gets a more extended treatment in 6.170–95, the speaker is a lustful old man somewhat like Januarie in Chaucer's *Merchant's Tale*. **58** *this*: a common use of the demonstrative in 'generic', quasi-definite (or zero) function (*MES* 174). **59** *bokes*: a vague allusion suggesting some indistinct authority; but the notion that sexual sin was less serious because arising out of a natural impulse (i.e. to procreate) might be associated with such influential writings as Jean de Meun's continuation of the *RR*. **62** *seuene*: the seven deadly or mortal sins that destroy sanctifying grace in the soul. This was a common topic in prose and verse writings prompted by the Fourth Lateran Council's prescription (1215) of yearly confession, which made examination of conscience and understanding of the categories and sub-divisions of sin obligatory. Stemming from the early C13 penitential treatises of Raymund of Pennaforte and Peraldus, and the late C13th *Somme le Roy* of Frère Lorens, the main examples in English are the *Ayenbite of Inwit, Handlyng Synne, The Book of Vices and Virtues* and (from the late 1390s) Chaucer's *Parson's Tale*. This last, the best contemporary commentary on **L**'s treatment of the theme and extensively cited in Passūs V–VII below, defines 'the chief and spring of alle othere synnes' in Augustinian terms simply as 'whan man loveth any creature moore than...oure Creatour' (*CT* X 388, 357). *none sonner*: a construction that understands a relative of comparison ('than which... [is])'. Mede's view of lechery as mitigated by its 'naturalness' is rejected by the severer contemporary moralists: 'fornicacioun...is deedly synne and *agayns nature*' (*CT* X 864); '[that] lecherie is kyndeli...siche veyn wordis þat excusen synne done myche harme among men' (*Select English Works of Wyclif*, II:76). But it would be mistaken to suppose (as does White 1988:92) that the Samaritan in 19.314 supports Mede's position in 59, though assuredly citing what spokesmen of 'oure wikked flessh' maintain (the distinction is properly explained by Tavormina 1995:194). **66** *peynten and purtrayen*: have her picture as donor included in the window-glass. Examples from this period are the figures of a gentlewoman in the N nave window at Waterperry, Oxon, the knights of the Clare and Despenser families depicted at Tewkesbury Abbey, and Sir James Berners, from West Horseley, Surrey (Baker 1978: pls. 45; 27, 31; 40).

(i) 68–74a 68 *defendeth*: inferred from the text cited at 74a. **69** *writen...dedes*: not that such deeds are *described* in the glass, but as the making of the window is such a deed, the naming (and, even more, depiction) of the donor such a 'writing'. **72** *ho þe catel ouhte*: here *Pe*'s '"to whom the money that is spent properly belongs", viz. the poor' reads too much into the text's statement that God knows who paid for the window and how much it cost. Whereas **B**'s *þi* makes clear that God also perceives the donor's 'greed' [to be honoured as a pious benefactor], this is less clear in **C**, where the referent of *here* is the greedy friars. If **L** has no Lollard-like 'objection to beautifying churches' (*Pe*), he presumably had none to donors' giving for this purpose rather than 'giving to the poor and distributing alms', but only to their pride in wanting recognition. **74** *God*: **L**'s frequent way of refer-

ring to Christ as utterer of precepts with divine authority (cf. 1.46 above and contrast A 251 below). **74a** '[And when thou dost alms], let not thy left hand know what thy right hand doth' (Mt 6:3).

B 70–2 70 *wel-dedes*: i.e. in providing the windows. **71** *Goddes men*: here specifically the friars. **72** Echoing *mercedem suam* from Mt 6:5 (see 311 below).

77–114 The parenthetical / digressive **77–85 (89)**, 'never clearly related to the context in **AB**' (*Pe*), seem only loosely joined through linking of the *lordes* warned against *couetyse* at 72 with *suche as kepeth lawes* at 78, who are urged to punish commercial malpractices in the city arising from the same *couetyse*. The addition **90–114**, redolent of the 'London' character of many **C** additions (Pearsall 1997), has a free-standing quality and seems awkwardly inserted here (115–20 would fit more smoothly after 89).

77–89 77 *bysouhte*: taken as intransitive by *Pe*; but it has three direct objects in 78 and means 'entreated', though what Mede entreated them to *do* is deferred until the verb's repetition at 115, after the digression-parenthesis is completed. *mayr*: the senior civic official of a town, whose 'chief rôle was as a magistrate responsible for fair trade practices' (*Bn*; see Poole I 251–6 and fig. 56). **B 76** *maceres*: taken by *Bn* to denote merely attendants who preceded dignitaries, by Alf*G* in the light of **C** as 'sheriff, bailiff, or sergeant-at-mace' (see MED s.v. *sergeaunt* 2 (c)). But **L**'s usage is loose: only the mayors themselves could properly be 'intermediary' between the king and the civic community at large (as defined here and at 1.155 above). **78** re-works Z II 189, perhaps one of **L**'s 'repertory' lines (see Appendix III), not re-used in **A** or **B**. *seri-auntes*: here the highly-paid and prestigious senior barristers (*servientes ad legem*) from whom the Common Law justices were selected (cf. Alf*G* s.v., *CT* I 309ff). **79** *To punischen*: a kind of 'predicative nominative' infinitive (*MES* 524–5) governing the three subjects in 78. *pilories*: see on 2.216. *pynyng-stoles*: likewise for punishment of breaches, esp. by women (see 5.131), of the assizes of bread and ale, by jeering, striking with rotten vegetables or ducking in the village pond. **82** *regraterye*: retail selling (esp. of victuals); legal but carefully regulated, and to be distinguished from the abuse of unlawful measure in 88–9. But **L** doubtless has in mind the practice of buying in rings from the wholesalers at depressed prices and re-selling dear at the expense of the poor purchaser, for which he has no good word (cf. 113). **85** *burgages*: tenements for rent, built in a 'row' (107) for several occupants (cf. the 'Rows' at Chester); then as now a major means of investing wealth from commercial profits. Their destruction by fire at 105 is seen as 'condign punishment'. **88** *þat...seled*: 'to the legal measure certified by the official seal' (see *Liber Albus* 233, 290; *English Gilds* 366–7; Lipson 1959:298–9).

90–114 This second major addition in **C**, 'on the suggestion of 121–6 [= B 93–6]' argues that the prayer of the poor may be answered by a vengeance of Biblical proportions that harms all alike, indicating 'the indivisibility of the community, in suffering as in true dealing' (*Pe*). The notion of indiscriminate divine *punishment* (paralleled in 11.62) may owe something to Lk 13:1–4; it finds its correlative in that of natural *benefits* extending to both just and unjust (21.435–6, commenting on Mt 5:45). **90–7** have been linked with John of Northampton's efforts in 1381–3 to reform the government of the City of London (Simpson 1993). **91** *thorw*[1–3]: the first and second denoting agency, the third, cause (as at 104). **93** *The whiche þat*: 'who'; a late, relatively rare construction (*MES* 199; also at 10.184). **95** *That*[1]: 'on those who'. *þat*: 'with the consequence that' (cf. *aftur* 103). **103** Cf. 11.62 below. **104** *breware*: see under gluttony at 6.225–33, where Coveitise's brewing wife Rose is a dishonest 'regrater' (cf. 82,113) and at 21.399ff. **105** *ybrent*: the construction fusing 'seen burgages burnt' and 'seen that...have been'. **106** *clemynge*: found only here in this sense (MED s.v. *clemen* v. 'stick'). **109** *for...siluer*: 'notwithstanding that money talks'; on the alliterative pattern cf. Pr 84. **111–14** *fre...freman...yfranchised*: all recorded here for the first time.

115–126 **118a** '[Take not away...my life with bloody men]: In whose hands are iniquities: their right hand is filled with gifts' (Ps 25:9–10), a text familiar from its use during the *Lavabo* prayer in the Introit of the Mass, contrasting 'innocence' (vs. 1; cf. 98) with 'vanity' (vs. 4); see further 287–9 below. **119** *for my loue*: 'for love of me', 'in order to have my favour'. **120** *aзeyne þe lawe / reson*: effectively the same, the revision bringing out the semantic closeness of the two terms. That **L** sees 'reason' as the divine law within man and all human law as based upon reason is shown in Alf*G* s.v. *Resoun* and in Alford 1988[1]. **121** *Salamon þe sage*: Solomon, son of David, king of Israel from *c.* 970–930 BC. His reputation for the wise sayings that form the core of the Book of Proverbs led to his later being ascribed several of the other 'Wisdom' writings. **123a** '[For the congregation of the hypocrite is barren]: and fire shall devour their tabernacles, who love to take bribes'. The collocation of *munera* 'bribes' with *mede* 123 indirectly provides a Latin 'gloss' on the lady's name at 119 (cf. Schmidt 1987:91). Ascribing the Job quotation to the presumed author of all the sapiential writings was perhaps prompted by the similar sentiment in such texts as Prov 15:27 'Qui autem odit *munera* vivet'. **124** *lettred lordes*: presumably the rulers and judges of 122. **B 100** *yeresyeues*: gifts taken by a royal officer on entering office, and renewed on New Year's day, often as a cover for bribes to connive at the giver's malfeasance; here applied to civic and manorial officers.

127–499 The *'Trial' of Lady Mede*. **127–54** describe the King's *preliminary interview* with her, in which minatory finger-wagging at 139–44 does not wholly disguise his ambivalence (cf. *litel* 130). **128** *þat ladde here*: the official of 3 above, whom **L** was reluctant to name as the actual clerk to the king's council (*Pe*). The device may thus reveal more than it conceals, but like the Rat Fable has wider non-topical significance.

(ii) 129–54 **129–30** The criticism is sharp when read in the light of 207, where the indulgence of corruption must be impliedly in part the king's responsibility. **131–2** make clear the foreconceit of Mede as a royal 'ward' requiring the king's permission to 'wed'. Allegorically, this means that reward in the kingdom should be governed by the king's will operating under the rule of divine justice or *Treuthe*, whose ultimate referent here and at 139 will be 'God'. **140** *castel of Corf*: the dungeons at Corfe in SE Dorset, long of ill-repute (*Pe*, citing Pugh 1968:128); but 'forcible enclosure as an anchorite' somewhat lessens the seriousness of the king's threat. **144** *teche*: i.e. through the discipline of enclosure (dependent on *Y shal* 140; the king, not the women, will instruct Mede). **145** *Conscience*: his certain hostility to such a marriage has been foreshadowed in **C** by his attack on clerical avarice and deception advanced to Pr 95–127. Theology has already warned that Conscience is of Truth's council (2.152), while Conscience has informed the king of False's plan to marry Mede (2.202–3) and denounced corrupt clergy as a threat to order in the kingdom (2.245–8). The present plan for Mede's future, presumably discussed in the *conseyl* (127) at which Conscience was not present, presupposes (not wholly unreasonably) that the remedy for her wantonness lies in marrying her to an honest husband, allegorically that 'pecuniary reward is in effect neutral, becoming good if given to the virtuous.'

(iii) 155–219 Conscience's *diatribe against Mede*, most of it retained from **Z** through **B** but lengthened by a topical ten-line addition (203–12), contends in contrast that she is irreformable: allegorically, that 'all forms of "payment" other than strict retributive justice are tainted'. **151** *louted*: the words 'and asked' are implied in the action. **155b** echoes Mede's phrase at 147 with an ironic resonance of the *Kyrie* response. **159** echoes 1.66 to associate Conscience with HC's stance against Mede. *In...tresor*: qualifying *monye*. **162** *зoure fader*: at the time of **ZA**, when Edward III was reigning, this would have been understood as Edward II, and his gifts to favourites as a form of *mede*. By the time of **B**, the natural referent was the Black Prince, Richard II's father, and by **C** this would have seemed even more likely. In **B**, *false biheste* 127 might be meant to signify Edward II's wrongful promises (of advancement) to his favourites; those made to Edward's supplanters with the help of 'meed'; or (with a more contemporary resonance) the promise of Pedro of Castile to pay the Black Prince for helping him to recover his throne (see McKisack 1959:144), a reading perhaps supported by C 162b. But topically speaking, the line is a 'living fossil'; in Mede's reply at 220ff the only king envisaged is Edward III. **163** *apoisend popes*: on the historical level perhaps alluding to Benedict XI's alleged death by poison (1306); but figuratively, to Constantine's legendary 'Donation' endowing the Church with landed property (see on 17.220–4), an act held by many ecclesiastical moralists to have 'poisoned' its spiritual nature (*Sk*). **164–5** *baud...helle*: in the light of 166a perhaps 'harlot anywhere' (MED s.v. *baud* n. (b)); but some wordplay could be involved, since Mede is figuratively one who 'goes between' the Church and the devil ('heaven and hell'). **166** *tayl...talewys*: an annominative pun may be suspected, Mede's public words being as 'promiscuous' as her private parts. **167a** is proverbial, but with obvious play on 'common woman'. Though ostensibly 'lady' and 'maid' (capable of high and pure uses), Mede (as money) is really 'open' to all who want her. **168** *musels*: the implication being that Mede gives these diseases to others she lies with (leprosy in particular was believed to be venereally transmissible). **175–6** *Fals... Treuthe*: here not the Devil and God but 'collective personifications' of the unjust, like Mede's would-be groom, and the just, like Piers later, who at 7.199 is offered and refuses *mede*. **178–9** Users of *mede* care nothing about excommunication, because they can be sure either of bribing the responsible episcopal officials not to impose it or of getting absolution for the initial offence from a co-operative confessor. **181–2** A single operation by Mede will accomplish as much in a month as the king's most urgent commands in four months. **182–4** The king's personal seal went (for example) with a letter authorising a Chapter to proceed to an election, or a bishop to appoint to a royal benefice. It could be circumvented by a provisor who had established a prior claim through a papal licence obtained by payment (hence through 'Simony and herself'). Conscience is warning the king that his authority may be powerless against the influence of money. **188** *forbodene lawes*: an active use of the p.pl. explained as due to confusion with *forbode* n. (*MES* 571). **189a** 'They do not thrive, because their dams are drabs'; an added Leonine hexameter of unidentified origin. Although this refers to clerics' bastards, blaming only the women for the inherited bad qualities could be a reflex of **L**'s intermittent anti-feminism. **191** *the whiche*: a usage of native origin but influenced by OF *liquels* (*MES* 198–9); frequent in **C** and found earlier at B 10.475, etc (see *IG*) but absent from **ZA**. **193–4** The figure is of a straight path being blocked by heaps of coin. **193** *lyth*: 'lies (down)'; 'tells lies'. **194** *fayth*: here a collective personification of '(the cause of) honest people,' as with *treuthe* at 11.17, and perhaps to be capitalised like *Treuthe* at 176. *forth*:

'free course, way'; a substantival use probably introduced by **L**. It is overlooked by MED but recorded in OED (s.v. *forth* C. *sb.*), which cites only one later ME example (obviously recalling this one): 'These men of lawe...withdrawe them to...lette falshede haue his forth' (*Dives and Pauper* VIII.vii.320/1). **195** *leet*: contracted form (SW and S) of *ledeth*, but perhaps playing on the near-homophone *letteth* 'hinders' (cf. 193). **196** *loueday*: a day set aside by the manorial court for a meeting to settle a dispute amicably out of court; the meeting itself; or the reconciliation resulting from it (cf. 11.17 and see Alf*G* s.v.). Spargo 1940 holds that 'love' in the compound has the specialised legal sense 'licence or permission [of the court]', but J. W. Bennett 1958 sees the term as formed on the model of the older 'lawday' (used in revision of B 10.306 at 5.158). Surviving only as a proper name, it answers to Lat. *dies amoris* and AF *jour d'amour.* Lovedays often involved mediation by a priest, monk or friar (B 5.421, 10.306; *CT* I 258); but they had a bad reputation as occasions for bribery and intimidation (see the quotations from Wycliffite writings in MED s.v.), as the parallelism in 195 implies. *Leute*: see 2.20 and Alf*G*; here personifying 'the course of justice' and contrasted with *Lawe* 198 'the process of law'. **C** is conceptually more coherent than **B**, though syntactically less so, since the antecedent of *ma3e* is better if 'law' than if 'loveday'. **198** *lordlich*: 'haughty', with an ironical glance at lords' interference in the course of law. **200–14** add a dozen new lines with topical relevance. **200–01** *bonde*: a revision significantly eliminating the highest class and, with 201b reflecting a harsher view of the *comune* in the wake of the Peasants' Revolt, but also deploring the destructive effect of money-values on otherwise loyal (*trewe*) people. **202** A verb 'causes' is to be understood after *and*. **207** *Vnsittyng soffraunce*: unseemly tolerance, 'turning a blind eye' to wrong-doing, here personified as Mede's sister; repeated at 4.189, where it implies wrongful granting of privileges to individuals under the king's private seal. *SkP-T* xxxiv finds an allusion to Richard II's unpopularity in 1392 and cites his unsuccessful attempt to raise money from the London citizens; but the lines do not support so late a reference. **208** *Marye*: the king's plight being grave indeed to need so powerful an intercessor. **209** *no lond*: perhaps alluding to the fact that in 1385 Richard II was at war with Scotland, and in summer 1386 supported Gaunt's expedition to Spain and faced a great French host preparing at Sluys for what seemed imminent invasion. *thyn owene*: Parliament impeached Richard's Chancellor Michael de la Pole in autumn 1386 and established a continual council to govern for a year. *the; thyn*: the sg. for *Pe* showing 'familiar contempt'; but though a pl. to *one* person indicates polite respect (Mede's pl. to the king at 220), the sg. need not import the opposite (e.g. Kynde Wit's sg. at Pr 148–50, with which contrast Mede's sg. to

Conscience at 224). Conscience's tone here is of urgent, intimate admonition and entreaty. **210** *knet*: cf. B 15.242; revising *coupleþ* B 165, it implies the same 'wedding' metaphor. **211** echoes B 19.458–9. **214** *maister*: referring to Mede's sway over the rich, but with a pun on the sense 'teacher' (cf. *lereth* 212). Cf. the Vernon Lyric 'Mercy Passes All Things' in Brown 1957, no. 95, ll. 249–50: 'Who is a maister now but meede / And pruide þat wakned al vr wo'. **215–19** The 'head of law' must allow the accused to 'excuse', displaying here the impartiality of the king in *WW* 218–20.

(iv) 220–82 contain *Mede's response*, not only a self-defence but an attack on her accuser. **220–44 221** *in whom*: the dependent personal relative in place of impersonal *wher* forcing a direct choice between the two disputants. **223** Mede gives no specific reference, but presumably understands the monetary settlement accompanying the Treaty of Brétigny. **224** 'Nor to offer you personal insults in a posture of stiff intransigence'. Alf*G* finds legal resonances in *deprauen* (as in *famen* 231), and the presence of these allegorical characters to state their case has analogies with a court trial *coram rege*. But as personifying opposed principles, their closest predecessors are Winner and Waster. **229a** 'I [now] can, as I [then] could'. **232** *kulde...kyng*: presumably alluding to the murder of Edward II, an act 'counselled' by opponents Mede opportunistically identifies as Conscience's followers. **233–55 (B 186–200)** Mede's reply expands a more historically explicit **B** passage unchanged from **ZA**, but still argues that persistence would have won a victory against France, and great wealth. The anti-war policy she attributes to Conscience as 'cowardly' (B 206) is now 'unwise' (243, 262 indirectly answering the king's *vnwittiliche* at 133) and also 'unjust' (244–9), since the king's followers deserved a share in the spoils. Mede's notion of a conqueror will be ironically echoed by Conscience's in 21.30–3, only to be contradicted by its re-interpretation at 21.50–62 in application to Christ. **233** *sixty thousand*: an 'indefinite large number', as at B 17.23. If Mede means the lives of men rescued by 'bought truces and ransoms' (*Pe*), her argument is fallacious, since peace with France would have saved even more. **239–40** *fortune; wyrdus*: an adroit conjunction of two (often contrasted) notions, making it seem that in rejecting a chance-presented opportunity the king defied his God-given destiny. **242** *heritage*: the basis of the campaign being Edward's claim to the French throne through the female line in 1337 (although he had already paid homage to Philip of Valois in 1329). Since even those who favoured peace would have seemed disloyal to question the claim's validity, in his reply Conscience does not. **243** *sulle*: in the Treaty of Brétigny of 8 May 1360, whereby Edward abandoned his claim to France in return for the cession of Aquitaine, Calais and Guisnes, and agreed to send back the captured

French king John for a huge ransom (Keen 1973:139–42). **244** *ducherie*: a sovereign duchy. Throughout the war, the English refused to acknowledge French suzerainty over the duchy of Aquitaine.

B 189–200 (A 176–87, Z 127–38) 189 'In Normandy it was not on my account that he suffered trouble'; by alluding to the campaign of 1359–60 Mede blames the King's 'conscience' (moral scruple) for his decision to end the war. **191–3** *cold...cloude*: the hailstorm and cold of 'Black Monday' (14 Apr. 1360) that contributed to Edward's decision to quit France. **195–6** Mede's claim that the pillaging suffered by the French people (whose pots and pans the English soldiers carried off) was due to the abandonment of the campaign gets a new 'spin' in **C 239–40**, which turn a recognition that the campaign was faltering (**B**) into a bold assertion that it was succeeding. *Caleis*: the port of embarkation, held by the English, and doubtless full of dealers ready to buy the utensils cheaply (and sell them back to the French at a profit).

245–84 245–56 provide a stronger and more detailed argument for persisting with the war than do the preceding versions. Since Mede claims that those who fought for the king expected to share in the spoils of victory, she plainly sees the motive of a foreign war as gain (little has changed). Though referring to events of the 1360s, this passage written in the late 1380s may reflect disillusionment in England, after military defeats in Aquitaine during the previous decade, about the failure of the war to bring any long-term economic benefit or political security (see on 209). **247** *ladde*: even more extravagant than *brol* (retained from **B** at 261), where only the king's kin are envisaged. **249** *as a man*: 'as befits a man [of consequence]'; on this 'normative' use of *man* cf. 267 and *manhode* at 230. **251b–52** 'or else make [his men] grants of everything they can win, so that they might gain best advantage from it'. A conqueror should reward his followers himself, or leave them to acquire their own spoils from the conquered. **254** *coueiteth*: an audacious pun; cf. Conscience's 'benign' wordplay at B 164. **255–6** *constable*: in this context not 'chief officer of a ruler's household or court' (MED s.v. 2 (b), citing the line, and Alf*G* s.v.) but 'a high (or the chief) military officer of a ruler' (MED s.v. 4, with apt quotation from *The Siege of Jerusalem* 881–2: 'To þe kyng wer called *constables* þanne,/ *Marchals*...men þat he to tristiþ', and see Sk's note *ad loc*, McKisack p. 265, Alf*G* s.v. *Marshal*). *marschal*: the king's commander-in-chief in the field, a term parallel in sense-development with *constable* (see OED svv.). Since Mede says that she would not entrust the (closely similar) duties of these officers to Conscience 'there [she] moste fyhte', a comma after *men* 256 would probably make this clearer. **262** *Vnconnynglich*: cf. 243; for 'cowardly' (B 206) see 241. **263** *a litel moné (siluer)*: actually three million crowns (in *gold*), never paid in full by the French.

A 196–276 form *this version's first major addition* and replace the vivid but conceptually somewhat uncertain 147–76 that conclude Passus III in **Z**. **266** *aliens*: in context perhaps referring to foreign mercenaries in the king's army. **269** *ȝerne...ryde*: i.e. on their service. **277** Internal rhyme here (and at 280–1 below) illustrates Mede's seductive rhetorical uses of *repetitio* (e.g. *mede* a dozen times; and compare also 275, 284 with B 220, 259). **279** *mede...prentis*: 'payment for training their apprentices' (on the sums paid, cf. Lipson 1959:414–16). The play of sound in *crafty...crauen, leueth...loueth* at 281 and the fourfold internal rhyme in 280–1 hint at a real ('Platonic') and not merely accidental affinity between the concepts of 'skill' and 'life' and that of 'meed'. **281–2** *mede...hire*: personified (cf. B 250) and better treated like B 227, where capitalisation formally recognises the word-play. **284** *me thynketh*: the repetition turning a Type III to a Type I line, while weakening (?intentionally) the King's assertion. *maistrye*: since she has won the debate, and deserves to rule.

(v) 285–482 *Conscience's rejoinder*, in **B** over twice and in **C** over three times as long as Mede's speech, decisively refutes her argument, supporting impassioned rhetoric with a quasi-scholastic structure.

B 230–58 separate two senses of the one word *mede* and propound a formal *distinctio* between 'reward' as God's proper recompense to those who 'work well' (= live a life of virtue) and the improper or 'unmeasured' reward the unjust give to wrong-doers, whom God will finally punish. This is supported by a bipartite scriptural *auctoritas* in the form of a question (234*a*) answered by another text (237*a*). Conscience does not rebut Mede's case point by point but answers 223–4 in 252–4*a*, 217–8 in 255–6 and 226 in 257–8 (on these lines see generally AlfQ p. 5, comparing the passage to B 7.40–51*a*). **234** *Prophete*: a Christian title for King David, the traditional author of the psalms (see Ac 2:25–35, esp. 30), based on his foretelling of the Messiah in Pss 15:8–11, 109:1, 131:11. **234*a*; 237*a*** 'Lord, who shall dwell in thy tabernacle? [Or who shall rest in thy holy hill?] He that walketh without blemish, and worketh justice' (Ps 14:1–2). **238** *of o colour...wille*: '[with his baptismal garment of innocence] spotlessly white [*sine macula* 'without blemish'], without hypocrisy or duplicity'. AlfQ, 6n highlights the phrase's legal connotations, citing the Latin vss in *CA* Pr ii: *Legibus vnicolor tunc temporis aura refulsit, / Iusticie plane tuncque fuere vie* ('Climate of law unclouded shone, / The paths of justice smoothly ran'); but it also has Biblical overtones (see Lev 19:19). **241** *enformeþ*: 'advises, gives [legal] counsel to' (AlfQ 7n10; MED s.v. 2). *truþe*: here and at 243 = 'justice' in a legal sense. **241*a*** 'He that hath not put out his money to usury, nor taken bribes against the innocent' (Ps 14:5, the *salmes ende*). The first two texts are translated after being quoted, the third before.

246–7 'A second meed, one without proper limits' (with *mesurelees* contrast *mesurable* 256). *desireþ...take*: the *maistres* craving and accepting such meed for wrongful 'maintenance'; but *take* may play on its antonym 'give' (the sense at C 3.350). **252** *plesynge*: 'a gift or offering (that will give them) pleasure', [rather than 'a sacrificial offering pleasing to God']; see MED s.v. (c), (a). **254** *hire...here*: the annominative wordplay underlining the semantic pun on *mede*: 'they get on earth the only enjoyable reward they will ever get'. **254*a*** 'Amen, [I say to you], they have received their reward' (Mt 6:5); Christ's condemnation of religious hypocrisy effectively applied to clerical greed.

285–313 285 *Nay...sothe*: translating a scholastic formula of denial (*nego*), adducing support from an authoritative Biblical text, and following it as in **B** with a *distinctio* introduced with *Ac* as an equivalent to the scholastic *sed contra* formula. **287–9** loosely paraphrase Ps 25:10 (B 249), quoted at 118*a* above and B 249 below. The 'large' or liberal-handed have 'gifts' in their right hands that they have won 'unlawfully' (= *iniquitatibus*) with their left. For a very full discussion of this passage see Adams 1988:217–32. **290–302** tactically define *mede* as 'payment in advance of work done', implying that such payment is neither wise nor just. **290** *mercede*: the King's objection at 342 that 'English was it never' holds for this word too, apparently coined by **L** from Latin *mercedem* and found only here, at 304, 332 and as a scribal variant in the **B** ms Cot at 20.76 (see *TN*). **293–5** The syntax is anacoluthic: 'It is neither reasonable nor just that (*That* 294)...nor that (*And for to* 295)...' **296–7** Pe's explanation, that 'a man should be prepared to work even if he has no certainty that his employer will survive to pay him his proper reward' is mistaken: the referent of *he* 296 is the *he* of 294. What is 'against right and reason' (on the legal resonances of which, see AlfG s.v.) is for the workman to take or demand payment 'before the doing', when *he* may not survive to finish the job. **299** *pre manibus*: 'in advance' [= *avaunt la main*], a term 'often associated with usurious or unethical agreements' (AlfG); also at 9.45, and showing **C**'s heightened interest in legal practice. **300** *Harlotes*: the collocation with *hoores* may suggest one who either frequents or employs the latter, and a specific contextual sense 'bawds' or 'pimps'. **307*a*** 'The wages of him that hath been hired by thee shall not abide with thee until the morning' (Lev 19:13); 'a commonplace in canon law' (AlfQ, citing Brinton 2:364), alluded to by Piers at 7.195. **308** *reue*: the one who would pay the workmen their wages. **311** An unusual macaronic T-type line; see on B 254*a* above. **313** *permutacioun....peneworth*: presupposing not 'exactly equal exchange value' but a 'just price' for goods that takes proper account of the labour that went to producing them.

314–406 distinguish ingeniously (in some 90 added lines) between two *terms*, the familar *mede* and the newly-coined *mercede*. **C** grounds its distinction, more elaborate than **B**'s, in the nature of language, with grammar understood as an analogically ordered system reflecting the *ratio* or proportional relation between the human and the divine. But **C**'s conceptual procedure derives directly from **B**'s unmediated notion of a correct and incorrect *ratio* 'relacioun' between deed and desert. On the complexities and difficulties in this passage see Overstreet 1984.

314–31 321 *hardy to claymen*: elliptical for 'are to be so audacious as to claim'; cf. 13.9. **323** *Solomon*: although the prior warning was to the *lege* (316), this one seems addressed to the King (and indeed no heir of Richard was to be king of England). But perhaps **L** is alluding to Richard's youthful household counsellors (Keen 1973:276) and suggesting a parallel between the king and Solomon's son Roboam, who 'left the counsel of the old men...and consulted with the young men that had been brought up with him and stood before him' (III Kgs 12:8). *grace*: favour (as at 330) and not, despite the context, 'grace' in the theological sense. **326** *refte...mynde*: not strictly accurate, since Solomon's kingdom was lost only by his heirs. Nor does *ryhte mynde* here literally denote sanity (as claimed by MED s.v. *right* a. 6 (a), citing this line) so much as moral righteousness (cf. *ryhte* 324). However, when III Kgs 11:9 states that *aversa esset mens eius a Domino*, the 'turning away' is a religious one, and Solomon's rejection of moral wisdom may be meant to signify a metaphorical descent into unreason. **327** *mysbileue...leue*: the semantic pun pointedly implying that the speaker's belief *is* true. *helle*: because '[he] follow[ed] strange gods' (III Kgs 11:2); *Pe* notes contemporary 'uncertainty' about this because the idolatry has no mention in the parallel (later) account in II Para 9. But Will's words at 11.221 suggest no uncertainty, though Ymaginatif at 14.192 in urging prayer for Solomon's salvation will appeal to the absence of any *scripture* specifying his fate, and to the immensity of God's mercy. **328–9** *So... so*: both words carrying stress and playing on the senses 'therefore', 'in this way'. *si...glose*: 'without an implicit condition [that the recipient remain faithful to God]'. *Pe* aptly cites God's conditional offer of *grace* to Solomon: 'si ambulaveris coram me...suscitabo thronum regni tui... Si autem aversi fueritis,...evellam vos de terra mea...' (II Para 7:17–19; cf. III Kgs 11:9 at 326).

332–406 propose an extended *distinctio* between *mede* and *mercede* by means of an analogy from grammatical relations, but initially define them simply as kinds of 'relation'. Of these *mercede* (the *second* 'relation' mentioned) denotes the direct or straight (*rect*) kind and *mede* the indirect. MED records *rect* as unique to **L** but illustrates only a grammatical sense that would necessitate translating *As* 335 (on which see *TN*) 'inasmuch as', thus deriv-

ing the moral 'ought' from the grammatical 'is' (value from fact). But the elaborateness of the analogy should not obscure the major ethical sense 'morally correct or upright' of *rect* at 366, which both OED and MED overlook and AlfG (despite recognising its cross-reference to *right*) leaves unsubstantiated. The basic *grammatical* sense of 'direct' applies to the nominative case, 'unbent' or uninflected, as opposed to the indirect or oblique cases, 'bent at an angle, inflected'. But while the argument illustrates an ethical *relacioun* that may be direct or indirect, this is conceptually prior to the analogy from grammar, in which the direct / indirect categories concern the relationships of nouns to their dependent adjectives. *Pe* explains that *mercede* (direct or proper reward) 'reflects the concord between God and man', whereas with *mede* 'the relationship is "indirect" and confused', though he concedes that since 'indirect relation' in grammar is not actually *incorrect*, 'some degree of propriety' is preserved for *mede*. But while the 'indirect relation' in grammar may not be confused, Conscience's analogy may (unintentionally) confuse, since in stipulating that a wage is *mercede* and payment for goods is 'exchange', he wants to exclude Mede from *any* rôle in human affairs. However, the coherence of the argument is ably defended with illuminating reference to the background of grammatical theory by Carlson 1991; and for a subtle analysis of the passage in terms of philosophical realism see Smith 1994.

333–42 333–4 The syntax is ambiguous, but *rect* must in this context apply to the nearer, *indirect* to the remoter antecedent. *reninde...hemsuluen*: rendered by *Sk* 'in a settled and secure (or regular) manner, agreeing with themselves (according to rule)', more closely by *Pe* as 'dependent on a firm and sure (concept of relation), in which both have a part' (the N form *reninde* is unusual in **L**). The metaphor of 'running on' suggests something like carriage-wheels over a road; but the notion of a 'basis' implied in *sikir* (cf. *fundement* 344) is not the relation itself (of *mede* and *mercede*) or its concept, but the condition that makes the relation possible and also 'resembles' it, in the way that adjective and noun achieve 'unity' and 'agreement' in the grammatical sphere. MED glosses *semblable* 3(c) as 'concordant', but with this example only, and presupposes a special 'grammatical' sense before the analogy from grammatical concord has been introduced. Under sense 2 'identical (in character) with', its illustrations cite the word with *wise*, *cas* and *manere*, but not with *relacion*. More naturally, it should therefore mean '(closely) similar to' (sense 1). Of the five other occurrences, the nearest to this (16.112), which states that poverty *is syb to Crist sulue and* semblable *bothe*, supports the latter reading. **337** *ayther...hem*: in grammar, the referents here are noun and adjective, which 'help' each other when they accord; but in the moral and religious sphere, they are the human will and the divine law which (when agreeing) generate the *retribucioun* 'reward' of final grace and heavenly happiness (cf. Carlson 1991). **339a** 'Be pleased, O Lord [for Thy name's sake] to grant eternal life to all of us who do good'; found in an early grace before meals (*Babees Book*, 382–5). The relevance of such a prayer here is to underline the 'habitual' character of Christian *lyuynge* (cf. 15.265). **340–2** Though the distinction between the two relations and the analogy that elucidates it is clear, the King not unreasonably wants this clerkly notion expounded in the vernacular (recalling Haukyn's request to Pacience at B 14.277).

343–61 343 *Relacioun*; *record*: the sense of 'a written account of legal proceedings kept as conclusive evidence' (MED s.v. *recorde* n. 5a) is worth noting as it reinforces the legal sense of *relacioun* 'the action of relating or narrating (an account....etc)' (AlfG 130) and 'reminds us of the historical basis of Christianity and the duty of the Christian to bear witness to it' (Martin in Vaughan 1993:173). **343a** 'Because it recalls a thing preceding it / its antecedent'. The formula explains the grammatical relation of a relative pronoun to its antecedent, as in Peter of Spain's 'Relativum *est ante latae rei recordativum, quia...relatio est ante late rei recordatio*' (Amassian and Sadowsky 1971:466). Such a fanciful etymology of *relatio* may have suggested use of grammatical analogy to explain a moral and spiritual *relacioun* (though Carlson 1991 throws light on the wider theological significance of Latin grammar in late medieval thought). A somewhat similar metaphor is found in a text by Henry de Harkeley in Lambeth Palace Library MS 61, ff. 143–147v (Kemp 1981:353–4). **344–5** 'Following (the course) and reaching down to the base of a stronghold, And (able) firmly (to) rise / ?project in order to strengthen the foundation (walls)'. The exact sense is uncertain, but 'direct relation' is envisaged as like foundation-course and buttresses that help support the walls (which themselves reach down to the base). Grammatical concord is imagined to 'strengthen' a linguistic, as a buttress strengthens a masonry structure. The rhetorical inversion of *fundement* and *strenghe* and the noun-verb conversion of the latter are noteworthy. **346** *In*: 'In respect of.' **347–50** *As...*: a second analogy to illustrate 'direct relation', which leads back ingeniously to the prior analogy from grammar. **347** *byleueth*: '(who) resides'. **348** *puyr treuthe*: 'absolute(ly guaranteed) uprightness (in dealing with him)'. **349–50** describe the attributes of the perfect earthly master, which are modelled on those of the heavenly master. **351** *hol herte*: a sincere heart (*cor integrum*) with faith, from which arises the second theological virtue, hope (cf. its re-appearance at 7.257 as the place where charity will make its home). **351–3** *Pe*'s explanation can hardly be bettered: 'Man is here the adjective seeking direct relation, or concord, with the substantive [God], out of which

concord will come salvation...God is...antecedent, since all ...true concord depends upon him; yet...self-sufficient and...not conditioned by the relationship'. As *Pe* goes on to say, **L** refers indiscriminately to the noun / adj., antecedent / relative pronoun relation, two of the four types of grammatical relation (the others being subject / verb, partitive or superlative / genitive). *relacioun...sauacioun*: the rhyme (*concordantia sonuum*), which can hardly be accidental (see Appendix I § 5 ii), aurally echoes the grammatical agreement of adjective and noun. **352** *Seketh*: '(that) seeks'. *sustantif*: as here punctuated, a noun, the reading preferred because this is what 'God' must be in the metaphor as a whole. But there may be an elaborate clerkly pun, if it is also an adjective, as in MED s.v. *substantif* adj. (c), since God must also be man's 'substantive salvation'. **353** *ground of al*: the divine substance as the basis of reality, echoing Anima's exposition at B 15.371 of grammar as 'ground of all (learning)'. As *prima substantia*, God is metaphysically 'antecedent' to all created being, which may be said to relate to him 'adjectivally' (attributively). **354** *rihte*: playing on the two senses of *rect*, 'direct' and 'right(eous)'. **355–9** The influence of the *crede* (359) on the metaphor's development is stressed in *Pe*'s 'Grammatical agreement...correspond[s] to concord with Christ' through belief in the Creed's key articles, such as the Incarnation: *Verbum caro factum est* 'And the Word was made flesh' (Jn 1:14); the Church: *Credere in ecclesia* 356 (*Sarum Missal* 592); the forgiveness of sins: *remissioun to haue = remissionem peccatorum*, already quoted at B 15.611; and life eternal: *lyue...withouten ende = vitam eternam* (12th clause of the Apostles' Creed). But while *Pe* (with MED s.v. *kinde* n. 14b., uniquely citing this line from before C15) correctly glosses *kynde* in context as = *gendre* '(grammatical) gender' (394), he overlooks its root sense of 'nature', on which **L** plays (divine *nature* becomes human flesh, but the nouns *verbum* and *caro* do not have the same *gender*). Also overlooked is the wordplay on *case* 356, referring to 'situation' (MED s.v. *cas* n. 19a *as against* 10, the grammatical sense) of the *trewe* man as a member of the Church, and on *nombre* 357. The last is obscure unless *rotye and aryse* does not refer to a *post-mortem* corruption (MED s.v. *roten* v. 1a) and resurrection but to the manifold post-baptismal sinning and repentance (ib. s.v. 2 (a)) of even 'þe saddest man on erthe' (10.49). AlfQ rightly links 355b with the eighth article of the Nicene Creed (*Missal* 591) *Et homo factus est* 'And was made man'; but he overlooks the specific relevance of the Johannine sentence (not identical with the credal clause), in which *Verbum* punningly affirms the divine *Word* as the ontological and grammatical 'substantive' to which humankind must 'adjectivally' accord.

362–72 362 *Indirect*: a relation improper in grammar because the adjective is made to pair promiscuously with plural and singular nouns of all genders (e.g. 'hi pueri et puellae sunt Angli'). **362–3** The sense and tone alike recall B 15.48–9. **365** *gode and nat gode*: some of the concords will be fortuitously correct, as some forms of 'meed' may be genuinely deserved; but the analogy is again confusing (see above), since Conscience has sharply distinguished *mercede* from *mede*. Perhaps *in which...nat gode* should be in brackets and the antecedent of *which* understood as *nombres* (with no semi-colon after) rather than *cache to and come to. and...wille*: 'and (yet) give them what neither of them (actually) wants'; i.e. the attempt to have it both ways results in having it neither way. **366–9** The strictly logical force of these two analogies from family relationships is dubious. Thus it may well be 'unreasonable' to reject one's father's surname while insisting on one's rights as his son, or to take a wife but refuse to accept her bad qualities with her good. Yet accepting a 'plurality of obligations' would seem to sit better with *rect* than with *indirect* relation, even if it is plain how promiscuous 'agreements' might lead to the incurring of such obligations. *Pe*'s comment that 'social contracts, like grammatical relations, are binding in all their parts' since 'the parties to the contract cannot pick and choose which parts they are prepared to observe' expresses the gist of the argument perhaps more connectedly than the wording of the text itself allows. **370–2** *indirect*: here defined as desire for a plurality of benefits without acceptance of a plurality of obligations.

373–406 373–81 define a threefold reciprocal relation of king and community by *relacioun rect* corresponding to the triple categories of grammar. **375** abruptly shifts viewpoint in the b-half to accommodate the alliteration: but these are all things the king requires the *comune* to do for him. **377–8** The three terms cover the ruler's duty: to preserve customary law, adminster it with equity and keep the good of his people in mind. **378** *Lawe, loue and lewete*: 'agreement' of the *comune* with the king (adjectival 'concord' with the noun antecedent) is made conditional on his offering them these. While the phrase recalls both B Pr 122 and C Pr 149 (cf. 17.126–31), a theological resonance is perhaps suggested by the collocation of *lewete* with love (= charity) and law (= faith). *lord antecedent*: cf. 353. **379** *heued*: the parallel with Christ (as head of the Church) reinforces the equation of royal with divine in *antecedent*, so that Conscience here seems to endorse the quasi-absolutist claims of the King-figure at B 19.475 to be *aller heed* 'head of all' as well as *heed of lawe* 473). **380–1** Constancy as well as impartiality in the king mirrors his divine model. **382–92** The attack on personal self-interest involves a play on the senses of *cas*: the *puyr indirect* are 'defective in respect of (grammatical) case' (386) and so careless of 'the outcome of a case [law-suit]' (388), as long as they gain personally. **387** *relatifs indirect*: relative pronouns that do not agree correctly with their antecedents (e.g. *vir* qui [*for* cui] *librum dedi* 'The man *who* I gave the book to'). **389** *peccunie*: from Lat through OF; first used by **L**. **391–2** *noumbre*; *acorde*: both perhaps playing on grammatical senses. Conscience's ideal outcome in a legal case is 'unity', a reconciliation of the parties to the dispute on the basis of reciprocal concession, not the outright victory of one (usually the wealthier) through ability to pay a lawyer or bribe a judge. **394–9** The three categories are exemplified in reverse order: *alle maner* = number; *o kynde* [unity of faith] = gender, and *soffre penaunce* = case. **395** re-uses A 11.306 with change only of the last lift. **395–6** have running alliteration and a 'wrenched' stress on *wymmén*. **400** 'For love of that Lord who died for love of us'. **401** *kynde*: a polysemantic pun on 'nature' and 'gender'. **401a** echoes the Athanasian Creed's 'Ita *Deus* et *homo* unus est Christus' (*Sarum Breviary* 2:484); the bare juxtaposition (elliptical for 'God (became) man') is later literally rendered by the compound *God-Man* at 12.115. **402** *noumbre*: 'company' and '(grammatical category of) number'. **402a** '[God is charity: and] he that abideth in charity abideth in God, and God in him' (I Jn 4:16; so also at B 5.487a (2), B 9.64a). **403–5a** 'And so humanity is, as it were, a noun that requires an adjective with three real inflexional endings; [for] God [who is] one is a Trinity: namely, Father, Son and Holy Spirit'. The formula recalls B 10.239–40a. **403** *man...mankynde...maner*: the pun revealing **L**'s 'Platonic' supposition of a 'real' relation between word and referent reflected in the felicitous homophonic overlaps between individual verbal items. **404** *hic et hec homo*: 'this human being (whether male or female)'; *homo* being a noun of common gender, the demonstrative can be both masculine and feminine. **405** *trewe*: because of God's nature as Truth (cf. *trewe Trinite* 11.151) but also 'genuine', 'authentic'. *termisones*: adapted from OF *terminaison* and found only here. It refers to the three distinct aspects or 'cases' (acc., gen., dat. / abl. of e.g. *verus* 'true') whereby the three persons of the Trinity may be thought to 'qualify' the *human* 'substantive' (through creation, incarnation and indwelling presence). **405a** *nominatiuo*: literally 'in the nominative'. *Pe* finds a pun on *in nomine*, 'in the name of [the Father, etc]', the opening words of the blessing when making the sign of the cross; but in context it is likelier to be on 'namely'. The nominative is the case of the *subiectum* 'the [verbal] subject' / '[divine] substance' which is 'one' but trinally 'inflected' by the three Persons. The final pun is of a piece with **L**'s manner throughout this remarkable passage.

407–35 407–8 *Regum...Absoloun*: C takes up the revision of **B** with an added example from II Kgs [= II Sam] 14–18, describing the tragic ambition of David's son. Absalom was killed while caught in the branches of an oak (18:14–15); but **L** deliberately suggests an execution by hanging, the fate to which desire for *mede* has

Commentary

brought many (in 408 *heo* rather than / as well as *How* bears stress). **408** *sethe*: 'then, next', i.e. in order of the argument, not of the Bible, the story of Saul and the *kyng* (Agag, king of the Amalekites) being in I Kgs [= I Sam] 15, which follows immediately after the Book of Ruth. *for mede*: Saul's sin was to obey the voice of the people, not God (ibid. vs. 24); but Conscience, perhaps on the basis of 15:19, interprets his retention of the spoils as greed (425 below). **410–11** See 1 Kgs 31:2–4. *sone*: presumably Jonathan, though all three of Saul's sons died (see 429). *his knaue*: David (I Kgs 16:17–23). *lambren*: the commonest form, a 'double plural' (like *children*) with both the OE *-ru* ending and standard *-en* by analogy (Mossé § 59). **412** *Regum*: for *Liber Regum* 'the Book of Kings'. **415** *for dedes of here eldres*: their hostility to the Israelites in the wilderness, for which God promised to destroy them (Ex 17:8–16). A 245 closely recalls A 2.51, which may have been removed in **B** for that reason. **420** *woman*: in the contextually restricted contrastive sense of 'unmarried woman' (not recorded in MED). A 251 *Crist*: a loose synonym for *God* occasioned by alliterative necessity, as at A 10.151, 156 (cf. *WPal* 3148); **B** and **C** avoid such imprecision. **423** *mede of money*: 'payment in cash' (cf. A 249 'millions in cash'). **426** *beste*: **C** closely follows I Kgs 15:15 in making this detailed revision. **427** improves in substance and style on B 275. **429** *sayde... deye*: interpreting God's 'rejection' of Saul and his refusal to 'spare' at I Kgs 15:26, 29 as a threat of shameful death. **432** *culorum*: (pronounced *clórum*) 'conclusion', **L**'s 'clerkly' formation from [*per omnia saecula sae*]*culorum* 'for ever and ever', the ending of solemn prayers like the Offertory at Mass. Here it signifies 'full implications' (cf. Alf*Q ad loc*, referring to the echo in *RRe* 72: 'And constrewe ich clause with the *culorum*'). These implications remain obscure, but the examples of Absalom and Saul might seem in different ways applicable to King Richard, one suggesting his martial inferiority to his grandfather Edward III and father the Black Prince, the other warning that he might lose throne, life and line through succumbing to Mede (434–5 were however already in **B**). **433** Cf. Pr 217–18.

436–82 *Conscience's prophetic lines*, much extended in **B**, are little changed in **C** (on the 'prophetic' character of *PP* generally and **L**'s relation with the Biblical prophets, particularly Isaiah, see Steinberg 1991). The Samuel-Saul-David motif having been present from **A**, no more immediately contemporary references can be securely conjectured, except that the **B** source of 457–66 presumably warned against renewal of the war with France in the summer of 1377 just after Edward III's death, which brought many calamitous defeats and setbacks (Keen 1973:257). More positively, the **B** expansion may be connected with the jubilee proclaimed in the the 50th and last year of Edward III's reign (Feb. 1377) and the widespread

hope of peace and prosperity in that of his successor Richard, David being 'the type of the ideal king' (*Pe*). But the prophecy, like that at 5.168–79=B 10.316–29, remains indeterminate as to time and is generally influenced by the 'messianic' model in Is 2:2–4 (*Bn*), to which Baldwin (1981[1]:20, 95n37) adds Jer 30:8–10, Amos 9:11–15 and interpretations of them in the *Glossa Ordinaria* (*PL* 114:44, 580). **437** echoes Pr 150 in understanding reason as the basis of justice and so as fitted to rule and order the state (Alf*G* s.v. *Resoun*; Alford in Kennedy *et al.* 1988:199–215). **438** At the time of **A** this would have been seen to refer to Edward III and his son the Black Prince, then in his thirties (Richard was not born till 1367). **440** *alle oure enemyes*: the topical referent of this revised last lift (if one is sought) being perhaps Spain, France and Scotland, which were all at war with England in the mid-1380s. **441** *o Cristene kyng*: an 'apocalyptic' touch, since England already had 'one' king, and there was little prospect of a single monarch ruling all Christendom. **445** *taketh*: 'takes (or gives) money'. *treuthe*: probably best capitalised (with referent 'God as Justice'). *transuerseth*: a solemn word, first instanced here. **446** *Lewete*: 'Justice', clearly distinguishable from the process of law itself. **447** *for*: 'in order to do' / '(because of being richly paid) for doing'; in an ideal society no money would be made out of law as a profession. *werie*: the form of this weak verb (like *maky* 452) is characteristically SW (Mossé, *HME* 79). **450** *letteth*: the subject is either 'evil' or 'Mede'. **451–2** express sentiments to be re-iterated by Reason at 4.144–5 as a real possibility if the king himself espouses *treuthe*. **451** *kynde loue*: a phrase suggesting the basis of society in a common bond of mutual human concern. **452** *maky...laborer*: 'force lawyers to work with their hands for a living'. **454** *and...glade*: semi-parenthetical in both texts, though *so* makes it clearer ('and as a result become glad'). **456** *Moises*: the great Lawgiver, appropriately associated with the reign of perfect justice expected with the coming of the Messiah (cf. 17.295–7). That some Jewish sages expected his return is asserted at 17.312. *þat...trewe*: elliptical in **C** for 'on account of the fact that...' **459** *smythye*: with passive sense after factitive *don*. **460a** '[And he shall judge the Gentiles and rebuke many people]: and they shall turn their swords into ploughshares and their spears into sickles' (Is 2:4a); a key Messianic prophecy read in the Office of the first week in Advent. **462** *speke of God*: i.e. as a preacher (unless these words anticipate a person like Piers Plowman). *spille no tyme*: revision to a positive injunction of **B**'s threat of self-destruction against the slothful. The prevention of the sin of sloth is envisaged later by Reason (5.127) and Wit (10.187) as a practical matter, not a millennial ideal. **463** *Placebo*: 'I will please [the Lord in the land of the living]' (Ps 114:9). *Dirige*: 'Direct my way, Lord, in thy sight' ('Dirige Domine Deus meus in conspectu tuo viam meam' [*Breviary* 2:273], based on Ps 5:9b). These words that begin the antiphons of the Office of the Dead at vespers and matins respectively were contained in the prayerbook called the 'primer' and will be cited by the Dreamer as among the 'lomes' he 'labours with' in his self-defence against the charge of idleness before Reason and Conscience (45–6). Bp. Brinton's ironic contrast of *placebo* with *dirige* (1:204) cited in Alf*Q* does not seem relevant here, since Conscience names both psalms to exhort the clergy to pray to God 'at all times', i.e. for those in the land of the living and of the dead alike. **464** *seuene psalmes*: nos. 6, 31, 37, 50 (the 'Miserere'), 101, 129 ('De profundis') and 142, called 'penitential' because specially concerned with sin and repentance. They could be said as a private devotion or on behalf of others, as Will states at 5.47–8. **B 311–12** *hunte*: '"hunt" only in a way pleasing to God [with prayer]'. *dyngen*: '"strike blows" [cf. B VI 141 for literal sense] only by "hammering away" at saying the psalms'. The phrase occurs in two alliterative pieces, the mid-C14th 'Papelard Priest' (ed. Smith 1951:44, Revard 2001) and the late C14th 'Choristers' Lament' (ed. Utley 1946, Holsinger 1999, Appendix). **467–75** prophesy an ideal state of affairs in which 'He that speaketh truth in his heart: who hath not used deceit in his tongue' (Ps 14:3) will preside as sole judge in a single court, and, in a realm wholly at peace with itself and its neighbours, no corruption in the law will hinder the operation of justice. **470–1** *recorde...most trewe acorden*: unclear in reference, but Baldwin takes Conscience's rejection of corrupt jury assises to signify preference for 'the autocratic process of "judgement by record", and not the normal processes of Common Law' (1981[1]:20, 95n36, citing *Stat. Realm* 15 Richard II c.2). **472** *Kynges court*: the Court of King's Bench (originally sitting under the king), the chief forum for criminal actions and appeals from the Court of Common Pleas (which handled civil actions and appeals from local and manorial courts). *constorie*: see on 34 above. *chapitle*: the court of a cathedral, monastic or collegiate chapter, hearing disciplinary offences. **473** *a court*: echoing the Ciceronian idea of the unity and uniformity of all true law based upon right reason (Alford 1988[1]:203n21). **476** The wordplay again reflects 'lexical Platonism': a wrong kind of 'smiting' will lead to being 'smitten'. **476a** 'Nation shall not lift up sword against nation: neither shall they be exercised any more to war' (Is 2:4b); completing the quotation at 460*a*. **477–82** are unchanged from **B** and have no clearly ascertainable topical reference. Such riddling prophecies were common (e.g. 'John of Bridlington', in Wright, *Political Poems,* I) and an 'apocalyptic' sense, 'seriously meant' (*Pe*) but vague rather than exact, seems intended (see Thomas Wimbledon's 1388 Sermon at Paul's cross, 895–8, and Bloomfield 1961:211–12). **477** *worste*: indicating the calamities preceding the end of the

world. **478** *sonnes*: more probably an extraordinary portent than (metonymically) a time six years hence. *ship*: perhaps emblematising the Church (the *navis* or *arca Christi*). *half a shef*: i.e. twelve, since a full sheaf had 24 arrows (Bradley 1910). The figure may be meant to evoke the twelve apostles who will judge mankind with Christ on doomsday (Mt 19:28) and *half* the number of the 24 'ancients' in Apoc 11:16 (of whom the other twelve may be the Major Prophets). **479** *myddel of a mone*: most probably alluding to the Paschal Full Moon of Easter Week, a mysterious dramatic revelation of which will bring about the conversion of Jews and Moslems alike. The Jewish Passover celebrated on the 15th day of the first month (Lev 23:6) was reckoned by the Synoptic Gospels as the date of the Last Supper (in Jn 13:1 this is the *eve* of the pasch). The image metonymically evokes either 'the events of the crucifixion' (*Sk*) or, more probably, Christ's example of humble charity which, if followed by all Christians, should lead to the conversion of the Jews. Galloway (1995:87–9) interprets the line in the light of a well-known riddle contained in ms BL Harley 3362 as interpreted according to the methods of the *Secretum Philosophorum*, an early C14th English treatise on riddles. This *aenigma* is a Leonine couplet *Lune dimidium solis pariterque rotundum, / Et pars quarta rote: nil plus deus exigit a te* 'Half of a moon and equally the round of a sun, And the fourth part of a wheel: nothing more does God demand from you'. Here, the 'half of the moon' (according to its shape) will be the letter C, the 'round of the sun' O and the 'quarter of *rota*' the letter R, giving the Latin word COR 'heart' as the answer to the riddle. Ingenious and entirely in **L**'s spirit, its relevance to the riddle of Patience at 15.163 seems more than arguable. But the phrase *myddel of the mone* is unlikely to mean anything except 'half way point of the lunar cycle, full of the moon' (see MED s.v. *middel* n. 4), strongly suggesting the same sense at its later appearance in the **B** form of Patience's riddle (13.156). **480** *Saresines*: in the light of 481, this must mean the Moslems. *Credo..:* 'I believe in the Holy Spirit' (from the Apostles' Creed). **B 328** 'Glory to God in the highest: [and on earth peace to men of good will]' (Lk 2:14). The scriptural source of **B** evokes the birth of Christ as the peace-bringing event, **C**'s key article from the Apostles' Creed points to Pentecost; but since both texts occur in the Mass (the latter being the opening of the *Gloria*), the peace-bringing power of the Eucharist (cf. B 13.259) clearly underlies Conscience's entire plea for peace. The *syhte* that will cause the Moslems to sing their credal song is the full moon that will inaugurate the new order, or the conversion of the Jews (*Pe*). But since it is unclear why either event in itself would convince the Saracens, the 'sight' of 'Christians living virtuously in peace and charity' (*Bn*) is more probably intended (**L** associates both 'holy men' and 'helpe of the Holy Goste' (17.185) with the conversion of the Moslems). **481** *Machameth*: regarded here as an apostate Christian driven to found his own religion by a failed ambition to be pope (17.165–82), who will one day be punished in the demise of Islam; hence the association with Mede, with her promises to advance clerks (3.35–7). **482** 'A good name is better than great riches' (Prov 22:1); see on 486*a*. The point is that Mede, for all her wealth, has a bad name that she canot shake off.

(vi) 483–99 483 *As...wynd*: a stock comparison (*Patience* 411, stanzaic *Morte Arthur* 1144). **484** *Sapiense*: **L**'s usual name for the *libri sapientiae* or 'Wisdom' books received by the medieval Church: Proverbs, Ecclesiastes, Wisdom and Ecclesiasticus, the first three regarded as the work of Solomon (see Davlin 1988:23–33). **486*a*** 'He that maketh presents shall purchase victory and honour' (Prov. 22:9). Mede both recognises the source of the Latin and adroitly answers Conscience's authority with a counter-citation from only a few verses later in the chapter; see 497 below. **487** Conscience courteously acknowledges Mede's cited authority before trenchantly denouncing her use of it as due to ignorance (a similar strategy of sarcasm is deployed in B 345, 347). **488** *lessoun*: suggesting (Alf*Q*) that the text is alluded to in its context as a *capitulum* at sext on Sunday (*Brev.* 2.64). **489; 493** *omnia...Quod...*: 'But prove ["put to the test"] all things: hold fast that which is good' (I Thess 5:21). The text provides 'sentence-names' in A 12.50–2 and is quoted by **L**'s Christ at 20.233*a*. **490–1** The 'line' was at the foot of the recto and the rest of it was at the top of the leaf's verso (so strictly the action in 491b would precede that of 491a). **494** A line either of standard type with *s* / *sh* alliteration or, with *shal* de-stressed according to the sense-pattern, of the rare Type IIb. B 348 may be standard or (with liaisonal stave in *if ye*) of Type IIIb with a-half counterpoint on *s*. **495** *teneful*: more 'lexical Platonism', this time across languages; those who do *not* hold on (*tenere*) to what is good will find the scripture that enjoins this become a text that causes pain (*teneful*). **B 351** is either extended Type IIIa with counterpoint or standard with the third stave liaisonal *þat ye*. **497** scans like a standard English line and completes the verse quoted in part at 486*a*: 'but he carrieth away the souls of the receivers'. It both exemplifies the pre-scholastic method of arguing by setting one authority against another and satirises the attempt of hasty, poorly-informed or (as in Mede's case) ill-intentioned laypeople to justify their conduct on the authority of Scriptural quotations torn out of context. **499** makes clear that to 'receive' Mede is to receive 'Guile', the earthly representative of the devil (2.70, 17.111), under whose sway she stands (A 2.24).

Z 147–76 This 30-line passage that concludes III stands in place of 86 lines progressively extended from **A** → **B** → **C** and should arguably be printed immediately

after Z 146. Rounding off Mede's answer to Conscience with a sustained and at points puzzling attack on him, it lacks both the King's provisional decision for Mede (A 215–6) and Conscience's powerful reply (217–76). Though leaving no trace in **A** (except of 169 at A 213), it anticipates the longer versions in thought and verbal detail. **148** *Northfolk*: an emblem of close-fistedness, as is presumably Greed's 'Norfolk nose' later at Z 5.98. The remote East Anglian county's educational backwardness is implied in B 5. 235, and a major satire on it is the Latin poem *Descriptio Northfolchie* (Wright 1838:93–106; see *R–B*, 17–18). *Normawndye*: alluding to her accusation at 144–6 of cowardly greed in abandoning the campaign for immediate monetary gains. *name was yfounde*: 'name / reputation [for prudential self-interest] was derived' (cf. *Foundour* at 176 below). **149** is taken by *R–B* as 'apparently a phrase for double-dealing', but just as probably it indicates his shrewdness about the value of his chattels. **150** The sense is 'Support now this person, now that, just as you please'. 150a resembles C 5.51. **151** *furst blamedest...shryue*: on this *R–B* observe that 'Conscience has not "blamed" the friars in this poem' but that having been 'rebuked by some authority, represented by Conscience' they 'have now been allowed to resume their old privileges, such as hearing confession'. 151–60, however, undeniably describe much of what happens in BC 20/22.230ff, where Conscience first 'forsakes' the friars (231), but later guarantees them their livelihood (249–50) provided they abandon speculative philosophy for practical charity, while 155 echoes Need's strictures at 20/22.231ff (for possible explanations of these '(pre-) echoes', see *TN*). **154** *couent couetyse*: the 'Platonic' wordplay is revealingly Langlandian. **156** *ant cumseth*: the subject *a* 'they' is understood. **158** A striking T-type line. *boted*: here some half-century before MED's earliest citation s.v. *boten* v. (2), with perhaps a homophonic pun on *boten* (1), 1(b) 'relieve'. *bewsoun*: analogous to *beau fitz*; a form of *bel sone*, with no pl. marker (see *MES* 57); a century earlier than the one citation in MED s.v. *bel* adj. (a). *bayard*: the familiar use of the name anticipating Z 4. 41 //. *stowlyche*: 'in fine style'; MED s.v. *stoutli* adv. 4, aptly citing parallel *WPal* 1950 *alle on stalworþ stedes stoutliche ihorsed*. **159** 'The thickest-woven brown [*burnet* < *brunet*] or white [undyed] woollen cloth for sale'. The *blanket* here is for wearing-apparel (cf. 9.254). **160** *bakken*: occurring elsewhere in this sense only at A 11.188; the noun *bak* (see *IG*) is rare outside **L** but found in *WPal* 2096. **161–2** The association of ideas is typical of **L**, as in the phrase *þe lecherie of clothyng* at 16.254 in a comparable attack on worldly and hypocritical clerks (with which cf. *in lykynge of lecherye...in wedes* at 6.176–7). *achoceth*: either *choken* with fused subject prn *a* or *achoken* with *a* omitted. **163–4** 'For lechery is sensual pleasure, and you also grossly inculcate [destructive] desire in clerk and layman alike'; for the possible pun on 'loss' and 'lust', see *TN*. **165–6** The thought is reminiscent of 21.454–6: 'The comune...counteth but litel...of conseyl... but if they sowne...to wynnynge.' **165** A line of Type IIIa or the rare Type IIa. **168** *at consayl*: 'in the Council' or 'in matters of an intimate and private nature'. *ful fewe*: cf. 3.199 //. **169** A counterpointed line of Type Ie (*aab / ab*). **170** The exact meaning is hard to determine, but clearly implied is the enrichment of friar-confessors by people suffering from a 'bad conscience'. Since Mede professes to see Conscience as the 'origin' of clerical greed in the sense of awakening scruples in rich sinners, the incoherence between this passage and her confession to a friar added at A 3.34ff would have required its removal. *robed*: with double reference; he has 'dressed' them in greed, and as a result of giving absolution for money they get the wherewithal to dress *themselves* in substantial clothes. **171** *soyleth*: the aphetic form of *assoylen* enabling a harsh homophonic pun on *soylen* 'soil, befoul'. *syluer... ouresylue*: the identical rhyme providing characteristic homophonic wordplay, with the sibilance of the Type Ib line aptly echoic. **172–3** argue that Conscience is the source of human action in the sense that he understands (*a wot hyt*) the nature of moral choices, whether good or bad, at their root. See the careful analysis of these lines in Brewer 1984:216n7. **174** *maistrye*: 'authority' (MED s.v. (c)) as well as 'power'; the idea survives at A 3.216 (not in **Z**). Mede with false modesty ascribes her duplicity to Conscience as her superior in human affairs. **175** 'God truly knows that without *his* knowing it, *I* can't accomplish anything of which *you* aren't the source and origin'. Mede's switch of addressee, from the king (apparently) at 167 to Conscience at 176, is paralleled, if less abruptly, at A 3.162 (*Nay, lord*) and 165 (*þou knowist*). **176** *foundour*: much earlier in this extended sense than the MED citations s.v. 4(b).

Passus IV (Z IV, V 1–18)

PASSUS FOUR is at 196 lines the shortest in **C**, following the longest, and describes the second half of Mede's 'Trial'. It presents allegorically the secular leadership's resort to the Church for wise counsel in the government of the realm: REASON will therefore emerge in V as personifying ecclesiastical authority in his *sermo ad status*. The Passus falls into: (i) the summoning of Reason (1–39); (ii) the Peace episode 40–107; (iii) Reason's admonition and prophecy (108–45); (iv) responses to it (146–65); (v) the king's rejection of Mede for Reason and Conscience as his councillors (166–96).

(i) 1–39 open with the King at Conscience's behest summoning Reason to advise him. **2** *sothe*; *bothe*: the internal rhyme suggesting the king's unrealistic and superficial

optimism: 'both' *cannot* serve him 'in truth'. **3** *Kusse here*: the kiss between former adversaries betokening reconciliation, something possible later between the Daughters of God (20. 463ff), because their 'conflict' is more apparent than real, but not here. The king naively desires the kiss of friendship to develop into that of love, the principles of conscientiousness and venality to 'marry' in his mind and domain. But Conscience as the practical application of *synderesis* (the knowledge of the first principles of moral action) should not be able to *sauhten* with the daughter of False. **4–5** *Nay*: the allegory enacts with precision **L**'s idea of Conscience as the soul's disposition to say yes or no to a particular line of action (*chepe or refuse* 16.189). *Pe* helpfully compares Alan of Lille's *Anticlaudianus* I viii–ix 'where Prudence defers likewise to the judgement of Reason'. *by Crist*: an oath here implying not irreverence (as with the brewer at 21.401) but serious purpose. The knightly speaker swears by his heavenly lord (cf. 8.19), whereas 'false' characters like Mede cannot invoke divine witness to their veracity. *But Reson...*: Conscience defers to Reason as the faculty of making general judgements in the light of the moral law (cf. 16.185). At the 'social' level of the allegory, **L**'s Conscience and Reason represent respectively the knightly and episcopal orders (this clarification coming only with **B**'s revision of A 5.11 where, as in **Z**, Conscience is confusingly a bishop). **7** *þat*: implying a verb of 'commanding' understood. **8** *consayle*: 'innermost thoughts', not 'advice'; Reason will advise *him*. **11** *acounte*: an apt term, since Conscience as God's *notarie* (16.190) will have to render a strict account to God on doomsday for the actions of the king and his subjects. **14** *Resoun*: personifying the intellectual principle that understands the *ratio* or divine order of the world; a norm in matters of moral praxis, both 'that which is apprehended and that which apprehends' (Alford 1988:204, an authoritative treatment of this complex idea). **17–23** The 'horse-riding' allegory is a counter-type to that of Mede's deceitful followers at 2.175–93. **17** *Catoun*: a symbol less of 'elementary learning' (*Bn*) than of 'everyday commonsense morality' or '(disillusioned) worldly prudence'. Aptly Reason's servant, he stands to him somewhat as Kynde Wit to Clergy, and is creditably associated with True-tongue. *Caton þe wyse* is approvingly quoted five times, only Study querying his *ooþer science* by comparison with Theology's more idealistic position at B 10.191–201 (deleted in **C**). 'Cato' denotes the *Disticha Catonis de Moribus ad Filium,* a C4th Latin collection in four books of two-line aphorisms in hexameters preceded by 56 prose phrases, attributed to 'Dionysius Cato' but of unknown authorship. With its edifying tone and simple Latin, it was useful as a basic school-text (cf. 7.34; see Galloway 1987, Baer 2001). **18** *Tomme Trewe-tonge*: the first personification with a self-characterising 'sentence-name'; already recommended as the ideal judge at 3.474. **20** *Soffre..*: his horse being the 'patient one waiting for evil to take its course', later named as Reason's special attribute and modelled on God's own *suffraunce* (13.194–200); an ideal 'suffrance' to be contrasted with the 'vnsittynge soffraunce' of 3.207. **21** *Auyseth..*: 'prudent foresight, to curb his will' (*Pe*); *providentia* is an aspect of prudence, and (Burrow 1990:141n9) taught by Reason's 'knaue' Cato in *DC* II.24: *Prospice qui veniant casus: hos esse ferendos; / nam levius laedit quidquid praevidimus ante.* The earlier forms *witty / wytful / witty-wordes*, surviving in *wittes* at C 23, place the same stress on the value of (listening to) words of wise counsel. **22** *wil...kyke*: ironically hinting at the Dreamer's refractory and argumentative character. **23** *wil*: the impulsive aspect of the soul requiring control by *suffraunce*; but the syntax (with *vpon* governing *Soffre...*) confusingly seems to identify the latter with the horse (will). This could be avoided by placing a comma after *vpon*, and reading *sette...vpon* as a phrasal verb with an implied object 'him' and *Soffre...* as the *complement* of 'saddle', as suggested by Burrow 1990:142 (see *TN* further). But the evolution of the earlier texts implies that the 'horse' *wil* is envisaged as being *transformed* into *Soffre...*(who is 'proleptically' so named) under the guidance of wise instruction; and this, despite awkward syntax, makes good theological sense. *peynted wittes*: suggesting that the horse's ornamental bridle signifies the persuasive eloquence sometimes needed to restrain 'wilfulness'; but unlike the example of *paynted wordes* at 22.115, the context here precludes an adverse sense. **27** The **C** alteration to *Waryn Wisman* qualifies the favourable overtones deriving from *Wisdom*'s association with Biblical *Sapience*. This character first appeared at B 4.154 and the contextual sense 'cunning and devious person' cited by MED s.v. *wise-man* (d) from *WBib* Job 5:14 (translating *sapientes* [Vg 5:13]) may be presumed here from Warren's association with *Wily-man*, who replaces **ZAB**'s more ambiguous Witty. **28–9** *Fayn...reed*: the lawyers turning to the authoritative spokesman of justice 'because they think that they have a special claim on Reason's help and advice' (*Pe*); but 29b shows why they will be disappointed. *that recorde sholde*: 'whose duty is to testify / declare (whether)'. **31** *Witty-man*: this **ZAB** figure's return in such company compromises his neutrality in **C**. *Wareyne Wryng-lawe*: a dishonest (?)barrister, perhaps identical with Wiseman, although in **B** the name Warren is given to Witty (67) as well as to Wisdom (154). A punning metonymic association of these characters' deviousness with the complexities of the burrows in a rabbit-warren cannot be ruled out, though 'Warren' was a common name and ME *wareine* (B Pr 163) denotes only the tract of bare land. **35–6** *wranglynge*: the symmetrical opposition with *leautee* (like *loue* with *wraþe*) suggesting 'engage in contentious law-suits'. **36a** 'Destruction and

unhappiness [are] in their ways: and the way of peace they have not known. There is no fear of God before their eyes' (Ps 13:3d); quoted in Rom 3:16–17 (*Pe*) during an argument on the inefficacy of the OT law to bring salvation.

B 29–41 // **ZA 29 29** *Cheker*: here the Exchequer of Pleas, a common-law court ancillary to the Exchequer and 'concerned with the enforcement of royal accounts and debts' (Baker 1971:35). *Chauncerye*: the Lord Chancellor's court of Chancery, now becoming 'a court of equity which served to correct the injustices of common law in individual cases' (Alf*G* s.v.) and dealt especially with grievances arising from other courts (McKisack 1959:199). Alf*G* doubts whether the *Pr* 91 ref. is to its equitable jurisdiction, and the most probable sense here is that Warren and Wily have financial liabilities to the Exchequer arising from a contract (*thyng*) and wish to be released from these by other means than payment in full, whether by appealing for special dispensation from the Chancellor's court, 'twisting' the legal process, or using bribes (B 31). See MED s.v. *thing* n. 11 (Alf*G* has no entry under *thing* but see s.v. *dischargen*); and see further Galloway 2001:122–5, Kennedy 2003:177. **32, 41** *knewe*; *knoweth*: Conscience 'recognises (the nature of)' but does not 'acknowledge (the worth of)'; a deliberate echo. The first use recalls B 2.47 and the second Christ's injunction in Mt 7:23 (*Bn*), with its resonance of Ps 13:4a.

(ii) 40–107 Mede's Trial modulates into a *Trial of Wrong*, who has injured PEACE and represents the same principle as her vanished would-be groom False; but Mede intervenes at 90. On the whole scene see Baldwin 1981:39–50, Simpson 1990:56–9 and Kennedy 2003:175–89, Giancarlo 2003:144–62. **40–63 41** *as...kennede*: despite conscience's being 'formed' upon the moral law of reason, specific decisions like 'recognising' *Wisman* may fittingly fall to the former; but over-strict interpretation of the psychological allegory should not be insisted upon. **42–3** The 'centrality' of Reason in royal governance (underlined by the identical rhyme) is more important than the topical referent of *sone* (at the time of **ZA** the Black Prince). In the illustrated MS Douce 104 f. 19 he is depicted here as a dignified seated figure, bearded and in riding-habit, with a hat, suggesting a judge (though 5.114 makes it clear he is a bishop). **45** *Pees*: personifying the spirit of amicable compromise that here may endanger the operation of legal justice (as later that of penitential justice at 22.335ff). He stands to Peace the Daughter of God (20.170) somewhat as the earthly institutional Church to the transcendent figure HC of Vision I (cf. on 17–23 above). *parlement*: not the Lords and / or Commons as a whole but rather (Baldwin 1981[1]:40–2) the Great Council of lords, a 'prerogative court' meeting under the king to hear complaints from private individuals, particularly against the administration of the law (*Pe*); see also 4.185.

This interpretation is challenged by Kennedy (2003:179–81), who argues for seeing Peace's action as exemplifying a 'common law' suit in Chancery. *bille*: a written petition (*libellus*) used to initiate a legal action, here one alleging 'assault on his person, property or land' by Wrong, which 'involved a criminal element' because 'the defendant was held to have committed a crime...against the King' (Stokes 1984:138–40). As allegedly perpetrated *vi et armis* and *contra pacem regis*, it would entitle Peace to seek a writ of *trespass* against Wrong (Alf*G* s.v., Baker 1971:82f). **46** *Wrong*: the earthly embodiment of the diabolic figure whom HC so named at 1.59; here perhaps referring more specifically to a class of civil and criminal *iniuriae* 'wrongs' against the king's peace (Alf*G* s.v.), those alleged including rape, theft, forcible entry and fraudulent sale. **46–8** tighten up **B** by making the three victims of rape represent the three female *status* of wife, widow and virgin in ascending order of moral gravity of the offence (see 18.56ff below). Both female type-names suggest purity and worth. **51–4** To Wrong's dishonesty and intimidation in **B** is added highway robbery, anticipating and replacing the description of Outlaw in B 17.99ff. **51** *Seynt Gyles doune*: the famous fair on St Giles's down near Winchester, mentioned at 6.211, 13.51. **57b** 'no matter what legal claim I made' (*Bn*). **58** *maynteneth*: supports with arms and payment; something made an offence by statute in 1377 (Kennedy 2003:182). **59** *forstalleth..*: he (forcibly) buys goods before they can come to the market-fairs, so as to re-sell for a profit at retail (see on 3.82) or avoid customs-dues (Alf*G* s.v.; Baker 1971:82f). Forestalling injured both wholesaler and purchaser, and the Edwardian statute against it was confirmed in 1378 (Kennedy 182n; see further Britnell 1987:89–102). *fyhteth...chepynges*: causing disturbances (to prevent the sale or bring the price down). **61** *tayle*: the tally-stick, an early form of duplicate invoice, marked with notches showing the amount due, and split so that both buyer and seller kept one half as a record of the transaction. Peace claims that Wrong never paid the money due. **64–107 65/6** The end-rhyme introduced in **B** replaces the identical rhyme in **Z** lost by revision in **A**. **67** makes clearer than **B** that Wisdom is a lawyer, whose services Wrong will pay handsomely for (with *largeliche* cf. 3.288–9). **68** *haue here helpe*: fitting better than *maken pees* **ZAB** (which sounds at odds with Wrong's subsequent defiance of Peace in 65–6) and making clear that he hopes to buy the court's mercy through the help of Mede. *handy-dandy*: a game in which one player shakes an object between his hands and then closes his fists, while the other must guess which hand it is in; so Wrong 'with closed hands' makes 'a privy payment' (cf. 22.265) to his lawyer to bribe the judges in his cause. **69** *the lord*: the king, as in **AB**. **72** The ambiguously semi-favourable presentation in B 69–73 // of the lawyers who

warn Wrong against the dangers of violent behaviour is removed in **C**. **73** *Mede*: money for bribery, personified as Lady Mede. **76** The tense-contrast between *knoweth* and *were* 77 leaves it uncertain whether this statement is from Peace or the narrator; but comparison with **ZA** favours the latter. **77** *Wyles*: replacing Wisdom is the cunning lawyer Wily-man of 31. **78** *o%ercome*: to be recalled in Greed's attempt to overcome Conscience at 22.122 (*Bn*). **82** *seuene*: a favourite indefinite number symbolic of the completeness of the sentence (as seven days complete a week). **83** *a wys oen*: presumably Wisdom, the leader of the quartet. **84** *Maynprise*: personifying the principle or action of release of a prisoner to a *mainpernour* (107 below) on payment of a surety (see Keen 2002:92). **B 91** 'Wit put forward a counter-argument likewise'; see *TN*. **88–9** 'It is better that a payment of compensation should wipe out the wrong done than that the wrong(-doer) be punished and this remain the best compensation [the injured party gets]'. **96** *waged*: doubtfully glossed by MED (s.v. *wagen* v. 1(d)) '?indemnify, compensate for injuries', but taken by Baldwin in the double sense of receiving 'security [that Wrong "will do so no more"] / payment for agreeing to withdraw the case' (ibid. 1(a); 3 (a)), so that what is accepted is 'a bribe to Peace and the king to drop the case' (1981[1]:49). However, Peace is unlikely to be so open; he means rather 'guaranteed', and merely seeks the king's consent to his accepting the indemnity. **98** 'In this way, provided the King will agree, all my claims are satisfied'. But despite Peace's willingness to accept monetary 'amends', justice has for the king a wider scope than the settlement of personal grievances, since he is in part the party injured by Wrong's crimes (cf. *myn hewes* 102) and 'for the sake of (his own) Conscience' is obliged to enquire further. **C** agrees with **ZAB** in submitting to Reason (personifying the rule of right) the decision on whether to take 'pity' [i.e. allow the 'amends' Peace wants], but replaces the concession to a reformed attitude in Wrong with insistence on retribution for evil-doing. **103** *stokkes*: a wooden punishment-frame confining a seated prisoner's head and ankles (cf. *pylo-rye* 2.216). **105–6 C** revises the **ZAB** understanding of reason as 'informing' (the king's) conscience to one of conscience 'counselling' the king (in the practical decision of judging Wrong), implicitly in the light of (reason as) the principles of justice.

(iii) 108–45 *Reason's diatribe*, like Conscience's at 3.155–214, takes a severely 'normative' position, refusing 'pity' [in effect = compromise] unless and until a series of stringent conditions are fulfilled.
108–17 These *impossibilia*, implicitly a programme for reform at all levels of society, if idealistic, are not in themselves incapable of being implemented. **111** *Purnele*: short for Petronella, a female diminutive of Peter;

the name of a saint at A 7.259, though here and at 5.128, 6.3 a type-name for a proud rich woman, and elsewhere in *PP* usually unfavourable in implication (see *Proper-Name Index* [*PNI*]). **112** 'And the practice of indulging children [metonymic for 'the practitioners'] be itself sternly disciplined', i.e. the parents should be beaten for *not* beating their children; more simply (with *chasted* = *chastising*), the one activity should replace the other. **113** 'And the piety of (reformed) lechers be celebrated as a major festival'; *harlotes* in the light of *harlotrie* 110 is unlikely to mean 'scoundrels' (*Pe*). In **ZAB** the sense is 'be treated as no great matter', i.e. because it will be so common. The notion that the holiness could be the harlots' *present* 'superficial piety' (countenanced by *Pe* as a possible **AB** reading revised in **C**) depends on the misguided *KaK–D* emendation *hethyng* after *A*-ms Ch, which is a scribal error (see *TN*). **114** *clerkene*: an analogical extension of the old gen. pl. weak declension ending (*HME* 52, *MES* 73). **115a** echoes B 19.418a. **116** *outryderes*: first found here in an English text, and echoed in *CT* I 166. **117** *Benet*: St Benedict of Nursia (*c.* 480–*c.* 550), the founder of Western monasticism. The centre of the Benedictine way of life is the saying of the Divine Office; but while the Rule required a monk to remain attached to his monastery, it did not stipulate enclosure. *Dominik*: St Dominic (*c.* 1172–1221), founder of the Order of Preachers (1217), which followed the Rule of St Augustine. *Fraunceys*: St Francis of Assisi (*c.* 1181–1226), founder of the Order of Friars Minor (1209). Neither Dominicans nor Franciscans had to remain in their convents, so presumably Reason means 'live by the rule instituted by their founders'.

B 120–2 120 *Recordare*: elliptical for 'sing *Remember,* [*Lord*]' or, punningly, 'remember to sing *Remember;*' a common opening to Offertory antiphons in the Sarum Missal (*Bn*). **121** *Bernard*: St Bernard (1090–1153), Abbot of Clairvaux, the most celebrated Cistercian. The strict rule of his Order (founded 1098) was designed to foster enclosed contemplative life within monasteries built in remote situations. **122** *prechours*: not necessarily the Order of Preachers (*Bn*) but (as at 5.42) all whose office is to preach (**C** confirms this).

118–45 118 *lerede men*: probably the clergy, the reference being to their moral instruction to laypeople. **120–1** widens the scope from religious to all needy people and replaces the criticism of bishops' lordly ways with an injunction to practical charity. *ben*: 'be (replaced by)', 'become'. **122** *Seynt Iames*: the shrine of St James the Apostle at Compostela in Galicia (*Galys* 124), NW Spain, a favoured European destination of English pilgrims (cf. *CT* I 466). **122b** greatly sharpens the vaguer **B**. The *spirit* of St James is to be 'sought' by doing the *corporal* good works he commended, e.g. 'to visit the fatherless and widows' (Js 1:27), the image anticipating that of Piers's

symbolic 'pilgrimage' to St Truth. **123** seems to echo the developed 'pilgrimage' metaphor of B 6.102. *Rome*: with the tombs of St Peter and numerous martyrs, the chief pilgrimage-centre after the Holy Land. **C** somewhat uncomfortably interlaces figurative Rome with literal Compostela as a pilgrimage destination in recommending 'spiritual pilgrimages' in place of literal ones. The implication may be that money expended by pilgrims to *straunge strondes* could be more meritoriously used to relieve the needy at home. **124** *for euere*: suggesting one final pilgrimage at the end of life; but the logic is awkward and a metaphorical sense may be intended, 'go on a perpetual "pilgrimage" by means of a life of penance' ('inner pilgrimage' is discussed in Dyas ch. 9). **125** Here 'Rome' signifies the Papal Court, which was actually at Avignon in SE France at the time of **ZA** but had returned to Rome by the time of **B** (though the anti-pope Clement VII still resided there). The people vaguely denoted will be those seeking benefits from the Pope and willing to pay for them. *ruyflares*: officials at the Curia who took money for their services to papal petitioners. **127** *graue*: stamped coins. *vngraue*: blank coin or bullion. **128** *forfeture*: doubtless the objection voiced being to the impoverishment of the country's economy by the removal of money from circulation. *ouerward*: perhaps suggested by the sound of *Douere* **ZAB** and generalising its sense. At Dover, the chief port of embarkation for France, travellers could be examined to see if they were carrying gold or silver abroad, something forbidden by law (Statutes of 1381–2, ii 17–18; Lipson 1959:531–3) to all except the groups mentioned. **130** *prouisour*: a tolerance of provisors seemingly at odds with the view of them as simoniacs at 2.182 //, unless Reason means here those who 'go to receive benefices or offices already given' (*Bn*). Like the other classes mentioned whose journeying may be personally obligatory or beneficial to the realm, they would need cash for expenses. *penaunt*: revising **ZA** as apparently contradicting the tone of *Rome-rennares* 125; someone on whom pilgrimage had been imposed as a canonical penance for some grave sin. **Z 119–31** Partly cut and partly transposed in revision of a passage obviously in draft condition (*Intro.* III, *Z Version* §3). The lines allow the possibility of intervening for Wrong in the event of a general transformation of society; but **A**'s deletion recognises that Wrong can never be converted. **131** *by þe Rode*: an oath conveying solemn resolution, not irreverence; used only here (but cf. also 179) and perhaps especially fitting, since Reason later preaches with a cross (C 5.13, B 5.12). **132** *barre*: the railing before the judge's seat at which counsel stood to plead, hence metonymic for the profession of advocate ('barrister'). The revision hints at a special animus against the latter. **134–5** recall Mede's supposition at 3.257–8. **136** *Wrong*: standing for every type of wrongdoer. **138b** improves on **B** in precision and substance. **139** 'Nor [should I] grant him mercy in return for payment...'; on the revision's awkward syntax cf. *TN*. **139b** Though this oath is found elsewhere (see *PNI*), it is contextually ironic, since the Virgin Mary is usually identified as the merciful intercessor, as at 7.287–90. **140–1** *Nullum...irremuneratum*: from the definition of the just judge in the *De contemptu mundi*, iii 15 of Pope Innocent III (1160–1216): 'Ipse est iudex iustus...qui *nullum malum* praeterit *impunitum, nullum bonum irremuneratum*' (*Sk* IV 83); both parts will be quoted again as 20.433. Reason's stand for inflexible retributive justice recalls that of Conscience at 3.332–3, 350–1 and anticipates the wording of Truth's Pardon at 9.286–7. But the present use of negative personifications entails a witty transposition of the original predicates: 'The man *No-ill* encountered *unpunished* / And urged that *No-good* go *unrewarded*'. **142** *confessour*: perhaps implying that observance of the principle may require absolution for the king's past faults in this regard (variants of the phrases occur in penitential writings cited by Gray 1986:53–60). **144–5** If justice is followed, lawyers will have to turn peasant-farmers and the king will find himself loved, instead of disliked for his *vnsittynge suffraunce* of wrongdoing (3.207–9).

(iv) 146–65 147b *kyndeliche..*: the revision of B 150b and excision of (added) B 151 deleting a sharp criticism of the king's clerical advisers. **148–55 (B 150–56)** The change removes the Dreamer's guaranteeing presence (new in **B**) and tightens the contrast between law and justice with a mordant pun on *ryhte* 150 and *ryhtful* 151. In **B 154** Warren represents the misuse of legal expertise for profit (with 156a cf. B 3.157, B 5.580–1) and in **B 155–6** the lawyers' willingness to suppress facts they know might prejudice a client's case is the converse of their refusal (at B Pr 212–16) to speak a word without being paid for it. **151–3** All right-minded people acknowledge the truth of Reason's case, Conscience and Kynde Wit (companions at Pr 142) thank him for his virtuous sentence, and everyone hopes from his words that humble innocence rather than cynical wealth will prevail with the king. The interpretation here offered will require adoption at 152–3 of *R–K*'s punctuation, with no stop in 152 but a semi-colon after *speche* 153. **155** *Mekenesse...mayster*: allegorically signifying that only humble expression of sorrow for injury done, and not monetary compensation without remorse, will suffice as grounds for a truly '*sitting* suffrance'. **159b** Mutilation was an archaic penalty for certain offences (with the oath cf. 8.290, B 4.146). **161** A pungent polysemantic pun on two senses of *commune*, 'the community' and 'the commonly-used'. In 161b an arresting n. + adj. compound-epithet must be in question, since *queynte* as adj. could hardly be de-stressed, and the half-line cannot contain three lifts. There is surely however a homophonic pun on *queynte* adj. 'cunning' as in Chaucer *CT* I

3276/7. **164–5** *capias...custodias*: 'Take Mede and guard her securely' is 'the standard formula in writs of attachment,' addressed [by the king] to the sheriff and served by his clerk (AlfG), here relayed by the latter to the officers as Mede slips out. *set...carceratis*: 'but not with those in prison'. The ironically 'unsitting' substitution by **L** himself (*pace* AlfQ) for the usual *in prisona nostra* hints that the king's threats at 3.140–1 are unlikely to be fulfilled: house-arrest is the worst Mede has to fear.

(v) 166–96 166 *to consayl toek*: i.e. 'conferred privately with', but with the implication of making them (permanent) members of his Council. **169** *chetes*: the 'reversion of land or its appurtenances to the king...upon failure of heirs to a tenant in fee simple [i.e. one holding directly from the king as feudal lord]'; and also 'forfeiture of the lands and goods of a felon' (AlfG), this second situation being the one referred to at 10.242–4. The text implies that lawyers can be bribed to substitute 'false heirs', e.g. by providing bogus documentation of identity or legitimacy. **173** *ȝow*: strictly Wrong, who is in need of bail; but his counsel are being addressed on his behalf. **B 179** *þe Marie of heuene*: a rare use of the proper name in a phrase with the definite article (*MES* 239), outside 22.221 perhaps unique. **174–5** *leautee*; *lele*: the king requiring that the common law be equated with a strict regard for the principle of justice (*for* is even stronger than **B**'s *in* 'governed by'; cf. *euene* 178) and administered by faithful and virtuous men. The unfavourable contrast between (uncompromising) justice and (compromised) *lawe without leutee* recurs at 12.94ff, where the insistence on *loue* as well as *leute* echoes *lyf-holy* 4.175 (an expression that may imply involvement of churchmen in the administration of justice). The revision, doubtless reflecting circumstances after 1381, replaces confidence in the communal sagacity of *moost folk* with reliance on trustworthy judges hand-picked for their loyalty and probity. **180a** *alle reumes*: the purpose of *alle* perhaps being to extend the reference to just rule *over* Ireland and the remaining English possessions in France; but its repetition in 182 (echoed by the king in *al* 183) implies relations *between* countries. **180b** is an uncommon case of three-stage linear revision from **Z → C**. **185–6** The revision sharpens the looser sense of **ZAB**. *Chaunceller*: the use of *cheef* indicating a parallel with the function of the Lord Chancellor of England, to whom the Chancellor of the Exchequer was a deputy. It seems to be implied at one level that the king of England is resolving to have a bishop as his chief minister of state (on a more abstract plane, Reason figures as 'chancellor' to the divine Wisdom in Nicholas Love's *Mirror*, p. 17 (AlfG s.v.)). *kynges justice*: Conscience will *judge* by the principles of equity in particular cases, just as Reason will *rule* by those of pure justice. **B 189** *Be... comen*: 'when my council has come.' **187a–90** Reason's reply is bracketed by the same phrase 'I assent', only with the qualifier 'but', a rhetorically tight utterance enclosing three strict injunctions that would seem to have had special relevance for Richard II. **187–8** *by so...partem*: 'on condition that you yourself *should hear the other side*'. The English conjunction is made to govern 188a and the subject *ʒowsulue* to fit with the Latin 2 pl. subj. in place of the usual imperative. **188** *Audiatis*: 'hear', in apposition with *yhere* 187 (hence the comma). This Roman law maxim was regarded 'as one of the self-evident propositions of natural law' (Alf*Q*). *aldremen and comeneres*: a set phrase specifically referring respectively to the chief officials of city wards, who were charged with holding the ward-mote (Pr 92), and the ordinary members elected to the common council of the city. **189** *priue lettres*: sent under the king's privy or personal signet or seal (in contrast to *letters patent* of public concern, sent under the Great Seal) and commonly granting a licence or favour. There may be an immediate allusion to a 1387 statute (11 Ric II c. 10, in confirmation of 2 Edw. III c. 8) that no such letters be sent in damage or prejudice of the realm, nor in disturbance of the law (Alf*G*); but the king had begun to use his personal seal as a warrant to the Chancery from 1383 onwards (Keen 1973:277). **190** *supersedeas*: 'you shall desist'; the opening word of a Chancery writ that stayed or stopped a proceeding in the common courts. While 'meant to protect individual rights...it was subject to abuses such as bribery, favouritism, etc.' (Alf*G*). **191** *loue...seluer*: i.e. 'if you rule justly, your subjects will be more willing to provide you financial subsidies.' **194** *Lumbardus of Lukes*: Lombards from Lucca (in N Italy), who after the expulsion of the Jews from England in 1290 became the chief bankers and moneylenders in the City of London and were especially useful to the king; Lombard St, just S of Cornhill, commemorates their residence there. For another criticism of Lombards, see Z 7.274. **196** *Resoun*: either the subject or the object of the verb; whichever way, only the just and upright are to be appointed to administer the realm. *Y wakede*: the second vision ends more logically with the dreamer waking, and so obviates the need for the poorly motivated waking at the opening of Passus V in **ZAB**.

Passus V

PASSUS FIVE, as concise as Four, has two balanced halves: (i) a *prelude* (1–108) introducing the Second Vision, and (ii) *Reason's Sermon* to the Folk (109–200), which precipitates the *Confessions* of the Deadly Sins in the next passus. The opening dialogue with two interlocutors foreshadows those described at 1 below and the one that initiates the Third Vision (10.1–60), 5.105–8 resembling the transition-passage at 10.61–7. **B** had added only about 20 lines to **A**, which remained the same length as the corresponding **Z** portion after halving Z 30–48 on the

great wind. **C**'s revisions have been necessitated by its expansion of **B**'s Sins-material from 400 to some 500 ll. and addition (from B XIII) of a 50-line passage on the origins of Sloth (7.69–118*a*). The *Confession Sequence* that fills **ZAB** V is now distributed in more manageable units over three shorter passūs (5–7) and embedded more firmly in the Dreamer's situation, turning the two waking episodes into a kind of didactic frame (on these changes see Russell 1982). The 'prelude' in certain respects replaces the exchange on *makyng* in B 12.10–28 but ranges more widely, and has attracted much attention as an ostensibly 'autobiographical' *apologia pro vita sua*. Middleton 1997 judges it **L**'s latest addition, reflecting provisions of the Statute of Labourers issued by the Cambridge Parliament of 1388. But little in Will's interrogation or replies could not have been written in 1382–7 (her main arguments are adequately answered in Wittig 2001:168–70). The 'historical' truth of **L**'s self-description is indeterminable, but the recognised convention of loosely modelling the narrator / dreamer-figure on the author (Kane, 1965[2]; Burrow 1993:82–108) certifies appearance and circumstances as likely to be authentic.

(i) 1–108 *The dialogue with Reason and Conscience.*
1–11 This waking encounter with personified abstractions resembles those with Hunger and Fever in A 12.59–98 and with Need in BC 20 / 22.1–50, containing rebuke and warning for the Dreamer and, through him, the audience. **1** *Cornehull*: a street in the City of London immediately S of the present Royal Exchange and Bank of England, and N of Lombard St (Du Boulay 1991: endpaper map). *Pe* notes the area's reputation as a resort for vagabonds, and cites the description in 'London Lickpenny' (Robbins 1959: no. 50, ll. 85–8). But as 'part of the city's commercial centre [it] always contained prosperous precincts' (Benson 2004:209, who has an illuminating account of medieval Cornhill [206–28]). **2** *Kytte*: a familiar diminutive of *Katherine*. If it has a meaning, it need not be as a type-name for 'a wife' (*Pe*, citing 7.303, and see *Vxorem duxi* following), but for a lascivious woman (MED s.v. *Kitte* n. 2(b), citing only *Beryn*). However, in 7.303 Actif may allude punningly to the name of his wife (and Will's own, B 18.428), who is *wantowen of maneres* 'undisciplined, wilful' (MED unconvincingly cites the latter under sense (d) 'lascivious'). *cote*: a dwelling of the poor (see *IG*). **3** *lollare*: a wasteful idler (MED s.v. *lollere* n.1), the earliest use of the noun in this sense being in B 15.213 (from *lollen* 'hang loosely', and confined to texts in the *PP* tradition). A possible pun on 'Lollard' (MED s.v. 2, a sense already in *CT* B 1173) cannot be ruled out; but this figurative use may be derived from a term for a hanging or trailing ship's rope (ibid. s.v. 3, *c*. 1356). **5** *made of*: commonly taken as 'composed verses about' (*Sk*, MED s.v. 5(b), *Pe*, Kane 1965[1]:64n1), in the light of which C

9.203–55 has been seen (by Scase 1987) as a specific piece of *makyng* about *lollares of Londone* that was separately circulated while **C** was being written (see *Intro*. III, *C*, §§ 21–2). But though there may be a secondary punning sense, in context *made of* (balancing *lytel ylet by* 3) more naturally means 'judge, regard' (Sisam 1962:233; MED s.v. *maken* 17 (a)). *Reason* is more likely to have 'taught' (5) the speaker to 'judge' than to 'compose poetry', and it is doubtful whether *lollers* who read clerkly satire would have given it a thought. This use underlies the phrase at 3.390 (and is how it was understood by the scribe of ms F, who substituted *rouȝte*). **6** *cam by*: 'acquired' (MED s.v. *comen* v. 4a. (e), a contextually apt sense proposed by Wittig 2001:270–1. But the association with *romynge* at 11 (rendered by Wittig 'moving in a desultory fashion') nonetheless implies a play on this phrasal use (earlier instanced at *WPal* 1688) and the literal sense 'pass by' found at 7.218, B 17.121. The idiom inevitably evokes an 'inward journey' like that described by Piers in 7.204ff, with its parallel expression *come into Consience* at 7.206 // **ZAB**. *Resoun*: in general terms 'the personification of the waking dreamer's own rational self-analysis...as well as the authoritative figure of Passus IV' (*Pe*); but the definitions at 16.186, 190 suggest here more specifically Will's examination of conscience in the light of moral law. Reflecting on his concrete moral decisions, he 'meets with' the principle of reason on which they are (or should be) predicated, which is *then* personified in the dream. **7–10** *hele...inwitt*: 'health of body and mind'; cf. 10. 182 and *TN*. **11** *Romynge*: a hanging participle (cf. B 18.299); it is Will who remembers. *aratede*: recalling the encounter with Reason in B 11.375.

12–34 12–19 specify three kinds of work: clerkly (12), 'crafty' (18a), and agricultural (13–19). **19** *Heggen*: either 'make / trim hedges' (*Sk*, *Pe*, MED) or the rare verb *eggen* 'harrow' (< OE *ecgan*; see OED s.v. *edge* v[2]) derived from *egþe* 'harrow' (= *aythe* 21.274), in which case it forms an alliterative doublet with *harwen*. The spelling *eggen* (in all **p** copies except MF) suggests that the *h* is inorganic, but is not decisive, though the verb's survival in rural usage favours the rarer lexeme. **21** '[So that] those who provide you a livelihood may be given some advantage [from doing so].' This construction with suspended subject pronoun, the infinitive as 'predicate nominative' (*MES* 524–5) is paralleled at 6.48, 21.233, 269; see *TN*. **24** *long*: 'tall'; alluding to the Persona's stature and punningly to one half of the author's surname, of which the second appears in 26a (he does *not* have 'lands'); for similar ironic self-references cf. B 15.152 and A 11.118 (*Pe* compares Hoccleve's *Regement of Princes* 981–7). **28** 'A compulsive spender or a time-waster' (*B&T-P*). **30** *Frydayes*: days of fasting, abstinence and alms-deeds, when the pious making their devotions would presumably be readier to give. *feste-dayes*: the many days of celebra-

tion, when the wealthier especially might be expected to feel generous. **31** *lollarne*: see on 4.114. **32a** '[God], Who will render to every man according to his works' (Rom 2:6; cf. Mt 16:27, Apoc 22:12). That the allusion is to Rom seems likely from the preceding verse's reference to 'the day of wrath...of the just judgement of God' (Rom 2:5). Alf*Q* traces the exact wording here to Hugh of St Cher's comment on Job 21:4. **34** *excused*: 'exempted (from working)'; the first use in this sense.

35–60a 35 *ȝong, ȝong*: 'very young indeed' (see *TN*). **36** *frendes*: 'family, relatives' (a ME set-phrase; see Olszewska 1973:205–7, who notes that in 12.157 the sense may be 'friends'). *scole*: 'university'. **37** *Holy Writ*: 'theology' (Bennett 1974:14). The context implies that Will had passed from the Arts into the Theology Faculty and was training for the secular priesthood (if he was a religious, he might have read Arts in the order's *studium* but would not have depended on his family for financial support). At Oxford, the Bible was studied during the first four years of the Theology course (Courtenay 1987:41–3). Bowers's preference for 'cathedral school' (1986:21–2) on the basis that the pl. form was used for the university in medieval times is mistaken; see MED s.v. *scole* n. (2), which shows the sg. as normal. **40** *foend...frendes*: echoes *frendes foende* 36 with polysemantic wordplay on *fynden*. The expense of the long university course required the support of a student's family or a patron (such as a bishop). **41** *longe clothes*: worn by clerks to distinguish them from laypeople; a wry hint at their aptness for one *long* (24) in stature as in name. **43a** 'In whatever vocation you have been called, [remain]'; loosely based on I Cor 7:20: 'Let every man abide in the same calling [i.e. type of work] in which he was called [sc. to be a Christian]' (cf. also vs. 24). **44** *London...opelond*: the present tense indicating alternating residence at the same period of time (on the reading see *TN*). Will receives hospitality (and possibly payment) in each household where he performs various clerical services (a line recalled at 16.286). **45–7** *lomes*: his 'tools of trade' are prayers of intercession. The 'Our Father', the psalms 'I will please the lord' (Ps 114:9) and 'Direct my way' (Ps 5:9), which are both parts of the Office of the Dead, and the seven penitential psalms (see on 3.463–4) all appear in the *prymer*, the standard book of devotion for laypeople (ed. Littlehales; see Duffy 1992:209–65). Will presumably said these prayers for (and perhaps with) his patrons. *Pater-noster*: on **L**'s understanding of this prayer see Gillespie 1991. **48** *here*: strictly redundant; for this duplicated possessive see *MES* 158 (and cf. 9.98). **50** *to be*: 'that I shall be / to make me' (on the infinitive as a predicate accusative see *MES* 527). **51** *on...begge*: i.e. he doesn't 'beg' at all [because he does a service for what he gets]. **52** *bagge or botel*: the visible attributes of the professional *loller*; free from them, Will associates himself rather with *Godes* *munstrals* (see 9.136–40). **54** *constrayne*: anticipating the Latin maxim at 60*a* and answering Reason's implied 'constraint' upon Will at 13–21 to do (mainly) 'servile' labour. **55** *Levytycy*: 'of Leviticus', inflected in the genitive after *of*. The allusion is probably not to Lev 21 (*Pe*) but to such injunctions in Num 18:20–4 (*B&T-P*) as that the tribe of Levi should 'possess nothing in their land' but be content with 'an offering from the tithes'. The parallel here between the 'ministry' of clerks in minor orders and that of the OT Levites (cf. 60) sits loosely with Will, who could lawfully claim only voluntary 'offerings', not the 'tithes' reserved for beneficed priests. **56** *of kynde vnderstondynge*: 'as commonly understood', i.e it is self-evident, stands to reason. **57** *swerien...*: i.e. serve on juries; distrust of their probity recurs at 22.162. **58a** 'Do not return evil for evil'. The nearest verbal source is the commentary on Lev 19:18 (the next vs of which is cited as 12.35), by Denis the Carthusian in *Op. Om.* 266 (Alf*Q*, who gives close parallels in I Thess 5:15, I Pet 3:9). **59** *hit ben*: on this 'formal' *hit* followed by a pl. vb (= 'they') cf. 8.217, 9.118 and see *MES* 132–3. **60a** 'The Lord is the portion of my inheritance [and of my cup: it is thou that wilt restore my inheritance to me]' (Ps 15:5, quoting Num 18:20); here cited in a less pragmatic context than at B 12.188. Though *hereditas* symbolises heaven, the verse's *b*-part may contain a hidden personal meaning for one who had renounced (or forfeited) an inheritance 'Crist for to serue'. *Clemencia....*: a maxim, possibly legal, of undiscovered origin. Despite a surface likeness to *Merchant of Venice* 4.1.179, it means not (*Pe*, Alf*G*) 'Mercy is not restricted' (which would require *constringitur*) but 'Mercy does not compel'. *B&T-P*'s 'it is perhaps intended to justify [clerics'] exemption from imposing legal or military sanctions on others' cannot be right, since clerics could only be required to 'impose' these if exercising *secular* office. The general reference is most probably to 'the privileges of tonsured clerks' (*Pe*); but a more specific contextual sense is: 'A generously lenient attitude (*clemencia*) [towards the obligation to earn one's livelihood] will not force [clerks to do such work as Reason described]'. The maxim authorises the sentiment in 54 and is illustrated by 61ff.

61–81 protest against the erosion of social distinctions (for **L**, guarantees of social order) following the Great Plague. The essential point is that if clerics (even unbeneficed ones) came only from the gentry, there could be no legal grounds for thinking that they should do servile work as when, right up to the highest levels in the church, they were being drawn from the estate of peasants (like Chaucer's Parson), and especially of serfs. **64** *frankeleynes*: free landowners below the knightly class; equated with 'ientel men' at 21.39. The one extant Langlandian life-record (*Intro.* V § 4) indicates that he came from this class, of which Chaucer's Franklin is the best-known lit-

erary example. **66a** *Thyse bylongeth*: a very terse phrase, omitting both *it* before the impers. verb and *to* before the pronoun (on the synthetic pronoun-dative without preposition see *MES* 97). **66b–67a** 'and [it is the proper task of] noblemen's relations to serve God and the Christian community [as clergy], as befits their social position'; on the punctuation, cf. Sledd 1940:379–80. **68b–9** envisage clerks who do not take holy orders performing 'clerical' and administrative duties for the nobility or the government. **70–81** *sythe*: governing all nine verbs before the main verb *hath be* in l. 80, *refused* etc being not linked main verbs but past participles dependent on the causal / temporal clause that introduces the sentence. In **73–4** *han be* is understood in 73a, *han* in 73b and 74b, where *ryden* is p.p. **71** Canon law prohibited the illegitimate from being consecrated bishop; but **L**'s objection extends to their appointment to the archidiaconate (often a stepping-stone to the episcopacy). *barnes bastardus*: 'bastard children', echoing 65a, with the second noun inflected adjectivally in the French manner (*MES* 277); against *R–K*'s preferred reading 'barons' bastards', see *TN*. **73–4** regard corruption of social harmony through the power of 'meed', and the departure of sanctity (80), as resulting from a series of abuses, simony being the last of them. **73** *lordes sones*: figuratively become the 'workmen' of newly rich merchant-traders by having to pledge their incomes to raise cash for the retinue and equipment needed for service with the king. This refers in part to events (**74–5**) affecting the previous generation; but there was war with France between 1369 and 1381, and against Scotland in 1385. Before the establishment of a national army in the 15th c., knights had to provide servants and equipment for war out of their own income; cf. the important new passage at 13.107–10 below. **76** expresses an opinion earlier voiced in A 11.201, a line not in **B**. **78–9** state that sons of the impoverished gentry have failed to win positions in the Church, which have gone to those using 'meed' to get them. **79** *Symondes sones*: those who sell and buy spiritual things; alluding to the sin of Simon Magus, who offered the Apostles money for spiritual power (Ac 8:18–24). In this period simony commonly denotes traffic in ecclesiastical preferment. **80** recalls Anima's assertion in B 15.92–102 that the return of virtue and charity requires reform of the clergy.

82–91 83 *consience*: the Dreamer's claim to know God's will for him echoing his statement in 6 above. **86–8** 'In truth man lives [*or*, man truly lives] not from the soil, or by bread, or food, as the "Our Father" testifies. It is *God's will be done* that provides us everything'. The source of the macaronic lines is the well-known 'Not in bread alone doth man live [*non in solo pane vivit homo*], but in every word that proceedeth from the mouth of God' (Mt 4:4, directly taken from Dt 8:3; quoted in full by Patience at 15.246*a*). Replacing the adj. *solus* by the ablative of the noun *solum* 'soil' furnishes a witty clerkly rejoinder to Reason's earlier implication that he should be doing manual (and especially agricultural) work. The '"word" from the mouth of God' that Will claims as sustenance enough for him is aptly one that he himself says for the providers of his *actual* food (46 above), but perhaps is here only synecdochic for prayer. The standard phrasing of the third petition occurs at 16.319, but the modified version here cited will recur at 15.252, where it receives a full 'commentary' in the form of an allegorical action (15.249–52) based on an original passage in // **B** to which the present addition is indebted. Another key scriptural text contrasting earthly with spiritual food that **L** may have associated with Mt 4:4 is Jn 4:34: 'Meus cibus est ut faciam *voluntatem* eius'. The present passage is a foretaste of the 'transcendentalised' food-imagery that in **B** first appears only at 14.29, and in **A** not at all. **89** *lyeth*: taken by *PeB&T-P* as 'applies, is to the point' (MED s.v. *lien* v. (1), 11(b)). But the MED examples cited in support differ from this one in having an indirect object following; and *Ac* 90 would have to mean 'On the contrary, but rather' (MED s.v. *ac* conj. 2(a)). The context suggests more that Conscience concedes Will's assertion at 84–5 but interprets Will's action as 'begging' and then denies that this is *sad parfitnese*. Evoking the tone and manner of a scholastic disputation ('I agree; but I maintain'), Will's own concession at 92a balances Conscience's *Ac* at 90, while his qualifying response at 94 (where *Ac ʒut* can only mean 'But nonetheless') answers it. The general sense of 89–91 is thus: 'You say that Christ tells you in your conscience what work you should do; and by the same Christ, I can't deny that what you say is true. But it hardly counts as solid virtuousness of life to beg in cities.' The points of substance here, Will's appeal to his conscience as a guarantee of his integrity and his interlocutor's acknowledgement of this appeal, are lost if *lyeth* does not mean 'is (saying something) false'. It is thus possible to reject *Pe*'s rendering while agreeing with him that 'Conscience points out that **L**'s theory of the perfect life is not what he practises'. **91** *obediencer*: a monk in charge of one of the administrative offices, such as cellarer or sacristan (Lawrence 1993:121–4). Conscience's acceptance of monks' 'begging' as compatible with *parfitnesse*, and his tacit exclusion of friars', are striking.

92–101 The Biblically-inspired analogy could suggest the recklessness of the compulsive gambler as much as the calculated risk-taking of the merchant-venturer; but **L** may mean that to the prudential mind the two are hard to distinguish. **93** *ytynt tyme*: on this theme cf. B 9.99, borrowed for Ymaginatif's added warning in 14.5 on Will's special responsibility not to misuse speech or time (see the valuable discussion in Burrow 2003). **94** *I hope as he*: either anacoluthic, beginning a sentence not to be finished, or else *as he* = 'like a man who', initiating a comparison

not with *hope* but with *I*. As in 99 below, *hope* carries the senses '(go on) trust(ing)' and 'expect'. **95** *loste... laste*: the chime that links the ideas signified encouraging perseverance by suggesting that a temporary setback may be the parent of a final success. **96** *bargayne*: with literal referent of the metaphor indeterminable, but possibly 'the final version of the poem', as the artistic and moral vindication of **L**'s 'twenty years largely wasted' (cf. Schmidt 2000:23–6). **97** *leef*: a traditional emblem of worthlessness; perhaps also signifying the single leaf of paper 'lost' when the writing on it is deleted, a loss that will seem worthwhile when the work is completed. *laste ende*: 'end of the day' but also the 'final reckoning', when the lost time may be overlooked by the Judge if the final product was a decisive good. (The text quoted at 98a is preceded and followed [Mt 13:39–40, 49] by solemn references to the end of the world and the last judgement). **98** *wordes of grace*: the use of *wordes* as a spelling-variant of *wyrdes* (see *TN*), itself a derivation from *worthen*, might have appealed to **L** the etymologist. But while 'happy fortune' fits the lucky merchant of the analogy and its Gospel source, 'grace-bringing words' better suits the maker Will (the true subject of the analogy) and ties in more closely with the Latin following. It is the hopeful individuals of the parables cited who inspire him to persevere with his poetry and the way of life that sustains it, which both involve uttering 'grace-bringing words'. **98a** (i) 'The kingdom of heaven is like unto a treasure hidden in a field. [Which a man having found, hid it: and for joy thereof goeth and selleth all that he hath and buyeth that field]' (Mt 14:44). (ii) 'The woman who found the drachma'; alluding to Lk 15:8–9. These two 'parables of the kingdom' are complementary: (i) describes selling all you have to buy one supremely valuable thing, (ii) finding no joy in all you have until you recover the one thing you have lost, which thus acquires more value than the rest. An analogy with the persona as clerkly maker would not be far to find: he hazards everything to get one thing right (his poem), but then gets no profit from what he has achieved (the 'B Version') until every last bit of it is to his satisfaction (the ongoing 'C Version'). **99** *So*: less 'therefore' than 'in that way [i.e. like the merchant]'. **100–01** *gobet*: echoing the *micae* 'fragments' in the story of the Canaanite woman (Mt 15: 27). *tyme...tyme*: 'a period of time...every moment of my (life)time'.

100–08 100–04 *bigynne...continue*: if Reason's 'No more time-wasting' admonishes, Conscience's 'Persevere' encourages. **105–8** resume the parallel text with **ZAB** V but reduce the crudity of their transition by making the passage one that better motivates the second dream (through sorrow rather than regret) and prepares for its central theme (sin and repentance). The various pious actions, which recall Haukyn at the end of B XIII and imply no lack of sincerity, are typical of the more demonstra-

tive kinds of medieval contrition (Vernet 1930:120–5). **105** reads, despite its deliberate repetition-with-variation (cf. *mette me / me mette* at 109–10), rather like a poetic 'catchword', and its removal would be a gain in economy. **107** *Pater-noster*: especially significant because of the medieval belief in the power of its seven petitions against each of the Deadly Sins and in its spiritual efficacy generally: 'This hooly orison amenuseth [lessens] eek venyal synne, and therfore it aperteneth specially to penitence...it avayleth eek agayn the vices of the soule' (*CT* X 1042; Gillespie 1994:107–11). **(ii) 109–200** *Reason's Sermon.* The structure of the vision in **B** as a fourfold action of sermon / confession / pilgrimage / pardon is illuminatingly analysed in Burrow 1984[1965]:79–101.
109–25 109–10 The opening of Vision Two amplifies through verbal repetition its echo of the opening of Vision One, a geographical supplementing of **ZAB**'s allegorical place-reference. *Maluerne Hulles*: recalling Pr 6 and in turn echoed at 9.295 by way of closure (though inconsistently, since the second dream occurs at or near Cornhill). Absence of further mention of the western locale suggests that the 'Visio' (= Pr–IX in its first form) envisaged an audience in the poet's home-region, but its **BC** continuations (with two dozen references to the capital and particular places in it) a London and national readership. **112–15** The **C** revision replaces the end-rhymes (different ones) of A 9/10, B11/12 with an assonantal echo of *prechede* 114 in *preuede* 115. But the substantive change is from Conscience as bishop in **ZA** (a function not coherent with his rôle as a knight able to marry Mede) to Reason as bishop in **B**, and then as supreme bishop in **C**, with Conscience intelligibly (if at the 'historical' level surprisingly) his cross-bearer. **112** *as a pope*: the conflict between this and his *addressing* the Pope at 191 below could be resolved by seeing him as 'a cardinal acting as papal legate' (*Pe*). But this is probably to be over-literal, since in the case of a personified abstraction 'rank' probably signifies allegorically 'importance'. Reason's higher position in **C** underlines his *universal* authority, the locale becoming both England (114) and the whole Christian world (111). **115** *preuede*: i.e. showed the truth of his claim by an appeal to a 'spiritual reading' of the 'book of Nature' akin to an exegete's of the book of Scripture (for a brilliant if overstated account of 'interpretation' as the poem's theme and method, see Rogers 2002). *this pestelences*: **C** preferring to describe attacks of the plague in the pl. (cf. 10.274, 11.60) and often with 'these', the force of which is both generic (plague is divine punishment for sin) and deictic (particular recent examples 'prove' this belief). After the Great Pestilence of 1348–9, three further attacks kept the subject topical (see on Pr 82); but by 1387 the 'proof by example' would be reminder more than demonstration. The unaltered re-

tention of this line from **Z** → **C** and the 'tempest' lines that follow imply as referent the outbreak of 1361–2. *was*: the subject being construed as a collective sg. (*MES* 62–3). **116** *south-weste wynde*: beginning on Sat. 15 Jan. 1362, lasting five days, and readily lending itself to the kind of moral *significacio* spoken of at B 15.482–3a. A figurative understanding of wind as an intelligible divine utterance is introduced as early as **Z** 34–6 after the line // to **C** 117, among seven lines deleted in **A** that provide the exemplum an apt commentary from *Holy Writ* [*that*] *wot muche bettre.* Storm symbolises God's anger against human pride in Is 28:1–3, 'Woe to...pride...the Lord is...as a *storm* of hail: a destroying *whirlwind*...'; Ezech 13:13, 'I will cause a *stormy wind*...in my indignation...and great *hailstones* in my wrath'; and Ps 148:8, 'hail, snow, ice, *stormy winds*, which fulfil [the Lord's] word'. Along with the concurrent second plague and the hailstorm of 'Black Monday' (14 Apr. 1360), the great wind seems to have furnished motifs and perhaps even occasioned the composition of Vision Two in its **Z** form. **117** *for pride*: 'on account of / to check pride'. This 'general roote of...the sevene deedly synnes' (*CT* X 386ff) was seen as inviting direct divine retribution, as by John of Bridlington: 'propter luxuriam et *superbiam* fient istae duce destructionis et pestilentiae' (Wright, *PolP* I:82). *PP* regularly associates pestilence with pride (8.348, 11.58–60, B 10.72), and its indiscriminate effect on rich and poor alike needed no labouring. *poynt*: natural disorders having a moral 'reason' and (secondarily) 'purpose' (MED s.v. *pointe* n. (1), 6 (f) and (d)). **Z** 34 Cf. *AW* 65/1: 'hwet is word but wind'. **118** *poffed*: hinting at what Z 40 makes explicit, that the *wynd of ys word* is the divine breath; as the MED exx. under *puffen* v. (a) show that the verb usually implies a human agent, a play on sense (b), found at 15.97, may be inferred. **119** *ensaunple*: for a later *ensanple...on trees* cf. 16.246, and for other 'natural' exempla B 7.128, 10.294, 11.324, 12.236, 15.472. These presuppose the 'sacramental' understanding of the world definitively expressed by Alan of Lille in 'Omnis mundi creatura' (*PL* 210:579; *OBMLV* no. 242). *do þe bettre*: the pregnant formula summing up the Vision's penitential intent, to effect attrition or repentance through fear of divine punishment (*drede...fordon*). This corresponds to simple conversion, not a higher stage in the life of virtue as will unfold in the *Vita* section later. **122** *hem alle*: despite **C**'s revision of **ZAB** *ye* to *we* 119, the pronoun's referent remains semantically disjunct, its immediate grammatical antecedent being the trees that emblematise diverse human types in the *felde of folk*, its more remote one his hearers. But *ous alle*, while more logical, might have seemed too sombre even for a penitential *sermo*. **125b** *to heuene*: 'to turn their minds to heavenly things'; likewise avoiding the repetition of B 11 in B 23 //. **126–45** now partly restate in a public sermon what Reason said to the King in his 'impossibilia' speech at 4.111ff. **126–7** recall Reason's stance towards the Dreamer at 26–8 above. *wastoures*: the pl. eliminating the first appearance of a personage who is to feature prominently at 8.149–78, but so as more exactly to echo the wording of Pr 24. In **ZAB** the sg. type-name signifies a caterpillar of the (rural) commonwealth, corresponding at a lower plane to the spendthrift of *WW*. **127** *tyme spille*: the eschatological character of 'honest work' is stressed in **C**, taking up the theme of 92–101. **128–33** describe three women who illustrate varieties of pride defined in penitential treatises. **128** *Purnele*: surnamed Proudheart at 6.3 (see on 4.111 above), with Wat's nameless wife embodying 'pompe and delit in temporal hyenesse and glori[ye] in this worldly estaat' (*CT* X 404), specifically as manifested in 'costlewe furrynge in hir gownes' (ibid. 417) and 'superfluitee...of clothynge' (431). **130** *Stoue*: a common name with no special meaning. **131** *Felyce*: the (?ironically) courtly name (cf. B 12.46) of a shrewish woman who exemplifies *inobedience, despit* or *janglynge* (*CT* X 395, 40). Timely discipline might save her from the punishment-stool reserved for scolds in the harsh world of village society (see on 3.79). **132** *Watte*: short for Walter; perhaps the same found with his wife in Betene's brew-house at 6.362. **133** *half marc; grote*: the value of a skilled workman's wage for a week (*Bn*); cf. the Wife of Bath in *CT* I 453–5. **134–5** The internal rhyme and assonance exemplify more 'lexical Platonism': the butcher is linked with his chopper and 'Betty' becomes her proper self when 'beaten'. *Butte* (or *Bette*): perhaps short for Bartholomew; a name given to a beadle and a butcher elsewhere. *Betene*: diminutive of Beatrice or Elizabeth; her sloth is 'ydelnesse...the yate of alle harmes' (*CT* X 713). *Sk* sees her as Butte's daughter, doubtless because children are mentioned in 136ff; but the only other Betene in *PP* is the *brewestere* of 6.352 who leads Glutton astray. **136–9** The **B** form (34–9) echoes a stanza preserved in *Fasciculus Morum* [*FM*], ed. Wenzel 1978:146, vs. 12. **137** *wynnynge*: well-to-do parents being commonly observed to indulge their offspring more. **C** omits the **B** line relating the collapse of discipline to parental indulgence of children who had survived the 1361–2 *mortalité des enfants* (so known because it especially affected children; see B 10.79 and McKisack 331). Also omitted is the common 'family' maxim (cf. Pr 203) having in the 'Proverbs of Hendyng' (Morris & Skeat 1873:36) the form *Luef child lore byhoueth* (and deriving from the b-half of the quoted Biblical verse). **139a** 'He that spareth the rod hateth his son: [but he that loveth him correcteth him betimes]'. The form of the Biblical a-verse's second part is closer to our 'spoil the child'. **142** *Lyue... leue*: 'Platonic' wordplay suggesting intrinsic relation between 'life' and 'belief'.

146–79 (B 10.292–329, A 11.204–13) move from briefly exhorting the secular clergy to warning the endowed religious at length in 35 lines expanded from B 10.292–308. Monastic foundations had been granted land and property by lay benefactors for the purposes of prayer and charity, and Reason's point here is that as the monks hold their lands from the crown, the king is entitled to take these over if they fail to observe their Rule. The lines were seen by some Reformation-period readers as a 'prophecy' of the Dissolution of the monasteries under Henry VIII (Crowley, *Address* in Sk *B-Text*, xxxiv; Jansen 1989); but they only advocate reform (Chaucer's more genial satire on the Monk in *CT* I 165–207 owes them several details). **C** here brings forward a passage from a longer critique of the clergy in B X to voice a positive ideal of enclosed religious life, with warm praise of monastic (and university) society, an attack on current failures in observance, and a warning of forcible change involving (without wholesale dispossession) a major redistribution of monks' wealth to the friars (173). **146** *Gregory*: Pope St Gregory the Great (*c.* 540–604), one of the four great Doctors of the Latin Church (21.317, B 9.73). Abbot at Rome in 585 and Pope in 590, he ardently promoted regular monasticism (then only a half-century old), exempting the orders from episcopal jurisdiction and making them directly responsible to the Pope (Lawrence 1989:19–22, 33). *grete clerk*: alluding to Gregory's learning, which had a pervasive influence on Western theological culture and spirituality (see Evans 1986; Straw 1988). *bokes* (*Morales* B 293): the vaguer **C** is more accurate; Gregory's massive *Expositio in Librum Iob, sive Moralium Libri XXXV* (the *Moralia*) expounds *Job* in the literal, mystical and especially moral senses. The only patristic work **L** cites by name, it seems to have affected his thought more deeply than any book apart from the Bible. **147** *reule*: Gregory wrote no Rule as such, nor is the 'fish' simile in the *Moralia*; but the sentiment accords with his stress on 'stability of mind' (Straw 66–89). He is also an apt authority on the conduct of English monastic life, since his Prior Augustine, whom he sent to evangelise the English in 596, set up England's first 'Roman'-style monastery in Canterbury (see B 15.444). **148–51** The semi-proverbial 'As a fish without water lacks life, so does a monk without a monastery', attributed to Pope Eugenius by Gratian (*Sk*), occurs in the C4th *Life* of St Antony (reputedly the original founder of monachism) that was a source of *Legenda Aurea* [*LA*] 21.iv (see B 15.269ff // C 17.6ff) and is quoted in *CT* I.179–81. The proverb's warning against wandering or instability is here adapted to attack the worldliness arising from the monks' involvement in mundane business. **152–3** A sentiment found in Bp. Thomas Brinton, 'si sit vita angelica in terra, aut est in studio, vel in claustro' (Orsten 1970) and also in Petrus Ravennus, 'Si paradisus in hoc mundo est, in claustro vel in scholis' (Kaske

1957[2]:481–3), L's wording seeming to fuse the two. **153** *cloystre*: synecdoche for the religious house and thence metonymic for the enclosed contemplative way of life. *scole*: 'university' (Bennett 1974:14). The strong monastic influence on the layout of early collegiate buildings at both universities is evident in William of Wykeham's New College at Oxford (1379), with its original cloister still extant. **C** removes both the stress on learning given by the identical rhyme of B 302/3 (part of the 'praise' passage added in **B**) and the negative *scorn*, which sits ill with *ese*. **155** A full-stop is justifiable after *lerne //* as completing the double statement about cloister and school; but a semi-colon may be preferable if the primary contrast intended by *Ac* 156 is between the more rigorous academic and the lax monastic communities. Strikingly, no corresponding criticism of *scole-clerkes* follows that of the monks (on the relations between these cf. Lawrence 1989:141–6, and on the state of monasteries at this period McKisack 1959:305–9). **157** *ryde...aray*: doubtless with a pun on the literal meaning (that when monks hunt they do not wear their long habits). **158** *ledares..*: understand *ben* before. *lawedays*: days for holding a session of the manorial or sheriff's court, at which monks as major local landlords might be envisaged as involved (the revision recognises that monks, as opposed to parsons and friars, were not conspicuous in love-days). *ypurchaced*: buying more land out of their surplus revenues. **159–60** could refer to hunting when riding *out* to scattered estates (*Pe*), since some great abbots travelling on business even took hounds in their train (*Sk*), but more realistically perhaps to hunting when riding *over* adjacent fields of the same religious house, as the notion of leading a pack would imply (cf. *CT* I 90–2, 207). **A 11.213** *Poperiþ*: a word found only here and securely glossed from its variants (*pryken, ryden*). MED s.v. derives it from *poppen* v.1. 'strike' (as with spurs), itself instanced only a half-century later. **161–2** The lordly monk expects his serving-man to behave towards him as to a knight (cf. 21.28). The antonymic paronomasia on *lord(eyne)* anticipates that at 8.46 (*quene / queene*): the monk is not a real lord, so his servant has not failed in 'courtesy', as perhaps the real lords *have* (towards their children). **164** *ryne...auters*: a commonplace in Wycliffite criticisms of the regular clergy (Wyclif, *Select English Works*, 1.308–9, 313–15), as noted by *SkPe*. The altars being those of parish churches where the monastic corporation was the legal rector, to whom the greater (or agrarian) tithe was due, it is being alleged that absentee rectors neglect the state of the parish church's roof. **165–6** Resident regular canons (see on 170) look to their own comfort rather than the charitable work that is their calling. **168, 171** The metaphor is one of an authoritative priest-figure hearing the monks' confession of faults and imposing an appropriate collective 'penance'. But as Reason's 'prophecy'

is an indefinite, quasi-apocalyptic threat that the regulars' pride and negligence will one day be punished by a 'king' (who could be Christ), it need hardly imply a sacral rôle for a secular monarch. **169** *as...telleth*: a formulaic stave-phrase also at B 9.41 and varied at 3.426, 18.222, the reference being to the text about beating at 177*a*. **170** *chanons*: canons regular (as opposed to secular canons attached to cathedral or collegiate churches), who followed a semi-monastic mid-C11th rule drawn up from writings uncertainly attributed to St Augustine (whence 'Augustinian' Canons). Unlike monks, they could be parish priests, and were subject to the bishop's authority (see further Dickinson 1950, Lawrence 1989:163–9). Only the form from Central French *chanoine* occurs for the regulars, AN *canon* (B 10.46) referring to a secular canon. **171** *Ad pristinum...*: 'to return to the original state', first used by Isidore of Seville (*PL* 83:899–902) to refer to a penitent cleric's restoration to his rights. Alf*G* finds *status* to mean (a) 'grace, in which the penitent has to his credit as much merit as though he had never sinned', (b) '"good fame", with the restoration of all legal privileges'. But neither seems relevant here, since the phrase has a quite different application, declaring (within a metaphorical context) that the endowed regulars will be required *as a penance* to 'return to an original state' of material simplicity (*Pe*, Baldwin in Alf*C* 75) that will help them recover the spiritual purity of their founders (cf. Scase 1989:88–9, 202n14). Although used by Wyclif in 1378, the idea of disendowing the possessioners was not necessarily linked with heretical positions at this period (Gradon 1982:188–9). **172** *barnes*: the direct beneficiaries, if lands their ancestors gave the monks reverted to the original owners. **172*a*** 'Some trust in chariots, and some in horses: [but we will call upon the name of the Lord our God]. They are bound and have fallen; [but we are risen and are set upright]' (Ps 19:8–9). The psalm's omitted b-verses make clear the double analogy with the 'blameworthy' clergy ensnared by worldliness who are brought to a fall (the horses are especially apt after 157–60) and with those who trust only in God for their livelihood. **B 10.320** *Beatus vir*: 'Blessed is the man [who hath not walked in the counsel of the ungodly]' (Ps 1:1). The *techyng* of Ps 1 is that those who rely on God will prosper, while the wicked will perish, and it supplies 'prophetic' backing for the expected dispossession of the endowed regulars. This psalm-opening is cited again at B 5.418 and B 13. 52. **173–7 (B 10.322–6)** The general (and more optimistic) sense of **C** is that the monks' disendowment will release wealth for supporting the friars, whose valuable missionary rôle in society seems to be compromised by dependence on begging for a livelihood. **173** *fraytour*: the refectory where they ate; friaries were often laid out on the same plan as monasteries save for a cloister (Lawrence 1989:304). Although the word is etymologically unrelated, its derived form was near-identical with *frater* 'friar'. **175** *Constantyn*: a loose metonym for the future king who it is hoped will bring this about. Emperor *c.* 306–37 AD, he was the first ruler to provide land and property for the maintenance of the clergy, who had hitherto lived by their work and the gifts of the faithful (see also on 17.220ff). **176** *Abbot...*: a generalised figure of monastic rule; the Abbess may be his 'niece' (a vestige of *godchildren* **B**) because the female branches of religious orders generally followed the male as subsidiary foundations, but perhaps also because abbesses often came from noble and gentry families that had connections with the Church, through which they secured advancement (Lawrence 1989:216–17). **177** *knok...wounde*: surprisingly violent language if thought of as coming from Reason; but the suspicion that fierce tensions lurked beneath the convent's surface gentility emerges later under the sin of Wrath at 6.128–50. *crounes*: if 'shaven crowns', then 'a poor alteration' (*Sk*), being inapplicable to women. The sense should be 'top of the head' not 'tonsure' (MED s.v. *coroune* n. 10 (a), not 11); but with a probable pun on sense 1 'monarch's crown', the witty image of 'crounes' being struck by a 'king' is well purchased. **177a (B 327a)** 'How is the oppressor come to nothing, the tribute hath ceased? [**B**] / The Lord hath broken the staff of the wicked, the rod of the rulers, / [That struck the people in wrath] with an incurable wound' (Is 14: 4–6)'. Though *Pe* is right that 'altering of the syntax by omission' makes the 'rod' the object of the divine blow that causes an incurable injury, this does not necessarily render 'the relation of the second half of 177 to the idea of monastic reform' difficult. For in the analogy, the 'oppressor' ('the king of Babylon') is presumably 'the Abbot of England' (= monastic lordship) and his 'tribute' the income monks get on their property, while the 'rod' is a metonym for their economic and social power, which would indeed be incurably injured by reform as radical as that envisaged. **178** *as...tolde* (*Caym...awake* **B** 328): both versions have an 'eschatological' flavour, but **C** imagines a spiritual renewal of the Church prior to the advent of the 'king' (who seems increasingly like Christ), while **B** looks to the coming of Antichrist, figured as Cain. There is an obscure allusion to unspecified 'chronicles'; possibly pertinent here is the renewal of the Church's 'clothing' envisioned in Eph 5:26–7 (and cf. Apoc 7:14).

B 322–7 The ambiguity in the imagery of the source-lines could be what prompted the **C** revision; for since the 'coffers' of **323** stand for the royal treasury into which monastic revenues would first revert, the notion that friars will get the 'key' to this might be thought to contradict **L**'s point. **324** *godchildren*: 'spiritual children' (*Sk*); see on 147. **325** *Abyngdoun*: in Berks (now in Oxon), one of the oldest and richest abbeys, levelled at the Dissolution. As 'the house into which the monks...

were first introduced in England' it is 'representative of English monachism' (*Wr*). Galloway (2001[1]:22–4) proposes to find a specific allusion to the Abingdon townsmen's attempt to 'impeach' the Abbot before the king's council in 1368 for infringing on their ancient liberties, and takes the phrase 'knok of a kynge' as corresponding to the legal term *impetitus* 'impeachment'.

180–200 Returning to **B** V, the revision continues the text's expansion by deepening the theological content of Reason's teaching. **181** *tresor*: the disillusioned word-play in **B** (*tresor / treson*) implying the people's possible unreliability is removed, perhaps because now realised in the 1381 uprising, which **L** may not have wanted thought of as a simple act of treasonable rebellion. *Conscience*: no exact allusion to specific words seems intended; but he had earlier urged the king against the pursuit of conventional *tresor* when arguing against Mede. **182–3** **C**'s counselling of accord between the different orders of society comes in the aftermath of the Peasants' Revolt and reflection on the reasons for it. *ryche*: presumably denoting secular and religious lords and the great merchants. *comuners*: craftsmen, tradespeople and peasants. **184–5** 'Let no machinations or greedy self-interest cause divisions between you and prevent the unanimity needed to discharge your responsibilities'. **184** *kyne counsayl*: 'kind of plan'; but as *kyne* is an archetypal spelling for *kene* 'sharp, harsh' (see 22.97), a semi-pun may be intended here, such counsel being likeliest to create dissension. **185** *That*: 'so that...not'; an idiosyncratic 'preclusive' use of *that* without *ne*. *ȝoure wardes kepe*: ambiguous in sense and reference, so as to allow some play on 'charges, responsibilities [i.e. to keep guard over]' (MED s.v. 2, citing this line) and 'city-wards [under your joint administrative care]' (ibid. 3 (b)). **186–8** The implied message is that everyone should keep his place, and that rebellion against the king's authority (not necessarily the same as the social status quo) is inspired by a devilish lie. *comune*: a more 'democratic' variant on the 'heavenly court' image at 1.104. **187** *Lucifer the lyare*: the stress on the Devil's lies, earlier introduced through his identification with Falsehood (1.60), is increased in **C**, as in the digression inserted at 20.350–8. It seems Reason finds diabolic influence at work in the 'lies' of those who provoked discord and rebellion against the king's authority, presumably the *wyse clerkes* (20.354) whose abstract arguments against private ownership (22.275–6) might have incited such as John Ball to teach the *lewed* disruptive doctrines of social equality. **189a** The repetition here of Conscience's injunction to the friars at B 20.246 may assume the audience's familiarity with UNITY as a 'nature-name' for the Church at the end of the B-Text. Although this sermon is addressed to all states and conditions of men, it may be implied that as the Church plays a special rôle in achieving social cohesion, its wealth is correspondingly a major source of divisiveness in the *comune*. **191–6 (B 52–5)** Reason's prayer to the Pope in **C** also has its admonition (B 51b) removed, no doubt in the same cause of fostering 'unity'. But it is unclear whether Wycliffite attacks on the highest ecclesiastical authority are being treated as analogous to (or even in part the source of) attacks on the authority of the state. **191** *haue pite*: hardly 'treat gently' (*Bn*), if the severe tone of B 19.432–3, 446–50a is borne in mind. The speaker in **B** is certainly here ascribing fault to the Pope, but the phrase fits less well in **C**, which shifts blame to secular rulers. **192–3** The injunction not to give pardons and indulgences to kings stipulates an end primarily to war between rulers (*alle...peple* being a single integral phrase), secondarily to antagonisms between rulers and their own people. **195b–6a** is not easy to interpret literally. Presumably not urging tolerance of evil-doing (cf. 4.94–104 above), it may be discreetly recommending pardon in perpetuity (i.e. no distraint upon their heirs) to those who took part in the Rebellion, and a more conciliatory approach than the harsh reprisals Richard's government took against the convicted rebels. But given that this is to be a 'penance', like that to be imposed on the monks (168–71 above), the king's own partial guilt seems inescapably implied. **B 52** *to kepe*: in your keeping (to administer), i.e. as rulers and judges (cf. B Pr 133). *Truþe*: Justice, as revealed by God. *youre coveitise*: '(the object of) your desire', with a punning implication as at B 3.164 (removed in revision) that, if they desire Truth, it will free them from that sin. **B 55** *Amen...*: 'Amen, I say to you, I know you not' (Mt 25:12); from the Parable of the Virgins, which appropriately teaches responsibility in one's office, with a possible reminiscence of Mt 7:23 'I never knew you', addressed to those 'that work iniquity'. **197** virtually repeats Pr 48. **198** *seynt*: both a title and an attribute 'holy' (as at 1.80, 11.204). The thought here is that the destination of a spiritual 'pilgrimage' should be God himself, here denoted by his primary 'nature-name' of Truth, like a saint the location of whose shrine may be known (as it is by Piers Plowman at 7.254). **199** *Qui...*: the formula-ending of many prayers and blessings, and appropriate here to Reason as a bishop concluding his sermon. If its well-known appearance in the Nicene Creed (*Brev.* 2:484) is being consciously echoed ('Et in Spiritum Sanctum...*Qui cum Patre et Filio* simul adoratur...'), then 'an identification of Truth with the Holy Spirit' (AlfQ) may indeed be intimated; but the poem's 'nature-name' for the Holy Ghost is *Grace*. Moreover, the early, fuller form of the line in Z 71–5, with its bracketing use of the 'Seek St Truth' phrase, clearly invokes the protection of Son and Spirit on those who seek (what can only be) the First Person, and this fits better with the pervasive use of 'Truth' to mean 'God (the Father)'. *þat...byfalle*: 'may good fortune come to those...' (a 'jussive' subjunctive).

Passus VI (ZAB V)

PASSUS SIX is the first of two in **C** dealing with the CONFESSIONS OF THE DEADLY SINS and the appearance of PIERS, which filled one passus in **B**. Though not dividing at the same point, it reverts to the more moderate size of **A**, breaking the massive B V into more digestible portions of about 450 (VI) and 300 lines (VII) each. It deals with Pride, Envy, Anger, Lust and Greed; but why Sloth begins VII instead of ending VI is not clear. **L** develops the Sins episode with over 100 lines of material from B XIII. He shortens Envy by 12 lines; leaves Gluttony and Sloth; but expands Pride by 50 lines, Lechery by 20, Wrath by 12 and Greed by 35. He thus obliterates the distinction in his earlier handling of the penitential theme between two separate phases of 'attrition' and 'contrition' (the Seven Deadly Sins; Haukyn's oblique 'confession'). But the loss in structural clarity is made up for by detailed improvements in expression. Haukyn's successor Actyf in C XV becomes a moderately virtuous character and, as a plausible contrast with the contemplative Patience, fitter to be the servant of Piers (who embodies both aspects). The passus falls into a brief prelude and six sections: (i) Pride 3–62; (ii) Envy 63–102; (iii) Wrath (103–69); (iv) Lechery (170–95); (v) Greed (196–307), followed by Evan the Welshman and Robert the Robber (308–14, 315–29), and Repentance's exhortation (330–48); (vi) Gluttony (349–440).

The moral scheme used derives from Gregory the Great's ordering, with the four 'spiritual' sins first and the three 'bodily' ones last: Pride, Anger, Envy, Avarice; Sloth, Gluttony, Lechery (Bloomfield 1952:105–21). It was familiar from vernacular works in the tradition stemming from the *Summa Vitiorum* of Peraldus (1236) and the AN *Somme le Roy* of Frère Lorens (1279). These included the early C14th English *Ayenbite of Inwyt* and *Handlyng Synne* and the later *Speculum Vitae* and *Book of Vices and Virtues* (see Pantin 1955 and Bloomfield generally). But easily the most accessible contemporary analogue is Chaucer's *Parson's Tale*, a schematic account of the 'parts' of Penitence and the capital sins in the sequence Pride, Envy, Anger, Sloth, Avarice, Gluttony, Lechery, a work that is close to *PP* in thought and phrasing and may reflect knowledge of it. **L** made some major changes in revising. **Z** treats Envy and Anger as a *joint* sin and **A** *omits* Anger. **B** *adds* Anger and ends with ROBERT THE ROBBER as a kind of 'summing-up' of all the sins before REPENTANCE returns to intercede for them all. **C** places Lechery after Anger, putting Robert (less subtly but logically enough) not at the end but after Avarice and a new character EVAN THE WELSHMAN. But no particular significance attaches to the final order where, after three of the five 'spiritual' sins (Pride, Envy and Anger), come a 'bodily' sin Lechery, the fourth spiritual sin Avarice, and the remaining bodily sins Gluttony and Sloth. The parallel version, where it differs, is discussed below *after* the initial commentary on the basic reference-text **C**.

1–2 PRELUDE: *Will's Repentance* **1** *Repentaunce*: envisaged here as an impulse of spirit ('ran') provoked by the sermon describing the effects of divine judgement, and personifying both remorse for sin and the recoil from sin that initates conversion of heart (on this very original creation, see Alford 1993). Despite the structural and conceptual change noted above, the **C** sinners are still moved to acknowledge and confess mainly out of a 'carnal' fear of punishment by an angry Lord rather than a 'spiritual' sorrow at offending a loving Father. **2** *Will*: the collective and individual *Animus* (16.182) that, *qua* guilty of all these vices, synecdochically 'represents' the folk of the field and is affected by the 'movement' of repentance. That the sinner-dreamer has the poet's presumed name is (even if fortuitously) an outstanding instance of the modesty-topos in medieval literature. But although reference to 'Will' in the third person here makes his symbolic rôle clear, the logically discordant (if dramatically striking) use of the first person at B 5.184–5 is abandoned, with a gain in clarity but some loss of tension (as often in the revision of **B** to **C**). *wepe*: recognised and encouraged in the period as an authentic outward expression of inward repentance (Vernet 1930:123–5), though its true meaning remains ambiguous for the beholder.

(i) 3–61 describe PRIDE, 'the beginning of all sin' (Ecclus 10:15); the only Sin allowed a proper name or presented as a woman (though both Envy and Anger include female examples). Gender is, however, indeterminate after the opening eight lines retained from **B**, and even these are not exclusive to a female speaker. All the capital vices had Latin names of feminine gender, but SUPERBIA was the one most commonly presented as a woman (see *vanagloria* in Katzenellenbogen 1939: figs. 8a, 9, 15, 16, 66). Awareness of the categorisations in the penitential literature is obvious from the correspondence between **L**'s account of Pride and the sins Chaucer specifies under Superbia (*CT* X 390–405), e.g. *inobedience* 15–17a, 19, *swellynge of herte* 7b–18, *contumacie* 20–1, *despit* 22–3, *arrogance* and *pertinacie* 24–9, *veyneglorie* 30 (cf. esp. *CT* X 404), *ypocrisie* 31–3, *avauntynge* 34, *inpacience* 35, *elacioun* 36–7, *insolence* 38–41, 42–6, *presumpcioun* 50–60. The closeness in thought is seen at ll. 28–30 'wysor / To carpe...proud in port' compared with 'to regard of...his konnyng, and of his spekyng, and of his beryng' (*CT* X 399). **3** *Purnele Proud-herte*: very briefly treated in **ZAB** but most expanded in **C**, with 30 lines from B XIII and 18 new. *platte...erthe*: a symbolic self-abasement 'putting down' her high and mighty airs. **6** *hayre*: worn in place of a soft undergarment to discipline desire for bodily gratification. **7** *affayten*; *fers*: terms fig-

uring wilful self-love as a wild hawk that needs strict training to be tamed. (*ParsT* 479–80 offers not a physical 'remedy' against pride but 'suffering to be missaid' as the third form of 'humility of heart'). **8** *holde*: i.e. 'I shall hold.' **10–11** *of alle... hated*: either '*from* all whom I have despised' or '*on account of* all my contemptuous hostility against people'. The latter is likelier as the mercy is sought from God (cf. 16), and so *hem* for *that* in **Z** need not itself favour the former reading. For *hated* here denotes scorn or contempt (MED s.v. *haten* v. 1(c), not 1(b), under which this line is cited), forming *part* of the sense of 'envy' < L. *invidia*. This probably accounts for the word's original presence in **ZA**, the revision of which removes possible confusion with that later vice. **ZA 86/53** *þat*: 'to whom'; on this oblique use see *MES* 97. **12** *Resoun*: i.e. at 117 above. **13** *sharpeliche*: both 'in unsparing detail' and 'vigorously' (MED s.v. *sharpli* adv. 2 (a) and (b)); heartfelt confession of sin is to be as painful as its *scharp salue* (22.307), the *hayre* donned as penance. *shak of*: like the furred gown of 4.111. **14–29** These new lines progress from breaches of the 4th commandment ('Honour thy father and mother') to 'authorial' self-rebuke for satire on the clergy. That little of this relates to the *Vanitas*-figure of Purnele understandably prompts *Pe*'s question whether 'a separate personification of Pride begins to speak at l. 14'. Certainly, what he calls 'the eclectic nature of the text' accounts for the disjunction between 14–60 and 3–11; but such lack of 'fit' is already present in the shift from the masculine Will at 2 to the feminine Purnele at 3 (and cf. on Envy at B 109, revising A 91). Moreover, as some heterogeneity is to be expected in the drama of vices in action, Pride must be a composite figure with traits appropriate to different sexes and occupations, not a unique individual. The illustration of an extravagantly dressed young man in ms Douce 104 at f. 24r, although placed opposite the opening 'Purnele' lines, depicts the later, more obviously male figure suggested by ll. 30–5. **19–21** may be an oblique authorial self-accusation for Anima's criticisms at B 15.92–5 (though these are not in fact removed in **C**). **19** *Inobedient*: taking up B 13.282 and more accurately locating it in relation 'to his sovereyns and to his goostly fader' (*CT* X 393). **21–6** are clearly echoed by Usk, *TL* I. v. 117–19: 'wening his owne *wit* more excellent than *other*; scorning al maner devyse but his own' (see *Intro.* V § 11). **26** *in...maneres*: applying to the scorning or to the making known of his / her name. **30–61** take up the HAUKYN section of B XIII, adding new lines at 38–40 and leaving only two unrevised; being based on the description of a man, they fit better if their speaker is male. **31** The false pretence to wealth or virtue is paralleled in *ParsT* 408–10 ('two maneres of Pride...withinne...and...withoute...that oon...signe of that oother'). **32** *Me (hym) wilnynge*: either an ethic dative 'desiring for myself' or a dative absolute phrase 'myself desiring', the participial adjective agreeing with the pronoun (*MES* 99–100, 115). The phrase is repeated as a nominative absolute at 41a without *me*. **36–41** describe *spiritual* pride taken 'in the goodes of grace...eek an outrageous folie' (*CT* X 470). **38** *secte*: probably in the light of *couent* 39 = 'religious order' (MED s. v. 2 (c)), the picture being of an itinerant whose lack of *stabilitas* would produce problems like those found under *Wrath* at 130, 162. **42** *And* (*Or* **B**): 'And / Or (that I was) the best...' **43** *strengest*: cf. 'pride...in his strengthe of body...is an heigh folye' (*CT* X 458). *styuest vnder gyrdel*: 'stoutest man alive' (*Pe*); but MED cites no other example of the phrase, and its positioning between 43a and 44 allows a *double entendre*, with *stif* here = 'potent' as well as 'valiant'. **45** 'And addicted to a way of living that no moral authority could commend.' **46** *fetures*: here clearly 'features' (MED s.v. *feture* n. (1) (b) or (c)), but in **B** either this or 'creatures' (ibid. 2 (b), as in its earliest use at *WPal* 2885–6: 'a mayde / fairest of alle fetures þat sche to-for hadde seie,' which is contextually ambiguous in the same way (contrast *WPal* 857 *so fair of alle fetures*). **47** *what*: i.e. charitable alms. **48** *They to wene*: 'so that they should suppose'; for the construction see on 5.21. **49–53** From boasting (as a branch of pride) comes exaggeration and thence outright lying. In 5.185–6 lying is connected with Lucifer's pride as the root of all sin, leading to his fall. **49–50** *And*: 'Even though (there was)...' *to telle*: dependent on *so bolde*. **52** *lyed on*: 'swore falsely by'. **59–60** 'I wanted people to know all that might occasion [particularly the] pride [I had] in getting people's praise' (**B**: 'that might please people and lead to his being praised'). Love of praise may come under *vauntynge* or *elacioun*; cf. 'desir to haue *commendacioun eek of the peple* hath caused deeth to many a busy man' (*CT* X 474). **60a** 'If I yet *pleased men*, I should not be the servant of Christ' (Gal 1:10); *and in another place*: 'No man can serve two masters' (Mt 6:24). A link between the two passages may be Mt 6:2: 'when thou dost an almsdeed [cf. 48–9 above], sound not a trumpet...as the hypocrites do...that they may be *honoured by men*'. **61** A variant of this semi-formulaic prayer for the sinner to be given the grace of repentance is repeated for Envy. While Repentance's responses illustrate the range of judgements open to confessors, from exhortation to refusal of absolution, these never fall to the indulgence shown by the friars who shrive Mede in IV and Lyf in XXII.

(ii) 63–102 The confession of Envy replaces the 27-line **AB** passage with a revised form of B 13.325–42 that subordinates physical and social detail to the internal aspects of this 'spiritual' sin. **C** follows its source down to B 5.87 and then makes a deft textual suture with B 13.325 at 69. On the **ZAB** lines about Lechery at this point, see at 170. **62–8 63** *Enuye*: still with the wider etymological sense of its ultimate Latin source *invidia* 'evil / wicked will',

as at 87 // Z 94 (MED s.v. *envie* n. (1), = 'malice' in *ParsT*), to which the opposed virtue is *charite* Z 96, as well as the narrower moral theological sense of 'sorwe of oother mennes wele, and joye of othere mennes harm' that *ParsT* 483 derives from St Augustine (*Enarrationes in Psalmos* 104:17). *heuy herte*: reflecting the ambiguous 'sorrow' the envious feel, i.e. *dolor* not *contricio*, chagrin not remorse (*carefully* AB 59/76 shows how much it was the former). **64** *mea culpa*: through my fault; from the *Confiteor*, the priest's opening prayer in the penitential rite of the Mass. In **A** Envy simply declares his guilt, in **B** curses (?his sins) with the Latin formula (in the ablative), in **C** no less incongruously uses it to curse his enemies (a line indebted to the omitted B 106 //). **65** *clothes*: Envy's allegorical attire, itself a reified verb-phrase (infinitive or imperative), may owe something to the metaphor of Haukyn's sin-stained coat around which **B** developed this section, or be ironically inverting the Pauline garb of virtue and girdle of charity (Col 3:13–14). **66** *wroth*: a provocative action of twisting the raised and clenched fist around in the face of the other. *Wrath*: the only instance of one personified Sin interacting directly with another. The linking of envy with anger its companion sin, foreshadowed in the rudimentary sketch at Z 91–4, is confirmed at AB 66/83, 97/116, what joins them being 'hate' (cf. B 99, 114 below). **68** *Chidyng*: cf. the 'chidyng and wikkede wordes' noted in *ParsT* 525.

B 77–118 Lines 77–85 remain unchanged from **A**, 85–92 are new, and only 84a and 87 survive into **C**. **78** *kaury-maury*: a word of unknown origin found only in *PP*. **80** *foresleues*: cut from the long woollen outer garment of a friar; so he may be an ex-friar or, more straightforwardly, in another manifestation a friar in a *frokke*. The accusation of envy made against friars (that will later occur at B 20.273–6 despite the warning from Conscience at B 20.246) is cut from the **C** confession here as possibly a cheap gibe ill-suited to a portrait mainly of a layman (the half-line recurs in a complimentary context at B 15.230 //). **86** *neddres tonge*: a vestige of A 69; cf. 'the venym of Envye' in *ParsT* 530. **88** *bakbitynge*: a vice distinguished into five sub-species in *CT* X 493–5. *berynge... witnesse*: a phrase first instanced here and denoting not slander but perjury, a means of getting 'one's back' for which envy is a main motive. **89** *curteisie*: kindness and good-will being qualities against which calumny is a specific sin; but Envy remains capable of a 'false' courtesy at B 100 below. **91** *Gybbe*: familiar for Gilbert, here a type-name for any male neighbour. **91–2** Envy's 'joye of oother mannes harm' gives him more pleasure than his own prosperity, and is thus a 'synne ayayns kynde' (*CT* X491–2). *wey...chese*: the Essex wey of 3 cwt as opposed to the usual two-plus (*Sk*). The massive cheeses of ewes' milk (*Bn*), costing twopence in 1399 (see MED s.v. *wei* n (2), 1 (a), (a)), were brought to market in Cheapside through Aldgate and Bishopsgate (see Du Boulay, end-paper map). **A 69–72** These physiological details of sour and bitter secretions that cause flatulence and prevent Envy from eating may have been deleted as anticipating the imagery of A 99 (retained in **B**), 100–02 (also in **C**). *verious*: juice of unripe grapes or crab-apples, used in cookery and medicine. **93–118** have been excised in revision perhaps because material from them repeated in the Haukyn section is absorbed by **C** and some is not wholly suited to this sin (see on 108–10, 114, 118 below). Nevertheless, they illustrate standard aspects of envy paralleled in *ParsT*: thus with 93 cf. 'accusynge, whan man seketh occasion to *anoyen his neighebor*' (513); with 95, 97 'discord that unbyndeth alle manere of *freendshipe*' (511); with 96 'Envye...is sory of alle the *bountees* of his neighebor' (489). **95** is virtually repeated at B 13.328, which is kept at C 72 below. **98** *speche*: removing the weak repetition of *tunge* in A 80. **101–2** On 'privy hate' or *malignitee* cf. *ParsT*: 'if he noght may, algate his *wikked wil* ne shal nat wante' (513). **106** *Crist...sorwe*: instead of prayer he 'curses men' (an idea retained in C 64–5). **107** *bolle...shete*: things of small worth; cf. 'gruc-chyng...agayns...los of catel' (*ParsT* 499–500). **108–10** seem more applicable to Greed than Envy (108 is very like Coveitise's admission at B 13.394–9 = C 6.281–5) and may have been dropped in part for that reason. **109** *Eleyne*: the switch to a feminine perspective is sudden, but unless this is a scribal error (see *TN*) the *his* of 111–12 will be a universal ungendered possessive. **110** *I wisshe*: a mark of covetousness rather than envy, which is strictly 'resentment at what another has' more than 'desire for it oneself' (see 116). **111–12** sum up the essence of this sin (see under C 63); with the laughter of *Schadenfreude* and the weeping of chagrin are contrasted the religious weeping noted at 2. **114** is substantially repeated at B 13.282, which fits in more aptly under Pride at C 6.35. **117** *loue-les*: the mark of envy also at B 13.332. *dogge*: an image recurring at B 5.257. **118** *bolnep*: repeating 83. *for bitter*: on this use of the adj. as noun with *for* see *MES* 381.

69–102 The **C** revision seamlessly joins B 5.87 to B 13.325. **69** *blame*: 'to find fault with'; on the plain inf. as a predicate nominative see *MES* 526. **70–1** place malicious gossip under the sin of envy (as at B 13.333). *by*: 'about' not 'through'; *Watte* (Walter); *Wille*: stock type-names, C's revision reducing the tongue-twisting quality of **B**. **73** *sleythes*: more appropriate than *strengthe* B 329, given that Envy is a coward. **74–5** describe a sin that destructively turns in upon itself when outward vengeance fails, the 'scissors' metaphor (suggested by the Latin *gladius acutus* of the second psalm-quotation) conveying the anguish of inward self-laceration. **75** *Lyke* (*As* **B**): 'As with'. *euen-cristene*: heightening the viciousness while avoiding the verbal repetition of 64–5 (*cursed hem* B 13.331b is pleonastic). **76** *Crist*: perhaps an inexact way

of referring to the Divine Teacher of the Prophet David more than a specific allusion to Christ's own prohibition of swearing (Mt 5:33–7). **76a** 'His mouth is full of *cursing*, and of *bitterness*, [and of deceit]: under his tongue are labour and *sorrow*' (Ps 9B (10):7). [And in another place]: 'The sons of men, whose teeth are weapons and arrows: and their *tongue* a *sharp* sword' (Ps 56:5). Both quotations aptly specify main features of envy. **77** *may-strie*: implying failure both to get one's way and to come out on top, hence frustrated expectation. *male(n)colie*: the sense shading from MED 3 (the emotional and spiritual sickness) to 4 (anger and gloomy anxiety), just as *angre* 79 implies both the inner state and the illness that attends it. The less common spelling without *n* shows the influence of mis-etymologising the prefix *male-* as 'evil, ill'. **78** *cardiacle*: for such palpitation caused by strong emotion cf. *CT* VI 313. **80** *twel-monthe*: perhaps alluding to the time since his last confession, this being obligatory once a year and usually made before the Easter Communion; cf. *ParsT* on the *rancour* that lasts 'from oon Estre day unto another' (551). **81** *Lechecraft...Lord*: spiritual healing through sacramental penance. On the pervasive image of grace as a holy medicine, cf. esp. the lines on Christ as *leche* at 18.138ff, 19.84ff, and for penance as medicine, B 17.96, 22.305ff. It is implied that Envy's physical symptoms will disappear if he receives medicine for the soul. *wycche*: here a maker of supposedly magical potions, rather than a sorcerer. **82–3** *ne can...To*: 'has no skill in comparison with...' **83** *Soutere of Southwerk*: an unknown but once no doubt familiar contemporary character. Southwark, just south of the Thames over London Bridge, was known for its brothels, breweries and alehouses (*CT* I 20), and lay beyond the reach of the strict City laws. *grace*: 'happy knack (of healing)', with ironic play on the theological sense (cf. 84). **B 13.340** *Shordych...Emme*: perhaps the person alluded to in Pr 226 which, present from **Z** through to **C**, may be the refrain of 'some low popular song' (*Sk*) that outlived its original subject (like the 'Mrs Porter' song in Eliot's *Waste Land*). The Lady Emma humorously named from Shoreditch, the area NE of Bishopsgate (Du Boulay, map), may have been one of those to whom Lechery resorted at times (189–91 below). **85** *chef hele*: echoing *cheef lyflode*, the revision at 68. The remedy Envy seeks for his sin is itself sinful, as consulting a 'witch' was strictly forbidden by the Church. **87** *euyl...euyl*: 'ill'; 'hard'; another piece of lexical Platonism, implying that just as the homonyms are semantically related, so are the conditions of soul and body. **88–90** The rhetorical question confounds physical and non-physical remedies, including the spiritually efficacious one of shrift's *scharp salue* (22.307). **88** *swellynge*: under Pride *ParsT* notes that 'Swellynge of herte is when a man rejoyseth hym of harm that he hath doon' (398); but as this well describes Envy's attitude at

B 111, his flatulent condition may be meant to signify the sin's 'condign' punishment. **89** *derworth drynke*: 'expensive cordial', perhaps including a tincture of gold (as in *CT* I 445), which was considered helpful 'agens cardeakle passioun' (Bartolomaeus Anglicus 16:4, tr. Trevisa 2:829). **C** avoids repeating the sense of *diapenidion* anticipated in B 121a. This rare word, which might have puzzled some readers, denotes a twisted thread of sugar used to relieve coughing. **91–2** The sense of 91 runs on to 92 and the revision improves precision and clarity, moving from the moderate hope of **A** through the incomplete and so potentially misleading **B** to the qualified two-stage penance in **C** (see 101–2). *ryht sory*: 'very / truly sorry', but also implying 'sorry in the right (properly religious) way' (MED s.v. *right* adv. 3(a), 9(a)). **93** *sory*: the first instance of a personified Sin 'carnally' misunderstanding a key theological idea (as Greed will 'restitution' at 237 //). **94** *megre*: revision of *mad* continuing the traditional motif of a vice given outward expression in its exemplar's physical appearance (cf. Pope's *Essay on Man* I. 217–8). Merchants are the only class for whom a specific form of sin is alleged to be not accidental but a trade. **95** is clearer, with the sinner as merchant acting as an agent for this sub-species of the vice, whereas in **B** it should properly be the Sin that designates a sub-species as its agent. **100** The internal rhyme neatly balances thought with action; (cf. 12.220, 18.292. 20.225, 258). **101–2** describe Envy's movement from remorse (*athynketh*) to seeking the grace of repentance as recommended at 91–2. *Lord...Lord*: simple affective *repetitio* with transposed lexical stress. **101b** *of thysulue*: not an objective genitive; hence, 'for the sake of that love which is yours by nature'.

(iii) **103–69** WRATH, defined in *ParsT* 535 as 'wikked wil to been avenged by word or by dede' (cf. 109b) and as arising out of envy (and also pride), seems to have been made a separate Sin in **B** so as to disengage the angry elements in *invidia* (see A 79, 97) from Envy's differentiating feature (see on 63 above). **104–17** are added, stressing the essence of Anger as the will to do bodily harm (see 109), whereas Envy's 'sword' is his tongue (cf. 77*a* above). In **C** a more general account of the fierce rebelliousness of this sin replaces **B**'s tendentious assault on the friars. **105** *wol*: on non-expression of the relative / personal pronoun see *MES* 204–5. **106** The same alliterative pattern recurs in 14.42 to express *invidia* as willed violence. **107** *to sle hym*: on the forms of manslaughter see *ParsT* 563–78. **110–13** *Inpacient...cause*: cf. *ParsT* on how the wrathful man 'blameth God of thyng of which he is hymself gilty' (580) and when 'amonested in his shrifte...wole he be angry' (584). **112** *somur...heruest*: if envy is incident to merchants, angry complaint could be specified as the husbandman's vice. **114–15; 117–18** The *repetitio* of 114a at 115a, shifting the stress from *alle* to *manere*, is typical of **C** (cf. on 101–02) as is the polyse-

mantic pun on by*fore* / *fore* (117b–118a). **116–17** 'Hearing harm' is not specified in *ParsT* but 'speaking harm' is, in the sin of 'double tonge, swiche as speken faire byforn folk and wikkedly bihynde' (644).

B 135–48 make the standard charge that friars' readiness to hear confessions encouraged by their successful sermons antagonises the parish clergy whose duty this is, and leads to that divisiveness within the Church adumbrated at Pr 64–5. The mendicants are regarded with some ambivalence; for despite **L**'s admiration for their founders' lofty ideals (see Clopper 1997), half a dozen major passages on them (2.220–42, 3.38–67, 10.1–60, 12.5–41*a*, 15.30–176, 22.230–384) offer almost nothing (if 5.173–5, 6.287–93 are excepted) favourable or friendly to the friars of his own day (Szittya, Du Boulay 1991:80–6, 134–6). But as **L** says little good about monks and parish clergy either, his emphasis on *Thyng þat al þe world woot* (12.36) may perhaps be best understood as part of the wider anti-clericalism of the period discussed by Scase 1989. **136** *gardyner*: of uncertain reference, possibly the master who instructed friars in preaching and hearing confessions. **137–8a** *lymytours*: a name applied later to the friar-confessor Sire *Penetrans-domos* at 22.347. The type is (for obvious reasons) the commonest butt of antifraternal satire, as in *CT* I 209, III 874. *lystres*: derived from OF *listre* 'reader' (< L. *lector*). Though *lector* usually signified a lecturer in theology (Lawrence 1994:128), *lystre* may denote contextually a friar who reads and preaches on a text, perhaps 'glosing' its hard moral demands 'to please lords' (as in B 20.355–72). *lesynges...lowe speche*: placed under *anger* in *ParsT*, these lies 'to the ese and profit of o man' (608) are presumably promises of 'esy penaunce' like those made to Mede in B 3.35–42. They produce an appearance of (false) humility, ironically anticipating B 16.6, where the leaves are *lele wordes*. The image suggests the potential for conflict in the Church arising from uncontrolled expansion of the mendicant religious foreshadowed in B Pr 66–7//. **140–1** *fruyt*: it is not obvious how friars' becoming confessors to *lordes* will make *folk* turn to them on such a scale as to antagonise the parish clergy. Perhaps the implication is that the nobility's favour encourages mendicants to preach critically about 'possessioners', so that ordinary people *in consequence* (hence 'fruit') prefer to confess to them, especially in Lent (and thereafter make their special Easter offering of alms to a friar rather than to the parson). Such sentiments as 'Thise curatz been ful necligent and slowe / To grope tendrely a conscience / In shrift' (aptly cited by *Sk* from *CT* III 1816–18) would understandably arouse the strife of which Wrath speaks. **147–8** *spiritualte*: their dispute about the value of parsons' earnings impoverishing both and forcing them to live on prayers and 'spiritual' things alone, or leaving one side with all the handsome donations from the faithful.

The text does not specify whether this refers to a present or future situation, or whether the friars want evangelical poverty for all or simply equal shares of the ecclesiastical cake (see on C 125–6 below). B 20.276ff suggest that **L** thought mendicants wanted the Church's wealth equally distributed amongst all the clergy. Compare *CT* III 1723, where the friar urges the people not to give alms to possessioners who have 'wele and habundaunce', i.e. the *spiritualte* or income from their benefice.

118–42 examine Wrath's life among the religious. **118** C alters **B** to make the quarrel one between friars and bishops, who object to their hearing confessions without permission. The religious orders were under the direct authority of the Pope, but as the mendicants' work was in the dioceses, it could here be implied that if the ordinary refused his consent, they might persist without official approval and even criticise the bishop for lack of zeal. **123** *beggares and barones*: mendicant friars and the lordly prelates. **125–6** Wrath's assertion refers to an anticipated state of affairs, but arguably (notwithstanding the note on B 147–8 above) this is already the sense of **B** and could be expressed by placing a stop after *ooþer* B 147 and a comma after *aboute* 149, the futurity being implicit in the present tense *reste*. An end to the strife Wrath foments between mendicants and 'possessioners' (including monks) will only come when one or other extreme solution is adopted. But at the end of the poem (22.384) Conscience proposes as a middle way the provision of adequate endowments to support the friars' ministry without any need for mendicancy. **127** *fortune*: glossing 'grace' in B 150 without repeating a phrase used at 83 by Envy. **130** *coek*: the 'convent-servant' figure effectively grows from *gardyner* B 136, but the latter has been removed in revision by **C**. **132** *pore ladies*: 'poor' because they vowed to own no personal property, 'ladies' because most nuns came from the upper ranks of society (Lawrence 1989:216–19) and had the same courtesy title *Dame* 'Madam' as their secular counterparts. Joan, Clarissa and Petronilla are all genteel-sounding names (though also borne by 'low' characters at 6.365, 366, 8.71 and possibly B 7.44). **133** *iangling*: spiteful gossip, one of the sins of the tongue (see *ParsT* 650) that lead to violence. These sexual insinuations refer to defects that would canonically debar a nun from becoming prioress. **136** *chapun-cote*: an undignified spot for the purpose, but perhaps hinting slyly at earlier dalliance with some *trede-fowel* in the same place. Purnele's situation would lead to her fitness for election being questioned at the convent's chapter-court. If the child's father were a priest, the case would come before the diocesan court and both might be declared *infamis* (see at B 166 below). **B 159** *chirie-tyme*: alluding to the licentious behaviour associated with the cherry-fairs held towards midsummer in the orchards. **137** The revision loses the *wordes / wortes* pun (Schmidt

1987:110) but avoids repetition of *ioutes* while creating the pungent irony of *sustres* and *lady* 138.

B 164–6 seem less Anger's sentiment than an authorial interjection 'voiced' through the immediate speaker, since it is echoed at B 19.162. **164** *Gregory*: here Gregory IX (Pope 1227–41), who forbade abbesses to hear nuns' confessions (cited *Bn* from *Decretals*, ed. Friedberg, ii. 887) because (the text implies) as mischievously gossipy women they could not keep them secret. **166** *infamis*: 'of ill repute', a term in canon law (Alf*Q*) for one formally pronounced guilty of *infamia* for serious irregularities (of which revealing the secrets of the confessional would be one), with resultant loss of the faculty to exercise holy orders.

143–63 By adding **143–50 C** replaces **B**'s clear 'religious' sequence of friars-nuns-monks with a 'three estates of womanhood' schema of (consecrated) virgins, wives and widows. No especially misogynistic animus need be suspected from this move to redress the sex-balance amongst the Sins. **144b–6** should perhaps be understood as in quotation marks; but the shift of Wrath from the standpoint of subject to that of observer is best sustained if the second pronoun at 147 is *she* not *Y*. **145** *Letyse-atte-Style*: a convenient type-name for (possibly) the wife of *Symme* at 207 below. **146** *haly-bred*: bread blessed and distributed after Mass to those who had not received Communion (i.e. most parishioners). One's position in the line to receive it, like the Wife of Bath's at the Offertory procession (*CT* I 449–52), could become a cause of dissension (cf. Duffy 1992:125–7). **147** *chydde*: under quarrelling *ParsT* 625, 630 cites such name-calling as 'thou harlot' and warns that a 'servant of God' should not wrangle (II Tim 2:24). **151–63** This favourable account may be meant to balance Reason's criticisms at 143–79 above by stressing that many monks pursue a life of tranquil order, disturbers of which are severely disciplined. **153** *Priour*: the head of a minor monastery (priory) or the deputy head of a major one (abbey). *Suppriour*: the Prior's deputy. *Pater Abbas*: the abbot (< Lat & Gk *abbas* < Aram. *abba* 'father'), having, as head of the monastic *familia*, the authority of a father over his spiritual 'children'. **154** *tales*: the penalty for malicious gossip being prison food and corporal punishment. *þe bare ers*: as illustrated in a representation of Patientia beating Ira at Southrop, Glos. (Kaske 1968: pl. 59c). **160** *otherwhile*: i.e. on special occasions such as feast days or founder's day, when he gets drunk and his pent-up anger pours out. **161–3** *flux...couȝe*: the slanderous utterances being like bouts of diarrhoea or vomiting that last for several days. **162–3** *couent*: the contrast between *eny* and *al* bringing out the nature of Wrath's injurious speech and justifying the *repetitio* so typical of **C**.

164–9 165 *Conseyl*: in *ParsT* 'biwreying of *conseil*, thurgh which a man is defamed' (645) appears among the 'synnes that comen of the tonge' (653). **166** *ouerdelicatly*: it not being obvious how concern with 'choice' drink promotes wrath, the idea may be rather of consuming *too much* from the range of drinks offered at a feast. *ParsT* includes under Gluttony 'whan a man get hym *to delicaat...drynke*' and also 'whan men taken to muche over mesure' (X 828–9). **167** *ne thy wit*: an improvement on **B**'s otiose second lift; as *ParsT* notes, 'dronkenesse bireveth hym the discrecioun of his wit' (825). **168** 'Be sober [and watch: because your adversary the devil, *as a roaring lion*, goeth about seeking whom he may devour' (I Pet 5:8). 'Soberness' here denotes seriousness of speech and behaviour as well as avoidance of drunkenness; but the connection between sins of the tongue's different powers (speech and taste) is made pointedly at B 10.165–8. The italicised phrase has special aptness to the sin of wrath. **169** *hym*; *his*: **B** *me*, *my*: misdiagnosed by *Bn* as scribal slips, but graphically reinforcing the persona's rôle as representative man at B 61, where use of the 3rd person brings out the dual sense of 'Will' as the name of both faculty and Dreamer.

(iv) 170–95 The brief confession of LECHERY in **B** is expanded to 25 lines with ten from B XIII and ten new lines at beginning and end. *ParsT* places *Luxuria* as the last of the deadly sins, after *Gula*, its 'ny cosin' (836); but **L**'s Lechery needs neither food nor drink as stimulus, though appropriately vowing to fast as a penance. Positioned between anger and avarice, sins of the spirit, this sin of the flesh is the only vice pursued for pleasure rather than just as a (largely painful) compulsion, and is the one by which Will is led astray at 11.179–82. But Lechery alone expresses regret (*Alas*) and recognises that his *lycames gultes* originate in the *gost*, i.e. that the essence of lechery is a wilful assent to disordered desire (see 181). **170** *Oure Lady*: as the patron and exemplar of chastity, the best intermediary between himself and Christ (cf. 7.287). The sense of B 5.72, 'to bring about a state of mercy on God's part towards my soul', is much more clearly expressed in C. **171–2** The assonances in the b-lifts of both lines bring out the desperate urgency of his plea. **172** *putour* (< AF *putour*): one who makes a profession of his sin (cf. 186, 189–90), unlike Haukyn, a simple fornicator. Depiction of lechery in its most destructive form, making money by corrupting both women and the men who use them, is perhaps in answer to Lady Mede's argument that 'frelete of fleysche' is 'synne as of seuene noon sonner relesed' (3.59, 62). But Lechery is also a corrupter of virgins (178) and so 'cause of manye damages and vileynyes' (*ParsT* 870). **173** *Saturdayes*: days of special devotion to the Blessed Virgin. Water and a single meal will curb his propensities on the eve of the sabbath (cf. Wrath's Friday penance at 155 above); but in **C** the promised fast is to be perpetual. **176** 'The sins of my body in indulging in lechery'. **177–81** are closely paralleled in *ParsT* 851–62,

which describe in sequence the *fyve fingres* of lust: 'fool lookynge' (177), 'vileyns touchyng in wikkede manere' (179–80, 187), 'foule wordes' (186), 'kiss[ynge] in vileynye (187)' and 'the stynkynge dede of Leccherie' (181, 188). **177** *waitynge*: warned against in Mt 5:28. *wedes*: the link between provocative clothing and lust is made in *ParsT* under Pride rather than Lechery, which notes how 'scantnesse of clothyng...ne covere[th] nat the shameful membres of man, to wikked entente' (422) and women 'notifie in hir...atyr *likerousnesse* and pride' (430). **181** *wil*: the flesh's will or assent to 'lust in action'. *werk*: an early euphemism for the sexual act (like *dede*10. 295). **182** *fastyng dayes*: for laypeople the Wednesdays and Fridays in the Church's penitential seasons, especially Lent (cf. later under Sloth at 7.25–6). *Frydayes*: as well as the abstinence from meat prescribed throughout the year, other penances recommended in honour of the day of Christ's death included refraining from (lawful) sexual relations. **182** *heye-festes euenes*: the vigils of major feasts like Christmas and Easter, to be similarly marked; but the *forboden nyghtes* B 349 were sometimes taken to include periods of pregnancy and menstruation. Lechery was forbidden at all times, but the speaker's declared indifference to the religious seasons points up the lack of any restraint upon his indulgence. **183** scans most effectively on vocalic grammatical staves, with the *l*-words as an under-pattern. **193** *oold*: implying that he is looking back on a life of sin, and suggesting that in B 13.354 *hir* pertains to the lechers seen prospectively in their old age. *þat kynde*: proving that his lust was an act of will, not Mede's 'cours of kynde' (3.60). **194** 'I enjoyed listening to (people) talk about (their) debauchery'. **195** *lewete*: the appeal to God's perhaps alluding to Christ's forgiveness of the Woman taken in Adultery, a story elaborated at 14.41–2.

(v) 196–348 At 150 lines, the presentation of GREED is the longest, the confession of HERUY the miser being extended and supplemented by those of EUAN THE WELSHMAN (308–14) and ROBERT THE ROBBER (315–29), fraud and theft respectively (on the change in Robert's function see Introductory note, end), and concluded by an exhortation to Greed. Gluttony and Sloth following him bring comic relief after an episode which, despite humorous touches, depicts Greed (the sole Sin to have three representatives) as especially serious because it threatens the entire Christian community. Its gravity is emphasised in Ecclus 10:9 and 10 (the latter verse cited at B 10.336*a*) and *PP* presents it as the greatest vice of the time. **L** follows a model pattern prescribed in penitential handbooks (on their influence see Gray 1986[1]), with Repentance as confessor interrogating and rebuking Greed three times (six times in **B**) at 233–9, 248–57, 286–307 and finally *refusing* absolution until he has made restitution.

196–205 196 *Coueityse*: 'desire to have (wealth)', whether to get or to keep. *ParsT* more narrowly distinguishes *Coveitise* as 'to coveite swiche thynges as thou hast nat' from *Avarice* 'to withholde and kepe swiche thynges as thou hast, withoute rightful nede' (744). Though the special sense of *auarice* at 191 is apparently contrasted with *coueityse* in 190, both terms occur interchangeably, the latter three times more frequently. **197** *Sire Heruy*: this character (who seems to have suggested Heruy Hafter in Skelton's *Bouge of Court*) is neither knight nor priest, so no plain reason for his title appears. The grotesque image of the miser, the most fully visualised of the Sins, reflects the medieval belief that inner nature reveals itself in physiognomy, gesture and even dress. **198** *bitelbrowid*: the sense 'grim-browed, sullen' in MED s.v. would connect the first element with OE **bitol* 'biting, sharp', which is phonologically possible but semantically unconvincing. More probably, Coveitise's shaggy overhanging eyebrows are being compared to the tufted protruding antennae of some insect (the common later understanding of the compound and the verb Shakespeare derived from it; see OED s.v. *beetle* a.). **199** *pors*: an emblem of Heruy's avaricious nature. **200** *ycheuelen*: a coinage or an idiolectal variant of *chiueren*, 'prob. a blend of *chillen* and *biveren*' (MED s.v.); a subject 'they' (= his cheeks) must be supplied as in **B**. **201** *yshaue*: cut so as to leave bristles sticking out as from bacon-rind after the meat has been removed; like the purse-cheek simile, an iconic emblem of miserliness that improves on **B**'s merely visual description. **202** *hat*: better than *lousy hat* B 192, which anticipates B 194. **203** *tore...twelue wynter*: the avaricious man's neglect of decent clothing is reiterated at 19.245–7, on the miserly rich. **204** *lous...lepe*: i.e there is so little material left that the louse would need to jump to get from one piece to the next; a variation on a semi-proverbial expression. **205** *He*: possibly a spelling-form for the feminine pronoun as in **AB**; but the louse's sex is not of pressing concern. *Walch*: metonymic for 'woollen flannel [made in Wales]', but doubtless reflecting a xenophobic English view of Welshmen as dishonest and mean instantiated in Evan at 308ff.

206–33 explore Greed's *commercial* frauds. **207** *Style*: cf. *Lettyse* at 145 above. **208b** affirms the apprentice's main obligation (repeated at 279). **209–10** *lerned...lessoun*: the sin being satirically envisaged not as an impulse or habit but as a skill, to be mastered in stages (cf. on 172). **209** *lye*: if with original vowel as in **A**, rhyming with *tweye* and with *waye* in the next line (and possibly with *Wy* in 211) to give an effect at once mnemonic and mimetic. *leef...tweye*: 'a page or two's worth [from the handbook of falsehoods]'. **210** *waye*: i.e. with fraudulent weights. **211** *Wy*: Weyhill near Andover, Hants, which had a week-long Michaelmas market for goods of every kind; Symme presumably dealt in foodstuffs. *Wynchestre*: where there

was also a great three-day autumn fair at St Giles's Down (4.51 above) under the patronage of the bishop. **212** *many manere marchandise*: cf. 'marchandise is in manye maneres....That...men haunten with fraude and...with lesynges...is cursed and dampnable' (*ParsT* 776, 779). **213** *grace of gile*: 'the devil's own luck', with some play on 'the grace of God', who is ironically invoked in 214b. **214** *this seuene 3er*: perhaps signifying only an indefinitely long period of time (cf. 233 below, 10.73); but also the normal length of an apprenticeship, Greed implying that without the help of guile he might have failed to qualify as a master of his art. **215–16** *drow...drawe*: more 'Platonic' wordplay. *Donet*: 'the elements [of fraud]'; named after Aelius Donatus, the C4th Roman author of a basic Latin Grammar used in schools. Having learned to *read* (= 'lie') with a grocer, Greed studied *grammar* (= 'deception') with clothiers. **216–22** Avarice Draper's trick was apparently to stitch two widths of expensive striped cloth (*raye*) together loosely with a large stout needle, fasten the sewn piece in a wooden frame (*pressour*) and pull lengthwise on the selvage side (*lyser*) so as to stretch it, increasing the size of the piece but also weakening it. To make the operation easier, his wife Rose (see 232) caused her yarn to be spun loosely (*oute*), involving the spinners in the fraud. **218** *bat-nelde*: glossed in MED s.v. as 'basting-needle'; but the variant *pak-nedle* in well over half the mss in all three traditions may suggest that the *bat-* element derives from OF *bast* 'pack-saddle' (the etymological root of *bastard*), as stated by OED s.v. **223–4** His wife's own deception of her gullible spinsters was to use a scale-balance 'pound' weight of 1¼ lbs; as they would have to put *more* wool in the pan to make it balance, she thereby paid for a quarter *less* than the weight of spun wool they brought her. Greed's own weighing-instrument was probably a 'steelyard', the bale being hung from the shorter arm of a lever and its weight determined by moving a counterpoise along a graduated scale inscribed on the longer arm, until balance was achieved. Although Greed's auncel measured accurately, it was ironically this device that was often banned by national and municipal regulations as open to fraudulent misuse (see C14th and C15th quots. in MED s.v. *auncel* n). So the text may hint at a more elaborate deception, whereby Greed used his *reliable* steelyard in order to 'con' his suppliers and purchasers into trusting that his wife's *false* scale-weights were also sound. **225–33** These brewery 'practices' follow a similar pattern of complex trickery. *Peny ale*: thin or small ale (cf. 21.403) sold at a penny a gallon. *poddyng ale*: thick ale sold at a groat or fourpence (the MED gloss 'cheap ale' s.v. *poding* n. (b) is misleading). The small ale stood in a separate barrel in the front shop, and customers who tried the best ale brought for tasting from the inner room paid the full price for this. But what Rose actually supplied was a mixture of the two, perhaps in 3:1 proportions (as with her weights), to evade detection. **229** *þer-aftur*: both 'thereupon' (after sampling) and 'accordingly' (in the belief that they were getting what they had tasted). **230b–31a** The revision improves on **B** by adding a further deception (*ʒut*): when she filled her customers' cans by cupfuls, she gave them *less* as well as *worse*. Between them, husband and wife make accomplished use of the *false mesures and met* (B 13.359) condemned in Deut 25:13–15. **231b** *craft*: playing on MED senses 2(b) 'skill in deceiving' and 6(a) 'trade'. **232** '...was her actual name [*sc.* and rightly was she so named]'. **232–3** *regrater... hokkerye*: though the former could be neutral before the 15th c., the latter always had unfavourable overtones, reflecting people's distrust of those who bought necessities wholesale to sell at a profit. Rose uses the quality of her own ale to conceal her trickery (cf. the *false gyn* of Chaucer's Canon [*CT* VIII 1160ff], who uses real silver when pretending to transmute mercury). **233** *elleuene*: another (alliteratively convenient) indefinite period (cf. 203, 214); despite his gains, Avarice still wears his tattered twelve-year old jacket.

B 224–35 (A 142–5, Z 97–103) The **B** passage is cut in **C**, possibly because repetitive (225a repeats 200a) and over-specific (226–7). **224** *so thee Ik*: an asseveration in Norfolk dialect that may be the residue and remnant of *Northfolk nose* Z 98 (an obscure gibe seemingly not derived from it). Presumably the meanness or dishonesty of Norfolk people is implied (see on Z 3.148 above, Mann 1973:166 on Chaucer's Norfolk Reeve). **226** *Walsyngham*: see on Pr 52. **227** *Bromholm*: also in Norfolk, a day's journey from Walsingham, so Greed could visit both in one pilgrimage. The Cluniac Priory (close to Paston Hall) had a famous miracle-working relic of the true cross, brought from Constantinople in the early 13th c. and kept in a 'patriarchal' style processional cross, before which he will pray for release from his *debitum* of sin (MED s.v. *dette* n. 4(a)). On the cross (which disappeared in 1537) see Wormald *JWCI* 1937:31–45 (esp. pls. 6a–c, 7a–b; an ampulla depicting it is in Alexander & Binski 223, pl. 77); and cf. the contemporary mention in *CT* I 4286. **232** *haddest...hanged*: on this use of the infinitive after an adjective see *MES* 538. **235** *Northfolk*: meaning that Greed knew *no* French (*Bn*), because he lived so far from London and its environs that education would be supposed scarce there. Though the county capital Norwich was the third city of England, Walsingham stands at Norfolk's 'furthest end', so if Greed lived nearby, he would have been 25m from it.

234–44 concern Greed's *financial* deceptions. **237** *rufol restitucioun*: with Greed's failure to understand the word, cf. Envy and *sory* at 93; both examples figure spiritual obtuseness under verbal ignorance. The lines improve on B 232–3, which declare theft more serious than fraud, but lack the warning that failure to make restitution will

damn the sinner even if he is never found out. **239** *vsurye*: strictly, lending at (exorbitant) interest; more loosely, lending for profit (see on 2.91), which was regarded as a grave sin. But Greed uses it to describe banned commercial practices, from coin-clipping to credit-transfer. **241** *Lumbardus...Iewes*: see on 4.192. **242** Since any heap of current pennies showed small individual variations, after isolating the lightest and weighing the others against it, he would remove tiny quantities from the heaviest so as to bring them down to its weight, and on a large enough scale, there was profit in the silver thus collected. This practice may be the 'horrible crime' described in a Commons petition of 1376 (*Rotuli Parliamentorum* 2:332). **243** (**B 240**) *loue of þe wed*: i.e. as opposed to charity towards the man. The loan is made in **B** from desire for the money to be got from selling the object pledged when it was forfeited, the *cros* being that inscribed on coins (Poole II, pls. 32, 34, and cf. 17.205). In **C**, it is for the pledge itself, which was more valuable than the loan or (the remaining wealth of) the man he made it to.

B 241–5 The sense of the elliptical B 240 is that Greed wanted the borrower to lose his security by failing to pay at the time agreed, and kept a written record in case this happened (241). The litotes of the macaronic 242 brings out his awareness of a charity he could have shown; but the irony works through *style indirect libre,* since knowledge of the psalm cannot be attributed to the *lewed* Greed as a 'character'. *Miseretur...*: '[Acceptable is the man that] sheweth mercy and lendeth' (Ps 111:5). Vs 9 shows that this psalm is concerned with charity to the poor, but **L** describes Greed's loan-making as directed towards the gentry in need of ready cash. **243** *chaffare*: either (a) he 'sells' (lends) goods (e.g. forfeited clothes or jewels from his pawn-store) and buys them back (to furnish the cash they want) at less than their true value (*Bn*), so as to conceal what is really interest charged on a loan (this is the *derne usurie* of B 2.176); or (b) *chaffare* denotes a loan of cash to buy such goods elsewhere, which then formed the pledge he would later buy back at less than their value. Either way, Greed would make a good profit. **245** again concerns the financial side of his operations. *Sk*'s note that in an ordinance against usurers (38 Edw III) they are said to describe *occulta usura* as 'exchange or chevisance' suggests that the two terms are euphemistic synonyms for usury. Or Greed, like Chaucer's Merchant (*CT* I 278–82), may be making a profit on the currency-exchanges involved in his capital-transfer operations.

245–52 continue with Greed's crooked *financial* activities. **245** humorously extends his coin-clipping of silver to his lending, his interest being imagined as a piece clipped off each gold coin he advances; but *Sk*'s more literal view of Greed as lending his clients clipped coin is not excluded. **246** *Lumbardus lettres*: bills of exchange used by Lombard bankers in Rome to facilitate payments due to the papal exchequer (e.g. from English clerics on appointment to benefices or sees). The money would be handed to their agent in England [viz. Greed], who then provided a credit-note for the sum, which could be disbursed by their office in Rome. If conducted honestly, the only gain for him should have been a fee for service. **B 248** *took it by taille*: for the use here MED s.v. *taille* n. 3(d) has 'receive it on credit' (the only other example of the phrase, at *CT* I 570, meaning 'bought on credit'). Greed acted as factor and received the client's money (in exchange for credit abroad); but because he handled the credit-note, he could alter it to make it worth less there than made out at home. However, the new C 247 (which prudently replaces B 248's explanation of how this fraud was done) understands Greed to *lend* the client all or part of the sum; and if **B** also implied this, *took* will there mean 'gave' (MED s.v *taken* v. 31a). Greed will again have doctored the bill of credit so that less was handed over in Rome than he had advanced in England, but would make his profit only *after* his client paid him back (another variety of *usura occulta*). **248** *mayntenaunce*: 'support' (MED s.v. n.2(a)), something useful for a money-man in a society dominated by the land-owning classes, whose backing would be helpful in running the *manoirs* he got through defaults on loans. **250** He brought down his social superior's status to that of a trader in textiles by causing him to forfeit or sell back goods bought by 'feigned sale' (*Bn*). **251** *gloues*: a typical gift-offering by an apprentice joining a master to learn a craft. The cream of the jest is that Greed will have amassed them as forfeited pledges, while his clients 'learnt' nothing of his 'mystery'.

253–7a C removes the questioning about charity and hospitality in B 253–8 perhaps because implausible from a confessor who had heard so much of his penitent's attitude and acts (Greed treats people like cats and behaves like a dog, hates his neighbours and is hated by them). C warns that Greed's wealth lies under a curse: his executors will misspend it (cf. B 15.138–45, omitted in revision) and his heirs get no benefit. **B** is theologically sound enough, with Repentance *wishing* that Greed, unless sincerely contrite, should not receive the grace to make satisfaction with his ill-gotten goods (i.e. by acts of charity), but is more severe than **C**, where the confessor simply does not 'believe or expect' that Greed's sin will be forgiven without satisfaction. B 260–3 seem to echo *WW* 440–4. **256** Even the successor of St Peter, to whom Christ delegated all power to forgive (see on Pr 128–9), cannot remit sin unconditionally (cf. on 320 below). In terms of the *partes penitentiae* 'stages of sacramental penance', even after contrition and verbal confession, complete forgiveness and pardon for sin wait on the act of satisfaction (see at B 14.16ff). **257** *sine restitucione*: 'without restitution'. While on a naturalistic level the Latin should be even less

intelligible to Greed than the English at 234, **C** is stressing his moral not his educational *lewednesse*, and the Latin formulae are presumably directed to the audience. **257a** '[If the other man's property can be returned but is not, the penitence is not real but feigned; and even if there is true penitence], the sin is not forgiven until the stolen goods are returned' (Augustine, Epistle 153, sect. 20, in *Opera*, ed. Migne, ii.662). The given sentence (quoted in **B** at *272a*) was a widely-cited maxim of canon law also found in sermons such as Brinton 1:27, *ME Sermons* 266 (see AlfG, Alford 1975:398, Gray 1986, Scase 1989:26). **258–85a** draw on B XIII, 258–61 dealing with Greed as *merchant*. **258–71 259** is echoed in 22.369 describing Friar Flatterer. **260–1** *Meddeled*: Greed's stratagems recalling on a larger scale his wife's petty deceptions (cf. the echo of 228 in 261a). *withynne*: (deep) inside the pile of goods (grain etc). **262–71** Greed's fraudulent activities as *farmer* grow directly into theft (265–6). **262** *hyne... beest*: alluding to the Tenth Commandment's prohibition against coveting one's neighbour's 'field, man-servant, ox, or ass,' (Deut 5:21, Ex 20:17). **267–71** *half-aker*: a normal small-holding of 16 furrows, a minimum capable of supporting a family. The fields lay in strips side by side divided by an unsown furrow, which offered Greed opportunities for adding covertly to his land. **268** *foet lond or a forw*: a foot's width was little in itself but (like the coin-shavings at 242 above) mounted up; since the field it ran alongside was a furlong (660 ft) in length, he could grab up some 3% of his neighbour's ground. **270** *over-reche*: cut his neighbour's corn on the other side of the furrow (something specifically forbidden in Deut 23:25).

272–85a return to Greed the *merchant's* constant concern with monetary rather than spiritual profit and loss. The whole passage, with its key-phrase at 279, implicitly comments on Mk 8:36: 'For what shall it profit a man, if he gain the whole world and suffer the loss of his soul?' **278** *Bruges*: at this time still a port, and a major centre of the Flemish cloth-trade, to which English wool would be sent. **279** *Prucelond*: Prussia, occupying most of present N Germany, 'the chief distributor of English cloth in Poland and West Russia' (McKisack 1959:359). **282b** The exact referent is unclear, perhaps 'anything in God's world that could delight the eye'. Greed cannot see properly because his eye is *nequam* 'evil', not *simplex* 'single' (cf. Mt 6:22–3). **283** *Paternoster*: the Christian's chief prayer, taught by Jesus in the part of the Sermon on the Mount preceding the *tesaurus* text. **285a** '[For] where thy treasure is, there is thy heart also' (Mt 6:21). The two verses before it, contrasting earthly and heavenly treasure, are directly relevant for understanding this passage. **286–307** Repentance's *refusal of absolution and his final warning* underline the seriousness of Greed's sin. **287** A possible T-type line revising one with cognative *þ / f* staves while turning the complimentary *good feiþ* into a mere asseveration. **C** disengages 'gold' from the powerful but not very lucid simile in **B** ('nor accept a penny from you as pocket-money, even if I were given a manuscript with leaves covered with a gold ground [*Bn*] for doing so'), which makes poor sense, since friars could not own such books as personal property. **290a** 'It is better to die than to live wickedly'; repeated at 17.40*a* (see on 1.142a and cf. 7.208–9). **293** *fyndynge*: friars are being obliquely admonished to follow Repentance and refuse absolution to 'false men' even if they offer handsome donations. **293a** 'Seek costly foods, another's slave you'll be; / Sup on your own plain bread, and you'll stay free' (source still unidentified). One friar who seeks such foods is the Doctor of Divinity of 15.66ff. **294** *vnkynde*: 'unnatural', because he preys on his own kind. **295** *by thy myhte*: 'as far as you are able'; if circumstances rule out exact restitution, he must make it up some other way, e.g. by charity. **296–300** The warning that those who knowingly accept money wrongfully obtained will 'share' in Greed's punishment as in his profits is directed in **C** not to a *werkman* (B 277) but to his parish priest (298, 304). It is assumed that the latter might have been persuaded by a rich tithe-offering to grant 'easy absolution' because, after the Plague, depopulation of parishes had reduced incumbents' income from that source. **298** On tithes, see at 8.101. **302** 'For behold, thou hast loved truth'; vs 8 of Ps 50, the fourth penitential psalm ('Miserere'), named at **B 276**: 'Have mercy on me, O God' (vs 3; and see B 13.53*a*). The *GO* interprets these verses as meaning that God will not compromise his truth (= 'justice') by leaving wrongdoers unpunished, but demands satisfaction from the sinner in the form of mercy shown to others. **B 276** *I mene*: the exact referent of *I* should be God (addressed in vs. 8), on whose behalf Repentance speaks; but if it is the latter, then *mene* is to be understood as 'am referring to (a text that speaks of) truth'. **303** *vsure*: Ps 50 makes no direct reference to usury. **305/7** The sustained *annominatio* on ers-, err-, *arste* associates both groups (who are later linked at 16.259). *ers-wynnynge*: on current debate about whether earnings from prostitution could be tithed cf. Wycliffe (*EW*, p.433); 8.71 would imply that they should not. The less severe general view of the prospect for whores taken here may owe something to Mt 21:31 (which, however, contrasts them with Pharisees, not usurers).

B 278–82a 278 *Cum...*: 'With the holy thou wilt be holy;...[and with the perverse thou wilt be perverted' (Ps 17:26–7). 'Construing' here involves more than translation: the text warns priests and religious against associating with the wicked for mercenary reasons if they would avoid their fate. **279** *wanhope*: Greed's reaction to Repentance's severity both echoes his threat at B 232 and prompts his injunction to pray for divine mercy, which

he declares illimitable. **282a** 'His tender mercies [*miserationes* Vg] are over [i.e. surpass] all his works' (Ps 144:9); repeated at B 11.139*a*=C 12.75*a* but removed here from its revised form (perhaps for that reason).

308–14 The introduction of EUAN THE WELSHMAN has no obvious explanation but is linked with the moving forward of the 'Robert' passage from after Sloth, the last Sin to confess in **B** (where, as *Pe* notes, it fits well as a warning against despair), to follow it immediately. Sloth's first two lines on repentance now form Evan's compound 'nature-name' (the first such in **C**) and the next two form the opening of his speech, which ends with his decision (alluding to the Mk 8:36 text cited under 272–85a) to renounce wealth for salvation. **308** *wonderly sory*: a sorrow, whether contrition (like Robert's at 316) or attrition aroused by Repentance's warning (which encouragingly replaces the *helle* threatened at 238 with *purgatorye* 299), accompanied by a resolve to make restitution at all costs. This suggests that Evan is a first manifestation of Greed, but now transformed by the incipient action of grace, while Robert in his new position is quite intelligibly the second. **309** *ȝeuan*: the form of the speaker's name perhaps punning on *ȝeuen* 'give'. On the textual problems of this passage see *TN*. It is here supposed that Evan's name is unlikely to have appeared in **Z**'s first lift and so to be derived from **C**, since the speaker's resolution to amend is immediately followed not by C 313–14 but by the equivalent of B 461–2 // A 234–5, lines spoken by Sloth that the final version excises.

315–29 The passage on ROBERT undergoes continuous revision, **A** omitting three lines of **Z**, **B** two of **A**, and **C** one of **B**. Additionally, it alters the sinner's cognomen, which could (offensively) imply a 'Platonic' link of the common name *Robert* with robbery, and re-directs his prayer from himself to heaven. In **B** it forms a transition from confession to absolution. **315** *Robert*: not an 'eighth sin' or (recalling the *Roberdes knaues* of B Pr 44) 'a generic name for a slothful waster' (*Bn*) but typifying *all* sinners as spiritually 'in debt' to God and so 'at his mercy' like the first thief Lucifer of 477. *the ruyflare*: recalling *riflede* 236 and establishing this character unambiguously as an avatar of Greed. *Reddite*: 'give back', echoing *Reddite ergo omnibus debita* 'Render therefore to all men their dues' (Rom 13:7); quoted by Augustine in the discussion of restitution from which *257a* is taken (*Pe*). The great importance of 'satisfaction' is later stressed by Conscience at 21.187–8. **316** *wherwith*: i.e. any good deeds to offset his sins; echoing 'And whereas they had not *wherewith* to pay...' (Lk 7:42). **318** *Caluarie*: the Roman name (Mk 15:22, Lk 23:33) for Golgotha ('place of a skull'), the hill of crucifixion outside Jerusalem. **319** scans weakly as an extended Type III on |ð| (*Tho, the*); but conceivably the anomalous *xa / ax* pattern produced by normal stressing on both a-half nouns may be meant (like stanza-group

XV in *Pearl*) to reflect symbolically its speaker's flawed spiritual state. Robert hopes that his prayer will likewise be received because he sincerely repents; but he lacks a good deed ('wherwith') comparable to his 'brother's' redeeming recognition that the robbers' punishment was just and that of Jesus unjust. In the two discussions at 11.255–63 and 14.131–55a, the Good Thief's salvation is ascribed in part to his acknowledgement of his guilt. In the earlier, Rechelesnesse (Will) adds that the thief *shrof hym* 'made his confession' to Christ (and thus received unconditional absolution, his mere acknowledgement constituting 'satisfaction'), while Ymaginatif affirms that those who implore God's grace will always receive it (14.131–2, and esp. // B 12.192). *Dysmas my brother*: the emblem of a last-minute penitence that won forgiveness and the promise of heaven from Christ himself. Only St Luke (23:39–43) distinguishes the characters of the two thieves. In ch. 10 of the apocryphal *Gospel of Nicodemus* (with which cf. also *LA* ch. 53, p.223) the one crucified on Christ's left hand is given the name Gestas and the one on his right the 'nature-name' Dismas (< Gk *dysmé* 'dying': cf. 'Longius' at 20.81); for the symbolism see on 2.5. **320** *mercy...man*: the **Z** form of this half-line is a 'repertory-phrase' used at 12.72 and elsewhere. *for* Memento *sake*: 'for (his words to you, "[Lord], remember [me when thou shalt come into thy kingdom]"' (Lk 23:42). **A 241–2 (Z 139–40)** The removal by **B** of these lines on hope, which interrupt the association between Dismas's case and Robert's, is a clear improvement. **321** *Reddere*: '[the wherewithal] to pay back (the debt of sin)'. **322** *wynne*; *craft*: the spiritual 'skill' that will 'earn' (profit for his soul). **323** *mitigacioun*: a legal term, appropriate to the convicted robber appealing to his judge; first recorded here with this referent, but in the Wycliffite Bible (MED s.v.) translating Vg *propitiatio* ['forgiveness' Douai-Rheims] at Ecclus 17:28 (vss 20–8 of this ch. are relevant to the passage). The ground of Robert's plea in his defence (anticipating Christ's to Lucifer in 20.415–38) is not the circumstances of his own case but the precedent of Christ's treatment of Dismas. **325** *byfel...feloun*: a paronomastic phrase cautioning against complacency. Robert's eventual salvation would, however, seem to be implicit in the Lord's words at 20.426–7, and its basis is his being Christ's 'whole-brother' (20.419) through his 'baptism'. **326** *wepte faste*: signalising Robert's contrition (see on 6.2) and associating him with Will as a type of fallen humanity. As such he bears the 'debt' of sin and totally depends on divine mercy (320) and pity (321). The contrast of these correlative but distinguishable attributes (rational and affective) of the one Saviour God at B 478–80 is removed in revision. **328** *That*: i.e. 'saying that'. *penaunce*: less august than *Penitencia*, the concretisation of the sacramental 'support' of the wayfaring Christian that Robert has dulled with disuse. Omission of B 476 may be a simple economy,

but the staff-image tellingly anticipates a life of penitential 'pilgrimage' as proper satisfaction for a life of sin. **329** *Latro*: 'thief', synecdoche for *latrocinium* 'theft'; the puns on *lateo* 'lie hid' and *latus* 'side' supposed by AlfQ seem implausible. *aunte*: apart from making the relationship unpleasantly incestuous, no reason for his bad 'aunt' appears, though it balances with his good 'brother' at 319 (and foreshadows Glutton's worthy aunt Abstinence at 439). That **L**'s Lucifer is 'that first grand thief' is clear from B 16.40–5, 17.103–11, 18.351–4.

Z 142–44 wittily cite a parable about indebtedness that concludes (vs. 9) with an injunction to 'make friends of the mammon of iniquity' (i.e. use ill-gotten gains for charity, so as to gain the intercessory prayers of those helped). Robert's wish to identify with the unjust steward (*caucyon* echoing *cautionem* 'bill' in Lk 16:6) must fail, since he has spent the money. **A**'s removal of these lines sensibly recognises that they do not apply to Robert's situation and that 142b may tend to lighten the tone inappropriately. **142** 'To dig I am not able; [to beg I am ashamed]' (Lk 16:3); remotely recalled in C 5.23–4, 51. **143–4** 'If I knew how to, I would wish prudently to put a payment of security in place / So as not to have to beg, borrow or end my days in despair'.

330–48 330 *Rode*: an apt oath since Christ's saving death on the cross, the basis of all sinners' hope, is especially suited to one who identifies with the crucified robber. **334** *Temese*: a local image of hot embers tossed over the side of a ship into London's river by night, as vivid as that of boisterous swimmers at 14.104ff (another passage about escaping from despair through trust in sacramental penance). **335** *drop water*: a mere drop from the river of divine mercy having the power to extinguish the 'fire' of sin; on the appositive genitive, see *MES* 84. **337a** 'All wickedness, in comparison with God's mercy, is as it were a spark in the midst of the sea'; widely cited in penitential writings (Gray 1986:59), homiletic works like the *FM*, sermons by Holcot and John of Grimestone (Wenzel, in Alford 1988:156), and popular moral treatises like the *Speculum Christiani* 73, 115: 'sicut scintilla ignis in medio maris, sic omnis impietas uiri ad misericordiam dei' (AlfQ). It was generally attributed to St Augustine, ultimately deriving from *Enarrationes in Psalmos* on Ps 143:2: *Unda misericordiae peccati ignis exstinguitur* 'By mercy's flood sin's fire is put out' (*PL* 37:1861). **338–42** The wordplay in **C** allows a double reference to Greed's spiritual bankruptcy, as a result of which any use of his wrongly acquired 'goods' even to survive will only harm his soul further. The omitted B 287 spells out that he would have to beg or labour to feed himself. **338** *vsurer*: the central figure Greed, left alone after Evan and Robert leave. **339** *marchaundise*: something not evil in itself but become so in his hands. **343–8** The practical difficulty of making restitution with ill-gotten gains is overcome by leaving it to the bishop to dispose of them for charitable ends. Repentance almost envisages the latter as a religious stockbroker investing capital for a client; but at the same time he stresses that the bishop, as God's 'steward', is responsible for his people's spiritual welfare. The removal of **B**'s homophonic wordplay on *lente*, paronomasia on *lette* and contrast between wisdom (*Oure Lordes good*) and wealth (*þe good...geten...wiþ falshede*) increases the solemnity, but with some loss of colour. **348** *What*: the instruction that the priests under his authority were obliged to give their parishioners, notably when preparing for their annual confession before Easter.

(vi) 349–440 The (failed) confession of GLUTTON is expanded from **AB** with only some half-dozen new lines, four on drunken oaths from the Haukyn passage (C 6.424–7=B 13.400–03). Its humorous liveliness, which perhaps prompted some 'farcing' of the **m** branch of **A** with lines from **B** (see *TN* on A 163) suggests that its popularity may have preserved the passage from revision in **C**. Like all the sins save Pride and Greed, Gluttony receives only a type-name; but proper-naming his sixteen drinking-companions provides a dense social background for his decline and fall. The 'moral comedy' of this scene arises from Glutton's falling foul of his habitual vice even as he is on the way to confess it, and so receiving condign punishment for his behaviour. **349–74 351** *Friday*: a day on which some penance such as fasting until noon was recommended in Lent, when this scene may take place (recalling the day at 438 serves to enclose the scene as if in a frame). The relation of the Glutton scene to the Easter weekend by Wilcockson (1998) would make this 'Friday' that on which the events of 318–20 above took place. **352** *Betene...brewestere*: possibly the wife of Butte (5.134), who may be the butcher abetting Hick at the 'new fair' (but the name was common); on the split genitive see *MES* 78–9. **356** *good ale*: Glutton really being an illustration not of gormandising but of drunkenness, the gravity of which *ParsT* notes when calling *Gula* 'desordeynee coveitise to eten or to drinke' because 'whan a man is dronken, he hath lost his resoun; and this is dedly synne' (*CT* X 818, 823). **357–9** Fennel and peony seed could be chewed without breaking the fasting-rule but (ironically) would arouse thirst and were used to ease bladder-pains, a consequence of heavy drinking (cf. 398). **360** *grete othes*: notably blasphemous swearing by the parts of Christ's body, as acknowledged at 426 below and criticised by Chaucer's Parson and Pardoner (*CT* II 1171, VI 472–6); they are later coupled at B 10.50. **361–74** The two-dozen occupations found among Glutton's cronies give a cross-section of London low life, C 368–9 adding some criminal types. **362** *Watte*: cf. 5.132–3. **365** *Claryce*: on the name cf. at 134. *Cockeslane*: between Holborn and Smithfield, a haunt of prostitutes. *Clerc*: the parish clerk, possibly to 'Sire Piers' (that he *is* Piers [*Bn*] is syntacti-

cally possible but contextually implausible). Probably in minor orders and so charged with ceremonial duties like leading the responses, censing and receiving the offering, his companion is Claryce (cf. *CT* I 3312ff, esp. 3334–6 on Absolon's fondness for taverns and barmaids). **366** *Sire Peres of Prydie*: signifying 'a grossly incompetent priest'; one who when he reached the words *Qui pridie quam pateretur* 'Who, the day before he suffered, [took bread]...', a solemn moment in the consecration prayer during the Canon of the Mass, was obliged to start again if he had not properly prepared the bread and wine (John Mirk, *Instruction for Parish Priests* l.1902, noted by Oliphant 1960:167–8 in establishing the phrase's meaning). If Sir Piers's parish clerk was someone like the 'Clerc' of 365, the negligence might be partly explained; but doubtless his own head (aided by Betene's ale) was *toty of his swynk* with his concubine Pernele. *Flaundres*: many London prostitutes hailing from a region that Chaucer depicts as prone to riotous excess (*CT* VI 463ff). **367** *hayward*: about as popular in the period as game-keepers later. *heremyte*: like the 'unholy' one of Pr 3. *Tybourne*: the chief place of execution, where a permanent gallows stood at the junction of present-day Oxford St, Edgware Road and Bayswater Road (cf. B 12.189). **368** *Dawe*: a typical labourer with his hands; mentioned again at 8.352. **369** *Of*: 'consisting of' (MED s.v. *of* prep. 10(a)); on the partitive genitive see *MES* 79–80. **370** *rakeare*: in **B** from Cheapside, one of the 26 city wards, where vegetable and animal refuse from the market-stalls would have quickly filled his rubbish-cart. MED s.v. cites a 1384 Gild record naming a Richard Maillour of Cheap ward, so **C**'s revision could be removing an allusion that offended a particular raker. **372** *Garlek-monger*: Godfrey's place of work is similarly deleted; but the garlic he sells will have been brought up from France by ship to this landing-stage (*hithe*) on the upper Thames estuary. *Gryffyth*: a typical Welsh name. **373** *vphalderes*: based at Cornhill, where Will resided (cf. 12.220). *herly...*: the adverbial phrase referring to the whole group installed for a long day's drinking. **374** *Geuen*: a Ø-relative ('who gave'). *to hansull*: a free cup to get the drinking off to a good start. **375–440** The barter-session (375–92) seems harmless enough in itself, but inevitably leads to heavy drinking by the two participants (symbolised by the 'greeting' to Glutton at 392). **376** *newe fayre*: perhaps derived from a London fair thus named, of ill repute because barter gave scope for deception and / or squabbling if one party was drunk. The relative value of cloak and hood is assessed by some of the chapmen present (perhaps the experienced *upholderes*) and whoever gets the better deal is to make up the difference to the other (in money or ale); Hick has help from Bette, but Clement seems to need none. The swearing (384) is due to the assessors' being unable to agree the value; but the thing is settled amicably when

Robin is made umpire and decrees that, since he regards the hood as worth more, Clement should bridge the value-gap by buying a round for Hick (and presumably the other two). The penalty if either has second thoughts is to pay for a gallon of ale for 'Glutton' (this may signify 'a drink all round'). The explanation is not pellucid in **AB**, which state at 175/325 that 'the one who got the hood should be paid whatever more the cloak was worth', though this could not be known in advance but awaited independent valuation by the chapmen. **C** makes laboriously explicit (380–1) that whoever gets one won't get the other, but if one is judged to be worth more, its owner will pay the difference to the other party. Part of the satirical point is that the experts' judgement proves unacceptable, and a neutral non-expert arbitrarily decides the outcome: this is not proper trade (*permutacioun apertlich* 3.313) but just an excuse for drinking (394 couples them). **395** *euensong*: in monasteries the sixth canonical hour, vespers, commonly celebrated in parish churches only on Sundays. The time varied with the season, but the service was marked by the lighting of lamps and candles (hence its other name *lucernarium*) and the ringing of bells that would be heard (by the sober) anywhere. Here the phrase means in effect 'till sundown, all day'. **397** *two grydy sowes*: as illustrated in a carving on a choir-stall in Little Malvern priory Church (Kaske 1968: 59, pls. a–b). **398** *Paternoster-whyle*: the length would depend on how slowly and devoutly he said the prayer, which might have formed part of his penance. Like 'evensong', it illustrates how for gluttons 'hire wombe is hire god' (*CT* X 820). **399–400** *ruet...horne*: a 'foul trump' that 'stank as the pit of hell' is described by Chaucer, *HF* 1654, perhaps recalling this scene; and cf. also *CT* VI 536. **401** *wexed*: MED s.v. *waxen* v. (2) (c), follows OED s.v. *Wax* v.², 2 in citing this (the only example), glossing it 'stop up [as with wax]'. But the line's ironic humour depends on the fact that the briars / furze would cause Glutton more pain if used to 'wax' his *ende* with the rubbing motion common to both polishing and the customary toilet-use. Hunters' horns were waxed to improve their tone, and the sense must be rather as in OED 1 '[polish with] wax', aptly citing *Master of Game* xxi (1400): 'A good hunters horne shuld be wele ywexede...after þat þe hunter þinketh þat it woll best sowne'. *weps*: straw or grass (not briars!) was commonly used for toilet purposes; see *ars-wispe* in MED s.v. *wispe* n. (c). **402a** Cf. the echo of this scene in 19.56 //, where being unable to *stepe ne stande* is (allegorically) the consequence of sin. **403–5** These comparisons with a performing dog and a trapper of birds (both highly trained) ironically highlight Glutton's drunken incapacity. **407** *thromblede*: first found here in **A**, and only here in this sense. **409–11** *knowes...lappe*: Clement gets him to his knees facing him and then Glutton vomits into his lap. **412** *Hertfordshyre*: unlike Norfolk, a county named

solely for alliterative convenience (cf. B 2.110). **416** The **B** revision reveals gluttony leading to the worst form of sloth, whereas **A** describes the fit of shakes following the drinking-bout. MED wrongly takes *exces*, a different lexeme answering to *surfet*, as a spelling-variant of *axesse* (a different word in **A**) and fails to record what is its earliest use s.v. 3. = 'intemperance'. *accidie*: glossed by MED as 'a spell of lethargy or apathy', citing only this example; but the pun on its main sense, 'the sin of sloth' is unmistakable, and the next Sin to follow (7.1) resembles his predecessor as the latter would look on awaking. **417** Glutton sleeps between Friday and Sunday evensong, a sign of his virtual transformation into Sloth. **420** *edwitede...synne*: **C**'s b-half showing reversion to the wording of **A**. *inwit*: the metrical stress on the second element highlighting this term's more general sense 'the rational power' (Quirk 1953); but since its moral colouring remains, it here virtually = 'conscience', which is what 'reproached' (*edwitede*) him. A 10.58–61 expresses **L**'s earlier view that drunkenness may quench awareness of right and wrong, but **C** shows Glutton moved by his own sense of shame (421 echoing A 208), rather than having first to be upbraided by his confessor. The reading of B 364 remains uncertain (see *TN*) and **C** may deliberately depict a sinner more susceptible to the 'ayenbite of inwit' than the total reprobate of **B**, whose conscience is almost extinct. **422–3** Glutton's prayer for pity replaces Repentance's admonition to purge his sins of speech and conduct by the 'verbal act' of confessing (B 366–7), for which he commends the penitent at B 379. In **C** the movement of repentance is thus spontaneous, rather than a response to priestly urging. **424–34** Glutton's inebriation leads to sins of inner and outer defilement by words and vomiting, and the comparison to a sick dog here is without the irony of 403–4. **C** omits the social harm caused by his waste of good food (B 374, with which cf. B 439). **426** In both **B** and **C** the first oath is blasphemous, the second a solemn one used improperly. **427** *falsly*: because too drunk to know what he was doing. Such defiance of the Second Commandment was seen as a direct offence against God. **428–33** Sins of eating before time, over-choicely or to excess are listed in *ParsT* 827–30 (and at 835 cf. 'to sitte longe at his mete'). The humorous but shrewd linking of gluttony with sloth in B 375–6 is replaced in **C** by typical *repetitio* of *foule* and the balance of excesses on feast and fast days dropped (neither a clear improvement). **428** *soper*: the evening-meal providing greater temptation to indulge, though excess at mid-day might be more serious, as it would prevent him from working (cf. Hunger's words at 8.274–5). **433** *bifore noen*: in effect eating the breakfast that the penitential regulations required him to forgo; but the sin is worse in **C** as it involves drink and bawdry. **B 379** *shewynge shrift*: 'making (your) confession'; a gerund governing a noun-object, as analysed in Tajima

2000:18–20. **437** *to verray God*: replacing the punning *faste* of B 382 ('to faste' / 'firmly'). His vow is presumably to keep from food before lunchtime on Friday, when abstinence from meat was always compulsory (hence *fysch*) but fasting so only in the penitential seasons. The penance that makes satisfaction for the sin is 'mesure…, that restreyneth by resoun the deslavee [uncontrolled] appetit of etynge' (*CT* X 835; cf. 1.32–5). **439** *Abstinence myn aunte*: for such 'relational' imagery cf. on 329. This authoritative figure is an abbess in B 7.133 and one of the seven sisters who serve Truth at 7.271. *ParsT* 832–3 notes that abstinence, the 'remedy' against gluttony, is spiritually efficacious only if accompanied by good will, patience and charity.

Passus VII (B V, ZA V–VI)

PASSUS SEVEN continues the Confessions of ZAB V and incorporates the rest of B V=ZA VI. It has six sections: (i) the Confession of SLOTH (1–68); (ii) a quasi-homiletic admonition to the rich (69–118*a*); (iii) Repentance's sublime prayer arousing hope among the sinners (119–153*a*); (iv) the penitents' setting out on 'pilgrimage' to St Truth and their encounter with the professional pilgrim (154–80); (v) the appearance of Piers Plowman to describe the way to *Treuthe* (181–281); (vi) the responses, mostly negative, to Piers (282–307). Adopted with little change from B 13.410–57, the 'admonition' (ii) considers SLOTH in relation to disreputable forms of entertainment that it contrasts with the figurative 'minstrelsy' of charitable acts. The effect is to make a vice that in its secular form corrupts society and government and in its spiritual form can induce resistance to conversion appear climactic or fundamental (see Wenzel 1960:135–47 and, arguing the centrality of *accidia* in L's thought, Bowers 1986).

(i) 1–68 1 *Sleuthe*: here identified with *accidie* as the condition *consequent on* gluttonous excess of drink (L's single use of that learned term at 6.416 lacks the full technical sense). This contrasts with Chaucer's use of 'sloth' not as the generic term but as a species of *Accidia* 'angwissh of troubled heart' (*CT* X 679) manifested in 'anoy of goodnesse' (*taedium boni*) or reluctance to do good. *ParsT* (like *PP*) understands the spiritual form of the sin as also physically enervating, for 'slothe maketh…feble and tendre' (689). **3** *stoel*: a faldstool or prie-dieu used for prolonged devotions. **4** *taylende*: metonymy for his need to evacuate; perhaps with an ironic pun on the homophone *taylende* (2) 'reckoning', alluding to his need for shrift. **5** *ryngyng*: i.e. of the church bells; confirming SLOTH's 'moral continuity' with Glutton, who was drunk asleep all Sunday till evensong (6.416–17). **6** *Benedicite*: 'Bless [me, Father, for I have sinned'; the formula for begin-

ning confession. *bolk*: the belch (*eructatio*) produced by the build-up of wind after drinking, sardonically recalling the verse *Eructavit cor meum verbum bonum* (Ps 44:2). But Sloth's only 'good word' is *Benedicite*, a frequent exhortation in psalms (e.g. 102:21). *knokkede*: a standard penitential gesture; cf. 5.106, Z 5.97. **7** *romede*: 'uttered a noisy yawn' (see *TN*); but if it is MED *remen* v. 1(b) 'yawn', the whole phrase resembles *he gon ræmien and raxlede swiðe* in Laʒamon's *Brut* 12972. *rotte*: echoing Sloth's 'other half' Glutton's lapse into his sin on the point of confession at 6.355–60, as Repentance's rebuke does that at B 5.365. **9** *drede*: i.e. of unpreparedness for death; from Sloth 'comth *drede* to bigynne to werke anye goode werkes' (*ParsT* 690). **10** *Paternoster*: its recitation commonly forming part of penance; cf. 5.107 and *ParsT* 1043: 'This hooly orisoun amenuseth [*reduces*] eek venyal synne, and therfore it aperteneth specially to penitence' (see further Gillespie 1994). Sloth is here a layman but at 30 will assume the persona of a priest. *syngeth*: i.e. at Mass, between the Canon and the Communion. Because of the power ascribed to it as a 'sacramental' (a sacred act made efficacious through the Church's intercession), laypeople were encouraged to learn the Latin Paternoster from childhood so that they could join in with the priest when he said it at Mass (see B 13.237). **11** *can*: i.e. by heart, through having heard them so often; the line associates the speaker with the wealthy hearers of harlotry at 81ff. *rymes of Robyn Hode*: the first vernacular reference to the folk-hero (Gray 1984:3–4; for texts and discussion see Dobson & Taylor 1976, Knight 1994). *Randolf*: the Earl (1172–1232), another hero of popular ballads, whose story is told in the Percy Folio MS. He is usually identified with the third earl (Alexander 1982:152–7). **12** *maked*: devotional lyrics or such narrative poems as the *Stanzaic Life of Christ*, *South English Legendary* and *Miracles of the Virgin* in the Vernon and Auchinleck MSS. **13** *voues*: to break a vow or make one frivolously being considered a serious sin; cf. Eccl 5:3–4. **14–15** *penaunce…sory*: wilful refusal to perform canonical penance, the third *pars penitencie* (satisfaction). It was regarded as voiding absolution, though failure to feel true sorrow was not thought so grave as to invalidate confession. The correct attitude to the sacrament is described by Piers in words directly echoing these lines at 7.243–6. **16** *in wrathe*: his sole prayer being to ask God to curse somebody. **18–19** The irony of Sloth's nature is that he is 'busy' only about 'idleness', in church and tavern; this line reinforces his affinity with Glutton. **20** *payne…passioun*: subjects that might move to contrition, and often commended to penitents by confessors. **21** Sloth is now shown in its technical sense of failure to do good deeds recommended as penance: here the omission of two corporal works of mercy (cf. Mt 25:36), a motif illustrated in a window at All Saints, York (Swanson

1989:300). *prisone*: here with a wider sense than *putte*, in **B** the parish lock-up, often located underneath the church (as at Sleaford in Lincs). **22–3** *likene...vnlikyng*: typical 'late' semantic wordplay, echoing the attack on bawdy minstrels at **B** 10.42. **C** starkly opposes ribald tales and malicious mockery to the supreme fiction of Scripture, replacing the **B** 407 reference to the popular *ludi* of Midsummer Eve (June 23) condemned by churchmen for licentiousness and irreverence towards sacred personages (see *MED*'s Mannyng, Rolle and Chaucer refs. s.v. *somer* n. (1), 3(c), and Wenzel 1989). **25** *Vigils*: times for fasting and watching in prayer, especially before major feasts. The other main *fasting-days* (involving abstinence from meat) were Fridays and Saturdays in Lent and the twelve Ember days marking the four seasons, i.e. the Wednesdays, Fridays and Saturdays after St Lucy (13 Dec.), Ash Wednesday, Whitsunday and the Exaltation of the Cross (14 Sept.). **26** *Lente*: Sloth's vice (compounded by lechery) is not intermitted even for the penitential season (cf. Pr 89). **27** Though failure to hear Sunday Mass was judged a grave sin, Sloth thinks his obligation discharged if the friars (at a church where perhaps he belongs to the fraternity) include his name in the community bidding-prayer (cf. Piers' expectation at 8.104 of such a mention from his parish priest for his lifelong payment of tithes). Friar Flatterer will later propose as much to Contricion, the type of those who 'wol nat suffre noon hardnesse ne penaunce'. *CT* X 679 and that passage favour this interpretation here. So does *MS* 630 'They haue a *memoire* of Mvm among alle other' (which *MED* s.v. *memorie* n. 2(c) misassigns in illustrating the phrase *haven memorie*). But as the **B** reading that **C** revises can only be conjecturally reconstructed, B 412 could mean 'recall [that there is a service at] the Friary church'. The point would then be that Sloth can arrive when the service is nearly over and still be held by his indulgent friar-confessor to have heard Mass. **B 413** 'Go, the service is finished', the priest's formula of dismissal of the people (from which 'mass' derives); 'sloth' is here negligent observance of the sabbath. **28** *seknesse*: with its concomitant fear of death; this illustrates the vice of tardiness, arising from 'a fals hope...that he shal lyve longe...that...faileth ful ofte' (*CT* X 719). **29** *ten ʒer... haluendele*: stronger than **B**, which alludes exactly to the duty of annual confession imposed by the Fourth Lateran Council (1215) and to neglect of the requirement that 'shrift moste be purveyed bifore and avysed' (*CT* X 1000ff). **30–4** The abrupt alteration of Sloth's identity typifies the plasticity of **L**'s allegory (cf. Pride's changing sex at 6.14). A similar portrait is found in *The Papelard Priest*, an alliterative piece of *c.* 1350 (edited in Revard 2001, Appendix). **30** *prest and persoun*: 'ordained and beneficed'. **31** *solfe ne reden*: ignorant of Latin and unable to sing the notes of the scale, so unequipped to

perform his services properly or develop spiritually by reading the lives of the Saints. **32** A line perhaps echoed in *CT* I 191–2. **B 419–20** The comparison may have been omitted as too complicated for an audience including priests like those criticised under sloth, or simply as over-specific for the purpose, which is to assert that he is 'illiteratus'. *Beatus vir*: 'Blessed is the man ...'; opening both Ps 1 and 111, but here more probably alluding to the former, the second verse of which requires the just man to meditate 'on the law of the lord' (with which *Canoun* B 422 corresponds). *Beati omnes*: 'Blessed are all they [that fear the Lord: that walk in his ways]' (Ps 127:1). *Construe clausemele*: referring to evensong, when these psalms would have been sung or said, though even a zealous parson would rarely have preached then. **33** Presiding at the manor court, especially on settlement-days (B 421; see on 3.195–6); going through tenants' accounts with the reeve might both help his *parisshens* and provide profit on the side. **34** *Catoun*: further heightening of the slothful priest's incompetence; he is ignorant of elementary Latin grammar (see on 4.17) and cannot read with understanding. **B 422** *Canoun*: the *Corpus iuris canonici,* the body of ecclesiastical law. *Decretals*: either generic for a collection of papal decrees or specifically the *Decretum* of the great Bolognese jurist Gratian (d. *c.* 1160). Although two separate works seem envisaged, Alf*G* is not wholly persuasive that *Canoun* = specifically Gratian and *Decretals* = the *Corpus*. The latter denotes the C12th gathering of earlier conciliar canons and papal decrees together with the C13–14th papal decretals determining points of canon law: the *Decretals* of Gregory IX (1234), the *Novellae* of Innocent IV (*c.* 1254), the *Liber Sextus* of Boniface VIII (1298) and the *Constitutions of Clement V* promulgated by John XXII (1317). The *Decretum* or *Concordia discordantium canonum* (*c.* 1140) was an analytical compilation used as an authoritative reference work (and often thought of as part of the *Corpus*) but not adopted formally as the Church's official law (Brundage 1987:233). **L** does not quixotically expect a parson to be an expert like the Doctor at 15.86, but *litteratus* enough to consult authorities when the need arose. **35–41** Sloth now metamorphoses into a dishonourable farmer who repudiates orally-agreed loans from trusting creditors but pays his own employees unwillingly and late (a sin against justice condemned in Lev 19:16, quoted at 3.307*a*). **35** *ytayled*: see on 4.61. **42–54** depict Sloth's decline into 'povertee and destruccioun...of...temporeel thynges' (*CT* X 721) through ingratitude and negligence. **42; 43; 45** *beenfeet*; *cortesie*; *loue*: forms of good that Sloth is as unapt to comprehend as to perform. The 'hawk' metaphor implies that he cynically appraises an act of disinterested goodwill to see what is in it for the giver (*he* always looks to his own advantage). **45** *luyred*: the lure was usually 'a bundle of leather and feathers resembling a bird' (*MED*

Commentary

s.v. *lure* n (1)), to which a piece of meat (= *ouht*) was sometimes attached. It was tied to a thong and swung round as part of training a hawk to return to the falconer. **47–8** *haue...speche*: i.e. both in forgetting to say 'thank you' and in not desisting from unkind remarks through remembrance of past kindnesses; sardonically punning on two senses of *sparen* 'refrain from' and 'save' (MED s.v. 2a, 5b). Burrow (2003:192–3), arguing with reference to B 435–9, would punctuate with a semi-colon after *sethe* 47 and *tyme* 48 so as to make *many a tyme* not an adverbial but a noun-phrase, yielding the sense: 'Have wasted many a moment of time in speaking or in failing to speak'. This misuse of time in relation to the gift of speech he persuasively shows to be specially apt to the sin of Sloth, illustrating from John de Burgo's manual for parish priests the *Pupilla Oculi* (cited from Wenzel 1960:197). **49–52** illustrate 'necligence, or reccheleesnesse, that rekketh of no thyng' (*CT* X 798), the serious consequence noted in 52b echoing 3.104–7 (which draws on first-hand observation). **53–4** Sloth's final transformation into a lazy vagabond who refuses to learn a trade and ends in beggary proves that if 'ignorance be mooder of alle harm...necligence is the norice' (*CT* X 710). **54a** The statement is quasi-authorial, not directly self-characterising as in its first appearance at 1.139a, the echo of which reminds that all the sins are implicitly those of 'Will' (6.2). **55** *swowened*: one harmful effect of sloth being 'sloggy slombrynge, which maketh a man be hevy and dul in body and in soule' (*CT* X 705). **56–68** formed the nucleus of the Sloth confession from **Z** onwards, and all survives save B 456–61 //, of which the first five lines are given to Evan, the last two omitted. **56** *Vigilate the veile*: 'Keep-Watch the Wakeful One'; a passing personification (unusually given words) of Sloth's near-extinct conscience, which produces tears sufficient to rouse him. The Latin name has resonances of texts on the need for alertness (lest death come suddenly), where sleep figures moral torpor, wakefulness spiritual awareness. These are Mk 13:33–7, 14:38 = Mt 26:41 (seeing sleep as vulnerability to temptation), I Cor 16:13, urging action, and I Pet 5:8, linking vigilance with sobriety (*sobrii estote, et vigilate*), a text preached to Glutton by Repentance at 6.168. Citing Wenzel 1967:102, *AlfQ* 13–14 notes that medieval commentators saw Mt 26:41 as warning specifically against *somnium accidiae*, the sleep of sloth. **58** *wanhope*: 'despair of the mercy of God, that comth...to muche drede...that he hath doon so muche synne that it wol nat availlen hym, though he wolde repenten hym and forsake synne...' (*CT* X 692). As with Greed at B 5.279, this is Sloth's end-condition, identified at 80 as its extreme form. **63** *auowe*: undoing his neglected vows (13). *foule sleuthe*: formulaic *repetitio* of 54b. **64** *Sonday*: making 'condign' satisfaction for his breach of the Third Commandment (Ex 20:8) by observing all three services (mat-

ins, Mass, evensong) on the sabbath; cf. Lechery's special attention to Saturday and Gluttony's to Friday (6.173, 338). *seuene зere*: cf. B 5.73, removed in // C 6.173. *but... make*: 'unless sickness cause it to be otherwise'; ironically repeating 7.28 (fear has been transformed through attrition to a firm purpose of amendment). **66–8** *matynes*: said at dawn and followed by Mass and dinner at noon; he will not drink between midday and evensong at 3.0 p.m. *þe Rode*: the vow being made before the crucifix on the screen below the chancel arch.

  B 5.456–61 (Z 5.124–30, A 5.229–34) will have come under Sloth originally because they deal with tardiness in restoring ill-gotten goods; but **C** improves in shifting them to the thievish Evan (see on 6.308–12). **B 460** *Rode of Chestre*: formerly on Rood Eye (Cross Island) in the River Dee at Chester; repeated by Piers at A 7.92, where // **BC** alter the oath. **461** Sloth's resolve is to use the money left after settling his debts to live virtuously rather than make satisfaction by a costly pilgrimage. These words adumbrate the major theme of 'true' pilgrimage as conversion of heart that will be developed in B VI = C VIII. **462–77 (Z 131–150, A 235–52)** See on **C 6.315–29**.

(ii) 69–118a consider the routes to sloth and specifically *wanhope*, regarded as the final stage of *Accidia* in *AI* (pp. 33–4), but digress into a diatribe against those who encourage idle entertainers, and an admonition to the rich to substitute the needy for such 'false' minstrels. In B XIII this ends the account of Haukyn's dire condition fittingly enough (he is a minstrel), but earns its place here as showing how works of charity can bring man to the opposite state of *welhope* (113) or confidence in final release from sin.

69–80 form a transitional passage of question followed by answer and prepare for the negative and positive exempla on false, true and figurative 'minstrelsy'. **69** *wheche been*: a shift to direct question recalling the didactic address of a *precheour of Goddes wordes* (87). But while the lines it introduces are perhaps 'not adapted to the dramatic situation' (*Pe*), they are hardly more abrupt than in their original location. *þe braunches*: the circumstances and acts that lead back / predispose towards the dark 'essence' of sloth, 'final impenitence', the unforgiveable 'sin against the Holy Ghost' (*CT* X 695). Sin was commonly symbolised as a tree with major branches and twigs (an image first found in *AI*, p. 17). Its conventional form occurs at B 15.74–5 (where the 'branches' grow *out of* the capital sins) and in *CT* X 388–9: 'everich of thise chief synnes hath his braunches and his twigges' (Katzenellenbogen 1989: ill. 66 depicts *Desperatio*, *Acedia* etc., the subdivisions of Sloth or *Tristicia*, as hanging fruits). **70** *Is*: elliptical for 'its origin is'; spiritual torpor leading to despair starts with lack of sorrow for sin, failure to do penance, and reluctance to hear or do good. **71** recalls

Sloth's admission at 14. **75** takes up B 13.350. *to* (1, 2); *of*: governed respectively by *likyng*, here 74. **77** *wordes of murthe*: 'amusing conversation', not bad in itself but implying lightness of mind when found with refusal to consider serious matters like one's mortality (cf. Eccl 7:5–7). **79** *carpeth*: replacing *telleþ* and echoing 76; an example of **C**'s typical *repetitio*.

81–118a 82 *foel-sages*: ideally 'sothseggers' (like King Lear's Fool) rather than *flateres and lyares*. But **L**'s animosity is explained by his wish to contrast *all* 'mysproud' jesters with skilled musicians (96) and religious preachers (87) and to recommend replacing them with another (metaphorical) type of 'minstrel', the poor (103). The passage is predicated on the higher classes' need to hear 'sad' words (grave truths from religious men) and see 'sad' sights (people in the poor estate that all must return to at the time of *deth-deynge*). **83a** '[Woe to you that are filled: for you shall hunger]. Woe to you that now laugh: [for you shall mourn and weep]' (Lk 6:25). The next verse is also relevant, intimating a parallel between these 'sage fools' and Luke's flattering 'false prophets', while the whole warning precedes injunctions to give generously to the needy. **85** echoes Sloth's words at 9 above. **86** *sorwe*: in hell. **86a** 'Those who consent [*sc.* to evil] and those who do [it] will be punished with the same penalty'; identified by Alford 1975 (following *Sk* and citing Lucas of Penna) as a canon-law maxim, also common in the 'penitential' tradition see (Alf*Q*): 'they that...*consenten* to the synne been parteners...of the dampnacioun of the synnere' (*CT* X 967). Presumably here the tellers of the bawdy *tales* (90) are the 'doers', their hearers the 'consenting partners'. **87** Despite the OT terms, the present tense shows that all three categories denote contemporary clergy. **89** *procuratours*: as later Piers is of the Holy Spirit (21.259; see Alf*G* s.v.). **92** *Dauid*: cited here as the model for 'God's minstrels' (David is discussed in Wurtele 2003). **92a** 'He that worketh *pride* shall not dwell in the midst of my house: he that speaketh unjust things [did not prosper before my eyes]' (Ps 100:7–8). **95** *mysproud man*: either the satirical *foel-sage* or another category of harmful companion (cf. the psalm quotation) like those at 11.38–41. **96** *kynges munstrals*: skilled professional musicians of the royal establishment, who were paid 20s. a year in Edward III's time (Southworth 1989:103). When coming to perform at the houses of bishops or the provincial nobility (Chambers 1903:i.53, ii.247), they would expect a warm reception for the respect due to their 'lord' (the king, but in the allegory God). **99** As the handicapped, sick and destitute are 'minstrels' sent by God, 'listening' to them (showing charity) will produce true *murthe* for the hearer (in heaven); cf. Mt 10:42 and 12.121–3. **100** *As*: 'for', 'inasmuch as' rather than 'just as', since Christ's words do not compare beggars to minstrels or refer to beggars at all, but to his disciples. A

later elaboration of the analogy at 9.128–38 calling God's minstrels his 'messengers' (9.136) refers to the infirm of mind who prompt charity, but affirms that they are *not* beggars. **100a** '[He that heareth you heareth me: and] he that despiseth you [despiseth me: and he that despiseth me despiseth him that sent me]' (Lk 10:16). The thought resembles Jn 5:23, 13.20 but **L** was more probably recalling Jn 12:48: '*Qui spernit me et non accipit verba mea, habet qui iudicet eum*'. **102** *solace*: playing on the senses 'entertain' and 'comfort (spiritually)'; see MED s.v. *solasen* v. 1(a), 2(a). **103** *for; thy*: alliterating on metrical allophones, each word carries strong sentence stress: 'in place of / in the rôle of' (so, unstressed, at 107); 'your'. **104–5** As the enjambement bears out, the final infinitive *for to saue* depends syntactically and semantically on both *to lere* and *suffrede*: Christ's passion, and poetic accounts of it (in works like those mentioned under 12 above), will profit the soul of the prudent rich man. **106** *geste*: the MED exx. s.v. *geste* n.1 are exclusively secular in reference save for **L**, whose four uses all differ. But here the revision (see *TN*) emphasises that the Passion story is 'not less but more heroic' than the martial tales a knightly audience might favour. **107** *bordiour*: paradoxical, unless wholly figurative, since the blindness is not a subject for mirth (contrast the comic remarks of the natural fools at 9.136, who are 'mery bordiours'). **108** *crye...*: intercede with God for the rich man (now or at the Last Judgement) by citing his generosity. **110–11** *til...seyntes*: '...offer great comfort to him who during his life...' *here*: 'receive', 'welcome'. **112–13** 'settle into a state of confidence that he will join the saints in heaven because he did such deeds'. **L** is of his age in seeing a person's last hour as crucial, a time of despair or joyful hope of salvation, but realistic in judging that sloth (defined as reluctance to do good) severely lessens the chance of a person's 'death-bed conversion'. **115** The image is of a musician conducting a procession of merrymakers into a banquet. *lythed*: revision of **B** to achieve the *repetitio* of 111 again typical of **C**. **116** *turpiloquio*: inflected as ablative after *with*; the same word that in Pr 40 associates the low satirist with Lucifer, users of vile language being those who sing the devil's tune. *lay of sorwe*: ironically, composed of *wordes of murthe* (cf. 77); but its transcendental 'meaning' is misery, whereas (a favourite paradox of the poet) the literal 'lay of sorrow' about Christ's passion will lead to *murthe* (cf. 12.202–20). **117–18a** The conclusion added in **C**, which rounds off the argument with an admonitory patristic text on the danger of patronising immoral *japeres*, makes the inserted passage seem even more like a miniature sermon. **117** Hell's pain is 'unending' as well as 'ceaseless', purgatory's prescribed a limit; but though both are intense, neither is understood as unjust (for the same sense of *wikke* see 11.275). **118** *þat*: '[those] who(m)', a 'Janus-faced' relative, the nominative being principal. **118a** 'To give money to actors [is much the same as offering sacrifice to devils]', part of a statement attributed to St Jerome by Petrus Cantor, '*Paria sunt* histrionibus dare *et demonibus immolare*'(*PL* 205:155). This warning should be read beside the strong criticism at B 9.92a of bishops whose wrongful giving deprives Christ's poor of their due.

(iii) 119–53a have REPENTANCE as a priest interceding with God for the sins of the people. But in strict allegorical terms his action serves to demonstrate how spiritual change engenders humility and thence receptiveness to the grace of conversion (witnessed in amendment of life). The speech, with its liturgical resonances, closely relates in theme and tone to the Passion-Harrowing sequence in 20.57ff, which it anticipates, e.g. at 134 (Bennett 1982:85–112). It is as richly veined with scriptural quotations as Passus XX, and its echoes of the Holy Week services (*Bn*) help to locate the great repentance scene towards the end of the season favoured for compulsory annual confession and orientate it towards Easter, which completes the liturgical cycle of redemption begun at Christmas. The later passage that 'recapitulates' this scene is explicitly set towards the end of Lent (21.385). **119** The 'Platonic' play on 'readiness' and 'counsel' is typical of **C. 123** See Gen 1:26. **124** *sykenesse*: i.e. in subjecting man to suffering and death. **125** *þe Boek*: the Bible's account of death coming into the world through the sin of Adam (Gen 3:16–19, Rom 5:12), against which is set the hope of eternal life through Christ's death and resurrection. **125a** 'O happy fault, [which was blotted out by the death of Christ]! O [truly] necessary sin of Adam, [which earned so great a redeemer]'; from the canticle *Exultet* sung at the start of the Easter Vigil service on Holy Saturday: 'O certe *necessarium Adae peccatum*, [quod Christi morte deletum est!] *O felix culpa*, [quae talem ac tantum meruit habere Redemptorem]'. Strang 1963:208 suggests that **L**'s inversions derive from a lost lyrical form of this text; but it is typical of **L** that his quotations are free and fitted to their immediate context. The canticle's 'necessary' implies that the Fall, though caused by Satan's enmity, formed part of God's providential plan to bring forth a greater good. **126–8** The fault was 'happy' because it led to the Incarnation, a first 'new creation' that exalts man even more than did his original creation in God's image. This idea is fully developed by Peace the Daughter of God in 20.207–37. **128** *with*: here and at B 488 = 'through the agency / in the person of', not 'together with'. The prayer is addressed to God the Father, making clear that not He but the incarnate Second Person died on the cross (though *all* divine acts are to be thought of as done 'through the will of the Father' and 'by the working of the Holy Spirit'). **128a** '[Do you not believe that] I am in the Father and the Father in me?' (Jn 14:10); 'he that seeth me seeth the Father also' (Jn 14:9). The quotations

(of which the first is repeated at 11.155a during Clergy's speech on the Trinity) underline that Christ (though truly man) shares his divine nature with the Father, whom he manifests to the world in human guise (*sute / sekte*). **B 487a** 'Let us make man to our image and likeness' (Gen 1:26); 'And elsewhere, He that abideth in charity abideth in God, and God in him' (I Jn 4:16). The creation of Adam is associated with the *second* 'new creation' (see on 126–8), that of the Christian through baptismal grace, making possible the supernatural life of charity that incorporates redeemed mankind in the life of God, *quoniam Deus charitas est* (I Jn 4:8; cf.1.82). As *Bn* notes, the second quotation is the source of the hymn *Ubi caritas* 'Where charity and love are, there is God' sung as an antiphon on Maundy Thursday at the ceremony of the Washing of the Feet. **129** *secte*: 'fleshly form': a revision removing the polysemous wordplay on *sute* (B 488), which also signifies 'cause, action-at-law' (*Bn*) and 'pursuit'. The legal and chivalric senses apposite to Christ's encounter with Satan in the Crucifixion (20.393–5, 443, 408) are replaced by a simple emphasis on the truth of his incarnation. But neither *semed* nor *fourme* 130 implies the deceptive or illusory, rather the 'sensibly actual' appearance concealing the 'metaphysically real' truth (though the effect on the 'false' Satan is to deceive *him*). **B 489** *ful tyme*: 'noon', perhaps further suggesting Christ's death as the coming to fulfilment of his historical life at '*plenitudo temporis* tyme' (Gal 4:4: see 18.127); cf. C 2.100, which conversely substitutes *noone* for *ful tyme* B 96. The Synoptic Gospels' *nona hora* 'ninth hour' (Mt 27:46 //) was 3 p.m; but the canonical office of None originally fixed for that hour came to be said after the principal monastic Mass of *midday* (132 below), and this was the word's main sense by the 13th c. **130** Whereas **C** stresses the reality of Christ's suffering, B 490–1 affirm that the Godhead remained impassible while the human nature united with it in the person of Jesus endured the pain. **B 491** *it ladde*: the pronoun is double-referenced, since Christ led mankind to salvation, and humanity ('his capul that highte *Caro*' 17.108) also 'led' or carried the divine nature. A sense 'endured' (MED s.v. *leden* 9(c)), with *sorwe* as object, is favoured in Mann's thoughtful discussion (1994[1]:44); but the *duxit* of 491a directs to the sense 'lead / carry (away captive)', with *secte* clearly the object. **130a** '[Ascending on high], he led captivity captive' (Eph 4:8, quoting Ps 67:19); sung as an antiphon verse on Ascension Day, and alluding to Christ's descent into *Limbo inferni* to release the souls of the just (a belief enshrined in clause 5 of the Apostles' Creed and based on I Pet 3:19 and Eph 4:9–10 9–10). The theme will be dramatically realised at 20.449. **131** refers to the 'darkening of the sun' between the sixth and ninth hour: *tenebrae factae sunt...Et obscuratus est sol* (Lk 23:44–5). *lees siht*: by *interpretatio*, 'became invisible' but literally 'became blind', since the sun is personified here, as later at 20.60. The phrasing echoes Rolle in his *Meditations on the Passion* (shorter version): *þe erþe þan trembled, þe sonne lost hys syʒt, þat al merk was þe weder, os it hadde ben nyʒt* (Ullmann 1884:462). *GO* states that 'the sun withdrew its beams either so as not to see the Lord hanging there or so that wicked blasphemers should not enjoy its light' (*PL* 114:348, following Bede on Mk in *PL* 92:290); and John of Hoveden writes that 'the sun refused to look upon / the suffering borne by the true sun' (original in *Poems*, ed. Raby, p. 188). On the rich Latin and vernacular poetic background to this motif, see Schmidt 1983²:185–8. **132** *mydday*: the normal time of dinner. The 'heavenly banquet' is here seen as celebrated at the time when on earth the Eucharistic *pignum* 'pledge' of that feast is re-enacted with the symbolic pouring out of the blood of Christ at the consecration of the wine. *Sk*'s doubt about making this connection, because Mass 'was more usually celebrated at an earlier hour,' is answered if what **L** had in mind is the major conventual Mass at noon (see on B 489). *most liht*: literally the sun's at full strength, but figuratively that of Christ the 'Sun of Righteousness' de-scending into the darkness of hell. *mel-tyme*: perhaps alluding to the legend in *St Patrick's Purgatory* (Day 1932:317–18, citing *SEL* pp. 216–17) that the blessed in the earthly paradise who have passed through purgatory are fed daily by a heavenly light. Wenzel (AlfC 164–5) notes a sermon passage used in *FM* that reads Christ's sacrificial death in the light of Cant 1:6 ('Indica mihi... ubi pascas, ubi cubes in meridie'). **133** Influence from the motif of the pelican sustaining its young with blood from its breast (*Pe*) conjoins with the well-known legend that the wood of the cross was made from the Tree of Life (Gen 2:30) and that its position on Calvary ('the place of the Skull') was directly above the grave of Adam, into whose mouth Christ's blood trickled. A C14th Italian crucifixion-fresco (Schiller 1972, II, pl. 504) comprehensively depicts the *arbor vitae*, the heavenly liturgy, the pelican (placed above the inscription) and the rock of calvary, while a C15th German Rood (ibid., pl. 489) also represents the tree of life. *tho*: the moment when Christ's blood was 'actually' shed, here envisaged as coinciding with that when it is made 'really' present at the priest's breaking of the Host. *forfadres*: all the patriarchs, beginning with Adam *oure aller fader* (B 16.205). Their participation in the feeding is graphically depicted in a wooden C13th German rood (Schiller 1972, II: pl. 479) where Adam holds a chalice to receive the blood. **133a** 'The people that walked in darkness have seen a great light: [to them that dwelt in the region of the shadow of death, light is risen]' (Is 9:2; qu. in Mt 4:16 with reference to the mission of Jesus). Read in the lesson for the Monday of the 4th week in Advent and the vespers of the Nativity, this text underlies the Introit of Christmas, associating

Christ's birth with his death as 'light-bringing' salvific events. Though not quoted in the Easter liturgy, it became the basis of patristic thought on Christ's liberation of the patriarchs from hell (*Bn* cites the *Sunday Sermons* of Pope St Leo, ii. 191), on which see *EN* 18:1. **134** *oute of The*: inspired by the Nicene Creed's description of the Son as 'Deum de Deo, *lumen de lumine*' (based on Jn 1:4–5, 9). *blente*: cf. 20.368. **B 496** *blewe*: the claim that 'strict syntax requires the action to be predicated of Lucifer' (*Bn*) is groundless, since *blewe* may be 2nd or 3rd pers. pret. (in the light of C 135 *brouhte* more probably the latter) and any difficulty must be semantic not syntactical. That the light, symbol of the divine power and presence, should 'blow' the souls out of hell is not much odder than that Christ's 'breath' should break hell's gates in 20.364 // (as *Bn* is aware), since this breath explains 'blew' (*Sk*). Fiery light and powerful wind together are traditional divine epiphanies from the OT to the Pentecost scene in Acts 2:2–3. For (uncompelling) speculation that the passage alludes to the theology of the generation of the Son by the Father and of insufflation by the Holy Spirit see Hill 1973:444–9. **136** *thridde day*: the morning of Easter Sunday being the third 'day' after the dawn of Good Friday, if this day is included. **137** *synful Marie*: Mary of Magdala, whose meeting with the risen Christ in the garden occupies half of Jn 20 (cf. 21.157–60). She was traditionally confused both with Mary of Bethany, sister of Martha and Lazarus (12.137), and with the un-named woman who anointed Jesus and had 'many sins forgiven her' (Lk 7:47). Since the 'seven devils' he had cast out of the Magdalen (Mk 16:9) were commonly allegorised as the deadly sins, she aptly emblematises the hope of forgiveness for the worst sinner (cf. 11.264–5). On the legend of Mary (*LA* xcvi) see Garth 1950 and Haskins 1993, and on the Magdalen hymns Szövérffy 1963. *Seynte Marye*: the usual ME style for the Blessed Virgin Mary (e.g. *CT* IV 2418), sometimes as part of *Oure Lady Seinte Marye* (*CT* VI 308). This appellation only became controversially contrasted with the title 'Our Lady' in Protestant usage at the Reformation. **138a** 'I came not to call the just, but sinners to penance' (Lk 5:32). Christ's appearance *first* to the Mary who typifies (converted) sinfulness rather than (unblemished) holiness is understood as offering special comfort to the truly penitent. **139–40** treat the evangelists as poets who composed the *geste* of Christ's heroic actions (see on 106, and cf. Lawton in Wallace1999: 478–9). *was don*: elliptical for '(related to what) was done' (*Bn*). *sekte*: with the same complex polysemy as at 129, 136. **B 501** *armes*: with both martial and heraldic senses (*Sk*), anticipating 20.21 where the referent is again 'humana natura'. **140a** '[And] the Word was made flesh, and dwelt among us' (Jn 1:14). **141** *by so muche..*: 'in virtue of the fact [that Christ now represents the human race he has become part of]'. **143** *fadur*: from 122 the prayer was to God the Father, from 129*a* to the incarnate Second Person, and now to the glorified Christ, in effect to God in his new relationship with mankind prophesied in the passage quoted at 147*a*. Formal Trinitarian exactitude is not to be looked for here, since for **L** it is the one God who makes and who becomes man (see 20.226, 230). **144–7*a*** affirm more clearly and explicitly than **B** that salvation is for those who are sincerely sorry for their sin. **147** *knowlechede*: understand 'our sins'. **147*a*** '[Whenever a sinner shall cry out], I will remember all [his] iniquities no more'; traced to pseudo-Ezekiel 33:12, by Marchand (1990), who notes that it was frequently cited in discussions on the necessity of confession and exhorting against the sin of despair. The possible source of this apocryphal OT passage is Jer 31:34b; certainly the whole of Jer 31:29–34 is relevant as a prophecy of the New Covenant established at the Incarnation. **148** *and... moder*: for the grammar see on 2.2. **151–6** This brief passage, dense with embedded and appended Latin, allegorises the awakening of the theological virtue of HOPE offered in baptism, lost by the *rybaudes* through persistence in sin, but now recovered through their formal repentance. A passing personification not to be simply identified with the *Spes* of XIX, Hope embodies positive trust in God that generates active will to do good. So as *welhope* (113), he signifies the metaphysical contrary to *wanhope*, the final stage of Sloth. **151** *horn*: understood by BnPe as suggesting the *tuba salutaris* 'trumpet of salvation' in the Easter *Exultet*'s opening sentence. But a verbally closer source is 'The Lord is...my protector and the *horn* of my salvation [*cornu salutis meae* = a powerful salvation for me],' from Ps 17:3, immediately after a reference to *hope* in God (*et sperabo in eum*), echoed by the canticle of Zacharias in Lk 1:69 (Alf*Q*). *Deus...*: 'Thou wilt turn, O God, and bring us to life: [and thy people shall rejoice in thee]' (Ps 85:7); the priest's prayer of general absolution (Burrow 1984 [1965]: 84) at the end of the public confession at Mass, after the *Confiteor* and the *Misereatur*. Though the context would suggest that Will and the repentant sinners have come to Mass and that **L** 'is here thinking of public liturgical, rather than private sacramental, penance' (Burrow), the two acts are complementary. Obligation to confess mortal sins personally to the priest remained, but those participating in the penitential rite of Mass could hope to be absolved from *venial* sins committed since receiving individual absolution at their last confession and receive help against falling into such sin (cf. *CT* X 385). **152–2*a*** 'Blessed are they whose iniquities are forgiven: and whose sins are covered' (Ps 31:1, the second penitential psalm). Assurance of sin forgiven is the 'breath' with which Hope fills his horn of God's life-giving presence in the Eucharist (a miniature scriptural allegory of the penitents' movement through Easter Confession to Communion that will be

dramatised in 21.367–93). The importance of this verse is shown by its return at 14.117*a*. and B 13.52–53*a*, 14.93. **153** *alle Seyntes*: illustrating the dogma of 'the Communion of Saints', which precedes 'the Forgiveness of Sins' as the 9th clause of the Apostles' Creed; allusion is to Lk 15:7 on the joy in heaven over one repentant sinner. **153*a*** 'Men and beasts thou wilt preserve, O Lord: O how hast thou multiplied thy mercy, O God!' (Ps 35:7–80).

(iv) 154–80 describe the response of the Folk as emotional rather than rational, though **L** eliminates the more dramatic symptoms of this (AZ 254 /152) to stress their ignorance and bewilderment: now *thei wilneth bettre* but are still *aboute þe mase* (1.8, 6). **155** echoes HC's farewell at 2.51. **156** *to go to Treuthe*: remembering Reason's parting injunction at 5.198 that urged them to repent. **158** *blostrede*; *baches*: rare words, the former found first here in this sense and associated with the blind irrational movement of animals (as in *Pur* 886), the latter earlier only in Laȝamon (MED s.vv. *blusteren* v. and *bach* n.(1)). *bestes*: echoing *iumenta* 153*a*, but suggesting pity for 'distressed sheep without a shepherd' (cf. Mt 9:36, Ps 77:52–3). **159–60** give a merciless caricature of the professional religious tourist ostentatiously sporting souvenirs from the chief pilgrim-shrines in Europe and the Near East. **Z 158** *palmere*: originally a pilgrim entitled to wear on his hat palm-sprigs sewn crosswise, as a sign of having visited the Holy Places; by now denoting 'a pilgrim who had travelled overseas' (*CT* I 13). **160** *paynyem*: because wearing the outlandish garb of *hethenesse*. **161** *bordoun*: a long staff carried by pilgrims travelling on foot. *liste*: perhaps for use as a bandage in case of accident (*Sk*). **164** *aunpolles*: lead or pewter flasks (*ampullae*) stamped with the saint's image (Alexander & Binski 1987:218–21, pls.43–53) and containing holy water from the shrine, in which the saint's relic had been dipped. **165** *Signes*: badges or insignia of having made a particular pilgrimage (Alexander & Binski pls. 54–67). *Syse*: Assisi, near Perugia, in Umbria, birth- and burial-place of St Francis. *shelles*: (Anderson 1971: pl. 60; Cutts 1925: pl. 163), commemorating a miracle of St James, through whose intercession a pagan knight saved from drowning in the sea emerged covered with scallop shells and was converted to the Christian faith (Cutts 169). *Galys*: see on Pr 48. **166–7** describe emblems of the pilgrimage to Rome (Sumption 1975:249–65). *crouch*: symbolising the martyrdom of St Peter. *kayes*: the crossed keys signifying Peter's spiritual authority (Mt 16:19). *vernicle*: a copy in cloth or metal of the napkin with which (according to her legend) St Veronica was believed to have wiped the face of Christ on the way to Calvary and on which his likeness was miraculously impressed; she was sometimes identified with the woman suffering from an issue of blood, whom Jesus cured (Mt 9:20–22). Gerald of Wales derived her name (probably a corruption of *Bernice* in Ac

25:13), from *vera icon* 'true image', the words inscribed under the Vernicle. The scene (Anderson 1971: pl. 38) became part of the Stations of the Cross performed in Rome (where the Vernicle was preserved in St Peter's) and is recorded in the *Legends of the Holy Rood* 170–1; but in the form **L** probably knew it (*LA* ch. 53), the incident occurs before the Passion (see further Lewis 1985). *bifore*: i.e. on his breast. **167–8** His 'carnal' attitude to pilgrimage is antithetical to Piers's spiritual understanding at 8.62–3. **170** *Sinoye*: Mt Sinai on the peninsula between Egypt and Palestine, where the great monastery claimed to preserve the body of St Catherine of Alexandria. *sepulcre*: Christ's tomb, the most sacred pilgrimage site, within the Church of the Holy Sepulchre in Jerusalem. **171** *Bedlem*: five miles S of Jerusalem, where the C4th Church of the Nativity stands over the traditional birthplace of Christ (Mt 2:1). All of these Holy Land sites were in the hands of the Turks, but intrepid pilgrims continued to visit them. *Babiloyne*: 'the Less' near Cairo (as distinguished from Babylon the Great in Mesopotamia), where 'a faire chirche of oure lady' (*Mandeville's Travels*, I 21) commemorated the time spent by Joseph and Mary in Egypt (Mt 2:14). **172** *Armonye*: where Noah's Ark had rested (Gen 8:30) on Mt Ararat (now in Turkey) and was still to be seen. *Alisaundre*: in Egypt, the main port of embarkation for pilgrims to the Holy Land and the place where St Mark and St Catherine had been martyred. *Damaskle*: capital of Syria, the legendary site where God created Adam before placing him in Eden (*Mandeville*, I..44; *CT* VII 2007; Comestor in *PL* 198:1053–1722). **176** *corseynt*: to the folk, 'saint' rather than 'saint's body [in a shrine]' (cf. Chaucer *HF* 117); but their very choice of term (MED s.v. *cor-seint* n.), implying a physical journey to a place like those the Pilgrim might have seen, shows them interpreting literal-mindedly Reason's injunction to seek 'St Truth' not 'St James or the saints of Rome' (metonyms for their shrines). Piers's response proves that he understands Reason correctly. **178–9** The pilgrim's ignorance of Truth's whereabouts echoes the charge against his ilk at Pr 47–50; but the harsh B Pr 50–2 having been cut, he is meant more probably as deceived than as deceiving. **179** *pyk*: like that in Cutts pl. 163, with the staff, hat and cloak part of the 'authentic' pilgrim's attire. **180** *ar now*: elliptical for 'before (you people) here just (have)'.

(v) 181–281 The sudden unprepared appearance of PIERS THE PLOUGHMAN opens the final section. His 100-line speech on the spiritual 'way' to Truth is only briefly interrupted twice by an entreaty at 199, but it provokes a set of cynical comments at 282–5. This is followed by two more substantial rejoinders, one negative and one positive, which round off the passus, initiate the second half of Vision Two and sharpen expectation of important events to follow.

181–98 181 *Peter*: a mild oath the thematic significance

of which will not be fully disclosed until 21.214, when Grace gives to Piers St Peter's NT rôle as guide and overseer of the Christian *comune*; but it is here appropriate as invoking the saint whose name he bears. *plouhman*: on the social status of the C14th ploughman, see Bennett 1937:183, Du Boulay 1991:44–51 and Dyer 1994. The best-known English literary type-portrait, in *GPCT*, is probably indebted to **L**, as is seen if B 545, 556–7 are compared with *CT* I 536, 538 and C 8.101–2 with *CT* 539–40. But Chaucer's giving his ploughman an idealised parson as brother eirenically counters the mutual antagonism dramatised in **L**'s Pardon Scene. Nothing in the text so far imports an allegorical reading, but a figurative relationship between ploughing and spiritual discernment was long established in commentary on the OT (e.g. Ecclus 6:18–20), and in the NT it symbolises religious commitment (Lk 9:62, I Cor 9:10, II Tim 2:6). *potte forth*: not necessarily implying pushing his head through a hedge on *over*hearing the question (*Bn*), but making better sense if Piers ('P.' hereafter) has heard the sermon along with the folk; for though P. never mentions REASON, 183 affirms his adherence to the principles formally expressed by the latter. **183** *Conscience*: first introduced in **C** as an unsparing opponent of 'carnal' religion, and properly acknowledged here as the source of P.'s moral and spiritual insight. But **C**, by removing the emphatic *re*-assertion of this point at B 7.134, offers no critique of clerical abuses beyond that of Conscience himself in Pr 95–124. *Kynde Wit*: see on Pr 141–7, which affirm both the priority of 'common understanding based on experience' to formal learning, and also its closeness to Conscience and Knighthood in providing for society's practical needs. **184, 189** *seruen*; *serued*: i.e. through his God-given calling as a ploughman (cf. *a potte me* 191; *hotep, deuyse* B 545, 547), which has a spiritual significance (cf. *withynne* 187) that the speaker holds certain. P.'s words affirm an unmediated acquaintance with Truth as a value through his faithful (*trewe*) practice of ordinary life in the world. **187** may scan with wrenched stress on *with-* or (more probably) on vowels, with natural word-stress and with sentence-stress on *his*; cf. the reversed form in 6.208, B 13.238. **188** *al...wynter*: 'many a long year' (*Bn*); despite 'olde and hoer' at 8.92, P. need only be in his fifties, and seems less decrepit than Will at 22.183ff. **189, 192** *to paye*: another example of **C** Version *repetitio*. **193–5** To speak of Truth as a just employer is situationally apt to P., who is rightly said to represent 'a peasant loyal to his manorial lord God in perpetuity' (Simpson 1987:99). At this point P.'s view of divine reward evokes Conscience's account of strictly just payment through 'wages' (*mercede* or *mesurable hire* 3.304=B 3.256) and corresponds to the theologians' *meritum de condigno* 'reward justly and absolutely merited' (Simpson, ibid. 93–60). But since P. claims to receive *hire* here and now

(193), he must believe not only that virtuous living is rewarded by God but that it brings its own recompense (a peaceful conscience), as well as assurance of divine favour (*paye*). **195** Cf. on 3.306–7; revision removes the (contextually inappropriate) allusion to the Vineyard Parable, where day's end symbolises death.

199–203 199 *mede*: a significant **C** substitution (reinforced at 202) of a dubious for a blameless term (*huyre* **ZAB**), in a field of discourse where even unintended ambiguity carries risks. **200** *bi...soule*: here, as at 4.137 and 8.102 (by contrast with B 6.117, 171), an oath that is thematically significant, not just expressive of anger. **201** *Seynt Thomas shryne*: at this time a veritable treasure-house because of pilgrims' grateful offerings. Abp. Thomas Becket (1120–70), who was murdered in his cathedral of Canterbury on Dec 29 1170, was canonised in Feb 1173, and his relics in the Trinity Chapel became the chief object of pilgrimage in England until the shrine's destruction by Henry VIII in 1538. The humour of P.'s paradoxical asseveration would not have been missed: as in *Pearl*, in the kingdom of *Treuthe*, a transvaluation of values must occur. The sin he here wishes to avoid would count as a form of simony.

204–81 P.'s elaborate 'signpost-allegory' of salvation (Frank 1953:237) conveys through its form a transcendental sense of 'the pilgrimage of human life', since as a 'figure of thought' *allegoria* bespeaks the spiritual dimension of historic existence and its record as narrative. It owes something to the French C13th poet Rutebeuf's *Voie de Paradis*, itself based on a work by Raoul de Houdenc (see Owen 1912, Nolan 1977:124). The somewhat mechanical *procédé* resembles the 'territorial' allegory in 2.88–96 (and similar homiletic expositions by the Minorite in 10.30–55, Conscience in B 14.15–28 and Anima in B 16.4–17); but the speech has didactic lucidity and is evidently grasped by its hearers. 205–30 describe how humility awakens consciousness of the divine imperatives (the Commandments); 231–59*a* how moral reformation in consequence of observing them lays the basis for a life of Christian devotion; 260–81 how, despite temptations to spiritual pride, the efficacious promptings of grace lead the pilgrim through ascetic discipline (the exercise of the virtues) to a state in this life that is a foretaste of beatitude in the life to come.

205–37 205 *Mekenesse*: specially connected with contrition, for which humility is a prerequisite (cf. B 4.142) and which alone earns not only royal 'grace' or favour (B 4.142) but also divine; cf. 'God resisteth the proud and giveth grace to the humble [*humilibus*]' (Js 4:6, I Pet 5:5, both quoting Prov 3:34, which has 'the meek' [*mansuetis*]). **206** *yknowe...sulue*: 'known by / recognised or acknowledged by' better brings out the presumed sense of the rather obscurely expressed B 562 'that Christ [who sees into your conscience] may know the truth

[about your spiritual state]' (for another rendering see Salter 1962:86n). Some allusion to the 'examination of conscience' preparatory to confession may be involved. **207–11** are based on Christ's summary of the two 'great commandments' of the Old Law in Lk 10:27, as given in Deut 6:5 and Lev 19:18 (cf. on 19.14*a*). **208–10** P.'s words paraphrase HC's injunction to Will at 1.140–4 (which she says derives from a *kynde knowyng* and constitutes truth), alluding to the text cited both there and at 6.290*a*. **209b** 'for fear [of some powerful man] or for entreaty'. **210–11a** *apayre / Otherwyse*: elliptical for 'harm / [nor treat] otherwise than'. **212** *brok*: the first watery barrier to be crossed, allegorically from the natural order into that of divine positive law. The b-half is not absolutely clear because elliptical, borrowing its verb from 213: 'until you find a kind of bridge across the brook.' *as it were*: because it is only a ford (a sense of *bridge* obsolete since OE). **ZAB** 'Be submissive (of speech)' may have been replaced because this is not one of the Ten Commandments, though it arises out of the virtue opposed to the root vice and is especially set against the 'inobedience' confessed to by Pride at 6.15–19. **213–15** Figurative 'immersion' in the habit of honouring one's parents is a 'baptism' in natural piety that prepares the individual for a successful and upright life. **L** stresses throughout the importance of early formation and the need for parental discipline, which produce strong limbs for running the race of virtuous living (the unquoted end of the 4th Commandment is relevant here), just as bad parenting does spiritual (and sometimes also bodily) injury to the children (cf. 5.138, 9.169). **215*a*** 'Honour thy father and thy mother, [that thou mayest be *long-lived*] upon the land which the Lord thy God will give thee]' (Ex 20:12). **216–17** This expanded form of the 2nd Commandment (a marker or signpost?) may have suggested to **L** his idiosyncratic device of a *compound personal name* based on a *command-sentence*, such as those later at 8.80ff. The injunction counters a sin to which the drunken Glutton is especially prone (6.425–7), though it comes under anger in *CT* X 587–99). **218–28** The next four 'places' are for avoiding. **219–20** are the 9th and 10th Commandments, directed against Lechery (6.192) and Greed (6.262–4). **220** *pat...*: 'in such a way as to cause them any harm'. **221** *bere nat*: 'anything' understood. *but if...owene*: elliptical for 'nothing'. **223** The 7th and 5th Commandments, especially relevant to Anger (6.107) and Greed (6.265–71). **224** *luft hand*: where the evil-doers are positioned; another echo of HC's words (at 2.5). In Rutebeuf's *Voie* (150–1) the Dreamer is directed to keep the habitation of pride on his left as he proceeds to the House of Confession; and fragment G of the early C14th alliterative *Conflict of Wit and Will* contains the lines: 'Þat bothe leute and loue louies with herte / And *leues on þat lefte hoende* alle lither redes' (ll. 5–6). **226–8** denote the 8th commandment, **229–30** perhaps also the 2nd. *ParsT* places all kinds of 'false swearing' under the sin of anger: 'Thou shalt swere sooth, for every lesynge is agayns Crist; for Crist is verray trouthe' (*CT* X 593). **231** *court...sonne*: envisaged as a fortified manor-house, the brightly shining court perhaps suggested by the Heavenly Jerusalem in Apoc 21:23 (cf. *Pearl* 1049–50). The image recalls the paradisal *tour* in the east of Pr 15 (see Davlin 2001:39–40 and ill. 2.7, from ms CUL Ee.iv.24, f. 35v). It may also owe something to Robert Grosseteste's allegorical poem *Château d'Amour* (Cornelius 1930:589; see *Sk* IV.i.150) and the tradition of interior dwellings represented by the C13th English *Sawles Warde* (on which see Mann 1994:200–03). This 'paradise within' is the state of sanctifying grace, that anticipates *in via* the heavenly condition of beatitude. **232** *mote*: a second watery barrier, suggesting baptism, through which man must pass from the OT domain of Law to the promised land of Grace under the new covenant (of Mercy). **233** *Wyt*: natural reason, here not unaided but informed by the supernatural faith infused through baptism, which enables man to resist the siege of unruly desire (*Wil*). The traditional opposition between these two sides of the human soul appears in *The Conflict of Wit and Will*. **234** *carneles*: the embrasures between the merlions or uprights in a battlement, where the castle's defenders stood. *Cristendom*: baptism in the wider meaning of 'membership of the body of Christ'; not yet clear in the more diffuse **Z**, which may be paraphrased 'The crenellations offer a trustworthy assurance of salvation to the Christian' but somewhat confusingly makes baptism the buttress. *kynde*: '(spiritual) substance', i.e. the soul. **234–5** *saue / ysaued*: identical rhyme drawing out the martial metaphor's secondary spiritual meaning. **235** *Ybotresed*: qualifying *wallyng*, not its immediate antecedent *carneles*. The name of the buttress is the 'right belief' necessary to salvation; alluding to the final words of the Athanasian Creed recited at Prime on Sundays and some feast-days, 'This is the Catholic faith: unless a man *believes* it faithfully, he cannot be *saved*' (*Brev.* II 46–8). This Creed is quoted again in the crucial words of the Pardon at 9.288. **236** *houses*: the many mansions envisaged within this 'inner' replica of the Heavenly City. *yheled*: homophonically punning on *helen* 'heal, make whole', given that 'love *covers* a multitude of sins' (I Pet 4:8, and cf. Ps 31:1, Hope's text at 152*a*), an idea associated with healing of spiritual wounds through *satisfaccion* at B 14.96. **237** *lele*: significantly replacing *lowe* (**AB**) as a mark of the Christian community. Emphasis on trustworthy speech is part of **C**'s robust antipathy to lies and treachery.

Z 66–78 (A 79–82) The original description harked back to the *tour* of ZA Pr 14 /15 and contained interesting (but digressive) topical details. Reduced from 13 to 4 lines, the passage may have been finally deleted because its stress on God's awesome power over the elements (perhaps suggested by Job 37:12) jarred with **L**'s desire to urge the accessibility of divine mercy. Reason's sermon having terrified the Folk into confessing their sins, P.'s task is to *encourage* their first steps towards a life of virtue aided by grace. **66 (79)** takes up Z Pr 103 / A I 12. **67 (80)** *day sterre*: echoing God's question in Job 38:32, with perhaps an allusion to his sovereignty over Lucifer whose name means 'day-star' (see Ps 109:3, Is 14:12 and cf. ZA 1.63/110). **68 L**'s notion of the moon as a mirror reflecting all mankind's thought seems to have no parallel. **69–70** With the linking of word and wind in this passage, cf. Z 5.34–40 above. **69** *word...wind*: a common Biblical image for God's sovereign power. **70** *blowe*: cf. Gen 8:1, Ex 14:21, 15:10. *be stille*: cf. Mk 4:39. *brethy softe*: cf. III Kgs 19:12. **71** *water...gloue*: perhaps echoing Is 40:12. **72** *fuyr...brenne*: the lightning, as in Ex 9:24, IV Kgs 1:10. **73 (A 81)** *Deth*: the opposition of Death to Life (= God) finds expression in the Crucifixion scene at 20.67, the subservience of Death to Kind (also = God) at 22.100ff. **74** *forst*: cf. Job 38:29. **75** *stere steren*: typical homophonic wordplay; *stere* may again, as in 67, allude to Lucifer. *steme*: cf. *CT* I 202. **77–8** *Wyndelesore*: alluding to Edward III's building works at Windsor from 1354 onwards (Walsingham, *Historia Anglicana* i. 288), which involved numerous workmen in 1365 (*R–B*, citing Salzman 1952:60). The master-masons were John Sponlee and (from 1360) William Wynford, pioneers of the Perpendicular style (Harvey 1984:280–1). **78** *spanne*: elliptical for 'a hand's-worth of work equal to it'; comparing earthly, external building with heavenly (and its homologue, interior) 'edification'.

238–59*a* 238 *barres*: either barriers without the gate or bolts to lock it (MED s.v. *barre* n. 1a, 4a); both should 'give way' easily in fraternal welcome. *bretherne of o wombe*: mutual consideration as typified by the (idealised) brotherly love of siblings, an OT norm of loyal affection, becoming in the NT a model of *charitas fraternitatis* (Rom 12:10) for those who through *cristendom* are *blody bretherne...of o body ywonne* (12.111). **239** *brygge*: the draw-bridge of earnest prayer. **240** *piler*: understood by *Bn* as one of the piers of the bridge across the moat (MED s.v. *piler* n. 1.j) or supporting a drawbridge; but the referent seems indeterminable. The later versions interpret the 'supports' of the spiritual life as penance and the intercessory power of the blessed united in purpose with the pilgrim or militant Church. This idea may derive from St Paul's description of 'the *house*...of the living God' as 'the *pillar* and ground of *the truth*' (I Tim 3:15). The earlier versions by contrast imagine the pillars (?supporting the gate-house) as like the Purbeck marble shafts common in early English C14th cathedrals (e.g. Wells or Lincoln), which took a polish. The image could have been dropped simply as repeating earlier

6.328 (= ZA 5.148/250). But although this is an effective symbol-allegory for the spiritual effect of penance on the soul, the reason for rejecting the architectural detail was perhaps its tacitly equating the ark of salvation with the Church as 'material organisation' rather than as 'spiritual organism'. **241** *hokes*: the fixed part of the door-hinge, let into the wall. **246** *parformed...*: reversing Sloth's sorry admission at 14. **247** *Amende-ȝow...Grace*: sanctifying *grace* being given to those who complete their confession by resolving to *amend* and by making due *satisfaction* through penance. P. urges the Folk to show that they have done this, are reconciled with the Church and now able to receive Holy Communion as a sign of it (the 'main' gate of heaven has as its additional immediate referent the door of the tabernacle where the Eucharist is reserved). The domestic *wiket* of the earlier versions, the everyday eating-imagery and the blaming of one or other partner finally disappear in the more solemn and abstract C 248–9. **B 603** *apples vnrosted*: because perfectly ripe, like all the fruit in paradise (labour, including cooking, being commonly seen as a consequence of the Fall). *eten here bane*: the death-bringing effect of the fruit (alluding to Gen 2:17) being reversed only when Christ (the 'Second Adam') comes to *drynken his deth-yuel* (B 18.53) on the cross, which was fabled to be fashioned from the wood of the Tree of Life. Paradise is here traditionally conceived as a walled garden with a wicket gate, a small gate in a larger one or a wall, like that in *CT* IV 2029–47 (see the 'Fall of Man' in the *Très Riches Heures du Duc de Berry* and Bosch's *Haywain* triptych). No *re*-admission is possible after the expulsion of Adam and Eve, who were condemned to die without hope; what the Redemption wins is the offer of entry into heaven. Mention of Eve (in the Latin) is thus due not to residual anti-feminism but to her theological significance as a type of Mary in the history of salvation. **249a** 'Through Eve [the gate of paradise] was closed to all, and through the Virgin Mary it was opened once again'; from the Antiphon of Our Lady sung at Lauds from the Monday within the Octave of Easter to the Vigil of the Ascension (*Bn*); see *Brev.* 1:dccclxx) As Eve's disobedience 'closed' heaven's gate to mankind, Mary's obedience to God's Word figuratively 'opens' it. But in patristic commentary on the sanctuary gate in Ezech 44:2 and the gate of justice in Ps 117:19 (*Pe*), the BVM was also herself figured as the *caeli porta* through which man might enter heaven and as the *regis alti ianua* 'gate of the high king' through which the Word entered the world (see the Candlemas and Assumption hymns 'Ave maris stella' and 'O gloriosa Domina' cited by *Sk*). **250–51** *leel lady*: the Virgin, 'who believed in the Lord' (responsory at Vespers of the Assumption). *vnlek...keye... clycat*: metonymic for the power to forgive sin, and usually associated with St Peter, but here emblematising the capacity to unlock the door of sanctification, and so effec-

tively making Mary co-redemptrix (cf. *vitam datam per virginem* in 'O gloriosa Domina'). *of grace*: 'by means of the grace [granted to her by God] / through her gracious kindness'; being herself 'full of grace' (Lk 1:28), she has been empowered to impart divine help and favour. **251** *keye*: found by *Bn* to recall David's in the Advent Vespers Antiphon for Dec. 20 'O clavis David' based on Is 22:22; here signifying Christ, whom the Virgin 'has' as her child. *thow...slepe*: the gloss 'i.e. in her womb' (*Pe*, following *Bn*'s 'felicitous reference to the immaculate conception') is not very apt, given the concessive *thow* 'even if'. The image suggests rather a noble chatelaine with full authority to admit or refuse entry to callers while her lord is resting. Technically speaking, Mary's intercessory (unlike her co-redemptive) power only becomes fully *active* after her assumption into glory. **254** The phrasing recalls St Augustine's 'in interiore animae habitat veritas' (cit. Spitzer, 1944:38), a figure echoed in *MS* 1225a 'in corde fidelis est habitacio veritatis', and there ascribed to *holy writte* (presumably in **L**'s sense of a patristic source). The basic theological idea is of the indwelling of the 'spirit of truth...[who] shall abide with you and shall be in you' (Jn 14:17) through *grace*, which **L** later employs as his 'nature-name' for the Third Person of the Trinity (21.214). *herte*: the centre of supernatural as of natural life because the seat of *Anima* 'soul' (cf. 10.175). **255–9a** 'Truth' is the subject of the three verbs in 255–6; and though 256 echoes B 607, 259 is closer in thought to A 97. All versions describe how Truth leads to Love, and knowledge of God's nature to ever more perfect performance of his will (growth in holiness). In **ZA** Truth teaches a law, in **B** unveils a vision, in **C** 'edifies' a habitation that becomes spiritually efficacious for others, a progression adumbrating the Dowel-Dobet-Dobest triad to come. **B 607–8** *cheyne of charite*: alluding to *charitatem...vinculum perfectionis* 'charity, the bond of perfection' (Col 3:14), an image that implies in context 'loving servitude' and 'love that binds [Christians together]' rather than a 'chain of office' (*Bn*). The actual phrase *vincula charitatis* occurs in the pseudo-Bernardine *Vitis Mystica* (*PL* 184:67), a work **L** seems to have known. *child*: an emblem of the simplicity and humility needed to enter the kingdom of heaven (Mt 18:3); cf. *Pearl* 721–2 and B 15.216 (*Bn*). 608 seems to *Bn* to 'make little sense in the context,' but the idea denoted is quite appropriately that of the complete obedience shown by Christ. *sires wille*: the Father's will, a main theme of St John's Gospel. **255** *payne*: not necessarily purgatory, since indwelling 'truth' helps the faithful believer to endure injustice and adversity here ('suffer' as God does). **256** *churche to make*: this virtue fashions an 'interior' equivalent of the visible Church whose exterior realisation in stone was itself commonly seen as an image of the Heavenly Jerusalem (Von Simson 1955:8–10); cf. I Cor 8:1: *charitas vero* *aedificat.* The symbolism, 'monastic' in flavour, reflects **L**'s sacramental view of a macrocosmic and microcosmic 'correspondence' between earthly and heavenly domains. **257–8** *hole*: playing on the senses 'healed', 'made whole' and 'sincere'; cf. *veritate et corde perfecto* 'truth and perfect heart' (Is 38:3). *herborwe; fynde*: perhaps denoting the contemplatives' intercessory prayer for the spiritual good of the faithful. **259** This triad seems an enigmatic periphrasis for the theological virtues in inverse order (charity, hope, faith). **259a** '(Whatever you ask in my name), (it shall be given to you)', a text conflating Jn 14:13 and Mt 7:7 (Alf*Q*).

260–8 warn against the spiritual pride (262) that menaces those whose advance in virtue makes them aware of others' relative sinfulness: a 'higher' (but deadlier) mutation of the vice described at 6.36–40. As these temptations incident to the spiritual life are treated not in penitential treatises but in ascetic writings such as *Ancrene Wisse*, P.'s awareness of them indicates the level of his religious maturity. **260** *Wrath-the*: 'Get(ting)-angry', i.e. 'pharisaic' resentment at one's neighbour's failings. In positive form, this command-name is syntactically clearer than the negative in **ZA**. **261a** anticipates the devil's siege of the soul at 10.134–5. **263** *boldnesse...beenfetes*: 'over-confidence in your own virtuous acts'. **264** *as dewe*: 'like dew in the sun', a typically vivid analogy (like the icicles at 19.194–5), but with a witty homophonic pun on 'as due'. **266** *hundret wynter*: 'a very long time (in purgatory)'; the heavy punishment for spiritual pride. **267** *to lete*: 'by thinking'; on this adverbial infinitive of cause see *MES* 536. **Z 101** may signify specifically the sin of Lust of the Eyes (one of Fortune's companions described in 11.175ff); or *wenche* may be used to draw an analogy with Eve (so called at Z 88) who tempted Adam *to lete wele by hymsulue*, whereby 'they lost [God's] love'. **268** *gifte*: some good deed(s) of the sinner, paradoxically imagined as like a 'bribe' to win God's favour (cf. 4.138). P. sees none such as possible and stresses the sovereign importance of grace at every stage of salvation, a teaching of St Augustine (as *Pe* notes) re-affirmed forcibly by Bradwardine against the so-called 'Pelagian' theologians in the 1340s. However, the assertion that after falling into grave sin one can regain God's favour only through a 'prevenient' grace that moves the will to repentance was not a distinctive tenet of Bradwardine's but the 'mainstream' teaching of Aquinas that became standard doctrine in the West.

269–81 269 *seuene sustres*: the seven Christian virtues developed in the soul through sacramental grace; customarily set as contraries to (and 'remedies' for) the seven capital sins. Distinct from the 'seven' composed of the four cardinal and three theological virtues, in this penitential context they are coherently opposed (as in *ParsT*) to the deadly sins treated in the Confessions: abstinence against gluttony; humility: pride; charity: envy; patience:

anger; chastity: lechery; generosity: greed (*CT* X 831, 475, 514, 658, 914, 810). The odd maiden out is Peace (*Pe*) unless, as the inner tranquillity that can counter sloth's 'angwissh of troubled herte' (*CT* X 676), she is to be equated with the 'seurtee or sikernesse...that...ne douteth no travaile...of the goode werkes that a man hath bigonne' (id. 734), i.e. the energetic diligence associated with sloth's usual remedy, fortitude. There is some overlap also with the twelve 'fruits of the [Holy] Spirit' (Gal 5:22–3), namely in the virtues of charity, peace, patience, kindness and chastity produced by the operation of sanctifying grace. The helpful maiden Peace returns as one of the 'Daughters of God' in 20.170ff, and an avatar of her companion Patience is the major (male) protagonist in Passus 15. (On possible influence from Grosseteste, see *Sk* IV i.152). **270** *porteres...*: for an illustration of these maidens defending a castle against the vices see Saxl 1942:104 (*Pe*). **274** *Largenesse*: specifically charitable giving, which was regarded as of great spiritual benefit. **275** The revision removes the (doubtless unintended) suggestion of possible release from hell, where *nulla est redempcio* (20.151a). **B 624** presumably refers to purgatory, or to the state of mortal sin, an interior constriction corresponding to the devil's 'pen'. **276** She ransoms and redeems souls suffering agony in purgatory, though the referent may properly include those wounded in the battle against sin while still *in via* who benefit from the intercessory prayer of the virtuous (cf. on 255–9). The line echoes in ironical answer Mede's dubious interventions at 3.173. **277** *sib*: a poetic figure of the individual's spiritual condition (like that of *aunte* at 6.329, 439); but at a deeper theological level, the 'relational' image intimates membership of the Communion of Saints, to which all in a state of grace are privileged to belong. **279 (B 627)** The revision eases the metre, perhaps to avoid ambiguously implying that possession of some virtue(s) cancels out one's remaining vice(s). For whereas 269–76 seem to envisage *each* virtue as able to secure a person's admission to heaven (e.g. 274), 279 requires 'relatedness' to them all, i.e. a completely sin-free state (cf. *eny gate* 281). The consistent position in *PP* is that any capital sin, if allowed to prevail, brings damnation (Js 2:10; see 13.121a). **280** P.'s asseveration recalls that of the King troubled by the difficulty of reforming society (4.177). *eny of ʒow*: '(for) any of you'; omission of 'inorganic' *for* (see *MES* 383–4) suggests that the phrase is being treated as a 'dative of person' (cf. *MES* 433–6).

(vi) 282–307 282–4 *cottepurs; hapeward; wafrestere*: professional thief and low entertainers. **284** *Wyte God*: 'May God know' = 'I'd have God know'. The female *wafrestere* (to judge by *CT* VI 479) may be assumed to sell not only cakes. **285** *frere prechynge*: an oblique tribute to the persuasive eloquence of the mendicants, renowned as outdoor preachers able to reach even those who never entered a church. **286** *3us*: 'On the contrary, you can!' **287** *Mercy*: a 'moat' at 232, but now personified and equated with Mary 'mother of mercy' (Office Hymn of the BVM). *myhte*: as chief intercessor before the throne of Christ at all times. **288** *syb...bothe*: through their identification (though sinless) with sinful humanity (cf. II Cor 5:21). **289b** 'Do not expect there is any other / it to be otherwise'. **290** *go bytyme*: i.e. not delay confession till the last moment, when the grace of repentance may not be offered. The Parable of the Supper warns against giving earthly concerns like possessions, work, or personal relationships priority over the demands of the Gospel. It replaces at a more plausibly 'average' level the (no doubt expected) refusals in B 639–42 of the Pardoner (afraid of having his credentials questioned) and the prostitute his companion. **B 640** *fecche my box*: presumably in order to get about his usual business, not use them as 'gifts' (cf. on 268 above) to bribe Truth's door-keepers. **291** scans on vowels or on *m* with liaised macaronic stave. *villam emi*: 'I have bought a farm [and I must needs go out and see it. I pray thee, hold me excused]' (Lk 14:18); rejecting P.'s invitation to a more active devotional life following the forgiveness of sins. **294** *falewe...*: cf. Lk 14:19. **298** *Actyf*: a personification of the practical life, destined to replace the B-Text's deplorable Haukyn in C XV, with most of his predecessor's viciousness having been peeled away in order to expand the portraits of the Deadly Sins depicted in C VI–VII. *hosbonde*: 'married man' (cf. the different sense at A 11.183, which this line recalls). Despite the appearance of 'Contemplation' at 304, 'Active' does not simply represent the 'active Christian life' of which Martha (Lk 10:41–2) was the traditional exemplar so much as 'the common body of sinning humanity' (*Pe*). **299** *wantowen*: glossed by MED s.v. *wantoun* a. as 'lascivious', doubtless in the light of the **p** variant *synnen*. But though possible here, the conjunction with *maneres* suggests that the sense 'self-willed', 'lacking self-discipline' is as apt (ibid. a, b), and the *maneres* pertain to her possessiveness. **303** *Kitte*: diminutive of Katherine, with contemporary overtones of lasciviousness (cf. Present-Day English 'moll'), as suggested by MED's quotation under *Kitte* n. (2) from *Beryn* 66: 'Goddis blessing have þow, Kitt! Now broke wel thy name!' **303a** '[And another said]: I have married a wife; and therefore I cannot come' (Lk 14:20). This text was often interpreted allegorically as signifying attachment to the pleasures of the flesh; but L's rueful use of a name presumably to be recalled as that of Will's wife in B 20.193–8 implies rather that the married state must inevitably hinder single-minded cultivation of the spiritual life (cf. I Cor 7:27–34). **304** *Contemplacioun*: personifying in passing the same aspiration to ascetic devotion later found in PATIENCE, whose words at B 13.159ff are echoed in 304b–05a. The present juxtaposition with Actyf anticipates the encounter of those characters in 15.191ff.

Passus VIII (ZA VII, B VI)

PASSUS EIGHT, dealing with the ploughing of the 'Half-Acre', is a complete allegorical action, but minutely 'realistic' in its social detail. It shows the least alteration from **Z** to **C** of any passus, chiefly **A**'s omission of **Z**'s six elaborating lines 196–201 and 20-line attack on false *leches* and **C**'s extensions on beggars; major revision and expansion begin again only with C IX. One immediate change is the opening with Piers's reply to Contemplation's remark on the difficulty of reaching Truth without a guide, which in all but **C** begins the passus, in **ZAB** with no ascribed speaker. The **C** form better prepares to focus on the character and actions of PIERS, who dominates VIII, and this links it more closely with C VII. The initial change is matched by a cryptic addition at the end in both **B** and **C** illustrating the longer versions' increased complexity. The passus divides into three sections and an epilogue: (i) 1–111 on P.'s organisation of the ploughing; (ii) 112–66 on his difficulties with those who will not work; (iii) the Hunger episode (167–341) forming the core of the passus; and the short 'prophetic' conclusion 342–53.

(i) 1–111. 1–55 *Piers's dialogue with representatives of the gentry* enables him to act as spokesman for the duties of all members of society. **1** *Perkyn*: a diminutive of Piers (cf. *Watekyn* 6.70). *Petur*: P.'s asseveration recalling 7.181 points to the faithful and impulsive ploughman's relationship with his name-saint the chief apostle, whose rôle is to feed the sheep of Christ (Jn 21:15–17; see the illuminating discussion in Burrow 1993[1]:77–80, 119–22). **2** *half aker*: the average area (2420 sq. yds) of a strip in the open-field system of farming (*Pe*); the minimum needed to sustain one household. P.'s authoritative status makes it doubtful whether this signifies his entire holding, so the size may be symbolic, with the 'typical' half-acre field (commonly understood as 16 furrows each of a furlong-length) a microcosm of this world and P. standing for the ploughmen of Pr 22–4, 145 (*Bn*). The usual peasant-holding for someone like Piers would be about fifteen acres (Dyer 1994:161). *heye weye*: a position indicating P.'s closeness to the folk as they 'bluster' down the pilgrim-routes that ran alongside such fields. A real ploughman could have gone (like Chaucer's in the *GP*) to Canterbury or Walsingham after completing the annual sowing. But (as *Bn* notes) P. puts his vocation to provide food before his avocation to guide others, his own example of 'pilgrimage' being to remain in his calling and discharge it faithfully. **4** *way*: the spiritual 'way' to Truth that P. described in 7.205ff; a well-established scriptural figure of the Christian life, e.g. *viam Dei in veritate* (Mt 22:16) and *via veritatis / iustitiae* (II Pet 2:2, 21). **5** *lady*: perhaps the *wyf* (55) of the knight who speaks at 19. *sclayre*: a veil covering the head, lower cheeks and chin, worn by women of rank (Poole 1958: pl. 108, Baker 1978: pls. 38, 45). **7** *ladyes*: i.e. all the women present; slightly confusing in **C**, since the task in 8 was not for the *worthily wommen* (9), whose long fingers would work with finer stuffs, but for the ordinary *wyues and wyddewes* (12). As spinning was a task of women below the gentry class, the sack-sowing is presumably intended for them. **10** *on*: 'on a ground of' or 'with (thread)'. **11** *Chesibles*: ornamental embroidery for vestments that showed off the skill for which English needlework or *opus anglicanum* was renowned (see the 'orphrey' in Poole pl. 107a; Christie 1938). **12** *Wyues*: in parallel with *men* at 17. **13** *Consience conseyleth*: a change from divine command at B 16 (alluding to Mt 25:36) to interior counsel that is as noteworthy as the less utilitarian tone, P. becoming a means to persuade rather than admonish the knightly class. **15–16** P.'s promise to go on ploughing makes it unlikely that he should later intend wholly to 'give up' the active for a contemplative life at B 7.118–30 // (lines significantly cut in **C**); at this stage the work he stresses is mainly physical. *for...heuene*: the polysemy allowing both an asseveration and the reason for his labour; not only 'out of love for God' but 'in order to win God's love' (cf. A 3.223, which further signifies 'because of the love God has for them'). **17** *molde*: taking up *lond* 15; presumably all work other than husbandry is implied. **19** *knyhte*: the political rôle of knights having already been treated in Pr 139–43, this section explores their part in keeping order in rural society as local Justices of the Peace. **20** *teme*: a homophonic pun on *teme* MED n. 1 (f) 'team of draught animals' and n. 2 'theme' or 'topic' (of ploughing). **22** *for...were*: 'as a kind of relaxation, so to speak' (cf. B 12.22). **C** improves on its somewhat quixotic predecessors, the knight's light but friendly tone affirming solidarity rather than an unrealistic reversal of functional rôles. **23–4** firmly repudiate any notion (such as the 1381 rebels proclaimed) of replacing the traditional social orders with a single class of 'commons' under the king. **25** *tho thow louest*: P's warm support of the knight's position (going beyond a tenant farmer's obligation to his landlord) and his use of 'thou' here imply a relation of loyal trust rather than a claim to equality (P. shifts to the expected 'you' at 35ff). **26–31** P.'s 'condition' is that the knightly (first) estate should protect the clerical (second) and labouring (third) estate against those who prey parasitically on society and against the 'natural' threats to the food-supply all need. **27** echoes Pr 24, where the labourers' vulnerability is heightened by the lack of reference to the knightly class. *wastores*: with precise referent not clear, but including those who refuse to belong to any of the functional groups recognised since Anglo-Saxon times. **28** *hares*; *foxes*: beasts of the 'warren' (tracts of land set aside for small game), which only manorial lords could

hunt. **29** *bore*; *bokkes*: beasts of the forest, which peasants were nonetheless permitted to hunt over warren (Bennett 1937:64). *myn hegges*: dividing his strip from his neighbour's and from the road. That they are 'his' indicates his status as a self-sufficient peasant tenant (see Lister 1982; Dyer 1994). **31** *diffoule*: the revision introducing a wry pun on *foules* 30. **33** *treuthe*: a very solemn word from a knight, whose duty HC specifies as *to fyghte and fende treuthe* (1.99), and to be taken as binding (cf. *CT* V 1479). **34** This line's evolution is noteworthy, **C** retaining **B**'s b-half, **B** and **A** only the a-half of their immediate predecessor. **35–55** This striking account of ideal knightly conduct bespeaks special authority in P. as Truth's servant rather than merely as a 'representative' of the third estate. **36–7** *tene...mersyen*: homophonic and semantic word-play (only the second pair are etymologically connected) indicating a lively awareness of the 'Platonic' power of verbal forms (Schmidt 1987:130–1). P. presumably does not mean that God *would* approve of causing deliberate distress to one's tenants. But as distress might indeed result from lawful impositions (*Bn*) like *tallage* (an arbitrary rate of rent), *heriot* (a customary claim on the best chattel of a deceased tenant) and *amerciaments* (discretionary fines), it is these that the knight is being urged to use with restraint. **39–40** P.'s advice accords with his own conduct at 7.200–3. **B 43** *one yeres ende*: taken by *Bn* as 'the end of one year or another, sooner or later'; but likening the privilege of rank during one's earthly life to a lease with a fixed date of *one* year is more telling. However, **C**'s motive for revision to a milder (and more intelligible) warning may have been not just the figure's lack of obviousness but the ambiguity of *perilous* B 44; for the **B** line confusingly echoes B 2.105, where the reference is to hell (and this too is deleted in **C**). **44a** 'Friend, go up higher' (Lk 14:10). The parable of the supper warns against all presumption, but here P. sees Christian humility as countering specifically pride that may arise from superior rank. The words are in Lk addressed to the humble man who has taken the lower place, and may elliptically be applied to the knight; but in the immediate context they appear to complete 44 and be addressed rather to the serf. This text's relevance to the feudal relation, though oblique, becomes more exact if read in the light of Js 2:6, which warns against oppressing the poor by force or law (see on 54), and more generally of Js 1:9–11. **45** *charnel*: the vault under the church for storing bones unearthed when the graveyard was dug over for new burials. Surviving charnel-houses are noted in Cook 1954:129–30. **46** *quene / queene*: a strong **B** addition further improved in **C** by arresting play on two words that differ in the sound-quality of the vowels but when written are as hard to tell apart in appearance as are royal bones from a commoner's (Schmidt 1987:113–4). The theme of Death the Leveller is a late-medieval literary commonplace, and this image, which goes back to St Ambrose, was widely used in preaching of the period (Fletcher 1993:350–4). **47** *corteys*: a significant addition (cf. 32) that softens the earlier text's austerity, suggesting fresh appreciation (in the wake of 1381) of how the common people were alienated by the nobility's purely authoritarian stance. A gentle and unassertive address was regarded by writers on chivalry as a feature of ideal knighthood (see *CT* I 46, 68–71 and Keen 1984:1–7). **48** *tales*: those recommended in **C** realistically including chivalric as well as didactic works. **51** On possible solutions to the line's metrical problem see *TN*. *suche men*: the 'japers' or 'false minstrels' attacked in Pr 35–40 (see Schmidt 1987:8–11); that P.'s opinion is the narrator's seems clear from comparison with 7.93–5, B 13.416–8. **Z 49** *messageres*: the contextual collocation implying the sense 'one who brings tidings in the form of an entertaining ballad' (MED s.v. *message* n. 1(a)). **53** This important addition, echoing the added Pr 138, may carry a generalised warning to members of the knightly class whose support for heterodox critics of the Church like Wyclif might have been read as weakening social and ecclesial order. **54** *Y assente*: representing the Knight's acceptance of P.'s 'prophetic' authority, in contrast with the disdainful attitude of the priest at B 7.131–2 (significantly deleted in **C**). *Gyle*: the C7th hermit-contemplative (*Egidie* 17.9), buried at St Gilles in S France; a popular saint in medieval England. His replacement of St James, the spokesman of '*doing well*' (cf. 1.180–2) who was appropriate to one thinking of pilgrimage (*Bn*), may intimate the knight's approval (like Conscience's for Patience at 15.184–5) of the ascetic simplicity that P. espouses. **55** *my wyf*: see on 5.

56–83 56b echoes 7.160 in its ostensive re-definition through a 'prophetic' donning of working-gear instead of the expected garb (scrip and staff) that symbolically enacts his rejection of conventional pilgrimage. On contemporary tensions between ideas of 'place pilgrimage' and 'life pilgrimage' see Dyas 2001:145–70. **58** *of*: 'pertaining to'. **59** *cokeres*: 'old stockings without feet, worn as gaiters' (*Sk*). *Kynde Wit*: echoing P.'s own claim at 7.183 that KW was his teacher. **Z 54** *clumse*: an adjective of probably Norse origin (OED s.v. *clumse* a.) related to the verb *clomsen*; the only known medieval instance, overlooked by MED. On this use of causal *for* with a semisubstantivised adj. see *MES* 381–2. **61** *buschel*: 8 gallons dry measure (enough to sow a half-acre), which could be carried in a wide shallow basket. *breed corn*: to be ground as bread-meal (for making 'whole-grain' loaves); here used as seed-corn. **62–3** *sethe...doen*: although in principle not necessarily meant ironically (i.e. 'if I do this, I *won't* then need to do *as palmeres doen*': see on 2), the new idea introduced in **B** that a life of *trewe* labour in the community suffices for salvation would preclude the need for literal pilgrimage. **64–5** are brought forward tell-

ingly from their position at B 103–4 // ZA (the end of P.'s speech) to complete the pilgrim-analogy. **64** *plouh-pote*: a stick with a pointed or forked end (Hassall 1954:fol. 6) used to clear the ground. Resembling the pilgrim's staff, it emblematises P.'s intent to 'guide' his fellow 'pilgrims' on the field by labouring in his calling. **65** *clanse*: clear of obstructions (see *TN*); the first recorded use with this referent. **66** *alle*: perhaps implying collective efforts on the common fields (Bennett 1937:44) or generally referring to those working the land. **67** *glene*: a revision eliminating the unintended ambiguity of *lesen* (MED s.v. 1, with which contrast senses 2 and 4). **68** *mery*: in the harvest feasting. **69** *crafty men*: the other main sector of the third estate (mainly in towns), skilled makers of specialised goods useful to all, for whom the special import of *treuthe* would be 'keeping to the standards laid down by the guilds'. **71–9** This added list of those excepted from sharing in the harvest seems meant to modify **Z**'s simple account of the well-integrated rural economy. The low characters enumerated ply their 'crafts of folly' (Owst 1961:371) typically in or around taverns like that described in 6.360ff or *CT* VI 465ff. **71** *iugelour*: 'Gesticulator...vbi harlott' (MED s.v. n. 1b, citing *Catholicon Anglicum* 68a). *Ionet...Stuyues*: possibly a stock name, since it recurs (once) in *Towneley Plays* 378/350; located in Southwark (home of 'Dame Emme'), outside the limits of the City's jurisdiction. The name is pronounced |sty:vəz| in **C** at least (MED s.v. *stive* n. 1) and refers to the small closets, heated by warm-air ducts, where the prostitutes met their clients. **73** P.'s hostility is ostensibly confined to *deceiving* friars, but the ambiguous breadth of *þat ordre* cannot be unintended, since no good is said of the mendicants anywhere in the poem. **74** The forceful added line illustrates polysemy without ambiguity in the normal sense. *lollares and loseles*: a coupling found in Clanvowe's *The Two Ways* (ed. Scattergood 1975:70). **75** *roust*: having a corrosive effect on the soul, 'rust' being a traditional homiletic image of sin (quots. in MED s.v. (d)). **76** *tolde me*: i.e. in the various scriptural texts echoed by this passage, which P. takes as a commission to 'prophetic' utterance. **77, 78a** 'Let them be blotted out of the book of the living: and with the just let them not be written' (Ps 68:29). The quoted text is correct in **A** but the **BC** modification integrating it more closely with 78 causes a lack of grammatical fit, as it needs an indicative mood for the verb after *Quia* (i.e. *scribuntur*) and is thus untranslatable. The psalm-text recalls Ex 32:32–3, and its eschatological overtones are clear from the use of the same image elsewhere, in Dan 7:10 and esp. Apoc 3:5 *non delebo nomen eius de libro vitae* (the 'book' holding the names of those who will be saved). P. seems to deny these characters the fruits of his labour because he finds their way of life incompatible with salvation. *dele*: the witty translinguistic pun generated from the Latin *del-*, *de l-* adding a 'Platonic' reason for avoiding the vicious to the Biblical authority of such texts as II Tim 2:15–17. **78** It was forbidden to accept tithe on immoral earnings (cf. 6.304–5). The 'just' to be rewarded at the Last Judgement are here associated with those who faithfully pay tithes (*Sk*; cf. 101). **79** *áscaped*: so stressed for the vocalic alliteration. *Bn* sees a reference back to the characters who disappeared from the scene at B 5.639–42; but *Sk*, following Whitaker, understands 'luckily escaped payment [*sc.* of tithes]', although 'it puts them in peril of their souls' (*Pe*). This is preferable, for the lines are dropped in **C** (which *cannot* therefore refer back to them) and P. does not name pardoners. The sense would appear to be: 'They (can count themselves lucky to) have got away with no heavier punishment (so far). May they find grace to repent (and live honestly, so as to be able to pay the tithes they owe and so be "written with the just")'. **80–3** P.'s family have allegorical nature-names rather than type-names like the bad characters just mentioned, the main change being his son's from **Z → A**. **80** *Worch...*: 'Act when the time is right to do so' and (alluding to Gal 6:10) 'Work while you have time to do so', both signifying 'Prudence'. **81** *Do...*: 'Disciplined obedience.' **82** *Suffre...*: 'Submission to authority'.

Z 64–8 This five-line injunction to industry and honesty has **L**'s stylistic 'fingerprint': no other poet produces alliterating 'name-lines' (though **C** improves by reducing the name to two lines). **Z 67** is recalled at 22.263, **68** at B 13.229a=C 15.204a. **68** *me*: either 'me' or 'people'.

84–91 incorporate at 86 the **AB** line 74 (82) omitted from the name, signifying 'Leave everything in God's hands as Scripture teaches'. Its new position slants P.'s admonition politically, perhaps associating his son with the younger generation of peasants who might have been among those most active in the uprising of 1381. The speech, which uses vocabulary close to Conscience's in Pr 95–127 and skilfully balances obedience to the king's authority with refusal to take the government and judiciary (who exercise it) at their own valuation, indicates P.'s moral standing, partly as for the poet's 'choric' mouthpiece. **86a; 90a** '[The scribes and the pharisees] have sitten on the chair of Moses. All things whatsoever they shall say to you, observe and do]: but according to their works do ye not. [For they say, and do not]' (Mt 23:2–3). This recurs in a similar context at 11.238a. **89** Strictly *hem* should be *hit* if *al* is sg., but if it = *alle* 'all things', then *hem* is acceptable. More probably, however, this is an elliptical construction: 'All they command you, allow them to (command you)'.

92–111 Despite the surface sense of **92–4**, reference to P.'s words at 64–5 suggests that he plans semi-retirement, not the complete 'rejection' of an active for a contemplative existence. **92** *myn owene*: enough saved through his lifetime's work to buy him food when he cannot grow his own. This indicates (contrary to what 303 would imply) that P. is not strictly a 'subsistence' farmer but has more than one strip to his holding. **94** *do wryte*: P.'s formal illiteracy requiring dictation of his will, in accord with his outward condition as an uneducated peasant. This fails to be at odds with his easy use of Latin scriptural quotations only because that is a purely symbolic device betokening *inward* closeness to the Gospel word. *biqueste*: on P.'s will see Perrow 1914:711–12, Bishop 1996:23–41. **95** 'In the name of God. Amen'; the standard formula for making a will. This was an act usual before setting out on pilgrimage, in case one never returned (*Bn*), but here signifies P.'s self-preparation for death. *I...mysulue*: declaring his will directly, not by proxy, and bequeathing (in order of importance) his soul, body and possessions. **96–9** reflect the common testamentary formula 'First, I bequeath my soul to God my creator' (*Bn*); but the language used is that of the feudal relation. P. returns what his 'lord' gave for the term of his life and trusts that at the individual judgement God will find his account in balance, his good deeds having discharged the penance due for his sins. **96** now scans better than **ZAB**, whether on vowels or on *sh / s*. **98** *crede*: neither the Nicene nor the Apostles' Creed, which do not refer to the individual judgement (at death). The allusion here may be to their mention of Christ as judge of living and dead on doomsday, and to the Paternoster's final petition. **99** *rental*: the record or register of rent due from tenant to landlord; here a figure for the creed, the last clause of which speaks of the eternal life promised to the just. Accompanying the stress on faith is P.'s trust that his good works will support his claim to salvation (cf. Js 2:22–6). Those in question here concern 'observance of the law', but 7.255–9a have shown the C-Text P.'s awareness of the greater demands of charity. **100** He will be buried in the churchyard and later his bones will be kept in the ossuary. *kyrke*: metonymic for the priest. **101** The greater or 'predial' tithe levied on the increase on grain-crops was given to the rector who, if not himself the incumbent, would give the latter a portion of it, or a stipend. The lesser tithe on the 'mixed' profits from livestock and on 'personal' profits from craft or trade went to the parish priest, even if only a vicar. The tithes on crops and animals were paid gross, those on craft and trade, net. *corn and catel*: probably referring to both tithes, *catel* here meaning '(income from) personal property or goods'. **102** *prestly*: like Truth (7.194), whose servant he is, and from whom he now expects final repayment. **103–4** *holdyng*: on this passive use of the present participle see *MES* 548. *masse...memorie*: the commemorative prayers (*Memento*) in the Canon of the Mass, perhaps those for the dead after the Consecration (*Bn*), and also those for the living before it, in which P. expects to be remembered by name. **105** *no more*: not implying that there *was* any more he had 'won' wrongfully. **106** *douhteres...childres*: on the authenticity of this unexpected collocation see *TN*. **107** *dette*: settlement of debts in making a will being imperative, failure to do so was regarded as a sin for which the debtor's soul would have to pay in purgatory. **108** *borwed...to bedde*: taken by *Bn* as alluding to Deut 20:10–13, though in fact that text enjoins a *lender* not to retain overnight a poor man's pledge (e.g. his cloak) against something he has borrowed and not yet repaid. The passage figuratively presents P. as free of all obligations and ready to leave this life with a clear conscience, his scrupulousness recalling his master Truth's at 7.195, and contrasting with the conduct of Wrong at 4.56. **109** uses a line that has already appeared at B 5.460, and is deleted in **C** at that point. *resdue... remenant*: the third portion of the net estate remaining after the widow had received one third and divided a second amongst the children. *Bn* sees this as 'equivalent' to 'the dead's part', which would cover overdue tithes and commemorative services or alms as specified by the testator. But P. must obviously be speaking metaphorically (cf. *pilgrym at þe plouh*); so *his* benefit from 'the dead's part' is to become 'dead to the world', by living more abstemiously and working for his neighbours. *Rode of Lukes*: a celebrated C8th wooden image of the crowned Christ on the cross in the cathedral at Lucca in N Italy; an unlikely object of pilgrimage for P. himself. **111** *pore and ryche*: the revision bringing out P.'s rôle of provider for all rather than 'champion of the poor' as in **B**, where 'the traditional bequest to the poor is transmuted into his labours for them' (*Bn*).

(ii) 112–66 offer a realistic description of contemporary agricultural practice. **112** *plouh*: literal, but also emblematic of *trewe* labours in the world (Lk 9:62). **114** *balkes*: the smaller ridges (produced by earth thrown up in ploughing, and now overgrown with weeds) rather than the wider unploughed strips dividing groups of furrows (see MED s.v. *balke* n. 2a and Poole 1958: I, fig. 2, pl. 1). **115** *apayed...payed*: typically 'Platonic' wordplay, 'satisfaction' and 'reward' being seen as reciprocal. **119** *hey prime*: the first break for refreshment, between dawn and noon. **120** P. stops either to supervise or to inspect their work, like a reeve (as he is later made in 21.259). **121** *huyred þeraftur*: 'paid accordingly'. **122** *ale*: usual at breakfast, often sweetened with honey. Ploughmen's food for the day was typically a loaf and a gallon of ale; but excess at mid-morning could make them like the gluttons at 6.395–6 (the ill-effects of over-drinking during the working-day have been warned against at B 1.25–6). **123** *trollilolly*: a refrain derived from *trollen* (MED s.v. v. 1 'rock', a word also first found in **L** with different sense at 20.332) and *lullai*; but it may be a meaningless cry of gaiety like modern echoic *tra la la*. The song recalls that of the bad workmen in Pr 225. **124** *in puyre tene*: an important revision in **B**, removing the unfortunate over-

tones of **ZA** *wrathe*. The phrase recurs at B 7.115, 16.86, with the effect of a *leitmotiv* in that version, and seems to denote the *ira per zelum* 'righteous anger' described in Gregory's *Moralia* (*PL* 75:726) and shown by Christ himself (*ST* II 2.158:2; III 15:9). But P.'s tendency to become quickly vexed (which associates him with Biblical personages like Moses and Peter) is almost eliminated in **C**. **127b** 'The devil take anyone who should care'; an execration paralleled in *PTA* 447. **129** *leiden...alery*: of uncertain origin, *alery* being possibly a cant word. The gloss 'acted as if paralysed' offered doubtfully in MED s.v. *aliri* cites the etymology proposed by Dobson 1947–8: 60 (OE *lima lyre* 'loss of [the use of] limbs'). But the explanation in Colledge 1957:111–13 convincingly shows (with the help of an illustration of a beggar from Bruegel's 'Fight between Carnival and Lent') that 'The object of the [*PP* beggars'] trick is to counterfeit a crippled or maimed appearance'. They do so not by sitting 'with the calf of one leg resting on the shin of the other' (*SkGl*) but by standing 'with the calf against the back of the thigh, so that it appears to be cut off' (*Bn*). This interpretation is supported by 135a and in turn supports *Sk*'s derivation of *alery* from OE *lira* 'fleshy part of the calf / thigh'. **135** *Lord...thonketh*: the humour of their hypocritical embrace of misfortune heightened by its deferral, the revised form suggesting that *lord...ye* in **ZAB** may have been intended as a parenthetical exclamation and not (*Bn*) as addressed to P. **136–40** vigorously re-write some rather slack **ZAB** lines and remove the echo in B 133 (itself a revision drawing on A 10.145 in the b-half) of the stock 'winner / waster' contrast, thus avoiding repetition of Pr 24. P. states firmly his belief that the prayers of the virtuous win practical blessings from God, already affirming the contemplative values later to be embodied in his *alter ego* Patience the Hermit. **B 131** // *(h)olde hyne*: echoing Lk 12:42. **137–8** are perhaps an indirect allusion to Prov 20:4b, quoted entire at 246a; but no specific scriptural warning against false beggars seems intended. *a-beggeth*: from *on* + the old verbal noun *beggath*, a construction later replaced by the gerund (whence 'a-begging'); see *MES* 581–2. **139–40** This double *repetitio* is a form of paronomasia with subtle expansions of sense in the move from n. to v. and a. to av. *wastours*: an attack possibly prompted by social conditions after the Black Death, when a massive labour shortage led to large rises in workmen's wages that the government unsuccessfully struggled to control (McKisack 1959:331–42, Ziegler 1971, ch. 15). Despite crop failures and dearth between 1350–75 (Frank 1990), some preferred not to work at all. **141** *teme to dryue*: i.e. 'work the land'; the 'text of Truth' alluded to may be II Thess 3:10. **142–3** *barly...broke...bolted*: the minimum needed to survive. This was prison fare, to judge by *RR* 2757 (barley being valued mainly for malt to make ale, which they will *not* have); so here P. boldly promises better food to prisoners than to idle wastrels. **146–8** evolve continuously through the versions (see e.g. Z 132 → A 135 → B 146 → C 146), with wholesale abbreviation to avoid repetition (e.g. A 133 of A Pr 28 //). The revision includes sincere mendicants but excludes monks. **146** *nones*: the standard régime for a fast day, which (as *Bn* notes) they always observe. **B 147** *þat han* 'those who have'; **A 137** *þat* 'for him who'; on non-expression of the antecedent, see *MES* 190. **148** *What...what*: more exuberant paronomasia. *what þat*: on this combination see *MES* 195.

B 139–51 are developed from A 127–8 and describe the duties a serf had to perform for his lord (*Bn*). They may have been omitted after 1381 as potentially provocative, ll. 143–4 simply as over-emphatic (the sense of 139–40 is used to better effect in the ironic new context of C 5.13–19). **144** scans with cognative spirants (*þ* / *f* / *v*). On **L**'s notion of divine forbearance as 'vengeance', cf. Reason at B 11.378. **148** *Robert Renaboute*: perhaps a wandering hermit (*Bn*) and, since *Robert* seems always a 'bad' name in *PP*, a dishonest one (see B 187). **149** *postles*: mendicant friars, and perhaps also itinerant preachers maintained by bequests and licensed to preach within particular 'limits' in a diocese. **151** *vnresonable Religion*: a form of religious life lacking in rational proportion (Alford in Kennedy 1988:214). *Bn* finds an 'evident allusion' to the sending of the 72 disciples in Lk 10:7; but P. no less evidently declares 'unreasonable' a life dedicated to preaching the Gospel without some guarantee of sustenance from the laity, and Conscience makes a similar point at 20.264–7.

149–50 *Wastour*: a type-representative of all who batten unscrupulously on others' labours. The annominative *repetitio* in *yfouhte, fyhte* removes the impropriety of *gloue* coming from a peasant. **149** *gan...yfouhte*: on this use of the perfect infinitive 'to express a hypothetical action simultaneous with that of a non-auxiliary finite verb' see *MES* 517. **151** *pyuische*: after two changes the term of insult restored to its initial form in **Z**; a rare word of uncertain origin (perhaps < Lat *perversus*), first found here. **152** *Bretener*: a group reputed for boastfulness, as shown by *AMA* 1348. **155** The near-identity with 68 cannot be accidental, since the AB 145/158 b-half differs from AB 61/67b, the intention presumably being ironic. The earlier line was P.'s promise to those who *did* work; the present is Waster's insolent demand for the same reward *without* work. **157** *couenant*: an agreement that expresses (with feeling) a vision of ideal relations between labourer and landlord in feudal society; see on 26–34 above. **158** *dere*: the price of goods inevitably rising with scarcity. **159** The new line states how the failure of religious sanctions finally leaves no option but force. **163–6** The Knight's threat of resort to the shire court, though stronger in **C**, is no more effective: Waster will

not wait around to be tried. **166** *pes*: a stock expression of worthlessness, but piquantly apt in the light of 176, where P. judges Wastour 'worth' only a pease-loaf (which yet is better than nothing).

(iii) 167–353 The Hunger episode, a dramatised allegorical meditation on II Thess 3:10 (*si quis non vult operari, nec manducet*) presents a drastic solution to the problem of ensuring enough affordable food for all. This problem is seen as caused by the failure of many to work the land, with resulting dearth. The character Hunger may be derived from Faim in *RR* 10133ff (see Kaske 1988; and on the allegory, Hewett-Smith 1996). Piers's dialogue with him may be understood allegorically as part of an interior debate between his conflicting impulses to severity and permissiveness. **168** The shift from 'typical' narrative making complete sense at the literal level to personification-allegory continues the mode announced in the Confessions Scene, where type-figures interacted with the personified sins. The personification Hunger had re-appeared at A XII 63–76, and this repetition may have been among the reasons for abandoning the attempted continuation. **170** *Awreke me*: signifying that P.'s only means of controlling the wasters is to deny them any food at all. *wil nat*: a change indicating not that the wasters' behaviour is any less destructive but that the knightly class, their morale shaken after the Peasants' Rising, are now less willing (or able) to enforce the Statutes of Labourers. For if they try and compel the idle to work when they do not wish to, they might be refused their services at times like harvest. **175** *barste*: p. t. subjv. in revised **C**, but indic. in **ZAB**. **B 180** *doluen*: '(dead) and buried', omission of *ded* sharpening the sardonic contrast with *doluen* B 190: to dig for one's food is better than to dig one's grave.

A 165–70 (Z 162–7) The excision of this grotesquely vivid (if at points confusing) allegorical sequence is a loss, though undeniably speeding up the action. **165** *benene bat*: a long loaf of bean-flour, costing 1/3 the price of a wheat loaf (*Bn*, citing *English Gilds* 366). **168** Doctor Thirst paradoxically *forbids* them to drink (too much), whereas in **Z** he encourages it. This revision is doubtless due to realising that barley- and bean-bread rapidly swallowed down would swell if much water was drunk, causing acute indigestion. For a similar change (from **B** to **C**), cf. on 20.53.

178–222 178 is virtually repeated at 192, a possible oversight that might have been put right before 'publication' (cf. 197 at 203). **179** *faytours*: false beggars and hermits, distinct from the wasters (cf. 208, 210 below), who work for Piers *before* they feel the pangs of hunger. **182** *potage...wyf*: a more generous (and realistic) touch, perhaps implying that P. feeds them for their efforts with what he would willingly eat himself, thereby welcoming them back into the *comune*. **186–7** remove B 189b's repetition of 187b, *duntes* replacing *doluen* (see above at B 180) in a similar contrast with *flapton*. **188** *he*: of uncertain reference (presumably Piers); the allegorical inappropriateness of Hunger 'healing' (A 179) when he inflicts the *duntes* (C 187) may be the reason for the change (but cf. 225). **189** *longes*: perhaps synecdochic for the less tasty offal generally not eaten. **195** *holde hewe*: cf. ZAB 120. **198** *daubynge*: applying clay to wattle fencing or huts for sheltering livestock. **199** *pynnes*: used as nails, in wheel-axles ('linchpins'), and to fasten roof-tiles. **200** repeats 7.190, showing that to follow P. is to become Truth's servant like him (cf. 195). **202** The T-type line emphasises how animal necessity has taken on the coercive authority of the impotent knightly class, and with it the title (*Syre Hunger*). **204** P., like his master Truth, renders to each according to his works (Prov 24:12, Mt 16:27), 'justice' paying no more or less than what is due. **208** *awroke*: completing what he asked for at 170. **209** scans as an extended vocalic Type III with counterpoint (*abb / ax*). **214–16** P.'s words show the Half-Acre scene re-enacting the pattern of the Deadly Sins sequence on the social plane; though the 'wasters' are given up, the beggars, who seem redeemable, are not sorry for their conduct, only afraid of its consequences. P.'s hope, however, is for a society like a large family, founded through Christ's redeeming act and united by brotherly love, without which disintegration will occur. **216** *filial*: found nowhere else in ME and possibly introduced here. **217** *blody bretherne*: a paradoxical idea, false if taken literally but true in a spiritual sense, since their common baptism is a sharing in the sacrificial death of Christ. The sacramental mystery involved is elaborated at 12.111 with far-reaching social implications. **218** Perhaps the most important scriptural source is Mt 5:43–48, a text linking love of one's enemies with being children of the God who provides natural blessings for good and bad alike. But also pertinent is the text 'Every one shall...say to his brother: Be of good courage' (Is 41:6). **221** *amayster...louye*: the **C** revision moving the urgent debate about the 'means' to a productive and harmonious social order from plain obedience to 'filial' service, and from a 'Mosaic' to a 'Messianic' conception of human relations. **Z 196–201** are vigorous but repetitive elaboration (e.g. Z 175–6, 203) and understandably therefore dropped by **A**. **223–302** The discourse of Hunger, who is largely abetted by P. in his three interventions, deals with the problem of providing justly for those who cannot as well as those who will not work, and for distinguishing between them. **223–34 225** *houndes...breed*: of beans and bran; so unappetising that it should persuade able-bodied idlers to work for better. **226** *abaue*: 'confound' (OED s.v. *abave* v); MED does not record this sense or cite this instance. **229** *fals men*: replacing an awkward reference to Fortune that might have implied a criticism of Providence.

231 *lawe of kynde*: the natural law, but also punningly 'the divine law', *kynde* (as will be revealed at 10.52ff) being another nature-name for God, who has created all men. In **ZAB** the appeal is grounded on the brotherhood of Christians through baptism (cf. 217); here the 'law of Christ' is seen expressed in his epitome of Truth's Commandments (Mt 22:37–40) as the 'eternal law' in which 'natural law is contained' (Aquinas, *ST* I, 2, 71:6). **231a** 'Bear ye one another's burdens: and so you shall fulfil the law of Christ' (Gal 6:2). Hunger interprets Paul's text (on helping fellow Christians overcome the 'burden' of their faults by offering them mild instruction) as an injunction to share their want through 'filial' charity.

B 223–5a envisage (unlike C 232–4) misfortunes that men bring on themselves through their own actions as sins that God will punish. **223** *nouȝty*: judged 'ambiguous at this date' by MED (s.v. *noughti* adj. (a), citing *Pur.* 1359). But *Bn*'s apt citation of *SS* 115 'nedful and *nawthi*, naked and nawth' (not in MED s.v. (c)) confirms here the sense 'in want, needy' otherwise instanced only in the R variant at B 7.70. **224** *vengeaunce*: i.e. where any retribution is due. **225** 'Even if they *are* doing wrong, leave it to God to sort things out'. **225a** 'Revenge is mine and I will repay [them in due time]' (Deut 32:35, qu. Rom 12:19, Heb 10:30 which have *vindicta* for *ultio*). This is **L**'s most often-cited Biblical text (B 10.206a, 368, C 17.235a, 21.449a), incorrect *vindictam* being a VL reading common in the period (Alf*Q,Sk*). Whereas **C** omits the important retribution-text, **B** probably implies awareness of Gal 6:5 ('For every man shall bear his *own* burden') as 'correlative' with Gal 6:1, which urges *not* condemning others' faults, through remembering one's own.

235–5a The sentiment preceding the quotation is altered in a more penitential sense, but with the same implication: charitable use of 'ill-gotten gains' will make satisfaction for sin and may gain the prayers of those helped. It is not suggested that P.'s gains are *untrewe* (cf. 105); but since all *tresor of erthe* is valueless when compared with *treuthe*, it should be used for others' good, the question of their 'deserts' being left to God. **235** *wiselich*: not just 'virtuously' but 'prudently' (cf. 223); Hunger does *not* advocate 'indiscriminate charity' (*Bn*, referring to Lk 6:27–38), nor can this be what P. has in mind at 236. **235a** 'Make unto you friends of the mammon of iniquity' (Lk 16:9).

236–315 *The dialogue between Hunger and Piers*. **237** *synneles*: i.e. give alms selectively (from even one's dubiously acquired riches); Hunger's appeal to three OT authorities and a rather OT-sounding Gospel parable shows that P. cannot think 'discriminate charity' might be sin. **240** *wyse men*: no immediate referent is apparent. The cognomen *geaunt* in **B** for *Genesis* refers to its being the longest book of the Bible (not counting Psalms) and the *engendrour* as it tells the origin of mankind (*Bn*). The clearer and more straightforward procedure in **C**, omitting the obscure *mnam* at B 238 // (but introducing two little-known *English* words at 242) and completing the quotations, suggests that readers might have found the macaronic syntax of B 232, 235 // difficult. **242** The first verb is unique, the second instanced in this sense only here; the construction requires understanding *we sholde*. **242a** 'In the sweat (and labour) of thy face shalt thou eat (thy) bread [till thou return to the earth, out of which thou wast taken]' (Gen 3:19). Inserted *labore* may have been prompted by Gen 3:17 *in laboribus comedes* (and cf. 261*a*). **243** *Salomon*: see on 3.121. **245** *sleuthe*: explicitly recognising idleness as one of the deadly sins (cf. 253, *CT* X 685). **246** *a-bribeth*; *a-beggeth*: see on 137–8; the identification of false beggars as failed labourers is confirmed by 9.203–10. **246a** 'Because of the cold, the sluggard would not plough: he shall beg therefore in the summer, and it shall not be given him' (Prov 20:4). To explain mistaken *yeme* 'winter' *Pe* suggests 'sympathetic association of winter and deprivation'; but 245 shows **L** aware that the text read *aestate* 'summer'. **247–58** The parable is told in Mt 25:14–30 and this reference may be recalling the specific mention of sloth in vs 26 *Serve male et piger* (*Bn*); but both the **ZAB** adj. *nequam* 'wicked' and the noun *mna* 'pound' come from Lk 19:12–27. **B 237** *mannes face*: alluding to the iconography derived from traditional exegesis of the 'four living creatures' in Apoc 4:7 (based on Ezech 1:10) as figures of the Four Evangelists (see on 21.263–7). Matthew was represented as a man because his Gospel begins with the human genealogy of Christ (see Schiller 1971:I, pl. 172). **249** *chele... hete*: signifying that the Christian should exercise his talents in all circumstances, including adversity. **Z 230–2** If this is a true autobiographical reference, it may reflect the fact that the author, though in minor orders, had not reached the rank of deacon, below which a clerk was not permitted to preach. See *Intro*, V § 4 and n. 8. **B 246–8** The rhyme-enclosed lines affirm almost catechetically that both nature and revelation require everyone to do some 'work', bodily or spiritual. *Bn* would have 'active and contemplative life' stand in parallel with husbandry and devotions, not as identical with them; though not exhaustive, these represent the two types of 'travail'. **259** *Sauter*: the psalm cited being concerned with the earthly blessings that will come to the just. **B 251***a*; **261***a Beati... manducabis*: 'Blessed are all they [that fear the Lord: that walk in his ways]. For thou shalt eat the labours of thy hands: [blessed art thou, and it shall be well with thee]' (Ps 127:1–2). **Z** is here closest to the full original Latin, which 238 translates (a feature more in keeping with authorial draft than scribal adaptation). **A** is a paraphrase stating that work here gets a reward here. **B** and **C** variously add a moral and spiritual dimension to both work (*feiþful / lele* labour) and reward. While correcting **A**'s one-sided-

ness (the psalm promises prosperity for *righteousness*), both nonetheless foreground what the psalm only implies (*labour*). Hunger's argument is: 'man must work; those who do not are punished here and hereafter; those who do are rewarded likewise'. **C** ignores the positive aspect of the psalm-text to end on a note of sombre warning. **263** *be*: 'will be'. **264–5** resume the two problematic categories of *beggares* and *boys* that trouble Piers. **267** *fisyk*: a more dignified term than *lechecraft*, ironically implying that the 'learning' true medicine requires is spiritual rather than bodily. **270** *ʒow*: hardly 'P.s "servants" rather than P.' (*Bn*) since 268b candidly admits that he too can give in to the pleasures of harvest plenty. **B 253** *my deere*: 'good friend', the affectionate tone indicating P.'s sense of his interlocutor's moral value to him. **269** *Of...woke*: 'for a whole week'. **271** *manged ouer moche*: strongly recalling A 12.72–6, the only other recorded occurrence of *mangen*. The opposite pole of 'want' that disciplines sloth is here seen as 'over-plenty' leading to the related vice of gluttony (see on 7.1–68). This doctrine, of moderation not of deprivation, is that of HC in I 33 (*Mesure is medecyne*) and shows how consistent is the moral position developed through such authoritative figures as Hunger (the *in*consistency in his presentation at A 12.72–6 may be one reason for **L**'s abandoning that passus; see *Intro*. III, *A Version*, x). **276** *Sire Sorfeet*: another passing personification, specified in **B** as an epicure guilty of 'delicacy' and 'curiosity' (*CT* X 830). **277** Cf. Glutton at B 5.377. **278–89** The Biblical exemplum lends homiletic weight to Hunger's moral admonition and may be contrasted with the clever *forbisne* used by the Friars Minor at 10.33ff. **B 266** *many maner metes*: recalling Ecclus 32–3. **278** *Diues*: commonly treated as a proper name, from the parable in Lk 16:19–31 of the rich man (*dives*) and Lazarus the beggar covered with sores, whose proper name conversely gave rise to the generic *lazar* for 'leper'. (Dives is cited again at 15.303 and 19.232 as an exemplar of *unkyndenesse*). Hunger's advice does not presuppose that P. is 'rich' but urges all with more than they need to give to those in want, who are their true 'neighbours' (cf. 9.71ff). The counsel needs careful interpretation, since Hunger is telling P. to feed from his table all who like Lazarus (a beggar) are really needy, but to give only the leftover scraps to the suspect characters who call. **280** *culde hym*: the harsh tone recalling B 20.151; Hunger is part of the reality of Kynde as 'mortality', also manifested as age and disease. **282** *Abrahames lappe*: i.e. heaven; so at 18.272–3 (*sinus* in Lk 16:23 is usually rendered 'bosom'). **284** *grat*: the form with retracted vowel avoiding confusion with the contracted form of *greten*. **288** *bord*: a trestle-table, folded up after use and placed against the wall. **290** Hunger attributes most illnesses to excess, i.e. the deadly sin of Gluttony, through which 'the humours in [the] body been distempred' (*CT* X 825; cf.

also *CT* VII 2836–9, Ecclus 37:32–4). **291** *Fisyk*: a brief 'professional' type-personification like *Cyuile* at 2.63. **291–2** *hodes...cloke*: evidence of physicians' large fees, often paid in part with a gift of robes by their rich clients. Physic's fur cannot keep him warm against the attack of old age in 22.176–7. *of Callabre*: trimmed with fine grey squirrel fur from Calabria in S Italy. **292** *communes legge*: recalling Reason's words to Purnele at 5.128–9. The ironic *repetitio* of *legge* 290 is a device typically favoured in the revision to **C**. **A** 257–8 A two-line critique replaces **Z**'s impassioned 18-line diatribe against bad doctors, retaining only **Z** 263–4 (and later 271–3 at 8.46a–48). This revision is misunderstood by Kerby-Fulton (1999:519) as indicating difference of authorship. **296** *destyné*: not a power in its own right but what is foreseen for an individual as his allotted time on earth. The notion here is that temperate living is likely to ensure a longer life than medical treatment.

Z 260–78 After Meed's attack on Conscience at 3.147–76, this is the longest passage of **Z** to be cut. Its complex and learned *distinctio* between true and false *leches* is also digressive and repetitive (271–3 recur as 8.47–9 apropos of lawyers), holding up the urgent dialogue between Hunger and Piers on the need for a morally balanced attitude towards the extremes of dearth and abundance to which the husbandman's way of life was subject. **260** *science...trewe*: cf. Gower on alchemy (*CA* IV 2598–9); Hunger's onslaught is upon ignorant practitioners, not on those who have properly qualified at the university, where a medical training took six years after completing the Arts course (Courtenay 1987:36–7). **261** accuses quacks of illiteracy (they cannot read even a manual of medicine). The tone of this line is very like that of **B** 15.375. **262–3** *hele / quelle*: for similar end-rhymes cf. **Z** 258/9 and **C** 8.343/4 (with identical rhythm), 9.92/3. **263** *maystres morthrares*: 'Masters of Murder' (cf. *doctour of deth* 20.402); for similar juxtaposed nouns cf. *maistres freres* at **B** Pr 62. **264** *lyares*: cf. **Z** 2.204–5, where Liar resides with the leeches. **265** *Ecclesiasticis*: ch. 38:1–9 deals with physicians and medicines as divinely ordained. The use of a single-word macaronic double-stave is characteristic. **267** 'Honour the physician for the need thou hast of him: [for the most High hath created him]' (Ecclus 38:1). The line scans as Type III on *n*. **268–70** are based on Ecclus 38:2, the phrasing resembling 14.85 (in a totally different context). **269** *ys*: perhaps better if 'thys', though the sense is acceptable. **271** 'Their reward shall be from kings and princes'; almost certainly from Hugh of St Cher's gloss 'id est, coram principibus et regibus' on Ecclus 38:3 (*R–B*; see further AlfQ). The notion that the cost of certain common necessities should be borne by king and lords is applied to lawyers' fees at **B** 7.42–3a (// in **Z** and **A**); but this earliest use in relation to doctors is closer to the source, as would be expected in a

first version. **274** *Lumbardes*: 'The Lombards notice that Londoners are gluttonous (and therefore prone to sickness) and see their opportunity to sell them medicines (which will turn out even more harmful)' (*R–B*, citing Thorndyke 1934:III, 526 on the Lombards' reputation for sorcery and poisoning). For London as a place of good eating see Pr 227–31. **276** *medecynes schapeth*: for similar phrasing cf. 'Shrift *schop* scharp salue' at 22.307. **277** *of the cardyacle*: 'by causing them heart-attacks [*sc.* through their toxic potions]'. **278** *Flemmynges*: residing in London, mainly in connection with the wool-trade. The line signifies 'people of all the different nations living there'.

297–341 The second half of this episode memorably evokes the cycle of the agricultural year, with its periods of want and plenty. 303–14 describe the 'hungry gap' before the next harvest (March to August), when the previous year's reserves were dwindling (Frank 1990:89–90) and the countryman's condition came near that of the urban poor all year round as described at 9.71–97. **297** *Poul*: a fitting name to invoke, since his teaching on work and feeding presides over the whole sequence (see on 141). *Pernel* **AZ**: St Petronella, the legendary daughter of St Peter (whence perhaps an apt saint for P. to swear by), who endured fever in order to grow in holiness, and fasted to death to avoid marrying a pagan lord (*LA* ch. 78). *poyntest...treuth*: part of the way to reality being through experience of *hoet hunger* (20.211). **299–300** The *repetitio* of *wel* in varying senses is typical of **C**. *awroke*: Hunger has done for P. what the knight (158) could not, and the past participle rounds off the sequence with an echo of the imperative at 170. **301** The only way to make Hunger (man's permanent companion) 'depart' is to feed him. **303–4** It is less likely that P. has only money enough to buy cheese, etc. (*Bn*), than that he has *no* money (to buy choice meats) but does have dairy produce, which he can provide himself (cf. *cow* 311), and oats for his cart-horse. **304** *grene*: unripe, because made (from the daily milk) for early eating. **306** *bred...peses*: the poor fare provided for beggars in 225 (the wheat having gone except for the seed-corn). **307** *ȝut*: he has not 'even' bacon and eggs, let alone fresh pork and poultry. **309–10** *parsilie*; *chiruulles*: cropped and eaten whole as salad-herbs (cf. *cresses* at 321 below). *sam-rede*: an improvement on *ripe chiries*, showing how hunger makes them eat the fruit (in early June) before it is fully ripe. **312** *drouthe*: of March (cf. *CT* I 2), the time for manuring the fields before the April rains (*Bn*). **313** *Lammasse*: < OE *hlaf-mæsse*; Aug. 1, the start of harvest-time, when a loaf made from the new wheat was offered at Mass. As this was also the feast of St Peter's Chains (see Ac 1:1–12), there is an apt parallel in the symbolism of P.'s release from 'imprisonment' by hunger. **317** *aples*: 'laid in hay or heather' (*CT* I 3262) to keep until the next September. **318** repeats 4.91 (ironically): this 'present' P. *will* accept or starve, since subsistence-farmers who depend on what they can put by have little money spare to buy food (but cf. on 92 above). **321** loses the witty 'poison'-image (on which see *TN*), doubtless to avoid the a-half's partially repeating 306b, 316. **322** *nyhed neyh*: either litotes ('by then harvest had come') or else this 'new' corn is the remains of last-year's, hoarded by merchants to sell dear and now released cheap to avoid a glut and provide space in barns (*Bn*). **324** *gode ale*: 'brewed from barley newly harvested' (*Bn*). **325–6** Another cycle of idleness begins with the arrival of plenty. *wandren*: dependent on *wolde*. **327** *clermatyn*: a choice bread of which nothing is known. *coket*: next in quality after *wastel* or cake bread (6.340), which came after *simenel*, the finest. **B 303** *ellis*: taken by *BnSch* as adj. = 'of other kinds' (MED s.v. *elles* adj. 1.b.) But the rhythm of the // lines and the unstress on the word suggest it is only an intensifier (ib. s.v. adv. 1a) used elliptically to mean that '(if not of the finest), their bread is (at the least) to be of wheat-flour alone.' **328** *halpenny ale*: 'feeble' ale like that drunk by the monks (6.159), costing half the standard brew (*peny ale* 332). **329** *brouneste*: thick, strong 'pudding ale', the darkest and dearest. **330** *Laborers*: taken by *Bn* to include crofters as well as unskilled town workmen of various kinds; cf. Gower, *Vox Clamantis* (in *Works* vol. iv) 5. 641. **331** *aday...wortes*: 'daily / the next day on yesterday's left-over greens'. **AB 292/307** *dyne*: here transitive (though **Z** has the same construction as **C**). **334** *chaut... pluchaut*: enticing cries from the cookshops (though not found earlier, the phrase sounds authentic), with perhaps some satire on the cooks' pretensions. **336** *ywrouhte*: making the discontented labourer's complaint about his wages one against his *destyné* (296) as ordained by God. **337** *Catones consayle*: see on 4.17. *gruche*: taking up a verb first used in **Z** (twice) but replaced in **AB** in both instances by *chide*. **337a** The second part of a Catonian couplet beginning *Infantem nudum cum te natura crearit*: '[Since Nature made you as a naked babe], Remember to bear the burden of poverty with patience' (*DC* I. 21). **338** *corseth*: not an outburst of bad temper but a rebellious challenge to authority. *iustices*: replacing *Counseil* so as to stress the royal judges' important rôle in punishing breaches of labour legislation during the unsettled period after 1381. **339** *lawes*: the Statutes of Labourers, beginning in 1349 and renewed again at about the time of **Z** in 1362, which required all workmen to take any employment available. Enforcement was at first successful, though the view voiced from **Z** onwards is that labourers' pay can be kept at a level in accord with the 'natural' (= divinely ordained) proportion between the value of goods and their price only through refusing excessive demands that subvert the providential social order. These laws designed 'to ensure a supply of cheap labour by pegging

wages [which nearly doubled between 1340–60] at pre-plague rates' (McKisack 1959:335) were much resented, and their restraint on peasants' economic aspirations contributed to the Rising of 1381. *lerne*: a revision with no change of sense; like *loke* here = 'prescribe'. **341** *statuyt*: a decree approved by parliament, addressed to all subjects and having the force of law, by contrast with an 'ordinance' passed by the king in council (Maitland 1974:186–8). The ironic figurative use implies a sanction more effective than those of the actual Statute.

342–53 This prophecy, spoken in 'authorial' voice but using a mode widely popular at the time and growing longer and darker in revision, seems intended (like much Biblical prophecy) as a moral warning rather than a prediction of disaster within a precise period of time. Thus 'before five years' would have indicated in **Z**, say, 1370, in **A** 1375 and in **B** 1383; but the alteration to 'few' in **C** safely covers the likelihood that some natural calamity would indeed befall. **343** *hiderwardes*: having temporarily quit the scene at harvest, but only to return in spring, in severer guise. **343/4** The rhyme's difference in **Z** is a strong indicator of its originality, the **A** revision both adding internal rhyme and eliminating the weak repetition of *werkmen*. **344** *water*: i.e. crop-destroying floods. **346** The grim message is to be inferred from the position of Saturn, the 'cold' planet farthest from Earth, which astrological lore associated with famine, flood and pestilence and (as in Chaucer) with social upheaval (*CT* I 2456, 2459, 2478). The *Prophecies* of 'John of Bridlington' (III c. 11, in Wright 1859:123–215) linked the pestilence of 1361–2 with 'the star most harmful to the earth and the bringer-in of plagues', while medieval astrologers believed that the Great Pestilence of 1349 had been 'brought about by an extraordinary conjunction of Saturn with the other planets, which happened scarcely once in a thousand years' (*Wr* p. xii). As *Bn* notes, the prophecy finds apocalyptic fulfilment at 22.80, where Kynde brings diseases 'oute of the planetes'. *sente*: 'sends [this message]'. **348–51 (B 325–27)** The **Z** and **A** Versions end the passus here. The two riddling prophecies added in **B** and **C** could well be read as direct utterances of the personified planetary power. **348** The coupling of pride and plague directly recalls Reason's words in the sermon *ad status* that opened Vision Two, and the line anticipates 22.98 / echoes B 20.98: Pride arouses the anger of God, who punishes it with plagues. **349–50** 'are', as *Sk* observes encouragingly, 'of course, inexplicable', and as 'mysterious prophecies' they may well be incapable of sure exegesis. But in 350–1 it is hard not to see an allusion to the Four Horsemen of Apoc ch. 6, usually taken to symbolise destruction, war, plague and famine; and this (as with the earlier and very similar prophecy at 3.478–82) would favour a wider 'apocalyptic' context of interpretation. **349** *Pe*'s judgement that the line contains a cryptic date-reference is supported by 350a, all the more if the referent of 350b is not geographical 'in all parts of the world' (*Pe*) but temporal 'on both sides of the full of the moon' (i.e. throughout the month in question). If *schaef* (in the light of 3.478) is the true reading here, it would seem to refer to a sheaf of *arrows* (Bradley 1910:342; Bloomfield 1961:211–12), of which the usual number was 24. The line thus yields the *three* successive figures 3, 24 and 8, of which the first divides the second by the last and the last divides it by the first. This may darkly suggest the idea that 'The first shall be last and the last shall be first', echoing an eschatological saying of Christ (Mt 19:30) that is immediately preceded by a reference to the *twelve* apostles judging the *twelve* tribes of Israel (= 24; cf. on 3.478 above). If a specific time is being intimated, this would be the third *hour* of the 24th *day* of the eight month, August. And if Bradley is right that the word 'ship' is here meant to evoke the conventional medieval outline of a ship (x), *three* ships ('xxx') will yield the numerical value 30, and by adding 30+24+8 a *year* [13]62 is obtainable. This is a significant Langlandian date, but its precise relevance to a text written in the 1380s remains unclear. Bradley, however, observes that the **p** reading *shaft* offers another numerical rebus 'l' (= 50), and with *vm* as = *viii* we have 30+50+8, giving another date [13]88. The closeness of this to **C**'s probable date of composition (1385–7) would make the 'apocalyptic' events foretold (war, and famine in place of plague) not past but to come, and preventable only by an act of divine remission. However, while such interpretations are authorised by, e.g., the famous numerical cryptograph in Apoc 13:18, they may (have) seem(ed) to many readers a little forced.

B 325–6 are in some respects more obscure than **C** (which may be an effort to 'clarify' matters to some extent). **325** *þe sonne amys*: connected with an eclipse by *Bn*, who notes after Bradley that a total eclipse occurred in 1377. *two monkes heddes*: understood by *Bn* as 'curious shapes in the sky', such as the eclipse might well have suggested, with 'a covert allusion to certain religious — or to apparitions'. The image seems better to merit *Sk*'s resigned comment (cited above) than does **C**'s numerological riddle (which for *Bn* 'increases the obscurity'). **326** *a mayde*: possibly an allusion back to Mede the Maid; the half-line echoes B 3.169 and the prophecy recalls Conscience's concluding denunciation of Mede in B 3.325–30. *multiplied*: 'be' is to be understood, and the past participle may apply to all the preceding conditions of the prophecy or (as preferred here) only to the 'maid', whose 'multiplication' would presumably signify the begetting of offspring (the alchemical sense suspected by Bradley is hard to fit in). In **B** the numerological significance (if any) of the figures 2 and 8 is not easy to discern. **351–3 351** states that after a return of the plague, followed by war, famine will be inflicted as a divine punishment.

352 *Dawe þe Deluare*: a representative labourer 'with no land to live on but his hands', who would therefore be the first to feel the impact of famine. **353** *trewe*: 'respite'; a merciful cessation of God's punishments. The punning juxtaposition of this word with 'Truth' in its other appearance at 20.462 suggests a similar intention here, namely that moral reform such as the Confessions have depicted is needed, if divine punishment such as Reason described at the opening of this vision (5.114ff) is to be avoided.

Passus IX (B VII, ZA VIII)

PASSUS NINE, the 'Pardon Passus' is the second instance of major structural change in **C**. Here concern over the hostility towards the Church shown in the 1381 Rising may partly explain the removal of two passages implying a challenge to clerical authority. These are the Tearing of the Pardon and the quarrel between Piers and the Priest, an ambiguous and presumably controversial episode added in **A** as the climax of the passus (**Z** proper having *ended* before the Tearing). The present Passus divides into three: i. the main part on the receiving of the pardon by Piers and the account of its contents (1–279, with a major addition beginning at 187); ii. the response of the priest (280–91); and iii. the epilogue on dreams, pardons and the need to do well (297–351). In **ZA** the first section is unbroken, but **B** expands the lines on begging with a discussion of whether charity should be discriminating or not (74–84). **C** replaces this with a passage on the same theme some nine times longer, contrasting the worthy poor with deceitful beggars and *lolleres* (71–161). It also inserts a 90-line passage on true and false hermits (187–279), with the continuation or second half of the latter starting where **A**'s 'Tearing' began (see at 175). These additions, even after the removal of B 115–38*a*, make **C** some 40% longer than **B**; otherwise, the three sections remain about the same length, as do their proportions (4:1:2). The excision of the Tearing destroys the dramatic intensity of the **B** conclusion, while the additions unbalance the *Visio* in a way that the 'autobiographical prelude' arguably does not (see on C V above). Given the new material's thematic relevance and outstanding quality, this hardly amounts to a major failure of artistic judgement. But that the changes, both negative and positive, were motivated by some anticipation of the audience's likely response seems probable.

(i) 1–279 *The Pardon*. **1–8** In all versions the Pardon is sent by Truth, and in the later ones it is not to be confused with any earthly document. But the earlier leave it unclear whether those who earn Truth's pardon by the way they live have also a right to a formal plenary indulgence from the Pope without performing a specific penitential act like pilgrimage (the ambivalent excursus on papal pardons at A 158ff does little to dissipate this confusion). **1** *Treuthe*: the master Piers has served all his life, who hears about his work and promptly responds to it as P. had said he would (presumably by the gift of a good conscience giving assurance of salvation). *herof*: the work on the half-acre; *K–F*'s reference of the word to Saturn's warning of famine to come (in 8.346ff //) is unpersuasive, since the ploughing (as well as bearing its purely literal sense) emblematises the just life that earns pardon. **2–7** The message is implicitly that of St Paul cited at 5.43*a* (I Cor 7:20–23). **2** *taken his teme*: both 'take his plough-team' and 'understand his argument' (MED s.v. *taken* v. 22a 'understand'). **3** *a pena et a culpa*: 'from punishment and guilt'. In strict theory, personal guilt for sins was forgiven through sacramental confession, and what a pardon or indulgence remitted was the canonical punishment imposed for sin (e.g. a period of fasting). This remission was usually to be obtained through an act of satisfaction such as almsgiving. But the Latin phrase came to be understood loosely as signifying also guilt for forgotten (mainly venial), unconfessed or imperfectly confessed sins, and it was generally held that to receive a pardon efficaciously required prior absolution from all grave sins. Temporal penance not fully performed at a person's death would have to be made good in the next life; so the function of commemorative masses and other intercessory prayers for which the deceased left money was chiefly to shorten the time that the soul would spend in purgatory. The brief definition in Alf*G* is thus slightly misleading in conflating these two aspects, since L's point is that a life of 'truth' will leave *no* punishment to be remitted (see further Dunning 1980 [1937]:109ff). In actuality, however, it was widely and mistakenly believed that a papal pardon in recognition of a major penitential act like a pilgrimage to Jerusalem or Rome not only remitted *all punishment* (thereby shortening time spent in purgatory) but absolved from *all guilt* without sacramental absolution (a misunderstanding that exposed the credulous to exploitation by such as Chaucer's Pardoner). But insistence on full confession (*pace* Hudson 1988[2]:405) is a major concern of the poet who, while understanding (and in principle accepting) the theory of pardon, is cool towards the practice. L's development of a figurative *pardon* sent by Truth thus logically complements the figurative *pilgrimage* undertaken by Piers, his exclusive point in both cases being the spiritual reality (repentance and forgiveness) mediated through an external institution. **4** *For hym*: reversing expected social order in beginning with the husbandmen who provide food for all. *ayres*: not that salvation can be inherited, but that the promise, like the one to Abraham (18.256), holds for P.'s descendants if they serve Truth like him. The language is made to resemble that of a charter in order to bring out the pardon's (at least formal) likeness to conventional documents of the type (cf. also *seal* at 27). **8** *perpetuelly*: holding now and hereafter (cf. *for euere* 4) if, as is tacitly understood, the recipients live a life of *treuthe*. **9–12** *Kynges and knyhtes*: even upright nobles requiring time in purgatory, because their office unavoidably taints them with some failure in justice or humility. **13** *Bishopis yblessed*: in contrast, by the dignity of their divine office, granted immediate entry to heaven and a share as the apostles' successors in judging mankind at doomsday (Mt 19:28; with *deys* cf. Vg *sedes*). The phrase ironically recalls Pr 76, which criticises negligent prelates. L's standard for episcopal excellence, however, being that of heroic martyrdom, his revision stresses the need not to fear the secular power of *lordes* (an ideal restated at 17.290–2). **14, 19** *fol of loue*; *lereth men*: corresponding roughly to **ZA** 14, denoting 'our duty towards God, and towards our neighbours' (*Sk*), and giving a fuller view than **B** of the episcopal 'mixed' life of contemplation and action (cf. B 6.248). The parallel **ZAB** lines allude to the two 'great commandments on which depend the law and the prophets' (Mt 22:36–40, and cf. 19.11–16*a*). The phrase *lereth men* is a rare direct echo of **A** in **C**. **20** *peres*: a proleptic pun seems possible in B 16 but less so here with *to* instead of *wiþ. alle...reule*: i.e. given rule in the next world by resisting the rulers of this one (cf. 10). **22–3** *Marchauntes...margine*: a more problematic category, because their motive is desire for profit (26); hence they are included as a concession, not by right. But though 'trade was dangerous for the soul' (*Bn*), what is here attacked is less the activity than the impiety and false swearing incident to it, and **L** may be assumed to have known the positive NT image of the merchant (Mt 13.450) as well as the hostile one (Apoc 18:11, 15). *many ȝeres...culpa*: i.e. off their time in purgatory, but not plenary remission, because the wholesale trader's way of life (as well as giving openings for serious crimes) was not self-evidently for the common good. **23** *Treuthe*: a revision removing the ambiguity that accompanies the irony of **ZAB**. *Pope*: perhaps implying that '[only] an ideal Pope would not, the actual Pope probably would'. **24** *haliday*: because selling on Sundays and feast days breaks the 3rd Commandment (Ex 20:8–11). **27** *secrete seal*: like the royal letters sealed with the privy seal, intended for their eyes only and not entitling them openly to defend their profiteering. **28–9** They are to turn their gains to benefits by works of general value to the community (maintaining hospitals, roads or bridges) and particular help to the neediest (the disabled, imprisoned, unmarried girls, orphan children, ?mendicant friars). On these works, many of which were provided for in bequests, see Thomson 1965 and Rosenthal 1972. **28** *boldly*: in the assurance that they can do some good even with the *mammona iniquitatis*. **37–40** These, the only words spoken directly by Truth, embody the Christian message of hope as *PP* understands it. **37** *Seynt Mihel*: often thought of as

Commentary

holding the balance that will 'weigh' souls at the time of judgement (cf. Jude vs. 9; and see Benson 2004:177–78). His protection was thus especially sought at the moment when the soul left the body and would be snatched at by the fiends, as described in *Prick of Conscience* 2216–373, 2902–19 (see Sheingorn 1995); the promise is an assurance that their prayer will be heard. **38** *despeyre*: effectively a gloss on **B**'s 'terminal fear' that undermines trust in divine mercy and engenders 'wanhope'. **ZA** 'whenever you die' acknowledges the possibility that sudden death (so common during the Plague) might prevent a final plea for grace. **39–40** The attitude to merchants has softened in **C** and the ban on 'professional' sins against *treuthe* is removed as perhaps out of keeping with the positive associations of a pardon. **40** The somewhat overweighted b-half removes the resonant identical rhyme of *ioye* in B 36/7. **42** *purchased*: through his confidential relationship with Truth.

    ZA 43–4 *Wille*: a breach of decorum, but less effective than at ZA 577/44 and with a touch of ironic lightness (cf. *mede*) out of keeping with the solemn tone of the scene. These lines imply that the poet-persona referred to in the 3rd person is a professional scribe who copies charters (as **L** himself might well have been, to judge by the insistence of 13.116–19). *here clause*: the part referring to them; as businessmen, they want a record of their quittance, for which they are prepared to pay handsomely.
43–57 The critique of lawyers, both shorter and less homiletically weighty than its immediate predecessor, replaces the modern-sounding proposal of 'legal aid' for those of low income with one of *pro bono* work by barristers. **44** *pat*: i.e. 'those among them who'. **44–5** *plede... pledynge*: the revision retaining the *repetitio* pattern of B 42. **45** *pre manibus*: 'beforehand', i.e. in advance of doing the work. Such payment, judged an usurious form of *mede*, had bad associations because sometimes done for immoral purposes (at 3.299 it is connected with prostitutes and quacks).
    B 39–51a 39 The key-stave is internal to the consonant group |pl|. **41** *innócentʒ*: stressed on the second syllable (as at 47), whereas the Latin stresses the third. *pat...*: 'who do not even know what evil is, [so do not suspect any].' **41a** Here as a commandment, 'thou shalt not take' but in Ps 14:5 (as quoted at 2.40a) a past-tense characterising statement '[he that hath not put out his money to usury], nor taken bribes against the innocent'. It is not clear from **B** alone whether reference is to lawyers taking inducements from people going to law against 'innocents' (e.g. in inheritance cases) or simply demanding pre-payment from their clients without consideration of the outcome. The second part of the quotation in **ZA**, from the gloss on Ecclus 38:2 noted under Z 7.271 above, affirms that lawyers should act for those who cannot afford fees and the State should pay them (*Bn* cites

ST II. 11.71), a sense to which *pre manibus* in **C** also points. **44–5** *Iohan*: 'a common fellow' (MED s.v. *Jon* (b)). Although it could also be 'Joan' (a type-name for a 'common woman'), prostitution was tried in the Church courts, not before a jury (whose members the lines presume open to corruption). **50–1** are removed in **C**, doubtless because repeating B 34–5. **51a** 'Lord, who shall dwell in thy tabernacle? Or who shall rest in thy holy hill?' (Ps 14:1); usually interpreted as referring to the temple of God in the heavenly Sion. *Bn* finds an allusion to Ps 14:5b (quoted in the **A** mss HW); but this merely sums up the five classes of righteous men specified in answer to the question asked at Ps 14:1.
51–69 52 *indulgences*: (intimations of) mercy from God, with perhaps an 'anti-pun' on the sense of 'formal papal pardon' (which would then be too late). **52–4** *ʒe...His... here*: a shift from direct address (echoing B 59) to impersonal generalisation that is more awkward than in **B**. *ful petyt*: only a slight remission of time in purgatory (cf. A 59). **56** *wit*: a surprising substitution for the expected *erthe*, ascribed 'to the frequent association of the five wits with the four elements' by *Bn* (with whom *Pe* agrees, suggesting *kynde witt* Pr 141 as the referent). But these 'wits' are the senses, not 'intellect(ual) knowledge', the argument here being rather that 'Human intelligence is a gift of God, like three at least of the four elements [*sc.* excluding *earth*, which was *not* owned in common], and is therefore free for all men to profit by. Just as we should afford the free use of [these] to all men, so should we give...advice and...counsel *even* to those who cannot afford...it' (*Sk*). This bold treatment of the faculty *wit* as an 'elemental' akin to a 'common' *tresor* enables a case by analogy for making its *fruits* ('knowledge') freely available to all. And if this notion of '*wit* got from others' (including an attorney's arguments in a law-court) as more than purely personal *catel* (cf. B 13.151) seems quixotic, the modern democratic institution of legal aid for the indigent shows it to have been prophetic. **B 53–4** *in commune*: recalling HC's teaching at 1.20. *Trupes tresores*: cf. C 10. 183. **A 57** *for prallis*: 'to be at our service'. **Z 67** *mercedem*: perhaps intended to recall *merces* at 47 (Alf*Q*). **Z**'s greater closeness to its source is a non-scribal feature supporting authenticity. **57** *alle...nedede*: cf. 1.21; 'necessary things' for 'common use' are (in modern terminology) a 'human right' (in **C** *alle* is more generous than **B**'s *trewe*). **B 59a** 'All things (therefore) whatsoever you would that men should do to you, do you also to them' (Mt 7:12). Christianity's 'Golden Rule' (cited again at 16.307) has special relevance for *legistris* because it was seen by canonists as the basis of natural law (Gratian *CIC* 1:1, cit. Alf*Q*). **55** *symonye*: since God's common gifts are akin to the religious goods ('of grace'). The revision removes the anacoluthon in B 53–6. **58–60** echo **8** in rounding off the list of those in the pardon and stressing again that

honest labourers have nothing to fear and everything to hope for. **60** *Pardoun perpetuel*: cf. 8; the change from **ZAB** *absolucion* may be to exclude misunderstanding of a *pardon*, an 'indulgence' outside the strict bounds of the sacrament of penance, to which absolution pertained. **61–9** The passage on genuine and false beggars allows in a mixed class just this side of the 'wasters' (who are excluded). Their position is suggested by Z 69 ('Unless they are included on the reverse of the document, on the outside, separately)', the thought of which anticipates 14.144. **62** *suggestioun*: they are guilty of *suggestio falsi* (see AlfG). **63** *begeth or biddeth*: the distinction is not clear (*or* may = *vel* not *aut*). **B 67** *wiþ*: 'along with, like' (*MES* 419). **69** 'Take heed whom you give [alms] to' (*DC*, Pr., sent. 17). Baer (2001:131) cites from Hazelton 1956:10 a C13th commentary on *DC* that glosses these words 'et retribue affectionis illius dignis…quia…"qui *dat* mimis et histrionibus sacrificat demoniis"' (the text quoted in abbreviated form at 7.118*a*).

B 71–85 are omitted in **C**, signifying a hardening of attitude towards beggars; but the new passage on the deserving poor (70ff) is by way of compensation. **71** *Clerc of þe Stories*: Peter Comestor (d. 1179), whose *Historia Scholastica*, the major medieval authority on Biblical history, re-tells the sacred narratives with comments and patristic allegorical interpretations (on Peter see Daly 1957, Sherwood-Smith 2000). **73*a*** 'Let your alms remain in your hand until you have taken pains to find out whom you should give to'; not from Comestor but varying a proverb '*Desudet* eleemosyna in manu tua, donec invenias *iustum*, cui des' common in penitential texts (Gray 1986[1]:59). It is linked (Scase 1989:198n112) with the Cato quotation in Peter the Cantor's *Verbum Abbreviatum* (*PL* 205:150), perhaps misremembered here (AlfQ). This important passage, cut in **C** but for line 70, adduces in quasi-scholastic form (*Ac*) an opposing patristic authority, clarifies the issue by analysis ending in a scriptural quotation (76–81*a*) and draws a practical conclusion (*Forthi*) clinched by another patristic text. **74** *Gregory*: see on 5.146. **75*a*** 'Do not choose (for yourself) whom to take mercy upon, for it may be that you will pass over someone who deserves to receive (your alms); for it is not certain for which (act) you may please God more [*sc.* giving to the unworthy or the deserving].' This is not from Gregory as stated (*Sk*) but from Jerome's Commentary on Eccl. 11:6 (a text of which *Bn* notes the relevance to Piers in the present context): 'Ne eligas cui *bene facias*… Incertum est *enim quod opus* magis placeat Deo' (*PL* 23:1103). **78** *yarketh…reste*: 'prepares a place of rest for himself [*sc.* in heaven]'. **80** *beggeres borwen…*: cf. Ps 36:21, which contrasts the sinner who borrows with the merciful just man who gives. **81** *Bn* aptly cites Prov 19:17. **81*a*** 'And why then didst thou not give my money into the bank [*mensam*], that at my coming I might have

exacted it with usury [*sc.* interest]?' (Lk 19:23; cf. B 6.237–45). *Bn* finds that 'its application appears to rest on the interpretation of *mensa* as the table from which charity is dispensed, and is hardly congruous with that of 6.2[37]ff'. But **L**'s discretely idiosyncratic use of the parable suggests both that money is better given to beggars than to *nobody*, since it is thereby 'invested on behalf of God' who will repay with interest, and implies that the penalty for *not* doing so will be grave. **82** *Forthi* …: a conclusion not following logically from the injunction to the givers, but standing in parallel with it: all should give to all who ask; but not all *should* ask. *gret nede*: i.e. total destitution; a phrase taken up at C 67, 161 and illustrated at B 20.20=C 22.20. **83** *Book*: 'Bible' (though the source here is patristic), anticipating 86, where the quotation *is* scriptural; the revision eliminates this oversight. **84*a*** 'He is rich enough who does not lack bread'; from Jerome, Ep. 125 (*PL* 23:1085). A parallel possible source is I Tim 6:8 (*Bn*; also relevant are vss.18–190). **85** 'Let the practice of reading saints' lives be your source of comfort'. *LA* describes early desert hermits living *Withoute borwynge or beggynge bote of God one* (17.8; *Bn*); but omission of this idealistic exhortation reflects the increased realism in **C**.

70–161 There follows, introduced by a line retained from **B**, the first part of **C**'s longest insertion. Though retarding the episode's progress and (taken with the removal of the Tearing) lessening the drama still further, it is remarkable for 'unsentimental compassion and raw truth' (Pearsall 1988:180; see also Shepherd 1983:175). This passage on people who are truly destitute and those who feign to be, and then the second on 'lollares' and false hermits (187–279), are quasi-digressions. The short one they replace (B 74–86*a*, debating whether to give alms to all who ask) was added to the diatribe against false beggars in the summary of Truth's letter at ZA 44–5. Only the first is integrated into the Pardon narrative resumed at 166, and what mainly links them is the idea that something worthy in itself may be rendered suspect by a corrupt simulacrum. Thus, against both the genuinely needy who do their best to live honestly and the 'lunatic lollars' (neither of whom beg) are opposed the false beggars and hermits who are capable of work but ask alms deceitfully. **L**'s animus may suggest that his earlier attacks on the latter had struck home, perhaps even drawn a hostile personal reaction.

71–97 deal with households whose poverty arises from losing the bread-winner or having many mouths to feed. **71** 'But if we consider the matter carefully, it is the most needy who are our neighbours'; a conception drawn from Christ's parable of the Good Samaritan (Lk 10:30–6) answering the question 'Who is my neighbour?' and one destined to play a large part in the definition of charity at 19.48–79. **72** Cf. 4.123 on these places as objects of spiritual 'pilgrimage'. *puttes*: see on B 5.406. *pore…*

cotes: landless cottage-tenants and (to judge from 83) widows (*Pe*), whose earnings come only from whatever poorly-paid work they can do at home. **74** *hous-hyre*: rent due because they have no husbands who can work for the chief lord and so get a cottage to live in free. **75–6** *to...with*: 'for making porridge with which to satisfy'; the twofold use of phrasal *with* before the direct object of *maken* is noteworthy. **79** *reuel*: from OF *ruelle* 'lane', the narrow space for the cradle between bed and wall. **81** *rusches to pylie*: to make rush-lights from the pith by dipping it in tallow (the candles of the poor), for their own use and for sale. **82** *ryme*: either a reference (the only recorded one) to alliterative or 'head-rhymed' verse as *ryme* or, simply, 'verse as opposed to prose' (MED s.v. *rime* n. (c) and (b)). **84** *And...of*: 'And the woe of...'; a comma would be better after *cotes* 83. **87** *at* (1): 'from'. *hym*; *here*: typical alternation of sg. and pl. *noon*; *eue*: i.e. at both daily meals. **89** 'What other things are needed by the man [*hym* understood] who...' **91** *And...perto*: 'And many to reach for [what he earns]...' **92–3** *as for*; *as*: 'as if it were'. *ytake / bake*: end-rhyme lending a formula-like feel. **94** *ferthing-worth*: 'more than 12 quarts; a sufficient quantity' (*Sk*). **95** *were*: 'would be [if they could get it]'. **96** 'This would indeed be a worthwhile form of alms-giving'. **L**'s proposal for 'social benefits' places poor families and the disabled before the religious orders, the traditional recipients of alms.

98–104 form an introductory flourish on feigned beggars, to be developed in 139–58. *Ac beggares...they... he...suche*: 'But as for beggars...(except for those who are...), if one of them...even if that sort die of hunger'. The tortuous syntax leaves unclear whether those in 99 are among the pub-haunters. **98** *with bagges*: in which they hide away food beyond what they need to live (cf. 139). *þe whiche...churches*: 'whose churches are the taverns'; a grammatical construction that 'fuses' *þe whiche* '(for) who(m)' (functioning as an ethic dative) and *here* 'their'. Frequenting taverns is insistently linked with failure in religious duties (cf. Gluttton at 6.417 above). **101** *lorélles*: with wrenched stress providing the third *r* stave. **103** *lymes*...: as they denied at 8.135 above. *lollares lyf*: for detailed discussion of *lollare* see Scase 1989:149–60, Wittig 2001:175–80. **104** *Goddes lawe*: see Ex 20:9, and cf. Gen 3:17b. *lore*: cf. II Thess 3:10.

105–27a *opere beggares*: mentally disabled, and so not to blame for not working, *lollares* but not *lorelles*. **108** 'And become more or less deranged with the phases of the moon'. **109** recalls Patience's characterisation of Charity at B 13.161–2 and the Dreamer's at B 18.1–2. **110** *moneyles*: a word occurring only once again, at 295. **111** *will*: the pointed (pre)-echoes noted suggesting a pun on this word. *witteles*: cf. again 15.1. **112** *Peter*; *Poul*: referring to their missionary journeys. **115–17** argue (as about the rich at 16.19–21) that the all-powerful God's

allowing something suggests that he has a purpose for it. **118** *Hit aren*: see on 5.59. **119** *sent hem*: both verb and pronoun have duplex reference ('he sent [the apostles]'; 'he sends [these mad people]'). *seluerles*: cf. Lk 9:3. *somer garnement*: deduced from Christ's injunction not to take two coats (Lk 9:3). **120** *Withoute bagge*: cf. Lk 10:4a. **120a** 'When I sent you without bread or scrip'; running together Lk 22:35, *Quando misi vos sine sacculo, et pera* and Lk 9:3, *Nihil tuleritis...neque peram, neque panem, neque pecuniam* 'Take...neither scrip, nor bread, nor money'. **121** *Barfot*: cf. *watschoed* 20.1. **123a** '[And] salute no man by the way' (Lk 10:4b). **124** *Matheu*: possibly misrecalling Lk 10:5 'Into whatsoever house [*domum*] you enter' (Alf*Q*). **125a** '[Deal thy bread to the hungry and] bring the needy and the harbourless [*vagos* 'wanderers'] into thy house' (Is 58:7); the bracketed text is quoted at 11.67a. **127a** '[Let no man deceive himself]. If any man [among you] seem to be wise [in this world], let him become [*fiat* for *fiet*] a fool, that he may be wise' (I Cor 3:18).

128–38 describe the duty of the rich to welcome genuine minstrels, if only for the sake of their noble patrons (cf. 7.96ff above), and compare the 'lunatic lollars' to them (at 137 repeating 107 entire) and the minstrels' patron to God. **134** *ȝut rather*: 'all the more readily'. **138** If they have sinned, God knows the truth of the matter; it is not man's concern. This undisclosed divine awareness is metaphorically represented by a royal letter under the privy seal granting a privilege or exemption.

139–61 bitingly characterise the way of life of vagabonds who are commonly confused with the previous class by being called 'lollars', though neither sick nor feeble-minded but deliberately idle. **140** *lollarne*...: 'of lollars and (of) ignorant hermits, (who...)'; on the archaic gen. pl. see at 4.14. **149** *sode mete*: 'cooked food' or perhaps 'boiled meat' (MED s.v. n. 2d; cf. Z 7.316). **154** *a begyneld wyse*: 'in the manner of a beggar'; found only in **L**, though the *AW* (MED s.v.) has *beggild*. The original sense may have been 'beggarwoman' (from *beg-* + the female suffix *-ild*) but neither here nor at 10.266 does it have feminine reference. There is no evidence that the Netherlandish order of *Beguines* which OED s.v. connects the word with were familiar in England at this period. **155** 'And knows any trade, should he wish to put it to use'. **157** *han*: either the verb without following indefinite art., or the latter with intruded aspirate. **158** *Goddes lawe*: see on 104. **159–61** The 'conclusion' by Piers lends authority to the narratorial condemnation (lollars must reform, beggars be truly needy). **160a** recalls the opening of the 'Beggars sequence' at 61 and the lines provide a juncture with the 12-line section on their tricks and vices retained from **B**. *Sk* ascribes 162–279 to Piers, so that his diatribe against negligent clergy prompts the priest's intervention at 280. But although this passage seems like a digression, when punctuated as here the intervention seems appropriate by way of response to 159–61; and it is not easy to read 163–65 as coming from Piers. **160b** *til...amended*: bringing out the ploughman's moral authority in determining who should be 'in' the pardon.

162–74 An attack that ends with a new line 'deleting' false beggars from entitlement to pardon and benefit from the common prayer of the Church. **L** dislikes them for serving Truth's enemy False and harming the prospects of the virtuous poor who depend on *trewe* men's charity to live, whether widows or contemplatives (or marginal clerks like himself?) **162** *banneth*: presumably because begging implies a lack of faith in God's goodness. **162a** 'I have been young, and now am old: and [**B**] I have not seen the just forsaken, nor his seed seeking bread' (Ps 36:25). Donaldson 1982 speculates implausibly that *derelictum* can be read as the noun, making the line satiric ('I have never seen a just derelict…'). *And elsewhere*: 'My strength is weakened through poverty' (Ps 30:11b). Both psalms are impassioned expressions of trust in Providence under trial and adversity. **163–5** are somewhat digressive and repetitive. **163** *preche*: so as to 'gloss' the scriptural text, which does not explicitly 'ban' begging. **164** *this*: a generalising quasi-definite use of the demonstrative (*MES* 174), not a reference to the folk present. **168** *of kynde*: 'by nature'; beggar-children, begotten out of wedlock like animals, are here held to inherit a bent to idleness, which becomes habitual following the abuse they suffer from their parents. **B 90 (Z 78, A 74)** is excised as perhaps unsuitably low-comic in the context (*wehee* is used in *CT* I 4066 of a horse running after wild mares). **169** *of here children*: making explicit what is awkwardly expressed in **B**'s sudden shift from pl. to sg. **170** *faiten*: by pretending that their children were born disabled. **171** **L**'s lack of sympathy for them arises from believing their disabilities to be self-caused (though this can hardly be true of the children). So austerely integralist a view of the family unit has an OT feel; but his divided attitude to the issue is suggested by Wit's argument at 10.236–47a.

175–86 This new form of the **ZAB** lines, expanded with a five-line parenthesis (178–82), ends with a macaronic containing the Latin that the Passus began with. But this *is* the end (however abrupt) of **Z**; and the Tearing scene added in **A** and retained in **B**, complicating the issue but rounded off with a musing epilogue on dreams and pardons, was plainly intended to give the *Visio* a conclusion at once more dramatic and more elegant. In **C** much more is to follow, beginning with lines on groups earlier omitted: the old; pregnant women whose inability to work makes the family poorer; those who have suffered misfortunes of natural or human origin. The passage makes its key idea a virtue that is to play a major rôle in the *Vita* because it earns divine mercy and complete pardon. *Patience*, especially as 'humble acceptance of suffering',

is seen as the product of true faith and therefore suffices (*sola fides sufficit*) to purge the soul of all remaining debt (cf. Pearsall 1988:181). Forming the passive counterpart to P.'s active work for his fellows in the Christian commonwealth, it is here found equally efficacious for salvation (in Z 90 even more so). A source for this notion that bodily distress meekly endured is spiritually purgative may be I Pet 4:1–2: 'for he that hath suffered in the flesh hath ceased from sins: That now he may live the rest of his time in the flesh, not after the desires of men but according to the will of God'.

187–279 The second major addition to Passus IX deals with 'false hermits', another category of *faitours* to be distinguished from a virtuous (at best, exemplary) group, the contemplative solitaries entirely devoted to *penaunce and pouerte* (B 15.270). The opening argument ('And alle holy eremytes…') follows the same procedure as at 128ff ('And alle manere munstrals…') and specifies this class of 'lollers' as *lewede ermytes* (192). **187** *holy eremites*: the successors of the *holy fadres* like Antony and Giles (B 15.272). **188–93** The sentence is not really incomplete (*Pe*), though the notion that 'they will not receive the pardon' is merely implied. For while it has two parallel subjects (*ermytes…thise lollares*), it is not anacoluthic. Punctuated (as is possible) with a comma after *Coueyten* 193, that verb may also be judged to have two parallel *objects* (*Al þat; þe contrarye*); but the latter is perhaps better explained 'as an adverbial phrase, with the force of "contrariwise"' (*Sk*). **188** *heye weye*: where the many who pass offer good prospects of alms; the model hermits by contrast *Woneden in wildernesse* (B 15.273), their solitude guaranteeing their sincerity. **193** *coterelles*: the *ouer-land strikares* who slink back to their *cotes* (151), misleadingly resembling the honest poor at 97. **196** *wonede whilom*: cf. 17.28. *lyons*: perhaps alluding to St Jerome, who is depicted in his cave with a tame lion at his feet; hermits with docile bears are not recorded. **197–202** stress the essence of the hermits' life as voluntary renunciation: they were not of low but high social class, *chose* poverty and either had income or worked to support themselves without imposing on others. **201** *were*: '(who) were' (Ø-relative). **203** *edifien*: glossed by MED s.v. 4(a) 'strengthen spiritually or morally', but this seems unlikely, since the point is that they *live* here (and construct their hermitages on the main road); so (as noted in Jones 1997:72n8) the sense will be 'build' (s.v. 1(a)), with an ironic 'anti-pun' on 'edify'. **205** *clerkes withouten grace*: perhaps like Will as he presents himself in Pr 3. **206** *Helden...hous*: for the phrase cf. B 15.142. **208** The sly implication is not that all friars are deceivers (cf. 8.73) but that, since those who deceive in friars' garb do well out of it, many *must* be. **210** *copes*: cf. Pr 54. **211** *oen of som ordre*: 'an individual belonging to some order or other'; read in the light of B 13.285, perhaps suggesting a (real or pretended) survivor of one of the obscurer orders suppressed in the C14th, though he is in fact its only 'member'. *profete*: 'used satirically' indeed (*Pe*), though a reference to Mt 7:15 seems out of place in this context. They are too *lewed* to set up as teachers, but not to ape the outward mannerisms of OT prophets (strange dress, behaviour and utterances) so as to impose on *lewed* hearers. **212** *þe lawe*: i.e. of the Church, though part of the meaning may be that feigned hermits in good health should do manual work as the Statute of Labourers required (cf. 245). *yf...trewe*: 'if (this) Latin (authority) is to be trusted'; a formulaic phrase (cf. 3.487). **212a** 'It is not permitted that we should make the law fit our wishes, but we should make our wishes fit the law'; untraced, but 'similar statements appear in Pseudo-Chrysostom's Commentary on Mt 23 and Innocent III's *De contemptu mundi* 2.4' (Alf*Q*), and the quotation is connected by Scase (214n59) with St Benedict's admonition against false hermits. **213–18** An ingenious deduction of the *lollares'* character from their name (or, proof of its aptness to their nature). **213** *Kyndeliche*: 'quite rightly', but also 'according to what they really are'. **214** *Engelysch...techynge*: implying that the verb, from which the noun indeed comes (MED s.v. *lollen* v.), was long familiar. But since **L** traces the sense 'loll about, move unnaturally' to the *fact* of lameness, *lollen* at **218** is not likely to allude punningly to Wycliffe's followers (as given by MED under 3 (b) 'to carry on as a Lollard' and as taken by *Pe* and also, with further speculations, by Kerby-Fulton 1999:523–4). The earliest use of *loller* with the referent 'Lollard' is *CT* II 1173, 1177, of the form *lollard* a 1395 close roll of Richard II (MED s.v. *Lollard* n. (a)). So despite suggestive contextual references to belief and law in 218, **L**'s insistence on the etymology (about which, in the light of his comment on *hethene* and *heeth* at B 15.458, he is unlikely to be wrong) and the strictness of the comparison (217a) indicate the correct meaning to be 'They lounge about idly in defiance of Christian doctrine and discipline' (cf. 104).

219–39 describe the civil and religious observance that the Church ordains for all members of society according to their estate. The best-known scriptural source for the doctrine of civil 'obedience' is Rom 13:1–6. **221** *religious*: perhaps not in its narrower sense but also including secular clergy who, being under formal obedience to their ordinary, have a 'rule' of life if not a Rule. **223–6** Cf. 5.65–6, 8.28–31. *fox...wolues*: their abundance in the woods and uplands making hunting a necessity and forming a main part of lords' perceived function in the rural economy. **227** *cese*: from both work and sport; it was obligatory to hear Mass on Sunday. **228** *mete*: the midday meal (dinner). **231** *haly...holly*: the emphatic chime stressing how Sundays and other feast-days were to be hallowed by attending all three services. **234** *Pouerte*:

allowing that the poor might find these observances difficult because of the pressure to work for basic needs. *trauayles*: those on necessary journeys might find themselves far from a church. **236–8** *this...dedly synne*: strictly only missing Mass on Sunday or a main feast-day; but regular non-attendance at the other Sunday services and breach of the fasting regulations ('this') were regarded as failure to fulfil the 3rd Commandment (Ex 20:8–11) and so potentially grave. **239** *acounted*: at the particular Judgement; cf. Pr 126–7.

240–54 This fine satire makes the serious point that such 'hermits' use their supposedly devotional manner of life as a cover for avoiding their basic religious duties. On hermits see Swanson 1989:271–3, Clay 1914: chs. 1–6 passim, Davis 1985. **240–1** *where*; *Yf*: 'whether'. *fer*: the assumption being that proper hermits would, if not ordained themselves, live in a community with a priest or near a church. **245** *þe lawe*: the Statute of Labourers. **246–7** *hem...he*: a switch from the collective to one typical individual. **246** *Y*: perhaps only representative, but the loss of normal narratorial distance heightens the sense of a digressive insertion. **247** *Come*: 'coming' (to dinner at some household); the form may be inf. or p.p. **248** 'He would have to be nothing less than an eminent divine or a venerable priest'. **249** *cloth*: russet; possibly his habit as a former friar. **250** *furste*: as an honoured guest like the *maister* of 15.39. **252** *syde...table*: cf. 14.139; this suggests that he may be an ex-friar, though never so distinguished as he now wishes to seem. **253** *wyn*: cf. 6.159–61 for the normal fare of professed religious and 15.66 for what they could get at a knight's table. **254** *blanked*: perhaps with the same sense as at Z 3.159, to fit with the white bread (both items implying 'the best quality'). **255–6** The accusation is like that of *vnsittinge soffrance* levelled at the king in 3.207. These *sottes* are not allowed to preach like the pardoner at Pr 78, but presumably stricter discipline is needed that would forbid them to go on wearing their habits. **257–8** *Simon...Vigilare*: 'It's as if the bishops were asleep; better wake up!' *Simon*: Simon Peter was regarded as the first bishop of Rome and (at least in high papal theory) his successors the popes as the immediate source of episcopal authority, which they delegated to the ordinary or territorial bishop. The quotation alludes to Christ's question in the Garden of Gethsemane: *Et ait Petro*: Simon, dormis? non potuisti una hora vigilare? 'And he saith to Peter: *Simon, sleepest thou? Couldst thou not watch one hour?*' (Mk 14:37). *charge*: a responsibility deriving from Christ's 'charge' or mandate (MED s.v. 7(a), first ex.) to Peter, 'Feed my sheep' (Jn 21:15–17), re-iterated in the Apostle's own injunction to priests to 'feed the flock of God' (I Pet 5:1–4) and 'watch' (*vigilate* 8). **259** *wakere*: ironically it is the wolves not the shepherds who 'keep watch'. *ben wroken*: 'have forced their way'; see *TN* on this apparently unique instance of the sense. **260** *berkeres*: allegorically, the parish clergy, who aid the bishops in their pastoral task. *as*: 'as if they were blind'. **261** '[I will strike the shepherd], and the sheep shall be dispersed' (Mk 14:27, quoting Zach 13:7). The NT reference is to the scattering of the disciples after Christ's death, the OT to the dispersion of the faithful remnant of Israel, a passage of Messianic intent. *þe dogge*: alluding to Is 56:10, quoted at B 10.287a. **262** *tarre*: mixed with lard for use against sheep-mange. The 'healing ointment' the people require for spiritual well-being is sound guidance in confession and good example from their pastors. **263** The best they can hope for however is that the archdeacon's summoner will, if bribed, stay proceedings against them over an offence (such as adultery) for which they have been summoned to the Church court; an invective against the desire for 'filthy lucre' (I Pet 5:2) corrupting the penitential system. *supersedeas*: see on 2.187. **264** *shabbede*: recalling A 8.17 (Kerby-Fulton 1999:524). *shyt wolle*: 'befouls the wool'; in the light of 266b the apparent contextual sense, although lexically the phrase ought to mean 'defecates (the) wool [of the sheep he has eaten]' (see *TN*). This 'has no literal sense' (*Pe*) unless the notion is that 'the proximity of evil clergy causes the laity to be spiritually defiled'. **264a** 'Under weak shepherds, the wolf befouls the wool, / The unprotected flock is torn by him'; *cacat* is glossed 'foedat' in Migne (= *fouleth* 266). The elegiac couplet is in Alan of Lille's *Liber Parabolarum* (*PL* 210:581), a work quoted at 20.452–3, and was a widely known proverbial saying (Whiting S241; Walther 30541; and cf. *CT* VI 101–2). **265** *herde*: i.e. the bishop. **266** *worye*: normally applied to the wolf; cf. 226. **268** *falsliche*: in a wrongful and deceptive manner (so the fleeces remain soiled). If *Pe* rightly interprets sheep-washing (on the basis of patristic commentary on Cant 4:2) as symbolising 'the purification of the soul of the faithful in the love of Christ', this protest will be against the compromising of sacramental penance by clergy whose bad confessional practice imperils the souls of the faithful. **269** *thy lord*: Christ, 'the prince of pastors', at the Last Judgement; the crucial source-text here is I Pet 5:2–4. **270** *moneye*: alluding to the large incomes of bishops, the purpose of which was in theory to further their pastoral work. **271** *weye*: implying that so many sheep will have perished that there will not be much wool. **272** 'Give an account of thy stewardship: [for now thou canst be steward no longer' (Lk 16:2); a text preached on by Thomas Wimbledon at Paul's Cross in 1388. Citing this parable is not just a warning but a threat: unworthy prelates will be punished in the next life, and may be dispossessed in this. **273–6** 'Your income, I believe, won't suffice to pay what you owe in that place where neither money nor mercy will avail you, but only "take this in return for the time *you* showed clemency for cash and broke my law"'. *lawe*: 'strict judgement by [the divine] law'. **277** *lacchesse*: a variety of sloth manifested by those 'newe shepherdes that leten hir sheep wityngly go renne to the wolf that is in the breres' (*CT* X 720). **279** This tart warning reaches a dramatic end and skilfully returns to the *pardon*, which had slid into the background at 188. The digression has in principle been heard only by the outer, not the inner audience; but in provoking the priest's response, it in a manner accounts for (the otherwise unmotivated) *iangelede* at 292.

(ii) 280–91 *Piers's Quarrel with the Priest* The important **A** *continuation* (89–100) from where **Z** broke off is kept entire and little changed in **B**, but cut by about two thirds in **C**. **280** *a prest*: a type-figure, inevitably suggesting the local parish priest, who had official authority to examine and pronounce on a pardon received by one of his parishioners. **82** The contents have clearly been communicated to the folk (e.g. the merchants at 41, who are entered in the margin with 'many years' after them); but their details and the lawyers' were in the private letter, and the present document with its two-line text is the Pardon itself. **283** alliterates either as standard on *b* with stress shifted to the proclitic particles or (reading more naturally) as Type Ie with counterpoint (*aab / ab*). *Y*: a graphic reminder of the narrating persona as eye-witness of (but not, as in **A**, participant in) events at this crucial point. **284** This memorable line is quoted at *MS* 655 (changing *two* to *three*). **285** *in...Treuthe*: 'as Truth's own testimony'; therefore needing no further authorisation. **286–7** '[And] those who have done well shall go into eternal life; but those who (have done) evil (will go) into eternal fire'. Clause 40 of the Athanasian Creed ends a passage (vss. 31ff) on the Last Judgement that includes under 'doing well' the corporal works of mercy mentioned at 71–97 (see Mt 25:34–40). As a direct citation from a major Creed of the Church, the lines re-inforce HC's teaching at I 129–33, which is itself grounded on Scripture (cf. Mt 25:34, 41). The credal clause grafts a modified form of the phrases *supplicium aeternum* and *vitam aeternam* (Mt 25:46) onto a clause derived from Jn 5:29: '...procedent *qui bona fecerunt, in resurrectionem vitae; qui vero mala egerunt, in resurrecionem iudicii*'. **288** *Peter*: not an address to the ploughman (cf. *Peres* 280, *Perkyn* B 131) but the saint's name used in an asseveration (see on 7.181). *no pardoun*: in the document considered as a (formal) pardon or any (actual) 'pardon' in the wording of its text, which the priest now translates and expands. **289** The scansion of this (Type III) line is awkward in deferring the first lift until *haue*. The words echo exhortations to turn from evil and learn to do good in Ps 33:15 ('Diverte a *malo*, et *fac bonum*') and Is 1:16–17 ('Quiescete *agere perverse*, Discite *benefacere*'). Their eschatological resonance recalls II Cor 5:10 on how before the *tribunal Christi* 'the judgement seat of Christ' everyone will receive 'according as he has done, whether good or evil [*sive bonum, sive* *malum*]'. *haue thy soule*: cf. 'The Lord will redeem the souls of his servants' (Ps 33:23). **291** *euele shal ende*: an improvement on **B** in referring to both the wrong-doer's last moments and his final destiny; cf.'The death of the wicked is very evil' (Ps 33:22).

B 115–38a (A 101–25a) Apart from some small revisions (e.g. of the obscure verbs in A 107 and the provocative quotation in A 123), **A**'s mysterious and compelling continuation of the (presumably complete) **Z** Version is unchanged in **B** but excised in **C**, for reasons that must remain speculative. **115** *pure tene*: used again of P.'s other powerful and unexpected action at B 16.86 (removed in **C**). Earlier interpretations are surveyed by Frank 1957:28–9, who interprets P.'s tearing (1951:317–31) as symbolising acceptance of the content of Truth's conditional 'pardon' and rejection of the need for or value of formal paper pardons. P.'s action 'does not imply a rejection of the message from Truth' but shows that the pardon's efficacy 'is not dependent on...a piece of paper' but is conditional on the way one lives (*K–F*). The scene has generated diverse and conflicting views. Woolf 1969 sees the pardon as a quasi-legal document that only becomes a true pardon after P. has torn it. Schroeder 1970 ([=Carruthers 1973:70], like Frank and *K–F*, does not think P. rejects the pardon, and interestingly compares the tearing with Moses' angry breaking of the tablets of the Law: 'iratusque valde [= *in pure tene*]...tabulas...confregit' (Ex 32:19), an act seen in patristic exegesis as typologically signifying the change from the old law to the new (ibid. 71). Baker 1984[1] finds the pardon's emphasis on good works shown to be inadequate later in the poem by comparison with documents such as those of Patience, Peace and Christ. The theology is examined in subtle detail by Baker 1980, Adams 1983 and Simpson 1990:71–88; and for recent discussion see Lawler 2000. **116–17** '[For] though I should walk in the midst of the shadow of death, I will fear no evils: for thou art with me' (Ps 22:4). The Latin (part-quoted again at B 12.291 apropos Trajan and good works) will scan as two alliterative lines of Types III and I respectively. Vs 6 of this great psalm of comfort ('And thy *mercy* will follow me all the days of my life') is also closely relevant to P.'s situation. For while the psalm-text refers to 'mercies' shown in this life and not the next, *pardon perpetuel* (9.60) may signify a guarantee of unceasing grace to the faithful *in via* attempting to live in *treuthe*. **118** *cessen*: not permanently (cf. *so* 118, 119) but in order to leave more time for prayer and penance. Receiving Truth's message arouses urgent realisation that 'doing good / well' goes beyond fulfilling one's 'active' social duties (8.110–11); and awareness of the limitless demand of charity sharpens one's sense of the need for immediate attention to *preieres and penaunce*. These may be here equated with the Pardon's *bona opera* (*Bn*), though in this period prayer was normally contrasted

with 'acts' such as the corporal works of mercy described in the vss preceding Mt 25:46, on which the Pardon text is based. This injunction to active love of one's neighbour, which constitutes the *second* of the two 'great commandments', P. is fully aware of (8.218–19). But now he will give first place to the spiritual 'work' that providing for the community's (and his own) bodily needs has prevented him from doing, so as better to fulfil the *first* great commandment, to love God (cf. 124a below). **119** *bely ioye*: replacing *bélyue* and altered in turn in the revision of A 112 at B 126b. **120** *plou3*: like the pike-staff of penance at 6.328, an emblem of 'active effort' (in the ascetic life). **121** *wepen*: prayer in the penitential spirit of the dominant psalm-influenced tradition, which was authorised by Jesus' own practice (Heb 5:7) and, since the time of St Bernard, directed principally to meditation on the passion of Christ. There may be a clerkly 'visual' pun on the sense '(spiritual) weapon' against temptation (cf. 21.219). **122** *payn*: the chime on pen*aunce* inevitably suggesting a homophonic pun on the senses 'bread' and 'penitential suffering' (MED s.v. *peine* n. 2a; for similar wordplay, cf. B 14.314). The figurative sense of *eet* will then be 'fed inwardly upon, drew spiritual sustenance from' (MED s.v. *eten* v. 3b Fig. (a)). **124** *esy*: a revision that removes the polysemy of *mete* A which, while uncertain both textually and lexically (see *TN*), is perhaps too much after *payn* (though *mete* itself is re-used at B 129). **124a** 'My tears have been my bread day and night' (Ps 41:4). **125** *Luc lye*: the evangelist's veridicity is repeated at A 10.120, a line dropped in revision. *Be fooles*: i.e. to be 'fools for Christ's sake' (I Cor 4:10) but wise in the sight of God (I Cor 3:19), because free from desire for *worldes blisse*. Lk 10:21 echoes the Pauline contrast in setting the *parvuli* against the *sapientes* as receivers of the secrets of God's kingdom. The uneducated Piers numbers himself with the 'little ones' amongst those who receive the pardon. **127** 'Be not solicitous [for your life, what you shall eat...]' (Lk 12:22); on medieval discussions of the text see Frank 1957:31–33, Scase 1989:61–4. Alf*Q* relates P.'s decision to Phil 4:6 *Nihil solliciti sitis*, which advises reliance on prayer. The text's citation by Patience at B 14.34a directly recalls this scene. **129–30** are based on Lk 12:24. *foweles*: cf. as an emblem of *lowe libbyng men* the lark at B 12.264=C 14.187. **132** *lettred a litel*: reminiscent of the phrase *simpliciter litterati* applied by the Cistercian William of Rimington c. 1385 to those with a smattering of Latin whom the Lollards led astray (Aston in Hudson & Wilks 1987:311). The priest's gibe seems provoked by P.'s reliance on what he hears as a tag-phrase picked up from listening to such people. **133** P.'s answer uses homophonic word-play on *abbesse* / *a.b.c.* to suggest through phonetic identity a real ('Platonic') relation between the rudimentary education / Christian understanding of the *simplices* and the virtue of ascetic self-control (see further Simpson 1986³:51; Schmidt 1987:86–7; Tarvers 1988:137–41). **134** Conscience teaches, as it were, at the grammar-school of the soul. On conscience as a 'book', cf. the description of a Cistercian lay-brother, 'simplex et illiteratus', who had 'pro codice, conscientiam' and yet grew spiritually by reading 'in libro experientiae' (Kirk 1988:17). **136** *diuinour*: 'theologian' in all its four appearances; but perhaps here punning offensively on '(idle) soothsayer' (MED s.v. 1). *Dixit …*: 'The fool hath said [in his heart: There is no God]' (Ps 13:1). The Priest, as well as criticising what he takes to be the Ploughman's 'foolishness' in attempting to expound Scripture, alludes to Piers's injunction to *be* a 'fool', without grasping its spiritual sense. **A 123** 'Because I have not known learning, [I will enter into the powers of the Lord: O Lord, I will be mindful of thy justice alone]' (Ps 70:15–16). The Priest's use of this quotation, mockingly inverting the Psalmist's faith in divine support against his enemies, is replaced in **B** by an equally strong but less subtle insult. **137** *Lewed lorel*: showing that P. has understood the sarcasm and replies even more directly by calling his critic (in the vernacular) a spiritual ignoramus. *litel*: smartly taking up the priest's own word at 132. **138** *Salomons sawes*: the Book of Proverbs. **138a** 'Cast out the scoffers, lest with them quarrels abound' [Vg: 'and…quarrels and reproaches shall cease'] (Prov 22:10). The verse occurs immediately after the one quoted by P.'s teacher Conscience at B 3.335*a* = C 3.486*a*.

292–6 292 *iangelede*: now somewhat out of place without the quarrel as in **AB**. **293** *thorw here wordes*: the noisy exchange that wakes Will being part of the 'realism' of dream-vision poetry (cf. the clamorous birdsong in Chaucer's *Parlement of Foules* 693–4). **294** *southe*: a detail indicating the dream's length; 'it is almost noon' (*Bn*), six hours from the first dream's 'inner time' of dawn (Pr 14) to the present 'outer time' of waking. This, too, 'realistically' corresponds to the time it would take to read out the two visions' 3000+ lines. **295–6** *Meteles… meteles*: the near-homonymy yielding a wryly 'Platonic' suggestion that dreamers may go hungry, to be later realised at 22.3.

(iii) *Epilogue* **297–351 297–301** form a transition between the end of the vision and the semi-ironic coda on the validity of dreams (302–16) and indulgences (324–45). These two sections are linked by a 7-line passage (317–23), beginning with *meteles* and ending with *pardoun*, that bases its authority for preferring *dowel* to the latter upon the former. Its significance is underlined by *concatenatio* and its being linked to 296 by running alliteration and to 298 by translinear alliteration. The syntax is somewhat elusive, for while in 299 *fol pencyf* could be the second object of *maked* 297, the two noun clauses of 300–1 cannot be further such objects, and so must be read as dependent on *studie* 'reflect deeply about what /

how.' **298** *so be*: 'describe what is really the case' rather than 'turn out prophetic'. **299** *pencyf in herte*: although the gloss 'thoughtful' (MED s.v. *pensif* adj. (c)) may be accepted here, the collocation with *herte* in quots. under (a) 'sorrowful' suggests an intended association with love-melancholy. This is confirmed by the tone of Will's later *love-dreem* after hearing Piers's name at B 16.18ff (a passage later drastically revised in **C**, which replaces P. with *Liberum Arbitrium*). **301** *two propre wordes*: presumably *Dixit insipiens* B 136; ironically ambiguous, since these words 'pertain to himself' as well as being 'appropriate' and 'goodly' (MED s.v. *propre* adj. 1(a), 3(a), 4(a)). But in **C** the referent is not these but the two pieces of 'construing' at 289–90, *wordes* there meaning 'utterances' (MED s.v. *word* n. 2a (a)).

302–16 302, 304 *Ac*: the import of this *pro / contra* quasi-scholastic formulation being 'Now…but on the other hand'. **303** *Caton*: standing for 'common-sense worldly judgement'; see on 4.17. *canonistres*: perhaps adduced here as exemplifying a clarity and certainty of interpretation at variance with the vagueness and ambiguity of dreams (Macrobius I. iii. 10). **AB 135 /151** quote the passage: Somnia ne cures, [*nam mens humana quod optans / Dum vigilat sperat, per somnum cernit ad ipsum* 'Disregard dreams, because the human mind / Sees sleeping what awake it hopes to find' (*DC* II.31). **A 135** *by hemseluen*: '(that) in their judgement'. **304** *Ac…bereth*: the syntax is strictly anacoluthic (as also in **AB**); but if *for* is taken in the formulaic manner suggested at 302, the sentence can be read: 'but on the other hand, the Bible testifies…' **305** *Danyel…dremes*: cf. Dan chs. 2–4; for discussion see Schmidt 2000:5–8. **306** *Nabugodonosor*: King of Babylon (6th c. BC). **C** corrects **AB**'s misattribution of a prophecy (139ff/155ff) directed not to Nebuchadnezzar but to Belshazzar, his successor and reputed son (the sg. at 307 would be more correct). *Bn* wonders if the change may be due in part to the 'implications for Richard II that might have been read into it'; but in the mid-1380s the threat to the King was less from 'uncouth knights' than from his own 'lower lords'. **B 155** *þi dremels*: confusing Daniel's explanation of Nebuchadnezzar's dreams (Dan 2, 4) with his interpretation to Belshazzar of the writing on the wall (Dan 5:23–8). **B 156–7** *vnkouþe knyʒtes… lower*: the Medes under Darius, 'lower' because not of the royal house of Babylon. **308–16** are a loose re-telling of Gen 37:1–11. **308–9** *mone…sterres*: despite the def. art., denoting no particular stars (Gen 37:9), but symbolising Joseph's mother, father and eleven brothers (315–16). **310** *iuged*: an interpretation not in the Bible, though **L** may have thought that Gen 37:11 ('his father considered the thing [*sc*. dream] with himself') implied Jacob's belief in Joseph's dream as a true prophecy. **311–12** describe their coming to Egypt to look for corn during a famine (Gen 42–5); it is actually Joseph who foretells the famine (to

Pharaoh: Gen 41:15–37). **315–16** replace the repetition in **B** of 165a at 167a but neatly repeat 312b at 315b with changed word-order and tense. Otherwise the lines alliterate vocalically on non-lexical words in a clumsy way reminiscent of the possibly draft lines at Pr 112–13. **316** *Israel*: 'he strives with God', the name (see *TN*) that God gave Jacob after he wrestled with the angel.

317–45 again follow a 'semi-scholastic' procedure (see on 302), beginning at 324 with *3ut* '(Now it is) nonetheless (the case that...)', leading up to *Ac* 330 'However (on the other hand...)' and concluding with *Forthy* 332 'Therefore...' and *At* '(For) at' **338**. This pattern is repeated in little within 321–3 ('For...So..'). **317** deliberately echoes 297 by way of summary. *Al this*: 'these Biblical examples and my own dreams.' **318** *And how*: governed by a verb implied in *studie*, 'And (reflect) on how the Priest asserted that "doing well" doesn't constitute a pardon'. The ironic sense 'that no pardon could be compared with "doing well"' is phantasmally evoked as a phrasal anti-pun (cf. the syntactical ambiguity of 319). *Dowel*: the first occurrence of a 'nominal verb-phrase' that is to provide a thematic structuring principle for the rest of the poem. **A 151–3** The leisurely 151–2 are dispensable; but 153 (with the cleric's *pure reson* counterweighing the Ploughman's *pure tene* at A 101) may have been removed as seeming to support the Priest, whereas **BC** *preuede* 'claimed [to find by experience of such things]' is fittingly ambivalent. **319** *demede*: with implied subject *I*; for though in principle in **AB** the Priest could be its subject and *indulgences* that of *passede* (an ambiguity allowed by the looseness of B 172), For C 321 removes any doubt that *Dowel* is the intended subject and governs all four objects. **320** *Bionales...*: legacies spent on such services that might have been better used (while the man was alive) in active 'doing well', thus obviating the need for them after his death (cf. 348–9 below). *lettres*: metonymic for the benefit to someone who supports the cause they promote (if the sense is as at B 5.640). **321** *dome*: again alluding to Mt 25:31–46 (see on 286–7). **323** *pardon and*: 'the pardon to be got from'. *Rome*: in // **B** 'the indulgence attached to visiting the basilica', i.e. *Seint Petres cherche* (*Bn*). **324** *hath þe Pope*: normal inversion after an adverb, not (as in *Ka*) a question. **325** *withouten penaunce*: if ironic, then hard to interpret precisely. There is no real contradiction between this and 328, as mistakenly judged in *Sch²*, which too closely associates 'pardon...with penance and prayer'. For the three categories are separate and distinct means of earning salvation (as might be brought out by punctuating with commas after each). 'L's view of indulgences' may then be read as 'orthodox enough' (*Bn*) if the sense of 324–5 is that 'a papal plenary indulgence [for some appropriate act of satisfaction] *is* able to save someone from purgatorial punishment [*penaunce*], if validly received [i.e. with

prior formal penance]'. Nonetheless, the mere survival from **A** to **C** of a phrase that risks misunderstanding and the exaggerated tone of 329 (which anticipates the friar at 10.31) may imply some reservations about the 'high' interpretation of the Pope's *plenitudo potestatis* derived from Christ's words to Peter quoted below. **326** *lettrede men...lawe*: theologians and canonists alike. **326a** '[And I will give to thee the keys of the kingdom of heaven. And] whatsoever thou shalt bind upon earth, it shall be bound also in heaven: [and whatsoever thou shalt loose upon earth it shall be loosed also in heaven' (Mt 16:19). The final bracketed part of this verse is the basis of the doctrine of canonical remission of punishment after death. **327** *so*: both 'therefore' and 'that is how'. **329** *Soules... dedly*: such a situation as when a dying sinner is absolved and through a major charitable benefaction receives a plenary indulgence for the temporal punishment he cannot now perform. **L** doubtless understands such apparent 'purchase' of pardon as an *in extremis* case (if by no means purely hypothetical) illustrating the 'mammon of iniquity' principle: that 'it is never too late to do well by yourself through doing well by others' (the point being to *do well*). **330–1** *to truste...so syker*: because active charity not only bespeaks an individual's humility, it benefits others, whereas this form of delegated piety does not. **333** *vp...tresor*: warning against the wrong inference that a virtuous use of money is a licence to sin in other ways. The word is resonant of its earlier charged occurrences, notably at 1.201–2. **335** Unless *nameliche* is a misreading for *manliche* (see *TN*) this line will require *maistres* to be trisyllabic and the pattern to be Type IIIa. **338, 341** *dede; dede*: the homophonic punning echo seeming to hint that what will matter to the dead at doomsday is what they did when alive (cf. *deth, dede* at 350–1 below). **338–9** *dome...acountes*: an image echoing that of Pr 126–7 and helping to draw together the *Visio*'s beginning and conclusion in a single eschatological perspective. **341** *day be day*: the judgement taking account not only of the end but of the course of each person's life, but concerning 'what' rather than 'how much' (342–3 scornfully dismiss the notion of quantity). **342** *provinciales lettres*: issued by the head of a religious order in a particular 'province' (e.g. England) and enabling lay people to participate in the spiritual benefits of its professed members, such as a mention in prayers for all members at Mass (cf. Wright *Pol. Songs* i. 256, ii. 21). The original idea behind religious confraternity was to share in the spiritual ideals of the order; but what **L** attacks here is a 'covetous' treating of salvation as a matter of *mede* rather than *treuthe* (as will become clear from Friar Flatterer's offer to Contrition at 22.366–7 below). **343** *fyue ordres*: the fifth order, first mentioned (*pace Sk*) in **B** not C, may be (as *Sk* thought) the Crutched Friars (*Fratres Cruciferi*, so named from the white cross emblazoned on their black habit), a non-mendicant order especially concerned with pilgrims and hospices. **342–5** The sentence is anacoluthic in all versions, but the sentiment is never in question: without good deeds, all the pardons in the world will prove worthless. This is not to condemn pardons as such, but a particular attitude of mind **L** seems to believe that they foster. **346–51** The convoluted concluding sentence encapsulates a prayer within an admonition and makes the object of the prayer the outcome of taking the counsel offered. **347–8** *And... That*: the verb *crye* is again to be understood after the first and before the second conjunction. **350–1** *deth...dede*: see on 338, 341. *reherce*: 'may be able to declare'.

Passus X (B VIII–IX, A IX–X)

PASSUS TEN initiates a Third Vision that in **C** fills the five passūs to XIV (XII in **B**, including an inner dream occupying most of XI) and at 1330 lines (1450 in **B**) forms the longest of the eight. Although the rubric ending IX is not securely authorial, the archetypal **C** *explicit* and **A** *incipit* both indicate a new start: this is the 'same' Dreamer's vision of the 'life' of doing well, better and best, beginning with the first of these. 'Life' here is at once 'life-story' (as of the saints in *LA*) and 'way or manner of life', both being explored through the Dreamer's search for a person 'Dowel' who lives it and is eventually to be identified as Piers / Christ. This is accomplished through the lively and often impassioned arguments of Will with type-figures and personified abstractions. The passus falls into three main parts. (i) a kind of 'prelude' to the dream describing an encounter with two Franciscan friars (1–60), is at 50 lines the longest waking-sequence after the 'autobiographical' episode (though unlike 5.1–108 it can be read as 'realistic' narrative). It is linked by a brief 'pastoral' reprise (61–7) of 1–5 to (ii), ll. 68–112, which consists of a calmer dialogue with THOUGHT. (iii) 128–311 is preceded by a short transition (113–27) where Thought introduces the Dreamer to WIT. The latter's discourse opens at a point corresponding to where A X / B IX began.

(i) 1–29 1–5 echo the Pr with references to clothing and summer (perhaps a symbol of Will's youth) during which his conviction (9.350–1) that Dowel is necessary for salvation drives his quest to 'give flesh' to this idea. **1** *russet*: the rough homespun worn by shepherds (the *shroudes* of Pr 2) and by the Minorites (called 'grey' friars after their garb of undyed wool), but also having associations with the Lollards (Hudson 1988:74–6,146–7). **3** *fraynede*: allegorically signifying his search for guidance; having seen Truth's pardon, he will try to find how to obey its injunction. **6–7** Will's rôle as 'representative man' is seen in the way his experience parallels that of the Folk in their quest

for St Truth at 7.157. *lasse ne more*: 'of whatever rank'; Will looks 'high and low' for Dowel. **8** *Friday*: a fasting-day (cf. 6.351), an apt time to meet mendicant religious vowed to ascetic self-denial. *two*: friars travelled in pairs (cf. B 12.19). **9** Franciscan theologians were amongst the greatest of the age, successive generations including Bonaventure (d. 1274), Duns Scotus (d.1308) and William of Ockham (d. 1347). On the Friars Minor in the 14th c. see Courtenay 1987:66–9, 185–90, 193–218. **11** *preyde hem*: echoing the request of the Folk to the Palmer at 7.169. **13** *frendes*: an initial attitude in keeping with his garb, which is like theirs; but Clopper 1997 overstates the case in thinking of the poet as a former Franciscan addressing a Minorite audience. **15** *courtes*: 'aristocratic households', like the one where Peace will say he met Friar Flatterer (22.345). **16** *cotes*: reflecting the Franciscans' mission to bring the Gospel to the urban poor. **17** *Do-euele*: a personified vernacular equivalent, never to recur, of the negative half of the Pardon formula *qui vero mala* [*egerunt*] (9.287). Will hopes they will be able to tell him what to avoid (as Piers told the Folk at 7.218–28). **18** *frere(s)*: the change from *Menours* works to widen the claim (which, while strong, need not be exclusive as Will takes it) to all friars instead of one order. **19** *hope*: the degree of unconscious arrogance in the claim depending on whether this ambiguous word is understood as 'believe' or 'hope'. **20** *Contra*: aggressive-sounding (at least in **C**, given the tone of 22b), but the normal abbreviated way ('contra dico') of stating the opposed position in a scholastic disputation (on the importance of this mode in **L** see Baker 1984). The procedure is preserved in *ST*'s standard formula *Sed contra* 'but on the other side of the question'. Like *ergo* at 28, this is its first appearance in a vernacular text, and it imparts a uniquely 'clerkish' tone to **L**'s writing. *despute*: 'argue the case', not implying quarrelsomeness; Will's interchange with the friars, his first real 'act' in the poem, differs from Piers's angry 'apposing' of the Priest after the latter had insultingly quoted a psalm-text at him (see B 7.136). His citation of authority follows the academic mode where controversial matters could be debated with calm courtesy, and it suggests that the *mony men* of 5 may be meant to include his teachers at the university or a religious *studium*. **21–9** Will's argument takes the form of a foreshortened syllogism: a major premiss of two propositions, the first assertoric (the scriptural dictum 21–4, treated as equivalent to a statement of fact) and the second (also bi-partite) apodictic (*whoso...euele*, necessarily true); a minor premiss (*Dowel...togederes*, again apodictic) linked by a copula; and a balancing two-part conclusion (*Ergo...freres* and its apodictic consequent *He...peple*). **21** *Sothly*: answering the friar at 18, with the force of 'It is a true proposition that....' *Septies...*: '[For] a just man shall fall seven times [and shall rise again: but the wicked shall fall down into evil]' (Prov 24:16). Will's opportunistic use of the first part of the verse is so like that for which Conscience rebukes Meed at 3.487 (after she has quoted from Prov 22:9b a commendation without the warning immediately following it) as to invite a cautious response to his challenge. The thought of the quoted verse is paralleled in Eccl 7:21, which omits mention of rising after sin, and 8:12, which warns against complacency, the greater pessimism of both passages according with the import of Will's truncated citation from Proverbs. **25–6** improve on the rhythm of **B** and the sense of **A**, deftly shifting the accent from the second to the first of the two words in the phrase. **25** The fourth lift is on *nat.* **26** spells out the meaning of 'not-well'. **27** Cf. 'But for to mowen don yvel ...ne mai nat ben referrid to good' (*Boece* IV. pr. ii. 247–9). **29** scans as Type I on *w* or as Type II on vowels.

30–60 'show', through an illustrative exemplum characteristic of the *ars praedicandi*, a more effective answer to Will than would be the purely analytical *distinctio* between senses of 'do well' and 'do evil' in a formal scholastic *responsum.* Clearly and memorably expounded so as to appeal to senses and emotions, the *forbisene* well illustrates the homiletic power of the mendicants. It is indebted to Augustine's Sermo 75, ch. iii (*PL* 5:247–9) on the account of Christ's stilling of the sea in Mt 14:24–33, which allegorises Peter's boat as the Church, the storm as temptation and the contrary wind as the devil who is trying to stop the disciples reaching the peace of heaven. *Pe* notes a Wycliffite sermon on Mt 24 (Arnold, iii. 375) attacking friars who apply the 'boat' image to themselves as the select vessel of salvation (cf. I Pet 3:20–1). **L**'s Minors refrain from doing so; but while not proving their contention that Dowel dwells with them, they demonstrate that occasional failures need not invalidate the claim they do make (18–19). *Pe* denounces their contention as 'a manifest falsehood'; but the friar's exposition takes full account of the text on which Will bases his argument, though quoting only the part that suits him. However, while he is neither presumptuous nor disingenuous (where Will is both), his subtle argument against *wanhope* fails adequately to recognise the need to avoid lesser offences and to see how the connectedness of venial to mortal can make of complacency the first step to presumption (these traits mark all the poem's friar-confessors at their worst). **33–5** *Lat bryng...*: a similitude that has something of the effect of a *distinctio* in that it accepts Will's major premiss (21–6), distinguishes between mortal sins and the venial sins of the just man so as to invalidate his minor premiss, and shows his conclusion not to follow. The result is to leave the friars' claim at 18–19 unrefuted (for an unusually positive reading of the friars see Strong 2003:255–75). *man...boet...water / water...bote...man*: the skilful inversion acting as a rhetorical substitute for the scholastic procedure of enumer-

ating and defining the key 'terms' of an argument. **36–43** correspond to **B** 45–50 // **A** 40–6 which, in describing the man's movements within the boat as necessary to prevent it capsizing (at 33–7 //), make sin appear inescapable, rather too promptly invoking a notion that Haukyn will find so 'hard' at B 14.322–3. **C** clarifies by assigning the boat a new meaning and arguing instead that to fall *within* the boat (= use the Church's sacrament of penance instead of despairing of God's mercy) preserves the just man. For his good works (*Dowel*) prevent him from falling *out* of the 'church' of charity that, as at 7.256–7, figures the state of grace (in // 35/30 the *stere*, like the pikestaff earlier, symbolises sacramental penance). The *rihtful mannes fallynge* (38, 41) is thereby distinguished from that of the *unrihtful* who forsakes the Church's ministry, and his good deeds (including his recourse to confession) are credited with power to protect him against mortal sin. Thus by the 'so' of *analogy* (38, 41), the friar arrives at the 'so' of *consequence* (43) and refutes Will's pessimistic contention that the just man 'falls out of joy' (52). **44–50** take up the earlier versions' understanding of 'the boat' as *oure body*, but now with the wider meaning of 'the conditions of our earthly existence'. They thus adapt **AB**'s conventional triad of man's three enemies, the world, the flesh and the devil, but blunt their sharp dichotomy between 'body' and 'soul' (or 'flesh'). **48–50** *That...lyf*: 'And so as a consequence, even the saint inevitably sins often during this life'. **B** 51 softens the bleak fatalism of **A** 47 with a phrase (*suffre...sleupe*) that indicates less 'laxism' (a mistaken emphasis of the Everyman *Commentary*'s note *ad loc*) than the notion of sin being (as in Julian of Norwich) *behovely* 'necessary / beneficial' (*Showings*, ch. 27) and divine sufferance as unfathomable. This idea is later developed in B 14.322–3 (lines removed in **C**) and is implicit in Ymaginatif's words at B 12.277–8=C 14.202–4, which need to be read alongside 21. **51–5** state that free will is given so that man can turn to sacramental penance during this life, where there is no evading sin. **C** is more optimistic than **B**, which in elaborating **A**'s brief reference to moral autonomy (*maistrie*) only increases the prospect of failure and the severity of punishment. **51** *foleweth*: cited as the only example of the sense 'urges' in MED s.v. *folwen* v. 5(e); but it could mean 'accompany' (ibid. 3(a)), with *To* 52 as elliptical for '(enabling him) to'. For while omitting **AB**'s negative view of freedom, **C** does not imply that freedom always and only prescribes *virtuous* action. *fre wit*: an obscure phrase possibly intended as a vernacular equivalent of *liberum arbitrium* 'rational free choice' (Schmidt 1968:168–9). The contrast between animals' unerring instinct as a kind of 'reason' to be contrasted with fallen man's frequently irrational behaviour is developed at B 11.34–49=C 13.143–6. **54** *rest...restitue*: 'Platonic' wordplay suggesting a connection between divine justice and peace of soul. **55** *lyf...lycames gultes*: not signifying 'sins of the flesh' as such; rather, that death is the price all men pay for the original sin of Adam *oure alle fader*. **56a–7b** are virtually made up from 1.136. *kynde knowyng*: 'direct, immediate understanding'; though subtle, the argument has not been recondite, and the ambiguity of *bettere*, which is either adv. or adj. as noun, allows some value to the Minorite's demonstration that he *knows* where Dowel 'dwells'. **59–60** betray a vacillating attitude to the friars, *me* restoring the politeness of **A** (in one of a very small number of such reprises in **C**) lost with **B**'s mocking shift of the benison to Will. But the persisting ambiguity of *meschaunce* reveals Will as unsatisfied by the argument. **61–7** form a transition between the dispute outside the dream (20) and that within it (114), the added B 63 associating the conventional 'May' elements with the opening motif of *wildernesse* 'spiritual desolation' in B Pr 12 (omitted in **C**). The lines' musicality, ironically recalling the elaborate manner of *WW*, is enhanced by running alliteration (61–2, 65–6, 66–7), assonance (62–3), internal rhyme (63–4) and pararhyme (64–6). **61** directly recalls B Pr 4, more mutedly C Pr 4. **62** *wilde wildernesse*: deliberate derivational paranomasia, comparable to Dante's *selva selvaggia* in *Inf*. I.5 (Calí, 1971:35). Both the Athlone emendations are wide of the mark (see *TN*). **64** The triple chime in this line closely echoes *SS* 8–9: 'in launde vnder lynde me leste to lende / And lenede'. **66** recalls *SS* 15: 'ffor muche murþe of mouþ þe murie moeth made'. **67** brings the 'birds' sequence full circle with the echo-word *blisse*, finally fixing the **A** form still fluid in **B**. *merueilousliche..*: repeating Pr 7 to indicate how this new section is a continuation of the *Visio* (BA 68/59 similarly echo BA Pr 11, though less closely).

(ii) 68–75 68 The scansion requires *me* to be rhetorically stressed; if it is not, a 'compensatory' extra stave may be found in *mysulue*. *muche man*: a mirror image of the dream-narrator, to judge by his self-description at 5.24 and his nickname *Longe Wille* at B 15.152 (removed in **C**). Self-seeing or autoscopy when awake is a known pathological condition, but (rather more interestingly) encountering a personified aspect of oneself as a 'double' has been recognised as a feature of *dream*-experience (Freud 1954:505–6). Without literary parallel, this may be yet another piece of 'dream-vision realism' (Hieatt 1967). **69–70** *kynde...knowest*: the echo of 56a hinting that the encounter within the dream may help Will to *lerne bettere* through looking into his own soul rather than seeking Dowel in the world outside himself. On *kynde name* see the very full account in Middleton 1990. **70–5** The sequence of four questions follows an echoing rhetorical pattern suggesting an internal 'dialogue of one': *that...That*; *knowest...knowe*; *wost...woet*; *Thouhte... Thouht...***71** *Wille*: a revision (like that at 1.5) perhaps presupposing an audience now familiar with *PP*, for in

all three appearances of *Wille* in **B** a personification of the faculty rather than the dreamer's *kynde name* may be signified. However, A 12.89 indicates an earlier intention to name himself unequivocally in the course of the Third Vision. **72** *Thouhte*: the mind as knowing and reasoning power (MED s.v. *thought* n. 3(a)); the vernacular equivalent for *Mens* at 16.183, as it is Chaucer's for Dante's *mente* (*Inf*. II 7–90) in *HF* 2.523 (Schmidt 1969:151n99). **73** *seuen ʒer*: either a vague indefinite period or having reference to the time spent in grammar-school learning how to think (from age seven to fourteen, the normal age for beginning university studies). His challenge amounts to saying: 'You have finished your secondary education; have you not yet learned to reason to some purpose?' **76–106** represent through personification-allegory an internal debate on the nature of Dowel produced directly by Will's reflecting on the data of his experience. **76** Thought's answer, introducing the Dowel-Dobet-Dobest 'Triad' for the first time, concerns more than Will had asked about, as if it were impossible to state a positive value without also conceiving its comparative and superlative degrees. On this section see Kean in Hussey 1969:79–84. **77** *thre fayre vertues*: inescapably hinting at the three theological virtues of Faith, Hope and Charity, though their concrete social reference is uppermost here. **78–81** *Dowel*: described as a sober and upright Christian labourer. The omission of A 71 is an improvement, since his special quality is to be *trewe* 'honest, upright' rather than *mek* 'humble' (a quality usually associated in *PP* with religious). **78** repeats HC's words at 1.84 and again at 80, somewhat weakly varied without enough difference in the sense of the b-phrase. **79** The emphasis on charity clearly evokes the character of Piers (and seems echoed in *CT* I 531–7). **82–92** *Dobet*: signifying both the knightly and mercantile classes (82–7) and the clergy (88–90), though the use of a single pronoun *he* makes insufficiently clear whether the latter are first denoted from 88 or earlier. **84** *helpeth*: the charitable rôle of knights and monks alike. **85–7** may describe a knight's or merchant's use of his own wealth (perhaps dubiously acquired) for productive charitable ends. **86** *Erl Auerous*: cf. 2.90–1; representing the greed and ruthlessness of the aristocracy, which true noblemen are urged to renounce. **87** *Mammona*: possibly a type-name for the acquisitive merchant-class from whom charitable works such as those prescribed in Truth's letter would be appropriate (cf. 9.28–36). The allusion is to Lk 16:9, quoted at 8. 235*a* and 19.248*a*. **88** *religion*: 'the religious life' (MED s.v. n. 1(b), the sense also at 9.221, 22.264 (OED cites this passage under 1(a) 'religious order'). But as **L** is unlikely to be *excluding* the secular clergy, the word may cover all worthy clerks in holy orders (a sense securely attested, however, only in the phrase *man of religioun*, as in *CT* I 477). This would answer *Pe*'s difficulty as to whether being a religious is just one or the only form the life of Dobet can take. *Sk* favours this sense on the basis of Wycliffite attempts 'to extend the meaning...beyond its old narrow limits'. But his citation of *religious* 17.47 as = *men of holy Churche* 'clergy generally' at 17.41 is doubtful; for in the light of 17.35, the latter more probably bears the contextually specific sense 'friars and monks'. *rendred*: 'recited, repeated [the text of]' (MED s.v. *rendren* v. (c)); referring especially to monastic life, which focussed on singing psalms and hearing scriptural readings. But since MED s.v. (d), citing this line as sole evidence, wrongly glosses it 'translated' the possibility of contemporary misreadings cannot be completely ruled out (though OED s.v. *render* vb. 6 shows this sense not found before the 17th c.). **90** '[For] you gladly suffer the foolish; whereas yourselves are wise' (II Cor 11:19). The speaker mistranslates *suffertis* as *sufferte* 'allow', replacing Paul's irony with his own rather than indicating 'Thought's limitations' (*Pe*), though Thought's discourse is, of course, 'limited' in its scope. These *insipientes* correspond to the 'fools' of B 7.125 and of 22.61 who have (like Paul) given up the 'wisdom' of this world for the 'foolishness' of the Gospel, and whom the 'worldly wise' are being recommended to support with their charity. **93–99a** *Dobest*: embodying episcopal authority, with its special responsibility of standing up fearlessly against immoral and lawless nobles. The lines adapt **AB**'s attempt at relating the Triad to the political order, with the supreme secular authority (advised by the bishops) seen as exercising final control over the first and second estates. **C**'s change of their rôle from a political to a purely moral one may reflect an awareness that Archbishop Sudbury (murdered in the Peasants' uprising) had incurred popular enmity not as a churchman but as Richard II's Chancellor, and a judgement that a bishop's freedom to give moral leadership is hampered if he is in the service of the Crown. No immediate contemporary reference can, however, be identified. **93–4** *bere sholde*: the change from an indicative to a modal here and at 98–9 intimates uncertainty as to how likely this hope is to be fulfilled. *crose...halie*: crosier shaped like a shepherd's crook (cf. 9.255–79), symbol of the bishop's function as pastor of souls. **95** *preuaricatores legis*: those who evade the law, especially by means of wealth or position; a phrase common in glosses on Ps 118:119 'I have counted all the sinners of the earth prevaricators [*Praevaricantes*]' (Alf*Q*). **99** *as God hihte*: all the injunctions of inspired Scriptural writers being ascribed to God indifferently, whoever the immediate author (e.g. St Paul at B 8.94). **99a** 'And fear ye not them that kill the body and are not able to kill the soul' (Mt 10:28); from Christ's warning to his apostles (whose successors the bishops are) to expect persecution for preaching the Gospel. **100–02** are a significant addition stating that Dowel and Dobet (laity and clergy) have formally set up an episcopal order (Dobest)

to rule spiritually and a monarchy to guarantee that rule by force, while acting always in accord with all three orders' judgement and advice. On *demede* 'adjudged' or 'established' see MED s.v. *demen* v. 8(a). **101** *to kull... That...*: 'to put to death lawfully / Those who...'; a sombre stress on the duty of the highest civil authority to punish those who disobey the highest religious authority, perhaps prompted by the excommunications of Lollards in 1382. The death-penalty for heresy was not formally prescribed in England till 1401, but had been accepted in Europe from the end of the 13th c.

108–12 form a transitional passage like that at 56–60, in which Will again asks for a more direct intuitive knowledge of the nature of Dowel and the rest (in **AB**, specifically of how they *act*). But whereas the friars leave, Thought remains, as he is the necessary *mene* (120) in the strenuous mental activity leading to *wit* 'understanding through knowledge' (MED s.v. *wit* n. 2 (c) and 3(a)). **108** *sauereth*: whereas at 56 Will could not *conseyue* 'grasp' the friar's argument, here he 'has no taste for' Thought's. The response reveals a growing 'wilfulness' that builds towards the outburst at 13.179ff below, but for the present he is in control.

113–27 form a second transitional *passage* concluding what was in **AB** effectively a transitional *passus* preparing for a major new one; but in **C**, which tends to eschew disproportionate length or brevity, it introduces the last two-thirds of the same passus. **113** *thre dayes*: an indefinite period (like 'seven years' at 73) or with the Biblical sense of the 'third day' as decisive (cf. I Cor 15:4), so that meeting Wit becomes the climax of a crisis. **114** *Disputyng*: cf. on 20 above. **115** *Wit*: knowledge or understanding derived from reflection on what is experienced, primarily through the *wittes* 'senses', or learned from others in an informal way (the formal way being 'clergy'). A limit on the word's semantic range may be established from its use at 16.187–8 to render *sensus*, 'the understanding of what one is told and the source of every practical art and skill.' **116–18** Wit's appearance is that of a modestly dressed scholar, physically like the Dreamer (whose *wit* he of course is). **119** *iangle*: their *matere* (the nature of Dowel) not being one that will produce a quarrel like that between Piers and the Priest (over the nature of the Pardon) but will be an orderly exchange conducted through the 'medium' of Thought (who disappears as if absorbed into his successor Understanding). **121** The approach is still semi-scholastic (*purpos*; *preuen*), Will testing Wit's powers (in a line added in **B**) by requesting a formal *distinctio* between the three concepts. **122** *What*: 'As to what'. **125** *oen*: the revision removing (presumably) undesired echoes of the semi-proverbial antithesis between Will and Wit ('emotion and reason'; see on Pr 174).

C Passus X 128–311, A Passus X, B Passus IX

(iii) 128–311 Except for one question at 151, WIT's 180-line speech is not interrupted by Will (who says nothing to deserve Study's rebuke at the opening of XI). It engages chiefly with the ordinary moral experience of lay-people in the family and society (see Tavormina 1995: 48–109 for a very full analysis of Wit's discourse). **128–58** Wit's starting point is man's situation as a material creature with a spiritual soul, and his traditional image of the Castle recalls the Friar's homiletic procedure in IX. While (as befits the speaker, a married layman) its flavour is secular rather than scriptural, its use in a spiritual allegory was long familiar from such works as *AW* (ed. Tolkien, 185/7). **128** *Sire*: a title relating this figure to Thought's earlier typology, with Dowel as the nobility, Dobest as the episcopate, and suggesting (somewhat awkwardly) that representatives of Dobet (the clergy?) should be descended from 'gentle blood' (a point earlier laboured at 5.63ff). The allegory signifies that Christians should receive elementary instruction in virtue from their natural parents, sacramental teaching from their priest, and wider authoritative guidance through life from their bishop. **129** *Kynde*: a new and arresting 'nature-name' for God the Father (cf. *Treuthe* earlier) in direct response to Will's demand for *a more kynde knowyng* at 109 (see 152–5). In technical language, Kynde represents *natura naturans* 'creating Nature' as contrasted with *natura naturata* 'created Nature' (on 'Kynde as God' see White 1988:60–88). **130** *ayer*: probably not 'air' (=*wynd* 131) but *aether*, the fiery 'upper air' above the earth, here treated as equivalent to the usual fourth element as the source of the body's heat. If the latter is the 'breath of life' of Gen 2:7 (Goodridge), called 'spirit' at 16.196 (cf. Wittig 1972:217n29), then this may be equated with the *aether*. **133** *lemman*: the image of God as a lover wooing the human soul, derived from patristic exegesis of the Song of Songs, was traditional in vernacular devotional writing. The classic chivalricised version in ME, with the soul as a 'lady' besieged by her foes 'inwith an earthen castle' is found in *AW* 198/18–20); see further Woolf 1962. *hymsulue*: because made in God's image and likeness (Gen 1:26, and cf. B 9.33, A 10.35). **134** *Anima*: the immortal Soul in its most comprehensive sense (16.199*a*), but with particular reference later (10.175) to its aspect as life-principle (16.181; see Schmidt 1968²). She is feminine as the 'object of desire' of both God and the Devil, not simply on account of the Latin noun's grammatical gender (for in B 15.23 Anima, the speaker who governs the whole passus, is male). *hath enuye*: not 'covets to possess' (*Pe*) but 'has malice [inspired by envy]', since she enjoys the love he has forfeited. **135** *Fraunce*: traditionally the national enemy; but the hostile

image does not bespeak Gallophobia, it simply evokes the stately pomp of French chivalry (see *Intro.* V § 33). *Princeps.*: 'the prince of this world', traditionally interpreted as signifying the devil (see A 10.62) and so used at 20.349*a*, quoting Jn 12:31 (see also Jn 14.30, 16:11). **136** *wyles*: especially the temptations of 'the world', i.e. *Pruyde of Parfyt Lyuynge* (11.176). **138** *marches*: perhaps specifically 'border territories' (MED s.v. *marche* n (2), 1(a), a good place for a defensive castle against marauders (on **L**'s acquaintance with the Welsh Marches cf. Breeze 1993²). Man is being thought of as placed near the 'boundary' between two regions (of angel and animal). **140** *þat lady*: royal or at least a royal ward, having a duke's daughter as a handmaid and a bishop as tutor. **143** *constable*: as in the early C13th *Sawles Warde* where *Wit*, who as 'God's constable' (*SW* 43) corresponds to **L**'s Inwit, has the outer and inner senses ('wits') as his household servants (*SW* 15–23). **144** *Inwit*: a term varying in sense from the general 'mind' or 'the collection of inner faculties' (MED s.v. 1(a), 3(a)) to something identical with 'conscience'. Its neutral sense of 'the rational power generally' (Quirk), in opposition to *outwit* 'outer sense', allowed the possibility that *inwit* could be misused, as at B 13.289. But that meaning is here excluded; for Inwit is *wise* 144. Attempts restrictively to correlate so common a word as *inwit* with a technical term of philosophy such as *synderesis* (Harwood & Smith 1970) are less persuasive in relation to **AB** than to **C** (see on 177, and contrast the possible contextual relationship between the coined phrase *fre wit* and the technical *liberum arbitrium* conjectured at 51). But **L**'s *conscience* may have a more exact meaning, being chosen instead of 'Inwit' to translate *consciencia* at 16.199*a*. **L**'s 'Inwit' is thus perhaps best understood as a non-specific name for the rational power under its practical (moral) rather than theoretical (speculative) aspect, intended by God to guide man's use of his senses (as a father governs his sons). Murtaugh 1978:15 not implausibly detects in **L**'s conception some influence from the Augustinian-Bonaventuran notion of moral understanding as involving direct illumination by God. **145** *sones*: the bodily senses in respect of their 'right uses' (cf. A 10.52–3 below), or as Wittig puts it 'the sensual powers of man precisely as ordered to higher ends while justly supplying the needs of man' (1972:217). In *SW* 43–59 Wit's supports against the devil are not his own sons but four 'daughters of God', here the cardinal virtues. *furste wyue*: 'the flesh in its unfallen state, when the senses were uncorrupted' (*Pe*), 'the old law' (*R–H*; see also Wittig 1972:217–19); it would be vain to ask who the *second* wife was (in *SW* 10 Wit's 'wanton wife' is *Will*). More neutrally, the figure may signify *sensualite* 'the natural capacity for receiving physical sensation' (MED s.v. (a)), described in *The Cloud of Unknowing* as 'a miȝte of oure soule, rechyng & regnyng in þe bodely wittes, þorow þe whiche we haue bodely knowyng & felyng of alle bodely creatures' (118/7). **150** *come or sende*: at the moment of separation from the body, *þe deth of kynde* 20.219. **A 25** This question, omitted in **BC**, is answered at A 38–9=B 49–50 but dropped from **C**, perhaps because of doubt whether *Caro* should be equated with human nature in its entirety or only with the (animated) mortal part (see on B 49). **155** anticipates 20.59, which makes clear that the *payne* is not man's alone but has been shared by the Son of God in *membres and face*. **157–8** allude to the taking of human nature by the Son in Christ, through which man resembles God even more than do the angels. The resemblance was traditionally held to reside in the *gost* of the Man originally created for eternal happiness (A 36–7) and now in the re-born soul of each baptised person who does not forfeit sanctifying grace through mortal sin.

B 32–52 The threefold expansion of **A**'s straightforward account through an elaborate but rather awkward analogy is abandoned in **C** for one simpler and more intelligible. **32a** '[For] he spoke, and they were made: [he commanded, and they were created]' (Ps 148:5). **A 34** The sense varies according as the stave-words are consonantal or vocalic: scansion on *w* makes the key-stave instrumental *wiþ*, on vowels the article *a* 'one single word' (i.e. *Fiat*). The latter seems preferable, but both are metrically clumsy and the line's omission is understandable since *al þing* repeats not only 31a but 28b. **34** *Eue... bon*: Gen 2:21–2. **35** *For*: an unexpected conjunction if the referent of *he* is God and the intended contrast one between God's 'singleness' and his use of a plural verb. But it is obviously in place if *he* refers to Adam (cf. Gen 2:18), for whom God made *Eue* 34 'because he was all alone by himself'. The same referent will also fit if *synguler* means 'unique [among creatures, through being made in the divine image]' (MED s.v. adj. 3(a), the sense at 6.36). The position of the mid-line pause tells against referring *hymself* to God, but the absence of a pronoun subject for *seide* argues for it: one of the awkwardnesses (another being the small-word staves of 36–7) that may have prompted removal of the whole passage. There is however an odd fitness in the ambiguity, which hints at the need for human plurality to mirror divine trinity. *Faciamus*: 'Let us make'; the opening of either Gen 1:26 'Let us make man to our image and likeness' (quoted in full at A 41*a* and earlier at B 5.487*a*) or of Gen 2:18 'And the Lord God said: It is not good for *man* to be *alone*: let us make him (*faciamus ei*) a help like unto himself", as seems more plausible in the light of 33–4. The *faciamus* phrase invited a 'Trinitarian' reading, as by Bede (*PL* 91:28–9): 'Faciamus, una ostenditur trium personarum operatio' (cf. also Raban Maur in *PL* 107:459), and some influence from the Victorine tradition has been suggested (Szittya 1986²). But in context it seems likely that the verb's pl. number (noted by *Sk*) is less important than its

sense, elaborated in 36–7, stressing not 'us' as opposed to 'me' but 'making' as opposed to 'saying' (the merely verbal act that sufficed to create the animals [32*a*]). **37** *wiþ*: here and at 42 meaning 'along with, as well as' not 'by means of' (cf. 51). **38–40** The tortuous analogy illustrates how as well as 'slime of the earth' (= *parchemyn*) from which he fashioned man's body, and his wisdom (*wit* 43), God needed to exert his *myȝt* to create man's immortal *goost*, something expressed 'instrumentally' by *penne* (see Schmidt 1980³; and for a different interpretation of the analogy, see Szittya 1986²). **41–2** *seide*: its sense repeated by, rather than translating *Dixit*; on the rationale of the reconstruction, which depends on the wider interpretation favoured, see *TN*. **43** 'He had to work actively as well as uttering his word, and thereby manifest his wisdom'. **46–7 (A 36)** *of þe (his) godhede*: 'by dint of his divine power'; *of* does not signify that man is a spark of the divine being but that his spiritual soul is akin to it because 'God is spirit' (Jn 4:24). **A 41a** See under B 35. **49** *Caro*: 'human nature', 'the body animated by the life-principle', as at B 17.108 (the confusing dichotomy at A 50 is removed in **B**). **C**'s rejection of both lines suggests unease over a word elsewhere connected with disordered desire (11.174); but its neutral use, like that of English 'flesh' (MED s.v. 5a), has Scriptural warrant, as at Jn 1:14 where *caro* denotes the human nature, body and soul, taken by the Word. Hill 2001, citing Biblical, Patristic and medieval sources (and comparing the use at B 18.409), argues convincingly that *caro* is synecdochic for 'humanity'. **52** *myȝt...mageste*: 'his sovereign power'.

159–71 Retaining only B 48, the revision shifts attention from the creation of man in God's image to the marring of that image through sin. The tone is sombre, and in place of the exultant 148th psalm of B 32*a* comes Ps 80 which, though it begins in solemn rejoicing, modulates into solemn warning at vs 12. **162** *sheweth nat*: 'does not favour' / 'reveal (himself) to'; see *TN*. **166** '[So] I let them go according to the desires of their heart: [they shall walk in their own inventions]' (Ps 80:13); see B 66*a*. **168** *goed*: a sardonic pun (cf. 177; for **L**'s complex play on this word see Schmidt 1987:134–8). **170** echoes 152; the *luther* men are rejected for loving created wealth more than the creator. **171** *The which*: defining the creative God (*Kynde*) in Johannine terms as love and eternal life (cf. Jn 10:10, I Jn 4:8). For St John's influence on **L** see Davlin 1996.

172–86 revise and deepen the 'naturalistic' **AB** argument in a 'spiritual' direction, keeping the notion of mental and sensory powers as divine gifts to man (174) but adding the 'infused' virtues of love and trust in God (*leute* here may = faith-and-hope), which provide the supernatural life of the soul. **175** The main sources of **L**'s psycho-physiology are the *De Anima* of Cassiodorus (*c*. 540) and the *De Spiritu et Anima* (C12th) of ?Alcher of Clairvaux

(Schmidt 1968²). In B 55–9 // A *Inwit* is 'the rational power' in its practical or moral aspect, the wording of B 59 suggesting however the inner law of 'conscience' in men, which is aided by but precedes the illumination brought by grace. His guidance of Anima can therefore be reconciled with his subordination to the religious authority Dobest (with *lat* B 58 cf. *is lad* B 16). However, the 'high' view of *inwit* in C 177 approaches the scholastic notion of *synderesis* (the soul's intuitive awareness of the first principles of moral action). So *grace* here perhaps signifies the 'actual' or 'prevenient' (as distinct from the sanctifying) grace given through the sacraments, which prompts good action and (it was thought) could exist in the unbaptised, as the Biblical examples show. **A 52–3** Cf. A 19–21. **177, 183** *tresour*: the term harking back to HC's teaching on Truth as the form of wealth that really matters (1.201). The underlying idea is that reason has an 'endowment' of moral intuition, which man can 'misspend' (176) through abuse of another divine gift, 'drink that does you good' (1.24). **178** *lykerous drynke*: repeating 1.25 and recalling HC's warnings at 1.25–40; association of these examples derives from Peter Comestor (Taitt 1976). **179** scans as a Type IIIb with a wrenched stress in the trisyllabic Latin form of the name *Herodés* providing the key-stave. The first stave *dede* alliterates translinearly with preceding *drynke*, the last stave of 178, as does the last stave *daffe* with the first of 180 (*douhter*). *Lote*: see on 1.25–31. *Noe*: on his drunkenness see Gen 9:20–7. *Heredes*: Herod Antipas, tetrarch of Galilee, who had protected the Baptist; inferred from the account of John's beheading in Mk 6:21–8 to have lost his *inwit* through over-drinking. **180–1** The dizzy syntax reflects the king's confused state: properly *bifore...gestes* modifies *daunsynge*, not *3af*. For the Gospel text makes clear that, while the king's rash promise was public (and therefore binding), the head was brought privately to Herodias his wife. *his douhter*: Salome, the daughter of Herod's wife by his brother Philip. **182** *hele*: good health and sound mind envisaged as all anyone could want; for the phrase cf. 5.10. **183** echoes the deleted B 7.54.

B 60–66a attack the morally corrosive effect of drink, repeating somewhat the argument of the Glutton sequence (B 5.366–7), which *glubberes* recalls. **61a** '[For many walk...whose end is destruction]: whose god is their belly; [and whose glory is in their shame...]' (Phil 3:[18]–19). **62** *hir soule..*: cf. B 7.113–4. **63** scans as Type I on *l* or as Type IIIa on *s* (cf. 71). **64a** '[God is charity: and] he that abideth in charity, abideth in God, [and God in him]' (I Jn 4:16). The unquoted end of the verse reminds how the abuse of Inwit can destroy the sanctifying grace that creates a 'church of charity' in the soul (cf. C 7.256–7). **65–6** *fordo...shoop*: because to quench reason in oneself is to unmake God's creation; anticipating the lines on murder at B 17.280–81 // (where Inwit

is again mentioned), as also that of God abandoning the morally abandoned at B 17.249–50a //, which likewise cites the *nescio vos*. **66** scans either vocalically on pronouns, with an exceptionally long prelude-dip of six syllables (including two lexical words) or, with greater ease, as Type IIIa on *s / sh* (cf. C 162). *liknesse*: found in reason, the power of moral judgement and self-control. **66a** 'Amen, I say to you, I know you not' (Mt 25:12). Verse 13 of Mt warns against the sudden arrival of death, which will find the drunkard unprepared for judgement.

184–6 C cuts **B**'s excursus on the decay of communal values and (unusually) looks behind **B** to **A**: 184 = A 58 and 185–6 rewrite A 69–70 rather than B 67–8.

A 58–75, B 67–71 The initial linking of the innocents with 'sots' and the ambiguity of *failiþ* (inwit is wanting in the one, extinguished in the other) make for confusion. But **A** goes on to distinguish quite clearly between the morally incompetent (58–65) and the morally adult (71–5) and between the drunk who fall under the devil's power and the innocents who do not sin even when they cause harm (*wykkide* 65). B 67–71 remove this unclarity but oddly lump together as incapable of rationally determining their lives the mentally defective with three groups of social poor (69 recalls A 8.32–3). Whether or not in response to readers' objections, C 185–6 wisely limit the point, while preserving in *folye* a polysemy free of real ambiguity. A 66–70 strikingly stress parents' responsibility for their children's anti-social behaviour and the obligation of the community (here, of the Church as its organ) to protect the young from crime and ?sexual expoitation (*folies* A 70 = C 185). A 75a echoes the wording of Z Pr 71.

B 72–94a offer a negative exemplum (see 93–4) contrasting the failure in charity of the Christian community's 'spiritual fathers' with the mutual care shown by Jews. **C**'s removal of this angry digression on a lordly and neglectful episcopate does not imply a more indulgent attitude toward the latter after 1381 (as the added C Pr 100–06 bear out), for the moral point is not weakened by concentrating on positive recommendations rather than hostile criticism. **72** re-uses Z 7.230. **73** *witnesses*: 'supporting texts'. *foure doctours*: the four great Western Doctors of the Church, Ambrose, Jerome, Augustine and Gregory. For their importance, see 21.268–74a. **74** *Luc*: Acts 6:1 refers to widows (Goodridge) but the true source (disallowed by alliterative necessity) is 'James the gentle' (1.180) whose injunction to help *faderlese children* and *widewes* (Js 1:27) draws on the precept of Deut 16:11–14 underlying the Jews' own *kyndenesse*. The rôle of *kyndenesse* in fostering unity within the Christian *commune* by economic means is explored in Galloway 1994. **77** An extended Type IIIb line with counterpoint (*abb / aa*) or a cognative Type Ia scanning on *pp / b*. **82–9 L**'s challenging praise of the Jews' solidarity and mutual concern is presumably inspired by reports (unless he had travelled in Europe), for they had been expelled from England in 1290. On **L**'s removal of these lines in **C**, see Narin Van Court, who argues that passages favourable to the Jews are 'revised, reduced, deleted or qualified in the last version' (1996:83). **85** *Iudas felawes*: that the Jewish nation was collectively guilty in perpetuity for the execution of Christ (and therefore condemned to the same fate as Judas) was an inference from Mt 27:25. This common belief, so alien to modern sentiment, accords with earlier OT ideas of racial guilt, the correlative of the Jews' belief in racial election; and the usual medieval understanding of this text seems endorsed by Faith's diatribe in 18.99–109a. **88** scans as Type IIIc (*ab / ab*) with cognative |dʒ| / |ʃ| alliteration. **91–2a** The notion of bishops who patronise low minstrels (rather than give charity to ragged beggars) as 'betrayers' of Christ is sharpened by awareness that Judas was the Apostles' purse-keeper (Jn 13:29), as bishops are keepers of the Christian community's possessions (for the collocation of Judas with 'japers' cf. B Pr 35). **92a** 'A traitor [worthy to be] set with Judas is the prelate who scants in distributing Christ's heritage'; *and in another place*, 'A ruinous giver is he who idly eats up what belongs to Christ's poor'. The Latin uses phrases from two passages traced by *Sk* to Peter the Cantor's *Verbum Abbreviatum,* ch. 47 (*PL* 205:135, 150); not quotations, and either drawn from another untraced source or recomposed (for the phrasing cf. B 15.244–6). **94a** 'The fear of the lord is the beginning of wisdom'; semi-proverbial (Ecclus 1:16, Ps 110:10, Prov 1:7, 9:10).

A **76–130** is (after Passus XII) the longest passage completely abandoned in revision to **B**, with only a little of the opening retained (79–81a) and many good lines never re-used, until **B** resumes with the discussion of marriage at 108ff. It defines the Triad as 'obedience (to the moral law),' 'sufferance', and 'humility', each closely linked with and following on from its predecessor. **76** *a duc*: referring back to A 11 (the image is dropped in the later versions). It actively destroys vice and enables virtue to begin and a parallel to the stages of penitence is unmistakable, with Dowel = confession and Dobet = satisfaction. *Dowel it makiþ*: though grammatically ambiguous, meaning 'fear of God generates (the will to) do-well', a sense in keeping with 80 and 118 as well as the general doctrine of Ecclus ch. 1 that underlies this passage. **78** *routen*: 'settle'; see MED s.v. v. (2) (c). **82** *For doute*: less 'out of fear' than 'as a consequence of fear': the doing-better (as 85 states) consists in awareness of possible (divine) punishment for sin as well as gratitude at having been justly punished for sin. *maister*: dowell being a discipline (Ecclus 1:34) that teaches virtue as well as avoidance of vice. **87** 'Thy rod and thy staff: they have comforted me' (Ps 22:4b); teaching the same lesson. **88–4a** The sense seems to be that if someone has

confessed his sins and is living by his (informed) conscience, he need seek nothing higher. **88** scans as Type IIa with a final cadence -*sélf dó wèl*. **90** 'The value of man's action is judged by his intention', a maxim of canon law cited in the *Summa Aurea* (1253) of the canonist Hostiensis: *Quicquid agant homines, intentio iudicat omnes* 'All men, whatever they may *do*, are judged by their intention' (Alf*Q*, proposing the reading; see *TN*). **91–4** form the poem's strongest assertion of the religious value of conscience enlightened by the Church's moral teaching. **L**'s omission of them could be linked with his later development of the idea of conscience's sense of right and wrong *possibly* conflicting with the words and judgements (at least of actual members) of the teaching Church, such as the Priest Piers quarrels with or the Doctor of Divinity in XV (B XIII) who angers Will. **94** *Goddis worde*: possibly Heb 10:26–7 (*Sk*); but the ultimate source is more probably St Paul's 'For all that is not of faith (*ex fide*) is sin' (Rom 14:23), where *fides* had long been understood as 'conscience'. *holiwrit*: the revered writings of the great Church Fathers, as distinct from the divinely inspired Biblical text (*Sk*; C 1.25 illustrates this use). **94a** 'The man who acts against (his) conscience is building (himself a house) in hell'; earliest attested in Gratian's *Decretum* (*CIC* 1:1088), and cited in Bromyard's *Summa Praedicantium* (1:130/1) s.v. *conscientia* as a gloss on the same text (Alf*Q*). Jean de la Rochelle (13th c.) uses this exact form in his *Summa de Vitiis* and Richard of St Victor, in his commentary on the *Song of Songs* (*PL* 196:481), a modified version of it in asserting that sins against conscience are mortal, citing Rom 14:23 (Schmidt 1967:366). The version in Alan of Lille's *Contra Haereticos* II xvi (*PL* 210:391) is not identical but could also be a source (Schmidt 1982:484). **95–102** The advice to *suffre and sit stille* defines Dobet as something to be received, not sought, and its warning against spiritual pride (101–2) echoes Piers's words at A 6.198–106. **98** 'As long as you live an upright life, care nothing for a villain's sneers / [What every fellow says is no concern of ours]' (*DC* III. 3). The line can be scanned as Type IIIa on *v*. **101** *herre*: 'something higher'. **102** *louȝnesse*: 'humility' (cf. 129), with a play on 'lowness' (inevitably 'lost' when one 'climbs'). **103–17** warn generally against restless instability, but in particular amongst those embarked on the religious life. **104** Whereas the common form of the proverb, 'a rolling stone gathers no moss', might argue against fixity in one's way of life, this witty variant argues *for* it in stating that a marble slab fixed in one place and trodden upon will keep its pristine condition. **105–6** Cf. A 11. 211, B 4.120. **107** *clergie*: a third authority added to the secular sages and folk wisdom. **108a** 'He who wanders from craft to craft / Belongs, be sure, to no craft'; learnedly varying the proverbial 'Jack of all trades and master of none'. A close analogue linking *genus* 'kind' with *ordo* 'religious order' is in Higden's *Polychronicon* I: 'Immo nonnulli *omne genus circumeuntes in nullo genere sunt, omnem ordinem attemptantes nullius ordinis sunt*'. Alf*Q* suggests a possible 'grammatical' context for the original (*genus* also = 'gender'); see Alford 1984. **111** *writen*: presumably as an edifying inscription in large letters on a wall. **112** 'Stay in whatever calling you were called to'; adapted from 'Unusquisque *in qua vocatione vocatus est, in ea permaneat*' (I Cor 7:20; see on C 5.43*a*). **115** *To... beryng*: 'so as to win heaven through the way you live [in that calling]'. **118** *to*: 'is to'. **119** *soueraynes*: '(true) elevation to a high rank (in heaven)'. This, the word's first occurrence, is overlooked by MED s.v. *soverainnesse* n. **120***a* '[Because everyone that exalteth himself shall be humbled: and] he that humbleth himself shall be exalted' (Lk 14:11, 18:14). Wit's advice recalls that of Piers, who cites the preceding verse to the Knight at C 8.44*a*. **121** *his dede*: acts of humble submission to God. **123–8** The metaphor envisaging Dobest as the sweet-smelling flower with rough root and thorny stem, from which the attar of charity will be distilled, is probably indebted to the imagery of *Canticles* (cf. Cant. 4:16, 5:13). **125–6** are recalled at C 13:22–3, 12.179–87. The 'wheat' image is also Biblical in its overtones, evoking the abundant crop growing in the midst of surrounding adversity (Mt 13:24–30). The 'rough, ragged root' image anticipates the walnut figure of 12.146–52. **129–30** assert what is asked for at A 8.182–3*a* above: humility (*Dobet*) wins grace to perform works of charity (*Dobest*). Wit's doctrine here is identical with Anima's in B 15.168–9 and shows how Will's interlocutors function as partial revealers of a truth that the poet has already grasped as a whole, not one he is fragmentarily aware of and seeking to acquire.

187–203*a* The newly composed account of the Triad takes them as 'living a virtuous life according to moral reason,' 'loving one's enemies' (the distinctive ethical precept of Christianity), and 'making peace between all nations as a basis for spreading the Gospel universally'. **B** is closer to **A**, seeing Dowel as obedience to moral law from fear of God, obedience from love of God, and total contemplative self-dedication to God. **193** *Bishopes*: a new 'heroic' view of bishops as exemplary imitators of Christ the Lord rather than of secular lords. **194** *For to*: overtly (and perhaps with deliberate irony) an infinitive of purpose, 'in order to seek worldly loss and martyrdom by fearlessly preaching the gospel'; but the intended sense must be 'even at the cost of' (no parallel is cited in *MES*). **195** The Synoptics do not specify *thre clothes* (a number *Sk* regards as indefinite), whereas Jn 19:23 implies four garments (excluding the coat) divided between the four soldiers. This detail is indebted to Ludolf of Saxony's *Vita Christi* II.112 (ed. Boland et al., p. 639) and to a patristic tradition that Christ wore three garments before the crucifixion, of scarlet, purple and white (Hill 1978:200).

hit were: see on 5.59. **196** *ruyfled*: (< OF *rifler*), first recorded in **L** and possibly introduced by him (Wilcockson 1983). **197** *for*: 'in order that', but with a secondary sense 'because of' (explaining why Christ was put to death), with *sholde loue* meaning 'if love was to'. *wexe*: 'grow (up) into'; a distant echo of the lost 'rose' figure in **A**. **199** *dere ȝeres*: 'years of dearth'. Wit's point is that these 'princes' should visit the poorest parts of their dioceses so as to 'cultivate' men's souls, sow the grains of virtues like fortitude (cf. 21.275–6), and enable them to endure their material distress better (cf. the thought at 16.322–7). **200–01** echo B 20.382. *tulie*: cf. B 19.263; on this important trope see Barney 1973. **202** *loueth; leueth*: the 'Platonic' pararhyme emphasising the dependence of man's faith on the love God has shown man in Jesus who, though destitute on the cross, was raised to glory. *sterue... clothes*: not literally true, as Christ's death shows. But Wit's paradoxical claim (implicit in Ps 33) may be that 'starving' is the price of the heavenly banquet, or that clerical princes' deprivations must be measured against those of their *Lord Prince Iesu*. Certainly 198 implies that proper use of their wealth would soften the impact of *dere ȝeres* on the poor. **203***a* '[The rich have wanted, and have suffered hunger: but] they that seek the Lord shall not be deprived of any good' (Ps 33:11); a warning to prelates (as to priests at B 11.280*a*).

B 95–107*a* The ascetic ideal of **B** is less specifically episcopal than in **C** and seems designed to cover ordinary laymen like Piers (cf. 105). It suggests the monastic régime that, in principle at least, sanctified each hour and left no room for *tynynge of tyme*. **97–8** *wiþdraweþ...To spille*: a use of the 'objective infinitive' in a sense ('from wasting') now expressed by the gerund. **98***a* 'Who errs in one word is in all ways guilty'. The quotation, adapted *ad hoc* from Js 2:10 to give a Type IIIa line, is quoted again (correctly) at B 11.308*a*=C 13.121*a* (see *TN*). The wider allusion is to Christ's warning in Mt 12:36–7 of the punishment that awaits idle words. **100** With the awkward placing of the adverbial phrase cf. on 180. **101** *spire*: on this image see Shoaf 1987:128–33. **102–4** On the notion of God as the lord of the minstrel, cf. 9.126. Here he is thought of as having given all men speech in order to sing his praises. **102** *game of heuene*: because the blessed will sing praise to God for eternity, and because poetry is a divinely sanctioned form of serious play; see Davlin's illuminating study (1989:59–60, 111–22). **103** *feiþful...fiþele*: a likely 'Platonic' pun, a well-tuned fiddle making 'faithful' sounds, as a well-disciplined tongue speaks true words. B Pr 51–2 finds lying akin to discord in music. **104** *tauernes*: where speech is 'spilled' in oaths and bawdy songs. **105–7** *To...to hem*: pleonasm bordering on anacoluthon: 'God loves all upright men and gives them grace'. *loude ouþer stille*: 'at all times'; taking up the image of the instrument, playing or silent.

204–58 contrast at length *trewe* and *fals* people, Seth's progeny and Cain's, the exemplum of Noah's flood (222–58) incorporating a troubled meditation (236–47*a*) on the issue of whether moral guilt can be inherited. **204–5** cannot be a question as *Sk* takes it (with *so...As* proposing a comparison); *As* must here mean 'such as' (*Pe*). 204a is near to A 132a in wording but the last lift echoes B 108b, while 205 retains B 109b and re-writes B 108a, keeping the line's Type IIIa pattern. This definition of do-well as an outward 'state' (faithful marriage) introduces the topical theme of wrongful sexual relations to which Wit ascribes the disintegration of the social fabric. **206–7** concentrate on the contribution of laypeople in providing saints and clergy, omitting both earlier versions' nobles and churls and their 'naturalistic' OT view of the marriage 'goods' as *proles* and *adiutorium*, the peopling of the earth and the provision of marital support. **C** also cuts **B**'s excursus on marriage, with its repetitions at 114a, 117a, and the 'paradisal' view of it at 118, the phrasing anticipating B 10.299 and the sentiment to be echoed in *Pur* 701–4 (Schmidt 1988:119–21). **B 117–18** *made...witnesse*: an allusion to Gen 2:18–24 as used at Mt 19:4–6. Since *witnesse* could imply 'present at' (*Sk*), the Marriage at Cana (Jn 2:2) may be intended to be recalled. **207** *maydenes*: i.e. virgin saints. The imagery of added 208–9 foreshadows the great figure of the tree of charity in 18.89–94, with virginity at the top. **208–9** are opportunistically adapted from Mt 7:18 (*Sk*) but vs 16 is also relevant, as that text's earlier and later citations at 2.28–9*a* and 10.247*a* indicate. **209** *sotil sciense*: because even the cleverest gardener cannot get sweet apples from a root-stock that naturally yields sour ones. Wit pessimistically implies that the best education cannot transform someone who is 'base' by heredity. **210** *no more to mene*: scarcely the contextual sense of the source-text's fruits ('deeds', not 'offspring'); but Wit's interpretation reflects one of the poet's strongest prepossessions. **211–12** That those born in wedlock have a 'lawful claim' to the grace by which men 'do well' sounds untypically unkind and also theologically unsound (the illegitimate, if baptized, being no more 'thralls' to sin than anyone else). But it might be charitably understood as presuming that 'unmarried parents are unlikely to baptise their children or teach them the faith' or, more speculatively, that 'the sanctifying grace imparted to Christian parents by the sacrament of marriage indirectly benefits their offspring'. **212** *lele legityme*: 'faithful lawfully-born people'. Wit at least acknowledges that if *all* the illegitimate can never do well, *some* of the legitimate may at times fail to do so. **214** '[Behold he (*sc.* the sinner) hath been in labour with injustice]; he hath conceived (in) sorrow, and brought forth iniquity' (Ps 7:15; Job 15:35, which adds 'and his womb prepareth deceits'; Is 59:4). *Pe* opines that *in dolore* is substituted for Vg *dolorem* (the form in the text

of // **AB**) under the influence of Gen 3:1 '*in sorrow* shalt thou bring forth children'. But the **C** reading is a known variant in both earlier traditions (see *TN*) and the change may be intended to stress the 'dolorous' issue of *careful concepcioun* more than the labour-pains that Gen imports (placing this quotation before the exemplum, however, frees the moral criticism from too close a dependence on the Biblical situation). The immediate context of the psalm-text (vss 14 and 16) could provide the basis for seeing 'lawless' sex as not only consequentially but intrinsically wrong: the 'arrows' of condign punishment for *ardentibus* 'them that burn [the lustful]' are suitably children who (like Cain) will carry on the cycle of wickedness. **215–21** allude to the tradition found in an OT Apocryphal text, the *Vita Adae et Evae* (ME trans. in Blake 1972:109–10), that Cain was conceived and born 'during the period of penitence and fasting to which our first parents were condemned for their breach of obedience' (*Wr*; see further Tavormina 1995: 84n59). Neither **A** nor **B** makes clear that this was why the 'time' was *yuel* or *cursid*. But **C**, though explicit, is not free of ambiguity, for 217a could mean 'without doing proper penance for their rash act [*sc.* of eating the fruit]' or 'without any regret for their rash act [of breaching the penance imposed for eating the fruit]'. What is clear is that the son's villainous character comes from the parents, their defiance of God's prohibition being like that of *sherewes* who couple outside marriage (for whom the *derne dede* is always *yuel*).

A 141–8, 151–6 are, despite a certain rhetorical vigour, rightly dropped in **B** as they are crude in feeling or expression (*wrecchide world*, *Crist / God*), slackly phrased (*se...likiþ* 149 after *whoso...knowen* 133) as well as repetitive and prolix (*Caym* six times, *cursid* four times, *Crist hatid*, *alle þat comen*, *Seþ and his sistir*, *couplide* twice, doublets in *wonen* and *libben*, *conseyuid* and *engendrit*). They are given final form at C 248–56 below; but from amongst the rejected lines 143a is reworked in another context at C 12.208 and 145b used twice at B 17.341//, B 19.218 //. **143** *aungel*: see Gen 3:23–4. **148** *Caym*: see Gen 4:1. **153** *Seth*: miswritten *Seem* at B 124. Adam's third son, born to take the place of 'Abel whom Cain slew' and father of Enos who 'began to call upon the name of the Lord' (Gen 4:25–6), is named in Lk 3:38 as the forefather of Joseph. **155** *alle þat comen*: Cain's descendants, who perished in the Flood (Gen 6–7); but symbolically 'Cain's kin' understood as the wilfully unrighteous in all generations (I Jn 3:12; Jude 11), who would be destroyed by God's anger (*Pe*). The verb here is preterite not present, but in // B 123 both verbs are tense-ambiguous. **157** *sente...aungel*: from Comestor's *HS*, Gen., ch. 31 as told in the C13th *Genesis and Exodus* poem based on it (ll. 517–54), an account going back to the lost Genesis commentary of the C3rd Greek Father Methodius of Olympus; see also Wilson, 1976:88–92.

Augustine in *The City of God* xv. 23 interpreted the sons of God and the daughters of men in Gen 6:2,4 as respectively the offspring of Seth and Cain. **161** *here werkis*: the coupling itself rather than the subsequent evil deeds of the offspring as cause of the divine anger.

219–21 This comparison from common life sees God as lord of the harvest: a feudal tenant (Adam) defiantly sows on a demesne fallow (Eve) and the crop (Cain) is cursed, because forbidden. The idea of the *hewe þat erieth nat* may be derived from Gen 4:12, where God tells Cain that any land *he* tills will be barren; the real-life referent would be a serf with no fields of his own who labours for wages. **220** *So...wreches*: because all illegitimate infants share Cain's curse and are marked out for destruction (Gen 4:11). This judgement, which affronts the modern notion of a child as a separate person with human rights, presumes instead the organic oneness of the family unit. It should be balanced by the assertion at B 78–9 of godparents' responsibility for the individual *litel barn er he þe lawe knowe*, which reflects the same medieval sense of 'collective identity' within the Christian *comune*. But the C doctrine (as at 246–7) is sterner than that of **AB**, which attack the coupling of the vicious and virtuous generations (the cause of the Flood), and make no overt link with the present-day situation.

222–35 describe the punishment of those who wilfully refuse to do well and the saving of an elect group to become the type and forerunner of the Christian Church. **224** '[I will destroy...from man even to beasts...: for] it repenteth me that I have made man [Vg *them*]' (Gen 6:7). The Bible text makes clear (as do 230–1) that the animals are cursed for the sin of man, under whose 'rule' they are (Gen 1:28): the 'subjects' share the lord's guilt as much as do his kin. The line is not translated here as in **AB** but at 255b–56a. **225** is repeated at 11.240, which relates the Ark to the Church and the Flood to the fiery deluge that will destroy the world (11.252). **228–9** *floed...bloed*: the trailed rhyme emphasising how the one is cause of the other, for the curse began when Cain made Abel's blood 'spring' and the pollution of the earth will end only with the 'washing clean' of his own 'blood'. **230** *Bestes...banne*: literally impossible, but symbolically including the humans (cf. the figurative use of *bestes* at 11.251). **235** *schingled ship*: with overlapping oak tiles; a common medieval English type. **236–47a** discuss in quasi-scholastic manner the problem of moral responsibility in the light of Biblical teaching and current legal practice. On the *pro* side is the OT supported by the law of England, on the *contra*, the NT; a *distinctio* resolves the clash of authorities by citing another NT text to elucidate or explain. **236, 238** *Here*; *hereageyn*: 'from this instance'; 'against (the maxim to be educed from) this instance'. **239** '[The soul that sinneth, the same shall die]: the son shall not bear the iniquity of the father, and

[**B**] the father shall not bear the iniquity of the son' (Ezech 18:20). *Pe* persuasively explains the 'mistake' (*Sk*) of *Gospel* (so at B 112a) by discerning 'a NT flavour' in the text and a prophetic foreshadowing of Christian moral standards in // Jer 31:29–30. Also relevant is Jn 9:1–3, where Christ implicitly endorses Ezechiel in denying that the blind man's physical ailment is due to his parents' sin, and Rom 2:6 which (quoting Prov 24:12b) states that everyone will be treated by God according to his own actions. No Biblical text is cited to support directly what the exemplum implied, but to Ex 20:5 (*Pe*), the rationale of which is explained at 220, may be added Pss 36:28b, 108:13–15, which see one's 'posterity' as one's 'property'. **242** *Westminstre lawe*: the common law administered by the royal courts. *worcheth....contrarye*: 'operates on the opposite principle'. **243–4** The heir to the property of an executed felon was deprived of the right of inheritance on the grounds of 'corruption of the blood', his chattels being escheated (forfeited) to the crown and his lands to his feudal lord. In theory 244 could mean 'It is for the King to decide what, if anything, the heir should be allowed to inherit'; but since felonies were 'unemendable' offences, they did not fall within the King's mercy (though this is how *Pe* takes *at þe Kynges wille*). **243** *thogh...and*: 'even if...if'. **245** *Ac*: 'But, against this' (= *Sed contra*). *glose*: taken (according to *Pe*) as 'a misleading gloss' by Wit, whose 'text-juggling...reveals the limitations of his understanding'. But this reading ignores the specific structure of Wit's argument. For the 'Gospel' authority referred to is not 239 but 247a (an actual 'Gospel' text), a *true* 'gloss' or clarification (functioning analogously to a *distinctio*) that enables Wit to explain how Scripture does not contradict itself. **245–7** may be paraphrased: 'The Gospel [which stated that sons should not suffer for their fathers' wrongdoing] provides its own commentary on that text (*ther*). And it veils what is the plain fact of the matter (*huydeth þe grayth treuthe*) under the fruit-tree figure that Christ used when speaking about offspring of this kind: namely that the offspring are always found to resemble the parents in natural disposition'. The unstated part of the argument would presumably run: 'If this text is true (and Scripture is always true if rightly interpreted), then it follows that the son would *not* really be paying for his father's sins but for those he would undoubtedly have gone on to commit himself (as Cain's descendants in the Bible exemplum did)'. **247a** '[By their fruits you shall know them]. Do men [*Numquid* Vg; here lit. 'Never (do men)'] gather grapes of thorns, or [**B**] figs of thistles? *And elsewhere*: '[Even so every] good tree bringeth forth good fruit: and the evil tree bringeth forth evil fruit' (Mt 7:16–17). Christ's saying does not really teach hereditarian determinism, because it *infers* the nature of the tree from the fruits it bears (i.e. judges men good or bad by whether they do well or ill). But that is how Wit takes it, and there are no grounds for thinking that he is being criticised for doing so. For although **C**'s stance has hardened (*neuere* C 247 against *selde* B 152), the **B** evidence (*I fynde* 147, *sestow* 152) is that Wit is appealing to common experience.

B 143–52 are abandoned for the more powerful legal example, leaving a residue of their fruit-tree imagery at C 208–9. The lines verge on the bizarre, whether *appul* 149 denotes 'apple' (Tavormina 1995:91n77 remarking that apples were grafted on elders for the sake of colour) or generally 'fruit'. If the former, then marriages for greed are seen as *vnkynde* like those of the Sethites, who were morally a different *species* from the Cainites ('elders' in a 'Platonically' semi-punning sense, as Cain was the elder brother). If the latter, then grafting a superior elder-slip on an inferior stock could never make the tree's fruit sweet (since the elderberry is by nature sour). Either interpretation supports the conclusion that 'it would seem less of a marvel if an evil man produced a child who was not also bad'. The argument, new in **B**, is less nuanced than the issue demands and inferior to what replaces it in **C**. **145** *in o degree*: less likely to be 'in one respect' (Sch, *B-Text Translation*), since the cited scripture does not qualify but deny the traditional OT view, than 'in the same way, in the same degree' (MED s.v. *degre* n. 7(a), under the phrase *in o degre*), i.e. 'The Gospel for its part is correspondingly opposed to that view'. **149** *ellere*: see on I 64, where Judas is the 'cursed' NT antitype of the 'cursed' OT Cain, whose brother Abel was held to be a type of Christ.

A 178–9 have been removed in **B** perhaps as illogical in blaming Cain for the marriage between (as the text says) Seth's children and his sister's children 'against the law of our Lord [i.e. incestuously]'. The sense 'both married *others* [i.e. the Cainites]' rather than 'each other' would be unidiomatic for 179. **L**'s point has already been correctly made at A 151–4, which makes the crime the union of the children of *both* Seth and his sister with the descendants of Cain.

248–58 replace AB 178–85 / 153–9 to explain why the human race was destroyed, and not just Cain's descendants. It is because, when the Sethites intermarried with them, everyone (by a sort of moral Gresham's Law) became corrupted (the main rhetorical stress is on *world* not *why*). The passage therefore warns against 'mixed marriages' between the virtuous and the vicious and makes the object of God's regret his creation not only of man but of marriage (seen in A 134 as 'þe riccheste of reaumes, and þe rote of Dowel'). **A** and **B** both directly compare these OT 'adulterations' of good with bad to *vnkynde* contemporary marriages based on parental greed and ambition (153–59/178–85); these lead to the adulterous begetting of bastard children, so that the vicious cycle of social decay goes on and gets stronger (on the 'apoca-

lyptic' overtones of these comparisons cf. Tavormina 1995:90). **C** defers this application to the powerful new lines 259–72. **249–56** The outer and inner *m*-alliterating lines enclose five interlaced lines on *k, s, s, k, s* that metrically mirror the theme of intermarriage between the families and perhaps hint at the final triumph of the virtuous line (the *s* / *k* = virtue / vice dichotomy is adumbrated in **AB**). **251** *Seth*: see on A 153 above. *seth*: the 'Platonic' pun hinting that he is so called because conceived *after* Cain. **253** *catel...byheste*: phrases giving the exemplum its topical application, i.e. that neither actual wealth nor the prospect of it (or of the moral reform of the suspect partner) should tempt virtuous parents to give their sons or daughters to *sherewes*. **254** 'Let his offspring beget offspring on his brother Cain's offspring'. **255–6** may be echoed in *Pur* 285: *Me for þynkeʒ ful much þat euer I mon made*. **257** *goode* (2): i.e. any 'goods' except 'goodness'; on this strand of wordplay see Schmidt 1987:136–7. **258** *via..*: 'I am the way, and the truth, [and the life]' (Jn 14:6). *avauncen*: spiritually, in the first place, but implying that those who seek to 'wed' good, not meed, will wed Truth or Kind, to whom Anima belongs (cf. 133–4), and will not want for their worldly needs (see 202–3a, B 178 and cf. Mt 6:33). The term foreshadows the image of Christ as the 'conqueror' of sin who endowed his followers with true nobility (21.31ff).

259–80 energetically expand the diatribe against avaricious marriage-making but keep almost unaltered the memorable seven-line core AB 186–96 / 162–72. The attack, despite affinities with contemporary sermons, is individual in stressing how impecunious gentry degrade themselves by rejecting virtuous, well-bred (and attractive) girls without dowries for rich women of inferior origins. The passage complements the similar complaint on the rise of low-born clerks who bribe their way to the top (5.63–81 above). **259** *thei*: i.e. the majority, not the *fewe*. **260** *and connynge chapmen*: 'and because of the shrewd [arguments of] tradespeople'; *and* would read better if *as*. **262** *heo*: indef. for 'a girl'; its antecedent is not *kyn(rede)*. **263–4** *gode...goed*: see on 257 above. *haue*; *haue* 'possess' and 'take', because they seek 'the moneye of þis molde' (1.42) not 'the tresore of treuthe' (2.201); cf. the similar play on *bonde* and *hosebonde* in 270. **264** The landed nobility wish to augment their (diminishing) wealth even at the cost of debasing their lineage. **266** *bond...douhter*: 'A pack-saddle quean, a slave, a tinker's whelp'; indignant hyperbole for 'someone of servile origin'. **267** *Ac late*; **269** *squier*: examples respectively of liaisonal and internal staves. **270** The wordplay stands out in sharper relief if the line is scanned with *beden* muted and the final lifts on *-hére* and *-bónde*. **272** *wexe*: perhaps alluding to the practice of offering to the Church one's own weight in wax (*Sk*), often in the form of a 'man of wax' (*Pe*); see MED s.v. *wax* n.(1), 2b (b), citing C Pr

99 (though this probably refers to votive lights rather than a wax image). Whatever the exact sense, he would clearly exchange his wife for her weight in wax or a small sum of cash. *Pe* wonders whether *wexe* is the p.p. of *wexen* and *or* should be omitted. But perhaps it is the malleability of wax that is the issue: the *morwe* after their wedding-night, the deluded groom realises that his monied low-born wife *can* of *iangelynge* but not of *cortesye*. **274–5** The revised b-half and the added line stress the hollow-ness of a troth based on avarice. *lyen lely*: 'lie, truly', 'truly lie'; see *TN*. **274** *this pestelences*: the pl. taking into account the attacks of 1361 and later as well as 1348–9, after which there had been a brief rise in marriages and births followed by a resumption of the preceding decline in population (Postan 1972:43). Wit's judgement that the 'quality' of gentry marriages had deteriorated in the post-Plague years may be compared with Reason's on the spoiling of children at B 5.36. **275** No major lexical contrast of *lyketh* with *louye* 274 seems intended; the sense is 'neither of them affords any pleasure to the other'. **276–8** The implication is that their mutual revulsion rules out fulfilling the first purpose of marriage, offspring. **277** *Haen þei..*: possibly a question (rhetorical). **278** *Done-mowe*: Little Dunmow in Essex, where a side of bacon was awarded to a couple wedded a year who could swear and prove they had never quarrelled or regretted marrying. The custom, dating back to the 13th c. and still kept up, is mentioned by the Wife of Bath, in an echo of these lines (*CT* III 217–18). *bote...helpe*: presumably to 'prove' by false testimony their entitlement to the flitch.

281–97 Wit's *conseyle* on marriage has three parts: a warning to all against marrying for the wrong reason, advice to the unwedded, and counsel to the wedded. **281–2** are half-composed of fixed phrases (281a = 9.346a, 282a = 260a) but re-invigorated by the lively wordplay on *coueytise* (Schmidt 1987:139). **282** *in...wyse*: not a strong half-line, but necessary for removing the contra-diction between the **AB** b-verse and the approval of *kyn-rede* 'good blood' as a factor in choosing a wife at 261. **283–4** propose 'similarity of nature' as the criterion for good marriage: the one protects against aged lust (Chau-cer's Januarie for May), the other against youthful greed (Jankyn for Alison of Bath). *maydones..*: virgins of either sex. **285** *more þe cause*: still idealistic, but less absolute than **B**. **286** *seculer*: 'lay' (MED s.v. *seculer* a. 1(d)), as opposed to clerical, not 'secular' as opposed to 'religious' (*Sk*). It is not being suggested that priests be permitted to marry. **287–8** *Wisely...lecherye*: echoing the Pauline text quoted below at 296a (and also vss 8–9), addressed to those *þat may nat contynue* ('sic *permaneant*, sicut et ego. Quod si non se *continent, nubant*'). **288** *lymȝerd*: a twig smeared with thick glue to trap birds, with an obvi-ous polysemantic pun on 'penis' (MED s.v. *yerd* n. (2), 5(a)). The image is echoed in *PPCr* 564. **289** *wepene*:

the figurative use occurs only here, but cf. *ballok-knyf* B 15.124. *kene*: 'sharp, strong', as of a dagger (MED s.v. *kene* adj. 3(a), 6(a)), but also 'sexually ardent', as at B 13.348 (ib. 6(b)), with apt citations from *WPal* 616 (*kene þouȝt*), 1011 (*kene kosses*). **290** *Awreke*: thereby turning the 'weapon' against the fiend. *Godes werk*: 'a divinely sanctioned act'; but with a pun on *werk* 'intercourse' (MED s.v. n.(1), as at 6.181 etc). The thought here may be echoed in *Pur* 697ff (Schmidt 1988:116–18). **290a** 'Thou lusty man, give not thy strength to whores: *The Gate of Death* is written on their doors'. **291** *out of tyme* (*in tyme* **B**): at the wrong / right time. **B 186** *vntyme*: e.g. those times named at B 13.349; see Brundage 1987:155–60. *bedbourd*: 'frolicking 'twixt the sheets'; a *hapax*, and a happy one in every sense. The conditions for lovemak-ing to be *Godes werk* are: to be free of mortal sin (esp. of a sexual kind), have real affection, and be properly married. The **B** reading is uncertain, but legitimacy in the act is stipulated. **295** *dede derne*: cf. *Pur* 697. The act is private between the spouses and their Maker who ordained it and works his purposes through it. **296** The revised form dissociates Paul's reluctant concession from the positive command alluded to by **B** (Gen 1:28, 2:24). **296a** 'It is good that for fear of fornication every man have his own wife' (I Cor 7:1–2). **299** *faytors*: the revi-sion removing **A**'s concern over the inheritance of land and titles by people of ignoble character (possibly those begotten on serving-women and passed off as a barren wife's offspring, with consequent dilution of the gentry stock). Wit's is a 'pre-Chaucerian' belief that nobility of character is inherited. This view is soon to be signifi-cantly modified by Trajan's assertion (12.110–17) that grace won by Christ makes all faithful believers *gentil* in a deeper spiritual sense. But C 5.65–81 have shown the narrator convinced of the reality and necessity of social divisions based on inherited rank (and the qualities ide-ally supposed to go with it). **300** *Vngracious*: 'lacking the grace / luck'; the theological sense is secondary, since this is spelled out in 304: until God grants them the prevenient grace to repent, they will never be 'graced' with either the good deeds required for salvation or the goods needed for a decent life in the world. *goed*[l]: playing on the senses 'wealth' and 'virtue', neither of which they are 'favoured' to obtain. **301** *wasten*: the sexual licence of the parents being presciently seen to spawn an alienated and destruc-tive 'underclass' destined for a bad end. **305–11** The final summary definition of the Triad, greatly expanded from **A**, sees *Dowel* as a life of obedience to the laws of Church and State, humility, innocence and benevolence (compat-ible with the Christian lay condition); *Dobet* as one of outgoing charitable action (that of the clergy); *Dobest* as one of abounding care for the whole *comune* (the true mark of the episcopal order). **310–11** make the important new point that the 'degree' of well-doing that people may achieve is in proportion to their (intrinsic) capacity: the more they are given, the more they are bound to give, and the better they become.

B 205–7 (A 217–8) *þe mody*: the 'proud prikere' of 135, the devil whose enmity to God is the chief threat to Anima. If the **AB** definitions imply an antithetical correlation of *drede* (faith) with 'the world' (= the sin of avarice) and *suffre* (hope) with 'the flesh' (= the sins of lust, gluttony, sloth), the undefined third (presumably the charity that grows from obedience and humility) stands against 'the devil' (= the sins of anger, envy and pride). **206** *wikked wille*: 'deliberate choice of evil', directly recalling the faculty in which well- and ill-doing alike are located (6.2). **207** In making explicit how the divine life in the soul is destroyed, the added line implies an equation of Dowel not only with virtue (the *habitus*) but also with the sanctifying grace (*gratia habitualis*) that creates it. *dryueþ away*: describing the failure of Duke Virtue's custodianship, a figure lost sight of in revision. It is through mortal sin that 'Mody' expels him from the Castle of Caro and wins possession of Lady Anima, a scenario to be enacted on a collective scale in the final passus of the poem.

Passus XI (B X, A XI)

PASSUS ELEVEN divides into: (i) Dame Study's diatribe (1–82), (ii) her dialogue with Will (83–105) and her reply (106–35), leading to his encounter with Clergy and Scripture (136–61). This ends with a rebuke from Scripture (162–5) precipitating (iii) the fall into an inner dream and the vision of Middle Earth (166–94), followed by (iv) the vehement outpouring by Rechelesnesse (195–317). Section (ii) cuts B 10.251–330, but the juncture of this shortened sequence with (iii), which takes over what in B XI is the first 'inner' dream (1–36), is unsatisfactory in leaving Scripture's hostility towards Will unmotivated. **B** has massively expanded **A**'s last completed passus by almost half, but **C** returns it to nearly the original length (about that of C X). The basic structure of (i) and (ii) as given in **A** is expanded in **B** largely with Clergy's long disquisition (B X 232–330). Of this, **C** omits the portion on Dobet and Dobest (251–90), including an attack on the clergy (although re-using some lines at C Pr 105–14), and shifts the criticism of the religious (B 10.291–327*a*) to C 5.146–179.

(i) 1–4 1 *wyf...Dame Studie*: personifying the disciplines preparatory to the study of philosophy and theology, i.e. at school, the study of grammar 'the ground of all' (17.107) and at university, of the seven Liberal Arts. But a deeper meaning is discerned by Harwood 1990 (who sees Study as both representing the teaching voice and as related to *lectio divina* in its spiritually formative function) and Zeeman 1999:193–5 (who also stresses how

'study' as *disciplina* in **L** signifies the intense effort, labour and difficulty of pursuing spiritual understanding). **2** *lene...lyf-holy*: the image, developing **A**'s b-half, suggesting a female religious instructing children in a priory school. Her allegorical 'marriage' to Wit plays on the senses of his name: as the 'knowledge' that the activity of study must unite itself to, and the 'faculty' (of understanding) that enables study to bear fruit. In her the acerbic tone of a strict schoolmistress-figure is humorously contrasted with Wit's (still firm but) more relaxed 'voice of wise experience'. **4** *starynge*: 'glaring' (cf. *wroth* 3); but **C** improves by removing the over-stated AB 6/7 and changing 'man' to 'men' at 7.

5–27 6 The charge against the Dreamer seems unfair, since he is no more 'flatterer' than 'sot' (B 8), and it obviously has a broader target (cf. 11). However, Will does (if ironically) describe *himself* as a fool (B 15.3) or as so judged by others (B 11.68) and as 'nearly out of his mind' (15.1). **7** *Nolite...*: '[Give not that which is holy to dogs]. Neither cast ye [your pearls before swine; lest perhaps they trample them under their feet: and turning upon you, they tear you]' (Mt 7:6). Study envisages not so much violence against the teacher from brutish pupils as defilement of the proffered wisdom by those who cannot see what it is. **9** *dreuele*: metaphorical for 'defile by disrespectful treatment', a sense borne out by 11.40. **10** *preciouse...prince*: perhaps echoed in the first and last lines of *Pearl*. AB **12** *paradis*: alluding to the belief (based on Gen 2:12 and richly elaborated in *Pearl* 73ff) that precious stones 'grew' in the Earthly Paradise. **12–13** The revision, in a tacit critique of *newe clerkes*, adds gluttony and lechery to avarice and pride as presumed motives for the pursuit of learning. *holynesse or hendenesse*: a coupling of religious and secular virtues as desired products of good education that recalls *SGGK* 653. **15** *cardet*: a metaphor from the combing-out of impurities in raw wool and the straightening of the fibres before spinning, by use of a metal tool furnished with teasel-hooks; it intimates that intellectual ability cannot now prosper unless 'dressed' with ambition and greed. **16, 18** The expansion of this troublesome line shows **C**'s liking for rhetorical *repetitio*, in contrast with the polysemantic punning on *serue* in A 22. **17** 'And put obstacles in the way of a just man's claim by settling the case out of court'. **18*a*** 'To those who know trifles and slanders, the law says "Enter"; those who know righteousness, it tells "Keep out".' This unidentified couplet highlights the corruption attacked in 4.148–50 / B 3.29–34, arguing that lawyers' careers depend on Lady Mede's favour. **19–20** describe how they win honour and wealth through manipulating the law or bribing juries. *yrobed...robbe*: more 'Platonic' wordplay; 'robed' specifically 'as a barrister' / 'judge'. **21** All three texts invoke the archetypical just man's moral authority, but (like the Psalter-citations following) they differ and are only partly from Job. **23** 'They spend their days in wealth. And in a moment [Vg *puncto* for *fine*] they go down to hell.' **B 25a** *Quare*...: 'Why then do the wicked live, [are they advanced, and strengthened with riches]?' (Job 21:7). *Bene*...: 'Why is it well with all them that transgress and do wickedly?' (Jer 12:1). **A 23a** 'Why doth the way of the wicked prosper?' (Jer 12:1, just before **B**'s *Bene*…, in **A** a variant of **B**'s Vg text). **A** is Jeremiah, **B** begins with Job and continues with Jeremiah, **C** is Job, possibly a deliberate correction. The source-chapters in both books ask whether the success of the wicked calls in question God's justice. **25** '[They] shall go into the generations of [their] fathers: and [they] shall never see light' (Ps 48:20). Vss 17–18 just before and the whole psalm are close to Job 21. *Et alibi*...: 'And in another place, "Behold these are sinners: [and yet abounding in the world they have obtained riches **B**]"' (Ps 72:12). **27a** 'For they have destroyed the things which thou hast made; [but what has the just man (done) **B**]?'

28–82 28 C does not specify *disours* or *iangleris* but shifts the critique from low minstrels to mocking clerks. **31** *he*: men like the author, who recounts *þe passioun of Crist* in XVIII–XX. **31** *ay...mouthe*: as does **L**, who cites it about once on every page. **32** *Treuthe*: a tacit allusion to the poet, who set out to tell of *treuthe and tricherye* (Pr 12). **B 33** *Tobye*: in a Vg book of *c.* 200 BC (Tobias = Tobit in AV Apocrypha). Its 'exemplary lives' of Tobias (cited at 11.70, 17.37) and his son provide models of household piety for 'lords at feasts' (34).

  B 38–50 (A 31–7) L's sharpest attack on the decline of minstrelsy (see Poole 1958:605–10; Southworth 1989:119ff; Schmidt 1987:5–11) into bawdy buffoonery. **44** *Munde þe Millere*: a type of the coarse, unspiritual man; cf. Chaucer's *janglere* who loved *harlotries* (*CT* I 560–1) and Mann 1973:160–1. *Multa* ...: 'God has done many [great things]'; loosely citing Ps 39:6. **46** *Seint Poules*: a canon there ranking among the wealthier clergy, with a large income from the benefices of which he might be rector. 49–50 Cf. the Vernon Lyric no. 95 (Brown 1957) ll. 133–4: 'Now harlotrye for murþe is holde, / And virtues tornen into vice'.

36–53 bitingly associate the higher classes' intellectual arrogance with lack of customary charity towards the needy. **36** *aȝen þe lered*: clergy perhaps present at table as at 15.39ff. **37** *Trinite*...: alluding to a story like Chaucer's Pardoner's Tale (*CT* VI), blasphemously applied to the Persons of the Blessed Trinity in speculations about the economy of salvation. *two*: the Father and Spirit. *thridde*: here the incarnate Son who is crucified. **38** *Bernard*: as almost a fifth 'Father' of the Church, a byword for theological orthodoxy, so that invoking his authority here is especially outrageous; see on B 4.121. **39** 'Reason presumptuously in probing the truths of religion / to prove the truth of their argument' (the latter alternative being

likelier in the light of 40b). **40** *dreule*: literally and figuratively, the 'pearls' here being the central dogmas of the faith; cf. 9. **42** *crye...ȝate*: avoiding **B**'s repetition of an earlier use at 9.80 (in a sequence omitted from **C**). **44** *go per God is*: euphemistic for 'drop dead;' but the added 45–6 turn the sarcasm against the speaker. **45** Either, 'in respect of those who utter such an order' or (from the suppliant's viewpoint), 'to those who ask alms in such dire need (it will be clear that...).' **47** *blisse*: ironic; the 'prosperity' is only temporal and will not become lasting if he uses it selfishly. **49** *riht*: 'very'; the insertion, making the line of T-type, evokes (by way of an 'anti-pun') only to exclude the notion that they are also 'righteous'. **B 66–7** are properly deleted as respectively repeating B 57=C 41 and anticipating B 70=C 53. **51** *Memento*: '[O Lord], remember [David: and all his meekness]' (Ps 131:1). **51a** 'Behold, we have heard of it [*that is,* charity] in Ephrata; we have found it in the fields of the wood' (Ps 131:6, with gloss). In the source the referent of *eam* is the Ark of the Covenant, which the Jews believed to house the divine presence and kept in a tabernacle-shrine before Solomon built the Temple; it here stands for holiness. *Ephrata*: otherwise Bethlehem, the city of David and the Messiah who it was expected would descend from him (see Mic 5:2); as the place of Christ's birth in a stable, an apt metonym for humility. The general point is that 'as the Ark was kept in the countryside, true Christian goodness will be found among simple people'. **52** *knyhtes*: a brave improvement on the weak **B** form.

54–69 54 *Freres and faytours*: guilt by alliterative association. Disturbing theological speculations characterised early C14th friar-theologians like Peter Aureole, a Franciscan, and Durandus of St-Pourçain, a Dominican (Leff 1958:272–9, Knowles1988:287–8). *questions*: 'theological conundrums'. *proude men*: possibly themselves. *pestelences*: perhaps (like 10.274 above) more recent (B 79) and prolonged attacks (60–1) provoking anguished uncertainty as to whether God wills or merely permits the innocent to suffer. **56** *Seynt Poules*: the great cross N of the E end of Old St Paul's, used for open-air preaching to large gatherings (cf. 15.70–1). *in...clerkes*: 'out of pure clerkly malice' (in allusion to bitter disputes between mendicant orders); or, as seems likelier, 'out of sheer hostility towards (the secular) clergy' (the friars themselves being 'religious' clerks; cf. 59, and *TN* further). The antagonism envisaged is between university theologians (more acute but no less arrogant than the lay would-be divines) and representatives of ecclesiastical authority like bishops and canons, whose acuity (like that of their modern successors) will have been dulled by routine administration. **57–8** *ne fre...ne sory*: implying that theological speculation undermines penance and charity, which for **L** go hand in hand. **60** *no power*: because the efficacy of prayer is related to the faith of the one who prays. **62** *gode men*:

more general than *girles* **B**, which directly evokes the *mortalité des enfants* of 1361–2, so called because specially fatal to children (McKisack 1959:131). Both idea and expression in **C** recall 3.103, the underlying notion being that since the *comune* is one, its innocent members suffer for the sins of the guilty ones. *togrynt*: a very rare word; the unique *forgrynt* that it replaces (unrecorded by OED or MED) may be a coinage. **63** *this...world*: 'these worldly wretches.' **64** *eny*: generalising the source of salutary fear beyond plague to death itself. **67a** 'Deal [thy bread **B**] to the hungry [and bring the needy...into thy house]' (Is 58:7). **68** scans as Type IIIb on *w* and vowels. **71a** 'If you have much [*copia* = *multum* Vg] give largely: if you have little, Take care even so to freely bestow a little' (Tob 4:9). **73–82** Six of these lines alliterate on *l* and two on *w*, the stave-sounds coming together in 82 to round off Study's speech, which concludes section (i) of the passus (80–1 echoing 7–10 at its opening). **76** *lettred man*: implying a well-to-do cleric, the phrase seemingly generated in revision of B 91. **79** recalls B 19.457.

B 92–136 combine spirited dialogue evoking contemporary debates on divine justice with details of manorial life (Colvin in Poole I:41–50; Girouard 1978:29–80, esp. 30; and see Tipping 1921: pls. 107, 206). The erosion of communal solidarity by the higher classes (through preferring domestic privacy) and of religious unity (in challenging the Church's teaching) are obliquely linked to suggest that ungenerousness and unbelief are 'reciprocal' vices. **C**'s excision of this major addition to **A** removes **B**'s telling association of theological presumption (fostered by friars' provocative sermons) with what the speaker views as lords' neglect of their social responsibilities. **94** *frere*: like Chaucer's in *CT* III 1709–60. **99** *for...sake*: an ironic homonymic pun, since they do it to shut out poor people in quest of scraps (42–5 above), not to help them. **102** *anoþer*: an heir (though it will finally make no difference whether miser or prodigal). **107** *worm*: see Gen 3:1–15. *in his blisse*: 'in his blessed state (which no imperfection could disturb)' or, 'in his happy place [Eden]'. **108–9** *biwiled*; *wiles*: dialectal variants (< AN) of *bigiled* and *giles*, words that will resonate in 20.322–7, 377–92a. **109–10** *helle...deep*: the sense is that 'Adam and Eve and their descendants after them were deprived of eternal life', not that 'all the just before Christ endure the torments of the greatest sinners'; so *helle* here = *limbo inferni*, the 'border land' of darkness adjoining Satan's domain (18.116–17). **112** *Of þat*: 'from / in relation to what'. **112a** See on 10.239. **114a** '[For] every one shall bear his own burden' (Gal 6:5). **115** *maistres*: ironic, their *glorie* 'vainglory'. **117** *Ymaginatif*: a unique preparatory reference to a character not introduced till the end of Passus XI, showing how each interlocutor serves a definite purpose in leading Will to understand 'Dowel'. But **C**'s deletion of this reference is small loss structur-

ally, since Ymaginatif will not actually explain why men must die (though he will defend the *clergye* attacked by the would-be *maistres*). **118** compresses two **A** lines into one, a feature marked in the revision of **B** to **C**. *Austyn*: see on 11.148. **118a** '[For I say...to all...], not to be more wise than it behoveth to be wise, [but to be wise unto sobriety and according as God has divided to every one the measure of faith]' (Rom 12:3); a critique of the demand for *kynde knowynge* by Will in 8.57–8, 110–11 //. As *Sk* notes, Augustine develops this 'theme' in *On Baptism* ii.5 (*PL* 43) when attacking the human temptation *aliquid sapere quam res se habet* 'to know a thing as in itself it is'. **119–20** recur (near)-entire at 126–7; the dense repetition-pattern (*wilneþ...wite* 124a, 126a, 133a; *wolde* 119, 125, 126, 129, 130) mimics a sustained catechesis. **121** Study firmly aligns herself with HC, whose tone and procedure at B 1.61–70 she recalls. **125** Study's anatomical curse vividly conveys her sense of how incongruous it is to probe the mysteries of Providence. **129–30** *as he wolde*: a stress on the supremacy of the divine will (honoured in the parenthesis), further implying the need to accept it through faith, not for the 'reasons' that 'arguers' seek and (as often as not) fail to find. Study may echo here Thomas Bradwardine's position in the 1340s against the followers of Ockham (Leff 1958:286–9). **131–2** *ablende...fro*: 'confuse men's minds as to the distinction between.' **134** *lyue*: the way to discover the meaning of the Triad being to *do* well, not try to define it.

(ii) 83–105 provide a transition between Study's attack on presumptuousness and statement of her own limitations and the need for Will (appropriately chastened) to progress to more advanced teachers. **83** *what ...menede*: signifying that if the will is to find *wit* 'understanding' (which as 'wedded to' can only be 'possessed by' *study*), it must submit to teaching, and not be headlong in its quest for answers. **84** *wittes*: 'wise judgements' (like those in Wit's allocution). **85, 87** *louted*: Wit's courteous bow teaches Will to show similar politeness to Study. **88** *ʒoure man*: Will's offer of allegiance reveals that he is ready for education, if it will bring real knowledge of the nature of Dowel (91). **92** *mekenesse*: the recognition of one's ignorance and the patient acceptance of instruction at the appropriate level. **93** *Clergie*: 'book-learning', with special reference to knowledge of the Bible. After a course of 'study' Will should be prepared to approach *clergie* (which is inseparable from God's written word, *scripture*). *cosyn*: here = 'brother-in-law', since he has married her sister (97). Wit, Study, Clergy and Scripture are all joined in a 'family-relationship' allegorically representing Will's progression through school to university. **94** *alle...of*: 'every theoretical and practical aspect of'. **96** *and ouer Skripture*: 'and (is placed in authority) over'; the 'authority' is that of the interpreting mind over the text, of *sententia* (theological interpretation) over *litera* (the grammatical relations of the words) and *sensus* (their immediate meaning); see generally Chamberlin 2000. 'Clergy' thus connotes 'formal religious doctrine' like that of a university textbook of theology such as Peter Lombard's *Sentences* (for a narrower interpretation see Harwood 1973[1]). *and ...trewe*: 'if the Bible texts copied by scribes could be relied on as accurate (for construing the *litera*)'. Study's concerns about inaccuracy are echoed by Rechelesnesse at 13.116–19. **97** *sib*: an aunt or older cousin. *þe seuene ars*: the Arts curriculum taken by all (except professed religious) before studying theology. Its classic form was the *trivium* 'threefold way', the mainly linguistic disciplines of grammar, rhetoric and dialectic or logic (which taught mastery in expression and reasoning); and the *quadrivium* 'fourfold way' of arithmetic, geometry, astronomy and music, mathematical subjects that taught the principles of scientific reasoning (on the Arts course see Piltz 1981:15–23). By the late 14th c. Arts graduates who were not seeking ordination, or those ordained but without a benefice (like Chaucer's Clerk) might go on to advanced work in philosophy based on Aristotle (*CT* I 294–5; Courtenay 1987:30–66). Holy Scripture or *sacra pagina* formed a main part of the higher ('post-graduate') course in divinity. **98** *wyf*: the Bible and the Fathers, the ideal 'marriage-partner', since the training in 'clergy' was for those seeking holy orders. *as hymsulue*: because Clergy's knowledge of doctrine and canon law derives from the Bible. **101** *kyndeliche*: meeting his condition at 91. Study's implication that there is no unmediated way to comprehend Dowel stresses the need for learning more than do parallel AB109 /154. But if she also tacitly challenges Piers's claim at 7.181–2 to direct knowledge of *Truth* (the presumed object of study), open conflict between her strengthened claim and the ploughman's bold defiance of the priest is avoided by **C**'s excision of B 7.131–8*a*. **103** *gold*: Will's preference for wisdom over gold, echoing Prov 8:10, shows that he has heeded HC's exhortation at 1.81, 201. **105** *tyme is*: signifying that after a period of instruction, Will can move on to the next stage.

106–35 The second part of Study's speech gives practical guidance for Will's journey, but also defines the limitations of her competence, which does not stretch to matters within Clergy's province. **106** *hey wey*: the direct route to knowledge of divine things, through patient endurance of the vicissitudes inevitable in the scholar's vocation, which will become a major theme of Patience's teaching. It imports simplicity of life and avoidance of greed, gluttony, lust, anger and sloth. *Soffre..*: a 'signpost-allegory' recalling Piers's earlier to the pilgrims at 7.205ff, though the verbal parallel is closer in B 163–9 // A 118–24 (cf. also the 'domain'-allegory in 2.88ff). **109–10** warn against the remaining deadly sins (pride having been overcome at

92). But while *enuye* might be expected here (see *TN*), *ire* is probably a rhetorical repetition-with-variation of *wrothe* and the list not meant to be comprehensive (that **L** did not think clerks immune to envy is clear from his account of its driving the friars *to scole* at 22.273). **A 118** *longe laude*: possibly a sardonic pun on the poet's name, more obvious than the anagram at B 15.152 (and possibly too obvious to be in good taste).

B 164–8 164 *left half*: cf. B 5.578. *large myle*: cf. *WPal* 1732. **165** *court*: cf. B 585=C 7.231. **165–8** Truth, sobriety and modesty are the 'spiritual' *trivium* to understanding. On soberness as a fruit of poverty (a recommended state for clerks), cf. 16.150. **168** *That...*: 'in consequence of which everyone will be happy to impart his knowledge to you.'

110–11 *slewthe / treuthe*: the end-rhyme underscoring the formulaic character of Study's 'passport' conditions. **111** *hit*: with immediate antecedent 'sloth', though presumably all the named vices are intended. **115** The revision makes for better allegorical sense. Instead of merely claiming authority as Clergy's initial teacher, Study cites Will's 'qualifications': he has done the common foundation course (*my bokes*) and is now ready to go on. **116–17** Study takes credit for copying the scriptural texts (*wrot* 'wrote down') and perhaps even understanding their *litera* (cf. on 96), but not for interpretation and exegesis (*Bible...yglosed*). **118–19** Logic, like Music, formed part of Arts, whereas Law was a higher-degree course. Possibly Study *is* laying claim to civil law, which had to be studied before canon law (Courtenay 1987:40), while implicitly assigning the latter (with theology) to 'Clergy'. **118** *Logyk*: training in which was usually followed by courses in natural and moral sciences (Courtenay 1987:31–2). **119** *musons*: translating OF *moison* (< Lat. *mensionem* or *mensura*), defined as 'the measures or note forms in mensural polyphony' by Holsinger (1999:127), who quotes a definition of *mensura* as 'habitudo quantitiva longitudinem et brevitatem cuiuslibet cantus mensurabilis manifestans' from the English musical theorist Johannes Hanboys, *c*. 1375. The time and rhythm of 'mensurable' music was noted down by various signs, in contrast with 'immensurable' music (i.e. plainchant). University study of this 'art' was largely theoretical, and was based on Boethius's *Institutio musica*, which touched on practice only in Bk IV (Chadwick 1981:84–8). **120** *Plato* (427–347 BC): also called a 'poet' at 308 and 12.175, 14.189 (and indeed he wrote some fine epigrams). But since 22.275, tacitly alluding to *The Republic*, shows awareness that Plato was a philosopher, *poete* here may signify 'sage' as at 14.92, where the referent is the Magi (the sense 'any ancient writer' in MED s.v. *poete* n. is found only in **L**). **121** *Aristotel* (384–22 BC): whose writings on the rules of argumentative reasoning (the *Organon*) formed the basis of logic (as the Bible that of theol-

Commentary

ogy). **122** *Gramer*: the first stage of the university Arts course, though its rudiments were taught in the 'grammar school', attended by *gurles* '(male) children' from eight to fourteen (Orme 1973, 1982; Courtenay 1987:15–20). **24–7** *craftes*: here various skills connected with Architecture which, though not a 'liberal' art, required at its higher levels a knowledge of arithmetic and geometry. Murtaugh 1978:68 finds a precedent for this more extensive list of skills in Hugh of St Victor's *Didascalicon* 2:1, with its view of the entire system of study as designed to restore the divine image in man. **124–5** *contreuede*: not a strong instance of *repetitio*, but the accent-shift in the key-stave from *-treuede* in 124 (a T-type) to *con-* in 125 serves to vary the rhythm. **127** *loke demme*: from poring over the fine detail of these 'crafts'. **128–35** *Teologie*: a discipline pertaining to Clergy not to Study, who finds herself out of her depth. The reservations in all versions may reflect unease about the bold speculations on the soul, providence and free will of *moderni* like Holcot, Buckingham and Adam of Woodham (Leff 1958:291–3). But **C** at 131, rather than warning against these, asserts that theology is not a body of organised 'knowledge' but a matter of loyal 'faith', thereby removing the hostility in AB 141 (186). **128** *tened...ten*: the vexation seeming to be multiplied by the 'Platonic' chime, as it would not be if written 'two hundred.' **131–2** The *repetitio* of *soth-* and *bileue* (the latter with form-class variation recalling **AB**'s *loue*) is semantically stronger than that in 124–5 above. **132** loses the ironic **AB** pun on *best* and *bettere*, which half-retracts what it only half-concedes: that the 'Queen of the Sciences' sets most value on the crowning 'theological' virtue, charity. **133** *a lykyng thyng*: an ironic echo of 10.288. *loth...greue*: developing the thought of the deleted B 206a. **B 185** *to sotile in*: perhaps alluding to the fine-drawn distinctions associated with the school of Duns Scotus, the 'Doctor Subtilis' (d. 1308). **132–5** **C**'s fourfold *repetitio* of *lou(i)e* (again with interwoven form-class variation) improves on its mantra-like sixfold **AB** source. **134a** anticipates 22.208a, 250b and echoes their source in **B**. **135** *doctour*: wittily paralleling the Triad-grades and the university hierarchy: above scholar, bachelor and master is a supreme teacher, at once 'precious' and 'beloved'.

B 191–219 (A 146–164) are excised in **C** as perhaps somewhat digressive and not wholly apt here. For Study both authoritatively supports Theology, which is not her proper province, and expresses (inappropriate) reservations about a respectable quadrivium subject, while taking ambiguous 'credit' for crafts dreamed up positively to mislead. **191** *ooper science*: here everyday moral wisdom, which lacks the special concern for others of the Charity taught by Theology. **192–3** 'He who in words would pretend, but in heart is no faithful friend - / Act like him, for your part: so art is beguiled by art' (*DC* I, 26). **194–6** paraphrase the Latin, strong proof (if any

were needed) that the **A** Version (which does not) cannot have been intended for an audience of *illiterati* (cf. *Intro.* V § 17). *gylours...bigile*: advice rejected here as the way to deal with one's fellow-men, but effectively invoked by Christ in the 'Harrowing' sequence (and incorporating at 20.392a a text close in sense to the Catonian couplet) as a way to deal with the devil. **197–8** *Ac...contrarie*: corresponding to the scholastic *Sed contra* (10.20), here setting a weightier (sacred) authority against a less weighty (secular) one. **199** *bidde...bidde*: replacing **A**'s plain statement with 'Platonic' wordplay hinting that 'command' and 'prayer' have the same (divine) origin. **199–201** *breperen*: cf. Mt 23:8, I Pet 3:8. *enemys...lene... good*: cf. 'But love ye your enemies: do good, and lend...' (Lk 6:35). **201** *do...yuel*: cf. Rom 12:21. *God hymself*: as inspirer of Apostolic teaching; less appropriate than in // **A**, where the words are Christ's own. **201a** '[And in *doing good*, let us not fail. For in due time we shall reap, not failing. Therefore], whilst we have time, let us *work good* to all men, but especially to those who are of the household of the faith' (Gal 6:9–10); cf. A 11.245a. This closely fits what follows, but as a text urging love of enemies and evildoers, less well than what it replaces. **A 154a** '[Woe to the world because of scandals. For] it must needs be that scandals come: [but nevertheless woe to that man by whom the scandal cometh]' (Mt 18:7); quoted in full at B 15.157a. **202–8** translate the Latin preceding (202–4) and following (205–6). **203–4** bring forward A 248–9 and are correspondingly deleted at that point. **206a** 'Revenge is mine, and I will repay [them in due time]' (Deut 32:35). The sense of only 206 is implied by the OT text, but since 205 is spelled out in Rom 12:19, which cites it and then the contextually apt Prov 25:21–2 (following it with the injunction translated at 201), that was probably the immediate source. **208** *science...soule*: a metaphor neatly bringing the argument back to the *artes*. **209–19** make some small but significant excisions from and improvements to **A**. **209** *Astronomye*: used indifferently in the period for the academic discipline of 'natural astronomy' and the pseudo-science of 'judicial astronomy' or forecasting from the heavenly bodies (='astrology'). The extensive overlap between the two is clear from 17.96–7, 21.245 (and well illustrated from Chaucer's Physician in *CT* I 414–18). *yuel*: possibly punning on the senses 'difficult' and 'bad', given the doubts at the mere mention of an 'art' that could lead easily to the more remunerative *astrologye*, as with Chaucer's Oxford clerk Nicholas (*CT* I 3191–97) or even to *magyk natureel*, as with his Clerk of Orléans (*CT* V 1273–96). 'Judicial' astronomy is also conjoined with the three mantic arts here named in Mandeville's description of the Great Khan's court (*Travels*, 154/2–3). **210** *Geometrie*: presumably not the respected second quadrival discipline (despite the reliance of magical conjuration on such complex geometrical figures as the pentangle) but *geomatria*, 'an occult art related to geo-mancy or a branch of geomancy' (MED s.v. *gemetrie* n. 2(b); see Herman 1991). *Geomesie*: 'divination by means of earth, dots and figures written in the ground' (MED s.v. *geomanci* n.); cf. *CT* I 2045n, Thorndyke II, 837–88. **211** *two*: the revision (perhaps responding to clerkly read-ers' protests) prudently safeguards astronomy from guilt by association. **212** *souereyn book*: the ultimate end of such studies, diabolic magic, subject-matter of the most advanced textbook in a notional academy of the occult. **213–14** refer to the deceits that attended the practice of alchemy (as revealed in Chaucer's *CT* VIII 1391–1425). **213** *fibicches*: a unique term possibly derived from *Pebi-chios*, an early alchemist and denoting '?some kind of alchemical manipulations or tricks' (MED s.v. *febic-ches*, citing R. Quirk). *in forceres*: i.e. secretly hidden away. *of...makynge*: fusing A 159b/160b, possibly as a concession to objections that Albert had been traduced here (see A 160–1 below). **215–19** Study rightly admits responsibility for *sciences* arising from *mis*direction of the 'virtue' she personifies, an activity that can never be a sufficient condition of true 'wisdom'; her duty is there-fore to warn against them as obstacles to *dowel*. **B** makes more robust Study's muted **A** farewell (A 165 recalling A 9.49b–50a). **217** *folk to deceyue*: an honest (if somewhat reprehensible) recognition that 'hydroptique immoderate desire for humane learning' [Donne] can lead astray. **218** *þise tokenes*: her recommendation of Will as now ready to begin Theology (allegorical shorthand for his having graduated in Arts). **219** *kyndely*: 'kindly, graciously'; al-though metrically in the a-half, crossing the caesura to form a phrase 'to know properly, in its true nature'. C 140 erases this dual meaning.

A 160–1 *Albertis makyng*: St Albertus Magnus, 'Doctor Universalis' (d. Cologne, 1280), the great Domin-ican theologian and philosopher, teacher of St Thomas Aquinas. He wrote widely on scientific topics, but was falsely ascribed various works on magic and alchemy. **161** *perimansie*: divination by looking at the flames of a fire. *nigromancie*: 'black' magic, the raising of demons and the spirits of the dead. This (usual) medieval spelling is by a false etymology, understanding *nigro-* as 'black' (it is a corruption of *necro-* 'dead'). *pouke*: an old unlucky name for the Devil (sanitised as Shakespeare's Puck); the line's removal seems an act of circumspection. **136–40** omit the point (A 176=B 229) that Will is hospi-tably received because he has native good sense and has done his educational groundwork. The drastic revision loses coherence by giving no reason why his hosts' good-will evaporates. **B 220–31** delete the redundant A 168 but remain leisurely (e.g. 222b repeats 221b, 224b is otiose). **140** reminds of the promise made at 101 in answer to Will's request at 91. **141–7** CLERGY's response to Will's enquiry and what

follows are among **C**'s least satisfactory abbreviation-revisions. SCRIPTURE's animosity had made more sense in **B** in response to the Dreamer's harangue (greatly expand-ing **A**) which, despite some palpable hits, could fairly be judged bumptious. **141** *Clergie*: the official voice of the Church, proclaiming through its ordained ministers the Biblical teaching formally articulated by theologians (see Harwood 1973[1]). Clergy tells Will to follow the moral law of the OT and believe in the key Christian dogmas of the Incarnation and the Trinity, equating the Do's with the theological virtues of doctrinal belief, heartfelt trust, and selfless love of God and neighbour. The correspond-ing **B** passage (232–50) stresses the community aspect of Christian faith and lacks the final definition of the Triad, but goes on with a lively and digressive account (B 251–339) prompting the question from Will that motivates Scripture's rebuke. **141** *coueyte*: stressing intention and (at 147) action, rather than the intellectual understand-ing the Dreamer seeks. **142** *Kepe...kepe*: a 'Platonic' play on co-polysemes linking obedience to divine law with protection against evil. **144–5** The generation of Christ is virginal and, though accomplished on behalf of the human race, needs the agency of no male person. While the wordplay (*mankynde...mankynde*) is on co-polysemes of one lexeme, it also exploits complex phrasal antithesis (between *for* and *withoute*, *on þe* and *of þat*) to underline that 'a man' (Christ) is the sole true intermediary between man and God. **146–7** is close to the Doctor of Divini-ty's definition at 15.126=B 13.116. *al*: tersely replacing B 233–42, from which 234a, 240a survive as 147a and 154a.

B 232–42 begin with DOWEL (*It*: 232) defined as 'ecclesial faith', *bileue* in and through the Church. **235** *grete...neuere*: cf. B 2.30, 9.28, 16.194; **C** avoids these formulae. **237** *dedly deep*: the tautology hinting at per-manent 'spiritual' as against purely 'natural' mortality (*þe deep of kynde*). **238b** 'which is the spirit (proceed-ing) from them both'; the '*Filioque*' doctrine, first pro-posed by Augustine in *De Trinitate* (see on 148). **239–40** *Thre...al...oon...ech*: 'number stands appalled' as Clergy confronts Will with the cognitive impenetrability of the chief Christian dogma, that the Persons are distinct; not three Gods, yet wholly divine. **240a** *Deus...*: clause 15 of the Athanasian Creed, recited at Prime on Sundays; En-glished literally in 241, but also translatable 'The Father is God, the Son is God, the Holy Spirit is God' or 'God (is) Father, Son (and) Holy Spirit'. **242** Deferral of the title 'Maker' to the end links the Trinity active in history with the eternal Godhead of 235.

A 182–203 give a taut and vigorous account of the Triad, traces of which remain in **B** (186 underlies B Pr 120, 193 is behind B 15.169, 196a becomes B 13.118=C 15.128a). If the speaker at 182 is Scripture, her riposte at 225 will seem less of a sudden intervention, and in this version Clergy will then say nothing. But since he has the corresponding speech in **B**, *she* could be diagnosed as an **r**-tradition misreading as *****heo of *he*, the preferable reading of **m** (see *TN* and Schmidt 2004). **182–7** define *Dowel* as the honest, faithful way of life of uneducated working people. **188–94** define *Dobet* as a life of active charity, strongly suggestive of the pastoral ministry of the clergy, whether secular or (199–203) religious. **188** *to...bred*: 'to distribute bread to beggars' (cf. Is 58:7 qu. at 11.67–67*a* above). **190** *seken...seke*: characteristic 'Platonic' word-play intimating that the sick are those whom we *should* seek out. **192** *þis*: either a pl. subject-form *þis* (common in **C** but not in **A**) or the complement of *þo* after pl. vb. *beþ* ('these are those who do better' / 'this is what those who do better are'). **192a** 'Behold how good and how pleasant it is for brethren to dwell together in unity' (Ps 132:1); associated by Brinton [1:58, 114] with the unity of the Church (Alf*Q*). **193a** 'Rejoice with them that rejoice: weep with them that weep' (Rom 12:12). **195–8** define *Dobest* as the life of the prelate, authorised to teach and govern clergy and laypeople alike. **196a** '[But] he that shall do and teach, he shall be called great in the kingdom of heaven' (Mt 5:19). **199–203** return through the linking idea of 'endowment' to Dobet as the life of monastics, whose *stabilitas* is essential to the work of alms-giving for which they were endowed with wealth and rectorial incomes. The speaker strikingly emphasies community and charity rather than learning or contemplation as distinguishing their vocation. **201** is recalled at C 5.76. **203** both recalls Lady Mede's friar-confessor and anticipates Sir *Penetrans-domos* in B 20.341.

148–55a 148 *Austyn*: St Augustine of Hippo (354–430). *þe oelde*: 'venerable / early (Father of the Church)'. *bokes*: his 15-book treatise *De Trinitate*, completed *c.* 419 (see Clark in Stump & Kretzmann 2001:91–102); it influenced **L**'s treatment of the theme. **150** *Patriarkes*...: cf. *De Trin.* XII vii 12–viii 13; the texts will be Gen 18:1–2 (Trinity), Ps 109:1–3 and Jn 14:11–17 (Father and Son; cited below). **151–2** *apperede...seyh*: not the sense of 'Ecce *apparet mihi* in ænigmate *Trinitas*, quod es Deus...' (*Confessions* XIII 5); but that passage underlies the legend that a pious woman, while Augustine was saying mass, had a vision of him before the throne of God 'de trinitatis gloria...disputantem' (*LA* 124:564). It is a measure of Augustine's authority that Clergy turns to his mystical experience (as well as the Gospel) to support the Church's teaching on the Trinity. **155a** 'I am in the Father and the Father in me'; *et qui...meum*: '[and] he that seeth me seeth the Father also' (Jn 14:10 / 11; 14:9).

B 244–9 B 244 This assertion of Augustine's purpose as being to confirm the faith of believers reflects his attack on the pride of intellectuals in mocking 'the mass of Christians who live by faith alone' (*De Trin.* IV xv 20). **B 246** *Crist...so*: either 'Christ declared himself to

be the authority [for this teaching]' or '...to be divine [as the Johannine text states]'. **B 249f** are echoed by a Lollard interpolator in *Jack Upland's Rejoinder* (Heyworth 1967:242–8).

156–61 156 is repeated entire at 14.155 below apropos of why some and not others are saved. **157** *alle*: spelling out what B 234 states but B 248 seemingly (and perhaps unintentionally) contradicts. **158** *fyn wit*: elliptical for 'intellectual subtlety *enough*'. **159** translates the following Latin, but the *repetitio* in *mouhte...mouhte* heightens the catechetical tone. **159a** '[We must realise that divine action is not marvellous if it is understood by human reason; nor] is there any merit in believing only what can be tested by experience'. This much-quoted saying from Gregory the Great's *Homilies on the Gospels* II:26 (*PL* 76:1197) is found, e.g., in the first lesson of matins on the Sunday after Easter (*Pe*). **160** Elliptical for 'Thus faith [is the first virtue], trust [the second] and love the third.' *leute*: 'trust [in God]'; on this term's distinctive contextual referent 'hope' (especially in relation to the triad) cf. Clutterbuck 1977. **161** *That*: either assuming the qualifier 'respectively' (as seems likelier) or understanding the theological virtues (whose character as nominalised verbs is very evident here) as collectively empowering men to attain all three degrees of the Triad.

B 251–329 Of these eighty (at times somewhat loosely written) lines on DOBET and DOBEST, **C** omits the first forty, leaving only a few echoes elsewhere (e.g. 279–82, expanded at C Pr 105ff and 286–7a at 9.260–1), and transposes the rest to 5.146–79. It develops from a series of admonitory maxims for a general audience into a diatribe against unworthy clerics (266–90), then specifically monks (291–329). **252** *bit*: e.g. in such texts as Mt 5:9–12. **255a** 'Seem what you are, or be what you seem' (Pseudo-Chrysostom, Homily 45 on Matthew [*PG* 56:885]); a frequently-cited adage (Alford 1975). The definition of Dobet as 'patient virtue' is close to that of Dobest by the Doctor of Divinity at B 13.118=C 15.128 (cf. on 146–7). **258** *Dobest*: exercise of rebuke (rightful only if one is righteous oneself) clearly fits with, though not strictly implying, formal authority in the Church. Clergy, like a preacher, translates or paraphrases the Latin before or after citing it. **260a** 'If to blame others thou desire, / Beware lest thou blameworthy be; / Thy lore becomes befouled with mire / When thine own faults bite back at thee'. This anonymous Leonine hexameter circulated widely (sometimes either line separately) and first appears in the Rylands Lat. MS 394 that also contains B 1 141a [B 5.44a] //, a manuscript perhaps known to **L** (see Alf*Q* and Pantin 1930). **262a** '[And] why seest thou [*vides* Vg] the mote that is in thy brother's eye; [and] seest not the beam that is in thy own eye?' (Mt 7:3). **264a** '[Thou hypocrite], cast out first the beam out of thy own eye; [and then shalt thou see to cast out the mote out of thy brother's eye]' (Mt 7:5). Clergy 'grimly' warns priests guilty of gross sins not to rebuke laypeople for lesser ones; but while he holds that their *dogma* 'teaching' may be inefficacious, he avoids the Wycliffite opinion that priests in a state of mortal sin could not administer valid sacraments. **266** *blind bosard*: a proverbial phrase for 'a stupid, ignorant or worthless person' (OED s.v. *buzzard* sb.[1]), of which this is the earliest cited example. The same word denotes 'buzzard', an inferior bird of the falcon family that cannot be trained for hawking, whence proverbially 'man [ne] may, for no dauntyng / Make a sperhauk of a bosard' (*RR* 4033, cit. MED s.v. *busard* n.). These 'blind buzzards' are like the 'dumb hounds' of 287 below. **268b** refers to both priests and parishioners; for the phrasing cf. *WPal* 2492 (*Many man by his miʒt*). **269** *This text*: the Latin of Mt 7:3–5. **270** *to..opere*: 'in order to bring salvation (effectively) to others.' **271–5** Clergy argues (somewhat tortuously) first (*For...yowselue*) that merely preaching the Gospel might have some value for the priest, even if it did no good to his hearers; next, that it now benefits no one (*Ac...Gospel*, the *lered* of 274 including the preacher) because he is *so* morally flawed he can't understand Scripture well enough even to preach on it. **275** *Marc*: not the only such misattribution; cf. B 6.237ff. **275a** '[They are blind and leaders of the blind. If the blind lead the blind, both fall into the pit]' (Mt 15:14). Clergy's point is that the parishioners will be '(mis)led' by the priest's living (hence 'blind to moral truth') more than by his preaching. **277** *festu*: possibly introduced by **L** from OF (< Lat. *festucam* Mt 7:3); otherwise found only in Wycliffite writings (MED s.v.). **279–82** draw on I Kgs, chs. 2–4, esp 4:11–18. **281–2** Ophni and Phinees, sons of the priest Heli, were guilty of lechery (I Kgs 2:22) and greed that 'withdrew men from the sacrifice of the Lord' (2:17), so the parallel with contemporary 'bad priests' is not obscure. **282** *Archa Dei*: the Ark of the Covenant holding the Tables of the Law, which was in the care of the priests (see on C Pr 107 and on 51*a*). But there may also be a punning allusion to Noah's Ark, a traditional 'type' of the Christian Church, which was entrusted to the keeping of the clergy (cf. C 245–54). **285** '[These things hast thou done, and I was silent]. Thou thoughtest unjustly that I should be like to thee: but I will reprove thee, and set before thy face [= "lay the charge before you" RSV]' (Ps 49:21). The psalm ominously warns that God will withdraw his favour from the sacrificial priesthood (a type of the Christian clergy) and give it to 'his saints' (= right-living laypeople) 'who set his covenant before sacrifices' (vs 5). **286–7** *burel clerkes...carpen now*: these 'homespun scholars' may include mockers like the 'heiʒe men' of 103–5 above who 'carpen as þei clerkes were'. Clergy's impersonal 'voice' facilitates the utterance of radical sentiments without 'blame'. **287a** '[His watchmen are all blind. They are all ignorant]:

dumb dogs not able to bark' (Is 56:10). Isaiah's referent is Israel as a nation; but Richard Fitzralph in an Avignon sermon (Walsh 1981:216), had applied his image to the negligent members of the clerical estate (it is developed further at C 9.260–1). **289** *preiere*: 'mere asking,' but with a pun on the co-polyseme 'prayer', which is presumed to gain efficacy from the petitioner's virtuous living. **291** *þis rule*: i.e. of *holynesse*. **292–327a** See at C 5.146–177*a*. **162–4** On these transitional lines, see again after **B 370**. They link Clergy's address to Will with an inner dream of FORTUNE that in **B** occupies most of Passus XI.

　　B 330–70 The forty lines that at this point expand **A 11.219–57** are here annotated first. **330** *dominus*: '(being) a lord', i.e. 'lordship, high social rank.' This is the (*faux*)-*naïf* question, provoked by Clergy's apparent equation of Dowel with a future reforming king, that arouses Scripture's ire. But since its deletion in **C** leaves her 'scorn' unexplained, it may be that some new lines were planned to motivate the latter. **A 223** See on C 8.86*a*; the quotation recurs at 11.238*a*=B.10.397*a*. Will provokingly takes *principes* to mean secular lords, not prelates, the 'princes' of the Church. **331** SCRIPTURE represents the written word of the Bible, hence her appeal to the *scryueynes* who copied the texts quoted at 336*a*, 337*a*. Her warnings against covetousness echo those of her sister Study at 161–2. **334** *reautee*: a word of which the only earlier occurrence is at *WPal* 5006. **335** *Poul*: the Pauline text in mind may be I Tim 6:6–10, 17–18, but *impossible* echoes rather Mt 19:24–6 (cited by Rechelesnesse at 11.203*a*). **336a** 'There is not a more wicked thing than to love money: [for such a one setteth even his own soul to sale]' (Ecclus 10:10). **337a** 'Money esteem, but not for its own sake' (*DC* IV.4a). The couplet continues *quam nemo sanctus nec honestus captat habere*, 'for virtuous men renounce the lust for wealth.' **338** *patriarkes and prophetes*: Job comes to mind, but also the Psalms, which praise 'God's poor' whose '*patience*...shall not perish for ever' (Ps 9:19). *poetes*: such as **L**'s anonymous contemporary who 'praises poverty with patience' at *Patience* 45. A 'spiritual' understanding of *pacience* is intimated by its collocation with *penaunce* in A 230. **340** *Apostles... witnesse*: a text especially apt being 'And we desire...that you become...followers of them who through faith and *patience* shall inherit the promises [*sc.* of eternal life]' (Heb 6: 11–12); cf. also Apoc 14:12. The blessedness of the poor is affirmed in the First Beatitude as given in Lk 6:20. **341–2** modify **A**'s overstated 'straw man' position by grounding the patient poor's right to heaven on a tacit understanding that (unlike the rich) they have had nothing here on earth; cf. 'Hath not God chosen the poor in this world, rich in faith and heirs of the kingdom...?' (Js 2:5). **342** is somewhat elliptical: 'whereas the rich cannot advance a claim [to salvation] as a right, but may only [appeal] to God to have pity and show grace'. The echo here of legal relations between subject and king, and the supra-legal character of divine compassion is unmistakable. **343** *Contra*: echoing 8 (10).20 and showing Will able to 'respond' scholastically to a theological assertion with a scriptural text that asserts the opposing view (and in a fairly radical form). *repreue*: 'refute' (answering *preueþ* 335); intellectually bolder than *wiþsigge* 'oppose.' **344** *Peter...Poul*: a deliberate riposte to Scripture's *Poul* 335. The authorities appealed to are not given here (though Scripture implicitly accepts their existence), and could be I Pet 3:21 ('baptism...now saveth you also...') and Gal 3:27–9 ('For as many of you as have been baptised in Christ...are...heirs according to the promise'). But while both texts may be taken to affirm the sufficiency (as well as necessity) of baptism for salvation, it was understood that the baptized must live out their Christian calling (by 'doing well'), and this opens a way for Scripture's reply. **345** *That is*: either, 'That is, (the) baptised are...' or, 'He who is baptised is...' **346** *That...extremis*: 'And *that* is (true, but) only in extreme cases...' Scripture too replies in scholastic mode, not directly denying Will's assertoric proposition (see on 10.29) but drawing a *distinctio* between (a) the narrow sense in which it *can* be absolutely true and (b) the wider sense in which it is not. Thus, when a Muslim or Jew at the point of death has no Christian at hand to perform the rite but receives baptism, he dies assured of salvation. *amonges*: 'in the case of...' or 'in the territories of'.

B 351–70 (A 240–57) 351 *Ac*: 'On the other hand, however...'; contrasting with (a), the wider case, (b), in which 345 is *not* true, i.e. for people born and brought up in a Christian society. **352–7** There is wordplay on both the senses of *confermed* 352 and the referents of *lawe*. In 352 the 'new law' of love is 'promoted' (MED s.v. *confermen* v. 7) and also 'ratified' (ibid. 1), in 354 it is at once the 'old law' that Christ fulfils and the new law that he establishes. Accordingly *That whoso* 353 can mean both 'Namely that / So that anyone who seeks eternal life...must [love]'. **353a** '[Therefore], if you are risen with Christ [*sc.* through baptism], [seek the things that are above]' (Col 3:1). **354** *and*: 'and in that way', as specified in **355–6** (which echo Mt 22:37–9, a passage quoted at A 11.242 and again at B 17.11–14 //). **A 242** '(Thou shalt) love [Vg *diliges*] the Lord thy God...[and] thy neighbour as thyself' (Mt 22:37, 39 run together). The first part is from Deut 6:5, the second a summary of the moral teaching of the 4th–10th Commandments. **357** *þat*: 'to those who believe (that they may) be saved', i.e. those who have faith must perform the works of faith. **A 243–4** *Godis word...enemys*: with reference to the distinctive Christian ethical precept 'Love your enemies' at Mt 5:43–4. **358–61** specify *Dowel* as almsgiving; but Scripture does not spell out the socially radical consequences of following Christ's precepts literally. **360** *bakkes*: rare outside *PP*

(though found in *WPal* 2096). **A 245a** See on B 10.201a. The sense of Gal 6:10 is paraphrased in A 246–50; but the eschatological vs 9 that precedes the Latin quoted is not developed till B 358–61. **362–3 B** alters **A** in specifying fellow-Christians and potential Christians; so Scripture, while affirming the Mosaic ban against killing one's fellow-men (on grounds of their 'likeness' to God), does not see the Gospel command of charity as answering to a 'human right' as now understood. Her priority is the moral renewal of Christian society and only then the conversion of pagans. **365** *þat ...liknesse*: 'that which is like my own likeness'; pleonastic for 'that which is made in my likeness' or (in the light of A 246b) 'that which is like (him who is) my likeness [i.e. the Son, who became a man].' **A 253** *ten hestis*: see Ex 20:1–17. **366** *tokene*: the chief such example in *PP* being God's command to Saul through Samuel to slay King Agag of Amalek (see A 3.238ff). *Non mecáberis*: i.e. for *Non moechaberis* 'thou shalt not commit adultery' (Ex 20:140); but since the speaker must intend 'thou shalt not kill', the error may be original (see *TN*). Donaldson, however, interestingly notes (1982:70) an echo of the collocation of adultery and killing in Js 2:11, following the important *offendit in uno* verse to be cited at B 11.308a (see also Goldsmith 1987:119–31); and AlfQ quotes from *FM* 681 an interesting comparison of adultery to manslaughter 'because husband and wife are one flesh'. **368** See C VIII under B 6.226. If this implies that capital punishment is forbidden to Christian authorities, **L** never states as much (cf. B 17.288–94=9.270–76, which envisage the severest divine punishment being for murder of the innocent). **369–70** do not translate any specific text but echo the familiar 'he shall render to a man according to his works' (Prov 24:12), especially as quoted in the eschatological contexts of Mt 16:27 and Rom 2:5–6.

11.162–13.215 The **C** revision distributes **B 10.371–475, 11.1–439** over two-and-a-half passus, reducing its dramatic intensity as well as its clarity and coherence in the interest of ascribing Will's angry speeches to Rechelesnesse, a personage whose substantial identity with the Dreamer becomes clear from 12.3–4. Lines 162–97 correspond to B 11.1–36, the opening of the first **B** passus that is entirely new (**A** having ended at 11.313). The revision here, which transposes as well as re-writes, involves loss of B 10.330–70=A 11.219–57 (discussed above).

162–5 162–4 now somewhat awkwardly link Clergy's address with Will's 'inner dream' of FORTUNE, which in **B** fills Passus XI. **162** recurs (with deliberate irony) at 13.130, where Scripture is the object, not the subject, of the same verb. **164** That this *Latyn* is meant to be (and is) understood by Will seems clear from his response at 166. **165** scans on *s* as a macaronic largely in Latin. 'Many know many things, yet know not themselves;' the opening of the *Cogitationes piissimae de cognitione humanae* *conditionis* (*PL* 184:485), misattributed to St Bernard (see on B 4.121). This work belongs to a monastic tradition that saw 'self-understanding' as the knowledge of God's image in the soul, and the 'knowledge' of merely external things as vain (see Wittig 1972:212ff; Bennett 1982:145–6; Simpson 1986³:49–51).

166–317 The second half of the passus consists mainly of the vision of FORTUNE and her satellites, followed by the long speech of RECHELESNESSE (195–307) and the responses of Plato and Fauntelete (308–17).

(iii) 166–94 166 *for...wrathe of*: either 'because of the anger of her words' or 'from anger at her words,' the latter being more apt in **C**, which gives no reason for Scripture's 'scorn.' **167** *wynkynge*: initiating a remarkable dream-within-a-dream in which Will's *alter ego* Rechelesnesse appears to personify the extreme aspects of his 'lower' self responding to the experience of Fortune (rather as later in the second inner dream *Liberum Arbitrium* will function as wise spokesman of his 'higher' self). *wonderliche*: removing B 11.6's echo of B Pr 11. **167–8** *mette / fette*: conspicuous end-rhyme marking Will's 'ravishment' from the outer-dream world of rational debate into an inner-dream world of emotional abandon. **168** *rauysched*: a word of ambiguous overtones (see MED s.v. *ravishen* v. 3) but always in *PP* with a negative sense (see *IG*). *Fortune*: the pagan goddess of worldly vicissitude, a 'merueylous monstre' who 'useth ful flaterynge famylarite with hem that sche enforceth to begyle, so longe, til that sche confounde with unsuffrable sorwe hem that sche hath left in despeir unpurveied' (Chaucer's *Boece* II, pr i, ll. 17–21); on *Fortuna* see Patch 1927 and Bartholomew 1966. Kaske 1968 draws attention to the iconography of Fortune's wheel at Kempley, Glos. and Leominster, and to an important depiction in the Arundel Psalter, which contains the inscription 'Vita decens seculi: speculo probatur' (165: pl. 60a). **169** *lond of longyng*: in part the allegorical terrain of worldly lusts (as the link with *loue* underlines), but less specific than *the launde...Lecherie* of B 10.163. For, as hinted by the phrase's sardonic inversion of the poet's *kynde name*, misdirected will 'ravishes' the soul into a *terra longinqua* 'distant land', where it becomes estranged from its defining object (God's image in the soul) and spiritually adrift in Augustine's *regio dissimilitudinis* 'land of unlikeness' (*Confessions*, vii, 10, 2; see Wittig 1972:232–4). **170** *myrrour...Myddelerd*: Fortune's mirror is the mutable world itself, particularly its transient pleasures (a like image occurs in Chaucer's Balade 'Fortune,' 10). But unlike the *speculum* of Nature in Alan of Lille's 'Omnis mundi creatura' (*PL* 210:579–80), as evoked by Kynde at 13.132, it 'reflects' only objects of selfish desire rather than acting as a *signaculum fidele nostrae sortis* 'a trustworthy token of our destiny' and a source of divinely guaranteed wisdom. Kaske 1968 traces L's contrast of the two mirrors to that

between the deceptive mirror of Narcissus and the true mirror of Nature in *RR* 20416ff, 17468ff. He also draws attention (p. 164) to Honorius of Autun's 'imago mundi, eo quod dispositio *totius orbis* in eo, *quasi in speculo* conspiciatur' (*PL* 172; 119–20). *Myddelerd*: the world of man in medieval cosmology being thought of as placed in the middle of the universe, 'between' heaven above its height and hell at its centre (cf. 1.127). **171** *wondres*: cf. Will's 'unholy' quest in Pr 4 *wondres to here*. **172** *and... coueytest*: 'and recognise what (it is) you (really) desire.' **173** *fayre maydenes*: 'pretty girls', her handmaidens lust and greed; their implied virginity is no less ironic than their congener's (Mede the Maid). **174** *Concupiscencia Carnis...Pruyde*: avoidance of the English derivate for the Latin here directing attention towards its source I Jn 2:16, which condemns 'all that is in the world' [= Fortune's domain] as 'the concupiscence of the flesh and the concupiscence of the eyes and the pride of life,' because 'the world passeth away and the concupiscence thereof: but he that doth the will of God abideth for ever' (ib. vs 17). *ParsT* (*CT* X 335) relevantly warns how 'concupiscence...wrongfully disposed or ordeyned in man...maketh hym coveite, by coveitise of flessh, flesshly synne, by sighte of his eyen as to erthely thynges, and eek coveitise of hynesse by pride of herte'. On the background history of this unholy triad, see Howard 1966:43–53. **176** *Parfyt Lyuynge*: 'luxury,' as pursued by the dissolute Lyf in 22.143 and by the protagonist of the early morality play *The Pride of Life*; but here with a tart 'anti-pun' (Schmidt 1987:111n8) on the sense 'life of moral perfection' later instanced at B 15.417 (cf. 13.231). **177** The revision to a T-type structure groups the chimed staves in the a-half, the new pun sustaining the passage's sardonic tone: whatever rejecting Clergy's 'lore' does for Will's 'looks', it does *not* promote his 'continence.' **180–1** The cloying indulgence profferred is mimicked by the repeated Type Ib lines and the fricatives of 183, 185–6. **183–4** *wille / nelle*: perhaps originally a perfect rhyme; 'I won't give up keeping company with you'. **186** *frende*: the ability of Fortune to become one's 'foe' (12.13) or to 'fail' (15.5) was proverbial, as shown especially in her replacement of youth, wealth and rank by age, poverty and loss of position (prelude to VISION FOUR). **188** *Elde*: the 'olde elde' of B 12.8, a sombre figure who in *PTA* 290 warns Youth and Middle Eld, 'Make ʒour mirrours bi me.' He is here what the Dreamer becomes in 22.183, after age has taken its toll of the vital powers, and makes an intermediate appearance in the second inner dream at 18.106. On medieval notions of Old Age, see Burrow 1986:150–62, Dove 1986:26–42, 103–17. **190–1** *fayle*; *forsake*: see 15.5, 22.195–8. **193** scans on spirantal 'metrical allophones' (*v*, *ð*), with *of Yes* liaised.

(iv) 195–317 195 *Rechelesnesse*: 'heedless disregard of one's spiritual state.' Stepping forth as suddenly as Piers in 7.181, he is in **B** one of three (followed by Plato and Fauntelete) to adopt extreme positions expressive of the Dreamer's wilful *likyng* (B 1.45). In C 200–307 he is given Will's entire **B** reply to Scripture's long lesson and dark showing (B 372); but some extended prefatory lines make clear his character as a desperate extreme of folly (*wanhope* 198; *rybaude* 199). *ragged clothes*: indicating either the ravages of Fortune's enmity or scorn of outward show (as at 16.349 where they are, however, the garb of Charity). **197** scans with an internal *t*-stave in *s̱toupe* and chiastic assonance. **198** *Sir Wanhope*: 'despeir of the mercy of God' (*CT* X 692–5); at 22.160 not a knight but a prostitute. *sib*: seen in 7.58, 80 as the end-stage of sloth (cf. *CT* X 692); here defiant indifference to one's final destiny (200), a variety of spiritual sloth 'related' to this enemy of the soul. **200** has a vocalic structural pattern and echoic counterpoint on |g|. *myn one*: the majority choosing the former (cf. 1.7–9, 66–7). **201** *þat ȝe seyn*: a reference to Scripture's attack on *richesse* and *reautee* in B 332–42 which has, however, been deleted in **C**. Clergy himself does not attack wealth in either text (except implicitly, through criticising the worldliness of religious). So unless taken as an 'intertextual' allusion (to **B**), it is an oversight on the revising poet's part. **203a** '[Only] in this way is it possible for a rich man to enter [the kingdom of heaven] — as a camel [might pass through the eye of a needle]' (after Mt 19:23–4; Vg has *dives difficile intrabit* and *facilius est camelum....transire*).

204–24 return to the line of argument first proposed in **A** and maintained, with only a few careful changes, in **B**. **204–9a** evolve from a natural-sounding form, expressing the speaker's conviction in **A**, through an ascription of the predestination doctrine to Theology in **B**, then in **C** to the Gospel as cited by Clergy, i.e. from Will's conclusion out of Scripture, through the theologians', to the formal teaching authority of the Church. Of the three, **C** is the most aggressively technical; but though **A** seems the most coherent with what has gone before, its clarity is deceptive, since A 281 could imply that nothing men do throughout life affects their final standing in God's eyes. **204** sarcastically echoes the wording and sound of 203. *Clergie saith*: not directly referring to something Clergy said but generally to what Will understands the Church to maintain about the NT doctrine of grace. Similarly, *ye tellen* B 373 denotes the Biblical teaching as doctrinally formulated by her theologians, not any actual words of Dame Scripture. **205** *man ymaed was*: relating a man's lot to the moment of his creation, whereas **A** elliptically declares him 'marked out [to be saved or damned]', a destiny that removes the necessity for either dowel or grace. *legende of lyf*: the *liber vitae* of Apoc 20:12. **206–8** The speaker's sense that 'since God is all-knowing, he must foresee the evil each person may one day do' is undiminished by his awareness of a distinction between God's

'permissive' and 'constitutive' will, what he knows (and so must be understood to allow) and what he ordains (and so must intend). *predestinaet*: 'pre-elected to salvation,' a technical term from theology. It is contrasted with *prescite inparfit* 'foreknown to be one who would sin', a direct derivation from Lat. *praescitus* used of those 'þat are to be dampnid or are now dampnid [having died]' (MED s.v. *prescite* adj.). Both terms are first recorded here and perhaps introduced by **L**; see further Von Nolcken 1988:85. *pult...*: 'violently thrust out of God's favour and beyond the reach of his grace.' **209** *Vnwriten*: first instanced here and echoing *non...scriptus* in Apoc 20:15 (*Pe*). It evokes the NT notion (drawing on Dan 12:1) that only those *fore-ordained* to be saved are recorded, whereas Piers at 8.77 has employed the more archaic OT idea that God initially writes down in the 'book of life' all men's names but later blots out those of the wicked, retaining only those who will be saved because they *have* 'done well' (Ex 32:32, Ps 22:29 [quoted at 8.77], Ps 138:16). *for* (*som*) *wikked(nesse)*: elliptical for 'as going to be evil' / 'for doing evil [at some future time]'. **209a** '[And] no man hath ascended into heaven, but he that descended from heaven, [the Son of man who is in heaven]' (Jn 3:13). Since in context this refers to the divine Son's real pre-existence and not to the notional 'heavenly pre-existence' of the predestined, the speaker's arbitrary and extreme interpretation may be meant to be seen as deliberately provocative. **210–24** cite exemplary cases from sacred and secular history of the truth of 209a (the 'proof by illustration' favoured by the *ars praedicandi*). The argument runs: these men were great teachers of wisdom; yet the Church denies they are saved; therefore they were predestined to be damned, whatever they did (cf. *wrong oper ellis* A 260b). But the only valid conclusion from the first two premises is that wisdom is not sufficient for salvation (cf. 14.192–3). **210** *by Oure Lord*: both an asseveration and an appeal to his words just quoted. **211–16** restate Conscience's argument at 3.323–6, omitting his crucial point that God forsook Solomon not in spite of his wisdom but because of his disobedience. **211** *Salamon...Sapience*: see on 3.121, 484. **212** *gaf...goed*: 'favoured him with wisdom and wealth'; as at 3.323–4 *grace* does not have its precise theological sense. *aftur*: the gift of wealth being added to the wisdom he asked for (III Kgs 3:9–14). **215** *wymmen*: the two harlots on whom King Solomon passed his famous Judgement illustrating that 'the wisdom of God was in him' (III Kgs 3:28). **216** 'Let it be neither mine nor thine, but divide it' (III Kgs 3:26). The way in which Solomon's psychological insight was displayed resembles Christ's in the incident of the Woman taken in Adultery (Jn 8:3–11; see 14.40–2). **217** *Aristotel*: regarded as simply 'the Philosopher' by Aquinas and as 'the master of those who know' by Dante (*Inf.* IV 131). If Solomon stands for practical wisdom, Aristotle (the exemplar of 'wit' outside the revealed dispensation, whose works formed the basis of higher study in the Arts Faculty) emblematises theoretical knowledge (including natural philosophy). *tauhte*: avoiding like **B** the ambiguous and even contradictory *wrouȝte* of **A**. **218–21** argue, in the form of another imperfect syllogism, against the pursuit of *clergie*: 'Solomon and Aristotle were wise; both are damned; therefore wisdom leads to damnation'. Once again, the *valid* conclusion from the minor premiss would be that 'wisdom' as such does not suffice for salvation (without grace). **219** *wordes...werkes*: a return to the sense and wording of A 269, perhaps through dissatisfaction with the ambiguity of B 384 *Of hir wordes* 'as regards / on the basis of their words.' The *werkes* would presumably refer to such matters as Solomon's wise judgements and Aristotle's guidance of the young Alexander; the re-phrasing eliminates the unacceptable suggestion in A 270b that they lived lives of great sanctity. **221** *And*: i.e. 'And yet'; not intimating opposition between *maistres* and *Holi Churche*; rather that although the university theologians recognise both men's wisdom, they agree with the Church's standard view. *in helle*: neither sage being traditionally included among the pre-Christian just in the *Limbo Inferni* (8.116), the borderland province of Hell. Aristotle was not as a pagan automatically denied 'actual' or 'prevenient' grace to assist his natural *grace of wit*; but according to spurious medieval traditions, he had (like Solomon) fallen prey to lust (see the illustration from 1310–20 in Camille 1996:pl. 88 of him being 'ridden' by Phyllis) and had committed suicide (see on B 12.43 below). In III Kgs 11:1–11, Solomon's idolatry (following upon lust) in his later years provokes God to take away his kingdom from his descendants. **222–4** embroider the specious argument with rhetorical wordplay on *werkes*, *wys* and repetition of *w*, the speaker leaving it unclear which 'works' are to be imitated and which are cause of their being damned (as well as mixing up sg. and pl. persons). **223** *That*: improving on the looseness of *And* A 277. *for*: with polysemantic wordplay on the senses 'because of' and 'in spite of' (MED s.v. *for* prep. 1(a), 9(a): see *IG* for other examples), effective in leaving the opponent no means of answer.

225–54 225–8 enable a better transition to 229–32 (preserved from **B**) through use of *For* 231. But the scholastic concession ('I am not saying *contra* to your position: I allow that those who follow what the books teach "do well"') is at once retracted by an assertion of the extreme 'Augustinian' view that a morsel of grace ranks above the mass of traditional religious learning: *Ac* 225 = 'Now', *Ac* 227 = 'All the same'. **230** *vngracious*: a mordant pun intimating that because clever people may lack God's grace, they must lack the capacity to please him. **231** *mony*: i.e. many 'witty' men, the argument here being that since most clerks seek learning for profit, not for

love of God, they in effect represent that 'wisdom of the world' that is 'folly' in God's eyes. **232** *goed*: the anti-pun ('property not goodness') gains force from the adjacent 'chime' (*annominatio*) on *God* (Schmidt 1987:114; with 232 cf. 1.177, B 9.178, 13.357). **232–3** Although the present punctuation is defensible, the stop could be omitted (making the syntax as in **B**) and a colon be placed after *meschief*, giving the sense '(when) mercy would be the most valuable "good" — mercy, which is granted only to those who have given mercy'. The allusion is to Mt 5:7, but the contextual meaning of *mercy* is 'charitable generosity shown in selfless use of one's learning'. The removal of B 395 and revision of the ambiguously parenthetical 397a are improvements (the homophone *seyen* 237 is a different lexeme); for a chief strength of Rechelesnesse's argument in **C** is that much of it is indisputable. **235–238** More rhetorical *repetitio* that not only draws ammunition from Scripture's own *connyng* to make the case against 'learning without love' (*witnesseth*; *Goddes word*) but also allows sardonic anti-puns on the ethical sense of *wel*. **235a; 238a** *Eadem..; Super...*: see on 1.173a and 8.86a above. **239–44** again exemplify homily-like *repetitio*; for the rationale of this application of the ark-image to the clergy, see on 10.224–5. **243** scans on *s* with a liaisonal first stave *his wyf*. **245** *leue*: for this revision of *lene* B cf. Pr 149. **245** In **C** both *folk* and *faith* economically govern *Holy Kirke*, but whereas in **B** the Church is the subject of the verb, in **C** it is more explicitly the clergy. The *Churche* form of the noun-phrase, with stress on *Holy*, now appears in line 248. **247–8** *Archa Noe...Holy Churche*: a standard typological interpretation: 'Ecclesia dicitur *arca*, quia, sicut arca Noe eos qui in ea erant defendit a diluvio, ita *Ecclesia* suos a mortis aeternae periculo' (Alan of Lille in *PL* 210:707). It goes back to I Pet 3:20–1, a text of sacramental rather than apocalyptic emphasis that makes the equation obliquely in comparing the water of the Flood by which 'eight souls' were saved to 'baptism, being of the like form' that saves 'all Christian souls'. *herborw*: anticipating the image of 'the house Unity' in 21.330 (cf. *hous* B 405). **B 405** *and...saue*: elliptical for 'and have the responsibility of protecting God's house(hold)'; **C** makes clear that 'Christian souls' are denoted. **250–1** *carpentares...bestes*: the 'proper' analogues being: churchmen ~ Noah's family, laity ~ the animals; but here the clergy are disturbingly equated with the Ark's builders, who were not saved. *vnder Crist*: the allusion to Our Lord's own 'craft' unsparingly highlights how, on account of their worldliness, clerks *fail* to 'build up' (edify) the Church. *Goddes foles*: both echoing the ironic sense 'fools to the world but wise before God' made explicit in 22.61 (but perhaps presumed as familiar from B 20) and playing annominatively on *foules* 'birds' (as at B 7.125–30). *fre bestes*: oxymoronic, since the 'lewed folk' are no more beasts, once liberated through baptism from the 'bondage' of sin. **251a** See on 7.153a; but whereas there the *bestes* are only implicitly equated with the Folk of the Field (cf. also 7.158), here the symbolic referent of *iumenta* is precise and the preceding words of the psalm-verse ('thy judgements are a great deep') clearly evoked by the eschatological context. Focus has now shifted from reform of the laity to reform of the clergy, and the poet's conviction 'that judgement should begin at the house of God' (I Pet 4:17) becomes relevant to the argument of this passage. **252** This notion derives from II Pet 3:5–12, which compares Noah's Flood with the 'fire against the day of judgement...of the ungodly'. *deth...ones*: either 'death and fire together' (with *deth* generic rather than specifically 'plague') or (more probably) 'deadly fire in one sudden instant'.

255–72 continue to argue from Biblical examples that mere faith can save not only without 'wisdom' but without 'do-well'. The probative instances mount from a common thief and a 'common woman', through a king driven by passion to kill a good man, to a (future) apostle who martyred Christians. But the proposition (suggestive of the 'Catholic' novels of Graham Greene) is again flawed: 'these "did worst" (not "best"), yet are saved; therefore to be saved one may (?must) live viciously, provided one has faith'. The argument ignores the crucial element of repentance, *followed by* good deeds: for even the Good Thief had a virtuous act (his rebuke of the Bad Thief's blasphemy [Lk 23:40–1]), and this was the fruit of (though uttered before profession of) his faith in Christ. The speaker here nonetheless has a point: that for all of them 'conversion' depended on the free proffer of divine grace, not on their own learning (or virtue). **255** *feloun*: see Lk 23:39–43 and on 6.319, and cf. 14.131–6. **256** *vnlawefulliche...lyued*: the 'positive' degree of 'do-ill', breaking the seventh commandment (the opposite of simple 'do-well' or keeping the law / comandments). **257** *shrof hym*: confession to and unconditional absolution and pardon from the 'great High Priest' himself (Heb 4:14), needing no penance in the form of (further) suffering or punishment (see on 262). **258** *sunnere ysaued*: on the strength of Christ's promise in Lk 23:43. In *GN* ch. 26 (ME version ed. Hulme 1573ff) the patriarchs liberated by Christ are surprised to meet the Good Thief in paradise. While his dramatic act of faith at the point of death would be properly interpreted as a limiting case, not a norm, Rechelesnesse as the spokesman of extremes is not disposed to take a balanced position. **258–60** Cf. 20.366–9. The choice of these figures is not arbitrary (they recur at 18.113–4): the first man, who is awakened from death by the blood of Christ (7.133), the great OT prophet of the Messiah (20.366), and the Messiah's forerunner. The text that probably underlies R.'s contrast of the Good Thief with the latter is Mt 11:11, 'he that is

the lesser [*v.l.* least] in the kingdom of heaven is greater than [John the Baptist]'. That Dismas *is* one of the 'least' will be maintained by Ymaginatif later at 14.131–48. **262** scans on vowels with an under-pattern of initial *p* sounds on the higher-ranking lexemes. *passioun*: the choice of this word suggesting that crucifixion with Christ (cf. Rom 6:6, Gal 2:19) constitutes a penance that needs no further *peyne*. **264** *Marie Maudelene*: traditionally identified with the 'woman...a sinner' who washes Christ's feet with her tears and is forgiven her sins (see on 7.137). Crucial to an understanding of R.'s argument is Christ's final words to the woman: 'Thy faith hath made thee safe' (Lk 7:37–50). **265** *denyede*: i.e. '(as she) said "no"' to'; **C** here (as with David) gives the sordid details **AB** only hint at. **266** Dauid's encompassing of Uriah the Hittite's death out of desire for his wife Bathsheba is told in II Kgs 11:14–17. Although losing **AB**'s fine gradational antithesis between *myȝte do* and *dede*, **C** provides one equally effective in its ironic *lelly...gyle / douhty...sleylokeste* paradox and its savage critique of ill-applied *connyng* by means of a graphetic 'Platonic' pun on *deuyned* (a visual transform of *denyede*). **269** *apostel*: not when he persecuted Christians; but the shocking juxtaposition of this title with *no pite* points up the impenetrable mysteriousness of divine election. R. here seems to echo disturbing contemporary speculations on such questions as 'Does God will only the good, or is a thing good only because God wills it?' **271** finally fixes this metrically troublesome line (which in **B** opens with a liaisonal stave on *pise ás*). Its great length (twice that of 269 or 270) formally mirrors Saul's abrupt but total spiritual transformation. **272** both obscures a truth (that grace abounded in these greatest of sinners) and suggests a falsehood (that they are saints because they did evil). **B 427–8** are rightly omitted in revision as repeating B 384–5. **273–5a** paraphrase the opening of the Latin quotation's omitted second part and offer a (not wholly satisfactory) revision of B 429–34, the form of which has been questioned (see *TN*). The **B** lines assert somewhat cryptically that two (seemingly unconnected) things are known to God alone: the fate of wise and virtuous men (or conceivably 'wise-and-virtuous men'); and whether people are to be judged on their good or on their evil acts and dispositions (the referent of *pere* 432 is 'God's hands', metonymic for his will). But the final conjunctival *for* does not readily follow; presumably the point of 434b is that 'the good *later* seen in Mary Magdalen, David and Paul shines all the brighter and better manifests the power of God's grace when contrasted with their former wickedness'. C 274–5 means 'Knows who deserves (what: whether bliss) for doing well or (pain) for doing evil'. Conceivably there is a pun on two senses of *for* 'because of'; 'in spite of' ('no one knows who is worthy [of heaven] — whether for his virtue or in spite of his sin'), as suggested by the following wordplay in 275 on *wele* '(heavenly) bliss' and *wykkede* (*pyne*) '(hellish) torment'. But the full scriptural text quoted does not support 'despite', stating rather that 'ill fortune and good befall all men alike in this life and so cannot be taken to signify divine (dis)favour'. **275** *he*: more probably reflexive than indefinite, since *no wyht woet wheper he is* answers to Vg *nescit homo utrum... sit.* **275a** 'There are just men and wise men, and their works are in the hands of God: [and yet man knoweth not whether he be worthy of love, or hatred. But all things are kept uncertain for the time to come; because all things equally happen to the just and to the wicked, to the good and to the evil...]' (Eccl 9:1–2). **B 434** may be scanned as Type IIa to avoid an over-weighted b-verse.

B 435–40 are cut in revision since they follow on directly from B 434 as part of an argument that **C** here omits. The colour-analogy is therefore not repeated at B 18.204–10, where Peace explains why suffering is necessary, but is used in variant form at parallel C 20.212–13. The argument moves from claiming that moral goodness could not be recognised without moral evil to contrast it with ('white cannot be perceived except in opposition to black') to asserting that we should tolerate evil men anyway, since even the virtuous are partly bad ('we are all neither white nor black but some shade of grey'). The ascription of 'complete white' to God alone implies that of 'complete black' to the Devil; and while this verges on dualism, the 'realistic' view of *man* it implies is scripturally based (440). **437** *goode*: see on 440 below. **438** 'When *must* steps onstage, there's nought but to *suffer* it'; a Latin-French macaronic scanning as a perfect Type IIIc line on vowels and *p*. This proverb, which is connected with the theme of judgement (AlfQ, s.v.), has the more usual form 'Quant *Oportet* vient en place, il convient que l'on le face', as in the *Roman des deduis* 3095–6 (cited Hassell 1982:183), and appears in an English poem on grammatical rules as 'And, when *oportet* cums in plas, / Thou knawys *miserere* has no gras' (Wright & Halliwell, ii.14, cited *Sk* II:163). **440** *Nemo bonus*: 'None is good [but God alone]' (Lk 18:19=Mk 10:18); Christ's reply to a rich man who addresses him as 'Good master', and whom he rebukes by asking 'Why dost thou call me good?' The implication in context is that only God may be called '(absolutely) good'. However, the use of *God* for Christ at 440 brings out that there *was* one man of whom 'bonus' could be strictly predicated, the divine Son (who is implied by the litotic *fewe* in 437). The text recurs at 15.137a.

276–307 276 firmly attributes the anti-clerical sentiment to R., who (ironically) bases his claim on his *reading*. The revision substitutes for the sharp contrast of *moup(es)* B 441, 445 the witty *clergie* of 283 to make the same point: that Christ replaced human learning by the superior wisdom of his Holy Spirit (A 301). The transition-

line A 293 ('And I cannot remember any more of what I learnt from my everyday practical experience') is well omitted in revision as both clumsy and inappropriate, since awareness that Christ did not commend learning is itself acquired from scripture (as C 276 acknowledges), not from *fyue wyttis techyng*. **280** 'When you shall stand before governors and kings [for my sake...be not thoughtful beforehand what you shall speak...For it is not you that speak, but the Holy Ghost' (Mk 13:9–11). **281** *clerkes* (*prestis*) *of pe lawe*: in context referring to the Jewish Scribes, though some readers of **C** might have thought of the ecclesiastical authorities, such as the Blackfriars' Council that condemned Wycliffe's doctrines in 1382. **283** *conclude*: like *disputen* B 447 a term showing how R. envisages his idealised *illiteratus* as able to engage the most accomplished scholastic theologian. It is not difficult to see why Lollard readers might have liked this. **284–5** allude to Ps 118:46, 'And I spoke of thy testimonies before kings: and I was not ashamed' (*Pe*). This text's keywords (*in testimoniis tuis in conspectu regum* echo those of 280 (*ante..reges...in testimonium*). **287** *wihtnesse*: an improvement on *wisedom*, affirming that theological victory is obtained neither by cleverness nor by compulsion. **288** *grace of fortune*: what is intended being apparently 'the divine gift of actual grace'; but the reading is unsure (see *TN* further). **290** *Austyn*: see at 148. *pat...wiste*: either parenthetical ('as far as anyone ever knew, he who said...was') or, as seems more idiomatic, completing the sense of *moste* ('for he who said the most that...knew...was...') (*Pe*). **B 453** *heizest....*: the chief of the Four Western Doctors of the Church, the *stottes* who harrow Piers's field in 21.268–74a. **291** *Saide*: '(Who) said.' *sarmon*: 'discourse', not 'sermon'. *for...clerkes*: an improvement in pointedness over **A**'s feeble and **B**'s flat b-half. **292** 'Behold, it is they, the uninstructed, who lay hold of heaven, while we the wise ones drown deep in hell'. This is loosely based on Augustine's *Confessions* VIII 8.1: 'Surgunt indocti, et *caelum rapiunt*, et *nos* cum doctrinis nostris sine corde *ecce ubi* volutamur in carne et sanguine.' Versions close to **L**'s circulated widely (AlfQ), so his omission of *sine corde* 'without heart' and substitution of 'hell' (= damnation) for 'flesh and blood' (= 'worldliness') may be of no particular significance; for **L**'s use of the quotation see further Benson 1976:51–4, Goldsmith 1987, and Lawton 1987;10n4 (citing the form in the Lollard *Lanterne of Lizt* 5, which has *in infernum dimergimur*). *idiote*: 'ignorant simpletons', the sense of the English equivalent 'idiot' at B 16.170, as opposed to 'one (culpably) ignorant' (B 11.316). *rapiunt celum*: alluding to Mt 11:12, 'regnum *caelorum* vim patitur, et violenti *rapiunt* illud' ('the kingdom of heaven suffereth violence and the violent bear it away'), and tacitly equating impulsive *lewed* believers like Piers with the 'violent' of Christ's words. *sapientes*: an uneasy echo of 275a.

294–307 The formula-like contrast between simple and subtle is underscored by *repetitio* in end-position of *bileue* (294, 296, 300) and in first position of *selde falleth* (301a, 305a), enriched alliteration (295, 297, 300), frequency of the stave-sound *p* (cf. B 463–5) and identical rhyme at 297–8. **C** improves by prudently adding *lele* to the *pore* and *lewed* of **AB** (perhaps in consideration of post-1381 conditions), avoiding the awkwardness of vocalic grammatical staves in A 313 and B 465, and condensing B 463–4 into one firmly conclusive line. **300** *penaunceles*: 'without having to spend time suffering there'; expressing what may be only 'the views of Rechelesnesse' (*Pe*), but hardly much bolder than the Pardon it recalls, which equated humble acceptance of suffering with loyal service of Truth as '*purgatorie* vppon this puyre erthe' (9.185). The difference in sense between the three versions is less than maintained by Johnson 1991:86–7, especially if the **p** reading *passen* is adopted (although the sense in either case could be that the poor simply need a kind of 'passport-check' in the place of purgation but are, like their emblem the messenger at 13.89–91, admitted to heaven without 'toll'). *parfit bileue*: perfect (i.e. pure and total) faith taking the place of **B**'s 'imperfect knowledge' and (necessarily 'worldly') manner of living. **300a** 'A short prayer pierces heaven'; neatly balancing 292 in both wording and imagery (*penetrat celum ~ rapiunt celum*). This proverbial phrase is based on Ecclus 35:21: '*Oratio* humiliantis se nubes *penetrabit*' ('The prayer of him that humbleth himself shall pierce the clouds' (AlfQ)). But since the *Paternoster* is specified at 299 (and cf. B 468), allusion to Christ's teaching it to his disciples (Mt 6:7–13) and recommending short prayers is the likely source (*Orantes autem, nolite multum loqui* 'when you are praying, speak not much'). Also relevant is Mt 23:12–14 (noted by *Pe*), where Christ criticises the Pharisees because they do not humble themselves, but 'shut the kingdom of heaven against men' (by their hypocritical example) and fail in charity while 'praying long prayers (*orationes longas orantes*)'.

B 466–8 are probably well removed, as seeming (inadvertently) to imply preference for an ignorant clergy, whereas the target is the spiritual arrogance of the learned, not their learning. **467** *Credo..*: 'I believe in God the Father [Almighty]'; this, 'þe furste clause of oure bileue' [i.e. the Apostles' Creed] (17.316) is also cited by Liberum Arbitrium at 16.322 as *clergie* sufficient for his ideal figure of 'Charity'.

301–03 This image of the clerical office reflects current social practice in the manorial economy; but it also alludes to the steward (= 'reeve') representing the Christian minister in the eschatological parable at Lk 12:31–48, which concludes 'And unto whomsoever much is given, of him much shall be required'. **307** *lene hem*: significantly adding to the teaching of pure doctrine an obligation to dis-

pense literal 'tresor' (= practical charity) as an equal duty of the clergy.

B 475–75a *soule to saue*: 'soul that is to be saved'; on this passive future use of the infinitive see *MES* 525. **475a** 'Go you [also] into my vineyard [and I will give you what shall be just]' (Mt 20:4). As at B 15.499 the workmen in the Parable are understood to symbolise Christian preachers; but **C** omits this quotation at both points.

A 312–13 conclude the main text of the **A Version** and are obviously intended to echo the lines of the SECOND VISION (A 8.87–80) corresponding to the point at which the **Z Version** ended. They are extended at B 463–5, which are then further expanded to round off B X. In conjoint **AC**-mss like TH²Ch this forms the point of juncture between the **A** and **C** Versions (see *TN*).

Passus B X *ends here, but the* **A Version** *is continued in* **mss RUJ** *by* **Passus XII,** *which follows immediately here in the text. The last ten lines of* **Passus C XI,** *which are printed after* **A XII** *opposite their parallel* **B XI 37–43** *(Vol. I, pp. 452–3), are commented on here.*

308–17 (B 11.37–43) 308–9 *Homo...disponit*: 'Man proposes, God disposes', a common proverb (Whiting M162), which Hugh of St Cher cites in commenting on its Biblical source, Prov 16:9: '*Cor hominis disponit* viam suam, Sed *Domini* est dirigere gressus eius' ('The heart of man disposeth his way: but the Lord must direct his steps' (AlfQ)). *poete*: see on 11.120 (and cf. 12.175, 14.189). **310–13** 'All those whom Truth [= God] guarantees as virtuous do not, to my mind, act foolishly if they follow the will of Fortune. Neither lust nor avarice will afflict you or lead you astray, unless that is what you desire'. Something like the speaker's equation of 'principled indifference to circumstance' with 'resigned acceptance of Providence' (and concomitant protection from worldly vices) might well be deducible from the true Plato's account of *The Death of Socrates*. The tone, moreover, does not seem ironic, though Rechelesnesse has hardly taken it in the intended spirit when using (at 196a above) the same words as 'Plato' at 311, and immediately goes astray now, as might be expected. **314** *farewel, Fyppe*: 'bye, bye blackbird!' *Fyppe* is a name for a sparrow, imitative of its chirp (and later to be treated as the proper name 'Philip' by Skelton). *Faunteltee*: a personification of culpable naïvety, very different from the care-free Charity described at 16.296 as *a childische* [= childlike] *thing*. **316–17** *me thouhte*; *Y counted*: the tacit identification of Rechelesnesse with Will now becomes overt.

A Version: Passus XII

The first 98 lines of A XII are here understood as an attempt, later abandoned, to continue or, more probably, complete the text found in A Pr–XI; their authenticity is argued in III, *A Version* §§ 69–74. 99–117, printed in italics, are taken as John But's addition. The lines offer (1) a continuation of the interview with CLERGY and SCRIPTURE (1–54) and (2) a condensed account of Will's encounters with HUNGER and then FEVER, who urges him to do well for the remainder of his days in order to get to heaven. Line 97 repeats A 1.119 and the passus abruptly ends.

1–11 Clergy's reply does not take up Will's final point in A 11.309–13 that the simple faith of the uneducated is a surer way to salvation than much learning, but protests at his contentious questioning and doubts his integrity and diligence. **2** *do...deuer*: referring to 11.182–218 and thus evidence that those lines are better assigned not to Scripture but to Clergy (see *TN*). **3–4** are somewhat elliptical: 'one who desires a higher state than is taught by the Bible (desires something that) surpasses the apostolic life and equals the condition of angels'. **3** *bettere...tellep*: i.e. than may be learnt from studying scripture (something implicitly called in question at 11.308 as leading men into heresy). **5** *seye*: 'observed (before). **8** *apose*: like *asoylen* 11 a term from academic debate. *so manye*: i.e. problems. **9** *tene...Theologie*: cf. A 2.79 //. **10–11** 'If I knew for certain that you wished to act on what you learnt, it would be my wish to resolve your every question'.

12–33 13 Scripture calls on Clergy not to instruct Will further until he has been confessed and baptised, a measure of how dire she thinks his 'presumptuous' state to be. **15** *kynde cardinal Wit*: in the light of 41–3, this should be Kynde Wit, Scripture's cousin (43), who was earlier mentioned in **A** only once at 3.260 (this is the only favourable use of 'cardinal' in *PP*). Transposing *cardinal* and *kynde* would improve the rhythm but the present word-order need not be corrupt, since it may play on the senses 'natural' and 'gracious'. **16–17** Both *pat*-clauses depend on *seyde*, one as a result-clause, the other as a noun-clause object. 16 shows characteristic *s / sh* alliteration, 17 scans as an extended Type IIIb with counterpoint (*abb / aa*). **18** *tellen hit*: i.e. what do-well is. **19** *Godes derling*: traditional; cf. 'dauið, godes ahne deorling' (*AW* 14b). **19–33** Scripture supports her *skele* 'argument' that 'Theology forbids its doctrine to be imparted to slothful sinners' with three Biblical texts in rising order of authority (David, Paul, Christ) and emphasis (*also* 19, *often* 22, *neuere* 25). **19a** *Vidi...*: 'I beheld the transgressors, and I pined away; because they kept not thy word' (Ps 118:158). **20–1** Scripture applies the psalm-verse to the Dreamer with a tart pun on his name; Dowel cannot be taught to anyone who clings to his sinful ways. *I seyde*: elliptical for 'I said, (nor shall I say)...' **22** *often*: incorrect, since Pauline reference to such words (if 22a is the referent of *hit*) is rare. **22a** *Audiui...*: 'I [he Vg] heard secret words which it is not granted a man to utter' (II Cor 12:4); to be re-used in a much more powerful context

at 20.438*a*. **23–4** comment on rather than translating the Pauline verse, which speaks of a private revelation, not the public teaching of the Church. *pat....hit*: 'tell what I heard'; for the phrase cf. C 7.17. **25–6** The use of *God* for Christ (as at A 1.24–5) heightens the presumptuousness of Pilate's *aposing*, and relates it to Will's (8). **27** *an hundred*: assuming (wrongly) that the interview took place in public (see Jn 18:33). **28** *Quid..*: '[Pilate saith to him]: What is truth?' (Jn 18:38). *verilyche...vs*: an addition making the question more sarcastic than it is in context. An echo of this punning macaronic is heard in B 15.60–1 = C 16.220–1. **33** 'But when he talks to me, I am what he says I am — [a scold];' a dry intra-textual joke (he does so only in the next line).

34–54 34 *pis skele ysheued*: contextually 'brought forth this argument', but with a pun on the sense 'showed reasonableness' (cf. C 6.25), as a 'scold' does not. **35** Clergy's action echoes the behaviour of another berated husband, Wit, at A 11.94–5 and, more distantly and humorously, recalls A 3.178 (*Sk*). **38–9** The gesture expresses his offer of allegiance to Scripture, as earlier to Study at A 11.101–2. *For eueremore after*; a phrase found mainly in **L** (see MED s.v. *euermor* adv 4(a)) and perhaps a small indicator of authenticity. **41** *Kynde Wit þe confessour*: Will in fact meets quite another 'confessor', Fever, whose 'dwelling' is not with Life but with Death. It remains unclear why KW is given this sacramental rôle, unless because it is a matter of self-evident good sense to acknowledge one's faults before embarking on a life of virtue (in the later versions, he is *contrasted* with Clergy as a source of knowledge of the truth). **42** *low*: a friendly response to Will's new-found humility; confession is a *sine qua non* of beginning to do-well. **44** *Lyf*: the principle of life (cf. A 10.46), not yet a 'nature-name' for God, 'the lord of life' (20.59) who is its 'transcendental' referent. **49** *clerioun*: an emblem of the simplicity required for spiritual progress, denoting either a young clerk (Will must 'go back and 'start all over again') or a schoolboy (cf. Is 11:6 'a little child shall lead them', and Mk 10:15). **50–2** *Omnia-probate*; *Quod...*: '[But] prove all things: hold fast that which is good' (I Thess 5:21); quoted in a sense nearer to that at 20.233*a* and very different from that of Lady Meed at BC 3.339–43 / 489–93. **50** *Omnia..*: personifications named from hyphenated Latin scripture-texts are rare in *PP* (cf. the one-word cases *Vigilate* at 7.56, *Multi* 12.48, *Pauci* 12.50). There is one similar Latin place-name at 16.331, but those at 18.4, 19.73 are made-up noun-phrases, not Biblical quotations. *pore*: implying a submissiveness to whatever God sends, as at 15.33 (and cf. 58 below), but perhaps also smallness of stature MED s.v. *povre a.* 5(a)). **51–4** Scripture's advice signifies allegorically that Will must meekly accept his unavoidable peccability, confess his sins and seek to make satisfaction by acts of virtue. **52** *burgh*: a town next to a large manor-house (*court* 57).

The allegory here is not unlike that at A 6.67ff or 10.1–11: the place (= persistence in virtue) is one reached after experience of both good and ill, a notion associated with similar use of the Pauline text at 20.233–33*a*.

55–76 58 The close echo of A Pr 62 suggests that XII was an attempt to conclude rather than continue the poem. **59** *fyrste*: i.e. hunger; the second is fever. **60** 'As I was growing up, towards the start of day'. The reference may be to a particular experience of dearth in his younger days. **61** This heavily-stressed indication of dazed helplessness echoes A 4.143. **63–6** anticipate the onslaught of age and illness upon Life in B 20.169ff. **64** *weye*: 'manner of proceeding'; Hunger is one way in which Will has come near to death. **65** Cf. A 7.164–70. *helpe*: i.e. with spiritual remedies and counsel, which can aid Will to endure but not avoid death. **71** 'A beggar's bagful — I bought the whole lot at one go' (perhaps implying that this is the food of a beggar-man Hunger has killed). **72** scans on vowels, with the verb in the opening dip, as at 3. **73** 'Because of the meals I had missed / to avoid losing any food that was there, I could not restrain myself'. **74–6** recall the Hunger episode at A 7.239–52.

77–98 82 *Feuere*..: 'Quartan Fever', with bouts every fourth day. **84** *Cotidian*: quotidian fever, with daily attacks; the earliest use (missed by both OED and MED). **85** *Tercian*: tertian fever, recurring every third day (in modern reckoning 'quartan' is applied to fever recurring at 72-hour, tercian at 48-hour intervals). *trewe drinkeres*: because causing great thirst. **86** *letteres of Lyf*: 'letters concerning / addressed to Life, (saying that...)'; with perhaps a sinister pun on the sense 'injurer' (MED s.v. *lettere* n. (1)). **87** *dedis*: 'documents' (announcing his coming demise), with wordplay on the senses 'effects' and 'deaths'. **88** scans cognatively on *g* / *k*, the first three words forming a dip. **89–93** Fever tells Will that his hour has not yet come; he will be given more time to 'merit happiness (in heaven)' by doing well. This final phase of **A** will in effect be re-written as BC 20 / 22. 199–211, where he is eventually told the meaning of Dowel (*loue lelly*). **90** scans vocalically with secondary *l*-alliteration and the fourth lift on *fór*. **96a** The image and pararhyme anticipate B 18.327. **97** recalls A 1.119.

99–117 JOHN BUT's conclusion falls into a) the death of Will and wishes for his soul; b) the identification of the scribe; c) the formal farewell and loyal blessing on the King. **99–105** are unlikely to be by **L**, since they mention 'other works about Piers Plowman and numerous other characters'. Unless these are **Z** and some other (lost) version, they are most economically to be assumed the **B** and **C** Versions written after **A**. Warner 2005:13 plausibly argues for punctuating with a comma after *bope* but is not convinced that the 'other works' mentioned must in consequence be taken to denote 'a category separate from *PP*' (17). At most, they *may* do so, for 102 could be

read quite naturally not as supplemental to but in parallel or apposition with 101, yielding the sense: 'Will composed what is written here and other works as well; [He composed works] about Piers Plowman and many [other] people too'. These 'many other people' need only be the numerous personages who appear in *PP*, not characters in some other Langlandian poem or poems supposedly being alluded to by But. **99** *Wille*: the author of the poem, whom the writer of these lines identifies with the protagonist of Passus XII and (presumably) of what precedes it. **103** *pis werk*: either just the text preceding *pat here is wryten* or including also the *oper werkes* 101. **104** *Dep...dent*: seeming to echo *Depes dyntes* in BC 20 / 22.105, though the phrase was traditional (MED s.v. *dint* n. 1c (c)). This the writer may have inferred as answering Will's prayer to Kynde at 20. / 22.201–3; but since the text at that point does not report Will's death, only his reconciliation with the Church, John But may have had personal knowledge of the poet's death. **105** *closed vnder clom*: a unique phrase but paralleled by *closed under clay* (see MED s.v. *closen* v. 6a). *Crist...soule*: a standard prayer for the dead at or after burial; it is balanced by the prayers for the living at 115–7. **106** 'And that is how John But would often pray [for the author], when he read these writings of his.' His identification as the King's Messenger who died in 1387 (Rickert 1913–14:107) is supported by Middleton 1988:243–66 (whose attribution of the whole Passus to him is rejected here). Other John Buts in the period are listed by Hanna (1993:160–3), but none seems a better candidate than Rickert's, and his affirmation of loyalty to the King may be more than conventional. **108** *Iames... Iop*: suggesting acquaintance with **B** or **C**, since Jerome is not *alleged* in **A**. **107** *busyly*: presumably with a different sense here; but perhaps corrupt (see *TN*). **109** *for... makyng*: 'dabbles in versifying'; apparently an echo of B 12.16. **113** reads as *aa / xa*, but a copyist may have transposed the b-lifts to prose order. The line would give a time before Richard's deposition in 1399 as the *terminus post quem* for **L**'s obit. **114–15** should not be pressed too hard to yield a precise date when there were lords who might *not* love Richard *lely in herte* (such could be found from 1384 on). But's protestation of affection may, however, be contrasted with Conscience's exasperation with the King in C 3.207–14. **116–17** are two Type Ic lines that skilfully slow down the pace so as to 'make a good end'.

Passus XII (B XI 44–284)

PASSUS TWELVE consists of (i) a *prelude* describing Rechelesnesse / Will's moral collapse, his disappointment by the Friar and his exchange with LEAUTE and SCRIPTURE (1–75a); (ii) a 'bridge' passage (76–89) on the appearance of Trajan; and (iii) an extended tirade on divine mercy, the virtues of poverty and the dangers of wealth

(90–249), which from 170 onwards is entirely new. Continuing beyond the end of XII and up to 130 of XIII, this is one of the more awkward structural changes, devised seemingly to reduce the long and dense B X–XI to more manageable size. In **B** the material of (iii) is given to Tra-jan; but C 13.129 confirms that the whole 280-line speech has been transferred to Rechelesnesse, who functions in part as the poet's quasi-dramatic mouthpiece, directly addressing an 'exterior' audience at 12.90, 221 (*lordes*), 13.25 (*lewede men*) and 13.64 (*wyse men*).

(i) 1–22 1 *Allas, eye*: 'Oh, the pity of it!' *Elde*: a reminder of a character who intervened from the wings at 11.188–94 but was silent during Rechelesnesse's long diatribe in 11.195–307 and the rejoinders of Will's bad counsellors. *Holynesse*: a conventionally appropriate companion to Elde (cf. 8.92–3) who has no further part to play. **2** On the traditional *wit / will* contrast, see at 7.243. Here the replacement of *likyng* **B** intimates 'Platonically' the relation between the dreamer's name and his chief propensity. **B 11.47** *fourty...more*: a basis, though somewhat slippery, for estimating Will's age (and by inference the poet's). If, contrary to modern notions, the dominance of Lust Of The Eyes is taken to begin from *birth* and the line is related to B 12.3, forty-five will be the Dreamer's total age (*Sk*); but the two references are not strictly parallel, since presumably we have imagination and memory from earliest childhood. More realistically in terms of the fiction, lechery's sway may be seen as extending from Will's abandonment of his studious search for Dowel, and 'forty-five' as loosely indicating the age *up to which* he languished under it. But the twofold mention may well be meant to hint at how old the author was at the time of the B-Text (see further Burrow 1993:92–3). **3** *me*: making clear that the Rechelesnesse in ragged clothes of 11.195 was but an oblique 'nature-name' for the narrator Will. **4/5** The rhyming revision (*were / frere*) refers to scruples as to how Will acquires wealth (the apparent sense of *good* 5, which is the referent of *hit* 6). But this is not necessarily the meaning in **B 50–1**, where the asymmetrical *mynde / dedes* contrast suggests rather that 'I continued to *think* about Dowel, although never acting it out'; and it is these scruples over how he may attain to virtue (53) that the wench assuages. **4** *reche / riche*: the sly pararhyme 'Platonically' hinting at the implied association of religious indifference with cupidity. **6** The new line, with its echoes of Lady Mede's 'easy' confessor at 3.42, 50, shows desire for money (shared by friars) as the clerk's main distraction from devoted study. **8** *fraternite... pardoun*: cf. 9.342–5, which couples these as equally useless on doomsday by comparison with Dowel. The words, recalling the friar-confessor's promise at 3.53–4, show Lust of the Eyes to be a true *damysele* (B 11.12) of Meed's patron Fortune. Her argument is that sin can be

pardoned without do-well and that *any* sin committed in acquiring money can be absolved by its judicious later use. **9** *Priour Prouincial*: the head of a mendicant order's whole 'province' (such as England). Having the status of a prelate, he might be prepared to grant pardons for a large enough donation. **10** *pol by pol*: 'each friar individually'. *pecuniosus*: for similar single Latin stave-words furnishing both lifts of a b-verse, cf. 2.191, 17.309, B 13.198. **10a** '[But] penance in the form of a payment of money does not suffice for spiritual faults'; a maxim of canon law, cited with slight variation in William Lyndwood's *Provinciale* of 1430 (AlfQ). Unattributable to the last speaker, it hangs suspended as if spoken 'aside' by Elde, the author, or the voice of conscience (cf. B 53), to which Will is not attending. **11–22** retain the core of **B** but remove the near-digression on burial and baptism (75–83). The passage takes Will in one line (12) from the condition of his summertime encounter with the mendicant masters in 10.9 to something like the decrepitude of 22.199–213. **12** *forȝat ȝouthe*: anticipating 22.155. *elde*: about 65 years, his notional age in the final passus. **15** is either an enriched Type IIa line (like B 63), with monolexical *cónféssede*, or a Ib, with the break after *Y*. *flittyng*: 'evasive', whereas in B 63–4 *flittynge...ayeins* chimes annominatively on the set phrase *fliten againes* 'oppose, contend against' (MED s.v. 2), suggesting that the friar tried to argue his way out of the original agreement (presumably, to give absolution on demand). **19–20** Cf. B 9.164. **20–22** The revision of B 74 *siluer* heightens the charge's formulaic quality, the repetition of *godes* forming a lexical triangle with the antithetical *rode* that friars should live by. **22** *Wher*: tartly punning on 'where' and 'whether', so as to accuse the friar not just of promise-breaking but of callous failure in his vocation, since burying the dead was the final 'corporal work of mercy' (added to the six in Mt 25:35–6).

B 75–83 76 *couent*: synecdoche for 'order' and more generally 'type of religious.' The 'Platonic' pun wrenches the verb from its neutral sense 'desire' (*IG* s.v. *coueiten*). *catecumelynges*: the idiosyncratic deformation of expected *catechumenes* (< Lat < Gk) 'a(ny) person newly receiving religious instruction,' with its diminutive suffix, links the term with children. Though *barnes* are not 'converts' in the usual sense, they must likewise (after baptism) be taught the elements of the faith (most actual baptizands would be infants). An instructional as well as a sacramental rôle may be envisaged for the friars; but the main point is that burial is a service that promises higher fees, gifts from the dead man's relations, and maybe legacies. Forfeiting the friar's readiness to absolve is the price Will pays for deciding to be buried not in the convent cemetery but in his parish church. The opinion his conscience prompts him to voice recalls Piers's words at B 6.91–5 (Conscience is the latter's instructor

601

at B 7.134). **78** *Baptiȝynge*: as understood here to cover the subsequent instruction implied by *catecumelynges*, coming under the first two 'spiritual works of mercy' (converting and instructing). **80–3** claim that of the two sacraments, confession is the less valuable because, while there is no salvation without baptism, there can be without confession, if the baptised person is contrite. **81a** 'Contrition alone can blot out sin'; a common theological maxim cited in variant form by Brinton (1:81), who follows Aquinas (*ST* III Suppl. qu.5., art. 2) in illustrating it from the Good Thief (Alford in Vaughan 1993:21–2), and one featuring in controversies over the importance of oral confession (Alf*Q*; Gray 1986[1]). The opinion itself (complementing the maxim at B 11.59 above) does not *lye* against the Church's requirement of (annual) confession. Confession is urged at B 14.16–32=C 16.25–34 by Conscience, even if he equates contrition with Dowel; for though heartfelt sorrow rendered the mortal sin venial, the obligation to confess it remained (cf. 12.174ff). That such sorrow *suffices* for salvation (as affirmed by Repentance at B 5.125 and by the Samaritan at 19.298) and that baptism is *necessary* for salvation are notions that would have been unquestioned, though both prove not without difficulties. But less important than the doctrinal implications of what he says is Will's combative tone in objecting to pecuniary exploitation of the sacrament. **82** refers to a child who *dies* in a state of Original Sin and who, while obviously incapable of 'actual' sin, is likewise incapable of the contrition necessary to save the unbaptised. The wording closely echoes Scripture at B 10.347 but may be meant to verge recognisably on the *in extremis* position she distinguishes at B 10.346 (cf. also B 15.33=C 17.121). **82a** '[Jesus answered: Amen, amen, I say to thee], unless a man be born again [of water and the Holy Ghost, he cannot enter into the kingdom of God]' (Jn 3:5). **83** is addressed at once from Will to the friars and (through him) by the poet to the learned members of his audience (cf. C 17.210).

23–50 In this section **23–41a** show detailed revision of B 84–106a in the direction of greater explicitness, as at 25–6, finer discrimination (the *treuthe / trewe* quasi-rhyme at 27–8), and dramatic propriety, as in eliminating the reference to *metels* (unless **L** envisages a 'lucid dream' in which the dreamer knows he is dreaming; with B 86 contrast B Pr 209–10. B 94–100 are now transferred to Will and 96–100 shortened to C 28–9. **23** *Leaute*: personifying equitable fairness and disinterested good faith (MED s.v. (a); cf. on Pr 149, 2.20–1) rather than 'law-abiding people' (Kane 1982:40) or 'strict adherence to the letter of the law' (Donaldson 1949:66n). Though already mentioned at 3.446, 4.156 as a foe of untruth and Mede, he here seems as much an aspect of the Dreamer as the embodiment of his ideal audience that he is in **B** (Schmidt 1987[2]:12–13). **27–9** The answer to Will's wish would come better from

Leaute as in B 87; but the sequence of *s*-alliterating lines subtly distinguishes between truth as fact and truth as integrity: only an honest man may utter discreditable facts about dishonest men. **27** *were treuthe*: 'would be the truth (if I were to say it)'. **30** See on B 10.285. The context in Ps 49 is significant in making God threaten the man who 'declare[s] [his] justices' (16) even while 'speak[ing] against [his] brother' (20). **31** *also*: 'likewise', 'in their turn', i.e. in reply to the psalmist's accusation of hypocrisy they will cite an even more authoritative warning against hypocritical judgement. **32** 'Judge not (anyone), [that you may not be judged]' (Mt 7:1). **33** *And*: 'Yes, (but)'. **35** 'Thou shalt not hate thy brother (secretly) in thy heart: but reprove him openly, [lest thou incur sin through him]' (Lev 19:17; cf. I Tim 5:20). The pl. *fratres* in B 88 is an adaptation to suit the 'implied referent' (Alf*Q* 19n33), the friars. **37** *retoryk*: 'poetry'; see Schmidt 1987[2]:108–41. **39** has the medial break after *nat*, whether *sum* is stressed or muted to give a T-type line. **41** *labbe..it out*: further from the Latin than **B** (but see *TN*). **41a** 'Praise moderately; blame more sparingly. [For too much praise deserves the same censure as too much blame]'; attributed to Seneca in Vincent of Beauvais, *Speculum Doctrinale* 5.69 and Alan of Lille, *Summa de Arte Praedicatoria* [*SAP*] 23 (*PL* 210:158). The Roman Stoic philosopher (*c.* 4 BC–65 AD) is quoted again at 16.141a.

B 96–100 are cut from **C** perhaps as irrelevant to an argument concerning public wrongs that affect the wider community. **97** *ech a lawe*: i.e. both civil and canon law permitting telling of the whole truth. **100** *synne*: presumably sins told under the seal of confession. Lewte is not authorising public exposure of individuals' faults; the text cited at 93=C 35 recommends not suppressing but taking up grievances face-to-face with one's fellow-Christians. **43** *matere*: the stern lesson that few will be saved. This would turn the many against religion if they heard it; but as the key-words remain in Latin, it can be grasped only by the few. **48, 50** *Multi*; *Pauci*: both words 'plucked' from the end of Scripture's preaching text (the parable of the marriage feast), 'For many [*multi*] are called but few [*pauci*] are chosen' (Mt 22:14). **50** *priueiliche*: not according to the Gospel; but perhaps meaning 'those chosen for salvation are known to God alone'.

51–75a The response of the clerk Will to this 'text' (51), as Kirk 1972:130 notes, both recalls (*tene*) and contrasts with (*tremblede*) the Plowman's to the 'text' of Truth's pardon (B 7.115), which led Piers not to *despute* but to *pulle it atweyne*. The debilitating effect of clerkly *wer* 'uncertainty' is ironically brought out by its 'Platonic' echo in *Where Y were*, the Latin *Utrum* 'whether' being a common opening to scholastic discussion of a *quaestio*. **53** *Holy Churche...fonte*: the most striking retrospective reference in the poem (to 1.72–3). Will understandably draws comfort from his associate membership of the

Communion of Saints, but remains doubtful about the sense of 'chosen': is it unconditional 'election' or only an offer of the means of salvation? (Cf. 60*a* and B 10.345 earlier). Scripture's *sompned* correlates with HC's *vnderfeng*, her *plihte* with *my biddyng to fulfille* (1.74). *R–H* 134–5 aptly note that in Augustine's interpretation of the parable, the marriage garment is not baptism but charity (to which baptismal grace opens the way). **56** *sismatikes*: anachronistic if taken literally; but Christ's 'call' is doubtless thought of as directly continued in historical time through the authoritative voice of his Church. **57–8** The powerful metaphor draws on the traditional image of Jesus as 'nursing mother' derived from texts like Is 49:15, 66:13 (Woolf 1968:189–90); for a possible source of the 'nurse' image Wenzel cites *FM* V, 7 (AlfC 162). The idea is vividly captured in the iconography of the 'Pelican in her Piety', which was fabled to feed its young with blood from its own breast; see Schiller II pls. 444, 451 (C13th), 504 (C14th). The present reference to Christ's blood as a healing remedy echoes 7.133 and seems directly derived from the penultimate stanza of the hymn *Adoro te devote* (traditionally ascribed to Aquinas): 'Pie pelicane, Iesu Domine, / Me immundum munda tuo sanguine, / Cuius una stilla salvum facere / Totum mundum posset omni scelere' ('O loving pelican, Lord Jesus, purify my impurity with your blood, one drop of which could save the whole world from all sin' (the original's *mundum / immundum* wordplay perhaps suggesting that on *saue* 57 'salve / safe(ly)'). But the context makes clear that the primary meaning is baptismal rather than eucharistic (cf. 60), and based on traditional interpretation of Jn 19:34 (see on 110–12 below). **58***a* 'All you that thirst, come to the waters...' (Is 55:1). The text, used to open the Introit at Mass on the Saturday following mid-Lent Sunday, had special relevance to catechumens being instructed for baptism or penitents preparing for absolution at Easter. Wordplay on *sicientes* and *scientes* 'knowing,' a reading found in Bromyard 2:347–2 (AlfQ), is discerned by *R–H* 135, but not strongly supported by the quotation's form or context. **59** *perto*: with implied referent 'saving grace' (*bote*), whereas in B 123 *pere* refers to its source (*breste*) or, more widely, 'salvation'. **60** *bouhte...tauhte*: the annominative chime bringing out the need first for faith in Christ's saving death and then obedience to his command to receive baptism. **60***a* 'He that believeth and is baptized shall be saved: [but he that believeth not shall be condemned]' (Mk 16:16). Read in the Gospel for Ascension Day, which ends the Easter season, the text concludes the sequence initiated by 58*a*. **62–6** The argument is that a Christian cannot *rihtfolliche* 'lawfully' renounce his religion, even if failing to practise it. For, after being freed through baptism from the devil's 'lordship', he is now a 'bondman' of Christ; and an attempt to escape from his new lord's service is like a serf's unauthorised flight from

the manor (the simile suggesting **L**'s endorsement of contemporary law and practice, which the 1381 insurgents were so strong against). **63–4** Villeins were not entitled to enter into legal agreements or to sell their moveable property without the lord's permission. The feudal analogy, with its tacit acceptance if not approval of servile status, would have won no friends among the rebels, who resented and wanted it abolished (see further on villeins, McKisack 1959:326–8, Keen 1973:189–98, Hilton 1969, and on the implications of this metaphor, Simpson 1990:122–4). **65** *rome fro home*: with this formulaic internal rhyme, cf. 60. **66** compares the apostate to a runaway serf who risks imprisonment if found. **67–8** *Reson; Conscience*: a coupling that recalls 5.11, where Will is *romynge in remembraunce* and, in answering Reason's 'rebuke', denies that he is a 'run-away' or 'caitiff' of any sort (5.82). Reason is envisaged as a 'moral reeve' who reckons up the dues of the lord's servants (cf. 3.308 and 13.34). **68** *acounte*: cf. 16.190. **69–70** He will pay for his lapsation by suffering purgatorial pains (believed to be akin to hell's in intensity though not duration) until the raising of the dead at the last day. **70** *rechelesnes*: this substitution for **B**'s third *arerages* is heavily ironic, coming from this speaker. *riht*: 'even until,' but punning on 'justly, lawfully'. **71** *and confessioun*: improving upon the inert *come and* of B 135 in fullness of sense and in sharpness, since *mouthe* must here suggest *oris confessio* more than just vocal prayer. The cautious orthodoxy contrasts with the boldness of B 11.81*a* (deleted in revision). **73–5***a* The first revision (74*a*) makes for syntactic explicitness, *heo* anticipating the Daughter of God at 20.118–9 who personifies the 'feminine' side of the divine Judge. The second (on *bothe* see *TN*) recognises humility as in origin a divine quality, discernible in Christ's Incarnation and Passion and closely linked with *mercy*, as at 1.168, B 18.115. *mekenesse*: the penitent sinner's (cf. 7.247), which precedes the granting of God's mercy, though here imagined not temporally but as 'tending obediently upon' (and so assisting) it. **75** *bokes...werkes*: a perhaps intentional secondary contrast, since Trajan is about to show the superiority of 'well-doing' over 'wisdom' (cf. the tension in *soethnesse...werkes* at 83). Scripture's parting words fittingly cite the 'Books' whose study she personifies. **75***a* 'His tender mercies [*miserationes* Vg] are over [surpass] all his works' (Ps 144:9); cited at B 5.282*a* but removed from its parallel in revision.

(ii) 76–89 are here treated as a 'bridge-passage' in C, spoken by Trajan, but in **B** as the opening of a long speech by him. On reasons for giving it to Trajan (who speaks of himself in the 3rd pers. from B 153–162) see *TN*; Rudd (1994:76, 179) notes the appropriateness of the examples used at B 189–95, 230–40, 248–56 to his character and status. **76** *bawe for bokes*: depending on the tone adopted, not necessarily implying rejection of scriptural authority

('Why refer to what "books" — even the Bible — say? I can vouch for this [God's mercy] from my own experience') so much as location of it in the *spirit* of Scripture, not its letter (cf. 98 below). *quod oen*: a memorable phrase clearly recalled in B at 319, which *closes* the speech and ratifies its ascription to the speaker of 76. *was...helle*: a sudden entry like Piers's at 5.537=C 7.181 (Rudd 1994:76); as Trajan is not *in* hell, the implied tense is pluperfect not preterite. The legend of his release from hell through St Gregory's intercession goes back to early lives of the latter, though the speaker himself refers us to **L**'s presumed source, the *Legenda Aurea* (B 160 below; on the background see Wittig 1972:249–54 and Whatley 1984[1]:50–6). The story as used here has been found by Gradon 1983, Whatley 1984[2] and Burrow 1993:8–14 to express an unorthodox, 'Pelagian' view of Trajan as saved by good works alone. But Simpson 1990:125–8 persuasively sees it rather as 'semi-Pelagian', with Trajan's *leaute* and *trewthe* meriting salvation not *de condigno* 'condignly' (or 'absolutely') but *de congruo* 'congruently' (in the only manner appropriate to one in his situation), 'by doing what is in him' (a position developed and elaborated by Ymaginatyf at 14.205–17). Trajan offers a limiting case, not a norm, and the theological extremism of this example recalls that of the Good Thief at 11.255–263, a factor that may have prompted transference of the long 'disputation' based on it from the Emperor to Will-as-Rechelesnesse. **77** *Troian(e)s*: a well-recognised form of Trajan's name (Wenzel 1996:184). Emperor of Rome AD 98–117, he was known for his justice, integrity and concern for the common people. *trewe knyht*: for similar 'chivalricisation' cf. 1.101ff. **78** *dwellen in helle*: more *repetitio* underlined by internal rhyme in revision. **79** *Gregori*: the revision, requiring scansion on 'cognate' staves (*k / g*), and improving by referring directly to the agent not to the account of *clerkes* (which is incongruous coming from one who cries *bawe* to books). **80–1** The sense is obscure because elliptical in the revision of B 144. **B**'s 'all the erudite theological arguments under the sun couldn't find grounds for my salvation' contrasts learning unfavourably with do-well (as pardons had been in 9.317–45). But **C**'s sense ('it was not my being baptized that saved me — because I wasn't — it was only my righteous conduct') is more audacious theologically, going beyond the 'sufficiency-of-baptism' argument of 60a to a 'non-necessity-of-baptism' position even more *recheles* than that of Rechelesnesse. This *is* 'Pelagian', unless *myhte...onlyche* is only affirming Trajan's *trewthe* as a necessary, not a sufficient condition for his release. **82** *this*: 'this fact' or 'my righteousness', or perhaps both (cf. B 151). **83** *soethnesse...werkes*: affirming that though Trajan was ignorant of Christian *veritas*, his *fidelitas* was homologous to formal faith, and evidence that he would have believed, had he known what to believe.

84–5 *wilnede wepynge*: the intensity of the saint's prayer being signalled by his tears (cf. B 262–3) which, in alluding to Heb 5:7, equate the Pope's 'high-priesthood' with that of his exemplar, the Supreme High Priest Christ. *Y were saued*: avoiding B 148b's implication that prevenient grace might be available for one no longer *in via*. The distinction between that supposition and **C**'s *of his goodnesse* is a fine one, perhaps relying on contemporary notions of God's *potentia absoluta* as transcending the normal (*ordinata*) channels of grace, the Church's sacraments. **86–7** are doubtless not meant to question the efficacy of ritual intercession for the dead but to say that Masses (as part of the 'ordinate' dispensation) would have had no relevance for Trajan, since he was in hell, where *nulla est redempcio* (20.151a). **88** 'Love, in the absence of true faith (was what), as the "religion" proper to me / bringing me justification (*rihtfoel*), saved me'. In this reading, the 'love [*sc.* of *trewthe*]' is Trajan's, a man supposed to have served God like those in Mt 25:37–40, who are unconscious of having done so (cf. also Mt 7:21). But if the 'love' = the 'goodness' of 85, then the sense will be that 'God's own boundless charity, answering (indeed perhaps prompting) the intercessory prayer (of Gregory) saved me, though I lacked formal belief in the true religion to justify me'. The revision's removal of the potentially ambiguous *truþe* in B 151, 155 'as open to the possible misinterpretation that T's salvation was owing to his orthodox faith' is noted by Green 1999:23–4. **B 151** *by lernyng of*: either 'through finding out about' or 'by dint of the "learning" [= knowledge of Christian truth] tacitly implied in my just conduct'. The second rendering (complementary rather than alternative) is supported by *soethnesse* 83. For a similar interpretation see Doxsee 1988, who sees a 'desire' for baptism as implicit in Trajan's love of *trewthe*. **89** *Sarrasyn*: here = *paynym* B 162, with no implication that Trajan shared any part of Christian belief, e.g. in one God (cf. 17.315–6). Elsewhere its usual reference is to Moslem Arabs (e.g. at 3.480).

(iii) 90–249 This enormous speech, continuing for another 130 lines in the next passus (= B 11.153–318), is finally ascribed to Rechelesnesse at 13.129, and so may be taken to *begin* at 90 (where in **B** the speaker is likely to be Trajan); but in both versions much of it sounds quasi-choric in nature and tone. **90–3** retain B 153, 157–8 but drop 154 (redundant as repeating 143) and add one summarising line to replace B 159–69, which are slightly repetitive (161b = 151b, 164a = 156a), digressive (168–9) and anticipatory (168–9 // B 12.72–3=C 14.37–8). **93** *leute*: repeated four times up to 98 (as love is seven times in B 170–80).

B 153–69 are spoken by Trajan about himself in the 3rd person as an example, and at 170 he is not beginning to speak but resuming. **155** *pure truþe*: 'utter integrity'. **156** *witnesse*: an overstatement, as Gregory prayed in hope, not certainty (**C** is less controversial). **159–69** are not without powerful moments, but omitting them makes for a tighter transition in **C**. **160** *legende sanctorum*: the macaronic title encompassing both its English name and the book's subject-matter. The *Legenda Aurea* 'Golden Legend' (*LA*) was completed *c*. 1265 by the Italian Dominican Jacobus de Voragine or Varazze (*c*. 1230–98; Abp. of Genoa in 1292). An immensely popular compilation of saints' lives and treatises on the Church festivals, much of it 'legendary' (see Reames 1985), *LA* is (with Gregory's *Moralia*) the only non-biblical book named by **L**, who relies on it in his accounts of various saints (as at 17.12, 21–4). **161** *leel loue*: contextually Trajan's, but also evoking God's reciprocal 'leaute'. **162** *peyne... paynym*: the 'Platonic' identical rhyme across the caesura pointing up his miraculous escape from the fate due to him as a pagan. **163** anticipates B 18.294, 322–3 and echoes Z 5.39. *truþe*: both Trajan's essential quality and the 'nature-name' for God / Christ cited at B 18.294; intimating that the virtue and the person are one. **165** *clergie*; *konnyng*: theology, which could not conceptually accommodate Gregory's *bone* with Trajan's unbaptized state. **166–7** *science...book*: in the ordinary sense neither, though the commandment of love *is* embodied in the written text of the Bible. **166** *Loue*: not strictly the 'theological virtue' of charity (the fruit of faith in God) but the Just Pagan's 'good-will towards men' that represents in terms of *de congruo* theology 'the best that is in him' (see on C 76). This is a notable advance from commendation of his perfect *justice*; but the association of truth and love has been foreshadowed by HC at B 1.148–51, here recalled. **168–9** *wrouȝte...wroot*: see Ex 32:15–16; cf. C 14.37–8.

94–109 94–100a move the stress in B 170–80 from love to *leautee*, from 'religion without love' to the more appropriate 'law without equity'. They tighten up the phrasing and eliminate otiose repetition (172a, 174a, 179b), but also lose the internal chimes of 176 and the effective rhetorical balancing of 176a / 179a. The eliminated **B** lines echo the sense of I Jn 3:17–18, 23. **100** *of his techyng*: referring to either the Apostle or the Lord. **100a** 'He that loveth not abideth in death' (I Jn 3:14). **101–2** shorten the somewhat wordy and repetitive B 181–8 (though losing the memorable 184–5, with their final assonance) and draw a double moral from the Gospel verses paraphrased in 103–9. These words echo HC's quotation from Js 2:26 at 1.186, and in giving them to Trajan, **L** may have recalled I Jn 3:10: 'Whosoever is not *just*, is not of God'. He proceeds here by a non-formal 'logic of negation': Trajan was not like Cain (who hated his brother); Abel was accepted by God; therefore Trajan, who did not hate his brothers, was accepted by God. Trajan can affirm that St John's *words* are *soþe* (B 175) because his own *werkes* are (B 147). **101** *pore peple*: that these 'represent'

Christ being implied in Mt 25:35. Trajan's 'love' for them is shown from his redress to a poor widow, which moved Gregory's compassion. But as he obviously had no love of his *enemies* during his life, he must be presumed to have learned this distinctive ethical precept of Christianity after his release from hell (cf. also I Pet on how 'the gospel [was] preached also to the dead'). **104** *knyhtes*: less close to the Biblical source-text, and losing the witty semantic wordplay on *kyn(nes)* at B 190. **104a** 'When thou makest a dinner...call not thy friends...[nor thy kinsmen nor thy neighbours who are rich: lest perhaps they also invite thee again, and a recompense be made to thee. But...call the poor, the lame and the blind. And thou shalt be blessed, because they have not wherewith to make thee recompense: for recompense shall be made thee at the resurrection of the just]' (Lk 14:12–14). **106–9** increase the *repetitio* (*paye* as well as *quite*) in place of the circumstantial detail of B 193a.

B 196–9 may have been omitted as potentially provocative or liable to misinterpretation after 1381; but a similar comment, affirming God's wisdom in creating men different in fortune and talent, occurs at C 16.19–21=B 14.166–7. **198** *of...riche*: made rich from his treasure-chests (i.e. of grace); for the image cf. 1.194–7. **199** *breþeren...blood*: like brothers born of the same parents. All men are descended from Adam; but through sin, social divisions have arisen. Baptism in the name of the new Adam, Christ, restores this original equality.

110–20a Christianity was 'born' through the saving death of Christ, into which Christians are baptized (Rom 6:3–5). **110** The allusion is to the blood and water that flowed from the pierced side of Jesus (Jn 19:34), which in the light of I Jn 5:6 was understood in patristic exegesis as symbolising baptism and the eucharist. **111** *blody bretherne*: 'brothers-by-blood' (*or* 'brothers through [Christ's] blood'), the Emperor's sentiment echoing the Plowman's (8.217–9) and anticipating Christ's at 20.418. **112** is a 'licensed' macaronic scanning *xa / ax* (Schmidt 1987:101–2). *As...vchone*: 'Each of us like noblemen, "like babes newborn"' (I Pet 2:2); spiritual re-birth through baptism frees men from the 'servile' status of sinners and makes them 'noble' (cf. on 62–6). The phrase occurs in the Introit for the Mass of Low Sunday (within the octave of Easter) and the Lesson of the day contains the passage from I Jn 5:6 cited above. **113** *but...make*: i.e. unless through sin we revert to the state of slaves. **113a** 'Whosoever committeth sin is the servant of sin' (Jn 8:34); cf. also vs 32. **114** *mennes sones*: a common OT phrase *filii hominum* found in e.g. Ps 4:3 (*Sk*), 'sons of Adam' only in Deut 32:8. The sense is 'human beings' but the implied contrast is with 'sons of God' (through baptism in Christ's name); cf. Gal 4:4–7. **115** *God-Man*: translating **L**'s own 'credal' phrase *Deus homo* at 3.401a. **116** *Redemptor*: here taken as Latin, though MED records it as an English word 50 years later; 'redeemer' does not appear till the late 15th c. The Bible uses it of God (e.g. in Ps 19:14), but though ascribing 'redemption' to him (e.g. Mt 20:28, Rom 3:24, Eph 1:7), not Christ, whose Resurrection **L** sees as proof of his divinity, entitling him to this name. **118** substitutes for the gentle, tolerant phrasing of B 208b–09, with their repeated *man*, a harsher reminder of coming judgement. **120a** See on 9.286–7; the Creed recalls the sombre warning of Truth's Pardon on the necessity of 'do-well'.

  B 210a–29a Most of this 20-line passage cut in **C** affirms the superiority of unlearned faith to logic and law (disciplines of the pre-Christian world that minister to the pride and avarice of modern clerks). But since the speaker's main theme is humility and the condition of poverty that favours it, these lines may be thought digressive. **210a** See at 8.231a. Gal 6:4, 9–10 certainly exhort to 'do-well', but 'in the spirit of 'meekness' (6:1), not with the monitory tone of C 120a (this text is cited at C 13.77a). **213** is cut here but re-phrased as C 15.80. **216–17** The reference is to Lk 7:37–50, where *mulier quae erat in civitate peccatrix* could be rendered 'a woman commonly known as a sinner'. The suggestion here is that since her sins were forgiven because of her faith (217) and not through baptism, *cristendom* 215 cannot be essential for salvation. But the parallel with Trajan is inexact, since the woman's faith is explicitly in Jesus, and the real likeness resides in her being forgiven 'because she hath *loved* much' (Lk 7:47), this love being understood as necessarily implying faith (in Christ), and Trajan's 'love [of *treuthe*]' conversely (if daringly) as implicit faith. **216** *commune*[1,2]: a dense pun on 'common / of the people' and 'in public'. **217** *Fides sua*: cf. 'Thy faith hath made thee safe' (Lk 7:50); leaving this crucial text in Latin underlines its special relevance for clerks. *sauen*; *saluen*: another complex interchange of senses, salvation being a way of bringing 'health' to the soul (cf. 229b). **218** *logyk or lawe*: the implied referents being probably 'theological reasoning' (cf. *lesson* 221) and 'formal religious observance'; but the latter is quickly collapsed into its habitual sense, perhaps with a wry allusion to the lucrative practice of canon lawyers. **218–26** For an analysis of *repetitio* in these lines see Schmidt 1987:55–7. **223b** 'you who do not care for lies'. **225–6** *Feiþes techyng...That*: the implied referent of 'Faith' being the speaker of the quoted words, Christ, who is the antecedent likewise. **226–6a** *Johan*: actually Matthew (7:2) or Luke (6:38); see on 1.173a. **229** *Gregorie*: a text still untraced to Gregory (an especially apt authority for Trajan to quote), though the sentiment is his. **229a** 'It is better to examine our sins than the natures of things'. The exact source is untraced, but *R–H* 140n72 cite an analogue attributed to Augustine in Peter Lombard's *Collectanea* (PL 191:1601): '*For it is better to know our weakness than the natures of things. For wor*thier of praise is the soul that knows its own weakness than one that, heedless of this, examines (*scrutatur*) the courses of the stars, the foundations of the globe and the heights of the heavens'. They also note its closeness to the sense of the line cited at B 11.3=C 11.165.

121–249 This long discourse on the spiritual advantages of poverty and the dangers of wealth gains a different meaning through being transferred from Trajan to Rechelesnesse. **B** chiefly instructs the great to be humble (none was greater than the Emperor); **C** defends exterior poverty against the scorn of the rich (none was poorer than Christ). **124–9** This encounter on Easter day is narrated in Lk 24:13–35, which gives no reason for the two disciples' failure to recognise Jesus (his wearing mean clothing is **L**'s contribution). They know him at the breaking of the bread (vs 30), which for **L** signifies not only that Christ is to be 'recognised' as really present in the Eucharistic rite but that genuine faith is discerned through / expressed in charitable action, such as sharing food (*hem bitwene*). **126** *pilgrimes clothes*: the simple dress of such as Piers at 15.34, the true 'pilgrim for the love of God', not the distinctive garb of the 'professional' pilgrim at 7.160. **129b** lessens the 'works' / 'words' contrast of B 236–7, stressing the need not to judge by outward appearance. **130** *ensample*: hardly the obvious one; but the general lesson of humility and 'pacience' is certainly there, since Christ rebukes the two disciples who had thought him 'a prophet, mighty in work and word' (vs 19) for failing to grasp that the Messiah must suffer. **132** *pilgrimes...alle*: one of the key tropes of medieval religious thought (*peregrini et hospites / advenas*), deriving ultimately from such texts as Heb 11:13–16, I Pet 2:11; another famous literary instance is *CT* I 2847–8 (see Dyas 2001). **133** *pore likenesse*: 'the appearance of a poor man'. **134** The revision relies on the force of a specific *ensample* instead of the general statement of B 241–2, which may concede too much to poor appearance and contradict the godliness among the rich later acknowledged at 16.351–2. But its sentiment echoes St Benedict's admonition to receive 'the poor and pilgrims...for in them Christ is received the more' (*Rule*, ch. 53). **C** now says only that Christ was as one of the poor, but nothing about his being often encountered among them. *Holy seyntes*: the disciples who knew Jesus in the flesh. B 244–5 are omitted in **C** doubtless as both partially inaccurate and as contradicted by Anima's rejection of begging at B 15.227. *Iohan*: presumably the Baptist (Mt 3:4) who, however, did *not* 'ask men for goods'. **135** *Matthew*: incorrect both here and at B 252, and in both cases probably induced by alliterative need rather than being ironically intended as the speaker's 'deliberate error'. **136** *pore...pore*: the literal poverty of Mary (if such is intended) may be an inference from Lk 1:48, where her 'humility' is primarily spiritual, that of Joseph from his failure to find room for them at the inn (Lk 2:7) 'because they were poor' (*LA* 41, the latter incident causing **L** some trouble at 14.90–1). **137** *Marie Maudelene*: identified with both Mary of Bethany and the unnamed woman who anoints Christ's feet at Bethany in the house of Simon the Leper (Mt 26:6) or of her sister and brother Martha and Lazarus (Jn 12:1–3); traditional since St Gregory the Great and re-stated in *LA* ch. 96, p. 408 (see on 7.137). **B 246** The revision removes not only a metrically awkward line with a strong dip in each half (the first containing the lexical word *aliȝte*), but also the variously problematic references to Jesus's mother (and therefore himself) as a 'Jew' (a term used elsewhere in *PP* to denote his opponents) and of 'pore gentel blood' (cf. 5.78). **139** 'Lord, hast thou no care that my sister hath left me alone to serve?' (Lk 10:40). **140** *God*: the full weight of divine authority being understood to inform Christ's answer (cf. 1.48). **142** *pouerte*: surprising if read literally (since the two women are sisters), but not if taken as 'poverty of spirit' (i.e. obedient humility), like that of the BVM. **140–2** *wel...betere*: the verbal echoing evokes the first two terms of the Triad (though the quoted Latin implies only a two-term opposition). **142a** '[But one thing is necessary]. Mary hath chosen the best part which shall not be taken away from her' (Lk 10:42). The 'best part' was traditionally interpreted as patient 'attending' on God, the contemplative as against the active life. **147b, 148a; 149a, 152a** The repeated formulaic phrasing recalls the manner of homiletic preaching (cf. 10.38a, 40a).

143–55a Poverty is further praised as providing freedom from care and the best conditions for penitential prayer and growth in holiness. The wholesale revision of B 11.269–84a (removing weakly repetitive lines like 270b, 272b, 280) adds 80 new lines on the superiority of poverty and the spiritual dangers of wealth, before resuming **B**'s critique of worldly priests. **144** *best* (*lif*): the exaltation of poverty by Rechelesnesse (Trajan) foreshadows Patience's praise of the state in XVI (B XIV). **149** *cornel of confort*: the loving mercy of God (152 below). The kernel (*nucleus*) is compared to Christ's divinity by Alan of Lille in his note on *nux* 'nut' (*PL* 120:871). **155a** 'Though poor, I play, but you, though rich, must brood' (Alexander of Ville-Dieu, *Doctrinale* 1091); cf. B 14.304a.

B 268–84a The argument here is that the OT doctrine of material sufficiency is spiritually inferior to the NT counsel of perfection through renouncing all possession. **269a** 'Give me neither beggary nor riches. [Give me only the necessaries of life]' (Prov 30:8). **L**'s variant wording (with *paupertates* for Vg *mendicitatem*) appears in *FM* 572. **270** *wiser...was*: cf. 'behold, a greater than Solomon here' (Lk 11:31). **272** *Luc*: a minor alliteratively-licensed inaccuracy (cf. B 252 above). **272a** 'If thou wilt be perfect, go sell [what thou hast and give to the poor]' (Mt 19:21); a text (minus the opening phrase) also found

at Lk 18:22. **278** *Dauid...Sauter*: alluding to Ps 36:25. **279a** 'Nothing is impossible to him who wills it'; a proverbial phrase (Walther 44445a1b) loosely derived from Mt 17:19 (which refers to faith, not will). **280** is repeated at 287 below. **280a** See at 10.203a. **284a** 'Judge me, O God, and distinguish my cause [from the nation that is not holy: deliver me from the unjust and deceitful man]' (Ps 42:1). Part of the Introit at Mass, the verse was especially associated with priests, a collection of treatises addressed to priests bearing this title (*Rolle*, ed. Allen (1927:93–113), cit.Alf*Q*). Deliverance from unworthy givers is sought in the *Lavabo* verses at the Offertory (Ps 25:10), taken from a psalm also opening with the words *Iudica me*.

156–78 156 *Holy Churche*: obviously not implying that this is the Church's teaching as opposed to Christ's (*efte* 162), since it merely amplifies the Gospel source of the following Latin. **161a** '[And] everyone that leaves [*reliquerit* 'hath left' Vg] [house or brethren or sisters or] father [or] mother [or wife or children or lands, for my name's sake, shall receive an hundredfold and shall possess life everlasting]' (Mt 19:29). **163** *segg...louede*: alluding to the account in Mk 10:21. **168a** See on B 272a above. **172a** 'So...every one...that doth not renounce all that he possesseth [cannot be my disciple]' (Lk 14:33, adapted). **173–8** constitute 'rhetorical amplification through random citation of learned "authorities"...probably little more than names to **L**' (*Pe*); echoing B 10.338–40, which is omitted at that point in **C**. **175** The line is repeated at 14.189. *Porfirie*: a voluminous Neo-Platonic writer (*c.* 232–*c.* 303) who espoused an ascetic contemplative life and, as the author of a treatise *Against the Christians*, may be here cited as an *argumentum a difficiliori*. *Plato*: see at 11.120. **176** *Aristotel*: see at 11.121. *Ennedy*: the Christian Latin writer Magnus Felix Ennodius (*c.* 473–521), Bp. of Pavia, author of hymns and epigrams. **177** *Tulius*: Marcus Tullius Cicero (106–46 BC); alluding perhaps to the austere Stoic philosophy expressed in his account of the 'Dream of Scipio', the last part of his *De republica* (cf. Chaucer *PF* 29–84). *Tolomeus*: Ptolemy, the Greek astronomer Claudius Ptolomeus (*c.* 100–179), whose *Almagest* in Latin translation had a preface with moral apophthegms by the Arab 'Albaguafe'. **178** *pacient pouerte*: both 'the patient endurance of poverty' and 'the state of poverty that exhibits endurance' (cf. B 14.101). These are linked in *Patience* 35–6.

179–211 argue that hardship fortifies and enables the Christian to produce more spiritual fruit, as hard winters encourage strong growth and abundant crops. The image of the farmer as a type of the faithful believer is in Js 5:7 (*Pe*), but the English distinction between winter and spring seeds is **L**'s. **180a** 'Unless the grain of wheat falling into the ground die, [Itself remaineth alone. But if it die, it bringeth forth much fruit]' (Jn 12:24–5); a text sung as an antiphon on the nativity of a martyr (Alf*Q*, citing *Brev*. 2:384) and seen by *Pe* as suggested to **L** by Lk 14:26. **187** *we lyuen alle*: the implication being that 'the blood of martyrs is the seed of the Church', and that all Christians benefit from the sacrificial lives of the saints. **199** *Fere*: probably 'danger' (MED s.v. *fer* n. (1).2; 'fire' would be possible (with raised SE vowel), though the word's usual (and presumably original) spelling in this text is SW *fuyr* (cf. 15. 166, and see Samuels 1985:241). **202–5** derive from Js 5:10–11 (*Pe*), which would perhaps support omission of the colon after *soffren* (see *TN*). **202** *this*: probably the pl. generic 'these', a common spelling in this text (*MES* 173) but possibly the sg. prn. 'this' as object. **208** *angelis...anger*: cf. A 10.143 with very different sense. **209** '[You shall be made sorrowful, but] your sorrow shall be turned into joy' (Jn 16:20).

212–49 use agricultural imagery to argue that material possessions ('sweet fruits') are really spiritual destitution and weaken men's ability to resist sin, while the 'easy' life of the rich ('fat land') predisposes them towards *alle vices*. **213** *Gospelle*: see at 217*a*. **215** The indirect form of the question in 215–6 would favour *after* here as a preposition 'concerning', though the source (Lk 12:20) shows the question to be direct, and the text here quickly moves into direct speech, concurrently evoking its adverbial sense. **217a** '[But God said to him]: Thou fool, this night shall thy soul depart [do they require thy soul of thee (Vg)]. [And whose shall those things be which thou hast provided? So is] he that layeth up treasure [for himself and is not rich towards God]' (Lk 12:20–21). *Tezaurisat...*: cf. also '[Surely man passeth as an image: yea and he is disquieted in vain]. He storeth up: and he knoweth not [for whom he shall gather these things]' (Ps 38:7). **219** *mothe*: cf. B 14.23. **220** *Hulle*: Cornhill, Will's place of residence (5.1), where second-hand clothes-dealers operated. The internal rhyme and final chime round off the mockery of the 'fool'. **227** *suche*: elliptical for 'is it with such'. **232** *ope*: '(heaped) on top of'. **234** *worth lygge*: 'will lie down (under its own weight)' (*Sk*). Taking *worth* as 'will be', *Pe* finds in *lygge* a form of an adj. unrecorded in MED but preserved in OED s.v. *ledger* adj. 5b, with a citation from Googe, not earlier than 1577 but very telling. **236** echoes B 14.73, which is removed in revision. **237** *how hit euere*: 'howsoever it'. **246–7** *hard...combraunce*: echoing the imagery and wording of 1.190–1. **248** *drede*: 'deference', with a tart pun on 'anxiety' (over losing it). **249** 'The wealth stored within them being the basic reason why there are robbers'.

Passus XIII (B XII)

PASSUS THIRTEEN (somewhat like books III and II of Chaucer's *Troilus*) is closely linked to XII, starting in the middle of a speech by Rechelesnesse (R.). XIII resembles XII in a certain symmetry, ending with the *start* of a speech by a new character that will continue through the *next* passus. Its emotional pattern is pyramidal, climaxing between 179–213 (where Will stands indignantly on a 'mountain'), then falling into a slough of embarrassed confusion (the 'ditch' of 235). In spite of its flowing dreamlike quality the three sections linked by transitional lines convey a sense of structural balance. (i) Ll. 1–97*a* continue RECHELESNESSE's diatribe against wealth and are new, the text parallel to Trajan's speech in **B** only resuming with the mention of unspiritual priests at 100 (for which a pair of link-lines 98–9 have been inserted) and going on for another 30 lines before the two parallel speeches end. The new material, now being designed not for the authoritative Trajan but for Will's 'doubled' persona R., mingles shrewd good sense with typical overstatements and mistakes of judgement (see on 11, 29, 77 and 114–15). (ii) consists of *a*) the vision of MIDDLEARTH (129–78), introduced by three connecting lines on KYNDE (131–3) and *b*) the dispute with REASON (179–213), also marked by such errors (e.g. at 191). (iii) Finally, there is the waking (214–18) out of the *inner dream* that began at 11.165, followed by the opening of a dialogue with a new interlocutor (YMAGYNATIF). The passus ends on a question from Will (219–48).

(i) 1–128 *Rechelesnesse on poverty and wealth* The rest of R.'s speech continues the praise of poverty (1–24), modulating into a comparison of it with wealth that modifies the original extremism through the extended exemplum / analogy of the Merchant and the Messenger (25–91). It concludes that poverty is spiritually superior (92–7*a*) and so preferable for priests, while importantly defining clerical 'poverty' as sufficiency, not destitution (98–128). **1–24** The two OT exempla cited argue better against wealth than for poverty, because in showing patiently-borne impoverishment rewarded by restoration of prosperity, they may prove too much, and cannot console those who were not rich in the first place. **1** *wel worth*: 'well may it be for'. *vnrobbed*: echoing *robbares* in 12.249. The thought here reflects that of the Latin line cited at B 14.304*a* and there removed in // **C**. **2b** repeats 12.144 but its logic is less than perfect, since presumably what saves the poor from being robbed is their lack of goods rather than their patience. However, **L** may simply see this virtue as what enables the condition of poverty to become a beatitude, not a curse. **4** Defying the OT (and modern) human expectation of getting richer over a lifetime's work, the saints grew progressively poorer through life, their ultimate exemplar being Christ himself (10.194–6). **4a** '[As sorrowful, yet always rejoicing: as needy, yet enriching many]: as having nothing and possessing all things' (II Cor 6:10). **5** *Abraham*: the story of how Sara was taken by the king of Gerara in the belief that she was Abraham's sister is told in Gen 20. **7** *for his*: 'because of his possessions.' **8** *pouerte*: in the sense of being deprived of his prize 'possession', his wife. *prince*: Abimelech; perhaps with an (unironical) echo of 3, for this 'prince' acts as an instrument of providence in teaching Abraham to trust God and not resort to deception. **11–12** *for he soffrede*; *criede hym mercy*: the speaker's (erroneous) interpretation of the scripture, where the 'kind king' in fact 'expostulates' with Abraham; but the happy outcome is indeed due to Abimelech's 'sincere heart' (Gen 20:6). **14** *gentele*: an epithet of alliterative convenience applied also to James and John (see *PNI*). **15** *the Book*: see Job ch. 1. **16–17** are composed from Job's reply to his wife: 'If we have received good things at [the hand of] God, [why should we not receive] evil [*mala* 'bad things']?' (Job 2:10). **18** Cf. 12.210 above *song*: L's way of assimilating Job's rebuking of his wife to the great psalm-verses of acceptance and hope (like Ps 112:5–8). **19** *newe*: both 'renewed' and 'new in nature', because now true 'spiritual joy' (cf. B 14.284–5). **20** *pacience*: Job is cited as the model of patience in Js 5:11, whereas Abraham in the NT is more commonly taken to exemplify faith. **22** *grayn*: the sense here, as at 12.186–7 above, is that humiliation (*greut*) can through the help of grace be the source of abundant virtue and even, if God so wills, be rewarded by further prosperity in this life. The underlying inspiration is again Jn 12:24–5. **23** *spredeth*: alluding to the abundant offspring of both (Gen 13:16, Job 42:16).

25–97a 25–31 are addressed to *lewede men* or *illiterati*, who risk drawing too extreme a conclusion about the dangers of wealth (perhaps **L**'s response to post-1381 conditions). But they argue that even if Dowel is compatible with wealth, Do-*better* belongs to (the patient acceptance of) poverty, which acts as satisfaction for one's sins. The deeper meaning of the merchant-messenger *ensaumple* offered to prove this is, however, something for *wyse men* (64). **27** *fylosofres*: echoing B 20.38–9. **29** *lyues*: the comparison of wealth with poverty recalling that of active and contemplative 'lives' at 12.142–5. *large weyes*: showing that the speaker, in his eagerness to right the balance, has forgotten the warning of Mt 19:23–4. **30–1** Cf. 9.183–6, 11.300. **32** *merchant...mesager*: two categories of traveller liable to be stopped at toll-bridges and ports (cf. 4.129. **34** The literal referent of *Resoun* is obscure and is presumably some sort of official at a customs-post; but the anagogical sense of the allegory is made quite clear at 66 (on Reason as 'reckoner' cf. 3.308). **36** is a line of awkward scansion, having in the a-half the second stave mute, and blank staves in *nede* and *ylet*, and in the b-half a 'strong' dip before the 'monolexical' *méssagére* (see *Intro*. IV § 38). **37–8** *paper*: the merchant's documents emblematising the long list of sins to which the rich are thought prone during their lifetime. *dettes.../ lette*: a rhyme hinting 'Platonically' at the spiritual effect of sins as a hindrance to heaven. *pryué*: alluding to sharp

practices that weigh on his conscience. **38** 'Will cause him to be left, I warrant, a mile behind (the messenger).' **41–50** It was forbidden to cross a wheatfield, and the *haiward* (44) was the manorial official empowered to enforce this. Reason, judging it futile to take a pledge (of future payment of a fine for trespass) from a messenger who cannot pay, but reasonable to do so from a merchant (who can), notes that the common-law right is sometimes supported by local regulations for the payment of toll. **43a** 'Nede hath no lawe' (22.100), a maxim of natural law (*CIC* 1:374) that had become proverbial (see Alf*Q*). The precise interpretation of this first allegory at 64–91 tells against supposing that 'the messenger, because he has no money to pay the fine, commits no offence in breaking the law' (*Pe*). The point being made is that (though the messenger *has* broken the law) it is not *wys* 'sensible' (43) to fine him for a minor tort, while the toll stipulated by *lawe* (49) does not apply to him anyway, so he 'is let through at once' (40) without a pledge (cf. 22.13). There is thus little support for Harwood's opinion (1973:289) cited by *Pe* that R. seeks 'cheap grace' and settles for 'sinlessness for want of opportunity'; for it has been made clear that poverty patiently borne not only avoids 'occasions of sin' but disposes to humility. Since R. does not say that the poor are licensed to break the law, only excused from the legal obligations of the rich, it is not relevant that 'haywards could be extortioners, and were much hated' (*Pe*), this 'hayward' being the agent of 'þe Kyng of Heuene' (66). **47** *hatt...gloues*: items often taken as pledges. **49a** 'And on top of that, be held up'. **51** *o... to*: 'on the one road that leads to'. *Wynchestre fayre*: see on 6.211. **60** *moneye*: explained at 69ff. **63** *as safly*: '(he could travel) as safely'.

64–97a are ostensibly addressed to those who can interpret the allegory accurately, but also set out to explain it to those who cannot: the merchant = the rich, the 'way' = a righteous life, the 'toll' = charitable works. **65–77** recall the 'marginal' words of Truth's pardon on the obligations of merchants at 9.22–36. **66** *Aren*: '(who) are' (the construction being parallel to the later Ø-relative clause at 79). **67** *euene*: a 'Platonic' echo of *heuene* 66, indicating that steady, 'just' adherence to God's law will lead them to him. **77** *Crist hymsulf...*: the words are in fact St Paul's. **77a** See on 8.231a., where the maxim is cited as stating the *lawe of kynde*. **79** *Beth*: 'And who are'. *boþe...lawes*: earthly and divine. **84** *contumax*: '(held to be) in contempt of court', esp. for failure to answer a summons. The sense in question seems to be the legal one (Alf*G* s.v.) rather than that of someone 'thurgh his indignacioun...agayns euerich auctoritee or power of... his sovereyns' (*CT* X 401; cit. *Sk*). **86a** See on 12.60a; the understood completion of the quotation is 'will be saved'. **88** *seel*: the sender's imprint being allegorically 'the king of heaven's mark' (17.77), the spiritual 'character' received by the baptized (cf. II Tim 2:19). *lord*: i.e. Christ, who sends him to the Lord (87) 'God' with the *tale* that he is a true believer. **89–91** *byleue...leue; gate.. gateward*: the first pun is polysemic, the second homophonic (for the image cf. 7.242). **90** *lawe*: 'regulation', playing on the literal sense instanced at 49 and implying subordination of church discipline to the 'law' of faith (86). *lette...gate*: unlike earthly laws subject to bribery (3.193). **92–3** A poor man complies with the law of charity by feeling for others what he hopes they feel towards him, and not asking for himself more than he can give them. **92** *of*: 'through'. **93** *as*: 'as for'. **94–5** evoke scripture to claim that the beggar's will is in effect his 'all'. **97a** 'Amen, I say to you, this poor widow [hath cast in more than all they who have cast into the treasury...]' (Mk 12:43–4; cf. B 13.197–8).

98–9 are transitional lines that sum up R.'s new parable-argument and neatly link (*For* 100) with the discourse on priestly perfection that the revision broke into at B 11.280 (see on 12.16). **99** *pouerte*: a condition not of destitution, but like that of Chaucer's 'povre persoun' who 'koude in litel thyng have suffisaunce' (*CT* I 478, 490).

The parallel text resumes with
C XIII 100 = B XI 285

100–28 reproduce (with improvement at 114–15 of B 301–2 and no major alteration) Trajan's attack on unprovided and ill-qualified priests. But they make R. sound somewhat like a spokesman for Wycliffe's 'Poor Priests' (*Pe* compares 16.110 and cites Leff 1967:527–9). **100** *Spera*...: 'Hope in God, [for I will still give praise to him: the salvation of my countenance...]' (Ps 42:6–7); especially appropriate to priests (AlfQ) as forming part of the Introit Psalm *Iudica me* at Mass, the text cited at B 11.284a. Peter Lombard saw this verse as warning against *pressuras saeculi* 'worldly preoccupations' (*R–H* 143). However, it is not Ps 42 that makes the promises of 101–2 but Ps 36: '*Trust in the Lord*, and do good, and dwell in the land: and thou shalt be fed with its riches' (vs 3); cf. also Ps 36:16, 'Better is a little to the just than the great riches of the wicked'. **103–6** argue that a priest should have a guarantee of material support ('title') from a lay or clerical patron (*he* 105), or from his ordinary (106), that will enable him to concentrate on his spiritual responsibilities without needing to find money, e.g. through serving in a chantry (cf. Pr 81–4); see Swanson 1985, Revard 1987:116–27, Du Boulay 1991:24. **106** *blessed... enbaumed*: when ordaining him priest. **107–15** compare priestly ordination with the dubbing of a warrior-knight, who also needs to be properly qualified. **108** *or...stren-the*: either (a) 'or [if he did not], maintained him for his prowess in battle' (with *kyng* as understood subject), or (b) 'or provided [in some way] for his needs as a man-

at-arms' (with *knyht* as subject). The reference at 110b to a knight's reputation for valour shows that the parallel between bishop and king does not stipulate a knight's financial *independence* any more than a priest's (as made clear in parallel B 291b), provided each has support from the one who 'ordains' him. **112** *connynge ne kyn*: a complaint against ignorant clergy (of possibly unfree origin) reflecting conditions after the Great Pestilence, which reduced the number of priests by up to two-thirds in some dioceses. **112–13** Given the positive emphasis at 103, 106, *title* here more probably means '(mere) name of priest' or '(merely) verbal guarantee of support', i.e. something purely formal, like a tonsure (which in B 299–300 is contrasted with learning and virtue). **B 299–300** 'He has, I believe, more expectation of getting a benefice simply because he's been ordained than because of his learning or acknowledged piety'; omitted in **C** either as awkward or as partly repeating 297. **114–15** are much stronger than the vacuous B 301–2, and 'Wycliffite' in tone, while remaining formally orthodox. *shendeth*: 'does injury to', in a sense not far from 'dishonours' (MED s.v. *shenden* v. 3(b); see *TN*). R. seems to locate the *vitium* not in the rite performed but in the one who performs it, so that the charter-analogy (unaltered in **C**), where *formal* error invalidates, is logically inexact. **120** *goky*: 'a silly cuckoo (< *gok*)'; instanced only here and in works influenced by *PP*. **121a** '[And] whosoever [shall keep the whole law but] offend in one point, is become guilty of all' (Js 2:10). The Latin forms a perfect alliterative line scanning on vowels (the other such lines are 1.142a, 3.496a, 10.90, 15.142, 20.112a, 21.173, B 7.116–7, 10.438 [Lat./Fr. macaronic]). In context the reference is to an otherwise virtuous man's one (major) sin; but the application would be more apt if the text read *vno verbo* (see *TN* on the earlier appearance at B 9.98 with *verbo* for *vno*, a variant that looks original there). **122** *For*: 'For the benefit of'. **123** 'Sing praises to our God, sing ye;... for [the] God [of Israel] is the king of all the earth: sing ye wisely' (Ps 46:7–8). R. takes *sapienter* to refer to the way the priest performs the liturgy more than to his spiritual understanding of it. **128** 'Ignorance does not excuse [bishops] or unlearned priests'; in **B** denoting bishops' (culpable) unawareness of ordinands' deficiencies, in **C** the fact that lack of education does not excuse a priest for ill performance of the liturgy or the bishop for ordaining him. The phrase is a maxim of canon law echoed in Abp. Pecham's *Constitutions* (Lyndwood's *Provinciale* I) and quoted by Bromyard (1.35/4): 'Ignorance does not excuse a priest in those matters which pertain to his office' (AlfQ). **B 316** *ydiotes*: the adj. (< the loan-word *idiote* n.) given a pl. ending as if French (see *MES* 277).

(iia) 129–78 *The Vision of Middle-earth* **129–33** The lines' transitional intent is indicated by their mid-sentence introduction of an entirely new motif with a subordinating conjunction (compare *Til þat* 131 with *and siþen* B 320). Ascription of the speech is clearer than in B 317–19, with its sermon-like acknowledgement of *digressio* and indeterminate *oon*, which echoes and should refer to the *oon* of B 11.140. **129** *rage aresenede*: ironic oxymoron 'placing' the preceding diatribe more critically than *dispute* in // B 319. **130** ironically recalls 11.162, which opened the rebuke precipitating the 'inner' dream. **131** *Kynde*: a benign character (see on 10.129) whose brief first appearance to help Clergy enlighten Will initiates the vision of MIDDLE EARTH. This focusses mainly on the non-human world and formally counterpoises that offered by Fortune at 11.170 (the echo of B 11.10 at B 11.322 is cut). L's treatment of the 'plenitude of creation' theme is indebted to the C12th philosophical and poetic traditions associated respectively with the School of Chartres and Alan of Lille, and also to the Victorine contemplative writers (White 1986:241–8). The vision's specific aim is to show the sexual drive as an instrument of God's purpose and not an excuse for licentiousness. The account in **B 321–5** is more didactically explicit than C 132–3. It identifies KYNDE as the Creator (325, a repetition of B 9.26 avoided in C), recalls man's origin (Gen 3:9), declares that nature's 'wonders' provide parables for his instruction, and 'Platonically' chimes near-identical lexemes (325) in anticipation of B 16.215 (cf. also C 17.153, 18.94). **132** *myrour.*: see on 11.170. *hym*: identity with the Dreamer being implied by the shift to *Y* at 134 (in **B** the vision is shown to the latter) and confirmed by the 'reckless' tone of Will's remonstrance at 184ff, and by verbal echoes like *resonede* 183.

134–78 139–41 *bothe*: bringing out the 'mingled' nature of earthly existence. **143** *Resoun*: here representing the divine *ratio* embodied in the cosmic order, with some influence from the understanding in Roman jurisprudence of 'natural law' as 'that which nature teaches all things' (Alford 1988:211). **146** Despite the offered punctuation (presupposing two lifts in the verb), the caesura may come after *anon* and the line be of Type IIIc, or Type I on vowels. **148** *ferddede*: the only recorded intransitive use. **151b, 153a** illustrate C's typical rhetorical *repetitio* (e.g. *nest* at 156, 159–60, the variations on *wonder* 137, 153, 158, 161). **152** *lykynge...flesch*: 'desire for sexual gratification'; cf. Z 3.163. **154** *out of resoun*: 'immoderately', because breaching the rational virtue of temperance. *rechelesliche*: ironically anticipating the motif of the Dreamer's discerning others' faults more readily than his own (B 386=C 207). **156/7** The rhyme heightens the formulaic character of the exempla. **165–6** Elaborate internal assonance / rhyme and fluid alliterative linking across the lines mirror the sense of order in nature seen in the earlier birds-passage at 10.63–7. **168** *Dompynges*: from *dompen* v. (MED s.v. (b)), possibly denoting the 'dive-dap' (moorhen or waterhen). **169** While the answer

is obviously 'from their Creator', its source is unlikely to be Job 39:13–17 (*Pe*), which remarks not on the birds' natural wisdom but on their *lack* of it; more relevant here is vs 4 of Ecclus 11, a ch. that influenced this passage. **170** *cauken*: from AF *cauquer* (< L. *calcare* 'trample'). **171–2** well illustrate 'Langlandian grotesque', the emblematic allusion to the rich, though muted, being elucidated at 14.178. Nature here functions as a 'faithful mirror of man's state', as in Alan of Lille's 'Omnis mundi creatura' (*PL* 210:579–80). **173–8** round off the vision of Middle Earth by recalling the opening (*see* 173=135; *colour* 178=138) and (more distantly) Pr 5 (*selcouthe*), with echoing phrases that again evoke the divine harmony through assonance and internal rhyme (174–7 on |ου| and |ευ|). **175** *Ne...on*: 'Nor what (I saw by way) of'.

(iib) 179–213 record Will's challenge to Reason and Reason's authoritative answer, which induces a rush of shame that wakes him from his deep dream of God's paradisal world. **179–82** are no more than a response to what Will saw at 139–42; but his objection in **183–93** assumes that since Reason does *not* accompany man, the supposedly rational part of creation (cf. 192), he cannot after all be wise. On Will's confusion of two senses of *resoun* (191), 'natural instinct' and 'rationality' (involving freedom to choose), see Schmidt 1969:148, and on the theodicy underlying this scene, idem 1986:33–5. The contrast between fallen man's sexuality and the animals' is drawn by Alan of Lille's Nature in *DPN*: 'almost all things obey my rule, excluding man alone by an anomalous exception' (*PL* 210:448). **185** *Wherefore and why*: recalling B 11.301, words of Trajan omitted at that point in revision. **187–9** *sorfeten...wedes...wordes*: both warned against in Ecclus 11:4, 8. **191** *al*: both an adj. 'all' (contrasting with *fewe*) and an adv. 'entirely' (modifying *reule*). **193** *leueth*: possibly punning on 'believes' and 'lives'. **B 373** *witty*: applied to God as at B 15.130. REASON is another 'nature-name' for God and so replies with unique authority, while also being associated with the power in man's soul that made him the Creator's image and likeness. **194–213** retain the essence of **B**'s moral argument: that mankind's defective state need not import imperfection in God, and is his concern alone. **194** *Reche*: reinforcing this characteristic that makes *Will's* 'nature-name' Rechelesnesse. **196** *Vch..*: signifying not 'everyone for himself' but 'mind your own affairs, not those of other people'; a position echoing B 10.263, where the *meuen mod* expression of 179 appears. **197** 'Strive not in a matter which doth not concern thee' (Ecclus 11:9). **B 378** superbly renders the French of B 384; but this oxymoronic line's omission in **C** seems due to a shift of emphasis towards *love* as what makes *soffraunce* (earlier criticised when *vnsittynge* at 3.207) a 'sovereign' virtue, supremely efficacious and 'sitting' for the king of kings. **198, 200** *soffreth*: 'puts up with' and 'suffers'; in both versions divine forbearance and suffering are to serve as models for man. **202** *soffrance*: the human virtue associated with God's mysterious tolerance of human sinfulness for his own hidden but ultimately 'reasonable' ends (cf. Ecclus 11:4, 14, 23). *for Godes loue*: distinguishing virtuous patience from craven acquiescence in wrongdoing. **B 382a** 'Be ye subject [therefore] to every [human] creature for God's sake...[for so is the will of God,...by *doing well*...as the servants of God... if, doing well *you suffer patiently*: this is thankworthy before God]' (I Pet 2:13–16, 20; cf. also Js 5:7–11). The omission before *creaturae* of *humanae* may, if intentional, signify that Will must learn to imitate the animals' *resoun* and so 'to tolerate the conditions of human necessity' (Kaulbach 1993:57). **203** *þe wyse*: i.e. 'Solomon', cited at 197. **204–5** 'Fine virtue is Patience, poor vengeance is Say-ill. Say-well and Suffer-well make a man speed well;' apparently proverbial (see Whiting S861), the thought being paralleled in *CT* V 773–80, which also translates the Cato tag quoted at 213 (*Pe*). **207** 'Before you blame anybody, consider whether there is anyone (including yourself) who deserves praise'. Reason's rejoinder echoes Leute's at 12.41a, which earned Scripture's approval, its 'Cato'-like prudence according with OT 'wisdom'. **B 386** *my lif*: 'the life of any man' as well as Reason's own observable 'behaviour' (for such double reference cf. on B 373 above). **208–9** argue that a man can no more create than he can christen himself: both require the action of another. **C** is milder in urging the Dreamer to reform his own life before others'. The revision replaces *lif* (at B 386, 389) with *repetitio* of *creature* at 208a, 209a and (with *variatio*) of verb-phrases at 208b, 209b. The omission of **B 394–9**, arguably digressive lines on bodily deformity as implying a criticism of divine perfection, improves the flow of Reason's argument that 'since *each* individual is imperfect, *none* should object that *all* are'. **B 396a** 'And God saw all the things that he had made, and they were very good' (Gen 1:31). **211** *matere*: presumably not implying that 'matter' *per se* is evil, but that man's 'fallenness' inevitably inclines him towards (especially sexual) sins he would be free from if he were pure spirit. **213** 'Cato agrees with me: "there's none from fault lives free"' (*DC* I. 5).

(iii) 214–48 open with the conclusion of the inner dream (Vision Three *b*) and return to the outer level of vision (Three *a*), which finishes at the end of C XIV=B XII. **214** *aschamed*: the violent access of feeling and surge of blood providing a psycho-physiological 'motivation' for the change of dream-state, which is not a true 'waking' but a receding from the stage at which greater things (*more* 216, 223) could have been dreamed. The phrasing recalls the moment when Will burst into tears and was plunged into the inner dream at 11.166 (on the association of states of emotional agitation with visionary experience, cf. *Pearl* 48–60, Carruthers 1998:170, 173). **217–218** The tone con-

trasts markedly with the confidence of **B**, the revision characteristically normalising the metrically licentious *s / ch* scansion of **B**. *grace*: here admitting of the theological sense, to hint that Will's access to deeper truth has been lost (like grace through sin) by his challenge to the divine wisdom personifed in Reason. **219** *was...wyhte*: a phrase repeated from B 18.229 and replacing one at B 408 that echoed B 11.140, 319. **220** *What is Dowel*: the question to be repeated by Will at 15.112 but here addressed *to* him (and echoing his words at 218); his answer (the fruit of experience) is not rejected. The word is stressed *Dowél* as at 218, not *Dówel* as at 221. **221** *al*: a little word, but with a large change in sense. Will's repetition here shows that he accepts Reason's injunction to imitate God (200), whereas in **B** the repeated *moore* of 410 is meant to resonate with 405 and 412. *soffre*: in its double sense; see at 198. **223** *þat Clergie can*: intimating that the meaning of the Church's teaching would have been disclosed if the vision had been accepted without questioning. **223–5** *conseyued mor...forsake*: reminiscent of the *Pearl*-Dreamer's similar realisation (1189–94) after a similarly abrupt awakening. **225a** *Philosophus...*: 'You might have been a philosopher, had you held your peace'; adapted from Boethius, *De Cons. Phil.* II pr. 7, 74–6, and found in almost this form in Bromyard I 450:2. *Et alibi...*: 'And in another place: "it has sometimes embarrassed me that I spoke, never that I kept silent"'; adapted from *nam nulli tacuisse nocet, nocet esse locutum* 'for harm comes from speaking, never from having kept silence' (*DC*, I.12b). **226** *Adam*: a rather ill-suited exemplum, since Adam's sin was not to *speak* (about the fruit) but to *listen* to what Eve said (cf. Gen 3:6). The passage generally recalls the warning against imprudent and unconsidered utterance in Ecclus 11:7–9. **227–8** may echo *DC* I .3: *Virtutem primam esse puta compescere linguam*; / *proximus ille deo est, qui scit ratione tacere* (Baer 2001:139). **228** is of T-type, the b-staves being cognative on *p / b*. *wisdom... of God*: in forbidding Adam to eat a fruit that would bring him death (Gen 2:17). **230** *wyte why*: echoing B 10.124 (deleted in **C**), while // B 419 recalls Lewtee at B 11.105–6, and 419b Reason at B 376. **231** 'Because of the arrogant self-confidence that comes from your extravagant style of life'. *parfit lyuynge*: with sense as in the name of Fortune's damsel at 11.176, but with a sardonic 'anti-pun' on the contrary sense instanced at B 15.417. **232** *Reson*: a significant addition, this weighty figure's refusal inevitably entailing Clergy's also. **233** *connynge*: a revision avoiding repetition of the point at B 435. **234** *shame*: probably personified here (and at B 431), as later at 244. The quality denoted is fear of others' disapproval and implies the Dreamer's return to his condition at 6.2, illustrating the importance of the 'affective' element in disciplining the will when a purely 'cognitive' training has proved ineffective. Some influence from Richard of

St Victor's *Benjamin Minor* chs. xlv–xlviii (*PL* 196:51, ME tr. in Hodgson 1958:142–3) may be suspected here. *shrewe* (*man* **B**): the strongest reproach ever used towards the Dreamer by any of his interlocutors. **235–41** allegorise under the figure of drunkenness the rake's progress that the speaker finds illustrated in Will. **235** *daffe*: here as at 10.179 applied to a drunk displaying insolence and lack of reason (but earlier to Will by HC at 1.138). **237** *thenne*: when he has fallen from Fortune's favour but does not yet realise what has happened. *recheth*: linking Will's intoxication with worldly pleasure to his extreme attitude towards the wisdom of providence. While the phrase echoes 194, this is the wrong kind of 'failure to care'. **240** *Nede*: an important figure later in the waking prelude to Passus XXII, where his hostile tone recalls his rôle here as an extrinsic initiator of shame. **244** describes the reflex of shame seen in others' attitude, that which causes the 'smart'. **247** *aroes vp*: implying that Will has felt acute mortification, acknowledged his faultiness, and acquired a new readiness to be instructed.

Passus XIV (B XII)

This short but dense Passus consists almost entirely of a single speech by YMAGYNATYF (Y. hereafter), who was introduced without being named at the end of PASSUS XIII when Will woke out of his inner dream. It pauses at 99–109, about mid-point, with a one-line question to Will (108), and is interrupted towards the close by a three-line objection from him (199–201) that Y. decisively answers, bringing the THIRD VISION to an end. C XIV is 80 lines shorter than B XII, with four main cuts at 16–54*a*, 81–96, 231–4 and 251–8. The chief of these is the first, Will's defence of his 'making' at B 20–8, which is compensated for by new matter on a similar theme earlier introduced at C V 92–104 (see Schmidt 1987:14–20, 142–3). Y.'s discourse defends *clergye* 'learning got from books' (specifically that concerning the way to salvation taught by the Scriptures) and 'the clergy' who have charge of it. He handles objections to the claim that knowledge of the Christian faith and acceptance of baptism are necessary for salvation, addressing the problem-cases of the Good Thief (131–48, 153–55*a*) and Trajan (149–50, 205–16), who were apparently saved without them. Ymagynatyf's argument employs vivid analogies based on experience that bear out his nature as the power of shaping mental images so as to draw spiritual understanding from them.

B 1–54*a* are considered first since they have been drastically revised and **C** is more conveniently commented on from where it takes up **B** to run continuously in parallel. Though in both versions Y. gives the Dreamer moral counsel, in **B** he does this much more explicitly through calling to Will's mind memories from the past,

thoughts of the present and imaginings of the future (e.g. of what it will be like to be old and unable to undertake penitential exercises for the sins of youth). **1** *Ymaginatyf*: a nominalised form of the adjective, signifying 'the ability to form images of things not experienced, e.g. of past or future events' (MED s.v. *imaginatif* adj. and n. 4 (c)). Corresponding to the *vis imaginativa* of late medieval epistemology, it encompasses acts now classed not under imagination but memory. In the tradition of 'monastic philosophy', however, *memoria* was considered not a passive but a 'shaping' and picturing power, especially in relation to the act of praying (cf. 16.184 and see Carruthers 1995). Literary personifications of imagination are rare, though one appears in the OF *Enseignement de la vraye noblesse* (cited in Keen 1984:152). L's figure has been convincingly seen as the power of actively or vividly representing [images] to oneself (Wittig 1972:271); personifying the mind's capacity to make similitudes (Harwood 1975:249); providing images and examples as means to understand the truth (Minnis 1981); and functioning as the *sensus communis* to co-ordinate sense-experience under the direction of prudence and, eventually, grace (Gallacher 1991:49). At the opposite ends of usage, the devotional and the scholastic, are White's identification in Y. of 'imaginative contemplation' as understood in the Victorine tradition, leading to wonder and love of God (1986), and Kaulbach's (1993) of the human potentiality for thought (and especially prophecy) as understood in the 'Augustinised Avicennism' of the period. Undeniable resonances of each account indicating a synthetic conception drawn from many traditions argue against seeking too specific a source. Wherever **L** situated imagination among the mind's functions, he did not include it with ANIMA's names in B XV. So perhaps Y. represents less a spiritual faculty than (in the broadly 'Aristotelian' tradition) one mediating between the bodily senses and the rational soul in order to furnish images from which the intellect 'abstracts' general concepts with which to reason (cf. Gallacher 1991, 1992). That *Ymaginatif*, who in principle stands nearer to 'the knowledge derived from experience', should discourse on the value of *clergie* 'revealed knowledge' is ostensibly paradoxical. But the Dreamer having proved unable to learn *directly* from Reason (questioning his 'wisdom' on the basis of his own observations of animal behaviour), and having 'contraried Clergy' (see on 100 below), it seems ironically fitting to have him learn the 'limited value' of experiential knowledge from a faculty whose starting-point is likewise the data of the senses. **3** *fyue and fourty wynter*: if taken as covering Will's complete age at this point, denoting (as at B 11.47) the peak of 'middle life', which was seen as a time of critical decision for man's spiritual destiny (Burrow in Heyworth 1981:21–41). **5** *And how*: 'and (to reflect on) how...' **6** scans on |ð| and

|w| as an extended Type IIIa with counterpoint (*abb / ab*). **9a** 'If not in the first watch nor in the second...'; after Lk 12:38: 'And if [the Lord] shall come in the second... or...the third watch and find them [watching], blessed are those servants.' As in Gregory's interpretation of this passage in his *XL Homiliarum in Evangelia*, Bk I, Hom. 13 (*PL* 76), three night-watches are here supposed. They correspond to youth, middle age and old age, when death and the individual judgement might come unexpectedly, and for which one must prepare (*R–H* 149 citing *GO* [*PL* 114:298]; see further Burrow 1986:69–70). **10–11** may have some personal significance known to the poet's earliest readers. The reference to the *pestilences* could betoken family losses; the *pouerte* agrees with the manner of life described in 16–17 and in C 5.1–4, 49–52; and A 12.81–7a record a (near-fatal) *angre*. **12** *baleyses*: natural affliction thought of as *virga Dei* 'the rod of God' (Job 21:9). **12a** 'Such as I love I [rebuke and] chastise' (Apoc 3:19, echoing Prov 3:12). In Lombard's *Commentary* (*PL* 191:243–4, cit. *R–H* 149n86) the 'rod' is interpreted as a light discipline, the staff as a stronger one (for older 'sons'). **13** *swiche...Iesus*: understood as prophetically applying to Christ's followers, who may expect persecution as a test of their faith. **13a** 'Thy rod and thy staff: they have comforted me' (Ps 22:4); a text encouraging the patient Christian to accept discipline as a sheep submits to the guiding blows of the shepherd: God's corrections become consolations (*Sk*). **16–17** *And;...and*: 'And yet'; 'when'. *medlest...makynge*: see Schmidt 1987:14–19. *seye...breed*: as a 'psalter-clerk', not qualified to celebrate Mass in a chantry (because not ordained priest), but authorised to recite the penitential psalms for the souls of the relatives of those who provide him sustenance. That this *may* reflect the poet's own circumstances is tacitly implied by his quoting from the psalms some 80 times severally. **17** *bokes ynowe*: semi-ironic, since books have clearly not given Will the *kynde knowynge* he has insisted on. **19** *peire freres*: alluding to the friars' custom of going about their mission in pairs, like those in 10.8 who answer Will's question about Dowel. **21–2** *þat... To*: running together two constructions to yield '(saying) that he should...' *solacen...make*: as Philosophy offers Boethius 'the sauasyoun of swetnesse rethorien' in *Boece* II pr. 141 (Rudd 1994:171). *sone*: alluding to the medieval view that the *Disticha de moribus ad Filium* (to give it its frequent title) was addressed by Cato to his son (Baer 2001:131) **22a** 'Give a place sometime to pleasure amid the pressure of cares / [That you might bear in spirit the burden of labour]' (*DC* III.6). **23–4** *holy men... Pleyden*: evoking the followers of St Francis, called *joculatores Domini* for their use of poems, tales and music in preaching the Gospel. **27** *wende...chirche*: i.e. adopt a contemplative life; the phrase 'foreshadows Will's arrival in Unity [at 22.212–13]' (White 1988:80). **27–8**

but; but: the semantic / metrical repetition-with-variation (mute and stressed co-ordinating / adverbial conjunction) is notable. **29a** '[And now there remain] faith, hope and charity, [these three]: and the greatest of these [is charity]' ((I Cor 13:13). **32** *lewte*: a quality, defining Dowel, that may here signify 'faith' in a wide sense of obedience to the commandments of God and the Church. Married man, monk and virgin all typify 'fidelity' to a chosen way of life that suffices for salvation, while the nine 'negative examples' following show what comes from varieties of infidelity. **35** *Riȝt so*: the first of three such arguments by analogical example (cf. 47, 51). **36** *Rome*: see on Pr 48. *Rochemador*: Rocamadour in Lot, S France, where the shrine of Our Lady was (and is) a favourite centre of pilgimage (illustrations in Jusserand 1899:338, 365). *but*: 'except' (i.e. not at all, since for a monk *stabilitas* is the 'main road'). **38** *continue*: used in this absolute sense of 'remain celibate' also at B 9.179=C 10.286 (MED s.v. *continuen* v. 6(b)). **39** *seint ferther*: the 'pilgrimage'-metaphor, with its wry pun on a non-existent 'St Further,' intimates that all the maiden needs for salvation is her virginity itself. **40** On the rhythm and alliteration in this line cf. B 2.33 above. *What made...lese*: answered in 45 (and repeated in 55), which also applies to the examples in 46–56a. *Lucifer*: see on 1.104ff. **41** *Salomon; Sampson*: whose loss of *sapience* 'knowledge of God' and *strengthe* '(divine) fortitude' was caused specifically by desire for foreign women rather than *catel* (III Kgs 11:1–10, Judges 16:4–21), though in 'Augustinian' terms, anything loved possessively may be so described. **42** *Iob*: whose loss of prosperity not being due to sin of any kind, *ioye* may signify the happiness ultimately restored to him (Job 42:12) more than the original wealth he 'paid a high price for.' **43–5** These four figures represent the summit of achievement in philosophy, science, literature and imperial conquest (*Wr*). **43** *Aristotle*: see on 11.121; held in popular legend to have fallen under the spell of a woman and said by Eumelus to have committed suicide (as did Socrates) by drinking hemlock (Chroust 1973, ch. 14). Like the next two, he presumably illustrates the moral weakness of natural intelligence (*kynde wit*) left to itself. *Ypocras*: the celebrated Greek physician Hippocrates (C5th BC), who was fabled to have died of dysentery sent as a divine punishment for murder (*The Seven Sages* 1040ff). *Virgile*: the great Roman poet (70–19 BC), bizarrely believed to have had himself cut to pieces in an attempt at magical self-rejuvenation, which failed (Comparetti 1966:367). **44** *Alisaundre*: Alexander the Great (356–23 BC), the archetype of earthly glory in medieval tradition and first among the 'Nine Worthies'; affirmed in his legendary history to have been poisoned (cf. *Kyng Alisaunder* 7850–93). The *combraunce* of *catel* is best represented by his case. *þat al wan*: with a possible grim secondary sense, punning on the homophonic noun-phrase ('that one who was utterly pale [after being poisoned]'). **46–8** These two instances prove the danger of over-valuing one's beauty as a 'possession' (*catel*). **46** *Felice*: heroine of the popular early C14th romance *Guy of Warwick,* who treated Guy with disdain when he wooed her and was left by him forty days after their marriage, the 'disgrace' presumably denoting what she felt as a result of this. **47–8** *Rosamounde*: 'fair Rosemund,' daughter of Walter, Lord Clifford, and mistress of King Henry II; allegedly poisoned by Henry's Queen Eleanor in 1177, she was buried at Godstow nunnery near Oxford. *bisette*: a reflexive *hir* is presumed by *Sk*, who makes 48a the inverted object; but an 'it' may be readily understood, though MED s.v. *dispenden* v. 1 (a) also cites (from Gower) an objectless use of this verb. **50** *wise wordes*: applying only to Solomon and Aristotle. **50a** 'Bad men there are, who about good speak well; [Reject the men, retain the truth they tell]'; from Epigram 169 by the C12th Anglo-Latin poet Godfrey of Winchester (Alf*Q*, citing Wright 1872:II 130). **53** *suffren*: 'indifferently accept the existence of' (with a polysemantic 'anti-pun' on 'suffer'); a similar point at B 15.138–45 is removed in revision. **54a** See on 1.195, where the reference is to specifically clerical avarice. Lk 6:38 ends with the warning at 1.173*a*, and the context implicitly evokes the verse after that quoted at 56a: '... unto whomsoever much is given [the rich, the fair or the wise]...much shall be required.'

(i) 1–109 move from a critique of the value of 'learning' and wealth to a defence of *clergie*, 1–16a forming Ymaginatyf's account of his own nature and of the Triad.

1–34 4 *Dowel*: Y. reminds Will of what he taught him before, his definitions of Dowel and Dobet coming not as answers to a particular question but as revived memories of what the Dreamer already knows (see on B 1 above). **7** *spille no speche*: recalling Wit's definition of Dowel at 10.187. **8–9** *tyne...tene*; *lowe...lawe*: hinting through the pararhymes that time wasted is opportunity lost for doing good, and that humility is the essence of obedience to the commandments. **13** defines love, morality and faith (the equivalents of the Triad elements) as 'facets' of a comprehensive whole, 'Charity', the modulated pararhymes (*louye, lyue, byleue*) 'Platonically' reflecting their referents' substantive relationship. **14** *Caritas*: 'Charity' (see on 2.37), appearing later as the fruit of the tree 'True Love' (of which *Kynde Loue* here is a synonym). The Latin term gains special resonance from such key Pauline texts as Col 3:14 (*Super omnia...charitatem habete*) and Rom 13:10 (on love [here actually *dilectio*] fulfilling the Law). **16a** 'It is a more blessed thing to give, rather than to ask [*accipere* Vg "receive"]' (Ac 20:35). **18** *weldeth*; *wel de*spene: more 'Platonic' wordplay, hinting at the 'ideal' relation posited between power and bounty. **18a** 'Those who know [God's will] and do not act [according to it] shall be beaten with many whips'; adapted from

Lk 12.47 ('servus qui...*non fecit* secundum voluntatem [domini sui] *vapulabit multis*'). **19–22** focus on disorder in Church and society and remove the potential ambiguity of B 57–8; for reference to the source (where Vg actually has *scientia*) does not favour giving *sapiencia* the meaning 'spiritual wisdom' as opposed to '(purely) intellectual or cognitive understanding' (*scientia*). **B 57a** '[...we know (*scimus*) that we all have knowledge (*scientia*)]. Knowledge puffeth up; [but charity edifieth]' (I Cor 8:1). The immediate Pauline context is important for correctly understanding **L**'s association of true wisdom with love: 'If any man think that he knoweth (*scire*) any thing, he hath not yet known (*cognovit*) as he ought to know (*scire*). But if any man love God (*diligere*), the same is known (*cognitus*) by him' (vss 2–3). The tacit logic of equivalence here is: if to love God is to be 'known' (acknowledged / understood) by him, then *e converso* to love ('acknowledge, obey') him is to 'know' (understand) him (a point reinforced at B 71b). **19–20** have a chiastic structure: *connynge → techares*; *rychesse → lordes. lewede men*: possibly alluding to the Lollard preachers, some of whom were laymen (though the term is sullied by association with *loreles*). **22** *Druyeth*: anticipating the figure of *graes* in 23–5; the abuses specified corrupt all, from peasants to prelates. **23–29** revise in the direction of greater metaphorical complexity and theological precision, tracing the operation of 'prevenient' grace, the arousal of the will to repent, and the 'softening' of the sinner's heart through the practice of virtues made possible by the gift of 'actual' grace. This excludes a full 'Pelagian' view that spiritually meritorious 'works' can proceed from human free-will without the action of grace, the imagery here more closely recalling B 1.152 and B 16.5–9. By contrast, B 59–61 locate the 'remedy' for pride of intellect and station in the 'patient poor' whose just living helps to heal the illnesses of society and the Church alike. **23** *grace...graes*: more 'Platonic' wordplay; nothing could be more natural than 'grass' (or less natural than 'grace'), yet the one answers homologically (as it does homophonically) to the other. **27a** 'The Spirit breatheth where he will [and thou hearest his voice...]' (Jn 3:8; see further at B 69a). The new rendering of *spiritus* as *Espirit* 27 highlights the Latin word's root sense of 'breath' and more readily enables the contrast of *spirat* with *inflat,* so that **C** keeps a residue of **B**'s conviction that the Holy Spirit especially favours the 'poor (in spirit)'. **28** *grace...grace...be*: i.e. 'the disposition to live virtuously cannot arise without (a specific intervention of) divine grace'. The meaning of *grace* (1) gains sharper outline in the light of the contrast at 33 below. **30–2** explain the origin of human learning in the senses, specifically sight, by which we read books (whence there need be no allusion to Jn 3:11 as found by *Pe*), and more generally experiential knowledge through 'natural intelligence'. The latter is properly a gift of nature, not of fortune (*Pe*), the gifts of fortune (= *wierdes*) being, e.g., position in society as determined by one's parentage. The notion that celestial influences shape character, one common in the period, was not held to necessitate strict determinism of the human will. **30** has contrapuntal staves in each half (*aab / ab*). **31** is a Type IIa with stress shifted to the prefix in *bygete*. **32a** 'What appears in this world is governed by what appears in the heavens'; a quotation (if such it is) of untraced origin. **33–4** fall short of perfect clarity, since *chaunce* may inadvertently suggest 'life-circumstances' (instead of 'what one has by nature'). **34** 'Clergy is knowledge acquired through natural processes of learning'.

B 64–9a 64 *siȝte and techyng*: in inverse order to their antecedents. **65a** '[Amen, amen, I say to you that] we speak what we know and we testify what we have seen' (Jn 3:11). In context, Christ appeals not to scripture but to 'direct' (= *kynde*) knowledge of God; but Y. exploits his text (which can only be understood through 'clergy') to support a contrast between 'learning from authority' and 'learning from experience'. **C**'s founding of *clergy* on sight provides a less subtle but more logical distinction (see on 30–2). **66** *of heuene*: because divinely revealed. **67** *of...peple*: 'through the observations [of natural things] made by a variety of human beings'. **68** *greet loue*: God's charity that makes him communicate knowledge of himself to his creature man (cf. Jn 3:16); but with a hint that human love, if strong enough (cf. Lk 7:47), can earn *grace*, 'God's favour','the supernatural means to live virtuously'. **69** *Knew neuere clerk*: grace as a supernatural gift being beyond the reach of learning and experience (85ff will nonetheless maintain the orthodox position that the clergy are divinely ordained as the ministers, though not as the source of grace). **69a** 'He knows not [thou knowest not *Vg*] whence he [the Holy Spirit] cometh and whither he goeth' (Jn 3:8); completing 63a. **35–71** are a defence of *clergie* or (the keepers of) sacred learning, as bringing salvation to sinners (35–42), instructing ignorant layfolk (43–57) and having charge of the religious cultus that sanctifies the people (58–71). **35–7** The revision is more awkward syntactically than B 70–1, since *clergie...for Cristes loue* must remain an integral phrase. But the important sense-change, perhaps reflecting revulsion from the 1381 rebels' attack on Church leaders, firmly installs (clerical) learning above the knowledge derived from experience. **35** *And ȝut*: 'Now, for all this'. **36** *clergi*: playing polysemically on MED senses 3(a) 'learning' (as at 35) and 1(a) 'the clergy'. **37–42a** remove the repetition of B 11.204a at B 73a and are more compressed, allusive and theologically dense, keeping the two scriptural exemplars but enforcing a more explicit understanding of Christ as the 'prophet' (Deut 18:15) who fulfils and ratifies the Mosaic

Law while seeming to challenge it. Yet at the same time it echoes the sound-pattern of the original in repeating **B**'s fourfold *Crist(es)* and relying on *k*-alliteration (though substituting an *s*-sequence for *w* at 40–2). **37** *Moyses witnesseth*: i.e. as the accepted human author of the Pentateuch. *God wroet*: alluding to the Commandments written in stone with 'the finger of God' (Ex 31:18). *and Crist... fynger*: not necessarily dependent on *witnesseth* so much as elliptical for 'and Christ *wrote*, using his finger' (after *Iesus...digito scribebat* in Jn 8:6). The syntactic parallel brings out not only how Christ is 'a law-giver like Moses' (*Pe*) but is like *God*, who gave Moses the Law in writing. **38** *Law of loue*: recalling HC's assertion in 1.45–53 that Truth gave this 'law' to Moses, a claim for the Mosaic law of *treuthe* 'justice' as being, when rightly interpreted, the same law taught by Christ. *Oure Lord*: the locution (evidently not used here from alliterative necessity) denotes Christ in its 20 other occurrences, save one at Z 6.46 (see *IG*). So its present reference to 'God' would seem meant to assert the ultimate oneness between the revelation of God as Truth in the OT and as Love in the NT (Christ will deliver 'tho that [he] louede' strictly 'by lawe' [20.369, 443]). *long...were*: in respect not of his eternal Sonship but of his temporal existence as Jesus of Nazareth. **39** *confermed*: i.e. the Commandments to love God and neighbour (Mt 22:37–40, cited at 19.11–20). *Holy Kirke made*: asserting the continuity of the Church of 'the new Israel' with the Assembly (Num 20:4, Deut 23:1) of the old Israel (Vg has *ecclesia* for both). **40** *in soend*: translating *in terra* (Jn 8:8). **42** adds the 'staff' and makes the Gospel's (married) woman a *strompet* (unless this is meant as sarcastically challenging her accusers, who are presumed able to recognise a prostitute). **42a** 'He that is without sin among you, [let him first cast a stone at her]' (Jn 8:7).

B 70–98 Although the retelling of the story of the Woman taken in Adultery (Jn 8:1–11) is prolix (cf. 75b, 76a, 80a, 81a), **70–81** are not without power in their insistent alliterating up to 83 chiefly on *k* (including its cognative *g* at 79) and *w*, to heighten the intensity of their six / fourfold repetition of *clergie*, *Crist(es)* and *womman*. **74–5** *auoutrye...deþe*: assuming (mistakenly) that the punishment for idolatry mentioned in Lev 20:2 was that enjoined for adultery (Lev 20:10), though Deut 22:23–4 specifies stoning for an espoused girl who is willingly unchaste. **77–80** Ymaginatyf (somewhat opportunistically) makes the 'learning' shown in the *caractes* the efficient cause of the act, though it is the mysterious but disconcerting *knowledge* revealed by Jesus through 'what he wrote' (not through 'the (f)act of (his) writing') that confounds the accusers. The interpretation of *Cristes writyng* as a list of the accusers' sins is found in Jerome's *Dialogue against the Pelagians* (PL 23:553). But *Sk* rightly traces this important parallel to Augustine's statement in Homily 33 on St John's Gospel, vii.6: 'Christ is the Lawgiver…What else does he signify when he writes on the ground? For the Law was written with the finger of God' (*PL* 35:1649). **81** *conforted*: a 'saving' (from physical and spiritual death) that prefigures the sacramental ministry of pardon. **84** *mansede…ende*: a warning to those excommunicated for some grave sin not to receive the last rites without confessing it; but obliquely aimed at the priest of immoral life who by celebrating Mass in a state of mortal sin 'eateth and drinketh judgement to himself' (I Cor 11:19). **85–9** propose that just as *clergie* (both 'sacred learning' and 'those ordained to apply it through their ministry') is a remedy 'comforting' the repentant, so its possession compounds the guilt of all who take their final communion unconfessed. **87** *yuele*: 'badly' (*av*) or 'in a state of sin' (*a*). **88–9** argue (in reverse order) that Christ's writing served both to prove the woman guilty of sin and to save her from it (as if aiming to ward off accusations of 'easy forgiveness'). The *expected* parallel would be between pardon for the woman and condemnation for her accusers, as in the retailing of the story at 78–9. **89a** 'Judge not, that you may not be judged' (Mt 7:1); an important injunction also cited in very different situations at 12.31*a*, 16.126*a*. **90–1** turn from the specific case of the viaticum to the general one of receiving the sacrament in a state of mortal sin. **90** *breperen*: a momentary slip prompted by the original context (I Cor 11:33). **92–8** This loosely-focussed section will be reduced to one line (C 43) introducing the dominant metaphor of 'blindness'. But the connective *Forthy* is logically weightier at B 92, which gives a double reason for honouring clergy, its making possible (through the sacraments) both absolution and sanctification. Practical knowledge handed down traditionally and that which is revealed both deserve honour because they come from God. **95** The 'mirror' of Middle Earth (C 13.132) is that from which man, by 'kind wit', learns to love his creator KYNDE *in* the world; that of the soul is (in principle at least) unveiled by the clergy, who instruct 'kind-witted' men' how to find CHRIST *through* the world (cf. B 15.162). There may be an echo here of Js 1:23–4; but these mirrors (of nature and scripture) are envisaged as reflecting divine truth itself, not just a man's outer self (see further Kruger 1991). **97** *logik*; *lawe*: dialectic as used to defend the faith / elucidate theology, and canon law, which both benefit *lewed men and lettred*. **98** *countreplede*: a legal term (AlfG) adapted from OF *contreplaitier* and, though suggested by *lawe* 97, used in a wider sense 'contradict'. **43–57** are carefully wrought of two negative similes introduced by *No more* and enfolding a positive (*riht as…riht so*), arguing that natural intelligence alone cannot lead men to Christianity and thus to the grace necessary for salvation. **45** A clerk who lacks books is aptly compared to a man without eyes, a trope more logically

anticipated at C 30 than at B 64. The connection of (scriptural) 'books' with 'eyes' will be later brought out in the 'broad-eyed' allegorical personification BOOK at 20.238–9. **46–7** refer clearly to the writers of Scripture and imply its literal inspiration. Men did the physical writing but received as it were a divinely-sent 'interior exemplar' to copy. **49** *lereth…to resoun*: 'instructs in wisdom' (the 'main road' to heaven). Y. here indicates why the *rude speche* (13.229) of Will's 'kind-witted' challenge to Reason (13.184–6) got such a dusty answer: intellectual presumption is the moral stumbling-block that the discipline of *lettrure* aims to remove. **50–1** read like an imaginary *reductio ad absurdum* of the effort to achieve salvation without *clergie*. But as *Sk* notes, they may allude topically to a real action of the blind King John of Bohemia who, though not wielding an axe in close combat, led his troops at the Battle of Crécy on 26 Aug 1346 and was promptly killed (Froissart's *Chronicles,* tr. Lord Berners, ch. 130). **54** *The whiche*: (membership of) the body of baptized Christians, the *arca* 'chest' / 'ark' that is the Church. *Cristis tresor*: sanctifying grace; the image earlier occurred at B 10.474, which was removed in revision at C 11.306. **55** *and lered*: removing any (doubtless unintended) suggestion that clerks may not themselves need grace and mercy (for confirmation of the thought cf. 71 below). The addition will not over-burden the b-half metrically if *the lewed and* forms the dip before *léred* (but see *TN* further). **58–71** offer a 'high' view of the sacredness of the priestly order. The *Saul* exemplum amounts to a rejection of the 'Wycliffite' view that the clergy could be deprived of their endowments for spiritual failings (64–6) and may even be implicitly warning the secular authorities against interfering with their prerogatives. **58** *Arca Dei*: 'the Ark of God' (see on Pr 108). The sudden shift in topic is not arbitrary, since the Ark of Israel was seen as a 'type' of the 'tabernacle' of Christ's human nature (Alan of Lille) and of the Eucharist (Bonaventure), of which the Christian priest was the custodian. *Leuytes*: ministers of the sanctuary in the early OT period chosen from the Tribe of Levi son of Jacob, who had special charge of the Ark of the Covenant (Num 1:50–1, 3:31, II Kg 15:24). Medieval Latin *Levita* was sometimes used by analogy for the Christian deacon (see MED s.v. *levite* n (b), and on 2.130); L's exemplum speaks figuratively about ordained Christian ministers in general. **60** *Bote hit (he) were*: 'only someone who was'. **61–3** The patterned language, with subtly varied repeated b-halves and frequent pararhymes, produces a tone of ritual solemnity (see *TN*) lacking in the more circumstantial B 118–20, which alludes to Oza's sudden death after touching the Ark to steady it (II Kgs 6:6). **61** Even the anointed king of Israel was but a layman, and 'sacrifice' (the ritual hallowing of a victim offered to God, a type of the Christian Eucharist) belonged exclusively to priests;

see I Kg 13:9, in which the prophet Samuel rebukes Saul for his sacrilege and ascribes his coming fall to it. **64a** repeats 43a with small variation to complete the argument. **65–8** prepare Will for his encounter with the Doctor of Divinity in 15.39ff and recall the last (and only earlier) incident of such *cheste*, the 'words' between Piers and the Priest at 9.293. **69a** 'Touch ye not my anointed: [and do no evil to my prophets]' (Ps 104:15); often cited to support the notion of clerical privilege (Alf*Q* citing Hugh of St Cher). In context it refers to the 'holy people' of Israel, but is here applied to the Christian priesthood, whose rite of ordination included anointing (see 13.106). **70–1** replace the (not obviously relevant) mention of knightly 'ordination' with a wider, apter claim. *vycary*: stronger than *kepere*, and used most commonly of the pope (MED s.v. *vicare* n. overlooks this and other early uses).

72–83a describe broadly 'secular' knowledge of this world, acquired through the senses and associated with the pagans, who lacked a divine revelation. **72** *a clergie...*: 'a kind of "learning" of their own'. **B 129** repeats B 64 (also changed), **B 130** allows that experiential knowledge involves both truth and error. **76** *here sotiltees*: 'the intricacies / complexities of these things'; the revision implies a similar sense for *hir wittes* in B 133 (MED s.v. *wit* n. 6(d) 'meaning, significance'). **78** *bokes*: in which they recorded knowledge gained through the senses and reason. **79** *kynde knowyng*: the final occurrence of this expression. Y.'s point is that empirical 'science', being based on mere sense-data, cannot give the knowledge of God vital for salvation (whence Will's mistake in asking for it at 10.109). **81** *Patriarkes and prophetus*: an a-half set-phrase, referring here (the quotation is from St Paul) not to OT figures but to the Christian Fathers, who criticised pagan learning. **83** *clergie of Crist*: 'the learning taught by Christ', 'revealed truth'. **83a** '[If any man among you seem to be wise in this world, let him become a fool, that he may be wise]. For the wisdom of this world is foolishness with God' (I Cor 3:18–1). Here *sapiencia* signifies not just 'natural science' but 'earthly knowledge that measures the things of God by its standards'. Earlier I Cor 2:13–15 contrasts the intellectual arrogance of the 'sensual man' with the humble wisdom of the 'spiritual man'.

84–103 sets natural knowledge against the (revealed) knowledge of God that Y. regards as the essence of *clergie*. **84–5** show rich verbal patterning of internal rhyme (*heuene...cleue*), assonance (*cleue...lepe*) and chime (*cleue...loue*) that counter the agitated surface sense. The underlying image may be that of a fruit falling from the top of a tree and being caught by a child. **84** *Holi Gost*: alluding to the angel Gabriel's words at the Annunciation (Lk 1:35). **85** depicts not only a 'descent' but the act of Incarnation itself, directly echoing HC's speech on the 'plant of peace' at 1.148–9 and verbally 'pre-echoing'

Christ's *descensus ad inferos* (20.249), which completes the redemptive work this first descent began. On the basis of Cant 2:8, patristic exegesis had developed a notion of the 'leaps' of Christ recalled here (Smith 1966:30). **86** *clennesse*: at least in its primary reference a metonymic periphrasis for the Blessed Virgin (*R–H* 152), the type of this virtue (cf. *Purity* 1070–88); but it may at the same time denote 'the clean of heart' (= the shepherds) 'who shall *see* God' (Mt 5:8). *clerkes*: elucidated as the Wise Men by the quotation following 88, with 97 below; but 86a may conceal a translinguistic pun on the familiar figurative sense of *pastores* as 'the clergy' (cf. 16.203 and MED s.v. *pastour* n. 2(a)). Evidence for seeing the *pastours* 92 as symbolising those who seek Christ in the 'manger' of the sacred text is cited from the exegete Bruno Astensis by *R–H* 153 and decisive patristic evidence is given by Twomey 1991. Though 'shepherds' are only in Lk and 'Magi' only in Mt, both accounts are combined here to demonstrate how low and great alike qualify in different senses as *clerkes* if they humbly seek *þe clergie of Crist*. **86a** 'The shepherds said one to another: [Let us go over to Bethlehem and...see this word...which the Lord hath showed to us]' (Lk 2:15). **87–8** more exactly distinguish those who received God's favour (the Virgin, the Wise Men and the shepherds) from the rich and noble. Thus whereas B 144–5 rather illogically contrast the 'most learned' Magi (who were also rich) with both the rich *and* the very wise, C 87–8 contrast only purity and wisdom with wealth and rank. A small stylistic improvement in revision is to promote the *repetitio* from the adverb to the semantically more important adjective. **88a** '[When Jesus was born in Bethlehem...] there came wise men from the east [to Jerusalem]' (Mt 2:1). Believed to be 'three' because of the gifts mentioned at Mt 2:11, they were accorded the status of kings by the 3rd c. (cf. 21.75–95) and were venerated as saints, their supposed relics being royally enshrined at Cologne Cathedral. **89** This sarcastic side-swipe (which may be thought to mar the tone of Y.'s discourse) gets an ironic edge from its having been the Franciscans who promoted the cult of the Christ-child and the devotion of the Christmas Crib. The implication is presumably that the friars have now abandoned material and intellectual humility alike. **90–1** These superficially surprising lines must be meant to dissociate Christ not from the poor but from professional beggars, for whom *PP* has not a good word to say. Doubtless the B form is intended to support the attack on the mendicants, who believed their way of life based on the Saviour's, in asserting that Christ's family was respectable though *pore*, 'humble' not 'destitute' (cf. B 11.246–7). The softening of the hammer-like plosives in B 146–7 and their provocative quotation / comment are improvements. **B 147a** *Set...diuersorio*: '[And... she laid him in a manger]: because there was no room [for them] in the inn' (Lk 2:7). *et...diuersorium*: 'and a beggar does not have [any use for] an inn'; an untraced addition intimating that (since they were evidently *seeking* an inn) Joseph and Mary cannot have been 'beggars'. **148** *poetes*: a word perhaps determined by alliterative necessity; this earliest use bears none of the meanings given in MED s.v. and must in context denote 'sage'. *appered*: directly to the shepherds (Lk 2:9ff), but to the magi in a *dream* (Mt 2:12), whence possibly **L** the dream-vision poet got his hint for *poetes*. **94** *song a song*: rhetorical *conduplicatio. Gloria…*: 'Glory to God in the highest: [and on earth peace to men of good will]' (Lk 2:14). **95** *rotte...reste*: a non-literal sense perhaps being intended in the light of 15.305–9; since the Gospel is preached to the poor (Lk 7:22), the rich are likely to ignore it. **96** *sheware*: 'revealer' (MED s.v. *scheuere* n. (b), but with polysemantic wordplay on 'mirror', as suggested by the third *Aȝenbite* citation under sense (d): 'Ac þe filosofes yknewen god be writinge ase be ane *ssewere* huerinne hy lokeden'. **97** *comet...comen*: 'Platonic' wordplay, since the 'comet' was what made the magi 'come'. *comet*: 'a sterre wiþ a liȝt blasynge crest above' (Trevisa in MED s.v.); a common understanding of the *stella comata* [20.247] that appeared over Bethlehem, as in *LA* XIV:91.

99–103 are transitional lines linking the first part of Ymaginatyf's defence of *clergie* to the second, a *responsum* to the Dreamer's objection that learning hinders rather than helps salvation. **100** *contraridest*: 'said "contra as a clerk" to', 'put the case against' (specifically at 11.255ff, 278ff), in maintaining that the ignorant and wicked are saved more easily than the clever and wise. **101–2** are significantly revised, having added the *luyther* (the 'Good Thief' of 11.255) to the merely *lewede* (of 11.298–300); they clarify the somewhat confusing 158 (though attacking *kynde wyt* in passing at 11.228, Will has mainly targeted clerical learning). **102** 'Than clever scholars with minds capable of comprehending [theological truths]'. **103** In good scholastic fashion Y. concedes that Will is partly right (*soth of somme*), before arguing that he is mainly wrong. This 'partial truth' of the Dreamer's position will later be illustrated in Vision Four from the Actyf / Doctor of Divinity contrast, which is greatly reduced in the C Version. *in what manere*: an informal equivalent of the scholastic *distinctio*, 'What you say is partly the case, but only in a qualified way (*secundum quid*), as I shall make clear'.

104–08 tighten the argument by cutting the (strictly) otiose B 165–8. Y. continues in a manner recalling the Friar in 10.32ff, whose *forbisene* of the 'wagging boat' perplexed the Dreamer's *kynde knowyng*. He uses an *exemplum probativum per analogiam*, a particular example of a general truth, as the basis of a second, specific truth on another level (which Will now shows himself able to understand): 'Knowing how to swim saves a man from drowning;

therefore *kynde connyng* is of great *practical* value. By analogy (*Riht so* 110), knowing the theology of penitence saves the sinner from despairing. Therefore *clergie* is of great *spiritual* value.' *Sk* finds the swimmer-image possibly imitated from the Boethian comparison of a man who has feet and can walk with someone who lacks feet and must creep (*Boece* IV, pr ii, 105). But though this might have provided a hint, **L** speaks not of a natural *power* and its (unnatural) absence but of a *skill* that does not come by nature, and must be acquired. **105a** is repeated at 19.58 and used in *Siege of Jerusalem* at 365a. **110** *resoun hit sheweth*: 'it stands to reason', but alluding to the Resoun Will challenged at 13.183. **B 166–8** The image of despair as a 'river' that will yet not dismay the penitent man may have been suggested by Ps 31:6b, of which vs 1 is quoted at 177a. *dide*: an early example of emphatic pleonastic *do* in a metrically prominent position.

(ii) 110–217 110–29 111–15 again echo 10.38–43: Y.'s example of the efficacy of sorrow for sin parallels the Franciscan Friar's of the distinction between mortal and venial sin. **114** *what is synne*: 'what acts are sins'; 'the (true) nature of (the state of) sin'. **115** *withoute*: 'even in the absence of'. The cause of 'comfort' is to know that contrition brings divine forgiveness, reducing a mortal to a venial sin without loss of sanctifying grace, though the obligation to confess it to a priest remains; see on B 11.81a and cf. the more qualified view of contrition at B 14.84–6, 92–3 (both deleted in revision). **116** *oen or tweyne*: Ps 6:7–9 and esp. Ps 50:19. **117** *contricioun... synne*: see Ps 31:3–5. **117a** 'Blessed are they whose iniquities are forgiven: and whose sins are covered.' This key text, first cited at 7.152, is specifically applied to 'contrition without confession' at B 14.92–3; but B 14.84–6 lay down the qualification that the penitent be too ill or weak to confess, and have lived as a faithful believer. **119** *floed*: see on B 166–8. **120** *Lente*: when confession before Easter communion was obligatory, and so some contrition prior to the act might be in place. **121** *hath no contricioun*: does not experience / express any sorrow until he gets to shrift (and can do as Repentance bids Sloth at 7.58–61). It is this that Y. doubts an uneducated *loresman* would be able to offer his *lewed* parishioners as a specific against 'wanhope'. **123–4** *parauntur...men*: reflecting **L**'s view of the low state of clerical education following the Great Plague. However explicit the Lateran norms on penitence, the seculars' theological backwardness left the field open for the expert ministrations of the friars. **124a** '[Let them alone: they are blind and leaders of the blind]. And if the blind lead the blind, [both fall into the pit]' (Mt 15:14; closely paralleled in Lk 6:39). The 'blind leaders' are ignorant clergy, the 'blind led' are ignorant laypeople, the 'pit' *þe put of helle* (B 10.369). **125–30** The defence of learning continues with a humorously 'minimalist' argument for education: that it can save not only a clerk's soul but his life in an emergency. **126–7** *þat*; *That*: 'the one who'; 'And the fact that'. **128** 'The Lord is the portion of my inheritance [and of my cup: it is thou that wilt restore my inheritance to me]' (Ps 15:5); a macaronic line that can be scanned as Type Ie (the famous Messianic psalm's opening '*Preserve* me, O Lord' is relevant in the context). An ability to read vs 5 of the psalm, 'quoted in the ceremony of tonsuring new clerics' (Alf*Q*), was a conventional test of literacy entitling a 'criminous clerk' to be tried in an ecclesiastical court (after conviction for felony by a secular court, but before sentence) and so escape hanging for such offences as theft. The 'neck-verse' was more usually Ps 50:1, but any psalm-verse could be prescribed. The basis of this privilege was the 1352 statute *Pro clero* which allowed a convicted clerk to be tried in the bishop's court by 'purgation', i.e. a supported oath of his innocence (see Swanson 1989:149–53). **129** *Tybourne*: in **B** the first recorded vernacular reference to Tyburn (see on 6.367 above); here metonymic for 'hanging'. **130** *lolled vp*: perhaps suggesting to some readers in the late 1380s a grim allusion to Lollardy (since heresy disbarred from 'benefit of clergy') but unlikely to do so in **B**, a decade earlier (see on 9.218). *saued*: the ironic exclamation leading naturally to the difficult case of Dismas, who did not save his life but his soul (though by faith, not 'learning').

130–55a deal with the problem posed by paradoxical instances of salvation *without* 'clergie'. **131–2** The syntax is either anacoluthic ('as for' to be supplied before 131 and 'that' before 132), or elliptical ('Was [*saved*])'. *toldest*: i.e. at 11.255–63. The argument Y. *answers* could be expressed as a syllogism: 'Dismas (= a criminal who could *not* claim benefit of clergy) was *lewed*; but he was saved; therefore *clergie* cannot be necessary for salvation'. Though logically correct, this is theologically misleading; for one (unique) example could hardly condone lifelong defiance of Christian moral teaching in expectation of the grace of final repentance. The argument Y. propounds is plainly not intended to disparage the Good Thief (the mystery of whose salvation is touched on at 153–5 below); but it counters Will's earlier extreme position, with its 'reckless' reliance on last-minute conversion and failure to see the need for constant striving after holiness. **134a** 'Is it my will that a sinner should die, saith the Lord God, and not that he should be converted from his ways and live?' The *VL* reading *peccatoris* [Vg *impii*] is more frequent (Alf*Q*), e.g. in the *N-Town* 'Death of Herod', l.1. **135–46a** recognise the perceived inequity of rewarding a felon equally with the greatest saint by positing a hierarchy of glory in heaven. Such a view at first glance contradicts that of the *Pearl*-poet (cf. Green 1999:371–2), whose baptized infant was raised to glory though she could neither sin nor do a virtuous act, whereas the Good Thief could respond to prevenient

grace in an act of faith, a kind of honorary 'baptism of blood' (see on 207–8 below), followed by confession and then 'communion' with Christ in paradise. Otherwise, though, their cases are symmetrical, both innocent child and repentant sinner dying soon / straight after their respective 'baptism'. **135** *noen hey blisse*: Y.'s acceptance (with modification) of Will's statement at 11.263 again exemplifies a quasi-scholastic *distinctio* procedure (cf. 103). **136** *aserued*: choice of this verb-form (see MED s.v.) enables a 'Platonic' polysemantic pun on senses 2 'deserve' and 1(c) 'minister to', the latter identical with the two verbs at 144, 147; equity requires equivalence of desert and service. **140** *beggare*: a slightly unhappy comparison in its (unintentional) suggestion that (in the *Pearl*-poet's phrases) the *gentyl cheuentayn* Christ is indeed a *chyche* or 'niggard' (and the ambiguity of 145 scarcely improves matters). The substantive point is that everyone in the hall, from beggar to chief guest, is fed on the same heavenly banquet. **142** *Iohn*: the Evangelist, widely seen as an exemplar of lofty contemplative spirituality *passynge alle opere* (21.267). *Simond*; *Iude*: the Apostles Simon the Cananean (Mt 10:4) or 'Zealot' (Lk 6:15) and Jude, brother of James (Lk 6:16), who share a feast day on Oct 28. **144** *soleyn*: wittily recognising the uniqueness of his case. **145–6** obviously can only apply to one *in via,* not to one *in patria*. Though *as þe lawe lyketh* does not mean that an ordinary thief lived under a suspended capital sentence, his prior conviction would raise a presumption of his guilt on any subsequent charge (a thief who escaped hanging might yet be branded with a 'T'). Here the analogy teaches the need to remember one's old offences in order to avoid complacency. **146a** 'Be not without fear about sin forgiven: [and add not sin upon sin]' (Ecclus 5:5); the following verses (6–9) warn against presumption, delay and the danger of sudden unexpected death. The inefficacy of sacramental absolution is not implied by this stress on the value of remembering sin for inducing humility and heightening moral sensitivity. **148** *resoun ne riht*: qualities essential to God as 'Truth,' which cannot be dispensed with in the next life. **149–52a** counter any notion that the Good Thief is in danger of ejection from heaven on a further offence (which would be impossible) by proposing a (somewhat whimsically) symmetrical relation between Will's two extreme examples of salvation without *clergie*: just as Trajan was 'only barely in hell', so Dismas is 'only barely in heaven' (but *vix iustus salvabitur* 203). **149** *nat depe*: because his only sin was ignorance of *revealed* truth. **151** *loweste*: the point made so vividly is moral rather than rigorously theological, with no suggestion that heaven has a 'limbo' corresponding to hell's and that the Good Thief is placed there. **152** *wel losliche he lolleth*: 'he dangles by a very loosely knotted rope'. The chosen verb is darkly ironic in its echo of 130, since the 'looseness' of

the Thief's tie with heaven is the very reason why he is not choked to death ('damned'). The referent is contextually certain to be the Thief, not Trajan (as is claimed by Middleton 1997:316n85). *as by*: 'from the standpoint of'. **152a** 'For thou wilt render [*lit*. he renders] to every man according to his works' (Ps 61:13). This is an important and widely quoted text on the retributive character of divine justice (see Alf*Q*), earlier found glossing heaven as the place 'There *ryhtfulnese* rewardeth *ryht* as men deserveth' (5.32*a*). **153–5a** 'Why' grace was given to one thief rather than the other is not a *quaestio* capable of rational solution, the *exemplum* enabling Y. to return (from a matter bearing on the order of *grace*) to the issue that first provoked Will's challenge to Reason (why the order of *nature* is thus and not otherwise). **155a** 'Why seemed it well to him? Because he willed it'; loosely adapted from Pss 113B:3 and 134:6 ('Deus...omnia quaecumque *voluit* fecit'); and cf. Bonaventure: '*quia voluit, et rationem ipse novit*' (on *I Sent*. 44 1.1: *ad* 4). *Pe* aptly cites here Peter Comestor on speculating about why the Fall occurred: 'If it is asked why God allowed man to be tempted...we say..."because he willed it". But if it is asked *why he willed it*, it is pointless to inquire into the *cause* of the divine will, which is itself the supreme cause of every cause' (*PL* 198:1075). In **B** this passage has been alluded to by Study (at 10.126–7) just after her anticipatory reference to Ymaginatyf's forthcoming 'answer' to Will's *purpos* (both are removed in **C**).
156–67 considerably abbreviate (e.g. B 220–1 at 158) the vivid but somewhat circumstantial B 218–34, which illustrate how 'angels-on-a-pinpoint' speculations foster in laypeople the vice of idle *curiositas* (about which see Neuhauser 1988). Y. is less abrasive than Study at B 12.124, where *whyes* '(divine) causes or reasons' also appears; and rightly, since Will has only wondered at the intricacy of nature and loved the Creator for it. **156–7** *whyes...how*: though seeming to suggest hostility to scientific enquiry, indicating the sense 'the reasons why, the origins and final cause' (cf. B 224), so that what is really being opposed is indulgence in unfettered theological speculation. **161** replaces B 228, a line of Type Id, with one of Type IIa, the pattern of B 227. **162** *and* (2): i.e. 'as well as all the other animals'; no more implying that man is a beast than *creature* B 225 implies that *Kynde* is a created being. **163** *kynde...saue*: referring to the innate knowledge of sexual functioning needed for the species to survive. B 230 makes clothing oneself (usually associated with *culture*) an expression of human 'nature', although Genesis describes it as taught to man only after the Fall. **164** *goed...wikke*: recognition of God as the ultimate 'author' of evil requiring prudent distinction between what he has willed and what he has permitted for his own unfathomable purposes. But the sentiment, superficially at odds with 134*a*, is a Biblical commonplace: see

Job 2:10 (cited at 13.16–17) and Is 45:7. **165a** '[For] he spoke, and they were made: [he commanded, and they were created]' (Ps 148:5); repeated at 15.263*a*. **166** This statement implies that what seems *wykke* is part of the original creation, not simply a consequence of the Fall; and it widens the issue from 'why Man fell' to 'why there is evil in the world', the major problem of theodicy. **B 230** *hem*: either 'themselves' or 'them' (= their genitals). **168–84** shorten the richly detailed but repetitive beast-allegory of B 235–58, with some loss of colour but a gain in immediacy. The tempering of animosity against the rich is theologically securer and morally more benign. **168** *longe-lybbynge*: importing less the longevity of the ancients than their amassing wisdom over a long period of observation of animal behaviour (the 'examples' that underlie the fables of *poetes* B 236). **170** *foul foulest*: 'Platonic' wordplay humorously pointing up the grotesque contrast between different aspects of the birds in question (which may puzzle the 'curious' mind), to show that advantages of one kind are balanced by deficiencies of another. **172** *popeiay*: improving in sense on the plain not gaudy *pehen* B 239 (at 174 the hen is apt, since it *is* slow). **173** *Bytokenen*: 'stand for', echoing *Ensamples token* B 236; as *Pe* notes, Y. 'answers questionings of the order of nature with moralised lessons from "natural history"'. **176** *ful hey*: piquantly ironic, since the bird indeed symbolises the 'high' condition of those with wealth. **178** *ledene*: the peacock's unmusical cry being the price it pays for its glorious appearance. *careyne*: denoting at B 253 the bird's corpse as buried, but here more naturally the flesh as food (cf. B Pr 189). The taste for eating peacocks was on the wane, and their place at sumptuous banquets largely decorative. **182** *kyn*: the speaker's objection being to the respect paid to wealth, an accident of fortune (whereas birth and intelligence are natural gifts); the sentiment recalls that expressed at 10.261. **183–4** more concisely distinguish nobles (*rentes*) and bourgeois (*shoppe*). *Thus*: 'That is the way in which...' (ironic, because the poet's praise is ironic). *poete*: uncertain in sense because the reference is uncertain; but (in contrast with 92 above) the parallel of *poetes*189 with *grete clerk* B 265 may imply here a generic meaning 'authoritative ancient writer' rather than a title like 'the Philosopher' (for 'Aristotle').

B 244–60 vividly if somewhat laboriously elaborate the comparison between peacock and rich man, beginning and ending formally with *Right so* (244, 260). **245** *taille... sorwe*: the wretched end of a rich miser's life impeding his soul's ascent to heaven, as the peacock's long tail impedes its flight. **248** *tail...plukked*: i.e. after the 'bird' is dead. **249, 251** *þanne*: a warning against the perilousness of last-minute repentance induced by fear of hell, not love of God. **252** *pies*: rightly removed in revision; to introduce another bird of ugly cry is confusing, since the *peacock*'s has already been called 'unlovely' at 243. The comparison, however, also implies that the dying miser's desperate prayer will be (symbolically speaking) unintelligible gibberish (cf. the use of this image in the *York Crucifixion Play* 256). **253–5** The memory of the miser will stink like the peacock's decomposing body and infect all those who 'have contact with him', i.e. 'behave in like manner' (though this could possibly allude to some obscure popular superstition about not wishing to be buried next to a miser). **254** *flaumbe*: 'will smell'; *Sk*'s 'contaminate', which would anticipate 255, has no support, the only other MED example (s.v. *flaumen* v. 4) signifying 'smell'. **256** *po feet*: that the peacock has 'foulest feet and riueled' is ascribed to Aristotle by Bartholomaeus Anglicus (*Batman vpon Batholome* xii. 31, cit. *Sk*), but these details are not in Aristotle's comment on the peacock in *Historia Animalium* VI.9. Fletcher 1991 notes that the peacock's ugly feet were a homiletic commonplace, citing examples from *FM* 64 and a C14th Worcester sermon. The allegorisation of the feet as 'false friends' here (like that at 185 below) could be original. *Auynet*: a generic term for a collection of beast-fables (*Wr*); Avienus was a C4th Latin writer of fables (cf. *Donet* for 'grammar'). Fable 39 in Robert's *Fabliaux* (on the peacock who complained of his voice) contrasts the fate of the unjust rich (who will be 'poor' after death) and the just poor (who will enjoy the 'riches' of heaven). **257** *fulfille...wille*: for an inverted form of the same internal rhyme in the half-line cf. B 3.265. **258** *and...witnesse*: 'though they themselves were witnesses'.

185–98 185–90 somewhat implausibly attribute preference for the lark (= the humble poor) to various pagan authorities 'at random' (*Sk*), for alliterative convenience (with *poetes* 189 cf. *logik* 266). But the main point developed is that, although these were wise in their way, even 'great clerks', such wisdom based on 'kind wit' could not guarantee their salvation. **185** *larke*: much favoured as a dish (see *WW* 350). **187** *is resembled*: a comparison (again perhaps original) in keeping with the 'examples and terms' (236) **L** finds typical of pagan natural philosophy. **189** *Porfirie and Plato*: part of an evident 'repertory' line; see on 12.175. **190** *logik*: a loose alliteratively convenient term for 'philosophical writings'; neither this nor B 266 seems to refer to a specific work on dialectic, but *logik* is synecdochic for Aristotle's authoritative œuvre. **B 265** Aristotle observes (*Hist. Anim.* IX, 25) that the lark is edible, but does not draw this or any other moral *ensample*. **191** *clergie*: theological source, e.g. such as Gregory, whose successful intercession for the just but ignorant Trajan proves the emperor *saaf*. The remark seems designed to elicit Will's response at 199–201. **192** *Sortes*: a corrupt form of Socrates (*c.* 469–399 BC), Plato's 'mayster' who 'deserued unrightful deth' (*Boece* 1.pr.3, 27). It is unclear whether he is mentioned for his wisdom or his justice, but the former seems likely. *scrip-*

ture: 'written [not specifically biblical] authority'. **194–8** The sense is: 'since the intellectual powers God gave these philosophers enabled them to write works of benefit to Christians, he must have intended their salvation, and so (it is fitting) that we should pray for it'. **194** *hope*: 'think' or 'believe' (governing *we ben yholde / That...*). **196** *And*: elliptical for 'And to be saved all the more effectively'. **198** *clerkes*: a revision that seems designed to provoke Will's denial.

199–201 This second speech of Will's is less compliant than his admission at 109 and presupposes an understood *Ac*: 'But *Christian* clerks assert in *their* books' (as opposed to *here bokes* 196). The strict requirement of baptism for salvation was not a theologians' opinion but the standard teaching of the Church (though special allowance was made for those before Christ who lived just lives); so exceptional rescues like Trajan's depending on recourse to God's *potentia absoluta* came close to threatening the necessity and sufficiency of the 'ordained' sacramental order.

202–17 The latent scholastic mode of Ymaginatyf's prior argumentation now becomes patent with his denial of Will's contention, supported by a Biblical *auctoritas* he will explicate as he attempts to integrate the case of Trajan (a just pagan who lived *after* Christ) into the existing paradigm of orthodoxy. **202** *Contra*: see on 10.20 where (as at B 10.343) the phrase is used by Will; here the Dreamer's own sympathetic imagination is being empowered to generate a 'solution' to the dilemma of how righteous non-Christians can be saved. **203** '[And if] the just man shall scarcely be saved, [where shall the ungodly and the sinner appear]?' (I Pet 4:18). *in die iudicii*: 'on the day of judgement'; **L**'s addition. **204** *Ergo saluabitur*: 'Therefore (it follows that) he will be saved'. The salvation is not *entailed* by *vix* ('its difficulty') but would seem to be *implied* by it; and the assertion signifies broadly that 'while insisting that salvation is hard even for the just, scripture also guarantees it, whereas the prospect for the sinful must be a faint one'. The basis of Y.'s case for Trajan is that the Emperor does not really count as the *impius et peccator* of St Peter's question. But while *Sk* is right that **L** 'lays a stress upon *vix*', this applies only to the first part of the quotation; the consequent (his addition) stresses *saluabitur* and assumes an unstated middle proposition. This is clear if the statement is formulated syllogistically: 'The just man will be saved, if with difficulty. Trajan was just. Therefore Trajan will be saved (though with difficulty)'. Y. is thus intimating that if 'Aristotel þe wyse' (193) and other pagan sages are not found *un*just on judgement day, a matter that lies hidden with God ('Sunt iusti atque *sapientes...*' 11.275a), then they *will* (we may hope) be saved, however narrowly. *no more Latyn*: i.e. no further scriptural *auctoritates*. **205** *trewe knyhte*: an echo of 12.77 reminding the audience of the special appropriateness of 'true' conduct to the knightly order. Most pertinent to the Emperor's case is the judicial incorruptibility laid down in 1.94–5, which had made him an exemplar of *trewthe*. **206** *the boek*: the *LA* (see on 12.77 above). **207–8** distinguish three varieties of baptism recognised by the theologians (Dunning 1943:45–54): the ordinary kind *of fonte*; the 'baptism of blood' of a martyr who might not have received the sacrament but 'seals' his faith by dying as a witness to Christ; and the 'baptism of fire', a mysterious infusion of sanctifying grace direct into the soul of a *trewe* man that generates (if tacitly) the 'righteousness' (*trewthe*) needed for salvation. Obviously, one who received this last kind (which had no sacramental 'outward sign') lacked *clergie* in the sense of 'formal knowledge of revealed truth' (in Trajan, troublingly, this lack even prompted hostility to Christianity). But while ignorant of the theological virtues, the Emperor in some manner practised the first of them, so that 'justification' could be 'imputed' to him (as is argued by Whatley 1984²). **L**'s attempt to reconcile the supposed conflict between the positions of Paul and James (Rom 4:9; Js 2:20–6), depends on his seeing 'works of justice' like Trajan's as exemplifying (and therefore as constitutive of) *fides implicita*. For a similar account of Trajan's salvation as effected through an implicit baptism of desire distinct from the explicit desire for baptism described by St Thomas in *ST* III.68, 2 see Doxsee 1988. **207, 209** *Ac*: taken here as having the force of *Sed* '(but) now' in scholastic disputation, rather than of *Sed contra* 'but on the opposite side'. Following Whatley (1984²), Burrow (1993) understands the first *Ac* as introducing a way of salvation *distinct* from the three baptisms and (preferring at B 282=C 207 the β reading *For* to *Ac* αC) translates it 'but however that might be'. **208** *al*: either 'everything that has been said is a matter to be firmly believed' or 'each of these three modes of baptism constitutes real faith'. **B 283** *þat*: having as antecedent either baptism of fire ('and that is sure faith') or the whole statement from *Ac* to *fullyng* (3) 'and that is [a matter of] certain belief' (corresponding to the first alternative for C 208). **208a** 'There came a divine fire [at Pentecost, as told in Acts 2:3, but recalling also Mt 3:11], not burning but illuminating [and gave them the gifts of grace]'; from a Pentecost Antiphon in the *Sarum Breviary*, 1:mvi, mxvi (Hort 1938:167). **209–12** The anacoluthic construction well conveys the speaker's sense of urgency. Y. argues that Trajan's *treuthe* is a homologue to the third type of baptism, as it 'illuminated' his mind to do justice, and claims that the God who is Truth will therefore commend Trajan's *fidelitas* as equivalent to *fides* and as qualifying him to join the *fidelibus* of B 290. **209** *treuth*: a near-personification of 'a righteous man', like those at 2.136, 3.176, 191. *trespassed neuere*: remote as was the chance of such indefectibility in the absence of baptismal sanctification, L seems insist-

ent that it can be and has been found, his motive being perhaps to allay anxieties about divine justice arising from the fact that many, through no fault of their own, have never known or will know God's revelation in Christ. **210** *lawe*: 'religious principles,' but with some allusion to Trajan's exemplary administration of Roman justice. **211** *wolde*: i.e. 'would [choose it and] live according to it'; the inappropriateness of *amende* B 286 is plain enough. **212** *Ne wolde*: either preterite 'God never wished...' or, preferably, jussive subjunctive 'May God never wish...' (in which case Y.'s position need not appear 'heterodox' [Green 1999:369–70]). *trewe God...treuthe*: the close collocation reminding that Truth, the first 'nature-name' for God to appear (Pr 15), expresses the divine essence as knowable to man through the 'inner law' of conscience. **212** *alloued*: understood by Whatley (1984²) as 'given credit for' [i.e. the will or intention implied by *trewe lyuynge*], even as 'reckoned as efficacious for salvation'. This may be to overstate the matter, but there is little at stake in the difference between 'reward' and 'commend' since either way Trajan *has* been saved. **213** *wher...nat*: 'whether it will actually turn out so or not'. The final outcome remains *in manu Dei* (11.275a) because the working of God's free unfettered agency ('potentia absoluta') belongs to the innermost mystery of the divine will. *the bileue...treuthe*: '[it is nonetheless the case that] the faith found in a just man is great' (or, less probably, 'great trust can be placed in righteousness'). *bileue*: the first of the three theological virtues, here judged 'implicitly' present in one who *lives* justly without conscious awareness of revealed truth. **214** *hope*: the second theological virtue, here thought of as derived from and dependent upon the 'faith' implied in righteous living (though the Triad is not named here, it is tacitly evoked). **214a** '[Well done, good and *faithful* servant]: because thou hast been *faithful* over a few things, [I will place thee over many things. Enter thou into the joy of thy lord]' (Mt 25:23). A lucid scriptural passage replaces the enigmatic riddle-text of B 290, but still needs to be interpreted in order that its relevance to Trajan's situation may emerge. In the Parable of the Talents, the 'few things' may be understood as corresponding to the secular dominion entrusted to the Emperor, which he administered with a 'faithfulness' (integrity) justifying his Lord's trust in him (cf. Harwood 1973:288). Trajan's practical righteousness corresponds to Langlandian 'hope' (*leute*), which receives as its reward *multa* 'many things'. The latter are here construed in 'feudal' manner as a generous 'extra' exceeding what the 'faithful servant' expects, nothing less than the gift of *caritas*, the third theological virtue (215), which wins Trajan the *gaudium domini* in heaven. **215** *yf...trewe*: a phrase of set type (with parallels at 9.212, 14.151, 15.239, 274, 17.5) having the sense 'since it is indeed the case that' and implying that if a pagan lives justly *without* revelation, his reward should be all the more generous. **216** *cortesye...couenant...carpe*: i.e. the 'bonus' should exceed the 'agreed wage'; and though God's 'covenant' with righteous non-believers does not constrain him to grant them heaven, if this 'lord' *is* true to his nature, he will do so out of sheer kindness, whatever theologians might deduce from texts like Mk 16:16, cited at 13.86*a* above (see Schmidt 1984). **217** *al... wol*: a resigned acknowledgement of God's sovereignty, echoing (in a more hopeful tone) Study's words earlier at B 10.129–30

B 290–5 291 'GOD is thus named as, so to say, "giving eternal life to his own", that is, to the faithful'. The key to the meaning of this quotation is an ingenious *interpretatio* of the Latin word DEVS as '*d*ans *e*ternam *v*itam *s*uis' found in a ms gloss in Evrard the German's treatise on rhetoric the *Laborintus*, ed. Faral 1924:65 (information from J.A. Burrow). The general sense may be paraphrased: 'God is wholly to be trusted, because the very letters of his NAME spell out his NATURE as the one who gives life to believers'. The exact source of this gladsome conceit is unknown, but the basic thought recalls Jn 17:2: 'ut omne, quod dedisti ei, det [Filius] eis vitam aeternam'. The promise of eternal life to the truly faithful forms a key part of the *dispensatio ordinata* mediated through Christ and the Church. **291** 'And in another place: "For though I should walk in the midst of the shadow of death, [I will fear no evils, for thou art with me]' (Ps 22:4). As this is the psalm of total trust in God quoted by Piers on tearing the Pardon at B 7.116–17, the effect here is to associate the *trewe* king / emperor with the *trewe* ploughman who will become in XIX–XX=XXI–XXII an emblem of the ideal Pope. This link is strengthened by the fact that the enigma-verse's phrase *aeternam vitam* echoes the first verse of Truth's pardon at B 7.110*a* (which promises the same reward to those who *bona egerunt*), thus in effect identifying Trajan as a 'pagan exemplar' of Dowel. The quoted psalm-verse needs to be read in the context of the preceding vs 3 ('He hath *led* me on the paths of *justice*') and the following vs 6 ('And thy *mercy* will *follow* me all the days of my life'). **292** 'The gloss on the basis of that verse concedes that a man of righteous life deserves a great reward'. The *GO* remarks on *mecum es* 'i.e. *in corde per fidem*, vt post umbram mortis ego tecum sim'; the source of this is Augustine's *Commentary* on the psalms (*PL* 36:182), noted by Davlin 1989:78. **293–5** Ymaginatyf's final commendation of 'wit and wisdom' comes somewhat unexpectedly after the praise of 'clergyless Dowel'. But its point would not be lost on a clerk, since it shows that *clergie* (informed by imagination as well as reason) has been required precisely in order to find a way to reconcile the salvation of righteous non-Christians with the Church's accepted teaching. **293** *wisdom....tresor*: specifically knowledge of *treuthe*, the tre-

sor praised by HC at B 1.208=C 201. **295a** closely recalls *so muche manhed & murþe* in *WPal* 97.

Passus XV
(B XIII, XIV 1–131*a*)

PASSUS FIFTEEN of **C** initiates VISION FOUR. In **B**, this vision *ends* decisively at 14.332 with Will awaking, and Vision Five begins with his falling asleep at 15.11 after a brief opening (15.1–10). The latter is neither a waking interlude nor a résumé of the preceding vision like the prelude to Vision Four, but a prologue summarising the Dreamer's life over a period of time between the episodes of Haukyn and Anima. An 'inner' dream (the second in the poem) is then made to form the deep heart's core of **B**'s Vision Five at 16.18–166; and from this Will wakes at B 16.167 into the containing 'outer' dream, which goes on to the end of B XVII. Though complex, the structure of **B**'s last five visions remains as coherent as that of the first three, thanks in part to the tight correspondence between vision- and passus-boundaries. Thus the Fourth occupies two passūs exactly (XIII–XIV), the Fifth three (XV–XVII) and the Sixth, Seventh and Eighth a single passus each (XVIII, XIX, XX). By contrast, **C** displays (at least superficially) a less clear organisation from XV to XIX, which may indicate a desire for a more dream-like fluidity of form (see on 28–9), or simply incomplete revision. Thus **C**'s Vision Four appears to run from 15.25 until 18.179, when the Dreamer awakes, though its action continues uninterrupted without his falling asleep again, and he wakes for a second time at the end of XIX. Close scrutiny of the revision suggests that **B**'s 'dream-within-a-dream' has been substantially retained. But as its opening is not formally indicated (it appears to be hidden away at about C 18.4–5), the fact that Will wakes at 18.179 is perplexing, though it corresponds to his 'waking' into the 'outer' dream at B 16.167. Nor is lucidity promoted by **C**'s abandonment of **B**'s tidy vision / passus correlation and (apparently arbitrary) decision to open XVI and XVII (at a point about halfway into the source of each, respectively B XIV and XV) with direct speech in reply to a speaker at the end of each preceding passus. The shortening of **B**'s XV recalls the splitting of B V into C V, VI and VII; but unsignalled transition to a deeper level of dream-experience risks creating confusion if, as is likely to happen, it passes unnoticed.

The first part of VISION FOUR opens with a prelude (1–24) and then divides into (i) the dinner at CONSCIENCE's house, from 25–185, linked by a five-line transitional passage (making clear Will's presence on the 'pilgrimage') and (ii) the opening dialogue between PATIENCE and ACTIVA VITA (HAUKYN of **B**), from 191–311. The two episodes narrated here focus on types of respectively *heigh clergye* (in the person of the Doctor of

Divinity) and *lewednesse* (in Actyf), between whom the Dreamer stands midway. The Vision begins as an attempt to reconcile Will with Clergy; but his bruising encounter with the learned friar confirms his rejection of the intellectual path to Dowel. He opts instead for an 'affective' approach to religious understanding ('seeing much and suffering more') in the company of his converse Patience, as a means to control the passions out of which most sins arise (on this see Simpson 1986[1]:14–19).

Prelude **1–24** are unusual in summarising the events of the preceding Vision (C XII–XIV, B XI–XII), from Fortune's entry in the first inner dream up to the disappearance of Ymaginatif. They retain B 1–10 intact but expand (and improve) most of 11–20. **1** *witteles*: a key word in the thematic development towards the *fooles* of XXI (see 18.179–80 //). Though Will is not about to go mad from the *wo and wrathe* that precipitated the inner dream (at 11.166), he has lost confidence in his reason after it has proved impotent before the mysteries of creation and the Creator. **2** *fay*: perhaps 'unfortunate, unlucky' or even 'stricken' (MED s.v. *feie* adj. 3(a), (b)), given Will's descent into near-destitution (5); but at 16.195 it means 'dying' or 'dead' (1a) and may imply here '(afflicted) with (a sense of) my life running out'. **3** *manere*: having a beggar's outward indifference to material welfare. **5–6** recall Elde's warning at 11.190 (now fulfilled) and spell out what is elliptically implied in B 6. *faylede*; *manaced*: seemingly parallel verbs and so, despite occurring in reflection on a dream that *foretold* this would happen, indicative (unlike subjunctive *lyuede* 7). **6–7** 'How Eld threatened me, saying that if I should happen to live to an old age, he would leave me in the lurch'. **10–18** use *repetitio* to link the key ideas of the summarising lines: *pore* (10, 11), *lewede*, *lord* (14, 15), *connynge* (18). **13–14** *al...boende*: 'all sections of society', generalising the sin of greed beyond the clergy, perhaps in the aftermath of 1381. **16** *curatours...incurable*: an angry pun 'Platonically' implying the dependence of the whole community's spiritual health on a virtuous clergy (a theme to be developed at 16.240ff). **18** *connynge*: a repetition (substituting for that of *bestes* in B 15–16) that shifts the sense from God's 'wisdom' to the 'instinctive knowledge' of animals by which they share in that wisdom, sardonically contrasted with *vnkunynge* 16. **B 15** *curteis*: see White 1986:244–6. **19** tones down the radicalism of B 17, which levels not only all men but all creatures. **20** removes the (unintended) restriction in B 16. **B 18** *creatures þat crepen*: cf. Ps 103–25, echoing Gen 1:25. **21–2** *iustus...vix*: 'That the just man before Jesus on Judgement Day / Shall not be saved, save by the skin of his teeth'. The lively new macaronics improve on the merely repeated B 19.

(i) *Conscience's dinner* **25–51***a* The opening recalls that of the waking interlude prefacing Vision Two, which occurred within a reverie of self-communing (5.9). For the indebtedness of this scene to traditional exegesis on Proverbs ch. 23, see Alford 1995, and to Mt 22, Lawler 1995; and cf. on 40 below. **26** *Clergie*: a figure not encountered since his single speech in Passus XI, to which Will had not been able to reply, though in B 10.330 his *faux-naïf* question (referred to by Ymaginatif at 14.100) was what provoked a tart rejoinder from Scripture. For discussion of the apparent incoherence at this point in the revision, see on C 11.162; B 24b shows Will, chastened by Ymaginatif's instruction, now ready to 'conceive more' (13.223) from Clergy and Scripture. **27–9** mimic the dream-like fluidity of the experience with its sustained verbal repetition (*rome...romede forth* twice, *Resoun* thrice). *Resoun*, the dinner-guest added in C, is especially relevant for the Dreamer's needs; for it is he, the companion of Conscience in Visions One and Two, whom Will finally *resonede* 'berated' at 13.183 after his *rage* against learning had remained unassuaged by Kynde's proffered evidence from experience (13.129–33). In **B** those present at Conscience's dinner are Clergy, his wife Scripture (who helps serve), the Doctor of Divinity, Will and the pilgrim Patience; in **C** are added Reason (as steward) and the pilgrim Piers. **27** *dyne*: an act symbolically marking Will's reconciliation with Clergy / Reason, whom he had offended by his *rude speche* 13.229. **30** *lyk*: ironically suggesting that he might *not* have been a friar (because he did not live up to the ideal), but of course *was*. **32** *woschen*: food being eaten with the fingers, the dust of the journey had to be removed. *dyner*: an afternoon meal, here at a knight's manor-house, with clerical guests at the high table and poor religious wayfarers receiving hospitality (rather than scraps) in the body of the hall (but not on the floor: cf. 42 below and 14.139–40 above). The arrangement is still clearly visible in the late-C14th halls of William of Wykeham's foundations at Winchester and Oxford. **33** *Pacience*: earlier the name of one of the seven sisters who watch over the posterngates at Truth's castle. This important virtue, an active personification only in Vision Four, wears the garb of a 'pilgrim-hermit' and combines an 'inner journey' (Wittig 1972) of thought and prayer with an outward one of dependence on God and charity (Godden 1990; on the figure of Patience see further Baldwin 1990:80 and the learned and provocative but unconvincing account in Aers 2004: 122–33). His separateness from Piers in **C** (confirming and confirmed by the present understanding of *Ilyk* at 34) tells against seeing him in **B** as more than an analogue of the Ploughman. **34** Piers seems to be in Patience's company and to have literally become the poor pilgrim he had planned to be figuratively at 8.93. On the crux *Ilyk* 'likewise' and its implications for the meaning of the passage see *TN*. **35** *for...*: 'for the love of Christ in heaven'. **37–8** contain two important small variants in repeating 31–2, *him* (referring to Piers, someone 'known' to Conscience) and *alle* (a general welcome foreshadowing Conscience's hospitable posture in XXI). **37** *welcomede hem alle*: cf. 'When thou makest a dinner... call the poor' (Lk 14:12–13). **39** *maister*: a synonym for 'doctor' (66), the highest academic degree (here in Divinity, the senior faculty in the medieval university; cf. Pr 60, 10.90). The line may allude to Christ's warning to his disciples against losing spiritual humility by accepting honorific titles: 'Neither be ye called masters: for one is your master, Christ' (Mt 23:10); cf. *CT* III 2184–8. *furste*: like the Pharisees in Lk 14:7, who 'chose the first seats at the table' (the Doctor has the place of honour, on the host's right). B 34 rather confusingly implies an order of seating, but presumably Clergy sits on Conscience's left and Patience remains below with Will (see *TN* further). *worthy*: 'honourable'; with an ironic pun on the co-polyseme 'morally excellent'. **40** *styhlede...styward*: close in sense and wording to *WPal* 1199: *þat oþer was his stiward þat stiȝtled al his meyne* and id. 3841. The servitorial rôle of Reason (previously seen as a bishop at 5.112–13) graphically conveys how the apostolic calling is to service, not rule; see Jn 13:13–16, which is close to Lk 14:7–11, a passage that lies behind this whole scene. **41** *mettes*: suitably enough, since patience is what Will lacked in his *rage* against Clergy and Reason, and what will be tested as he listens to the Doctor speak. **42** *syde table*: a trestle table aligned with the length of the hall below the *deys* or platform for the high table (66). **43–5a** express allegorically how the priestly exponents of the Church's learning are ideally nourished on the Gospels and the writings of the Fathers (as more fully enacted later in the Ploughing allegory at 21.262–74). **45** *Austyn*: see on 11.148; allusion is to his commentaries on Scripture, such as the Tractates on the Gospels and Epistles of St John. *Ambrose* (339–97 AD): bishop of Milan, friend and mentor of Augustine; author of widely used hymns and important treatises on the sacraments and on ethics. As two of the Four Doctors of the Western Church (cf. 21.268ff), both are suitable 'meat' for this Doctor to 'chew on' (see Mann 1979:26–43). **45a** '[And in the same house, remain], eating and drinking such things as they have: [for the labourer is worthy of his hire...]' (Lk 10:7). Christ's instruction to his disciples to accept hospitality from a single household during their preaching mission was cited by friars as justifying this aspect of their manner of life. **46–51** improve on **B**'s complicated contrast of one kind of literal food with another (luxurious with plain), instead clearly opposing 'this food' (spiritual sustenance such as Christ speaks of in Jn 4:34) to the literal 'food of more cost' preferred by the Doctor. The rapidly unfolding metaphor resembles that at 1.145ff in density and complexity, and the portentous moral is underlined by having the lines alliterate exclusively on *m* and *s*. **46**

myhte...chewe: 'didn't find to his taste'. **B 40** *man*: a junior friar accompanying the Doctor, as later at 22.341 (at 10.8–9 the pair are *both* 'masters'). *maner flessh*: 'plain, simply-prepared meat'. **47** *of more cost*: on the ironic suggestions, cf. *worthy* at 39. *potages*: something more elaborate than at 8.185, where it is ordinary labourers' food. **48** *pat...myswonne*: presumably not implying that his present host lives off ill-gotten gains but that the friar, like his predecessor at 3.38, customarily offers those who follow Mede 'easy absolution' in return for support of various kinds. **49–51** *sour...bittere...salte*: the final taste of their food proving unpleasant at the time of reckoning, unless they heal the offence with penitential intercession. *vnsauerly ygrounde*: i.e. if the spices have not been crushed finely enough to blend in the cooking. **50** *Post mortem*: 'after death'. Possibly 'the allegorical name of the mortar' is 'the whole expression from here to *teres*' (*Sk*); but the translinguistic echo of *mortem* in *morter* (and perhaps *mortrewes* 47) 'Platonically' implies a real link between wrongful enjoyment in this life and rightful retribution in the next. Alf*Q* interprets the phrase as 'in purgatory'; but purgatory is not mentioned, and if there is an allusion to 'sinful receipt and abuse of bequests ("*Post mortem*")' (Scase 1989:105), given the belief that heaviest punishment befell those with spiritual gifts they failed to use, the threat may be rather of damnation unless they pray for the souls of benefactors who *myswonne*. **51** *synge*: i.e. intercessory masses and penitential psalms. **51a** 'You who sup on men's sins — unless you pour forth tears and prayers on their behalf, what you devour with relish, you will retch up in pain'. The source is unknown, but the image and other details derive ultimately from Osee 4:8–11: 'They shall eat the sins of my people [*Peccata populi mei comedent*] and shall lift up their souls to their iniquity. And there shall be like people like priest... And they shall eat and shall not be filled...they have committed fornication...and wine and drunkenness take away the understanding'. Here the referent of *They* is probably *sacerdotes* 'the priests', as taken by Gratian (*CIC* 1:391, cit. Alf*Q*); but as used in the C13th anti-mendicant prophecy 'Insurgent gentes' (Kerby-Fulton 1990:156–7), the phrase is aimed at the friars. The image also appears in Huon de Méri's *Tournoiment de l'Antichrist* (*Sk* after Warton; see Owen 1912:104–7). Here the contextual allegorical sense of 'eat sins' will be 'profit from the vices of', i.e. by giving absolution in return for donations. **52–8 52** *as Resoun radde*: Reason is still counsellor to Conscience as at 4.5 above. **54** *breed*: a scriptural text, illustrating the doctrine of Deut 8:3 earlier appealed to by Will (see on 5.86–8). **56** *sour loef*: the sense here not unfavourable as at 49, since this leavened bread will be spiritually nourishing. *Agite penitenciam...*: 'Do penance: [for the kingdom of heaven is at hand]' (Mt 3:2); the message of John the Baptist, already found in the OT in Job

21:2 and Ezek 18:30, and repeated in the NT in Ac 2:38 and Apoc 2:5 (Alf*Q*). Conscience will prescribe penance again at 21.67, and its importance has been accepted by Will in the passage cited under 54 above. **57** *Dia perseuerans*: 'the potion of perseverance', playing 'Platonically' on the Gk *dia* 'medicinal drug' (used at 20.47) and Lat *diu* 'long', in allusion to Christ's assurance that 'he that shall *persevere unto the end*, he shall be saved' (Mt 10:22), and perhaps echoing his promise of the 'meat... which endureth (*permanet*) unto life everlasting' (Jn 6:27). See further Schmidt 1987:92, 1992:xli–ii, and *TN* for defence of the reading.

B 51–4 are removed in **C** as perhaps too metrically unwieldy and verbally complicated, with their array of quotations (mainly from Pss 31 and 50) laid out like items of food on a plate. As these and the other penitential psalms were specially prescribed for recitation during Lent (Alf*Q*), the scene may be meant to contrast the pilgrim-hermit's literal self-denial with the mendicant Doctor's facile verbal asceticism. **52** *he*: Conscience, in whom the act of penitential 'feasting' takes its origin. **52, 53a**² *Beati quorum*; *Et...peccata*: 'Blessed are they [whose iniquities are forgiven]: and whose sins are covered' (Ps 31:1). *Beatus vir*: 'Blessed is the man [to whom the Lord hath not imputed sin]' (Ps 31:2). *makyng*: the happy condition of being forgiven viewed (a trifle illogically) as the 'product' of *not* having sinned; but the absolved state in *PP* is, in line with orthodox teaching, thought of as restoring the condition of innocence (cf. B 14.96). 'Beatus vir' begins Ps 1, but as the second penitential psalm (already quoted), Ps 31 is the likely source here. **53a**¹ *Miserere*...: 'Have mercy on me, O God, [according to thy great mercy. And according to the multitude of thy tender mercies, blot out my iniquity]' (Ps 50:3); the central fourth penitential psalm. The prayer for forgiveness is served on the same platter as the offer of forgiveness, an assurance that sacramental penance is immediately efficacious. **54** *derne shrifte*: confession being an intimate transaction between the sinner and God; the dish is covered, so no one else can see what is in it. *Dixi...tibi*: 'I said: I will confess [against myself my injustice] to [the Lord. And thou hast forgiven the wickedness of my sin]' (Ps 31:5b). Annual confession was particularly encouraged before Easter. This scene shows Patience accepting the discipline that he will urge on Activa Vita in B 14.15–24 (a passage removed in revision to **C**).

59–77 60 Contrition is meant for all as the 'food' that sustains a sincere spiritual life. **61** *pytaunce*: a little portion (discreetly ordered by the host in **B** and provided by the 'cook' in **C**) appropriate to Patience, whose special vocation is to fasting and self-denial. **61b–61a** 'For this shall every one that is holy pray [to thee] in a seasonable time' (Ps 31:6). The contextual referent of *this* is 'forgiveness' or 'the grace of repentance' and that of *seasonable time*

'now, always' or more specifically 'the penitential season of Lent'. **62** *conforted*: 'cheered (with food, refreshment)'. *bothe*: 'as did'; the friendly service of this pair contrasts with their attitude earlier when Will impatiently disputed with them. **63** '[A sacrifice to God is an afflicted spirit]: a contrite and humbled heart, O God, thou wilt not despise' (Ps 50:19). **66a** '[Woe to you that are wise in your own eyes, and prudent in your own conceits]. Woe to you that are mighty to drink wine' (Is 5:22). The bracketed verse before the one quoted has special relevance to the Doctor's situation, as will appear. This Isaian 'woe' is linked with another familiar Pauline text against gluttony (Phil 3:18–19) in goliardic verses ascribed to Walter Map in his *De Avaritia et Luxuria Mundi* 89–90: 'Vae! vae vobis fortibus ad bibendum vina, / quorum deus venter est, hominis sentina' (Wright 1841:165). **71** *Poules*: the Doctor's sermon at St Paul's Cross outside the Cathedral (inside before the Dean, in **B**) having focussed on the Apostle's own sufferings, that in **C** more on the need for all Christians to suffer for love of God. **73** *how pat...what*: 'about Paul, and what suffering...' (anacoluthic). **74a** '[In labour and painfulness],...in hunger and thirst, [in fastings often...]' (II Cor 11:27). **B 67a** 'Thrice was I beaten [with rods]...' (II Cor 11:25)... '[And] of the Jews five times did I receive forty [stripes save one]' (II Cor 11:24). **77** 'There is danger in false brethren' (after II Cor 11:26).

78–85 are more obviously parenthetical in **B** (because of *write* B 71, with its breach of decorum) than in **C** where, with no intrusion of Will-the-author, the sentiments could arguably form part of Will-the-Dreamer's mutterings to his *mette* and continue without break at 86. **C** softens the tone, conceding that it could quote an elaboration on the Pauline text but will refrain so as not to upset brother-Christians, whereas **B** insists on giving the inflammatory text in Latin for the benefit of the *litterati*. **78–9** *Holy Writ...fals frere*: an opportunistic (and anachronistic) perversion of the Pauline *falsus frater* that uses St Francis' humble self-designation as 'brother' to attack the whole *secte* of mendicants. **80** The sentiment recalls that of Trajan at B 11.213, a line from a 20-line passage revised out at that point. **82** *fyue*: 'five (orders of)'. **83** *this*: the text quoted in **B** *with* introductory 'gloss'. **B 73a** 'Let everyone be on guard against a brother [= 'friar'], since, as they say, "there's danger in false brothers [friars]"'. No exact source is known, but similar utterances appear in anti-mendicant writings (Alf*Q*).

86–107 86–7 admiringly enunciate the friar's academic qualifications only to deflate them with a parenthetic gibe at his other less commendable kind of 'greatness'. **88** *vs pore*: echoing Trajan on the Christian gentry's duty of hospitality to the poor 'when [they] maken festes' (12.103). No direct judgement on the host can be intended, since he has invited a learned (and presumably devout) religious, and 'none kyne riche' (12.104). But since **L** later makes the hospitable Conscience evince blindness to the plausible 'falseness' of (at least some) mendicants at a crisis in the defence of Unity (22.242), he may have judged the knightly classes especially susceptible to the suave address of highly educated friars. **90** *wille*: the tart pun on his name bringing out the still unreformed character of the Dreamer, whose wish, even as toned-down in **C**, too readily recalls Envy's at B 5.102. **B 83** *Mahoun*: 'the Devil' (as at 20.293); the name of a pagan god (corrupted from *Mahomet*) popularly supposed to be worshipped by the Moslems. **93** *iurdan*: originally a vessel with bulb-shaped body and narrow neck widening at the top, used by physicians for urine specimens (whence applied to a chamber-pot). A coarse allusion to the Dominican William Jordan (Marcett 1938) may be allowed since it is Will who is speaking, though that would be hard to reconcile with Leaute's rules for moral satire in 12.33–41*a* (which are called forth in response to Will's anger against another friar). The contextual relevance of the dispute between Jordan and the anti-mendicant Durham monk Uhtred of Boldon is urged by Middleton 1987:31–2n. **94** *purgatorie on erthe*: penitential sufferings that will shorten a person's time in purgatory (cf. 9.185). **95–6** *Lat be...se*: advice to act on what Will asserted was Dowel: 'To se moche and soffre al' (13.221). **96** *may*: 'can (eat)'. **97** *penaunce*: Patience's humorous pun serving to counter, while sympathising with, his *mette*'s indignation. **98** *gothelen*: harshly recalling Glutton's porcine rumblings at 6.397. *gynnen*: '(he will) proceed to'. **100** *preuen hit*: implying that the Doctor has dialectical skill enough to argue a conclusion favourable to himself from the unlikeliest premisses. *Pocalips*: alluding to the goliardic *Apocalypse of Golias* attributed to Walter Map, which has a description of greedy abbots (Wright 1841:341–80). *Aueroy (Auereys* **B**): either Aurea, a Spanish solitary who drank only what she could distil from cinders, or Avoya, a saint fed with bread from heaven (*Sk*); or an imaginary saint (the **B** form echoing *Auarice*) suited to the Doctor, whose own 'passion' would presumably result from over-indulgence. Middleton (1987), favouring Marcett's proposed link with Friar Jordan, suggests that the name is a corruption of 'Averroes', the Spanish Moslem Aristotelian philosopher (*c.* 1126–98) whose preference for physical science over spiritual and moral had been supposedly espoused by the Dominicans, and that its use shows the Doctor to represent a purely carnal understanding of moral apologetics. But this does not fit well with 'Passion', and identification of the 'saint' remains uncertain. **103** *take...at*: in its earlier use at 12.77 clearly meaning 'appeal to' but here, in the light of B 94 *testifie of*, rather 'deliver testimony concerning'. *trinite*: taken as '*the* Trinity' by *Pe*; but *a* here (as at 111) indicates as referent rather the 'Dowel' Triad. **104** *of* (*after* **B**): 'concerning'; **C**'s removal of the punning *repetitio* on *after* is noteworthy.

108–38 110 *carpede*: presumably on 'the life of Dowel'. **111** *me* (*vs* **B**): a small revision showing Will's important rôle in this scene; Conscience's look down from the high table is an invitation to him to speak. **112** *Dowel... Dobest*: Will's question is the one Patience recommended at 107. **113** *dronke*: the deadly parenthesis demonstrating how much louder actions speak than words. The scene recalls Map's satiric parody of the sacred rites: 'Dum coenas celebrat abbas cum fratribus...vinumque geminis extollis manibus...calix inebrians in manu strenui' (*Golias* 361–7). **114–15** cover the prohibitive Commandments and express (in negative form) the same doctrine as Gal 5:14 (*Pe*), that 'all the law is fulfilled in one word: *Thou shalt love thy neighbour as thyself.*' This verse from Lev 19:18 occurs shortly after that quoted at 12.35 in the Leutee scene. **117a** echoes Study's words at 11.65 shortly after attacking friars who preach at St Paul's (11.54–69). *passeth*: either 'do, perform' or 'excel in, surpass' (MED s.v. *passen* v. 13 (d)). The sense 'transgress' (ib. 10a) would require *R–K*'s reading *nouthe* for *nouhte* in 116 (rejected in *TN*). **118a** '[Blessed be the Lord God of Israel]: because he hath visited and wrought the redemption [of his people]' (Lk 2:68); from the canticle of Zachary. Since the mission of all Christian preachers is 'To give knowledge of salvation to his people' (Lk 2:77), the sarcasm in this reference to the friar's visit (and 'redemption') is hard to miss. **119** *syke freres*: both these and the *yonge children* (?novices) of B 110 doubtless protesting if offered only 'penitents' food' while the doctor fed on *mortrews and poddynges*. **120** *in die iudicii...*: 'on judgement day', a standard Biblical phrase (e.g. Mt 12:36). The idea of 'Dowel' (Good Works) 'accusing' those who fail in the corporal works of mercy (of which the first was to feed the hungry) alludes to Mt 25:31–46 and echoes the earlier reference to Dowel as intercessor on Doomsday at 9.338–45. **B 111** *permute*: a witty choice of word, given its specialised canonical sense 'exchange of benefices between two clerics, one receiving compensation for the difference in value' (something regarded as simony; see Alf*G* s.v.). Will means that he stands to gain, at least in a material sense. **122/3** The full final rhyme (echoed by the identical rhyme at 126/7) restores a sense of 'courteous' calm to the dinner-table conversation by inviting repetition of the question, but without suggesting a provocative answer. **125** The answer, however, differs from his first casual reply and shows the Doctor rising to the challenge as he proposes 'obedience (in laypeople), instruction (by the clergy), and the union of obedience and instruction in a higher class of cleric'. **128a** '[But] he that shall do and teach, he shall be called great (in the kingdom of heaven **B**)' (Mt 5:19). The text was earlier cited by Scripture at A 11.196*a* in defining Dobest as 'a bishop's peer'; but the Doctor (ironically unapt an exemplar though he may be) more probably means learned mendicants like himself than the episcopal order as a whole. Alan of Lille's *Summa* evokes this text to warn: 'Qui enim docens non facit, Christo contradicit' (*PL* 210:184). **129** *þou*: the intimate pronoun used to Clergy (by contrast with the formal ȝoure to the Doctor at 123) suggesting familiarity such as that of a country knight with the parish priest of his church. **130–8** Clergy's reply, removing some of the obscurities of **B**, is adroitly adapted to prepare for the striking intervention of Piers. **130–1** 'As far as I am concerned, definition of Dowel is not a topic to be raised for discussion outside the theology faculties'. **B 120–1** The Seven Arts are at 11.97 Scripture's *sib*, a term not usually applied to one's children and (even if the constraints of metre are recognised) one inconsistent with their being *her* children (*Sk*). The inconsistency is certainly conceptual, as the Arts do not follow but precede Scripture in the order of studies. *castel...lif*: recalling Wit's allegory at 10.128ff where, under the authority of Dowel, Inwit and his *five* sons defend the *lady* Life. **132** Though it is not clear where Piers has been sitting, his presence at the end of the hall (ȝent) contrasts strongly with the B-Text's mere mention of him as *oon Piers*, 'a certain Piers' at 124; and Clergy's reluctance to analyse Dowel is now due to 'love' for Piers, not simply deference towards his objections. *inpugnede ones*: since **134** alludes broadly to such earlier passages as 7.196 (Truth as humble and faithful), 237 (love and *lele* / *lowe* speech), 8.43–4*a* (humility), 214–19 (love and fidelity), Clergy seems unlikely to intend one specific utterance of the Plowman (could such a passage be found). Perhaps he is meant to be recalling Piers' quarrel with the priest in B 7.130–38*a* (excised, however, in **C**) or the powerful case for love and against learning made by Trajan, Piers's surrogate. All three elements come together in the Emperor's speech (12.131, B 11.166) and *lowe herte* appears in the Pardon (9.184, B 7.62). **135, 137** *preue*(*th*): Piers's position being based on authority rather than reason; but since Christ himself is cited, the 'text' is assumed without argument to be the essence of reason. **136** 'Thou shalt love [the Lord thy] God [with thy whole heart] and...thy neighbour [as thyself]' (Mt 22:37, 39); 'Lord, who shall dwell [in thy tabernacle?]' (Ps 14:1); see on 2.38–9*a*. As *Pe* notes, vv 3–4 of this psalm answer the question with a definition of Dowel in part identical with the Doctor's first at 114: 'He...that worketh justice...*nor hath done evil to his neighbour*'. **137***a* '[And Jesus said to him: Why callest thou me good?] None is good [but one, that is God]'. **138** *lele...treuthe*: indirect reference to the 'double-natured' God whose sovereign transcendence Christ intimates by insisting that *he* should not be called 'good'.

B 122–30 122 Clergy finds difficulty in reconciling the idea of right action as understood by moral philosophy (based on Aristotle's *Ethics*, to which the Arts course immediately led) and religious morality as taught by the Church. **124** Clergy's reticence in the face of Piers's objection seems to imply knowledge of Trajan's impassioned response to Scripture at 12.76ff (at which Clergy must be presumed present). *vs alle*: philosophers and theologians alike. **125** *saue loue one*: a sentiment like Trajan's at 12.94–6, even the wording echoing his 'ley þer a bene / Or *eny science* vnder sonne'. **128** *infinites*: 'limitless, boundless things' (Middleton 1972:169–78).

139–66*a* The two versions diverge considerably at this point and the revision, while equally dramatic, becomes even more obscure in its use of *aenigma*. **139–49** Piers's words are offered to 'prove' the assertions Clergy attributed to him and said he *could* prove; so in effect this passage of **C** not so much replaces as completes B 131–5*a*, where Conscience appeals to Patience's experience (of suffering) as a source of knowledge of Dowel. **139** *Pacientes vincunt*: 'the patient (or, 'those who suffer') conquer'; a phrase, quoted three times in each version, derived from the apocryphal *Testament of Job* 27:10 (Baldwin 1990:72). Paralleled in Chaucer (*CT* V 773–5: 'Pacience...venquysseth' and, recalling 13.198, *CT* X 658–60: 'Pacience...maketh a man lyk to God'), the thought is Stoic in origin and echoes the Dreamer's 'philosophical' definition of Dowel at 13.221. But it has a clearly religious resonance here, evoking NT texts that explicitly link this virtue with Christian Dowel: '[God] will render to every man...who, according to patience in good work (*patientiam boni operis*) seek[s]...eternal life' (Rom 2:6–7). Baer 2001 notes the similarity of thought to *DC* I.38: *Quem superare potes, interdum vince ferendo / maxima enim morum semper patientia virtus*. **140** *perpetuel pees*: synecdoche for *God*, which word glosses it in 141. Peace is a divine attribute in Ps 84:11, both 'peace of God' and 'God of peace' are common Pauline locutions (Phil 4:7, Rom 15:33), and it is conjoined with Patience at 7.273. *þat Y saide*: the maxim of 139, or what Clergy reported in 134ff. **142** 'Learn, teach, love God (your enemies **B**)'. As Alf*Q* notes, this has the character of a school maxim, to which **L** may have added 'enemies' from Mt 5:44 and 'God' from Mt 22:37. **B 140** *Loue*: a fleeting personification of Patience's beloved (and Peace's at B 18.181) that foreshadows the allegory of the Tree of Patience / Charity as Anima will describe it at 16.9–10. **143–4** *enemy...coles*: from Prov 25:21–2, quoted at Rom 12:20 by St Paul with the comment: 'Be not overcome by evil: but overcome evil by good'; the complementary command not to be unkind to one's fellow-Christian is taught by the Samaritan, a more fully 'emergent' version of Piers, at 19.217. Hot coals symbolise in context the 'mortification' of someone receiving only kindness in return for injury; but they were commonly interpreted as the heat of love that melts an enemy's hardness of heart (as in *AW* 206/10). **144–9** memorably convey the paradox of how human action is 'transformed' when its motive

Commentary

is charity (on the operation of this curious 'figure of thought', which might be called *transsumptio*, see Simpson 1986:161–83). **146** *eft and eft*: recalling Mt 18:20–1, 5.39, with the difference that in **L** the *suffering* of (literal or figurative) hostile blows undergoes 'transsumption' into the *giving* of (purely figurative) 'blows of charity'. **150–1** Piers's sudden departure distantly recalls that of Jesus at Emmaus (Lk 24:31) and is the first hint in **C** that he is a *figura* of Christ, a hint confirmed by the important final mention of him at 16.338 before his re-appearance at 20.8. But Piers here clearly possesses the same identity as in Vision Two and exists on the same allegorical plane with the Dreamer and the other personified figures, as Reason's ability to accompany him attests. **152** *ran after*: the immediate attraction of the personage who embodies Justice to the one who embodies Love anticipates a similar pursuit of the Samaritan by the Dreamer, Faith and *Spes* at 19.81. In the light of **B**'s ending, **C** might even hint at the need for the episcopate in a divided Christendom to 'follow' or 'look for' an *ideal* 'pope', if he can be found. Reason's disappearance from the poem leaves Conscience to work alone (Whitworth 1972) in the final two visions, which will concentrate on the spiritual integrity of the individual within the Church. *riht...yede*: 'went straight off with [Piers]'; the uncomfortable under-sense 'justice departed with [Reason]' cannot be decisively excluded. **153** *no mo*: the 'staff' having withdrawn, and of the guests, bishop and 'pope' departed, leaving only knight, priest, hermit, dreamer (and theologian) to continue the discussion. **154** *Pacience*: taking Piers's position (and his place), though not yet asked formally by Conscience to speak. **155** *litel thyng*: 'little'; '(something that is a) small thing'. *coueyteth*: simply 'desires', without the subtly punning *repetitio* of **B**. **156** *and...to*: 'if I really set my mind to it'. Patience's brag has nothing to do with 'diplomacy as opposed to war'; his way to 'win' France is to 'lose' the greedy desire to win it, the motto-phrase re-quoted at 158a proclaiming this paradoxical notion of 'conquest' to be that of Christ as later explained by Conscience at 21.50. **158** *a partye*: either (understanding *to* after *take*) 'a part (of authoritative tradition)' or (taking the phrase as *take...of*) 'partly, in part'. **160** *tonge*: metonymy for 'words of contumely', alluding to Mt 5:11. **161** *pacience*: here making explicit the referent of *it* B 164, as a 'little thing' (vouched for by the speaker who exemplifies the virtue) to be carried interiorly in all circumstances. Its closeness to heavenly charity is brought out by the gloss-citation 166a, which implies a view of the latter as essentially (not just accidentally) love that 'suffers all' (cf. I Cor 13:4, 7: 'Charitas *patiens* est,...omnia *suffert*,... omnia sustinet'). **163** *cart-whel*: an image alluding to the emblematic 'Wheel of the Virtues' familiar in the period as an allegorical diagram (Kaske 1963:55–7) in which PATIENTIA is situated in the corner made by the spokes.

crow croune: possibly a crow's skull used as a charm, although the term 'head of the crow' is an alchemical term of art for the process of calcination (MED s.v. *hed* n. (1), 9(d)). Galloway 1995:94–6 ingeniously interprets the phrase in terms of the esoteric riddle-tradition of the early C14th English *Secretum philosophorum* to mean 'head [= *caput* or first syllable] of the Latin word for "crow" (*corvus*)', i.e. *cor* 'heart', and the '*cor*ner' of the cartwheel to signify a 'fourth part of the *rota* or wheel' i.e. the letter R which, when added to C and O, gives COR. This explanation, which does not force the lexical sense overmuch, is rather more persuasive than his reading of 3.479 (see above and further on B 156 below), and accords well with the general meaning of the passage. 'Patience carried everywhere in the heart' is certainly what the speaker seems to have in mind. **166** *ne be*: elliptical for 'nor (will he) be'. **166a** '[Fear is not in charity: but perfect] charity casteth out fear, [because fear hath pain]...' (I Jn 4:18).

B 149–72a express the mystery of 'patient charity' in a riddle which, though entirely recast in **C**, remains enigmatic in the revision. **149** This perhaps self-evident assertion becomes in **C** a general statement of the contrast between true love and selfish desire. **150–1** *coueiteþ* (1, 2): the subject of a benign 'transsumption' of meaning like that noted under B 144–9. **151** *Kynde loue*: 'natural', 'true' and 'kind / gracious' are all meanings of the epithet in this phrase, which earlier occurred at 3.451; eight variants of the word *love* appear in 140–50. *speche*: a friend's precious conversation, the only 'possession' of his that true affection desires. **152–7** The basic image is that of a bundle tied with a strap on which is inscribed the tag of 152b. The riddle is correctly given by *Sk* 'the general solution...Charity, exercised with Patience' and the passage interpreted as 'a general reference to the great events of Christianity' (more particularly, the redemptive events of Passion Week that provide the ground-pattern of Vision Six). Detailed discussions by Smith 1961, Kaske 1963 (rev. 1969), Goodridge 1966:299–308 and Schweitzer 1974 provide more or less satisfactory attempts to 'undo it' in detail, and Baldwin 2001:102–4 attempts to relate the riddle to particular events in the peace-process between England and France in June 1377. **152** *half... lyne*: playing on both the grammatical and liturgical associations of the Latin b-half. One allusion is to the phrase *Tene hanc lampadem* 'hold this lamp' from Priscian's *Grammar* 'illustrating grammatical "rulership" by the *ex vi transitionis*' (Kaske 1963:240–1), the other to *half* of the priest's words to the baptizand during the solemn ceremony of the Easter Vigil, *Accipe lampadem ardentem* [*et irreprehensibilem: custodi baptismum tuum: serva mandata*] 'Hold the burning light that cannot be taken away; [keep your baptismal vows; observe the commandments]' (*Sarum Manual*, cited Schweitzer). The lit lamp is in the exegetical tradition a symbol of holy charity (see on 1.184). Galloway, however, sees the 'lamp' here not as an allusion to the grammatical expression but as a metaphoric substitution for 'moon' in the *Lune dimidium* phrase of the Harley 3362 riddle discussed under 3.479, and renders 152a as 'the "half-a-lamp" line in Latin' (1995:91). But this is unacceptable, for grammar, syntax and metre all show that L's compound is not 'half a lamp' but 'half a lamp-line', and the indefinite *a* cannot be rendered 'the'. Another interpretation of *laumpe lyne* (Bradley 1910), as referring to the cord by which a lamp was suspended, conjectures a Latin word *cordella* as the key to the riddle, 'half' of this word being *corde* 'hert', an apt referent for *perinne* in 153 (and in harmony with Galloway's comment cited under 161 above). *Ex...*: '(drawn) from the (grammatical) power of transitivity', that 'by which [in Latin] a [transitive] verb "rules" [governs] its direct object in the accusative case' (Kaske 1963:236). The terminology for analysing syntax called *regimen* is discussed by Bland 1988, one given source (130–1) being Villedieu's *Doctrinale*, a work L cites at 11.267=C 12.155a. The exact interpretation of this compressed figure is hard to establish, but the general sense seems to be that 'the baptismal vows should "directly govern" Christians' actions and provide a secure "fastening" for the virtue (patience) that will sustain them through life'. The allegorisation of grammatical relations in B 13.151 anticipates that of the elaborate 'direct and indirect relation' in the *mede / mercede* figure of C 3.332–405a. Given the equal importance of the liturgical as of the grammatical context, *transicionis* may plausibly be taken as a punning allusion to *transitus* 'passage', i.e. the Hebrews' crossing of the Red Sea in Ex 12:11 (Schweitzer 315). This is the key event for the religion of the Jews, recalled in the Passover, and for Christians commemorated in the Holy Saturday liturgy as a 'type' of Christ's passion, death and resurrection. Galloway's interpretation of this phrase as 'the force of *transitio*' that 'may evoke the multiple procedures and "transitions" [of the riddle-tradition]' (1995:94) may register as over-ingenious. But Baldwin's rendering of the Latin phrase as 'from the passing over of power' and as perhaps referring 'to the transition of royal power (*vis*) from one reign [Edward III's] to the next [Richard II's]' must be impossible, since the phrase is *ex vi transitionis* not *ex transitione vis*. **153** *perinne*: here and at 158 having as referent *kynde loue* 151 (as *Sk* recognised), as does *herwith* 157. **154–5** 'As a symbol of [Holy] Saturday, which originally established the calendar [of the Christian year], together with all the significance of the [Mass of the] Wednesday of the following [Easter] week; the full of the moon providing the power of both [days]'. Baldwin's interpretation (2001:103–4) of Wednesday as 24 June 1377, the day on which the Treaty of Bruges (1375) expired and Saturday as 20 June 1377, 'the last complete day in the life of Edward III' carry lit-

tle conviction. But she is undeniably right that Patience's speech is urging on the government a 'patient foreign policy' in relation to France, which renewed hostilities in June 1377. **154** *signe*: perhaps with specific reference to the *sign* of Confirmation (Schweitzer), another sacrament customarily administered on the vigil of Easter (from the date of which the Church's moveable feasts were reckoned). **155** *wit*: 'meaning', i.e. the fulfilment of Christ's promises in the Second Coming and the Last Judgement, together with the necessity of Christ's suffering, as stated in Ac 3:18 (read in the Epistle of the day). **156** *myddel... moone*: the Paschal full moon, a metonym for the Christian Easter; the event from which stems the efficacy of baptism and confirmation, sacraments 'governed' directly by the *vis* 'power' of Christ's *transitus* 'passover' from death to life (Kaske 1969:245). *The myddel of the mone* must mean 'half-way point of the lunar cycle, full of the moon' (see MED s.v. *middel* n. 4); so Galloway's attempt (1995:87) to see it as equivalent to 'half of a moon' in the 'Oxford' riddle cited at 3.479, which has no lexical support, cannot be accepted. **157** *it*: i.e. *Charitas patiens* (I Cor 13:4), 'Charity, exercised with patience' (*Sk*). **158** *Vndo it*: 'Undo the bundle' / 'Resolve the riddle'. **164** *it*: as in 157. **164a** 'Charity fears nothing'; see on C 166a. **167–76** keep the essential sense of **B 165–72**, but remove some of the awkwardness of expression. The tone of the *impossibilia* recalls that of a text like Mt 21:21 (on faith) or I Cor 13:7 (on charity); in the end, patient charity is invincible and will reveal its power to those in power (for an interesting comparison of L's posture with that of Wycliffite critics of Church involvement in war, see Somerset 2001). **B 168–9** *my3t...redels*: 'the power (that is the solution) of this riddle [i.e charity]'. The suggestion of E. Kirk (cited Somerset, 110n1) that it is the *Fiat voluntas tua* of B 14.49 is atttractive (if that comes somewhat late to be a gloss on a riddle 350 lines earlier); but 'obedience to the will of God as exemplified in the Passion' could well be regarded as the supreme act of *charitas patiens* shown by Christ towards mankind. *wicchecraft... wit*: because such influence, though commonly thought of as acquired through magic, is really a form of wisdom. **172** *dido*: found only here as a common noun; the name of the Queen of Carthage whose tragic story in Bk IV of Virgil's *Aeneid* moved Augustine to tears (*Conf.* I xiii 1). Its original use in **B** was perhaps suggested by Patience's *quene* at 170, and the Doctor's bright answer may imply, 'What you say has as little chance of happening as poor Dido had of getting Aeneas to stay with her when Jove was against it'. **173** *wit...worlde*: deliberately rejecting Patience's contention, but going further to deny that wisdom (even 'worldly') plays any part in the real world of passion-driven politics. **174** *Pope...enemyes*: an allusion to the Great Schism of September 1378, which was preceded by armed conflict at Rome between Pope

Commentary

Urban VI and a mercenary army supporting the cardinals who sought to depose him. Freshly topical at the presumed time that **L** wrote **B** (1378–9), the Schism was to last another thirty years; and during the period of composition of **C** Urban led a major campaign against his former ally the King of Naples (1383–4). **B 176** *kynges*: Charles VI of France and Richard II of England. Political tension between the two countries during the Schism was heightened by English acknowledgement of Pope Urban and French support for the Avignonese anti-pope Clement VII, who was excommunicated by Urban VI in November 1378. The close entanglement of the two issues is seen in the last major C14th incident of the Hundred Years War, England's intervention in the Flemish revolt against French rule, culminating in the disastrous 'Crusade' of 1383 against the Clementists, led by Henry Despenser, Bishop of Norwich (McKisack 1959:145–7, 429–33; Houseley 1983). **C**'s excision of this line and revision of *peple* 77 to *parties* **C** 175 may reflect the truce with France of Jan. 1384, which lasted a year, and thus point to a date for the composition of this Passus round 1384–5 (when hostilities were renewed, they were largely confined to the struggle for supremacy in Spain). **175–6** *putte...conseyle*: a gesture of complacent superiority that will meet an unexpected check (albeit toned down in **C**).

B 179–99 179b expresses a commonly held view (see Pr 47–50), while failing to distinguish the speaker as an inner or spiritual 'pilgrim' (like Piers at B 7.120–1, who also chose penitential 'food') from such as the 'professional' pilgrim at B 5.515ff=C 7.159ff. *lye*: referring to his unrealistic claims for the power of patience at 166–78 (for assessments of these see Baldwin 2001 and Somerset's 'Response'). **180** *loude...curteisliche*: i.e. in rejecting the Friar's low-voiced (and discourteous) 'sidelining' of Patience. **182** *go*: in face of the Doctor's dismissal of the 'pilgrim', a surprising decision by the host to share Patience's journey (allegorically, adopt his manner of living). The omitted 17-line passage explicitly rejects 'learning' (keen intellect) for 'suffering' (good will) and heightens the emotional tone. The effect is to make Conscience seem reminiscent of such austere contemporary 'Lollard knights' as Sir John Clanvowe, author of *The Two Ways*. The tension in the interchange between knight and priest (Clergy), marked by the repetition of one speaker's phrases by the other (183a, 188a; 190, 202a), foreshadows a breach that lasts till the moment Conscience will call (in vain) for Clergy's help at 376, when it is too late. **184–8** Clergy's incredulous rejoinder shows him less worldly-wise than the Doctor, but still (despite his expressed respect for Piers 124–30) sceptical of Patience's seeming independence of institutional authority. **185** *yereȝeues*: implying that he will become a wandering minstrel (like Haukyn, whom they will soon meet). *rede...redels*: an etymological pun that stands out

if the line is read as T-type; clerkly interest in riddles as a part of rhetorical study is noted by Galloway 1995:93. **186** *bring yow*: an eirenic offer to meet the distinguished layman's desire for the pure milk of scripture to sustain his religious life. *book...lawe*: perhaps JOB, the 'last word' on the theme of 'patience'; an open but tactful hint that the knight (note the polite *ye* 184 as against Conscience's *þee* at 189) needs for this purpose nothing he could not learn from the Scriptures that are in Clergy's charge. But though Conscience seems driven by the same desire for *kynde knowyng* 'direct first-hand acquaintance' of Dowel as was Will, he seeks it not in books but in *preue*, i.e. in 'seeing much and suffering more' (B 11.421). **190** *proud*: Conscience 'speaks fair' to make clear he is not rejecting one 'sect' (friars) for just another (hermits), but responding as befits the spiritual 'timbre' he discerns in the two representatives of these ways of life. **191–2** *folk here*: the indefiniteness conveying a chilly politeness, since the *folk* can only be the Friar, just as *wight* 193 (echoing *wye* 191) can only be the Hermit. But the fourfold repetition of *wil* in 191–4, the half-rhyme on *fulle / wille* (countering Clergy's on *lawe / knowe* 186/7) and the emotive words *mood* and *moorne* leave no doubt that Conscience is firmly choosing the affective / volitional over the intellectual / cognitive as the best way to Dowel (on this key contrast see Simpson 1986:1–23). **193** *goode wil*: the importance of *bona voluntas* (Lk 2:14) to **L**'s thinking on the mystery of 'prevenient grace' (*gratia gratis data*) is preserved in C 14.24–5. Its synonymy with *trewe wille* here points up the crucial relevance of this concept to the situation of 'virtuous pagans', a point already made by Ymaginatyf at B 12.286–7=C 14.211–12 (with which cf. B 11.146–8=C 12.82–5). *was...fulle*: 'could never have an adequate price put on it'. **194** *tresor...wille*: the clear echo of Holy Church's words on *treuthe* (B 1.207) betokening less a shift in the poem's direction than a belated discovery through experience (*kynde knowyng* B 142–5) of their real meaning. **195** *Maudeleyne*: often identified with the 'woman...in the city, a sinner' of Lk 7:37–50 who anoints Christ with ointment and is forgiven 'many sins...because she hath loved much' (7:47); on 'Mary Magdalen' in *PP* see on 7.137. **196** *Ȝacheus*: the rich tax-collector, 'a man that was a sinner' (Lk 19:7, paralleling Lk 7:37), whose dramatic disposal of his *tresour* is here judged less valuable spiritually than that of 'Maudeleyne' or the poor widow. *Dimidium...*: 'The half of my goods I give to the poor; [and if I have wronged any man of any thing, I restore him fourfold]' (Lk 19:8). **197–8** are omitted in revision here, having been used in the passage on poverty at C 13.96. **197** *poore widewe*: in Lk 21:1–4; like Mary Magdalen (as described later at 17.21–2), signifying passive acceptance of and total dependence on the divine will. **198** *gaȝophilacium*: 'the treasury' (Lk 21:1). **177–85** carefully revise **B 199–205**, adding fullness and weight to Conscience's speech, dropping the end-rhyme *frere / ere* and making small changes in tone, as with the harsh 'Platonic' self-rhyme Lett*rure* / lett*eth*. But since the words to Clergy are easily audible (not whispered as in **B**), they must (like *fol monye* 182) be meant as an oblique rebuke to the Doctor. The decorous **B** farewell (*curteisliche*; *first* 199) is replaced by the abrupt *sone*, a new asseveration-line added (179), and the good-humoured conclusion to the parting removed. **183** 'They can't recognise the nature of true patience (when they see it) / patience for the gracious thing it is'. **185** *to fynde*: 'discover the whereabouts of' and 'achieve (for myself)', but both implying that it cannot be found with the secular clergy or the religious orders.

B 203–15 203 *no congie*: because expecting to see him again betimes. Allegorically, this represents the priest's expectation that the lord of the manor will quickly tire of his pious whim and come back to his old friend and counsellor. 205b ominously anticipates Conscience's urgent cry at 20 (22).376, which will be followed by his second, desperate decision to 'become a pilgrim'. **205** *forwalked*: a rare word recorded only here and in *WPal* 2236 (also with *wery*). *wilne*: '(that you will) desire to have me advise you'. **206** *soop*: Conscience's acceptance here of his need for priestly support is completely dropped in **C**. **207** *oure partyng-felawe...bope*: a union of clergy and nobility (estates often at odds) in a spirit of loving charity could, he claims, achieve universal peace and 'conversion' of unbelievers. The possible pun on this phrase ('the fellow with whom we take our leave of each other') suggested in Simpson 1986³:64 is contextually improbable, since Conscience is about to *leave* Clergy and *accompany* Patience, and the condition proposed by *If* is an ideal one (hence the subjunctive). **212** The amicable repetition of Conscience's conciliatory phrase *That is soop* does not weaken Clergy's resolve to remain with his given duties in order to 'strengthen' the Christian community, simple and subtle alike ('sacramental confirmation', though reserved for the bishop [B 15.456], *may* also be implied under the *devoir* of the ordained clergy as a whole). But since he understands Conscience's intention (212), his tone in 215 must be taken as neutral, not sceptically ironic.

186–90 form a transitional passage between the two major episodes of Vision Four. **186a** The ironic echo of Pr 49 here and at 191 points the contrast between different kinds of 'pilgrim' and 'pilgrimage'. *grete wille*: 'intense commitment'; a phrase found otherwise only at 12.85, describing the fervour of Gregory's prayer for Trajan's salvation. That the Dreamer is inspired to identify his name with his action in a spontaneous response to the immediate situation need not imply the poet's unqualified endorsement of Conscience's action (here as later at the end of the poem) as normative. **187** *as...vitayles*: the com-

parison's ordinary meaning is 'transformed' (Simpson 1986²); for since Patience is not 'as' ordinary pilgrims, his food will not be 'as' theirs, but the sort he was content to be served at the dinner (cf. 57, 61 and 63 above). *hym and Consience*: patience and conscience are 'friends' in ch. v of Augustine's *De Patientia*: 'patientia amica est bonae conscientiae' (*PL* 40:611–27). **190** These vices are later coupled at 22.297, while the topographical allegory recalls that at 2.90.

(ii) 191–311 The *second episode* of Vision Four, that of Acтiva Vita (Haukyn or *Actyf* in **B**), crosses the passus-boundaries to occupy half of C XVI (all of B XIV). Despite significantly altering **B**'s conception of Actyf (through transferring the descriptions of the sins on Haukyn's soiled coat to the Confession-sequence in Vision Two), **C** retains intact its threefold thematic purpose. This is, first, to contrast with the satirical portrait of a learned friar the more sympathetic (self-)portrait of a 'lewed' layman who, if also 'carnal' (though rather less in **C** than in **B**), is not closed to the call to penitence. Second, to offer Conscience a *preue* of how Patience, like his divine exemplar (13.198), 'suffers' sinners by encouraging rather than condemning their efforts to break free from the grip of vice. Third, more widely, to shift the focus of the poem's concern with salvation from the problem of learning that occupied Vision Three to the experience of *charitas patiens* incarnated in Christ, whose vɪᴛᴀ will dominate the rest of the poem. The dialogue, opening with a question from Patience (197–8), is advanced by another three from Actyf (248, 276, 281–2) that break it into more manageable sections, is followed by Patience's massive homily on patient poverty, and ends with a final two questions expressing Actyf's (and in part the reader's) not unreasonable incomprehension (16.114,116). **194** *he*²: possibly referring to Patience; but if to Actyf, then the adverb marks how great the change in **L**'s conception of him is. **195** *Actiua Vita*: not 'the Active Life as opposed to the Contemplative Life' of contemporary religious discourse (cf. B 6.248) but 'a practical life based on and judged by purely temporal conceptions of goodness' (Maguire 1949 [1969]:195, 200). **196** *Peres prentys...*: the basis of this claim to a connection (allegorically, of the purveyors with the producers of food), one closer than in // B 238, being that Haukyn makes his bread from the corn Piers grows. It affirms the status of people like him as honest working members of the community. **197** *dere frende*: the warmth of Conscience's address here to be contrasted with his sceptical coolness towards Will at 5.89–91.

200–33 200 *wafrer*: a maker and seller of ordinary *wafres*. In the immediate context, however, these appear to be the special wafers used for the Eucharistic host, and *godes gestes* are the communicants (Pe), an addition linking Actyf's rôle more directly with the Church's responsibility for 'feeding' souls. The Latin terms *wafferarius* and *menestrallus* were near-synonymous, since many wafer-sellers customarily provided entertainments (respectable or low) such as Haukyn says he *cannot* (see MED s.v. *minstrel* 2. 'servant, functionary', and cf. Southworth 1989:8–1). **201** *lauhe*: figuratively, since they take pleasure in his fare. **202** *payn*: the choice of the French form suggesting that these are fancy breads like those named at 8.327. **203** *robes*; *gounes*: gifts given only to the most distinguished of 'lords' minstrels', such as the King's (see Bullock-Davies 1978 and Southworth 1989, ch. 4). **204–9** Actyf unrealistically laments his lack of rich rewards for any of a jumble of crude and refined forms of amusement. **204** *lye*: make satirical gibes and innuendoes (about public figures), like the modern 'stand-up comic'. **207** *Farten*: the ability to do this at will was cultivated by low *japeres*, as shown in the marginal illustrations of certain medieval manuscripts. **210/11** The identical rhyme underlines his resentment at their refusal properly to recognise his services (such rhyme similarly heightens the catechetical flavour of the statement at 16. 265/6, 316/17, 17.39/40, 150/1). **214** Parallel **B 237** specifies the Paternoster (said at Mass before the distribution of Communion), a fitting prayer on behalf of the community's food-providers because its fourth petition is 'Give us this day our daily bread.' **216** The wider generality of **C** both removes **B**'s invidious collocation of tonsured clerics with false beggars and makes the important point that Actyf provides for all men, like his master Piers (8.24–5) and Piers's master Truth (21.433–6). **217** *Fro...Mihelmesse*: 'from one end of the year to the next'; the Feast of St Michael the Archangel (Sept. 29), a quarter-day, here also marks the end of one agricultural season and the start of another. *drynke*: a rhetorical exaggeration, obviously. **218** *þe Pope*: figuratively, in that Actyf and his kind provide for every level of society up to the highest, a fact that licenses him to complain about the 'practical' ineffectivenesss of the Church's ministrations. *Sk* takes this as an allusion to Peter's Pence, an ecclesiastical tax paid to the Pope by all; but the sum seems too small to support Haukyn's point. **B 244, 246** play on two senses of *provendre*, 'prebend' and 'provender' (for the Pope's mount, presumably better food than the bean-flour Hunger recommends for beggars at 8.225). But the jest is idle, for while Haukyn might (in hard times) realistically provide 'horse-bread' as a sideline, he could never be entitled to a clerical living. **220** *bulle*: the lead seal (*bulla*), stamped with the heads of SS Peter and Paul on one side and the reigning pontiff on the other, and attached to a papal pardon; 'solid' enough, but lacking any power to put an end to the plague. Actyf seems here to voice the disbelief engendered (as commonly happens) by natural disasters and scandals in the Church among laypeople who looked for material benefits from spir-

itual remedies received in a physical form. **221** *luythere eir*: expressing the belief that plague was caused by corruption of the atmosphere. **B 250** *bocches*: dark-coloured tumours ('buboes') in the groin or arm-pit; the commonest symptom of the bubonic plague, incurable and leading swiftly to death. **222** The wordplay on *bere* (like the *repetitio* on *myhte* in 220, 222) conveys the *lewed* Haukyn's disillusion, which parallels the *lered* Doctor's political cynicism at 173 above, though not excluding the possibility of self-criticism (227ff). **223a** '[And these signs shall follow them that believe]: In my name they shall cast out devils (**B**)...and they shall lay their hands upon the sick: and they shall recover' (Mk 16:17–18). **B 254** *as...sholde*: deliberately equivocal in tone, like the Dreamer-Narrator's remark at 9.327, poised between sullen doubt and a hunger for faith. **224** Actyf articulates an unwillingness to do anything for his fellow-Christians until the head of the Christian community does something for him. **226** *þe power*: 'the power of the keys' (see on Pr 136). *pot...salue*: an image of the healing power Christ gave to the Apostles. Actyf's initial point is that if Peter's successor, the Pope, possesses spiritual power (as Christians are expected to believe), then this should also enable him (as it apparently does not) to heal diseases, as did Peter. **226a** '[But Peter said]: "Silver and gold have I none, but what I have, I give thee. In the name of the Lord [Jesus...], arise, and walk"' (Ac 3:6). No more than his master Piers's psalm-quotations at B 7.116–7 and 124a do these scriptural texts imply that Actyf is *litteratus* (16.116 makes it plain he is not). They function rather to convey symbolically his beliefs about Peter's power and the Sodomites' sinfulness: their content is Actyf's thought, their form directed to the capacities of the poem's 'literate' readers. **227–33** express an anti-mechanistic view of healing, one dependent on conversion of heart, that is hard not to see as authorial, just as the view of pride as punished by plague and dearth is of a piece with the stern prophecies of Reason and the narrator at 5.115–7 and 8.342–53. **231a–33** are adapted from B 14.75–7 and better integrated with the moral argument than **B 261–3**, which loosely connect the need to 'amend' with the need to work if one is to feed oneself. **231a** 'From too much bread and wine worst sins arise'; adapted from Peter Cantor's *Verbum Abbreviatum* CXXXV, 300: 'Et *abundantia panis* causa fuit *peccati* Sodomorum' (*PL* 205:331), and found in Brinton's Sermon 48 (p. 216); cf. also Comestor, *HS* (in *PL* 198:1099). It derives from Ezech 16:49, which significantly adds to excess of food both pride and sloth (*otium* 'rest' 233, = *ociositas* in B 14.76a) as causes of Sodom's sin (though lechery was more commonly linked with *gluttony*, as in *CT* X 839). A variant form of the quotation appears at B 14.76a.

B 261–460 Commentary *on the* transferred parts *of this* 200-*line passage omitted here will be found under* **C VI** *and* **VII**

B 261–460 261–71 Removal in **C** of these lines vividly localising Haukyn in place and time (along with his personal name and vices) transforms the new character Actyf from a fly-blown exemplar of quotidian viciousness into a blunt yet tolerably well-intentioned layman. But though avoiding some repetition and redundancy (e.g. 281 at 303, 295 at 297, 299b at 313b), the change entails loss of poetic richness and thematic subtlety. For Haukyn's capacity to achieve a measure of self-recognition serves dramatically in **B** to differentiate 'contrition' or repentance through sorrow (B 14.16–17a, 320–32) from the Deadly Sins' (often comically ignorant) 'attrition' or repentance from fear in B V. **262** *corn*: synecdoche for 'wafers'; referring to Haukyn's pre-dawn labours at the oven, not (by ellipsis) to Piers's work in the fields. **265** *no3t longe ypassed*: less than a decade, if the accepted dating of **B** (which the lines help to establish) is correct. **266** *Stratford*: Stratford-atte-Bowe in East London, residence not only of Chaucer's Prioress (*CT* A 125) but of many bakers supplying bread for the city. Places their carts stopped at included (according to Stow, p.159) Cheapside and Cornhill (*Wr*). **267–8** The beggars depend on *broke bred* (A 12.70–1), whereas the labourers can buy other food. **270** The year 1370 suffered a great dearth of corn partly because of lack of rain in the early growing season. **271** *Chichestre*: John de Chichester, a wealthy goldsmith, Mayor of London in 1369–70. **272/3** The terminal rhyme in effect marks off as a separate section of the passus a 'portrait' of Haukyn given variety by direct speech at 308–11, 329–42, 363–99 and 405–6; a question from Conscience at 314–15; shifts of narrative perspective to Will at 343 and Patience at 355; and a full-scale *digressio* (410–57) on the origins of sloth that quickly becomes an attack on the nobility's patronage of 'the fiend's disciples' and culpable neglect of 'God's minstrels'. In its first part, 275–313a, pride (including vanity and hypocrisy) is described as it appears on Haukyn's 'coat'; in the second, 314–409 deal with envy, lust, greed, gluttony and sloth; only anger is omitted, and therefore contributes no material to **C**'s revision of the Sins. **273** *Haukyn*: nowadays only a surname, but in origin a familiar form of Harvey or Henry (cf. *Watekyn* 6.70, *Perkyn* 8.1). Harley 1981:97–9 interestingly suggests that it may be a rhyming variant of 'Dawkin', a diminutive form of David, the archetypal repentant sinner, minstrel and exemplar of the active life. **274** *cote...bileuep*: 'a tunic of orthodox Christian faith'; Haukyn's soul, allegorically figured as the white christening robe he was wrapped in at baptism (the scriptural background is discussed in Alford 1974:133–8). **275** *moled*: alluding to the 'spotted garment

[*tunicam maculatam*] which is carnal' of Jude 23 (Frank 1957:71n). **279** 'Pretending to inner or outer qualities that he did not possess'. **285–91** contain details that bring Haukyn's portrait disturbingly close to the Dreamer's own self-depiction (285a recalls B Pr 3, 287 applies to much of the poem's satirical writing, and 291 recalls B 11.414). The references to *wit* in 289 and 292–3 that strengthen this link are removed in revision, to leave Actyf a more *lewed* type of figure. **290** *as...name*: 'How best to get a reputation for sexual prowess'. **313** *and...hymselue*: 'and (serve as a means to win their) praise for himself'. **313a** '[For do I now persuade men, or God? Or do I seek to please men?] If I [yet] pleased men, I should not be the *servant* of Christ' (Gal 1:10). 'And in another place: "No man can *serve* two masters... [You cannot *serve* God and mammon"]' (Mt 6:24). The texts are connected through this common theme: Haukyn's 'gospel' is *secundum hominem* 'according to man' (Gal 1:11) since, although he claims to serve Piers as his 'prentice', his behaviour reveals his true 'master' to be the spirit of this world. **323** *leue...chide*: '(and with) a tongue quick to quarrel'. **340** *of Shordych Dame Emme*: some notorious contemporary character, doubtless she of the workmen's song at Pr 226. Shoreditch lay just N of Bishopsgate outside the City wall. **357** *good...God*; **370** *gaderen...good*: on these significant chimes see Schmidt 1987[2]:135. **379** echoes B 1.192. **390–1** The sense of these difficult lines (cut in **C**) seems to be that 'even when performing a kind act, he clung inwardly to his grasping and loveless avarice.' As well as the contrast between the (reluctant) outward act and true inner attitude, the use of the polysemous *conscience* pointedly warns how the 'negative scruples' that the unconverted experience (about what they might lose through kindness) vitiate 'charitable' works and make them a further occasion for sin. It seems to be intimated here that only when restored to a state of grace can men produce acts which are truly virtuous, because arising from heartfelt love of God. **400** recalls B 5.307. **410–57** are transferred entire with small changes to C 7.69–118a (q.v.); they bring the argument round again through denunciation of the *mysproud man* (436) to the theme of the metaphorical 'minstrels' whose services comfort men at the hour of death. **458–60** return to where Haukyn was left at 409 as Conscience begins his characteristically 'courteous' enquiry into why Actyf has neglected to clean the stains of sin from his soul by making sacramental confession (see B 14.18). At one level, this encounter represents a way of broadening the knight Conscience's experience of the common man in preparation for his rôle as leader in Passūs XXI–XXII. The experience is made possible by the mediation of the hermit, the spiritual guide who moves between different levels of society.

B XIV *begins;* C XV *continues*

B 14.1–28 continue the dialogue of Conscience with Haukyn that will conclude at 320–32; both passages are deleted as part of **C**'s transformation of the latter from *l'homme moyen sensuel* to a morally more neutral type of the common man. Also much altered is Patience's almost lyrical assurance to Haukyn of spiritual sustenance, which ends by tellingly contrasting dearth, over-abundance and sufficiency (70–4). **2** *slepe þerinne*: suggesting spiritual slothfulness, of which unwillingness to change one's working clothes at night is an apt figure; allegorically, the robe of Christian living is to be worn at all times. **3a** 'I have married a wife; and therefore I cannot come' (Lk 14:20); the excuse of one of those invited in St Luke's Parable of the Supper, occurring shortly after the verses (12–14) quoted at 11.190*a*=C 12.104*a*, which lie behind 13.442–54=C 7.101–13. Alford (1974:133) interprets 'wife' allegorically as 'concupiscence'; but the collocation with servants and children suggests more widely 'preoccupation with the things of this world'. **5** *laued*: intermittent bouts of reform occasioned by illnesses and commercial setbacks, from which Haukyn always slips back into his old ways. **16–28** aim to show how Confession properly carried through will not only cleanse the 'garment' of the soul but enable a man to keep it 'clean' (in a state of grace). They draw on the standard penitential doctrine as found in the *SAP* of Alan of Lille, who states that *tria* 'three things' must be present for confession to be *vera* 'authentic': *cordis contricio, oris professio, operis satisfactio* (*PL* 210:173; see also Alf*Q*, and cf. *CT* X 106–9). Though these *tria* do not tally neatly with the Triad, contrition appears here as a (vital) preliminary *disposition*, loosening the impacted dirt from the coat (= the sloth that impedes initial recourse to the sacrament). Dowel is then the first properly good *action*, to confess (= washing the fabric clean). Dobet corresponds to a second action, the priest's giving of absolution (= restoring the original hue by steeping), which strengthens the penitent's will to virtue through the pouring-in of sanctifying grace. Finally Dobest (= the drying of the garment in readiness for wearing) signifies the expression of this renewed will in meritorious acts that discharge the debt of sin and protect the soul against defilements by the flesh, the world and the devil. This fluid but slightly confusing exposition is revised and clarified at C 16–31*a*, which exactly equates the graded Triad with the three parts of penitence (as described in *CT* X 106–9). **16–17** *of...make*: 'to construct something out of contrition'. **17a** 'Heartfelt sorrow (for having offended a loving God)'. **18a** 'Verbal confession (to a priest)'. **22** 'Making full satisfaction for the sin forgiven' (by prayer, almsgiving, devotions, pilgrimage). **23** *mope*: from Mt 6:19–21, the last verse of which was quoted at B 13.399*a* above (Alford 1974). **28**

Activa Vita: a second occurrence of Haukyn's Latin cognomen (first used of himself at 13.225), but with deeper theological resonance, now more properly denoting a (normative) life of grace possible for laypeople who *be labour sholde lyuen and lyflode deseruen* (C 5.42; cf. B 6.248). This new reliance on *þe grace of God and hise grete helpes* (13.399) to 'walk worthy of the vocation in which [they have] been called' (Eph 4:1) is not to be seen as mechanical but as a real liberation from *vnkynde desiring* (356). **29–36** Coming after the account of sacramental confession, Patience's *paast...for þe soule* (29–30) may *suggest* the Eucharist; but what it *refers to* is God's word and patient acceptance of God's will (as confirmed by revised C 237–8). **34** and the following texts echo B 7.126–30, underscoring the close link between Patience and his avatar Piers, from whom the first two are virtually borrowed. **34a** '[Therefore]...be not solicitous [for your life, what you shall eat....Behold] the birds of the air, [for they neither sow, nor do they reap...and] your heavenly Father feedeth them' (Mt 6:25–6); immediately following the verse quoted at 313*a*. L's *celi Deus* runs together *Pater...caelestis* (Mt) and *Deus* (in // Lk 12:24). *Pacientes*: see on C 15.139. **35–8** C's omission of this amusing interchange tends to flatten Actyf into something of a 'yes-man' and forfeit the telling connection between the *vitailles* Patience offers Haukyn and the penitential *mete* he himself ate in the first action of Vision Four. **37–8** *poke...vertues*: see 13.217–20.

C 234–52 Patience's reply to Actyf's last point at C 231 warns that since pride is so deeply rooted in human nature, it does not need wealth and plenty to nourish it, so dearth alone will not suffice to quell it. His own 'virtuous' remedy aims to heal rather than hurt, a measure of the difference between penitence based on fear and penitence based on 'verray sorwe' (see *CT X* 128–30). **238** *me hyder sente*: patience being the fourth of the twelve fruits of the Holy Spirit (Gal 5:22). **239** *yf...trewe*: both 'if what we believe is correct' (the usual sense, as at 14.151) and 'if our faith is genuine' (reminding that Christ's promises are not fulfilled automatically but in relation to the believer's disposition). In // B 39 the phrase is more tellingly a rejoinder to Haukyn's sceptical play on *leue* 36, which is echoed in *Leue...bileue* 246. **240** *here*: 'on this earth' rather than 'their'. **243** *cryket*: probably the salamander, fabled to live in fire (the Trevisa quot. in MED s.v. *criket* n. makes both points). *corleu*: the quail (*coturnix*), in exegetical tradition often a symbol of spiritual pilgrimage and the need to rely on faith in God (Spearman 1993:242–58); perhaps with some echo of the quails sent by God in Ex 16:13. **246a** 'Whatsoever you shall ask the Father in my name, it will be given to you' (adapted from Jn 14:13). 'And in another place: "Not in bread alone doth man live, but in every word that proceedeth from the mouth of God"' (Mt 4:4). The context of the first quotation is Christ's appeal to the Apostles at the Last Supper to believe in him, so that 'the works that I do, [they] also shall do' (vs 12). That of the second is Christ's rebuke to Satan during his fast of forty days, the scriptural model for the season of Lent; the citation of Deut 8:3 reminds the Israelites that during their forty years in the wilderness God fed them with manna and quails. Both the second text and the following *Paternoster* petition at 252 are used in the later-composed self-defence by the Dreamer at 5.82–8. **248** The rhythm of Actyf's mild enquiry ironically recalls that of Glutton at 6.357. **250** *pece*: continuing the metaphor of prayer as 'spiritual food' dramatised at 59–65. Patience's way of speaking has been anticipated by Piers at B 8.118–24a; but **C**'s removal of that passage weakens the link between these figures that is so strong in **B** (see on B 34) and was affirmed by **C**'s making Piers the first to utter Patience's motto-phrase (at 139 above). **252** *Fiat...*: 'Thy will be done', the third petition of the Lord's Prayer (Mt 6:10), quoted again by Liberum Arbitrium as a source of spiritual 'feeding' at 16.319, as is the fourth at 16.372a (see on B 168–9 above). A systematic association is made by Alan of Lille (*SAP* ch. xv) between seven types of patience, the seven petitions of the Paternoster and the Seven Beatitudes (*PL* 140–3). On the significance of the Paternoster in *PP*, see Gillespie in Minnis 1994:95–119.

253–75 form perhaps the frankest statement of the pilgrim hermit's philosophy of 'reckless' dependence on God alone for *lyflode*, and willing acceptance of deprivation. Taken as a whole, it may be understood less as rejecting earthly existence than as radically subordinating it to the spiritual life that lies beyond death. Moreover, the *social* radicalism of its conclusion shows that Patience is not denying the goodness of creation but asserting that man's sin is responsible for men's sufferings. **254** *claumsen; drouthe*: first recorded here in these senses. **256** *pacientes...*: see on 139 above. **262a** 'One who cares for Christ will not covet this world'; the first part of a Leonine couplet that continues *sed quasi fetorem spernens illius amorem* 'but scorn the love of it like a sickening stench'. Taken from the *Cartula*, one of the grammatical texts making up the *Auctores Octo*, and also found as the *Carmen Paraeneticum* in *PL* 184:307 (Alf*Q* 88), it is based on I Jn 2:15, 'If any man love the world [*Si quis diligit mundum*], the charity of the Father is not in him', an important passage that underlies 11.162–97. **263–5a** are couched as a quasi-syllogistic argument: 'God gave creatures life by his breath (= word) alone; therefore he must also keep them alive by his breath (word); if so, man too can be sustained by his word'. In strict logic the conclusion does not follow, since 'to be given life' is contained under 'to live' but not *e converso*. The argument's authority depends rather on the meaning of the scriptural texts adduced, which state that since God created all life by his word, he *must* have

both the power (and the will) to sustain it by his word. Patience takes literally the second part of the Matthean text quoted at 246a but ignores the first part, which tacitly modifies its extremism. **263a** '[For he spoke] and they were made' (Ps 148:5). **265a** 'Thou openest thy hand: and fillest with blessing every living creature' (Ps 144:16); part of a commonly used grace at meals (*Latin Graces* in *Babees Book,* ed. Furnivall 1868:382). **266** *founde*: three asymmetrically functioning examples from the OT and Christian legend; in the first and third, people favoured by God are fed by him; in the second, those who offend God are punished. *fourty wynter*: the period of the Israelites' 'journey in the wide wilderness' (Jos 5:6; cf. Ex 16:35). **267** *floed...dronke*: see Num 20:11, Ps 77:20 The rock struck by Moses is taken by St Paul (I Cor 10:4) as a 'figure' of Christ who is the sustenance of his people. **268** *Elies tyme*: see III Kgs 17:1ff. The prophet Elias (Elijah) 'closed heaven' by the command of God 'for three years and six months' (Js 5:17) to punish Achab king of Israel for idolatry. **270** *tylede*: on the basis of the *Sk* text *of no mete telden* explained by MED (s.v. *tellen* v. 1a (a)) as an ironic way of saying 'had nothing to eat'. But this gloss, like the **p** reading it is based on, is an error (see *TN*), since the verb (as is clear from B 67) is the same as at 266. **271** *Seuene slepen*: seven young men of Ephesus who were said to have remained asleep in a cave from the persecution of Christians under the Emperor Decius (*c.* 250) to the time of the Eastern Emperor Theodosius II (448); see *LA* ch. 101. They were cited first as proof of the resurrection of the dead, later as exemplifying God's miraculous preservation of his faithful. **273** *mesure*: the cardinal virtue of Temperance (to be described at 21.282–9). B 74 makes the witty point that 'moderation by its very nature can *never* be over-valued (become too costly), so that it cannot *ever* produce scarcity.' After extreme arguments for total dependence on God, Patience reverts to the moderate (and surprisingly modern) point of Holy Church at 1.33, that it is sins of excess like gluttony and greed on the part of the few (the rich) that produce scarcity for the many (the poor). **275** 'I will give to you according to your asking'; adapted from Ps 36:3–4: '[Trust in the Lord, and do good, and dwell in the land: and thou shalt be *fed* with its riches. Delight in the Lord]: and he will give thee the requests (*dabit tibi petitiones*) [of thy heart]'. The relevant NT parallel to this statement (which complements the 4th Paternoster petition) is less likely to be Mk 6:22 (*Pe*) than Jn 14:14. **B 72** *vnkyndenesse...makeþ*: 'a topos of medieval economic theory...Caristia ['dearth'], which is not in Vg [Alf*Q*], occurs in writs and ordinances...directed against victuallers who in order to drive up prices created artificial scarcities' (Alf*G*).

B 75–96 are cut here and partly transferred, 75–80 to C 15.231–3 and 81–96 (in much modified form) to 16.25–35. **76a** *Ociositas*: 'idleness', 'sloth'; see on C

15.231a above, which omits this. **77–80** are clearly if somewhat awkwardly expressed: 'Because (*For*)...(But) did...vengeance fell on them in such a way (*so*) that they sank...' **77** is a metrically clumsy line, understandably deleted. **78b** repeats B 1.28 (removed in **C**). **81–96** make (when read aright) a strong plea for recourse to sacramental confession, and 83 is only a little more explicit than standard penitential teaching on the power and worth of contrition-with-intent-to-confess (*CT* X 309 quotes the same Ps 31:5–6 cited at 93). Their deletion in **C** could be due to clerical readers' objection that emphasis on inward sorrow (though salutary) might inadvertently produce the opposite effect to that intended, but more probably to **L**'s awareness of the discrepancies between what they say and B 16–28. In Patience's three-stage move towards the act of confession (i.e. faith, contrition and conscience), the last presumably signifies the active awakening of the penitent's 'sad purpos to shryve him' (*CT* X 128). **81** *sheltrom*: 'protective battle-formation' (going back to the ancient English interlocking shield-wall); alluding to the *armatura Dei* of Eph 6:11–17. The figure is of a *collective* mode of defence, because the faith is not merely an individual's 'existential' commitment but that of the Church in which the baptized person shares (the moat of communal tears at 19.280–3 will carry a similar significance). **82** *conscience*: possibly alluding to Conscience's remarks at 16ff; but the collocation with faith and contrition at 87 argues against capitalisation here. **87** *Dowel*: at one with Conscience's analysis at 16.28; for since contrition arising from faithful assent to the Church's teaching and issuing in a resolve to confess is now equated with Dowel, so by implication Dobet becomes confession itself and Dobest satisfaction, as at C 16.25–35. **88** *surgiens*: a figure anticipating that in the dramatised allegory at 22.311ff. The three elements constitutive of Dowel can 'operate' on the sick soul, not just 'physic' it. But while weakening the illness, they do not destroy it, as maintained by Will at B 11.81a and by Ymaginatif at B 12.177 (89–91 however, which now ascribe destruction of sin to the act of confession, still insist on inward contrition *accompanying* it). **91** 'Through confession to a priest, sins are slain'; paralleled in Brinton 2:437, 'Peccata per confessionem delentur' (Alf*Q*). **92** *dryueþ it doun*: a figure from cutting off a weed above ground (cf. *roote* 94). **93** *et...*: see on B 12.177a. **96** *wounde*: returning to the 'surgeon' metaphor of 88.

276–82 276 The question, which assumes that patience' is what 'fed' the Israelites, Elias and the Sleepers, and serves to introduce the main theme of the next passus, is better integrated with the preceding discourse than Haukyn's about the whereabouts of *Charity*, a subject not hitherto mentioned. The latter echoes ironically the question of the Folk about the whereabouts of *Truth* at B 5.532–3 // (a point reinforced by *truþe* at B 99); but

Patience's answer recalls that of Piers rather than the Pilgrim. **277–8** The sense of this passage is that a will marked by a gentle spirit of reconciliation and harmony is conducted to heaven by Charity, here in effect identified with the patience that suffers every danger (I Cor 13:4,7). *wille*: the new explicit emphasis on the affective-volitional preparing the ground for the appearance of Liberum Arbitrium as Haukyn's *ledare* at 16.156. **279** *charite chaumpion*: taking up a memorable phrase at B 8.46, from an 8-line passage deleted by **C**. **280** *pore pacient*: 'poor person who has patience (enough)'; the first adjective is substantival, the second is the epithet. **282** 'Than spending one's wealth in a just and proper way'; what matters being not how wealth was obtained, but how it is spent. **283** 'Yes, but *is* there such a man? We'll praise *him* soon enough!' A split quotation from verses on the dangers of wealth and the rareness of virtuous rich men: '[Blessed is the rich man...that hath not put his trust in money nor in treasures]. Who is he, and we will praise him? [For he hath done wonderful things in his life]' (Ecclus 31:8–9). **284** *to...ende*: 'all over the globe' / 'till the crack of doom' (cf. 18.175). **B 107** *fel*: understand *ne fel* (*ne* borrowed from *ne dredde* 106) as in // **C**. **288** *of this ryche*: 'from among these rich people' rather than 'in this kingdom'. **289–90** *preue...haue*: 'prove that he should have'. *puyr resoun*: 'simple justice', the legal sense confirmed by *lawe* 290 and *iuge* 291. **291** *þat*: 'he who'. **292–6** Patience draws an analogy from observation of *kynde* 'the natural order' (B 119) that (like Ymaginatif's *ensample* of the peacock and the lark at 14.168–90) forms the basis of an ethical deduction. 'Even animals do not experience winter all year, so why should some men suffer the "winter" of hardship all their life? It therefore "stands to reason" (as well as being "a matter of strict legal right") that they should be granted *blisse*.' **300** In revising, **C** supplements **B**'s polysemantic verbal punning (on *som...som*) with homophonic phrasal wordplay (*elliswher...were*) so as to hint 'Platonically' that the very nature of things as ordained by God requires suffering in this life to be balanced equitably by joy in the next. **301** *þat*: '(for) who(m)'. **303–11** are more sombre and final in tone, and less sympathetic to the 'misfortune' of the wealthy (in having their 'payment' [heaven] in this life and losing it in the next), than are B 122–31a. For the latter's tacit implication that if all were equal in life, none need risk suffering 'beggary' after death, amounts to a questioning of Providence. **303** *Dyues*: 'Mr Rich'; see on 8.278. *douce vie*: the French phrase and the French derived *deyntees* (like the Latin name *Dives*) lexically mirroring the rich man's detachment from (and indifference to) the situation of his wretched opposite Lazarus. **304** *beggare*: because now destitute of all except suffering, a punishment ironically 'condign' (cf. also 309). **305** is like B 124 in alliterating on vowels; but though it likewise stresses the same homophone twice, **C** (perhaps in awareness of the vocally tricky *hir hire heer* of B 128) replaces the empty homonyms of B 124 with different lexemes menacingly coloured by the polysemantic pun (on 'here') in the second *here*. The suggestion is that even good deeds, if done in a state of sin, are spiritually fruitless for the rich: 'whan we doon deedly synne, it is for noght thanne to rehercen or drawen into memorie the goode werkes that we han wroght biforn' (*CT* X 237). **306** *ledes*: the ominous rhyme-echo of *dedes* 305 hinting at the transience of any treasure except *treuthe,* the Pardon having long ago pointed out that only those who '*do* well' will '*have* well' (9.289). **311** 'They have slept [their sleep: and all the men of riches] have found nothing in their hands' (Ps 75:6). 'And in another place, "As the dream of them that awake, [**B**] O Lord, *so* in thy city thou shalt bring their image to nothing"' (Ps 72:20). In the full form, the 'dream' denotes the rich men's life of *wele,* 'death' their awaking from it, the 'city' the place whence they will be judged to *purgatorie or helle* as the *puyre pore thynges* they are.

Passus XVI
(B XIV 132–XV 255)

PASSUS SIXTEEN continues to dissolve **B**'s bond between the structural units of passus and vision, carrying on directly with Patience's instruction to Actyf. It divides in half at about 156, with the appearance of *Liberum Arbitrium* (LA). But since this fails to coincide with a new vision as in **B**, the Fourth Vision in **C** goes on until 18.179, only implicitly indicating an inner dream at the point parallel to B 16.18–19, and with almost no revision between 37 and 155. From 210–83 LA delivers a diatribe against corruption in the Church, provoking Will's clerkly rejoinder on Charity's absence from the contemporary world, and from 284–372a a fervent homily on the nature of CHARITY that recalls and develops from Patience's disquisition on POVERTY in 43–155. This long instruction, lasting through 17.1–321, is punctuated by five (mainly) short questions and interjections from the Dreamer at 314–15, 334–7, 17.1–3, 125, 150. But most of XVII comprises a single speech like its source B XV where, after the Dreamer's 'charity' intervention at 148–62, ANIMA's vast discourse is broken by four similar instances of question / rejoinder / exclamation at 151–64, 175, 195, 197.

(i) **1–155 1–21** describe the spiritual danger of riches, omitting a passage (B 145–54) that tries to accommodate earthly wealth and heavenly reward with the justice of God, leaving the situation of the rich less hopeful in **C** (cf. also the omission of B 168–73). **4** *deyeth...to dyne*: 'does he die...who dines'. **9** is metrically acceptable as it

stands, but the incompleteness of the thought suggests a possible lacuna in Cx, which could be adequately filled by B 141b (see *TN*).

B 142–57 develop a semi-syllogistic argument by analogy from the world of experience in the half-acre and contemporary conditions of wages and desert. Rich men cannot justly get 'paid' twice, but if they use their wealth to help the poor, they get a second payment as a bounty (not a wage). However, since they rarely do that, wealth remains a serious danger; so *if* the rich receive heavenly reward, it is not as a 'just due' but only as a generous 'extra' for good service. **B** thus affirms the 'camel through the eye of a needle' view alluded to at B 212a, that their salvation (though not impossible) is very hard because of entanglement in worldly selfishness. **143** *at þe laste*: at death (as spelled out in the repetition at 147). **144** *Mathew*: alluding to Mt 19:23–4. **144a** 'From delights to delights is a difficult crossing'; based on St Jerome's *Epistola ad Julianum*, which has 'difficile, imo impossibile est...' (*PL* 22:965). **145** *rewarde*: playing polysemantically on the other main sense at 148, to hint at a 'Platonic' connection between human and divine munificence. **146** *lawe*: both secular and religious. **147** *curteisie*: an echo of B 12.177 resonant with theological significance, denoting the 'habitual grace' that protects the rich from the dangers of wealth, especially at death. **C** places this notion of 'courtesy more than covenant' (cf. 151) earlier, in Ymaginatif's account of how the just pagan is saved (see 14.215–6). **148** *double richesse*: 'a double helping of wealth'. **151** *cote*: a pointed choice of reward, since Haukyn complained at 13.228 of getting 'few robes' from earthly lords. It may be analogically implied that the sanctifying grace given through absolution, in returning him to the state of original righteousness conferred by baptism, is the 'courteous' gift of a second *cote of cristendom* (B 13.274). **153** *double hire*: ingeniously equating the lot of the rich with that of the rest, since all receive forgiveness and happiness. **154** *Here... hir*: for the stave-pattern cf. 124 and C 15.305. **155** *bokes*: whether the allusion is to *LA* or to ascetic writings, the scarcity of righteous rich men seems certain.

10–21 The seasonal analogy resumed from 15.292–301 is more rationally handled in **C** as the vehicle ('summer') is introduced *before* the tenor ('happiness'). **13** *myssomur*: around June 21, the summer solstice, and June 24, the Feast of St John. This marked the 'hungry gap' or period of scarcity between the last of the previous season's corn and that of the new harvest (Lammastide), when there would be little to spare for beggars (Frank 1990:89–90); cf. also B 178. The assimilated form (if original) may hint a sly pun on 'miss-summer'. **17** *somur somtyme*: the homophonically punning phrase from 15.299, here repeated in a prayer. **21** *for þe beste*: affirming that it is not from the 'nounpower' of God that wealth is unevenly spread, but for a providential reason (to give rich people opportunities for acts of charity).

22–36 22 *vs alle*: a striking revision; all need God's mercy and the virtue of humility, and **B**'s special concern for the souls of the rich may have appeared insensitive in the aftermath of 1381, when the authorities resorted to oppression but had no remedies to offer for social ills. *rode*: where the divine pity was supremely shown; recalling 1.164–6. **25–42** connect the wealth / poverty dyad with the confession triad through imagining sacramental penance as a kind of spiritual wealth that confers the power to endure literal poverty and, because equally accessible to all Christians, makes them in a sense all equal. **25–32** take up B 14.22, which was excised at that point in **C**. **25–6** *clanse...kulle*: cf. B 14.16–17, 91. **31a** 'Heartfelt contrition, oral confession, satisfaction through works'. **33–4** mimic echoically through internal rhymes the basic idea of 'sacramental wealth' through 'the abundant riches of [God's] grace' (cf. Eph 2:4–8) as a 'spiritual levelling' that makes all Christians potentially 'equals'. The Triad interpreted in terms of the grades of penitence creates a new spiritual hierarchy to supersede the 'carnal' one based on riches. **35** *charite*: perhaps personified, as a shared name for Christ and the Christian who is in a state of sanctifying grace. *chartre*: presumably of manumission from the 'serfdom' of sin (cf. on *acquitaunce* B 190 below). **36** *domesday*: recalling the intercessory rôle of Dowel described at 9.350–1.

B 168–95 Of these lines, **171–80a** are arguably dispensable because repetitive, 172 repeating 13.162 and 173 the sense of 171a, 179 that of 175; but omission of **174–80a**, with its skilful rhetorical patterning and delicate wordplay (*fulle...carefulle*, and *Conuertimini* 'Platonically' echoing *Conforte*), is a real poetic loss. **168** *rupe...men*: presumably through granting them grace to save themselves by acting *rewfulliche* towards the poor. *rewarde*: with perhaps a play on its other sense (cf. 145), since the rich have an opportunity to 'pay' the poor out of what God has given. *prisones*: visiting prisoners was recognised as a 'corporal work of mercy', but few could see the poor (see 174) as also figuratively 'imprisoned' by their want. **169** *ingrati*: 'ungrateful' in both legal and theological senses, 'refusing to reciprocate one's lord's kindness' (AlfG 73–4) and therefore (anticipating 170) 'ungracious', i.e. 'rejecting God's grace and so rejected by Him' (cf. B 17.254=19.220). Similar wordplay occurs in the *Floretus*, one of the *Auctores Octo* texts: *Non sis ingratus domino si vis fore gratus* 'Be not ungrateful to the Lord if you would be pleasing to him' (AlfQ). **179** *in þi riche*: a pun is possible here; for since both poor and rich may enter Christ's *kingdom*, he might be able to comfort the distressed 'in' or through the generosity of the *rich*, thereby comforting 'all'. **180a** 'Be converted to me, and you shall be saved' (Is 45:22). **181** *in...gen-*

tries: 'in virtue of his nobility of nature'; *in genere* 'in the kind or genus of'; a term in grammar and logic. **184** 'To receive baptism in the name of the Trinity'; cf. Mt 28:19. **185** *kynnes synnes*: the emphatic internal rhyme underlining the categorical assurance given by the sacrament. **186** *fille...folie...falle*: pararhyming *annominatio* hinting not that sin is trivial but that it is (in Julian of Norwich's term) *behovely* 'necessary' (*Showings*, ch. 27, p. 405) and so men should not be oppressed by a sense of hopelessness but always look to the mercy promised by God. **188** *as many sipes*: cf. Mt 18:22. **189** *pouke*: Walafrid Strabo in his *Expositio in Johannem* observes that 'homo percussus a *diabolo* qui credit *passionem Christi* liberabitur' (*PL* 114:906). *plede*: envisaging the Devil as counsel for the prosecution against man. *punysshe*: by making the sinner suffer from 'scrupulosity', the anxiety that he is not truly forgiven and reconciled to God. **190** *acquitaunce*: 'a document in evidence of a transaction...such as a release' (MED s.v.), here release from sin, obtained through baptism and penance. 'To be able to show a sealed release or acquittance was crucial; otherwise the law regarded a person to be still in debt' (AlfG). In the *Stanzaic Life of Christ* the Latin rubric after 6408 (on Christ's granting 'manumission' to mankind) defines *manumissio* as *litera acquietancie quando natiuus redimitur* 'a letter of acquittance when a serf buys his freedom' (ed. Foster, p. 215). **190a** *Pateat...*: 'Let it be manifest, etc.'; the first words of a deed, recalling a royal letter patent (192) declaring that the accused is released under surety (from Christ). *Per...*: 'Through the Passion of Our Lord [Jesus Christ]'; indicating the source of the reconciling sacraments' efficacy. This metaphor may derive from Col 2:14, which describes the forgiveness of sin through Christ's Passion in terms of the deletion of a document of accusation against the sinner. It is taken up again when the 'patent' becomes the tablet of the Old Law that awaits the 'seal' of *cros and Cristendom, and Crist þeron to honge* (B 17.10, 6). **191** *borwe*: mainprise, on which see Keen 2002:91–3 who, however, does not discuss this acquittance (cf. Steiner 2000:101–2). **192** *parchemyn*: the material of a letter patent from the king, figuring the disposition of humility needed for the saving power of Christ's Passion, accessible through the sacraments, to be 'written down' or made operative for man's soul. **194** *decourreþ*: from OF *decorir* 'to run or flow away from'; probably used by **L** to mean 'shun, avoid'. Kane 2000:50–1 takes the verb as derived from Lat. *decoriare* 'scrape clean from' (for which there is likewise no other ME instance); but though the sense would fit well with *principalliche...but*, the sudden shift to imperative pl. is unprepared for. The omission of the figure in **C** may register awareness that the line was obscure.

37–112 38 *preyeres*: a well-advised revision; since 'a piece of the Paternoster' was what Patience offered Haukyn at

49 (and cf. 372*a*), it would be unfitting to question its efficacy here. *Rome*: see on Pr 48, 4.123. **40–1** *writeth... freres*: i.e. the names of donors, as promised by the friar-confessor to Meed at 3.51–4. *fals*: if provided by absolved sinners who have no purpose to amend. **42** *in comune riche*: 'collectively wealthy' / '[live] in a society that is wealthy because each of its members desires the well-being of all'. This need not imply that all property must be owned in common, a theory of pagan origin attributed to the friars at 22.276 and repudiated at 277–9 as against God's law. It cannot be doubted that **L** knew the practice of the early Jerusalem community (Ac 2:44–5) was the basic model for religious orders and admired the spirit of mutual aid in *cloistre* and *scole*. But the b-verse stresses that Christians must *will* the common good above private or personal advantage, 'so distribution should undo excess' and 'all became poor' (Baldwin 2001:108), i.e. 'had enough'. Underpinning the social ideal advanced here is the same conception (see on 25–42) of the sacramental graces won by Christ as spiritual goods Christians share in, the 'common wealth' of the *holy comune in heuene* (5.86), on which the Church (Unity) is meant to be modelled. **43** *seuene synnes*: an account of the Deadly Sins attacking the individual soul that is transitional between the 'enacted' representation of them as types of 'Sinner' in Vision Two and as personified enemies in Vision Eight that *assailen* the Christian *comune* sheltering in Unity (21.337ff). The specific argument propounded here is that sin must be a greater threat to the rich than to the poor because vices are 'armed' by wealth, but 'disarmed' by patient poverty. In fact, although seven appear (in the order Pride, Anger, Gluttony, Covetousness, Avarice, Lechery and Sloth) the fourth and fifth are two aspects of Greed while Envy, a likelier vice of the have-nots than of the haves (except *in scole*) is prudently omitted as doubtless weakening the case. **44** *fend followeth*: cf. 1.38. **47** *pore...ryche*: behind this realistic recognition that honour is valued by *all* human beings may lie the example of the technically 'poor' Doctor of Divinity (still present in Patience's and the audience's mind) who is 'maed sitte furste, as for the moste worthy' (15.39). **50–1** *fer...heuene*: Patience's placing of *wit*, a 'gift of nature', above wealth, a 'gift of fortune' (cf. *CT* X 452–43), may be thought to contradict Ymaginatif's linking of both as 'encumbrances' (14.17). But the collocation of wit with *wisdom* and of wisdom with *heauen* here suggests that the phrase denotes neither, but a 'gift of grace,' specifically the first of the Holy Ghost's seven gifts (Is 11:2); whence the indigent wise man's prayer is sooner heard than that of the wealthy fool. **53** The rich man's progress is slowed by changes in direction or gradient because of the weight of his goods ('worldly concerns impede spiritual growth'). **B 212***a* See on C 11.203. **54***a* 'For their works follow them' (Apoc 14:13); referring to the saints who

from their labours rest (vs 13). **55** *Bataúntliche*: possibly coined by **L** from OF *batant*. **56** The joy is the reward not of the poverty itself but of the patience it is borne with. **B 215***a* 'Blessed are the poor [in spirit]; for theirs is the kingdom of heaven' (Mt 5:3). The wording may be influenced by Lk 6:20, which omits *spiritu*; but that is surely implied, since 215 and 220 make clear the necessity of the *patientia sanctorum* (Apoc 14:12) that brings heavenly 'rest' (cf. the identification of poverty and patience with respectively the first and last of the Beatitudes in *Patience* 34–45). **58** *mayster...man*: alluding to the arrogant behaviour of nobles' retainers. The phrasing recalls B 13.40, reminding that one can be proud of intellectual as well as material 'wealth', while conversely spiritual 'poverty' (humility) is possible, if difficult, for the literally rich. **60** *none*: because humility, the root of Christian virtue, is the specific against pride, the root of all sin (cf. *CT* X 475), and literal poverty disposes to meekness. **61** recalls Rechelesnesse at 13.2. **63** *breed...drynke*: avoiding the implication in *broke loues* 'scraps of bread' B 222 that beggary (cf. A 12.70) is being tacitly recommended. But since (against this) the change of *asken* B 229 to *begge* does suggest 'destitution' rather than 'basic sufficiency', it could be that poverty here is intended to signify only 'dependence on others for one's livelihood'. **64** *at werre*: the hostility between pride and humility (43), elaborated in traditional 'psychomachic' terms as a physical struggle between the deadly sins and (patient) poverty. **66** *wrastle*: an extended metaphor throughout which the vehicle is amusingly at odds with the tenor, since the poor man 'wins' the match by *not* wrestling (= 'getting angry'). *he*: i.e. Wrath. **68** *he*: i.e. again Wrath. **73** *glotonye*: i.e. even if he is able to indulge in drinking, he still has to 'pay' for it by sleeping on cold bed-straw. **76** *his...synne*: hendiadys for 'his great sin of gluttony'. **78 C** substitutes for **B**'s benign sympathy 'condign punishment': whether or not discomfort engenders contrition, it diminishes pleasure. **79–89** treat both aspects of Greed separately (see on 6.196), notionally making the total of sins up to seven, despite the omission of Envy. **84** *layk...neuere*: so the bout would be cancelled after the contenders had been measured. **88** *boest*: i.e. for the thief; but the poor man is better off because he has nothing to attract a burglar. **93** *serue nat*: fail in his religious observance. **95** *gretteste help*: cf. Haukyn's reliance on charms at 13.341–2. **96–7** Since the poor man always 'serves' another, he belongs to Christ's own liveried retinue, whether he is virtuous or not (cf. Js 2:1–6); and even where he *fails* to serve God (through sloth), his poverty means that he bears the Saviour's 'badge'. **99** *of puyr rihte*: 'as a matter of sheer justice' (cf. 15.290); categorical, where **B** is more tentative. **101** An unusual double-staved line with alternative scansion on *m* or vowels. **101–3** perhaps allude to the example *par excellence* of St Francis of Assisi, the son of a rich merchant, who renounced his wealth at the age of 24. **105** *paramour*: 'beloved'. The contrast in sense with 'husband' seen in Gower *CA* 4.1269 is negated here: as her *make* she feels for him *kynde loue of þe mariage* 'the affection natural and right towards a spouse', as noted by *Sk*, who finds an echo of Eph 5:31 (citing Gen 2:24). **110** *So hit fareth*: 'That is how it is', i.e. such a person greatly deserves love (from God). *persone*: possibly punning on 'person' and 'parish-priest' (cf. 13.99–102 above). **111** *weddeth*: as St Francis weds the Lady Poverty in the C13th Latin allegory the *Sacrum Commercium*. **112** *syb... semblable*: Christ's poverty as a model being stressed by mendicant rigorists.

113–55 113 *angryliche*: the only sign in **C** that Patience's unworldly idealism might set a nerve jangling in the representative of the common man. **114** *What is pouerte*: a translation of the question *Quid est Paupertas?* introducing the quoted Latin original that follows in answer. **B 274–5** 'For God's sake, Patience, you keep on singing the praises of poverty — but what exactly is it?' (For the contemporary social background to this discussion see Shepherd 1983, Aers 1983, Pearsall 1988, and the perceptive account of the oxymoronic character of the medieval concept of poverty in Scott 2001:141–53). **115–15a** 'Poverty is "a hateful good". It is the removal of cares; possession without calumny; a gift of God; the mother of health; a path free of worry; mistress of wisdom; business with no losses; [it is], amidst fortune's uncertainty, happiness without anxiety'; from the *Gnomae* of Secundus Philosophus, quoted by Vincent of Beauvais, *Speculum historiale* X, 71 and by others (AlfQ). Chaucer's paraphrase in *CT* III 1195–1200 may show the influence of **L** (e.g. the necessary association with patience at 1197–8) and the whole quotation appears as the Latin gloss to this passage in the Ellesmere MS. **115** scans as a macaronic Type Ib with cognative b-verse staves. *odibile bonum*: the oxymoron highlighting the contrast between poverty's superficial unattractiveness and its spiritual worth (see B 286a). Except for *donum Dei* (see on 134a), poverty's 'points' are of broadly non-Christian origin and not *prima facie* antithetically opposed to the seven sins severally but especially focused upon greed, envy, anger and gluttony. **116** *construe*: Actyf's perplexity amusingly recalling the King's at Conscience's learned 'grammatical' analogy of *mede* and *mercede* (3.340–2), and providing a motive for Patience to elaborate in ways that draw his exposition closer to the preceding one of the deadly sins, though they hardly qualify as a 'proper [strict] construing' of the Latin. **B 279** *by...vnderstonde*: 'so that you may understand'; see MED s.v. *bi* conj. 2b, citing only this example. **120** *goed*: rhetorical *repetitio* of co-polysemes, hinting 'Platonically' at the metaphysical oneness of ethical and logical categories. *greue a litel*: corresponding to **B**'s account of *odibile bonum*, which **C** does not cite directly

(in **B** the Latin 'points' come before, in **C** after their exposition in English). The subtle comparison of poverty with contrition in B 282–5 serves to link the Stoic ascetic values of the definition with the Christian penitential doctrine of B 14.81–96; but **C** is perhaps wise to confine the moral teaching wholly within the practical terms Actyf might readily understand. **B 286** *cura animarum*: 'the care of souls', i.e. a force that brings spiritual strength and encouragement. The canonical sense of 'the exercise of a clerical office...by a person legitimately appointed for the purpose' (AlfQ) seems to have no relevance in this context, but the expression's ambiguity may partly account for its deletion (on its relation to *remocio curarum* see Schmidt 1987:111). **122** *sothe to declare*: i.e. as a juror at the assise. **126a¹** *Nolite*...: 'Judge not, that you may not be judged' (Mt 7:1); an opportunistic use of the 'commandment', which warns against individual 'judging' of one's neighbour's character, not against performing one's civic obligations. But a poet familiar with legal matters would be aware that medieval jurors often found on a defendant's (real or supposed) character rather than the facts of the case. **127** 'Poor people seldom become very well-off except through coming into a lawful inheritance'. The play on *rihte / rihtfole* recalls that on *wel* at B 278. **128** *wightes*: specified as a characteristic vice of the covetous at 6.258 and 19.246. *vnselede mesures*: like Haukyn at B 13.359; measures used by brewers and taverners had to to be sealed with the alderman's seal to attest their true capacity (*Sk*). The suggestion here seems to be that dealing honestly is likely to leave a man poor. **130** 'It's hard to raise a loan if people know you're badly off'; but in a society with inordinately high interest-charges, there were advantages in not falling into the 'credit-trap'. **133** *folies*: gluttony, lechery and sloth. **134** *collateral*: possibly alluding to the legal notion of 'collateral warranty' (AlfG); but a non-technical sense of the term (first used here) seems likeliest, these spiritual advantages being to the poor man unexpected gains or 'blessings in disguise'. **134a** *Donum Dei*: probably from the opening of St Augustine's *De Patientia* (*PL* 40:611), which states that 'Patience is so great *a gift of God* that it is even ascribed to Him who grants it to us' (Schmidt 1969:28, Orsten 1969, Baldwin 1990; and cf. 13.198–200). Augustine is explicitly acknowledged at 151. **136a** 'Mother of health' because poverty protects from excess, the cause of many illnesses (cf. 8.290–4); but since too *little* food would also undermine health, 'poverty' must denote 'sufficiency' rather than 'want'. B 299–300 make clear that the temptation is probably lechery (see *TN* on 136). **137** *pees*: because freeing from anxiety about violent assault ('wrath'). *pase of Aultoun*: a road or 'pass' on the Surrey-Hampshire border, at this time forested; a notorious haunt of outlaws (cf. B 17.103) who lay in wait for merchant-trains travelling to the fairs near Winchester (see 6.211,

13.51). **141** 'Given that he has no idea whom he might encounter by night'. **B 304a** 'The povre man, whan he goth by the weye, Bifore the theves he may synge and pleye' (Juvenal, *Satires* X, 22 as translated by Chaucer in *CT* III 1193–4). The reading with *paupertas* for original *vacuus* is found in Bromyard, *SP* I:86/1 (AlfQ). **141a** *Seneca...*: the Roman Stoic philosopher (*c.* 4 BC–65 AD), tutor of Nero. The exact source of this line (which will scan in both versions as a Type IIIb) is untraced; but the sentiment is in keeping with those in his Epistles 2 and 8 and with various remarks in the tract *De Paupertate* made up of quotations from Seneca's writings. **144** echoes B Pr 51, and the truth / treasure dichotomy is reminiscent of Holy Church's teaching in 1.81. Truth provides the poor man a perfect 'tuning-fork' for his speech in that, being free from cupidity, he is free to say what he really thinks. **147** *no loes*: 'not caring' about loss is a mark of the humility from which charity grows (cf. 288, where it is a mark of charity itself); seeking no material gain, he does not risk the *damnum* 'loss' of his own soul. *wynne*: either as the direct end of his *chaffare* or as a 'return' from others on his 'outlay' of unselfishness. **149** *here*: presumably the pronoun, with referent 'soul' (as is clear from // B 313 and would be clearer in **C** with *his* omitted). **151** *Austyn*: see on 134a above. **152** 'That true patient poverty meant humility in this life'; adding the more important positive part of Augustine's teaching, that the purpose of removing worldly anxieties is to free the soul to 'mind the things that are above, not the things that are upon the earth' (Col 3:2). **153** The added 152 removes an ambiguity in **B**, which might inadvertently imply lack of concern for *spiritual* 'business', the only proper *sollicitudo* (cf. also Rom 12:11). **153a** The ninth point echoes and is the fruit of the first (121a): removing the wrong kind of *cura* brings the right kind of *felicitas*.

B 320–32 One of **C**'s chief structural omissions, in **B** ending the Fourth Vision with a dramatic emotional climax that plausibly motivates Will's awakening in the best tradition of medieval 'dream-vision realism' (see Hieatt 1967:89–97). **321** *for Dowelis sake*: 'because I could not do (anything for do-) well.' **323** *Synne...euere*: a sentiment echoed by Julian of Norwich (see on 186 above). *sory*: with polysemy perhaps intended, since Haukyn's melancholy is caused by thinking of 'the blight man was born for', though he also seems to repent with a new and comprehending contrition. **324** *wepte...eighen*: recalling earlier 'conversion' tears, those of Will (whose surrogate he in some manner is) at B 5.61, of Robert at B 5.463 and of Longeus at B 18.91. **326** *Swouned*: an extreme reaction reminiscent of such as Margery Kempe of Lynn (*Book*, p. 219). As with Will's faint at B 16.19, its removal may suggest doubts about emotional demonstrativeness as a true measure of spiritual sincerity. **327–8** Haukyn's judgement that possessions or superiority over others

minister to pride shows him as having fully accepted Patience's teaching at 59–61 above. *lordshipe*: here any kind of ownership of land. **330–1** *shame...couere*: his sinfulness being such that he should never be entitled to wear the clothes he coveted (at B 13.228–30), except for decency's sake. **331** *careyne*: the contemptuous term seeming apt because it is to *corpus mortis huius* 'the body of this death' (Rom 7:24) that Haukyn now realises he was enslaved. The whole of Romans ch. 7 (on man's 'carnal' incapacity to *perficere bonum* 'accomplish that which is good' has great relevance to this scene. **332** *wepte...awakede*: i.e. both at the noise within the dream (like that at 18.179 below) and at the intensity of the emotion, which Will shares empathetically with his surrogate Haukyn. The reverse-sequence (*falling* asleep through a strong access of his *own* feeling) has been illustrated at B 11.4–5 and will be again at C 5.108.

B XIV *ends here and* B XV *begins, running parallel with* C *to the end of* XVII

(ii) 156–372a contain the first part of an extended dialogue between Will and LIBERUM ARBITRIUM, who does most of the speaking. This large and significant revision divides B XV (which is only a little shorter than B V) towards mid-point, and redefines the relation between the Dreamer and his alter-ego Actyf, in whose 'free will' he now encounters an image of his own 'inner self'. The new structure is less monolithic but also less elegant than in **B**; for there Anima's passus-long monologue prepares for the Sixth Vision (an inner dream) to occupy (and lead to an awakening nearly coincident with the end of) Passus XVI, neatly balancing the opening's introductory material. **C**'s less tidy shape may be meant to reflect the fluidity of the dream state more accurately, but it makes for difficulty of comprehension and could be due to incomplete revision. The main structural boundary occurs clearly enough at the end of C 18.179; but another less explicit one seems intended at C 18.4, corresponding to the start of the inner dream in **B**. The re-naming of **B**'s ANIMA as Liberum Arbitrium may arise from an altered understanding of the traditional Isidorean powers of the soul (see Sanderlin 1941; Donaldson 1949:188–96; Schmidt 1969²; Harwood 1973²). But making him Actyf's 'leader' links this movement more closely to the encounter preceding it (Patience is presumed present throughout this dialogue, though never speaking again after 162).

156–71 The sudden transition lacks smoothness, as the new personage abruptly supplants Actyf (who never returns), and the 'interior' character of his interchange with Will is less obvious than in the dialogue with Anima in **B**. **156** *ledare*: a neutral term, but always positive in **L**, as is probably confirmed by the later Latin definition in 191–2. *Liberum Arbitrium*: 'Free Choice' more than simply 'Free Will', stressing the moral knowledge that gives rational decisions their 'freedom' rather than the 'existential' autonomy that *may* defy 'the dictates of that reason [or] recognition and observance of the will of God, [which] is for [man] true freedom' (*Pe*). The added definition at 199*a* (on which see Schmidt 1969²:134–43, Harwood 1973²:680–95), removes the ambiguity in the English at 191 and puts this beyond doubt. One motive for introducing a personification of the Soul's 'rationally determinative' power may be to counterbalance the affective/volitional thrust of the main arguments advanced in the Third Vision. **157** *Consience...Clergie*: because truly 'free' choice will be informed by both the innate moral sense and the teaching of the Church. **160** *Liberum Arbitrium* (LA) clearly supports Patience on the superiority of poverty, but his phrasing draws upon the omitted conclusion to B XIV. Thus the echo of B 14.327 in 158 is one of the poem's more striking 'intertextual' moments, almost as if Actyf's 'deep self' were speaking about his shallower ('Haukyn') self. **161** *preyde Pacience*: Will's new-found courtesy sits ill with the rebuke to him at 210 below (uncancelled from B 50). **162** The referent of *oper name* is obscure, since the Dreamer does not yet know any of his interlocutor's 'other names'; perhaps Patience means, 'Ask him by what other name he is known'. **164** *creature*: not by 'creation' (as all men are created by God) but by his 'new creation' through baptism. **166** *a party*: 'partly, in part', since not all who possess free choice are Christians. **167** *Peter the porter*: because traditionally thought of as gate-keeper of heaven, and represented in iconography as holding 'the keys of the kingdom' given him by Christ (Mt 16:19; cf. Pr 128–9). *fauchen*: his traditional iconographic emblem (see Baker 1978:pl.19), since as a Roman citizen St Paul was believed to have been executed by beheading with a sword

B 15.1–15 2 *Er*: implying that the knowledge eventually comes, when Will asks Kynde what *be best to lerne* (20/22.207) and receives the answer 'Love'. **3** *wit*: both 'knowledge' and 'understanding'. *fool*: contrasted with the dull 'daffe' of B 1.140 and looking forward to its ironic 'Pauline' use at the point where Will joins the 'fools' (the followers of Conscience) who seek refuge in Unity (22.61). At 10 Will's failure to show conventional 'respect of persons' leads perforce to his being held a worldly incompetent. **4** *lakkede my lif*: condign punishment for the behaviour Reason condemned at B 11.386; but the suffering it produces prepares him to receive further disclosures. **5–6** echo Js 2:1–3, an important vindicating authority for L's entire enterprise. *and*: implying 'because'. **7** *persons*: like the *grete syres* of Pr 177. **10** *folk*: the *peple* on whom Holy Church comments at 1.5–9. *raued*: reflecting the judgement of 'the world' on those who give first place to 'the things that are above'. **11** *Reson*: the authoritative figure whose wisdom Will

'rebuked' at B 11.372; having 'suffred', he is ready to 'conceyue moore þoruʒ Reson' (B 11.411–12), who will now have 'ruþe' on him. *rokked*: implying that the Christian 'fool' is a kind of 'child'; as Will is to learn shortly, Charity is a 'childissh þyng' (B 15.149). **12** *sorcerie*: because raising bodiless spirits was the province of magicians; cf. *coniured* 14, where there may be humorous wordplay on MED sense 2(a). *wiþalle*: both 'to be sure', as at closely parallel B 18.115 (MED s.v. *with-al* adv. 1(c)), and 'altogether, completely' (1(a)). *sotil*: the soul (as noted by Simpson 1990:172n) being called 'subtilis et invisibilis' in the pseudo-Augustinian *De Spiritu et Anima* (*PL* 40:789). **13** *tolde*: an inward 'telling', since the soul has no bodily organs. **14–17** The insistent *k* alliteration underscores the catechetical character of this interchange.

171–80 are added to explain the new character's nature and function. **172–3** vary the phrase *somtyme* by shifting the stress from the first to the second element; 172 *may* be Type IIIa (see *TN*), 173 is probably IIIc. **174** *Layk*: i.e. '(consent to) engage in (some act)'; a submerged metaphor from 'play at a sport'. **175** *do wel or wykke*: making plain that both the virtue and its antithesis depend on the agent's free consent. *a wille with a resoun*: a loose but memorable rendering of the volitional and rational elements in *Liberum Arbitrium*; see further Harbert 1990. **178–9** 'It's like the way wood and fire support each other, and the same applies to [man's material nature and his] spiritual will'. LA will fit well enough in this figurative dichotomy if regarded as synecdochic for 'soul'. **180** presumably denotes the state of full possession of one's mental faculties.

181–99*a* provide a comprehensive analysis of the soul's multiple aspects by giving it ten (nine) different Latin names (see Schmidt 1969:151–2). Eight denote its vital, cognitive and affective powers, one a virtue of its volitional power (*love*), and one its condition in separation from the body (*spirit*). All are defined, but *Anima*, *Animus* and *Liberum Arbitrium* are given no vernacular equivalents, though presumably only the last lacked one (on the coined phrase *fre wit* as a possible such name see on 10.51 and Schmidt 1968¹:168–9). **181** *Anima*: the soul as life-principle, 'animans' (see earlier on 10.134 and Schmidt 1968²:363–4). **182** *Animus*: the appetitive and volitional capacity. **183** *Mens*: the mind in its active reasoning function, perhaps meant to recall the personification *Thouhte* at 10.72ff (*thought* is Chaucer's equivalent at *HF* 523 for his source Dante's *mente*). **184** *Memoria*: 'recollection,' in the sense of the spiritual function of 'calling to mind [God, one's past sins, one's benefactors etc]'. This is the only sense of English *memorie* in **L**, who more often uses *mynde* (MED s.v. n. (1), 2 and 3a) for 'memory' (see A 11.216 and cf. MED s.v. *memorie* n. 2(a), 4(b)). **186** *Racio*: a term with legal-moral resonances and a special association with justice fully explained in Alford 1988[1]. **187** *Sensus*: both 'sense-perception' (whence *welle* 'source') and 'understanding of the meaning of language' (whence *telleth*). The Latin term often answers to (*kynde*) *wit* in **L**'s customary usage (see on Pr 141–7 above). **189** *chalenge...chepe*: semi-figurative uses that signify acts of choosing to do or not do something. **190** *Concience*: see on Pr 95. *Goddes...notarie*: because divinely implanted in the soul, with the power and responsibility of 'reckoning' or evaluating all one's moral acts. **191** *gode...ille*: ostensibly expressing an 'Augustinian' understanding of free-will (see Schmidt 1969[2]:141). But if it is possible that *do* is meant to take *gode dedes* as its exclusive object and *do nat* only to govern *ille* (*dedes*), this syntactic ambiguity will find itself resolved in the purely positive conception of LA as given in the Latin definition at 199*a*. **193** *lelly*: in accordance with 'love' truly understood as charity. **196** *spirit*: the common formal term (= native *goest*) for the immaterial soul when separated from its body (as in Mt 27:50, Lk 24:39, I Pet 3:19). **197** *Austyn*: author of treatises on the soul; but the allusion here may be to the *De Spiritu et Anima* (see Schmidt 1969:143–4), which was ascribed to him in the period. *Ysodorus*: St Isidore (*c.* 560–636), Bp. of Seville, whose encyclopaedic *Etymologiae seu Origines* is **L**'s direct source for everything here except for **C**'s LA, which he may have added from Godfrey of Poitiers (Schmidt 1969[2]:142–3). **199*a*** *Anima...Spiritus est*: 'The SOUL chooses for itself a variety of names according to its varying modes of operation. As giving life to the body, it is *Soul*; as willing, *Intention*; as knowing, *Mind*; as bringing to mind things past, *Memory*; as judging, *Reason*; as perceiving, *Sense*; as loving, *Love*; as turning from evil towards good, *Free Choice*; as breathing (the life-breath), *Spirit*' (Isidore, *Etymologies* XI.i.13). Like Patience's nine-fold definition of Poverty at 115–15*a*, this *divisio* (nine-part in **C** as well as **B** if *Mens* was accidentally omitted by **L**), is accompanied by an English paraphrase (181–96), here before not after the Latin. The influence of St Bernard's conception of free-will as reflecting the image of God in man is persuasively argued in Donaldson 1949:189ff. But the wording of the newly added clause on LA directly echoes Godfrey of Poitiers's '[liberi-arbitrii] est declinare a malo et eligere bonum', a formulation that itself conflates Ps 36:27 ('Declina a malo et fac bonum') and Is 7:15 ('reprobare malum, et eligere bonum'). For an analysis of this list see Schmidt 1969[2]:151–2.

200–39*a* **202** 'Prelate, Pontiff, Metropolitan [= primate of an ecclesiastical province], Bishop, Pastor'. **206** *and of myn*: a rebuke at odds with Will's having been *encouraged* by Patience to 'assay' LA's names (162), and perhaps reflecting imperfect revision at this point. **208–9** express a 'Faustian' craving for knowledge of everything, theoretical and practical (*sciences*; *craftes*). In exceed-

ing what is possible for a created being, it resembles Lucifer's *superbia* understood as desire for an omniscience leading to omnipotence. **211*a*** See on 1.111*a*. **212** *aзeyns...resoun*: 'against every law of nature and of reason'. **213** *creature*: used not *proprie* of Christ but loosely as = 'being', or else with specific reference to his human nature (as divine, he would 'conne al'). **214** *Salamon*: see on 3.121. **215–215*a*** 'Just as it is not good for a man to eat much honey, so he that is a searcher of majesty [*sc.* that of God] shall be overwhelmed by [his] glory' (Prov 25:27). On the reading *opprimatur* 'let him be overwhelmed', see *TN*. **216** The translation-response recalls Patience's words at 118 and reminds that the one whose 'leader' LA is remains the *lewed* Actyf. **218–19** do not improve on the compressed but pungent **B** 58–9, since the repeat of *worche* 218*b*, though skilfully stress-varied in the T-type 219 as *wél wórche*, is less telling than the sense-varied *do* of **B** 59 with medial pause before *double scape* (a notion correlating with that of 'double reward' at **B** 14.148). These lines do not cite but tacitly evoke Lk 12:47–8, which is quoted at **B** 12.56*a*=**C** 14.18*a*. **220–1** 'Blessed the man who does the Bible scan / And turns words into works as best he can'; from St Bernard's *Tractatus de Ordine Vitae* (*PL* 184:566), whose scriptural source is Mt 7:24: 'Omnis...qui audit *verba* mea haec et *facit* ea, assimilabitur viri sapienti...' (Alf*Q*). **223*a*** 'Craving for knowledge deprived man of the glory of everlasting life'; from St Bernard's *Sermo* IV *in Ascensione Domini* (*PL* 183:311). The two quotations set against the Dreamer's (supposed) intellectual pride the spiritual humility, faith and love that St Bernard archetypally represents (Leff 1958:134–5; Stiegman in Evans 2001:129–39). LA's argument, somewhat ironically, echoes that of Will's *alter ego* Rechelesnesse at 11.276ff. **224–5** improve on **B** 64–5 (which repeat **B** 57) by correcting the awkwardly asymmetrical analogy between 'honey' and 'the reasoner' (instead of 'the knowledge derived from reason'). This revision replaces a warning against the worldly arrogance displayed in scholastic speculations on God's 'absolute' and 'ordained' power (*myзtes*) with one against plain intellectual disdain like the Priest's towards Piers at **B** 7.131–2. **226** *þat*: 'those who'. **B 67** *likynge*: 'desire [for such knowledge]', with a probable pun on 'licking' (i.e. of the *hony* that symbolises it) and a 'Platonic' linking of desire with the body (*licame*). *licames coueitise*: that *sapientia carnis* 'wisdom of the flesh' which is 'an enemy to God' (Rom 8:7). **227** '[For I say, by the grace that is given me],...not to be more wise than it behoveth to be wise, [but to be wise unto sobriety and according as God hath divided to every one the measure of faith]' (Rom 12:3). At 22 syllables, the longest line in the poem, scanning on *s* or *p* (see *TN*); // **B** 69 is a simple Type IIIc. **228** *Freres*: see on 11.54. *prechen*: an accusation not easy to substantiate from surviving examples of friars' sermons to lay people, and more guardedly expressed in **C**, which allows that points made in addresses to (say) a university audience might reach the non-*litterati* indirectly, as over the host's table in a lodging. **229** *insolibles and falaes*: taken by MED (following *Sk*'s preference) as adjectives qualifying *motyues*. But while such post-positioned French *s*-pl. endings amplify the same construction and may contribute towards an effective satirical point, it is more natural to take both as noun plurals (*Pe*), translating scholastic Latin *insolubilia* 'logical paradoxes' (on which see Spade 1975, 1982) and *fallaciae* 'logical fallacies'. The real cause of concern is the problems for believers produced when dialecticians speculate on dogmas of faith, in a form such as: 'God is all-good and so cannot do evil; but God is all-powerful and so can do anything; therefore God can and cannot do evil. *Quod est insolubile*'; or, 'Christ was God, so could not die; but Christ was man and so could die; therefore Christ could and could not die. *Quod est fallacia*'. **B 71** *vnmesurables*: perhaps suggested by *mensuram fidei* in Rom 12:3 (see at 227). These 'matters' moved for debate exceed the 'measure' appropriate for 'telling of the Trinity' (which is that of reverent faith). On the French adjectival form see *MES* 277. **231** substitutes simple rhetorical *repetitio* of *ten* for **B**'s 'Platonic' punning on *bileue...bileuen*, which subtly implies a link between faith and intellectual self-restraint. However, as well as being syntactically clearer than B 72–3, the adverbial phrase *ten sythe* (pointedly balanced against *fyue wittes*) economically modifies both *teche* and *were*, intimating that frequent *repetition* of basic truths is far more worthwhile than a quest for novelty. **B 74b–75** are well omitted; for though giving a neat descending pattern of 'ten, seven, (five)', they repeat B 14.219 and B 13.410=C 7.69. **234** *helynge*: perhaps 'clothing [themselves]' (MED s.v. ger. (2) 2(a)), as this corresponds to *haterynge* B 78; but the commoner sense 1 'roofing' would be as apt. **239a** 'Do not be respecters of persons'; a near-quotation from Js 2:1, which itself echoes Deut 1:17 ('nec accipietis cuiusquam personam') and Prov 24:23. While Ac 10:34 'Non est *personarum acceptor* Deus' may be verbally closest (*Pe*), it refers to God, not men. The 'judgement' context of the OT originals leads AlfQ to opine that **L**'s phrase was a legal maxim. But as the reference here is to friars' cultivation of the rich rather than the poor, a source that is conceptually closer if verbally remoter might be Lk 14:11–14, which 'records' what Christ said.

B 81a–85 **81a** 'Let them all be confounded that adore graven things' (Ps 96:7). 'And in another place: Why do you love vanity, and seek after lying?' (Ps 4:3). **82** *glose*: Cassiodorus on Ps 4:3 (*GO*), identifying 'graven things' with *lies* and false earthly goods that cannot fulfil what they promise (*PL* 113:849). The same authority's *Expositio in XX primos Psalmos* quotes without attribu-

tion the Augustinian comment on Ps 4 cited by *Sk* contrasting truth (which makes blessed) with *vanity* and *falsehood* (= love of worldly goods). **83** *If...wit*: 'If I'm grossly misrepresenting you because of my ignorant lack of understanding...' *brennyng*: a vivid asseveration like Book's later at B 18.254 (20.264). Heretics were already burnt at the stake in France, but in England not before the execution of the Lollard William Sawtrey a little before the statute *De Heretico Comburendo* of 1401, which confirmed a (long unused) canonical penalty.

240–83 severely attack the worldliness of contemporary priests and ascribe current moral decline to the laity's disillusionment with their hypocrisy. **240–53** paraphrase the Latin quoted at 271. **240** *holy writ*: not Scripture but authoritative traditional writings, as of the Church Fathers (cf. 1.125). **242** *enspireth*: 'fills with (religious) zeal'. **246** *ensample...trees*: cf. the earlier moral emblem of trees at 5.118–22; an inverted anticipation of the Tree of Charity at 18.9ff. **249** *stokkes*: an improvement in accuracy, since the root's disease will reach the branches from the trunk. **251** *to reule*: 'in which to govern'. **253–4** *leue... leue*: 'Platonic' *concatenatio* stating a condition for spiritual renewal in the Church. The image seems to echo St Bernard in *Sermones in Cantica Canticorum* 51.2: 'Itaque nec sine flore fructus, nec sine fide opus bonum' (cit. Stiegman in Evans 2001:149n58). **254** *lecherye of clothyng*: a metaphor pointing to the part played by fashionable dress in arousing admiration and desire; see 267–8 and B 15.123–4, and cf. *CT* I 156, 193–4, 262–3. **256** recalls 15.117; **257** echoes 10.78, 80; **259** adapts B 85. **260–2** The ellipsis here follows a complex construction (with incidental loss of tense-sequence in *amenden*): 'Laymen would be reluctant not to follow your teaching and renounce sin, more as a consequence of your example than (they would fail to do this) as a consequence of your not practising what you preach'. **263** scans cognatively on *p / b / p*. *braunche*: cf. *CT* X 393. **264–5** *in Latyn*: as in the C13th *Summa virtutum de remediis anime* where images of dunghill, wall and wolf-like behaviour all appear 'clustered in a passage on hypocrisy' (Wenzel 1984:94–6, and id. in Alford, ed. 1988:169). *dong-hep... snakes*: the nesting of snakes and worms in the warm interiors of dung-hills being a fact of natural history. This dunghill / snow image is found 'moralised' in *AI* 81: 'non uayr body ne is bote...ase a donghel besnewed'. But while the archetypal emblem of hypocritical deception is the 'subtle' serpent of Gen 3:1, the vice's best-known association with snakes is in John the Baptist's expression 'brood of vipers' addressed to the Pharisees and Sadducees (Mt 3:7), which seems to have been associated by **L** with Mt 23:27. **265/6** The identical end-rhyme reinforces the passage's homiletic-instructional tone. **266** *wal*: alluding to the 'whited sepulchres...full of...all filthiness' of Mt 23:27. **268** *enblaunched*: a loan-word found first here and only once later, and lexically at ease with the macaronic line's French stave-words. *bele paroles*: the fine words of their eloquent sermons which, like the whitewash on the surface of tombs, hides spiritual deadness within; to be contrasted with the *lele wordes* of B 16.6 (on these phrases see Schmidt 1983:139–41). *bele clothes*: in this context of 'hypocritical whitening', perhaps alluding ironically to the priest's alb (signifying 'integrity') and his *Asperges* prayer of purification before Mass ('lavabis me et super nivem dealbabor'), as much as to the inappropriate apparel implied by 254. The relevance of Js 2:2 (cited Alf*Q*) is not clear, since the rich man of that passage is neither hypocrite nor priest. **269** *lambes*: on vesting with the alb, the priest prays to be made white (*dealbatus*) with the blood of the Lamb, and there may be a learned anti-pun concealed here, since *dealbare* is Medieval Latin for 'whitewash' (see MED s.v. *whitlymen*). *wolues*: a Gospel image of 'false prophets' in sheep's clothing, the religious equivalent of the *wastours wolueskinnes* who destroy Piers's field in B 6.161. **270** *Iohannes Crisostomus*: St John Chrysostom (*c.* 347–407), Patriarch of Constantinople and Doctor of the Church; the widely-circulated homilies misascribed to him are classed as by 'Pseudo-Chrysostom'. **271** 'Just as all good comes out of the Temple, so does all evil. If the priesthood possesses integrity, the whole Church flourishes; but if it is corrupt, the faith of all withers up. If priests live in sin, the entire people turns to sin. Just as, when you see a tree pale and withered, you know it has something wrong with its root, so when you see a people undisciplined and irreligious, it is certain that their priests are diseased'. This passage from the Latin translation of pseudo-Chrysostom, Homily 38 on St Matthew (*PG* 56:839), is commenting on Mt 21, where the image of the barren fig-tree is at vs 19.

B 119–27 119 *lewed...Latyn*: this long and explicit warning to clerics, even fuller than that at B 13.71–3*a*, is veiled *only* by its being in Latin. **121–4** specify costly adornments judged unfitting for clerics to wear (cf. *CT* A 159–62, 195–7). **123** *Sire...Geffrey*: the common courtesy-title (= Lat. *Dominus*) for a priest (see also 6.366). **124** *ballok-knyf*: a fashionable ornamental dagger with a knobbed (testicle-shaped) haft (see Poole 1958:I, fig. 59c). **125** *porthors...plow*: recalling Piers's figurative use of 'plough' at B 7.120. *Placebo*: see on 3.463=B 3.311. **126–7** attack priests who insist on payment for their spiritual services. **272–83** affirm the 'poetic' justice or condign punishment whereby wealth that a man has unjustly obtained is spent unworthily after his death. This is a different attitude to the use of 'the mammon of iniquity' from that at 8.235–35*a* and 19.247–8*a* (each an injunction, not a description of the actual state of affairs). Laymen bequeath money to bad clerics, who leave it to people unwilling to use it to help the souls of the former. **272–3** Translinear 'trailing' rhyme

strengthens the protest and allows a mordant pun on 'provide' and '(later) discover to be' for *fynde*. **273** *Vnkynde curatours*: cf. 1.188–91. **275** 'God who is wise would never wish anything other than that...' **278** *þat*: 'that what'. **B 135** Bequests left to unworthy priests in the expectation of their prayers deprive the poor (*Goddes folk*) of a share in 'Christ's goods' (= wealth bequeathed to the Church). **280–1** *leue...Leueth...lyuen...loue*: the *concatenatio* transformed into *annominatio* as the staves move through the sequence of vowels; cf. 356. **B 147** *goode meteȝyueres*: the noun always accompanied by this adjective.

284–372*a* explain CHARITY through the actions of a personification of this virtue, **284–313** beginning with a sketch, on the basis of I Cor 13:4–7, of its passive or purely spiritual side. **284** The probing question about the nature of charity is triggered by a casual and 'unweighted' use of the word (like the riposte to a similar use of 'wille' at B 150). **286** echoes 5.44; **287** repeats 5.40 and 11.277. **B 152** stresses the length of the speaker's experience (*lyued* implies 'lived long'), C its social range (there seem to be echoes here of the 'autobiographical' passage). *Longe Wille*: 'Tall Will', 'Perseverance' (= *longanimitas*, the seventh fruit of the Holy Ghost); a memorable phrase intimating both his stature and his persistency. When forming an anagram with preceding *lond*, it also yields what has been taken as the poet's *kynde name*, in a manner reminiscent of the Preface to John of Bridlington's *Prophecies* (Wright, *Pol. Songs* 1859:127) explaining a verse '*Cantu* cantabit *ariae* plebs et jubilabit' ('The people of "Sing-an-air-ville" [Canterbury] / with the-singing-of-an-air will sing and rejoice'). **155** may just mean literally that 'they only give when certain of repayment (but otherwise never, however great the need)' or may relate more directly to expectations that their almsgiving will be re-paid by God in heaven. **289*a*** '[Charity...] is not puffed up, Is not ambitious, [seeketh not her own **B**]' (I Cor 13:4–5). **292** *nyme*: an infinitive dependent on an understood preceding *wolde*, omitted in revision. A similar auxiliary such as *wende* is needed before *fynde* and *thynketh* 294, which break the tense-sequence and ought to be preterite. **293** *sektes*: cf. 355; no Dominic, Francis or Clare is to be met with nowadays in the orders they founded. **294** *but figuratyfly*: i.e. *neuere sooþly* (B 162), only with the same relation to a body that a mirror-image has. **294*a*** 'We see here [*nunc* Vg] (through a glass) in a dark manner; but then face to face' (I Cor 13:12). The Pauline 'mirror' may signify the Creation or Scripture, both of which reflect, though dimly, the 'face' of God. **295** 'And I believe that is, as far as we can tell, how things really stand in relation to charity'. **296** *childische*: having the trusting innocence of 'newborn babes [who] desire the rational milk without guile' (I Pet 2:2); something very different from *fauntelte* (B 15.150). **296*a* (B 149*a*)** '[And Jesus calling unto him a little child,...said:...

Unless you [be converted and] become as little children, [you shall not enter into the kingdom of heaven **B**]' (Mt 18:2–3). That humility is the basis of charity echoes B 5.607, 11.208; saying so here serves dialectically to oppose spiritual 'childlikeness' to the childishness 'put away' by St Paul in I Cor 13:11 (the preceding verse). LA seems to urge mature Christians with a *fre liberal wille* ('open and generous, and so truly "free"') to be content to believe (in a childlike way) what they cannot see with their eyes and should not (in a childish way) ask to see. **B 164** 'In my opinion, Charity isn't something you get by force or by payment, as a prize or as a purchase'. **298** *russet*: as worn by friars and by the addressee (cf. on 10.1). **299** *cammaca*: a word from Arabic and ultimately of possible Chinese origin. **B 168** *Tarse*: Turkestan or Tartary (a region of Central Asia west of Chinese Sinkiang); first used here or at *SGGK* 571 (and cf. Mandeville's *Travels*, 24/17 linking 'cloth...of tartarie or of camaca'). **300–01** *glad...sory*: cf. Rom 12:15, quoted at A 11.193*a*, a line deleted there from **B** but retrieved for use here (B 169*b* also echoes Rom 12:14). **301–2** *childerne / Lawhe*: an image of approved (childlike) guilelessness. **304** 'It never occurs to him that anyone would lie on oath'. **306** *For... God*: 'such is his (own) reverent awe of God'. **306a** See at B 7.59*a*, where **C** deletes. **308** *likene...scorne*: 'do imitations of people in order to mock them'. **309–11** recall Patience on *caritas* at 15.159–60. **312/13** *þat ilke / Þat*: 'the sort of person who'.

314–34a 314–15 The implication of Will's question, which verbally echoes Reason's to him at 5.26–7, is that to exercise practical charity presupposes economic independence. **316–34a** LA's reply resumes Patience's teaching earlier on charity and on humility as the spiritual essence of 'poverty': as Charity's resources are spiritual, he can always draw on these even when he has no material means to succour those in need. **316/17** The identical rhyme added in revision underlines the quasi-catechetical character of LA's replies. **318–19** These two fleeting personifications of Charity's spiritual helpers affirm the oneness of OT and NT understandings of divine fidelity or *treuthe*. **318** *Aperis..*: 'Thou openest thy hand'; see on 15.265*a*, quoted before Patience illustrates from the case of the Seven Sleepers the efficacy of absolute dependence on God . **319** *Fiat...*: 'Thy will be done [on earth as it is in heaven]' (Mt 6:10); the third petition of the Lord's prayer and the same 'pece of þe *Paternoster* þat sholde fynde vs alle' offered by Patience to Actyf at 249–52. **320** *Credo...*: 'I believe in God the Father Almighty'. The revision here, perhaps in response to doctrinal turbulence in the 1380s, completes the list of the Church's four chief prayers that are the 'spiritual food' of Charity with the opening clause of the Apostles' Creed: sincere devotion must be complemented by right belief. **B 180** *Spera...*: 'Trust in the Lord, [and do good]' (Ps 36:3); a psalm of total trust in God,

on which see further at 13.100. **321** *purtraye...peynten*: a metaphorical evocation of the Rosary devotion; it envisages the Lord's Prayer as providing the 'outline' of faith in 'God the Father Almighty' that is 'coloured in' by the 'Hail Marys' focussed on the lives of Mary and Christ. The Rosary's three sets of five Mysteries for spiritual meditation (joyful, sorrowful and glorious), each contain ten 'Hail Marys' preceded by an 'Our Father' and followed by a 'Glory be'. *Auees*: from '*Ave Maria, gratia plena*', the opening of the prayer in Latin (Lk 1:26). **322** *pilgrimages*: symbolic ones like that of Piers 'atte plow for pouere mennes sake' (B 6.102); the wording echoes Reason's at 4.123 and Truth's at 9.34–5. **323–4** The provision of food and clothing were the first and fourth, visiting the imprisoned was the sixth of the 'corporal works of mercy' based on Mt 25:35–6. *pore men and prisones*: two separate categories, but regularly associated (and even identified) by **L** (see B 14.174). No nourishment was provided for prisoners save what was brought by *frendes* or by visitors as an act of charity. **B 183** is slightly obscure. If *hir* is a subjective genitive, the 'pardon' is something they give to their visitor, i.e. he obtains remission of *his* sins through the opportunity *they* provide. This meaning seems tonally at variance with the disinterestedness of Christian charity as defined at 157 above (*non querit que sua sunt*). However, if *pardoun* bears not its religious but its legal sense (MED s.v. 2 'release from penalty', not 1 'forgiveness of sins'), **L**'s point will be that those whom Charity visits find 'release' (relief) from the pain of their 'imprisonment' (literal or figurative) through the *bodily foode* or *goostly foode* that he brings. **324–7** Whereas **B 184–5** intimate that the mere fact of his visit and concern (*Thouȝ* 'even if') will have value, the revision (less subtly perhaps) stresses how Charity brings them, together with material help, the religious message that their condition provides an opportunity for the imitation of Christ. **329–34a** After active good works, Charity turns to the contemplative side, weeping religious tears for the innocence lost in *ȝouthe* (metonymic for the sins of his own youth). An echo may be detected of the life of St Francis, a rich gallant before his conversion, who is named at 353–5 below. The 'washing' metaphor is that used by Conscience to Haukyn at B 14.16–28 (a passage excised in **C** perhaps to avoid confusion as well as repetition), and in the present allegory the soul is figured as a garment. The activity described here, however, is not sacramental confession but the *purgatio* that forms the first stage of the contemplative life; after sins have been forgiven, spiritual humility is to be renewed by regular acts of inner 'compunction'. **330** *hem*: the referent here (as at 331–2, B 192) being the 'accompanying attitudes' (vain self-regard, etc) of Pride (synecdochic for 'sin'), these strictly should be 'clawed' off (B 14.17) rather than 'laved'. But possibly **L** had in mind how spiritual writers like St Bernard believed that *amor carnalis* (= human love of Christ's humanity) could overcome the *vita carnalis* ('fleshly existence'), not destroying it but purifying and redirecting it towards *caritas* (*Sermons on Song of Songs* 20.9, cit. Stiegman in Evans 2001:148n26). **331** *Laboraui...*: 'I have laboured in my groanings, every night I will wash my bed: I will water my couch with my tears]' (Ps 6:7); from the first of the seven penitential psalms included in the Primer, the chief prayer-book used by lay people. This phrase provides the name of the spiritual 'laundry', anticipating the grange *Lavacrum-lex-Dei* at 19.73. **332** *breste*: the metaphorical source of his tears, and the referent of *hit* (revising *hem* B 190, which has the 'appurtenances' as referent). Striking the breast is the classic gesture of penitential sorrow (cf. 7.59–60, and Lk 18:13). **333** The stained breast is washed clean with tears; *hit* here too is altered from *hem* B 190 to make the 'washing' image fit better with the personal pronoun in the following Latin. **333a** 'Thou shalt wash me, and I shall be made whiter than snow' (Ps 50:9); familiar from the *Asperges* rite before Sunday Mass and conventionally associated with penitential tears, as by Brinton 1:84 (Alf*Q*); cf. on 268–9 above. **334a** is from the *Miserere*; see on 15.63.

336–38a 336 repeats 5.29, where Reason asks Will if this is indeed what he does. The sub-text may signify 'become a mendicant hermit (like Patience)'. **338** slightly moderates the negative tone of Anima's rejoinder at B 198, suggesting the same caution about criticising the official Church that is observable in the C line added earlier at Pr 138. The citation-gloss on 'Piers the Ploughman' is one of the most challenging moments in the poem; for discussion of the probable influence from Augustine's *De Trinitate* Bk XV, see Simpson 1986:9–13. **338a** 'And God saw their thoughts' (adapted from Lk 11:17 'Et ipse vidit cogitationes eorum' or the similar Mt 9:4). **L**'s arresting use of *Deus* for *ipse* makes explicit the divine nature of Jesus (to whom *Ipse* refers) and intimates that 'Piers' might be a 'guise' of Christ, just as the humanity of Jesus was of God (cf. Jn 14:9). The nuanced elaboration of this audacious idea at B 212 is omitted in **C**. **B 201–8** This attack on religious caterpillars may have been cut as both digressive and repetitive (204a=B 13.302a).

B 209–15 proclaim that Charity cannot be recognised by his outward appearance, learning (or lack of it), words or actions but only by his inner intent, something (*þat* 211) unknown to any human being except Piers, the Peter who 'is' Christ. **210** *wordes...wil*: a structurally important theme, on which see Burrow 1969:111–24 and the pertinent reference to Is 11:3 in Burrow 1993:120n4. Anima's loosely 'anti-intellectualist' position recalls Richard Rolle's in the Prologue to *Incendium Amoris*, p.147. **212** *Petrus...*: 'Peter, that is, Christ'; on this phrase see Huppé 1950:163–70, Davlin 1972:280–92 and for discussion of interpretations, Alford 1988[2]:55–6. Two

identifications are made here, of Piers with 'Petrus' and of 'Petrus' with Christ, the ambiguous term being the middle one, the Latin form of 'Piers' that inevitably suggests reference to the Apostle Peter. Separating the two names with *id est* invites a reading of the second as a gloss on the first, and hence their implicit identification at some level. The phrase itself has been thought to echo St Paul's allegorical interpretation of the rock (*petra*) from which Moses struck water in the wilderness: '*petra* autem erat *Christus*' (I Cor 10:4). This depends on accepting (Burrow 1993:121) that **L** deliberately substituted *petrus* for *petra* by way of allusion to Christ's punning promise to St Peter in Mt 16:18: 'tu es *Petrus*, et super hanc *petram* aedificabo ecclesiam meam', the scriptural basis of the Popes' claim to supreme jurisdiction in the Church (i.e. Christ the rock of salvation is present in Peter the rock of the Church). The particular divine power of seeing into men's hearts (Ps 7:10, I Par 28:9) is demonstrated in St Peter's detecting of Ananias's secret motivation (Ac 5:3–4), which Comestor (*PL* 198:1659) notes he did *praevidens in spiritu* 'through prophetic insight in the spirit' (Burrow 1993:121–2, acknowledging Goldsmith 1981:35–6). **215** *in ...*: 'on those who favour them'; a phrase with legal resonances (Gray 1986:60, Alf*G*). **216** *champion*: answering Will's denial at 164 above; Anima's use of the word involves a *transsumptio sensus* of the kind instanced at B 13.145 above.

339–72a 339–40 significantly alter B 210, rejecting appearance and words (but *not* actions) as reliable indicators of inner 'will' or intent. 339a repeats B 11.237 (on Christ at Emmaus). **340a** '[Though you will not believe me], believe the works' (Jn 10:38); Christ's works 'speak' for themselves and should suffice to create faith in those sceptical of 'mere' words. **342a** '[And when you fast], be not as the hypocrites, sad' (Mt 6:16). **344** *graye*: the colour of undyed wool, as worn by Franciscan friars. **345** *hit*: the implied referent is his clothing; but since one would scarcely give gilt armour to the needy, it may be indefinite ('he gave [alms])'. **346** *Edmond*: St Edmund the Martyr (*c.* 840–869), King of the East Angles, killed by invading Danes and interred at Bury St Edmund's. *Edward*: the Confessor (*c.* 1005–1066), the last Saxon king of England, who built and is buried at Westminster Abbey. Both were reputed to have lived a life of virginity. **347** *And...and*: 'And charity in an eminent degree was... and they were'. **348** *syngen and rede*: as a priest or deacon (cf. 5.68–9). **349** *clothes*: revising *wedes* here as at 12.126 (B 11.234). **351** *riche robes*: those of a prelate or great abbot. **352** *ycrymyled*: perhaps a form of *crimplen* 'curl, plait' as taken by *Sk* in IV I (p.348) and MED s.v. (a), which cites this as the earliest example (though all the others have medial *p*). Alternatively, it is a coinage from OF *cresmeler* 'anoint with holy oil' (*Sk* Gl s.v. and n. in IV II, p. 894) and alludes to *unge caput tuum* 'anoint thy head' (Mt 16:17, quoted at 342a above), to warn against judging outward austerity as a reliable sign of inner charity. **354** *Franceys tyme*: some 150 years earlier (see on 4.117). In the late 14th c. the Franciscan order was riven with dissension between the rigorist 'Observants' (1368, heirs of the earlier 'Spirituals' who had been condemned in the 1320s) and the 'Conventuals', who accepted the accumulation of property. **357a** 'Blessed is the rich man that is found without blemish' (Ecclus 31:8). The verse following this has already been quoted at 15.283. The present speaker's position may seem more optimistic about the rich than that of Patience the hermit, but in fact complements rather than rejects it, recalling B 14.145–54. **358–367** describe various public milieux in which charity is or is not to be encountered. **358; 360** *court*: the royal court; a law court. **361** virtually re-uses B 5.88 (on sins of envy), which is removed in **C** at that point. **362** *constorie...commissarie*: both criticised strongly at 3.34, 178–9. **363** *here lawe*: the complaint against the protracted nature of proceedings in the courts Christian echoes that against common-law courts in 3.198. **364–7** re-phrase in milder form the angry protest against ungenerous prelates in B 244–8. **366** *cardynals*: in **L** the objects of nothing but obloquy for their greed, notably at 21.225. **367** *coueytyse*: perhaps personified, like *auaris* at 365. The semi-formal repetition of the two terms may be meant to highlight their distinct special senses ('desire to keep'; 'desire to get'). **368** *coueyteth*: an ironic echo of 367, not unlike the wry humour of *eileþ* in B 251. **B 254a** 'In peace in the selfsame I will sleep [and I will rest]' (Ps 4:9); said regularly at compline and as an antiphon at matins on Holy Saturday (AlfQ). The exact referent of 'the selfsame' is not clear (it may be the 'light of God's countenance' mentioned at vs 7); but its connection with the resurrection of the just and with the peace and rest of heaven is made plain at B 18.186 below. **372a** 'Give us this day our daily bread' (Mt 6:11); another 'piece of the Paternoster', expressing Charity's dependence on 'God alone'. **B 255** recalls Z 1.127, a line perhaps stored up in a part of **L**'s 'repertorium' (*Intro.* V §§ 29–30).

Passus XVII (B XV)

PASSUS XVII directly continues the dialogue with LIBERUM ARBITRIUM, making the division from XVI purely formal (even *borweth* 1 echoes *borwe* 16.372), and it does not end until 18.105. The Passus itself divides roughly into two halves, (i) 1–121 and (ii) 122–320. Its main theme is the essential reality of the Church as a 'spiritual organism' constituted by Charity, something shown supremely in its leaders' readiness to witness to Christ at the cost of their lives. This is contrasted with its actuality as a 'material organisation' subject to ambition and greed, which obstruct its mission of peace and salvation to the Christian and non-Christian world alike. LA's discourse is interrupted by Will's opening scepticism at 1–3 about whether charity exists, and his questions at 125 and 150, on the Church as charity and on whether pagans possess charity. The rest of B XV to which XVI corresponds is kept, except that 30 lines on the nature of the Church at 122–49 replace some 70 on the Church's mission (416–89a).

(i) 1–121 1–24 correspond to B 15.268–97, but only about seven lines remain unrevised. Answering Will's objection that this ideal is never found in experience, LA cites the Desert Fathers who, though hardly typifying normative spiritual life, serve as *exempla ab extremis* against the worldliness of contemporary churchmen. **1** *no such*: with no immediate referent in the passus, but denoting Charity as described in 16.288–72. **3** 'And, moreover, sometimes angry, without necessarily being to blame for that.' **5** 'He falls short of the highest level of charity'; on *cheef charite* cf. 16.347. **5a** '[Charity] beareth all things' (I Cor 13:7). **6** *Holy writ*: 'sacred tradition'; here specifically the *LA*. **8** links the argument with the end of the XVI (372).

B 258–71 begin with a deeply-felt defence of humble and peace-bringing charity that sees human suffering as providentially willed for a positive purpose, and go on to a detailed account of the hermit saints. They echo HC's eloquent praise of divine Love (1.160–9) and Reason's observation on how God 'suffers' (B 11.378–81), but alter the sense of that verb from 'tolerate' to 'endure'. A possible reason why **C** cut these lines is that 271b repeats 259a and has already been re-used at C 6.114. **267** See on 15.139. **268** *Verbi gratia*: 'By way of example'. *and*: 'and (cited)'. **269** See on B 11.160. The chapters of *LA* used are 15 (Paul the Hermit), 21 (Antony), 56 (Mary of Egypt), 96 (Mary Magdalen) and 130 (Giles). **277** *leons*; *leopardes*: emblems of the nobility, from whom Anima implies contemplatives should not seek support (this having caused the problem of the monks' possession of so much property). **C**'s removal of the line suggests a softening of attitude towards this group after 1381, when they suffered the rebels' hostility. **282** *sondry tyme...book*: see *LA* p. 583.

9–36 9 *Egide...To his selle*: 'to Giles's cell' (anticipated indirect object). St Giles (d. ?700), a popular saint in medieval England, was said to have lived as a hermit and monk in Provence and to be buried at present-day St Gilles, Rhône. According to St Jerome's *Vita Pauli*, Antony was his guest when a raven brought bread. *hynde*: the allegorical *significacio* of the 'mild beast' (B 280) is uncertain, either the monks (cf. B 468 below) or the Church generally, considered as custodian of 'Christ's goods'. **10** *selle selde*: 'Platonic' wordplay linking solitude with self-denial. *be*: '(itself) to be'. **12** *Antony*: St Antony of Egypt (?251–356), an early Desert hermit and the reputed founder of monasticism. *Arseny*: St Arsenius

(d. 449), a Roman nobleman, a follower of Antony. **B 283** *on a day*: 'once a day, daily'. **13** *Paul primus heremita*: 'Paul the first hermit', a phrase from the opening of his life in *LA* p.94. Most of what is known about St Paul of Thebes (†*c.* 340) is from Jerome's Life. **15–16** *frere Austynes...ordre*: the Augustinian Friars or 'Friars Hermits' (on the French adjectival *-s* ending see *MES* 276), who claimed Paul the Hermit as their founder. Several congregations following a common Rule said to be based on the precepts of St Augustine united to form the Order in 1256. Suspicion that this much-debated claim (Arbesmann 1943, Sanderlin 1943) might be untrue (*gabben*) seems excluded by *LA*'s reliance here on the friars' own tradition. **17** St Paul the Apostle's trade was tent-making (Ac 18:3); but like Chaucer (*CT* VI 445), **L** confuses him with the Hermit, who wove baskets (*PL* 23:28). **19** *Peter...Andrew*: see Mt 4:18. **21** St Mary Magdalene was believed to have come to Marseilles where, after converting the pagans, she lived 30 years in solitude on the 'heavenly banquet' of angels' song (*LA* 413), glossed here as 'contemplative love and faith'. *mores...dewes*: a tradition preserved in the early C14th Rawlinson lyric 'Maiden in the moor lay' (Sisam, p.167). **23** *Marie Egipciaca*: St Mary of Egypt, a C5th hermit (*LA* 247) who, like her namesake, having been a prostitute lived 47 years in penance and mortification. *thritty wynter* by confusion with the Magdalene. **24** *thre litle loves*: the *tres panes* she had brought with her (*LA* 248). **28** uses B 273, with annominative repetition as in 10.62. **30–1** Such events are common in the lives of the Desert Saints, e.g. the lion that 'mildly' (*mansuete*) helps Zosimas dig a grave for St Mary of Egypt (*LA* 249) and, most famously, St Jerome's amiable beast (*LA* 653–6). *foules*: betokening 'righteous' laymen whose duty it is to provide for contemplatives (in // B 306–7 the b-half noun-phrases are the verb subjects, *mylde* corresponding to *mansuetus*). From the fact that *LA*'s 'fierce beasts' (B 305), though 'courteous' to the saints, did not bring food, the speaker infers that they signify 'lords and ladies' (B 309) and such as merchants (cf. 46), who should not be relied on, as their wealth may be unjustly gained (C 36).

B 313–14 *foweles...briddes*: 'true' trusting believers are compared to birds, doubtless in allusion to Mt 6:26. But though this use of *foweles* allows a play on 'fools' (as with the converse pun in *Goddes foles* at 11.251), the whimsicality of the present lexical contrast with *briddes* may explain the lines' deletion.

37–64 37 *Holy Writ*: the book of Tobias, chs. 2–3. LA turns the story of Tobias's scrupulosity about the kid (here 'lamb') that his wife got for her weaving into a lesson to churchmen not to offer spiritual gifts (such as prayers of intercession) in return for material ones of dubious origin. His argument is that only an example like Tobias's *from* churchmen will succeed in altering the behaviour of

rauenours. **B 312** *yborwed*: a euphemism for 'extorted'. **39/40** The identical rhyme as usual heightens the exemplum's catechetical flavour. **40a** 'Take heed, lest perhaps it be stolen'; 'And elsewhere, "[O Lord, do with me according to thy will]...for it is better for me to die, than to live [badly]"' (Tob 2:21; 3:60). The addition of *male* 'badly' in the second quotation is by contamination with a *worde* 'proverb' (Usk *TL* I VII 61) that **L** may have ascribed to Tob (see on 1.142a). **42** *riht...riht*: 'Platonic' wordplay underscoring the absolute character of *treuthe*. **48–9** The first metaphor for grace may echo 16.248, if the reading adopted is *grene-leued* (but on the revised reading see *TN*); the second (*chield*), perhaps inspired by *refrigescet charitas multorum* in Mt 24:12, is related to images like that of grace as softening moisture at 14.23–5. On its eschatological overtones cf. Tavormina in Edwards 1994. **51** *parfite patriarke*: not technically one of the patriarchs of ancient Israel, but given an honorific title here (and at 20.151) for exemplary patience and humility. Authorship of the Biblical book was uncertain, and sometimes ascribed to Job himself. **52** *To make*: not directly; but the text can be so applied. *mesure*: the ascetic 'temperance' appropriate to professed religious. **53** *Nunquam...steterit*: 'Will the wild ass bray, *says Job*, when he hath grass? Or will the ox low when he standeth before a full manger?' (Job 6:5; *Numquam* 'never' is an error for the interrogative particle *Numquid*). *Brutorum...tua*: 'The very nature of brute beasts is a condemnation of you, since with them common [shared / ordinary] food suffices; your evil has originated from excess'. This second quotation probably comes from a commentary on Job such as the one *Sk* cites by Bruno Signiensis (*Expos. in Job* vi. 5, p. 329): 'Or else, let the very animals [*bruta animalia*] teach you, who don't go on bellowing or lowing when they have their fill of what they need'. The passage recalls 13.143ff, esp. 150. **54–8** form a significant outburst against pious laypeople who deprive their dependants in donating to religious orders. **59a** See on 7.215a. **62–4** replace the sarcastic attack on 'poore freres'. **62** alludes to the proverb 'Charity begins at home'. **64** *haste*: i.e. have means to do so.

B 326–45 undergo complete revision in **C**, criticism of contemporary religious yielding to praise for the early Church's bountiful clergy. **326** 'He hath distributed, he hath given to the poor' (Ps 111:9; quoted as part of St Paul's commendation of cheerful and generous giving in II Cor 9:9); for the second half of this psalm-verse see **C** 66a. **327** *it are*: see on 5.59. **328** *buyldynge*: of great 'preaching churches' like the London Blackfriars and Greyfriars (see on 3.52). **335, 339** Rhetorical *repetitio* underlines the speech's homiletic character. **338** recalls the Thames reference at B 12.160, and use of a similar analogy at C 6.334 may explain its removal here in **C**. **341–2** have characteristic repetition-with-variation (*riche ben, riche bén*). **342a** *Quia...*: 'For it is a sacrilege not to give to the poor what is theirs' (Peter the Cantor, *VA* ch. 47, in *PL* 205:147). *Item idem...*: 'The same [authority] also [says], "to give to sinners is to sacrifice to devils"' (ib. col. 149). *Item...*: '[He likewise says], "Monk, if you are in need and accept, you are giving rather than receiving; but if you are not in need and (yet) accept, you are stealing"' (ib. col. 152). *Porro...*: 'Further, a monk is not in need if he has what suffices for nature' (a reminiscence of I Tim 6:8); cf. C 7.118*a* and B 9.92*a*.

65–93 continue the critique of avarice with a pointed contrast between the model generosity of early clerics and the greed of contemporary 'false Christians' (not only but especially clerics). **65** *Laurence*: see at 2.129–30. **66–6a** *manhede...manet*: possibly an unusual 'Platonic' pun of a translinguistic kind. **66a** 'His justice remaineth for ever and ever' (Ps 111:9), the second part of the verse quoted as B 326, sung as a versicle on the feast of St Lawrence; for the biblical and liturgical context see Tavormina 1987:245–71. **67** *Goddes men*: here not 'the clergy' but the *pauperes Christi* (for the poor as God's special care see Ps 33:7–11). **70** *That*: 'Of which'. *here part*: sentiment and phrasing recalling 3.245; alms for the poor are a 'treasure' won by Christ's 'conquest' of men's hearts. **71** *of...lawe*: the duty of OT Jews to give tithes to the Levites (Num 18:26, Heb 7:5) being the scriptural basis of the Church's claim to the same. **72** *Purnele*: a type-name for a priest's concubine, as at 6.366. **73–84** The comparison of man's soul to a coin was traditional (Raw 1969:156–7). **73** *Loscheborw*: Luxembourg shillings and pence, light counterfeit coins the importation of which was forbidden as treason by Edward III in 1346 and later. **75** *þe printe*: the indelible 'character' held to be imparted to the priest's soul by his ordination. **77** *Kynges...Heuene*: on the group-genitive see *MES* 78–9. *marke*: here the sacramental 'character' conferred by baptism (*follynge*); but where the phrase occurs at // B 351 *crowne* (with its pun on 'tonsure' and the 'crown' symbol on coins) signifies Holy Orders. **85–6** stress the perceived inefficacy of churchmen's intercessory prayers for peace (86 recalls 15.230), B 354 the collapse of fellowship in society. No topical allusion appears, but sin is more persuasively aligned with failures in the natural order via the declining competence of human agents.

94–121 95 *no byleue*: their lack of confidence in their technical skills inducing the same harmful anxiety as the doctrinal errors of theologians. **97** *byfore...aftur*: ascribing some measure of predictive capacity to judicial astronomy (see on B 10.209). **98–9** improve on B 360–2 in substance and precision. **98** *þe seuene sterres*: either the planets then known (*Pe*) or the Pleiades, in the constellation Taurus (a star-cluster when obscured would better indicate weather conditions than the widely scattered planets). **101** 'From the nature of the seed-corn the commercial value of the crop'. **102** *and*: i.e. 'and what'.

106 *clymat*: 'one of the regions of the earth dominated by certain zodiacal signs' (MED s.v. n. 1(b)); but the sense (c) 'often considered with respect to its weather' seems relevant, since weather-forecasting is in question. **107** *Gramer*: a discipline (see on 11.122) described by Isidore of Seville as the source and foundation ('origo et *fundamentum*') of the liberal arts (*Etym.* I.1.372). A complaint by Bp. Grandisson of Exeter in 1357 about the decline of grammar-teaching is cited by Moran (1985). **109** *versifye...endite*: on these two parts of *ars rhetorica* see Murphy 1974:135–93; Schmidt 1987²:21–7. **110** *construe*: the proper skill taught by *ars grammatica*. **B 375** *any langage*: i.e. French, the decline of which Trevisa observes in 1387 (Sisam 1962:149); on L's knowledge of and use of French see Schmidt 1987²:102–7. **110–16** deplore the fall in educational standards from the most elementary level to the highest. **111–12** *Gyle...Flaterere*: an attack on the readiness of educators to debase standards (through venality, cowardice or stupidity) that has lost none of its timeliness. *þe seuene ars*: see on 11.97. **114** *quodlibet*: 'a question proposed for disputation on any academic topic' (MED s.v.). Presided over by a *maistre* in a higher faculty, these took place twice a year in Advent and Lent (AlfQ; see Piltz 1981:148–9 and Wippel 1982). **115–16** 'It would seem a miracle to me if they did not prove deficient in philosophy — assuming there were philosophers alive who were willing to give them a strict examination'. The tense-sequence is less clear than in B 382–3 (on C's textual crux see *TN*). **117–21** assert that even if priests (culpably) mangle religious services, no blame falls on the laity attending who are (sincere) believers. **120** *Corpus Cristi feste*: the solemn commemoration, on the Thursday after Trinity Sunday, of the institution and gift of the Eucharist. Established *c.* 1263, it was celebrated by the 14th c. with processions and performances of religious plays. **121** *sola fides sufficit*: '[To strengthen the sincere heart], faith alone is enough', from vs. 4 of the hymn *Pange, lingua* (ascribed to St Thomas Aquinas) sung at Lauds on this day. L may derive *soethfaste byleue* 119 from *cor sincerum*; but Aquinas's point is that what *sheer faith* suffices for is 'accepting Christ's real presence in the sacrament (despite the defectiveness of the senses)', not 'salvation (despite the defectiveness of the priest)'.

(ii) 122–320a The important added lines **122–55** (half of them alliterating on *l* on account of the twelve-times recurring keyword 'love') attempt to explain how the theological virtue of CHARITY is substantially constitutive of the Christian Church as a 'spiritual organism' (cf. Tavormina 1994). **118** *hastite*: formed from *hasti a.* and first instanced here (earlier than the citations in MED). **122** *doen...wel...bettre*: almost accidentally alluding to the Triad, but more significantly echoing 92: '[if men did their duty as nature does, they would prosper materially]; if priests did their duty properly, laymen would thrive spiritually' (cf. 16.241–3). **123–4** The reference of *For...so* is to a *sola fides* posited as being given to an unbeliever on the point of death. Its linkage with **122** is oblique, however, since it cannot be that priests' good example might arouse faith in 'Saracens'; rather the elliptical meaning is 'For (given that even) pagans can be saved through a death-bed conversion, how much better would Christians' prospects be with a virtuous clergy to guide them!' **125–31** A crucial passage triggered by the question on the nature of Holy Church (one Will never addressed to HC herself). **126–9** A definition of HOLY CHURCH rather than strictly of Charity: 'Life, love and trust; one moral law based on a single religious faith; trust and true belief entwined together by love; Christians of every kind joined firmly together by a single purpose; [whether] giving, selling or lending — [doing] all without any falsehood or deceit'. The C-Text's emphasis on unity and orthodoxy appears to have been developed out of the idea of the Church as UNITY in B XX, perhaps as a response to the disunity produced by heresy and dissent in the 1380s. **130** *Loue-lawe withoute leutee*: 'a religion of love that is not founded on right morality.' **133** *here...diuerseth*: 'their religions differ (from ours / one another).' **134** scans either on |g| (as Type Ia or T-type) or on vowels as Type Ia; it echoes B 15.605, which is removed at that point. **136** *Ac*: perhaps 'It is, however, the case that' rather than 'but', since it is not being maintained that Jews and Saracens who worship 'with good heart' (*corde sincero*) love 'unlawfully', only that *here lawe diuerseth*. **137–40** bring out vividly the ambiguity of the supreme lexeme. 'Love' that is contrary to morality is condemned; only love based on obedience to God's will can issue as the charity that brings salvation (a tacit figuring of 'law' as the underground source of a spring, 'love'). **140a** 'Love God for his own sake, that is, for *truth*'s sake; / And your enemy for the sake of the commandment, that is, for the *law*'s sake; / And your friend for love's sake, that is, for the sake of *charity*'. The quotation (if such it is) remains unidentified; its substance, which is traditional, is paralleled elsewhere in the poem (AlfQ) and fully glossed by 141–3. But though truth, law and charity undeniably correspond to the theological virtues, they are here assigned their determining character in relation to their respective *objects* (God, enemy and fellow-Christian) and do not answer closely to the hierarchical Triad. The first line echoes A 11.242 and B 15.583 (*Dilige Deum et proximum*) but, perhaps prompted by Mt 5:43, LA distinguishes the expected *proximum* 'neighbour' as *inimicum* and *amicum*. The second recalls B 13.137, where Patience equates such love with Dobest. The third echoes B 13.149–51, on how *kynde loue* or *amor* can be transformed through grace into supernatural

caritas. **142** *entierely*: 'whole-heartedly', as in Patience's eloquent exhortation at B 13.143–8. *Goddes heste*: Christ's 'command' is the 'law' of the New Covenant (see Mt 5:44). **143** *thy fayre soule*: the soul as man's closest 'friend' recalls Patience quoting his *lemman* 'Love' at B 13.141–2. Much of LA's teaching re-works Patience's key deliverance on charity and (coming from him) must aim to reveal how deeply that teaching has entered Will's own *fayre soule*. **148** The stress on charity as involving true or proper *self*-love 'so...as to avoid sin and be kind to all' (*Sk*) is a measure of how far **C** (with its new material) has moved towards true interiority. *be cher ouer*: 'take loving care about', *cher* being evidently chosen not for the alliteration's sake but for its etymological tie with *charite*, than which nothing can be more 'dear.' Whether or not *Sk* is right that **L** mistakenly supposed native *chary* to derive from OF *cher*, a link with the *chierte* form of 'charity' seems plausible, and the present construction with *ouer* is cited by OED (s.v. *chere* a.) from the C15th *Dives et Pauper*. **149** LA's tone and phrasing recall Conscience's at Pr 138. **150/1** Identical rhyme heightens the catechetical character of the interchange. The question is crucial, as charity is a fruit of grace, which came only through faith in Christ and through the sacraments. Its answer concedes that Moslems *may* possess charity 'of a sort', a love of God based on the creature's natural veneration for the Creator. The revision (perhaps prompted by deeper reflection on the case of Trajan) alters Anima's judgement at B 389 that non-Christians may be saved through a sincere *faith* 'in some ways resembling ours' (392). **B 390–1** are deleted perhaps because repeating B 309, which // **C** retains. **153** The phrasing picks up on the lexical *annominatio* at B 16.215, which **C** deletes at that point. **B 392–3** are adapted from *LA*: 'But [Moslems] agree with Christians in believing in one sole all-powerful God who created everything' (p. 828; see also on B 605). **393** *For*: 'inasmuch as', i.e. *if* the clergy lived as they taught, they might win over those who share Christians' faith in one God; see Schmidt 1987[2]:73.

156–85 157 *Legende*...: referring to the account of Mahomet in the 'Life of Pope St Pelagius' forming ch. 181 of *LA* (pp. 827–31). The story is also told in the *Speculum Historiale* (*c.* 1260) of Vincent of Beauvais (IV.40), a Dominican contemporary of Jacobus de Voragine, whose expression 'chronica' (p. 827) may denote Vincent's work. **158** *a mene*: 'a (merely human) mediator' (*Sk*). **159** *Makemeth*: after 'Magumeth', the form of which may be influenced by the legendary tradition that he was 'pseudopropheta et etiam *magus*' (*LA* p. 827). *Messie*: as in *LA* pp. 828–9, which states that Mahomet declared *himself* to be the promised Messiah (not that *the Jews* so proclaimed him, as translated in Ryan & Ripperger 751). **160–4** argue that Moslems live by natural law and also by a positive law (the Prophet's teaching) that is for them what the

Mosaic Law is for Jews. **161** *kynde...cours*: the echo of Lady Mede's *cours of kynde* (3.60) may be adventitious, for what is invoked to account for such Moslem practices as polygamy (*LA* p. 830) is the 'natural law' customs that Christian theologians held to have been superseded by the Law of Moses. **162** warns that where 'the *lawe* of kynde' is not restrained and over-ruled by a higher positive law, Mede's '*cours* of kynde' will prevail and moral order be unable to subsist. **163** *Beaute...*: 'Beauty without goodness', part of a well-known proverb (Whiting B 152); Fair Rosamund (B 12.47–8) would be a case in point. **164** *sanz cortesie*: 'without good breeding'; the unique choice of the courtly French language for these macaronics wittily reinforces the claim about the inadequacy of untutored nature. **165** *a man ycristened*: not stated as such in *LA,* which describes how a certain *gret clerk*, disappointed in his ecclesiastical ambitions, comes to Mahomet and shows him how to become a religious leader. L may have run together these two characters. **166** *cardinal of court*: 'in Romana curia' (ibid). *Pe* observes that L 'could have got all he needed from a popular handbook of exemplary stories like the *Alphabetum Narrationum*'; but the explicit reference and verbal details confirm *LA* as his chief source. **167** *pursuede*: translating *LA* 'cum...honorem...*assequi* non potuisset'; but *to haue be pope* may recall the description of a (Christian) magician greedily desiring to achieve high station and become pope ('exaltari magus hic et *pontificari* / Affectans auide') in another *Life of Mahomet*, by Hildebert of Lavardin. This C12th Latin poem cited by *Wr* may be the 'historia ipsius' referred to in *LA* (p. 827). **168** *Lossheborw*: 'impostor'; see at 73. **169** *souhte...Surie*: taken by *Sk* as alluding to the flight from Mecca to Medina in 622; but this is too specific, and L more probably refers to Mahomet's departure from Christian Palestine into pagan Arabia. **170–82** The version of the story as told in *Speculum Historiale* XXIII.40; in *LA* the trick with the dove is taught to Mahomet by the unnamed 'clericus quidam valde famosus'. **179** *God sulue...lyknesse*: a claim to divine authorisation modelled on the account in Mt 3:16 of how Jesus at his baptism received 'the Spirit of God descending as a dove' (it is invoked as the emblematic bringer of divine peace at 246–9). *coluere*: on the weak vocalic genitive sg. see *MES* 72. **183–6** argue by the logic of *e converso*: if a false preacher could successfully mislead, surely true ones could undo his work? **C** removes the symbolisation of greed as a dove in B 414 (problematic, given its association with guilelessness in Mt 10:16).

B 411–89a As part of the (conjectured) transposition of material in the revision of B XV (see *TN* on 187–251 and 188–257), this homiletic excursus rich in vivid parabolic detail has been excised, perhaps as digressive and repeating earlier material (see on 418, 423 and 431). However, 420b, 423a, 429 and 431 will be re-used at C 4.117,

17.48, 17.230 and 8.333. 416–50 deal with the contribution of personal holiness in the effort to establish peace in society and convert the heathen, 451–89 with ways of bringing faith and sustaining it. **411** *so*: 'to be thus'. **417** distantly recalls A 12.4. *parfit lyuynge*: i.e. their way of life which, if properly observed, equals the apostles'. **418** *ministres*: i.e. religious clergy (cf. *hem* 421); seculars would have 'title' to maintenance. **420–1** Antony represents the class of hermits (see on C 17.12); Dominic and Francis the order of mendicant preachers; Benedict and Bernard the monastic vocation (see on 4.117, B 4.121). **423** The metaphor of grace as growing among the humble echoes B 12.60–1, the phrase *be grene* B 102. **424** *fynde*: understand *hem* 'themselves'; the connection of the sense 'discover' to the verb's co-polyseme 'provide' at 422 hints 'Platonically' at a causal correlation between humility and healing. The key-stave is cognative *diuérse*. **425** *The bettre...*: as desired by Haukyn at B 13.248ff. **427** *Alle*: envisaging peace not only between nations but in society at large. *trewe*: specifically 'faithful to their vocation'. **427a** 'Ask and it shall be given you'; referring to prayer (cf. Jn 16:23, cited at C 7.259a). **428** The proverb is not recorded elsewhere. **428a, 430a** 'You are the salt of the earth. [But] if the salt lose its savour, wherewith shall it be salted?' (Mt 5:13). This scriptural insistence on the absolute need in the clergy for *holinesse and honeste* (= the power to 'save' souls) underlies Anima's categorical teaching at 92–5. **434** *heighe wey*: both 'direct route' and the *alta via* to heaven (*Boece* IV, m.7.70). **437–41** may echo Thomas Brinton's Sermon 91 (ed. Devlin 2, 413–14): 'Cogitent igitur...patres mei...*sal terrae*...quod si turba apostolica in omnem terram exiuit....*quanto magis* ipsi...laborarent vnanimiter...ut hostes nostri Iudei... transferentur in regnum filii Dei'(Warner 2003:128). **437** *Elleuene*: properly twelve (as *Sk* notes), counting Matthias, who was elected to replace Judas (Ac 1:25–6). **439** *Sholde*: i.e. be converted. *alle maner men*: implying people of different religions, just as 'all the world' signifies geographical terrains. **441** *saue*: with some play on the senses 'preserve (from corruption)', as at 428, and 'save (from sin)'. **443–44** *Gregory*; *Austyn*: see at C 5.146–7. St Augustine (d. 604/09) was the first archbishop of Canterbury. *þe kyng*: Ethelbert of Kent, converted to Christianity in 597. **445** *rede*: chiefly in Bede, *Historia Ecclesiastica* I. 23–2.3. **448** *Moore þoruȝ miracles*: the emphatic repetition here (echoing Haukyn at 13.256–7) points to the modern clergy's lack of the strong faith needed to work 'miracles' (of spiritual conversion: cf. Lk 17:6), however learned their sermons. **451–60** The comparison of a catechumen's baptism to the 'fulling' of cloth and domestication of wild animals seems inappropriate to the christening of an infant. But Anima correctly sees 'Christian initiation' as extending to confirmation, which took place when the child was older (though dependent on the availability of a bishop to administer the rite). **452–4** To prepare woven wool for tailoring involved raising the nap with teazles arranged on a frame, thickening the cloth by moistening and adding fuller's clay, then beating and pressing. **456–7** *and...hepene*: not strictly correct theologically, since a baptised infant who died was held to be in a state of grace *as to heueneward*. However, Anima may mean only that before confirmation (which ideally required prior instruction in Christian faith and morals), a child who had reached the age of reason remained in effect 'helpless' to perform the virtuous acts necessary for salvation. The passage may reflect the contemporary infrequency of confirmation; and while this was not confined to remote parishes after the Great Plague (see Swanson 1989:277–9), such considerations may have prompted the 'wilderness' analogy. **457** *hepene*; *heuene*: revealing 'Platonic' tension at the semantic level between these metrical homophones, with a hint at the need for transformation of one into the other through the 'fulling' process of Christian initiation. **458** *is to mene after*: i.e. is derived from (the etymology is correct); an allusion to the historical fact that outlying country districts were the last to be Christianised, as is registered in the parallel development of the Latin-derived synonym 'pagan' (< *paganus*, 'countryman'; see OED svv. *heathen, pagan*). **460** *vnresonable*: applying *analogice* not *proprie* to animals, which lack 'reason' in the usual sense. **461–84** form an elaborate beast-allegory only tenuously linked with the Parable of the Wedding Feast, but provide an opportunity to distinguish between the categories of instructed and upright laity, devout contemplatives and ordinary unlettered folk guided by the clergy's teaching and example. Though the analogy is characteristic, its quirkiness, whimsicality and lack of logical clarity could account for its removal. **461** *Mathew*: see Mt 22:1–14. *R–H* (p. 188n29) note that Bede interprets the *altilia* as the apostles; but in the present context the term seems rather to imply the Christian people at large, who are fed by the word and sacraments of Christ. **463** *foweles*: barnyard fowl, not mentioned in the parable. **463a** 'Behold, [I have prepared my dinner]; my [beeves and] fatlings are killed, and all things are ready' (Mt 22:40). **464** The calf is counted as one of the ritually pure animals at Lev 11:3, Deut 14:4 (*Sk*); and at B 16.229 Abraham will feed his angelic visitors with *calues flessh*. **465–9** are not easy to interpret as an analogical 'argument', but loosely, the calf signifies purity of life in the clergy, which nourishes the common people (*folk* 464, 471); they themselves are nourished by the milk of mercy and truth, as are the contemplatives (468), and upright laymen are sustained by love, justice, mercy and truth. **471–9** Ordinary uneducated people are compared to chickens and the clergy to their keeper, from whom they learn to live a life of Christian charity. **480–4** The giver of the feast stands for God. **481** *of*: '(who) of';

on the unexpressed subject-pronoun (Ø-relative) see *MES* 205. **482** *wederes*: cf. Reason's assertion at B 5.14–20. **485–8** *who...Thei wol*: 'those who...will'. **487** 'Without a tenth of the work honest men have to put in to get what they want'; the proportion ironically echoing the 'tithe' paid by laypeople to their priest. **488** *write*: the breach of decorum reminding the audience that ANIMA is a mouthpiece for the author's criticisms. **489–89a** *Mathew and Marc*: see 461 and 491. *Memento...Effrata*: see on 11.51. The psalm speaks of David's desire to care for the things of God above all else, and his trust in divine protection if he does so. Though the relevance of such zeal for 'English clerks' seems clear, the main point may be that to find *eam* (= 'charity' [11.51a], but more loosely 'receptivity to the Gospel') in heathen lands, would be an incentive for mission.

187–320a argue that 'apostolic' bishops of old lived ascetically and willingly gave their lives for the faith, and if their successors followed their example, they would convert the Moslems. But they have been corrupted by greed ever since Constantine endowed the Church, as appears from the case of the Templars (see on 209), whose fate is a warning to avaricious clerics. (On the transpositions of **B** material here, see *TN* to C 187–251; commentary on the parallel **B** lines will be found under **C**.)

189–93 189 *Nasareth...*: representative names of titular sees *in partibus infidelium*, territories in Palestine and Syria under Moslem control. Bishops appointed to such sees, most of whom were friars (Warner 2003:112), rarely went near them, as the prospect of death was assured. **191** 'Go ye into the whole world and preach [the gospel to every creature]' (Mk 16:15); spoken just before the Ascension, after Christ rebukes the disciples for their lack of faith, and followed by his assurance that God will protect and empower them in their task of evangelising the world. **193a** 'The good shepherd giveth his life for his sheep...[But the hireling...leaveth the sheep and flieth...]' (Jn 10:11). These texts (the second repeated at 291a) show martyrdom as the price of properly discharging the apostolic office. **B 499a** 'Go you also into my vineyard [and I will give you what shall be just]' (Mt 20:4). This parable (here linked with such passages as Mt 9:37–8, Jn 4:35) is more often connected with proportionality of 'reward' and 'works' (as in *Pearl*) than with evangelisation of the world.

B 500–31 For commentary on these lines, see below on **C 17.252–82.**

194–232 194 *riht holy*: an improvement in precision in making the referent the hermits and missionary saints, not virtuous men generally. **197** *boek...consience*: 'nothing to read but their own innermost thoughts'. The trope of conscience as a written register of one's good and bad actions and thoughts to be publicly opened on the Day of Judgement may come from Alan of Lille's *SAP* (*PL*

210:118, 181), but it originates in Jerome's Commentary on Dan 7:10 (see Schmidt 1982:482–4, and Wilson 1983:387–9). **198a** 'But God forbid that I should glory, save in the cross of our Lord [Jesus Christ]' (Gal 6:14). **200–01** *rede...rede...rode*: self-rhyme linking adjectival with verbal *rede*, which itself repeats *rede* 194, but with a bitterly ironic sense-difference; heroic virtue is only 'read about' (in the past), whereas squalid venality is something to 'speak about' (in the present). The choice of 'red' for the coin (see on 3.47) starkly contrasts it with the blood-stained cross of Christ. **202** The added line condemns the use of money to 'buy' spiritual benefits in the contemporary church. **204–5** LA ascribes not only simony but war, and the distress that follows from it, to greed (a similar attitude to Chaucer's in 'The Former Age', ll. 60–3). **205** *couetyse...cros*: the noble bore a cross on the reverse. *corone*: i.e. the crown they seek being not the 'crown of justice' (II Tim 4:8), which may require martyrdom and is symbolised by the clerical *croune* 'tonsure', but the 'corruptible crown' (I Cor 9:25) of worldly success represented by the gold coin. The noble's obverse had a crowned king's head; but since the reverse's cross was also surrounded by crowns, **L**'s point may be that worldly churchmen choose the 'crown' but reject the 'cross' that goes with it (see Poole 1958:I, pl. 34e). **207** *grotes*: see idem, pl. 35a. **209** *Templers*: the great religious order of Knights Templar, given a rule in 1129 drawn up by St Bernard. The order was suppressed by Pope Clement V in 1312 under pressure from King Philip the Fair of France. **210–13** voice a widespread contemporary belief in the Templars' corruption, which they admitted under torture but which is now generally discredited. Ironically this attack on greed would have been better directed against the French king, who coveted their vast wealth in his domains. **211** *tresor...treuthe*: evoking a contrast first made in 1.135 by HC, who sees 'truth' as the distinctive ideal of knights (1.90–100). *dar nat*: perhaps alluding to the French charge against the Templars 'of cloaking under oaths of secrecy a system of organised vice and communal sacrilege' (Keen 1975:217). **215** *dampne dos ecclesie*: 'bring down condemnation upon the wealth the Church has accumulated through endowment'. The Latin phrase is either a quasi-personification or a metonym for 'those who hold the Church's temporal wealth', as at 223. **215a** 'He hath put down the mighty from their seat' (Lk 1:52). Spoken by the supreme exemplar of humility, the Virgin Mary, and familiar from its daily use at Vespers, this text underlines how greed is not being condemned as a separate sin but as a specific manifestation of the 'pride of life' held to afflict the clergy. **216–19a** seem to threaten that a faithful alliance between social groups who have overcome their own internal dissensions will strip the clergy of riches and force them to live simply on what the laity provide them. They overlook how the

Church's wealth, which brought many positive benefits (e.g. educational), came from generous lay benefactors, and tend to confuse possession with greed. But the depth of LA's disillusionment with the institutional church is suggested by his ready assumption that the motives of those favouring disendowment would be disinterested. **219** *Leuitici*: the OT Levites here standing for the priesthood (see on 14.58). **219a** 'By first-fruits and tithes'; traced to Num 18 by AlfQ. L has run together Num 18:19 and 21, which prescribe respectively the first-fruits for priests and tithes for the Levites; but he uses 'Levite' figurally for the Christian clergy generally (as well as for 'deacons' specifically, as at 2.130). **220** *Constantyn*: see on 5.175. *dowede*: according to the fabricated C8th 'Donation of Constantine', whereby the Emperor granted Pope Sylvester I (314–35) perpetual primacy over the other churches of the empire and secular dominion over Rome and its Western provinces (see Southern 1970:91–3, and for contemporary citations, Smalley 1960:154–7). The story that an angelic voice was heard crying *Hodie venenum est effusum in ecclesiam Domini* 'Today poison is shed forth upon God's Church' goes back at least to the 13th c. It appears in *B*-mss OC[2] after 15.558, is cited in Higden's *Polychronicon* IV 26 and Gower *CA* Bk ii, and was favoured by Wycliffe (e.g. *Dialogue* IV, 18), who insisted on disendowing the Church as part of its reform. This inflammatory passage, which comes closer to Wycliffe's preaching in London in 1376 than any other in the poem, is associated with contemporary anti-possessioner polemic by Scase (1989:90). **222** *hye...crye*: the plangent internal rhyme heightening the speaker's anguish about an act from which he judges most of the Church's troubles to spring. **223** *Dos ecclesie*: i.e. 'the Church, by accepting endowments...'; see on 215. **225** *moste perto*: 'is needed for this'. *amende*: what worldly clerics have considered (202) the means to further the Church's position in society having become the problem for both the Church and society. **226** The thought, not fully expressed (but elucidated by the added lines 228, 233–8), seems to be that 'it is hard for prelates to pray sincerely / effectively for peace between those in conflict' either because of 'pre-occupation with looking after estates' or because 'as landlords, they may themselves be in civil or armed dispute about property'. **227** The exhortation here widens the call for dispossession beyond the religious orders (as in the 'prophecy' at 5.168–79) to the whole clergy. The underlying belief in material poverty as disposing towards 'spiritual poverty' or humility is paralleled in Wycliffe's tract on 'The Poverty of the Saviour' (c. 1378), but has a long and by no means 'heterodox' history (Gradon 1982). Hudson (1994:101) finds at B 15.563–6 a 'clear echo here of' the demands of Ball and Tyler during the Peasants' Revolt; but **L**'s 'echo' could be simply of a widely expressed opinion also voiced by Wyclif and the rebels (see *Intro.* V §§ 7–10 above). *dymes*: from OF *disme* < Lat *decima*); a policy advocated in Wycliffite writings (e.g. Arnold 1869:147, Matthew 1880:364–96). **233–49** develop an impassioned protest against war into a prayer for the true dove of heaven to bring about through sincerity what Mahomet with his false dove achieved through deceit. **233** *For...parfyte*: anacoluthic, since 236 reads *His* not *Hire*. *þe Pope formost*: perhaps alluding to Urban VI's wars against the anti-pope Clement VII in 1379, or against the King of Naples between 1383 and 1389, when Urban died, or (nearer home) the Despenser Crusade of April 1383 (see McKisack 1959:431–2; Houseley 1983). **234** *with moneye*: possession of wealth making war possible, just as desire for wealth causes it. **235–5a** *Luk*: an error; the OT text (Deut 32:35) is quoted in the NT at Rom 12:19, Heb 10:30; see on B 6.225a. **236** *with his pacience*: 'accompanied by patience [towards his enemies]'; echoing Patience at B 13.165–72a and Conscience at 13.207–11 (cf. Baldwin 2001:106–8). **238** *with alle prestes*: either 'along with the rest of the clergy' or 'with all those clerics who are at present his enemies [i.e. those who support the anti-pope].' *pax vobis*: 'peace be to you', Christ's first words to his Apostles at their last meeting (Lk 24:36, Jn 20:19), used by the priest in greeting the people after the 'Agnus Dei' at Mass. The allusion implies that the clergy have betrayed their Lord in not handing on his gift of peace to the world. **239–42** are not an accurate summary of how Islam spread among 'Sarrisines of Surie' (it was indeed *thorw mannes strenghe*) but reflect his source's claim that Mahomet won over through *sanctitatem simulatam* 'feigned holiness' those whom he could not overcome *per potentiam* 'by force' (*LA* 829). **242** *pacience*: coupling it with *gile* not to undermine the goodness of patience but to show how even the wicked can draw advantage from this most virtuous of virtues. **249** practically repeats B 2.187, which is accordingly revised at C 2.197. **250–320a** deal with the difficulty of converting non-Christians and the qualities needed for bishops in the apostolic work of building up the Christian *comune*. **250–61 250–1** Small revisions (*thus*; *now*) smooth the transition between the new material preceding and the section of // **B** with which **C** resumes (at Vol. I, p. 602; for comment on the major transposition of **B** material at 252–82, see *TN* on C 187–251). The syntactical ambiguity of *peple...That*, which could be a relative or a restrictive clause (leaving the intensity of the observation indeterminable), is perhaps best reflected with no punctuation after *amende*. The referent is probably 'the Christian people' (since **L** writes *amende* not *torne*) rather than non-believers collectively. **252** *scribz...Iewes*: presumably not meaning that the 'scribes' are *not* Jews; a carelessness (uncorrected in revision) perhaps resulting from alliterative necessity. **252** *lippe*: Islam being

seen (because monotheistic) as a partial, imperfect form of Christianity rather than as a religion in its own right regarded by its adherents as superseding Christianity. **B 502a** 'Seek and you shall find' (Mt 7:7), understanding in the original context 'an answer to your prayer'. Here the object could be 'that this is so' or, simply, 'the non-Christians, [whom you will find receptive to your efforts]'. **255** *alle paynymes*: here specifically 'all Moslems' (Bk IV of Alan of Lille's *Contra Haereticos* (*PL* 210:421) is directed 'contra paganos seu mahometanos'); but the ME term (< OF *paienisme*) normally implies 'non-Christian [other than Jew or Moslem]', as at B 11.162. **257** *shewe*: i.e. to God, in his rôle as mediator. **258** 'So those people live by one (and the same) faith (with us), but believe in a false mediator' (see *TN*). **259** *tho rihtfole men*: either specifically the Christians in Moslem lands, who have no clergy to minister to them, or generally all monotheists of good-will who have no one to preach the Gospel to them. **260–1** repeat with small variations 188–9 above. *perel*: i.e. to their souls, for not fulfilling their apostolic vocation. *Neptalym...*: names that are mere ciphers, as these places had no Christian missionary presence. **262–82** correspond to B 510–31 with a few small changes that remove repetition (e.g. B 521) or obscurity (B 524). **264–5** The ambiguity here entails no real contradiction: 'Christ performed miracles to show by a powerful "argument" that men are not saved through argument but through grace.' This assertion is of a piece with the poem's insistence that only the faithful witness of apostolic evangelisers (extending to 'miraculous' readiness for martyrdom) and not appeals to authority or subtle disputation could convince unbelievers of the truth of Christianity or lead lax believers to repent. **267** *metropolitanus*: '"chief bishop" of all the world; Jerusalem being the original Christian metropolis' (*Sk*). The unexpected application of this dignified ecclesiastical title to Christ (explained in the next line) brings out by implication the high demand made on prelates who *wilne þe name* (190). **268** *baptisede*: alluding to traditional interpretation of the water that came out of Christ's pierced side (Jn 19:34, I Jn 5:6) as a 'figure' of baptism, the sacrament of initiation into his death and resurrection (Rom 6:3–4; cf. Lk 12:50). See the *Homilies on St John's Gospel* of Augustine (1888:434) and Chrysostom (1889:319), cited in Weldon 1989:52–3. *bissheinede*: the 'illumination' is of the soul, both in the sense of 'enlightening' with divine wisdom and 'making bright or glorious' with divine grace. The blood is imagined as like the gold sometimes used to represent it in C14th works of art such as the Despenser retable in Norwich Cathedral or Duccio's *Maestà* (Davlin 2001:80n44; Alexander & Binski 1987:711). **272** illustrates the wide range of countries where missionaries in earlier times gave their lives for the faith. *Ynde*: held to have been evangelised by Thomas the Apostle, whose traditional place of martyrdom is near Madras ('Upper India' in *LA* 39). *Alisandre*: 'Blessed Alexandria, made bright with this triumphal blood' (*LA* 266), the place where St Mark perished in the Neronian persecution. *Armonye*: where St Bartholomew the Apostle was martyred at Albana (*LA* 546). *Spayne*: where those put to death *c.* 304 in the persecution under Diocletian included the protomartyr St Vincent of Saragossa (*LA* 117–20). **274–5** St Thomas Becket was murdered by knights of Henry II in his own cathedral church at Canterbury. **276** Cf. *The Simonie* 39 (Auchinleck text): '[Seint Thomas] was a piler ariht to holden vp holi churche' (cited by Warner 2003:122). **277–9** affirm that 'St Thomas is an example [of martyrdom] and *not* of wandering about the country and interfering in the affairs of local clergy' (see *TN*). **278** The 'pointed personal allusion' suspected by *Sk* is doubtful, pl. *suche* denoting the whole category of titular prelates. **280a** 'Put not your sickle into another man's corn'; a maxim in canon-law and penitential texts deriving from Deut 23:25 and used 'as the *auctoritas* prohibiting confessors from hearing the confessions of those...under another's jurisdiction' (Gray 1986[1]), and see Alf*Q*). The image of unconverted people as corn to be harvested is Biblical (cf. Mt 9:37–8, Jn 4:35); but there may be a sardonic allusion to the stealing of parsons' livelihood. **281** *amonges Romaynes*: including in the 1st century Peter and Paul (under Nero), in the 2nd Ignatius and Justin, in the 3rd 'Lawrence the Levite' (65 above). **282** *were*: the careful choice of the verb-mood contrasting a necessary condition with a fact (*was* 281).

283–92 rewrite B 569–77 to stress how the ideal Christ-like bishop is servant more than spiritual ruler. **284** *prouynce*: an exhortation implying poor pastoral care especially in the remoter parts of dioceses (cf. 292). **285** *Feden*: with 'spiritual sustenance' (B 572). **285a** 'By your staff's shape, let this be still your rule: / Drive, lead and goad your flock, heed law in full'. These Leonine verses (cited in Walther, *Initia* 8828), resembling those copied in BL MS Lansdowne 397, f. 9v (*Pe*), are anticipated at 10.93–5, which elaborate the symbolism of the bishop's crosier. **286** *enchaunten*: the only favourable use of this word, the crosier here being arrestingly imagined as a conjurer's rod. **287–92** draw an apparently original comparison between a priest / bishop and a knight / king as defenders of the whole community. **291a** See on 193a.

B 569–77 569 *cros*: the emblem here defining the bishop's responsibility, not that of authority (*crose* 10.93) but that of service, the cross worn on his breast or the processional one carried before him. **573** *Ysaie*: Isaiah, 'the Great Prophet' of the OT (8th c. BC). *of yow*: utterances of OT prophets applied 'in figure' to the Christian clergy, in a way illustrated earlier from the Psalms at 13.122–3a, 14.69–71. *Oʒias*: Osee [Hosea], a significant 'Minor Prophet' of the early 8th c. BC. The first passage has an un-named man refusing to become king because he lacks

the wealth; the second, spoken by God, is here implicitly ascribed to the bishop. Hosea may have been confused with Malachy because their prophecies are similar, Hos 5:1 threatening priests in terms close to Mal 2 and 3 (in correcting **L**'s wrong ascription to Osee, *R–H* p. 189 misprint 'Mal' as 'Matt'). **575a** '[I am no healer and] in my house there is no bread nor clothing: make me not ruler of the people' (Is 3:7). **576** *for swiche*: 'in relation to / on behalf of'. What in context is a command from God to bring tithes to the temple is here made to relate to the use of the people's offerings to relieve *nedy folk*. **577** 'Bring all the tithes into the storehouse that there may be meat in my house' (Mal 3:10).

293–306 slightly shorten but greatly revise B 578–99, with loss of some powerful writing. **293** *of oure tonge*: i.e. bishops who preach in English and books written in English. **295** *Oure Lord*: 'God', not 'Christ'. **296** *maister...Messie*: i.e. the Mosaic Law is to hold good until the arrival of the divinely anointed deliverer foretold by Isaiah and Jeremiah (Is 9:6–7, 11:1–5; Jer 23:5–8, 33:14–26), whom Christians recognise in Jesus. **299–300** *saued*: the repetition bringing out how Our Lord's message of salvation from sin was underpinned by his acts of healing ('salvation' from disease). **301** *myracles...made*: as affirmed by Jesus himself a little before performing this one (Jn 10:37–8). **303** *Quadriduanus coeld*: 'dead for the space of four days' (Jn 11:39). **L**'s view of the crucial significance of this miracle for Christian faith is shown by the line's repetition in the second account of it at 18.145, where the last lift (the same as in B 16.114) takes up the second (*rome*) from B 594. **304** *soercerye*: an accusation made in Jn 7:20, 8:48, 10:20 *before* (not after) the raising of Lazarus (see 18.151a). **305** *studeden...struyden*: the self-destructive character of malice enacted 'Platonically' by the transformation of 'stud*eden*' through 'struye' into 'struy*den*'. **306** *brouhte*: with *he* understood as in B 597; alluding to the destruction of Jerusalem in 70 AD, an event widely seen by medieval writers (e.g. in the alliterative *Siege of Jerusalem* 725–9) as divine retribution for the Crucifixion. **307** *ʒut*: both 'nevertheles' and 'even now.'

B 578–99 582 *stoon...stonde*: the rhyme-echo 'Platonically' enacting the commandments' permanence. **583** 'Love God and your neighbour', from '*Diliges* Dominum *Deum* tuum [ex toto corde tuo]...*et proximum* tuum [sicut teipsum]' (Lk 10:27), a text combining the *Iewen lawe* of Deut 6:5 and Lev 1:18 (where *amicum* = *proximum* in OT terms). **590–1** This miracle (Mt 14:15–21) was understood as fulfilling the Isaian prophecy of abundance in the Messianic age. **593–4** are replaced in **C** by two virtually identical with C 18.144–5, suggesting that the later lines awaited final attention, as this is the kind of exact repetition the revision tends to avoid. *stank*: a detail from Jn 11:39, removed as perhaps lowering the tone. **593a** '[He cried with a loud voice], "Lazarus, come forth".' **597a**

denotes in its final appearance 'suffering unto death', since Christ's *pacience* 'conquered' through his Passion. Anima's teaching re-inforces that of Conscience, Patience and Piers. **599** 'When the Holy One of Holy Ones shall come, your anointing shall come to an end'; a verse relating the end of the Jews' special relationship with God as his 'anointed people' to the death of Christ 'the Lord's Anointed' and the destruction of 'the city and the sanctuary', followed by 'the appointed desolation' (Dan 9:26). Derived from Dan 9:24, its wording (*Pe*) comes from the pseudo-Augustinian homily *Contra Judaeos* (*PL* 42:1124), which was read in a lesson for the 4th Sunday of advent (*Brev.* I.137). It is used in **C** at 20.112*a*. On the background see Cohen 1983.

307–20a continue on the rejection of Christ and on the prospects for preaching the faith to non-believers. **307** *Sarrasynes*: not strictly correct, since the Moslems saw Jesus as one of the great prophets, as **L** could have known from *LA* (p. 828). **309** *pseudo-propheta*: a phrase occurring during Christ's 'apocalyptic' prophecy of the destruction of the Temple (Mt 24:11, 24), which warns against deceivers and cites Daniel at vs 15; it was made familiar through its use in anti-mendicant writings (Szittya 1986:56). **312** The possibility that Moses would accompany (or actually be) the expected Messiah figured among Jewish expectations concerning this mysterious prophetic figure; but the notion has been projected onto the Moslems, who have no apocalyptic expectation of the return of Mahomet. **B 604** *Grekes*: not the Eastern Christians (MED s.v. *Grek* n.1(c), only from late 15th c.) but loosely used for 'non-Jewish non-Christians' (s.v. 1(b)), i.e. descendants of the pre-Christian 'Greeks' (Gentiles), who are distinguished from Moslems and Jews but supposed (like them) to be monotheists. **315–16** The thought here is close to that of Alan of Lille in *Contra haereticos* IV, 1: 'those called Saracens or pagans agree with Christians in affirming one God who created the universe, but with the Jews in denying that there is trinity in the divine unity' (*PL* 310:421). **316** 'I believe in God the Father Almighty' (first clause of the Apostles' Creed). **318** 'And in Jesus Christ [his only] Son, [Our Lord]' (2nd clause). **319** 'And [I believe] in the Holy Ghost' (7th clause). **320** 'the forgiveness of sins' (10th clause). **320a** 'The resurrection of the body and the life everlasting' (11th and 12th clauses).

Passus XVIII (B XVI)

PASSUS EIGHTEEN falls into (i) the Tree of Charity episode (1–178), concluding with the formal end of VISION FOUR and (ii) the encounter with Faith (179–292), which begins VISION FIVE and answers to the second part of the 'outer' dream (of Vision Five) in B 16.167–275. (i) is extensively altered, removing Piers and adding a passage on contemplatives (60–80) in harmony with the revision's loftier and more spiritual tone. **C** abandons **B**'s bold but clear structure for a smoother if more elusive transition, so that any intended 'inner dream' in C XVIII that finished at 178=B 166 should have begun at 16 (a more likely point is 4, the entry into the secret place of the 'heart'). However, the dramatic break initiating the inner dream in **B** is neither needed nor possible; for whereas in **B** Anima is replaced by Piers, in **C** both figures coalesce into Liberum Arbitrium, who remains throughout with Will as custodian of the Tree. (ii) closely follows **B**, but with extensive re-writing.

(i) 1–178 The Tree of Charity episode occurs in a 'quasi'-inner dream that ends with Will's being woken by the shouts at the arrest of Jesus in Gethsemane. **1–30** begin with an 'inward journey' (in Wittig's phrase) into 'the country of the heart' and have a more mysterious and suggestive quality than **B**'s 'prelude' (B 1–17). **1** *Leue...leue*: wordplay 'Platonically' linking Will's faith in the 'representative' power of his own Soul with LA's 'affection' for him (cf. 17.143). **2** *Charite*: last mentioned at 17.286, after forming the theme of the dialogue in 16.284–372. **4** *contre*: recalling the allegory at 15.190, but even more the heart as journey's end at 7.254–9*a*, where it was the seat of truth and the site of charity. *Cor-hominis*: 'the heart of man'; not a 'common phrase' in the Bible (AlfQ), though 'heart' by itself is, and denoting man's deepest centre of both understanding (I Kg 3:9) and will (Prov 6:18, Ps 44:21). The passage AlfQ cites as 'most pertinent to the context' (I Cor 2:9) speaks actually of what *cor hominis* has *not* conceived rather than of what is revealed to it. Perhaps more pertinent might be Prov 20:5, 'Counsel in the heart of a man (*cor viri*) is like deep water: but a wise man will draw it out' (as LA does from the well of Will's consciousness in this scene). **5** The image of the garden as a meeting-place with God derives ultimately from Gen 3:8ff, but as a place of *love*-encounter from Cant 4:12, 5:1 (the relevance of the *GO* commentary on Cant. for interpreting this sequence is argued by Hanna 2010). *pryuatees*: as the locus of man's secret thoughts (Ps 43:22). **6** *in þe myddes*: alluding to Gen 2:9, 3:3, where the Trees of Life and of Knowledge stand. *ympe*: recalling the tree whose 'ground' is 'free wil, ful in th[e] herte' in *TL* III vii 10, and suggesting that Usk may have read the C-Text while still in progress. On the tree-image see generally Smith 1966, and also A. J. Bowers 1975, Aers 1975:79–109, Salter 1988, Lewis 1995, Benson 1997:8, 2004:168–9. **7** scans as Type IIIb on |g| with final stress on *Ymagó* or, more naturally, as a licensed macaronic (*aa / bb*). *Ymago-Dei*: a title used of Christ in II Cor 4:4 (AlfQ); but the Genesis context evoked by *erber* would seem to allude to the account of man's creation 'in the image of God' (Gen 9:6). **9** *Trewe-loue*: an explicitness that seems designed to ward off ambiguity, the fruit's Latin name demanding a careful translation-gloss, and with *trewe* (like *kynde* at 14.14) here signifying 'real, essential'. (For the *English* term reciprocally defined 'aright' as charity, see MED s.v. *treu-love* n. 1(b)). *Trinite*: the tree's divine origin recalling the Incarnation passage in 1.147–53. But the point of naming the three-personed God is to match each enemy of Charity against a divine Person: the 'world' with the world's creator, the 'flesh' with God-made-flesh, the 'spirit of evil' with the Holy Spirit. **10** *louely lokynges*: the smiles of a mother to a child before it has speech, or of lovers before they have first spoken; for the phrase cf. *SS* 72. **12** scans cognatively on |k| |g| / |k|, with the lexical word *calleth* as key-stave. **14** *Caritas*: see at 14.14. *Cristes oune fode*: Christ's *cibus*, the will of God (Jn 4:34), and Christ as *cibus animae* (Jn 6:57). **15** *alle soules*: what solaces them being the *werkes* of 12, which the living may offer for their relief. **16** *si3te*: a toned-down version of *swowned* B 19. **17** *Y...sithe*: using a phrase from A 12.48. **20** *schoriares*: a more exact term than *piles*; found only here and at *TL* II vii 87. **25–8** The exposition is more didactic than at B 24, where Will's question concerns the function, not the nature, of the supports. **25** *plonte*: recalling 1.147, where it emblematised Christ. **29** The Gregorian 'three winds' allegory of the soul's enemies in *Moralia* 13.25 (*PL* 75:980), noted in *R–H* 193 and Woolf 1968:408, is paralleled in Alan of Lille's 'four kinds of *pride*' that 'blow through the world like winds' (*PL* 120:133) and in Bonaventure's 'winds of *pride* and vainglory' that blow down the house of [man's good] intention (*PL* 184:665). On these winds' connection with worldliness see 31, and on their 'condign punishment' of the sin of Pride, cf. 5.116–7. The Three Temptations' re-appearance in this 'charity' inner-dream recalls their incursion in the 'concupiscence' inner-dream at 11.162–97, which was induced by *wrathe*, as this 'contemplative' dream is by *joye* (*R–H* 193). **30** *hit...myghte*: 'so that its strength should not fail'.

B XVI 1–25a The one-to-one symbolisation in Anima's speech is an 'allegory of equivalence' (Carruthers 1973:38) like that of Piers at 7.204ff. But Piers's own explanations of the Tree (a visible *shewynge* with a meaning) differ from his earlier 'signposting', which gave visual form to a purely inward 'journey'. **2** On the split or group genitive see *MES* 78–9. *Haukyns loue*: Will's 'What is charity?' at 15.149 having recalled Actyf's 'What is poverty?' at B 14.275, his taking-over of Haukyn's rôle is here underlined by his acceptance of Anima's teaching on behalf of all ordinary people. **4** *trie*: used of Truth and his tower at B 1.137, Pr 14, an epithet connecting the 'fruit' with the 'treasure', the divine as 'known' with the divine as 'loved'. **5** *Mercy*; *rupe*: two distinct concepts, one rational, the other affective (Burnley 1979: Index s.vv. *mercy, pitee*). **6–7** The leaves-and-blossoms imagery here thematically inverts

that of the false leaves and blossoms produced by Charity's antithesis Wrath at B 5.136–9 (a passage removed in revision), as the *plonte* at C 25 reverses that at 7.228. The iconography of virtuous and vicious trees was traditional (see *R–H* 194, Salter 1988 [1971]:262–3, Katzenellenbogen 1989, Benson 1997:7–8). **6** *lele wordes*: those of the Church authorised by its Lord, as in 'The vine's leaves are the words of Jesus' from pseudo-Bernard's *Vitis mystica* (*PL* 184:651); on *lele wordes* see Schmidt 1983:139–41. **7** *buxom speche*: cf. 'A peaceable tongue is a tree of life' (Prov 15:4). **8** *Pacience...tree*: theologically coherent, since patience *is* the support on which the fruit grows. In *Vitis Mystica* humility [= **L**'s Patience] is called *radix crucis* (*PL* 184:733) and is so depicted in the tree of virtues in Katzenellenbogen 1989:fig. 67 (where the fruit is *Caritas*). But since the custom of language is to use the same name for the tree as for its fruit, the revision is clearer. **9** The probable source of the Tree of Charity image (Goldsmith 1981:59; Dronke 1981:214) is Augustine's *arbor caritatis* in his commentary on I Jn (*PL* 35:1993, 2020, 2033). **11** *saulee*: see *TN* on 17.24. **12–13** *growep...growep*: the *concatenatio* intensifying the catechetical tone; cf. the *complexio* of *growep* at 13a:15b and the purely dramatic *repetitio* of *Piers* at 17/18. **13–14** The allegory of the body as a garden may ultimately derive from Gen 2:9, where the Tree of Life corresponds in position to the heart; but the metaphor of the 'gardin þe herte' is already found in *AI* 232/18. **16** *Liberum Arbitrium*: see on C 16.156. **17** *piken...weden*: apt images for LA's function of rejecting the bad as described at C 16.199a. **18** *Piers...joye*: marking the fulfilment of Will's desire to see Piers again that was implicit in *ful pencyf in herte* at B 7.146, a line it echoes. But the bold paralleling of his reaction to Piers's name with a devout contemplative's at that of Jesus might have provoked objections that prompted the revision. *pure*: 'sheer' and 'spiritually refined'. **20** *loue-dreem*: an exploitation of the love-vision convention reminiscent of *Pearl* 59–60, where the emotion precipitating the dream is grief. The compound phrase is unparalleled in the sense 'love-dream', the OED ex. under *love* sb. 15 from 'Swete Ihesu now' (*Minor Poems of Vernon MS*, p.449, l. 20) being a misclassification (now correctly glossed in MED as 'joy of love' s.v. *love* n.(1) 4b). The Vernon lyric's sense is accepted for the present phrase by Kane, who renders it 'ecstatic experience of the love of Christ' (1989:286n31). But given that what follows is the second 'inner dream', from which Will *wakes* at 167, the sense 'love-dream' must be primary, even allowing for a polysemantic pun (for rejection of the reading *lone dreem* see *TN*); cf. further Schmidt 2000:7–9. **24** Will's first words to Piers in the poem. **25** *wite...wite*: 'Platonic' *annominatio* strengthening the link between 'knowledge of God' and 'God's protection of man'. **25a** 'When *the just man* [VL, *he* Vg] shall fall he shall not be bruised, for the Lord putteth his hand under him' (Ps 36:24).

31–52 dramatise the deep enmity of 'the world' against charity, *concupiscentia mundi* against *voluntas Dei* in I Jn 2:15–17, and man's need for the support of the Trinity in his fight against evil (a foreshadowing of Pride's final siege of Unity). **31** *World*: corresponding loosely to *superbia vitae* 'the Pride of Life' at 11.176 (see on 29), whence arises Covetousness of the Eyes, the 'fair sights' that arouse desire for possession. **34** *Potencia Dei Patris*: 'the power of God the Father', the *propre myзte* (see 54 below) of the First Person. Augustine refers in *De Trin.* Bk VI to I Cor 1:24 on 'Christ the power [*virtutem*] and wisdom of God' (Alf*Q*); yet as **L** does not seem to mean 'power shown in deeds' (*virtutem*) but 'power as capacity to create' (*potencia*), to make the latter's referent the *Second* Person would produce incoherence (cf. on 41 below). **35** *Flesch*: corresponding to *Concupiscencia Carnis* at 11.174. *flouryng tyme*: youth, when sexual desire is strongest. **37** *norischéth*: with wrenched stress on the third syllable (see *TN*). **39** The imagery suggests that when lust destroys charity, it leaves 'merely nominal adherence to the Church's teaching' (*bare stalke / leues*), rather than 'the bare text of God's scriptures' (as in Salter 1962:75, and cf. Aers 1975:91–2). **40** *Sapiencia...*: 'the wisdom of God the Father'. The Patristic association of the VERBUM of St John's Prologue with the personified SAPIENTIA of Proverbs 8:22–31 and Wisd 7:24–6 is most fully elaborated in the C15th *Macro* morality play of *Wisdom who is Christ*. **41** *The which*: drawing on the same Pauline text (I Cor 1:17–25) that finds God's unfathomable 'wisdom' exemplified supremely in the 'foolishness' of the Cross (a fit plank to 'ward' the tree of true-love). The deletion of B 38 dissociates the redemptive *power* (B 37 indeed echoing *virtutem* in I Cor 1:24) from man's actions and locates it entirely in the Son of God, whose 'penaunce' is not for any sin of his own. **44** *laddere*: the traditional 'ladder of vices' (Katzenellenbogen 1989:73n), inverting the *scala virtutum*. *ronges*: the 'steps' up towards strife being lies and falsehoods, as in the description of wrath's engendering at 6.138–42. **48** *this lordeynes*: with implied referent more probably as in // B 48 than in C 46. *lithereth þerto*: the revision introducing one of **L**'s happiest homophonic puns, 'to cast [lies, etc] at' (s.v. MED 1, < *lithere* n. (1) 'a sling'), 'to act wickedly' (s.v. 2, < *lithere* a. 'wicked'). **51** *Spiritus Sanctus*: 'the Holy Ghost', clarifying and (over)-simplifying B 46–52. In C the Third Person is denoted asymmetrically with the first two appellations, *Spiritus Sanctus* replacing **B**'s *Liberum Arbitrium*, which occurs where a Latin divine title would be expected (Murtaugh 1978:25) and more subtly distinguishes between the 'agent' free-will (the human faculty that responds to grace) and the 'instrument' grace (the bestowing of which is 'appropriated' to the Spirit, and equated with 'right

belief'). The explanation could be perhaps that a Latin 'nature-name' such as *Gratia Dei Patris* might have produced confusion through failing to affirm the crucial Western Trinitarian doctrine that the Spirit proceeds from the Father *and* the Son. **B**

  B 47a–66 47a *Videatis..*: 'See [by this that] "He who sins against [*VL*; 'speaks against' Vg] the Holy Ghost, it shall not be forgiven him"' (Mt 12:32). *hoc...repugnat*: 'this is the same [as saying] that "one who sins through free will does not resist [sin as he should]"'. The unidentified maxim seems to take the 'sin against the Holy Ghost' as wilful refusal of the 'sufficient grace' given to resist the sins that destroy charity. **53–66** focus on the nature of the *postes*, whereas **C** re-directs interest from the three Divine Persons to the three 'degrees' into which humanity is disposed. **53** echoes Will's words to Anima at B 16.1; but as Will is to learn from Piers that the proper study of mankind is man, his theological curiosity is aroused only to be checked. **54** *propre myзte*: the distinctive 'power-in-act' appropriated to each Person of the Trinity (respectively creation, redemption, sanctification). **56** *woxen...growed*: speculations about the generation of the Three Persons and the source of divine being; mysteries (as Piers will indicate) for devout meditation, not problems for intellectual probing. **60** 'That may indeed turn out to be the case'. By contrast with **C**, the three *piles* seem to 'grow' like trees, a feature *Pe* finds reminiscent of 'the three stems, also symbolic of the Trinity, which grew from the seeds planted by Seth, were found by Moses...and went to the making of the true Cross'. However, the relevance of this is unclear, since **L** presumably means that the one term *tree* may be predicated 'equivocally' of both God (goodness itself) and Man his image, who reproduces God's goodness in the *herber* of his heart. **61–3** may have been replaced because they lack perfect coherence. Piers describes the 'ground' the tree grows from, instead of saying what it is called, then claims he *has*; but ANIMA *named* it (as 'Patience') at 8, and the 'Trinity' that it *meneþ* 64 is not its 'name' or *significans* but its transcendental *significatum* 'referent' (the tree is in fact never named by Piers in **B**). The passage both dramatises man's intense desire to know about the being of God and affirms the need to rest content with analogical understanding: divine love is best 'known' through experiencing human charity, the image of God in man.

53–105 expand **B** 53–74 into a categorical exposition (not necessitated by the original account) of the three ways of life in which charity can reach different degrees of perfection. **53** re-uses B 22, deleted at that point. **56** *thre degrees*: a parallel with the Three Persons (*of o greetnesse* B 59 and *iliche grete* C 62); but not to be pressed. The tree of human life, with a man standing in it, is depicted in an early C15th spiritual encyclopaedia (Saxl 1942: pl. 22c). **59** may be scanned as Type IIa or as Ic with stresses on *is, al, o* and *Y.* **60** recalls 12.225, introducing a contradictory notion not resolved till 100 (*Pe*). On a natural level, sweet fruit is ripe fruit, therefore nearer to rotting than is unripe fruit (which is not sweet). But at a 'transcendental' level, virginity effects a transformation (a figure of thought described in Simpson 1986[2]) of the earthly state of affairs, managing to be sweet without becoming ripe, and never sour (because never unripe). **63** *suynge smale*: 'in regular gradation' (*Pe*); but the sense is rather of *successive sameness,* i.e. 'real apples are not all equally big, equally small or equally sweet'. **64–6** recall 1.116–17. *sonne...sonnore*: with a homophonous 'Platonic' pun ('copious grace brings quickly to perfection'). **67** *by oure kynde*: 'in relation to our (human) nature'. **68** *Adam...tre*: LA's tree is primarily metaphorical ('the tree of human nature'), but secondarily metonymic, for by tasting forbidden knowledge Adam left the guilt of his original sin to his 'fruit' or offspring. **69** *variable*: contrasted with the 'fast' or firm quality of truth, and so 'prone to falsity'. **71–80** form an addition that could doubtless have been more clearly expressed (for discussion see Tavormina 1995:118–40). They envisage one (normative) mode of active life, the married state and parenthood (78–80), but two of contemplative — continent widowhood (77) and consecrated virginity (73), arranged in ascending order of excellence. The 'grades of chastity' are specified in the pseudo-Bernardine *Vitis mystica* ch. 18 (*PL* 184:672); see also Bloomfield 1958:227–53. **72** *The whiche*: with antecedent *maydones*, glossed in 74 as both religious and other celibate clergy (not strictly 'contemplatives' alone); but if a colon replaced the stop after *sonne* 75, better to reflect the fluidity of ME syntax, then the widowed life could also be included (77). *seweth*: the Spirit, unlike the earthly sun, being able to move so as constantly to give these 'apples' warmth (grace) to 'ripen' or mature them spiritually. *sonne*: extending to the Holy Spirit the figure's commoner association with Christ as the Light that 'shineth in darkness' (Jn 1:5). The Spirit is 'sol' and 'radius' in a C13th *Veni Creator Spiritus* (Dreves-Blume 1909, *Jahrtausend* [*JLH*] II:169 = *Analecta Hymnica* [*AH*] XXI:52), 'lux beatissima' in the pentecostal sequence of 21.211, and 'ardens ignis' in another sequence (*JLH* II:64=*AH* X:34). **74** *men*: not in apposition, so understand '(and) men'. **77** *is lyf*: '(which) is a life'. **80** *That... hit*: 'which', with (redundant) supplementary object, a fusing of relative and co-ordinate constructions. **82** *as...techeth*: a polite quasi-scholastic appeal to learned authority in arguing *per contra*. **83** scans as a Type IIIa line on |t| (-*tiua*, -*témpla*-). 'Active Life and the Contemplative Life' puzzle the Dreamer, because LA has not invoked the familiar dichotomy of physical and spiritual *work* found at B 6.248 but three degrees in respect of the *exercise or restraint of* sexuality, a special kind of 'work' (see *IG* s.v.). **84** scans either as Type IIb on fricatives

and |s| or as Type Ie on |g|. **86** *multiplieth*: see Gen 1:28 and Wit's praise of matrimony at 10.204–7. **87** *bettre... gode*: an evocation of the Triad now in relation to the 'grades of chastity' paradigm. A similar analysis of 'the relative values of active and contemplative lives, with accompanying defence of the merits of the active life rightly lived' is noted in *Dives and Pauper* [*c.* 1410] 1/1, 65–9 by Tavormina 1995:139n50. **88/9** Identical phrasal rhyme underlines how the comparison requires the fruit to be seen *as in* 'from the perspective of' heaven (either *as* yields the same sense, which is not the simple comparative adverb understood by Tavormina 1995:139). **88** *Wydewhode*: regarded in the NT as favourable to prayer and closeness to God (e.g. Lk 2:36–7), its superiority to (second) marriage affirmed in I Cor 7:8–9. **L** mentions consecrated widowhood only once elsewhere (14.143), but urges charitable help for those who may wish to avoid re-marriage so as to achieve it (A 8.32). *more worthiore*: on multiple comparatives see *MES* 281. **B 69** *Continence*: a personified metonym for holy widowhood; its sense here is not, as wrongly glossed by MED s.v. 2(a), 'moderation in sexual intercourse (as between spouses),' but (b) 'abstinence from sexual intercourse' (as stated at C 77 and used at C 73). *kaylewey bastard*: possibly a grafted or cultivated dessert pear (*poire de caiollel*) from Cailloux in Burgundy; the comparison is obscure, beyond suggesting its excellence. **90** *euene with angelis*: a phrase 'Platonically' playing on its homophone *heuene* to intimate at once that virginity is 'for the angelic order the heavenly state' and 'the equal of the angelic condition' (a different co-polyseme of *euene* is later linked punningly with *heuene* at 22.270). *pere*: both 'equal' and (more mutedly than at B 71) 'pear'. **91–9** expand the praise of virginity. **91** *Hit*: i.e. Virginity (89); the tortuous attempt to make this refer to marriage in Tavormina 1995:126–39 is a misreading of the text. *furste fruyte*: in the religious sense 'first-fruit' (an earlier use than MED records s.v.), hence 'the choicest' (see 94). **93** 'Signifying that the Supreme Being aimed to honour the fairest being' (virginity being a necessary attribute of humankind in its original state). **94** *creature...creatour*: as at B 16.215 (revised out at that point), the *annominatio* hinting at the nearness of the one to the other. *furste*: with priority in rank, since they are equal to angels, and in time, since they are the first to see God. This latter 'eschatological' meaning of virginity reaches beyond the beatitude-promise (Mt 5:8) to the account of the 144,000 virgins in Rev 14:4 as 'the *firstfruits* to God and to the Lamb'. But there may also be an allusion to the supreme exemplar of virginity, whose Assumption into heaven is celebrated in 'Auguste in a hyȝ seysoun' (*Pearl* 39). **97/99** *on erthe* / (*as*) *of erthe*: paralleling the repeated *as in heuene* 88/9, though now the analogy implies that the way one lives in this life will be exactly reflected in the next. **97** *on erthe*: referring to *their* time on earth, since (except for Martha and Mary) neither category was prominent among Christ's followers during *his*. **98** *is*: the sg. with two pl. nouns, assuming them to be a collective or categorial subject and anticipating sg. *fruyte...hit* (99–100). **99** *as of erthe*: 'from the point of view of our life here' (cf. 88); the image is of choice fruit placed before a king. **B 70–1** *kynde*: in the light of C 99 'best, most excellent' (MED s.v. *kinde* adj. 5(c)), because 'truest [to its species]'. **71** *aungeles peeris*: 'the equals of angels / pears fit for angels [i.e. even choicer than the widow-*kayleweys*]' (see Biggs 1984:426–36 on the patristic sources of this image). **100** *swellynge*: from concupiscence or (its frequent consequence) pregnancy. The virginal state enjoys instead of 'the heat' of desire only the 'heat of the Holy Ghost', sanctifying grace. **101–5** allegorically express Will's desire for experiential knowledge of human existence in all its dimensions. They recall his words and LA's reply at 16.207–9, 212–13; but here within the 'quasi'-inner dream (an answer to his wish), he receives no rebuke. Owing to the replacement of Piers by LA and the transference of his actions to Elde, the passage holds less scope for drama, the echoic anger of the human Ploughman now being ascribed to his divine exemplar. But the Langlandian grotesque, a blend of humour and sublimity, remains.

106–17 enact the process of human development towards death (whence the aptness of Elde's 'shaking' the tree), though they run together the 'synchronic' falling (of the individual) with the 'diachronic' Fall (of just men from Adam to John). **107** *the rype*: '(so that) the ripe ones might fall.' **108** *Elde*: see on 11.188. *to...-ward*: on *to-ward* separated by its noun-object (*MES* 413) see at 16.144; the 'crop' is where virginity is placed. **108–10** The sounds uttered have a humorous fitness. *crye* 'cry out' (not 'weep'), because reluctant to be touched; *wepte*: as befits a widow; *foule noyse*: the unmusical clamour of a shrew (a touch of 'clerkly' anti-feminism heightening the strangeness of this passage). On the Bosch-like quality of **L**'s art see Salter 1988:263–6. **111** scans either as Type Ia on |d| (like B 79), with a six-syllable onset and a first stave by liaison of *hadde_eny*, or as Type IIa on vowels, the latter being perhaps preferable. **113–14** *Adam...Baptiste*: including patriarch, 'judge' and prophet, and extending from the first man, in the age of nature, to the last righteous man before 'the second Adam' Christ, in the time of grace. **116** *in ...Inferni*: 'in the borderlands of Hell', where the just remained until Christ led them out (20.364–9). Alf*Q* finds **L** here 'at variance with Church doctrine' (which was never very definite on this point). But as the 'Limbo Patrum' was often thought continuous with Hell (*ST* III, 52, Suppl. 69:4, 5), Satan may be understood to have a nominal (not a real) 'mastery' over the Patriarchs. *Their* 'darkness' is lack of the Divine Light that is soon to break in on them (cf. Adam's words in *LA* 54:243), and their 'dread' a continu-

ing apprehension until they are liberated; but their *pleyinge* (273) clearly implies that they are not in torment.

118–37 118–23 signify that 'in the depths of the divine majesty' 118 (a stock phrase needing no source), 'anger' was provoked by the Devil's act, in consequence of which the Father as Power 'grasped' the Second Person to pursue and punish mankind's enemy. This sense for *lauhte* 119 is apt on the literal plane, but since the verb means 'assumed [human nature]' at 19.125, that would seem implied at the allegorical level. The difficulty of the phrase *Libera Voluntas Dei* (which corresponds to *Liberum Dei Arbitrium* at 20.20) is that it designates the *divine* will, Liberum Arbitrium the human power. What is clear nonetheless is that *þe Fadres wille* is expressed through the Second Person (*þe myddel shoriare* 119) who becomes man (*Filius* 'the Son' 121) by the 'grace and help' (B 51–2) of the Holy Spirit; in this way the Trinity works as one to redeem mankind through the Incarnation (see Hill 1975:531–2). **B 86–9** *for pure tene*: recalling the memorable use at B 7.115, a passage also removed in revision. Piers remains firmly human, while suggesting the potential in human nature to incarnate the eternal Word. The ambiguous syntax of 87–9 allows for *Filius* to be in apposition with 'Piers' or (more probably) with *pil* (as direct object of *hitte after*), a double sense barely possible in the revision at 120–22, which leaves a residue of syntactic-semantic difficulty (see *TN*). Hill (1975) detects an echo of the Communion prayer *Domine Jesu Christe* (in *Sarum Missal* 26–7), the phrase *by þe Faderes wille* echoing *ex voluntate Patris* and *frenesse of Spiritus Sancti* the words *co-operante spiritu sancto*. **122** The application of this earliest use of the word *ragman* (MED s.v. *raggeman* n. (b)) to Satan is **L**'s own (cf. 'Ragamoffyn' as a devil's name at 20.281). **123** *fals biheste and fruyt*: the promise to Adam and Eve of being as gods if they ate the forbidden fruit (Gen 3:1–6; cf. 20.320). The symbolism is deeply ironic, since Satan has both used fruit to deceive man and has won man's 'fruit' (offspring) as a prize. *furste*: beginning the period of his 'maistrie' over man. **124–5** See Lk 1:26–38; the Spirit speaks through the archangel when he proclaims his coming act (Lk 1:35). **126** *a iustices sone*: as Son of God, the Supreme Judge; there may be some play on *sonne*, since the title 'Sun of Justice' was applied to Christ as Messiah (Goldsmith 1981:6, 93n16). *iouken*: commonly used of birds (esp. hawks roosting) and alluding to the traditional image of Christ as a heavenly bird who descends to earth for a time (see Hill 1975:532, and Cervone 2008:277–82). The association of the divine 'eagle' with the sun of justice is clear from the whole verse alluded to: 'Et orietur...Sol iustitiae, et sanitas in *pennis* suis' (Mal 4:2) and Alan of Lille's observation: 'Christ is called "eagle" because with irresistible penetration of mind he pierces the secrets of the *sun of justice*' (PL 210:706). *chaumbre*:

cf. 'chambre of the Trinite' in William Herebert (Brown, *C14th Lyrics* 1957:32) and the Sequence on the nativity of the BVM, st.19 quoted by Alan of Lille in his *Distinctiones* (*PL* 210:980), that calls her 'totius trinitatis / nobile triclinium [couch]' (*AH* I.269). **127** *plenitudo temporis tyme*: '[But when the moment] of the fullness of time was come, [God sent his Son...]' (Gal 4:4–5). The 'moment' is that of Christ's death; but the pointed conjunction of this text with *Iesus...chaumbre* at 126 suggests the influence of Fortunatus's 'Pange lingua', which was sung on Good Friday at the Adoration of the Cross: 'And so when came the fullness / of the sacred time [*sacri plenitudo temporis*], / The Son who made the world was sent / down from his Father's clime / And went forth clothed in flesh assumed / within a virgin womb' (st. 4). **128–9** 'When Old Age should knock down the fruit, or when it should attain to ripeness, and Jesus have to joust for it, to settle by combat who was to get it'. **129** Since the sense of *j(o)uste* is figurative, a play on words (originating in the homophony of *justes / justice*) may be intimated ('(do) justly' / 'deal justice'). The decisive combat with Satan will be a 'judicial duel,' an action at once legal and chivalric. **131** could scan vocalically as Type Ie with a mute stave on (a)*doun*, but a preferable scansion is cognatively on |t| |t| / |d| with *adóun* as key-stave (for a similar pattern but with |t| as key-stave sound see 20.325 //). **133a** 'Behold the handmaid of the Lord: be it done to me [according to thy word]' (Lk 1:38). **134** *wenche*: a bold use of this slippery term (see *IG*), not elsewhere recorded in relation to the Mother of God, that proclaims her (outward) ordinariness (cf. 20.116). *fourty wokes*: the length of normal pregnancy, as in William of Shoreham's reference to 'Al hyre ioyen of *uorti woken*' (*Poems* 118/110). But as a number with significance in the Bible (the 'Wilderness years'; Jesus's desert fast) it suggests also a period of symbolic preparatory waiting for man's salvation preceding Christ's birth. **B 101–2** The (not quite decorous) implication that the Saviour displayed aggressive potential in the womb may account for the revision at C 135–6, which clearly refers to his youth. **136–7** *barnhoed...come*: alluding to the occasion when the twelve-year old Jesus disputed with the Doctors of the Law in the Temple (Lk 2:42–52) before his coming of age (which here figuratively = the dubbing of a knight). *bold... yfouhte*: 'bold enough to have fought'. In **B** the elliptical sense is 'knew enough about fighting to have fought'. **138–51a** describe Christ's miracles of healing, which evoke both faith and hostility. **138** *lechecraeft*: a metaphor for Jesus as a trainee physician, and not entirely lucid (whether with Piers Plowman or Liberum Arbitrium as his 'teacher'). It may have been prompted by Gal 4:1–7, which describe Christ as 'made under [i.e. subject to] the law' (vs 4), like one 'under tutors and governors until the time appointed by the father' (vs 2, referring to men generally but here applied to Christ). **B 104–5** The

'leechcraft' is initially that of learning how to dress battle-injuries (a recognised knightly accomplishment, as in the *Histoire de Guillaume le Maréchal* ll. 1789–92), and the situation envisaged is that of an older knight acting as *mestre* to a younger (Burrow 1993:73–4). **139** The Latin phrase now signifies the climax (*hy tyme*) of Christ's life, his Passion, seen as initiated by his public ministry. **142a** '[The blind see], the lame walk, the lepers are cleansed...' (Mt 11: 5). **B 110a** 'They that are in health need not a physician, but they that are ill' (Mt 9:12); Christ's reply when the Pharisees ask why he consorts with *peccatores* 'synfulle' (whom he treats as spiritually 'sike'). The revision largely removes the metaphor in these lines (on which see Schmidt 1983:146–8), except for an echo in *clansed* 143, which answers to *mundantur* 142a. **B 111** *menyson blody*: alluding to the woman with an 'issue of blood' who was healed by Jesus after touching the hem of his garment (Mt 9:20); see also on 7.167. **144–5** See on 17.302–3, which these lines virtually repeat, the rhyme neatly contrasting the death natural to man with the supernatural life given by Christ. **146** *miracle*: not an improvement on *maistrie* B 115, which linked Jesus's miraculous act to the divine 'instruction' he received, the raising of Lazarus being his 'graduation-exercise' as a 'master' of the redemptive *ars*. The clear echo of these lines in B 18.276=C 20.299 is also foregone; but the replacement of *maistrie* by *miracle*, *selcouth* and *wonder* may be intended to avert an over-literal response to the metaphor. *mestus...*: 'Jesus became sad' (Mt 26:37); from the Garden of Gesthemane narrative, replacing 'wept' (Jn 11:35) in that of the raising of Lazarus. At B 115 the chime-echo of *maistrie* in *mestus* 'Platonically' hints at the close union of divine power with human vulnerability in the person of the incarnate Son. **147** *yes...why*: the internal rhyme both echoing and differing from that of B 116, **C** intimating the deeper significance of this 'sign' and that Christ's sorrow is not just for the loss of a friend but for all men's subjection to death because of sin. **148–9** elaborate Jn 11:45 and 12:42 in the light of Jn 19:7. **147** The stock-phrase repeated here audaciously associates Christ with the three 'types of the common man' it is used of earlier, Will, Robert and Haukyn (6.2, 326, B 14.324). **148** *seyde þat tyme*: an inference from Jn 11:45, 12:11. **151** Despite this collocation, *Mahond* stands for 'Satan' (152) and not the founder of Islam (always 'Mahomet' in **L**). **151a** 'Thou hast a devil'; the exact form of Jn 7:20 and 8:48, in both of which Jesus is called mad (in the usual Biblical phrase meaning 'possessed'). But in only the third occurrence (*demonium habet*), just before the Raising of Lazarus (Jn 10:20), does the question arise of whether Jesus works wonders through the devil's agency. This accusation is provoked by his claim to have power over death (Jn 10:17–18), when speaking of his own resurrection, which the raising of Lazarus prefigures (Jn 11:23–6).

152–78 The halving of this 45-line stretch of **B** sacrifices vivid detail but keeps the substance intact, though with significant changes of emphasis. **152–3** condense four lines having repetition (B 124 of 109) and (in 121) prematurely voicing a theme that will be developed (in its proper place) at 18.104. **152** *saueour*: playing ironically on the sense of spiritual and physical salvation anticipated at B 109. **154** harks back to the form of B 15.590, a line omitted in revision at that point. **156** *Vnkynde*: because ungrateful for his various deeds of 'kindness'. *vnkunnynge*: in failing to recognise in these deeds the Messiah prophesied. **157** *ouerturned*: a small act but used (somewhat provocatively) at 163 as foreshadowing a much greater one, the meaning of which his listeners cannot grasp. **158** is a vocalic Type IIa having an unusual pattern of lifts, without intervening dips in the a-half: *hém oút álle* (cf. 22.307). **159** paraphrases the Latin at B 135a. **B 135a** 'My house shall be called the house of prayer; [but you have made it a den of thieves]' (Mt 21:13, quoting Is 56:7). In Mt this is said on Palm Sunday (and directly stirs up the Jewish rulers against Christ), in Jn during an earlier visit to Jerusalem at the beginning of his ministry. The two Gospel accounts may have been combined in order to connect this scene with the resurrection-motif pervading the story of Lazarus in Jn 11 (cf. on 146). **160–1** The ostensible referent of *hit* must be the *hous* so that, though Christ means the willing sacrifice of his life, his hearers' misunderstanding is hardly surprising (the source-account in Jn 2:13–22 is much clearer). **162** *iustice*: of uncertain reference, all the Evangelists making the official charge against Jesus before the Roman governor the political one of claiming to be King of the Jews. But since the accusation here is that before the Sanhedrin, the council of Jewish religious leaders (Mt 26:61), *iustice* (as at 178) may signify the High Priest and others authorised to judge in purely religious cases. **163** The a-verse cannot mean 'overturning [of the tables] *in* the Temple' but must refer to Christ's prophecy that he would re-build the 'temple' [of his body] if it were destroyed. *bitokened*: as noted in Jn 2:21; elliptical for 'the overturning symbolised his [crucifixion, the re-building his] resurrection', and what the overturning more widely 'betokens' is the end of the old dispensation. **164** *Enuye.*: repeating 6.87 and doubtless importing 'envy' as well as hatred. *Iewes*: with religious not racial reference; used by **L** (when re-telling NT material) in the regular Johannine sense of 'the religious leaders opposed to the mission of Jesus'. **165** *pans* (*siluer* B 143): see Mt 26:15. **165a** '[But they said: Not on the festival day], lest perchance there should be a tumult among the people' (Mt 26:5). **166** *Of*: 'from, through'. *Iudas þe Iew*: a regular collocation (see B 10.128, 15.264); more than an alliterative convenience, it aims to associate the disciple's treachery with that of the people he 'sells' Jesus to (cf. B 9.85), who are assumed

to share his fate (see on 164). **167** *Pasche*: Passover, the principal Jewish religious festival, commemorating the Exodus from Egypt, and celebrated on the night of the 14/15 in the month Nisan (here = the day after Good Friday). Although B 140 specifies *Þursday* as the day of the Last Supper, the Synoptic Gospels treat this meal as a Passover meal. **B 145** *Tu dicis*: 'Thou sayest it' (i.e. 'As you yourself say'), replacing Christ's reply *Tu dixisti* (Mt 26:25) to Judas's question 'Is it I?' with his words in answer to Pilate (Mk 15:2). **169** *Aue, raby*: 'Hail, rabbi. [And he kissed him]' (Mt 26:49). This is Judas's pre-arranged signal for the arrest of Jesus (Mk 14:44), as 170 explains. But the revision sacrifices the verbally complex digression on the insincere kiss at B 147–8, with its rich wordplay on three distinct homophonic lexemes (*to*), and its echoes tolling through 'tolde' and repeated 'tokne' (itself repeated in 'to *kno*we'). **170** *to be knowe*: 'in order that he [Jesus] might be recognised in that way', but with an ironic suggestion that the 'false kiss' will become a metonym for Judas's own treachery. **171** *sayde*: perhaps signifying 'spoke', since the Jews are not directly addressed till 176. **173** *kissyng*: the common salutation among friends in England at this time (cf. A 11.177). The revision is more appropriate, since Judas would not have been laughing. **B 155** *galle*: an ironic forewarning of the drink that will be offered Jesus on Calvary (Mt 27:34). **174** *myrrour*: a negative one, unlike St Thomas at 17.277. **175** The revision extends the condemnation from Judas to the whole class of friend-betrayers. **B 157** states that Judas shall be the worse for it (in becoming an example of how to destroy a friend through falsity). *worþe... þiselue*: the idea of evil 'recoiling' on itself, implicit in the Vulgate's verb-subject inversion of B 157a and the containment of *ve* in '*ve*nit'. **175a** '[Woe to the world because of scandals]. For it must needs be that scandals come; but nevertheless woe to that man by whom the scandal cometh' (Mt 18:7); in context not addressed to Judas, though the 'hanging' reference in Mt 18:6 may have suggested applying it to him. **177** See Jn 18:8.

B 160–66 This 'foreshadowing summary', with its ominous assonances, may have been cut because it reduces the tension of the coming drama through anticipating the chivalric account of the combat at B 18.28ff (itself an anticipation), 'giving away' its outcome (one not, of course, unknown to the audience) at B 18.35. **161, 163** The phrases composing 161b and 163b stand in apposition, person, act and name evoking joy for 'all', as Piers's did for one at 18. And the collocation of name and emotion, in echoing the latter, intimates how (despite the *difference* in name) person and mission are mysteriously one, as will be shown at B 18.25 (the importance of the name JESUS will be elaborated at B 19.18–22). **166** *Deide... day*: negative 'Platonic' *transsumptio* that in its creative wordplay discloses the creative power of the Word.

(ii) 179–292 The Encounter with Faith takes place on a less profound level of dream-consciousness than the vision of the Tree of Charity. This is indicated by the retention of *wakede* from B 167 at 179, which argues for interpreting the preceding sequence as a deep (effectively 'inner') dream despite the lack of a 'swoon' at 4 like that at B 19. Unusually for **C**, Will's motivated awakening by *moche noyse* (see Schmidt 1986:25–6 and n9) is *more* dramatic than in **B**. The interchange following is an exposition through question-and-answer. The only 'vision' seen (Abraham's of the Trinity) will be an event *recalled* from the past, to be re-evaluated in the light of present understanding.

179–87 Vision 5*a* ends explicitly here in **B** at 167 and (virtually) in **C**. **180** The disappearance of *Liberum Arbitrium,* unlike that of his predecessor in **B**, is total, a clarification that foregoes the Piers-persona's rich capacity for progressive development. **B 170–1** *ydiot*: a word describing Will's sense of having lost rational self-control (cf. *frentyk* C 179) and affirming the continuity between the obsessions of his waking (B 15.10) and of his sleeping life. An 'idiot' is what the Dreamer seems to the world, even as he comes to understand spiritual truth (cf. I Cor 1:25, 3:19). The urgent pursuit for Piers (*souзte*) actualises Will's desire at B 7.146 and will be recalled in Conscience's equally urgent quest at 20.386. **181** *waited*: contrasted with *souзte* in B 171. Will cannot 'seek' his own faculty (because it has disappeared within his soul's *erber of pryuatees*) but must now turn for further enlightenment to the history of Christ's redemptive acts as unfolded, at the more 'communal' plane of the liturgically-oriented outer dream, in the scriptural readings of the Missal. **182** *mydde-Lentones Sonenday*: the fourth in Lent, called 'Laetare Sunday' after the Introit of the day, 'Rejoice, Jerusalem' (Ps 121:1). The time of Abraham's appearance follows the liturgical sequence: he is the subject of the day's Epistle (Gal 4:22–31), which understands his two sons Ishmael and Isaac *per allegoriam* as signifying the Old Covenant and the New respectively. **B 175** is deleted as otiose, **174** as repeating B 5.525. **185** *with Fayth* (*of Abrahames hous* **B**): the inversion retaining ('with'; 'of') a separateness between the quality and the man, since the Biblical figure is a real person of 'exemplary' virtue, not the personification of an idea. **186** *heraud of armes*: one with the expertise to descry from a distance and accurately proclaim the blazons of those entering the tournament ground. **B 178–9** are properly removed because a 'quest' is more suitable to Will than to Faith, who as a 'herald' would wait for knights to arrive, not go out in search of them (but *seke* remains at 269, possibly with the sense 'ask about' (MED s.v. *sechen* v. 4(a)).

188–239 re-write **B**'s account of the Trinity with less assurance but perhaps more subtlety. As what follows

is continuously revised, it makes for clarity to break the commentary into smaller sections and deal *suyrelepes* with the two parallel texts.

188–96 188 revises B 181 in the words of B 17.27, at the cost of some repetition. *persones*: the choice of word implying the *interpretatio* of the emblem. *pensel*: 'a pennoncel or streamer identifying an individual knight' (MED s.v. *pencel* n. (1), (b)). The 'device' differs from that in B 181 in representing the persons as *departable*, signifying their unity not synecdochically by *lyþ* but metonymically by *pensel*. **189** *speche*: i.e. the Word, the Second Person. *out of alle*: hinting at the generation of the Son, the double procession of the Spirit and the 'circumincession' or mutual interpenetration of the Persons (the *perichoresis* or 'dance' around the 'still point' described in T. S. Eliot's *Burnt Norton* II). **190** stresses total unanimity without conflict. **191** *se vpon*: 'consider theoretically'. *solus Deus*: '(one) only God'; despite the exact verbal parallels at Mk 2:7, Lk 5:21, 18.19 cited by AlfQ, the sense here is not 'God alone' but 'the sole God' as in the *Deus solus* of Ps 85:1 (*Pe*). **192** *suyrelepes... sondry names*: names *resulting* from the true distinction between Persons, not creating it; an indication of Will's metaphysically 'realist' view of religious truth. Though recalling his question on the soul's names at 16.201, this shows more tentativeness and respect. **195** The **C** line could be an extended Type Ia on |θ| with a mute stave on *þat* and vocalic semi-counterpoint (*hált ál*) or, in the light of the **B** line 188 under revision (which makes *a* the key-stave), a Type Ia (or Ic) line scanning on vowels. If the latter scansion is preferred for **C**, the word *a*, despite its semantic weight, must be treated as mute; but this is optional in **B**, which may be T-type (*-sóne, -sélue*). *halt al*: a rôle more commonly that of the Father, who 'contains' the whole Trinity. **196** *in alle*: conceiving the Spirit as divine immanence; *al* 'everything' and *alle* 'all (individual) beings' have 'the creation' as implied referent.

B 181–90 181 *noon...ooþer*: recalling B 57, as elements of the inner dream now 'surface' in the outer. **183** affirms both the unanimity of the persons and their self-sufficient divinity, a paradox hard to reconcile rationally with an 'appropriation' of functions that is not also a division of powers. **184** *makere*: 'Creator', the name of the Father as the generator who is not generated. **186–7** The special titles of the Son as knowable *veritas* (Jn 14:6) and guardian of rational beings derive from his nature as *Verbum* and *Sapientia* 'Word and Wisdom of the Father', revealer of God's hidden nature as Trinity. **189–90** *light*: source of understanding, as in *JLH* II:165, vs 2. *Confortour*: the *Consolator* sense of 'Paraclete' (Jn 14:16), which also means 'Advocate'; see the Pentecost hymns in *JLH* II 161, vs 2; 162, vs 1; 164, vs 8. *alle blisse*: the *beata gaudia* brought by *spiritus paraclitus* (*JLH* II:154). **197–239** form a (varyingly successful) attempt to throw light on that *myrke thyng* the mystery of the Trinity (an object of trusting faith rather than *kynde knowynge*) by two analogies, of a lord and his servant, and of the human family of husband, wife and child.

200–14a compare the Trinity's act of self-disclosure to that of a lord who operates through an agent (for possible influence from Abelard here see Szittya 1986²). **202–3** 'Power, and a means to make known his own power, that of himself and that of his agent, and what both experience / undergo' (see *TN* further). **205** *seruaunt*: the term *servus Dei* 'servant of God', common in the OT for a prophet (I Par 6:49, Dan 6:20); but most relevant here is Phil 2:6–7, which state that Christ was 'in the form of God' but took on 'the form of a servant' for his redemptive work. **206–10** The relational image, which anticipates the second analogy in 215–39, is based on the theological emblem of the Church as the 'Bride' of Christ, whom he loves and who brings forth 'issue' (the saved). The immediate scriptural source is Apoc 21:2, 9, where the New Jerusalem (itself a 'type' of the Church as the City of God) is further figured as the Bride of the Lamb (Christ). **208** *Patriarches and prophetes*: OT 'servants of God' but placed with the apostles of the New Dispensation because the Church (like the Tree of Charity) has its roots in the past and extends to the end of time, so that the faith in God of the just before Christ (and the Messianic hope it engendered) are implicitly faith and hope in the Son who alone saves. **209–10** clarify B 199–200 by advancing B 210 to make more explicit how an 'incarnational trinity' (Christ the Head, the earthly society of the baptised co-terminous with the Christian world, and the Mystical Body that includes the blessed) may symbolise the Holy Trinity and the orthodox ('Trinitarian') faith. **211–14a** assert that the one Creator-God exists in Trinity (in 213 the a-half stresses fall best on *is*). That he made man in his likeness (212) inevitably raises an expectation (fulfilled in the next analogy) of a 'trinity' in mankind. **213–14** *bereth...werkes*: especially man himself, the Creator's chief 'work' (cf. the closely parallel Ps 8:6–7). While the world's proclamation of God's *triune* nature is not obvious, **L** may envisage it as divided into land, sea and sky, and 'created things' into lifeless, animate and spiritual, or 'animate creatures' into birds, beasts and fishes. **213** *A thre*: 'a trinity' or 'in trinity'. **214a** 'The heavens show forth the glory of God: and the firmament declareth the work of his hands' (Ps 18:2); a verse only loosely relevant to the argument about the created universe revealing the Trinity.

215–39 endeavour to show how humanity itself 'proves' (better, evidences) the divine triunity. For detailed discussion of this passage see Tavormina 1995:140–66.

215–26 215 *thre persones departable*: the three distinguishable divine Persons, seen as (necessarily) reflected in humankind, which is complete or perfect only when

male and female unite to engender offspring. *Y...by*: a claim less to demonstrate formally the truth of a proposition from data than to 'assay' the validity of a belief by submitting it to the test of experience (so as to acquire a *kynde knowynge*). **216** *o God*: the unity of the divine nature (shared by the three Persons) is shown *analogice* by the descent of human beings from Adam, so that they *aren bote oen in manhede* (220). **217** The phrasing is close to Bonaventure's 'Eva, quae fuit ab Adam sive de Adam deducta' in his Commentary on Bk I of Lombard's *Sentences*, 12.1.3, in *Op. Omn.* I:223 (Galloway 1998:130n16, citing Clopper 1997:119). **219** scans either as Type IIb on |ð| and |θ| and vowels, or as a vocalic Type Ib with a four-syllable onset. A vocalic scansion would seem preferable, since the first alternative would require a mute third stave in a Type II line, something **L** avoids. **221–6** The link between these lines and the foregoing is presumably the notion of unity as 'completeness'. A sterile union falls short of the norms of 'perfect' marriage, just as humanity would have been incomplete with only a male, or with a male and female but with no issue. **222** *Bible*: not a specific text; but the injunction at 223a accords with the 'Biblical' conception of an Israelite's duty to obey the divine command in Gen 1:28 (echoed as late as Lk 1:25). **223** *acorsede alle couples*: not, according to Tavormina (1989:155n81), a statement that individual childless couples are 'unblessed', since 'the command to multiply applies to the species as a whole'. But though this assertion need not be taken as universally intended, it remains dramatically apt in the mouth of Faith (Abraham), to whom God's *specific* 'promise' was of a child by his wife (Gen 15:2–6). **223a** 'Cursed is the man who has not left offspring in Israel'. The quotation appears in a lesson for St Anne's Day (*Hereford Breviary* II.266), addressed by the high priest to Joachim, father of the Virgin Mary, in the Temple (Tavormina 1989²:117–25).

B 201–19a offer a more complicated analogy, which though itself a little *myrke*, essentially takes the three *status* seen (B 68–78) on the Tree that 'signifies' the Trinity (B 63) as constituting a 'collective human trinity' (203). This division derives from the familial 'trinity' of father, mother and child (205–6). But the ingenious (and somewhat tortuous) comparison of the *status* to the *heavenly* Trinity fails to articulate the analogy of the third state, virginity, with the Spirit (which is not made explicit till C 18.74–5). **201** *in pre leodes*: an allusion to the three men who visited Abraham at Mamre (Gen 18:2; B 227) and were traditionally understood as an OT prefiguring of the Trinity revealed in the NT. **206** *of hem þope*: a happy 'betokening' by the 'human trinity' of the orthodox (Western) doctrine (*trewe bileue* 210) of the 'Double Procession' of the Spirit from Father and Son. **207** The mutual love of parents and child likewise figures that of the divine Persons. **208** *oon singuler name*: not the *same* name predicable univocally of God and Man, but one 'special' name predicable equivocally of *both* (i.e. *man-hede* 'humanity' of Man and *godhede* 'divinity' of God). But **L** may be punning on another sense of *singulere* 'unique' (MED s.v. 3(a)), if he also means to evoke the condition of the God-Man Christ who unites *heuene and here*. 211 *Might*: the generative power 'appropriated' to a father / the Father (see on 18.34=B 30). 212 Strictly, the subject of *bitokeneþ* is *might*, but obviously it is *marriage* that 'symbolises', power being predicated 'literally'. *trewely*: in part because the first human pair were given a 'marriage' blessing by God in the words 'Increase and multiply' (Gen 1:28). *dorste*: repeated at 214 and expressing awareness of the audacity of the analogy. 213 *He*: an emphatic nominative instead of the expected accusative *Him* (see *TN*). 214 *widewe*: because separated by death (which occurs just after he utters the cry quoted) from his 'other half', the divine nature 'wedded' to his human nature. 214*a* 'My God, my God, why hast thou forsaken me?' (Mt 27:46, quoting Ps 21:2). 215 *creatour weex creature*: the sense is that 'matrimony "becomes" widow-hood', power becoming powerlessness, through the death of the Creator'. The morphemic *annominatio* 'Platoni-cally' highlights **L**'s arresting ascription of Incarnation to God's analogical 'need' to experience the suffering and mortality that define creatureliness, so that his limitless perfection may be (paradoxically) 'completed' through limitation (cf. B 18.221–4). **L**'s wordplay recalls Walter of Châtillon's 'factor fit factura / et *creator creatura*' (ed. Strecker, no. 10, st. 3).

227–40 treble B 220–4 in the effort to elucidate the place of the Third Person, who had been left out of **B** (something perhaps remarked on by an attentive early reader). They achieve this chiefly through omitting the awkward *stat□s* analogy (though the elaborated 'marriage' model is not without difficulties) and insisting on an appeal to experience (240). 228 *in hymsulue*: in apposition with *in God Fader* 227. *simile*: the word, only half-naturalised, perhaps echoing Gen 2:18 ('faciamus ei adiutorium *simile* sibi'), to suggest how Eve was both 'in' Adam and resembled him, and to compare her emergence from his side to the Son's leaving the 'bosom' of the Father' (Jn 1:18) at the Incarnation. 230–33 liken the 'springing' of the child from the first pair to the 'double procession' of the Spirit; but this *simile*'s weakness is that whereas they had further children, He is unique. 231 *spyer*: echoing the 'Eve-out-of-Adam' image to suggest consubstantiality more strongly than the slightly subordinationist 'Abel-out-of-Adam-and-Eve' image. 232 *of hem bothe*: perhaps better taken not as an adjectival possessive phrase but as an integral adverbial phrase qualifying *Is* 233 = 'proceeds / has his being from them both.' 233 involves a harsh shift from sg. subject (*Spirit*) to an implied pl. (*Thei*); for *were* could not be sg. (and so also subjunctive) if the 'double

procession' is eternal (*ay*) and necessary, not contingent and a 'consequence' of the Incarnation (see *TN*). 234–6 are somewhat elusive, but not unintelligible (see *TN* and at *Intro*. II § 133), though the comparison enforced by *as...So* is hardly exact, what is offered being a parallel under the guise of a likeness. But the thought becomes clearer if *mankynde* is seen as the 'human trinity' that is an analogue of the 'divine trinity' (see on B 201–19): 'Just as it is obvious that three persons — a man, his wife and their true offspring — are of absolutely one and the same human nature, so the Son of God is God, and the Trinity subsists in three persons'. 235 This insistence that the child be the 'legitimately begotten' offspring of married parents (an illegitimate child breaching both positive and natural law) is in place coming from the speaker; for Abraham sent away his servant's son Ishmael because only Isaac, as the child of promise, counted as his 'true' issue (Gen 21). But the sentiment is also of a piece with less specifically ascribable utterances, such as Wit's at 10.204–14. 237–8 The phrasal rhyme that seems to mimic the thematic content suggests a homology (cf. *encountre* 239) between divine and human trinities, as the verbal antithesis of *cam of* and *goth to* their complementarity. 237 scans as Type Ib on non-lexical words (*Ín, áren, ó, álle*) or, preferably, on |m| with two staves in *mátrimónie* and contrapuntal alliterating vowel staves (*áren, álle*). The line's breach of logic is only apparent, since the first man's name signifies equivocally both '(hu)man (nature)' and 'Adam' who, with Eve and Abel, 'came out of' it. 238 *alle thre*: the primary grammatical subject of *is* (like *Sone* in 236). 239 '"Three set against three" in the case of both the Godhead and humanity'. *Pe* notes that *treys* is an AN term for a throw of three in the dice-game of 'hazard' (MED s.v. *trei* n.(3)); but Tavormina (1982:162n) suspects a contracted form of *trey-as* 'three-ace', a two-dice throw of three and one. Though 'an excellent linguistic symbol of tri-unity', this requires greater metrical prominence for both *treys,* and scansion on *tt / d* as a macaronic Type IIa (with a cognative liaisonal stave in *quod_hé* or *Godhéde*). But with unwrenched stresses in the two opposed b-half terms (the key-notion being the mirror-symmetry of human and divine), preference would be for palatal-stopped Type IIe or IIIa (with cognative main staves -*cóuntre-*, [*quód*], *Gód*). Perhaps nothing more precise is intended than a 'matched throw' that illustrates how an 'adventurous' Creator seeks 'equality' with his creature by becoming human so that man may become divine. 240 scans as Type III counterpointed and enriched (*abb / aa*).

B 220–4 222 *gendre of a generacion*: 'a species (springing) from a single act of generation'; somewhat loosely expressed, for though Adam's progeny 'proceed' from him, *he* was created, not generated. The phrase applies better to the Trinity (see Tavormina 1989[1]). *bifore...*

heuene: an asseveration (cf. 1.140). **223** *So*: inaccurate, because the analogy ignores the usual theological opinion that essence and existence are identical in God, but distinct in creatures. The 'necessity' of a child's relation to its parent differs from that of the Second and Third Persons to the Father in being 'consequential', not 'ontological' (see on C 233). *Fre Wille*: adapting from Augustine (*De Trinitate* X, XII. 19, XV and XXI) the analogy between the Spirit and the human faculty that chooses and loves (cf. his *frenesse* at B 88 and association with *Liberum Arbitrium* at B 50–2). **223a** 'The Spirit proceeding from the Father and the Son'; the standard Western understanding of the dogma as expressed in the Athanasian Creed: 'Spiritus Sanctus a Patre et Filio...procedens' (Alf*Q*, p.105). **224** *alle* (1): loosely expressed, since *bothe* would be better.

241–69a bring the personification of Faith's 'historical' identity into focus as he retells the Biblical story of God's covenant with the Father of the Chosen People. The approach is doctrinal, with Abraham's experience seen as the first revelation of God's triune nature, but also typological and sacramental, his acts of circumcision and sacrifice being understood as figures of Baptism and the Eucharist. That Abraham's encounter is with one God 'gangynge a thre' is carefully sustained by the shifting number of the pronouns, e.g. *hym* 243, *they* 244 (Davlin 2001:93).

241–53 241 *somur...porche*: suggested by Gen 18:1; but the echo of Pr 1 and 10.2 hints at the general idea of 'new beginnings'. **242a** 'Three he saw and worshipped one'; from a Quinquagesima Antiphon (*Brev.*1:dxli) often cited in proofs of the doctrine of the Trinity (Ames 1970:56), and based on Gen 18:2 ('apparuerunt ei *tres* viri...quos cum *vidisset*...cucurrit...et *adoravit*'). Alan of Lille observes that 'in the three who appeared, [Abraham] understood trinity; and because *he adored one*, he understood a unity in the Trinity; and thus he is understood to have adored a God both three and one' (*PL* 210:404). In the 'liturgical' time-scheme that underlies Passūs XVIII–XXII and has reached the Fourth Sunday of Lent in 'dream-time', this scene forms a 'prelude', since the fiftieth day before Easter is the Sunday before Ash Wednesday, when Lent begins. The OT readings of the whole week concern Abraham, those of the day itself dwelling on God's covenant with him that provides the substance of this section, and the day's hymn is one to the Trinity. **B 229** The details are from Gen 18:6–7. **247** *tokenes*: properly referring to circumcision, the *signum foederis* 'sign of the covenant'; but here related typologically to the patriarch's obedience in offering Isaac, and to God's providing the ram for sacrifice and swearing by himself to multiply Abraham's offspring for ever (Gen 22:13–18). The importance of Abraham extends beyond the OT rite of initiation to his figurative significance as 'father of faith' and his offering

as foreshadowing Christ's at the Last Supper and the Mass (see 264). *whan tyme cometh*: improving on the vagueness of B 230 and anticipating the encounter in Limbo (20.366). **249–50** both have unusually long 'preludal' dips and their first lift on the pronouns *hym* and *his* (with Isaac and God as referents). **251** *allowe*: alluding to St Paul's interpretation (Romans 4:3, citing Gen 15:6, 9) of Abraham's obedience as 'imputing' righteousness to him or 'justifying' him through his faith.

B 233–35 233 *bi hym*: with referent either God or Isaac; Abraham's 'will' as regards both is precisely the issue. *wol*: carefully balancing *wille* to bring out that God's attitude towards man depends in part on man's attitude to God. **235** The OT placing of the Covenant of Circumcision (Gen ch. 17) *before* the offering of Isaac is not incompatible with the Pauline view of this rite as a *signaculum iustitiae fidei* 'seal of the justice of the faith which [Abraham] had, being uncircumcised' (Rom 4:11). But L, taking the offering of Isaac as the *main* 'token' of that faith, places circumcision after it (*siþen*), signifying typologically that individual faith *precedes* baptism into the 'new Israel' of the Church. The *sone* of 252 could denote Ishmael (Gen 17:23–6), but *siþen* indicates the same *sone* as at C 248, Isaac (Gen 21:4), and B 234–5 put this beyond doubt. Presumably the point is that only Abraham's 'true' issue can be a fit type of Christ in the 'human trinity' model proposed as an analogy for the divine one.

254–69a 254 The bleeding at circumcision foreshadows that of Christ on the cross, which generated sacramental baptism (21.325 echoes the wording here). **255** *his bileue*: 'faith in him' (objective genitive). **257–9** *lyf...Mercy*: though neither promise is made to Abraham in Genesis, he here stands as a 'type' of the believer in the New Dispensation for whom these promises hold, subject to faith and repentance (the 'confessional' phrasing of 259–60 directly echoes 12.72). **B 242a** 'As you once promised to Abraham and to his seed'; a variant of the last verse of the *Magnificat*, based on Lk 1:46–55 and forming the regular first canticle at Vespers. **261–5a** As *Sk* notes, Abraham's sacrifice (Gen 15:9) has been confused with that of Melchisedech (Gen 14:18–19). But the 'confusion' may be intentional (*somewhat hit bitokneth* 264), since the 'altar' and 'worship of the Trinity' seem meant to prefigure the Mass where, during the Consecration prayer *Supra quae*, Melchisedech's sacrifice is mentioned (after Abraham's) as a type of Christ's. **261** *a sente me*: without authority in Genesis. **264** *so*: 'in this manner'; such stress on the elements that will be used in the Eucharist is part of the Church's seeing in 'the father of all them that believe' (Rom 4:11) a figure of Christ the perfect High Priest (as borne out by Abraham's 'prophetic' pre-consciousness that Christianity will extend God's revelation to all mankind). The entire presentation here is deeply influenced by the argument of Rom 4:16–25. **265a** '[And other sheep I have that are not of this fold: them also I must bring]... and there shall be one fold and one shepherd' (Jn 10:16); the main Gospel statement that Christ's mission is to unite the Gentiles and the Chosen Race as one people of God. **266–9a** condense B 249b–50a and omit 251 (a line repeated at B 18.324, but there retained by **C**). **266** Not only does Abraham's awareness of his rôle as a *figura* of the Christian believer pertain to his allegorical character as Faith, his words and actions are accommodated to the liturgical cycle's re-telling of salvation history, and find no parallel in the typologically-structured Miracle Plays. *here*: 'while alive on earth' (so at 269). *helle*: 'Limbo' (where he now dwells); for this sense of 'hell' see at 116. **269a** 'Behold the Lamb of God...[who taketh away the sin of the world]' (Jn 1:29). The Baptist's words convey his prophetic sense of the Messiah's redemptive mission as universal. But their image of 'Christ the Lamb of sacrifice' (correlative to Abraham's 'Christ the Shepherd') coheres with Faith's 'proleptic' allusion to the Mass, being the words the priest speaks as he holds up the Host before administering Communion.

270–92 enable Abraham to complete explaining his task as 'herald' of Christ's Incarnation and its purpose: to win back the 'fruit' that through the 'death of kind' caused by the Fall must fall into the Devil's hands (111–17). **270–3** are a fine specimen of 'grotesque sublime' in their allegorical 'realisation' of 'Abraham's bosom' (Lk 16:22), varying somewhat from the Biblical source's *chaos magnum* 'great gulf' between the place of the damned and the place 'afar off' where Abraham rests (Lk 16:26, 23). **271–2** *bosom*; *lappe*: synonyms translating Lat. *sinus*, which also meant a 'bay' or 'gulf' (resembling the open lap in shape). *blessede*: in his capacity as Father of those to be 'blessèd'. *lazar*: a word derived from the proper name of the beggar in the parable at Lk 16:19–31; denoting (MED s.v.) 'a poor person afflicted with a loathsome disease (often leprosy)'. Lazarus became the patron saint of lepers, and that **L** understood *lasar* as 'leper' is clear from 18.142, translating *leprosi* in Mt 11:5. **275** *I wolde ywyte*: renewing the inquisitiveness rebuked by Anima at 16.210, but receiving a more positive answer from Abraham. **278** *present*: the fruits of the tree (the just who have died before Christ), envisaged as a 'gift' intended for God but seized by the Devil without hope of redemption through ordinary means. The sense of their lying in the Devil's *daunger* (< L *dominationem* 'power') is in tension with their being at ease (*pleynge*), their situation seeming more like house-arrest than imprisonment. **279–86** The position envisaged is of remaining without freedom till the 'better pledge' (of Christ's life) has been paid, which exceeds any claim that even the just have upon God. A strict legal relation is judged to exist between God and the Devil and to govern their coming dispute for the posses-

sion of humanity; but Faith himself is (quite fittingly) unaware of the flaw in Satan's claim that Christ will expose in 20.370–92. For full discussion of this theme see Marx 1995. **281** *maynprise*: no simple payment of bail being able to effect their release. **282** *Crist...name*: in // B 265 a resonant re-working of B 161, a line omitted from **C** in revision. But the sense of 'Christ' as the right name for Jesus *after* he has conquered death is clear in context and will be made explicit at 21.62. **283** *þe deueles power*: in B 266 repeating B 10.237, also removed in **C**. **285** *or ligge*: 'or else we shall have to lie'; the *or...til* construction does not propose an alternative to deliverance by Christ, but repeats it. **286** *Lollyng*: a term more ambiguous in tone than *pleynge* 273, since their lot (if unrelieved) would resemble an eternal execution (cf. 14.130). *suche a lord*: not 'a lord such as' but 'that same lord' (MED s.v. *swich* adj. 1a (a)). **288** *myhte* (1, 2): the lexical-rhetorical noun → verb 'conversion' (polyptoton) underlies the Dreamer's sense of sharing Faith's frustration at mankind's plight in the grip of evil. But the **B** line's echo of B 420–5 (like Haukyn, Will weeps 'religious tears') is lost in **C**, since those lines have been removed in revision. **289** As at 13.219, a new character (*another*) who is to dominate the opening of the next passus is introduced at the end of this one. **290** The acceleration of the action is marked from this point and will continue at 19.50, 333–4. **291–2** *whennes...whoder*: increasingly urgent questioning that now concentrates on establishing the origin and purpose of all the speakers to be met. **292** *wolde...tolde*: internal rhyme producing through echo an effect of closure, and preparing for the passus to follow.

Passus XIX (B XVII)

PASSUS NINETEEN replaces vision with action and dialogue but is no less intellectually demanding than XVIII, with personification allegory supported from below by a typological one. It falls into (i) an encounter with *Spes*, who is figured by Moses (1–47), leading to an enactment of Christ's parable of the healing of the wounded man in Lk 10.29–37 (ll. 48–95). This is linked by the Dreamer's enquiry (96–107) to (ii) the Samaritan's discourse on God's *kynde* and the sin of *unkyndenesse* that blocks the operation of grace (108–334). It has expository and homiletic sections of roughly equal length: (a) an extended bi-partite *simile* (161) comparing the Trinity to a hand (113–167) and to a torch (169–225), then (b) a denunciation of *unkyndenesse* (226–334). The main change is to omit B 17.84–90 (perhaps as too complimentary to Will), 103–24 (a prophecy of 'Outlaw's' defeat not free of repetitions and redundancies), and 161–66 (some leisurely elaboration). B 17.180–352 remain (if with much local revision), but 234–48a add a condemnation of those who live luxuriously in indifference to the needy.

(i) 1–47 1 *Spes*: 'Hope'; the second virtue in St Paul's great 'list' at I Cor 13:13. *spie*: 'one who searches for someone / something' (MED s.v. 1(e)), with perhaps some allusion to Moses' spying of the promised land from afar off (Deut 34:1–5). *SPES* is not identified by name with the Hebrews' lawgiver as Faith is with their progenitor at 18.183. But though his figural relation to the 'theological' virtue of Hope, having no explicit NT basis, is necessarily more oblique than Abraham's to Faith, it is unmistakable (Lk 24:27 names him as the first to foretell Christ). *spere*: a probable translinguistic pun on F *espier* 'spy' (a word etymologically unconnected with the native verb *spere*) and *espeir* 'hope' (St Jacques 1977:483–5). There may also be a play on *spyer* 'sprout, scion' (18.231), hope being a virtue that 'grows out of' faith. *knyʒte*: developing Faith's 'herald' image (18.186); *Spes* is envisaged as in pursuit of a 'knight errant' expected at the jousts but not yet arrived. **2** *maundement*: 'commandment', with a play on the sense 'writ' (MED s.v.1(b), 2(a); see Keen 2002:77). *Synay*: where the Ten Commandments were given (Ex 19:20; see on 7.170). **3** *alle reumes*: because the Commandments largely embody the precepts of the natural law (hence 'right and reason': cf. 21.481 and Alf*G*). L seems to think of even the non-Christian world as monotheist and to have no conception of a purely 'secular' society. **4** *lettre*: his *writ* (**B 3**), 'an administrative document used to order a particular action', here understood as involving 'a proclamation of law' (Keen 2002:77, 79). *Latyn... Ebrew*: the original Commandments being in Hebrew, but the reference to Latin signifying their translation for non-Jews into the official language of the Roman Empire, in which they are quoted at 22.279, B 10.366. The Bx line scans either as Type IIIc (on vowels and |w|) or as Type I on |r| with an internal stave in *writ* (see *Intro.* IV § 45); but the form of revised **C** as a Type Ib line and the fact that the *r*-staves would fall on lexical words recommends the latter. **5** *sey*: probably 'say' (cf. 23), but possibly with a play on 'saw' (cf. 29), alluding to Moses' vision of God on Sinai (Ex 19:20, 24:16). **6–7** The letters have not yet received their authentication, which is what 'nay' refers to; but as 'letters patent' (cf. 12), they are open to all, for the Commandments are not 'privy counsels' but universal laws (contrast Truth's 'secret seal' at 9.27). **6** *lettres*: plural because they are written on two tablets of stone, or because in both sacred languages. **7** *seel*: to validate the document; Christ's death will confirm God's promise of salvation to his people. **8** *croes*: often the form of a seal. *to hange*: after the Crucifixion, which will ratify man's hope of salvation by making available the sacraments of the Christian Faith. **9 (B 7)** Both lines have the same thematic and contrapuntal stave-sounds, but **C** scans as a Type Ie (*aab / ab*) and **B** as an extended Type IIIa (*abb / ab*). **10** *lowe...lygge*: the act of 'affixing the seal' (= the nailing of Jesus to the cross) will effect the

destruction of Satan's power, as will be seen in Passus XX. **11** *we...knowe*: 'so that we might know what the law says'. **12** *patente*: a newly promulgated royal edict addressed to the whole realm, which carried the Great Seal of England and was openly displayed for all to see. *roche*: alluding to the stone tablets on which the Law was written (Ex 24:12, 31:18). **13** *two wordes*: here 'a twofold command' (MED s.v. *word* n. 4 (a)). **14** 'Thou shalt love...God...and [love] thy neighbour [as thyself]' (Mt 22:37). The first part cites Deut 6:5, the central text of the Jewish religion, covering the content of the first two commandments. The second summarises the other eight, dealing with moral conduct, and recalls Lev 19:18 as quoted at Lk 10:27, which has *proximum* 'neighbour' for original *amicum* 'friend'. **15** *good gome*: reminiscent of 9.283–7, where Will reads the words of Truth's pardon, the first major 'divine document' in the poem. **16** *glose*: Christ's comment on the entire OT teaching. *gult penne*: metonymic for gold illumination, on the basis of the metaphor of the 'letter'. **16a** 'On these two [commandments] dependeth the whole law and the prophets' (Mt 22:40), i.e. they sum up the ethical teaching of the OT. **19–22** assert that the writ, though not *yet* sealed, is already effective, as if to say that those before Christ who 'loved God and their neighbour' *are* 'saved' (conditionally). Though in Limbo (cf. 24, 18.270–3), they will be released when his crucifixion 'seals' the document and makes it law. **20** recalls Truth's Pardon, esp. in its form at B 7.112–4. **21** *charme*: a metaphorical usage; but strict Jews wore the text on their heads (Deut 6:8), and medieval Christians often carried charms containing prayers (Duffy 1992:73), even if the practice was not approved (*CT* X 607). There is an ironic echo of the charm obtained from a 'wise woman' that Haukyn (13.341–2) relied on for *boote* instead of *Goddes word*. **23 (B 20)** The scansion of both lines may be vocalic, **C** an extended Type IIIa, **B** Type Ib; or each line may be read as a Type IIa on |s| with *saide* in **C** (or *þis_heraud* in **B**) as third stave. **25** These OT military champions extend from Mosaic times to the 2nd c. before Christ. *Iosue*: Joshua son of Nun, successor to Moses (Deut 34:9) as 'servant of the Lord' (Jos. 3:7, 24:29), whose devotion to the Commandments is shown when he renews and writes down the Mosaic covenant (Jos. 24:25–6). *Iudith*: the widow of Bethulia whose courageous beheading of the Assyrian general Holofernes is told in the apocryphal Book of Judith of the C4th–2nd BC. An exemplar of faith and piety (Jud 8:6–8, 16, 9:17), her song of thanksgiving formed the canticle at Lauds on Wednesdays. *Iudas Macabeus*: the pious hero (d. 161 BC) of I and II Maccabees. These last two books of the Latin OT were valued for affirming belief in resurrection and the efficacy of prayer for the dead (II Mac 7:9, 12:43–5, the latter said in the anniversary of the burial Mass) and their relevance in this context is clear from vs 45: 'they who had fallen asleep with godliness had great grace laid up for them'. **27** *Where...trewe*: 'Which if either of you can / Can either of you (be trustworthy)?' The question asks why, if *faith* in the Trinity together with repentance suffices for salvation, *love* of (one) God and one's neighbour is necessary? **30** virtually repeats 18.188, while its B 27 form is repeated exactly at C 98. **32** *sory*: '(were) sorry'. **33** *somme; somme*: the homophonic pun mockingly hinting at Will's incredulity. **35** now scans as revised on |s| not |v|. **36** *aspyed*: 'looked over / out'; the word plays on his rôle as *spie* (1). **38 (B 35)** may scan on |g| but furnishes a more effective set of contrasts on vowels, giving usually non-lexical *o* and *on* full semantic value (cf. *al(le)* in 39) and a first stave in *God-héde*. In **B**, *in* strictly belongs with *beleeue*, as *louye* takes a direct object. But Bx's order of the verbs can be justified, since 'belief' precedes 'love', and sound theology thus prevails over correct grammar. **C**, by contrast, with the line in its new position at 42, adopts the grammatically correct order, *belief* in (one) God having already been predicated at 38–9. **41** *as oureselue*: filling out the words omitted from the quotation at 14. **B 37–41** offer two examples from common experience to suggest that religion may just be too difficult for the ordinary man to understand, let alone to obey, so the 'simpler' it is, the 'easier' it will be to follow. **42** revises a syntactically awkward B 35 ('to believe in and to love'). The echo of 17.135 reminds that without its 'hard' doctrine of the Trinity (and its related doctrine of the Incarnation), Christianity comes much closer to Judaism and Islam. **43** *and for lered*: a change in the direction of intellectual humility recalls that at 14.55. **44–5** keep the objection ('to believe in the Trinity and love one's enemies...') but omit **B**'s observation that the second of these is *harder* than the first, and that Christianity's central ethical demand (Mt 5:44, explicitly extending Lev 19:18) is the chief obstacle to its acceptance. This, *pace Pe*, is surely in Will's mind; and Goodridge (p. 42) is mistaken that Will's problem is his inability to reconcile the doctrine that faith justifies with the command to good works and charity, a 'Pauline' dichotomy absent from the text. **46–7** Will's dismissive words to *Spes* (which in **C** also apply to Faith) clearly cue the arrival of one who will show that, however difficult, it *is* possible to *vse* 'practise' charity. What is not immediately clear is how this personage relates to the 'hard' teaching that forms half of his exposition; but he will emerge in Passus XX as the divine Son whose mission is to reveal the true nature of God to man, and the two crucial doctrines (Incarnation / Trinity; love of enemies) as inextricably connected.

48–82 The ultimate source of the SAMARITAN EPISODE is Lk 10:30–6, but it owes much to patristic exegesis as transmitted by medieval commentators on the liturgy of the 13th Sunday after the Octave of Pentecost (Saint-

Jacques 1969:217–30, Bennett 1981; Wailes 1987:210–12). The dramatised parable demonstrates concretely how efficacious religion must combine true belief and 'true' living, faith in the Trinity and service of one's neighbour, and how only through the Incarnation of one of the three 'lovely persons' can man receive the grace and example that equip him 'to love a shrew'. Though he has no abstract allegorical name, it is easy enough in the light of the preceding to divine the Samaritan's double function as a persona. 'Biblical', but not a 'straight' historical character like Abraham and Moses, this fictive type-figure serves as an oblique analogue *both* of Christ and of his faithful servant Piers (the 'transcendental' Plowman) in whom grace has actualised the divine 'image' (see Murtaugh 1978; Raw 1969). The Samaritan's supernatural Charity differentiates him from Faith and *Spes*, who are powerless to cure humanity incapacitated by sin. In the Gospel parable, the Priest and Levite reveal the limits of the OT religion. Bennett 1981 notes how allegorised representations of the Parable, in both literary and iconographic sources, were familiar in the period and show it to have been understood as a paradigm of the Fall and restoration of man. **L** has prepared for his specific identification of Priest and Levite with the Jews' progenitor and liberator respectively by his earlier stress on Abraham's sacrifice (a priestly function), and here by Moses's law-giving (historically the rôle of the Scribes rather than the Levites). A disturbing parallel may even be hinted at between Abraham / Moses and the contemporary Church establishment, with the 'outsider'-figure of the Samaritan possibly suggesting the devout layman of perfect integrity (Piers). This already complex pattern **L** further complicates by correlating the esteemed first two *Theological Virtues* with OT personages who can do nothing if they lack the third and highest Virtue, Charity. The normally expected relation between these virtues, all of them held to be infused by divine grace through baptism, was one of *interdependence*: being faith and hope *in Christ* (I Tim 1:1), they were the *fulfilment* of their OT types. But while ultimately reconcilable with the teaching of I Cor 13, **L**'s bold presentation arouses locally some intellectual and dramatic tension. **49** *Samaritaen*: a member of a race descended from the inhabitants of the ancient Kingdom of Israel whose 'impure' religion (mixed with some pagan practices) was regarded by Jews with hostile contempt. The Gospel parable shows those whose religion *is* ritually and doctrinally pure as nonetheless incapable of 'using' towards *their* 'neighbour' the 'law of love' taught to their leader Moses (cf. B 1.151). *muyle*: an apt rendering of Vg *iumentum*, since **L**'s re-telling blends the parable narrative with that of Jesus's entry into Jerusalem on an ass (Lk 19:35ff) to be recounted in 20.19. The unique 'Langlandian grotesque' will later be shown in making a humble beast of burden replace the powerful *destrier* ridden by this 'knight' (cf. 52), an instance of how 'earthly honest things' (in this case the supreme secular 'icon' of the age) must undergo a spiritual 'transformation of meaning'. **50** *rihte way*: judged by Bennett (1981:18) an echo of Christ's words 'Thou hast answered right' to the lawyer he addresses the parable to (Lk 10:280. **51–2** The Lucan narrative makes clear that the traveller, the priest and the Levite (though not necessarily the Samaritan) were travelling *towards* Jericho. But **L** has them all going to Jerusalem (50), evoking the Gospel account of Christ's journey to his Passion (Jericho being named in Lk 19:1 as the town where Jesus stops on his way). **52** *ioust*: taking up a hint dropped as early as 1.152–3. Its prime religious source may be the Easter Sequence *Victimae paschali*, vs 3; but the image of Christ as a knight doing combat with Satan was established in medieval vernacular literature (see under 20.77). **53** *at ones*: more dramatic than in Lk 10:31–3, where the three pass the man successively at intervals. **54–5** improve the somewhat prosaic B 54 and their a-verses now echo 10.62a and 68a, evoking (as **B** does not) Will's state of moral perplexity at that earlier encounter. The traveller is understood in Hugh of St Victor's *Allegoriae in novum testamentum* (*PL* 175:814–5) as designating 'mankind gravely wounded by the evil of original sin' (*R–H*), the priest and levite as the 'fathers of old' who lived holy lives but were little able to heal the wounds of sin, and the Samaritan of course as Christ. In the C12th Lambeth homily *De natali Domini* cited by *Sk* (Morris, *OE Homilies* 1868:I, 78–85), the Levite is specifically Moses; and Bennett 1981 notes how St Bernard in his Sermon VII (*PL* 183:23) includes Abraham and Moses among several men who passed by the wounded traveller. **L**'s interpretation is redolent of the discourse of salvation theology (57a, 58b, 69b) and, as *Pe* notes (referring to discussions in Owst 1933:57–66, Coghill 1944:351–7, *R–H* 1951:2–3, 204–8, Salter 1967:5–7, Smith 1966:74–93), his handling of the parable can be usefully analysed in terms of the four levels of scriptural exegesis. **54** *theues hadde ybounde*: **L**'s addition, drawing on the common idea of persistent sin as incapacitating man from free action. The *latrones* (the devils or their instruments the deadly sins) are agents of 'that first grand thief' Satan. **55** *they*: '(whom) they'; on the Ø-relative see *MES* 205. **56a** recalls Glutton at 6.402. **57** *semiuief*: directly answering to *semivivo* in Lk 10:30; the word's one other appearance, in *Beryn* 2202 (MED s.v.), could be echoing this Langlandian coinage. **58** On the phrase see at 14.105. **60** 'And was unwilling to go anywhere near him' (the distance of 'nine plough-lands' is typical humorous exaggeration). The original significance of the 'passing by' in the parable is that the traveller might have been dead and, since touching a corpse incurred defilement, it shows both 'religious' men to place ritual purity above the law of

love (or *kynde*: see on B 72). By contrast, the 'impure' Samaritan does not recoil from handling and helping the desecrated image of the God both he and the Jews worship. **61–2** *ybosted...yholpe*: cf. 22, making clear that the 'carefole' man's 'care' is sin. **66** *lyard*: more grotesque humour, the mule becoming a grey horse as the 'joust' metaphor unfolds (by 72 its colour in **C** has changed to brown, returning to grey at 333). **68** *poues*: evidencing the physical contact the others avoided; this is the 'kynde knowynge' Will has been seeking, experiential knowledge of man's need by a *creatour* who becomes *creature*. **71–2** *wyn...oyle*: suggestive of the three healing sacraments (of baptism, absolution and unction). The wine is here used to cleanse wounds, not to drink; but *atamede* hints at its symbolic significance, and in the light of *embaumed* (88), the eucharist's healing as well as feeding power (*dronken*) is intimated. The Samaritan's act was often interpreted as prefiguring administration of the sacraments to someone whom simple faith and the observance of the moral law cannot help recover fully: restoration to God's favour comes only from the grace of Christ given through the 'mysteries' he instituted. **72** *on...sette*: an action seen by Bede to signify 'believing in Christ's incarnation, being initiated into his mysteries [sacraments], and at the same time being guarded against the onslaught of the Enemy' (*PL* 92:469–70). **73** *Lavacrum...*: 'the bath of the law of God', signifying the baptismal font (*Sk*); Alan of Lille in *SAP* XXX (*PL* 210:170) speaks of the *lavacrum baptismi,* doubtless echoing the *lavacrum regenerationis* of Titus 3:5, glossed 'Baptismum' by Hugh of St Cher (7:235b). The 'law of God' will cover the 'way of living' to which a Christian is committed by baptism, particularly the Mosaic Commandments as interpreted by Christ the new Moses in the Sermon on the Mount. *grange*: 'barn or outlying farmstead' (Vg *stabulum* 'stable', 'inn'); interpreted by Bede (*ibid.*) as the Christian religion found in the *Ecclesia praesens* where pilgrims on the way to their eternal *patria* are refreshed (cf. B 119). *Pe* (following Smith 1966:79) notes an anticipation of the barn of UNITY at 21.319. **B 72** *Lex Christi*: a phrase occurring in Gal 6:2: 'Bear ye one another's burdens and so you shall fulfil the law of Christ [*legem Christi*];' it is called the 'lawe of kynde' at 8.231a (cf. B 11.210a) and Christ is described as commanding it at 13.77. Alf*Q* observes that the Pauline verse was cited in glossing the Samaritan's action (e.g. by Hugh of St Cher 6:195) and was much discussed in the C14th (Coleman 1981:28). **74** The circumstantial details have no apparent allegorical significance, unless to imply the original separateness of the Christian community from the society in which it found itself. **75–7** indicate how the spiritual care of Christians falls to the ordained clergy until the Second Coming of Christ, who will reward his faithful ministers at the end of time (the vaguer *aʒeynward* is less confusing than **B**'s *come fro þe iustes*, which is bound to suggest the Resurrection). **75** *a-lechynge*: 'a-healing', < *on* + verbal noun. *to...myhte*: 'so that he should recover, if it was possible'. **76** *toek*: the construction takes a dative second object (cf. 2 above), but omission of usual *to* (stylistically one too many in this line) seems to follow the parallel construction with its commoner synonym *give*. The polysemantic *annominatio* on *toek...take* improves the somewhat vapid B 77b. **78** *lyard he bystrideth*: the phrase recalling Z 3.158. **79** The revision removes the split-preposition construction of B 80, with which cf. 16.144 above (*MES* 413).

B 82–3 82 recalls *WPal* 5169 *hou þei* sped *hem to* spayne spacli *þerafter*; for the polysemantic *annominatio* in *spedde...spede* cf. on 76). **83** may be prompted by the account of Moses's talking to Christ on Mt Tabor (Mt 17:3) and Christ's speaking of himself ('beginning with Moses') on the way to Emmaus (Lk 24:27).

83–95 convey a sense of friendly intimacy unlike that between Will and any of his previous dozen interlocutors. The Samaritan's Piers-like courtesy (cf. 8.14–15 above), though less striking than in B 86–7, bespeaks his nature as the 'hidden' Christ. But as revelation is 'progressive', his Trinitarian teaching at 108–225 is presented as continuous with Abraham's at 18.199–239, though stressing not the metaphysics of triunity but the mystical bond between the virtue he embodies and the divine nature. Sins against charity strike at the centre of that nature and 'paralyse' the proffer of sanctifying grace, thereby leading to the specific 'sin against the Holy Ghost'. This is seen as extending from 'inhumane treatment of the needy' to 'wilful murder of the innocent', which destroys the grace of repentance whereby man has access to the divine life. At its deepest symbolic level, the Samaritan's discourse resumes the great penitential theme of the poem's earlier parts in sacramental terms, alluding to the phases of conversion and absolution that culminate in the Easter Communion, and implicitly equating the 'fruit charity' with Christ's presence in the Eucharist. **81** *sewede*: implying both Will's speed (explicit in B 84), which enables him to outstrip the two old men, and its cause, his direct response to St Paul's *Sectamini charitatem* 'Follow after charity' (I Cor 14:1). **B 87** echoes Will's poignant question at B 15.151; the answer is 'Here, in Christ'. Bennett (1981:23) convincingly finds an echo of Jn 15:15. **84** *medicyne*: on the image of Christ as physician and its structural significance in the poem see St-Jacques 1991. **85** *festred*: the earliest use, overlooked by MED. **86–8** scarcely improve on B 94–6, which memorably evoke demonic child-sacrifice, the better to force attention upon Christ's redemptive action as extending from his birth to death (cf. on 94). **86** *bloed...barn*: perhaps suggested by the thought that Jesus began his ministry to man when as an infant he bled the same blood he would shed on the cross: 'in his

circumcision...this pouring out of [Christ's blood] was the beginning of our redemption' (*LA* 82). **88–95** proceed in an order fitted to an ideal 'norm' for the time (christening in infancy and spiritual growth over a lifetime): 'Man cannot be saved without being baptised in Christ's name, believing firmly in Christ's saving Incarnation, resisting sin with the help of penance, and receiving the food of life in the Eucharist'. **88** *enbaumed*: as part of the rite of baptism (see on 72); yet **C** more comprehensively sees Christ's blood as not only cleansing (baptismal remission of 'original' sin) but as healing ('penitential' absolution from 'actual' sin). **B 95** Since the believer is baptized into the saving death of Christ (Rom 6:3–4), release from sin by Christ's blood is implicitly equated with this sacrament (I Jn 1:7; cf. also I Pet 1:2). But the most relevant scriptural context is provided by Jn 19:34 where, in the standard patristic understanding, the blood and water symbolically prefigure the first sacrament (see on 17.268). **90** The startling image of child-eating relates the greatest sacrament (the Eucharist) likewise to the infant Jesus by a sort of 'logic of backward inference'. This audacious way of speaking, where the unutterably sublime verges on the repellently grotesque, is modelled on Christ's own words in Jn 6:54–7, as noted by Bennett (1981), which alienate some of his disciples. But for **L** the high Eucharistic teaching of the 'pris' evangelist (21.267) is the spiritual centre of the Christian faith (see Schmidt 2006:306). **91** *plasterud*: taken up from B 96 to be applied not to Christ's suffering for sinners but to his followers' own resistance to sin through the power of grace (patience is the fourth 'fruit' of the Holy Spirit). **92** *this way*: the *semita vitae* or journey of life; the *wildernesse* of B 99 (eliminated from **C**) evokes more the perplexing 'region of unlikeness' of B Pr 12. **93 (B 101)** revises to Type Ia or Ic a **B** line of either extended Type IIIb with semi-counterpoint on |f| (scanning *abb / aa*) or (less probably) of Type Ia on *s* with a liaisonal stave *his felawe. such*: an improvement on *Feiþ...þiself* in B 101–2, which is theologically acceptable as indicating the necessity of Faith and Hope to protect against evil, but not in (apparently) affirming the adequacy of the Jewish religion. The conceptual discrepancy between these two dimensions of **L**'s double-named personification personages (Lawton's term 'actants' [1987:14–16]) may have been brought to his attention by critical readers, and is removed in revision. So is any hint of presumption in the somewhat Dantean 'thyself' and the (unintentionally) ambiguous reference in *oure werkes* at B 102, presumably denoting the acts of charity without which faith and trust do not suffice for salvation (I Cor 13). **94** *litel baby*: taking up B 96, but to be 'fed on' only 'in faith'. **94–5** *þat...That*: the double object of the verb, yielding the sense 'whose'. *lychame*: i.e. in the Eucharist, faith in Christ's Incarnation being a seamless whole from his birth to his death (cf. on 88), liturgically re-enacted from Christmas to Easter.

B 103–23 Excision of this realistic little allegory (foreshadowed at B 14.301–2) may have been prompted by its theological incoherences (see on C 93) and its anticipations of the next passus which, while arousing expectation, reduce tension. **103** *Outlawe*: an apt image for Satan, the rebel ejected from the 'holy comune' (5.186) of heaven, living outside God's order and preying on his people. **106** *hym...on horse*: contrasting the speaker with Faith and *Spes*; though a traveller on horseback might *escape* Outlaw Satan, a mounted 'knight' was a positive threat he would be wise to fear. **108** *Caro*: 'Flesh', last heard of as the 'castle' where Anima lived (B 9.49). The word evokes Jn 1:14 and probably has here the wider sense 'human nature' suggested by Hill 2001:216. The interpretation, familiar from liturgical commentaries (St-Jacques 1969), went back to Bede: '[The Samaritan's] beast is the flesh (*caro*), in which [Christ] saw fit to come to us' (ibid). **109** *in Inferno*: represented by the dark ditch into which the outlaw flees (cf. B Pr 15–19). **110** 'But within three days from now': in form a realistic 'chivalric' promise, but directly alluding to the time that Christ will lie in the grave (cf. B 18.42). **112** The words mean that for any who trust in Christ, the Devil's power is broken, not that the Devil will be powerless against any who sin wilfully. **112a** '[I will deliver them out of the hand of death. I will redeem them from death]. O death, I will be thy death; [O hell, I will be thy bite]' (Osee [Hosea] 13:14, and cf. I Cor 15:54–5, which alludes to it). The verse, which is repeated at B 18.35*a*=C 20.34*a*, implicitly understands Death and Hell as persons, and is liturgically associated with *Christ's* death, appearing as the first antiphon at Lauds on Holy Saturday. **113** *forster*: the rôle in which Faith after Christ's victory over death will direct men to the right path through the 'wilderness'. The idea here seems to be that Abraham's 'prospective' trust will reach fulfilment as the theological virtue Faith infused at baptism. Bennett (1981:25) notes the duty of a forester to keep the edges of the highway clear of trees and branches that might shelter brigands lying in wait. **114** *kennen out*: the prime task of Faith being guidance in what to believe about the things of God (*teche* 117). **116** *hostilers man*: an image from the parable being enacted, but needing to be read 'inversely' as personification- rather than symbol-allegory (Frank 1953), the virtue of hope bringing needed comfort to those for whom faith is not enough in the struggle against sin. **118** *lede*: the traditional rôle of Moses. *lettre*: the document of B 17.9 that contains the rule of life sufficient for salvation but has not yet been 'ratified'. **119** *bileue*: the *Lex Christi* of B 72. **120** *salue*: 'salvation', the goal of the Samaritan's journey to Jerusalem; the ointment is specified at 123, and the words indirectly reaffirm what the sacraments of healing intimated at B 70–1. **121** *come*

ayein: referring to Christ's post-resurrection appearance to the Apostles, when he gives them his spirit (Jn 20:22–3); but the 'salve' may be more narrowly understood as 'grace' (cf. 122), which will be released for *alle sike* on Pentecost Day (B 19.209 //).

96–107 rehearse the lesson Will has learnt from Faith and Hope. **98** virtually repeats 30, but in the form of B 27 (whereas B 127 *revises* the b-verse of 27), accentuating the effect of his speech as a 'lesson learnt'. **101** *for his loue*: 'for love of Him' (objective genitive). **103–7** express not a Mosaic but a Christian view of humility (influenced by Mt 7:3–4, Lk 18:13; Mt 5:11–12, 39.44) that reverses the self-conceit shown by Haukyn at B 13.287, 295–6. **105** *And*: 'And (to believe myself)'.

(ii)a 108–30 109 *as...o God*: 'according to *the way in which* A. taught you to believe in the One God [i.e. in God-as-Trinity]'. The Samaritan elides the teaching of Faith and Hope separately recounted by Will at 99–102: faith in divine (tri)unity and love of neighbour being inseparably bound together. **111** *Kynde Wit*: an unexpected reference to this elusive semi-personification of 'the knowledge derived from experience', evoking a mental world left far behind since the (quasi)-inner dream began at 18.4, but only to emphasise the distance between divine mysteries (Truth dwells in a high tower) and what commonsense expects or comprehends. The replacement of 'conscience' B 136 by 'eny kyne thouhtes' removes what could be a source of tension arising from L's having used 'conscience' (which *should* always follow reason) to denote the conscientious scruples of someone unable to believe a doctrine that seemed against reason. The Samaritan's reply, like Ymaginatif's earlier, comes as two extended analogies of a hand (113–168) and a candle (169–77), the latter moving by an easy transition to describe the action of divine grace upon man. These rely on feeling and imagination rather than logic in attempting to answer such 'arguments' as that the dogma defies the principle of contradiction (cf. Alan of Lille in *PL* 210:401). **112** Anti-Trinitarian monotheism was not a current Christian heresy, so the Samaritan's real concern may be the objections of the Jews (whence his insistence that Abraham had knowledge of the Trinity). These Alan of Lille addresses in Bk. III of his treatise bearing the general title 'Against Heretics', first with scriptural and rational 'arguments' (*auctoritates et rationes*), then through analogies (*similitudines*), including one of a candle. *thien hoend*: see generally on this image Biggs 1991. **113** *bigynnynge*: connecting not God's own 'origin' but the Trinity's self-revelation with the 'origin' of the universe, prior to which (and during which) the 'fist' was ('and still is') folded or clenched. **114a** 'Folding the world fast in his fist', applied to the 'three-fold High deviser and designer' in the C6th Marian hymn 'Quem terra, pontus, aethera' sung at Matins in the Office of the BVM (*JLH* I:41, vs. 4). The Biblical sources of the image include Isaiah 40:12 (*Sk*) and Prov 30:4. **115** *fuste*: borrowed from *pugillo* in 114*a* but developed in typically idiosyncratic fashion. The clenched fist is an Augustinian 'natural sign' of *power* (the attribute appropriated to the Father at B 16.211–13); and in medieval art a hand with finger(s) outstretched often 'betokens' God's action: see Schiller I pl. 235, II pl. 531 (single hand with three spears), 527 (three hands). **116** *fynger*: as *Pe* notes (citing Bartholomaeus I. 21. 30), a traditional name of the Son; but see on 140*a*. **117** *as...paume*: 'as one does in the case of one's palm'. **118** *pethe*: in the light of // *purely* B 142 signifying more 'essence' than 'strength' (MED s.v. *pith* n. 2(a) not 3) and thus earlier than the recorded uses in this sense. Because the a-verse re-writes B 142*a*, C 141 avoids being repetition. **119** 'To perform whatever function the hand has strength and skill to accomplish'. **120** Parallel B 144 virtually repeats B 16.212, which **C** removes. **123** The basis of this apparently original thought may be that God 'touches' the world directly through the Word, by first creating and then by redeeming it (Jn 1:3, 10–11). **124** recalls *Cursor Mundi* 18940: 'Gaf to þaim þe haligast / Alkin wiit to *tuche and tast*'. *at techyng of*: the Divine Son being thought of as having undergone *kenosis* 'self-emptying' (Phil. 2:7) to become the obedient Jesus of history; an allusion to the power of the Holy Ghost overshadowing Mary (Lk 1:35). **B 149a** *Qui*...; **C 125a** *Natus*...: 'Who was conceived of the Holy Ghost, Born of the Virgin Mary'; the fourth and fifth clauses in the Apostles' Creed. The revision makes better sense, since the Son's birth, not his conception, is the main subject. **127** *huyde*: perhaps suggested by Is 40:12 ('Quis mensus est *pugillo* aquas...?'), which is strikingly linked with Dan 5:5 in a Trinity Sunday sermon by Jacobus a Voragine in Lambeth MS 43, col. 278 cited by Galloway (1998:138). The basic (and not quite satisfactory) assignation of fist, fingers and palm to the Persons severally may be original. **127a** 'For I, [if I be lifted up from the earth,] will draw all things to myself' (Jn 12:32). This is clearer in **B**, which can be made to refer back to the Son's action (the words being Christ's); but the 'drawing of all things' may signify God's resumption of Creation at the end of time. Better is the revision of B 154–6 which (though not at odds with physical fact) untheologically suggest that the 'palm' is the *source* of the Trinity, whereas the Spirit should proceed from Father and Son.

B 160–3 160–1 echo 'aquas et caelos palmo ponderavit...molem terrae...' in Is 40:12 (Galloway 1998:138n28) and they may be recalled in *Patience* 206–8. **160** will scan either as Type Ia on |w| with a mute key-stave or as an extended Type IIIb on vowels with semi-counterpoint on |w| and first stave on either *halt* or a rhetorically-stressed *al* (*abb / aa*). Whichever pattern is recognised, the metri-

cal structure of the b-half is identical: *wiþínne hém þrè*. **163** scans as Type IIIa on |t| with a liaisonal first stave (*it_is*) or, preferably, as Type Ia on |n| with a trisyllabic prelude dip. **131–52** affirm how all Three Persons possess 'full' godhead ('þe same myhte' 149) equally (131, 136, 141), **153–68** how God's grace is incapacitated by man's deliberate sin against his nature as Love. **132** *furste*: prior not in order of dignity but conceptually, and in order of time only insofar as God was initially known to *man* as 'Creator' and as 'One' before his final self-revelation as Three Persons, which had to await Christ's appearance in time (hence *ar* 133). **134** retrieves the form of A 10.28 (from the description of Kynde) to emphasise again that God is the originary source (as *fader*) of uncreated and (as *formeour*) of created being. **134a** 'Thou art Creator of all things', from the Compline hymn 'Jesu salvator saeculi', st. 2 (*Brev*. 2.234). **135 (B 169)** scans either as Type Ia on |w| with a four-syllable prelude dip and with the caesura before *and* or, preferably, on vowels as Type IIa with a 'supplemental' stave in position five. The **B** line may be either a vocalic Type Ic with mute key-stave or else a standard Type Ia on |m|. The latter is preferable since potency (*myȝt*) is associated closely with creative action (*makynge*) in the b-half, whereas **C** stresses the sempiternity of the Father's power. **136–40a** lack some clarity since they compare the Son with the thumb, implying an unintended analogy of the fingers with the Father (who is figured by the entire hand in an inclusive sense). **139** *be ne myhte*: a paradox (that the Father *depends* on the Son) resolved at 140, which states that the Father could not operate (*holde*; *hente*) without the *agency* of the Son, through whom he made the world. **B** expresses the same thought in calling the Son the *science* 'Wisdom' of the Father (cf. Wisd. 7:24–7). Though appearing to contradict the 'fullness' of power affirmed of each person (149), the explanation is that *failed þe Sone* presumes what is not even an 'ideal' but an *impossible* condition. **140a** 'Finger of God's right hand', from st. 3 of 'Veni creator spiritus' (*JLH* I:80), the hymn sung at 21.211–12. There, however, its referent is the Holy Ghost, whom the Pentecost Hymn quite logically calls the 'finger', thereby understanding the Son as the 'right hand' and 'God' as the Father 'containing' the Trinity as a whole. The motif is clearly illustrated in Schiller I: pls. 356–7, where the Spirit descends on Christ as a dove directly below the outstretched index finger of a right hand. L's idiosyncratic departure from the customary use of the 'hand' image could have been prompted by the famous 'prooftext' *Sede a dextris meis* (Ps 109:1), which Alan of Lille in *CH* says 'pertinet *ad Filium*, qui existens Deus, sedet *a dextris* Domini, id est aequalis Patri' (*PL* 210:404). **142** The 'natural' function of the clenched fist is to strike, of the fingers to handle. **147** *greued...grype*: 'pained with what they grasp'; the Spirit is imagined as the Trinity's 'feeling' aspect, the *amor medius* 'Love between Father and Son' (*JLH* II:191, vs.5) that suffers from the sinner a direct *injuria* (like that to a King when a criminal breaks his peace). **149–50** *of...o God*: cf. 'Unum esse deitatis / Et *eiusdem potestatis*' (*JLH* II:191, vs. 2). **158** An economical fusion of B 190a and 193b allowing omission of 192 (as over-particular) and 191 (as repeating 186). **B 192** *toshullen*: taken as the p.p. of a verb the simplex of which is glossed 'break' by MED, rejecting the *Sk*, OED derivation from OE **scelan* (p.p. **scolen*) 'peel'. But *kynde wit* may well wonder whether someone with four fingers and thumb broken *could* 'help himself in many kinds of ways'. **161** 'On the basis of this analogy I find grounds for believing...' *simile*: a term from rhetoric here used to mean 'an analogy for use in an argument'; recalling Alan's *CH*: 'by a likeness (*similitudine*) the same [the doctrine of the Trinity] is proved' (in *PL* 210:406). **162** *in*: 'against' (167), a usage conditional upon the Latin quotation's *in* (cf. 'sinnyng in the Hooly Goost' at *CT* X 694). **163** *elleswhere*: i.e. in purgatory. **163a** See on B 16.47a; repeating Piers's teaching in a **B** passage removed from **C** at that point. A deliberate, free act of evil involves rejection of grace and contempt for the divine goodness, attitudes which, persisted in to the end, send the sinner straight to hell. *R–H* 208 understand the 'irremissible' sin as denial of faith and loss of hope leading to despair; but B 215–17=C 181–3 present it as wilful sin against charity. **165 (B 200)** scans either vocalically as Type Ia on *is* (1, 2) and *as* or, preferably, on |f| as Type IIa, with *For* as stave one and a supplemental |f| stave in position five. **168** *quenche*: 'extinguish', providing a transition to the image of the *torch* (cf. *R–H* 209).

169–225 use an *argument* and a dominant *image* that are ascribed to Augustine by Jacobus a Voragine, though deriving partly from Tertullian (Galloway 1998:139). The patristic comparisons familiar from medieval hymns (e.g. *aenigma radius* in *JLH* II:191, vs. 5), are all with the *sun*, its ray and its heat, not a candle and its wax and flame, to which there are closer analogues in Bartholomaeus XIX, 63:10 (*Sk*) and *LA* 164–5 (*Pe*). Images of candle *and* sun are, however, juxtaposed by Alan of Lille specifically as *similitudines* that 'prove' the doctrine of the Trinity: 'The Father is called spiritually...light, because he shines from himself...and because from him shines the light that illuminates, the Son, and the light that enkindles, the Holy Spirit' (*PL* 210 406–7). But it is **L** not Alan who envisions the 'sin against the Spirit' as a 'quenching' of the *lux inflammans* and who brings together 'divine light' and its 'extinction' by wilful sin. It may be assumed therefore that while the double *similitudo* is 'deeply rooted in clerical materials' (Galloway 1998:138), it is the poet's own imaginative synthesis of reading and experience, *kynde wit* and *clergye*. **169** *torche*: a large candle of twisted hemp soaked in wax. *taper*: wax candle. **174** *this*: a collo-

quial use of the demonstrative for the definite article; see *MES* 174. **176** revises to a T-type a **B** line of the rare linetype IIb. *fyn loue and bileue*: infused by grace in baptism and penance, the sacraments that 'cleanse from sin'. With *fyn loue* compare *fyn hope* at 85: 'excellent, pure, refined, noble', this is God's unmerited love that alone can heal fallen man. **178 (B 212)** scans as Type Ia (*sómtỳme*) or as Type IIIc (*sôm týme*). **180–1** mean that the divine life which can never be entirely quenched is blocked when opposed by man (cf. Jn 1:5, 11). The 'fire' in the wick that continues to smoulder is the obverse of the 'spark' of a repentant person's sin that can *not* remain alight in the river of unlimited divine forgiveness at 6.333–7a. **181** *grace withouten mercy*: a paradoxical phrase, since one sense of *grace* was 'mercy' (see *IG*); God's *kynde* cannot change, but its help to *unkynde* man can be blocked by deliberate resistance. **183** *lycame and*: a revision making clear that murder is envisaged (265–7); the univocal application of *leel* to 'body' and 'life' is noteworthy. **187** *togyderes*: the whole Trinity being the source of grace (divine life), the Spirit its form and agent. **191** *blowe*: the first of three witty inversions, here of the usual image of the Holy Ghost himself as *spiramen* 'breath' (*JLH* II:191, vs 3); for now the 'breath' is man's free assent (i.e. the will to 'love and believe' that makes for repentance) in the work of redemption. **192** *flaumeth he*: a second inversion, making the Spirit's fire 'melt' the 'solid' power of the Father and Son, and proving L's 'grotesque sublime' sturdily underpinned by *kynde wit*. For since ice is water in another state, God's 'true' nature as merciful love rather than severe justice may be communicated through this image without offence to sense and reason. *Sk* aptly cites from Morris, *OE Homilies* (1868) ii.150: 'The tear of compassion is warm like the water of snow that trickles down in the sun's heat' (original in Latin). **194** *hete.. sonne*: the same Alanian metaphor for the Spirit (*solis... calor* in *PL* 210:407A) as at 18.75, there denoting 'sanctifying', but here 'habitual' grace. **196** *the...Trinite*: clearly the object of *melteth* 197, and thus denoting 'Potencia-Dei-Patris', with *al* being adverbial. But the syntax allows this phrase to be read also in apposition with the subject (*al* now becoming pronominal, and having reference to the Three Persons); for Love is, in the last resort, the 'sublime power' of God. **198** *wex*: a third unexpected inversion; with the human will now required to immolate itself like a candle-end flung on a sinking fire. **200** *derkenesse*: symbolically signifying 'sin', both echoing the canticle of Zachary said at Lauds (Lk 1:79) and foreshadowing 20.365. **204** *þat...deyeth*: recalling Trajan at 14.211, a passage where the Spirit's power as illuminating grace is invoked. *þat*: 'for someone who'. **206** An unusual T-type with the caudal b-staves anticipated in the a-verse after a muted a-stave in position 2. **208** *cortesye*: 'gracious generosity [beyond one's desert]'; also echoing the end of the Trajan passage (14.216). **209–10** The speaker's authority for this claim is 1.164–9, where Christ forgives even those who do *not* ask him pardon. **211** *fuyr at a flynt*: a cry for mercy from one who refused to show any. **212** *tasch*: i.e. 'willingness to repent'. **213** recalls Pr 195 and is echoed in *CT* VIII 781. **214** *flaume make*: i.e. 'bring mercy and grace'. *faile...kynde*: 'if what its very nature requires is absent' (fire needs something to burn); an example that shows common experience to argue against the possibility of forgiveness for the unforgiving. **215–225** warn against trusting in external 'religious' acts while remaining at heart *vnkynde* 'uncharitable' to one's fellow Christians. **215–16a** repeats 181–2a, a measure of the importance attached to the idea expressed here. **216a** 'Amen, I say to you, I know you not' (Mt 25:12); addressed by the Bridegroom (a parabolic *figura* of Christ) to the wise and foolish Virgins whose 'oil' represents deeds of active charity that prepare them for the arrival of their lord (cf. on I 183–4). **217** scans either on lexical words in |k| or, preferably, on vowels with *al* as key-stave, the important prefixes *vn-* and *em-* (*euene-*) bearing sentence-stress, and a secondary alliterative pattern on |k| (for other 'dual-scansion' lines cf. 19.3, 23, 38, 280 and B 17.3). **218** *Dele*: an echo of I Cor 13:3. The spiritual attitude envisaged is little more strained than that of its (deliberately) hyperbolic Pauline source, since those presumably intended are rich people who can 'buy' pardons while remaining unkind to their kind. **219** *Pampilon*: referring to indulgences for remission of sin granted by the Bishop of Pamplona in Navarre for issue by the Abbot of St Mary's Rounceval at Charing Cross (the house of Chaucer's Pardoner in *CT* I 670), a dependency of the Augustinian hospital of Our Lady of Roncesvalles on the pilgrim route to Compostella. These would be granted for actually 'seeking St James' or for a monetary composition for the same. The house had a bad reputation for pardon-mongering (Bloomfield 1956). **220** *ingratus*: '(personally) unkind, cruel', though the use of the Latin word was perhaps suggested by St Paul's description in II Tim 3:2ff of the *ingrati* who 'resist truth' (cf. 230a, from Christ's warning against those without true inward religion). The presence of *dele* at 218 precludes the sense 'ungrateful, mean' of *ingrati* at B 14.169, used of the rich who refuse alms to 'men þat it nedede'. **223** *blowynge of vnkyndenesse*: recalling the imagery of 'wicked winds' in 18.29ff and inverting the wind of love spoken of at 191. The very strong word *vnkyndenesse* (White 1988:95–110) here denotes the spiritual 'wind' of hell that blows fiercely against the clear flame of divine love. **224** *where*: 'whether (or not)'. **225** 'If I speak with the tongues of men, [and of angels, and have not charity, I am...nothing]' (I Cor 13:1–2). The famous Pauline passage is less an attack on uncharitableness than a declaration that salvation is impossible without charity; so a more relevant

(tacit) authority for seeing *vnkyndenesse* as a destructive force that quenches the divine light may be I Jn 2:9–11. **(b) 226–76** form a diatribe against 'unkindness' directed especially towards the wealthy (see on 218). **228** scans either on |k|, with two stresses in *crístene* or on vowels, with *Y* as second stave (mute) and two stresses in *é(m) crístene* (cf. 217). **230a** 'Not every one that saith [to me], Lord, Lord shall enter into the kingdom of heaven: [but he that doth the will of my Father...]' (Mt 7:21); a warning against formal religion without 'do-well'. **231–48a** This elaboration of **B**'s perfunctory warning to complacent rich men may result from seeing the events of 1381 as a summons to social reform rather than the occasion for repressive reaction that it became. **232** *Diues*: sometimes taken as a proper name for the selfish 'Rich Man' (*Dives*) of Lk 16:19–31 already alluded to at 18.272. This second Lucan parable is cited to show not that Dives's wealth was ill-gotten but that he used it selfishly; and reference to the original makes clear that he is not condemned by 'a newe lawe' (19.34) but by that of Moses (Lk 16:31), who taught the love of neighbour the Samaritan Parable was told to illustrate (see on 49). **235** *as men rat*: an assertion with no explicit scriptural basis, but an important part of **L**'s warning that since lawful possession of wealth does not justify ignoring the higher law of divine justice, the lot of those who win *un*lawfully then fail to spend 'well' is desperate indeed. **238a** 'He feasted sumptuously and was clothed in linen'; adapted from Lk 16:19. **240** *Godes*: an objective genitive, here = 'to, against'. **241** With this minatory internal assonance and rhyme compare 265; Dives is not in limbo. **242** scans either as Type Ia with six-syllable prelude or as Ic with stave one found (unusually) in *with*. **242–3** *atymye..lyue*: 'might properly enough go about living like a lord'. **245–6** *ȝut...ȝut*: 'moreover... still further'. **247** *sitte*: i.e. at table; the implication being that if they ate as befits their wealth, there would be some left over for the needy, whereas their miserliness mars all. **248** echoes 16.274, where the thought concerns not *good* use of ill-won wealth but its inevitable *mis*use by the vicious. *frendis*: i.e. in heaven, who will intercede for him after death. **248a** See on 8.235a. **250** The sense is less that money should be given to the Church than to the 'needful poor', who are in a special sense *hise* 'God's' (cf. 12.133–4). **251–63** are effectively a commentary on I Tim 6:9–10 and equate *vnhyndenesse* with *vnkyndenesse*, the sin against God's own nature as life-giving love, both as literal murder and as the 'killing' of a man's reputation by slander so as to obtain his wealth. It is this that forges a link with the foregoing address to the rich: the 'thieves' are not all outlaws, nor the 'banks' they lurk under only of earth. **256** *Vnkynde Cristene men*: an arresting oxymoron highlighting the special unnaturalness of such a sin amongst believers; cf. *sed vos fraudatis...fratribus* (I Cor 6:8). **257** *for his mebles*: making clear that the metaphorical 'slaying' is not 'murder of the soul through evil example' (*R–H* 210) but slander, which ruins a man's livelihood through destroying his reputation. **258** *hath to kepe*: a clear allusion to 'your members are the temple of the Holy Ghost, who is in you, whom you have from God' (I Cor 6:19). **259** *loue*: the divine life of sanctifying grace identified with the Holy Spirit. The argument refers at once to the physical 'life' of the good man and the virtues ('fruits of the Spirit') that make him good. **260–1** neatly develop from 169: as the true 'mirror-image' of the Trinity, a virtuous man can be fitly compared to the same light-giving candle; cf. 'Sic luceat *lux* vestra...ut videant *opera* vestra *bona...*' (Mt 5:14–16). **261** scans as Type IIIc on |r| and |t| (*ab / ab*) with the first stave by liaison in *Or_élles* or on |t| as Type Ib with first and third stave (mute) in *to* and a 'compensating' fourth stave to supplement the latter. *to...Trinite*: 'such as are lit in honour of / as an image that duly honours the Trinity'. **262** *morthereth...man*: an act especially heinous because it destroys the physical 'temple' that houses the supernatural life of the Spirit. **267** *þat Crist dere bouhte*: 'that which Christ bought at so dear a cost'. The argument now defines the supreme sin as 'destroying the life of one redeemed by Christ', not only the 'good' but any (or perhaps any baptized) person. **268; 269** *mercy* (2); *mercy*: the divine 'mercy' as personified in Christ and (mirrorwise) in the redeemed person; a striking analogy to the notion of the Spirit's 'love' as personified in the 'good' man (259). **269** *anyente*: possibly introduced by **L** from Fr. *anienter*. **270** Though technically not one of the moral virtues, Innocence here signifies something more positive than 'freedom from guilt', and in its allusion to Abel implies the moral purity associated not only with infants but with those specially 'near' to God, like the virgins (cf. *priueoste* at 18.98). **271** *hit*: the understood referent being 'the act', but metonymically the agent. **272** *forschupte*: 'deformed, mutilated' (MED s.v. *forshapen* v.) according to well-supported glosses; but 'unmade' (*Sk*) better hits off the contextual sense of 'negating' the Creator's work. **272a** 'Avenge the blood of the just!' Alluding to Apoc 6:10, the phrase runs together the texts cited in Alf*Q* from the versicle for Holy Innocents' Day 'Vindica sanguinem nostrum' (*Brev.* 1.306) and the antiphon 'Vindica...sanguinem sanctorum tuorum' followed by the versicle 'Justorum animae' (*Brev.* 1.239). That there is an allusion to the blood of 'Abel the just' (Mt 23:35, Heb 11:4; cf. Gen 4:10), the first man to be murdered and a familiar type of Christ (Heb 12:24), seems certain. But the liturgical echo is equally clear, with no formal distinction made between the guiltlessness of murdered children and that of the 'good man' (the feast of the Innocents follows two days after that of Stephen the first martyr). **273** The exact referent of *verray charite* would seem not to be the virtue *per se*, since its supreme exemplar Christ asked

forgiveness not vengeance for his murderers. Rather, the virtuous and the innocent who are murdered could be envisaged as 'embodying' or 'personifying' the divine love (cf. on 268–9), and destruction of this love demands retribution as part of justice. The text invoked may be Rom 12:19 (citing Deut 32:35), which at once urges forgiveness for wrongdoing and promises that God will punish it. **274** *Charite...is*: recognising in 'Charity' the Church's inner essence as a 'spiritual organism', and so identifying the sin against the Spirit as also a direct attack on Christ. For the doctrine in this line, which improves on B 292 in depth and precision, cf. Piers's words at 7.256 expressing the poem's basic conception of the 'mystical body of Christ' as realised within individual believers in a state of grace. The verbal echo of Piers's *charge* in *chargeth* strengthens the conceptual link between these two passages. **275** *laste ende*: 'the (individual's) moment of death' (as implied by Will's *nouthe* at 277–80), or 'the Last Judgement'; still ambiguous, but clearer than B 294 *pere*. **276** *lyf*: a careful synonym for 'person' that ironically highlights the evil of extinguishing 'life and love' (259) and warns against the consequence.

277–98 277 *pose*: the question broaching less Will's own immediate concern than the issue of the moral value of 'death-bed repentances', as a counter-case to the *Pearl*-Dreamer's view of the supposedly 'easy' salvation of those dying in infancy. The 'optimistic' view is reflected in *CT* X 94. **282** *repentaunce*: the sinner's conversion, which 'converts' divine justice to pity, as described at 193. **283** *selde yseyn*: not that God *cannot* offer the grace of final repentance (294), but that a hardened sinner is unlikely to change enough to be able to alter the course of justice. With its appeal to experience (cf. 20.153), this passage between 282–8a contains a dozen terms from the language of the law courts. *sothnesse...witnesse*: both 'to tell the truth' and 'where witnesses tell the truth (and judges aren't bribed)'. **284–5** *be*; *Be*: 'be found'; '(And) be'. **286** *þat partye*: i.e. the 'dead' man (hence the difficulty of any 'accord'); but if the 'murder' was of a man's reputation, then forgiveness and compensation are theoretically possible. **288** *That...equitee*: 'So that each party may get what is his just due'. The king's mercy (remission of the lawful punishment) cannot properly be given without the agreement of the injured party, who is envisaged at 271ff as demanding retribution. The severity of the Samaritan's argument here will be echoed by that of Truth and Righteousness at 20.145–51a, 195–206; but 297–8 obscurely adumbrate the miraculous 'letters' sent by Love to Mercy and Peace at 20.184–91. *holy writ*: 'sacred tradition'. **288a** See on 6.257a; St Augustine's maxim contains a dire warning that explains why to 'murder a good man' is such a heinous act. **290** *til... synne*: i.e. at death, when they have no more power to do wrong (cf. *CT* VI 286, which quotes this familiar saying, and *CT* X 92). **292** *mercy...mynde*: a harsher view of the prospects for repentance than that at 6.339, but some measure of how much graver the sin against the Holy Ghost is than greed (or any other). **293** *hope*: 'expectation', which can be qualified by 'good' or 'ill'. The sight of the evils he has done blocks out the thought of God as anything but the sternest judge (a state of mind later dramatised by Marlowe in Dr Faustus's last soliloquy). **294–8** re-state Scripture's words at 12.73–5*a* and recall Repentance's to Greed at B 5.281–2*a*. **294** *And...myhte*: 'and not because God isn't fully able...' **296*a*** See on B 5.282*a*. **297–8** '...it is restitution that will make this happen, in the form of heartfelt *sorrow*, which serves as *satisfaction* for those who are not in a position to pay what is due to justice'. This remarkable elision of the first and third *partes penitentiae* proves both the authority and the *kyndenesse* of the speaker. It tempers the warning to those who *euele lyuen and leten nat* with an echo of the promise to the truly repentant at 201–10, and it provides a crumb of comfort even for the desperate sinner, if not an actual guarantee of 'prevenient' grace.

299–334 The final part of the Samaritan's homily reduces the intensity that has reached its peak at 298 by using homely proverbial images of the 'picturing-model' type (Aers 1975:13–14) that serve to distinguish clearly between different spiritual conditions and to warn against falling into the one that leads to despair. **299** *thre thynges*: recalling the didactic method of HC expounding another 'three things' in B I 20ff. The best-known version of the exemplum, as *Sk* noted, is in a widely-cited passage from Pope Innocent III's *De Contemptu mundi* I, 18: 'There are three things that drive a man from his home: smoke, dripping water, and a wicked wife'. This is based on Prov 19:13, 27:15 (which *compare* the wrangling wife to the dripping roof), 10:27, which uses the smoke image, and 21:19, which declares the wilderness preferable to a quarrelsome woman. But two other likely sources are Map's *De Uxore non Ducenda* (ed. Wright 83) and another late C12th text, Peter Cantor's *Verbum Abbreviatum* (in *PL* 205:331), which offers similar (not the same [*Sk*]) interpretations of the 'three things' as his: *carnis tentatio* for the wife, *peccatum ignorantiae* for the smoke and *suggestio extrinseca* for the dripping water. **L** changes the order and significance of the second and third of the 'three things'. **300** *oune house*: 'domo propria' (Map). *Holy Writ*: with dual reference to the medieval authorities and to their Biblical source. **301** *wikkede wyf*: 'mala uxor' (Innocent). **306** 'It mars his sleep even worse than his wife or the wet' (a sardonic comparison of the 'wicked' wife's insistence to the drip of rainwater). **310** Elliptical for 'who should bring (and did not)', i.e 'for not bringing'. **311–16** cover all sins of the flesh resulting from the propensity of fallen human nature to give in. Awareness of the difference between weakness and

wickedness is evident from the careful use of *kynde* in 313, 322 to show how sins arising from these two sources are forgiveable, while those due to *vnkyndenesse* are not, as wet wood, though kindled, *cannot* 'foster' a flame but suffocates it. However, the phrasing (*cleueth on hym*) also recalls 7.303 and implies a sexually demanding as well as a nagging wife, while 314 with its echo of Mede's words at 3.59–60 also suggests specifically sexual sins. The passage expresses the imagined speaker's own laxism (cf. the Samaritan's use of *lihtliche* at 323), but its echo in 315–16 of 208–10 is nonetheless encouraging. **318** *seeknesses...sorwes*: recalling Ymaginatif's words on the power of *angres* to punish for sin and arouse conversion, but less warning against the loss of faith shown by Envy at 6.77–85 than encouraging the sufferer not to be too hard on himself. **319*a*** '"[My grace is sufficient for thee]: for power is made perfect in infirmity"' (II Cor 12:9); referring to the power of divine grace to enable men to make their weakness an occasion for developing the needed virtues (here, patience). **324** *euele may suffre*: recalling B 12.8, which is removed in **C**. **326** *coueytise and vnkyndenesse*: a significant coupling, seeing in unbridled greed the sin furthest from the boundless generosity of God. **327** *contrarie*: a different kind of 'oppositeness' from that of the afflicted who *contrarien* (322). **328–32** seem to argue that whereas the 'vnkynde' *reject* love, the afflicted and the fallen remain capable of inner or verbal generosity of some kind, which initiates their recovery. **331** anticipates 21.185 in its entirety. **332** *that...amende*: 'so that his own life may thereby improve'. **333–4** *prikede / awakede*: half-rhyme sealing the end of the passus (cf. the similar use of internal rhyme to end at 18.292 above). *awakede*: in B 352 ending the *outer* part of Vision Five (which began at B 15.11). But since there is no new dream at the corresponding point in C 16.156, the one that Will woke out of at 18.179 may be the presumed / implied 'inner' dream beginning at 18.4 (see *ad loc* on this problem). The 'outer' dream (if such it is) that he wakes from at 19.334 must therefore be the one that began at 15.25.

Passus XX (B XVIII)

PASSUS TWENTY (Vision Six) is the last fully revised portion of **C**; but it adds only some 45 lines, mainly on the devils' attempted resistance to Christ (281–94, 308–11), and omits B 255, 351–2, 355–7. The *additions* include 45, 212–13, 216–17, 314, 338–40, 346 and a not entirely happy semi-digression on lying, the sin of which Satan is seen as arch-exemplar (350–8). The many *verbal changes*, though minor, are mostly improvements and show no hesitancy, e.g. at 2, 34, 46, 48, 50, 53, 55, 61–2, 75–9, 86, 90, 93, 95–8, 100, 154–6, 186–9, 250, 303–7, 336, 345, 347, 360–1, 369, 379–85, 434–6, 458–9. The Passus contains echoes of a number of texts which are noted in detail to bring out the wide-ranging nature of **L**'s treatment of this sequence. The origins of its narrative material are mainly Latin: the canonical scriptures; the Easter liturgy (St-Jacques 1967); ch. 54 of *LA* (*Sk*), which **L** certainly used; and the latter's direct source the 'Gospel of Nicodemus' (*Evangelium Nicodemi*, hereafter *EN*). This last is the name given from the 13th c. to the Latin version of an apocryphal Greek Gospel of about the 5th century. It is made up of two works by separate authors, the *Gesta Pilati* 'The Acts of Pilate' and the *Descensus ad inferos* 'Descent into Hell' (which survives in two Latin versions, A and B). The first of these texts is an elaborated synthesis of the canonical Gospels, the second an imaginative work purporting to be the testimony of the sons of Simeon (Lk 2:25–35), who were released from hell when Christ rose from the dead and who witnessed the liberation of the patriarchs. **L** also shows awareness of the late C13th English verse-adaptations of *EN*, the *Harrowing of Hell* (*HH*) and *Gospel of Nicodemus* (*GN*), on the background of which see Izydorczyk (1997), as well as AN poems by Nicholas Bozon (*Vn rei estei jadis ke aueit vne amy*) and Robert Grosseteste (*Le Chasteau d'Amour*). The Debate of the Four Daughters of God that **L** inserted into his account is not part of the 'Harrowing' story but derives from a homiletic tradition widely popular in C12th France. First found in a sermon by St Bernard of *c.* 1140 (*PL* 183:383–90), it goes back to a lost Latin translation of the *Bereshith Rabbah*, a Hebrew *midrash* (commentary) on Genesis (Tveitane 1980).

As well as uniquely combining elements of the sublime and the earthy, Passus XX (as first noticed in Waldron 1986:75–6, discussing the B-Text) reveals a complex patterning and carefully balanced argument. Its *two linked main sequences* have a 'triptych'-like structure, each flanking an episode that forms its thematic and dramatic centre: (i) CHRIST'S CRUCIFIXION (his seeming defeat by Death) and (ii) the HARROWING OF HELL (Christ's real victory over Death). This novel design enhances the poetic spaciousness and theological perspective in what becomes, following successive reductions and sub-divisions of earlier passūs in **B**, the longest passus in **C**. The central portion of (i) occupies ll. 35–94 (b); it is 'framed' by (a) a tense interchange between Will and Faith (8–34*a*) prompted by the Samaritan's arrival in Jerusalem (which links Vision Six with Vision Five), and by (c) Faith's stinging rebuke to the Jews his descendants for rejecting Christ (95–112*a*). Before (a) comes a brief *prologue* (1–7) on Will's increasing alienation from worldly affairs as his thoughts focus on the liturgical mystery that reaches its doctrinal and emotional peak in Passion week. **L**'s final treatment of the Crucifixion in ll. 35–94 (Bennett 1982:85–112) combines its scriptural and literary sources with striking originality (Marx

1995:100–13). Sequence (ii) occupies ll. 113–478 and its 'central episode' (b) the HARROWING OF HELL (271–451), is framed by (a) the 'debate' of the FOUR DAUGHTERS OF GOD at ll. 116–270*a* (with its brief lead-in lines on the Dreamer's quasi-Dantean 'descent' into Limbo) and (c) their reconciliation (452–70). Further enclosed in (a) at 238–68 is a *sub-episode* (a¹), the intervention of BOOK to attest Jesus as Messiah, ending in a nuanced transition from what the Daughters *hear* to an event the audience *witness* with them (269–70*a*). The splendid central scene (271–451) divides into 1) the Devils' panic-stricken reaction to Christ's summons to open hell (274–94); 2) their 'frantic colloquy' (295–349*a*), a parodistic mirror-inversion of the 'Daughters' dispute' (Russell 1984:239); and 3) Christ's great speech (370–446*a*) justifying God's action as one not of force but law. This last is linked to the 'Devils' debate' by the 'Liar-digression' (350–8), is prefaced by Christ's liberation of the souls of the just (359–69), and closed with an elegant two-line transition to the sequence's outer frame (c), the *reconciliation* of the Daughters in a cosmic round-dance that echoes the divine harmony (452–71). The entire passus ends with an *epilogue* (471–8) in which joyful bells, heralded by dream-music balancing the pre-dream *prologue*'s organ and choir, wake the Dreamer for the first matins and mass of Easter Morning. In complexity of organisation, sustained dramatic irony, clarity of exposition and variety of style, Passus XX represents the summit of **L**'s art, and it could have served as not only the climax but as the conclusion of the whole work.

PROLOGUE 1–7 **1** *Wollewaerd and watschoed*: Will's shirtlessness indicating his poverty (MED s.v. *wolleward*). But as the phrases coupled commonly describe penitents' garb (cf. *Prick of Conscience* 3512: 'And fast and ga *wolwarde*, and wake' [*Sk*]), 'wetshod' may indeed signify 'barefoot', the manner of the original Franciscans. *R–H* 212 note the contrast with his unholy hermit's apparel in Pr 2–3. *wente...aftur*: echoing *wente aweye* 19.334 and hinting a sense of Will's journey as one he does not expect to return from. **2** *recheles*: recalling the spokesman of total dependence on God last named at 13.129 and his sentiments at 13.94–5, 98, 101–2. **4** *wilnede*: his desire being for vision rather than instruction, spiritual wisdom more than theological learning. *eefte*: the adv. going with both verbs. **5** *lened me to*: echoing the beginning of Will's dream-visions at Pr 8b; but since 'Lent' is nearly over, perhaps also importing 'relied upon', i.e. 'lived in a penitential manner [befitting my advancing age]' ('lent myself to' [*R–H* 212] is unidiomatic). **B 6** is omitted perhaps because its tone conflicts with that of *gretly* following; earlier *rotte* at 14.95 had indicated not openness to, but ignorance of heavenly revelation (the angels' song), and at 7.7 was comically unedifying. *Ramis palmarum*: 'with palm-branches', short for *Dominica in r. p.* 'Palm Sunday' (so named after the responsory phrase 'Cum *ramis palmarum*: Hosanna, clamabant in excelsis'). Holy Week, the sixth and last of Lent, began with clergy and people processing round the church carrying blessed palm-branches and singing the hymn *Gloria, laus* on re-entering. **6** 'Glory, praise [and honour to thee, Christ, Redeemer King, / To whom their noble cry *Hosanna* Israel's children sing]'; the opening verse and antiphonal response of the hymn. *greetliche*: its use with *dremede* unparalleled and the exact sense uncertain, but perhaps (as in *WPal* 1248) 'with deep and powerful feeling' (MED s.v. *gretli* adv.), or else referring to the lofty content of this passus (contrast its one other occurrence at 11.313). But *long tyme* (5) and *faste* (B 6) also imply the length of time spent in single-minded pursuit of the vision's profound meaning. **7** *Osanna*: 'Save, we beseech Thee'. This Hebrew word, found only in the accounts of Christ's entry into Jerusalem (Mt 21:9 //) read in the first Palm Sunday Antiphon, underlies the *salvum me fac* of Ps 117:25–6, from which the Gospel acclamations quote; repeated in the Palm Sunday liturgy, it concludes the *Sanctus* at every Mass. *by orgene*: possibly a portative instrument accompanying the procession rather than the main one played in the church. But an organ seems intended, since the liturgical chant recalls the familiar ending of the last psalm, sung at Lauds on Saturdays: 'Laudate eum...choro...et organo' (150:4); see *TN* further. *oelde*: 'adult' rather than 'aged', contrasted with the *gurles* of 6 (perhaps singing antiphonally in a choir). **B 9** *ofrauʒte*: 'obtained possession of', i.e. 'redeemed' (though most recorded instances mean 'reached to'). But whether the antecedent of *þat* is 'Christ' or 'his passion', the meaning is much the same, and the b-half's echo of B 7.147 faintly audible. The somewhat strained sense may account for the line's deletion. **(i) 8–112a** THE CRUCIFIXION SEQUENCE **(a) 8–34a** *Will and Faith* **8** The loss of partial resemblance to the actually encountered Samaritan is made up for by the partial recognition of Piers. Both effects are attributable to the interval between the Fifth and Sixth Visions, which has given the Dreamer time 'to studie / Of that [he] seyh slepynge' (9.297–8). **9–12** are deliberately paradoxical, the figure being both like and unlike knight, Samaritan and ploughman, yet by a conceptual *transsumptio* the true 'heavenly' norm of chivalric *kynde* (on 'earthly things which signify the supernatural' and the positive reflections in 'earthly concepts' of 'their eternal counterparts' cf. the valuable discussion in Waldron 1986:72). Weldon 1987[2]:119 interestingly compares the unrecognised Jesus to the 'fair unknown' of chivalric romance. **9** *asse bak*; *cam prikye*: an endingless 'positional genitive' and infinitive of manner after *comen*; see *MES* 73, 536–7. *boetles*: 'without boots' but not 'without remedy' (*boet*)

for man's sin, which depends not on 'piercing with' but on 'being pierced by' a spear; an echo of 1.152–3 and a foreshadowing of 20.80–8. **10** Cf. 'Withouten stedes and hors of prys / He haþ ouercome his enemys' (from the C14th *Meditations on the Life and Passion of Christ*, 1605–6, based on the C13th Latin *Philomena* of John of Hoveden, XIX 52). **12** *galoches*: possibly an alliterative synonym for 'shoes' (of the kind that could be pattern-cut) rather than signifying the specific type with wooden soles and leather fastening thongs. A knight armed for battle would have steel 'sabatouns' (*SGGK* 574; Cutts 1925:350, pl. from BL MS Royal 2. B vii); so this is peaceful footwear (like that worn by the figure being dubbed at court in Keen 1984:pl. 14). **13** 'O, Son of David!' Faith here momentarily speaks for those of his descendants who recognise in Jesus the promised 'Rex justus salvator' riding on an ass (Zach 9:9, quoted at Mt 21:5) and accordingly utters his 'herald's' cry to alert the spectators. Though immediately prompted by the context of Mt 21:9 //, the words are addressed to Jesus (*Fili* being vocative as in the Palm Sunday Antiphon); but since they are also those spoken by the blind men Christ heals *secundum fidem* at Mt 9:27–9 (Alf*Q*), they may be meant to evoke that stark image of 'blind' faith. **14** *heraud of armes*: see Keen 1984:136–7 on their duties. *auntrous*: the adj. used nominally (here pl.), paralleled only in *Ywain and Gawain* 3399. *ioustes*: single combats between mounted knights, often for a prize (here mankind). **15** *Olde*: referring not to their personal 'age' but to the ancient times they lived in, and contrasting the Jews who welcomed Jesus as the Saviour with those of the present time who still look for another (17.295–7). **15a** 'Blessed is he that cometh in the name of the Lord' (Mt 21:9, 23:39); ending the Antiphon *Pueri Hebraeorum* sung during the distribution of palms before the procession, and forming the second part of the *Sanctus* at Mass. Christ's own 'Messianic' sentence (Mt 23:39) is a direct allusion to his Second Coming. **17** *sholde iouste*: 'was going to joust'. For the full working-out of this metaphor see Waldron 1986:66–74, who shows *L*'s indebtedness to two allegorical crucifixion poems in AN by the C14th Franciscan poet Nicole Bozon, and Warner 1996:129–43 on the contribution of the tradition of 'Round Table' sermons. Even more important is the devotional tradition represented in the *Meditations* and the *Philomena*. **18** *þat...claymeth*: as prophesied at 18.129–30. *Pers...Plouhman*: on the split genitive see at 2.2. **19** *preynte*: a wordless sign recalling Piers's look that silences Will's questioning in B 16.64–5 (removed in C); on such signs see Burrow 2000. **20** *Liberum-Dei-Arbitrium*: a composite 'nature-name' suggesting both the figure who showed Will the Tree of Charity and the *Libera Voluntas Dei* of 18.129, there the equivalent of Piers in // B 16.86 and here corresponding to 'Jesus' at B 18.22. The referent is the divine Word who unites with human nature in the person of Christ (for whom 'Piers'/ 'Jesus' is an outer vesture) to make possible the one-to-one combat with Satan. *vndertake*: alluding to the Prophets' promise of a Saviour to Israel (e.g. Isaiah, chs 40–1). **21** *of his gentrice*: 'out of the nobility that is his by descent' (cf. B 14.181 and the quotation from Oliver de la Marche in Keen 1984:150). *Pers armes*: his human body, not the *conysaunce* described by Faith at 18.188, which might give his identity away and frighten his adversary off. Outlaw Death must be 'beguiled' into thinking he is fighting an adversary he can defeat. **22** *haberion...natura*: cf. '*þis haberion* is *þy* body fre' (*Meditations* 1603, = *loricam carnis* in Hoveden XIX 61). **23** The motif of the disguised Christ as a chivalric figure appears in the AN poems attributed to Bozon, *Vn re esteit iadis ke avait vne amye* and *Coment le fiz deu fu armé en la croyz*, both found in the commonplace book of his fellow-mendicant William Herebert, ms BL Addl. 46919 (the former printed by Wright from BL Cotton Julius A V in Langtoft, ii 426–37, ll. 17–24; also in Jubinal II, 309). The first has been proposed as a specific source by Gaffney 1931, the second by Bourquin 1978:702–7; see further the discussion in Waldron 1986. *consummatus Deus*: 'supreme God' (*Pe*) but, though recalling the insistence on the Son's full divinity at B 17.172–3, also ironically anticipating the 'supreme' or consummating moment of his *human* existence at 57 below. **24** *plates*: on plate-armour, a late C14th development, see Poole 1958:I, 324–5 and pl. 53b, Keen 1984:221. The metaphoric *transsumptio*, based on the radical claim that Christ's 'kingdom' is not of this world (Jn 18:36), widens the gap between tenor and vehicle, since a ploughman would wear a simple woollen jacket (as in **B**), not armour. **B 25** *paltok*: cf. Walter of Châtillon, I.7: 'Dei prudentia.../ cum in substantia cerni non potuit, / nostre *camisia* se carnis induit' ('God's wisdom, that in substance went unknown, / A shirt of flesh put on, and that our own)'; and see also Wheatley 1993:135–42. *prikiare*: ironically contrasting this rider's humility with the pride of the two others this word is used of (10.135, B 10.307). **25** *in..*: 'in the divine nature he has from the Father'; a stock expression for which no source need be sought. **26** *or*: not implying 'logical' alternatives, but rather a set phrase as at B 15.389, hence, 'the Jews generally or the scribes of the Jews in particular'. 17.252 nonetheless seems to imply that **L** sees them as a separate (racial or religious) group among Christ's opponents. **28** *Deth*: a 'nature-name' for the embodiment of evil, first mentioned in C Pr 17 as the ruler of hell (*dux mortis* in *EN* 423, *LA* 243). He is the 'last enemy' of I Cor 15:26 (and see on 34*a*). The opposition here between a personified Death and Life (which inspired the later ME poem of that name) is indebted to vs 3 of the Sequence *Victimae paschali laudes* by Wipo of Swabia (11th c.) sung before

the Gospel on Easter Sunday: '*Mors et vita* duello / Conflixere mirando: / *Dux vitae* mortuus regnat vivus' ('Death and Life in wondrous duel strive: / The Lord of Life has died, yet reigns alive'). **27** *fals doem*: referring primarily to the unjust sentence of death passed upon Jesus the second Adam, secondarily to the curse of death laid on man (through the Tempter's 'falsity') for the first Adam's sin. **29** contains 15.19b and an a-half earlier used at B 14.32 but excised at that point in // **C**. **30** *Lyf*: a personification drawn from the Easter Sequence, and hence a contrasting nature-name of the quality characterising the WORD in Jn 1:4 (the allusion is to Christ's prophecy in Mk 8:31). *lyeth*: Death's claim being ultimately a 'fals doem', which Truth will controvert decisively. *to wedde*: as a gage thrown down in fulfilment of the 'undertaking' at 20 (cf. Mede's use of the phrase at 3.258). **31** *That...to*: 'that he will walk' (anacoluthic). **32** is either IIb or, like 18 more certainly, Type Ia. **34** largely retains **B**'s sense in the b-half: 'and bring eternal death to death' (also possible for B 35; see *TN*). **34a** '[I will deliver them out of the hand of death]. O death, I will be thy death: [O hell], I will be thy bite' (Osee 13:14). Already part-quoted at B 17.110*a* (removed in revision), it is here imagined as spoken by God, but with contextual relevance for Life's chivalric 'vaunt' to his enemy. Christ the Lion of Judah (Rev 5:5) will 'bite down' the fatal Tree of Good and Evil (20.206) that brought 'bale' into the world and from which the Doctor of Death harvests his poisonous wine, in return for Man's fatal 'bite' from its fruit. The 'death / bite' pun is possible only in Latin, so the whole quotation is needed: 'swallowing down death [*deglutiens mortem*] that [men] might be made heirs of life everlasting' (I Pet 3:22). The text is used in Alan of Lille's discussion in *CH* of Death's loss of 'jurisdiction' over man, cited at 36 below. It is illustrated along with its companion text from I Cor 15:54–5 in Schiller II pl. 531, and even more strikingly in pl. 385, which shows a lion-headed shoot from the cross 'biting down' Death.

(b) 35–94 describe CHRIST'S CRUCIFIXION in a free-flowing and richly macaronic style that keeps to the fore the words and imagery of the Holy Week readings. **35** '[Pilate], sitting in the place of judgement'; based on *sedente illo pro tribunali* (Mt 27:19). **36** *demen...rihte*: 'pass judgement on the claims of the two'; perhaps suggested by Alan of Lille's 'Because the presumption was unjust, when Death assaulted one over whom he had absolutely no legal claim, he rightly lost the jurisdiction he had obtained over man' (*PL* 210:419). **37** *iustice aʒeyns Iesus*: an ironic echo of *Iesus a iustices sone* at 18.126 that points up the difference between earthly and heavenly notions of right. **38** *court*: used loosely for those present before the *tribunale* (Mt 27:17–22). *Crucifige*: 'Crucify (him)' (Lk 23:21, Jn 19:6), read on Wednesday and Friday of Holy Week. **39** *pelour*: one who makes an *appeel* 'charge or accusation before a judge' (Alf*G* s.v. *appel*); corresponding to the two 'false witnesses' (Mt 26:60–1) who make the deposition of 40–5 before the Sanhedrin. As the Trial before Pilate had no 'accuser' figure, **L**'s version (which does not exonerate the governor) makes the event more like an anarchic English lynching than a Roman judicial process. **40** *despised*: i.e. 'it', the verb being transitive and not constructed with *of*. **41–5** are based on Mk 14:58 (and cf. Jn 2:19–21). **46** *Crucifige*: not given to any individual in the Gospels. *wycchecrafte*: a detail from *EN* II. para. 1 (*magus*), 4 (*maleficus*); cf. English verse *GN* (MS Addl. 32578, ed. Hulme) ll. 215–16 (*bywichid*). **47** *Tolle..*: 'Away with him: Away with him: [Crucify him]' (Jn 19:15). **47–8** are based on Mt 27:29 / Mk 15:17; the paradoxical 'garland' image appears in the early C14th *Northern Passion* 1110: 'Yiet a nomen þornes kene / And made him a *gerlond*' and the 'coronam de spinis' is represented as a victory-garlond in the early iconography of the *crux invicta* (Schiller II pls. 1, 9). **49** *enuye*: 'sheer malice', perhaps echoing the chief priests' *invidiam* suspected by Pilate at Mk 15:10 (a text read on Tuesday of Holy Week). **50** 'Hail, Rabbi [Master]' (Mt 26:49), the words of Judas to Christ in Gethsemane, which strikingly replace the 'Ave rex Iudaeorum' of Mt 27:29, making those who insult Jesus his own people, not the Roman soldiers. *redes*: with which the soldiers beat his head after placing one such in his right hand in mockery of a sceptre (Mt 27:30). *shot vp* (*þrew* **B**): the precise action envisaged is not clear in either version. **51** *thre nayles*: the manner of representing Christ's crucifixion standard in Western iconography after about 1250 (Schiller II pls. 480–532); cf. *AW* 129/2–3; Furnivall, ed. *Pol. Poems* 111; *Joseph of Arimathie* 262. The number may be symbolic in an indeterminate way, like the *thre clothes* at 10.195–6. *naked*: the (historically correct) early tradition (Schiller II 91) found in Berchorius, *Op. Omn.* (Cologne 1731:340) and mostly avoided in later depictions (see Schiller II pl. 310). **52–3** *pole*: a reed in Mt 27:48, Mk 15:36, a hyssop stick in Jn 19:29. *poysen*: the drink offered to Christ on the cross (a different mistake in each version); see Hoveden's 'the venomous people offer him a drink' (*Cythara*, st 33, ed. Raby) and 'for wine poison (*pro vino virus*) you would offer him' (*Canticum Amoris*, xxix 195). In **B** the drink is meant to hasten Christ's death, in **C** cruelly to prolong it. The first interpretation is found in devotional writings such as the Latin prose *Meditaciones* (ed. Stallings 1965:115), the English verse *Meditations*, and Hoveden's *Philomena* sts 194–5 (see Schmidt 1983[2]:176–85; Ruffing 1991); the second appears in *LA*. One expresses the wish of Satan, the other that of Hell (cf. Goblin's words at 335). **54–5** *hymsulue...rode*: based on Lk 23:35; the vocative form of B 54 is closer to Mt 27:40. **55** *Yf...sone*: a fusion of Lk 23:35 ('si hic est *Christus*') and Mt 27:40 ('si *Filius Dei*

es, descende de cruce'). **B 55** *kynges sone*: suggested by Mt 27:42 ('si *rex Israel* est, descendat nunc de cruce') and perhaps by *Meditations* 1868: 'Whi sleþ venym þe kynges sone?' **56** *thenne...leue*: conflating Mt 27:42 ('descendat...et credimus ei') and Mk 15:32 ('descendat... ut videamus, et credamus'). *Lyf*: a 'nature-name' for God, the 'lord of life' (59), whom they cannot recognise in the dying figure of Jesus (see on 30 above). **57** '[Jesus...said]: It is consummated. [And bowing his head, he gave up the ghost]' (Jn 19:30). The words refer both immediately to the end of Christ's ordeal and beyond that to his completion of the eternal plan of *consummatus Deus* (23): 'opus consummavi quod dedisti mihi' (Jn 17:4). In the liturgy of Good Friday this text, marking the most solemn moment, is followed by silence. **59** may be exceptionally a line with three lifts in the b-verse, symbolically representing a unique closure, or normative with *leyde* muted or with *his eyes* as part of a 'strong' pre-final dip. *lord...liht*: a title running together two divine 'nature-names' given at 20.306, 403 (cf. *Philomena*, sts 64–5) and supremely ironic in its echo of 10.155 as the title of 'God grettest'. Especially relevant among the images of Christ as Light in St John's Gospel are Jn 12:35–6 (alluding to his coming death) and 46. *leyde...togideres*: a phrase unparalleled as a way of saying 'lowered his eyelids / closed his eyes'. Kaske 1968 refers to depictions of Christ's half-closed or closing eyes in C14th windows at Preston, Glos. and Mamble, Worcs. **60** and **62b** re-enact the earlier crucifixion account (at 7.131) based on Lk 23:44–5, which was read at Mass on the Wednesday of Holy Week: 'tenebrae factae sunt....Et obscuratus est sol'. **61–5** are based on Mt 51–2, but **L** seems to have creatively (mis)read *velum templi* 'the veil of the Temple' as *vallum templi* 'rampart, wall' in the light of Mt 27:51–2 (and cf. *GN* ll. 691, 705–6). **61b–2a** *euene...to-roef*: 'in duas partes.... et petrae scissae sunt' (Mt 27:51). *hard roch*: echoing 19.12; the tearing of the Temple curtain was understood by the Fathers as symbolising the end of God's Covenant with the Jews, who had rejected his Son. The splitting of the Temple *wall* (fulfilling Christ's words at 18.160 and verbally recalled by the revision *to-cleue* at 112) is here perhaps meant to be associated with Moses' breaking of the Tablets of the Law in anger against the Hebrews for rejecting God (Ex 32:19). **63** adds an element of paradox in contrasting the 'quik' earth with the 'dede' men; the Gospel source is Mt 27:51–3. **64** Cf. *GN* l. 709. **65** *tempest*: a familiar Biblical symbol of God's anger (see on 5.121–2); here virtually a mythicised struggle between divinity and chaos symbolised by upheaval of all the elements, with one nameless 'dead body' being made a substitute for the herald Faith, who cannot see what is happening. **66** *bataille*: specifically interpreted as a 'civil duel of law' by Baldwin 1981[2]:66–72 (cf. the interesting comparison with the judicial duel in *Ywain and Gawain* in Clifton 1993:126–8). But the basic image of a conflict between death and life comes from vs 2 of the Easter Sequence (see at 28); the outcome is left uncertain to create tension for the events that follow Christ's death. On the iconography of *Mors* and *Vita* see Schiller II 114–15 and the important pl. 385. **69–70** The sound-repetitions in '*Son*eday', and '*Godes sone*' hint at further 'theopoetic' wordplay in '*sonne*-rysynge': the *sol iustitiae* and the *iustices sone* are one. Dawn is the time of the resurrection given in Mt 28:1–2, Mk 16:2. **70** *Somme*: based on the statement in Mt 27:54 of the centurion 'and the[m] that were with him', and interpretable as expressing awe at the earthquake rather than faith in Christ as in // Lk. *so fayre*: suggested by the quieter statement that 'the centurion...seeing that crying out *in this manner* he had given up the ghost...' (Mk 15:39). **70a** 'Indeed this was the son of God' (Mt 27:54). **71–2** An invented linking of the concern of Christ's enemies to ensure his death (Jn 19:31) with their reported charge (Jn 7:20) that he cast out devils by Satan's power (see on 18.150–51*a*). *soercerie*: cf. 17.304, stating that the Jews suspect Jesus of raising Lazarus by magic (whence their worry here). The term is not sharply distinguished from *wicchecraft* (used interchangeably at 46), but more strongly associated with raising the dead. **73–9** re-work the Gospel source, here mainly Jn 19:31–5, so as to give the 'gentries' of Jesus as the reason why he receives a spear-thrust from a knight and not the same insulting treatment as the thieves from a *cachepol*. **74** *so...lawe*: meaning little more than 'as the common [Roman] practice was, [to crucify several malefactors together]'. **75** *craked...legges*: so as to hasten their death (*armes aftur* is an addition). **77–9** The descent from *Godes body* to *knyht* somehow produces not bathos but ennoblement: as a man, the champion who has fought by the laws of chivalry deserves honourable treatment from his enemies (the present statement that he was a knight will form the basis of Conscience's words at 21.28). **78** *Kynde*: with primary reference to God, but with a secondary sense of 'the nature of things, what was fitting for someone who had *the kynde of a knyhte*' (11). **80–94** The story of the *blynde knyhte* (following *GN* 626) who reluctantly pierces Christ's side undergirds the thematic stress on *gentries*, the 'nobility' granted the Chosen People but which (as both 'redeeming grace' and 'social rights') the Jews have lost through 'ignoble' treatment of their rightful king by descent from David. **81** *Longius*: 'Longinus miles' (*EN* XVI 4), a name derived from Gk λονγχη 'spear(man)' (= Lat *lancea*) in Jn 19:34, and given him in *GN* ll. 625–30. In *LA* 202–3, St Longinus is the Roman centurion of Lk 23:47 (*videns signa quae fiebant...credidit* echoing *videns quod factum fuerat*); see also Comestor, *HS* (in *PL* 198:1633–4) and for the background, Peebles 1911, Kolve 1966:218–21, and Burdach 1974. **82** *place*: suggesting a jousting arena with the

ruler watching; but as Pilate was not present at the Crucifixion, reference here may be to prior events before the judgement-seat (Jn 19:13). **83** *mony teth*: a peculiar nonce-variant on the idiom *maugre his chekes*, perhaps darkly alluding to the *LA* statement that 'his teeth were torn out' for refusing to worship idols after his conversion. *was made*: by the Jews in *GN* 625, at Pilate's order in *LA*. **84** *Iouste*: the *bataille* being over, it is a dishonourable act to inflict wounds on a dead knight's body. *blynde Iewe*: L's alteration (he is a Roman centurion in *LA*) serving to illustrate this people's spiritual blindness, which he figures specifically as a lack of *gentries* (Clifton 1993:125 aptly notes how his literal blindness symbolically corresponds 'to the blindness of those who executed Jesus, not knowing what they did' [Lk 23:34]) and rightly stresses that in the *bataille* he 'cannot represent Satan...only the influence of Satan on the souls of men'). Longeus's es-sential *gentries*, revealed once he realises what he has done, proves that L does not regard the Jewish lack of faith in Christ as insuperable (see further on 88). **85–7** *alle they...Bote*: Longeus alone knowing neither that Jesus is dead nor that he is a 'knight' of royal descent. **87** *herte*: as in the earliest representation (c. 430), where Longinus thrusts his lance into Christ's heart (Schiller II pl. 323); C14th iconography shows a spear-wound in the right side (Schiller II pls 509, 518). The sacramental significance of the Saviour's *herte*-blood (cf. 21.58 below) as miraculously healing seems plain. **88** *vnspered*: a sovereign instance of L's serious wordplay, metaphorical and symbolic at once; the wounded hero's blood seeking not vengeance but virtue, and its effect being both to heal the body and inspire faith (see further Clifton 1993:126–7). But while the immediate written source *LA* describes how Longinus by chance touched his eyes *de sanguine Christi per lanceam decurrente* (see Schiller II pl. 525), agency is here ascribed to Christ's blood, as at 7.133. The scene may be viewed as exemplifying the Samaritan's words at 19.86–8, for in offering his knightly submission Longeus implicitly seeks to be *ybaptised* (see further Schmidt 2010:214–16). L's making him a Jewish 'knight' may be influenced by the iconographic motif of the blindfolded 'Synagogue' with a pennoned lance that breaks when Christ dies, as in Schiller II pl. 529 (Synagoga is usually female, as in Mâle 189, Schiller II pl. 450, but male in Schiller II pl. 528). At a more literal level, it may be a (somewhat bizarrely) ironic inversion of the Jewish leaders' cry 'His blood be upon us and on our children' at Mt 27:25. **89** *fil...knees*: for an interesting connection of this action with response motifs of 'kneeling and naming' in relation to the metaphor of Christ as knight, see Weldon1987[2]:119, and for illuminating association of Longinus's kneeling with the service of Good Friday, Weldon 1989:60–65. **91** *forthenketh*: as in the C13th OF *Passion*, source of the early C14th

English *Northern Passion* (II.61), a text often accompanied in manuscripts by the *Harrowing*. **92–4** erupt in a spate of serious puns characteristic of the later versions (*do*; *licame / likynge*; *rihtful / riht*). **92** The cry for mercy is also a tacit prayer for the sacramental grace that will confirm his faith (this whole speech may be compared with Robert the Robber's at 6.323–4). The poem is silent about how Longinus's conversion bore fruit in missionary work and a martyr's death in Caesarea of Cappadocia *c*. 58 AD (*LA*). **93** offers not feudal service but surrender of all he owns as a forfeit for his crime. **94** *riht with þat*: 'immediately' and 'rightly thereupon'; the weeping is an appeal from Christ's *riȝt* 'justice' to his *ruthe* 'pity'. **(c) 95–112a** *Faith's denunciation of the Jews* for rejecting his and their saviour stresses that their action was as ignoble as it was wrong-headed (the small revisions at 95, 97 underscore the crime against Christ's *gentries*). The severe tone of Abraham Father of the Jews is clearly related to their *lack of faith*, not their race (as is confirmed by the preceding instance of the mercy shown to the Jew Longeus, who believes). **98** *dede...dede*: the *annominatio* exposing this deed stands as an extreme form of the *failure* of Priest and Levite to act towards another stripped and wounded man (in the parable of the Samaritan). **101** *gre*: the paradox of Christ's victory effectively 'chivalricised' in Longeus's submission. **102–3** *chaumpioun... recreaunt*: an action customarily taken as signifying cowardice, to judge by the tone of *CT* X 697, which describes the despairing man as 'lyk the coward champioun [not *victor* but *combatant*] recreant, that seith "creant" withoute nede'. There may be an etymological pun on *recreant* 'giving up one's religion', since the Jew Longeus in acknowledging his 'defeat' by divine Love *acquires* faith in his conqueror. **104** *derkenesse ydo*: i.e. by the Light's descent into Hell (to defeat Death) and his subsequent resurrection (to show how Life has *þe maistrie*). This association of Death with the darkness of hell is anticipated by the early revision at Pr 1–8. *Deth...yvenkused*: vividly illustrated in Schiller II pl. 531, where a 'Trinitarian' hand thrusts three spears into Death, Satan and Hell. **105** *lordeyns*: an 'anti-pun' on etymologically unrelated 'lord' (it is < OF *lordin*) may be suspected, since what their 'vileyns' behaviour has cost them is 'lordship' (spiritual election by God *and* the right to own land). **106–10** The Jews had been expelled from England in 1290 and, being without civil rights in most European states where they could reside, they had to live by money-lending, which the Lateran Council of 1215 had allowed them. But since the Jewish law forbade 'usury' (see on 110), contemporaries often saw their disabilities as condign punishment brought on the whole race (no more a nation after AD 70) by their own wish after Pilate's refusal to condemn Jesus (Mt 27:24–5), rather than as a (remediable) human injustice. (On the conditions of European

Jews in the period see Cohn 1972:76–81, Cohen 1983, Stow 1992). The central irony of the passage is that the Jews' progenitor Abraham was himself allowed to live in Canaan, and their law-giver Moses to authorise re-settlement of this 'promised' land, by conquest; so 'a father's curse' in effect reverses 'God's blessing' to him and his descendants at 18.255–7. **109** *as bareyne*: 'as if totally unproductive' (OED s.v. *barren* 4), i.e. unable to raise crops, rear livestock or engage in trade (the instance is misassigned by MED s.v. *barain* adj. 5 'destitute'). The word's use here may assume the Scholastic conception of money as 'barren' in nature, i.e. not a form of true property but only a medium of exchange, use of which was held to be adequately repaid by return of the original sum to the lender. Further reason for resentment against Jews was inevitable when, through taking interest, they made 'breed of barren metal' (*Merchant of Venice* I iii 132). *vsure*: see on 2.91; their 'ability' to practise this fitted in with Christians' need for money that other Christians were forbidden to lend them (the hypocrisy this gave rise to was to be excoriated by Marlowe in *The Jew of Malta*). Medieval writers say no good about a people they regarded not simply as 'unbelievers' but (95, 113) as *false*; and that the whole race had deceitfully *betrayed* Christ is implied in the Good Friday Collect asking God to deliver them not only from spiritual *obcaecatio* 'blindness' but from *perfidiam* 'treachery'. **110** Lending at interest was formally proscribed at the Second Council of Lyons (1274); but *alle lawes* may allude to Ex 22:25, Deut 23:19–20, which only forbids such lending to other (poor) Jews. **111** *Daniel*: an OT book especially important in Christian disputes with the Jews about the Messiah because Jesus's adoption of its term 'Son of Man' (7:13–14) in the Synoptic Gospels was understood as an oblique self-designation as the Messiah (see Schiller I 19, pl. 33). **112a** See on B 15.598a, an earlier use to describe the 'undoing' of Jewish hopes of a kingdom, removed at that point in revision. The Daniel passage (9:24) stating how '[vision and prophecy may be fulfilled and] the Saint of Saints may be anointed (*ungatur Sanctus sanctorum*)' was a key anti-Judaic text, discussed by Alan of Lille in *CH* in his proof that Christ was the expected Messiah (*PL* 210:411–12). **(ii) 113–478** THE HARROWING OF HELL SEQUENCE is preceded by a brief *transition* into what resembles another 'inner dream' (113–15), concluded (471–8) by Will's literal and spiritual awakening, and framed within the debate of THE FOUR DAUGHTERS OF GOD (116–270; 452–69). The scriptural source of this last motif is Ps 84:11, which is finally quoted at 467a, and among writers who use it, only **L** positions the argument at this point in salvation history (Traver 1907:147; discussions of its development are Traver 1929, Mäder 1971 and Tveitane 1980). Each of the Daughters has a leading trait: Truth's courage, Righteousness's firmness, Mercy's gentleness and Peace's patience paralleling the complementarity of the four Cardinal Virtues, Fortitude, *Justice*, Temperance and Prudence. Their debate's two halves (between Mercy and Truth at 113–73, Justice and Peace at 174–237) are abruptly followed by Book's intervention, dissolving into 'vision' at the Latin command spoken by Christ's voice (269–70*a*). It is not resumed but it is resolved (at 462) with another Latin cry, that of angels affirming Christ's triumph. L does not so much dramatise a debate in the 'heart' of God, as understood by the C12th Julian of Vézelay (Tveitane 1980), as articulate the contradictions attending human attempts to understand the divine purpose. Popular in later drama (*The Castle of Perseverance* 95–111; the *N-Town Play* I 111–23), the motif is not found in the liturgy itself like that of the 'duel' of Life and Death (though the image of 'darkness' provides a linking element). The chief Latin source, St Bernard's Sermon I on the Annunciation (*PL* 183:383), which is much later than that of the Devils' debate (already in *EN* XVIII–XX), is a fruit of the special emphasis on Christ's humanity that marked the 'new devotion' of the early Gothic period. This is drawn upon for illustrations in a mid-C12th English Bible (Schiller I pl. 35), and the four figures are later depicted as part of the paradoxical image of 'Christ crucified by the Virtues' (Schiller II pls. 453, pairing Justice / Peace and Mercy / Truth above and below the cross; Saxl 1942:pl. 25b). The motif's first appearance in a vernacular text is in the AN *Château d'Amour* of Robert Grosseteste (ed. Murray; ME translations ed. Sajavaara). L may also have known an early C14th English variant, the Parable of the King and his Four Daughters in *Cursor Mundi* 9517–9752.

113–15 *A Transition* **113** *ferly*: the marvellous events culminating in the darkness at Christ's death. *false Iewes*: a measure of Will's self-identification with Christ (against whom the *vyl vilanye* has been perpetrated), but echoing a wider contemporary anxiety that Jews might actually repeat their first 'wounding' of Christ by desecrating his sacramental body in the Host, as in the mid-C15th 'Croxton Play of the Sacrament' (in *Non-cycle Plays*). **114** (*with*)*drow* (*me*): an action both literal and potentially symbolic, this deeply spiritual vision lacking only a formal indication that it is an 'inner dream'. *derkenesse*: evoking also the liturgical stress on mourning in the Office of Tenebrae said in the darkened church on Wednesday, Thursday and Friday of Holy Week. *descendit...*: 'He descended into Hell' (article 8 of the Apostles' Creed); an allusive periphrasis for 'the depths of hell'. The outward disappearance of the sun's light at Christ's death provides an awe-inspiring entry into the infernal domain where there is 'darkness and dread and the devil master' (18.117). **115** *seyh sothly*: the adverb affirming the truth less of the narrator's personal witness (cf. 116,

120) than of the dream's content, which rests on authority. *secundum scripturas*: 'according to the sacred writings'; a phrase from the Nicene Creed said at Sunday Mass, but evoking its original source I Cor 15:4, which affirms that the key events of Christian faith fulfil OT prophecy. Insertion here of the *descendit*-phrase from the other familiar creed (it is absent from the Nicene) aligns the elaborated narrative of the apocryphal *EN* with that of the canonical scriptures, which contain the seeds of the story in I Pet 3:18–20.

(a) 116–270*a* *The Debate of the Daughters of God* 116 *west*: the direction of sunset and of death (Russell 1984:139). In cathedrals the Last Judgement portal stood on the west or main front (e.g. Chartres in Schiller I pl. 62), and in parish churches the Doom was depicted in the west window, as at Fairford (Baker pl. 17) or on the chancel arch facing west (Benson 1998:18–20). Mercy's symbolic association with the Last Things portends what is hoped will be the final attitude of the Creator to his creatures. *wenche*: possibly neutral, but usually implying low social status. Its ironic conjunction at 119 with *buyrde*, a term from alliterative high style used of Lady Mede at 3.15, is a striking example of L's 'grotesque sublime', superbly explored in Coghill 1988 [1962]. **117** *to hellewárd*: i.e. 'downward' (MED s.v. *helle* n. 1 (g)), the metrically required stress on the suffix favouring a polysemantic pun on *ward* 'stronghold' (MED s.v. n. 3(a)). Though in Pr 16–18 hell lies westward, and in 1.111–13 northward, the sisters seem to approach from all 'the round earth's imagin'd corners' towards a *centre* beneath which Hell lies. But *Sk*'s sense of the scene's resemblance to a stage-play where actors come from the four quarters and meet in the middle of an open space, though justifiable, lends no support to his inference that *helleward* means 'eastward'. For this 'stage' is no wooden platform but a theatre of the mind, and the directions' symbolic meanings are therefore crucial. **118** *Mercy*: a personification of the *misericordia* that is 'aboue Godes werkes' (Ps 114:9, qu. at 12.75*a*, 19.296*a* and cf. 6.337*a*). *mylde*: the revision modifying the complete verbal repetition at B 115b of B 16.91b without concealing the allusion to the Blessed Virgin Mary, the 'mater misericordiae' who at 7.285 is signified by Mercy the 'mayden, hath myhte ouer hem alle'. **119** *benyngne...speche*: retaining the verbal echo of B 16.7 in B 18.116. **121** *eest*: the most important symbolic 'direction', as the location of Truth's tower (see on Pr 14–15), and thus the only proper place for her to come from. **122** *Treuthe*: the *veritas* of Ps 84:11, God's self-revelation, under the limitations of time, history and language, as the object of human understanding. This, the first 'nature-name' the poet assigned to God, has special authority, even if the 'whole' truth of the divine nature is not known to the speaker and can only be grasped as a harmony eventually realised by the reconciliation of all four sisters. **123** *vertue*: a hint at the cardinal virtue *fortitudo*, the *myht* especially associated with God the Father. A parallel between the daughters and the cardinal virtues is suggested by their depiction in a mid-C12th crucifxion enamel (Schiller II pl. 446).

124–73 *Mercy and Treuthe* are regularly coupled in the Psalms, e.g. at 24:10, 88:14. **125** scans either as Type IIa with *of* mute or, perhaps preferably, as Ia or Ic with *of*, here meaning 'about', as a full-stave, thus facilitating repetition with variation in following 126 (123), where *Of* is unstressed. *this grete wonder*: the darkness above and the light below. The subject of the Harrowing is taken from Part II of the *EN*, ll. 1160–1536 in the ME translation. The version in *LA* 242–5, observing that the canonical Gospels say nothing about what Christ did in Limbo, refers to *EN* as authority for the story, along with an unspecified sermon of 'Augustine' (not used by **L**) that it retails at length (identified by Marx 1997:218 as pseudo-Augustine, Sermo 160 *De Pascha*). **126** *þe day roued*: 'day was breaking'; not the outer natural dawn of Easter morning (still to come) but the supernatural light before hell, which seems associated with the 'day' that 'withdrew' at 60. **127** *lihte*; *leem*: the doublet echoing *lux... luminis sempterni* (*LA* 243) or *illuxit...lux magna* (*EN Descensus* [Latin B] , XVIII.1). The light shining in darkness that cannot overcome it inevitably evokes the Biblical image of the Son's divine radiance (Jn 1:5). **130–1** A 'Platonic' association of the stave-syllables seems intended, given the earlier use of 'mercy' as a nature-name for the Virgin (see on 118). **132** *speche*: Gabriel's 'thou shalt conceive...Because no word [*verbum*] shall be impossible with God' and Mary's answering 'be it done to me according to thy word' (Lk 1:31, 37; 38). In iconography the virginal conception is often represented as taking place through the ear (Schiller I pls. 108, 111). **133** *grace...Gost*: cf. Lk 1:28–30, 35. **134** *wommane wem*: the loss of virginity (with Mary as referent); but **L** may more widely understand the stain of original sin contracted by all at conception (Ps 50:7, a verse following that quoted at 420*a*), but from which Mary was held to be free. On the weak subjective genitive in *wommane* see *MES* 73. **135** *witnesse*: referring to the prophecies (141) that this would happen, above all Is 9:2, quoted at 7.133*a*, foretelling this very event (7.134–5), and again here at 366. **136** *thritty*: the 'ideal' age (perfect manhood) traditionally said to have been Christ's at his death; it is more precisely specified (perhaps not accidentally) at line 3*32* below. **137** *Deyede*: a Ø-relative with *Who* understood. The homophonic play on *dey* and *day* echoes that at B 16.166 and recalls the *lyf / liht* collocation at 59. *mydday*: the ninth hour (*nona hora*), commonly reckoned today as 3 p.m., but understood as noon (see on 7.132) by **L**, who connects the earthly sun's disappearance with the heavenly Son's *aureus solis color* (*EN* XVIII.1, *LA* 243) be-

fore the gates of hell. **138** *clips*: no simple covering-over with clouds but a unique planetary occurrence. Earlier crucifixion iconography often depicts the lesser and the greater light in the corners (Schiller II pl. 435 shows sun and moon weeping). **139** *In menynge*: the natural event having symbolic significance, as at 15.245, 5.121–2 above, because the 'book of nature' (see Alan of Lille in *PL* 210:579, Raby *OBMLV* 242) is the first part of God's ordained revelation to man. *merkenesse*: firstly that of the patriarchs in Limbo, but more widely of all humanity; Christ's resurrection brings a 'light' to the Gentiles and Jews as in the prophecy (Lk 2:32) that Simeon recalls at *EN* XVIII.2, *LA* 243. **140** re-presents as coming what was recalled in Repentance's great prayer at 7.134, reminding how liturgical ritual combines diachronic and synchronic axes, narrating salvation history and enacting an 'existential' drama. **141** The most specific prophecy concerning the second tree is Is 11:10, 'In that day, the root of Jesse... the Gentiles shall beseech: and his sepulchre shall be glorious' (qu. Rom 15:12). Although the symbolic image of the 'Jesse Tree' was commonly connected with the Incarnation, it is found 'combined with the tree-Cross as the *arbor vitae*' in the remarkable 'Jesse Cross' illustration in a mid-C14th *Speculum humanae salvationis* (Schiller II 135, pl. 442). **142–3** The notion of the 'tree of Christ's cross' (Ac 5:30, 10.39; I Pet 2:24) as the means to 'lift up' Man subjected to death through eating the fruit of the 'tree of good and evil' derives from the *Pange lingua*, sung during the ceremony of the Adoration of the Cross (and directly quoted at 164*a*). The tree's becoming the subject of the victory shows influence from the Good Friday liturgy's metonymic treatment of the 'crux fidelis', the alternating response to the verses. But the figurative theology of Venantius Fortunatus's great hymn is enriched from the medieval legend telling how the wood of the Cross grew from the seeds of the first *tre* in Gen 2:17 (see *Legends...*1871, *Legend...*1894). On the *arbor vitae / arbor crucis* iconography, see Schiller II 132–6, pls. 431 (C11th) and 443 (C14th), both including Adam and Eve; Saxl 1942:pl. 27b. **142** *tynt...wynne*: cf. 'To undo the loss inflicted by that wood' (*Pange lingua*, st. 2). **143** *deth*: the expected antithesis would be *lyf*, but the essence of the Christian paradox lies in this ultimate *transsumptio*, wherein the referent becomes the 'obedient' (and thence 'redemptive') death of Christ. **144** *walterot*: a humorously 'Platonic' nonce-creation from the elements of *troteuale* (a word of unknown etymology that MED cites four times from Mannyng's *Handlyng Synne*), rendering the 'nonsense' Truth accuses Mercy of even *more* nonsensical. The insulting tone, which makes the argument parody the calm politeness of scholastic disputation, is not without a touch of 'clerkly' anti-feminism. **146–7** The syntax is ambiguous, allowing *leue* to be indic. pl. governed by the noun-phrase subject in 145–6 or, as more likely, imper. sg. addressed to Mercy, with the noun-phrase as anticipated object in apposition with *hem* 147. **147** *brynge*: 'could bring'; a 'subjunctive of unreality' (*MES* 455). **149** *truyfle*: perhaps meant to recall *troteuale* (though not derived from it). *Treuthe...sothe*: a (deliberately) banal b-half with an ironic echo of Piers's words at 7.244; Truth's 'pre-Easter' *tokene* is the solemn OT certainty of 151*a*. **150** corresponds closely to its source *Sic qui descenderit ad inferos, non ascendet* 'so he that shall go down to hell shall not come up' (Job 7:9) and implies that Job, as one of the suffering patriarchs, can speak from experience. But the speaker is unaware of the words' ironic deeper sense: for *Christ's* 'descensus ad inferos' is that of one who has already 'descended' (to earth from heaven) and therefore will 'ascend' (from hell to earth); see on 11.209*a*. The same sentiment is ascribed to Solomon in the Towneley 'Harrowing' play (XXV/295–7). **151** *Iob*: strictly neither a patriarch nor a prophet, so not a 'perfect' example with which to rebut Mercy's claim to authority at 141. **151***a* 'For in hell there is no salvation; [have mercy on me, O God, and save me]'; from the Office of the Dead, Nocturn 3, response 7 (*Brev.* 2:278). This paraphrase from Job 7:9 was widely cited in vernacular literature (e.g. *Prick* 7248) and in the penitential tradition (AlfQ). **152–64***a* *Mercy's reply* is (in good sermon fashion) an *argumentum per analogiam* ('For...and so...and as...so...'), its thrice-repeated instrumental preposition *thorw* (153, 159, 162) answering Truth's repeated 'never' (147, 150). **153** *experiense*: an earlier use than any recorded in MED, appealing to what Will has constantly sought as *kynde knowyng*. **154** The folk-belief in the contrary action of similars (on which see Bartolomaeus Anglicus 1249–50) had an 'experiential' basis, the lethal / recuperative action of herbal drugs (e.g. those derived from belladonna and digitalis) depending on the dosage and manner of administration. Mercy's implication that there are two kinds of death, corporeal and spiritual (one temporary, the other not necessarily eternal), will be taken up by Christ at 373–5. On the important link of this idea with Holy Church's *tryacle* figure at 1.145 see St-Jacques 1991:114–15. **155** *bote*: a 'remedy' for death won through death (itself the punishment for sin, not a means to *further* punishment), by God's sharing man's mortality through the Incarnation. **156** *scorpioun*: an apt choice for the analogy, as its barely visible bite made it an emblem of deadly treachery, and therefore of the Devil. **157–9** A common belief, found in Lanfranc's *Chirurgie* 344/11: 'scorpiouns...ben brent þat we mowe vse hem in *medicyns*'. **158** 'Until, dead, he is placed against the injured spot'. The *vertu* of Christ's death has already been learnt 'thorw experiense' in the healing of Longeus' blindness (symbolically, the consequence of sin) when he pierced Christ's already dead body (cf. 98). The image of Christ himself as the 'healing medicine' echoes the

Johannine understanding of his Cross as the 'antitype' of the brazen serpent set up by Moses in the desert, which cured from serpent-bite all who looked on it (Num 21:8–9); cf. Alan of Lille's *Distinctiones* citing Jn 3:14–15: 'Serpens...dicitur Christus' (*PL* 210:942) and Fortunatus in the stanza quoted at 164*a*: *Et medelam ferret inde, Hostis unde laeserat* 'Fetching healing from the place Where hostile malice left its trace'. **159** *vertu*: a deliberate 'anti-pun' as well as a play on co-polysemes; the hidden 'virtue' or strength that God as *parfit practisour* will draw from Satan's *dede* is unknown to the devil and obviously not due to *his* exercise of 'virtue'. **160** *this deth*: Christ's. But as ironic ambiguity is of great significance in this context of divine disguising and table-turning, the noun-phrase may also be resolved grammatically as '*this* shall destroy death', the antecedent of 'this' being the scorpion Christ (see on 158), and the whole of 161 then standing in apposition to *deth* 160. **161** suggests almost as strongly as B 158 Death's separate, near-dualistic existence alongside Satan over against God / Life, a way of thinking evidenced in the later iconography (Schiller II pls. 531, 532, 536). **163** *goed ende*: balancing the implied good beginning, the Creation (cf. Gen 1:31). The Apocalypse (21:1) strongly emphasises the creation of 'a new heaven and earth'. **164** *goed sleythe*: the wordplay operating as at 159, with oxymoron a pointer to God's final transformation of diabolic evil (which lacks substantial reality) into divine good. **164***a* '[That God by stratagem should foil / The shape-shifting Destroyer's guile'; from *Pange lingua*, st. 3. The *ars* is the Son's assuming human form, as Satan did a serpent's, with the difference that Incarnation is no disguise but a mysterious reality (including acceptance of death), a 'sleight,' yet not 'guile'.

165–173 *Righteousness and Peace* **166** *nype...north*: the region of 'biting cold', darkness and wintry night, here freed of the specifically diabolic associations of 1.110ff but in the OT often where 'evil and destruction' will come from (Jer 1:14, 4:6, 6:1). As in the OE *Wanderer*, cold is a 'natural' symbol of the end of time, pointing to the Judgement in which *justice* will reign. *nype*: possibly a back-formation (earlier than that of 1551 in OED s.v. *nip* sb. 1) from the verb *nyppen* at 6.104 (also first instanced in L) derived from OE *genip* 'darkness' or (*Sk*, MED s.v.) **hnipa* 'crag, peak' (peace and justice are both associated with mountains and hills in Ps 71:3, and in 84:12 'iustitia de caelo prospexit'). **167** *Rightwisenesse*: Justice, one of the Cardinal Virtues (21.219); a prime attribute of God in both OT and NT (Dan 9:7, Job 36:3; Rom 3:21). **168** Righteousness's seniority to Mercy in age and wisdom is obvious enough, her seniority to Truth less clear. That the eldest sister somehow reflects God's unrevealed essence and Truth his self-revelation in time seems out of keeping with her palpably limited knowledge at 192ff below. **169** is the only other Type Ib line alliterating on *s*, recalling Pr

1. The pararhyme with *soth* and half-rhymes with *bothe, yclothed, opere* create an effect of calm and reassurance. *southe*: the 'sikerore' region, according to HC (1.116). **170** *pacience*: 'an heigh vertu certeyn' (*CT* V 773) that promotes peace between human beings. It has a theological character in relation to the God who 'soffres' and as the fourth of the Twelve Fruits of the Spirit (Jn 14:27; Gal 5:22). But a further association of Peace's special 'clothing' or 'outward sign' *patience* with the Cardinal Virtue of prudence is suggested by Prov 14:29, a text cited by Chaucer's Dame Prudence (*CT* VII 1510). **171** *Loue*: an oblique 'nature-name' that is now empowered to take the place of 'Truth' in consequence of the full and final revelation in Christ that 'God is Love' (see on 1.82 above). In contemporary iconography it is represented metonymically by the singular motif of 'Caritas [*or* Ecclesia] embracing / piercing Christ on the Cross', as illustrated in Schiller II pl. 447 and most strikingly (because she embraces Christ *in the midst of* the Four Daughters) in the C14th stained-glass image in Schiller II pl. 453. Relevant to Love's 'mediatory' relation with the Daughters (through his 'love-correspondence' with Peace) is Alan of Lille's comment (*In cant. cantic.*) on the text *media charitate constravit propter filias Jerusalem* (Cant 3:10): 'Charity is, so to speak, the other virtues' mediatrix and form,...illuminates and informs the rest, and relates equally to them all' (*PL* 210:76). So too is his interpretation of 'Jerusalem' as 'the mind of Christ in which is the vision of "the peace which surpasseth all understanding" [Phil 4: 7]'. Love's 'desire for Peace' aptly figures God's wish to reconcile the world to himself through Christ (II Cor 5:18–19).

174–237 174 *When...oper*: elliptical for 'when Peace [and Justice] approached each other'; the B 171 form has Peace being intercepted by Justice as she approaches the *other* two sisters. **175** *in*: the small revision of *for* removing **B**'s unjustified anticipation of an understanding that Righteousness does not yet possess, and making her bow an act of ordinary courtesy (see further on 466). **177** *garnementes*: such as a lover or bride wears; echoing Ps 44:9–12 and Is 52:7. **179** *merkenesse*: the dark enveloping them in Limbo, now pierced by the light of Love. **181** In the revision, the song of Mercy (see *TN*) provides the music for Peace to dance to; in B 178 the verb *haue* is two-way-facing, the subject being either *Adam...Moses* or *Mercy* (with sense either 'obtain' or 'take'). *Moises*: making clear that *Spes* was always to be understood as a *figura* of the hope of salvation from sin offered by the Commandments, rather than the 'historic' Moses who saw the vision of the 'promised land' [of heaven] but never entered it (he is still in Limbo). **183a** '[For wrath is in his indignation; and life in his good will]. In the evening weeping shall have place: and in the morning gladness' (Ps 29:6)'; to be read in the context of vs 4,

where the psalmist's praise of God for 'saving his soul from hell' makes the psalm especially apt for the vigil of Easter, the time of the action to be narrated. **187** As the office of condemning man was granted to the two elder sisters Justice and Truth, so that of 'saving' him is to the two younger. The rôle of Mercy and Peace as speakers for the defence is very explicit in the revised form of 186–7. *maynprisen*: see on 2.208, and the valuable discussion in Keen 2002:91–4. **190** *patente*: the New Covenant 'sealed' in Christ's blood and sent to Peace as an open letter to all mankind; fulfilling (as well as ratifying) that of *Spes* at 19.12, it is the same *acquitaunce* relied on by Patience at B 14.190*a* (not in // **C**). In keeping with the episode's pervasive 'legal' character, the patent combines the language of a charter of enfeoffment (offering entry to heaven) with the action of a writ of mainprise (offering the prerequisite release from hell), the first clause (190b) making the grant, the second (191b) the warranty (Keen 2002:91); see further Steiner 2000:106–7. **191** *In... requiescam*: 'In peace in the selfsame I will sleep and I will rest' (Ps 4:9); the understood referent of 'selfsame' is presumably 'the presence of God', and Love's letter is properly addressed to *Peace* because Love itself is what HC called the 'plant of peace, most precious of virtues' (1.147). Sung at Compline in Lent and (divided as versicle and response) at Matins on Holy Saturday (*Pe*), the verse denotes in its liturgical context Christ's own 'rest' in the tomb before his resurrection, and thus stands as an analogue to the imperfect *requies* of the just in Limbo, which is soon to become *pax* (the vision of God in heaven). **191** *And...duyre*: 'And to guarantee the lasting validity of this document'. There may be a pun on two polysemes of *dede*, since an 'action' (Christ's crucifixion) is what has permanently validated the 'document', and his sacrificial death needs no repeating (I Pet 3:18). **192–3** The tone of pitying incredulity, together with her condescending use of 'low' terms (*rauen, dronke, chewe*) suggests an elder sister convinced of her superior rationality and (taking into account Mercy's appeal to 'experience' at 153), the sheer weight of cause-and-effect ('if...then'). At 193 she repeats as a question what Truth stated at 147. **195** *bigynnynge...world*: a superficially puzzling phrase that echoes 19.113 and contains an implication unknown to the speaker. *doem*: the valid (but incomplete) OT view (Gen 2:17) of the divine plan for man. **197** *downriht*: the adverb here perhaps answering to Vg's emphatic *morte morieris* 'die the death'. Though there is only one *deth of kynde* (natural death), the speaker may imply *peyne perpetuel* (spiritual death) as well: the forfeiture not just of immortality (as in *Purity* 245–6) but of *any* hope of reconciliation with God after the loss. *euere*: a revision of **B**'s more accurate (and moderate) *after* 'as a result' that highlights Righteousness's imperfect understanding of even the Old Law, making her anticipate verbally

Lucifer at 303–4 and, more generally, the *Spiritus Iusticie* of 21.299–310 (which while acting *euene trewe* acts only *eueneforth his knowyng*). **199–200** The internal rhyme in the b-verse and the emphatic pararhyme in the next a-verse underline the catechetical tone (Peace responds in kind at 225). **201** *loue*: a concession to Mercy's claim that Love is the power behind *ȝone lihte*, but also an assertion that the Fall was a wilful abandonment of that Love for a different teaching and love. **203–6** have strong associations with the language of the courts, and figure the two elder sisters as judges sitting on the bench to proclaim the law of heaven's King in all its rigour (*resoun, recorde, preyer, boteles bale*). **204** *is*: better than *be*, since they are not passing the sentence but recalling it.

207–37 *Peace's plea* **207** *preye*: 'petition'; its substance is the necessity, for both man (214) and (somewhat surprisingly) for God (216), of first-hand knowledge of suffering and death, and the verb *witen* is repeated ten times in Peace's speech. The same ground appealed to by Mercy at 153 is now supported and ratified by God's own wish to know *kyndeliche* 'through experience' (i.e. in his Son the man Jesus). The claim that such 'knowledge by contraries' (happiness, repletion, colour, light, wealth) is part of the divine plan is now extended *analogice* in the manner of the preacher, more than *logice* in that of the clerk, from the sensory domain (where the analogy is persuasive) to the moral (where it is doubtful). For Peace's argument risks blurring the distinction between God's choosing to experience what he is free to and man's choosing to know what he was forbidden to. **210** *woet*: 'really understands'. **212–13** take up (in inverted order) B 10.435, which is omitted at that point in revision. **213** scans either as Type Ia on |w|, with mute key-stave, or as an extended Type III on vowels with counterpoint on |w| and main stresses on *álle* in both halves. **216** is best scanned as a Type IIIc on vowels and |s| or as a Type Ie with blank second stave (*God*) and mute third stave. *ysoffred of*: 'undergone experience of'; contrasted with 'consented' in 222, 228, but both occurrences intimating 'suffered' (231, though even here not explicitly). **217** *wist*: the 'limitation' on God's capacity arising from his unlimitedness (i.e. it is impossible to God *as* God); but that this is not absolute is shown by the fact (and arguably necessity) of the Incarnation. *sour...*: an apt metaphor, since death came in from tasting fruit. **222** *sorwe of deynge*: thereby identifying entirely with Adam's race, since to be human is to have to die. The scriptural basis for the doctrine of Christ's *kenosis* 'self-emptying' to take the form of one 'enslaved' to death is Phil 2:6–11. **224** is unusual in replacing a macaronic line (if with one of somewhat weightier import). *moreyne*: the plague-image well suggesting the suddenness of the encounter with Death, and recalling so early a passage as A 12.81ff. The knowledge that we must die may teach us to live with restraint even more effectively than will want

(*modicum*). **224** *mete with*: 'encounter', as at 18.182, but in B 215 possibly with some play on the sense 'equate' (MED s.v. *meten* v. (1)), as at B 4.143. Peace offers a negative version of HC's 'measure is medicine': learning the evil of *too much* ('sin') through experience of *too little* ('suffering'). **225** has internal rhyme modelled on the Latin 'Leonine' line as at Pr 152–7. **227** *hym*: an emphatic 'popular' pleonastic use; see *MES* 137–8. *furste*: an important addition indicating that the Fall was part of God's providential plan. **229** *ther-thorw*: i.e. by 'felyng', as God, who knows only *wele*, will come to know *wo*. The final answer to the Dreamer's quest for direct knowledge of God is found in this assurance of God's direct knowledge of Man: *wyte* becomes *kyndeliche to knowe* 'to know by experience / as in itself it really is' through the intermediary of *fele*. **230** *auntred*: a resumption of the chivalric metaphor introduced at 14. The Son's becoming Man involves a transformation of all the categories, since this is an 'auntur' that cannot be lost, and can be 'won' only by losing. (On L's use of the chivalric metaphor see Gaffney 1931, Waldron 1986 and Warner 1996). *Adames kynde*: more specific than *mankynde* in stating that Christ is the 'second Adam'. **231** God's 'knowledge' in heaven of man's suffering on earth is not yet a *kynde knowynge*, but it is what makes him desire such *knowynge*. However, the Incarnation seems hardly conceivable without 'pre-compassion' on the part of the Son, in whose image man was made (cf. the tone of 372). *in...places*: the adverbial phrase qualifying 'God's knowing', not 'Adam's suffering.' **233** *þat*: with antecedent *he* 232. **233a** See at 3.489. The application of this injunction to Christ is audacious but encouraging, since he can actually fulfil it. **234–7** are richly paradoxical: folly 'teaches', Peace proclaims the necessity of war, and men must lack prosperity to understand it. The 'Platonic' pun in 237 builds on the popular etymology that understood the exclamation *wei-la-wei* as meaning 'weal away'.

a¹ **238–68** The *Book episode* continues the fusion of comic and sublime, 'personifying' not an idea but an object (it has an article at 245), as in the prosopopœia of the OE Riddles and *The Dream of the Rood*. Yet this 'book' is the loftiest of all, God's own word, here *holiwrit* in its wider sense of both Scripture and patristic tradition (MED s.v. (a) and (b)), the latter especially as preserved in the service-books of the Church. **238** *two brode yes*: symbolising the Old and New Testaments, the literal and spiritual levels of interpretation (Kaske 1959:127), or (recalling Alan of Lille *In Cant. Cantic.* on the two eyes of the BVM) the active and the contemplative lives (*PL* 210:81). See also White 1995. **239** *bolde*: 'audacious' and 'forthright', as his oath and first words prove. **240** *Goddes body*: a common 'great oath', often with eucharistic reference (MED s.v. *bodi* n. 5), and not a little incongruous in a *beaupere*'s mouth. *bere witnesse*: an assertion that gains authority from the custom of swearing oaths on the Bible in court. **241** *blased a sterre*: see Mt 2:1–10. The verb has hitherto been used only in the torch-simile in 19.189, which re-surfaces in the echo of 19.260–1 at 248. **242** *That*: 'of such a kind that'. **243** *Bethleem þe citee*: (Lk 2:4); a word-order common in ME with ancient cities (*CT* I 939, VII 2147). **244** *saue*: as told to the shepherds in Lk 2:11 (the prophecy made to the 'wise' in Mt 2:2 was of a king). But the earlier Christmas narrative at 14.84–98 (verbally recalled at 249b) likewise unites as a single manifestation of *claritas Dei* 'God's radiance' (Lk 2:9) the appearances of the star to the Magi and of the angels to the shepherds, which are found severally in Mt and Lk. **245** The elements' witness to the Saviour's birth goes back to St Gregory the Great's C6th commentary on Mt 2:1–2 (Kaske 1959:119); their witness at Christ's death is found in Pope St Leo's Sermon 8 on the Passion, read as the ninth lesson in the third nocturn of Matins on Good Friday: *unam protulerunt omnia elementa sententiam* 'all the elements gave unanimous judgement'. In recalling HC's reference to the elements at 1.17, the line effectively links the divine work of creation (246) with that of redemption (244), revealing how the events that attest Christ's godhead extended from his birth through his ministry to his passion and death. *hereof*: effectively, 'to his divinity.' **246** *God...wrouhte*: acknowledging the Jesus who was to be put to death as being the divine VERBUM through whom 'omnia...facta sunt' (Jn 1:3). *welkene*: the 'upper air' or aether of the region above the moon; sometimes used for the element of 'pure fire', as in the listing of all four at B 17.161 (MED s.v. *ether* n.) but not here, where it denotes 'air'. **247** *Tho...*: the angels, whose association with the star relates to **L**'s running-together of the complementary Lucan and Matthean accounts of Christmas and Epiphany. *stella comata*: the specially-created 'long-haired star' (*stellam eius* 'comet' 14.97), understood in medieval interpretation as what the Magi saw (*ME Sermons* 227, cit. Alf*Q* 111; clearly thus depicted by Giotto *c.* 1305 in Schiller I pl.288). **248** See 19.261, which uses the same mute stave *to*. **249** The divine 'torch' inevitably suggests the 'High Holy Ghost' (14.84–5) who splits heaven so that Love can leap out 'into this low earth' (see the dove-nativities in Schiller I 183, 198 of mid-14th and early 15th c.). **250** *druye*: a small addition serving to link the Redeemer's subjection of the water under his feet with the Creator's mastering of the waters in Gen 1:9, Ex 14:29, 15:8. **253** 'Lord, [if it be thou], bid me come to thee upon the waters' (Mt 14:28). St Peter's words ironically contrast him with Christ, since he *fails* to walk on the water. **254–5** The sun's refusal to look on her creator's suffering is a major motif in Latin and vernacular devotional writing (Schmidt 1983[2]:185–88). In medieval iconography the sun is more usually depicted as a man and the moon as a woman (e.g. Schiller

II pls. 381, 385); that *sonne* is feminine here (*heresulue*) and elsewhere in later ME (Schmidt ibid. p. 187) may be a survival from OE literary tradition (*MES* 46n1). **256** *heuynesse*: the earth's, though the syntax allows it to be Christ's, and *soffre* to be both transitive and intransitive. The choice of word mutedly echoes (by way of an 'anti-pun') the 'love-heaviness' of I 148–9. **257** recalls 63 above. *quyk*: an eschatological, not animistic suggestion, evoking the Pauline idea of the whole creation 'groaning' in anticipation of the final consummation of things (Rom 8:93). But it seems appropriate enough that a 'wide world' held in the hand of the Trinity (B 17.159–62) should 'quake' when that hand is 'herte...in the myddes' (19.153). **258** *helle*: not mentioned in Mt 27:51; but the conjunction with *roches* 257 may be a recollection of the 'rock' and 'gates of hell' in Mt 16:18, the death of Christ being the birth of the Church that will continue his work of subduing Satan's kingdom. *holde~tholede*: the sonorous internal rhyme bringing out the profound theological antithesis between Christ's power and his suffering. **259** *Symondes sones*: named in *GN* as Carinus and Leucius (Lentinus) and identified as the sons of Simeon, the 'just and devout' old man who utters the *Nunc dimittis* in Lk 2:29–32. Raised at Christ's descent into Hell (which immediately follows the moment of his death and therefore implies they were among the *dede men* of 64 above), it is their written account of the events that is claimed as the source of the *GN*. **259a** '[And he had received an answer from the Holy Ghost], that he (*sc.* Simeon) should not see death [before he had seen the Christ of the Lord]' (Lk 2:26). Simeon's privilege is mirrored in that of his sons, who are released *from* Death at the moment of Christ's death. For the positioning of this verse here cf. *EN* (Latin A) XVIII:2. **260** *hit*: that the elements' witness proves Jesus 'Christ, and Christ God's son' (55). **261** *Iesus (Gigas)...geaunt*: a description that presents Christ's breaking down of Hell-gates as a typological fulfilment of Samson's carrying-away the Gates of Gaza (Jg 16:3; see Anderson fig. 11, Schiller II pls. 428, 488 from *c.* 1370, Kaske 1968:168). Kaske 1957 finds a reference to the common interpretation of Ps 18:6–7 ('Exsultavit ut *gigas* ad currendam viam; a summo caelo egressio eius') as referring to Christ's indomitability and more-than-human origin and nature. *gyn*: glossed for **B** 'siege-engine (figurative)' in MED s.v. *ginne* n. 4(a); but unless the allusion is to his cross, there is probably a polysemantic pun on sense 2 (a) 'trick, ruse'. For Christ's victory is not, like Samson's, a feat of physical strength but (in apparent weakness) one of superior wisdom, and his *gyn* (< L. *ingenium* 'intellect') is 'his double nature, true God and true man...whence he is called a *Giant*' (Hugh of St Cher, 6.138v, cit. Alf*Q* 111). **264** *brente*: alluding perhaps to heretics' punishment for teaching false doctrine (cf. Anima at B 15.83), and assuredly 'condign' for any *book* found to tell lies (cf. *CT* III 790–1). *bote*: 'unless' (Donaldson 1966:265–6) as against 'but' (Kaske 1959:136). *to lyue*: 'to life' (Kaske ib. 134–5; considered by Wittig 1986 an infinitive, but this is the same construction as at 398). Donaldson takes the verbs in B 255–6 as 'subjunctives, becoming infinitives [at 257]' (ib. 269); but both verbs in B 257=C 266 may be intransitive, with 'will' understood and their respective senses 'become dislocated' and 'split apart' (svv. 1b(a); 3(a)). **B 255** No reason appears for this line's excision, unless that the risen Christ possessed *more* than 'man's' powers, and a special reference to his mother seemed otiose (the Gospels do not mention an appearance to her). **266** *ioye vnioynen*: a 'Platonic' play on near-homophones, suggesting that since true joy 'gynneth dawe' from faith in Christ's divine power, the false 'joy' of his adversaries will come apart like a badly made piece of furniture (the MED gloss 'destroy' s.v. is too imprecise, given the conjunction with *vnlouken*). **267** *And bot*: still dependent on the main verb in 264a; Book is solemnly foretelling their destruction and damnation unless they believe. *newe lawe*: not itself a Biblical phrase but corresponding to *testamentum novum*, the 'new covenant' that supersedes the old (Heb 8:8 [citing Jer 31:31], 22).

269–70a provide a second skilful *transition* (cf. 113–15), this time from the debate outside to the debate inside hell. Somewhat confusingly, from the standpoint of infernal geography the *Limbo Patrum* where the just are held is now envisaged as enclosed by the Devil's walls, as if in an outer courtyard, whereas earlier it had seemed a territory adjacent to (but under the sway of) hell. **270a** 'Lift up your gates, O ye princes', [and be ye lifted up, O eternal gates' (Ps 23:7). In the dialogue between Christ and Satan at B 315–19a (a major casualty in the revision to C) the remaining verses of this royal processional psalm are drawn upon, vividly evoking the liturgy of Holy Saturday, when Ps 23 was sung in the second nocturn at Matins. The psalm's 'palace gates' are conflated with the *portae inferi* of Mt 16:18 (so *EN* A. XXI:1) and the 'brazen gates' of *EN* A 21.2 (*LA* 244).

(b) 271–94 describe in ironically physical terms the *Defence of Hell*. **271** The theme of 'the Light of Christ' (*Lumen Christi*) is dominant in the vigil service of Easter (especially the canticle *Exultet*), which is insistently echoed: 'This night, of which it is written [cf. Ps 138:13]: And the night shall be lit up like the day [*nox...illuminabitur*]'. The phrase's more distant allusion is to the lightning and thunder (the most familiar combination of 'voice' and 'light') in Ex 19:16, which herald a theophany. More immediately, it recalls the *vocem virtutis* of Ps 67:34, the voice of God resounding in Job 37:2–4, and shaking the doors in Is 6:3–4, and the *vocem magnam* proclaiming the Devil's defeat and Christ's triumph in Apoc 12:10. The *liht* / *Lucifer* opposition (as at 359) seems deliberate,

if B 1.112 // is recalled (cf. the *York* 'Fall of the Angels' 49–50). **272** *Principes*: the Latin investing Christ's command with a liturgical solemnity that heightens its irony; hereafter, the true *Princeps* 'speaks no more Latin'. **273b** translates the Latin quoted at B 318 and omitted in // C. **274** *Satoun*: a character elsewhere in *PP* presumed identical with the chief of the rebel angels (and cf. *N-Town* Passion I, 1–3), but here *distinguished* from 'Lucifer' as one of three (or possibly four) major fiends who may be meant to 'correspond' to the Daughters of God. In *EN* A. XX.3 (and *LA* p. 243, which is based on it) Satan is *princeps et dux mortis* and doubtless identical with Lucifer (Marx 1997:244–5). *Helle*: answering to *Inferus*, a personification of the place as in *EN* (deriving from Apoc 20:13–14); but here seemingly a metonymic title for a major devil, possibly Lucifer, who replies at 295 (on the devil's names see further Russell 1984:247–9). **275** Satan presumably means not that Christ's glorified soul entered hell in the days of his flesh but that he recognises coming from this 'lyht' the same 'stif vois' (B 15.593) he once heard summon Lazarus. (On the relation of the latter's raising from 'the pains of hell' [*Towneley* XXXI 204] with the Harrowing of Hell, see Pilkinton 1975:51–3). **277** Christ's assault is seen as like that of a medieval king besieging the gates of a fortified city, and the martial imagery of the added passage 281–94 (recalled in *Paradise Lost* VI 570ff) heightens the ironic incongruity of the devils' material defence against so irresistible a force as light and the purely spiritual 'lord' it manifests. Satan's military tactic is to provide inner protection for the chief devils, and to station lesser fiends on the battlements to do the fighting. **278** *per...is*: presumably heaven (which is what Christ intends), though Satan seems unaware that Lazarus is in the world of the living. *lihtliche*: 'easily', but with an unintentionally humorous homophonic pun on the effortless ease with which the heavenly *liht* performs its office. **279** *parled*: a word possibly introduced by **L** from OF. **280** The main allusion is to Isaiah's great prophecy, quoted in part at 20.366 (see at 7.133a). **281–4** introduce a note of grotesque comedy suggesting affinities with (and possibly influence from) the way in which this episode was treated in the earliest Miracle Plays (these are not extant, but cf. the early C15th *York* XXXVII = *Towneley* XXV). **281** *Ragamoffyn*: found only here as a contemptuous name for a lesser demon, with the etymological sense 'ragged lout', and once earlier as a surname (MED s.v.). *barres*: the *vectes ferreos* of *EN* [A] XXI.1. **282** *Belial*: from the Hebrew for 'wickedness' or 'destruction'; an ancient name for a false god, but used of the Devil in this addition's probable source II Cor 6:14–15: 'Or what fellowship hath *light* with darkness? And what concord hath Christ with *Belial*?' He appears in the Miracle Plays (e.g. *N-Town* 23/5), and this insertion may be a response to contemporary readers'

'Who he?' on first encountering B 322. *beelsyre*; *dame*: the notion of 'families' among demons further heightening the parodic inversion of the Daughters; perhaps suggested by *filii Belial* at Deut 13:13 where, however, the referent is human (cf. *kyn* at 288). **284** *blente*: see Mercy's words at 140; the devils who dwell in 'darkness and dread' fear as a destructive weapon the light that mankind will welcome (cf. the ironic echo of *blente* 284 in *blende* 292). **285** perhaps refers to movable wooden louver-slats worked from below with a chain. **286** evokes a castle in the latest style: hell's dungeon is an inverted version of the Tower of Truth. *louer*: (< Fr *l'ouvert*), 'a lantern-like structure placed on the roof over the central hearth, with side openings for the escape of smoke' (Wood 1965:277; and see Salzman 1966:219–22). An early C15th louver survives at Lincoln College, Oxford (*RCHM Oxford* pl. 121). *loupe*: cited in MED s.v. n. (2) (a) as 'loophole...for the protection of archers, gunners. etc' (as at *SGGK* 792). But the word's conjunction here with *louer* (MED s.v. *lovere* n. (1)) suggests that this (earliest) example should instead come under (b) 'an opening for ventilation, a louver' (effectively a synonym); for if the devils are to hide *inside* in darkness, it is light coming from above (not through battlement-loopholes) that they would fear. **287–8** The internal and end-rhymes underline the sense of ritualised panic. **287** *Astarot*: originally 'the (moon)-goddess of the Sidonians' (III Kgs 11:33), usually coupled with Baal among the 'strange gods', as in Jg 2:13; a devil-name found in the Miracle Plays (*Towneley* XXV 107). **288** *Coltyng*: an unparalleled devil-name, probably invented as a patronymic (< *colt* + *-yng*) for this expendable 'fiendling'. *kyn*: 'tribe', extending the relational metaphor of 282. **289–94** describe forms of artillery, old and new, deployed against a supposed force of besiegers (Poole I pl. 12b). **289** *Brumstoen*: sometimes used in repelling sieges (*Siege of Jerusalem* 675), and abundant in hell's 'stagno ardenti igne et sulphure' (Apoc 21:8) to provide explosive materials for the cannon (the resemblance of which to hell-mouth needed no spelling out). *boylaunt brennyng*: two juxtaposed participles, the first with the rarer French ending, mimicking the speaker's desperation. **290** An ironic recall of the bold *transsumptio* at 15.143–4. **291** *bowes of brake*: 'cross-bows of the largest size and strongest tension' (*Sk*), worked by a crank or lever (*brake*); see Poole I fig. 41. *brasene gonnes*: an up-to-date touch, perhaps influenced by knowledge of the King's authorising large supplies of ordnance and ammunition for the Tower in 1382–7 (Poole I 161–2, fig. 48). **292** *sheltrom*: the infantry formation, originally with over-lapping shields and often a wooden platform-cover, which Satan (with comic literalism) expects to be used in the assault. His aim is presumably to smash this, fire the fragments and pick off the attackers as they run out and stumble on the iron obstacles. **293** *Mahond*: popularly

thought to be a pagan deity (*Towneley* IX 9, 122), but for **L** another devil-name (MED s.v. 1 (d)), at 18.151 translating Vg *demonium*. *mangonel*: heavy artillery piece like the *trébuchet* (Poole I fig. 42).

295–349a Since it is no use physically resisting Christ, Lucifer's ultimate 'line of defence' is *legal*: his 'rights' over a mankind justly condemned for sin and sentenced to die and go to hell for ever. According to the main Patristic 'devil's rights' theory of atonement, the Devil had been granted (B 283) possession of mankind after Adam's sin. This could be lawfully removed only if he tried to seize a sinless soul (the 'abuse of power' theory as formulated in Augustine *De Trin.* XIII [*PL* 42:1025–31]) *or* if such a soul were offered in place of the souls of men (the 'ransom' theory). Marx (1995) holds that this theory was modified rather than repudiated in the new 'atonement' theory of Anselm (*Cur Deus Homo*), who argued that since the Devil had deceived man, he had no right of possession over man, only (as argued by Simpson 1990:213), the power of a gaoler allowed him by God in respect of man's enthralment to sin. The aim of the Incarnation was that Christ should win back ('redeem') mankind from the Devil and effect a reconciliation ('atonement') between God and man. The 'compensation' (*amendes* B 18.343) he offers is not to the Devil (who has no true right to it) but to God (the 'satisfaction' theory). Marx 100–13 shows that while **L** is familiar with the older theory (as found in *EN*), he is basically in accord with the Anselmian understanding. This view has been vigorously disputed by Green (1999:362), who considers the notion of Lucifer's 'title' to mankind as unfounded not a rejection of but 'a weak form' of the pre-Anselmian soteriology. However, as Simpson convincingly maintains (1990:215), Langland does not promote but 'does, nevertheless, shape his narrative around [the 'Devil's rights'] theory, precisely as a way of refuting it, and...insisting on the legal aspect of the Atonement'. **297** echoes (with rich dramatic irony) 19.20, where *Spes* proclaimed how obeying God's law is the perfect protection against death. **298** *perelles*: i.e. the moral trap of being called a tyrant (in over-ruling his own law). **299** *robbeth*: ironically exposing his lack of self-understanding. *maistrie*: i.e. force, like the king's use of 'prerogative' to overrule the ordinary courts' judgement (rather than to supplement the insufficiency of existing precedent for the just settlement of a particular claim). But unbeknown to him, the word accurately predicts Christ's 'mastery' of the very legal argument Lucifer relies on. **300** *riht... resoun*: 'a well grounded right in law'. Lucifer's appeal is to the common-law principle of unevadable precedent (endorsed by Truth and Righteousness), implicitly as against those of equity (in its embryonic beginnings in the court of Chancery), which invoked a wider concept of fairness in judgement (Birnes 1975; Kennedy 2003). **301**

A claim contested by Christ at 372 below. *bothe...ille*: the devil's own excessive claim already (unintentionally) creating space for an 'equitable remedy'. **303–5** repeat Righteousness's words at 196–8; so Lucifer's claim might seem strong (see Simpson 1990:214–16). **304** *here dwelle euere*: Lucifer's 'unwrast' interpretation of the *þretynge* in Gen 2:17, the correct one being God's in 3:19 (which pronounces death, not eternal punishment). **309** *sesed*: a legal term; on the devil's 'seisin', see Alford 1977:944–5. *seuene thousand*: a figure perhaps metrically determined; usually (in relation to the supposed date of the Fall) 4000 (see Gray, *Selection*, no.2) or 4,600 (*York* 'Harrowing' 39–40, *Towneley* XXV 27–8)). **310** *neuere...now*: a misunderstanding of the law (as Christ makes clear at 375), which gives Lucifer no such 'right'. Consequently, the precedent he appeals to (the essence of customary law) and its length (something of weight in medieval courts) are irrelevant (see further Alford 1977²). **B 282** *Soopnesse*: see on 2.200; perhaps not formally a personification so much as a definition. **311** echoes Book's words at 240; despite the irony of the Father of Lies relying on God's veracity, the absolute truth of Scripture was common ground between all medieval disputants.

312–49a Save 312–13, 329–31, 335–7 these lines (divided between Satan, Gobelyn and a 'Devil' who may be Lucifer) are extensively revised in both substance and expression. **312** *That*: the precise antecedent being perhaps their long possession, which is certainly a fact. *doute*: a small revision allowing the fruitful double sense that the reason for Satan's 'fear' is the 'dubiety' of the devils' case. **314** *on his londe*: Lucifer has committed trespass as well as fraud. **316** is more elegantly expressed than B 288, which misleadingly suggests (*hem*) and then denies (*hirselue*) that Satan tempted Adam. **316a** 'Woe to him that is alone: [for, when he falleth, he hath none to lift him up]' (Eccl 4:10); referred to Eve's supposed wilfulness in going off by herself, so that she was alone when the Devil tempted her (cf. Milton, *PL* IX 380ff). **317** *aftur to knowe*: 'that after [eating the fruit] they would know'. **318** paraphrases Gen 3:5, 318b ironically repeating 301b, which states the consequences of their 'knowledge'. **319** *treson and tricherie*: 'falsity and deceit' (as in *SGGK* 4–5), given the known intention of the tempter here (and at 323). But part of his 'promise' was undeniably fulfilled, in that their eyes were opened, though they also died the death (Gen 3:4–7). *troyledest*: a rare verb (< OF *troiller*), elsewhere only in the *Trental of St Gregory* (c. 1350) 1, 11: '[Þe fend] *truyled* hire wiþ his tricherye'. **320** *bíhéstes*: a very striking 'monolexical' b-half (see *Intro.* IV § 38). **322** Arguably this line should be given to the same speaker in **B**. *gyle*: a word that with its derivatives echoes insistently round the walls of hell through the rest of the passus. **323** *Gobelyn*: already a proper name c. 1325 ('Of Rybaud3', in Wright, *Political Songs* 1839:238), but adapted from a

word of unknown etymology meaning a demon or incubus. Wenzel (in Alford 1988:163) relates him to 'a demon popularly called *goblin*' in *FM* VII.16 who specialised in leading travellers astray; but his rôle here seems too important for 'a puckish sprite'. In B 294 'the Devil' could have been meant to be distinct from Gobelyn, and the change of *Certes* to *Forthy* at C 325 provides the latter a more heroic function as executive officer in the field, while Lucifer (who originally tempted Eve) now lurks in headquarters planning a counter-attack. **324** *trewe title*: valid legal claim, *titulus iuris* (AlfG). Alford (1977²:945) notes that Gobelyn's point is that of a canonist, recognising that the devils do not possess man 'in good faith' but through fraud. *maketh*: 'invalidates it'. **325** *Treuthe*: God's first nature-name (see at Pr 15), now derived to the Son *e deitate Patris*. **326** The exquisite irony in God's 'deception' of Lucifer arises from his assuming the likeness of his own likeness (cf. Gen 1:27), whereas Lucifer's was performed under the disguise of another species. Where God's 'sleight' honours man, Lucifer's debases the serpent. **327** *in...weye*: 'in the form of a man' / 'in carrying out his plan of action' (cf. *way* at 298). **328** *gome*: on the *s*-less positional genitive see *MES* 72–3. **329** *thritty*: cf. *HH* 74–5 and see on 136. **331** *askede... answere*: during the Temptations in the desert (Mt 4:3–10). Gobelyn alludes to the recognition of Christ's divine origin by 'unclean spirits' (Mk 3:11–12) whom he commanded 'not to make him known'. The text suggests that for **L**, God's 'deception' is to make the fiends see Jesus simply as a holy man whose good work must be frustrated (though in **C**, Gobelyn's suspicions (333) make him more active in seeking to prevent Christ's death). **B 299–300** *slepynge*: a notable early 'hanging participle'; the speaker of course went to Pilate's wife ('Claudia Procula') in *her* slumber, not his (L perhaps remembering Gobelyn's original nature as an incubus who pressed down upon his sleeping victim). The story, an elaboration of Mt 27:19 that ironically ascribes the Roman governor's and his wife's scruples to (unsuccessful) diabolic intervention, earns a play to itself in the York Miracle cycle (XXX, ll.158–76; see Kolve 1966:228–30). *done*: 'make of' (= kind of), here with uninfl. gen. (*MES* 86). **333b** repeats 19.236b.

341–49a are spoken by Satan (cf. 350), who is distinct from Gobelyn and Lucifer, and improve in clarity on B 306–14. **342** *grete lihte*: the *lucem magnam* of Is 9:2 (qu. Mt 4:16). The association of Christ's soul with the divine *Shekinah* or 'glory' evokes such texts as Ezech 43:2 and esp. Heb 1:3, which describes him as 'splendor gloriae et figura substantiae [Dei]'. **344** *abyde...sihte*: cf. Ps 5:6. **345–7** See on B 1.111–19; the C revision at that point omits the 'lies' motif for a digression on 'northern men'. **349a** 'Now shall the prince of this world be cast out' (Jn 12:31); spoken by Christ here in *EN*, and cited in a ser-

Commentary

mon of Pope Leo read in Lesson 8 at Matins on Good Friday. This may be a free-standing 'speakerless' quotation like 438a below; but it is ironically piquant to have Satan cite an (as yet unwritten) scripture against Lucifer (*princeps huius mundi* is used of the Devil at 10.135 and in a separate unparalleled text at A 10.62). The devils are not to be cast out of hell or even banned from the terrestrial region, but to lose their uncontested dominion over it.

350–69 350–8 The lively digression on liars may have been prompted by reflecting on 'dishonest' utterances of clergy and lawyers that were thought to have encouraged the commons' violent action against royal and ecclesiastical authority in the Rising of 1381. But it reduces the intensity of the scene and loses some splendid alternating Latin / English lines that make **B** read almost like a liturgical drama. **352** *at þe laste*: on Judgement Day. *lyares here*: 'people who tell pernicious falsehoods in this life'. **354** virtually repeats 9.51, again in a context of final judgement. **356a** 'Thou hatest all the workers of iniquity: thou wilt destroy all that speak a lie' (Ps 5:7). **357–8** This disarming interjection lowers the tone by comparison with **B**, but is perhaps aesthetically defensible as a *reculer pour mieux sauter* before the sublime scene to follow. **B 316–19a** *Quis...virtutum*: 'Who is this [King of Glory? The Lord of hosts, he is] the King of Glory' (Ps 23:10); quoted in *EN* 21:3, *LA* 244 where David (its supposed author) answers Hell's question. The great royal processional psalm, usual at Prime on Mondays, was sung at Matins on Holy Saturday (see vss 7–10 entire). **360** *lord*: Lucifer's use of the title (repeated three times before 371) tacitly recognises his coming defeat. **361** translates *virtutum* concisely but omits **B**'s wordplay for the dismaying affirmation anticipated at 342. **362** *Dukes... place*: an ironic courtesy from 'the King's Son'; cf. Alan of Lille's 'O vos *principes tenebrarum*, attollite portas...' (*PL* 210:907), 'duke of dethe' (*GN* 1453). *anoen*: more urgent than *prest* at 272 above. *ȝates*: Alan (ibid.) interprets *portas* as 'potestas diaboli qua detinebat captivos in inferno'. **363** *Kynges...Heuene*: see on 2.2. **364** *breth*: a metonym for 'spoken word' (as at 15.263) but directly implying that Christ blew the gates in; see B 5.495–6 and Z 5.39, which **L** seems to draw out of his 'repertory'. **366** *populus...*: see on 7.133a. **367** *Ecce...*: the Baptist's prophecy at 18.269a now fulfilled. **368** *Lucifer...ablende*: echoing 7.134 so as to bring out the circling recurrence of the liturgical cycle based on the solar year.

370–446 *Christ's vindication of the Redemption* A direct speech of Christ to the Devil is not found in *EN* or *GN* but in the ME *Harrowing*, which is virtually a drama. The indebtedness of **L**'s feudal language to Grosseteste's treatment is emphasised by Waldron (1986:79–80). **370–1** *soule(s)* and *bothe*: to be read with stresses in each line. The repetition is ripe with irony: for it is Christ's possession of a human body and soul through his Incar-

nation that will enable him to dispossess Satan of his supposed 'right' over man. *to saue*: the change in sense from B 329 defers the outcome till the end of Christ's speech. **372** *þe bet*: '(the) better for that / than you.' **373** *resoun...mysulue*: 'simple justice and my own edict'. **374** The verbal repetition of B 280 in B 332 is here avoided by rewriting of the latter as C 305. **375** forms the crux of the legal issue: Lucifer (like Daughter Truth at 145–51a) has misconstrued a 'point of law', the nature of the punishment inflicted by God on man. The correct interpretation awaits the perfectly just judge who is also perfectly equitable through 'wyt[yng] what al wo is' because he 'woet of alle ioye' (233). **376** *dedly synne*: as when 'man turneth his herte fro God...that may nat chaunge... to thyng that may chaunge and flitte' (*CT* X 266, after Augustine *De libero arbitrio* 1.16). This is the sin that brought man death; but the familiar theological term is at once questioned by the speaker's claiming that Adam's sin was not self-suggested, a change that adds precision and removes **B**'s near-repetition of 18.90. **378** *my palays Paradys*: as depicted in the C13th *Mappa Mundi* at Hereford Cathedral (Kaske 1968). **B 338** *lusard*: the shape of the serpent in some iconographic depictions, e.g. the Rheims Cathedral Eve (ill. in Russell 1984:258); **L** may envisage a serpent (378) with hands (cf. Prov 30:28 on the lizard). *a lady visage*: an idea popularised by Peter Comestor (*HS*, Genesis 21): '[the devil] chose some sort of serpent having the face of a girl' (see further Bonnell 1917). In the 'Fall of Man' from the *Très Riches Heures du Duc de Berry* (*c.* 1420) at Chantilly and in the left panel of Bosch's *Haywain* triptych at Madrid (*c.* 1500) the 'visage' resembles Eve's own, and in both the whole upper body is human (and female). **381–2** *Аȝeyne...leue*: 'in defiance of my love [for them] and without my permission to do so.' *Olde...falle*: cf. Prov 28:18, Ps 9:16. *be*: 'should be', as an inference ('based on a sound principle' B 340) from 385a. *gylours...gyle*: on the 'folk-lore' aspect of Christ's trickery of Satan the trickster see Ashley 1982:133–4. **383–5** derive from Ex 21:26–7. **385a** 'Eye for eye, tooth for tooth' (Ex 21:24, inverting the Vg order); the legal principle of retribution (*lex talionis*). **386–7** 'Thus a living man must lose his life when he has destroyed a life, so that one life shall pay for another': see Ex 21:12. In citing this authority, Christ appeals to the law against the prosecutor; on his rôle more of an 'advocate' than judge, see Birnes 1975 and Baldwin 1981[2]. **B 344–5** make explicit that mankind is *owed* to God by Satan (because he was slain by 'Death'), and they come near to stating that Satan 'caused' Man's Fall, rather than merely making it possible by deceiving him into disobeying God. This doctrinally delicate point is abandoned in revision for the simpler and clearer assertion that Christ's life, which was not forfeit for sin, now 'quits' or makes recompense for Satan's (qualified) 'right' to the *justi* in limbo. **388** *Ergo*: a sign that the speaker must defeat the Devil in argument, to show (for an alert and serious readership) that divine authority resides not in sheer power but in true justice ('right and reason' 395). The passage may therefore be understood as robustly affirming God's *potentia ordinata* in the face of contemporary questioning: 'Therefore my soul shall pay for man's, and only (that which is) sin will henceforth go to (the abode of) sin'. This utterance leaves open, as Julian of Norwich would later, whether Hell will *finally* possess any occupants other than the devils for whom it was created, or who created it (see further Watson 1997[2]). **389–90** *mysdede...fordede*: presumably a deliberate echo; Christ will make 'amends' for Adam's disobedience, which empowered Death to destroy (in him and his race) the original entitlement to eternal life that the death of Jesus will now restore. *mysdede*: the preterite is more circumspect than the perfect of B 342, which could suggest that Christ will pay for 'every (person's every) sinful act' (rather than 'the entire consequence of one sinful act') and thus undermine the Samaritan's firm teaching in 19.270–6 by implying that wilful sin without repentance could be overlooked. *to amenden*: a 'predicative infinitive expressive of futurity' (*MES* 525), here replacing a finite future (or perhaps volitional) in B 342 (cf. 2.84, 98ff). **391** *quykie and quyte*: 'give life to and make recompense for'; the satisfaction of the claim of divine justice will be accompanied by the gift of heaven. *queynte*: echoing the 'torch' image in 19.168ff; it is assumed that the just from Adam to the Baptist have sought God's mercy, not rejected it 'wickedly and wilfully' (19.269). **392** spells out, in close correspondence to the following Latin, that God's 'guile' (*grace*), is a deception without deceit. *392a* confirms Mercy's citation of the text at 164*a*; the immediate context of Fortunatus's hymn is relevant to Christ's present claim that his action is just because 'the true order of things demanded that in the work of man's salvation craft should undo the craft exercised by the betrayer in his many shapes.' **393** *aȝeyne þe lawe*: Christ's case being (obliquely) addressed as much to Righteousness (representing a possible theological position: see 195–204) as to Lucifer, both of whom took their stand on strict law. L's closeness to Grosseteste (*Château*, 1068–71) is noted by Waldron 1986:70n8). **394** states that Christ has come only for the just (the 'lege' who lived 'subject to his laws', i.e. obeyed his commandments) and is not acting by *force majeure*. A pun on *souereynliche* by *maistrie* is nonetheless inescapable: Christ *has* exercised 'supreme mastery' in correctly interpreting the divine decree that both he and Lucifer are bound by. **395** *raunsome*: with the root sense of 'release (a prisoner) by payment' here to the fore, since part of Christ's 'gracious guile' is to make the 'payment' of his soul one that Lucifer must accept but cannot keep (for closely similar wit in relation to a

ransom, cf. *WPal* 1248–51: 'But gretly y þonk god þat gart me achape, / & dede þe wante þi wille for þou wrong outest. / but, sire, in þe same seute sett artow nouȝ, / & I am prest þi prisoun to paye þe my ransum'). *my lege*: 'my lawful subjects, [not yours]'; the act observes the laws of chivalry, it is not spoliation following conquest. **395a** 'I am not come to destroy the law but to fulfil' (Mt 5:17); from a passage emphasising observance of the law in its entirety. **396** *grace*: Christ's act being in essence not a deception at all; for since Lucifer's claim to absolute lordship of man (= his eternal *damnation*) is ill-founded, God no more needs to trick him out of it by superior guile than to force him out of it by superior power, but offers man eternal life through pure generosity. **B 351–2, 356** are omitted perhaps because repeating B 337; but the balanced irony of 355, 357 is thereby lost. **397, 398** *and alle*: reminding of the 'apples' on the Tree of Charity at 18.112. *a tre*: see on 142–3; the senses of *a* are at once 'a single' and 'one and the same'. **B 361a** '[He hath opened a pit and dug it]: and he is fallen into the hole he made' (Ps 7:16). The reference has an ironic appropriateness, since the 'pit' (= prison) of hell is presented as a literal not a figurative place. **399–400** The implied figure is of the sea or a tidal river; though dropping the text quotation, C 399 here draws on vs 17 of the same psalm: '*Convertetur* dolor eius in caput eius'. **401–2** The 'bitterness' is the cup of death 'brewed' for the second Adam by the Devil, which Lucifer will now have to drink forever. Cf. the 'cup of death' imagery of the English C14th *Meditations*: 'Of deþes cuppe he [Christ] dronk a drauȝt / þorw which he haþ oure lyf ylauȝt' (881–2) and see the discussion in Ruffing 1991:105–8. **403** *lyf, loue*: not an accidental collocation, since Christ gives those who love him a life that overcomes death (cf. 59), and continues to live in and through those who believe in him. For the equation of love with the essence of the Church as spiritual organism, see on 7.256–7, and on the Latin and vernacular sources and background of the imagery, see Schmidt 1983[2]:181–4. *loue...drynke*: the present image being of (man's) love as something Christ desires (the only drink that will satisfy his divine thirst), but as also implying a reciprocal offer of his love as the *vinum spirituale* 'the hot wine of sweet love' (Rolle, *Incendium* 279; *Mending* 129) that will sustain man's life on earth. **404** *as it semede*: a statement hardly intended to be gnostic but meaning that Christ's death was not the final defeat it appeared to be to his enemies. **405–7** A remarkable addition affirming that Christ died not for the powerful and educated few but for the powerless and ignorant many, identifying himself with the 'pore symple of herte' spoken of by Anima (B 16.8). The a-verse will be echoed by Need at 22.19. **406** *comune coppes...soules*: the image of the *poculum mortis* here undergoing a complete 'sacramental' *transsumptio*, as well illustrated by representations of ECCLESIA holding a cup beneath the wound in Christ's side to collect his blood, such as the mid-C14th 'Jesse Cross' in Schiller II pl. 442. *depe helle*: an ironic reminder to Lucifer that his 'deep clergyse' has been defeated by the 'foolishness' of the cross. **408** *for...sake*: the adverbial phrase going with both preceding verbs, as cause and object respectively. **408a** 'I thirst' (Jn 19:28). The context makes clear that Christ's word on the cross is in fulfilment of the scripture of Ps 68:22; but it is also linked with his words to Peter in Gethsemane (Jn 18:11). The common OT symbol of *thirst* as 'desire for God' seen in Ps 41:3 (which Alan interprets as 'desiderium' in *PL* 210:947) is here transposed to Christ in a striking example of *communicatio idiomatum*. The allegorical interpretation of *sitis* as a 'love-thirst' for the souls of men was developed in devotional and mystical works of the 12–13th c., e.g. in the *Vitis Mystica* of Pseudo-Bernard: 'we believe that his thirst was a most burning desire for our salvation' (*PL* 184:662). The thought is itself genuinely Bernardine, as in the *Meditation on the Lord's Passion and Resurrection*: '*Sitio*, I thirst. For what? For your faith, your salvation, your joy' (*PL* 184:744). **409–10** The added line contrasts worldly values (as emblematised in luxurious beverages) with celestial, providing a prolonged pararhyming chime through *fulle*, *valle* and *vale* that connects Christ's desire for souls with the decisive outcome of his effort at the end of time. **411** *ventage... Iosophat*: 'Yahweh has judged', the name of the valley near Jerusalem where it was believed that the Last Judgement would take place. The prophet's grapes of wrath in the source-text (Joel 3:12ff; cf. Apoc 16:19) on the coming destruction of the wicked are transformed by Christ into a metaphor for God's merciful love towards mankind (see further Lunz 1972). **412** *riht...resurrecio mortuorum*: 'wine newly pressed [from grapes] fully ripened, the resurrection of the dead'; on the English phrase see Wirtjes 1987. *must*: cf. *Vitis Mystica*: '*Musto* quippe illo nobilissimo *charitatis* Dei' (*PL* 184:738). The chief reference is to the figurative 'wine-harvest' at the end of time, when God's plan will reach fulfilment with the rising of the dead for judgement (a scene vividly depicted in an Apocalypse scene from Bodl. MS Auct. D. 4. 17, f. 13r reproduced in Saxl 1942:pl. 32). On this motif the best comment comes at the end of the same work (ch. 46): 'The SPOUSE drinks his own *wine* from the vine in his vineyard, the CHURCH;...drinks the *blood of the ripest grapes*, *the souls of his saints*, pressed and separated from the lees in the wine-press of the cross, in labour and thirst, cold and nakedness, vigils and other spiritual exercises.' The Latin phrase summing up the foundation of Christian belief comes from I Cor 15:12–13 and provides the 11th clause of the Nicene Creed. **413** *kynge...angeles*: alluding to the 'apocalyptic' conception of Christ's Second Coming in glory as an everlasting king (Dan 7:13) and judge (Mk 14:62), with

a crown (Apoc 14:14) and with angels (Mk 8:38). **414** *out...soules*: i.e. 'the souls of all men who are there'; it is not implied that all men are in hell (some would be in purgatory), but that the fate of many coming to judgement remains to be decided. **415** *fendekyns*: a coinage; not perhaps quite an affectionate diminutive, but perhaps a pitying recognition that even minor demons like Ragamuffin from dysfunctional diabolic families (281–2) might have a remote chance of getting out of the pit. **416** The revision of this half-line (like that in 429) does not automatically imply the doctrine of *apocatastasis* or universal salvation, which had been condemned at the Second Council of Constantinople in AD 543; but equally it does not rule out a final offer of grace to the fallen angels as impossible for an all-powerful God. For without trivialising evil or cheapening the cost of redemption, **L** has re-imagined the redemption in terms of the older 'glory-centred' theology of *Christus victor*. The result is a Lord of Life with 'auntrous' and royal qualities that outweigh the period's dominant late-medieval 'passion-centred' theology of *Christus patiens*, which will re-surface dramatically in the final passus. **417** *kynde*: 'very nature', soon glossed 'nature as man'. **418–20** affirm that Christ *may* pardon all men and *will* pardon all baptised Christians. The basis of this (not self-evidently 'orthodox') statement is the intense conviction pervading *PP* that God, as man's 'father and brother' (7.143), cannot be less loving than a human parent or sibling, any more than he can be less just than a human king. Waldron (1986:73) aptly notes the 'reciprocity' between Christ's words here and those of Piers at 8.217–18. **419** *hole brethren*: 'entire brethren', through divine adoption in baptism, as opposed to 'half-brethren' through their shared human nature (see 436 below): humanity makes men brothers of Christ as man; baptism, brothers of Christ as God. For if only the baptized are strictly God's adopted 'children' by grace (Gal 4:5), the Incarnation has established grounds for considering all Adam's offspring Christ's 'brethren' by *nature* (cf. I Cor 15:21–2). **420a** 'To thee only have I sinned' (Ps 50:6). The 'legal' force of this maxim resides in the very nature of sin as an offence against God, which he may remit if he so wishes (and that he does is implied by *Nolo mortem peccatoris* at 14.134a). **421–5** describe a startling appeal to the 'experience' argument invoked by Mercy at 153. **422** *Ofter than ones*: inasmuch as mankind has already suffered one 'hanging' (*death*), and so should not be punished with a second (*damnation*). Now as then it is a principle of the common-law tradition that a person cannot be punished twice for the same offence. **424** *thief*: a change perhaps meant to recall Robert the Robber (6.315–24) and his 'brother' the Good Thief crucified with Christ, the King who indeed gave him (eternal) life when he 'looked on him' (Lk 23:43). *deth oþer iewyse*: 'execution or condemnation to be executed' / 'death or some other punishment' **B** (see *TN* further on the problems of this reading). **425** *Lawe*: here the ancient custom of pardoning a criminal who had survived hanging and had the good luck to have the king pass by; possibly alluding to the pardoning by Edward III of Walter Wynkeburn at Leicester in 1363 (*Sk*). *he...hym*: the respective referents being determinable from 428, though the contextual ambiguity is suggestive. **428** Christ's acceptance of the constraint of human custom (*lawe*) is a measure of how closely the Incarnation identifies him with man. **429** *dede...ille*: an alteration (which can hardly have seemed uncontroversial) appealing less to the notion of God's unlimited power than to the necessary limitedness of all human judgement in ignorance of the sinner's interior state, which is accessible only to God (the best gloss on this is the next two lines). **430–1** recognise that an earthly court cannot pass a perfectly just condemnation, since only an all-knowing judge can consider every mitigating circumstance relevant to equitable judgement of an individual. **430** *Be... abouhte*: 'if it be at all adequately paid for [i.e. by Christ's sacrifice]' (*Pe*) cannot be right, since *enythyng* would be inapplicable to that 'full and perfect sacrifice'. **L** must therefore refer to such people's virtuous acts, which are known to God alone: against the *boldenesse* of their *synne* must be set that of any *beenfetes* (7.263) to their credit. **431** *of*: altering a somewhat opaque original 'through' into 'from out of, on the basis of', which also allows the daring alternative sense 'I have the power to turn my justice into mercy [not arbitrarily, but on taking everything into account]' (cf. 19.196–7 above). *and...trewe*: 'while at the same time preserving the veracity of everything I have said in the Scriptures'. **432** recalls the words of the Pardon (9.286–7). *Holy Writ*: not scripture in the quotation itself, but doubtless evoking texts such as Mt 16:27 or Rom 2:6. *wol*: not implying constraint upon Christ but presuming that his *wordes* and *workes* will accord. *wreke...ille*: cf. 19.270–6. **433** See at 4.140. **434–5** 'And so [though] I wish to take vengeance on wrong-doers, for all my sharp anger [as God], my nature [as man] will exert restraining pressure on my will'. Christ's point is that though man's offence against an infinite God is in a sense 'infinite', he himself as a finite man can only feel a finite anger (*ire* answering to *ira* in the unquoted second part of the text following). *here*: at the place of judgement. **435a** 'O Lord, rebuke me not in thy indignation, [nor chastise me in thy wrath]' (Ps 6:2 and 37:2); another 'speakerless' quotation (the sentiment cannot be Christ's), like the resounding one to follow at 438a. **B 392–3** express a ground of traditional hope (the purgatorial 'work' of suffering that will satisfy justice), replaced in **C** by total reliance on grace. *til...hote*: 'until a command *Spare them* bid it be otherwise'; adapted from the first lesson of the Office for the Dead (Matins, first nocturn), taken from Job 7:16: '*Spare* me, Lord, for my days are nothing' (see Alford

1972). **436** *halue-bretherne*: much more precise than **B**, and with reference presumably to non-Christians, *monye* delimiting those who (like Trajan) lived just lives according to their conscience (cf. Rom 2:14–16). **437–8** 'For while you might see your kinsman go cold and thirsty, you could not behold him bleed without feeling pity' (see on 418–20 above). The passage plays on the 'unspoken' sense of *blood*: Christ, having bled for mankind, can feel compassion for its suffering (cf. *Pearl* 1135–44). **438a** 'I heard secret words which it is not granted to man to utter' (II Cor 12:4). This enigmatic 'speakerless' quotation (on which see Donaldson 1982) is associated in St Gregory's *Moralia* (*PL* 76:630), commenting on Job 39:29, with I Cor 13:12 (Goldsmith 1981:97). If the voice is meant to be the poet-visionary's, the verb's first-person subject identifying him with St Paul would seem to involve allusion to the apostle's privileged 'visions and revelations of the Lord' (II Cor 12:1). The words' content remains mysterious (so they are called 'secret'); but the context implies that they concern the boundlessness of divine mercy, a persistent theme of the poem (19.294–8 anticipate this passage). For a very acute discussion of theological problems arising out of this text see White 1995. **439–40** *in*; *and*: small but crucial revisions linking God's absolute justice with his judgement upon hell (the angels who fell were tempted by one of their own) and his mercy with his incarnation (man fell tempted by a superior spiritual being). **B 398–400** *al mankynde*: not necessarily implying that all men *will* be saved but (if the contrast of *mankynde* and *vnkynde* is related to B 389–90) then certainly 'a hope hanging therein' that they *may* be. **442a** 'Enter not into judgement with thy servant: [for in thy sight no man living shall be justified]' (Ps 142:2); vs 3 following could be spoken by one in hell. **443–5** The intricate verbal patterning (*lawe...low*; *lede... ledis*; *louye(ede)...leued*, with the threefold *l*-alliteration followed by a sudden plosive outburst on *b*) endows with ritual finality Christ's final words to his adversary. **446** *bonde...chaynes*: an action based on Jude 6 which, with II Pet 2:4 (its source), is one of the few NT references to the fate of the rebel angels; cf. the elaboration in *EN* B. 24.4. **447–51** effect a third *transition*, this time from 'deep derk helle' (B 1.115) to the upper region where 'most shene is þe sonne' (455). This is the proper abode of the Four Daughters of God, who are now fully enlightened as to 'what this wonder means' (129) and inspired to share in the heavenly concert. **447** *Astarot*: chief of the 'fiendkins' (see on 287), whose panic recalls the *smale muys* of Pr 166 and Mede's terrified followers at 2.249. **448–9** echo Col 2:15: 'et expolians principatus, et potestates traduxit confidenter, palam triumphans illos in semetipso'. **450** The angels' song that announced the start of Christ's redemptive work (Lk 2:13–14) now marks its completion. **451** '[The angels quake to see / Man from death's doom made free]: Flesh sins, flesh frees from sin; / God reigns, God's flesh within'; from vs 4 of 'Aeterne rex altissime' (for a translation insisting on *dei caro* as 'the humanity, body and soul, of God' cf. Hill 2001:217). Though sung on the vigil of the Ascension, forty days later, it fits well in a scene initiating the *triumphus gratiae* (vs 1) that the feast celebrates.

(c) 452–70 resume the *Debate of the Daughters of God* suspended at 270. Only three speak, but Mercy can afford to remain silent after the eloquence of her spokesman Christ. **452** *of ...note*: 'a song in Latin'. *poetes* (*poesie*): applied by **L** (the first writer to use either) solely to learned Latin poetry, in this case verses by Alan of Lille (see Schmidt 1987[2]:145). **453** *Clarior...amor*: 'Sun after storms often we brighter see, / Love also brighter after enmity'; from Alan's *Liber Parabolorum* (*PL* 210:581–2) and found in this exact form (with *nebula* for correct *nubila*) in the collection *Auctores Octo* (Alf*Q*). The quotation echoes a Biblical verse of some relevance in this context: 'For thou art not delighted in our being lost; because *after a storm* thou makest a calm, and after tears and weeping, thou pourest in joyfulness' (Tob 3:22). **455** *shoures*: with some play on the sense '(storm of) blows, battle' (MED s.v. 5), as in *WPal* 4514: '& many a *scharp schour* for þi sake þoled'. **458** Her appeal is naturally enough to the one who sent her the 'letters' that would explain 'what this marvel signifies'. Love's irresistible power and Peace's unbreakable patience are to be the *maistres* ('teachers' as well as 'governors') of man's life on earth. **462** *Trewes*: the light-hearted pun showing this sombre sister who called Mercy's 'trewe tale' (135) a 'truyfle' (149) joining the revelry and conceding, in another piece of sacred wordplay, that 'soeth by Jesus' (as Righteousness also grants at 466) goes deeper into the mystery of God's *kynde* than rigid adherence to 'truth'. **463** *Cluppe...kusse*: the kiss of peace being the symbol of reconciliation for Christians, exchanged at every Mass. The origins of the 'reverence' the Daughters now show each other is the Cross that Will urges his family to reverence with a kiss at 473–4 (for the phrasing, cf. the reconciliation of William and Alphons in *WPal* 4526). *in couenaunt*: 'as a sign of our agreement'; but with more than a little resonance of the 'new covenant' of which 'Jesus [is] the mediator' (Heb 12:24). **465** recalls Gabriel's words to Mary at Lk 1:37; the Incarnation has 'made possible' man's release from hell. **466** *reuerentlich*: cf. her greeting to Peace at 175; she now understands the meaning of her younger sister's 'rich clothing' of divine patience. **467** *per secula..*: 'for ever and ever', 'world without end', the standard concluding formula of longer prayers in the Mass, but with an echo of Heb 13:20–21. **467a** 'Mercy and truth have met each other: justice and peace have kissed' (Ps 84:11). The deferral until now of this crucial verse, from which the whole allegory of the

Daughters arises (Traver 1925:44–92; Owst 1961:90–2), imparts a clinching authority to the argument. **468** On **L**'s presentation of the Easter triumph see Vaughan 1980:87–153 and Harbert in Phillips 1990:57–70. *Te Deum laudamus*: 'We praise you, God'; the great hymn of rejoicing, in rhythmic prose, sung at the end of Matins on Easter Sunday morning and on greater festivals. **469** *Loue*: the mysterious and much-anticipated figure whose brief entrance provides music that tunes the dancing and harmonises the four aspects of the divine Providence; the earthly presence of the risen Lord who has now returned to heaven. The image recalls depictions of angels singing and playing musical instruments, as in the *Très Riches Heures* (Schiller I pl. 292). **469a** 'Behold how good and pleasant it is [for brethren to dwell together in unity]' (Ps 132:1). The statement foreshadows **L**'s presentation of the community of believers under the 'nature-name' of UNITY in Passus XXI; cf. the discussion of this text in Brinton's Sermons 2:58, 114 (Alf*Q*). **470** *caroled*: 'danced in a ring'. The secular dance aptly (if boldly, given its associations) expresses the communal joy at Easter, while symbolising in its circular shape the cosmic harmony of 'sacred mirth' at the fulfilment of the divine plan for humanity.

EPILOGUE **471–8** The exultant coda of Passus XX is linked to the dream by the sounds of music, which express how 'terrenis coelestia, humanis divina junguntur' (*Exultet* canticle of Easter Saturday), passing from the heavenly 'symphony' of the Daughters into the familiar earthly summons to awake and worship. **471** *rang*: the bells rung on Easter morning in the parish churches of London linking the music that accompanies the mystic circle of the vision (a figure of eternity) with the linear human life that continues from year to year and will terminate in individual death and the final end of historical time. (On the Easter bells, the first to be rung since the start of Lent, see St-Jacques 1977[1]). Being woken by a sound within the dream is a feature found earlier at 18.179, but a sound from the waking world outside is paralleled in Chaucer's *Parliament of Fowls* 695. **472** *Kitte; Calote*: as much (and perhaps as little) fictions as Will himself, though some wryly humorous lines are devoted to the former at 22.193–8 that might have carried a special resonance for the original audience. The possible pejorative associations of these two names are explored in Mustanoja 1970:51–76. **473; 476** *Godes resureccioun / blessed body*: the unusual phrases robustly conveying **L**'s understanding of the 'theology of glory', the act on which Christian faith is based having for him only one author (cf. Rom 4:24, 6:4, Col 2:12 I Thess 1:10, I Pet 1:21). **474** *crepe...*: the penitential ceremony of 'creeping to the cross' (Duffy 1992:29), that took place on Good Friday (and survives as the rite of the Veneration of the Cross); also sometimes performed on Easter Sunday

(Harbert 1990:68). Will's summons to this devotional act aptly expresses how the continuance of Christ's victory over death requires his followers to share in the suffering that made it possible. *iewel*: because a symbol of Christ himself, 'our joy and jewel' (B 11.184). Harbert's insistence that 'it is a cross that he goes to kiss, not a crucifix' (ibid.) separates the suffering from the glory, something which for **L** can only occur at the end of time (cf. the imagery of *Pange Lingua* vs. 1: *gloriosi / Laueam certaminis* 'the laurel wreath of a glorious strife' and the theology of Gal 6:14). **475** This added line stresses the unique value, among all the relics revered by Christians, of the True Cross that had been stained with the blood of the incarnate God. Most churches possessed a supposed fragment of it, to be venerated annually at Eastertide and at the feast of the Invention of the Cross (May 3). **477** The significance of the Cross as the potent symbol of Christ's conquest of evil had been a familiar part of Christian tradition since the Dream of Constantine, in which he was said to have seen a great cross in the sky with the words *in hoc signo vinces* 'you will conquer by this emblem'. **478** *grisly goest*: a phrase also found in a somewhat less solemn context in *WPal* 1730. After celebrating the victory of Christ as 'Lord of Light', this magnificent passus ends with a climactic paradox: if the shadow of Christ's cross frightens the fearsome occupants of 'deep dark hell', its substance must be of incomparable power indeed.

Passus XXI (B XIX)

XXI and XXII contain only light revision and either awaited further changes or were regarded as finished. Though the contrast with the energy of revision in XX suggests a sudden cutting short, little here would seem to need alteration, and these passūs bring the **C** Version, like its predecessor, to a satisfactory (if troubled) close. XXI is structurally less complex and emotionally less elevated than XX, more didactic and expository (the calm before the storm), but lucidly planned and executed. It falls into three main sections, the echo of the first line by the last bringing the passus full circle. (i) 1–199 form the encounter with CONSCIENCE (a key figure in the last two passūs), introduced and ended by a repeated formulaic half-line at 12a (the entry of Jesus) and 208a (the coming of Grace). Its PRELUDE is a four-line waking scene of Will's visit to Church on Easter morning (as anticipated from the end of XX) and the singular yet strangely familiar vision of PIERS-CHRIST (5–8). The vision opens (9–25) as a *dialogus* in the poem's customary mode that quickly becomes an authoritative discourse by Conscience like those of Anima and Will's other interlocutors, most recently the Samaritan in XIX. Conscience offers an 'inner narrative' that substantially re-tells the life of Christ, dealing from lines 149–99 with the events

after his Crucifixion, leading to his Ascension, the last event narrated in any gospel (Mk 16, Lk 24), its distinctive standpoint being an understanding of Christ as successively knight, king and conqueror or emperor. This section parallels the liturgical sequence from Christmas to Easter, the Age of the Son. (ii) 200–336 continue the outer narrative with the descent of the HOLY GHOST, propelling a recapitulation of the Gospel account onwards to events told in the Book of Acts. Conscience introduces the Third Person of the Trinity (the Paraclete) under the poem's final divine 'nature-name' of GRACE and invites the Dreamer to kneel and be caught up in the scriptural-devotional action, thus blurring the border between 'inner' and 'outer' narratives. This Pentecost sequence is the Age of the Spirit active in Christian history, which points forward eschatologically to the end of history. Section ii's account of the founding of the Church emphasises Grace's granting of two gifts: to PIERS (a figure now strongly suggestive of the Apostle Peter and his successors) the power of pardon (i.e. spiritual dominion), and to the rest of society the earthly and spiritual gifts needed to do well. The allegory of the spiritual 'sowing' and the building of the BARN OF UNITY represents the Church's outward expansion through time, sustained by Scripture (the Four Gospels) and Sacred Tradition (the Four Doctors), authorities **L** has coupled throughout as *holiwrit*, and both incorporated in the annual cycle of readings used in liturgical worship. (iii) 337–484 describe the preparation of Unity under Conscience's leadership to withstand the siege of PRIDE (337–93), with the resistances and challenges to ideal Christian oneness of heart offered by different orders of society, from Commons to King (394–484). This section, which brings events firmly into the authorial present, answers to the liturgical time after Pentecost (from Trinity Sunday to Advent) and then the season of Lent once again. It also recapitulates in reverse the action of Vision 1 and (to some extent) of Vision 2, in particular Passūs VI–VIII and III–IV.

(i) 1–199. PRELUDE **1–8 1** *Thus Y wakede*: an opening that recalls the major section-division at 10.1 (Vision 3) and, like that of XXII, hints that the work's main argument is drawing to a conclusion. *wrot*: a verb the repetition of which at the end of the passus will indicate the character of the whole experience as something recorded for posterity and now being completed. **2** *derely*: in honour of the chief feast of the Church's year, so perhaps 'in my best clothes'. **3** *holly*: as urged at 9.231. *hoseled*: reception of the sacrament at Easter was compulsory for all. If it may be assumed that Will has made his confession, it is not necessarily implied that he misses communion by falling asleep, as contended by Weldon: 'Non-participation in the Eucharist symbolises the dreamer's spiritual deficiencies, which are compensated for and mitigated by the dream which follows...the body of Christ-Piers, the "host' he had evaded by falling asleep during the mass' (1987:275). For a dream need occupy little real time, and there is no sign in the text (nor is it plausible) that Will seeks to 'evade' communion, any more than that he immediately seizes up his writing-materials on waking (484). The dream is rather a profoundly 'eucharistic' vision, entirely appropriate at a point before the formal reception of communion. **4** *in myddes of*: 'at the mid-point of', when the assistants brought the bread and wine up to the priest for the Offertory. A point between the reading of the Word and the Canon is thematically fitting for a vision of Christ, though in pictorial tradition this more usually occurs during the Consecration when, according to the legend of the 'Mass of St Gregory', Christ as Man of Sorrows was seen poised above the Pope (Schiller II pls. 805–7). **L**'s version recalls the less familiar image of Gregory kneeling before the Man of Sorrows, which in a striking Swiss wall-painting of *c*. 1400 follows an unambiguous image of Christ as Artisan (Schiller II 226 and pl. 691). Most relevant here, given the liturgical setting, is the variant called the 'Eucharistic Man of Sorrows' (Schiller II pl. 760). **6** *Peres*: the sudden presentation of the Plowman with the marks of the passion and exactly resembling ('riht lik') Jesus resumes and makes explicit the earlier partial resemblance ('semblable somdeel') at 20.8, despite Will's uncertainty at 10–11. *peynted*: suggesting the devotional sculptures of the time painted in bright colours. **7** *cam...cros*: recalling B 5.12, where Reason preaches divine wrath and the need for repentance; but what is seen proclaims the triumph of mercy witnessed in XX. The best-known examples of Christ carrying his cross *after* the Passion, like Bellini's and Giovanni di Paolo's (Schiller II pls. 710, 713), are C15th; but the image probably existed earlier (ibid. 688).

9–14 9 *Conscience to kenne me*: the traditional function of this power, as **B**'s echo of line 7.134 (removed in // **C**) suggests. The discreet visual allusion to the iconographic motif of *Christus in torculari* [*crucis*] 'Christ in the Winepress [of the Cross]' derives from patristic commentary on Is 63:1–6, a key text that opens with the same question *Quis est iste* asked by Lucifer at B 18.316. Elaborated in works of passion-mysticism like *Vitis Mystica* (*PL* 184:739: see on 20.412 above and cf. Schmidt 1983²:181–2), it metamorphosed from an emblem of divine vengeance into one of divine mercy, the blood now being that of Christ and not of his enemies. Doctrinally this image (like that of the bleeding Lamb in *Pearl* 1135–40) serves to intimate his *compassio* or co-suffering with the members of the Mystical Body of which he is the head. Superimposing the 'chivalric' element drawn from another devotional tradition therefore restores some of the martial quality of Isaiah's *propugna-*

tor, with an effect of startling paradox. The 'winepress' image became a popular motif in art (Schiller II 228–9, pls. 808, 810–12); but the knight / ploughman aspects seem to be of **L**'s creating. **10ff** Will's questions to Conscience recall the interchange with Faith at 20.17–34. **11** *paynted*: the repetition from 6 pointing up the fictive character of this vision, which evokes images like those in wall-paintings of the time (on the significance of these for **L** see Benson 2004:157–201). **12** *armes*: echoing 20.21. The 'Arma Christi' (instruments of the Passion) formed a familiar iconographic motif (Schiller II pls. 654–7); but *armes* here metaphorically denotes the 'insignia' that enable Christ to be recognised by a 'herald' with the eyes of Faith. **13** *colours*: Christ's 'armorial' *gules on argent* may allude obliquely to the crusader knight's red cross on white (and cf. the short lyric in Gray 1975, no. 20). *cote armure*: recalling Will's question at 18.187. **14b** proclaims Christ both his people's champion and the benign 'conqueror' of their hearts, like the kingly wooer in *Ancrene Wisse*. 'Conquest' forms part of the theological theme of 'Christus triumphans', in which the Cross symbolises his victory over sin and death.

15–68 15 *Crist*: the Gk for Hebrew *Messiah* 'the Anointed One', by which title the Son's rôle in salvation history is specified as 'both the divinity that anoints and the humanity that is anointed' (*ST* III 16.5). Denied to Jesus by the Jews who rejected him, and by their descendants (cf. 17.307–14, 20.55), it is the *nomen credentium* insistently used by St Paul, though (with a few exceptions such as Mt 1:16, Jn 1:17) not by the Evangelists, who speak only of 'Jesus'. On these two names see Bernard's *Sermo I in vig. nat. Dom.* (*PL* 183:88). **16–18** allude to Phil 2:10 quoted at 80*a* below. On the significant 'pattern of kneeling' in this passus see Weldon 1989. *prophecied*: referring to the expectation in the Psalms and Isaiah (46:24) of God's salvation through a Messiah; no actual OT prophecy concerns the personal name *Jesus* ('Yahweh saves'). **18** *þe...Iesu*: 'the divine name, Jesus' (which replaces God's OT name YAHWEH), 'the name of Jesus, God'. **19** *Ergo*: because the man who bore it has now been revealed as divine. **21** *deueles*: alluding to its use by the disciples in driving out evil spirits (Mk 9:37–8) and in the Church's rite of exorcism. *hit*: the name JESUS (not the title CHRIST), the object of a devotion popularised by Richard Rolle in his *Emendatio Vitae* (see Schmidt 1986:31–2). The feast in honour of the Holy Name (Aug. 7) began to be celebrated by the mid-14th c. and a special Mass was in existence by the 1380s (Pfaff 1970:66). **22** *saued*: see I Cor 6:11. **23** Will's insistence recalls his attitude to Liberum Arbitrium / Anima's many names; but here his curiosity receives no rebuke as at 16.205. **25** *Iesu*: the vocative case; used as a simple alternative form of the name at 44. *ioye*: brought simply by uttering the name, according to Rolle in his *Form of Living* (ed. Ogilvie-Thomson 18/610–20). **26–30** all scan on *k*, underscoring the 'catechetical' tone of the lines. **26** *kunne resoun*: an allusion back to Will's encounter with Conscience and Reason in 5.1–104. **27–30** The three grades inevitably suggest the Triad, here to be understood perhaps in relation to Christ's ministry, passion, and resurrection / ascension to glory. **32** *lordes of laddes*: the uniqueness of the conqueror (as evinced in the history of England) being the power to transform the social order by dint of his total control. The notion of divine grace 'freeing and ennobling' the slaves of sin has Scriptural origins (Rom 8:21, I Pet 2:9) and is echoed in the doctrine of 'theological nobility' [that of God's elect] taught by the C14th legist Bartolus of Sassoferrato (Keen 1984:149). **34–41** elaborate in more measured terms the denunciation of the Jews by Faith at 20.95–112*a*. They express the common medieval view that Christian baptism confers both spiritual and legal 'freedom' and that the Jews' legal and social disabilities (Cohn 1972:79–80; Gilchrist 1969:111) were the result of rejecting Jesus as the Messiah (as they were certainly the usual consequence of the Jews' unwillingness to give up their religion). **36–7** *worlde*: the referent being essentially 'Europe' or Christendom, since the Jews were spared these disabilities in Muslim lands. **38** *þe Baptist*: see Lk 7:29–30; implying that since many Jews followed John, who acknowledged Jesus as Messiah (Jn 1:26–37), it did not contravene their Jewish faith to do likewise. **39–40** could mean simply that Jews who received baptism in Christ's name were freed from sin; but the mention of Christ's being baptised (by John) seems pointless unless the referent of *follyng* 39 is the baptism performed by John. This would imply **L**'s awareness that John's disciples who became followers of Jesus were not baptised (a second time) in his name. *frankeleynes*: a term answering to *generosus* in the TCD ms 212 note on Stacy de Rokayle (see *Intro.* V §4). **41** *ycrouned...Iewes*: alluding to the crown of thorns and Pilate's mocking inscription above the cross, which were transformed into symbols of lordship after the resurrection (in the NT the divine title 'king [of kings]' is applied to Jesus only in Apoc 17:14). **42–3** 'It is fitting for...a conqueror to maintain [and protect] his bounty and his dominion with the revenues from his act of conquest / conquered territory' (MED s.v. *conqueste* n. 1(a), 2); the conqueror's chief duties are largesse and protection. Of the two verbs in 42b, *kepe* strictly governs the first and *defende* the second noun in 43 (a line that scans as a Type IIb with a monolexical stave-word *cónquéste* in position 2 and 3). **44–5** 'He brought them the means of justification by teaching them the law of eternal life [faith in himself as redeemer]' (cf. Jn 17:3); this is Christ's 'large'. **46–7** *fended hem*: Christ's protection against his people's foes, seen as deliverance from disease, sin and error (see Jn 4:52, Mt 9:20–2, Mk 5:1–14, 10:1–12). **48**

gentel prophete: cf. 'propheta magnus' (Lk 7:16). **50** *conquerede he on cros*: a general theological formulation, but also evoking the emblematic 'knightly' submission of the representative 'believing Jew' Longeus at 20.93 above. **51** echoes 20.28. **52** *regnede*: Christ's sovereignty being exemplified, even before the Ascension, in his conquest of hell. **53** *quyke...dede*: echoing the 6th clause of the Apostles' Creed. **55** *cherles*: a 'social' term substituted for the usual 'prisoners' in keeping with the metaphor of sin as slavery and liberation as ennoblement. **57** *bonde him*: an idea deriving from Apoc 20:1–3 (and cf. *EN* B 24). **58** *herte blood*: recalling 20.87–8; the blood from Christ's heart ('side' Jn 19:34) was traditionally interpreted as symbolising the sacrament of baptism by which 'all folk are made free' (cf. 12.110–11). **62** *Crist to mene*: not necessarily implying belief that the name signifies 'conqueror' (*Sk*) so much as the 'superlative degree' of the 'knight, king, conqueror' triad and is hence uniquely fitted to the 'Lord's Anointed' who was son of God as well as of David (Ac 2:36, I Cor 1:24). **63–8** recapitulate the teaching of Rechelesnesse at 12.205–11, of his *partyng-felawe* Patience on *Passio Domini* at B 14.189–93, and of Anima at B 15.270–1.

69–95 69 *cam...name*: for this type of internal rhyme within the b-half cf. 19.265. **70** *Faythly*: found in this sense (MED s.v. *feithli* adv. (c)) only here and at *WPal* 209 (*f. for to telle*). **71–95** re-tell the Infancy story to prove that Jesus was 'knight and king's son', stressing the recognition of his noble origin by the traditional representatives of the Gentile world. **72** The Magi ('Kings') in C14th nativity paintings are sometimes shown led by an angel, as by Giovanni Pisano (Schiller I, pl. 287), while in Giotto's 'Adoration' (ibid. pl. 288) an angel holds the gold vessel and the first king kneels. **74** An elaboration of the Lucan account common in late medieval pictorial representations (e.g. Schiller I, pls. 202, 206). **74a** 'Glory to God in the highest' (Lk 2:14); the text that opens the *Gloria* at Mass. **75–9** are based on Mt 2:11–12. **75** *Kynges*: after *LA* 89, which assigns the *sapientes et reges* their traditional names of Caspar, Balthasar and Melchior. The royal status of those who bring Christ gifts for which they ask neither thanks nor return (thus in effect 'tribute') adumbrates his appointed rôle as 'conqueror'. **79** *kyngene*: on the subjective genitive from the OE weak ending see *MES* 73. *by... angelis*: an inference from Mt 2:12 in the light of verse 13. **80** *word...speke*: at 16–20 above. **80a** '[God hath given him a name...above all names: That] in the name of JESUS every [knee] should bow, of those that are in heaven, on earth, [and under the earth]' (Phil 2:9–10). The 'earthly knees' here include those of the kings of the earth. **81** See at 74 above. The 'heavenly ones' recognise Christ's divinity at his birth, the 'infernal ones' do not, their submission coming only after his entry into hell (20.449–50). **82** *wit... world*: not *sapiencia mundi* but 'every kind of knowledge

703

under the sun'. **83** The Magi are imagined almost in folktale terms as fairy godfathers bringing the royal child 'gifts of character' that he will need to fulfil his calling. These symbolised qualities recall the Four Daughters and anticipate the seed-symbolism of the cardinal virtues, e.g. 'Reason' suggests both Truth (cf. 90) and Prudence; but they are especially appropriate to a king-conqueror (cf. Pr 153–7). **L**'s allegorisation alters the Biblical order of the gifts and differs from that of *LA* 93, which not unexpectedly sees *gold* as a 'tributum' of love to Christ's 'regia potestas', *incense* as a 'sacrificium' of worship to his 'divina majestas' and *myrrh* as a burial-offering 'ad sepultura mortuorum' acknowledging his 'humana mortalitas'. **85** *Magi*: pleasingly if incorrectly etymologised as 'quasi in sapientia magni' in *LA* 88, which also recognises its parallel senses of 'magician' and 'sorcerer'. The common view was that the Magi were Mesopotamian or Persian *secretorum inspectores* 'students of the occult' or astrologers (*LA* 89). Their esoteric learning enabled them to understand the significance of 'his star in the east' as the *signum* (cf. Gen 1:14) of a divine king's birth, and thence to offer him precious gifts of mystic signification. **86** *Resoun*: not *intellectus humanus* but *divina ratio* (the quality personified in the authoritative figure of 13.194ff), in apt recognition of Jesus as the *Logos* incarnate of Jn 1:14. *sense*: a 'Platonic' pun may be hinted by the aphetic form, since what a 'sensory' mode conceals (the mystical meaning of the gift) is revealed to the light of spiritual understanding. **88** Medieval jurisprudence stressed the close bond between equity and justice, reflecting 'the basic premise of natural law theory — that the rules governing human conduct should be in conformity with the natural order. Reason is the name given both to that order and to the faculty that apprehends it' (Alf*G* 134). *reed gold*: see on B 2.16. **89** 'It is to gold that justice is compared, because both are imperishable'. Gold was regarded as the perfect metal and a fit emblem of immortality because (unlike iron or copper, say) its appearance and chemical properties survive contact with the four elements. *Lewetee*: 'Justice'; see Alf*G* s.v. II and on Pr 149. **90** *richeles*: the emendation (see *TN*) removing the apparent 'contradiction' (*Sk*) in 90. *to...treuthe*: the more natural reading is to take both terms as synonyms for Reason; but Lewetee and Resoun are probably parallel subjects, *riht* glossing the first, *treuthe* the second. **92** *Pyte*: a word having the range of *pietas* (see on Pr 157); a near-synonym of *reuthe* 83 and *mercy* 93, which are mutually distinguishable as respectively affective and rational in the period (Burnley 1979, Index s.vv.). **93** *mirre is mercy*: a 'Platonic' pun, the connection being the use of myrrh to anoint the dead, an act of compassionate piety (cf. Jn 19:39). *mylde speche*: especially in passing judgement; the opposite of harshness or severity. **94** *Ertheliche honeste thynges*: 'natural objects of honourable use'; the key-phrase encapsulating

L's 'sacramental' vision of the world. *was*: sg. because the gifts are one gift offered 'at ones'. **95** *thre kyne*: i.e. from three different countries.

96–107 summarise the ministry of Jesus, which is then expounded in terms of the Triad as acts of power (108–23), compassion (124–82a) and pardon (183–199). **96** *for all*: i.e. because, though they were gifts for a king, Jesus had yet to earn that title by his own acts. The lesson is that though Baptism makes all Christians members of a 'royal priesthood', they cannot enter into their inheritance without actively 'doing well', as their Lord had to. **97** *comsed...man*: the implied reference being to his qualifying as a skilful knight, a stage towards winning his kingly title. **100** *wyles and wit*: alluding to Christ's mastery in argument (see e.g. Mt 22:35–46). **101** *whoso... hit*: 'if one might make bold to say'; a filler-phrase (cf. 3.235). **102** *soffrede*: in the desert (Mt 4:2). *hudde hym*: see Jn 8:59. **103** *fauht*: perhaps alluding to his driving the money-changers from the Temple with a whip. *fley*: to escape from his enemies (Jn 10:39). **104** *gaf goed*: perhaps referring (as Christ did not give alms) to the 'good wine' of the Wedding at Cana (Jn 2:1–10); see 108. *hele*: on Christ's miracles of healing cf. 18.140–45. **105** *Lyf and lyme*: see Mk 5:22ff; Mt 12:10–13. *as...wrouhte*: cf. 20.449. **107** *alle hem*: alluding to the Harrowing of Hell but echoing the eschatological 20.414.

108–23 describe and in the expository manner of catechesis (cf. 116 repeating 110) symbolically interpret Christ's turning of water into wine. **108** *iuuentee*: a fancy of **L**'s in keeping with his '*Christus victor*' triad (27–30). The scriptural source describes Jesus with disciples and implies his full maturity (Jn 2:2); but **L** makes Cana a 'wonder' of the Lord's *enfances*, performed 'before' (and impliedly 'for') his Mother. Unless meaning simply 'a Jewish celebration' (cf. 115), the phrase *Iewene feste* would seem to make 'this beginning of miracles' (Jn 2:11) a *public* 'sign' at the start of Jesus's mission, asserting his claim to be the Messiah (the Gospel account makes clear that it was quite the opposite). **110** *of his grace*: 'out of gracious kindness'; for Jesus's apparent reluctance, cf. Jn 2:4. **111–14** The general sense of the allegorisation (perhaps of **L**'s devising) is clear, but the expression *wyn is likned...*a little awkward, since properly water should correspond to 'lawe' and wine to 'lyf-holinesse' (of which the sublime test is love of one's enemies). **112** The Old Law forbade wrong against all and allowed (though without encouraging) retribution against enemies, but it did not urge *love* for them. This, the distinctive ethical teaching of the New Law, was defined by Wit as 'do-better' at 10.189–90, but tacitly correlated with 'do-best' by Piers at 15.144. Christ's comment at Mt 5:43 assumes a common contemporary understanding of Lev 19:18 which that text need not itself assume. **113** *consayleth*; *commaundeth*: normally contrasted as precepts for the *perfecti* and the *incipientes* respectively; but Christ's injunction at Mt 5:44 is a universal command like those that preceded it. **117** aims (rather inelegantly) to state that he was called not only Jesus but 'Christ', i.e. in recognition of his Messiahship revealed in the miracle. **118** *fauntekyn*: inappropriate, given Christ's actual age, unless the term is to be taken as referring to his lack of public position and his still being known (Mk 6:3) as *filius Marie* 'Mary's son' (it is she who asks him to perform the act). **120** *bileue*: not questioning that she did (Jn 2:5 presumes Mary's complete faith in Jesus), but openly confirming what she believed in her heart. **121** *Grace*: the first use of this new 'nature-name' for the 'high Holy Ghost' (14.84) working in and through Jesus. *of no gome*: 'not by any man'. **122** *no wyt*: not from the learning Jesus had to acquire in a normal way (such as knowledge of Scripture), but from his nature hidden 'in deitate Patris'. *thorw word one*: recalling the Creator's *dixit* (15.263*a*), so as to indicate Christ's divinity. **123** *Dowel*: treated as a noun here ('embarked upon [the knightly life of] DOWEL'). **124–82***a* Christ's ministry, Passion and resurrection are all treated under DOBET (kingship), accommodated with the new parallel triad enunciated at 27. This makes good sense, since the sending of the Holy Ghost obviously = the Conqueror's distribution of his 'large'. But it remains an imperfect correspondence, given that the *act of conquest* (the defeat of Satan's kingdom) takes place *before* the resurrection / ascension. So it is best to see the stages as continuous, rather than disjunct. **124–62 124** scans either as Type IIa on |w| or as Type IIIb on vowels. *wexen...absence*: figuratively speaking (see on 118), referring to his departure from Nazareth. The account is re-shaped to accord with **L**'s imagining of Jesus as a Percival-like figure leaving his mother's household to perform the acts of war against Satan's dominion on earth that will win the kingdom rightfully his as the son of God. **125** *lame ...blynde*: see Mt 11:5. *liht*: not a mere alliterative necessity, but stressing how those miraculously healed could now fully 'see' who Jesus was. **126–7** Cf. B 15.590, and see Mt 14:17–20=Mk 6:38–44, Lk 9:13–17. **129** scans either as Type IIIb (with natural stress-pattern) or (stressing *was*) as Type Ie with an enriched final lift. *Dobet...wente*: suggested by *Bene omnia fecit* 'He hath done all things well' (Mk 7:37). **130** See Mk 7:32–5. *doynges*: deliberately stressing Christ's *acts* of kingly 'maistrie' (cf. *word one* at 122). The NT sees illnesses as signs of Satan's sway over man, and to overcome them as requiring *greater* power than that exercised over the non-human world in the wine-miracle. **132–3** See Mk 9:26–31; the people recognise in Jesus the promised Messianic king by observing his actions. **133** *Fili...*: 'Have mercy on us, O [Jesus] Son of David' (Mt 9:27, 15:22; cf. 21:9). This cry of the blind men / the Canaanite woman is associated here with the accla-

mation of the crowds at Christ's entry into Jerusalem on Palm Sunday, and both of them with that of the women after David's defeat of Goliath a thousand years before Christ (see next). Jesus is called 'son of David' as a title of honour (because he is the Messiah) and also because his legal father Joseph was of the house and lineage of David (Mt 1:6, 16). **135** *Saul...*: '[And the women sung as they played. And they said]: Saul slew his thousands, and David his ten thousands' (I Kgs 18:7). **136** The people's recognition of Jesus parallels that of the women who acknowledged his 'ancestor' David. **137** *nempned... Nazareth*: 'called him [Jesus of] Nazareth, King of the Jews' (see Mt 21:9–11=Lk 19:38, Jn 12:13); the *titulus* placed above the cross in Jn 19:19 (the Synoptics omit the name). **137–9** *no man...Iesus*: after the Feeding of the Five Thousand (Jn 6:15). **138** *cayser*: here in part for alliterative convenience, but doubtless appropriate as anticipating Christ's universal spiritual *imperium*. **138** *Iuda*: the ancient kingdom of David, in Roman times part of the province of Judea, with an imperial governor but no native king. **139** *iustice*: an office occupied in reality by the Roman governor (cf. 20.37). **140** *Cayphas*: the Jewish high priest, chief mover in the plot to put Jesus to death (Mt 26:3–4). *enuye*: implied as a motive for their hostility in Jn 11:47–50. **142–3** The crucifixion (Pilate's act) is here ascribed to the moral agency of Christ's enemies among the Jews, as is his burial (which in Jn 19:38–42 is ascribed to the Council-members Joseph of Arimathea and Nicodemus, who were secretly his disciples). **144** *knyhtes*: the guard placed at Christ's tomb by the Jewish religious leaders (Mt 28:62–6). **145** *profetes*: alluding to Ps 15.10, understood at Ac 2:27 and 13.35–7 as applying to Christ. **147–8** *goen...deuyned*: not part of the psalm-prophecy but spoken by Christ at Mt 26:32. **148** *Marie*: a separate appearance of Jesus to his mother not being recorded in the Gospels, this addition is presumably on the basis of *LA* 241–2, which affirms the 'common belief' and cites St Ambrose in support. **149–56** are based on Mt 28:11–15. **150–1** The phrasing (confirmed by the end-rhyme) clearly recalls the account of the nativity scene at 74. *day spronge*: an echo of Christ's incarnation-title of 'dayspring' that hints at his resurrection as a birth to a new life (see Mt 28:1). **152** 'Christ, rising again [from the dead, dieth now no more. Death shall no more have dominion over him]' (Rom 6:9); sung as a Vespers anti-phon during Eastertide. **154** *preyed...pees*: 'begged them to keep silent'. **155–161** The fourfold repetition of *cam* and the annominative com*pany* seems deliberate. **156** *bywiched*: recalling the accusation at 20.71–2 as colour for the fabrication put abroad. **157** *Marie Maudeleyne*: the first to see Jesus after his resurrection (Mk 16:9, Jn 20:14). **158** *Galilee*: see Mt 28:10; the account also contains echoes of the Easter Sequence ('Sepulcrum Christi viventis...Scimus Christum surrexisse'). *in...manhede*:

complementing *Verray man* at 153; the risen Jesus is now manifestly the divine Son. **159** *lyues and lokynge*: 'alive and in full possession of his faculties'. *aloude cride*: see Jn 20:18. **160** 'Christ has risen', the Easter Sunday greeting. **161a** 'Thus it behove[s] Christ to suffer and [so] to enter [into his glory]'; a conflation of '*Nonne oportuit haec pati Christum, et ita intrare* in gloriam suam' (Lk 24:26) with '*sic oportebat Christum pati* et resurgere a mortuis' (Lk 24:46), the latter verbally concording with *resurgens* 160 (Alf*Q* after *Pe*). **162** ironically inserts 'clerkly' anti-feminism (cf. B 5.166) in a solemn context, while echoing the Jewish reluctance to credit women's testimony in Mk 16:11 and Lk 24:11. The line is seen by Richardson 2000:180 (citing [p. 164] 'cum mos sit mulierum / Cuncta revelare' from the C12th Latin *Lamentations of Matheolus*1596–7) as 'a mocking application of proverbial misogyny'.

163–99 163–82a are based on the account in Jn 20:19–29. **163–5** The Gospels record only Peter (Lk 24:12) or Peter and John (Jn 20:2–10), not all the Twelve, going to the tomb to investigate. **165** *Taddee*: the apostle (Mt 10:3, Mk 3:18) commonly identified with the author of the Epistle of Jude and the brother of James 'the Less'. According to the 'Passion of SS Simon and Jude', he was martyred in Persia with his companion Simon 'the Zealot' (*LA* 710). *Thomas of Ynde*: said in early tradition going back to the C3rd 'Acts of Thomas' to be the evangeliser of India, who was martyred there (*LA* 39). **166** *wyse weyes*: referring to their prudent self-concealment 'for fear of the Jews' (Jn 20:19). **167–8** Christ's entry into the locked dwelling is a peaceable version of the breaking through hell's gates at 20.364–5, the repeated *al* bringing out his effortless power. **169** *Pax vobis*: 'Peace be to you' (Jn 20:19); read as the 'Alleluia' verse at Mass on the Sunday after Easter, and providing the greeting of the celebrant to servers and people before every Communion. **170–1** are resonant with spiritual meaning; Christ is 'teaching' Thomas to *believe* by entering deeply into the 'heart' or innermost purpose of his coming in the flesh (for the symbolic positioning of the spear-wound, see on 20.87 above). The scene is superbly illustrated on the Syon Cope of *c.* 1300, a masterpiece of *opus anglicanum* now in the Victoria & Albert Museum, London (Camille 1996: pl. 77). **172a** 'My Lord and my God'; the only explicit acknowledgement in the Gospels of Christ as God, rounding off and experientially 'proving' the opening affirmation at Jn 1:1. **174** *Y bileue*: an inference from Christ's words to Thomas at Jn 20:29. **176** *lyuynge...lokynge*: cf. on 159. **179** *Yblessed...euere*: an addition bringing out Christ's gratuitous kindness or 'courtesy' in giving Thomas more than he deserves (the source contains no such blessing). **182** *Y...hem*: a special assurance to the Dreamer (cf. B 15.162) and to the audience of the value God attaches to belief founded on trust rather than physical evidence. **182a** 'Blessed are

they that have not seen and have believed' (Jn 20:29). **183–99** are based on Lk ch. 24 and Ac ch. 1, but differ from the scriptural accounts in stressing the forgiveness of 'actual' sin through sacramental penance rather than of original sin through baptism. They compress the events described in the liturgical lectionary from Easter to Ascension Thursday forty days later, which follows Ac 1:3, in the light of the account in Lk 24:50–1, which places the Ascension on the evening of Easter Day (see 192–3 below). **183** *Dobest*: specifically the commissioning of the Apostles, as the first step in the founding of the Church, the act of dobest itself. **184** *Peres*: here as at 202 below unequivocally identified with the Apostle Peter (Burrow 1993[1]:119–22), the spiritual 'ploughman' of all lands awaiting salvation (on the evangelical 'ploughing' motif the fundamental study is Barney 1973). **185–8** The power to *forgive* sin is granted solely to the bishops and the clergy under their authority, who receive it by a line of ordination reaching back to the Apostles. But the capacity to *be forgiven* is offered to all who are willing to confess their sins and 'satisfactorily meet the terms of Piers's pardon'. The sense of *knowleched to paye* as 'agreed to pay' is convincingly supported in MED s.v. *knoulechen* v. 7(g) by a 1343 ref. combining the two words, a legal usage not noted in Alf*G*. **188** *Redde quod debes*: 'Pay what you owe' (Mt 18:28); not without ironic humour, the words of the Unjust Servant in the parable here being turned against him. **189–90** are based on Christ's words to St Peter at Caesarea (Mt 16:19); see on Pr 129–30. **189** *his...payed*: 'the terms of his pardon met'. **190** *elles*: i.e. in heaven; Peter's acts of granting or witholding absolution will be ratified by God. **191** *dette*: not 'the sin of debt' but 'the binding obligation to make satisfaction for sin'; Peter and his successors cannot grant pardon for nothing. **192–9** echo the end of the second clause of the Apostles' Creed; on 192–3 cf. Lk 24:50, Ac 1:9. **194–5** *reddit...*: 'pays what he owes'. Line 196, glossing this, stresses that satisfaction must accord with strict equity. **197** expands 9.21 in lines that echo the wording of B 7.112–14. **199** may be scanned as Type Ia with caesura after *wonye*, as a T-type, or best as Type IIb dividing after *wo* and providing the most solemn conclusion to Conscience's *carpyng*.

(ii) 200–335 The *Grace Sequence* deals with the Founding of the Church and carries the liturgical time swiftly forward to Whitsun's celebration of the Descent of the Holy Ghost 'in spirit and power' on the 120 disciples (Ac 1:15). The final scene with Conscience describes this event, which fell on the fiftieth day after Passover. It is also an allegory of the (inward) experience of devout Christians communally re-enacting that of the disciples (preface to Mass of Pentecost), and the poetry draws deeply on the language and imagery of the seasonal readings.

200–13 201 *perto*: continuing the worship of Christ's

cross begun at 20.475–6. Still at 325 below the cross remains the 'structural form' of the Church as the Mystical Body of Christ. **202** is a Type IIIa with two lifts in *Páraclítus* or, preferably, a Type Ia variant with mute second stave and internal first stave in *Spíritus*. That serviceable Latin lexeme scans with |sp| at 304, with |s| at 277, with |p| at 458 and on its final syllable with |t| at 466. *Paraclitus*: 'the Comforter'; based on the Johannine conception of the Holy Ghost as 'advocate' and 'strengthener' of believers (Jn 14:26, 15:26, 16:7). The phrase occurs in the Pentecost Vespers hymn 'Beata nobis gaudia' (st. 1) and 202–5 are influenced by the wording of st. 2; but the Spirit's action as Comforter is most fully elaborated in the Whitsun Sequence 'Veni, sancte spiritus'. *Peres...felawes*: this second appearance again contextually implying St Peter and his fellow apostles (cf. Burrow 1993:77–80). **203** *lihtnynge*: an imaginative variant (lightning is also forked) on the *dispertitae linguae tanquam ignis* 'parted tongues, as it were of fire' of Ac 2:3 (cf. 206), with some recollection of *ignis vibrante lumine* from the 'Beata' hymn, st. 2 (*JLH* 154). *lihte*: 'Platonic' wordplay relating the fire from the skies to the heaven-sent Spirit; but **L** stresses its illuminating as well as enkindling force (as in the Pentecost Sequence). **204** See Ac 2:4–11; the ironic echo of 16.208–9 reminds that God is the source of all *sciences and sotil craftes*, which must be learnt in humility and faith. **205** *wondred*: Will shares the 'amazement and wonder' (Ac 2:7, 12) of the Jews who hear the apostles preach after receiving the Spirit. **206** *lihte*: figuring the divine (as at 20.127) by an overwhelming radiance that arouses awe in those who behold it. **208** The a-half repeats 21.12 above (see introductory note), symmetrically 'signing off' the Dreamer's instruction by Conscience. *messager*: because sent by Christ to bring the Apostles knowledge and understanding of all they have to preach (Jn 13–15); cf. Mahomet's claim at 17.177–80. **209** scans either as Type Ia on |g| with a four-syllable prelude-dip or as Type Ic on cognative *k / g*, the first stave being |k| in *cometh. fro...God*: cf. Jn 15:26, the basis of the Western doctrine of the Double Procession, but a text interpreted by Eastern theologians as supporting their objection to the *Filioque* clause. Following Truth and Kind for the Father and Christ for the Son, the final divine 'nature-name' Grace (for the Holy Ghost) comes as no surprise, his rôle as bringer of all grace having been explained by the Samaritan at 19.181–217; see sts 1 and 7 of the hymn quoted at 211. **211** *Veni...*: the C9th Vespers Pentecost Hymn, ascribed to Raban Maur, which inspires much of the action and imagery in section iii of XXI (see *JLH* I, 80). **212** *many hundret*: evoking the interior of a great church such as St Paul's.

214–62 214 Grace's accompanying of Piers accords well with the latter's intimate knowledge of him displayed at 7.242ff, when he was seen more in terms of his action in

prompting men to penitence and the pursuit of *treuthe* or righteous living. *Peres the Plouhman*: the third appearance of the name now explicitly equating not Christ (as *Sk* holds) but Christ's apostolic vicar with his own successors in historical time, the popes and bishops (of whom the poem's eponymous hero is the type) and *pari passu* the first Christian community with the worshippers assembled to celebrate the feast. **215** *Conscience*'s allegorical rôle in this summoning of the *ecclesia* is not precisely determinable; but in the light of his first and persistent signification, he is likely to suggest the secular authority in its capacity of 'joint' religious leader with the clergy. **216** *today*: the liturgy associating each day of Pentecost week with one of the Seven Gifts of the Holy Ghost enumerated in Is 11:2, beginning with Wisdom on the Sunday itself. **L**'s elaboration at 230–62 departs from this list in both sequence and content, extending the Spirit's bounty to the whole range of necessary human activities ('tresor to lyue by' 218; 'alle craft and connying' 254), and blurs the distinction between religious and secular. For the argument that **L** envisages his ideal community as modelled on the parish fraternities of various occupational membership, see Simpson 1993. *grace*: not in the strict theological sense of the 'supernatural' gift (distinguished as 'prevenient', 'actual' and 'habitual') but as something nearer to 'talents or endowments' (254 below). **217** *his*: understanding 'to every individual of every kind'. **218** is a Type Ia sub-variant with *to* mute in both the second stave, as the unemphatic infinitive particle, and in the key-stave, where as the preposition 'until' it puns polysemantically. If both are mute, two of the four stresses fall on annominating lexical words, providing a contrapuntal pattern on *l*; but possibly *to* (2) is meant to be a full stave. The line recapitulates rather than merely repeats Wit's declaration at 10.182–3: *tresor* (repeated in a semi-catechetical manner at 226) exists in the new dispensation on a more exalted level. **219** scans as either a Type Ia on |w| or, as preferably here, with natural stress on lexical words, as Type IIIc on |w| and |f| (cf. 227 below, where *with* is best stressed in this Type Ia line with its necessarily muted key-stave *when*). **220** *Auntecrist*: a Johannine expression used for those who deny Christ's incarnation, Messiahship and divinity (I Jn 2:18–22, II Jn 7–11 cf. 4:3). It covers both Jews and Christian heretics already actively at work (II Jn 4:3), whose presence has an eschatological significance ('it is the last hour', I Jn 2:18). St Paul in II Thess 2:3–9 (without using the name) speaks in similar terms of 'the man of sin, the son of perdition' who seduces into error, envisaging him as a diabolic wonder-worker whose appearance will precede the Second Coming of Christ. On medieval developments of this figure see Cohn 1972:33–6 and Emmerson 1982. **222** *false profetes*: foretold by Christ himself (Mt 24:24), the same phrase denoting heretics and schismatics in II Pet 2:1 and I Jn 4:1. **224–5** *Pryde*: the chief sin, thought of as assisted by Greed (a single vice, often second in the list of the Deadly Sins), denoted comprehensively by both the 'cardinals' who advise him (cf. 19.326). *Vnkyndenesse* here = *avaritia* or miserliness. **227** *wepne*: on the weapons of spiritual warfare see I Cor 10:4. **228–9** The elucidation given in 230ff indicates that these graces are the talents that make possible the skills of practical life. Worthwhile and useful activity is certainly thought of as a remedy against sin; but on a wider scale the line attests **L**'s vision of 'Unity' as a social ideal encompassing both secular and religious values. **229** *Ydelnesse*: indolence predisposing to amorous indulgence; he is porter of the garden gate in *RR* 1273ff / *CT* I 1940. **229a** '[Now] there are diversities of graces, [but the same Spirit...of ministries, but the same Lord...of operations, but the same God]' (I Cor 12:4). The spiritual charisms Paul refers to are 'transsumptively' interpreted by **L** as 'earthly honest things' (234). **230–4** describe the work of those who use speech to explain, argue and instruct, all tasks that meet real needs. **231** An echo of the opening (Pr 21), modified to emphasise the importance of justice in the pursuit of one's living. **233** *They... lyue*: on this 'predicate nominative' use of the infinitive see *MES* 524–5. **235** *syhte*: as used in activities like the scribe's or the architect's. **236** Perhaps the craftsman's skill in making and the merchant's in assessing the quality of goods are meant. **237–8** refer to farming and fishing; cf. 17.20. **239–40** are among the few fully revised lines in the passus. **241** *deuyne*: 'find out about, investigate (mathematical) matters'. **245** *astronomye*: see on B 10.209 and MED s.v. n (1). **246–8** Knights are envisaged as enforcers of justice in society who should use 'forcible means' to recover goods stolen by force; the example of the Knight's failed courtesy at B 6.164–8 proves this the only 'law' that law-breakers will heed. **248** *with*: 'by means of'; the sense 'against' given by MED (s.v. *with* prep. 1b.(a)) would deprive the line of its sardonic bite. The 'grace' in question here corresponds to the recognition at 1.91–100 of an obligation to compel rather than persuade when circumstances demand it. *Foleuiles lawes*: 'rough justice', a phrase found only here. Despite a possible pun on 'Foolville' ('Fool Town'), *Sk*'s preferred conjecture of a proper name 'Folville' is well supported by Stones (1957) and Bowers (1961). The allusion is to the practices of the Folville clan, a notorious criminal gang active in Leicestershire in the 1330s. See further Green 1999:165–205. **249** *longyng...Cristene*: monastic and solitary contemplatives (cf.16.110–12), not 'the poor' (Hewett-Smith 2001:240). **251–5** may allude to the conflict and rivalry amongst the contemporary London gilds (see Simpson 1993). The sentiment recalls Trajan at B 11.213–14. **256** *myldest of berynge*: cf. Mk 9:33–4, Jn 13:13–16. **257** *crowneth...kyng*: the quality that is to pre-

vail in the governance of the Christian community and be assisted by practical wisdom ('craft' virtually = *prudentia*). **259–62** recall and recapitulate Passūs VII–VIII. But Piers's 'ploughing' is now wholly spiritual, since he will administer Grace's moral economy and 'cultivate' justice in the Christian *comune*, his rôle emblematising those of the pope and bishops as successors of the Apostles. **260** refers to the bishop's duty as *prowour* or 'overseer' (the literal sense of *episcopus*) of the system of penance, from confession to pardon. *registrer*: literally the clerk of an ecclesiastical court (Alf*G*). He receives an 'account' of what those 'on earth' have done to make adequate satisfaction for their sins (for the Latin phrase see at 188). **261** *prowour*: a variant of *purveiour* (MED s.v. n 1(b)). **262** *to tulye treuthe*: for the scriptural origin of the metaphor cf. I Cor 9:10–11, which envisages the preaching of the Gospels in term of ploughing, sowing and harvesting.

263–74a On the image of *spiritual ploughing* see R–H 17–19 and Barney 1973. The figure recapitulates 'mystically' the original sequence of literal ploughing in Passus VIII, where Piers attempted to create an orderly and productive régime to meet the community's need for food. **263** *foure grete oxen*: as seen on f. 170r of the Luttrell Psalter, reproduced in *R–H* title-page and Blanch 1969:21, and discussed in Camille 1987; also (with two beasts) f. iiib in Cambridge, Trinity R. 3.14 (frontispiece to Vol. I). A full team usually had eight, but the number here is evidently symbolic. The image of the four Gospel writers as oxen pulling the plough of evangelization appears (*R–H* 18) in a commentary on Lk 9:62 attributed to St Jerome: 'quatuor boves, id est, quatuor evangelistae' (*PL* 30:591). The traditional symbolisation, also going back to the 5th c., derives from the 'four living creatures' round the throne of God in Apoc 4:6–10 and was familiar in iconography of all types (Mâle 1961:35–7; Katzenellenbogen 1939: fig. 69; Schiller II 108–9, pl. 442 [*c.* 1350]). **264** *large... lou-chered*: perhaps alluding to the meek appearance in depictions of the bull that is St Luke's emblem (as in the very early image in Schiller I pl. 425) or, more obliquely, to his Gospel's special emphasis on the Virgin Mary's humility (Lk 1:48–52). **265** *Marc*: emblematised by a lion. *Mathewe*: his emblem a man (see on B 6.237). **266–7** *Iohan*: specially honoured for the theological depth of his Gospel (for his influence on *PP* see Davlin 1996). John's emblem is an eagle (often fashioned into the lectern supporting the Gospel book), because of the loftiness of the bird's flight and its fabled ability to look directly at the sun (an allusion to the description of the Word as the Light in Jn 1:4–9). **268** *stottes*: heavy work-horses often used for harrowing; an apt metonym for the arduous interpretative labours of the Four Great Doctors. **269** *erede*: ploughing understood allegorically by Raban Maur (*PL* 111:610–1) as the preaching of the Gospel through which the 'earth' of human hearts is prepared to receive the 'seeds' of the virtues. *they to harwen*: 'it would be their task to harrow' (for the construction see on 233). The action of reducing the tilth to a finer and smoother condition before sowing is a fit emblem of the Fathers' exegetical work on the Bible. **270–1** The four named had a special authority in the Western Church, were revered in the monastic as well as the scholastic traditions of Biblical study, and had a general and in some instances strongly specific influence on **L**'s understanding of doctrine, moral teaching and spirituality. **270** *Austyn*: see on 11.148. *Ambrosie*: see on 15.45. **271** *Gregory*: see on 5.146. *Ieroem*: St Jerome (*c.* 345–420), translator of the Hebrew and Greek scriptures into what became the standard Latin text (the Vulgate), and erudite commentator on a large part of the Bible. *þe gode*: alluding to his ascetic life as a hermit-monk at Bethlehem. **272–4a** Their Commentaries used Scripture to interpret itself, a comparative method with its roots in the practice of St Paul (e.g. in Gal 4:22–31). Jerome adopted the literal, Augustine and Gregory the allegorical approach. **273** *handwhile*: scant exaggeration, since the three great contemporaries commented on most of the Scriptural texts, while Gregory later synthesised, developed and transmitted their achievement to the medieval Church. **274** *aythes*: a word of extreme rarity (< OE *egþe* 'harrow'), as is its cognate verb *heggen* (see on 5.19). *oelde...newe*: perhaps an allusion to Mt 13:52; the 'thesaurus' of the OT (like that of the pre-Christian Cardinal Virtues) retains its moral and spiritual value even under the time of Grace. **274a** 'That is, the Old Testament and the New'; Alf*Q* (comparing B 15.212) finds that this 'suggests the language of a biblical commentary'. Scripture itself will help exegetes penetrate and smooth over the sometimes rough and difficult sense of particular Biblical texts and passages.

275–310 describe the sowing of the *Cardinal Virtues*. **275** *graynes*: since the virtues are the 'food' of the soul. The image has been traced to Homily I.3 on Ezechiel (*PL* 76:807–9) by one of the *foure stottes*, St Gregory, which with Jerome's Commentary forms the gloss in *GO* (Kaulbach 1993:136n119), and to Gregory's *Moralia in Job* II.49, ll.37–9, which describes the Spirit as forming the four cardinal virtues in the mind; see also Hugh of St Victor, *Summa Sententiarum* III xvii (*PL* 176:114), cited by Burrow 1993[1]:69. *cardinales vertues*: treated as if French, with the adjective having a plural inflection (see on Pr 132), but as a normal English phrase at 339. The notion of the four chief virtues of practical reason on which the other virtues 'turn' (*cardo* = 'hinge') was taken from Plato and Aristotle into the mainstream medieval view of divine revelation as building on the ground of human nature created in the image of God (*ST* I–II qu. 61). The traditional order moves from wise foresight, through the moderate way of life it makes possible, to the capacity to endure hardship, and finally to the ability

to judge without fear or favour. The virtuous circle thus turns from one cognitive through two affective virtues to a second cognitive virtue now informed with the knowledge derived from experience (*kynde knowynge*). Christian understanding of the cardinal virtues (something particularly important for those entrusted with secular or religious governance) was influenced by the list of the Spirit's seven gifts to the Messiah in Is 11:2–3, the wording of which is echoed in the names 'spiritus intellectus...spiritus fortitudinis' (see Burrow 1993[1]:69). Of these seven, 'consilium', 'fortitudo' and 'pietas' are seen by Aquinas as 'corresponding' respectively to prudence, fortitude and justice. **276** *sewe...soule*: not a new image in *PP*, but recalling 14.23–7a. As *Creator Spiritus* (211 above), the Third Person is fittingly made the author of the natural (cardinal) as well as the supernatural (theological) virtues. The sowing is performed by Grace as an example for his 'prowour' to imitate, clearly indicating that the Church's mission is not simply individual and other-worldly but aims to transform society as a whole. **277** 'The Spirit of Prudence': the virtue of planning and foresight (< *providentia*). Though called *spiritus intellectus* at 466, it signifies not 'speculative understanding' but sagacity or 'practical moral insight', with which it was often linked (Eph 1:8; cf. Prov 8:12, 14:8ff). Personified as 'Dame Prudence' in Chaucer's *Melibee*, it is never a purely 'secular' virtue, and is commended in Christ's exhortation to measure the 'cost' of discipleship (Lk 14:28–32). **278** The 'seeds' are imagined as growing in the soul and bearing fruit in wise foresight. **280–1** illustrate prudence from everyday experience, pointing up the virtues' affinity with *kynde wit*. **282** 'The Spirit of Temperance': more than mere moderation, this is restraint and self-control, much valued by the ancient Stoics but also seen as the basis of Christian asceticism and as a remedy for anger, greed and pride. Among the virtues, it is close to both the 'abstinentia' and 'patientia' urged in II Pet 1:6 and the 'modestia' and 'continentia' that are among the Spirit's 'fruits' in Gal 6:23, and its special importance will emerge later in the speech of NEED at 22.6ff. **284** *swelle*: with either repletion or rage; the possessor of this virtue will be able to handle *utraque fortuna* 'good hap or ill'. **288** *curious cloth*: attacked as a sign of extravagant pride in *CT* X 416–20. **289** *Maister Iohan*: an ironic 'learned' title for a skilled 'master chef'. **290** 'The Spirit of Fortitude': not the *wihtnesse of handes* of 247 but the courage to endure pain and distress without yielding. **296** *plede...pacience*: 'go to law only by patient acceptance'; *al* is either nominal or adverbial. *Parce...*: '[I have done with hope. I shall now live no longer]. Spare me, [Lord]' (Job 7:16); the text part-quoted by Christ at B 18.393, and in the Commentary on Cato's distich 'Parce laudato' (Alf*Q*). Job is the prime OT exemplar of patient fortitude, but the quotation comes from a passage that can hardly be called 'murye'. **297** *Caton*: see on 4.17. **298** 'Be [glad and] of stout heart when you are unjustly condemned' (*DC* II, 14). The text has *libens* before *cum* and the couplet concludes *nemo diu gaudet qui iudice vincit iniquo* 'None rejoice long who through a false judge win'. **299** 'The Spirit of Justice': the capacity to judge oneself and others with fairness, a virtue especially suited to those in public office. Described by Conscience as the 'chief seed' at 409, in a sense it incorporates the discernment of prudence, the fearlessness of fortitude and (as 'equity') the moderation of temperance, providing (as *treuthe* or *rihtwisnesse*) an organising concept of the poem (Stokes 1984:1–31; AlfG 76–7). **302** *gyle...priueyly*: as at 2.70ff. **303** *thorw*: 'by [those sitting in judgement]'. **304–9** lay down the need for adherence to the law and judicial impartiality in adminstering it, even if the wrong is done by the highest in the land. **L**'s apprehensions about the likeliest source of interference seems prescient. **308** *dede*: a grim 'Platonic' pun, hinting that death might be the price of such scrupulous justice under a tyrant. **310** *eueneforth his knowyng*: 'to the best of his ability'; because the judge's knowledge of the truth should be his sole guide in making a just judgement. **311–36** describe through the figure of 'harrowing' the development of Christian theology. **311** Harrowing prepared the soil by removing troublesome weeds and covered the sown seeds to protect them against birds. **312–13** Though the 'natural' virtues of reason need the help of Scripture (interpreted by the Fathers) to grow, the task of destroying evil in the world falls to *Love*, the 'plant of peace' (1.147) that has now been 'sown' on earth through the Incarnation of Christ described in 69ff. **314** *cammokes*: the tough-rooted weed *Ononis spinosa* or *resta bovis* 'rest-harrow', which 'arrests' or obstructs the harrow's movement. *wedes*: '(other) weeds'. **317** *alle þat conneth*: 'all you who possess practical understanding'. Those addressed are not the clergy specifically but the Christian people at large, whose practice of the virtues should be directed by the Church's teachings. **320** *hous*: an image for the Church perhaps suggested by the capacious medieval tithe-barn (like the one still extant at Great Coxwell in Oxfordshire), which resembled in shape the mendicant 'preaching-church'. A patristic source for the idea appears to be Augustine's Sermo 73 (*PL* 38:471). *herborwe in*: an inf. verb-phrase allowing the object to stand at the line-end. **323–30** allegorically present the Church not as a material organisation but as a spiritual organism, the 'Mystical Body of Christ'. In accordance with traditional thought, the Cross (metonymic for the Passion) is made its central foundation (an idea that found its physical counterpart in the cruciform ground-plan of larger Christian edifices). **323** *cros*; *croune*: 'tokens' of the Passion signifying how the Christian community must suffer like its Lord in order to win the 'crown of glory' that the personified female figure of Ecclesia often wears

in depictions of the Crucifixion (Schiller II pls 446, 450). **325** *bapteme and bloed*: hendiadys for 'baptismal blood'; alluding to patristic understanding of the blood and water from Christ's side as emblems of the sacraments, especially baptism (see on 12.110–11, 21.58). *bloed...rode*: for the Leonine internal rhyme across the caesura, cf. Appendix One § 5.ii.(c). **326** *morter*: the bond holding together the members with their Head, the divine mercy shown in Christ's dying for mankind and the Church's sharing in his redemptive suffering. **328** *wateled and walled*: 'made a wall of wattle-and-daub' (a rural building-method using woven branches and lime-mortar). **329** *alle Holy Writ*: perhaps here signifying the authoritative patristic tradition. *roof*: Scripture 'covering' the harvested virtues against the elements and so protecting the Church against false belief, but not forming its foundation, which is Christ himself (Eph 2:20). **330** *Vnite*: a synecdochic 'nature-name' (itself *an Englisch*), unity being one of the 'marks' of Christ's mystical body as described in Eph 4:1–16. As an oblique designation of the Church for whose unity its Founder prayed (Jn 17:11), the name would have had special poignancy in 1378, when Christendom was divided by the Great Schism (see *Intro.* V § 15). The idea of 'unity' as a protection against the deadly sins, and much of the local imagery and verbal detail, are convincingly traced by Wilkes (1965) to *Ancrene Wisse* (ed. Day, 109–10). **331** *And...doen*: see 183 and cf. 279. **332** *cart*: for an earlier allegorical cart (of vices) see 2.190. *Cristendoem*: both 'baptism', which cleanses from original (as confession from actual) sin, and 'the Community of Christians' into which the baptized are initiated. *sheues*: human souls as a spiritual 'harvest' to be reaped by preaching the Gospel; cf. Mt 9:37–8, Jn 4:35. **334** *hayward*: the person assigned to watch and protect the crops against 'pickers and thieves' (cf. 5.16, 13.44). The ordinary clergy are envisaged as having a stable ministry to the local community (the parish), the prelates as having a wider call to evangelize. **L** does not see the latter's rôle strictly as missionary, except for bishops *in partibus*, but stresses the need for diocesan visitations in order to 'feed' the people with 'ghostly food' (see 17.277–92, B 15.572, and cf. I Pet 5:2–3). **335** See on 19.36 above. **336** covers both faith and morals, doctrine and edification, 'truth' and 'love' (cf. B 1.76, 16.6). *londe of bileue*: for another such allegorical terrain, cf. 11.169.

(iii) 337–484 deal with the *preparation for the Siege of Antichrist* that occupies the final Passus. It resembles that for the Harrowing of Hell in XX, and the tone of lines like 340 suggests a darkly ironic inversion of Christ's effortless triumph (20.364) over those who resisted him. The Deadly Sins first encountered in distorted human guise in Vision 2 now return in nakedly diabolic form to assail the barn of Grace, their eventual triumph reversing the fragile success of the original Piers in Passūs VII–IX.

337–93 describe the building of *the spiritual defence-works*. **337** *Now...plouh*: this 'spiritual ploughing' recalling the 'literal ploughing with a spiritual significance' at 8.110–12. *Peres*: signifying at the existential plane Christ's 'faithful pastors and teachers' (*Sk*), but at the historical, 'all who resist the enemies of Christianity'. These range from the first to be identified as Antichrist, the Roman Emperor Nero (when the Piers-figure correlates closely with St Peter), to all bringers of heresy, schism and worldliness into the Christian *comune*. *Pryde*: the root of the Deadly Sins and their determined leader. While assuredly an emblem of the contemporary clergy's material-mindedness, he perhaps typifies historically less the persecutions of the pagan Emperors (which hurt Christians but failed to corrupt the spiritual *ecclesia*) than the Church's more perilous temporal success under Constantine, after these persecutions had ceased. **340** The virtues are understood as a crop still growing in *þe londe of bileue*. **341–2** The simplest and most satisfactory solution to the problem of the number of villains present would probably be to see only two, Pride's sergeant-at-arms (sg.) and his spy (see *TN*). **341** *Surquidou(r)s*: an embodiment of arrogance or presumption, 'whan a man undertaketh an emprise that hym oghte nat do, or elles that he may nat do; and this is called *surquidrie*' (*CT* X 403). *seriaunte of armes*: officer (usually armed) attending on the king; a class at this time in ill-repute for extortions and oppressions (AlfG). **342** *Spille-Loue*; *Speke-euele-bihynde*: 'command-names' like Amend-you, Dowel (or Modern English 'spoilsport' and 'killjoy'). The second, a gloss on the first explaining how back-biting and slander destroy charity, recalls Wrath at 6.115–17. **345** *Sire*: the title (contemptuously) acknowledging his 'priestly' status. **346** *broke*: as a result of the dissension to be caused by arrogance and slander in the Church; words well fitting both the heresies and schisms spoken of in the Epistles (e.g. I Cor 1:10–11, 14:33) and contemporary animosities between the supporters of Pope and antipope. **347** *come out*: a sign of defeat and surrender. *caples tweyne*: for another allegorical horse cf. B 17.108. That these particular *caples* are made to draw the cart of Belief serves to underline the crucial link between righteousness and orthodoxy. For **L** corrupt conduct and false belief (vice and heresy) both flourish when the sacrament of penance is abused. **350–1** The individual's conscience will become morally confused by mistaken guidance from his confessor, and in consequence the body of Christian believers will progressively go astray. The referent of *Conscience* may ironically include the conscientious priest confessing a penitent previously misled by one less scrupulous. **351** *Cristene or hethene*: a grim warning that the conduct and faith of Christians will have so decayed that the distinction becomes blurred. **352–3** *marchaunt*: a single example illustrating how and where

moral uncertainty can generate serious consequences for society as a whole. **354–7** The allegory enacts the nobility's special temptation of luxurious self-indulgence, the 'lord' being a type-figure later named at 22.312 as the recipient of a Friar's emollient ministrations. **358–62** Conscience's advice is that strength lies in unity and that dissension among Christians will help only the enemies of the Church. The contemporary resonance of the lines will have lessened only slightly a decade after the B-Text, since the Schism was still unresolved and the Lollards (who opposed obligatory confession) were gaining adherents (cf. Pearsall 2003:19). His stress on the need for Grace in order to oppose sin implies in this context the necessity of the sacraments (the usual channels of grace), something also challenged by Wycliffite teachers. **360** *pees*: recalling St Paul's reference to '*unity* of the spirit in the bond of *peace*' (Eph 4:3); a quality vital for the survival of the Church. L's 'prophetic' awareness reflects the deepening impact of the Schism as well as echoing scriptural warnings against divisions (cf. I Jn 2:19). **362** *goen agayn*: i.e. set out from Unity to *attack*; they must therefore go on the defensive. **363–6** A close association with Conscience has been evident from as early as Pr 141–6. Since *kynde wit* 'intuitive good sense' is conceptually 'prior' to the moral reasoning that issues in a concrete judgement of *conscience*, his 'teaching' (cf. 3.436) may be understood to 'inform' the constable of the situation (MED s.v. *techen* v. 2(b)) and of the urgent need for an 'outer' spiritual defence (made up of pious works). **364** *comaundede*: the actual command coming from the 'officer' Conscience (367), with Kynde Wit as a sort of NCO conveying what needs to be done. **365** *diche depe*: recalling the abode of Wrong in B Pr 15–16; the onslaught of infernal powers on earth demands a matching resistance. **366** *Holi Churche*: the Church Militant, the whole body of Christian believers. *holinesse*: not impossibly with a 'Platonic' pun. The 'hole' is hollowed out for a spiritual stronghold that is an earthly simulacrum of Truth's tower, vividly expressive of the common medieval understanding of a cathedral church as an earthly 'replica' of the heavenly Jerusalem (cf. Von Simson 1956:8–11). *pile*: an image traced by Wilkes (1965:334–6) to *AW* (see at 380 below). **368** The Church's outer structure as a sacred society must imitate its inner nature as a spiritual edifice; hence the *moche moet* will correspond to that described at 7.232, the outward tears that fill it paralleling the repentance experienced inwardly. The passage recapitulates 10.128–36, where Anima within the Castle of *Caro* was represented as besieged by the Prince of this World. **369** *hem*: its 'ordained' defenders. **370–5** recapitulate various moments in Visions 1 and 2 (e.g. 2.59, B 5.641), as the world depicted reaches forward to the actual present and increasingly comes to resemble the *Visio*'s Field of Folk. **370** *comune wommen*:

because 'professional' sinners; Conscience does not contradict the teaching of Mt 21:31–2 and the recognitions at 18.143, B 11.216 of harlots who *will* 'repent and refuse sin'. **372** *sisour*; *sompnour*: a pair associated with the archetypal 'common woman' at 4.161–2 and condemned throughout *PP* (see 2.59, 3.170). **373–4** bring out how 'their sin's not accidental but a trade' (false testimony that a guilty person was innocent); heavily-stressed *sothly* highlights sarcastically their true awareness of their sin against truth. *with...helden*: recalling 2.179–80. **377** *wexe*: implying a change of metaphor (to that of a growing plant); but the notion of sanctity as the 'water' of spiritual life, outwardly manifested as 'religious tears', is soon resumed. **378–9** Prayer, pilgrimage and alms-giving are the traditional works of 'satisfaction'; the personal penances will include fasting and other forms of self-denial of a less visible kind. **380** recalls the action of Repentance in Passus VI, beginning with Will's weeping. *walled water*: the magnified image recalling such Biblical parallels as 'Let tears run down like a torrent day and night' (Lam 2:18). Wilkes aptly cites *AW* (ed. Day, pp. 109–10): 'ase ofte as þe ueond asaileð ouwer castel & te soule buruh, mid inwarde bonen worpe ut uppon him schaldende *teares*…þu hauest forschalded þe drake heaued mid *wallinde watere*…kastel þæt haueþ deope dich a buten & water þe iðe dich þe kastel is wel kareleas aȝen his unwines…ah habbe ȝe depe dich of deope edwurdinesse & wete teres þerto' (Wilkes 1965). Although *wallinde* here must mean 'boiling' rather than 'springing', the verbal and contextual affinities are arresting. **382–3** The purgation effected during the penitential cycle aims to restore the Church each Lent to its pristine condition at its founding. For the idea of holiness as especially associated with chastity, cf. 18.95–6 above, *Purity* 7–16 and Alan of Lille's praise in *AP* of the blessing of a pure conscience 'that purges the mind of uncleanness' and is 'the image of eternal life' (*PL* 210:139). **385** *lord of lust*: the principle of sensual pleasure as something governing men's lives, the *exercitus carnis* 'army of the flesh' seen by Alan of Lille as fighting against the soul (*PL* 210:141, quoting Gal 5:17). *Lente:* The poem's 'liturgical time' has now shifted back (or forward) to the Lenten season with which the redemptive sequence began at 19.1. It commences and climaxes in the space of 386–7, as the Christian community perform an *anamnesis* or 'calling to mind' of Christ's redemptive death and resurrection. **386** *dyneth*: a figure evoking Biblical images of the Messianic banquet; the food is to be not, as at Conscience's / Reason's dinner (B XIII / C XV), the *words* of scripture but the consecrated 'bread of heaven'. **387** *labored...Lenten*: the discipline of self-denial recapitulating at a higher plane the bodily labours commended in Hunger's sermon to Piers (8.250–63). **388** *bred yblessed*: the Easter Eucharist, which was seen in a special way as the reward of

Lenten abstinence (cf. I Cor 5:7–8, the Communion verse for Easter Sunday). *Godes body*: the normal phrase for the sacred elements (cf. B 12.85), asserting their identity with the crucified Christ (cf. 20.77, 476, which the phrase echoes); a stronger sign of **L**'s rejection of Lollard beliefs than recognised by Pearsall 2003:13. *þervnder*: cf. *sub panis specie / Velaris divinitus* from the Corpus Christi sequence hymn 'O panis dulcissime' (*JLH* II, 210). **389** *Godes word*: the words of consecration instituted by Christ at the Last Supper (Mt 26:26–8). **390** states elliptically that Grace gave the ordained priesthood the *power* to consecrate the Eucharist and all Christians the *capacity* to receive it (cf. on 185–8). **391–3** propose a frequency of communion (perhaps also tacitly assuming confession before it) more like the clergy's than the once-yearly reception usual for laypeople (Duffy 1992:93–4). **393** *Redde...*: see on 188.

394–461 report the opposition Conscience meets with as a series of tense exchanges, first with the *comune*, next with a fractious brewer and an uneducated (but very vocal) vicar, and then (462–84) at the opposite end of the social scale, a nobleman and a king. **394–5** echo Christ's words at Mt 5:23–4 (together with I Cor 11:27–9 the scriptural basis for requiring confession before *housel*). The sacrament of 'communion' between Christ and the believer requires accord between the latter and all other Christians, an aspect of the rite especially stressed in the period, with its close-knit pattern of social organisation (Duffy 1992:127). **397a** 'And forgive us our trespasses'; the fifth petition of the Paternoster. **398** *assoiled*: obligatory confession before Easter Communion offering an opportunity to settle grievances between neighbours or more widely in the *comune*. **399** *Bawe*: ironically recalling Trajan's interjection at 12.76. *breware*: connected by profession with both the provision of drink and the deceits and abuses that went with it, as described in 6.225–31 above. **399–400** *be...Iesu*: the ironic syntactical ambiguity underlining the speaker's wrong disposition. **400** The 'justice' involved here is the sale of goods at a price reflecting their true value. **402** *at on hole*: i.e. pretend that both qualities are drawn from the same barrel of (superior) ale; a trick like that of Greed's wife Rose the Regrater at 6.225–33. **403** *Thikke...ale*: see on 6.226. **404** *hacky aftur*: found only here; it is possibly a phrasal verb, or else *aftur* may mean 'in accordance with'. **408–9** *Saue...ysaued*: with 'Platonic' wordplay depending on the emendation (on which see *TN*). **409** Though justice is here declared the 'chief' of the four cardinal virtues, a subtle claim for Temperance will be put by Need at 22.23ff. **411** *we*: a small revision bringing out the interdependence of everyone in Unity, and how the failings of one affect all. **412** *lewed vicory*: a shrewd observer like the prudent mouse of Pr 196ff. The acerbic commentary of this second 'lower-class' figure (whom Conscience significantly does not rebuke) articulates the *comune*'s grievances, his criticisms of the shortcomings of the highest orders in the Church recalling the narrator's at Pr 134–7. The ill-educated vicar's real-life counterparts would have been the priests rapidly ordained without proper training to make good the massive loss of parish clergy after the Black Death (see on Pr 82). Gasse 1996 relates the vicar to the earlier priest at 9.280=B 7.105 and sees him too as an object of satiric scorn. **414** The speaker's ignorance of what the Cardinal Virtues are intimates economically both his lack of learning and the absence of these qualities from the society of the time. *Cardinales Vertues*: the French form allowing a tart pun on 'virtuous cardinals'. **415** *a...hennes*: one of many such phrases ('bean' 12.94, 'pie-crust' 9.345) denoting a thing of little value; semi-proverbial in ring but not paralleled. **416–26** The attack on cardinals expresses resentment at their grand manner and cost to the ordinary diocesan clergy who had to contribute to their maintenance. Cardinal legates in England exercised 'extensive authority...with their own miniature curia, including a penitentiary' (Swanson 1989:150) and contemporary criticism of their luxurious living rivals that of the Avignon Papacy itself (Ullmann 1948:7n). There may be a specific allusion here to Cardinal Simon Langham (d. 1376), who was papal nuncius to England in 1371–2 and 1373 (Barney 2006). **418** *pelure...pelours*: a 'Platonic' pun relating luxury to legitimised extortion; the half-line recalls 4.115. **419** is the poem's only macaronic Type IIb line. *clamat cotidie*: 'cries out daily'; this is 'a formula used to initiate proceedings against a public enemy' (Alf*Q*, Alf*G*). **424–5** mordantly express ironic praise, suggesting that they both 'will and will not' be corrupted by the company of the Jews. **425** *Auenoun*: the papal residence until 1377, when Gregory XI removed the curia to Rome (though still intending to return there, when he died in April 1378). As the centre of papal taxation and litigation it required the ministrations of several curial cardinals, who raised the loans they needed from moneylenders, possibly including Jews (Gilchrist 1969 s.v. 'Avignon'). In 1379 a Jew transported to Avignon (which belonged to the papacy) the cardinals who supported the anti-pope Clement VII (Bennett 1943²:63); but the text need not be specifying these, as opposed to Pope Urban's supporters. *Cum sancto...*: see at B 5.278. **426** *Rome*: where the cardinals had their titular churches, the important relics of which were in their keeping. *as here reule wolde*: the 'rule' being their general responsibility as the Pope's immediate helpers in administering the universal Church. The speaker's objection is to the presence of cardinals as papal legates and nuncios (fiscal officers collecting papal taxes) in other countries, including England. *relikes*: sarcastically intimating that some of the holiness of these important relics of Roman martyrs and

saints might rub off on them. **427** *in*: '(should remain) in'; as desired by the King at 4.186. **428** *gredest so of*: cf. at 362, 389ff. **429** *newe plouh ...olde:* 'the ploughs of B VI and XIX respectively: the old plough for the growing of wheat on the half-acre and the new one for the cultivation of the virtues on the manor of Grace' (Burrow 2007:124). **430** *Emperour*: presumably not in a juridical but in a religious sense of 'supreme spiritual ruler'. The vicar, for whom the Pope's dominion stretches over the souls of all believers, is clearly no follower of Wycliffe, who had himself, however, written to Pope Urban VI a more or less conciliatory letter in 1378 (*Fasciculi* 341–2; Workman ii.315 for date). But his criticisms echo Wycliffe's in their negative contrast of papal conduct with Scriptural standards and in their admonitory repetition of 'Christian' (446–8). *alle...Cristene*: implying that such a Pope could work for the conversion of the Moslems, Jews and heathens with hope of success.

431–51 turn from cardinals to contrast the ferocity of the actual pope with the forebearance of a true *servus servorum* worthy of the name of Peter / Piers. **431–2** probably allude to Urban's use of mercenary soldiers against Clement VII in April 1379 (Bennett 1943:63; cf. *Intro.* V § 20). **432** *suche*: his Christian subjects who support the antipope. **433** *pat...doynge*: 'who follows the example of God in the way he conducts himself'. The vicar imagines an 'ideal pope' as guided by Reason's teaching at 13.194–200 and clearly implies that the reigning Pontiff would give far more effective spiritual leadership if he exercised *spiritus fortitudinis* through patiently enduring his enemies' opposition instead of asserting his rights by seeking to crush them through force (see on 467). **434** '[Love your enemies: do good to them that hate you... That you may be the children of your Father who is in heaven], who [maketh his sun to rise upon the good and bad and] raineth upon the just and the unjust' (Mt 5:44–5). **437–9** conflate the present allegorical sense of Piers's ploughing with the literal sense as enacted in Vision 2. The Pope, clergy and faithful laypeople must work for the good of all, including the worst, while keeping a proper distinction of dignity in the sacramental community between themselves and the wasters and prostitutes (who are not, however, excluded from Unity). **443–4** echo the words of Study at B 10.129–30. **444** *soffreth*: cf. 13.200, which gives another reason for putting up with evils. *til som tyme*: not implying that all *will* repent, only that they may (and at times and in ways known to God alone); a more benign interpretation of God's 'syttynge' sufferance than that in the parable of the cockle and wheat to which allusion is perhaps made (Mt 13:24–43). **445** *the Pope*: the obvious referent being Urban VI, whom England acknowledged. **446** *And*: 'Even though'. *pe Kynge*: with no specific reference being necessarily intended, only the Pope's standing claim to immediate universal spiritual jurisdiction unlimited by the temporal authority. **449a** 'Thou shalt not kill' (Ex 20:13), quoted at Lk 18:20; 'Revenge is mine' (Deut 32:35). In **B** there is a summary echo of B 10.366–8 (a passage **C** omits), which juxtaposes the quotations. Both Testaments concur in reserving to God the right to punish by force; but while **L** clearly has the clergy in mind, he does not necessarily deny its use to the civil power (cf. on 248). **452–61** insist that cardinals' ingenuity in acquiring *wele* has led all to care only for getting rich, by whatever means. **460** The climax of the complaint is that in the hypocritical moral ethos engendered by the clergy's example, virtues are manipulated as disguises for the concealment of vices.

462–84 *The response of nobility and king.* **462** *lord*: a type-figure, one with or cousin to the pleasure-loving noble later to be met with at 22.90–2. **463** *of my reue*: and thence from his tenants, from whom the reeve collected manorial dues. The lord presumably means that under the guise of prudent management he extracts the last ounce from his feudal dependents (whatever their conditions of life at any given time), an attitude Piers warned against at 8.36ff. **466** *Spiritus Intellectus*: 'the Spirit of Understanding', an ironic synonym for Prudence (see on 275), as the lord obviously 'understands' what is to his advantage. It is taken as a synecdoche by Alf*Q*, who cites from *FM* 589 'understanding of present things' as one of the three elements of prudence, and the discussion of the cardinal virtues in the Proem to Cato's *Distichs*. **467** The 'spirit of fortitude' here is nearer to 'aggression' than to the 'endurance' specified at 292–6. *fecche hit*: cf. 242. *he*: the person from whom the reeve reckoned the payment due. **468** *bi his corone*: by his authority as king; that the phrase is an oath and does not mean 'with reference to his crown' (*Sk*) seems supported by parallel 462. The king's speech concludes, from the proposition that he is head of law, that all he does is lawful (cf. the cry of the Commons at B Pr 145). **469–70** echo the words of the coronation oath of medieval English kings, but significantly omit all reference to ruling *justly*. **471** *to lyue by*: on this phrasal infinitive used as noun-subject (with 'the means' understood) see *MES* 523. **472** *heed*: either 'source' or 'controller' or both; in either case, the claim is to absolute authority. **476** *ȝow two*: addressed to the clergy and the people; the king is lawfully entitled to tax both. **476–7** Though nothing on these lines is said at 304–10, the king evidently considers himself (as supreme judge) to be above the judgement of all others and hence *potentially* above the law. For he fails to mention his duty of observing the ancient laws and customs of the realm as stated in Edward II's coronation oath, to which Conscience alludes at 480–1 below (see Maitland 1908:100–01 for further clarification of the issue, and Baldwin 1981, Firth Green 1995:232–7). **478** *borwe neuere*: and therefore need not 'pay what he owes' (since he owes nothing).

hoseled: cf. 394–8. **480–1** *defende...rewme...treuthe*: Conscience's 'condition' echoes the coronation promises of King Richard's great-grandfather Edward II to confirm the ancient customs and laws of England, to defend 'the laws and righteous customs which the community of the realm shall have chosen' and to do 'equal and right justice and discretion in mercy and truth' (on the oath see Richardson 1949 and 1960). The 'condition' is meant to exclude any conflation of public authority with personal power, the crucial issue in the later years of Richard II. **482** *thy lawe*: the constitutional precedent he cites in support of his claim. **482a** 'What's yours is yours to keep and defend, and not to seize for your own end'. An analogue is found in the *Summa de Vitiis* of Peraldus cited by Wenzel 1974:367: 'Likewise, if slaves' possessions are said to belong to their lords, this is in the sense only that they are to be defended by him, not plundered [*ad defendendum et non ad depredandum*]'. **483** *fer hoem*: 'a long journey home'; the suggestion is of a return from the cathedral to his village-parish. **484** brings the vision full circle by closely echoing line 1 of the Passus.

Passus XXII (B XX)

PASSUS XXII opens with an important waking Prelude (1–50). The remainder is given over to *Antichrist's Siege of Unity:* (i) the preparations (51–73); (ii) the siege itself, with counterattacks (74–142); (iii) the Lyf-Elde episode with the Dreamer (143–211); (iv) the Confession crisis, followed by the entry of Friar Flatterer (212–386); and (v) a Finale, the departure of Conscience, with which the poem abruptly ends (381–7). Will's falling asleep after a rebuke, and the beginning of Vision Eight, recall the opening of **C**'s Vision Two after its allegorised predream encounter with two somewhat aggressive personified figures at 5.1–108. The Need Episode (1–50) can now be seen to echo that revised opening, which was perhaps designedly added in the light of what had already been done in B XX. Both instances are interior dialogues of the waking self, in the earlier one complacent in plenty (5.6–9), in the later wretched with want. NEED, personifying the 'necessitous deprivation' (Burrow 1993:95–100) mentioned by Piers at 9.62–3=B 7.66, is vocal in asserting the common right of all to share in the earth's produce that (as noted in Simpson 1990:233) was recognised by HC in I 17–19. His argument is regarded with suspicion by Adams (1978:273–301), who connects Need with the Antichrist of the following dream and with the *egestas* of Job 41:13 as understood in Gregory's commentary, and sees him as voicing the questionable views on poverty and mendicancy associated with friars. Simpson (1990:232–4) also sees Need as encouraging 'the poor, and Will in particular...to manipulate temperance', a view shared by Godden (1990:162–4). Yet this is surely not what he is doing by urging temperance even in a situation of 'necessitous deprivation'; and when Need appears within the dream at 232, he insists on the friars' adherence to the poverty they profess. This however has led Frank (1957:113–14) to interpret Need's speech as an ironically intended warning against the theory of poverty espoused by the friars. Here Frank is partly misled by reading *bydde* for *byde* at 48, and Simpson (239–40) makes the same mistake, as does Barney (2006:195, 204), who is misled by failure to recognise the irony in *begge* at V 51 (but see *TN*). In fact Need does not support begging and does oppose (what he regards as) the friars' covetousness, much as Conscience (233, 246) opposes their envy. For earlier and later discussions of this controversial figure and the themes articulated by the episode see Carruthers 1973:160–66, Hewett-Smith, 2001:33–53, the studies cited in Kim 2002:160n and most fully and insistently Barney 2006:186–96. A more positive interpretation of Need in the light of traditional treatments of the 'paupertas crucis' motif will be found in Schmidt 1983[2]:188–92, and of medieval natural law doctrine on the common ownership of earthly goods in Mann 2004:3–29.

Prelude **1–50** NEED's rebuke articulates the Dreamer's own misgivings about the way of life described at 5.42–52, in which material necessity (in age) results from failure to do paid (physical) work. But his earlier robust reply to Reason at 5.82–8 is replaced by an oblique (and quietly subversive) defence of his position as conforming with Temperance. Need first claims (6–22) that 'winning' (obtaining) the bare necessities, even by dubious means (*sleithe*), is acceptable if it is the only way to survive and if it respects the cardinal virtue which, as it controls and moderates the others, *cannot* be 'manipulated'. Though Simpson is right to stress the importance of law for **L**, in a situation of extreme need natural law takes precedence over positive law, because no man-made decrees can be just that deprive man of the prospect of life, a gift of God. The 'law of kind' (the urge to preserve one's life) thus becomes indistinguishable from the 'law of reason' (the requirement to respect others' property), *insofar as it observes* TEMPERANCE. **4** *noen*: dinner-time; see on 2.100. *Nede*: personifying a condition always for **L** associated with feelings of shame, whether the want is self-caused, as at 13.240, or results from adverse fortune, as at 9.84–7, where the noon meal is again mentioned. **7** *to lyue by*: i.e. the minimum necessary for survival. **8** *techyng... tellyng*: not that Temperance *enjoins* 'taking', but will justify it if this virtue's precepts are followed. *Spiritus Temperancie*: see on 21.282–9; commended as protecting against the colourable excesses to which prudence, fortitude and justice were shown as exposed at 21.455–79. **10** *nede*: either grammatically identical with *nede* at 9

or the nominal adjective *nedé* meaning 'needy (person[s])'. *ne...lawe*: 'is not subject to the constraints of (positive) law'. It translates the Natural Law maxim *Necessitas non habet legem* earlier quoted at 13.43*a* in an addition insisting that a messenger who passes through a cornfield (and perhaps picks ears of corn) is not obliged to give a pledge to the hayward. Alf*G* 103 aptly cites *Dives et Pauper* 2:141, with its allusion to Mt 12:1–8, and Szittya 1986:270, 277 notes the phrase's special association with friars (for a standard discussion of the idea, see *ST* IIa–IIae, lxvi, a. 7, also a. 8 and q. lxxvii–viii). The implication of the parallel is that the Dreamer's harmless (if materially unproductive) mode of existence is like the errand-bearer's, in that he 'carries' the 'message of eternal life' to society by constantly writing about it. Thus he tacitly defends his poetic 'work' as partaking in Piers's cultivation of the field of Truth with the 'ploughshare of the tongue' (Barney 1973). The 'sleight' by which he 'comes to cloth' and 'drinks at a dish' is his *makynge*, the life of non-manual work that he defends in the Prelude to V. *dette*: i.e the 'debt' of sin. One in extremity who contravenes (positive) law to save his life does not sin if he takes only what he needs: so he does not 'owe' anyone anything. **11** *thre thynges*: these (food, drink, clothing) recall 1.20–4, where HC (like Need here) enjoins moderation in using gifts ordained by God *of his cortesye* 'bountifully' for the benefit of all (*in comune*). The burden of this timeless moral message concerning what are now called 'human rights' is that those who deny their fellow human beings these basic needs (whether through force, economic control, or law) are the ones who offend divine justice. **15** *synegeth*; *wynneth*: a 'Platonic' anti-pun signalised by the internal rhyme; for this kind of 'winning' is not a form of 'sinning'. **17** The personification generates a potent and paradoxical figure: a man reduced to dire need *has* no 'surety' in the usual sense. **18** *lawe of kynde*: perhaps with a dual reference, depending on whether the implied human subject of *wolde* is the needy man or other people. For it signifies both the natural instinct of self-preservation found in all creatures and the *lex naturalis*, the principles of moral reason forming part of man's nature as the image of God. **21** *Cardinale Vertues*: see on 21.275ff above. Need's claim is that temperance (unlike the other three virtues) intrinsically cannot be perverted, because one cannot by definition be too temperate. It is tacitly endorsed by the pragmatic Vicar in his not including temperance among the 'fayre vertues' that can be made to seem 'vises' (21.459); but it also recalls the idealists HC on *mesure* at 1.34–5 and Patience at B 14.74; and it is close to the teaching of Alan of Lille in *AP*: 'O what a glorious virtue is *temperance*, which makes virtue hold *the middle*, lest it should fall into *diminution* or develop into *excess*' (*PL* 210:162); cf. 27. Since Need's claim could arguably be extended to 'ideal' (as opposed to 'actual') justice, fortitude and prudence considered as each a 'mean' between extremes, and so as each a form of *mesure* (with all virtue being 'temperate' in its essence), his argument does not perforce entail 'depreciation of the other virtues' (*Pe*). **23–32** criticise the cardinal virtues other than temperance, here tacitly equated with Need and elevated in status as conducing to humility, which God himself displayed in the Incarnation. **23** *bi ver to*: 'by a long way comparable to'; cf. Conscience's comment on the primacy of Justice at 21.409. **25/6** The identical end-rhyme underlines the catechetical quality of the exposition. **29** scans as a macaronic Type IIIa with two lifts in *Iústicie* (cf. 21.477). *shal*: 'is constrained to'. **33** distinguishes between *insight* into the nature of things (true wisdom, a gift of the Spirit) and *foresight* about likely future outcomes (prudence), which can always prove mistaken. *ymaginacioun*: cf. 21.278–9. **33a** See on 11.308–9. **35–50** are marked by emphatic *traductio* of *need* and its derivatives over a dozen times. **35–7** The argument here echoes Patience's about the value of Poverty at 16.69–70. **35** *nexst hym*: cf. 18.98; because need removes any material obstacle between the soul and God. **36** *as*: '(is) as'. *louh...*: a comparison used in describing Dobet at 10.83. *þat*: '(of) that (which)'. **37** 'For of necessity Need makes the needy feel humble of heart'. **38** *Philosopheres*: such as Diogenes the Cynic (4th c. B.C.), cited as an authority on poverty in Chaucer's 'Former Age' 35, the 'wise men' who praise poverty at 12.143–5 and those mentioned at 12.175–8. Asceticism as the means to wisdom was central to such Christian 'ways' of holy living as the eremitic, the monastic and later the mendicant (cf. B 15.416–22). **40** *goestliche*: its position after the mid-line break favouring the sense 'really' (MED s.v. *gostli* adv 3(b)) rather than 'as a spirit' (ibid. 1 (c), citing this example); the stress is unequivocally on the physical truth of the Incarnation. **41** *nedy*: through abandoning his boundless 'wealth' as God for the limited condition of human existence. But on Christ's birth into a poor family, see 12.135–6, and on his praise of poverty 12.156–72; and for key scriptural texts on the special blessedness of 'the needy and the poor' cf. Pss 39:18, 40:2 and 68:30. **42** *the Boek...places*: the Gospels make little of Christ's personal poverty, but record his judgement of wealth as an obstacle to holiness in Mk 10:17–31. The desert of the Temptation is among those 'many different places' (taking the phrase as modifying *was* not *saith*) where his 'wilful' privation reached an extreme (Mt 4:1ff). **41–3** The inspiration for relating the idea of *paupertas Christi* to the cited Gospel text may be the pseudo-Bernardine *Vitis Mystica*: 'The king of kings... who alone lacked nothing...became so poor that, as he himself bears witness, he was found to be poorer than *the foxes...and the birds*...Poor in his birth, poorer in his life, poorest of all *upon the cross*' (*PL* 184:638–9). **43** *on...*

rode: not scripturally correct, the words being spoken to a scribe who asked to be Christ's disciple (Mt 8:20=Lk 9:58). But their appropriateness to Christ's ultimate 'poverty' on the cross may have licensed the misattribution, already found in the first version of Rolle's *Meditations on the Passion* (Horstman I, 1895:88), a work in the main 'affective' tradition. Also plainly recalled here is Mt 16:24, on 'bearing one's cross daily', and in a broader sense the Christian ascetic aspiration to 'crucify' every desire for worldly 'wele'. Need's speech draws not only on learned Bernardine-Franciscan devotional writing but on the vernacular tradition represented by Rolle, the C13th *Southern Passion* (1605ff) and the Harley 4196 text of the C14th *Northern Passion* (804ff); see Schmidt 1983²:174–96. **47** Thought and wording recall the paraphrase of Jn 16:20 at 12.211–12 but are also close to the 'Meditation A' (*De Passione secundum Ricardum*) ascribed to Rolle: 'it falleth to him that is grete to *suffre gret thinges* but soone thilke gret peynes shal be gone and after *shal ioye comme* withowten ende' (ed. Ogilvie-Thomson 65). **48** *abasched*: claiming on Christ's authority that the indigent should not feel shame or even embarrassment at their plight (as do the decent upright poor of 9.86–7). **48/9** The climactic identical rhyme imparts catechetical finality to Need's injunction. **49–50** The unparalleled extremity of divine love teaches all to endure their (comparatively) lesser privations, the crucified Saviour (1.167–9) being their 'example'. The thought here is close to that of a Latin passage ascribed to Augustine in the margin of Hoccleve's *Regement of Princes* 1079–85: 'Consider the Saviour's life from the time of his birth to his death on the cross, and you will find in it nothing save the marks of poverty'.

(i) 51–73 The *Eighth Vision* begins with Antichrist's siege of Unity. **53** *A(u)ntecrist*: see on 21.220. L here develops Mt 13:24–30, 39, with some influence from the early C13th French allegorical poem *Le Tournoiement d'Antéchrist* (Owen 1912:145–7; Jung 1971:268–89). His use of this figure lends a broadly 'apocalyptic' character to the attack on Unity, since Antichrist was thought of as a harbinger of the Second Coming of Christ; but no 'prophecy' of specific events need be intended. (On the 'apocalyptic' dimensions of the poem and their implications for its form see Bloomfield 1961). L's outlook seems closer to the 'reformist apocalypticism' described by Kerby-Fulton 1990 (recalling the reading of Frank 1968) than to the chiliastic 'end-time' apocalypticism of Emmerson (1981:193–203), which sees Antichrist's coming as ushering in the Last Judgement. **52** *mette ful merueylousely*: the introductory phrase to the final dream mirroring that of the first (Pr 9). **53–4** recall the eschatological imagery of Reason's speech at 5.120–2. *crop of treuthe*: as sown by Piers at 21.311; cf. 21.262. **55** *fals*: recalling (like *gyle* in 57) Meed's wooer in 2.42, who was also 'a devil's offspring'. *sprynge and sprede*: echoing 13.23 and 16.242 on the growth and extension of goodness and holiness. *nedes*: not now the bare necessities Need spoke of but the unruly desires from which greed, envy and the other capital vices arise. **57** *growe*: the metaphor inverting positive earlier images of love and grace as plants (1.147, 13.22–3, 14.23ff, 17.47); after uprooting the virtues, Antichrist sows his own seeds of evil. *a god*: Antichrist's status as a false god depending on people's mistaking him for the representative of the true God. While no direct identification with a leader of the Church (such as the Anti-pope) is made, his strongest support is shockingly asserted to lie amongst clerics. Antichrist, Pride and *Lyf* (the diabolic, the worldly and the carnal) stand as an unholy trio set against Grace, Piers and Conscience, who signify heavenly, ecclesiastical and secular right order. **58** *Freres*: the most explicit condemnation of the 'corrupted' mendicants since the warning at Pr 56–65, which may now be seen as being fulfilled. *copes*: echoing the charge made as early as Pr 59 (and already in **Z**) of a kind of vain covetousnesss among them. **59** *religious*: used habitually by **L** for monks *as against* friars (see *IG* s.v.). **60** scans as a standard Type Ia line, reading *welcóme*. In this word, metrically necessary wrenching of stress occurs in five instances, normal accentuation on the first element in three (see *IG*). *tyraunt*: a word used earlier of False and his accomplices at 2.211 (another example of how the final vision 'recapitulates' the first). But the presentation here suggests the head of an invading army going about the country to raise support (69ff). **61** *foles*: the spiritually wise who are unwise in the sight of the world for not wishing to 'spede' through 'gyle'; see on B 7.125. **62–3** They find 'the shorter life the better' (15.262), while waiting for the promised end 'in longing to be hence' (21.249). The élite remnant of ascetic 'pilgrim-hermits' like those of Pr 25–30 may be envisaged. **63** *Leautee*: collectively standing for all (perhaps especially lay) people who live in accordance with *treuthe*; see on Pr 149. Friend of Holy Church, enemy of Mede, critic of the friars, Leautee vigorously affirms the right and duty to expose 'falsenesse and faytrye' (12.34) among clerics. **65** *þat* (1): an indefinite sg. for pl. 'those' understood. *mylde...holy*: without the sharp contrast between layman and religious contemplative intended at B 15.306–7 (revised in // **C**). **67** *hem*; *here*: i.e. 'false folk'. **68** *here*: i.e. 'these kings'. **69** *at*: 'serving under'. **70** The chief Deadly Sin holds 'pride of place' as his leader Antichrist's standard-bearer in the attack. **71** *a lord*: one like those favoured by Mede at 3.57 and perhaps to be identified with the 'lord of lust' of 21.385 and with *Lyf* at 143. **72–3** *kepar...gyour*: his rôle here seeming closer to a bishop's than a secular lord's, though his name permits equivocal reference with univocal sense.

(ii) 74–164 The *Defence of Unity* begins with Conscience appealing to *Kynde* to help the Church (understood as co-extensive with all sincere believers) against what is now conceived more as a concerted onslaught by the forces of evil than as the individual's habitual yielding to weakness as in the Sins-sequence in Vision 2. **74** *foles*: Pauline irony, the worldly-unwise gladly adopting their enemies' mocking appellation. **75** repeats the invitation addressed to 'all Christians' at 21.359. The failure of *al þe comune* to answer the call to Unity may signify allegorically the ongoing dissension occasioned by the Schism, which in dividing the Church strengthens its enemies. **76** *crye... Kynde*: recalling the threat from *Princeps huius mundi* to the individual soul enclosed in the Castle of Caro at 10.134–6, though the Barn of Grace here is a purely spiritual organism and the threat to it collective. Conscience's 'cry' to Kynde (76) is less a direct request for punitive calamities than a forceful attempt (78), as in Reason's sermon at 5.114–22, to arouse men's instinctive dread of age, illness and 'the death of kind' (20.219) as a means of bringing them to repent of their sins. **77** The contemporary ordeal of the Church existentially recapitulates that of the early Christian community in the time of St Peter, its 'eschatological' dimension being something realised in everyday experience throughout every age. *Foles*: 'Fools that we are'. **79** *Beliales childrene*: human beings who have rejected God and embraced sin; see on 20.282. **80–7** distantly remember the approach of Death in the abandoned ending of **A** (A 12.62ff). This sequence also 'recapitulates' Piers's summoning of Hunger in 8.167–70, though here the instrument of chastisement is not famine but disease. **80** *Kynde Conscience*: juxtaposition of grammatical subject and object to bring out their closeness and suggest how men's moral sense is sharpened by taking proper account of mortality. KYNDE is the poem's 'nature-name' for God, author of endings as well as beginnings. *planetes*: an allusion to the notion of illnesses being influenced by planetary 'aspects' at birth, but also to that of a major malign conjunction as the origin of macro-cosmic catastrophes (see on Saturn at 8.346). **81** *forreours*: because making preliminary inroads on the body in preparation for its demise; with this list of ailments cf. at 6.78–9. *feueres and fluxes*: suggesting a gastro-enteritic infection. **83** *radegoundes*: a disease (*gutta rosacea*) marked by inflammation and swellings (MED s.v. *red-gound* n). **L**'s spelling may suggest he thought that cure of the disease was sought through the particular intercession of St Radegund, the ascetic C6th abbess of Poitiers (*Sk*) who ministered to 'women covered with various kinds of leprous spots' (*LA* 953); but there is no direct evidence for this association. **84** *bocches*: implying in the light of B 13.250 plague-boils (*bubones*); the citation of this instance as figurative in MED s.v. *bocche* n. is wrong. **85** *Freneseyes*: attacks of delirium thought to be caused by an imbalance of the humours. *foule eueles*:

a recurrent set phrase (3.96, 16.136 and 21.46) possibly indicating a specific ailment, though there is no positive evidence for the 'epilepsy' suggested by MED s.v. *ivel* n. 5(b). **86** *Hadde*: '(Which) had'. **87** *a legioun*: the large figure for deaths evoking the aftermath of epidemic plague, when even survivors' resistance to lesser ailments was weakened by secondary infections. **89** *Deth*: see on A 12.63. L's DEATH says nothing but wreaks havoc on the population. The *Mors* who in Apoc 6:8 rides a pale horse was commonly interpreted as 'Plague', and in this quasi-apocalyptic context Death is perhaps meant as a version of the adversary *Mors* mastered by LIFE (Christ) in 20.67–9 (though the *Lyf* of 143 is very obviously to be distinguished from the latter). Iconographic representations of the Triumph of Death, a motif particularly popular in the early 15th c., are discussed in Tristram 1976:158–83. **91** *Conforte*: Lust's first line of defence against the approach of Death, who finds in his opposite number Old Age a foe with the power to lessen the efficacy (and attractiveness) of physical pleasure. **92** *alarme*: a military call to arms (< It *all'arme*); Kynde leads a counter-attack for Conscience against the forces of Antichrist, his officers being Elde and Death, his fighting-men the bodily ailments. *vch lyf*: 'everybody'. **93** *munstrals*: as if at a free tournament over open ground, a scene ironically illustrating how the Death who seemed to defeat Christ in a joust now sides with his Church against the sensual and proud. **95** *Elde*: the sombre figure first met at 11.190–4 (and perhaps recalled in Chaucer's Old Man of *CT* X. 713ff), whose warning to Will in the dream of Fortune is now realised; see also at 18.106ff. **96** *baner*: cf. 70, 91; if worldliness is essentially embodied in the 'lord' (= the Pride of Life), his adversary is Death, and the standard-bearers of the two hosts are respectively Comfort and Age. *bi riht*: as 'nearest' to Death; the task was an honourable one. **97** The violent ferocity of this scene, which draws on the imagery of the Book of the Apocalypse, recalls OT passages like that paraphrased at 3.416–24. *kyne*: the spelling, if original, supports annominative play on *kynne* 'kinds'. **98** *pokkes*: pustules of smallpox; distinguished from the large *bocche* of the pestilence. **99** *corupcions*: infectious diseases whose grim symptoms are a sign to the living to do penance in time. **100** Death is imagined as a mounted warrior whose single blow immediately strikes the enemy into the dust / into dust. The pregnant phrasing hints at the fulfilment of the warning in Gen 3:19 (*in pulverem reverteris*), which is used on Ash Wednesday in the rite of imposition of ashes. On the motif of the Triumph of Death in Europe in the half-century after the Black Death see the illustration of the fresco by Traini in the Camposanto at Pisa of *c.* 1350 (Meiss 1951: pl. 85). **101** echoes the imagery of the Dance of Death known to have been depicted in the Pardon Cloister at Old St Paul's. **103** *euene...euere*: 'Platonic' wordplay equating Death's blow with perma-

nent loss of control and movement. **104–5** *lady...duntes*: on this motif cf. such ME lyrics on the *Ubi sunt* theme as 'Where beth they...' (Brown *C XIII Lyrics*, no. 48). **106–9** intimate that the prayers of conscientious believers obtained an intermission of the diseases, enabling those whose sin had occasioned them (5.115–17) to repent. **106** *his*: with referent Kynde. **108** *priueyliche*: in the confessional; no humiliating public avowal is demanded. **109** *to se*: an infinitive either of purpose, 'to see (if) the people (would) amend' (cf. 107), or of cause, 'at seeing' (*MES* 536, citing B 2.117); but if the latter, not necessarily 'ironical' (*Sk*), since the 'few' might (initially) have repented.

110–64 *The Rallying of the Vices.* **110–13** The siege resumes with the reviving complacency (expressed in renewed dissipation) of those who have survived the disasters. The assault of these confident DEADLY SINS recapitulates in reverse their earlier avatars' repentance in Vision 2. **110** *Fortune*: here apparently a male character (unless *he* 111 is a B-Ø error for *heo*), whereas earlier Fortune was female, as commonly in medieval literature (see at 11.168ff, and Patch 1927). **111** *Lecherye*: also male, in contrast to Fortune's companion *Concupiscencia Carnis* at 11.179ff. **113** *greet oest*: that lechery is the commonest 'sin as of seven' was cheerily maintained by Mede at 3.58–60. **115** *priue*: ironically contrasting with 108. **116** *ydelnesse*: see on 21.229. **117** *bowe...arwes*: the traditional attributes of Cupid, classical god of desire (as in Chaucer *PF* 211–17, *RR* 923ff); but their presence in a military allegory is especially apt. **118** *fayre biheste*: recalling the arrow 'Faire-Semblaunt' carried by Cupid's squire in *RR* 963. *fals treuthe*: though the sense of *treuth* here is 'troth' or 'love-promise', the blunt oxymoron strikes home. **119** *vntidy tales*: 'louche gossip', the enemy less of ascetic holiness than of ordinary decency.

121–42 The lines on GREED recapitulate the extended account in Vision 2 (6.196–307), but with clear echoes of the Mede episode in Vision 1, esp. 3.77–127, and a heightened sense of this endemic vice's strength and persistence. **121–3** *Couetyse...Auarice*: for the distinction in sense, see at 6.196. **123** *hungriliche*: revealing how this special foe of Temperance is an inordinate desire that fails to satisfy; the poem's misers hoard without enjoying. **126** *Symonye*: see at 2.63. **127** A precise referent for this revision cannot be ascertained, but if Pope Urban VI (himself a reformer of prelatical excesses) is meant and if Antichrist *is* equated with the Antipope, then L may have in view attempts to bribe his opponents (for or against him). But at a more general level, the criticism seems directed against higher clerics who side with the *princeps huius mundi* in order to hang on to their wealth and status. **128** *temperaltee*: see on *spiritualte* at B 5.147. **129** *Kynges consail*: sometimes functioning as a final equitable court of appeal (see Kennedy 2003:179ff). **130**

knokked: a more explicit statement of what *kneled* **B** iron- ically implies (bespeaking corruption through the 'force' of bribery) and better in keeping tonally with *kene* 129, *baldeliche* 132 and the 'jousting' metaphor of 132–5. *Court*: the law courts, where conscientious testimony is vital for justice to flourish. 131 *Goed Faith*: at 10.148 one of the sons of Inwit (an avatar of Conscience) appointed to guard the soul 'till Kind come or send'. *Fals*: given the surname 'Faithless' at 2.42. *to abyde*: reversing his igno- minious flight through 'dread' of strict justice at 2.220. The picture now is of a darkening world very different from the ideal society hoped for at the end of Vision 1. 132 *noble*: replacing the expected word *spere*; but the metaphor of money as a weapon against 'faith' or hon- esty here recalls 3.194. A sardonic pun here on the senses 'enlightened' for *brihte* and 'noble(man)' for *noble* (MED s.vv. a. 5(b)), n. (1) (a)) cannot be excluded. 133 *wit... Westministre Halle*: metonymic for the senior justices of the King's Court, who sat there (see on 3.13). It is not implied that the money has been licitly spent on fees for the most learned counsel. 134 *iustice...iustede*: a trench- ant 'Platonic' pun that hints at the ease with which judges can be 'borne down' by a heavy bribe. 135 *ouertulde*: a word appropriate to the allegorical context of jousting ('tilting'). *on amendement*: i.e. 'in payment for amending your judgement in my favour'. 136–7 recall 2.61–2. 136 *Arches*: metonymic for the appeal court of the Canterbury province held at St Mary le Bow Church in Cheapside (see on 2.61). 137 *Syuyle*; *Symonye*: see on 2.63. *Offi- cial*: see on B 2.174. 139 *Departen...come*: alluding to the marriage vows pledging 'good faith' for life: 'to have and to hold from this day forward...till death do us part'. *deuors*: the assumption being that the Official will falsify the grounds (e.g. consanguinity) of the annulment (see on B 2.176). 141 *were Cristene*: so that his power could be turned to good use instead of bad.

(iii) 143–82; 183–211 The LIFE episode, seamlessly joined with that of the Dreamer's encounter with ELDE (183–211), brings out Will's inescapable Haukyn-like involvement in the Sins until the point where he renounces them for the narrow way into Unity. 143 *dagge*: a sign of worldly vanity to contemporary moralists, who criti- cised 'the cost of...the degise endentynge...and...dagg- ynge of sheres' because 'the moore that clooth is wasted, the moore moot it coste to the peple for the scarsnesse' (*CT* X 416–18). 145 *wastour*: 'idle good-for-nothing'. 146 *Lyare*: earlier encountered at 2.9 as a companion of False. The contrast may be simply between 'bond' and 'free', but as with all the terms used by Lyf, their values are reversed morally, a licence to sin being called 'free- dom' and a willing acceptance of the moral law 'bond- age'. 147 *folye*: a term willingly accepted by Conscience and his followers at 61 that sums up how spiritual values appear to the worldly wise. **150b** recalls 21.193, with its

reference to the *Parousia*, the Second Coming of Christ. It is not necessarily implied that the end-time has come, but rather that when it does, it will be like this, so that Kynde's action in the Plague is to be interpreted propheti- cally as an apocalyptic sign of the Last Days. 151 *saue... one*: not of course an explicit affirmation that all consci- entious Christians will escape death, but its eschatological character confirmed by its echoing a statement in I Thess 4:16 that at the Parousia the just will be taken alive into heaven. The moral point is uppermost: that since the hour of Christ's Second Coming is unknown, believers must stand prepared at all hours. 152 describes Lyf's act as resembling that of a military leader halting in his advance to pick up a prostitute. 153 *Hele*: good health and the sense of well-being that comes with it (cf. the Dreamer at 5.7, 10). *heynesse of herte*: the vice rejected by Purnel Proudheart at 6.8. The present protagonists deliberately reverse the repentance of the Deadly Sins in Vision 2. 155 *forȝete ȝowthe*: either 'forget that you are no longer young' or 'forget the sins of your youth' (which should be repented in age before the onset of death); see *TN* further. 156 *Fortune*: here female again (cf. 110 above). The emblem of both sensuality (11.168) and of transi- ence (15.5), Fortune's treacherousness is shown in her using Lyf's short respite from death to distract him from repentance. 157–8 allegorise the genesis of a particular deadly sin from the union of natural vitality and thought- less surrender to sensuality. 159 could scan on *w* but (given the metrical stress on *was* in 158) is probably to be read as an extended Type III line with counterpoint (*abb / ax*). The repetition of this pattern at B 163 may have prompted revision in C. 160 *Wanhope*: somewhat sur- prisingly a woman here (having been male at 11.198); but 'marrying a punk' seems appropriate enough as an act of desperation or sheer sloth. **160b** The echo of 21.438b is ironic, given the name of this 'wench'. 162 *Tomme Two- tonge*: the antithesis of Tomme *Trewe*-tonge (Reason's servant at 4.18), and standing for a class found hopelessly corrupt at every appearance. For the origin of the name, cf. the statement in Ecclus 5:11 that 'omnis peccator pro- batur in *duplici lingua*'. *ateynt*: possibly 'convicted...for perjury or...false verdict' (Alf*G*); but as such conviction would have put an abrupt stop to Tom's career, 'corrupt, perjurious [but *not* found out]' (MED s.v. *atteynen* v. 3 (b)) seems likelier. 163–4 Though the siege-engine is large, the distance it could hurl projectiles is somewhat exaggerated. 167 *good hope*: like the *wel hope* of 7.113, based on good deeds done in life and the positive expec- tation of forgiveness arising from these. The situation of Lyf here is that described by the Samaritan at 19.291–3. *hym*: with double referent, 'eld' being the state in which both 'hopes', one prompting to, the other away from con- fession, conflict. The allegory depicts the subject reject- ing the temptations (especially sexual) that distract the

Commentary

old, despite illness and impotence, from preparing well for their coming death. **169** *Fisyk*: on this avaricious and cynical figure see at 8.291. **172** *glasene houe*: a proverbial phrase (Whiting H624); cf. MED s.v. *houve* n. (c) citing from *c.* 1300 'Þ[ou] madest me an houue of glas', and *TC* 5.469. The physicians' nostrums do not protect against danger, but may even increase it. **173** *lechecraft*: an untrustworthy physic, to be contrasted with the sober way of life recommended by Hunger at 8.270ff and the true (spiritual) healing offered by Christ at 18.138–45. **174** *dyaes*: from Gk δια 'through, made of', and standing for 'a drug made of (some specified ingredient' (cf. *diapenidion* at B 5.122); the first recorded use of the prefix as an independent noun. Lyf's material weapon ('drugs') is used against Elde's spiritual weapon ('good hope'). **175** has a complex metrical pattern *aab / [a]ba*, settting Elde's vocalic sounds against the liquids associated with Lyf. **176–7** *fisician...aftur*: poetic justice in the light of 8.291–6 (this physician cannot heal himself), and ironically echoing 18.161. **180** *in ...hente*: 'expecting better fortune on the basis of his [present] good health, he plucked up courage'.

183–211 *Will's Encounter with Elde*. **183** *myn heued*: the Dreamer-Persona's startling reference to his own body bringing him into the forefront of the narrative. On *Elde* as a figure who urges repentance and warns of approaching death, see Burrow 1981. *ʒede*: the result of Elde's riding over the supine Dreamer being to leave him bald. **186** *vnhende ...the*: 'may discourtesy go / may [it] go discourteously with you'; *vnhende* is either an (unparalleled) nominal form of the adj (*Sk*) or the adv (MED s.v.). **189** *leue*: the repetition from 188 putting it beyond doubt that this is the same word, and not *leef* 'dear' (*Sk*). **190** Use of Leonine rhyme here anticipates the 'Goliardic' flavour of the following passage on Will's impotence. **191** *boffeded...wangteeth*: recalling Hunger's treatment of Waster and the Breton at 8.173–5. **193–8** A possible source of this ruefully mock-ironic passage is Walter Map's *Golias de conjuge non ducenda* 149–56: 'Omnem suscipiet virago masculum / omnemque subdita vincit testiculum. / Quis potest conjugis implere vasculum? / nam una mulier fatigat populum. / Insatiabilis vulva non deficit, / nec unam feminam vir unus reficit; / iccirco mulier se multis subjicit, / et adhuc sitiens non dicit *sufficit*' (Wright 1841:83). **193** *reuthe*: the tone of the next line showing the 'sorrow' to be chiefly on her own account. **194** *in heuene*: so that she could marry someone younger and more virile. **195** *fele*: on its sexual sense cf. 20.131. **196** *a nyhtes...naked*: the usual custom being to sleep wearing no night-clothes. **197** *maken...wille*: cf. B 2.148 above. **198** *Elde and heo*: more clerkly anti-feminism, implying that she is partly responsible for his condition. **199–203** are reminiscent of *CT* VI 720–38; 'the death of kind' would be a welcome relief from the 'care' of decrepit age.

201–11 The *Dreamer's dialogue with Kynde* concludes his encounters with figures of divine authority (Holy Church, Reason and Piers / Liberum Arbitrium in Visions 1, 3 and 5). His interlocutor's message is (unsurprisingly) to take refuge within the Church, the *schola amoris*, as the best place in which to 'learn to love'. **203–4** *Awreke*: 'heavenly vengeance' upon the body's enemy, age, properly taking the form of spiritual preparation for death. The Dreamer has learnt from 'worldly' experience what the ascetics of 21.249 made their deliberate choice in life. **205** *sende for the*: echoing 10.150; the messenger that Kynde will send is Death, now conceived more positively than as first at A 12.81–7. **206** *ar...thennes*: before the time of death. **207–9** This crucial interchange, which contains the germ of such later allegorical dramas as *Everyman*, serves to set in perpective the temporal skills and qualifications that will not help man 'in his most need'. The 'best craft' here is not distinct from the one commended by Christ to Mary 'Magdalen' at 12.142*a* above, since spiritual poverty or disengagement from worldly concerns is the ideal condition for learning the craft of love. **207–8** *beste...alle othere*: recalling Patience's '*Dilige*, and Dobest at B 13.139. **210–11** echo Patience's promise at 15.159–66 that perfected love of God and neighbour (the craft of charity 'mastered') overcomes such fears as those about bodily necessities.

(iv) 212–27 *The Resumption of the Siege*. **212** *conseil of Kynde*: the divine voice communicating to the soul through the medium of ordinary human experience, which awakens the conscience to a sense of the need for repentance. **213** *Vnite*: here a 'nature-name' for the 'church of charity' in the heart, the state of spiritual union with God through confession followed by holy communion and the entry on a renewed life of active virtue. **214** *constable*: the same office in the Church community as INWIT performs in the soul of the individual Christian at 10.143ff. **215** *geauntes*: the Seven Deadly Sins. Though the term was used of Christ in his assault on Hell, the proverbial reputation of 'giants' was for wickedness. Alan of Lille's *Distinctiones* (PL 210:803) relates them to the *obstinati*, citing Job 26:5 'Gigantes gemunt sub aquis'; and the Wycliffite Bible gloss on Prov 21:16 understands *gigantum* as 'of men yuele rulid, ether of fendis' (MED s.v. *geaunt* n. & adj. 1(b)). The image may distantly echo the siege of Thebes by seven giants or that of heaven by the giants in *Boece* III Pr 12:144. **216** *helden aʒeyn*: 'stood in support (of A.) against'. **218** *prestes*: corrupt clerics, first seculars then religious, exemplars of both sloth and greed. **219** recalls the description of a worldly priest at B 15.121–7 (a passage removed at that point in revision), such attire emblematising lust and vanity. *paltokes*: unsuitable dress for one who should wear the clerk's 'long clothes' (5.41). These short jackets of fine cloth such as satin, usually worn with hose, are like the *hayneselyns* attacked by Chaucer's Parson 'that thurgh hire shortnesse ne covere nat the shameful membres of man, to wikkede entente' (*CT* X 421). *pissares*: 'cocky swaggerers', their knives probably of the type mentioned at B 15.124 (see *TN* for defence of this reading and fuller explanation of the phrase). **221** Swearing by Mary is common in *PP*, but the oath with the definite article is paralleled only in the phrase 'by þe Marie of heuene' at B 4.179. *march of Ireland*: presumably a byword for bibulous uncouthness. Satiric comment on Irish priests is found as early as *The Owl and the Nightingale* 322 from the late 12th century. **222** *cache suluer*: i.e. for saying religious services (cf. B 15.126–7). **223** *Then...ale*: 'at no more than the price of a drink'. **225–6** The image of 'great oaths' like those here and in the text cited by *Sk* (*WSEW* 3: 332) as sharp weapons tearing the body of Christ was a homiletic commonplace, as in *CT* VI 472–5. **226** *nayles*: those used to crucify Jesus. **227** *holynesse*: at 21.383 the water in the moat, but here loosely understood as part of the barn's outer defence-works.

228–41 *Conscience's summons of help: Nede.* **228** The summons to *Clergie*, personification of the sacred learning that enables secular clerics to discharge their duties properly, is answered (in their absence) by the chief contemporary exponents of such learning, the friars, who were not slow to 'preuen inparfit prelates of Holy Churche' (6.119). The passage seems to imply that the educational shortcomings of 'ydiotes preestes' (B 11.316) after the Plague (see at Pr 82) contributed to the success of the (highly educated) mendicants. **231** *crafte*: the one referred to at 207 and at 250–2 (cf. B 15.422–2, a passage removed in revision). **232** *Nede*: a figure ironically well-fitted to voice the discrepancy between the friars' profession and their practice (see the headnote; for the phrasing, see at 4). **233** *cure of soules*: presumably not full responsibility for parishes; but their superior preaching often prompted their hearers to make their confessions to the friars, with the consequences foreseen at 56–65 (for an earlier account of the antagonism between parochial clergy and mendicants removed in revision cf. B 5.137–50). Need's remarks have been found to echo not only the anti-mendicant criticisms of such as Fitzralph, but also points made within the internal Franciscan reformist tradition (Clopper 1990). **235** *to fare wel*: because they are as worldly as other clerics, but desire the reputation for holiness that goes with a habit of ascetic poverty. *folk...riche*: cf. B 5.137–9. **237** The a-half's assertion that friars should eat their chosen 'food' of poverty ominously echoes Righteousness's words at 20.205. **239–41** reject the argument that 'since friars flatter because of their poverty, they would not flatter if they were not poor', maintaining instead (on the basis of their having freely chosen poverty) that 'since those who must beg from poverty lie the more readily to avoid its dis-

comforts, let them live like beggars or, having renounced material happiness, like the angels'. While initially he turns down the friars' help (231), this proves unacceptable to the magnanimous knight Conscience; but events prove his trust misplaced. **239** *he þat laboreth*: the seculars, the monks or laypeople; but reference to the latter seems contextually inappropriate. **240** *forsoke*: according to the rule of Francis and Dominic, who followed the example of the 'holy hermits' (9.201–2). **241** *angeles fode*: a phrase used of the Eucharist (*panis angelicus*), or as a proleptic metonym for Christ, as in the 'panem angelorum qui de coelo descendit' of the *Vitis Mystica* (*PL* 184:646). But its likeliest referent here should be 'loue and lele byleue' (17.21–2), eked out (as by Mary Magdalen) with roots and water. Need's assumption is that if the friars trusted in God alone, he would not leave them without food (cf. the 'authorial' attack on *beggarie* at 9.162–5, citing Pss 36:25 and 30:11b).

243–72 *Conscience's admission of the Friars into Unity*, though guarded by qualifications that go some way to meet Need's misgivings, is shown to be an error. This is some measure of the poet's disillusionment with their pretensions to evangelical charity and zeal. **243** *corteysliche*: recalling the Knight at 8.161 rather than Conscience's own earlier, less tolerant self in the First Vision (3.155). *calde...freres*: allegorically representing the historical welcome given the mendicants by popes, kings and nobility into the formal structure of the Church, especially after 1256, when the dispute about the friars' position was settled in their favour by Alexander IV. **246** *in vnite*: a polysemous phrase meaning 'in a state of [spiritual] unity with the whole Church, between your order and other orders, and within your own order'. The admonition alludes to rivalries between seculars and mendicants; between Franciscan and Dominican styles of theology and mission; and within the Franciscan order itself *c.* 1370, when the Observants insisted on poverty and the Conventuals accepted property and papal privileges. Conscience's sympathies lie with the former, to judge by his exhortation, but this seems contradicted by 384 below. **249** The third of these *necessaries*, possessing a place to live (something implied by HC's *vesture* at 1.24), was what most troubled rigorous interpreters of evangelical poverty (cf. B 15.325–30). **250** repeats Kynde's advice to Will at 208 and so would appear to be authoritative. The command (*lerneth*) is not part of the condition (*leue*) but follows it separately. *logic*: perhaps with the wider sense 'philosophy' (as at 14.190). But Conscience's requirement that they give up this discipline may allude to the fact that its greatest C14th masters were indeed friars, like the Franciscan William of Ockham (who however supported the rigorists against Pope John XXII on the question of poverty). The contextual implication is that such study is at odds with the practice of charity, though the overt criticism of logic by Trajan at B 11.218–29 (which the B-Text here would be echoing) has been removed in revision. **251–2** Francis of Assisi renounced his family wealth, but not study, as he was never himself a student; and while the young Dominic sold his books to help the poor during a famine, he also authorised the founding of a *schola* for his friars attached to the University of Paris in 1217, one that proved of major importance to the development of theology. Conscience's stance (which resembles St Bernard's towards Abelard in the 12th c.) is one of opposition to the university mendicants' deep involvement in theological debates, which Anima / Liberum Arbitrium denounces as undermining the faith (B 15 70–2=C 16.228–30). **253** *coueiteth cure*: a piece of ironic wordplay, Conscience at once warning the friars against desiring pastoral responsibility and recommending restraint as the 'cure' for the over-recruitment consequent upon their success as preachers. **254** *mesure*: understood as 'a rule of reason that limits', in accord with a correct judgement of the 'proper' number of any class of entities, natural or human. **255** *hit*: the implied referent being 'all created things'. *serteyne...syker*: the notion that the number of every class of being should be fixed and determinate stemming from a view of the creator as a 'cosmic architect' who allows no arbitrary alteration or excess. **256a** '[Praise ye the Lord...] who telleth the number of the stars: [and calleth them all by their names]' (Ps 146:4). **262** scans as IIIc or as Ie with cross-caesural counterpoint on *b*. **266** refers back to the two categories mentioned, soldiers and monastics. *lawe*: the relation of numerical limit with equity is discussed by John of Salisbury, *Metalogicon* 2:20. **267** *A...certeyne*: 'A definite number for a definite purpose'. **268** *kynde wit*: 'simple common sense'. **269/70** Identical end-rhyme imparts a catechetical tone to the speech, which concludes with the eighth repetition of the keyword 'number' in ll. 253–72. **269** *wage*: plainly figurative, since friars were no more paid wages than were monks. *wexeth*: a reflex of their growing numbers. Although the mendicants in England formed, at some 2000, perhaps only a third of the regular clergy (Swanson 1989:83), their presence in towns would have made them much more 'visible' than the monks, who remained in their monasteries. **270** *euene*: apparently the earliest instance of this sense, but not cited in MED s.v. *even* adj. 5. The allusion is doubtless to the notion in Apoc 7:4 that there is a fixed (and 'even') number of the blessed, the homophony with *heuen* providing some noteworthy 'Platonic' wordplay. *withoute nombre*: not specifically mentioned in Scripture, but expected far to exceed that of the elect. In the 'darkness and dread' of hell, where there was *nullus ordo* (Job 10:22), the number of the damned would be impossible to count. **271–2** The source of Conscience's worry is that (unlike the monks') the mendicants' total number, being hard to discover, has

'no order'. The nature of the friars' mission meant that at any given time not all members of a convent would be resident, so no 'natural' limit was imposed on them by the number of religious houses available. According to the Biblical and neo-Platonic notions of *nombres proporcionables* (Wisd 11:21, *Boece* III m. 9, 18–19; Chadwick 1981:75, 234), 'limitlessness' would be interpreted as a sign of chaos and evil. **273–6** *Enuye*: not yet encountered among Antichrist's host at 215ff, but the 'giant' identified by Conscience (246) as the mendicants' special vice and the root both of their desire for influence and their resentment of the possessioners' advantages. *scole*: the friars' quest for pre-eminence in the university (cf. 250) here being traced to the vice ('enmity' or 'hatred' as well as 'envy') most directly opposed to love. **274** *lawe*: Canon Law, which with logic was unfavourably contrasted by Trajan with the 'law of love' at B 11.227. *contemplacioun*: 'consideracioun or speculacioun in þe resoun' (MED s.v. 2(a), citing Pecock), the present use ironically conjuring up by way of a polysemantic 'anti-pun' the commoner sense 'meditation on things divine' specified as the goal of 'monks and monyals' at 18.74. **275** *of; by*: 'out of / about'; 'by reference to'. Neither philosopher (see on 11.120 and 16.141*a*) taught pure communism, though Plato (*Republic* III 416e) restricted his Guardians' property to the 'necessaries', while Seneca (Ep. IX 3) held that greed had destroyed the Golden Age, when possession was believed to have been shared (cf. Chaucer, *Former Age* 5–15). The doctrine of primeval common ownership was attributed by Froissart to John Ball, a leader of the Peasants' Revolt (*Chronicles*, tr. Berners 1913:251), who was not unsympathetic to the mendicants (McKisack 1959:421); but such ideas have not been found in their extant sermons (Owst 1961:288). **277–94** form a narratorial interjection reminiscent of Will's outburst at 15.105, though less clearly distinguishable from the 'authorial' voice. **277** *lewed*: the friars' popularity with 'lewed peple' (B 15.70–2) making their excursions into novel social doctrine (like John Ball's) seem to the authorities a threat to the existing order. **278** *Moyses hit tauhte*: 'taught it to Moses / Moses taught it'. **278a** 'Thou shalt not covet thy neighbour's goods' (Ex 20:17); cited as a maxim of canon law (Alf*Q*) in Richard Fitzralph's polemic against the friars' claims to jurisdiction (Scase 1989:24–31). **280** *euele...yholde*: inasmuch as the people themselves enable the friar-confessors to 'covet' (successfully) the parson's 'goods' (his parishioners). **281–7** The syntax is somewhat loose but the sense is clear enough: shame (as commonly at this time) is seen as an integral part of the penitential process, and flight from it to the anonymity of a friar-confessor as undermining the moral influence of the sacrament. **282** *curatours*: whose task is to 'take care of' souls (by 'knowing' their condition) and to 'heal' them by absolution; see 14.70, 326–7 below, and cf. MED s.v. *curen* v. 2, 3(a). **283** scans cognatively as a standard Ia line on |b| |p| / |p|. **285** *Westmynstre*: metonymic for the royal courts of justice, where the suitors pretend to take the money under colour of pursuing a legal claim, only to squander it while asking for repayment to be waived or postponed. But an insincere confession to the friars, it is intimated, will no more remit sin than a misspent loan will settle an outstanding suit at law. There may be an allusion here to the abuse of the Westminster Sanctuary by debtors fleeing their creditors, with an echo of the 1378 statute governing its use (Baldwin 1982:106–8). **288** *be bifore*: 'be quick to make the most of it'. **290–4** claim that jurymen and executors purchase absolution and intercessory prayers from their friar-confessors with some of the misappropriated money, while they spend the rest on themselves. **294** *soffren...dette*: i.e. by not disbursing what the deceased bequeathed for charitable purposes in order to make satisfaction for their sins and shorten their time in purgatory. **295–324** *The Crisis of Contrition*. **296** *to...scole*: 'made provision for friars to study philosophy at the university'. Some of these contemporary friar-philosophers are discussed in Leff 1958:279–94 and Coleman 1981:151–8. **298** scans vocalically as a Type IIa line with a 'supplemental' stave in position five (see *Intro.* IV § 45), *In* 'within', 'inside', having full sentence-stress. **299** *Pees*: an appropriate gate-keeper, able to neutralise the harm of scandal-mongers and malicious gossips; but one whose eirenic posture proves vulnerable to a flatterer's subtle address. **302** *at þe ȝate*: the significance of Hypocrisy's closeness to the entrance of the Church being that he wounds those whose task is to form the conscience of the Christians within (cf.16.263–9). **303** For the phrasing cf. *WPal* 1218. **305–24** The Confession Crisis occurs when the sinners, represented by Lechery, recoil from the severe formal penance (figured as a biting treatment applied by a doctor) that their confessors enjoin. **305** *leche*: the old native word (repeated by Conscience at 319), carrying overtones of the necessarily painful nature of sincere shrift, but also echoing the metaphor as used of Christ in 18.138ff (see St-Jacques 1991). **307** contains a strikingly mimetic a-half with clashing stresses and falling rhythm in the third lift: ´´´ `. **308** On the scansion see *TN*. **309** *redde...*: see on 21.188. **311** *Yf*: 'to find if'. *in the sege*: 'present at the siege' (so at 314), i.e. outside the barn, since 'Lyf' is within it. Paradoxical as it might seem (at the literal level) to seek medical help from amongst those *outside* Unity, at the allegorical a distinction is being drawn between the occupants of the Barn ('fools' vowed to holiness, including virtuous examples of the parish clergy) and those outside (who should be opposed to the besiegers but are soon discovered to be of their part). Lyf belongs with the former only inasmuch as

during Lent his thoughts turn customarily to changing his ways (he becomes a 'seasonal fool'). But like Lady Mede (who got 'easy penance' from a friar), he is a pliable character, always looking for a painless remedy. *softur*: on the adverbial use of the adj. here and at 315 see *MES* 315–16. **313** *fastyng...Fryday*: a usual, fairly mild penance for sins of the flesh, given to Gluttony at 6.351 and to Lechery at 6.174. Because of the link commonly perceived between 'thise two synnes...so ny cosyns' (*CT* X 836), fasting was deemed a fitting discipline for the irregular motions of the flesh, especially during Lent. *deye*: cf. 6.129 on the difficulty some felt in doing bodily penance. **314** *can*: 'knows how to'; the verb also (as 'know') directly governs *fysyk*. **315** *more*: 'knows more'. *fayror*: i.e. than Shrift. The allusion is to the confessional expertise of the friars, whose preaching had much increased use of this unpopular sacrament; cf. Bonaventure's 'Quare fratres minores praedicent et confessiones audiant' (*Op. om.* 8:375–83). **316** That 'Lyf / Lechery' should be unaware of (or indifferent to) the true nature of someone named *Flatrere* makes good allegorical sense; but the similar ignorance of Contrition and his 'cousin' Conscience (358) may hint that a 'blind-spot' of the pious gentry was susceptibility to the winning address of highly-educated mendicants. *is*: '(who) is (both)'; on 'non-expression of the subject pronoun' (Ø-relative clauses), see *MES* 204–5, which notes it as especially common in poetry. *fiscicien and surgien*: able to treat both diseases and wounds, and thus supposedly a complete master of the healing art (penitential theology and its practical application). The deeply ironic echo of 18.140–1 seems unmistakable. **317** *Contricion*: here personifying the important prior stage of penance; but his unwareness that a flatterer is hardly the right person to cure hypocrisy is disturbing. **319–21** The vehemently stressed negatives underline that the existing penitential system provides adequately for the confession and release of even the gravest sins (like incest, sacrilege and murder); friars, it is implied, can offer nothing further. **321** *Piers...alle*: the Pope as the ultimate recourse of the excommunicate, able to override any lower authority's decision to withhold absolution. **322** 'And may grant full remission, unless prevented by a refusal to make due satisfaction'. *dette*: see on 21.191; the internal rhyme emphasises how the only true obstacle to forgiveness lies in the will of the sinner. **323–4** The tone of these lines is as unclear as Conscience's apparent *volte-face*, some word like 'however' needing to be understood, along with his supposition that *any* kind of confession might be better than complete avoidance of sacramental penance. *soffre*: a word ambiguously echoing both the divine tolerance of 13.198–200 and the *vnsittynge suffraunce* of 3.207. Just as Conscience's earlier stiff opposition to Mede at 3.155–6 was modified by a concession at 4.4–5, so here his declaration of principle is undermined by the *hendenesse* that is always willing to find good even in one suspected of being untrustworthy. At the plane of personal allegory, it seems suggested, an individual's moral faculty can make wrong concrete judgements if the 'rede' of right Reason is weakened. The passage is obscure, but the reader may be intended to recall Christ's mysterious 'suffrance' of Judas's treachery as recounted in Jn 13:27. For a general discussion of Conscience see Jenkins 1969:124–42, and on the problem of his admission of Friar Flatterer, Simpson 1990:241–2 and Harwood 1992:136.

325–54 *The arrival of Friar Flatterer.* **325–30** describe how the Friar obtains, from a local magnate who knows him, a letter of recommendation to the ordinary for the right to hear confessions within his diocese (the latter's consent may obliquely imply some obligation to the lord for his own position). For an analysis of the following scene see Schmidt 1983:161–83. **326–7** *curen...curatour*: 'to heal like / exercise the powers of'. The polysemantic wordplay brings out **L**'s sense of a theological as well as lexical link between the priest's ministry of spiritual healing and possession of the temporal rights that go with his office. **331** This rôle of Peace is foreshadowed in Eph 4:3, where Paul exhorts 'to keep the *unity* of the Spirit in the bond of *peace*'. **333** *profyt*: a term (distantly echoing Pr 57) the ambiguity of which is disguised by its association here with the positive idea of health. **336** *yf thei*: either 'for them to' (*hard* = 'difficult') or 'if they are to' (*hard* = 'painful'). **338** On a general plane, the claim to acquaintance with Conscience acknowledges the fact that scrupulous penitents *were* attracted to mendicant confessors and found them (at some point) helpful. On the more direct level of the poem's 'action', it finds support from 15.31, possible evidence that this 'knight' is one who regularly 'welcomes' friars at his table. Friar Flatterer may even be meant to be associated with the Doctor of Divinity's silent 'man' (he too has a *felawe*). *and...bothe*: possibly implying that as a knight who may have inflicted injuries in war, Conscience has himself benefited from this or some other friar's 'salves' in confession. **341** *felawe*: see on 10.8, 12.19. *Penetrans-domos*: 'Piercer-of-homes', alluding to the text 'in novissimis diebus...erunt homines...habentes speciem quidem pietatis...ex his enim sunt qui *penetrant domos*, et captivas ducunt mulierculas oneratas peccatis, quae ducuntur variis desideriis...' (II Tim 3:1–6). The Pauline text was commonly invoked in writings against the friars (Scase 1989:32–9), and in 1255 the secular master William of St-Amour's polemical tract on 'The Perils of the Last Days' accused them of breaking into the *domus conscientiae* 'the dwelling of conscience' (Szittya 1986:305). But the context, the evocation of 'foolish women' (like Lady Mede) and the metonymic symbolism of *oute* at 347 below make it hard to doubt the presence of 'clerkly' sexual innuendo in the phrase. **342–3** *fisyk*; *craft*: contrasting 'theoretical knowledge of penitential

theology' like that of the Franciscan friar at 10.30ff and 'effective practical skill in dealing with penitents' like that of Chaucer's Parson (*CT* I 515–23). **345** *thus ycoped*: i.e. under a similar guise as a confessor (and cf. Pr 61 for an instance of a literal reference). **346** *leche*: '(spiritual) physician'; but in context the *annominatio* with *lechour* seems unavoidable (see Schmidt 1983:143–4). *oute*: 'not at home', thus leaving 'my lady' and 'our women' exposed to the fraternal attentions of Flatterer Prickhouse. **348** *salued*: presumably the verb *salven* 'treat with medicaments' (as at 306), though if it were *saluen* 'greet' (not found elsewhere in *PP*) the satire would be no less pungent (ibid.141–3). *so*: 'in such a way', 'to such a degree' (MED s.v. 1a (a), 8 (a)). **349** *Hende-Speche*: another attribute of the graciously-disposed knight Conscience, personifying the courtesy obligatory for Christians (16.242–3). Unhappily, it admits the persuasive friar possessed of the same quality (*thorw* 355) when the suspicious roughness of Peace might have been preferable. **350** *make...chiere*: 'greet them with a smile'. **351** *here here*: i.e. in confession; understand 'such things as may, perchance, bring it about that...' **352–3** *Couetyse...Pruyde*: two of the other sins (along with Lechery and Sloth at 156–66) most incident to him. The speaker's hope is that the friar's example of voluntary poverty will inspire Lyf to renounce luxurious indulgence. **353** *be adrad of Deth*: like the Dreamer at 200 and in contrast to Fortune, who makes Lyf's survival of the Plague grounds for thinking he might 'drive away Death' (174), like 'this wreches of this world' of 11.63–4 (lines anticipating the present scene). **354** *acorde...oþer*: echoing the King's attempt at 4.2–3 to reconcile Conscience with Mede.

355–73 355 *thorw*: 'by means of'; with its dual referent ambiguously suggesting that the 'entry' is effected through the mutual courtesy of the friar and the knight, who forgets his experience of mendicants at the dinner in Passus XV (the important lines B 13.191–2 having however been removed in revision, the link becomes 'intertextual' rather than 'intratextual'). A parallel to the friar's admission has been found in Prudentius's *Psychomachia* 667ff (Barney 1979:82–104). **357** *welcóme*: stressed as in 15.31. **358** *cosyn*: an allegorical relationship, recalling that of Study and Clergy, which might be expected to be less indirect, with conscience as the *parent* of contrition. **359** *Conforte*: though innocently intended, replete with unconsciously ironic resonances of Lyf's house of revelry at 182, as is confirmed by its appearance at 372. **359/60** The 'rich' rhyme here would seem to hint at desperation more than determination. **360** *plastres*: the penances, some perhaps literally physical (like fasting, or the hairshirt of Purnel at 6.6–7). **361** *lat*: '(he) lets'; on 'non-expression of the 3rd person subject pronoun' see *MES* 138–42. **362** *Lente to Lente*: the severity of the penances being evident from their allowing no respite even for the festive seasons. **363**

ouerlonge: the Friar's echo of Conscience's own criticism hinting at a tacit complicity in the relaxation of austerity that the latter favours. *amenden*: another 'innocent' word with unfortunate overtones of venality (cf. 135). **364** *gropeþ*: a word equivocally referring to the surgeon's and the confessor's intimate examination. **365–8** The Friar's promise to Contrition recalls that of Lady Mede's confessor at 3.38–44. 'Payment' purchasing the intercessory prayers of his convent will take the place of the arduous penances imposed by the parish priest and, it is implied, permit Contrition to share in the complacent delusions of Lyf (whose spiritual self he signifies). *payement...preye*: the internal rhyme associating material and spiritual realms in an audibly *vnsyttinge* manner. **366** *holde to*: 'obliged to (pray for)'; an 'offer that cannot be refused'. **367–8** Friar Flatterer undertakes to include Contrition and his lady in the prayers offered by the whole convent for those who have membership in it. *fraternite*: see on 3.54. **368** *a litel suluer*: how little is not clear, but it seems that this friar is not asking (like his predecessor and avatar in Vision 1), a major benefaction for a 'perpetual licence' to go on sinning, so much as a 'sweetener' for his good offices in formally mitigating the penitent's obligations. Unlike Mede's substantial gift recorded in window-glass, this 'payment' will be a secret between Contrition and Sir *Penetrans*. **369** *gedereth*: suggesting a large-scale operation that takes the friars right through society, commuting strict canonical penances in return for payment. *gloseth*: cleverly interpreting Contrition's sins (along the lines that Mede suggested finds support in 'books' at 3.59) as less grave than they were judged by his customary 'penitencer' (22.320). **370–1** *crye...wake*: austerities like those espoused by Piers at B 7.120–24*a*, endorsed by his 'prentys' Haukyn at B 14.324–32 (both passages removed in revision), and seen as practised by the ideal figure of Charity in B 15.186–93*a*=C 16.328–34*a*. But it is clearly not to be assumed that Conscience, whose request for 'comfort' at 359 seems to imply a *tempering* of penitential severity, would approve the 'clean forgetting' of contrition (370) offered by the Friar as 'comfort' at 372. **370** *forȝete*: 'forgotten (how) to'; implying not only that a specific obligation is neglected but that a virtuous habit is undermined (*woned* 370). **371** *wake*: a standard penance being to keep vigil in prayer (cf. the personage *Vigilate* at 7.56 who urges Sloth to active 'breast-beating'). **372** *confort*: here signifying 'relief from the rigours of mortification' rather than 'spiritual consolation arising from a good conscience'. *contricioun*: specifically the continuing sense of a *spiritus contribulatus* and *cor contritum* (Ps 50:19) that was thought to constitute the essence of penitence, is expressed in acts like those at 21.380–1, and alone justifies his name; he is now no longer 'himself'. **373** *kyne synnes*: for the tone of this concluding internal rhyme cf. on 322, 324 above.

374–80 374 *Sleuth*; *Pruyde*: waiting in the wings (see 149ff) and now renewing the assault, with an access of new strength from Contrition's descent into spiritual torpor. **376** *efte*: see at 328–9. He earlier received no help from the regular clergy (whose inadequacy had prompted his recourse to the friars) and their silence now testifies to the dire condition of the institutional Church. **377** The guardian of the entrance (*ȝate*) is the sacrament of penance; if this is rendered inefficacious, Christians are unable to receive the Eucharist, the sacrament that establishes Unity Holy Church as a 'spiritual organism'. **378–80** On the possibility of revision here see *TN*. The **C** form is both stronger in itself and better in keeping with the idea that Friar Flatterer has administered a 'benign' sleeping potion to neutralise the salutary fear of sin that the entire poem insists is indispensable to repentance. The essence of the friar's 'flattery' is to convince the sinner that he is not such a bad fellow after all. In this way the 'inevitabilist' and 'mediocritarian' stance of the Friars Minor found so unsatisfactory by the Dreamer at 10.49–50 is shown decaying into a moral insensibility that threatens to fulfil the prophecy of B Pr 66 (the ferocious **C** revision of which is now explained). **379** *enchaunted*: the unfavourable earlier uses of this word at 2.43 and at 17.176 (in connection with flattery and heresy respectively) indicating a sombre view of the friars as potential agents of the Antichrist, 'corrupted in mind, reprobate concerning the faith' (II Tim 3:8). **380** *dwale*: a bitter narcotic made from gall dissolved in wine with such (potentially poisonous) herbal ingredients as hemlock, henbane or deadly nightshade (see MED s.v. 4 (a)). Its function as a pain-killer makes it ironically appropriate here; but as the 'sleep' induced is a symbol of spiritual ignorance, a grim pun on the sense 'deception', 'error' (ibid. s.v. 1 (a)) seems likely in the context.

(v) 381–7 *Finale.* **381** *pilgrime*: an echo of Conscience's earlier resolve at B 13.182, a passage removed in revision to **C** (and more distantly of Piers's resolve at B 7.120). A second disillusionment with the prospect for spiritual renewal offered by the mendicant orders leads the figure of the conscientious knightly layman to recommence his urgent personal search for Piers, the sole 'kynde' exemplar of truth and charity in the world. **384** *þat freres hadde*: if this is dependent on *seke* 383, understand 'and [to look for some way in which] friars might be endowed [for their mission]'. The responsible spokesman of Christian laypeople now sees it as a prime problem of the Church that 'need' (in the sense of lack of assured income) is what induces the friars to lower the spiritual threshold and encourage people in general and the gentry in particular to evade the stricter demands of their faith as traditionally understood. But that Conscience rejected the unrealistic solution proposed by Need at 236–41 and sought some relaxation of traditional penitential rigour (359–62) has shown that he still valued the work a reformed mendicant movement might accomplish in the world. *fyndynge*: argued by Dolan 1988:37 to refer specifically to the Franciscans. The term, as Frank argues (1957:117), attests L's wish for 'some kind of reform…of the friars' and 'establishes a certain limit for interpretation of the more obscure elements in the conclusion'. **385** *countrepledeth*: a term importantly associated with Conscience in two lines added in revision (Pr 138 and 8.53). Without necessarily carrying the 'legal' force discerned by Simpson (1990:243), it reveals the speaker's sense of the dangerous power of mendicant learning and eloquence when used to advance a bad cause. **385–7** The conclusion of the poem has proved controversial: see Frank 1950 and the representative discussions in Harwood, Simpson and Godden, who all find it 'dark and despairing' (Godden 1990:164). The end is perhaps intended to be a deliberate challenge to interpretation, but it would seem mistaken to think of L's Conscience at the end of the existing form of **C** as personifying the intention of the conscientious layman literally to 'leave' the Church, let alone set up 'an ordre by hymselue' (B 13.285). This would be out

of keeping with his upright and loyal nature, especially as brought out by the added **C** lines insisting on 'Holy Church's rights' at Pr 138 and 8.53, which are obviously subsequent to the completion of B XX. The possibility therefore cannot be excluded that the ending was to receive further revision, perhaps on the scale of the text up to Passus XX. However, the circumstance of Conscience's apparent deception by the friars, on the other hand, remains a disturbing acknowledgement that human limitedness can only cry out for divine grace, and go on hoping for less flawed human vessels through which that grace may be mediated. The final collocation of KYNDE, PIERS and GRACE ('nature-names' for the Father, Son and Spirit) brings the work to its close with an impassioned plea to God for success in finding a true leader for the Church, an 'angelic' pope who might bring about the reform of the material organisation needed to save the spiritual organism. **385** *me avenge*: the sense is more 'do justice for me', 'vindicate me' than 'take vengeance [on my enemies]'. **386** *Piers þe Plouhman*: the articulation of the name functioning as a valedictory 'title' for the poem at its end.

D. BIBLIOGRAPHY OF WORKS CITED

The Bibliography includes all books and articles that are referred to by short title or author / date in sections A–C and a selection of the other main works consulted but not specifically mentioned (where revised and reprinted, they are cited in their latest published form except where otherwise stated). It is arranged under two main headings, **Primary** and **Secondary Sources**, the latter sub-divided into Reference Works; Textual, Linguistic and Metrical Studies; Critical and Interpretative Studies; Historical and Background Studies. The place of publication is London, unless otherwise specified.

I. PRIMARY SOURCES

A. Manuscripts

For a descriptive list of the *Piers Plowman* manuscripts see section A, *Introduction*, I, *The Manuscripts*. Studies of the manuscripts cited there by short title are given under II. B below.

B. Printed Primary Sources

1 Printed Facsimiles

Bennett, J. A. W., ed. *The vision of Pierce Plowman, now fyrste imprynted*. 1505 [1550].
Benson, C. D. & Blanchfield, L. S. *The Manuscripts of PP: the B Version*. Cambridge, 1997.
Brewer, C. & Rigg, A. G., eds. *PP: A Facsimile of the Z-Text in Bodleian Library, Oxford, MS Bodley 851*. Cambridge, 1994.
Chambers, R. W. *et al. PP: The Huntington Library Manuscript (HM 143) reproduced in Photostat*. San Marino, 1936.
Doyle, A. I., ed. *The Vernon Manuscript: A Facsimile of Bodleian Library, Oxford, MS. Eng. poet. a.1*. Cambridge, 1987.
Matsushita, T. *PP: the A-Text. A Facsimile of the Society of Antiquaries of London MS 687*. Tokyo, 2007.
——*PP: The Z-Version. A Facsimile of Bodleian Library, Oxford MS Bodley 851*. Tokyo, 2008.
——*The Vision of PP: The A-Text. A Facsimile of Trinity College, Cambridge MS R. 3. 14*. Tokyo, 2010.
——*The Vision of PP: The B-Text. A Facsimile of Trinity College, Cambridge MS B. 15. 17*. Tokyo, 2010.
——*The Vision of PP: The C-Text. A Facsimile of Huntington Library, San Marino MS Hm 143*. Tokyo, 2010.
Pearsall, D. (with Scott, K.), eds. *PP: a Facsimile of Bodleian Library, Oxford, MS Douce 104*. Cambridge, 1992.

2 Electronic Sources

Adams, R., Duggan, H., Eliason, E., Hanna, R., Price-Wilkin, J. & Turville-Petre, T. *The PP Electronic Archive, Vol. I: Corpus Christi College, Oxford MS. 201 (F)*. CD-ROM. Ann Arbor: University of Michigan Press, 1999.
Turville-Petre, T. & Duggan, H. *The PP Electronic Archive, Vol 2: Cambridge, Trinity College, MS B. 15. 17 (W)*. CD-ROM. Ann Arbor, Michigan. 2001.
Heinrichs, K. *The PP Electronic Archive, Vol 3: Oxford, Oriel College, MS 79 (O)*. CD-ROM. Woodbridge, Boydell & Brewer for the Medieval Academy of America and SEENET. 2005.
Duggan, H. & Hanna, R. *The PP Electronic Archive, Vol 4: Oxford, Bodleian Library, MS Laud Misc. 581 (L)*. CD-ROM. Woodbridge, Boydell & Brewer for the Medieval Academy of America and SEENET. 2005.
Eliason, E., Turville-Petre, T. Duggan, H. *The PP Electronic Archive, Vol 5: London, British Library, MS Additional 35287 (M)*. CD-ROM. Woodbridge, Boydell & Brewer for the Medieval Academy of America and SEENET. 2005.
Calabrese, M., Duggan, H. & Turville-Petre, T. *The PP Electronic Archive, Vol 6: San Marino, Huntington Library, MS Hm 128 (Hm, Hm²)*. CD-ROM. Woodbridge, Boydell & Brewer for the Medieval Academy of America and SEENET. 2008.

Bibliography

3 Editions of *Piers Plowman*

Bennett, J. A. W., ed. *PP: The Prologue and Passus I–VII of the B-Text*. Oxford, 1972.
Kane, G., ed. *PP: The A Version. Will's Visions of Piers Plowman and Do-Well*. 1960. 2nd edn. 1988.
——& Donaldson, E. T., eds. *Piers Plowman: the B Version. Will's Visions of PP, Do-Well, Do-Better and Do-Best*. 1975. 2nd edn., 1988.
Knott, T. A. & Fowler, D., eds. *PP. A Critical Edition of the A Version*. Baltimore, 1952; repr. 1964.
Pearsall, D. *PP by William Langland. An Edition of the C-Text*. 1978; repr. with corrections, Exeter 1994.
Rigg, A. G. & Brewer, C., eds. *PP: The Z Version*. Toronto, 1983.
Robertson, E. & Shepherd, S. eds. *William Langland. Piers Plowman*. Norton Critical Edition. New York & London, 2006.
Russell, G. & Kane, G., eds. *PP: The C Version*. 1997.
Salter, E. & Pearsall, D., eds. *PP: Selections from the C-Text*. 1967.
Schmidt, A. V. C., ed. *William Langland. The Vision of PP: A Critical Edition of the B-Text*. 1978; repr. 1987 with added Glossary. 2nd (revised) edn. 1995.
Skeat, W. W., ed. *The Vision of William concerning Piers Plowman, together with Vita de Dowel, Dobet, et Dobest, Secundum Wit et Resoun*, by William Langland. 5 vols. I: Text A, EETS o.s. 28 (1867); II: Text B, EETS o.s. 38 (1869); III: Text C, EETS o.s. 54 (1873); IV, i: Notes, EETS o.s. 67 (1877); IV, ii: General Preface, Notes and Indexes, EETS o.s. 81 (1885).
The Vision of William Concerning Piers the Plowman by William Langley (or Langland). 1869. 2nd edn rev. 1874.
The Vision of William Concerning PP in Three Parallel Texts. 2 vols. Oxford, 1886; repr. 1954.
Whitaker, T. D., ed. *Visio Willí de Petro Plouhman Item Visiones ejusdem de Dowel, Dobet, et Dobest*. 1813.
Wright, T., ed. *The Vision and the Creed of Piers Plowman*. 2 vols. 1842; rev. edn. 1856.

4 Translations of *Piers Plowman*

Covella, F. D. *The A-Text. An Alliterative Verse Translation*, intro. D. C. Fowler. Binghamton, NY. 1992.
Donaldson, E. T. *PP: An Alliterative Verse Translation*, ed. E. Kirk & J. Anderson. 1990; repr. ed. E. Robertson & S. Shepherd. New York, 2005.
Economou, G. *William Langland's PP: The C Version: A Verse Translation*. Philadelphia, 1996.
Goodridge, J. F. *Piers the Ploughman*. Harmondsworth, 1959; 2nd edn. 1966.
Schmidt, A. V. C. *PP: A New Translation of the B-Text*. Oxford, 1992.

5 Editions of other Texts

i ENGLISH WORKS

Ancrene Wisse. The English Text of the 'Ancrene Riwle': 'Ancrene Wisse', ed. J. R. R. Tolkien. EETS o.s. 249 (1962).
The English Text of the 'Ancrene Riwle': Cotton Nero A. xiv., ed. M. Day. EETS o.s. 225 (1952).
Ancrene Wisse: Parts Six and Seven, ed. G. Shepherd. Rev. edn. Exeter, 1985.
Audelay, John. *Poems*, ed. E. K. Whiting. EETS o.s. 184 (1931).
The Babees Book; see F. J. Furnivall, *Early English Meals and Manners*.
Barr, H. ed. *The Piers Plowman Tradition*. 1993.
Bartholomaeus Anglicus. *On the Properties of Things*. John Trevisa's translation of *Bartholomaeus Anglicus De Proprietatibus Rerum*, ed. M. C. Seymour. 2 vols. Oxford, 1975.
Batman vppon Bartholome. 1582.
Bennett, J. A. W. & Smithers, G. V., eds. *Early Middle English Verse and Prose*. Oxford, 1966.
Blake, N., ed. *Middle English Religious Prose*. 1972.
Brown, C., ed. *English Lyrics of the XIIIth Century*. Oxford, 1932.
Religious Lyrics of the XIVth Century. 2nd edn. Oxford, 1957.
Burrow, J. A. & Turville-Petre, T., eds. *A Book of Middle English*. 2nd edn. Oxford, 1996.
Geoffrey Chaucer, *Troilus and Criseyde*, ed. B. A. Windeatt. 1984.
——*Works. The Riverside Chaucer*, ed. L. D. Benson. Oxford, 1988.
Clanvowe. *The Works of Sir John Clanvowe*, ed. V. J. Scattergood. Cambridge, 1975.
The Cloud of Unknowing and the Book of Privy Counsel, ed. P. Hodgson. EETS o.s. 218 (1944).

The Conflict of Wit and Will, ed. B. Dickins. Kendal, 1937.

Cursor Mundi, ed. R. Morris. 7 vols. EETS o.s. 57, 59, 62, 66, 68, 99, 101 (1847–93).

Death and Liffe, ed. J. M. P. Donatelli. Cambridge, MA. 1989.

'Deonise Hid Divinite' and Other Treatises on Contemplative Prayer related to 'The Cloud of Unknowing,' ed. P. Hodgson. EETS o.s. 231 (1958).

Dives and Pauper, ed. P. Barnum. 2 vols., EETS o.s. 275, 280 (1976, 1980).

Dobson, R. B. & Taylor, J., eds. *Rymes of Robin Hood*. 1976.

Early English Meals and Manners, ed. F. J. Furnivall. EETS o.s. 32. 1868.

English Gilds, ed. Toulmin Smith & L. Toulmin Smith. EETS o.s. 40 (1870).

English Medieval Lapidaries, ed. J. Evans & M. Serjeantson. EETS o.s. 190 (1933).

Genesis and Exodus, ed. R. Morris. EETS o.s. 7 (1865).

Gower, John. *The Complete Works of John Gower*, ed. G. C. Macaulay. 4 vols. Oxford, 1899–1902.

Gray, D., ed. *A Selection of Religious Lyrics*. Oxford, 1975.

Greene, R., ed. *A Selection of English Carols*. Oxford, 1962.

The Romance of Guy of Warwick, ed. J. Zupitza. EETS e.s. 42 (1889).

Herebert, William. *The Works of William Herebert, OFM*, ed. S. R. Reimer. Toronto, 1987.

Hoccleve, Thomas. *Regement of Princes*, ed. F. J. Furnivall. EETS e.s. 72 (1897).

Hudson, A., ed. *Selections from English Wycliffite Writings.* Cambridge, 1978.

Jack Upland, Friar Daw's Reply, and Upland's Rejoinder ed. P. L. Heyworth. 1968.

Joseph of Arimathea, ed. D. Lawton. New York, 1982.

Julian of Norwich. *A Book of Showings to the Anchoress Julian of Norwich*, ed. E. Colledge & J. Walsh. Toronto, 1978.

Kempe, Margery. *The Book of Margery Kempe*, ed. S. B. Meech & H. E. Allen. EETS o.s. 212 (1940).

Kyng Alisaunder, ed. G. V. Smithers. 2 vols. EETS o.s. 227, 237 (1952, 1957).

Laȝamon. *'Brut'*, ed. G. L Brook & R. R. Leslie. 2 vols. EETS o.s. 250, 277 (1963, 1978).

Lanfranc. *Lanfrank's Science of Cirurgie*, Part I, ed. R. Fleischhacker. EETS. o.s. 102 (1894).

The Lanterne of Liȝt, ed. L. M. Swinburn. EETS o.s. 151 (1917).

The Legend of the Cross, ed. A. S. Napier. EETS o.s. 103 (1894).

Legends of the Holy Rood, ed. R. Morris. EETS o.s. 46 (1871).

Love, Nicholas. *A Mirror of the Blessed Life of Our Lord Jesus Christ*, ed. L. F. Powell. 1908.

The Macro Plays, ed. M. Eccles. EETS o.s. 262 (1969).

Mandeville, Sir John. *Mandeville's Travels*, ed. P. Hamelius. 2 vols. EETS o.s. 153, 154 (1919–23).

Mannyng, Robert. *Robert of Brunne's 'Handlyng Synne' and its French Original*, ed. F. J. Furnivall. EETS o.s. 119, 123 (1901–03).

Meditations on the Life and Passion of Christ, ed. C. D'Evelyn. EETS o.s. 158 (1921).

Michael, Dan of Northgate. *Dan Michel's 'Ayenbite of Inwyt'*, ed. R. Morris. EETS o.s 23 (1866). Vol. ii, Introduction & Notes by P. Gradon. EETS o.s. 278 (1979).

The Middle English Harrowing of Hell and Gospel of Nicodemus, ed. W. H. Hulme. EETS e.s. 100 (1907).

Middle English Sermons, ed. W. O. Ross. EETS o.s. 209 (1940).

Minor Poems of the Vernon Manuscript, ed. C. Horstmann & F. J. Furnivall. 2 vols. EETS o.s 98, 117 (1892, 1901).

Morris, R. & Skeat, W., eds. *Specimens of Early English*. Oxford, 1873.

Morte Arthure: A Critical Edition, ed. V. Krishna. New York, 1976.

Le Morte Arthur, ed. J. D. Bruce. EETS e.s. 88 (1903, repr. 1959).

Mum and the Sothsegger, ed. M. Day and R. Steele. EETS o.s. 199 (1936).

Non-cycle Plays and Fragments, ed. N. Davis. EETS e.s. 1 (1970).

The Northern Passion, ed. F. Foster. 2 vols. EETS o.s. 145, 147 (1913–16).

The N-Town Play, ed. S. Spector. 2 vols. EETS s.s. 11,12 (1991).

Old English Homilies and Homiletic Treatises, 1st series, ed. R. Morris. 2 vols. EETS o.s. 29, 34 (1868).

The Parlement of the Thre Ages, ed. M. Y. Offord. EETS o.s. 246 (1959).

Pearl-poet. *The Poems of the Pearl Manuscript,* ed. M. Andrew & R. Waldron. 1978; rev. edn. Exeter, 1987.

Pierce the Ploughmans Crede, ed. W. W. Skeat. EETS o.s. 30. (1867).

The Plowman's Tale, in W. W. Skeat, ed. *Chaucerian and Other Pieces* (Oxford, 1897) 147–90.

The Plowman's Tale: the c. 1532 and 1606 Editions of a Spurious Canterbury Tale, ed. M. Mc. Rhinelander. New York, 1997.

The Pricke of Conscience, ed. R. Morris. Philological Society, 1863.

The Promptorium Parvulorum: the First English-Latin Dictionary, ed. A. L. Mayhew. EETS e.s. 102 (1908).

The Prymer or Lay Folks' Prayer Book, ed. H. Littlehales. 2 vols. EETS o.s. 105, 109 (1895–7).

R. H. Robbins, ed. *Historical Poems of the XIVth and XVth Centuries*. New York, 1959.

Rolle, R. *English Prose Treatises of Richard Rolle of Hampole*, ed. G. G. Perry. EETS o.s. 20 (1866).

Yorkshire Writers: Richard Rolle of Hampole and his Followers, ed. C. Horstman. 2 vols. 1895–6.

The Fire of Love and the Mending of Life (tr. by Richard Misyn, 1434–5), ed. R. Harvey. EETS o.s. 106 (1896).

[Rolle] *Meditationes de Passione Domini*, ed. H. Lindkvist. Uppsala, 1917.

Writings Ascribed to Richard Rolle, ed. H. E. Allen. New York, 1927.

English Writings of Richard Rolle, ed. H. E. Allen. Oxford, 1931.

Richard Rolle: Prose and Verse, ed. S. J. Ogilvie-Thomson. EETS 293 (1988).

St Erkenwald, ed. R. Morse. Cambridge, 1975.

St Erkenwald, ed. C. Peterson. Philadelphia, 1977.

Sarjent, H. J. & Kittredge, G. L., eds. *English and Scottish Popular Ballads*. Boston, 1932.

Sawles Warde, in Bennett & Smithers (1966) 246–61.

The Seven Sages, ed. K. Brunner. EETS o.s. 191 (1932).

The Siege of Jerusalem, ed. R. Hanna & D. Lawton. EETS o.s. 320. Oxford, 2003.

The Simonie, ed. D. Embree & E. Urquhart. Heidelberg, 1991.

Sisam, K., ed. *Fourteenth Century Verse and Prose*. Oxford, repr. 1962.

The South English Legendary, ed. C. D'Evelyn & A. J. Mill. 3 vols. EETS o.s. 235, 236, 244 (1956–9).

The Southern Passion, ed. B. D. Brown. EETS o.s. 169 (1927).

Speculum Christiani, ed. G. Holmstedt. EETS o.s. 182 (1933).

A Stanzaic Life of Christ, ed. F. A. Foster. EETS o.s. 166 (1926).

The Towneley Plays, ed. A. C. Cawley & M. Stevens. 2 vols. EETS s.s. 13,14. Oxford, 1994.

Usk, Thomas. *The Testament of Love*, in W. W. Skeat, ed. *Chaucerian and Other Pieces* (Oxford, 1897) 1–145.

William of Palerne, ed. W. W. Skeat. EETS e.s. 1 (1867).

William of Palerne: An Alliterative Romance, ed. G. H. V. Bunt. Groningen, 1985.

William of Shoreham. *William of Shoreham's Poems*, ed. M. Konrath. EETS e.s. 86 (1900).

Wimbledon, Thomas. *Wimbledon's Sermon: Redde Rationem Villicationis Tue: a ME Sermon of the 14th Century*, ed. I. K. Knight. Pittsburgh, 1967.

Wordsworth, W. *Prose Works*, ed. W. J. B. Owen & J. W. Smyser. Oxford, 1974.

——*The Prelude: 1799, 1805, 1850*, eds. J. Wordsworth, M. H. Abrams and S. Gill. New York, 1979.

Wright, T., ed. *The Political Songs of England, From the Reign of John to that of Edward II*. Camden Society 6, 1839.

——*Political Poems and Songs Relating to English History*. Rolls Series. 2 vols. 1859–1861.

John Wycliffe. *Select English Works of Wyclif*, ed. T. Arnold. 3 vols. Oxford, 1869–71.

The English Works of Wyclif hitherto unprinted, ed. F. D. Matthew, EETS o.s. 74 (1880).

Wynnere and Wastoure, ed. S. Trigg. EETS o.s. 297 (1999).

The York Plays, ed. R. Beadle. 1982.

ii LATIN WORKS

Alan of Lille. *Alani de Insulis Opera Omnia*, ed. J-P. Migne. *PL* 210. Paris, 1855.

Alexander of Ville-Dieu. *Das* Doctrinale *des Alexander de Villa-Dei*, ed. D. Reichling. Berlin, 1893.

Aquinas, St Thomas. *Summa Theologica*. 6 vols. Madrid, 1961.

Auctores Octo cum Commento. Jacobus Myt, 1514.

Augustine, St. *Augustini Opera Omnia*, ed. J-P. Migne *PL* 32–47. Paris, 1861–65.

Homilies on the Gospel of John, ed. P. Schaff. 1888.

Bede. *Venerabilis Baedae Opera Omnia*, ed. J-P. Migne *PL* 90–5. Paris, 1862.

Historia Ecclesiastica, ed. B. Colgrave & R. A. B. Mynors. Oxford, 1969.

St Bernard. *Sancti Bernardi Opera Omnia*, ed. J. Mabillon. *PL* 182–5. Paris, 1859–60.

Opera, ed. J. Leclercq, C. H. Talbot & H. M. Rochais. 8 vols. Rome, 1957–77.

Bible, Vulgate. *Biblia Sacra iuxta Vulgatam Clementinam,* ed. by A. Colunga & L. Turrado. 4th edn. Madrid, 1965.

Glossed Bible Facsimile. *Biblia Latina cum Glossa Ordinaria*, 1480/1. Intro. K. Froelich & M. T. Gibson. 4 vols. Brepols-Turnhout, 1992.

Bible, English. *The Holy Bible: Douay-Rheims Version*. New York, 1941.

Bible, Old Latin (*Vetus Latina*). *Bibliorum Sacrorum Latinae Versiones Antiquae, seu Vetus Italica*, ed. P. Sabatier. 3 vols. Rheims-Paris, 1743–51.

Boethius. *Tractates & Consolation of Philosophy*, ed. H. F. Stewart & E. K. Rand. Cambridge, Mass., 1918, rev. edn. 1968.

Bonaventure, St. *Opera Omnia*. 10 vols. Quaracchi, 1882–1902.

Brinton, Thomas. *The Sermons of Thomas Brinton*. 2 vols, ed. M. A. Devlin. 1954.

Bromyard, John. *Summa Praedicantium*. 2 vols. Venice, 1586.

Bruno Signiensis, *Expositio in Librum Job*. Venice, 1651.

Cato, Dionysius. *Disticha Catonis*, ed. M. Boas & H. J. Botschuyer. Amsterdam, 1952.

Chobham, Thomas of. *Thome de Chobham Summa Confessorum,* ed. F. Broomfield. Namur, 1968.

Chrysostom, St John. *Homilies on the Gospel of St John and the Epistle to the Hebrews*, ed. P. Schaff. 1889.

Corpus Iuris Canonici, ed. A. Friedberg. 2 vols. Graz, 1955.

Corpus Scriptorum Ecclesiasticorum Latinorum. Vienna, 1866-.

Denis the Carthusian. *Dionysii Cartusiani Opera Omnia*. Montreuil and Tournai, 1896–1912.

Dreves, G. (rev. Blume, C.), eds. *Ein Jahrtausend Lateinischer Hymnendichtung: Eine Blütenlese aus den Analecta Hymnica*. Leipzig, 1909.

Faral, E. *Les Arts Poétiques du XIIe et XIIIe Siècle*. Paris, 1924.

Fasciculus Morum: A Fourteenth-Century Preacher's Handbook, ed. S. Wenzel. Pennsylvania, 1989.

Fasciculi Zizaniorum Magistri Johannis Wyclif cum Tritico, ed. W. W. Shirley. Rolls Series, V. 1858.

Glossa Ordinaria, ed. J-P. Migne. 2 vols. *PL* 113–14. Paris, 1852.

The Gospel of Nicodemus, ed. H. C. Kim. Toronto, 1973.

Gower, John. *Vox Clamantis*. See Gower under I above.

Gregory the Great. *Sancti Gregorii Opera Omnia*, ed. J-P. Migne. 4 vols. *PL* 75–9. Paris, 1849.

   Moralia in Job, ed. M. Adriaen. CCSL 143. Turnhout, 1979.

Hervieux, L. *Les Fabulistes Latins, III: Avianus*. Paris, 1894.

Higden, Ralph. *Polychronicon*, ed. C. Babington & J. R. Lumby. 9 vols. 1865–86.

Hildebert of Lavardin. *Hildeberti...Opera Omnia*, ed. J-P. Migne. *PL* 171. Paris, 1893.

Hugh of St Cher, *Postillae in Universa Biblia*. 7 vols. Lyons, 1667.

Hugh of St Victor. *Hugonis de Sancto Victore Opera Omnia*, ed. J-P. Migne. 3 vols. *PL* 175–7.

Innocent III, Pope. *De Contemptu Mundi*. See Lotario dei Segni.

Isidore of Seville. *Etymologiarum sive originum libri XX*, ed. W. M. Lindsay. 2 vols. Oxford, 1911.

Jacobus a Voragine. *Legenda Aurea*, ed. T. Graesse. 3rd. edn. Leipzig, 1890.

The Golden Legend tr. by G. Ryan & H. Ripperger, 1941, repr. New Hampshire, 1991.

John of Hoveden. *Nachtigallenlied* [*Philomena*], ed. C. Blume. Leipzig, 1930.

The Poems of John of Hoveden, ed. F. J. E. Raby. 1939.

John of Salisbury. *Metalogicon*, ed. C. C. J. Webb. Oxford, 1929.

Knighton, Henry. *Knighton's Chronicle, 1337–1396*. ed. G. H. Martin. Oxford, 1995.

Liber Albus. The White Book of the City of London, ed. H. T. Riley. 1861.

Peter Lombard. *Petri Lombardi Opera Omnia*, ed. J-P. Migne. 2 vols. *PL* 191–2. Paris, 1854.

Lotario dei Segni. *De miseria condicionis humane*, ed. and tr. R. E. Lewis. Chaucer Library, 1978.

Ludolph of Saxony. *Vita Jesu Christi*, ed. A. C. Boland, L. M. Regallot & J. Carnandet. Paris and Rome, 1865.

Lyndwood, William. *Provinciale*. Oxford, 1679.

Macrobius. *Commentary on the Dream of Scipio*, tr. W. H. Stahl. New York, 1952.

Map, Walter. *The Latin Poems commonly attributed to Walter Mapes*, ed. T. Wright. Camden Society, 1841.

Meditaciones de Passione Christi Olim Sancto Bonaventurae Attributae, ed. M. J. Stallings. Washington, D.C. 1965.

Migne, J-P., ed. *Patrologiae Cursus Completus. Series Latina*. 221 vols. Paris, 1844–64.

Petrus Cantor. *Opera Omnia*, ed. G. Galpin. *PL* 205. Paris, 1855.

Petrus Comestor. *Opera Omnia*, ed. J-P. Migne. *PL* 198. Paris, 1855.

Prudentius, Aurelius. *Works*, ed. H. J. Thomson. 2 vols. Cambridge, Mass., 1949–53.

Rabanus Maurus. *B. Rabani Mauri Opera Omnia*, ed. J-P. Migne. 6 vols. *PL* 107–12. Paris 1864.

Raby, F. J. E., ed. *The Oxford Book of Medieval Latin Verse*. Oxford, 1974.

Rolle, Richard. *Incendium Amoris*, ed. M. Deanesly. Manchester, 1915.

   Emendatio Vitae: Orationes ad Honorem Nominis Ihesu, ed. N. Watson. Toronto, 1995.

Rotuli Parliamentorum Anglie, 6 vols. n.d.

Sacrum Commercium, ed. S. Brufani. Medioevo Francescano, Testi, I. Assisi, 1990.

Sarum Breviary. Proctor, F. and Wordsworth, C., eds. *Breviarium ad Usum Insignis Ecclesiae Sarum*. 3 vols. Cambridge, 1857–86.

Sarum Manual. J. Collins, ed. *Manuale ad usum percelebris ecclesie Sarisburiensis*. 1960.
Sarum Missal. F. H. Dickinson, ed. *Missale ad usum Sarum*. Oxford, 1861–83.
Schneemelcher, W. *New Testament Apocrypha*. 5th edn. 1987.
Thurot, C. *Notices et Extraits de divers manuscrits latins, pour servir à l'histoire des doctrines grammaticales au Moyen Age*. Paris, 1869, repr. Frankfurt, 1964.
Tischendorf, C., ed. *Evangelia Apocrypha*. 2nd ed. Leipzig, 1876; repr. Hildesheim, 1966.
Walsingham, Thomas. *Historia Anglicana*, ed. H. T. Riley. Rolls Series, 2 vols. 1864.
Walter of Châtillon, *Die Gedichte Walters von Châtillon*, Vol. I, ed. K. Strecker. Berlin, 1925.
Walther, H., ed. *Proverbia Sententiaeque Latinitatis Medii Ævi*. 6 vols. Göttingen, 1963–9.
Wright, T. ed. *Early Mysteries and other Latin Poems*. 1838.
    The Anglo-Latin Satirical Poets and Epigrammatists of the 12th. Century. 2 vols. 1872.
——& Halliwell, J. *Reliquiae Antiquae*. 2 vols. 1841–3.
Wycliffe, John. *Dialogus sive Speculum Ecclesie Militantis*, ed. A.W. Pollard. Wyclif Society, 1886.

iii FRENCH WORKS

Bozon, Nicolas. *Deux poèmes de Nicholas Bozon*, ed. J. Vising. Gothenburg, 1919.
Deguileville, Guillaume de. *Le Pélerinage de Vie Humaine,* ed. J. J. Stürzinger (1893)
    Le Pélerinage de L'Ame, ed. idem (1895).
    Le Pélerinage Jesucrist, ed. idem (1897).
    The Pilgrimage of the Lyfe of the Manhode, ed. A. Henry 2 vols. EETS o.s. 288, 292 (1985, 1988).
Froissart, Jean. Tr. Lord Berners. *The Chronicles of Froissart*, ed. G. C. Macaulay. 1913.
Gervais du Bus. *Le Roman de Fauvel*, ed. A. Langfors. Société des Anciens Textes Français 31. Paris, 1914–21.
Grosseteste, Robert. *Le Château d'Amour de Robert Grosseteste*, ed. J. Murray. Paris, 1918.
    Le Mariage des neuf filles du diable, ed. P. Meyer, in *Romania* 29 (1900) 54–72.
    The ME Translations of Robert Grosseteste's 'Château d'Amour', ed. K. Sajavaara. Helsinki, 1967.
L'Histoire de Guillaume le Maréchal, ed. P. Meyer. Paris, 1891–1901.
Huon de Méri, *Li Tornoiemenz Antecrit*, ed. G. Wimmer. Marburg, 1888.
Jubinal, M., ed. *Nouveau Recueil*. 2 vols. Paris, 1839–42.
Langtoft, Peter. *The Chronicle of Pierre de Langtoft*, ed. T. Wright. 2 vols. 1866–68.
Lorris, Guillaume de & Jean de Meun. *Le Roman de la Rose*, ed. F. Lecoy. Paris, 1965–70.
Robert, A., ed. *Fabliaux inédits*. Paris, 1834.
Rutebeuf, *La Voie de Paradis*, ed. E. Faral & J. Bastin. Paris, 1959.
    Œuvres complètes de Rutebeuf, ed. A. Jubinal. Paris, repr. 1974.

II. SECONDARY SOURCES

A. Reference Works

a. Bibliographies

Colaianne, A. J. *PP: An Annotated Bibliography of Editions and Criticism 1550–1977.* New York/London, 1978.
Middleton, A. 'XVIII. *PP,*' in Hartung, A. E., ed. *A Manual of the Writings in Middle English 1050–1500*, vol 7. New Haven, Conn. (1986) 2211–34, 2417–43.
Pearsall, D. *An Annotated Critical Bibliography of Langland*. New York and London, 1990.
Proppe, K. '*PP*. An Annotated Bibliography for 1900–1968', *Comitatus* 3 (Los Angeles, 1972) 33–90.
The Yearbook of Langland Studies (Michigan, 1987–): 'Annual Bibliography'.

b. Dictionaries, Concordances, Glossaries and Grammars

Alford, J. *PP: A Glossary of Legal Diction*. Cambridge, 1988.
    PP: A Guide to the Quotations. New York, 1992.
Hassell, J. W. Jr. *Middle French Proverbs, Sentences and Proverbial Phrases*. Toronto, 1982.

Kane, G. *Piers Plowman: Glossary.* 2005.

Kurath, H., Kuhn, S. M, Reidy, J., & Lewis, R., eds. *Middle English Dictionary*. Ann Arbor, Michigan, 1964–2001.

Matsushita, T. *A Glossarial Concordance to William Langland's The Vision of PP: The B-Text*. 3 vols. Tokyo, 1998–2000.

——*A Glossarial Concordance to William Langland's The Vision of PP: The Z-Text*. Tokyo, 2009.

——*A Glossarial Concordance to William Langland's The Vision of PP: The A-Text*. Tokyo, 2009.

——*A Glossarial Concordance to William Langland's The Vision of PP: The C-Text*. Tokyo, 2010.

Mossé, F. (tr. J. Walker). *A Handbook of Middle English*. Baltimore, 1952.

Mustanoja, T. *A Middle English Syntax. Part I: Parts of Speech*. Helsinki, 1960.

Oxford English Dictionary. Oxford, 1971.

Whiting, B. J., ed. *Proverbs, Sentences and Proverbial Phrases from English Writings Mainly before 1500*. Cambridge, Mass., 1968.

Wittig, J. S., ed. *A Concordance to the Athlone Edition of 'PP'*. 2001.

B. Textual, Linguistic and Metrical Studies

Adams, R. 'The Reliability of the Rubrics in the B-Text of *PP*,' *MÆ* 54 (1985) 20–31.

'Editing and the Limitations of the *Durior Lectio*,' *YLS* 5 (1991) 7–15.

'Editing *PP* B: the Imperative of an Intermittently Critical Edition', *SB* 45 (1992) 31–68.

'L's *Ordinatio*: The *Visio* and the *Vita* Once More', *YLS* 8 (1994) 51–84.

'Evidence for the Stemma of the *PP* B Manuscripts', *SB* 53 (2001) 173–94.

'The R/F MSS of *PP* and the Pattern of Alpha / Beta Complementary Omissions: Implications for Critical Editing', *TEXT* 12 (2002) 109–37.

Barney, P. 'Line-Number Index to the Athlone Edition of *PP*', *YLS* 7 (1993) 97–114.

'Line-Number Index to the Athlone Edition of *PP*: the C Version', *YLS* 12 (1998) 159–73.

Barney, S. 'L.'s Prosody: the State of the Study', in Tavormina and Yeager (1995) 65–85.

Benson, C. D. & Blanchfield, L. S. *The MSS of PP: the B Version*. Cambridge, 1997.

Black, M. 'A Scribal Translation of *PP*', *MÆ* 67 (1998) 257–90.

Blackman, E. 'Notes on the B-Text of *PP*,' *JEGP* 17 (1918) 489–545.

Blair, C. 'The Word "Baselard"', *Journal of the Arms & Armour Society* 11 (1984) 193–206.

Bowers, J. M. '*PP*'s William Langland: Editing the Text, Writing the Author's Life', *YLS* 9 (1995[1]) 65–102.

'L.'s *PP* in Hm 143: Copy, Commentary, Censorship', *YLS* 19 (2005) 137–68.

Bradley, H. 'The Word "Moillere" in *P the P,*' *MLR* 2 (1906–7) 163–4.

'Some Cruces in *PP*', *MLR* 5 (1910) 340–2.

Breeze, A. '"Tikes" at *PP* B. XIX. 37: Welsh *Taeog* "Serf, Bondman"', *NQ* 238 (1993[2]) 442–45.

Brewer, C. 'Z and the A-, B- and C-Texts of *PP*', *MÆ* 53 (1984) 194–219.

'Some Implications of the Z-Text for the Textual Tradition of *PP*.' Unpublished D.Phil. thesis. Oxford University, 1986.

'The Textual Principles of Kane's A-Text', *YLS* 3 (1989) 67–90.

'Authorial vs. Scribal Re-Writing in *PP*,' in Machan (1991) 59–89.

'George Kane's Processes of Revision', in Minnis & Brewer (1992) 71–92.

Editing 'PP': The evolution of the text. Cambridge, 1996.

Britnell, R. H. '*Forstall*, Forestalling and the Statute of Forestallers', *EHR* 102 (1987) 89–102.

Brooks, E. St J. 'The *PP* MSS in Trinity College, Dublin', *The Library*, 5th ser., 6 (1951) 5–22.

Burrow, J. A. 'The Structure of *PP* B XV–XX: Evidence from the Rubrics', *MÆ* 77 (2008) 306–12.

——'*PP* B XIII 19', *NQ* 55 (2008) 124–25.

——'*PP* B: Paragraphing in the Archetypal Copy', *NQ* 57 (2010) 24–26.

Cable, T. 'Middle English Meter and its Theoretical Implications', *YLS* 2 (1988) 47–69.

'Standards from the Past: The Conservative Syllable Structure of the Alliterative Revival', in J. B. Trahern, ed. *Standardizing English: Essays in the History of Language Change in Honor of J. H. Fisher*. Tennessee Studies in Literature 31 (1989) 42–56.

The English Alliterative Tradition. Philadelphia, 1991.

Calabrese, M. '[P] *the* [P.]; the Corrections, Interventions, and Erasures in Huntington MS Hm 143 (X)', *YLS* 19 (2005) 169–99.

Carnegy, F. A. R. *An Attempt to Approach the C-Text of PP*. 1934.

Cerquiglini, B. *Eloge de la variante: Histoire critique de la philologie*. Paris, 1989.

Chambers, R. W. and Grattan, J. G. 'The Text of *PP*: Critical Methods', *MLR* 11 (1916) 257–75.

'The Text of *PP*,' *MLR* 26 (1931) 1–51.

Clopper, L. 'L.'s Markings for the Structure of *PP*,' *MP* 85 (1988) 245–55.

'A Response to Robert Adams', *YLS* 9 (1995) 141–6.

Colledge, E. 'Aliri', *MÆ* 27 (1958) 111–13.

Crawford, W. R. 'Robert Crowley's Editions of *PP*: A Bibliographical and Textual Study'. Unpub. Diss. Yale University, 1957.

Dahl, E. 'Diverse Copies Have it Diversly: An Unorthodox Survey of *PP* Textual Scholarship from Crowley to Skeat', in Vaughan (1993) 53–80.

Davis, B. P. 'The Rationale for a Copy of a Text: Constructing the Exemplar for BL Add. MS 10574', *YLS* 11 (1997) 141–55.

Dobson, E. J. 'Some Notes on ME Texts', *English & Germanic Studies* I (1947–8) 56–62.

Dolan, T. P. '*Passus* in FitzRalph and L.', *ELN* 23 (1985) 5–7.

Donaldson, E. T. 'MSS R & F in the B-Tradition of *PP*,' *Transactions of the Connecticut Academy of Arts & Sciences* 39 (1955) 177–212.

'The Grammar of Book's Speech in *PP*' [1966], repr. Blanch (1969) 264–70.

Doyle, A. I. 'Remarks on Surviving MSS of *PP*', in Kratzmann and Simpson (1986) 35–48.

——& Parkes, M. B. 'The production of Copies of the *Canterbury Tales* and the *Confessio Amantis* in the Early 15th Century', in M. B. Parkes and A. G. Watson, eds., *Medieval Scribes, Manuscripts and Libraries. Studies Presented to N. R. Ker* (1978) 163–210.

Duggan, H. 'Final –e and the Rhythmic Structure of the B-Verse in ME Alliterative Poetry', *MP* 88 (1986[1]) 119–45.

'Alliterative Patterning as a Basis for Emendation in ME Alliterative Poetry', *SAC* 8 (1986) 73–105.

'The Authenticity of the Z-Text of *PP*. Further Notes on Metrical Evidence', *MÆ* (1987[1]) 25–45.

'Notes towards a Theory of L.'s Meter', *YLS* 1 (1987[2]) 41–70.

'L.'s Dialect and Final -*e*', *SAC* 12 (1990[1]) 157–91.

'Stress Assignment in ME Alliterative Poetry', *JEGP* 89 (1990[2]) 309–29.

'Notes on the Metre of *PP*: Twenty Years On' in J. Jefferson and A. Putter, eds. *Approaches to the Metre of Alliterative Verse* (Leeds, 2009) 159–86.

'The end of the line', in Burrow & Duggan (2010) 67–79.

Edwards, A. S. G. 'The Early Reception of Chaucer and L.', *Florilegium* 15 (1998) 1–22.

'Two *PP* MSS from Helmingham Hall', *Transactions of the Cambridge Bibliographical Society* 11 (1999) 421–6.

Fisher, J. '*PP* and the Chancery Tradition' in Kennedy & al. (1988) 267–78.

Fletcher, A. J. 'The Essential (Ephemeral) WL: Textual Revision as Ethical Process in *PP*', *YLS* 15 (2001) 61–84.

Flom, G. T. 'A Note on *PP*,' *MLN* 23 (1908) 156–7.

Fowler, D. C. 'A New Edition of the B-Text of *PP*,' *YES* 7 (1977) 23–42.

'Editorial "Jamming": Two New Editions of *PP*', *Review* (Blacksburg, Va.) 2 (1980) 211–69.

Galloway. A. 'Uncharacterizable Entities: the Poetics of ME Scribal Culture and the Definitive *PP*,' *SB* 52 (1999) 59–84.

Green, R. F. 'The Lost Exemplar of the Z-Text of *PP* and its 20-line Pages', *MÆ* 56 (1987) 307–10.

Greetham, D. C. 'Reading in and around *PP*,' in P. Cohen, ed. *Texts and Textuality* (NY, 1997) 25–57.

Greg, W. W. *The Calculus of Variants*. Oxford, 1927.

'The Rationale of Copy-Text', *SB* 3 (1950) 19–36.

Griffiths, J. and Pearsall, D. eds. *Book Production and Publishing in Britain*, 1375–1475. Cambridge, 1989.

Grindley, C. 'The Life of a Book: BL MS Add. 35157 in an Historical Context', Glasgow PhD. Diss. 1996.

'Reading *PP* C-Text Annotations: Notes towards the Classification of Printed and Written Marginalia in Texts from the British Isles 1300–1641', in K. Kerby-Fulton & M. Hilmo, eds. *The Medieval Professional Reader at Work*. 2001.

Hailey, R. C. '"Geuyng light to the Reader": Robert Crowley's Editions of *PP* (1550)', *PBSA* 95 (2001) 483–502.

'Robert Crowley and the Editing of *PP* (1550)', *YLS* 21 (2007) 143–70.

Halamari, H. & Adams, R. 'On the Grammar and Rhetoric of Language Mixing in *PP*,' *NM* 103 (2002) 33–50.

Hanna, R. 'The Scribe of Huntington Hm 114', *SB* 42 (1989) 120–133.

'Studies in the MSS of *PP*,' *YLS* 7 (1993) 1–25.

'MS Bodley 851 and the Dissemination of *PP*,' in *Pursuing History* 195–202.

'On the Versions of *PP*,' in *Pursuing History* 203–43.

Pursuing History: ME Manuscripts and their Texts. Stanford, 1996.

Harley, M. P. 'The Derivation of *Hawkin* and its Application in *PP*,' *Names* 29 (1981) 97–99.

Hill, T. D. 'Green and Filial Love: Two Notes on the Russell-Kane C-Text: C 8.215 and C 17.48', *YLS* 16 (2002) 67–83.

Horobin, S. '"In London and Opelond": The Dialect and Circulation of the C Version of *PP*', *MÆ* 74 (2005[1]) 248–69.

'The Scribe of Rawlinson Poetry 137 and the Copying and Circulation of *PP*', *YLS* 19 (2005[2]) 3–26.

'Harley 3954 and the audience of *PP*', in D. Renevey & G. Caie, eds. *Medieval Texts in Context*, New York (2008) 68–84.

'Adam Pinkhurst and the Copying of British Library, MS Additional 35287', *YLS* 23 (2009) 61–83.

'The Scribe of Bodleian Library MS Digby 102 and the Circulation of the C Text of *Piers Plowman*', forthcoming in *YLS* 24 (2010).

——& Mooney, L. 'A *PP* Manuscript by the Hengwrt / Ellesmere Scribe and its Implications for London Standard English', *SAC* 26 (2004) 65–112.

——& Mosser, D. W. 'Scribe D's SW Midlands Roots: A Reconsideration', *NM* 106 (2006) 32–47.

——& Wiggins, A. 'Reconsidering Lincoln's Inn MS 150', *MÆ* 77 (2008) 30–53.

Jansen, S. L. 'Politics, Protest, and a New *PP* Fragment: the Voice of the Past in Tudor England', *RES* 40 (1989) 93–9.

Jefferson, J. A. 'Divisions, collaboration and other topics: the table of contents in CUL ms Gg. 4. 31', in Burrow & Duggan 2010 :140–52.

Johnston, G. K. W. '*PP*, B-Text, Pr 78–9', *NQ* 204 (1959) 243–4.

Kane, G. 'Poetry and Lexicography in the Translation of *PP*,' *Medieval and Renaissance Studies* 9 (1982) 33–54.

'The "Z Version" of *PP*,' *Speculum* 60 (1985) 910–30.

'The Text', in Alford, ed., *Companion* (1988) 175–200.

Review of Schmidt, *PP: A Parallel-Text Edition*, in *NQ* 43 (1996) 315–21.

'An Open Letter to Jill Mann about the Sequence of the Versions of *PP*,' *YLS* 14 (1999) 7–33.

'Word-Games: Glossing *PP*,' in S. Powell & J. J. Smith, eds., *New Perspectives in Middle English Texts: A Festschrift for R. A. Waldron* (Cambridge, 2000) 43–53.

Kennedy, E. J., Waldron, R. & Wittig, J., eds. *Medieval English Studies Presented to George Kane.* Woodbridge, 1988.

Kerby-Fulton, K. 'Langlandian Reading Circles and the Civil Service in London and Dublin, 1380–1427', *New Medieval Literatures* 1 (1998) 59–83.

'Professional Readers of L. at Home and Abroad: New Directions in the Political and Bureaucratic Codicology of *PP*,' in D. Pearsall, ed. *New Directions in Later Medieval Manuscript Studies* (Woodbridge, 2000) 103–29.

'"L. in his Working Clothes?" Scribe D, Loose Revision Material and the Nature of Scribal Intervention', in A. J. Minnis, ed. *ME Poetry: Texts and Traditions. Essays in Honour of D. Pearsall* (Woodbridge, 2001) 371–92.

'The Women Readers in L.'s Earliest Audience: some Codicological Evidence', in S. R. Jones, ed. *Learning and Literacy in Medieval England and Abroad* (Turnhout, 2003) 121–34.

——& D. Depres, *Iconography and the Professional Reader: The Politics of Book Production and the Douce 'PP'.* Minneapolis, 1999.

Kiernan, K. *'Beowulf' and the Beowulf Manuscript.* Ann Arbor, Michigan, 1996.

King, J. N. 'Robert Crowley's Editions of *PP*,' *MP* 73 (1976) 342–52.

Knott, T. A. 'An Essay toward the Critical Text of the A Version of *PP*', *MP* 12 (1915) 129–61.

Lawler, T. 'A Reply to Jill Mann, Reaffirming the Traditional Relation between the A and B Versions of *PP*,' *YLS* 10 (1996) 145–80.

Maas, P. *Textual Criticism.* Oxford, 1956.

Machan, T. 'Late ME Texts and the Higher and Lower Criticisms', in Machan, ed. *Medieval Literature: Texts and Interpretation* (Binghamton, N.Y. 1991) 3–16.

Mann. J. 'The Power of the Alphabet: A Reassessment of the Relation between the A and the B Versions of *PP*,' *YLS* 8 (1994[1]) 21–50.

Minnis, A. J. & Brewer, C., eds. *Crux and Controversy in Middle English Textual Criticism.* Cambridge, 1992.

Mitchell, A. G. 'The Text of *PP* C. Prologue l. 125', *MÆ* 8 (1939) 118–20.

'Notes on the C-Text of *PP*,' *London Medieval Studies* 1 (1948 for 1939) 483–92.

Moore, S. 'Studies in *P the P,*' *MP* 11 (1913) 177–93; 12 (1914) 19–50.

Mustanoja, T. F. 'The Suggestive Use of Christian Names in M.E. Poetry', in J. Mandel and B. A. Rosenberg, eds. *Medieval Literature and Folklore Studies: Essays in Honor of F. L. Utley.* New Brunswick, N.J. (1970) 51–76.

Oliphant, R. 'L.'s "Sire Piers of Pridie"', *NQ* 205 (1960) 167–8.

Olszewska, E. S. 'ME "Fader and Frendes"', *NQ* 218 (1973) 205–7.

Onions, C. T. 'An Unrecorded Reading in "PP"', *MLR* 3 (1907–8) 170–1.

Parkes, M. B. 'The Influence of the Concepts of *Ordinatio* and *Compilatio* on the Development of the Book', in J. J. G. Alexander & M. T. Gibson, eds., *Medieval Learning and Literature: Essays Presented to R. W. Hunt* (Oxford, 1976) 115–41.

Bibliography

Patterson, L. 'The Logic of Textual Criticism and the Way of Genius: The Kane-Donaldson *PP* in Historical Perspective', in Patterson, *Negotiating the Past: The Historical Understanding of Medieval Literature* (Madison, Wis., 1987) 77–113.

Pearcy, R. J. 'Langland's *Fair Feld,' YLS* 11 (1997) 39–48.

Pearsall, D. 'The Ilchester Manuscript of *PP,' NM* 82 (1981) 181–93.

'Editing Medieval Texts: Some Developments and some Problems', in J. McGann, ed., *Textual Criticism and Literary Interpretation* (Chicago, 1985) 92–106.

Perry, R. 'The Clopton MS and the Beauchamp Affinity: Patronage and Reception Issues in a West Midlands Reading Community', in W. Scase, *Essays in Manuscript Geography: Vernacular MSS of the English West Midlands from the Conquest to the Sixteenth Century* (Turnhout, 2007) 131–59.

Revard, C. '*Title* and *Auaunced* in *PP* B. 11. 290', *YLS* 1 (1987) 116–21.

Rouse, M. & R. H. '*Ordinatio* and *Compilatio* revisited' in M. J. Jordan & K. Emery, eds. *Ad litteram: Authoritative Texts and their Medieval Readers*. 1992.

Ruggiers, P., ed. *Editing Chaucer: The Great Tradition*. Norman, Oklahoma, 1984.

Russell, G. H. 'Some Aspects of the Process of Revision in *PP,*' in Hussey (1969) 27–49.

'Some Early Responses to the C Version of *PP,' Viator* 15 (1984) 275–303.

'"As They Read It": Some Notes on Early Responses to the C Version of *PP,' LSE* n.s. 20 (1989) 173–89.

——& Nathan, V. 'A *PP* MS in the Huntington Library', *HLQ* 26 (1963) 119–30.

Samuels, M. L. 'L.'s Dialect', *MÆ* 54 (1985) 232–47; with corrections in *MÆ* 55 (1986) 40.

'Dialect and Grammar', in Alford, ed. *Companion*, 201–21.

Sargent, M. G. 'What do the Numbers Mean? A Textual Critic's Observations on some Patterns of Middle English Manuscript Transmission', in M. Connolly & L. Mooney, eds. *Design and Distribution of Late Medieval Manuscripts in England* (New York, 2008) 205–44.

Scase, W. 'Two *PP* C-Text Interpolations: Evidence for a Second Textual Tradition', *NQ* 232 (1987) 456–63.

Schaap, T. 'From Professional to Private Readership: a Discussion and Transcription of C15th and C16th Marginalia in *PP* C-Text Oxford, Bodleian Library MS Digby 102', *Studies in Medieval and Renaissance History* 16 (2001) 81–116.

Schmidt, A. V. C. 'The C Version of *PP*: A New Edition', *NQ* 225 (1980) 102–110.

'The Authenticity of the Z-Text of *PP*: A Metrical Examination', *MÆ* 53 (1984) 295–300.

'A Misattributed Speech in *PP*, A XI 182–218', *NQ* 249 (2004) 238–40.

'*Ars or Scientia?* Reflections on Editing *PP,' YLS* 18 (2004) 31–54.

Sebastian, J. Review of Turville-Petre & Duggan, *PP Electronic Archive Vol. 2, YLS* 15 (2001) 219–27.

Shepherd, S. Review of Duggan et al., *PP Electronic Archive Vol. 1, YLS* 14 (2000) 199–207.

Skeat, W. W. *Parallel Extracts from Twenty-nine Manuscripts of PP*. EETS 17 (1866); reprinted in revised form as Index VII in EETS edn. of *PP*, IV ii 831–62.

Sledd, J. 'Three Textual Notes on C14th Poetry', *MLN* 55 (1940) 379–82.

Smith, M. 'L's Unruly Caesura', *YLS* 22 (2008) 57–101.

'L's Alliterative Line(s)', *YLS* 23 (2009) 163–216.

Spargo, J. W. 'Chaucer's Love-Days', *Speculum* 15 (1940) 36–56.

Spearman, A. 'L.'s "Corlew": Another Look at *PP* B XIV 43', *MÆ* 62 (1993) 242–58.

Stanley, E. G. 'The B Version of *PP*: a New Edition', *NQ* 221 (1976) 435–7.

Tajima, M. '*PP* B. V. 379: A Syntactic Note', *NQ* 245 (2000) 18–20.

Taylor, S. 'The F Scribe and the R MS of *PP B,' ESt.* 77 (1996) 530–48.

'The R MS of *PP B*: A Critical Facsimile'. Unpub. Ph.D. diss. Univ. of Washington, 1995.

'The Lost Revision of *PP B', YLS* 11 (1997).

Thorne, J. R. & Uhart, M. C. 'Robert Crowley's *PP,' MÆ* 55 (1986) 248–54.

Turville-Petre, T. 'Sir Adrian Fortescue and his Copy of *PP,' YLS* 14 (2000) 29–48.

'Putting it Right: The Corrections of HL ms HM 128 and BL Additional ms 35287', *YLS* 16 (2002) 41–65.

Uhart, M. C. 'The Early Reception of *PP.*' Unpub. Ph.D. diss. University of Leicester, 1986.

Vaughan, M. F. 'The Ending(s) of *PP* A' in Vaughan (1993) 211–41.

Warner, L. 'The *Ur*-B *PP* and the Earliest Production of C and B', *YLS* 16 (2002) 3–39.

'*PP* B XV 417–28a: an Intrusion from L.'s C-Papers?', *NQ* 249 (2004) 119–22.

'John But and the Other Works that Will Wrought (*Piers Plowman* A XII 101–2)', *NQ* 250 (2005) 13–18.

'The Ending, and End, of *PP* B: the C Version Origins of the Final Two Passus', *MÆ* 76 (2007) 225–50.

——*The Lost History of* PP: *The Earliest Transmission of Langland's Work*. Philadelphia, 2010 (forthcoming).

Weldon, J. F. G. 'Ordinatio and Genre in MS CCC 201: A Medieval Reading of the B-Text of PP,' Florilegium 12 (1993) 159–75.
Westcott, B. F. & Hort, F. J., eds. The New Testament. 2 vols. Cambridge and London, 1881–82.
Wilcockson, C. 'A Note on "Rifling" in PP B. V. 234', MÆ 52 (1983) 302–5.
Windeatt, B. A. 'The Scribes as Chaucer's Early Critics', SAC I (1979) 23–35.
Wittig, J. S. 'The ME "Absolute Infinitive" and the Speech of Book', in Groos et al. (1986) 217–40.

C. Critical and Interpretative Studies of *PP* and related works

Adams, J. F. 'PP and the Three Ages of Man', JEGP 61 (1962) 23–41.
Adams, R. 'L. and the Liturgy Revisited', SP 73 (1976) 266–84.
    'The Nature of Need in PP,' Traditio 34 (1978) 273–301.
    'Piers's Pardon and Langland's Semi-Pelagianism', Traditio 39 (1983) 367–418.
    'Some Versions of Apocalypse: Learned & Popular Eschatology in PP,' in Heffernan (1985) 194–236.
    'Mede and Mercede: The Evolution of the Economics of Grace in the PP B and C Versions' in Kennedy & al. (1988) 217–32.
Aers, D. PP and Christian Allegory. 1975.
    Chaucer, Langland and the Creative Imagination. 1980.
    'PP and Problems in the Perception of Poverty: a Culture in Transition', LSE 14 (1983) 5–25.
Sanctifying Signs: Making Christian Tradition in Late Medieval England. Notre Dame, Indiana, 2004.
Alexander, J. W. 'Ranulph of Chester: An Outlaw of Legend?' NM 83 (1982) 152–7.
Alford, J. 'PP B XVIII 390: "Til Parce It Hote"', MP 69 (1972) 323–5.
    'Haukyn's Coat: Some Observations on PP B XIV 22–27', MÆ 43 (1974) 133–8.
    'Some Unidentified Quotations in PP,' MP 72 (1975) 390–99.
    'The Role of the Quotations in PP,' Speculum 52 (1977¹) 80–99.
    'Literature and Law in Medieval England', PMLA 92 (1977²) 941–51.
    'The Grammatical Metaphor: A Survey of its Use in the Middle Ages', Speculum 57 (1982) 728–60.
    'More Unidentified Quotations in PP,' MP 81 (1984) 146–49.
    'The Idea of Reason in PP', in Kennedy et al. (1988¹) 199–215.
    Ed. A Companion to 'PP'. Berkeley, Los Angeles, London, 1988².
    'The Figure of Repentance in PP', in Vaughan (1993) 3–28.
    'L's Exegetical Drama: the sources of the Banquet Scene in PP', in R. G. Newhauser & J. A. Alford, eds., Literature and Religion in the Later Middle Ages: Philological Studies in Honor of Siegfried Wenzel (Binghamton, NY, 1995) 97–117.
Allen, J. B. The Ethical Poetic of the Later Middle Ages. Toronto, 1982.
    'L.'s Writing and Reading: Detractor and the Pardon Passus', Speculum 59 (1984) 342–62.
Amassian, M. and Sadowsky, J. 'Mede and Mercede: a Study of the Grammatical Metaphor in "PP" C IV 335–409', NM 72 (1971) 457–6.
Ames, R. M. The Fulfilment of the Scriptures: Abraham, Moses and Piers. Evanston, Illinois, 1970.
Arn, M-J. 'L.'s Triumph of Grace in Dobest', ESt. 63 (1982) 506–16.
Ashley, K. M. 'The Guiler Beguiled: Christ and Satan as Theological Tricksters in Medieval Religious Literature', Criticism 24 (1982) 126–37.
Astell, A. W. Political Allegory in Late Medieval England. Ithaca, NY. 1999.
Baer, P. 'Cato's "Trace": Literacy, Readership, and the Process of Revision in PP,' Studies in Medieval and Renaissance History 16 (2001) 123–47.
Baker, D. N. 'From Plowing to Penitence: PP and C14th Theology', Speculum 55 (1980) 715–25.
    'The Pardons of PP,' NM 85 (1984¹) 462–72.
    'Dialectic Form in Pearl and PP,' Viator 15 (1984²) 263–73.
    'Meed and the Economics of Chivalry in PP,' in D. N. Baker, ed. The Hundred Years' War: French and English Cultural Studies. Albany, NY 2000.
Baldwin, A. The Theme of Government in Piers Plowman. Cambridge, 1981¹.
    'The Double Duel in PP B XVIII and C XXI', MÆ 50 (1981²) 64–78.
    'A Reference in PP to the Westminster Sanctuary', NQ 29 (1982) 106–8.
    'The Triumph of Patience in Julian of Norwich and L.', in Phillips (1990) 71–83.
    'Patient Politics in PP,' YLS 15 (2001) 99–108.

Barney, S. 'The Ploughshare of the Tongue: the Progress of a Symbol from the Bible to *PP*,' *MS* 35 (1973) 261–93.
    Allegories of History, Allegories of Love. Hamden, Conn. 1979.
    The Penn Commentary on 'Piers Plowman', Vol. 5: C Passus 20–22; B Passus 18–20. Pennsylvania, 2006.
Barr, H. 'The Use of Latin Quotations in *PP* with Special Reference to Passus XVIII of the B-Text', *NQ* 33 (1986) 440–8.
    'The Relationship of *RRe* and *MS*: Some New Evidence', *YLS* 4 (1990) 105–33.
    Signes and Sothe: Language in the PP Tradition. Cambridge, 1994.
    Socio-literary Practice in the Fourteenth Century. Oxford, 2003.
Barratt, A. 'Civil and Theology in *PP*,' *Traditio* 28 (1982).
Barron, C. 'WL: A London Poet', in Hanawalt, ed. *Chaucer's England: Literature in Historical Context* (Minneapolis, 1992) 91–109.
Bennett, J. A. W. 'The Date of the A-Text of *PP*,' *PMLA* 58 (1943[1]) 566–72.
    'The Date of the B-Text of *PP*,' *MÆ* 12 (1943[2]) 55–64.
    Chaucer at Oxford and at Cambridge. Oxford, 1974.
    'L.'s Samaritan', *Poetica* 12 (1981) 10–27.
    '*Nosce te ipsum*: some Medieval and Modern Interpretations', in Bennett, *The Humane Medievalist*, ed. P. Boitani (Rome, 1982) 135–72.
    Poetry of the Passion. Oxford, 1982.
    Middle English Literature, ed. D. Gray. Oxford, 1986.
Benson, C. D. 'An Augustinian Irony in *PP*', *NQ* 23 (1976) 51–4.
    'The Function of Lady Meed in *PP*,' *ES* 61 (1980) 193–205.
    '*PP* and Parish Wall Paintings', *YLS* 11 (1998) 1–38.
    Public PP: Modern Scholarship and Late Medieval English Culture. Pennsylvania, 2004.
Benson, L. & Wenzel, S., eds. *The Wisdom of Poetry: Essays in Early English Literature in honor of M. W. Bloomfield*. Kalamazoo, Mich., 1982.
Bertz, D. 'Prophecy and Apocalypse in L.'s *PP*, B. XVI–XIX', *JEGP* 84 (1985) 313–28.
Biggs, F. M. '"Aungeles Peeris": *PP* B 16.67–72 and C 18.85–100', *Anglia* 102 (1984) 426–36.
    '"For God is after an Hand": *PP* B 17. 138–205', *YLS* 5 (1991) 17–30.
Birnes, W. J. 'Christ as Advocate: the Legal Metaphor of *PP*', *AM* 16 (1975) 71–93.
Bishop, L. 'Will and the Law of Property', *YLS* 10 (1996) 23–41.
Blanch, R. J., ed. *Style and Symbolism in PP: a Modern Critical Anthology*. Knoxville, Tennessee, 1969.
Bloom, H. *Poetry and Repression: Revisionism from Blake to Stevens*. 1976.
Bloomfield, M. W. *The Seven Deadly Sins*. Michigan, 1952.
    'The Pardons of Pamplona and the Pardoner of Rounceval: *PP* B XVII 252', *PQ* 35 (1956) 60–8.
    '*PP* and the Three Grades of Chastity', *Anglia* 76 (1958) 227–53.
    PP as a Fourteenth Century Apocalypse. New Brunswick, 1961.
Bourquin, G. *PP: Etudes sur la Genèse littéraire des Trois Versions*. Lille and Paris, 1978.
Bowers, A. J. 'The Tree of Charity in *PP*: Its Allegorical and Structural Significance', in E. Rothstein & J. Wittreich, eds. *Literary Monographs*, vol. 6: *Medieval and Renaissance Literature* (Madison, Wisc., 1975) 1–34.
Bowers, J. M. *The Crisis of Will in 'PP'*. Washington, D.C. 1986.
    '*PP* and the Police: Notes toward a history of the Wycliffite Langland', *YLS* 6 (1992) 1–50.
    '*Pearl* in its Royal Setting', *SAC* 17 (1995[2]) 111–55.
    'Dating *PP*: Testing the Testimony of Usk's *Testament*,' *YLS* 13 (1999) 65–100.
    Chaucer and Langland: The Antagonistic Tradition. Notre Dame, Indiana, 2007.
Bowers, R. H. '"Foleuyles Lawes" (*PP* C 22.247)', *NQ* 206 (1961) 327–8.
Braswell, M. F. *The Medieval Sinner: Characterisation and Confession in the Literature of the English Middle Ages*. Rutherford, N.J., 1983.
Breeze, A. 'The Trinity as a Taper: a Welsh Allusion to L.', *NQ* 235 (1990) 5–6.
    'A Welsh Addition to the *PP* Group', *NQ* 238 (1993[1]) 142–51.
Bright, A. H. *New Light on 'PP'*. 1928.
Burdach, K. *Der Gral: Forschungen über seinen Ursprung und seinen Zusammenhang mit der Longinuslegende*. 2nd edn. Darmstadt, 1974.
Burnley, J. D. *Chaucer's Language and the Philosophers' Tradition*. Cambridge, 1979.
    'Langland's Clergial Lunatic' in Phillips (1990) 31–8.
Burrow, J. A. 'The Audience of *PP*', *Anglia* 75 (1957), repr. in id. *Essays* (1984) 102–16.

'The Action of L.'s Second Vision', *EC* 15 (1965) 247–68, repr. in *Essays* 79–101.

'Words, Works and Will: Theme and Structure in *PP*', in Hussey (1969) 111–24.

Ricardian Poetry. 1971.

'L. *Nel Mezzo del Cammin*', in Heyworth (1981) 21–41.

'Autobiographical Poetry in the Middle Ages', *PBA* 68 (1982) 389–412.

Essays in Medieval Literature. Oxford, 1984.

The Ages of Man. Oxford, 1986.

'Reason's Horse', *YLS* 4 (1990) 139–44.

Langland's Fictions. Oxford, 1993[1].

Thinking in Poetry: Three Medieval Examples. 1993[2].

'Gestures and Looks in *PP*,' *YLS* 14 (2000) 75–83.

'Wasting Time, Wasting Words in *PP* B and C', *YLS* 17 (2003) 191–202.

'Lady Meed and the Power of Money', *MÆ* 74 (2005) 113–18.

'The Two Ploughs of Piers Plowman (B XIX 430)', *NQ* 252 (2007) 123–24.

——& H. N. Duggan, eds. *Medieval Alliterative Poetry: Essays in Honour of Thorlac Turville-Petre*. Dublin, 2010.

Calí, P. *Allegory and Vision in Dante and Langland*. Cork, 1971.

Cargill, O. 'The Langland Myth', *PMLA* 50 (1935) 36–56.

Carlson, P. 'Lady Meed and God's Meed: The Grammar of *PP* B 3 and C 4', *Traditio* 46 (1991) 291–311.

Carruthers, M. *The Search for St. Truth*. Evanston, Illinois, 1973.

——& Kirk, E., eds. *Acts of Interpretation: the text and its contexts 700–1600. Essays on medieval and renaissance lierature in honour of E. T. Donaldson*. Norman, Oklahoma. 1982.

'Imaginatif, Memoria and "The Need for Critical Theory" in *PP* Studies', *YLS* 9 (1995) 103–14. *See* Schroeder, M.

Cassidy, F. G. 'The Merit of Malkyn', *MLN* (1948) 52–3.

Cervone, C. M. 'Christ the Falcon', *NQ* 55 (2008) 277–82.

Chamberlin, J. *Medieval Arts Doctrines on Ambiguity and their Place in Langland's Poetics*. Montreal and Kingston, 2000.

Clifton, N. 'The Romance Convention of the Disguised Duel and the Climax of *PP*', *YLS* 7 (1993) 123–8.

Clopper, L. M. 'L.'s Trinitarian Analogies as Key to Meaning and Structure', *Medievalia et Humanistica* n.s. 9 (1979) 87–110.

'The Contemplative Matrix of *PP* B' *MLQ* 46 (1985) 3–28.

'L.'s Franciscanism', *ChR* 25 (1990) 54–75.

'*Songes of Rechelesnesse*': L. and the Franciscans. Michigan, 1997.

Clutterbuck, C. 'Hope and Good Works: *Leaute* in the C-Text of *PP*', *RES* 28 (1977) 129–40.

Coghill, N. 'God's Wenches and the Light that Spoke: some notes on Langland's kind of poetry,' [1962], repr. in D. Gray, ed. *The Collected Papers of Nevill Coghill, Shakespearean and Medievalist* (Sussex, 1988) 199–217.

Cole, A. 'WL's Lollardy', *YLS* 17 (2003) 25–54.

Coleman, J. *PP and the Moderni*. Rome, 1981.

Cooper, H. 'L.'s and Chaucer's Prologues', *YLS* 1 (1987) 71–81.

Cornelius, R. D. *The Figurative Castle*. Bryn Mawr, Pa. 1930.

'*PP* and the *Roman de Fauvel*', *PMLA* 47 (1932) 363–7.

Craun, E. D. *Lies, Slander and Obscenity in Medieval English Literature*. Cambridge, 1997.

Davies, R. 'The Life, Travels and Library of an Early Reader of *PP*', *YLS* 12 (1999) 49–64.

Davlin, Sr. M. C. '*Kynde Knowynge* as a Major Theme in *PP* B', *RES* n.s. 22 (1971) 1–19.

'"*Petrus, id est, Christus*": P. the P. as "The Whole Christ"', *ChR* 6 (1972) 280–92.

'A Genius-Kynde Illustration in Codex Vat. Pal. Lat. 629', *Manuscripta* 23 (1979) 149–58.

'Kynde Knowynge as a ME Equivalent for "Wisdom" in *PP* B', *MÆ* 50 (1981) 5–17.

'*PP* and the Books of Wisdom', *YLS* 2 (1988) 23–33.

A Game of Heuene: Word Play and the Meaning of 'PP' B. Cambridge, 1989.

'*PP* and the Gospel and First Epistle of John', *YLS* 10 (1996) 89–127.

The Place of God in PP and Medieval Art. Aldershot, Hants. 2001.

Day, M. '"Mele Tyme of Seintes": *PP* B, V, 500', *MLR* 227 (1932) 317–18.

Dolan, T. P. 'L. and FitzRalph: Two Solutions to the Mendicant Problem', *YLS* 2 (1988) 35–45.

Donaldson, E. T. *PP: The C-Text and its Poet*. New Haven and London, 1949.

'L. and some Scriptural Quotations', in Benson & Wenzel (1982) 67–72.

Bibliography

Donna, R. B. *Despair and hope: A Study in Langland and Augustine*. Washington, D.C., 1948.

Doob, P. R. *The Idea of the Labyrinth from Classical Antiquity through the Middle Ages*. Ithaca & London, 1990.

Dove, M. *The Perfect Age of Man's Life*. Cambridge, 1986.

Doxsee, E. '"Trew Treuthe" and Canon Law: the Orthodoxy of Trajan's Salvation in *PP* C-Text', *NM* 89 (1988) 295–311.

Dronke, P. 'Arbor Caritatis', in Heyworth (1981) 207–43.

Du Boulay, F. R. H. *The England of 'PP'*. Cambridge, 1991.

Dunning, T.P. 'L. and the Salvation of the Heathen', *MÆ* 12 (1943) 45–54.

'The Structure of the B-Text of *PP* ', *RES* n.s. 7 (1956) 225–37; repr. in Blanch (1969) 87–100.

Piers Plowman: An Interpretation of the A-Text, 2nd edn. rev. and ed. by T. Dolan. Oxford, 1980.

Dyas, D. *Pilgrimage in Medieval English Literature, 700–1500*. Cambridge, 2001.

'A pilgrim in sheep's clothing? The nature of wandering in *PP*,' *ELN* 39 (2002) 1–12.

Dyer, C. '*PP* and Plowmen: A Historical Perspective', *YLS* 155–76.

Eaton, R. 'L.'s Malleable Lady Meed', *Costerus* 80 (Amsterdam & Atlanta, Ga., 1991) 119–41.

Emmerson, R. K. *Antichrist in the Middle Ages*. Seattle, 1981.

Erzgräber, W. *William Langlands 'PP'. Eine Interpretation des C-Textes*. Heidelberg, 1957.

Fletcher, A. J. 'Line 30 of the Man of Law's Tale and the Medieval Malkyn', *ELN* 24 (1986) 15–20.

'A Simoniacal Moment in *PP*,' *YLS* 4 (1990) 135–8.

'The Hideous Feet of L.'s Peacock', *NQ* 236 (1991) 18–20.

'The Social Trinity of *PP*,' *RES* 44 (1993) 343–61.

Preaching, Politics and Poetry in Late-Medieval England. Dublin, 1998.

Fowler, D. C. *P the P: Literary Relations of the A and B Texts*. Seattle, 1961.

'A Pointed Personal Allusion in *P the P*,' *MP* 77 (1979) 158–59.

'Star-Gazing: *PP* and the Peasants' Revolt', *Review* 18 (1996) 1–30.

'Annotating *PP*: The Athlone Project', *TEXT* 10 (1997) 151–60.

Fowler, E., *Literary Character: The Human Figure in Early English Writing* Ithaca, NY, 2003.

Frank, R. W. 'The Conclusion of *PP*,' *JEGP* 49 (1950) 309–16.

'The Pardon Scene in *PP* ', *Speculum* 26 (1951[1]) 317–31.

'The Number of Dreams in *PP*,' *MLN* 66 (1951[2]) 309–12.

'The Art of Reading Medieval Personification-Allegory', *ELH* 20 (1953) 237–50.

Piers Plowman and the Scheme of Salvation. New Haven, 1957.

'The "Hungry Gap", Crop Failure, and Famine: the C14th Agricultural Crisis and *PP*,' *YLS* 4 (1990) 87–104.

Gaffney, W. 'The Allegory of the Christ-Knight in *PP*,' *PMLA* 46 (1931) 155–68.

Gallacher, P. J. 'Imagination, Prudence, and the *Sensus Communis*', *YLS* 5 (1991) 49–64.

'Imaginatif and the *Sensus Communis*,' *YLS* 6 (1992) 51–61.

Galloway, A. 'Two Notes on L.'s Cato: *PP* B. I. 88–91; IV 20–23,' *ELN* 25 (1987) 9–13.

'The Rhetoric of Riddling in Late-Medieval England: The "Oxford" Riddles, the *Secretum philosophorum* and the Riddles in *PP*,' *Speculum* 70 (1995) 68–105.

'Intellectual Pregnancy, Metaphysical Femininity, and the Social Doctrine of the Trinity in *PP*,' *YLS* 12 (1998) 117–52.

'Making History Legal: *PP* and the Rebels of C14th England', in Hewett-Smith (2001[1]) 7–39.

'*PP* and the Subject of the Law', *YLS* 15 (2001[2]) 117–28.

The Penn Commentary on 'Piers Plowman', Vol. I: C Prologue–Passus 4; B Prologue–Passus 4; A Prologue–Passus 4. Pennsylvania, 2006.

Gasse, R. 'L.'s "Lewd Vicory" Reconsidered', *JEGP* 95 (1996) 322–35.

——'The Practice of Medicine in *PP*', *ChR* 39 (2004) 177–197.

Giancarlo, M. '*PP*, Parliament and the Public Voice', *YLS* 17 (2003) 135–74.

Gilbert, B. B. '"Civil" and the Notaries in *PP*,' *MÆ* 50 (1981) 49–63.

Gill, S. *Wordsworth: A Life*. Oxford, 1989.

Gillespie, V. 'Thy Will Be Done: *PP* and the *Paternoster*', in A. J. Minnis, ed., *Late-Medieval Religious Texts and their Transmission: Essays in Honour of A. I. Doyle* (Cambridge, 1994) 95–119.

Godden, M. *The Making of Piers Plowman*. 1990.

Goldsmith, M. E. *The Figure of Piers Plowman*. Cambridge, 1981.

'Piers' Apples: Some Bernardine Echoes in *PP*,' *LSE* n.s. 16 (1985) 309–25.

'Will's Pilgrimage in *PP* B', in M. Stokes & T. L. Burton, eds., *Medieval Literature and Antiquities: Studies in Honour of Basil Cottle* (Cambridge, 1987) 119–31.

740

Gradon, P. 'L. and the Ideology of Dissent', *PBA* 66 (1982 for 1980).

    '*Trajanus Redivivus*: Another Look at Trajan in *PP*,' in D. Gray and E. G. Stanley, eds. *ME Studies Presented to Norman Davis* (Oxford, 1983) 71–103.

Grady, F. '*PP, St Erkenwald*, and the Rule of Exceptional Salvations', *YLS* 6 (1992) 63–8.

Gray, D. 'The Robin Hood Poems', *Poetica* 18 (1984) 1–39.

Gray, N. 'L.'s Quotations from the Penitential Tradition', *MP* 84 (1986¹) 53–60.

    'The Clemency of Cobbleres: A reading of "Glutton's Confession" in *PP*,' *Studies in English* n.s. 17 (1986²) 61–75.

Green, R. F. 'John Ball's Letters: Literary History and Historical Literature', in Hanawalt (1992) 176–200.

    'Friar William Appleton and the Date of L.'s B-Text', *YLS* 11 (1997) 87–96.

    A Crisis of Truth: Literature and Law in Ricardian England. Philadelphia, 1999.

Groos, A. et al., eds. *Magister Regis: Studies in Honor of R. E. Kaske*. New York, 1986.

Gwynn, A. 'The Date of the B-Text of *PP*,' *RES* 19 (1943) 1–24.

Hanna, R. *William Langland*. Aldershot, 1993.

    'Annotating *PP*,' *TEXT* 10 (1994) 153–63.

    'Emendations to a 1993 "Vita de Ne'erdowel"', *YLS* 14 (2000) 185–198.

    London Literature, 1300–1380. Cambridge, 2005.

——'The Tree of Charity — again', in Burrow & Duggan (2010) 125–39.

Hanawalt, B. 'Ballads and Bandits: C14th Outlaws and the Robin Hood Poems', in idem (1992) 154–75.

    ed. *Chaucer's England: Literature in Historical Context*. Minneapolis, 1992.

Harbert, B. 'Langland's Easter', in Phillips (1980) 57–70.

    'A Will with a Reason: Theological Developments in the C-Revision of *PP*,' in P. Boitani & A. Torti, eds., *Religion in the Poetry and Drama of the Late Middle Ages in England*. Cambridge, 1990.

Harwood, B. J. 'Clergye and the Action of the Third Vision in *PP*,' *MP* 70 (1973¹) 279–90.

    '*Liberum-Arbitrium* in the C-Text of *PP*,' *PQ* 52 (1973²) 680–95.

    'Imaginative in *PP*,' *MÆ* 44 (1975) 249–63.

    'Langland's *Kynde Wit*,' *JEGP* 75 (1976) 330–6.

    'Langland's *Kynde Knowyng* and the Quest for Christ', *MP* 80 (1983) 242–55.

    'Dame Study and the Place of Orality in *PP*,' *ELH* 57 (1990) 1–17.

    '*PP* and the Problem of Belief*. Toronto, 1992.

——& Smith, R. F. 'Inwit and the Castle of *Caro* in *PP*,' *NM* 71 (1970) 48–54.

Hazelton, R. 'Two Texts of the *Disticha Catonis* and its Commentary, with special reference to Chaucer, Langland and Gower'. PhD. Diss. Rutgers University, 1956.

Heffernan, C. '*PP* B I 153–8', *ELN* 22 (1984) 1–5.

Heffernan, T. J., ed. *The Popular Literature of Medieval England*. Knoxville, Tennessee, 1985.

Hench, A. L. *The Allegorical Motif of Conscience and Reason, Counsellors* University of Virginia Studies 4, 1951.

Henry, A. 'Some Aspects of Biblical Imagery in *PP*,' in Phillips (1990) 39–55.

Herman, J. P. 'Gematria in *PP*,' *Connotations* I (1991) 168–72.

Hewett-Smith, K. M. 'Allegory of the Half-Acre: the Demands of History', *YLS* 10 (1996) 1–22.

    '"Nede ne hath no lawe": Poverty and the De-stabilisation of Allegory in the Final Visions of *PP*,' in Idem (2001) 233–53.

——ed. *William Langland's PP: A Book of Essays*. 2001.

Heyworth, P. L. '*Jack Upland's Rejoinder*, a Lollard Interpolator and *PP* B. X. 249f', *MÆ* 36 (1967) 242–8.

——ed. *Medieval Studies for J. A.W. Bennett Aetatis Suae LXX*. Oxford, 1981.

Hieatt, C. *The Realism of Dream-Visions*. The Hague, 1967.

Hill, T. D. 'The Tropological Context of Heat and Cold Imagery in Anglo–Saxon Poetry', *NM* 69 (1968) 522–32.

    'Some Remarks on the site of Lucifer's Throne', *Anglia* 87 (1969) 303–11.

    'The Light that Blew the Saints to Heaven: *PP* B V 495–503'*, RES* ns. 24 (1973) 444–9.

    'A Liturgical Allusion in *PP* B XVI 88', *NQ* 220 (1975) 531–2.

    'Christ's "Thre Clothes": *PP* C.XI. 193', *NQ* 223 (1978) 200–3.

    "Satan's Pratfall and the Foot of Love: some Pedal Images in *PP* A, B and C', *YLS* 14 (2000) 153–161.

    'The Problem of Synecdochic Flesh: *PP* B.9.49–50', *YLS* 15 (2001) 213–18.

Holsinger, B. W. 'L.'s Musical Reader: Liturgy, Law and the Constraints of Performance', *SAC* 21 (1999) 99–141.

Hort, G. *PP and Contemporary Religious Thought*. 1938.

Howard, D. R. *The Three Temptations*. Princeton, N.J., 1966.

Hudson, A. 'The Legacy of *PP*,' in Alford, *Companion* (1988[1]) 251–66.

 The Premature Reformation: Wycliffite Texts and Lollard History. Oxford, 1988[2].

 '*PP* and the Peasants' Revolt: A Problem Revisited', *YLS* 8 (1994) 85–106.

 'L. and Lollardy?', *YLS* 17 (2003) 93–105.

Hughes, J. *Pastors and Visionaries: Religion and Secular Life in Late Medieval Yorkshire.* Woodbridge, 1988.

Huppé, B. F. 'The A-Text of *PP* and the Norman Wars', *PMLA* 54 (1939) 37–64.

 'The Date of the B-Text of *PP*,' *SP* 38 (1941) 36–44.

 '*Petrus, id est, Christus*: Word Play in *PP*,' *ELH* 17 (1950) 163–70.

Hussey, S. S. 'L., Hilton and the Three Lives', *RES* n.s. 7 (1956) 132–59.

 'L.'s Reading of Alliterative Poetry', *MLR* 60 (1965) 163–70.

——(ed.): *PP: Critical Approaches* (1969).

Izydorczyk, Z., ed. *The Medieval Gospel of Nicodemus: Texts, Intertexts and Contexts in Western Europe.* Tempe, Arizona, 1997.

Jenkins, P. 'Conscience: The Frustration of Allegory', in Hussey (1969) 124–42. *See* Martin, P.

Johnson, D. F. '"Persen with a Pater-Noster Paradis oþer Hevene": *PP* C 11.296–98a', *YLS* 5 (1991) 77–89.

Jones, E. 'Langland and Hermits', *YLS* 11 (1997) 67–86.

Jones, H. S. V. 'Imaginatif in *PP*,' *JEGP* 13 (1914).

 '*In somnium, in visionem*: the Figurative Significance of Sleep in *PP*,' in L. Houwen and A. Macdonald, eds. *Loyal Letters*: *Studies in Medieval Alliterative Poetry and Prose* (Groningen, 1994) 239–300.

Jung, M-R. *Etudes sur le poème allégorique en France au Moyen Age.* Berne, 1971.

Jusserand, J. J. *PP: A Contribution to the History of English Mysticism.* 1894; repr. New York, 1965.

Justice, S. 'The Genres of *PP*,' *Viator* 19 (1988) 281–306.

 Writing and Rebellion: England in 1381. Berkeley & Los Angeles, 1994.

——& K. Kerby-Fulton, eds. *Written Work: Langland, Labor, and Authorship.* Philadelphia, 1997. *And see* Kerby-Fulton.

Kane, G. *PP: The Evidence for Authorship.* 1965[1].

 The Autobiographical Fallacy in Chaucer and Langland Studies. 1965[2].

 'Music "Neither Unpleasant nor Monotonous"', in Heyworth (1981) 43–63.

 'The Perplexities of WL', in Benson & Wenzel (1982) 73–89.

 'Some C14th "political" Poems', in Kratzmann & Simpson (1986) 82–91.

 Chaucer and Langland: *Historical and Textual Approaches.* Berkeley & Los Angeles, 1989.

 'Reading *PP*,' *YLS* 8 (1994) 1–20.

 'L., Labour and Authorship' (review article), *NQ* 243 (1998) 420–5.

Kaske, R.E. '*Gigas* the Giant in *PP*,' *JEGP* 56 (1957[1]) 177–85.

 'L. and the *Paradisus Claustralis*,' *MLN* 72 (1957[2]) 481–3.

 'The Speech of "Book" in *PP*,' *Anglia* 77 (1959[1]) 117–44.

 'L.'s Walnut Simile', *JEGP* 58 (1959[2]) 650–4.

 '"*Ex vi transicionis*" and Its Passage in *PP*,' *JEGP* 62 (1963) 32–60, repr. in Blanch 228–63.

 '*PP* and Local Iconography', *JWCI* 31 (1968) 159–69.

 'Holy Church's Speech and the Structure of *PP*,' in B. Rowland, ed. *Chaucer and ME: Studies in honour of R .H. Robbins.* 1974.

 'The Character Hunger in *PP*,' in Kennedy & al (1988) 187–97.

Kaulbach, E. *Imaginative Prophecy in the B-Text of 'PP'.* Cambridge, 1993.

Kean, P. M. 'Love, Law and *Lewte* in *PP*,' *RES* n.s. 15 (1964) 241–61, repr. Blanch (1969) 132–55.

 'L. on the Incarnation', *RES* n.s. 16 (1965) 349–63.

 'Justice, Kingship and the Good Life in the Second Part of *PP*,' in Hussey (1969) 76–100.

Keen, J. A. *The Charters of Christ and 'PP': Documenting Salvation.* New York, 2002.

Kellogg, A. L. 'Satan, Langland and the North', *Speculum* 24 (1949) 413–14.

 'Langland and Two Scriptural Texts', *Traditio* 14 (1958) 385–98.

——& Haselmayer, L. A. 'Chaucer's Satire of the Pardoner', *PMLA* 66 (1951) 251–77.

Kellogg, E. H. 'Bishop Brunton and the Fable of the Rats', *PMLA* 50 (1935) 385–98.

Kennedy, E. D., Waldron, R. & Wittig J. S., eds. *Medieval English Studies Presented to George Kane.* Woodbridge, 1988.

Kennedy, K. E. 'Retaining a Court of Chancery in *PP*,' *YLS* 17 (2003) 175–89.

Kerby-Fulton, K. *Reformist Apocalypticism and 'PP'.* Cambridge, 1990.

'"Who Has Written this Book?" Visionary Autobiography in L.'s C-Text', in M. Glasscoe, ed. *The Medieval Mystical Tradition in England* V (Cambridge, 1992) 101–16.

'L.'s Reading: some Evidence from MSS containing Religious Prophecy', in C. Morse, P. Doob & M. Woods, eds., *The Uses of MSS*: *Essays in memory of J. B. Allen* (Kalamazoo, 1992) 237–61.

'L. and the Bibliographic Ego', in Justice & Kerby-Fulton (1997) 67–143.

Piers Plowman, in Wallace, ed. *CHMEL* (1999) 513–38.

——& S. Justice, 'Langlandian Reading Circles and the Civil Service in London and Dublin, 1380–1427', *New Medieval Literatures* 1 (1997) 59–83.

Kim, M. 'Hunger, Need and the Politics of Poverty in *PP*,' *YLS* 16 (2002) 131–68.

King, J. N. *English Reformation Literature*. Princeton, 1982.

Kirk, E. D. *The Dream Thought of* PP. New Haven & London, 1972.

'"Who Suffreth More than God": Narrative Re-definition of Patience in *Patience* and *PP*,' in G. Schifforst, ed. *The Triumph of Patience* (Orlando, Fla., 1978) 88–104.

'L.'s Plowman and the Recreation of C14th Religious Metaphor', *YLS* 2 (1988) 1–23.

Kirk, R. 'References to the Law in *PP*,' *PMLA* 48 (1933) 322–8.

Knight, S. *Robin Hood: A Mythic Biography* (Ithaca, NY, 2003)
[Mentions L and Folvilles]

Kolve, V. A. *The Play Called Corpus Christi*. Stanford, 1966.

Kratzmann, G. & Simpson, J., eds. *Medieval English Religious and Ethical Literature: Essays in Honour of G. H. Russell*. Cambridge, 1986.

Kruger, S. F. 'Mirrors and the Trajectory of Vision in *PP*,' *Speculum* 66 (1991) 74–95.

Dreaming in the Middle Ages. Cambridge, 1992.

Kuczynski, M. *Prophetic Song: the Psalms as Moral Discourse in Late Medieval England*. Philadelphia, 1995.

Lawler, T. 'Conscience's Dinner', in Tavormina and Yeager (1995) 87–103.

'The Pardon Formula in *PP*: Its Ubiquity, its Binary Shape, its Silent Middle Term', *YLS* 14 (2000) 117–52.

Lawlor, J. 'The Imaginative Unity of *PP*,' *RES* n.s. 8 (1957) 113–26, repr. Blanch, 101–16.

PP: *An Essay in Criticism*. 1962.

Lawton, D. 'Lollardy and the *PP* Tradition', *MLR* 76 (1981) 780–93.

——ed. *Middle English Alliterative Poetry and its Literary Background*. Cambridge, 1982.

'The Subject of *PP*,' *YLS* 1 (1987) 1–30.

'Alliterative Style' (1988) in Alford, *Companion* 223–49.

'The Diversity of ME Alliterative Poetry', *LSE* n.s. 20 (1989) 143–72.

'Englishing the Bible, 1066–1549', in Wallace, ed. *CHMEL* 454–82.

Leader, Z. *Revision and Romantic Authorship*. Oxford, 1996.

Levy, B. S. and Szarmach, P. E., eds. *The Alliterative Tradition in the C14th*. Kent, Ohio, 1981.

Lewis, L. 'L.'s Tree of charity and Usk's "Wexing Tree"', *NQ* 240 (1995) 429–33.

Lindemann, E. 'Analogues for Latin Quotations in L.'s *PP*,' *NM* 78 (1977) 359–61.

Lister, R. 'The Peasants of *PP* and its Audience', in K. Parkinson & M. Priestman, *Peasants and Countrymen in Literature* (1982) 71–90.

Lunz, E. 'The Valley of Jehoshaphat in *PP*,' *Tulane Studies in English* 20 (1972) 1–10.

Mäder, E. J. *Der Streit der 'TöchterGottes': Zur Geschichte eines allegorischen Motivs*. Bern, 1971.

Maguire, S. 'The Significance of Haukyn, *Activa Vita*, in *PP*,' *RES* 25 (1949) 97–109; repr. Blanch, 194–208.

Mann, J. *Chaucer and Medieval Estates Satire*. Cambridge, 1973.

'Eating and Drinking in *PP*,' *E&S* 32 (1979) 26–43.

'Satiric Subject and Satiric Object in Goliardic Literature', *Mittellateinisches Jahrbuch* 15 (1980) 63–86.

'Allegorical Buildings in Medieval Literature', *MÆ* 63 (1994²) 191–210.

Marcett, M. E. *Uthred de Boldon, Friar William Jordan and PP*. New York, 1938.

Marchand, J. W. 'An Unidentified Latin Quote in *PP*,' *MP* 88 (1990–1) 398–400.

Martin, P. *'PP': the Field and the Tower*. 1979.

'*PP*: Indirect Relations and the Record of Truth', in Vaughan (1993) 169–90. *And see* Jenkins, P.

Marx, C. W. *The Devil's Rights and the Redemption in the Literature of Medieval England*. Cambridge, 1995.

Matheson, L. Review of *William Langland* by R. Hanna, *YLS* 8 (1994) 192–4.

Mehl, D. 'The Audience of Chaucer's *TC*', in S. Barney, ed., *Chaucer's Troilus: Essays in Criticism* (1980) 211–29.

Geoffrey Chaucer. Cambridge, 1986.

Meroney, H. 'The Life and Death of Longe Wille', *ELH* 17 (1950) 1–35.

Middleton, A. 'The Idea of Public Poetry in the Reign of Richard II', *Speculum* 53 (1978) 99–114.

'Two Infinites: Grammatical Metaphor in *PP*,' *ELH* 39 (1972) 169–88.

'The Audience and Public of *PP*,' in Lawton, ed. *ME Alliterative Poetry* (1982) 101–23.

'The Passion of Seint Averoys [B.13.91]: "Deuynyng" and Divinity in the Banquet Scene', *YLS* 1 (1987) 31–40.

'Making a Good End: John But as a Reader of *PP*,' in Kennedy et al. (1988) 243–66.

'William Langland's "Kynde Name": Authorial Signature and Social Identity in Late–Fourteenth Century England', in L. Patterson, ed. *Literary Practice and Social Change in Britain, 1380–1530* (Berkeley, Los Angeles and London, 1990) 15–82.

'Acts of Vagrancy: The C Version "Autobiography" and the Statute of 1388', in Justice & Kerby-Fulton (1997) 208–317.

Mills, D. 'The Rôle of the Dreamer in *PP* ', in Hussey (1969) 180–212.

Minnis, A. J. 'L.'s Ymaginatif and late-medieval theories of imagination', *Comparative Criticism: A Year Book* 3 (Cambridge, 1981) 71–103.

——ed. *Late-Medieval Religious Texts and their Transmission: Essays in Honour of A. I. Doyle*. Cambridge, 1994.

Mitchell, A. G. 'Lady Meed and the Art of *PP*,' (1956), repr. in Blanch (1969) 174–93.

Morgan, G. 'The Meaning of Kind Wit, Conscience and Reason in the First Vision of *PP*,' *MP* 84 (1987[1]) 351–8.

'L.'s Conception of Favel, Guile, Liar and False in the First Vision of *PP*,' *Neophilologus* 71 (1987[2]) 626–33.

'The Status and Meaning of Meed in the First Vision of *PP*,' *Neophilologus* 72 (1988) 449–63.

Murtaugh, D. M. '*PP* ' and the Image of God. Gainesville, Fla. 1978.

Narin van Court, E. 'The Hermeneutics of Supersession: the Revision of the Jews from the B to the C-Text of *PP*,' *YLS* 10 (1996) 43–87.

Nolan, B. *The Gothic Visionary Perspective*. Princeton, 1977.

Orme, N. 'Langland and Education', *History of Education* 11 (1982) 251–66.

Orsten, E. M. 'The Ambiguities in L.'s Rat Parliament', *MS* (1961) 216–39.

'*Patientia* in the B-Text of *PP*,' *MS* 31 (1969) 317–33.

'"Heaven on Earth"—L.'s Vision of Life Within the Cloister', *American Benedictine Review* (1970) 526–34.

Overstreet, S. A. '"Grammaticus Ludens": Theological Aspects of L.'s Grammmatical Allegory', *Traditio* 40 (1984) 251–96.

Owen, D. L. *PP: A Comparison with some earlier and contemporary French Allegories*. 1912.

Owst, G. R. 'The "Angel" and the "Goliardeys" of L.'s Prologue', *MLR* 20 (1925) 270–9.

Literature and Pulpit in Medieval England. 2nd edn. Oxford, 1961.

Pantin, W. A. 'A Medieval Collection of Latin and English Proverbs and Riddles, from the Rylands Latin MS 394', *BJRL* 14 (1930) 81–114.

Papka, C. R. 'The Limits of Apocalypse: Eschatology, Epistemology and Textuality in the *Commedia and PP*,' in Bynum, C. W. & Freedman, P., eds. *Last Things: Death and the Apocalypse in the Middle Ages* (Philadelphia, 2000) 233–56.

Pearsall, D. 'The Origins of the Alliterative Revival', in Levy and Szarmach (1981) 1–24.

'The Alliterative Revival: Origins and Social Backgrounds', in Lawton (1982) 34–53.

'Poverty and Poor People in *PP*,' in Kennedy et al. (1988) 167–85.

'"Lunatyk Lollares" in *PP*,' in P. Boitani & A. Torti, eds. *Religion in the Poetry and Drama of the Late Middle Ages in England* (Cambridge, 1990) 163–78.

'L.'s London' in Justice and Kerby-Fulton (1997) 185–207.

'L. and Lollardy: from B to C', *YLS* 17 (2003) 7–23.

——ed. *New Directions in Later Medieval Manuscript Studies*. York and Woodbridge, 2000.

——& R.A. Waldron, eds. *Medieval Literature and Civilisation: Studies in Memory of G. N. Garmonsway.* 1969.

Peebles, R. J. *The Legend of Longinus in ecclesiastical art and in English Literature*. Bryn Mawr, 1911.

Perrow, E. C. *The Last Will and Testament as a Form of Literature*. Transactions of the Wisconsin Academy of Sciences, Arts & Letters 17 (1914) 682–753.

Phillips, H., ed. *Langland, the Mystics and the Medieval English Religious Tradition: Essays in Honour of S. S. Hussey*. Cambridge, 1990.

Pilkinton, M. C. 'The Raising of Lazarus: a Prefiguring Agent to the Harrowing of Hell', *MÆ* 44 (1975) 51–3.

Quirk, R. 'L.'s Use of *Kind Wit* and *Inwit*,' *JEGP* 52 (1953) 182–9.

'"*Vis Imaginativa* "', *JEGP* 53 (1954) 81–3.

Raabe, P. *Imitating God: The Allegory of Faith in PP-B*. 1990.

Raby, F. J. E. '*Turris Alethie* and the *Ecloga Theoduli*', *MÆ* 34 (1965) 226–9.

Raw, B. 'Piers and the Image of God in Man', in Hussey (1969) 143–79.

Raymo, R. 'A ME Version of the *Epistola Luciferi ad Cleros*', in Pearsall & Waldron (1969) 233–48.

Revard, C. 'The Papelard Priest and the Black Prince', *SAC* 23 (2001) 359–406.

Richardson, G. 'L.'s Mary Magdalene: Proverbial Misogyny and the Problem of Authority', *YLS* 14 (2000) 163–184.

Rickert, E. 'John But, Messenger and Maker', *MP* 11 (1913–14) 107–116.

Risse, R. G. 'The Augustinian Paraphrase of Isaiah 14:13–14 in *PP* and the Commentary on the *Fables* of Avianus', *PQ* 45 (1966) 712–17.

Robertson, D. W. & Huppé, B. F. *PP and Scriptural Tradition.* Princeton, N.J., 1951.

Rogers, W. E. 'Knighthood as Trope: Holy Church's Interpretation of Knighthood in *PP* B.I', *Sewanee Medieval Studies* 9 (1999) 205–18.

  Interpretation in 'PP'. Washington, D.C., 2002.

Rudd, G. 'The State of the Ark: a Metaphor in Bromyard and *PP*,' *NQ* 235 (1990) 6–10.

  Managing Language in PP. Cambridge, 1994.

Ruffing, J. 'The Crucifixion Drink in *PP* B.18 and C.20', *YLS* 5 (1991) 99–109.

Russell, G. H. 'The Poet as Reviser: The Metamorphosis of the Confession of the Seven Deadly Sins in *PP*,' in Carruthers & Kirk (1982) 53–65.

Ryan, W. 'Word Play in Some OE Homilies and a Late ME Poem', in E. Atwood & A. Hill, eds. *Studies in Language, Literature and Culture of the Middle Ages and Later.* Austin, Texas, 1969.

Rydzeski, J. *Radical Nostalgia in the Age of PP: Economics, Apocalypticism, and Discontent.* New York, 1999.

St-Jacques, R. 'L.'s Christ-Knight and the Liturgy', *Revue de l'Université d'Ottawa* 37 (1967) 146–58.

  'The Liturgical Associations of L.'s Samaritan', *Traditio* 25 (1969) 217–30.

  'Conscience's Final Pilgrimage in *PP* and the Cyclical Structure of the Liturgy', *Revue de l'Université d'Ottawa* 40 (1970) 210–23.

  'L.'s Bells of the Resurrection and the Easter Liturgy', *English Studies in Canada* 3 (1977[1]) 129–35.

  'L.'s "Spes" the Spy and the Book of Numbers', *NQ* 222 (1977[2]) 483–5.

  'L.'s *Christus Medicus* Image and the Structure of *PP*,' *YLS* 5 (1991) 111–127.

Salter, E. *Piers Plowman: an Introduction.* Oxford, 1962.

  '*PP* and "The Simonie"', *Archiv* 203 (1967) 241–54, repr. in Salter, *English and International*, 158–69.

  '*PP* and the Visual Arts' (1971), repr. in *English and International*, 256–66.

  'The Timeliness of *Wynnere and Wastoure*', *MÆ* 47 (1978) 30–65, repr. in *English and International*, 180–98.

  'L. and the Contexts of "*PP*"', *E&S* 32 (1979) 19–25.

  English and International: Studies in the Literature, Art and Patronage of Medieval England, ed. D. Pearsall and N. Zeeman. Cambridge, 1988.

Sanderlin, G. 'The Character "Liberum Arbitrium"', *MLN* 56 (1941) 449–53.

  'John Capgrave Speaks up for the Hermits', *Speculum* 18 (1943) 358–62.

Sargent, H. J. and Kittredge, G. L., eds. *English and Scottish Popular Ballads.* Boston, 1932.

Scase, W. *PP and the New Anticlericalism.* Cambridge, 1989.

  '"First to reckon Richard': John But's *PP*,' *YLS* 11 (1997) 49–66.

Schmidt, A. V. C. 'A Note on the A-Text of *PP*, X.91–4', *NQ* 212 (1967) 355–6.

  'A Note on the Phrase "Free Wit" in the C-Text of *PP*, XI 51', *NQ*. 213 (1968[1]) 168–9.

  'A Note on L.'s Conception of "Anima" and "Inwit"', *NQ* 213 (1968[2]) 363–4.

  'Two Notes on *PP*,' *NQ* 214 (1969[1]) 168–9.

  'L. and Scholastic Philosophy', *MÆ* 38 (1969[2]) 134–56.

  'L. and the Mystical Tradition', in M. Glasscoe, ed. *The Medieval Mystical Tradition in England* I (Exeter, 1980[1]) 17–38.

  'L.'s Structural Imagery', *EC* 30 (1980[2]) 311–25.

  'L.'s Pen / Parchment Analogy in *PP* B 1X 38–40', *NQ* 225 (1980[3]) 538–9.

  'L.'s "Book of Conscience" and Alanus de Insulis,' *NQ* 227 (1982) 482–4.

  'L., Chrysostom and Bernard: A Complex Echo', *NQ* 228 (1983[1]) 108–10.

  'The Treatment of the Crucifixion in *PP* and in Rolle's *Meditations on the Passion*', *Analecta Cartusiana* 35 (1983[2]) 174–96.

  '*Lele Wordes* and *Bele Paroles*: Some Aspects of L.'s Word-Play', *RES* n.s. 34 (1983[3]) 161–83.

  'A Covenant more than Courtesy' [*recte* 'A Courtesy more than Covenant']: a Langlandian Phrase in its Context', *NQ* 229 (1984[2]) 153–6.

'The Inner Dreams in *PP*,' *MÆ* 55 (1986) 24–40.

'"Latent Content" and "The Testimony in the Text": Symbolic Meaning in *Sir Gawain and the Green Knight*', *RES* n.s. 38 (1987[1]) 145–68.

The Clerkly Maker: Langland's Poetic Art. Cambridge, 1987[2].

'*Kynde Craft* and the *Play of Paramorez*: Natural and Unnatural Love in *Purity*', in P. Boitani and A. Torti, eds. *Genres, Themes, and Images in English Literature*. Tübingen, 1988.

'L.'s Visions and Revisions', *YLS* 14 (2000) 5–27.

'"Elementary" Images in the Samaritan Episode of *PP*', *EC* 56 (2006) 303–23.

'The sacramental significance of blood in *PP*', in Burrow & Duggan 2010 : 212–24.

——& Jacobs, N., eds. *Medieval English Romances*. 2 vols, 1980.

Schroeder, M. C. '*PP*: The Tearing of the Pardon', *PQ* 49 (1970) 8–18. *And see* Carruthers.

Schweitzer, E. C. 'Half a Laumpe Lyne in Latyne" and Patience's Riddle in *PP*,' *JEGP* 73 (1974) 313–27.

Scott, A. 'Never noon so nedy ne poverer deide: *PP* and the Value of Poverty', *YLS* 15 (2001) 141–53.

'*PP' and the Poor*. Dublin, 2004.

Shepherd, G. T. 'Poverty in *PP*,' in T. H. Aston et al., eds. *Social Relations and Ideas: essays in honour of R. H. Hilton* (Cambridge, 1983) 169–89.

Shoaf, R. A. '"Speche that spire is of grace": a Note on *PP* B.9.104', *YLS* 1 (1987) 128–33.

Simpson, J. 'From Reason to Affective Knowledge: Modes of Thought and Poetic Form in *PP*,' *MÆ* 55 (1986[1]) 1–23.

'The Transformation of Meaning: a Figure of Thought in *PP*,' *RES* 37 (1986[2]) 161–83.

'The Role of *Scientia* in *PP*,' in Kratzmann & Simpson (1986[3]) 49–65.

'"*Et vidit deus cogitaciones eorum*": A Parallel Instance and Possible Source for L.'s Use of a Biblical Formula at *PP* B XV 200*a*', *NQ* 231 (1986[4]) 9–13.

Piers Plowman: an Introduction to the B-Text. 1990. 2nd edn. Exeter, 2007.

'The Power of Impropriety: Authorial Naming in *PP*,' in Hewett-Smith (1991) 145–65.

'"After Craftes Conseil Clotheth Yow and Fede": L. and London City Politics', in N. Rogers, ed. *England in the C14th: Proceedings of the 1991 Harlaxton Symposium* (Stamford, 1993) 109–27.

'Grace Abounding: Evangelical Centralization and the End of *PP*,' *YLS* 14 (2000) 49–74.

Reform and Cultural Revolution: The Oxford English Literary History 2, 1350–1547. Oxford, 2002.

Smith, A. H. 'The ME Lyrics in Additional MS 45896', *London Mediaeval Studies* 2 (1951) 33–49.

Smith, B. H. 'Patience's Riddle: *PP* B XIII', *MLN* 76 (1961) 675–82.

Traditional Imagery of Charity in PP. The Hague, 1966.

Smith, D. V. 'The Labors of Reward: Meed, Mercede and the Beginning of Salvation', *YLS* 8 (1994) 127–54.

Smith, G., ed. *Elizabethan Critical Essays*. 2 vols. Oxford, 1904.

Somerset, F. 'Response' to Baldwin, 'Patient Politics in *PP*,' *YLS* 15 (2001) 109–115.

Spalding, M. C. *The Middle English Charters of Christ*. Bryn Mawr, 1914.

Spearing, A. C. 'Verbal Repetition in *PP* B and C', *JEGP* 62 (1963) 722–37.

Criticism and Medieval Poetry. 2nd edn. 1972.

Medieval Dream-Poetry. Cambridge, 1976.

Spitzer, L. *L'Amour Lointain*. Chapel Hill, 1944.

Steiner, E. 'L.'s Documents', *YLS* 15 (2000) 95–115.

Steinberg, T. L. '*PP' and Prophecy: an approach to the C-Text*. New York, 1991.

Stock, L. K. 'Will, Actyf, *pacience* and *Liberum Arbitrium*: Two Recurring Quotations in L.'s Revision of *PP* C-Text, Passus V, XV, XVI'. *Texas Studies in Literature and Language* 30 (1985) 461–77.

Stokes, M. *Justice and Mercy in PP: A Reading of the B-Text Visio*. 1984.

Strang, B. '*PP*, B-Text, Passus V, 491–2', *NQ* 208 (1963) 286.

Strong, D. 'The Questions Asked, the Answers Given: L., Scotus and Ockham', *ChR* 38 (2003) 255–75.

Sullivan, Sr C. *The Latin Insertions and the Macaronic Verse in '*PP*'*. Washington, 1932.

Swanson, R. N. 'L. and the Priest's Title', *NQ* 231 (1986) 438–40.

Szittya, P. R. *The Antifraternal Tradition in Medieval Literature*. Princeton, N.J., 1986[1].

'The Trinity in L. and Abelard', in Groos, A. et al (1986[2]) 207–16.

Szövérffy, J. '"Peccatrix Quondam Femina": A Survey of the Mary Magdalen Hymns', *Traditio* 19 (1963) 79–146.

Taitt, P. 'In Defence of Lot', *NQ* 216 (1971) 284–5.

Tarvers, J. K. 'The Abbess's *ABC*', *YLS* 2 (1988) 137–41.

Tavormina, M. T. 'Kindly Similitude: Langland's Matrimonial Trinity', *MP* 80 (1982) 117–28.

'*PP* and the Liturgy of St Lawrence', *SP* 84 (1987) 245–71.

'"Gendre of a Generacion": *PP* B. 16.222', *ELN* 27 (1989[1]) 1–9.

'"Maledictus qui non reliquit semen": The Curse on Infertility in *PP* B XVI and C XVIII', *MÆ* 58 (1989[2]) 117–25.

Kindly Similitude: Marriage and Family in PP. Cambridge, 1995.

——& R. F. Yeager, eds. *The Endless Knot: Essays in Honour of Marie Borroff*. Cambridge, 1995.

'The Chilling of Charity: Eschatological Allusions and Revisions in *PP* C 16–17', in R. Edwards, ed. *Art and Context in Late Medieval English Narrative: Essays in Honour of R. W. Frank, Jr.* Cambridge, 1994.

Taylor, S. 'Harrowing Hell's Halfacre: Langland's Mediation of the "Descensus" from the *Gospel of Nicodemus*' in Frantzen, A. J., ed. *Four Last Things: Death, Judgment, Heaven and Hell in the Middle Ages. Essays in Medieval Studies* Vol. 10 (Chicago, 1994) 145–58.

Thorne, J. B. 'Piers or Will: Confusion of Identity in the Early Reception of *PP*,' *MÆ* 60 (1991) 273–84.

Traver, H. *The Four Daughters of God*. Bryn Mawr, 1907.

'The Four Daughters of God: A Mirror of Changing Doctrine', *PMLA* 40 (1925) 44–92.

Trigg, S. 'The Traffic in Medieval Women: Alice Perrers, Feminist Criticism and *PP*,' *YLS* 12 (1998) 5–29.

Tristram, P. *Figures of Life and Death in Medieval English Literature*. 1976.

Turville-Petre, T. *The Alliterative Revival*. Cambridge, 1977.

Tveitane, M. 'The Four Daughters of God: A Supplement', *NM* 81 (1980) 409–15.

Twomey, M. W. 'Christ's Leap and Mary's Clean Catch in *PP* B. 12.136–44a and C. 14.81–88a', *YLS* 5 (1991) 165–74.

Ullmann, J. 'Studien zu Richard Rolle de Hampole', *Englische Studien* 7 (1884) 415–72.

Utley, F. L. 'The Chorister's Lament', *Speculum* 21 (1946) 194–202.

Vasta, E. *The Spiritual Basis of 'PP'*. The Hague, 1965[1].

'Truth, the Best Treasure, in *PP*,' *PQ* 44 (1965[2]) 17–29.

Vaughan, M. F. 'The Liturgical Perspectives of *PP* B XVI–XIX', *Studies in Medieval and Renaissance History* 3 (1980) 87–155.

ed. *Suche Werkis to Werche: Essays on 'PP' in Honour of David C. Fowler*. East Lansing, Michigan, 1993.

'The Ending(s) of *PP* A', in Vaughan (1993) 211–41.

Vershuis, A. '*PP*, Numerical Composition and the Prophecies', *Connotations* 1 (1991) 103–39.

Von Nolcken, C. '*PP*, the Wycliffites and *P. the P.'s Crede*', *YLS* 2 (1988) 71–102.

Waldron, R. A. 'Langland's Originality: The Christ-Knight and the Harrowing of Hell', in Kratzmann and Simpson (1986) 66–81.

Wallace, D., ed. *The Cambridge History of Medieval English Literature*. Cambridge, 1999.

Warner, L. 'Jesus the Jouster: the Christ-Knight and Medieval Theories of Atonement in *PP* and the "Round Table" Sermons', *YLS* 10 (1996) 130–43.

'Becket and the Hopping Bishops', *YLS* 17 (2003) 107–34.

'L and the Problem of *William of Palerne*'. *Viator* 37 (2006) 397–415.

Watson, N. 'Censorship and Cultural Change in Late-Medieval England: Vernacular Theology, the Oxford Translation Debate, and Arundel's Constitutions of 1409', *Speculum* 70 (1995) 822–64.

'Conceptions of the Word: the Mother Tongue and the Incarnation of God', *NML* 1 (1997)[1] 88–124.

'Visions of Inclusion: Universal Salvation and Vernacular Theology in Pre-Reformation England', *Journal of Medieval and Early Modern Studies* 27 (1997)[2] 145–87.

'The Middle English Mystics' in Wallace (1999) 539–65.

Weldon, J. F. G. 'The Structure of Dream Visions in *PP*,' *MS* 49 (1987[1]) 254–81.

'Sabotaged Text or Textual Ploy? The Christ-Knight Metaphor in *PP*,' *Florilegium* 9 (1987[2]) 113–23,

'Gesture of Perception: the Pattern of Kneeling in *PP*,' *YLS* 3 (1989) 49–66.

Wenzel, S. *The Sin of Sloth*: Acedia *in Medieval Thought and Literature*. Chapel Hill, N. Carolina, 1967.

'The Source of Chaucer's Seven Deadly Sins', *Traditio* 30 (1974) 351–78.

Verses in Sermons. Fasciculus Morum *and its Middle English Poems*. Cambridge, Mass., 1978.

'Medieval Sermons and the Study of Literature', in P. Boitani and A. Torti, eds., *Medieval and Pseudo-Medieval Literature*. Cambridge, 1984.

'Medieval Sermons', in Alford, *Companion* (1988) 155–72.

'*Somer Game* and Sermon References to a Corpus Christi Play', *MP* 86 (1989) 274–81.

'L's *Troianus*', *YLS* 10 (1996) 181–5.

'Eli and his Sons', *YLS* 13 (1999) 137–52.

Bibliography

Whatley, G. 'The Uses of Hagiography: the Legend of Pope Gregory and the Emperor Trajan in the Middle Ages', *Viator* 15 (1984[1]) 25–63.

 '*PP* B.12. 277–94: Notes on Language, Text, and Theology', *MP* 82 (1984[2]) 1–12.

Wheatley, E. 'A Selfless Ploughman and the Christ/Piers Conjunction in *PP*,' *NQ* 238 (1993) 135–42.

White, H. 'L.'s Ymaginatif, Kynde and the Benjamin Major', *MÆ* 55 (1986) 241–8.

 Nature and Salvation in PP. Cambridge, 1988.

 'Book's Bold Speech and the *Archana Verba* of *PP* Passus B XVIII', *BJRL* 77 (1995) 31–46.

Whitworth, C. W. Jr. 'Changes in the Roles of Reason and Conscience in the Revisions of *PP*,' *NQ* 217 (1972) 4–7.

Wickham, G. Early *English Stages:1300–1600*. 2 vols. 2nd edn. New York, 1980.

Wilcockson, C. 'Glutton's Black Mass: *PP* B-Text Passus V 297–385', *NQ* 243 (1998) 173–6.

Wilkes, G. L. 'The Castle of Unite in *PP*,' *MS* 27 (1965) 334–6.

Wilson, E. *The Gawain-Poet*. Leiden, 1976.

 'The "Gostly Drem" in *Pearl*', *NM* 69 (1968) 90–101.

 'L.'s "Book of Conscience": Two ME Analogies and another possible Latin Source', *NQ* 228 (1983) 387–9.

Wirtjes, H. '*PP* B XVIII.371: "Right Ripe Must"', in M. Stokes and T. L. Burton, *Medieval Studies and Antiquities: Studies in Honour of Basil Cottle*. Woodbridge (1987) 133–43.

 '*PP* B XVIII 364–73: the Cups that cheer but not Inebriate', in D. M. Reeks, ed. *Sentences: Essays presented to Alan Ward*. Southampton, 1988.

Wittig, J.S. '*PP* B Passus IX–XII: Elements in the Design of the Inward Journey', *Traditio* 28 (1972) 211–80.

 '"Culture Wars" and the Persona in *PP*,' *YLS* 15 (2001) 167–201.

Woolf, R. 'The Theme of Christ the Lover-Knight in medieval English Literature', *RES* n.s. 13 (1962) 1–16.

 The English Religious Lyric in the Middle Ages. Oxford, 1968.

 'The Tearing of the Pardon', in Hussey (1969), 50–75.

 Art and Doctrine: Essays on Medieval Literature, ed. H. O'Donoghue. 1986.

Wordsworth, J. 'Revision as Making: *The Prelude* and Its Peers', in R. Brinkley & K. Hanley, eds., *Romantic Revisions* (Cambridge, 1992) 18–42.

Wurtele, D. 'The Importance of the Psalms of David in WL's *The Vision of PP*', *Cithara* 43:1 (2003) 15–24.

Young, K. *The Drama of the Medieval Church*. Oxford, 1933.

Yunck, J. A. *The Lineage of Lady Meed: the Development of Medieval Venality Satire*. Notre Dame, Indiana, 1963.

Zeeman, N. 'Studying in the Middle Ages — and in *PP*,' *New Medieval Literatures* 3, ed. D. Lawton, W. Scase & R. Copeland. Oxford (1999) 199–222.

 'The Condition of *Kynde*,' in D. Aers, ed. *Medieval literature & Historical Enquiry: Essays in Honour of Derek Pearsall*. Cambridge (2000) 1–30.

 '*PP' and the Medieval Discourse of Desire*. Cambridge, 2006.

D. Historical and Background Studies and Works of Reference

Adair, J. *The Pilgrim's Way*. 1978.

Adler, M. *The Jews of Medieval England*. 1939.

Alexander, J. & Binski, P. *Age of Chivalry: Art in Plantagenet England 1200–1400*. 1987.

Anderson, M. D. *History and Imagery in British Churches*. 1971.

Arbesmann, R. 'Jordanus of Saxony's *Vita Sancti Augustini*, the Source for John Capgrave's *Life of St Augustine*', *Traditio* 1 (1943) 341–53.

Ashworth, E. J. *The Tradition of Medieval Logic and Speculative Grammar*. Toronto, 1978.

Aston, M. 'Wyclif and the Vernacular' in A. Hudson & M. Wilks, eds. *From Ockham to Wyclif* (Oxford, 1987) 281–330.

Baker, J. *English Stained Glass of the Medieval Period*. 1978.

Baker, J. H. *An Introduction to English Legal History*. 1971.

Baker, T. *Medieval London*. 1970.

Baldwin, J. F. *The King's Council in England during the Middle Ages*. 1913.

Barber, R. *The Knight and Chivalry*. 1970.

Barron, C. M. 'The Parish Fraternities of Medieval London', in C. M. Barron & C. Harper Bill, eds., *The Church in pre-Reformation Society* (1985) 13–37.

Bartholomew, B. *Fortuna and Natura*. 1966.

Baum, P. F. 'The Medieval Legend of Judas Iscariot', *PMLA* 24 (1916) 481–632.

Bean, J. M. W. 'The Black Death: the Crisis and its Social and Economic Consequences', in Williman (1982) 23–39.

Bennett, H. S. *Life on the English Manor*. Cambridge, 1937.

Bennett, J. W. 'The Medieval Loveday', *Speculum* 33 (1958) 351–70.

Bolton, J. T. *The Medieval English Economy, 1150–1500*. 1980.

Bonnell, J. K. 'The Serpent with a Human Head in Art and in Mystery Play', *American Journal of Archeology* 21 (1917) 255–91.

Boon, K. G. *Rembrandt: The Complete Etchings*. 1977.

Boyle, L. *Pastoral Care, Clerical Education and Canon Law, 1200–1400*. 1981.

'The Curriculum of the Faculty of Canon Law at Oxford in the First Half of the C14th', in *Oxford Studies presented to Daniel Callus*. Oxford, 1964.

Brundage, J. A. *Law, Sex and Christian Society in Medieval Europe*. Chicago & London, 1987.

Bull, M. *The Miracles of Our Lady of Rocamadour*. 1999.

Bullock-Davies, C. *Menestrellorum multitudo: Minstrels at a Royal Feast*. Cardiff, 1978.

Bumke, J., tr. W. T. H. & E. Jackson. *The Concept of Knighthood in the Middle Ages*. New York, 1982.

Bursill-Hall, B. L. *Speculative Grammar of the Middle Ages*. The Hague, 1971.

Camille, M. 'Labouring for the Lord: the Ploughman and the Social Order in the Luttrell Psalter', *Art History* 10 (1987) 423–54.

Gothic Art. 1996.

Carruthers, M. *The Book of Memory: a Study of Memory in Medieval Culture*. Cambridge, 1990.

The Craft of Thought. Cambridge, 1998.

Catto, J., 'Wyclif and Wycliffism at Oxford 1356–1430', in Catto & Evans, eds., *Late Medieval Oxford*, 175–262.

——ed. *The Early Oxford Schools: The History of the University of Oxford*, gen. ed. T. H. Aston, vol. 1. Oxford, 1984.

& R. Evans, eds., *Late Medieval Oxford: The History of the University of Oxford*, gen. ed. T.H. Aston, vol. 2. Oxford, 1992.

Chadwick, H. *Boethius*. Oxford, 1981.

Chambers, E. K. *The Mediaeval Stage*. 2 vols. Oxford, 1903.

Cheney, C. R. *Notaries Public in England in the Thirteenth and Fourteenth Centuries*. Oxford, 1972.

Chettle, H. F. 'The Friars of the Holy Cross', *History* 34 (1949) 204–20.

Christie, A. G. I. *English Medieval Embroidery*. Oxford, 1938.

Chroust, A-H. *Aristotle*. 2 vols., 1973.

Clark, M. T. '*De Trinitate*', in Stump & Kretzmann, 91–102.

Clay, R. M. *The Medieval Hospitals of England*. 1909.

The Hermits and Anchorites of England. 1914, repr. Detroit 1968.

Cohen, J. *The Friars and the Jews: the Evolution of Medieval Anti-Semitism*. 1982.

'The Jews as Killers of Christ in the Latin Tradition, from Augustine to the Friars', *Traditio* 39 (1983) 1–27.

Cohn, N. *The Pursuit of the Millennium*. 1972.

Comparetti, D., tr. E. F. M. Beneche. *Vergil in the Middle Ages*. 1872; Eng. tr. repr. 1966.

Conway, C. A. 'The *Vita Christi* of Ludolf of Saxony and Late Medieval Devotion', *AC* 34 (1976).

Cook, G. H. *Medieval Chantries and Chantry Chapels*. 1947.

The English Parish Church. 1954.

Courtenay, W. J. 'The Effect of the Black Death on English Higher Education', *Speculum* 55 (1980) 696–714.

Schools and Scholars in 14th century England. Princeton, N.J. 1987.

Cross, F. E. & Livingstone, E. A., eds. *The Oxford Dictionary of the Christian Church*. Oxford, 1997.

Cutts, E. L. *Scenes and Characters of the Middle Ages*. 1925.

Daly, S. R. 'Peter Comestor: Master of Histories', *Speculum* 32 (1957) 62–73.

Darwin, F. D. S. *The English Medieval Recluse*. 1944.

Davis, V. 'The Rule of St Paul, the first hermit, in late medieval England', *Studies in Church History* 22 (1985) 203–14.

Dickinson, J. C. *The Origin of the Austin Canons*. 1950.

Du Boulay, F. R. H. & Barron, C., eds. *The Reign of Richard II: Essays in honour of May McKisack*. 1971.

Duffy, Eamon. *The Stripping of the Altars: Traditional Religion in England 1400–1580*. New Haven and London, 1992.

Dyer, C. *Standards of Living in the later Middle Ages*. Cambridge, 1989.

Emmerson, R. K. *Antichrist in the Middle Ages*. Seattle, 1981.

Evans, G. *The Thought of Gregory the Great*. Cambridge, 1986.

——ed. *The Medieval Theologians*. Oxford, 2001.

Finucane, R. C. *Miracles and Pilgrims: Popular Beliefs in Medieval England*. Totowa, N. J., 1977.

Freud, S. (tr. Strachey). *The Interpretation of Dreams*. 1954.

Friedberg, E., ed. *Corpus Iuris Canonici*. 2 vols. Leipzig, 1879–81; repr. Graz, 1959.

Gallais, P. & Riou, Y.-J., eds. *Mélanges offerts à René Crozet*. 2 vols. Poitiers, 1962.

Garth, H. M. *St Mary Magdalen in Medieval literature*. Johns Hopkins, 1950.

Gee, H. & Hardy, W. J., eds. *Documents Illustrative of English Church History*. 1921.

Gilchrist, J. *The Church and Economic Activity in the Middle Ages*. 1969.

Girouard, M. *Life in the English Country House*. New Haven, 1978.

Glorieux, P. *La Littérature quodlibétique*. 2 vols. Paris, 1925–35.

Glunz, H. *History of the Vulgate in England*. Cambridge, 1933.

Hamilton Thompson, A. *The Historical Growth of the English Parish Church*. Cambridge, 1913.

Harding, A. *The Law Courts of Medieval England*. 1973.

Haren, M. *Medieval Thought: the Western Intellectual Tradition from Antiquity to the Thirteenth Century.* 1985.

Harvey, J. *Henry Yevele: The Life of an English Architect*. 1944.

    English Mediaeval Architects: a Biographical Dictionary down to 1550. Gloucester, rev. 1984.

Haskins, S. *Mary Magdalene: Myth and Metaphor*. 1993.

Hassall, W. O. *The Holkham Bible Picture Book*. 1954.

Hatcher, J. *Plague, Population and the English Economy 1348–1530*. 1977.

Helmholz, R.H. *Marriage Litigation in Medieval England*. 1974.

Henisch, B. A. *Feast and Fast*. Pennsylvania, 1976.

Hill, R. M .T. '"A chaunterie for soules": London chantries in the reign of Richard II', in Du Boulay & Barron (1971) 242–55.

Hilton, R. H. & Aston, T. H., eds. *The English Rising of 1381*. Cambridge, 1984.

Holmes, G. *The Good Parliament*. 1975.

Houseley, N. 'The Bishop of Norwich's Crusade, 1383', *History Today* 33 (1983) 16–20.

An Inventory of the Historical Monuments in the City of Oxford. Royal Commission on Historical Monuments, England. 1939.

Jolivet, J. 'Quelques cas de "platonisme grammatical" du VIIe au XIIe siècle', in Gallais & Riou, eds. II 93–9.

Jusserand, J. J. *English Wayfaring Life in the Middle Ages*. 1899.

Kaske, R. E., with Groos, A. & Twomey, M. *Medieval Christian Literary Imagery: A Guide to Interpretation*. Toronto, 1988.

Katzenellenbogen, A. *Allegories of the Virtues and Vices in Medieval Art*. 1939; repr. Toronto, 1989.

Keen, M. *England in the Later Middle Ages*. 1973.

    Pelican History of Medieval Europe. Harmondsworth, repr. 1975.

    Chivalry. New Haven and London, 1984.

Kemp, E. W. 'History and action in the sermons of a medieval archbishop' in R. H. C. Davis & J. M. Wallace-Hadrill, eds., *The Writing of History in the Middle Ages: Essays presented to R.W. Southern* (Oxford, 1981) 353–4.

Kirschbaum, E. & al., eds. *Lexicon der christlichen Ikonographie*. 8 vols. Rome, 1968–76.

Knight, S. T. *Robin Hood: a Complete Study of the English Outlaw*. Oxford, 1994.

Knowles, M. D. *The Evolution of Medieval Thought*. 2nd edn. Ed. D. E. Luscombe & C. N. L. Brooke 1988.

——& Hadcock, R. H. *Medieval Religious Houses: England and Wales*. 2nd edn, 1971.

Kreider, A. *English Chantries: the road to dissolution*. Cambridge, Mass & London, 1979.

Kretzmann N., Kenny, A. J. P. & Pinborg, J., eds. *The Cambridge History of Later Medieval Philosophy*. Cambridge, 1982.

Lawrence, C. H. ed., *The English Church and the Papacy in the Middle Ages*. 1965.

    Medieval Monasticism. 2nd edn, 1989.

    The Friars. 1994.

Leff, G. *Medieval Thought: St Augustine to Ockham*. Harmondsworth, 1958.

    Heresy in the Middle Ages: The Relation of Heterodoxy to Dissent, c.1250–c.1450. 2 vols. Manchester & N.Y., 1967.

Lewis, F. 'The Veronica: Image, Legend and Viewer', in Ormrod (1986) 100–119.

Lewis, C. S. *The Discarded Image*. Cambridge, 1964.

Lipson, E. *The Economic History of England, Vol. I: The Middle Ages*. 1915 (12th edn. 1959).

Loewe, R. 'The Medieval History of the Latin Vulgate', in G. W. H. Lampe, ed., *The Cambridge History of the Bible*, II (Cambridge, 1969) 102–54.

Lunt, W. E. *Financial Relations of the Papacy with England, 1327–1534*. Cambridge, Mass., 1961.

Macy, G. *Theologies of the Eucharist in the Early Scholastic Period*. Oxford, 1984.

Maitland, F. W., ed. H. A. L. Fisher. *The Constitutional History of England*. Cambridge, 1908 (repr. 1974).

Mayr-Harting, H. & Moore, R. I., eds. *Studies in medieval history presented to R. H. C. Davis*. 1985.

McKisack, M. *The Fourteenth Century, 1307–1399*. Oxford, 1959.

Mâle, E., tr. D. Nussey. *The Gothic Image*. 1961.

Meiss, M. *Painting in Florence and Siena after the Black Death*. Princeton, 1951.

Moran, J. A. H. *The Growth of English Schooling 1340–1548*. Princeton, N.J. 1985.

Murphy, J. J. *Rhetoric in the Middle Ages*. Berkeley, 1974.

Myers, A. R., ed. *English Historical Documents, 1327–1485*. 1969.

Neuhauser, R. 'Augustinian *Vitium Curiositatis* and its Reception' in B. B. King & J. T. Schaefer, eds., *St Augustine and his Influence in the Middle Ages* (Sewanee, 1988) 99–124.

Noonan, J. T., Jr. *Bribes,* New York, 1984. pp 275–9.

Orme, N. *English Schools in the Middle Ages*. 1973.

Ormrod, W. M. ed. *England in the 13th Century*. Woodbridge, 1986.

Pantin, W. A. *The English Church in the Fourteenth Century*. Cambridge, 1955.

Partner, P. *The Murdered Magicians: the Templars and their Myth*. Oxford, 1982.

Patch, H. R. *The Goddess Fortuna in Medieval Literature*. 1927.

Pfaff, R. *New Liturgical Feasts in Medieval England*. Oxford, 1970.

Piltz, A., tr. D. Jones. *The World of Medieval Learning*. Oxford, 1981.

Poole, A. L., ed. *Medieval England*. 2 vols. Oxford, 1958.

Popper, K. R. *The Logic of Scientific Discovery*. Rev. edn. 1980.

Postan, M. M. *The Medieval Economy and Society*. Harmondsworth, 1972.

Pugh, R. B. *Imprisonment in Medieval England*. Cambridge, 1968.

Putnam, B. H. *The Enforcement of the Statute of Labourers*. New York, 1908.

Radford, U. M. 'The Wax Images found in Exeter Cathedral', *Antiquaries Journal* 29 (1949) 164–8.

Reames, S. L. *The Legenda Aurea*. Madison, Wisconsin, 1985.

Reuter, T., ed. *The Medieval Nobility*. Oxford, 1978.

Richardson, H. G. 'The English Coronation Oath', *Speculum* 24 (1949) 44–75.

'The Coronation in Medieval England: the Evolution of the Office and the Oath'. *Traditio* 16 (1960) 111–202.

Rickert, M. *Painting in Britain: the Middle Ages*. 1954.

Rosenthal, J. T. *The Purchase of Paradise: Gift-Giving and the Aristocracy, 1307–1485*. 1972.

Roth, C. *A History of the Jews in England*. 3rd edn. Oxford, 1964.

Roth, F. *The English Austin Friars, 1249–1538*. New York, 1966.

Rotuli Parliamentorum. 6 vols, 1767–83.

Russell, J. B. *Lucifer: the Devil in the Middle Ages*. 1984.

Salzman, L. F. *Building in England down to 1450*. Oxford, 1952; revd. repr. 1966.

Santarcangeli, P. *Le Livre des Labyrinthes*. Paris, 1974.

Saxl, F. 'A Spiritual Encyclopaedia of the later Middle Ages', *JWCI* 5 (1942) 82–142.

Schiller, G. *Iconography of Christian Art*. 2 vols. 1971–2.

Sheehan, M. M. *The Will in Medieval England*. Toronto, 1963.

Sheingorn, P. '"And Flights of Angels Sing Thee to Thy Rest": The Soul's Conveyance to the Afterlife in the Middle Ages', in K. L. Scott & C. G Fisher, eds. *Art into Life*. East Lansing, Mich. (1995) 155–82.

Sherwood-Smith, M. C. *Studies in the Reception of the 'Historia Scholastica' of Peter Comestor*. Oxford, 2000.

Shinners, J. & Dohar, W. J., eds. *Pastors and the Care of Souls in Medieval England*. Notre Dame, Indiana, 1998.

Shrewsbury, J. F. *A History of Bubonic Plague in Medieval England*. Oxford, 1975.

Smalley, B. *English Friars and Antiquity in the Early 14th Century*. Oxford, 1960.

The Study of the Bible in the Middle Ages. 3rd edn. Oxford, 1983.

Southern, R. W. *Western Society and the Church in the Middle Ages.* Harmondsworth, 1970.

Southworth, J. *The Medieval Minstrel.* Woodbridge, 1989.

Spade, P. V. *The Medieval Liar: a Catalogue of the Insolubilia Literature*. Toronto, 1975.

'Insolubilia', in Kretzmann et. al., 245–53.

Spargo, J. W. 'Chaucer's Love-Days', *Speculum* 15 (1940) 35–56.

Statutes of the Realm. 11 vols. 1810–28 (repr. 1963).

Stiegman, E. 'Bernard of Clairvaux, William of St. Thierry, the Victorines', in Evans (2001) 129–55.

Stones, E. L. G. 'The Folvilles of Ashby Folville, Leicestershire, and their Associates in Crime 1326–41', *Transactions of the Royal Historical Society* 7 (1957) 117–36.

Stow, J. (ed. C .L. Kingsford). *A Survey of London*. 2 vols. Oxford, 1908.

Stow, K. *Alienated Minority: The Jews of Medieval Latin Europe*. Cambridge, Mass., 1992.

Straw, C. *Gregory the Great: Perfection in Imperfection*. Berkeley, Los Angeles & London, 1988.

Strutt, J., ed. Cox, J. *The Sports and Pastimes of the People of England*. 1903 edn., repr. 1969.

Stump, E. & Kretzmann, N., eds. *The Cambridge Companion to Augustine*. Cambridge, 2001.

Sumption, J. *Pilgrimage: An Image of Medieval Religion*. 1975.

Swanson, J. 'The *Glossa Ordinaria*', in Evans (2001) 156–67.

Swanson, R. N. *Universities, Academics, and the Great Schism*. Cambridge, 1979.

    'Titles to orders in medieval English episcopal registers', in Mayr-Harting & Moore (1985) 233–45.

    Church and Society in Late Medieval England. Oxford, 1989.

Talbot, C. H. *Medicine in Medieval England*. 1967.

Tawney, R. H. *Religion and the Rise of Capitalism*. 1926.

Thompson, A. H. *The English Clergy and their Organisation in the Later Middle Ages*. 1947.

Thompson, D. *A Descriptive Catalogue of Middle English Grammatical Texts*. New York, 1979.

Thomson, J. A. F. 'Piety and Charity in late medieval London', *Journal of Ecclesiastical History* 16 (1965) 178–95.

Thorndyke, L. *A History of Magic and Experimental Science*. 6 vols. New York, 1923–64.

Tipping, H. A. *English Homes, Vol. I*. 1921.

Toulmin, S. & Goodfield, J. *The Fabric of the Heavens*. Cambridge, Mass., 1963.

Tristram, E. W. *English Medieval Wall Painting: the C13th*. 2 vols. Oxford, 1950.

Tuck, J. A. 'Nobles, Commons and the Great Revolt of 1381', in Hilton & Aston (1984) 194–212.

Ullmann, W. *The Origins of the Great Schism*. 1948.

    Law and Politics in the Middle Ages. Ithaca, N.Y., 1975.

Vale, M. *Piety, Charity and Literacy among the Yorkshire Gentry 1370–1480*. York, 1976.

Vernet, F. *Medieval Spirituality*. 1930.

Von Simson, O. *The Gothic Cathedral*. 1956.

Wailes, S. L. *Medieval Allegories of Jesus' Parables*. Berkeley, 1987.

Walker, D. M., ed. *The Oxford Companion to Law*. Oxford, 1980.

Walsh, K. *A C14th Scholar and Primate: Richard FitzRalph in Oxford, Avignon and Armagh*. Oxford, 1981.

——& Wood, D., eds. *The Bible in the Medieval World*. Oxford, 1985.

Warren, A. K. *Anchorites and their patrons in medieval England*. Berkeley, Los Angeles & London, 1985.

Webb, J., ed. *A Roll of the Household Expenses of Richard de Swinfield, Bishop of Hereford [during] 1298–90*. Camden Society, 1854.

Williams, A. 'Relations between the mendicant friars and the secular church in England in the later 14th century,' *Annuale Medievale* 1 (1960) 22–95.

Williman, D., ed. *The Black Death: the Impact of the Fourteenth Century Plague*. Binghampton, N.Y., 1982.

Wippel, J. F. 'The Quodlibetal Question as a Distinctive Literary Genre' in *Les genres littéraires dans les sources théologiques et philosophiques médiévales*, Publications de l'Institut d'études médiévales, 2nd ser. vol. 5 (Louvain, 1982) 7–84.

Wood, M. *The English Mediaeval House*. 1965.

Woodcock, B. L. *Medieval Ecclesiastical Courts in the Diocese of Canterbury*. 1952.

Wood-Legh, K. *Church Life in England under Edward III*. Cambridge, 1934.

    Perpetual Chantries in Britain. Cambridge, 1965.

Workman, H. B. *John Wyclif: a Study of the English Medieval Church*. 2 vols. Oxford, 1926.

Wormald, F. 'The Rood of Bromholm', *JWCI* 1 (1937) 37–45; repr. in J. Alexander, T. Brown & J. Gibbs (eds), *Francis Wormald: Collected Writings* (2 vols., 1988) 123–38.

Wunderli, R.M. *London Church Courts and Society on the eve of the Reformation*. Cambridge, Mass., 1981.

Ziegler, P. *The Black Death*. Harmondsworth, repr. 1971.

E. INDEXICAL GLOSSARY

The **Indexical Glossary** includes all separate words appearing in the texts in Vol. I; rejected variants recorded in the Apparatus or discussed in the *Textual Notes* are listed in a Supplementary Index. Grammatical words are illustrated extensively so as to bring out their full range of senses; but coverage of these, as of the commoner lexical words (*be, have, come* etc) is necessarily selective. Other lexical words are cited in all their independent appearances. Reference in the first place is to the **C** Version; where a word is not found in **C**, it is cited from **B**, and where not in **B**, then from **A**. All the unique words of **Z** are likewise listed, but the more wayward spelling variants of items otherwise found in **A**, **B** or **C** only where they may present particular difficulty. Instances of words in lines exactly or closely parallel to **C** are not recorded unless the line in question occurs at some distance from the **C** (or occasionally **B**, or **A**) original that is the point of reference. In the sequence of numbered references it is always stated whether a text other than **C** is in question; if two or more such follow in succession, the version is specified in bold type (**B, A, Z**) for the sake of clarity.

The order followed in each entry is as follows: the lemma in **bold** type, with spelling variants, if any; the word's grammatical class in *italics*; its forms, where any are given, in brackets; the gloss; the line-reference. Concise grammatical explanation as required is given in italics within round brackets, and further explanatory comment, where appropriate, is placed in square brackets. For convenience, entries will often include extensive examples of set or characteristic phrases in which the given lexeme appears, particularly where it is one with numerous indexed references. Additional information, e.g. specifying the referent, is also sometimes supplied, but no attempt is made to expand the glosses into full dictionary entries, and lexicographical detail must be sought elsewhere (the more difficult cases are discussed in the notes). The order of senses follows that used in the MED, with figurative meanings being given within each sequence of referenced literal senses on first occurrence. Where particular words are discussed from a textual or interpretative point of view in the *Textual Notes* the letter 'n' is appended to the cited line-number, where in the *Commentary*, 'c' is similarly appended.

The order of words is strictly alphabetical, except that in a few instances a derivative is moved up or down a position or two so as to follow immediately upon its radical and thereby enable the lexeme's semantic range to be more conveniently grasped. Each head-word is given in the spelling that occurs most commonly, but where the latter does not coincide with the first referenced gloss, the variant form is noted by being bracketed after the main form (e.g **althow** 2.121 bracketed after **althouh**). Words are listed in their standard lexicographical citation-form, whether or not this is instanced in the text, e.g. infinitives for verbs, such as *thuruen* (although only *thar* appears) and nominative sg. for nouns.

For the sake of simplicity, the following graphemes are treated as identical. Yogh (ȝ) as velar spirant |ɣ| is treated as equal to *gh* in medial and terminal position; in initial position as the palatal glide |j| it is treated as equivalent to consonantal *y*, with which it appears in the latter's normal alphabetical position; as |z| it is placed with *s*. Vocalic *i / y* are treated as one letter, but words beginning with consonantal *i* representing initial |dʒ| are grouped together at the end of the sequence. Where two common spellings exist in the texts, e.g. in words beginning with both *k* and *c* (such as *connen / konnen*), preference is given to the forms dominant in the C-Text. Cross-reference is made for the form not adopted for the head-word so that occurrences can be readily traced. Thorn (þ) and *th* are treated as one letter. The consonantal and vocalic values of *v* are distinguished in the same way as those of *i* described above: thus words with initial |v| occur in a group together at the end of the entry. This letter has the peculiar added feature of using non-initial *u* for |v|, e.g. *vuel* 6.20. Where *u* has this value, its order is always that of *v* in the modern alphabet, wherever it occurs; thus, e.g. *hauen* appears after < *hauk* → *hauthorn* > but before *hawe*.

Latin and French words are grouped in a separate list, but a few words of indeterminate status appear in the main Glossary, even if this means that they appear twice (e.g. *simile, q.v.*)

The following ABBREVIATIONS are used:

a	adjective	*masc.*	masculine
acc.	accusative	*meton.*	metonymic (sense)
app.	apposition		
art.	article	*n.*	noun
assev.	asseveration	*num.*	numeral
assim.	assimilated		
attrib.	attributive	*ord.*	ordinal
auxil.	auxiliary		
av; avl	adverb; adverbial	*parenth.*	parenthetic
		p.; p.p.	participle; past participle
card.	cardinal	*part.*	particle
coll.	collective	*p.t.*	past tense
comb.	combination	*pers.*	person(al)
comp.	comparative	*person.*	personified
cpd.	compound	*phr.*	phrase
conj.; conjv.	conjunction; conjunctive	*pl.*	plural
constr.	construction	*poss.*	possessive
contr.	contracted	*pr.*	present
correl.	correlative	*prec.*	preceding
		pred.	predicative
dat.	dative (case)	*pref.*	prefix
def.	definite	*prep.*	preposition(al)
dem.	demonstrative	*prn*	pronoun
dir.	direct	*prnl.*	pronominal
ellip.	elliptical	*ref.*	reference
emph.	emphatic	*refl.*	reflexive
et p.	*et passim*	*rel.*	relative
ex.	example		
excl.	exclamation	*sel.*	selected
		sg.	singular
fem.	feminine	*spec.*	specific(ally)
fig.	figurative (sense)	*subj.*	subject
foll.	following (followed)	*subjv.*	subjunctive
Fr	French	*suff.*	suffix
fut.	future	*sup.*	superlative
gen.	genitive	*tr.*	transitive
ger.	gerund	*trs.*	transposed
imp.	imperative	*uncontr.*	uncontracted
impers.	impersonal	*uninfl.*	uninflected
indef.	indefinite		
indic.	indicative	*v*	verb
inf.	infinitive		
infl.	inflected	Ø	zero reading
interj.	interjection	†	conjectural reading
interrog.	interrogative	*	word recorded only in *PP*
iron.	ironic (sense)	#	word first recorded in *PP*
It	Italian		

a¹ *a* (*as def. num.*) one 1.27, 3.473, B 3.258; *a* (*as indef. art.*) a Pr 1 *et p*; = a certain 12.77, 15.103, 17.158, 205, 258, 20.305, **B** 12.76, 18.193; (*before proper name*) 7.137, 303, (*foll.*) **al** ~ a whole 6.80, 8.269, 10.2; **vch** ~ every 6.245, 7.307, 12.106, B 13.68, **which** ~ what 9.300, 19.231, 20.127, which A 11.68 (*sup.*) ~ 20.475, (*av.*) ~ 22.87; *with n. of multitude / quantity / kind, foll. by Ø* **of:** ~ **doseyne** 4.38, ~ **drop** 6.335, ~ **galoun** B 5.336, ~ **payre** 6.251, B 12.19; ~ **seem** 3.42

a² *pers. prn* (*unstressed*) he Pr 72 *et p.*, Z Pr 121; she 2.17 *et p.*, Z 1.17; they 3.89, Z 5.154

a³ *prep.* on 2.56, 3.51, 259, 11.255, 14.131, 141, 15.19, 18.182, 20.44, 349, 21.237, B 16.189, 17.106, 18.314, A 4.32; in 3.51, 259, 9.154, 11.164, 13.147, 18.213, 242, 19.151, 193, A 5.215, 8.115; to A 9.58

a-⁴ *pref.* (*forming av*) = on 7.13, 52, 8.138, 197, at 6.236; ~ **daye** a day, daily B 8.44; = in 6.44, 7.26, 19.75, 22.196; at, by 19.174

a⁵ *excl.* ah, oh! 1.41, 20.13, Z 5.140

abaschen *v* be upset, lose one's composure [through shame *etc*], *p.p.* ~**ed, -et** ashamed 6.17, 9.86, 22.48, B 10.286; at a loss 15.164, B 10.445

abaten *v* lessen (difficulty of digesting) A 7.169; alleviate B 12.59

abauen *v* confound 8.226

a.b.c. *n* alphabet, a.b.c. B 7.133

abbesse *n* abbess [superior of convent of nuns] 5.176

abbot *n* abbot [superior of monastic abbey] 5.176, B 10.325

abedde *av* in bed 6.44, 7.26, 10.262, 265, 273, B 5.389

abeggen Z 7.66 *see* **abuggen** *v*

(a)-beggeth *av* (a-) begging 8.138, 246, Z 7.220

abyden *v* remain 1.132, 2.199, 250, 4.35, 9.40, 10.227, 22.79, 131, A 9.96; wait 8.288, **B** 11.377, 15.313; linger 10.63; continue A 7.138; endure 20.344, 22.46; *pr. p. a* *abydyng(e) steadfast 18.136, 21.295, 22.142

aby(y)en 20.446, B 3.251, **abyggen** 2.141 = **abuggen** *v*

abite *n* dress, habit Pr 3

abiten *v* bite / nip off 18.32

ablenden (*p.t.* **ablende**) blind 20.140, 368, † B 10. 31.

***abosten** *v* arrogantly defy 8.152

abouhte *p.t.* 10.262 *etc; see* **abuggen** *v*

aboute(n)¹ *av* around, about 7.162, B 11.17, A 6.73; in all directions 9.107, A 2.39; from all quarters 2.172; from place to place Pr 31, 5.29, B 2.177, A 10.105; here and there B 15.328; everywhere 4.183; this way and that 10.46, B Pr 151, *in phrr.* **al** ~ to everyone 2.158, 232; **comen** ~ come into existence A 10.217; *av as a* surrounding, neighbouring 10.12, 20.337, B 2.86; round about B 5.145; *in phrr.* **ben** ~ be diligent / active 4.77, 10.191, B 13.369; **comere** ~ visitor A 2.43; **rennere** ~ vagabond A 11.202

abouten² *prep.* enclosing B 5.586; (clasped) around Pr 178; in attendance on 2.62; near 19.58; about, upon

6.180, 8.173, 15.164, 22.191; throughout, all over 1.91, B 12.254; at approximately (the time of) 7.132, 9.246, 16.13, 20.69, 137, B 15.283; involved with 1.6, B 7.119; concerning 13.227, B 13.252, ? 1.88*n*

abouen¹ *av* at a higher level 18.87, *in phr.* **bringen** ~ bring to prosperity 13.21; *av as a* on top 21.281, B 5.192

abouen² *prep.* superior (in authority / rank) to 10.141, 21.473, B 8.95, Z 3.174; beyond, surpassing 12.75, 16.34, 19.102; over and above B 14.151

a-bribeth *av* a-scrounging 8.246

abroed *av* forth widely 15.263; out wide 9.143; (forth) away from home **B** 2.177, 5.139

absence *n* absence 21.124

absolucioun *n* remission B 7.63

abstinence *n* self-denial, *esp.* fasting, (*person.*) 6.439, 7.271

abuggen (*p.t.* **abouhte** 10.236, *p.p.* 20.430) pay for [at the cost of labour / suffering] 2.141, 8.41, 83, 16.219, 20.446, **B** 3.251, 12.42; pay the penalty 10.236, 13.15, 20.430; pay interest on B 13.376

ac *conj.* but Pr 78 *et p.*; nevertheless 10.51; but on the contrary/ rather 3.233, B 10.121; except / but (that) B 8.55; however Pr 62, A 5.247

acale *p.p. a* afflicted with cold 20.437

accidie *n* (the) sin of / bout of sloth 6.416

accion *n* right to go to law, grounds for a suit 1.94; act(ion) 5.196

accordyng *pr.p.* A 10.91 *see* **acorden** *v*

ac(c)usen *v* charge, indict 2.245, 3.219; *and see* **cusen** *v*

achocen *v* choke Z 3.161*n*

acombren *v* encumber, burden 2.52, Z 7.91; oppress 21.221; weigh down 1.31, 190, 197; *see* **(en)combren** *vv*

acordaunce *n* (grammatical) agreement 3.336, [394*n*]

acordaunde *pr.p.* 3.394 *see* **acorden** *v*

acorden *v* come to agreement 3.392, 6.385, 11.315, 13.213, 19.287, 22.304, B 13.122; be reconciled 5.183, 22.354; agree 3.273, 471, (grammatically) 355, 361, 371, *pr. p.* in (grammatical) agreement (with) 3.394*n*; concur [in judgement] (with) 4.87, 8.243, 9.69, 12.162, 20.242, **B** 3.319, 4.158, **A** 4.144, 10.88, Z 4.125; conform (with) *pr. p.* A 10.91

acorsen *v* excommunicate 22.263; interdict 20.96; declare anathema 18.223; damn Pr 127; condemn B 18.107; *p.p. a* wicked, execrable B 15.412. A 10.155

acountable *a* responsible 13.66

acounte *n* account, reckoning 7.40, 13.34, 21.465, A Pr 91; (*fig.*) final reckoning acquitaunce B 14.190. settle accounts 4.11, 7.33, 11.302, 13.34, (*fig.*) 12.68, Z 7.75; take account of, esteem 3.392, 8.159, 10.96; regard 9.239; value (at) 21.415

acoupen *v* accuse (of sin) B 13.459

#acquitaunce *n* document of acquittal B 14.190

actif *a* active [= practising the life of activity in the world] **B** 6.248, 13.226, A 11.183, (*person.*) 7.298, 15.215 *et p.*, **B** 13.239, 273, 458, 14.26, 320, 16.2

acumbren *v* Z 7.91 = **acombren** *v*

acuth *pr. sg.* Z 7.242 *see* **aken** *v*

aday *av* on the next day, ? daily 8.331

adaunten *v* put down 3.440

ad(d)ere *n* serpent 20.315, 326, 378

#**adiectif** *n* adjective 3.335, 342, 360, 393, 404

a-do *n* business 5.163

adoun(e) *av* down Pr 64, *esp. in phrasal vv.* 1.91, 3.43, 4.88, 8.29, 10.95, 18.50, 20.28, 22.132, **B** 5.7, 9.205, 10.329, 16.73, 17.65 *etc*

adreden *v* (*p.p.* **adrad**) frighten 21.307, 22.353

adrenchen *v* (*p.t.* **adreynten**, *p.p.* **adreynt**) drown 10.163, B 10.407; inundate 10.248; befuddle 22.378

af(f)ayten *v* train 8.30; discipline 6.7, B 11.384

afe(e)ren *v* frighten, make afraid 1.10, 4.66, 8.128, 179, 11.282, 15.166, 19.82, 20.123, 477, 21.206, 22.166, **B** 11.63, 15.384

afeld(e) *av* (in)to the fields 4.144, 8.198, 312, B 6.142

afellen *v* (*p.t.* **afelde**) bring down, destroy 3.162

aferes *n. pl.* affairs, doings 6.152

affiaunce *n* trust 18.255

af(f)raynen *v* ask B 16.274, ~ **at** enquire (of) 20.16; *see* **fraynen** *v*

afyngred *p.p.* (< *of-hungred*) very hungry 9.85, 11.43, 50, 16.15, 17.68, B 6.266, A 12.59

afore *av* in advance B 14.134; earlier Z 5.28; *prep.* in front of B 5.12, 23, **as** ~ in the sight of B 12.79; ahead of Z 2.160

afrounten *v* insult 22.5

after¹ *av* after A 12.39; following Pr 52; in succession B 2.102; after that 12. 215, 14.85, 20.41, B Pr 140; in consequence 3.103, B 3.314; afterwards Pr 50, 9.181, 12.204, 215, 20.230, 22.103 *etc*, B 1.68, A 12.35; later B Pr 218; hereafter, to come Pr 207; accordingly 12.150, A 12.7; as well 11.118, 13.13, 15.26, 169, B 3.262, 5.110;

after² *prep.* after 2.106, 10.303, 12.200 *etc*; following B 5.261; towards Pr 14; for 1.123, 189, 8.279, 13.73, 14.120, 16.276, 18.180, 22.387, B 3.71; next to A 1.110; about B 13.95, A 12.79; in keeping with 2.27; according to 3.470, 9.110, 14.123, 127, 17.160, 19.19, 21.123, 22.247, A 12.94; in the likeness of B 17.138;

after³ (*conj.*) ~ (**that**) according as 22.30, A 7.195

afterward(es) *av* next, after that B 10.224, A 11.181

afuyre *av* on fire 16.178

afurst(e) *p.p.a* (< *of-þyrst*) afflicted with thirst 9.85, 11.43, 16.15, 20.437, A 12.82

agayne (**aʒe(y)n(e)(s))¹** *av* back (again) 3.331, 6.309, 7.268, 20.399, 21.247, **B** 6.43, 17.121; again 9.29; in return 22.172, B 10.201;

agayne (**aʒe(y)n(e)(s))²** *prep.* in front of 3.193; towards

B 4.44; contrary to 17.280, 20.377, A 10.160; against (= in opposition to, in defiance of) 3.188, 409, 445, 7.73, 8.341, 9.26, 65, 16.214, 238, 19.266, 20.262, 393, 21.362, 22.72, 113, 154 *etc.*, **B** 5.608, 6.314, 8.46, 9.127, 10.39, 13.132, 15.68 *etc*, Z 6.75.

agasten *v* (*p.p.* **agast(e)**) frighten 2.221, 21.301, B 13.268; frighten off B 14.281

age *n* age 18.246; old age 22.189; *in phrr.* **myddel** ~ B 12.7; **of** ~ old enough 10.252, 22.159, **of twelue wynter** ~ twelve years old 6.203

ageyn(e)(s) B 6.314, A 10.160 *etc*; *see* **agayne** *av*

aglotyen *v* satisfy (with food) 9.76

ago *p.p., in av phr.* B 15.231 *see* **ygon** *v*

agrounde *av* on the earth B 1.90; *and see* **ground** *n*

agu(w)e *n* acute fever 6.79, 22.84

agulte *n* guilt, fault 21.305

agulten *v* sin 17.44; offend 6.17, 19.278, **B** 14.7, 15.391

aye Z 4.32, **aʒe(y)n(e)(s)** 7.73, 8.341, **B** 4.44, 10.201 *etc*; *see* **agayne** *av, etc*

aʒeynes *conj.* as soon as 21.319

aʒeynward *av* again, once more 19.77

ay *av* always 12.102, 115, 13.58, 14.133, 214, 16.62, 17.146; all the time B 8.49; eternally 18.233; for ever B 9.48; constantly 11.31, 15.247, 16.94, 20.400; every time 5.95, 10.40; in each case 8.219, Z 3.150, ~ **the lengere** in each case, the longer 13.4, the more often 3.136

#**aiel** *n* forefather, ancestor B 15.322

ay(e)r (**eir**) *n* air 1.126, 10.130, 15.221, B Pr 128, 14.44

aylen (**eilen**) *v* ail, afflict 8.134, 270, B 15.251

ayr (**ey(e)r, heyr**) *n* heir 3.321, 431, 5.59, 163, 6.255, 9.4, 10.86, 18.246, **B** 2. 102, 15. 322, A 10.210

aysches (**askes**) *n.pl.* ashes 3.125

*****aythe** *n* harrow 21.274

ayther (**either**) *prn* each of two **B** 13.348, 16.207; both 16.346, Z 5.91; each B 18.74; of each one 12.140, B 13.348; *as a* each, both 19.288, B 13.177; *in phrr.:* ~ **of hem bothe** each of the two 16.197; ~ **oþer** each other 6.188, B 7.139, A 10.179; ~ **... oþer** each one... the other 6.149, 16.65, **B** 5.147, 9.86; **here; oure; yow** ~ **oþer** each of (the two of) them 22.354, us 6.188, you †B 14.36; *conj.* either (**or...eyþer** either ... or B 17.136)

aken *v* (*p.t. subjv.* **oke**) ache B 6.255, should ache **oke** 19.160

aker *n* arable field [of acre size], *in phr.* **half** ~ 6.267, 8.2, 3, 113, 123

aknowen *v* acknowledge, *p.p.* **aknowe**, *in phr.* **ben** ~ acknowledge, admit 9.86

al(l) (*pl.* **alle** Pr 56, B Pr 103, A 2.137) *a* all Pr 10, 3.473 *et p.*, *with prns* = them all, all of (them *etc*) *a* **hem** ~ Pr 68, **vs** ~ 7.124, **they** ~ 20.85, **we** ~ 12.132, **yow** ~ B 1.14; ~ **þat** 19.244, B 5.233, ~ **þise** B 9.71; (*placed after n / prn*): 2.219, 9.309, B 3.12, *before n* B 11.198;

whole, ~ **a** a whole 8.269, the whole of Pr 50, the entire Pr 192, A 7.134; *in n. phrr.* ~ **nacion** every nation 18. 102; ~ **þe reame** Pr 192, 5.114, 125, 11.59, B 15.524; ~ **þe world** the whole world 21.430, 22.49, B 15.437, Z 5.40; everyone Pr 100, 104, 12.36, 21.220; ~ **(thy** *etc*) **lyf-tyme** the whole of (your) life (long) 1.75, 2.32, 6.239, 436, 440, 7.215, 8.25, 10.169, 11.256, 15.198, 18.200, 20.3, 22.366, **B** 5.476, 13.142

al(l)(e) *n* (*gen. pl.* **al(l)er(e)** 21.474, B 16.205) everything Pr 13 *et p.*, B 3.269, Z 2.164; all things B 10.355, Z 5.36; all creatures 15.296; all people, everyone 2.249, 16.19, B 3.242; *in prnl and avl phrr.* **oure aller** of all of us B 16.205; **ouer** ~ everywhere B 9.55; **youre alere** of all of you 21.474; **wiþ** ~ moreover B 15.288

al *av* all, entirely Pr 28, B 2.125, A 7.183, Z Pr 28; purely, simply 7.139, 10.237, 12.51, B 4.150, A 10.179, Z 5.43; quite, absolutely B 2.164, A 7.170, Z 5.105; (*as emph. part.*) 8.124, 11.4, 13.166, 20.290, B 16.18; *in phr.* ~ **aboute** right round Pr 178, 7.162, 21.365; everywhere 4.183, in all directions 13.134; to everyone 2.158; ~ **aloude** out loud 6.23

alay *n* alloy of base metal B 15.348

alayen *v* alloy (*fig.*), debase 17.79, B 15.352, 353

#**alarme** *interj.* to arms! 22.92

alday *avl phr.* time and again 17.96

aldreman *n* alderman [member of govering body of city] 4.188

ale *n* ale [beer brewed without hops] 6.159, 228, 392, 433, 7.51, 67, 8.122, 328, A 10.60; **bred and** ~ 7.51, 9.156, **feble** ~ 6.159, **good** ~ 6.356, 374, 8.324, 16.73, 22.223, **halpenny** ~ 8.328, **peny** ~ 6.226, 8.332, 9.92, **poddyng** ~ 6.226; **thikke...~ thynne** 21.403; ale-house / - drinking Pr 43, 7.19, 9.194

a-lechyng *ger. av* 19.75 *see* **lechen** *v*

aleggen *v* B 11.89, A 12.107 *see* **allegen** *v*

alere *n. gen. pl. see* **al(l)(e)** *n*

alery *av* twisted across, ? bent backwards 8.129*n*

aliche B 16.57 = **yliche** *av*

alien *n* foreign resident 3.266

alyday Z 6.47 = **holyday** *n*

alyhten (aliȝten) *v* alight, come down (upon) 11.143, B 11.246

alyue *a* alive 22.110, B 8.113; **o lyue** A 2.14 *see* **lyf** *n*

alkenamye *n* alchemy B 10.214

allas *interj.* alas! 12.1, 17.56, ~ **þat** 16.1

alle *a, n. pl.* Pr 20 *etc*; *see* **al(l)(e)** *a, n*

al(l)eggen *v* adduce [text] as proof 12.31, A 12.107

aller *n. gen. pl.* B 16.205 = **alere**; *see* **al(l)(e)** *n*

alles Z 1.101 = **elles** *av*

alleskynnes *gen. phr.* of every kind Z 3.172

allouable *a* permissible 17.130

allouaunce *n* allocation of funds [for expenses], repayment 9.269; acknowledgement, approbation 15.290, B 11.220

al(l)ouen *v* commend 12.141, 16.143, B 15.4; esteem 16.143, B 10.432, 434; recognise as valid 17.136, 18.82, 14.212*n*; permit 3.74; tolerate 3.204, 7.95; reward 8.250, 12.196; hold to (someone's) credit 18.251

almarie *n* cabinet 16.87

almesdede *n* charitable work, *esp.* almsgiving 7.72, 241

almesfull *a* generous in almsgiving 6.48

almesse (almusse) *n* alms 8.133, 9.141, 191, 13.78, 17.47 (*pl.*), **B** 3.75, 7.73, 15.84, 311, 419, (*spec.*) food from table for distribution to poor B 6.146; act of charity 9.96

almest (almo(o)st) *av* almost 3.208, 22.227, B 4.174

almy(g)hty (almyhten Pr 218) almighty, omnipotent 1.110, 5.99, 14.98, 17.135, 20.465, B 15.393; *in phr.* ~ **God** B 10.431, **God** ~ Pr 218, 1.26, 6.426, 7.217, 13.101, 15.281, 17.152, 18.96, 211, 216, 19.38, B 5.132, 7.80, 9.64, 93, 190, 10.124, 15.295, **A** 10.132, 12.26; **Lord** ~ 17.135, 19.42

almusse *n* 9.96 = **almesse** *n*

alofte (olofte) *av* (up) on high 1.112, 6.423, 20.44, 147, B 1.90, (up) above **B** 12.219, (*fig.*) Pr 157; up(right) 6.409

alogh B 12.233 = **alouȝ** *av*

along *av* out, lengthwise 6.216

alongid *p.p.a* desirous, eager A 7.251

alosen *v* praise 19.103

aloft(e), alowed *av* out loud 6.23, 20.360; with a loud voice 2.131, 21.159

alowed *p.p.* 3.204 *see* **al(l)louen** *v*

als *av* as 16.350, **B** 4.195, 6.36, A 2.122

alse *av* 17.92, B Pr 217, 3.46, 72, 5.226, 7.233, **A** 3.211, Z Pr 59 = **also** *av*

also *av* too, also, likewise Pr 46 *et p.*; (just) as 16.345, 21.441, B 3.331, A 11.95; so, in such a way †B 10.367

althouh (althow) *conj.* although 2.121, 12.146, 14.46, 20.373

alway, alwey *av* always, at all times 10.28, 16.96, B 15.313

am *1 sg. pr.* 1.72 *et p.*, (*without prn subj.*) 19.278, 20.129, B 5.599 *see* **ben** *v*

amayst(e)r(y)en *v* master, get control of 2.161, 167, 8.221

ameddes 9.122 = **amydde(s)** *prep.*

amendement *n* correction, ? improvement 3.122; **on / vp** ~ by way of compensation, [for taking trouble] 22.135; repentance 6.102; conversion B 10.363

amenden *v* put right 4.86, 12.74, 13.199, 17.202, 19.295, **B** 3.57, 94, 6.272, 10.60, 439, 11.104, 377, 12.95, 13.208; repair 3.65, 9.30, 31, 33, 19.160, 20.389, 22.363; improve B 12.286; heal 20.157; make amends for 4.92, 19.203; relieve **B** 9.83, 10.60, 11.209, 14.188; restore (peace in) 4.182; reform [morally] 1.77, 2.103, 141, 246, 3.100, 135, 6.61, 169, 7.121, 8.79, 9.16, 160, 237, 10.304, 15.229, 16.261, 17.50, 225, 250, 19.316,

332, 21.445, 22.109, **B** 5.132, 7.15, 10.123, 268, 11.424, 12.7, 15, 194, 14.20, (*person.*) 'Be converted' 7.243, 247; save, redeem 1.163, 7.127, 16.23, 18.288, **B** 13.409, 15.249; discipline Pr 212, 5.170, B 3.94

amendes *n* reparation, amends 4.84; (*person.*) 2.120 *et p.*; compensation 4.97, **B** 5.325, 18.343; **to** ~ in satisfaction B 18.328

amercyen *v* (impose a) fine (on) B 6.39; *see also* **mersyen** *v*

amydde(s) *av* in the middle [of it] B 13.83, 247; *prep.* in the middle of 6.334, 9.122, 10.33, 14.137, B 16.14; amidst 10.67, B 10.407; through the midst of 13.42; straight in the A 7.166

amys *a* wrong, amiss 19.295; in a disordered state B 6.325; *av* wrongly 1.172; amiss 13.199, Z 7.45

amonge *av* along with [it] B 14.238

among(es) *prep.* among 3.49 *et p.*, Z 7.287; in among 22.112; in the company of 6.241, 434, 9.189, 10.28, 11.34, 17.28; between 21.252; amidst 17.288, B 11.365; with Pr 131, B 10.48

amorteysen *v* alienate in mortmain 17.55

amorwe *av* (on) the next morning 3.307

amorwenynges *av* in the mornings B 11.338 (**amorwenynge** 13.147)

amounten *v* add up [to saying] A 3.86

ampulle *n* B 5.520 = **aunpolle** *n*

an¹ *indef. art.* (*before vowel and silent* h) Pr 3 *et p.*

an² *prep.* in 3.70, 7.217, 9.281, 14.7, 14, 16.186, 19.4, **B** 13.402, 17.116; on 2.134, 5.186, 6.124, 12.42, 17.222, 18.106, 21.192, **B** Pr 13, 11.107

an³ *v* = **han** ~ Z Pr 99, *conj.* = **and** Z Pr 91 *etc*

ancre (**anker**) *n* anchorite / anchoress Pr 30, 3.140, 8.146, B 15.214, A 10.136

and (**ant** Z Pr 5 *et p.*, **an** Z 1.41) *conj.* and Pr 5 *et p.*; and yet Pr 162, 16.103, B 14.12; but Pr 195; if 2.204, 3.44, 4.34, 6.289, 8.160, 9.71, 238, 11.96, 12.194, 13.56, 15.156, 19.208, 22.14 (1), 210, **B** 2.193, 4.88, 5.90, 9.81, 10.360, 11.100, 12.240, 13.110, 15.427, 16.73, A 11.218; even though Pr 120, 3.114, 6. 49, 21. 446, B 10.407

angel *n* angel 9.37, 10.156, 11.150, 12.208, 14.92, 15.302, 17.222, 18.90, 20.413, 450, 21.72, 74, 79, 81, 150, 22.241, **B** Pr 128, 131, 9.124, 16.71, **A** 10.143, 157, 12.4, 95

anger, angre *n* anguish, affliction 6.79, 114, 12.208, 16.150, 19.320, 21.292, **B** 12.11, 15.259, 271; wrath A 10.143

angr(y)en *v* afflict, trouble 16.85, B 5.116

#**angrylyche** *av* petulantly 16.113

anhengen *v* hang 1.64

anhouren Z 6.42 = **honouren** *v*

any *a, n* 17.282, 21.305, B Pr 156 *et p.*, A 2.32 *et p.* = **eny** *a, n*

#**anyent(is)en** *v* utterly destroy 19.269, 20.386

†**animal** *n* animal B 10.242

anker 8.146 = **ancre** *n*

#**annuel** *n* payment for annual commemorative-service Z Pr 63

ano(e)n, ano(o)n(e) *av* at once Pr 113, 1.114, 6.338, 9.163, 13.40, 214, 217, 240, 18.106, 19.66, 20.362, 22.35, 136, B 16.19, A 12.35; presently 3.320, B 9.131; soon B 11.46; *conj.* ~ **as** as soon as Pr 111, 21.18; ~ **riht** *av* right away 4.150, 7.293, 15.52, 22.17; immediately B 11.337

anoyen *v* offend, irritate B 2.167; harass A 3.176; trouble B 5.93

another *prn* a second (person) 13.35, 18.289, 21.270, A 12.35; another Pr 199, 6.38, 17.104, B 9.84; another person, someone else 3.319, 7.293, 301, 18.197, 20.47, B 10.102; anyone else 6.24, 9.123; someone 3.295; one more 1.105; *a* a second B 3.246; another B 14.131

answere *n* answer, reply 20.331

answeren *v* answer, reply B Pr 140, 11.251, 18.315, A 12.62; give an answer [in explanation] B 10.117, [to interrogation] **A** 11.299, 301, 12.29, [in dispute] B 15.381; be accountable B 5.293

#**antecedent** *n* (grammatical) antecedent (*fig.*) 3.353, 361, *a* 3.378

apayen *v* please, satisfy 2.45, 8.115, 9.178, 15.64, B 6.195; *see* **payen** *v*

apayren (ap(p)eyren) *v* (do) harm (to) 3.163, 7.210, 8.229, Z 2.3; damage [by reducing] 5.144

(a)p(p)aray(l)le (parail) *n* dress, wearing-apparel 6.30 (B 13.278), 10.117, 12.126, 133, 17.72

(ap)parailen *v* clothe, attire Pr 25, 2.224, 7.160, 8.56, **B** Pr 23, 2.171, 215, 5.516, 6.57, 11.240

a-parceles *n. phr.* as (distinct) parts 19.98

apart *av* privately 6.383; ~**ye** separately 15.54

ap(p)e(e)l *n* formal charge 19.286; appeal [to a higher court] 2.186, [for protection] 2.244

apeyren Z 2.3 = **apayren** *v*

apenden *v* belong 1.97, B 1.45, Z Pr 55

ap(p)eren *v* appear 11.151, 14.92; show, reach 16.83; present oneself Pr 188, 3.149; be symbolised (by) 21.92

(a)pertly(che) *av* plainly, manifestly 3.313, 5.117, B 1.100; openly, in public B 5.23

apeward *n* ape-keeper [juggler with trained monkey] B 5.631

(a)poisenen *v* (kill by) poison 3.163; corrupt fatally 17.224; grievously harm B 3.82

ap(p)osen *v* confront with question 3.5, 5.10, 14.154, 15.94; (put a) question (to) 1.45, 15.193, 16.161, **A** 11.298, 12.26; dispute (with) B 7.139; ask question(s) A 12.8

ap(p)ostata *n* apostate, violator of the code of one's order 1.98, Z 1.65

(a)postel *n* apostle 9.20, 11.32, 150, 12.34, 13.3, 18.177,

208, 21.147, 155, 169, **B** 10.340, 15.417, A 12.4; (**Peter þe**) ~ 20.251, (**Poul þe**) ~ 11.269 *etc*; (*fig.*) 9.118; (itinerant) preacher B 6.149

appel (appul) *n* fruit 10.208, 20.305, 374, **B** 12.232, 16.73, A 10.141; apple 8.317, 18.62, **B** 5.603, 9.149, (*fig.*) 18.68, 70, 18.122, ~ **tree** 18.61, B 18.287

appelen *v* accuse (formally) B 11.421

appetit *n* appetite (for food) B 6.263

(ap)purtinaunce *n* subsidiary right / privilege (*iron.*) 2.108; appendage, accessory 16.330

Aprill *n* (the month of) April B 13.269

aprochen *v* approach 18.139, 20.174

apropren *v* acquire right to endowment and income (of) Z Pr 58

ar¹ *av, comp.* **arre** Z 4.4 the sooner, (*sup.*) **arst(e)** first (of all) 6.307, A 4.29; *and see* **or**¹ *av*

ar² *prep.* before 5.122, 17.61, *etc*; *and see* **or**² *prep.*, **er**²*prep.*

ar³ *conj.* before Pr 164 *et p.*; *and see* **or**⁴ *conj.*, **er**³ *conj.*

ar(e)(n) *pr. pl of* **ben** *v* Pr 93, 126, 11.237, B 3.80, 17.165, *etc.*; *with* **hit** *and pl. subj. following* there are 8.217, 15.288, A 7.49, Z 7.263; they are 9.118, 126; (*trs*) ~ **hit** are they 15.309

aray *n* order, *in phr.* **riden out of** ~ (*fig.*) behave in disorderly manner 5.157; clothing 2.16

arayen *v* (*refl.*) get ready 4.16; robe B 5.11

araten *v* reprove, berate 5.11, 12.37, B 11.375; scold B 14.163

#arbitrere *n* arbitrator, **be ~s** through the mediation of a third party 6.381

arc(h)a(u)ngel *n* archangel 1.107, 21.150, B 1.108

archidekne *n* A Pr 92 = **erchedekn** *n*

arch *n* arch, **in þe Arches** [*meton.* for the ecclesiastical court of appeal for Canterbury held at St Mary of the Arches (le Bow)] 2.61, 186, 22.136

are *pr. pl.* 8.217 *et pl.*; *see* **ar(e)(n)**, *pr. pl.*

arechen *v* get hold of, hand 20.281

aredy *a* prepared 6.97, 7.119, Z 6.69

aren *pr. pl.* Pr 93 *et p.*; *see* **ar(e)(n)**

arerage *n* B 10.470 = **arrerage** *n*

arere *av* back (wards) 6.404, B 10.139

areren *v* make, set forth A 2.48

areso(u)nen *v* rebuke, berate 13.129, 183, 194, 245, B 12.217

arguen *v* dispute 16.113; expound an argument 11.121

arguere *n* disputant, critic B 10.118

argument *n* (formal) argument [in a disputation] 19.112, B 15.381

aryht *av* in the right way 17.157

arysen *v* (*contr. pr.* **ariste** 12.232, *p.t.* **aroos** 6.62 *etc*) get up 5.15, 6.62, 386, 391, 8.125, 13.247, 15.28, 20.281, **B** 6.263, 8.35, Z 4.158; rise [from the dead] 20.264, 21.52, 152, B 10.353, A 8.172, [from sick-bed] A 7.132, [from sin] 3.357, 10.52, 14.111; grow up 3.452;

originate (from) 11.234, 12.232, 17.139, 19.250, A 10.119, 121; be obtained A 8.47; occur 8.345; take place A 5.188

arm¹ *n* arm 16.82, 20.76, **B** 9.165, 15.122, *pl.* = embrace 7.26, A 12.42

arm² *n* (*in* **armes** *pl. only*) armour B 5.501; battle, *in phrr.* **iugement of** ~ trial by combat (*fig.*) 18.129, **seriaunt of** ~ (royal) officer commanding an armed force (*fig.*) 21.341; armorial bearings, coat of arms (*fig.*) 21.12, (*also*) B 5.501; *in phr.* **heraud of** ~ herald [at tournament] 20.14, (*fig.*) 18.186, 22.94

armen *v* (*p.p.* **y-armed**) arm, equip with weapons 21.144, (*fig.*) 21.354, 22.116

armure *n* armour (*fig.*) 1.153, *in phr.* **cote** ~ coat of arms (*fig.*) 21.13

arn *pr.pl.* 9.137, 10.298, B Pr 98 *etc*; *see* **ar(e)(n)** *pr.pl.*

arnde *n* A 3.40; *see* **er(e)nde** *n*

†arne *p.t.* B 16.136 = **ern** *p.t.*; *see* **rennen** *v*

arre *av comp.* the sooner Z 4.4

aro(e)s, aroos *p.t. see* **arysen** *v*

(a)r(r)erage *n* debt, arrears, *in phrr.* **casten in** ~ find (sb.) short in his accounts 12.68, **fallen / rennen in** ~ fall behind with payments / run into debt 9.272, 11.301, 12.65, 15.288, B 5.242

ars *n. pl.* 11.97 *see* **art** *n*

arst(e) *av* first, soonest 6.307, A 4.29

art *n* (*pl.* **ars, art3**) art, discipline, *in phr.* **the seuene** ~ the seven branches of higher study (at university) 11.97, 12.95, 17.114

art 2 *sg.pr.* art, are 1.80 *et p.*

article *n* article [of Creed] B 10.233

artow *assim. 2 sg. pr.* (= **art thow**) 13.225, 16.210, 18.184, 20.360, B 19.408

arwe *n* arrow 3.478, 22.117, 226

arwen *v* daunt, make fearful 3.236

as *conj.* as Pr 8 *et p.*; such as Pr 30, 220 *etc*, B 3.89, A 8.169; as for example 3.374, 6.276, 8.261, 13.51, 155, B 13.402, Z 7.91; = as if Pr 2, 66, 3.54 *etc*, B 5.100; = though 13.184; *av* = like Pr 3, 2.28, 3.387, 4.194 *etc*, B 10.350, A 10.212, Z Pr 37 inasmuch as 7.100; *in phrr.* ~ **by** to judge by, according to 3.306, 9.214, 11.268, 13.27, 97, 14.152, 201, 17.157, 21.456, B 14.155; as if from 8.88, 17.152, as if through 16.108; ~ **for** as if as 2.146, 9.92, 12.197, 15.39, 171, 18.205, 22.20, with regard to 7.191, B 15.457; ~ **in** in respect of 6.32; ~ **þee** as if to treat you B 13.171; ~ **to** in regard to 6.36, in comparison with 14.83; ~ **who seiþ** as if to say B 9.36; ~ **whoso** like someone who B 15.337; (*pleonastic for emph.*) 3.62, 6.32, 36, 11.265, 285, 12.81, 191, 17.149, 202, 18.88, 99, B 2.58, A 10.206, Z 2.131; (*as intensifier with av*) ~ **3erne** right away 7.36 (~ **quyk** B 14.190, **swiþe** ~ B 3.102, ~ **tyd** B 13.319, 16.61) (*in comb.*) **theder** ~ where...to 1.118; **ther** ~ where B 2.92

asayen 3.5= **assayen** *v*

ascapen 8.79 = **askapen** v

ascuth *3 pr. sg.* Pr 21, 1.34, *imp. pl* 6.56 = **asketh** *see* **asken** v

as(s)elen v seal [with official mark to authenticate] 2.114, 19.6, 9, Z 3.84

asentaunt *a.* willing Z 3.152; *and see* **assenten** v

aseruen v deserve, merit 14.136

aseth (asset3) n adequate satisfaction 19.204

as(c)hamed *p.p.a* filled with shame 6.421, 13.240, 22.284; mortified 13.214

asyde *av* sideways 6.404; out of the way, apart 19.59, 63, 22.152; off to one side A 11.95

askapen v escape 2.215, 3.61, 8.79; avoid B 3.57

asken v ask (question) (of) 6.353, 17.204, 18.78, 20.330, 22.332, **B** 3.236, 10.310, 11.408, 12.233, **A** 11.178, 12.27; (~ **of**) enquire (of sb.) (about sth.) 1.46, 10.5, 11.104, 18.24, 20.125, **B** 13.309, 16.65, A 12.11, ~ **after** enquire concerning 7.180, 12.215, A 12.79, ~ **at** 6.56; (make) request (for) 22.188, **B** 7.75, 10.203; ~ (**of**) beg, pray for [grace, mercy *etc*] (from) 6.14, 8.319, 9.237, 14.56, 132, 17.256, 18.260, 19.280, 19.268, 21.131, B 14.229, 17.334; demand 3.272, 275, 299, 301, 4.97, 7.36, 8.78, 15.291, 16.291, B 14.260, A 1.178; call for 1.34; claim 3.245, 13.49, 16.101, 17.70, 20.387, 21.482, 22.266, *ger.* request, claim 21.482; seek A 1.100; require Pr 21, 3.335, 404, 5.67, 18.78, 19.273, 20.417, 442, 21.231, 479, **B** Pr 120, 2.27, 18.348

askes *n.pl.* B 3.98 = **asyshes** n

aslepe *av* asleep 2.53, 5.108, 21.5, 22.51, **B** 11.5, 15.11

asoilen v 12.6, A 12.11 = **assoylen** v

asondry *a* separate B 17.165

asparen v spare B 15.140; *and see* **sparen** v

(a)spelen v save 6.431, 13.76

aspyen v (*p.t.* **aspy(e)de** 9.207, 21.337) observe (secretly) 4.53, 6.152; examine 2.235, 19.36; find out 2.46, 3.109, 12.143, 14.167, B 6.129, A 11.226; seek B 16.170; discover 8.232, 9.207, 21.303, B 8.127, Z 7.274; descry, catch sight of 15.153, 21.337, A 12.103

assay n trial, testing B 10.255

as(s)ayen v try 6.356; try out B 16.106; examine 3.5; find out 16.162, 20.71, B 16.74; have a go 8.22

assail(l)en v attack, besiege 13.62, 21.227, 22.126, 297, 375; afflict 2.297; tempt 20.330

assche n ash-tree Z 5.45

asse n ass ~ **bak** back of an ass 20.9

asselen v 19.6 *see* **as(s)elen** v

assemblee n gathering B Pr 218

assemblen v come together B 2.57

assent(e) n mutual agreement 16.108, B 9.116; sentiment, opinion B 4.187

assenten v assent, agree Pr 190, 2.68, 155, 170, 3.153, 4.98, 187, 190, 8.54, 10.106, B 4.182, 188, A 4.89; consent 19.266; approve 8.36

assignen v indicate, specify B 4.126

as(s)oylen v absolve [sacramentally] Pr 68, 3.42, 50, 180, 358, 6.168, 257, 294, 9.4, 12.16, 19.162, 21.186, 191, 398, B 5.272, Z 3.171; solve, explain 11.156, 14.155, B 11.221; answer, resolve 12.140, 17.114, B 3.237, A 12.11

ast *2 sg. pr.* Z 3.156 = **hast**; *see* **hauen** v

asterten v avoid 13. 211

astronom(i)en n astronomer 17.96, 21.245

astronomye n (the art of) astronomy 21.245, B 10.209

aswagen v lessen, relieve 6.88

at *prep.* at 2.68, 3.490, 5.29 *etc*, B 4.131; at the value of 5.97, 8.166; behind 22.69; from Pr 205, 2.176, 3.254, 375, 7.56, 292, 12.57, 13.158, 15.103, 19.211, 21.402, 22.19; in 20.416, B Pr 85; in time of 5.129, 10.190, 11.233, 15.5, 22.20; of 1.203, 3.26, 6.56; on 6.324, 9.21, 154, 321, 351, 11.252, 12.110, 16.54, 21.197, B 7.17, A 2.40; to 3.417, 7.214, 9.87, 16.63 *in phrr.* ~ **þe ale** Pr 43, **þe barre** 3.448, ~ **bedde** A 2.52, ~ **ese** 3.44, **þe freres** 7.27, **þe furste** 2.210, ~ **herte** 9.183, ~ **heste** 3.148, ~ **ynne** 10.4, ~ **large** 22.192, ~ **lykyng** 15.168, ~ **þe newe feire** A 5.171, ~ **... nombre** 22.255, ~ **ones** 11.252, 13.31, ~ **þe stuyues** 13.74, ~ **wille** Pr 38, ~ **worthe** 14.66; *in names* = living at / by ~ **þe-Noke** A 5.115, ~ **þe-Style** 6.207

at(t)achen v arrest 2.211, 252; sequestrate 18.278; vouch for 11.310

a-taken v catch in the act, *p.p.* 3.139

atamen v broach 19.70

ateynen v find false or corrupt 22.162

athynken v (*impers.*) cause remorse, grieve 6.100, B 18.89

aþrest *a* afflicted with thirst A 12.82

atyer n fine apparel 2.15

atymyen v attain, manage 19.242, 246n

atiren v dress up, attire B 2.19, 166

a-to *av* in two 8.64, 20.75, 21.340

atones *avl phr.* B 17.53; *see* **ones** *av*

atte *prep. phr.* (= **at the**) 3.34, 4.132, **B** 5.197, 6.102, 115, 10.52, 11.118, **A** 7.48

attese *prep. phr.* 1.19 = **at ese**

attyf Z 7.235 = **actif** *a*

attre n poisonous, rotten matter B 12.255

atw(e)(y)n(n)e *av* in two Pr 114, B 7.115; apart 18.190

auctour n **B** 10.245, 15.120, 374 = **autor** n

audiense n a hearing 7.93

auditour n auditor, accountant 21.464

au3te *p.t.* **A** 2.21, 5.71, 7.123, **aughtest** *2 sg.* A 1.73 = **ouhte(st)**; *see* **owen** v

auht (ou3t, ouht) *prn* anything 6.111, 7.35, 8.235, **B** 11.49, 13.300, 416; something 7.45, 15.12, = everything 7.123; *in phrr.* **ar come** ~ **longe** before very long 17.214, **by** ~ (**þat**) as far as 7.283, 12.143; *av* at all 7.176, A 8.61

auncel (auncer) n weighing-balance 6.224

aungel A 10.143 *etc*, B Pr 128 *etc* = **angel** n

aunpolle *n* flask, ampulla 7.164

aunte *n* aunt 6.128, (**Abstinence**) 6.439, (*Latro*) 6.329

au(e)ntur(e) *n* chance, luck, *in phrr.* **an** ~ in case, lest perchance 3.70, 433, 8.40, **B** 3.72, 13.72, **good** ~ by good luck 8.79

aunt(e)ren *v* (*refl.*) venture, dare 10.218, 20.230, 22.175

auntrous *a as n* adventurous (knights) 20.14

auter *n* altar [of church] 5.164, 17.279, B 5.108, A 3.50, [of sacrifice] 18.263

autor (aucto(u)r) *n* authority 11.149, B 10.245; (Latin) writer B 15.374

auaylen (availlen) *v* help, be of use to 9.7, 274, 19.83, 22.179, B 10.272

auaryce (auaris) *n* avarice, (the sin of) greed 1.191, 2.91, 16.365, B 15.247, A 8.40, (*person.*) 16.85, 22.123

auarous(e) B 15.85 *see* **auerous** *a*

avauncen (avaunsen) *v* benefit, cause to prosper 10.258; promote 1.187, 3.36, ? 13.103 (*or* appoint), A 4.116

avengen *v* avenge 22.385n; (*refl.*) avenge oneself 6.74 (B 13.330); take vengeance upon 3.93

auenture *n* B 3.72, 13.72 *see* **au(e)ntur(e)** *n*

auer *n* wealth, property 6.32

auerous *a* avaricious, greedy 1.187, 16.279, B 15.85, *a as n* 14.21

auysen *v* (*refl.*) reflect, consider 17.54, (*person.*) 4.21

auoutrye *n* (the act of) adultery B 12.74

auowe *n* solemn vow 7.63, **B** Pr 71, 5.398; *and see* **vowe** *n*

avowen *v*[1] affirm 3.312, 15.115, 20.224, Z 3.162

auowen *v*[2] vow B 5.382

away (awey) *av* away 4.100, 10.229, 14.117, 17.144, 19.334, 22.56, 174, B Pr 166, **A** 4.93, 7.183; off, away 3.422, 4.60, 7.221, 8.118, 10.136, 12.240, 18.49, 155, 19.291, 21.156, **B** 5.107, 14.83, Z 7.59; aside 22.168, B 17.89; to the side B 5.108; along 19.52; *in phrr.* **fer** ~, **wel** ~ far and away, very much **B** 12.262, 14.209, 17.43; (*as predicate*) removed 12.148; absent, missing 19.138, B 1.190

awey 2.225 *etc* = **away** *av*

a-werke *av* to work 8.197

awayten *v* waylay 10.301; watch stealthily 4.52, B 13.361; attend to 6.279; find out 17.63, B 10.332; look for B 16.257; wait / watch for B 16.138

awaken *v* (*p.t.* **awaked(e)** 5.1 *etc*, B 16.167, **awoke** 9.293, *p.p.* awaked 22.1) awake 2.103, 5.1, 9.293, 13.215, 15.1, 272, 16.77, 19.334, 22.387; wake up 7.8; wake, rouse Pr 214, (*fig.*) 15.308; arise 6.103, 139, 394; spring up 8.344

awreken *v* (*p.p.* **awreke** 2.206, 17.4, **awroke** 8.208 *etc*) avenge 2.206, 8.158, 170, 208, 300, 17.4, 22.203, (*refl.*) vent (oneself) 10.290

ax *n* axe 3.458; battle-axe 14.51

axen *v* 7.180, A 11.178 = **asken** *v*

#axesse *n* attack of fever A 5.203

bab(e)len *v* mumble, mutter AB 5.8

baby *n* baby 19.94, B 17.96

#baburlippid *a.* with thick protruding lips 6.198c.

bacbiten *v see* **bakbiten** *v*

bache *n* valley 7.158

bacheler *n* (bachelor) knight 20.87, B 16.179; bachelor (of divinity) Pr 85, 9.248, A Pr 90

baco(u)n *n* bacon 6.201, 8.332, 9.148, 10.280, 15.68, 101

bad(e) *p.t.* 2.158, 219 *et p.*, A 12.106, **baed** 22.377; *see* **bidden** *v*

badde *a* wicked, vicious 9.16, B 10.280; ~**lyche** *av* poorly 4.55, 17.197; #~**nesse** *n* wickedness B 12.48

baed *p.t.* 22.377 = **bad(e)** *p.t.*

baer *p.t.* 18.115 *et p.*; *see* **beren** *v*[1]

ba(e)r *a* 22.184 *see* **bar**

bagge *n* bag, sack Pr 42, 5.52, 7.163, 9.98, 120, 139, 154; wallet 10.85; money-bag (*meton.*, = money) 22.142

bayard *n* (bay) horse [*as name*] 4.56, 8.178, 192, 19.72, B 4.124, Z 3.158

bail(l)if (bayl(i)e) *n* bailiff [sherrif's under-officer] 2.60, 3.2

bak(k)(e) *n* back 6.69, 9.154, 169, 20.9, **B** 2.172, 3.196, 199, 13.317, **A** 8.15, 12.70; cloak, outer garment [to cover back] 13.71, B 10.360

bakbiten *v* slander, detract [from someone's good name behind his back] 2.85, *ger.* 6.95, 16.361, B 5.88; **bakbitare** *n* detractor 18.46 (B 16.43)

baken *v* (*p.p.* (y)bake(n)) 8.178, B 6.292) bake 8.178, 192, 317, 333, **B** 6.182, 282, 15.432, ? roast 9.93n, B 15.462n

bakere *n* baker Pr 222, 3.80, 4.120

bakken *v* clothe A 11.188, clothe oneself Z 3.160

bakstere (baxter) *n* baker B Pr 219, 3.79

balayshen *v* beat with rod 6.157

bald(e)li(che) 16.55, 18.115, 22.70, 132, 328, Z 7.61 = **boldely** *av*

baldore, ~ere *comp.* 4.102, 9.334 *see* **bold** *a*

bale *n* wrong, misdeed 4.85, 88, 89, 20.206; evil A 10.147; sin 12.58; death, the life-destroyer (*semi-person.*) 20.34; misery 13.21, 141; ~ **deeþ** (*semi-person.*) baleful death B 18.35

baleyse *n* rod [for flogging] 11.123, (*fig.*) scourge, tribulation B 12.12

baly Z Pr 38 = **bely** *n*

balk(e) *n* ridge of unploughed land 8.114n

balled *a* bald 22.184, (*fig.*) crafty, glib 11.38

*ballok-knyf *n* knob-hafted knife B 15.124n

bande *p.t.* 6.218; *see* **bynden** *v*

bane *n* destruction (of life) 8.350, A 6.93

baner *n* banner, military standard 22.69, 96; (bishop's) banner [*sc.* the Cross] A 8.15

banyer *n* standard-bearer B 15.435

banisshen *v* drive away A 3.274

bank *n* bank, slope B Pr 8; embankment B 17.103

bannen *v* curse 1.58, 10.230, 11.192; condemn 3.143, B 15.252; reproach B 10.7; strongly forbid 9.162

bapte(w)me (baptisme) *n* (the sacrament of) baptism 12.60, 14.201, 20.418, 419, **B** 11.82, 14.184, Z 6.63; = the water from Christ's side [symbolizing baptism; *see* Jn 19.34] 21.325

baptisen (baptiȝen) baptise B 16.250, = (administer Christian baptism to) **B** 10.345, 11.77, 79, 80, *(fig.)* 17.268, 19.88, *ger.* **baptiȝynge** administering baptism B 11.78

baptist *n* baptist 10.181, 21.38, *etc. see* **Iohan, St** (the Baptist)

bar *p.t.* 2.3 *et p.*, **baren** *pl.* 6.415, B 5.107 *see* **beren** *v*[1]

bar(e) *a* bare 6.150; naked 6.157; devoid of hair 22.184; *(as intensive)* the very 18.39; ~**fot** *a* barefoot 9.121, 20.9

bareyne *a* barren, unproductive 20.109

bargayn *n* business transaction 2.92, Z 2.97; purchase, bargain 5.96; agreement (to barter / sell) 6.394

barke *n* shell, husk 12.147, 148

barly *n* barley-meal 6.225, ~ **breed** 8.142, A 7.169; barley-sheaves Z 7.170

barn(e) (bern) *n* offspring, descendant 3.188, 5.70, 172 (B 10.321), 17.58, *in phr.* ~**es bastardes** bastard offspring 5.71; (young) child 8.306, **B** 9.78, 165, 15.455, A 10.147, *spec.* = the infant Christ 2.3, 19.86, 90, 20.136, 241, 243, B 12.146, A 12.117; young person B 11.77; person 14.126, B 11.82, A 12.117; *pl.* people, *in phr.* †**barnes of Israel** children of Israel B 10.279

barnhoed *n* childhood, ? warriorship *(fig.)* 18.136

baro(u)n *n* lord, nobleman Pr 220, 5.172, 6.123; peer, great baron 22.129; baron [noble ranking between knight and earl] 3.261, **B** 10.320, 13.166; judge B 3.321

barre *n* barrier [outside gate] *(fig.)* 7.238; the Bar [rail before judge's seat in law court] 3.448, 4.132, 169, 9.45, **B** Pr 212, 4.169; bar [for bolting door] 20.281, 364

barren *v* (*p.p.* **ybarred**) bar 20.284, 21.167

barste *p.t.* 8.175; *see* **bresten** *v*

#**bas(e)lard** *n* (fashionable) dagger [worn at the girdle] 3.457, B 15.121, 124, A 11.214

basket *n* basket 18.155

bastard *n* bastard 2.24 (Mede), 2.144 (Fals), 6.133 (Ione), 5.65, 9.168; *a* illegitimate 5.71*n*; ? grafted, ? cultivated B 16.69

bat *n* clod, lump 18.92; loaf A 7.165

bat *contr. pr.* Z 4.47 = **bet(eth)**; *see* **beten** *v*

batayle *n* Pr 108, 112, 8.49, 14.50, 17.288, 22.262; warfare 3.475, 8.350; (single) combat 20.66, B 16.164

*****batauntliche** *av* with noisy eagerness 16.55

baþen *v* bathe B 17.95

*****bat-nelde** *n* pack-needle 6.218*c*

batren *v* thump, slap B 3.199

#**baud(e)** *n* procurer 8.72; procuress 6.189; go-between A 3.45; ?harlot 3.164

*****baudekyn** *n* little go-between A 3.40

baw(e) *interj.* *(expressing scorn)* bah! 12.76, 21.399

baxtere A Pr 98 = **bakstere** *n*

be *inf.* Pr 54, *p.p.* Pr 62, 3.259 *etc*, *subjv.* Pr 104, 150, *etc*; *see* **ben** *v*

be (by) *prep.* 12.145, B 3.15, Z 8.69; close to 7.218, 8.2, A 5.136; of 10.241, 14.72, 18.195; on 10.232, 20.316, B 18.45; to 1.116, 20.7, 169; in 9.214, 243, 11.74, 12.37; along 22.188, 22.1, B 10.305, Z 1.109; past 5.6, 11.108; alongside 2.180; with 3.40, 4.62, 7.30, 11.126; in relation to 13.229, 14.141, 16.110, **B** 1.28, 4.71, 10.187, 12.210; with reference to A 12.108; in regard to 6.36, 7.267, B 11.153, 418, A 11.209; in the case of B 15.73; through 1.158, 3.413, 7.54, B 1.139, A 10.157; for 6.40, 16.120; by means of 2.4, 6.381, 10.105 *etc*, B 7.128, A 7.21; on the basis of 2.122, B 10.332, 344, **A** 8.153, 11.196; according to 1.86, B 6.251, A 8.135; in accordance with Pr 78, 1.90, 2.147, **B** 3.7, 10.386, **A** 10.91, 11.276; concerning 3.287, 6.70, 162, 10.165, 11.11, 13.111; from the example of 3.142, A 11.275; from 4.154, 17.104, 22.275; = to the extent of 7.141, 19.60, A 4.29; in, on 6.373; during 7.64*n*, 111, B 6.101; *for phrasal vv.* **setten** ~ *etc, see main entries; in phrr.* ~ **dayes...** continually 9.222; **day** ~ **day** 9.341; ~ **fer** 22.315; ~**... myhte / power** according to one's power 6.295, 9.17, B 10.268, A 5.75; ~ **siht of** by the witness of 1.200, 2.115; ~ **that** from what 16.295, by that time 8.314, 322*n*; ~ **þis day** today 7.9, 8.302, (?*oath*) 4.172; *in oaths:* 3.141, 8.234, A 2.92, Z 4.152; *conj. in conjv. phr.* ~ **so** provided that 4.98, 5.39, 6.331, 12.4, 15.256, 21.450, 22.222, B 12.166; ?**so that** 14.279*n*

beaupere *n* elder, reverend father 20.239; venerable priest 9.248

beaute *n* beauty 13.10, B 12.48

beche *n* beech-tree 5.120

become *p.t.* A Pr 91, 7.181 *see* **bycomen** *v*

bed *imp. sg.* Z 7.45; *see* **beden** *v*

bed *n* (*dat.* **bedde**) bed Pr 44, 6.415, 7.4, 8.108, 9.145, 254, 19.303, B 10.65; *in phrr.* **a- (on)** ~ in bed 10.273; **at** ~ **and at boord** = in all conjugal duties and relations A 2.52; *in cpds.* # ~ **bourde** *n* bed-play, sexual relations 10.293; ~ **chaunbre** *n* bed room 6.228; ~ **rede(ne)** *a* bed-ridden 7.107, 9.34, A 7.130, Z 7.197*a as in* 9.177, B 6.191

bedden *v* provide with a bed, *p.p.* 17.197; (*refl.*) go to bed B 2.98

beddyng *ger.* bedding, somewhere to sleep Z 7.199; bed 16.73

bede *n* prayer 7.16, **B** 5.8, 12.28, ~**(s) biddyng** saying of prayers 12.86, 21.378, *in phr.* **peire** ~ set of rosary-beads B 15.122; command Z 1.56, 2.60

bedel 2.111, 3.2 = **bydel** *n*

bed(e)man *n* messenger, spokesman 3.43, 48; bedesman [one who prays for another, *esp.* religious] 3.274, B 15.205, 427

bedredene *a* 7.107 *etc*; *see* **bed** *n*

beden *p.t. pl.* 3.28, 15.27, 20.53, 21.143, *p.p.* 2.56; *see* **bidden** *v*

beden *v* (*p.p.* **bede(n), boden**) offer 10.270; invite 2.56

beel-syre 20.282 = **belsyre** *n*

beem *n* beam, plank B 10.264, 276

been *inf.* 5.15, *pr. pl.* 7.69; *see* **ben** *v*

beenfeet *n* good deed 7.42, 263

beer *inf.* 22.91; **beere** *p.t.* B 5.138, *subjv.* B 15.121; *see* **beren** *v*

beest B 3.267 *etc* = **best** *n*

beet *p.t.* 8.175, 20.282, 22.191 *see* **beten** *v*

***befloberen** *v* muddy, soil B 13.401; *see* **flobren** *v*

before *av* 21.115, A 7.226; *prep.* 2.100, 13.124, 15.211, A 8.39; *see* **byfore** *av, prep.*

begeneld 10.266 = **begynneld** *n*

begen *v* 9.63 = **beggen** *v*

begere 3.274 = **beggare** *n*

beggare *n* beggar 2.173, 3.274, 5.65, 6.49, 7.54, 99, 8.193, 201, 210, 224, 279, 326, 9.61, 98, 161, 171, 12.117, 13.71, 94, 14.140, 15.297, 16.13, 55, 89, 350, 22.239, 241, B 3.219, 6.194, 7.80, 82, 10.360, 11.276, 13.267, 15.341, A 12.71, *in phr.* ~**s and biddares** Pr 41 (*trs*), 8.210, 9.61, B 15.205, ~ **of kynde** natural beggars 9.168*n*; destitute person, pauper 6.123, 125, 16.103, 364, B 4.124, 9.90, 10.84, 11.197, 199, 13.303, A 10.115, 11.188; rascal, knave 8.265, 12.113, 15.304 (*with prn*)

#**beggarie** *n* (the practice of) begging 9.162, 165

begged Z 7.220 = **(a)-beggeth** *av*

beggen *v*¹ *v* beg (for) 5.29, 51, 90, 174, 6.313, 9.62, 121, 161, 189, Z 3.160; ask for alms (for) 9.86, 10.186, 16.70, 336, 22.238, B 6.192, 15.328 *in phrr.* ~ **(and) / or bidden** 9.63, B 6.236, 11.276, 15.256, 16.370, **borwen** 16.372, Z 5.144, *ger.* 17.8, 27

beggen *v*² Z 4.78 = **byggen** *v*

***begynneld** *n* beggar 9.154*c*, 10.266

#**begynnere** *n* originator A 10.53

begynnyng *ger.* first stage A 10.80

begon *v* beset, overcome, *p.p.* A 2.24

begruchen 8.155 = **bigruchen** *v*

beȝonde (biyonde) *av* beyond, *in phrr.* **fro** ~ from abroad 3.145, **of** ~ abroad, in foreign lands B 4.128

byhyhte *p.t.* 3.30 *see* **bihoten** *v*

beheld *p.t.* Pr 14, 13.156, Z 4.159 *see* **byholden** *v*

behynde 16.49, A 5.74 *see* **byhynde** *av, prep.*

behoten 8.301 = **byhoten** *v*

behouen A 8.116, 10.74 = **bihouen** *v*

beygh (*pl.* **beyus**) *n* necklace, collar Pr 178, 180, 191

beyre *prn* (*gen. pl. of* **bo**), *in phr.* **þer beyre** of both of them 20.36

bek(e)ne *n* beacon, signal fire 19.230

bekennen A 11.165 = **bykennen** *v*

beknowen 5.92 = **byknowen** *v*

belauȝen *v* laugh / rejoice about, *p.t.* A 8.107

beleue 8.97, 15.239, 16.230, **beleuen** 7.125, 11.132 = **byleue(n)** *n, v*

bely *n* stomach Pr 42, A 12.70, 74, *in phr.* ~ **ioye** pleasure in eating B 7.119, A 8.112

belyen *v* (*p.p.* **bylowe(n)** 9.181 *etc*) tell lies against, accuse falsely 9.181, 20.355, B 2.22, 5.408, 10.22, A 5.76

belle *n* (church) bell 22.59; (ornamental) bell Pr 180 *et p.*

belouȝ *p.t.* A 8.107 *see* **belauȝen** *v*

***belouren** *v* scowl / frown at A 8.107

belowen *p.p.* A 5.76 *see* **belyen** *v*

belsyre *n* grandfather 2.121, 20.282; forefather 10.236

belwen *v* bellow B 11.341

be(n) *v* (*pr. sg.* **am** 1.72, **art** 1.80, **best** (*with fut. sense*) 7.235, Z 7.238, **beth** B 10.345, †A 11.197, **is** Pr 40, *pl.* **ar(e)(n)** Pr 93, 126, (*after sg. subj.* 5.59, B 9.121, **ben** A 10.210), **ben** Pr 87, **beth** 3.28, A 6.110, **buth** 9.160, *imper. pl.* **beth** 1.171, (*with prn.*) be 3.85, *subjv.* Pr 104, *pl.* Pr 202, *p.t.* **was** Pr 15, *pl.* **were(n)** Pr 53, *subjv.* Pr 2, *p.p.* **(y)be(n)** Pr 62, B 11.242, A 11.195) be Pr 1 *et p.*; (*subjv.*) may be Pr 150, is 1.124; let it be 3.422; if... / are 5.165; let us be Pr 202; *in constrr. without* **to** = to be 3.28, = (he *etc*) will be 2.104, + *p.p.* = once (sth.) is done 3.247, 389, 8.211, 20.104, 21.189; *with p.t. of* **hauen** = would have been 6.214 *etc*; (have) exist(ence) 18.217; become, be made 5.71

bench *n* bench [at table] Pr 200, 6.361, **syde** ~ bench at side table 9.252; *in phr.* **Kynges** ~ court of ~ [= highest law court] A Pr 95

benden *v* bend, stoop 10.37

bene *n* (*gen. pl.* **ben(e)en(e)** A 7.165 / Z 7.162) bean 8.177, 226, 306, 317, 326, B 6.182, 194, A 7.169, made of beans A 7.165; (*fig.*) = thing of little value 12.94

benefice *n* ecclesiastical living 3.33, B 3.314, Z 3.32

beneth 18.85 = **bynethe** *av*

benigne *a* gentle, kind 18.11, 20.119, B 16.7; *av* ~ **lyche** with good will 14.57

benyson *n* (priest's) blessing B 13.236

berd *n* beard 6.201

bere *n* bear 9.196, B 15.299

beren *v*¹ (*p.t. 2 sg.* **bere** B 3.196, **bar** A 3.183), *3 sg.* **ba(e)r** 7.161, 18.115, *pl.* **beren** 6.415, Z Pr 53, *p.p.* **(y)bor(e)(n)** 1.58, 2.144, 14.31) carry 2.177, 3.422, 4.60, 126, 6.344, 415, 7.161, 163, 221, 8.108, 288, 9.139, 10.93, 13.54, 15.162, 222. 16.176, 18.115, 155, 271, 20.476, 21.49, 22.70, 96, 117, 286, *ger.* 8.198, B 3.41, 5.107, 6.142, 14.304, 15.97, Z Pr 53, 7.61, (*fig.*) A 8.15; support 2.3, 20.476; wear Pr 178, 16.97, 21.71, B 15.569; bear (weapon) 3.457, 475, 14.50; hold B 6.166; maintain, bear B 15.171, ~ **witnesse** 2.85, B

7.51 *etc*, *ger.* 16.361, B 5.88; thrust (through) 20.87, (down) 22.132; have [name] 3.143, 16.201, 17.261; give birth to B 9.165, *p.p.* **(y)bore(n)** 1.58, 2.144, 14.31, 90, 20.136, 241, 21.71, **B** 15.455, 17.123; bear [leaves, fruit] 2.28, 16.247, B 16.70; **beryng(e)** *ger.* behaviour, conduct 21.256, 22.116, **B** 10.256, 11.300, 13.277, A 10.115; demeanour B 15.202

beren *v*² bellow 13.150

berye *n* grape 2.28

berken *v* bark 9.261

berkere *n* barking dog 9.260

bern¹ 18.280, A 3.250 = **bu(y)rn(e)** *n*

bern² 17.58 = **barn(e)** *n*

bern(e)³ *n* barn 4.60, 8.179, 12.216, 21.346, 360, Z 7.61

berne 3.237, 422 = **brennen** *v*

berthe (burthe) *n* birth 14.93, 20.248, 21.81

berw *n* hill 7.226

beseken A 11.99, *ger.* A 11.108 = **bisechen** *v*

beside *av* nearby A 2.42

best *2 sg. pr.* 7.235, Z 7.238 *see* **ben** *v*

best(e) *a. sup.* best 6.41, 345, 10.191, B 13.314; finest 3.426, 6.228, 8.329, B 5.267; most excellent 21.436, B 13.171; most advantageous 3.383, 5.38, 11.233, 22.207, **B** 13.290, 14.30; *a as n* B 6.299, A 5.136, (= the best thing) 1.201, 4.9, 83, 8.19, 220, 12.144, 14.91, B 1.42, 4.30; one's best 3.252; *in phr.* **for the ~** as the best (thing) 12.144, 15.128, 17.297, A 11.154, in the best interests of (someone / everyone) 7.125, 12.168, 16.21, B 10.367, 11.197; **of þe ~** of the best quality A 2.127, **to þe ~** (in the) best (way) / to the best end B 5.124, A 8.62

best(e) *av* best 8.120, 9.248, 12.106, B 5.24; most B 6.87, A 11.195; most thoroughly 5.43; most highly 8.250(2), B 15.156; *in phr.* **don ~** 10.110, 16.34, B 9.97, **þe ~** in the most advantageous way A 10.95; **~ liken** be most pleasing 9.28

beste *n* living creature [*incl.* man] 10.230, 14.162, 15.264, **B** 9.32, 13.15, A 10.27; animal 7.158, 10.233, 11.242, 13.143, 180, 186, 191, 14.80, 169, 15.18, 244 *et p.*, B 10.32, A 10.175; (*spec.*) = (wild) animal 9.224, 13.136, 16.10, 17.28 *et p.*, **B** 6.140, 7.90, A 10.67; = (farm) animal (*pl.* cattle, livestock) 3.420, 426, 7.186, 8.189, 9.269, 11.251, 14.88, 21.264, B 3.267, **A** 3.252, 4.153, 7.181, 11.310

bestryden Z 3.158 = **bystriden** *v*

bet(te) *av* better A Pr 63; *in phrr.* **don ~** 14.10, 16.34; **þe ~ the more** satisfactorily B 11.174, A 10.82, the more successfully 7.239, 8.42, the more properly 20.372; **ben þe ~** be better off 5.96

bet *p.t.* Pr 115, *p.p.* A 4.80 *see* **beten** *v*

beten *v*¹ (*contr. pr.* **bat** Z 4.47, *p.t.* **be(e)t(te)** Pr 115, 8.175, *p.p.* **(y)bet(e)(n)** 4.89) beat, flog 5.135, 7.60, 8.81, 11.123, (*fig.*) B 12.12; punish Pr 115, 4.89, 5.169, 8.163, 22.27; chastise 13.239; strike 20.98, B 16.127;

belabour (with blows) 4.102, 6.141, B 4.59, *ger.* (*fig.*) 15.149; flail, thresh Z 7.170; lay low 3.237; overcome 20.262; beat [cloth in cleaning] B 14.19, (*fig.*) 16.332

beten *v*² repair A 8.30; relieve 8.246

bet(t)(e)re *a* better (than), superior (to) 1.135, 2.11, 6.243, 381, 12.145, 16.50, 177, 231, 18.87, 19.310, 20.344, 22.16, 319, **B** Pr 191, 1.208 15.73, A 12.3, Z 7.55; greater 3.164; easier 16.88; more valuable 18.284, B 12.294; more powerful B 17.173; *a as n* the superior 12.142; superior 2.30, B 11.381, *in phrr.* **no ~** nothing better 1.8, 14.210, 15.125, B 4.193, **þe ~** the better 15.262, better off 4.86, B 15.425, A 7.210, **neuer þe ~** no better off 4.89

bet(t)(e)r(e) *av* better 1.143, 7.275, 10.57, 71, 11.217, Z 5.35, (*ellip.*) (to do) better 8.162; more satisfactorily 5.145, 9.36, B Pr 66, A 11.165, 206; more successfully 14.196, A 11.31; more fittingly Pr 120, B 13.51; more thoroughly 1.136, 5.142, 10.57, B 11.385, A 8.121, Z 3.169; more easily Pr 163, B 5.419; **þe ~** the better 10.137, the more successfully Pr 33, 3.424, **wel þe ~** much / all the better A 7.138, *in phr.* **do (þe) ~** 5.119, 14.11, 17.122, **B** 1.34, 9.96, A 10.89; more 11.132, 210, 14.136, **B** 5.232, 11.253, 16.231, A 6.35, 12.31, **þe ~** the more B 10.187

beteren *v* give advantage / benefit (to) *p.p.* 5.21

beth *imp. pl.* 1.171 *et p.*, *3 pl. pr.* 3.28, 16.200 *et p.*, Z 3.158, *3 sg.* (*with fut. sense*) 19.86

betrauaillen 15.211 = **bytrauaillen** *v*

bette¹ 8.42 = **bet** *av*; **bette**² *p.t.* B 6.178 *etc*; *see* **beten** *v*¹

betwene *av* 10.120, *prep.* A 7.165, **betwyn** A 5.55, 10.206 = **bytwene** *av, prep.*

beuerege *n* drink (to seal bargain) 6.394

bew-pere 9.248 = **beau pere** *n*

#bewsoun *n.pl.* fine fellows Z 3.158n

by¹ Pr 78 *et p. see* **be** *prep.*

by² Z 2.57 = **be(n)** *v*

bible *n* book B 15.89; **þe ~** the Bible 3.426, 484, 5.169, 8.238, 10.88, 11.116, 18.222, **B** 6.234, 7.137, 9.41, 10.279, 327, 11.269, 392, Z 7.269; copy of the Bible B 13.186; *in phr.* **þe boek ~** the Book of Scripture 9.304, B 10.88

bicam *p.t.* 7.127 *et p.*; *see* **bycomen** *v*

bycause (of) *avl phr.* by reason of B 3.100

byc(c)he *n* bitch 6.403

bycomen *v* (*p.t.* **bycam** 7.127 *et p.*, **bicom** B 10.138, *pl.* **bycome** 12.111, A 1.112 *etc*) go to 15.151, B 5.642; become 7.127, 11.145, 12.111, 13.19, 17.267, 18.135, 20.60, 221, 21.38, 22.41, **A** Pr 91, 1.112, 2.32, 7.181; ~ **(to)** be fitting / suitable for 3.264, 5.61, 21.42

bid *contr. pr.* 17.62 *see* **bidden** *v*

biddare 8.210, 9.61, Z Pr 37 = **bidder(e)** *n*

bidden *v* (*contr. pr.* **bid** 17.62, **byt**, **bit** 3.306, 20.270 *etc*, *p.t.* **bad(e)** 2.158, 219, *pl.* **beden** 3.28, *p.p.* **beden (boden** B) 2.56) ask 6.344, 14.29, 22.286, B 3.219;

make a plea for B 8.103; pray 7.16, 142, 239, 14.57, 196, 19.217, **B** 5.227, 10.199 (2), 11.263, 12.9, 17, 28, 13.237, 15.323, A 12.106, Z 7.240, ~ **of** pray for 7.60; supplicate 19.209; ask for alms, (go) beg(ging) (for) 9.63, 16.350, 370, 17.2, **B** 6.236, 7.79, 82, 11.276, 15.256; command, direct 3.306, 8.227, 11.45, 15.78, 17.190, 20.270, **B** 4.187, 9.15, 92, 10.199 (1), 252, 12.54, 15.185, 219, Z 7.269; advise Z 2.41; urge 7.247, 8.227, B 15.312, Z 7.248; invite 2.56, A 1.138; wish 6.69; **biddyng** *ger.* praying, prayer 12.86, 16.350, **B** 11.152, 15.425; entreaty B 5.584; command, bidding 1.74, 3.417, 10.98, 16.63, 20.416, B 1.110, A 9.93, Z 1.23

bidder(e) (biddare) *n* one who asks for alms, beggar Pr 41, 8.210, 9.61, B 13.242, 15.205

bydel *n* beadle, under-bailiff 2.60, 111, 3.2

byden *v* (*contr. pr.* **byt** Z 7.135) remain B 9.134; remain in, endure B 18.309*n*; continue (working) Z 7.135; wait patiently 22.48, *pr. p. a* **bydynge** = steadfast B 20.142

bidowe *n* short curved sword or long broad knife A 11.214

bidrauelen *v* cover with spittle, *p.p.* B 5.191 (*and see* **dreuelen** *v*)

#**bidroppen** *v* besprinkle B 13.321

byfallen *v* (*p.t.* **byfel** 6.325, **byful** Pr 7, *subjv.* **byfulle** 6.27) happen 9.313, 10.8, 17.97, 18.167, 21.243, 22.351, B 7.167; befall, happen (to) B Pr 6, ~ **of** 6.325, B 9.159; (*subjv.*) may befall 5.199, 20.97, might / should befall 6.27, Z 4.135; belong / pertain to 1.48, 20.379; befit 13.108, **B** 11.293, 15.104, 16.60; be the duty of 9.129

byfore[1] *av* in front 7.167, 20.127, 22.184, **B** 13.316, 17.105; ahead 16.54, B 15.435; = openly 6.117*n*; in a superior position 12.142, **ben** ~ be forward, take advantage 22.288*n*; earlier 5.109, 21.115, A 7.226; previously 22.371, B 16.140; in advance 3.302, 4.21, 16.3, 7, 17.97, 21.16, 55, 148, 244, B 14.142; *in phr.* ~ **and / ne bihynde** anywhere B 15.153, (*trs*) ? 6.117*n*

byfor(e)[2] *prep.* in front of 5.106, 9.254, 22.96, B 13.82; before 15.211, B 13.74; in(to) the presence of Pr 197 *et p.*, 13.124, A 8.39; in preference to 17.60, 201; before (= prior to) 2.100, 6.433, 18.167

byg(ge) *a* sturdy 8.224, 18.136

bigan *p.t.* 1.103 *et p.*; *see* **bygynnen** *v*

bygare Z 2.53 = **buggere** *n*

bygat *p.t.* 1.29 *see* **bygeten** *v*

bigerdel *n* purse 10.85

bygeten *v* (*p.t.* **bygat**) beget 1.29; conceive, *p.p.* 10.210, 14.31 (*and see* **byȝete** *n*)

†**biggen** *v* dwell, *pr.p.* **biggyng** B 5.128

byggen (bu(y)ggen) *v* (*p.t.* **bouhte** 2.3, *p.p.* **ybought** Pr 191) buy Pr 183, 6.225, 8.303, 9.28, 16.72, 18.158, B 5.244, 7.52, A 12.71, Z 3.160, *ger.* 21.236; make

purchases 3.86, 7.35; acquire, obtain 3.33, 82, 85, 4.85, 5.96; pay for 6.229, B 13.193; pay (penalty for) 15.304, ~ **the tyme** (interest on loan) 6.247; get hold of 18.165; redeem 2.3, 8.217, 12.60, 19.267, **B** 9.65, 11.207, Z 5.93

byggere A 2.44, 11.212 = **buggere** *n*

bigilen *v* deceive, delude 20.164, 323, 326, 327, 380, 382, 392, B 10.195; defraud 3.92, 95, 11.17, 14.5, B 13.361; perplex 17.107; lead astray (into sin) 1.37, 11.313, 15.79, 16.45, 20.162, B 10.120, 127

bigynnen *v* (*p.t.* **bigan** 1.103, *pl.* **bigonne** B 5.338, *subjv.* B 14.149) originate (with) 6.341; bring into existence 1.103, 17.134, 19.113, 20.163; begin, start 5.100, 102, 6.180, 349, 394, 7.6, 8.164, 9.243, 17.62, 20.183, 310, 399, 21.110, 116, **B** 2.74, 13.347, 14.149; set about 7.122, 20.48, 21.214, 327

bigynnyng *ger.* beginning (of existence) 18.204, (of the world) 19.113, 20.195, (of man) 8.239; origin 14.159, 19.113, 20.195

*****byglosen** *v* persuade with specious arguments 20.380

bygon Z 2.28 = **begon** *v*

bygonne *p.t.* **B** 5.338, 14.149 *see* **bygynnen** *v*

bigruchen *v* complain (at) 8.68, 155

byhe(e)ld *p.t.* 9.283, 13.156, 16.350, B Pr 13, **bihelte** 13.134 *see* **biholden** *v*

byheste *n* promise 10.253, **fayre** ~ fine promise 12.13, 22.118, **fals** ~ deceiving promise 18.123, 20.320, B 3.127

bihyhte *p.t.* 6.5 *etc*; *see* **bihoten** *v*

byhynde *av* behind 15.7, 21.342, *in phrr.* ~ **or bifore** secretly or openly, anywhere 6.117, (*trs*) B 15.153, **leuen** ~ abandon 15.7 **putten** ~ push aside B 14.208, *as pred. a* in the rear **B** 15.436, 17.105; overdue 7.39; *prep.* behind 6.69, 9.283, 16.49

byhofte *n* benefit, use 12.189

biholden *v* (*p.t.* **byhe(e)ld** 9.283, **bihelte** 13.134) look Pr 14, 13.134, B 7.138, 11.9; catch sight of 9.283; see 13.156, 16.350, B 5.109, Z 4.159; look to 19.67

bihoten *v* (*p.t.* **bihyhte** 6.5 *etc*) promise 3.30, 6.5, 7.68, 8.301, 18.246, 258, 20.317, 375, 22.111

bihouen *v* (*impers.*) be necessary 7.294, **B** 17.315, 18.400, A 8.116; be compelled to B 8.34; (*pers.*) need 9.89, **B** 5.38, 9.71

byiapen *v* deceive 1.63

bykam *p.t.* 13.19 *see* **bycomen** *v*

bykennen *v* commend (to) 2.51, 10.58, A 2.31

bikeren *v* contend, fight 22.79

byknowen *v* (*p.t.* **byknewe(n)** 11.257, 21.149, *p.p.* **byknowe** 3.36) know 3.36; make known Pr 210; recognise B 18.24; admit 21.149; acknowledge 5.92, 13.10; confess 6.206, 11.257

bile *n* bill B 11.357

byleue[1] *n* (religious) faith 11.296, 14.213, 16.230, 17.87, 126, **B** 11.218, 220, 13.211, 15.347, 392, *in phrr.* **false**

~ 21.47, **ferme** ~ 14.208, B 17.133; **good** ~ 11.307, **lele** ~ 12.88, 15.246, 17.22, 127, 158, B 15.438; **parfit** ~ 11.300, 17.266, B 14.193, **rihte** ~ 11.294, **soth-faste** ~ 11.131, 15.188, 17.119, 18.51, **trewe** ~ 18.210; (*spec.*) (the virtue of) faith 11.160, 19.176, 191; faith (in God) 18.255; = the Christian religion (**þe ~, oure ~**) 7.73, 9.218, 12.45, 17.294, 316, 18.255, B 10.204, **Holy Kirke** ~ 13.89, B 17.119, **londe of** ~ 21.336; creed 21.348, B 5.7; trust, confidence 17.95; belief B 11.299; = what I / we believe 8.97, 14.151, 15.239, B 7.176

byleue² 5.21, 21.236 = **bilyue** *n*

byleuen *v*¹ (*imp.* **byleef** 11.143) (~ **in, on**) believe (in) 1.78, 2.75, 3.356, 7.235, 10.192, 11.132, 17.135, 187, 255, 269, 286, 19.28, 42, 44, 96, 20.268, 21.182, **B** 10.121, 232, 234, 14.86, 15.393, 394, 395, 15.571, 578, 17.35, 42; believe, have faith 13.86, 14.13, 16.357, 17.123, 133, 18.250, 19.32, 35, 110, 21.174; accept as true 11.152, 157, 21.178, 182, **B** 13.274, 15.476; place one's trust in 10.169; hold as certain, think 7.125, 14.122, **B** 6.88, 13.254

byleuen *v*² dwell 3.347; remain (? leave) behind 12.214; leave off 8.176

bilyen B 5.408, 10.22 *see* **belyen** *v*

bilyue *n* livelihood 1.18, 5.21, 8.260, 16.336, 21.236

bylyuen 10.169 = **byleuen** *v*¹

bille *n* (written) petition / complaint 4.45, B 13.248

bille Z Pr 75 = **bulle** *n*

bylongen *v* belong 1.43; [as right] B Pr 110; be incumbent on / the duty (of) 5.66, 9.230, 11.157, B 10.357; be due (to) 9.262, B 9.78; be proper for 18.201; be an attribute of B 17.164; pertain to 19.144

bylouen *v* love, admire, *p.p.* 3.267, Z 5.96

bylowe(n) *p.p.* 9.181; B 2.22 *see* **belyen** *v*

†**bilowen** *v* (*refl.*) humble (oneself) B 6.227

bymenen *v*¹ mourn B 15.147

bymenen *v*² (*p.t.* **bymente** 20.16) mean, signify Pr 217, 1.1, 56, 20.16, 172; symbolise B 15.480

*****bymolen** *v* stain, spot B 14.4, 22

bynam *p.t.* B 6.240 = **bynom**

bynden *v* (*p.t.* **bo(e)nd(e)** 19.72, 20.446, *p.p.* (**y**) **bounde(n)** Pr 193, 21.57) tie up 19.54, 20.100; wrap 7.161; bandage 19.72; bind (with fetters) 20.33, 446, B 2.208, (*fig.*) A 10.56; trim [chest] with bands Pr 97; make subject (to law) B 3.353; impose penance Pr 129, 21.190

byneth(e) *av* lower down 6.180 (B 13.347), 18.85; underneath B Pr 15

bynymen *v* (*p.t.* **byno(e)m** 8.254, *p.p.* **bynomen** B 3.314) take away (from) 3.320, 8.254, B 3.314

bionales *n. pl.* masses said over a two-year period 9.320*n*

byno(e)m *p.t.* 8.254, 13.9 *see* **bynymen** *v*

biquasshen *v* (*p.t.* **biquasshe**) shatter B 18.248

biqueste *n* will, testament 8.94

biquethen *v* (*p.t.* **byquath / byqueþe**) bequeath 15.12

birch *n* birch-tree Z Pr 9

bireuen *v* take away (from) 8.258

birewen *v* repent, regret B 12.249

byschytten *v* shut up, (*p.t.*) 2.223, (*p.p.*) 21.167

bis(c)hop *n* bishop Pr 76, 78, 81, 85, 3.185, 4.120, 193, 5.70, 6.344, 9.255, 10.98, 141, 193, 12.227, 13.106, 124, 127, 16.200, 201, 364, 17.217, 277, 283, 294, 22.320, 328, **B** 2.177, 6.149, 11.301, 15.138, 456, 574, A Pr 90, 94, Z Pr 53, *in phrr.* **~es bayardes** B 4.124, ~ **crose** 10.93, ~ **lettres** 9.320, B 5.640, ~ **names** B 15.509, ~ **pere** 10.141, ~ **selys** Pr 67

bysechen, biseken *v* (*p.t.* **bysou(g)hte** 1.165 *etc*) entreat, beg 1.56, 3.77, 115, 4.107, 6.16, 92, 319, 386, 7.120, 142, 11.86, 18.141, 22.106, 170, A 12.11, *ger.* entreaty A 11.108, Z 4.121; pray for 1.165, 4.90, 6.10, 273, 323, 12.8, B 5.281, A 12.116; pray (to) 17.154, 244

bisegen *v* besiege 22.215

byseye *p.p.* 22.202 *see* **bysen** *v*

biseken 6.92, 7.120, A 12.116 = **bysechen** *v*

bysemen *v* befit 9.248

bysen *v* deal wih, treat 22.202

bysetten *v* bestow, invest 6.254, 345, B 5.260; employ B 12.47

bisherewen *v* scold, curse B 4.168

bishut *p.p.* 21.167 *see* **byschytten** *v*

bisy (besy, busy) *a* (pre)occupied 1.6; industrious 15.224; concerned **B** 7.119, 126, 14.34; **~liche** *av* diligently 11.155; earnestly A 12.106; ? carefully, scrupulously A 12.107; **~nesse** *n* anxiety 16.153

byside(s) *prep.* next to 6.54, 20.74; from 19.74

biside *av, in phr.* ~ **forth** in addition B 17.73

bisitten *v* afflict B 2.141, 10.359

#**bysloberen** *v* soil (with saliva) 7.1

bismere B 5.88, 19.296 = **busmare** *n*

bysnewed *p.p.* snowed-over 16.265

bisperen *v* lock up (in chest) B 15.143

bysou(g)hte, bisowte *p.t.* 1.165, 3.115 *etc*; *see* **bysechen** *v*

bis(s)h(e)inen *v* illuminate 17.268

bistowen *v* bestow, give B 7.73

bystriden *v* mount 19.78, Z 3.158

bisweten *v* (*p.t.* **biswatte**) cover with saliva (*lit.* sweat) B 13.403

byswynken *v* (*p.t.* **biswonke**) work for, obtain by toil 8.224, 260, 22.293, B 15.487

byt *contr. pr.* 3.306 *etc*, B 3.75, A 11.151, Z 7.269 *see* **bidden** *v*

bite *n* mouthful 20.206

bytechen *v* command (to) 15.184

byten *v* (*p.t.* **bo(o)t** B 5.83) cut 21.340; bite 6.141, B 5.83; smart 22.362; eat 15.54; *pr.p.a* (*fig.*) **bitynge in** severely critical of 9.16

#**bitelbrowed** *a* with beetling (prominent) brows 6.198*c*

bitere 22.27 = **bittere** *av*

bythenken *v* think up 6.107

bytyden *v* (*contr. pr.* **bitit,** *p.t.* **bytydde**) happen to, befall 3.156, 13.212, 14.61, 62, **B** 2.118, 3.167, Z 7.281

bytyme *av* in good time 7.290

bytok(e)nen *v* represent symbolically 14.173, 18.26, 210, 264, 19.120, 123, **B** 15.465, 16.212; presage, be a sign of 12.204, 18.163, 20.130, B 7.155; *and see* **tokenen** *v*

bytrayen *v* betray **B** 10.128, 16.150; deceive, lead astray 1.66, 7.58, **B** 1.39, 11.302

#bytrauaylen *v* get by labour 8.242, 15.211

bitt(e)r(e) *a* bitter(-tasting) 12.147, 148, *a as n* (= bitterness) B 5.118; harsh B 12.12; grievous 4.181; severe 15.50, **B** 11.152; fierce 20.66; *av* dearly 13.15, 15.304, 20.446, **B** 3.251, 10.280, (*comp.*) **bittorere** 16.219; severely 22.27; **~liche** bitterly, harshly 3.143, 11.192; **~nesse** *n* bitterness (*fig.*), = wickedness 20.401

*bytulyen *v* gain by tilling 8.242

bytwene *av* in between Pr 19, 6.157; (*prep.*) between 3.165, 381, 4.43, 8.157, 10.277, 16.84, 17.248, **B** 5.72, 97, 9.186, 13.175, 176, A 7.165, *in phr.* **mene** ~ 10.120, **B** 3.76, 7.197; amongst 12.127

bywichen *v* cast a spell upon 21.156

†biwilen *v* deceive by cunning B 10.108

byȝete *n* (truly) begotten / legitimate progeny 2.144n; offspring B 2.41

†biyeten *v* take possession of B 10.320

biyonde B 3.110, 4.128 *see* **beȝonde** *av*

blak *a* B 10.435; murky 16.266

blame *n,* **to** ~ at fault 3.305, 5.132, B 8.55; to be censured 13.241, B 14.1; **~les** *a* free from reproach 13.127, ~ **worþy** guilty, blameworthy B 10.260

blamen *v* rebuke, scold 3.435, 5.172, 13.239, **B** 10.7, 15.252; find fault with 6.69, 95, A 5.74; censure 9.162, 165, 12.38, B 10.258, 260, 286, Z 3.151; hold to blame 3.439, 13.124

blanket (blanked) *n* (white or undyed) woollen cloth Z 3.159; blanket 9.254

blase *n* flame 19.179

blasen *v* burn vigorously 19.186, 199, (*fig.*) 189, 223, 230; shine brightly 20.241

blasen *n* coat of arms B 16.179

blaunmanger *n* creamed stew 15.101

bleden *v* (*p.t.* **bledde(n)**) 18.254, 20.438, 21.107, 325, A 12.117; cause to bleed A 7.167

blenchen *v* turn aside 7.226

blenden *v* (*p.t., p.p.* **blente**) blind 7.134, 20.284, 292

#bler-eyede *a* with watering eyes 19.308

bleren *v* cause to water, *p.p.a* watery 6.198, ~ **yes** cause eyes to water, (*fig.*) = hoodwink Pr 72

blessed *p.p.a* blessed (by God), holy, pious Pr 76, 7.135, 9.13, 10.181, 11.242, 14.15, 16.201, B 11.167, Z Pr 53; sacred 20.476, 21.146; pleasing to God 17.163,

Z 7.238; (chosen to eternal) blessed(ness) 11.248, A 10.115, *a as n* 7.135, 17.59; consecrated 21.388; happy, fortunate 16.153, B 14.36, (*comp.*) 12.145

blessen *v* bless, bestow (God's) favour on 18.91, B 19.182, (*invoc.*) 8.260, 21.179, 180, 440; make sign of 12.127, 18.271; ask God's blessing (on) A 11.151; consecrate 3.185, 13.106, 12.127; say thanks for 14.126, 18.254, (*invoc.*) 8.260, 21.179, 180, 440, B 11.163

blessyng(e) *n* divine favour A 7.236; (formal papal) blessing 15.220, 229, B 13.250

bleten *v* bleat 17.38

blew (bloo) *a* pale, blue-grey 3.125

blew(e) *p.t.* 6.399, 7.152, B 5.496 *see* **blowen** *v*

blynd(e) *a* blind 7.107, 8. 128, 143, 201, 9.97, 99, 177, 260, 14.50, 15.149, 17.38, 20.80, 84, 87, B 16.124, A 7.178, Z 7.197, *a as n* the blind 8.188, 18.142, 20.98, 21.125; unable to see 19.308; spiritually blind 7.263; giving out no light 19.229

blis(se) *n* (state of) happiness / well-being / good fortune 11.47, 13.141, 228, 14.80, 15.292, 296, 297, 20.347, 416, B 10.107n, 11.26, 16.190, **worldes** ~ B 7.126; the blessedness of heaven, beatitude Pr 29, 7.135, 9.40, 11.263, 12.160, 14.78, 16.100, 20.347, 21.54, **B** Pr 106, 1.113, 9.47, 10.464, 11.167, 14.85, 154, 215, 15.175, 481, 16.180, 17.32, **A** 2.30, 4.91, 11.313, Z 7.76; *in phrr.* **hey ~, more** ~ a high(er) degree of beatitude 14.135, B 6.47, **Lord of** ~ blessed Lord B 11.188; (God's) glory 1.103, 11.203, 14.96, B 3.232; ceremony B 3.103; rejoicing 3.11; joyful singing 10.63, 67

blisful *a* blessed B 2.3

blissed(e) B 11.167, A 10.115, **blissen** 18.254, A 11.151 *see* **blessed** *p.p.a,* **blessen** *v*

blythe *a* joyful, glad 2.171, 3.28, Z 3.39

blo(e)d (blood) *n* blood 18.254, 19.272, 448, ~ **of gees** 15.68, [= the blood of Christ] 7.133, 12.60, 110, 17.268, 19.86, 88, 20.88, 21.58, 325, [in Eucharist] 19.90; *in phr.* **flesch and** ~ human form 1.151, **~(s) (c)hedyng** bloodshed 15.157; shedding one's blood [= martyrdom] 14.207; (*spec.*) the 'humour' blood A 10.55, 56, 61; (blood) kin, family 3.261, 20.418, 419, 437, 438, B 11.199; lineage, race 10.229, **gentil** ~ people of gentle birth 5.78

blody *a* bloody, **menyson** ~ B 16.111; covered with blood 4.74, 6.150, 21.6, 13; (related) by blood 8.217, 12.111, 117

bloo *a* pale, bluish-grey B 3.98

blosme *n* blossom (*fig.*) 18.10, 11, B 16.7, 35; **~n** *v* (*fig.*) flourish B 5.139

blostren *v* wander aimlessly 7.158

blowen *v*[1] (*p.t.* **blew(e)** 6.399, *p.p.* **(y)blowe(n)** 5.120) blow 5.120, 19.179, 310, 21.340, B 5.496, Z 6.70, (*fig.*) 18.36; ~ **to** blow upon (*fig.*) 19.191; *ger.* (*fig.*) 19.223; play [horn] (*fig.*) 6.399, 7.152

blowen *v*[2] blossom (*fig.*) 18.101, *ger.* B 16.26

#**bo(c)he** *n* plague-sore 22.84, B 13.250

bocher(e) *n* butcher Pr 222, 3.80, 6.378

bode *n* command A 2.51; message A 3.251

boden *p.p.* B 2.55 *see* **bidden** *v*

body(e) *n* body 5.33, 38, 12.22, 111, 13.134, 16.176, 177, 195, 17.146, 20.100, 337, 21.143, 146, **B** 5.83, 118, 12.48, (**dede**) ~ 3.105, 20.66, B 18.97, *in phrr.* ~ **half** front half B 13.317; **Godes** ~ 20.77, 476, [= Eucharist] 21.388, B 12.85, 86, 90, (*in oath*) 20.240; [*as opp. to* soul, = the 'flesh') 10.37, 47, 12.207, **B** 8.48, 14.284, 317, 15.425, *in phrr.* **labour of** ~ B 14.129, **lykynge of** ~ fleshly pleasure 9.202, 11.12, 16.102, **lust of** ~ 21.355, ~ **and soule** 1.58, 9.40, 20.301, 21.180, B 6.251, (*trs*) 1.146, 7.128, 12.89; person, self **B** 13.290, 16.124, anyone B 10.260, **no** ~ **B** 10.256, 16.83, **som** ~ one person 22.27

bodily *a* for the body B 15.575

bodyward, into þe *avl phr.* into the stomach A 7.167

bo(e)k(e) *n* book 17.197, **B** 5.267, 10.302, *in phr.* **to** ~ to studying 14.126, 157; (authoritative) writings, written authority 3.59, 5.146, 7.182, 11.115, 148, 154, 155, 228, 276, 12.75, 76, 13.128, 14.45, 46, 78, 169, 196, 201, 15.181, 17.294, **B** 10.427, 458, 12.17, 273, 14.155, 15.278; **the** ~ the written authority B 15.342, = the Bible Pr 129, 3.306, 5.38, 6.76, 7.125, 9.120, 127, 162, 10.23, 11.67, 13.15, 15.222, 17.59, 19.236, 21.71, 22.42, **B** 3.251, 6.251, 7.83, 10.252, 11.275, 12.65, (*person.*) 20.240 *et p.*; *in phr.* **the** ~ **Bible** the book of Scripture 9.304, = book (of the Bible) 1.180, 18.222, B 13.186; **Sapience** ~**s** the Book of Wisdom B 3.333; [= (*spec.*) the *Golden Legend*] 14.206, 15.269, 271, 17.27, B 15.282; = the books of law A 2.80; = service-book, psalter B 15.122; (*fig.*) = source of knowledge 12.98, **B** 5.146, 10.212, 11.167

boend *p.t.* 19.72 *see* **bynden** *v*

boende 15.14 = **bond(e)** *a*

boer 13.150 = **bor(e)** *n*

boerd 15.175 = **bord** *n*

boest 16.88, 21.252 = **boost** *n*

boet *n* boat 10.33, 39, 47, 227, B 8.36

boetles *a* without boots 20.9

boffaten (boffeden) *v* buffet, strike (with hand) 8.173, 22.191

†**boȝen** A 7.165 = **bowen** *v*

boy(e) *n* fellow (*contempt.*) Pr 78, A 11.61; churl, 12.113; low / common fellow 20.77, 79, 98; rascal 8.265, 9.194; jester 9.127

boylen *v* boil *pr. p.* **boylaunt** 20.289

boyste *n* box A 12.69

boke Pr 129 *et p.* = **bo(e)k(e)** *n*

bokke *n* buck [male fallow deer] 8.29

bold *a* daring, courageous 18.136, 21.295, B 16.179, *a as n* Z 4.142; confident 20.239, B 10.135, 258; presumptuous, forward Pr 202, 4.55, 8.201, 224, 18.46,

20.77, A 9.93, (*comp.* 4.102, 9.334); rash 6.34; impudent 2.87, 6.49, B 13.303, A 11.61; powerful 22.142, A Pr 90; mighty B 13.290

bold(e)ly *av* confidently 9.28, 16.55, 21.478; freely 18.115, Z 7.61; insolently 22.70; vigorously 22.132; promptly 22.328

bolden *v* embolden, cheer B 3.199

bold(e)nesse *n* gravity 20.430; assurance 7.263

bole *n* bull 13.150

bolk *n* belch 7.6

#**bollare** *n* tippler 9.194

bolle *n* drinking-bowl / cup 6.419, 20.407; bowl 7.163, B 5.107, A 7.167

bollyng (bollnyng) *n* swelling 8.226

bolnen *v* swell B 5.118

bolten *v* fetter 8.143

#**bommen** *v* guzzle 6.229, A 7.138

bon *n* bone 9.169, *pl.* limbs Z 5.142, body 8.100, 9.157, *in phr.* **gon on** ~ **es** walk about (alive) 20.337

bond *n* fastening (of straw) 5.14; fetter 21.57

bond(e) *a* of servile status 10.266, *a as n* 3.200, 10.270, 15.14

bonde *p.t.* 20.446, 21.57 *see* **bynden** *v*

bondage *n* (*coll.*) bondmen A Pr 96

bondeman *n* bondman, villein [customary tenant] 5.65, 70 (*gen. pl.*), 6.201, 8.42; ~ **of thorpes** Pr 220, ~ **of tounes** A 10.138

bone *n* prayer 12.86; command 3.417

boord *n* A 2.52 = **bord** *n*

boost *n* arrogance 16.64, A 1.111, ~ **of pride** in B 3.314; noise (= cause for boasting) 16.88; noisy argument 21.252

boot[1] B 8.36 = **boet** *n*; **boote**[2] B 7.28 = **bote** *n*

boot *p.t.* B 5.83 *see* **byten** *v*

bord *n* plank 10.225; side of boat 10.40; dining-table 8.276, 288, 15.175, B 13.36, *in phr.* **at bedde and at** ~ = at all times A 2.52n; ~**les** *a* without a table 14.140

bordiour *n* jester 7.107, 9.127, 136

bordoun *n* (pilgrim's) staff 7.161

bore *n* boar 8.29, 13.150

bore *p.p.* 14.31, 21.71 *see* **beren** *v*[1]

borewe 1.74 = **borw** *n*[1]

borewen 6.247, 16.129 = **borwen** *v*

borgeys Z Pr 59 = **burgeys** *n*

borgh *n* B 7.80, 10.135 = **borw(h)** *n*[2]

born *p.p.* 1.58, B 12.146 *etc; see* **beren** *v*[1]

bornet *n* fine brown woollen cloth Z 3.159

borre *n* bur, (*fig.*) hoareseness 19.308

borw[1] borough 2.92; town 9.189, B 2.98, A 12.52, Z 7.130; ~ **town** *n* town incorporated by royal charter 3.112

bor(e)w(h)(e) *n*[2] surety, guarantor 4.85, 18.280, 22.13, 248, **B** 7.80, 10.135; sponsor 1.74; **vnder** ~ under the protection of a surety B 14.191

borwen *v* borrow 2.176, 4.55, 56, 6.247, 342, 7.35, 8.108, 16.129, 313, 370, 372, 17.1, 21.478, 22.286, *ger.* 17.8, 27, **B** 5.253, 7.79, 13.376, 15.256, 312, (*fig.*) 6.342, B 5.289; stand surety for B 4.109

bosard *n* buzzard, (*fig.*) **blynd** ~ stupid oaf B 10.266c

bosch *n* bush 13.156

bosken *v* (*refl.*) hasten 3.15, 10.227

bosom *n* lap 18.271; bosom [front inside part of robe] 15.162

bost A 1.111 = **boest** *n*

bosten *v* brag, speak arrogantly 2.85, 6.34, **B** 13.281, 306, 15.252; (claim) boast(fully) 19.61

bostere *n* braggart B 13.303

bot(e) *conj.* Pr 36, 2.136 *etc*, *as prep.* 2.175, *av* 6.93 *etc*; *see* **but** *conj., prep. and av*

bote *n* good, advantage 15.229; remedy 4.85, 88, 89, 12.58; relief B 13.341, 14.116; cure 8.178, 192; salvation 20.476, B 12.86; repair B 7.28; *in phr.* **to** ~ in addition 16.108, B 14.238; *a* ~ **les** irremediable 20.206

botel *n* (leather) bottle / flask 5.52, 9.139, 19.70

#boten *v*¹ provide with boots Z 3.158

boten *v*² be added to [so as to equalise value] 6.381

botenen *v* cure 8.188

bothe *num., n* both 1.28 *et p.*, B 2.68, *in app. with prn.* **hem** ~, **they** ~, **vs** ~, **we** ~ both of them / us 2.90, 6.125, 8.24, 20.168, B 13.207; *after infl. prn.* **here** ~(**er**) 2.67 (B 2.68), **oure** ~, ~ **oure** 20.371, 6.181 of both of them / us; *a* both Pr 76 *et p.*; (*in deferred position*) 3.40, B 5.375, Z 6.3; (*emph.*) ~ **two** the two of them 13.28, B 2.55, Z 2.215; *as av* too, as well Pr 10. *et p.*, B Pr 116, A Pr 100, Z 3.163; *as correl. conj.* ~...**and** 2.252 *et p.*, B Pr 163, Z 1.18, (*with more than two subjs.*) = not only...but also **B** 15.489, 17.161

boton *n* stud B 15.124

botresen *v* buttress, support 7.235

botte Z 7.162 = **bat** *n*

bouken *v* cleanse with lye 16.332, B 14.19

boun A 2.51, 124, 3.245 = **bow(e)n** *a*

bounchen *v* strike (*fig.*) Pr 72

bounde(n) *p.p.* 21.57, A 10.56 *see* **bynden** *v*

bounte(e) *n* virtue 17.163; (chivalric) valour 8.49; reward B 14.150

bour *n* private room 3.11, 15, 6.228, **B** 2.65, 3.103, 139, Z 4.159; dwelling-place A 10.55

bourden *v* jest 16.200

bourdeour B 13.448; **bourdyor** *n* 9.127 = **bordiour** *n*

bourly *a* stout, excellent, *sup.* ~**okest** Z 3.159

bourne *n* stream B Pr 8

bowe¹ *n* bow 20.291, 22.117

bowe² 16.247 = **bow(h)(e)** *n*

bow(e)n *a* ready 2.173; willing **A** 2.51, 3.245

bowen *v* bow 21.17; submit 4.181, 10.270, 15.149; drop down 10.37, B 8.48; bend (down) 13.134; go B 5.566, †A7.165

bow(h)(e) *n* bough, branch 5.134, 16.247, 248, **B** 5.575, 15.98

box *n* jar B 13.195; case 9.263 [*with play on* jar], 13.54, B 5.640; collecting-box Pr 97, B 15.214

braek *p.t.* 20.364 = **brake**

#braggen *v* brag, boast noisily 6.34, 8.152, B 13.281

#braggere *n* braggart B 6.154

brayn *n* brain [as seat of mind] A 10.54, 56

braynwood *a* mad, crazed A 10.61

brak(e) *p.t.* Pr 114, 12.127, **B** 1.113, 10.282, 11.163; *see* **breken** *v*

brake *n* winch [of crossbow] 20.291

braken *v* vomit 6.430

bran (bren) *n* bran B 6.182, 282

bras *n* bronze Pr 183; (utensils of) brass / bronze 20.291

brasene *a* made of bronze 20.291

brast *p.t.* B 6.178 = **barste**

#braulen *v* wrangle, *ger.* 16.361

#braulere *n* quarrelsome person 18.46

braunche *n* branch, (*fig.*) = (sub)-species (of sin) 7.69, 80 (B 13.410, 421), 16.263, B 15.75

braw(e)n *n* meat 15.68, 101; boar's flesh B 13.63

brech *n* drawers 6.157

bre(e)d *n* bread 5.174, 8.306, 326, 9.120, 200, 11.67, 12.127, 15.54, 211, 18.262, **B** 12.85, 13.236, 242, 261, A 11.188, Z 7.199, *in combs.* ~ **corn** grain for making bread 8.61; ~ **yblessed** (= Eucharist) 21.388; **bake** ~ B 13.267, **barly** ~ 8.142, A 7.169, **broke** ~ A 12.70, **haly** ~ 6.146, Z 8.75, **hors** ~, **houndes** ~ 8.225, **whete** ~ B 6.137, 7.121, **whyte** ~ 9.254; ~ **and ale** 7.51, 9.156, ~ **and clothes** 22.248, ~ **and drynke** 16.63, B 13.252, ~ **and water** 6.155; food 5.174, 8.224, 16.63, 22.248, **B** 7.83, 84, 12.17, 85, *a* **#bredles** without food 9.121, 16.13

brede *n*¹ breadth 2.93, 3.259

brede *n*² roast meat Z 7.199

breden *v*¹ (*p.t.* **bredde(n)** 13.165) breed 13.165, B 11.358, *ger.* (manner of) breeding B 12.218; rear young **B** 11.347, 12.227; live ? B 2.98c

breden *v*² grow stout ? B 2.98c

breef *n* letter of authorisation 22.328

bre(e)re *n* briar 2.28; branch covered with prickles 6.401; dog-rose stem A 10.124

breiden *v* hasten B 17.69

breken *v* (*imp.* **brek** Z 6.50, *p.t.* **br(a)(e)k(e)** Pr 114, 20.313, 364, *p.p.* **(y)broke(n)e** Pr 69) break Pr 114, 2.87, 9.276, 334, **B** 5.575, 10.282, (into fragments) 18.155, B 14.222; tear **B** 5.107, 9.92; distribute (bread) 11.67, 12.127, A 11.188, Z 7.287; break into 16.88, 20.313, 21.346, A 9.79; be broken into / break open 16.88, 20.364; cripple 5.33, 9.169, 177; break down, destroy 8.29, 20.262, 21.340, B 11.163, ~ **vp** 4.60; ~ **out** escape from 12.76; fail to keep Pr 69, 9.236, 241, 20.320, **B** 1.113, 5.241, *ger.* 5.169

breme *a* vigorous, powerful B 12.223, *sup. comp.* A 10.55, 56

bren B 6.182 = **bran** *n*

brennen *v* (*imp.* **bern** 3.422, **bren** B 3.267, *p.t.* **brente** 19.310, **brende** B 17.328, *p.p.* **(y)brent** 3.105, B 5.267) burn (*tr.*) 3.105, 422, 20.264, B 3.267, Z 6.72, *ger.* B 15.83; (*intr.*) 12.69, 19.179, 199, 223, 230, 310, 20.289, ~**ynge aguwe** acute fever 22.84; make pure by fire, refine B 5.267

brest(e) *n* breast 5.106, 7.6, 60, 12.57, 16.332, Z 5.97; heart A 5.99

bresten *v* (*p.t.* **barste**) crush 8.175

Bretener *n* Breton 8.152*n*, 173

bretful *a* brimful Pr 42

breth *n* breath(ed) utterance 15.263, 264, 20.364

brether(e)n(e) *n.pl.* brothers [by blood-relationship] 7.238, 9.315, 21.255, B 10.199, 11.199, A 11.191, (*fig.*) B 11.207, 18.394; **blody** ~ (*fig.*) 8.217, 12.111, 117, 20.418, **halue** ~ 20.436, fellow human-beings / Christians 15.81, B 12.90; fellow religious 16.293, B 5.178

brethyen *v* Z 6.70, *ger.* (exchange of) breath B 11.357

bretil *a* fragile, brittle 10.47

breuh-wif *n* female brewer 6.353

breuet *n* letter 13.54; letter of authorisation B Pr 74, 5.640

brewen *v* (*p.t.* **brew**, *p.p.* **browe**) brew 6.225, 20.401

*****brewecheste** *a* trouble-brewing B 16.43

brewere *n* brewer Pr 222, 3.80, 104, 4.120, 21.399, 407

brewestare *n* brewer 8.329, 9.189, B Pr 219; female brewer, alewife 6.352

brewhous *n* brewery-tavern 9.98

brybour *n* thievish impostor 22.262; *and see* **a-bribeth** *av*

brid *n* bird 9.200, 10.63, 13.156, 162, 15.292, **B** 11.357, 12.223, 14.44, 15.284, 314, *in phr.* ~**es and bestes** 11.242, 13.136, 14.80, 169, 15.292, B 12.218

bridale *n* wedding celebration 2.56, B 2.44

brydel *n* bridle B 4.22

brygge 7.239 = **brugge** *n*

bry(g)ht(e) *a* bright, shining Pr 178, 183, 3.457, 17.277, 20.100, 22.132; vivid, brilliant **B** 12.221, 14.19; *av* brightly 21.436; ~**nesse** *n* radiance 13.10, 20.284

bryngen *v* (*p.t.* **brouhte** 3.10, *p.p.* **(y)brouh(t)e** 3.2, 8.61, 15.11) bring 1.74, 2.214, 3.10, 4.56, 7.86, 7.135, 8.61, 317, 350, 9.200, 15.54, 211, 17.32, 19.84, 310, 20.34, **B** 10.309, 12.89, 13.52, 186, 15.308, A 12.87; introduce 11.169, 19.34; convey B 14.85, **A** 2.138, 10.147, Z 6.63; *in phrasal vv.* ~ **above** make prosperous 13.21; lead 3.408, 7.80, 11.194, 14.78, 17.236, 20.147, B 15.75, 426; lead out 9.260, B 11.152; ~ **(a)doun** overcome 3.43, 4.88, 20.28, 143, 340, 20.28, 21.51, B 9.205; ~ **a slepe** put to sleep A 9.58, ~ **forth** produce Pr 67, 1.18, 2.66, 3.188, 9.168, 10.276, 11.36, 15.61,

18.79, **B** 9.151, 13.236; give birth to 13.166, 18.223, A 10.147, (*fig.*) 2.31; display 6.141; ~ **(hit) to hepe**, ~ **herto** bring it about, succeed in (doing) 10.191, 193, 4.177; ~**in** bring into 6.415, 7.4, 8.163, 10.33, 17.181, **A** 3.144, 5.74; ~ **into world** give birth to 20.134; ~ **out of** release from 18.280, 20.265, 22.201, B 5.227; make (sb.) lose 21.285; ~ **to care** cause harm to 19.55; ~ **to louhynge** turn to laughter 20.460; ~ **to nauhte** destroy 2.139, 3.200, 17.306, B 14.95

#**brocage** *n* arrangement through an intermediary 16.107; business deal 2.92

broche *n* splint 19.212; brooch Pr 73, B 15.121

brochen *v* stitch loosely 6.218

brocour *n* B 3.46, 5.244 = **brokere** *n*

bro(o)d(e) *a* wide 7.161, 10.33, 20.238, B Pr 8, Z 2.47; extensive B 13.243; stout (? wide-spreading) 5.120, Z Pr 9; broad-headed 22.117, ~ **hokede** wide-barbed 22.226; broad-bladed B 3.305

brode *av* extensively 5.167

brok *n* brook, stream 7.212, (= water) 8.142

broke(n) *p.p.* 9.177, 18.155, 21.346, **A** 9.79, 12.70 *see* **breken** *v*

brokelegged *a* lamed in the leg 8.143, 188, 12.76, Z 7.197 (~ **sshankid** A 7.130)

brokere, broko(u)r *n* agent 2.60, B 5.244; purveyor 6.95; go-between 2.66, B 3.46

brol(le) *n* brat 3.261

brood 7.161 *etc*; *see* **bro(o)d(e)** *a*

brother *n* brother Pr 107, 1.62, 12.171, A 3.243, **Caymes seed his** ~ Cain his brother's offspring 10.254, (*fig.*) 7.143, **B** 5.466, (= fellow Christian) 10.263; *and see* **brether(e)n(e)** *n pl.*

brouken *v* drink 12.58, 20.401

broun *a* dark (= strong) 8.329

browe *n* eyebrow A 12.12

browe *p.p.* 20.401 *see* **brewen** *v*

brugge *n* bridge 7.212, 239 (drawbridge), 9.32

brumstoen *n* sulphur 20.289

brusshe *n* brush B 13.460

bruttenen *v* destroy 3.237, *ger.* destruction 15.157

buggen 4.85, 9.28, 16.72, 21.280 *etc*; = **byggen** *v*

buggere *n* purchaser B 10.306

buggynge *ger. see* **byggen** *v*

buyen 15.304 *see* **byggen** *v*

buylden *v* build B 12.227, *ger.* B 15.328

buyrde *n* lady 3.15, 20.119; damsel 21.135

bu(y)r(e)n(e) *n* man 6.247, 18.280, **B** 3.267, 11.361, 12.65; *pl.* people 18.11, Z 5.38; soldier 15.157; lord, baron 3.473

buyrielles *n sg* the grave 21.146

bulle *n* papal bull [edict of pardon] 3.184, 9.337, 15.220; (document of) pardon 9.42, 61, 160, 283; episcopal edict Pr 67, B 5.640

bummen A 7.138 = **bommen** *v*

bungen Z Pr 80 = **bounchen** *v*

burel *n* coarse woollen cloth (*fig.*, *attrib.*) = half-educated, ? lay B 10.286*n*

burgage *n* house in town [held by burgage tenure, directly from king or lord without feudal obligation] 3.85, 105

burgeys *n* (*sg. & pl.*) burgess (freeman / citizen of town) Pr 220, 3.200, 14.91 (*gen.*) **B** 5.128, 15.202, 342, **A** 3.144, 10.138

burg(h) B 2.98, A 12.52 = **borw** *n*

burien *v* bury 12.22, 21.143, **B** 11.65, 67, 74, 12.253, 13.9; bury the dead B 11.76, *ger.* B 11.78

burionen *v* sprout, burgeon B 15.75

burn B 3.267, 11.361, 12.65 = **bu(y)r(e)n(e)** *n*

burthe *n* birth 20.248, 21.81

buschel *n* bushel [= 8 gals.] 8.61

busy B 13.252, **busiliche** 11.155, A 12.106 *see* **bisy** ~ *a, av*

busken Z 4.159 = **bosken** *v*

busmare *n* calumny 21.295, B 5.88

but(e) *conj.* (*with subjv. clause*) unless Pr 64 *et p.*, B 4.142, A 4.96, except 10.120; (*with* **that** *and conditional cl.*) except that 3.396, unless †15.120; only that †15.220; (*with inf.*) except 5.9; (*with av.*) except 16.294; than (that) 10.210, 16.275, (*in constr. with* **yf**) unless 1.176 *et p.*, B 2.129, A 9.96, ~ **(...) hoso** unless one 7.306, 10.39; but (rather) (*with cl.*) 1.79, B 6.311, A 3.253, (*with inf.*) 8.335, B Pr 206; (*with n. phr.*) 1.99, 3.304, 17.265*n*; *in correl. conj.* but also 21.117; however 6.10, B 3.180, A 12.5; and, furthermore 12.200, B 5.470, A Pr 5; (*as av.*) only Pr 204 *etc*; nothing but 11.9, 13.239, B 11.429, Z 5.34; *as prep. with n.* except 1.21, 13.65*etc*, 9.289*n*, B 5.235; anything except 7.77; *as quasi-a.* only 2.200, 4.61, B 8.82

buth 3 *pr.pl* 9.160; *see* **ben** *v*

buttre *n* butter B 5.438

buxum *a* obedient 3.417, 9.220, 16.63, B 1.110, **Z** 1.23, 6.41; submissive B 15.202, A 2.52; willing 15.224, B 6.194; modest, mild 20.119, **B** 5.566, 16.7; ~ **liche** *av* humbly 14.57, B 12.194; graciously 17.283; ~ **nesse** *n* humility 16.64; kindness 7.238, B 10.302; obedience 20.320, **B** 1.113, 4.187

caas B 10.348 = **ca(e)s** *n*

cabane(e) *n* tent B 3.191; cell A 12.35

cac(c)hen *v* (*p.t.* **cauhte** 13.214, *p.p.* **cauht** Pr134) get hold of 10.301, B Pr 207, 14.239; pick up, ? filch 22.14; capture 2.204; catch 14.174, 18.170, B Pr 189; snatch (at), pursue 3.364; take 6.408, †B 2.36; obtain **B** 11.173, 13.299; get 3.388, 6.78, B 12.221; ~ **of** get (sth.) from A11.87; receive Pr 134, 14.86, 21.128, ~ **colour** blush 13.214; drive, chase 14.117, A 7.128, 183

cachepol *n* catch-poll [minor law officer] 20.46, 75

ca(e)s *n* state of affairs 9.48 (?*or spec.* suit, law-case),

22.14, B 10.348; event 3.432, **in** ~ in the event that 9.155; (grammatical) case 3.336, 346, 356, 386, 388*c*, 394, 398*c* (*with pun on* condition)

cayren *v* wander Pr 31; proceed B 4.24; (*refl.*) betake oneself 6.350; convey B 2.162

cayser *n* emperor 3.314, 318, 22.101, B 9.111, A 11.219; lord 21.138; *and see* †**cesar** *n*

caytif (kaytif) *n* wretch 6.206, 8.244, 12.66; poor man 14.90; scoundrel 10.222, 20.96, 99, 21.406, Z 7.261; *a* worthless 13.109; poor †A 10.68; ~**liche** *av* wretchedly 3.241; meanly (clad) 12.129; ~**tee** *n* vileness 9.255; *and see* **cheytyftee** *n*

cake *n* flat cake, loaf 8.305, Z 7.107; ~ **breed** *n* ? griddlecake B 16.229

cald(e) *p.t.* 1.4, *p.p.* Pr 132 *etc*; *see* **callen** *v*

calf *n* calf 8.311, B 15.465, 466, **y** ~ with calf Z 3.149, **calues flessh** veal **B** 15.464, 16.229

callen *v* (*p.t., p.p.* **cal(l)(e)d(e)**) call out B 17.74; call on 21.9; summon 3.3, 127, 149, 4.17, 20.472, 22.305, **B** 4.171, 15.593, A 12.49; invite 12.105, 22.243, B 13.31; (call by) name Pr 132, 1.4, 4.161, 5.162, 7.176, 9.213, 249, 10.69, 11.174, 175, 12.114, 14.14, 16.181, 199, 18.11, 12, 14, 19.51, 20.96, 21.15, 23, 85, 117, 136, 330, 22.5, **B** 7.91, 10.287, 11.173, 15.430, 16.135, 245, **A** 4.140, 10.25, 148, 12.84, **Z** 2.169, 6.41; greet B 1.4; **do** ~ have announced 3.34

cam *p.t.* Pr 95; *see* **comen** *v*

cammaca *n* fine (? silken) fabric 16.299

cammok *n* rest-harrow 21.314, Z 7.91

can[1] *pr. sg.* 2.236 *et p.*, *pl.* 1.190, 8.267, 11.18, 228, 14.11, 15.174 *see* **connen** *v*

can[2] *p.t.* (*modal v.*) did, proceeded to 15.191, 19.71

candle *n* candle 3.106; taper 19.186

cano(e)n (canoun)[1] *n* canon law 15.86, B 5.422; #**canonistre** *n* expert in canon law 9.303

cano(u)n[2] *n* cathedral canon B 10.46, A 11.33; *and see* **chano(u)n** *n*

canst 2 *sg. pr. see* **connen** *v*

cantel *n* portion 14.163

capel (capul) *n* riding horse 4.24, **B** 2.162, 17.108; cart horse 21.333, 347

capon *n* capon 4.38, B 15.473

cappe *n* hat 7.173

caract *n* written character B 12.78, 88, 91

carden *v* comb [wool for spinning] 9.80, (*fig.*) spruce up 11.15

cardiacle *n* heart-disease 22.82, Z 7.277; heart-pains / palpitations 6.78

cardinal *n* cardinal Pr 134, 16.366, 17.166, 21.225, 416, 420, 423, 452, ~ **wit** A 12.15

cardinal(e) *a* (*pl. form* **-es**) cardinal, chief [of the virtues] Pr 132, 21.275, 318, 339, 396, 410, 414, 423, 455, 22.21, 73, 122, 304

care *n* sorrow, misery 1.57, 20.265; vexation 22.165;

distress, hardship 3.201, 372, 19.55, 20.276, 22.201, **B** 13.161, 14.175; harm 18.173; misfortune B 9.153; anxiety 20.223, B 2.151

car(e)fol(e) *a* sorrowful B 13.266; wretched, miserable B 9.158, 11.294; *a as n* wretched 11.42, 18.267; distressed 1.197, 12.105, 19.65, 21.128, B 14.179

carefully *av* wretchedly B 5.76

careyne 14.178, B 14.331 = **caroyne** *n*

caren *v* care 1.124, 9.109, 21.384; worry 22.150; be solicitous 15.259, B 2.162

caryen *v* carry 9.151, 21.332, A 6.32, Z 6.20

carnel *n* crenel, embrasure 7.234, †20.288

caroyne *n* corpse 8.100, 16.195; carcass B 12.253; (wretched) body B 14.331; flesh B Pr 189, 14.178n

carolen *v* dance and sing a *carole* [round dance] 20.470

carpen *v* speak, discourse Pr 209, 2.27, 4.32, 6.29, 7.76, 79, 11.52, 13.178, 15.110, 191, 16.270, 17.69, 18.219, 282, 21.69, 177, 200, 22.334, **B** 10.51, 104, 13.58, 180, 15.301, A 12.33, *ger.* B 10.140, manner of speaking 16.339; say 14.216, B 11.215; tell 2.203; object 19.111, B 10.106; find fault B 10.287, *ger.* carping talk B Pr 204, cry out B 10.58

carpentare *n* carpenter A 11.135, *(fig.)* 11.250

carpentrie *n* the craft of carpentry 11.125

carse *n* cress, *(fig.)* = jot, anything 11.14

cart *n* cart, wagon B 13.266, (= hay-wain) 5.13, *(fig.)* 2.190, 192, 21.332, 333, 348; *in cpds.* ~ **mare** 8.311, ~ **way** 3.167, **~whel** cart-wheel 15.163

carten *v* work as a carter 5.62

cartere *n* cart-driver 9.205

cartsadlen *v* place cart-saddle [small saddle for cart-horse] upon B 2.180

cas 3.336 *et p.* = **ca(e)s** *n*

cast *n* skill 3.20

castel *n* castle, fortified tower 1.4, 3.140, *(fig.)* 10.129, 143, **B** 9.49, 13.120, A 10.22, 25; dungeon-stronghold 1.57, A 11.189

casten *v* (*contr. pr.* **cast** 9.151, *p.t.* **caste** Pr 143) throw 6.375, 14.104, B 16.128, Z 7.277; hurl 15.144, 20.289, B 16.42, 75; put 8.58; place B 15.401; place forcibly 4.81, B 8.102; ~ **vp** lift B 11.408; devote, apply 6.264, B 13.357, *(refl.)* apply oneself 9.151; provide B 6.16; think about 22.121; intend, plan 21.281, B 15.333; plot 11.16, 18, 21.141, B 16.137; ordain Pr 143; reckon (to be) 12.68; write, draw up B 13.248; *ger. phr.* **castynge of ei3en** looks, glance B 11.187

cat *n* cat Pr 168, 185 *et p.*, B 5.254

#catecumelyng *n* catechumen B 11.77n

catel *n* property 3.322, 425, 7.219, 8.157, 9.181, 10.195, 253, *in phr.* **coueytise of** ~ 10.260, 282, 12.243, 247, 16.109, B 9.157; goods B 7.22; money Pr 210, 3.72, 4.78, 5.129, 6.288, 8.230, 9.90, 13.107, 17.212, 22.209; income (from property) 8.101; treasure B 10.323; wealth 10.170, 12.216, 19.245, **B** 10.29, 11.211; *in*

phrr. ~ **and kynde wit** wealth and native ability 14.17, **lordes** ~ B 10.471, **losse of** ~ B 14.7, **trewe** ~ honestly earned wealth 19.240, **worldly** ~ material wealth 21.293, = reward 21.77; cattle, livestock B 3.273; possession **B** 12.294, 13.151; provisions [*sc.* food] B 15.428

*cateles *a* without property / money A 10.68

caucyon *n* surety-payment Z 5.143

caudel *n* hot drink, (*here* = mess) 6.411

cau(g)ht *p.p.* Pr 134, 18.170, 19.186, **~e** *p.t.* 6.408, 13.214, 21.128 *see* **cac(c)hen** *v*

*cauken *v* tread the female, mate 13.170, 14.161, B 12.228

*caurymaury *n* rough cloth A 5.61, (B 5.78)

cause *n* cause 5.190, 9.255, B 12.224, 225; reason [for sth.] 3.316, 9.255, 16.205, 20.138; reason [for action], motive 10.285, 21.23, 63, B 11.173; justification 3.364, 17.131, 136, 19.322; side, case [in argument] B 13.126; responsibility 6.113; *in phrr.* **by** ~ **of** as a result of B 5.183, **by** ~ **to** in order to B 11.173, A 12.32

caue *n* pit B 12.253

cene *n* supper B 16.140

certeyn(e) *a* fixed, definite 19.33, 22.255, 265, *in phr.* **som(me)** ~ prescribed sum 19.33, B 13.377; indubitable B 10.429; sure 3.85, 9.165, 19.221

certeyne (*a as*) *n* fixed number 22.258, 267 (1); definite amount B 13.377; particular (order) 22.267 (2); **of** ~ as a secure sustenance B 6.151

certes *av* certainly, truly 9.331, B 2.152, A 9.18; surely, to be sure 5.22, 13.221; of course 13.246; indeed 9.257, 18.58

cesar (= **kayser**) *n* emperor 3.329n.

ces(s)en (sesen) *v* desist from, leave off 9.227, 14.41, 22.107, 109, B 7.118; stop 2.165, 4.1

chacen *v* rush, hasten B 17.52

†chafen B 12.125 = **chaufen** *v*

chaffare *n* trade, business Pr 33, **B** 5.225, 15.164; transaction involving exchange 6.379, B 5.245; merchandise, goods in trade 2.60, **B** 5.131, 243, 13.380

chaffaren *v* (engage in business or) trade for profit 5.94, 6.252, 8.249, 12.229, 16.147, **B** 6.238, 15.165, 16.129; gain through trade B 15.107

chayere *n* raised seat [of office] Pr 114

chayne *n* chain, fetter 20.446, B 17.111; ornamental chain (*fig.*), = 'bond' B 5.607

chalengen *v* rebuke 6.156; object to 6.136, *in phr.* **wiþouten chalangynge** without question B 15.344; (lay) claim (to) Pr 91; (make) claim / demand 16.189, B 15.165; scold, *ger.* **chalengynge** 6.68, B 11.423

chaleniable *a* open to objection 13.116

cha(u)mbre *n* private room 2.65, 7.93 (B 13.434), 236, **B** 3.10, 4.124, 10.100, Z 4.158; bedroom B 4.124; *(fig.)* womb 18.126

champion B 8.46, 15.216 = **cha(u)mpio(u)n** *n*

Chancerye *n* Chancery [office of Lord Chancellor of England] Pr 91, B 4.29

changen 6.146 = **chaungen** *v*

chano(u)n *n* canon [cleric living under canonical rule] 5.156, 170 (B 10.318), 17.55, A 10.113

chapeleyn *n* priest (officiating in a chapel) 1.185, 8.11; bishop's assistant priest 13.127

chapitre (chapitle) *n* (body of members of a) convent-chapter 3.472, B 5.159 ~ **hous** chapter-house 6.156

chapman *n* merchant, trader Pr 62, 5.136, 6.235, 379, 10.260, 12.229, B 15.85

chapun-cote *n* capon-shed 6.136

charge *n* (burden of) responsibility 9.96, 258; blame A 10.73

chargen *v* burden 9.73, ? 22.237; enjoin 5.136, 7.256; insist on, treat as important 19.274; care (about) 16.147, 288; appoint A 10.23; entrust (with) Pr 87, ? 22.237 (*or* burden)

charite *n* (the theological virtue of) charity Pr 87, 1.183, 185, 15.279, 16.284, 347, 17.49, 62, 64, 140, 148, 150, 151, 286, 19.276, **B** 1.194, 5.264, 12.30, 31, 15.156, 250, 343, 344, 16.3, 17.293, A 1.164, Z 5.96, (*person.*) 7.256, 272, 16.288, 295, 348, 18.2, B 14.97, 100; *in phrr.* **cheef** ~ 16.347, 17.5, **cheyne of** ~ B 5.607, **children of** ~ 18.207, þe **fruyt** ~ B 16.9, **ful** ~ B 15.153, **Holi Chirche and** ~ Pr 64, 2.140, 16.35, 19.274, †**leel** ~ B 9.188, **loue of** ~ 16.283, **parfit** ~ B 15.148, **puyr** ~ 11.65, **B** 10.314, 15.79, *pur* ~ for charity's sake 8.169 *et p.*, **trewe** ~ 2.37, **verray** ~ 19.273; ~ (þe) cha(u)mpion 15.279, B 8.46; (people's) love / affection 16.147, B 13.110; charitable act 17.231; (what is given out of) charity 1.189, 2.140

charme *n* magic spell (for healing) 6.85, (*fig.*) 19.21, B 17.21

charnel *n* charnel-house 8.45

chartre *n* deed granting rights 2.69, A 2.35; legal document 13.116, 119; legal contract 12.63, (*fig.*) agreement 16.35; charter of foundation 5.166

chast(e) *a* virgin(ally pure) 1.175, 185, 16.347, (?*av*) 18.77

chastite *n* chastity, sexual purity (*person.*) 7.272; sexual abstinence 1.183

chastel *n* castle 2.89

chastilet *n* little castle B 2.85

chasten *v* discipline Pr 212, 13.234, 19.301, 312, B 6.51; reprimand A 11.198; chastise, punish 4.112, 5.136, 8.344

chastisen *v* punish Pr 110, B 4.117

chatel *n* personal property, chattels 12.63

chat(t)eren *v* rant 2.89, 16.68

chaufen *v* grow warm 17.49; inflame (*fig.*) 14.68

chaumbre 7.93, 236, 18.126 = **cha(u)mbre** *n*

chaumbrere *n* confidant B 14.100

cha(u)mpio(u)n *n* chosen warrior 20.102, B 15.164; (supreme) champion, protector knight 15.279, **B** 8.46, 15.216

chaunce *n* good luck 6.85 (B 13.342); (a matter of) one's luck / fate 14.33

Chaunceller *n* chancellor [king's chief executive and administrative officer] 4. 185

Chauncerye B 4.29 = **Chancerye** *n*

cha(u)ngen *v* change, alter (*tr.*) 5.81, 13.179, 22.361, B 16.129; (*intr.*) (for the worse) 6.146, (for better) 12.211

chedyng *ger.* shedding, *in phr.* **bloed** ~ [*sc.* as a martyr] 14.207

cheef *a* highest, supreme 4.185, A 10.72; foremost Pr 62; principal 6.68, 85, 7.272, 21.475, B 10.100; pre-eminent, most important 15.279, 20.102, 21.409, ~ **charite** 16.347 charity in the highest degree, ~ **iustice** judge of the supreme court 13.116, ~ **lord** immediate (feudal) lord 9.73; *a as n* leader B 14.100

chees *p.t.* 13.3 *see* **chesen** *v*

cheeste B 13.110 = **cheste** *n*[1]

cheyne B 5.607, 17.111 = **chayne** *n*

cheynen *v* fetter 1.183; *pr. subjv.* chain up [entrance] 20.285

cheytyftee *n* destitution 22.236; *and see* **caytiftee** *n*

cheke *n* jaw B 5.162; cheek 6.150, 199, 8.173, 9.208, 15.87, 109, B 5.82; *in phr.* **maugre(e)...chekes** despite all (sb.) can do 8.38, **B** 4.50, 6.158, 14.4

#**cheken** *v* (*pr. subjv.*) barricade 20.285

Cheker *n* Exchequer [royal court of accounts] Pr 91, 4.185, B 4.29

chele *n* cold 22.236, B 1.23, 10.59, *in phr.* **in** ~ **and in hete** at all times 8.249

chepen *v* bid to buy B 13.380; (*fig.*) = choose 16.189; *ger.* ~**yng** market 4.59, 8.322

cherche B 7.173, 10.252 (*uninfl. gen.*), A 12.17 *see* **churche** *n*

chere *n* mien, countenance, expression 11.188, 22.114, B 11.186, A 11.2, Z 3.39, **glad** ~ friendliness 6.374, B 16.155; *in phr.* **maken...~** show (...) expression 4.160, 17.30, 22.350; **chered** *a* with a (...) expression 21.264, 22.2

cher(e) *a* dear 17.125, *in phr.* ~ **ouer** deeply concerned about 17.148

cherie *n* cherry 8.310, 12.223, ~ **tyme** time of cherry harvest B 5.159

cherl *n* bondman 8.45, 12.63, 20.107, 21.35, 37, 22.146, B 9.111, A 3.247; slave 21.55; boor 1.29; villain B 16.121 (*with play on* bondman); fellow 6.410

cher(is)sen *v* indulge, *ger.* 4.112

cherubyn *n* cherubim 1.105*n*

chese *n* cheese 7.51, 9.150, **Essex** ~ B 5.92, **grene ~s** 8.304

chesen *v* (*p.t.* **chees** 13.3, *pl.* **chosen** Pr 33, 22.236, *p.p.* **(y)chose(n)** 6.379, 12.53) choose 6.379, 16.198, (as) a way of life Pr 33, 20.205, 22.236; decide 16.174; elect to eternal life 12.53; *p.p. as n* 12.54

chesible *n* chasuble 8.11

cheste *n*[1] strife, contention Pr 105, 2.89; quarreling 10.277, 14.68, B 13.110

cheste *n*[2] chest, ark 14.68

chete *n* escheat [reversion of estate to lord] 4.169

cheuen *v* fare Pr 33, (*impers.*) 16.68; succeed 6.252; thrive 8.248, 20.107

cheuentayn *n* head, lord 21.475

cheuesaunce *n* way of acquiring (sth.) 22.16; agreement to lend money with (concealed) payment of interest 6.252, B 5.245, Z 2.71

#cheuisshen *v* guard against A 10.73

chewen *v* eat 8.286, 15.46; consume 1.189, 2.140; subsist 20.205, 22.237

chibol *n* spring onion 8.310

chidare *n* troublemaker 18.46

chyden *v* (*contr. pr.* **chy(h)t** 1.175, 16.288, *p.t.* **chydde** 6.147) rail 3.223, rail against B 11.406; nag 7.301; dispute 3.389; quarrel 1.175, 6.147, 20.205, 464, B 13.323; complain 8.335, 340, 12.229, 16.68, **B** 4.52, 13.380; *ger.* fault-finding 6.68, B 11.423

chief Pr 62, 7.272, 9.73, 13.116, 20.102, B 5.87, A 10.72; B 14.100 *see* **cheef** *a; n*

chieftayn B 19.476 = **cheuentayn** *n*

chield 17.148 = **child** *n*

chield *p.p.* 17.49; *see* **chillen** *v*

chiere 22.350 = **chere** *n*

chyht *contr. pr.* 1.175 *see* **chyden** *v*

child(e) *n* (*pl.* ~**erne** 10.277, ~**ren(e)** Pr 105, 3.396 (*gen. pl.* 4.112) ~**res** 8.106) child 1.175, 3.420, 6.156, B 5.38; baby 6.136, **with** ~ pregnant 9.176, 20.133, 22.348; *pl.* children Pr 115, 4.112, 5.136, 138, 8.106, 9.73, 89, 169, 10.259, 12.118, 158, 16.301, **B** 3.268, 9.68, 155, 11.384, 14.3, 15.248, **A** 3.247, 7.267, 10.103, 179, Z 7.201; schoolboys 17.107; descendants 20.107, **B** 3.260, 16.121; offspring 5.65, 10.277, B 16.221, (*fig.*) 18.207, 208; = people Pr 105, 111; (adopted) children of God 17.291, B 12.12; (spiritual) children 17.291; followers 22.79, B Pr 35; *in phr.* **wymmen and** ~ 3.396, 9.226

childhod *n* childhood A 10.73

childisch(e) *a* childlike 16.296, B 15.149

chillen *v* grow cold, *p.p.* **chield** grown cold 17.49; *ger.*, **for** ~ to prevent...from growing cold 8.334

chymenee *n* fireplace B 10.100

chyn *n* chin 6.200

#chine *n* chink, crack 20.285

chirch(e) Pr 64 *et p.* = **churche** *n*

chirie-tyme *n* B 5.159 *see* **cherie** *a*

chiruul *n* chervil 8.310

chyt *contr. pr.* 16.288 *see* **chyden** *v*

chivaler *n* man-at-arms, knight 20.102

*chyuelen B 5.190 = **ycheuelen** *v*

chop *n* blow 10.277

choppen *v* strike Pr 64, 14.68, A 3.247

chose(n) *p.t. pl.* Pr 33, 20.205, 22.236, 237, *p.p.* 12.53; ~**e** *p.p. as n* 12.54 *see* **chesen** *v*

churche (cherche, chirche, kirk) *n* church (= local church-building) 2.231, 3.64, 5.12, 30, 60, 104, 6.272, 288, 354, 365, 7.65, 8.11, 45, 100, 9.189, 228, 241, 21.2, **B** 1.180, 5.1, 103, 11.65, 12.27, 13.9, 16.129, **Seint Petres** ~ B 7.173, **Sent Poules** ~ Z 2.80, (*fig.*) = spiritual temple 7.256; = the (Christian) Church [as teaching, governing and sacramental body], Holy ~ Pr 64 *et p.* (*see* **Holy Churche** *for full refs.*), *person.* 1.72; = the Christian clergy, *in phrr.* **curatours of** ~ 16.279, **folk of** ~ Pr 118, **lawe of** ~ 9.218, 326, 14.152, **legates of** ~ 7.81, **love of** ~ 9.104, **men of**~ 17.41, **prechours of** ~ 16.250, **prelates of** ~ 6.119, 16.243, 22.229, **princes of** ~ 10.198, = the community of Christian believers (**Unite Holy** ~) 21.366, 22.75, 245

circumcisen *v* circumcise 18.252

cyte(e) *n* city Pr 177, 3.90, 112, 203, 5.90, 20.243, B 14.80, ~ **of Londoun** B Pr 160

Cyuyl(l)e *n* Civil (Roman) law, (*person.*) B 2.116 *et p.*; *and see* **Syuyle**

clayme *n* demand 4.98

claymen *v* demand 3.377, 17.71, B 14.142; (lay) claim (to, by right or title) 3.321, 374, 10.212, 12.59, 15.290, 16.99, 17.58, 71, 18.201, 20.18, 372, 21.446, 22.96, **B** 7.156, 10.321, 342, 18.344; declare (oneself) 21.446; ? claim to possess 1.89

clannesse *n* (moral) purity, integrity 7.76 (B 13.417), 21.382, **B** 14.11, 15.465; virginity 14.86, 88, B 14.300

clansen *v* clear 8.65; purify 16.25, B 18.392; purge, absolve 3.358, 18.143, 19.177

claumsen (clomsen) *v* become numb 15.254; *and see* **clumse** *a as n* Z 7.54

clause *n* clause 17.316, B 7.106; sentence 4.147; (short) text 11.249; letter (? *or* clause) A 8.44

*clausemele *av* clause by clause B 5.420

clawe *n* claw (= nail) 6.149, Pr 172 (**clee**)

clawen *v* claw, lacerate B Pr 154; scrape B 14.17; clutch Pr 172; grasp 19.157, (*fig.*) B 10.283

clee Pr 172 = **clawe** *n*

cleef *p.t.* B 18.61 *see* **cleuen** *v*[2]

cleer *a* bright 7.231; pure B 12.221

cleymen B 7.156, 10.342 = **claymen** *v*

cleken *v* Z 3.36 cluck (*or* = **clokken**)

†clemat B 15.370 = **clymat** *n*

clemen *v* gutter 3.106

clemp *p.t.* 18.108 *see* **clymben** *v*

clene *a* (*comp.* **clenner**, *sup.* **clennest**) unmixed 8.327; pure 3.23, 10.294, (*sup.*) 18.94, ~ **lyuyng** 21.382, 461; clean **B** 14.2, 12, 15.190, (*fig.*) **B** 14.185, †18.392; chaste B 1.195; ~ **moder** virgin mother 2.51, 7.155; ~

consience good, right conscience 9.26, **A** 6.27, 10.88; upright 21.382, 461, **B** 10.259, 11.300, (*comp.*) 13.296; ?elegant 20.122n; refined (*sup.*) 18.95, (*comp.*) 21.253; wholesome (*sup.*) **B** 14.44, 16.70; ~**nesse** *n* **B** 14.11, 300, 15.465 = **clannesse** *n*

clep(i)en *v* speak **B** 10.246; call (by name) 6.149, 21.117, 22.182; summon 11.18; invite 12.55, 104

clerc 5.54, 6.365, **B** 7.71, 13.248, Z 7.265, (~**us** *pl.*) Z 3.170 = **clerk** *n*

clere *av* brightly 19.223

clerg(i)(e) *n* the clergy 15.170, 21.470, **B** 3.165, **A** 11.65, (*person.*) **B** Pr 116, 3.15; learning 11.278, 283, 12.99, 14.30, 34, 35, 43, 70, 71, 72, 83, 191, 16.234, **B** 11.144, 165, 12.66, 71, 77, 81, 83, 85, 92, 15.209, 380, (*person.*) Pr 151, 11.93 *et p.*, 13.129 *et p.*, 14.100, 15.26 *et p.*, 22.228, A 12.1, 13, 35; doctrine 16.320, **B** 12.171; wisdom A 10.107

#clergialiche *av* in a scholarly way 8.34

clergyse *n* learning 20.405; the clergy Z 3.100

clerioun *n* young cleric A 12.49

clerk *n* cleric, member of the clergy 1.88, 121, 2.58, 246, 3.44, 49, 4.114 (*gen. pl.*), 146, 5.54, 56, 61, 63, 179, 7.91, 9.205, 210, 247, 11.306, 12.228, 14.54, 86, 199, 216, 16.263, 270, 279, 337, 17.69, 120, 175, 208, 214, 19.238, 20.354, 21.382, 417, 428, **B** 10.106, 112, 396, 411, 12.98, 233, 13.116, 14.180, 15.68, 104, 198, 331, 412, 443, 580, **A** 4.105, 10.137; = (higher) ecclesiastic 3.150, 12.228, 22.68, **B** 4.189; secular cleric 11.56; cleric (in orders below priest) **B** 13.11, 15.117; lawyer, ~ **of the lawe** learned lawyer 11.281, ~ **of þe Kinges bench** royal justice A Pr 95; parish clerk 6.365; educated person 11.236, 14.114, 118, *in phr.* ~ **and / or lewed** 'clerk or layman', educated or uneducated 6.29, 16.290, 22.68, **B** 10.51; learned man, scholar Pr 141, 3.27, 35, 210, 5.146, 6.76, 82, 7.182, 11.137, 156, 236, 291, 295, 12.162, 14.11, 45, 52, 64, 88, 97, 100, 114, 155, 198, 17.166, 21.271, **B** 3.347, 7.154, 10.104, 286, 466, 12.265, 15.82. 90, 211, 356, 372, 414; university student 10.20; student 3.276, **B** 10.196, 12.21; secretary (of records / accounts) 2.59, 3.179, 4.164, 21.465, **B** 10.471, A Pr 91; (*fig.*) 16.190; (royal) official 3.3, 16, A Pr 95; *in phr.* **connynge** ~**es** 3.37, 14.102, **B** 10.458, A 11.273, **knyhtes and** ~**es** 3.44, 49, (*trs*) 7.96, 11.52, A 4.105

*****clerkysh** *a* clerkly, apt for a scholar 6.42

clerliche *av* completely **B** 18.392

#clermatyn *n* a fine white bread 8.327

cleuen *v*¹ (**on**) cling to 7.303; hold together in 17.128; inhere in 19.313; devote (oneself) to **B** 11.224

cleuen *v*² (*p.t.* **cleef**) split **B** 18.61

cliaunt *n* (lawyer's) client 3.392

clycat *n* locking latch 7.251

clyf *n* hill A 1.4

*****clyketen** *v* (shut locking) latch 7.265

clymat *n* region of the earth [considered with respect to its weather] 17.106

clymben *v* (*p.t.* **clemp**) climb 18.106, 108; aspire A 10.101

clingen *v* shrivel up 15.254

clippen *v* grasp 19.157; (*pr. subjv.*) embrace 20.463

clips *n* eclipse 20.138

clyuen **B** 11.224 = **cleuen** *v*¹

cloches *n. pl.* clutches Pr 172; *and see* **cluchen** *v*

cloystre *n* monastery 4.116, 5.151, 153, 154; monastic building, cloister 3.64, 6.163, **B** 6.147

cloke *n* cloak 6.375, 380, 388, 7.166, 8.292, 9.139, **B** 3.296

*****clokken** *v* limp 3.37

clom *n* clay A 12.105

clomsen **B** 14.51 = **claumsen** *v*

closen *v* close, shut (up) Pr 132, 7.264, 265, 15.268, 21.168, ~ **with** close...with Pr 133; **do** ~ have confined 3.140; enclose 10.132, 172; cover over **B** 18.135; = bury A 12.105

cloth *n* cloth 5.18, 8.13, **B** 6.14, **lynnen** ~ **B** 14.56, **wollone** ~ 6.221; clothing 4.114, *in phr.* **corn and** ~ / **breed and** ~**es** food and clothing 8.145, 15.259, 22.248; cloth garment 10.195, 22.16; garb 9.249, 21.288, *pl.* **clothes** 5.41, 8.58, 263, 10.203, 12.126, 16.268, 349, 19.238, 22.7, 143, **B** Pr 199, 6.16, 11.431, A 8.43, Z 7.48, 199, (*fig.*) 6.65, **B** 14.177, 329, *in pl. phrr.* **bele** ~**es** 16.268, **broke** ~ B 9.92, **holde** ~ Z 7.48, **longe** ~ 5.41, **pilgrymes** ~ 12.126, **B** 13.29, **raggede** ~ 11.195, **wyde** ~ 18.270

clothen *v* dress Pr 54, 1.3, 2.9, 5.2, 9.210, 15.81, 19.243, 21.258, **B** Pr 62, 5.78, 13.273, (*fig.*) 5.179, 20.170, 174; provide clothes for 9.90, 13.83, 16.324, 17.196, 22.209, **B** 4.119 *ger.* **clothyng** garb, clothing 9.208, 12.129, 16.339, 20.175, **B** 14.157 *in phrr.* **continance of** ~ Pr 26, **lecherye of** ~ 16.254, **rich** ~ 20.175

clothere *n* cloth-maker 11.15

clotus Z 7.199 *see* **cloth** *n*

cloude *n* cloud 10.159, 14.73, 20.456, **B** 3.193, Z Pr 16

cloustre 3.64 = **cloystre** *n*

clout *n* rag 2.230; lining **B** 13.63

clouten *v* patch 9.80, **B** 6.59

cluchen *v* close (fingers) into a fist 19.122; clutch 19.157; *see* **cloches** *n*

#clumse *a* (*as n*) numb(ness) Z 7.54n; *and see* **claumsen** *v*

cluppen 20.463 = **clippen** *v*

coblere *n* cobbler, shoe-repairer 6.375

cock *n* cockle 9.95

coek 6.130 = **coke** *n*

coeld 17.303, 18.145 = **cold** *a*

coest 3.372, 384 = **cost** *n*²

coffe *n* mitten 8.59

cof(fe)re *n* chest (for valuables) 5.129, 12.216, 16.87, 89, **B** 13.301, (*fig.*) 14.54, **B** 10.323, 11.198

coghen **B** 17.327 = **cou(ʒ)en** *v*

coyne (koyne) *n* image (on coin) 1.46, (*fig.*) 17.80, 81

cok *n* cock, ~ **es fether** = thing of no worth 21.415; (pea) cock 13.171

coke *n* cook Pr 227, 3.80, (*fig.*) 5.175, 6.130

#coken *v*¹ cook (*fig.*) 15.60

coken (koken) *v*² make haycocks 5.13, 21.239

cokeney *n* (?small) hen's egg 8.308*n*

coker *n* legging 8.59

cokere *n* haycock-maker, harvestman 5.13

#coket *n* bread of fine flour 8.327

cokewold(e) *n* cuckold 4.59, 6.134

col *n* cabbage B 6.285

cold(e) *n* cold 9.109, Z 7.200; **for** ~ because of the cold 8.244, 15.254, 16.77, B 13.161; to keep off the cold (from) 13.71, **B** 3.191, 6.60, against the cold Z 7.53; *a* 1.124, 9.93, 16.73, B 13.262, Z 3.157

cold *a* cold 1.124, *quadriduanus* ~ four days dead 17.303, 18.145

cole *n* coal 9.142, (*fig.*) 15.144

coler *n* (ornamental) neck-chain Pr 179, 209, B Pr 204

#collateral *a* concomitant 16.134

collen *v* embrace B 11.17, A 11.177

colloppes (colhoppes) *n. pl.* bacon and eggs 8.308, 15.68

colomy *a* grimy B 13.356

colour *n* colour 13.138, 175, 18.21, 20.212, B 12.221; specious argument / appearance B 15.209; coloured dye / pigment 21.242; armorial bearings 21.13, (*with play on* 'specious appearance') 21.354; (*fig.*) manner, guise B 3.238

colouren *v* colour, speciously present 21.349; make (sth.) appear 21.461

coltur *n* coulter [vertical-cutting plough-blade] 3.460, 8.65 (B 6.104)

coluer(e) *n* dove 17.173, 175, (*gen.*) 179, 246, B 15.406, (*fig.*) 414

com *imp.* 7.218, *p.t.* 2.30 *et p.*; *see* **comen** *v*

coma(u)ndement *n* command 3.409; precept 16.126; commandment 11.142, 16.231

com(m)aunden *v* command 13.77, 21.113, **B** 6.16, 11.180; order 2.210, 4.6, 8, 81, 195, 8.88, 15.53, 21.364, 367, *p.t. 2 sg.* Z 3.154; ordain 1.20

comaundour *n* master A 3.274

combraunce *n* trouble 5.190; misfortune 12.247, 18.173, B 12.45; distress 20.276

combren *v* overcome 1.67; **burden** A 10.93; *and see* **acombren** *v*

comely *a* beautiful 20.122; fit(ting) B 15.451

comen *v* (*imp.* **com** 7.218, *pl.* **cometh** 21.386, *p.t. sg.* **cam** Pr 95, **com(e)** 2.30, *pl.* **cam** 18.4, **come(n)** Pr 71, 10.206, *pr. subjv.* **come** 4.8, *p.t. subjv.* 7.169, 22.329, *p.p.* **(y)come(n)** 3.455, 5.63, B 4.189) come Pr 71 *et p.*; should come 17.296, 21.423, 22.329, B 17.83; get to arrive 12.49, 18.127, 137, A 4.21; arise 13.234; call 5.50, 9.125; be created B 12.127; *in phr. vv.* **~aȝen**

attack 22.72, 220, approach B 4.44; **ar** ~ **auht longe** before very long 17.214; **~by** pass 7.218 (1), (through) B 17.121, ?acquire 5.6n; ~ **in** arrive (at) 6.231, 15.189, 17.173; enter 6.337, 7.218 (2), 9.253, B 11.50, take part in 13.84, 16.359; be (put) in A 7.287, ~ **into** arrive in 7.206, 18.4, B 3.303; ~ **of** be descended (from) 2.30, 3.60, 6.58, 10.206, 222, 14.182, 21.123, B 9.123; originate (from) 14.45, 79, 18.237, 21.25, 254; ~ **til** attend 8.98; ~ **to** arrive on B 2.26; reach 3.364; get to 6.307, 7.231, B 5.413; obtain 9.156, 21.69, 22.14, 16, 209, B 10.351; attain to 14.53, 157, 15.72; ~ **togyderes** match (in contest) 16.79;

comen 18.143 = **comune** *a*

co(m)menden *v* praise 11.278, 14.117, 16.285; approve B 4.158; **to** ~ to be commended 14.35

comenere *n* burgess, citizen [*spec.* member of town council] 4.188, B 15.331; one of the common people 5.183

comere *n* caller 2.240, ~ **aboute** visitor A 2.43; *and see* **nyhte-comare** *n* 21.144

com(e)sen *v* originate 1.158, 160, *ger.* origin Z 3.172; begin 21.97, 106, 123, Z 3.156, *ger.* beginning 20.223, origin Z 3.172; proceed to 4.24, 8.337, 10.20, 14.202, 21.97, 22.212, B 3.104; undertake, *ger.* 11.94; utter Z 7.36

comet *n* comet 14.97

comfort 22.182; **comforten** 6.281, 20.265, 21.128 *see* **confort(en)** *n, v*

comyn 3.167 = **comune** *a*

comyng(e) *ger.* (Christ's`) coming (into the world) 18.267, 20.444

commen 12.169 = **comune** *a*

comissarie *n* bishop's legate 2.190, 3.179, 16.362

commune 21.370, B 5.641; B Pr 113 *et p.*; *see* **comune** *n, a*

compacen *v* design 21.242; establish B 10.180

#compacience *n* compassion 15.89

compaignie B 5.641, 11.422, 13.161 = **companie** *n*

companie *n* band 21.155, B 13.161, Z 2.163; body of followers 22.120; (social) gathering 16.342, 21.160; fellowship 22.182; company 13.244, **folwen ~, suen ~** keep company (with) **B** 5.641, 11.422; **compenable** *a* companionable 16.342

compas *n* compass (for measuring) 11.125

compasen B 10.180 = **compacen** *v*

compeny 22.182 = **companie** *n*

comsyng *ger* see **com(e)sen** *v*

comune *n* people, community, nation Pr 95, 143, 144, 147, 1.155, 3.206, 374, 377, 384, 4.176, 5.20, 75, 180, 186, 17.289, 21.215, 394, 419, 469, 475, 479, 22.78, **B** Pr 115, 9.89, 10.29, 272, 12.294, 13.262; common people, populace 3.201, 468, 4.30, 76, 161, 8.84, 9.10, 15.170, 17.216, 308, 21.155, 382, 454, 22.30; free citizens [meeting as court] 16.360; fellowship 5.186; *pl.*

comunes the common people B Pr 114, A 3.66; sustenance Pr 143, 5.144, 8.292, 21.417

comune a common, in phr. ~ profit common good Pr
167, 184, 201, 4.119; of the whole community in phr. ~
helpe 3.244, 4.176n; open to all 3.167; in phrr. ~ court
Court of Common Pleas, ? county court 2.22, 3.472; ~
fode food shared by all, ? ordinary, normal 21.410n; ~
lawe law of the land 20.74; ~ peple common people
2.58, 11.297, 21.7, 132, 423; þe ~ speche the familiar /
well-known expression A 11.241; ~ woman prostitute
18.143, 21.370, B 11.216; a as n, in phr. in ~ (shared)
in common 1.20, 16.42, 22.276; universally B 10.356;
in public B 11.216

comunely(che) av usually 16.139; frequently, commonly
14.19, 21.314; in general 11.295

conceyuen (conseyuen) v conceive 10.215, 220, 13.149,
151, 20.132, B 9.121, 11.357; comprehend 10.56,
13.223; utter 8.32

concepcion n procreation, mating 13.145; offspring B
9.158

concience 3.254, (person.) 15.26 et p., 16.190, 21.26,
22.106 = consience n

concluden v confute 11.283

condicion n, in ~ on condition 21.480

confermen v ratify 14.39, B 10.352; (administer sacrament of) confirm(ation to) B 13.214, 15.456

confessen v (refl.) (make one's) confess(ion of sins)
6.337, 12.5, 19.279; hear confession (of) 5.168, 12.15,
17.280, (fig.) B 10.316

confessio(u)n n (formal) confession of sins (to a priest)
10.53, 12.71, 14.115, 16.26, 21.333, 348, 351, 22.213,
329, B 14.187

confessour n confessor [= one who affirms Christian
faith under persecution] 10.206, 12.198, B 12.203; [=
priest who hears confessions] 3.38, 4.142, 146, 5.194,
22.372, B 11.70, 14.18, A 12.41, 77

conformen B 11.180, 13.209, 15.343 = confo(u)rmen v

confort n consolation 7.110, 16.134, Z 6.62 (? or trust);
relief 22.372; pleasure (person.) 22.91, 182; benefit
5.75, B 4.151; strengthening 12.149, 152

confortable a consoling B 14.282

confortatif a cheerful B 15.219

conforten v inspire with spiritual strength 17.50, 18.73,
B 11.264; reassure B 12.175; encourage 14.118, B
12.21; abet 22.67; refresh 15.189, 196, B 14.147,
179, 180; cheer (up) 2.164, 3.16, 27, 18.267, 20.265,
22.243, B 13.22; relieve 14.115; console 1.197, 6.281,
14.70; minister to 9.48, 15.196, 16.324, 22.359; succour 8.230, 9.97, 15.147, 21.128, B 12.81, 14.175;
entertain 15.62, B 13.58

confortour n bringer of strength / refreshment B 16.190

confounden v cause harm to 5.190

confo(u)rmen v (refl.) consent, agree 3.397; submit to B
15.343; dispose B 11.180, 13.209

confus p.p.a discountenanced B 10.138

congie n leave, farewell B 13.203

conieyen (congeyen) v take leave of 15.177; order to
leave, dismiss 3.219, 4.195, 11.163, 16.367

conyng n rabbit B Pr 189

conyon n fool, oaf A 11.87

conysaunce n heraldic device 18.187

coniuren v solemnly charge B 15.14

connen (konnen) v (pr. sg. can 2.236 et p., pl. can 1.190,
3.496, 8.267, 11.18, 228, 14.11, 15.191, conne(n)
8.69, 13.125, 14.11, 17.316, conneth Pr 35, (subjv.)
conne 14.111, 21.480; p.t. couthe Pr 196, coude A
2.188, 8.44, 12.73, assim. 2. p. sg. p.t. †coudestow A
6.21; ger. connyng 11.283, pr. p. 10.260) be able 3.218
et p., A 11.185; have ability 6.82, 8.69; be capable of
6.58; know how to Pr 35, 3.496, 8.129, 14.111, 21.401;
have mastery of 2.236, 16.209, 17.114, 22.231, Z 7.49;
have knowledge of 7.157, 8.267, 16.213, B 2.227;
know 3.3, 16.205; recognise, come to know 11.101,
†A 12.32; grant A 8.44

connyng ger. skill 11.285, 14.106, 15.133, 21.235, 254,
B 13.293; knowledge, understanding 11.295, 14.34,
36, 15.18 (2), B 10.472, 11.165, 211, 12.66; learning 11.228, 13.112, 233, 14.19; science, (branch of)
knowledge 11.94, 15.133; wisdom 11.283, 15.18 (1),
21.461, B 11.300; prudence 21. 235, A 10.50

connyng(e) a skilful 6.42; clever, shrewd 10.260, B
11.70; learned 3.37, 14.102, 114, B 10.458, A 11.273

conqueren v acquire by force of arms 3.244 (p.p.), 254; ~
on win victory (over) 3.250; (fig.) be victorious 21.50

conquerour n conqueror [= one who subjugates a peo-
ple] 21.27, 30, 43, 99, 106, (fig.) 21.50, 53, 62, 97;
victorious leader 21.14

conqueste n conquered territory 21.43

conseyl, consayl n assembly Pr 167; council 11.18;
(meeting of) (royal) council (of advisers) 3.127, 156,
4.119, 5.144, 16.358, 22.30, 68, 129, B 4.189; adviser,
counsellor, be of ~ be counsellor to 16.359, B 4.193;
be in the confidence of 2.152, taken to ~ take into
one's confidence 4.166, 15.176, B 13.178; counsel,
advice Pr 208, 3.7, 253, 375, 6.76, 8.337, 11.100, 317,
16.238, 367, 17.56, 21.38, 79, 258, 297, 317, 358, 396,
455, 22.21, 212, 242, B 9.115; plan, scheme 2.119,
5.184; secret / private matter(s) / concern(s) 4.8, 6.165,
21.162, B 5.166, Z 3.168n; wise judgement 22.147

conseilen v counsel, advise Pr 201, 3.232, 241, 253,
262, 4.106, 5.180, 6.29, 8.13, 9.346, 10.281, 14.5, 43,
64, 19.228, 21.201, 215, 394, 465, 22.74, B 11.224,
15.343; give (divine) counsel 12.169, 21.113, 394, persuade, prevail upon 1.62

conseyuen 10.56, B 9.121, etc = conceyuen v

consenten v agree to give 2.90

cons(c)ience n (inner) attitude of mind / feelings 3.71,
B 13.391n; ? conscientiousness B 14.87; conscience

2.52, 5.83, 9.26, 17.197, 216, **B** 14.82, 189, 17.136, **A** 10.88, 91, 93, 11.309, (*person.*) Pr 138 *et p.*, B 7.134, Z 3.147; scruples 12.5; *in phrr.* **as in** ~ truly 17.149, **bi here** ~ in fairness, 'in all conscience' 6.385

conspiren *v* plot secretly B 10.19, 422

constable *n* constable, king's high or chief military officer (*fig.*) 3.255n; = warden of royal castle (*fig.*) 10.143, 22.214; = officer of the king's peace 2.210, 4.81, B 2.207, Z 2.188; justice of the peace 3.467

constillacioun *n* planetary / lunar position (in relation to the ascendant zodiacal sign) 14.31, A 10.146

cons(is)torie *n* consistory [bishop's] court 3.34, 178, 472, 16.362, (*fig.*) the court of God [judging mankind at the last day] Pr 127

constraynen *v* compel 5.54; restrain 20.435

constru(w)en *v* translate 4.142, 9.281, 16.116, **B** Pr 144, 5.278; explain 4.147, 7.34, B 5.420; interpret 17.110, B Pr 61; (pass) judge(ment on) B 2.36, A 8.134; practise A 11.19*n*

contemplacio(u)n *n* contemplation (of divine things) 18.73, 77, (*person.*) 7.304; rational speculation 22.274

contemplatif *a* contemplative (= devoted to contemplation of God) B 6.248

contenuen 5.39 = **contynuen** *v*

continaunce (**continence**) *n* outward show Pr 26; looks 11.177, Z Pr 25; meaningful look 6.165, 11.163, 15.121

continence *n* sexual abstinence 18.73; (state of) sexual abstinence (within widowhood or marriage) B 16.69

contynuen *v* persevere 5.104, 10.286, B 12.38

contraye 8.206, 21.314 = **contre(ye)** *n*

contrarie *n* opposite 1.121, 9.193, **B** 10.198, 395, 12.50; reverse 10.242, 17.106; contrary [element] 19.327, B 17.271; opposition 17.161

contrarien *v* oppose, act against 17.149, 19.313, B 5.54; violate 17.251; feel resentment 19.322, contradict Pr 59, 2.22, 14.100

contre(y)(e) *n* region, place 8.206, 9.111, 10.12, 269, 17.164, 21.136, 22.56, **B** 13.224, 16.170, 17.114, 121, (*fig.*) 15.190, 18.4; area of jurisdiction [ecclesiastical] 22.329; country, realm 2.56, 3.238, 17.164, 21.420, 22.224, B 15.519, A Pr 95; shire A 2.43; town 19.51; country district Pr 31, 10.15, **sysores of c** ~ **s** district jurors 2.63; the countryside 21.314

#**contrepleden** Pr 138 = **countrepleden** *v*

#**contrerollor** *n* keeper of the counter-roll (= accountant) 11.302

contreuen *v* plan, devise 14.160; establish Pr 144; fashion 11.124, 125; discover 14.73; scheme 6.39, 11.16, B 16.137

contricio(u)n *n* contrition [religious sorrow for sin] 10.53, 12.71, 14.115, 117, 121, 16.25, 21.348, 350, 22.213, **B** 11.81, 14.16, 82, 84, 87, 92, 282, (*person.*) 15.60, 21.333, 22.317 *et p.*

contrit *a* contrite, filled with sorrow for sin B 14.84

conuthe *pr. pl.* Z 8.13 = **conneth**; *see* **connen** *v*

conuerten *v* reform 18.143; convert 17.186; transform 20.188

cook 5.175 = **coke** *n*

co(o)me *p.t. subjv.* 17.296, 21.423, 22.329, B 17.83

cope A 5.59 = **coupe** n^2

cope *n* cope [sleeveless clerical cloak] Pr 54, 59, 8.185, 9.210, 247, 22.58, Z 3.153

#**copen** *v* provide / dress with (in) a cope 2.240, 3.38, 179, 6.288, 22.345, (*fig.*) Z 3.156

copien *v* copy A 8.44

coplen 2.190 = **couplen** *v*

coppe *n* drinking-cup 3.23, 5.161, 6.389, 20.406; *av* ~ **mele** a cup(ful) at a time 6.231

corecten 21.305 = **cor(r)ecten** *v*

corleu *n* ?quail 15.243*n*

corn *n* (crop of cereal) grain 5.17, 8.31, 101, 244, 322, 17.173, 21.320, **B** 6.140, 15.401, **A** 6.32, 7.128, Z 7.65, 108; corn-fields 13.45; (as food) bread 15.259, B 13.262, A 7.183; **breed** ~ wheat-grain 8.61

cornel *n* kernel 12.149, 152

corner *n* angle (formed by spokes) 15.163

coro(u)ne 17.205, 21.468, B 2.10 *see* **croune** *n*

corps B 13.9, 19.151 = **cors** n^1

Corpus Cristi (feste) *n* the feast of Corpus Christi 17.120

cor(r)ecten *v* set right by rebuke 21.305; punish B 10.283

correctour *n* one who rebukes / punishes (for misconduct) B 10.283

cors *n* body [dead] 15.11, 21.151, [living] 16.181, B 1.139

cors 13.145 = **cours** *n*

corseynt *n* saint [*lit.* 'holy body'] 7.176

*****corse-men** *n. phr* 'curse-men' 6.65*n*

corsen *v* curse, invoke evil upon 6.64, 8.338, 22.68, **B** 10.466, 13.331, 15.171; utter an imprecation 19.309; excommunicate 3.178, *ger.* 8.159; *p.p.a* **corsed(e)** damned, accursed 10.220, 229, 231, 250, A 10.140, 146, 148; wicked 17.212, 19.255, 21.406, 435, 470, B 6.160, Z 2.163; ill-fortuned, wretched 3.106, (*comp.*) 21.420

corteys *a* well-bred, polite 4.17, 8.47, B 13.459, A 4.105; gracious, generous 14.160, 16.255, B 13.15, A 3.59; ~**liche** *av* politely 8.161, 15.121, 194, B 13.31, 46, 180, 199; graciously 3.9, 129, 4.42, 152, 8.32, 161, 21.177, 22.243, 356, A 11.177; respectfully 2.164

cortesye *n* (refined / good manners 10.267, 17.164, B 10.310; courteous behaviour B 5.89; generosity, kindness 3.314, 7.43, 17.220, B 11.439, Z 2.7; loving-kindness, merciful graciousness [of God] 1.20, 19.208, 21.452, 22.106, B 12.77, 14.147; gracious gift 14.216; respect B 15.303

corupcion *n* disease 22.99

corue *p.t.* (*2 sg*) Z 3.153, ~**n** *3 pl.* 8.185 *see* **keruen** *v*

cosyn *n* kinsman 11.93, 22.358, **B** 2.133, 12.93, A 12.41, 43, 53

cost *n*¹ disposition (? *or* expense) 3.72*n*

cost *n*² expense ? 3.72, 372, 384, 15.47, 19.238

costen *v* (*p.t.* ~ed(e), -e) cost Pr 209, 210, B 13.383

coste *n* region 10.12, B 2.86; quarter (of the heavens) B 18.113

costnen B Pr 205 = **costen** *v*

costume 14.73 = **custume** *n*

cote *n*¹ small cottage 4.123, 5.2, 9.72, 83, 151, 10.16, 14.90

cote *n*² tunic 16.299, **B** 5.109, 11.283, 14.151, (*fig.*)**B** 13.274, 314, 355, 403, 458, 14.17, ~ **armure** tunic with heraldic devices (*fig.*) 18.187, 21.13

*****coten** *v* provide with tunic 3.179

#**coterel** *n* (lesser) cotter, subtenant 9.97, 193

#**cotidian** *a* daily-recurring A 12.84

cottepors *n* cut-purse, thief 7.282

coude *p.t.* **A** 2.188, 12.72 = **couthe**, *2 sg.* †**coudestou, coudest thow**; *see* **connen** *v*

couden (**couth** Z) *p.t. pl.*; *see* **kithen** *v*

couen 19.309 = **couȝen** *v*

couert 1.104 = **court** *n*

cough (**cowh**) cough B 20.82 (22.82)

couȝen *v* cough 19.309; clear throat 15.110; vomit 6.163, 411

counforten A 11.189 = **conforten** *v*

counsayl 5. 184, **counseil** B Pr 144 etc = **conseyl** *n*; **counsei(ll)en** B Pr 115 etc, A 10.97, 11.222 = **conseilen** *v*

counte(e) *n* county, earldom 2.90

counten *v* number, reckon Z 3.168; regard, esteem 3.178, 9.303, 10.261, 11.177, 317, 12.198, 13.238, 14.83, 22.147, 222, A 7.154; take account (of), care (for / that) 9.109, 21.306, 447; make reckoning A 4.11; *and see* **acounten** *v*

#**co(u)ntrepleden** *v* plead in opposition to (a demand) 8.53, 88; argue against Pr 138, 22.385, B 12.98

countreseggen *v* contradict 11.225

coupable *a* (found) guilty 19.284; guilty (of sin) B 12.88

coupe *n*¹ guilt (for sin) 6.327, 350, A 5.59

coupe *n*² drinking bowl 3.23

coupen *v* slash (for decoration) 20.12

couple *n* married pair 18.223, B 9.162; pair (of male and female animals) B 9.141

couplen *v* unite in marriage B 9.126, 128, A 10.156, (*subjv.*) 158; join in league 4.146, **B** 3.165, 10.162; put on a leash B Pr 207; (be) hitch(ed) [to a vehicle] 2.190

courben *v* bend, kneel B 1.79, 2.1, Z 1.24

#**courrour** *n* courier, messenger A 12.84

cours *n* movement (of planets) 17.104; sequence 3.346; (proper) conduct, ? progress 3.388; process 3.60, 13.145; way 17.161

court *n* enclosed yard B 15.473; manor-house 10.15, 22.345, **B** 8.15, 13.23, (*fig.*) 7.231, B 10.165, A 12.57; royal residence Pr 168, 16.358, 18.95, A 4.29, Z 2.163; royal household Pr 204, 215; heavenly court of God 3.455, B 15.21, 22; (of judgement) 16.166; royal council 21.427, 22.130; papal court, curia Pr 134, 17.166, B Pr 111; law court, (royal) court of justice Pr 158, 2.22, 202, 3.34, 468, 472, 473, 20.38, 21.306, **B** 2.63, 4.166; manorial court 7.33; ? county court 16.360; church tribunal 3.34

courteysly(che) 2.164, 8.32, 161, = **corteysliche** *av*

courtepy *n* short jacket 8.185, B 5.79

couthe 17.196 = **kuth** *n*

couth(e) *p.t.* Pr 196 *et p.* (*2 sg.* **couthest** 10.74, 18.2) B 1.116, A 4.142, Z 5.143 *see* **connen** *v*

couth *p.t.* Z 8.44 *see* **kithen** *v*

coueiten *v* covet [*esp.* goods], desire unrightfully Pr 31, 3.425, 362, 5.151, 7.219, 9.48, 193, 10.281, 11.109, 16.144, 291, 15.155, 19.182, **B** Pr 29, 11.76, 13.150, 14.309, 15.159, A 3.248; desire strongly, long (for) 3.254, 398, 401, 10.109, 11.18, 141, 12.61, 170, 15.72, 16.199, 368, 17.80, 228, 19.182, **B** Pr 189, 3.164, 10.337, 11.125, 13.151, 15.175, 254, 17.216, 22.253, A 10.101, 12.3; desire sexually (*fig.*) 20.171; yearn for 11.172, B 15.469, 17.122

coue(y)tise *n* covetousness, greed (y desire for wealth) Pr 59, 103, 1.67, 190, 2.52, 247, 3.72, 201, 210, 430, 5.184, 10.260, 282, 12.243, 247, 16.109, 17.205, 208, B 9.157 *in phr.* **counte of** ~ 2.90, **custumes of** ~ 3.206; **licames** ~ B 15.67; (*spec.*) the deadly sin of Greed 2.90, 4.33, 11.15, 15.13, 190, 17.214, 18.32, 19.256, 326, **B** 10.281, 13.356, 391, A 2.32, Z 3.154, 156, 170; (*person.*) 6.196, 16.79, 81, 367, 21.225, 22.141, 220, 297, 352, B 15.414, Z 5.97; ~ **of Yes** 11.175, 312; (strong) desire (*with pun on* 'greed') 4.114, 16.222, **B** 5.255, 14.11, A 7.183

coue(i)tous *a* covetous, greedy for wealth 6.206, 16.42, A 3.59, *as n* 14.21; eager for B 13.184

couena(u)nt *n* binding agreement 8.157, (*fig.*) = divine pledge 14.216; pact (of peace) 20.463; agreed payment B 14.151; condition, *in phr.* **in** ~ **þat** on condition that 6.389, 8.26, 21.187

couent *n* religious community (living under a rule) 6.39, 130, 162, 22.60, **B** 5.136, 11.76, Z 3.154; (the) convent(ual buildings) 5.151

coueren B 14.331 *see* **keueren** *v*

couerour *n* repairer / provider of roof 5.175

couetyse 3.72 *et p.*, **couetous** 6.206 *see* **coue(y)tise** *n*, **coue(i)tous** *a*

cow *n*¹ (*pl.* **kyen** B 6.140) cow 8.311, 13.149, **B** 6.140, 15.466, Z 3.149; *in cpds.* ~ **calf** female calf B 15.469, ~ **kynde** female of (any) cattle 13.149

cow (**ko**) *n*² chough A 7.128 (Z 7.125)

cowardly *av* in a cowardly manner B 3.206

cowh 22.82 = **cough** *n*

cow(h)en *v* 6.411, 15.110 = **couȝen** *v*

crabbed *a* ill-tempered 14.100, B 10.106

crachen *v* scratch [with claws] Pr 200, B Pr 154, [with fingernails] 6.140; comb [cloth to raise a nap] B 15.453; snatch, tear away 12.80

cradel *n* cradle 9.79

craft *n* power B 1.139; skill 6.322, 7.190, 9.90, 155, 16.188, 21.254, 22.206, 207, 343, B 5.25, (*person.*) 21.257, 258; ingenuity 3.20; (business) acumen 21.235; trade, craft Pr 144, 2.236, 5.20, 6.322, 7.190, 11.124, 8.200, 9.90, 155, 15.194, **B** Pr 222, 5.547, 7.31, 19.254; profession 4.170, 22.231; branch of learning 15.133; art, (applied) science 16.208; ? craft guild 21.251*n*; way, means 2.4; trick 6.231, B 10.21; activity 8.58, B 17.171

crafty *a* skilled in / master of a craft, ~ **men** 3.279, 8.69, A 11.185, ~ **connynge** skill in a craft B 13.293; skilfully wrought Pr 179

craftily *av* ingeniously 10.132; skilfully B 19.242

#**craym** *n* cream 8.305, 321

craken *v* break 20.75

crammen *v* cram, stuff full Pr 42

crampe 22.82, B 13.335 = **crompe** *n*

crauen *v* ask 16.55, †B 11.439, 13.165; ask (to have) 3.274, 276, 279, **B** 13.242, 15.254, 17.122; implore 12.151, B 14.187; beg 6.49, 15.35; demand (as one's due) 8.101, 21.479, B 15.165

creatour *n* (the) Creator [God] 10.152, 17.153, 18.94, **B** 11.325, 16.215

creature *n* created thing 17.153, B 16.215; creation 16.164, 165; living creature 13.133, 18.94, 21.17, 22.151, **B** 11.397, 13.18, 16.190, A 11.246; (order of) living creature 1.104; person, 'body' 6.294, 10.215, 13.209, 14.5, 43, 157, 15.225, 16.170, 213, 19.284, 20.122, 132, 21.217, 375, **B** 11.180, 12.83, 225, 276, 14.175, 180, 15.171, 195, 211, A 12.110; *in phrr.* ~ **vnder Crist** anyone anywhere 13.208, 14.159, **Cristene** ~ Christian person 15.274, 21.375, **B** 9.80, 84, 10.356, 362, 15.578, **Cristes** ~ 16.164, 165, B 11.198, **vncristene** ~ non-Christian 12.79, B 11.154; **vnkynde** ~ in-human person 19.182, 216, B 5.269

creaunt *a* (confessed as) vanquished, i.e. submitting [to Christ] in faith 14.132, 153; *and see* **recreaunt** *a*

crede *n* Creed, *spec.* the Apostles Creed 3.359, 8.98

crepen *v* (*p.t.* **crepte** A 12.35, **crope** (*pl.*) Pr 200, *2 sg.* B 3.191) crawl 15.20, B 13.18, (*fig.*) B 16.28; creep Pr 200, 1.190, 22.44, [on knees as devotional act] 20.474; withdraw cautiously B 3.191, A 12.35, insinuate (oneself) 17.280

cresse (carse, kerse) *n* 8.321, **welle** ~ water cress 6.292; (*fig.*) thing of no value (? *with pun on* 'curse') 11.14

cryant 14.153 = **creaunt** *a*

crien *v* (*p.t.* **cri(e)d(e)** 1.76, *pl.* **criden** 21.213) shout out

Pr 227, 17.222, 19.270, 20.13; ~ **on** shout at 7.57, **B** 11.70, 18.39, A 12.13; scream 6.140; cry out 4.157, 6.4, 64, 17.222, 21.213, 22.140, B 18.262; ~ **after** summon 22.90, B 15.279; demand B 15.254; call (upon) 22.78, 165, 376; wail 11.42, 18.108, B 9.80; lament tearfully 22.370; beg (for) 6.337, 7.155, 9.346, 13.12, 15.35, 17.246, 19.208, 279, 20.89, B 14.331; ~ **(to)** supplicate (in prayer) 2.1, 3.93, 6.170, 7.147, 155, 19.270, 22.201, **B** 5.106, 17.222, *pr.p.* Z 5.153; proclaim 7.108, 21.159, 364, B Pr 143; command publicly 4.164

cryket *n* house-cricket, ? salamander 15.243

crimylen *v* ? curl / plait, ? anoint (with oil) *p.p.* 16.352n

Crist *n* Christ, *in oaths*: **by** ~ 2.204, 246, 3.283, 4.4, 79, 99, 5.89, 7.282, 304, 8.19, 21, 167, 264, 308, 9.213, 11.141, 15.130, 179, 16.290, 21.401, 22.268, 381, **B** 5.163, 9.162, 10.343, 13.189, 272, 314, 14.12, 15.301, A 4.144, Z 7.108; *in imprecations*: ~ **ȝeue hem sorwe** 19.309, B 5.106, **so me** ~ **helpe / spede** 4.11, 10.108, **B** 4.104, Z 7.200; *in assevs*: ~ **haue his soule** A 12.105, **for** ~**es loue** 15.35, 16.164, B 15.523, **for** ~ **sake** 14.5, B 12.92, **vnder** ~ anywhere (alive / in the world) 11.156, 12.80, 13.208, 14.155, 159; *in phrr.* **Cristes owene beestes** (= the Christian people) B 10.409; ~ **clergie** (= spiritual wisdom) 12.99; ~ **court** 16.166; ~ **creature(s)** 16.164, B 11.198; ~ **cros** 17.203; ~ **fode** 18.14; ~ **good(es)** (= the Church's wealth) **B** 9.87, 15.104; ~**lawes** 17.251; ~ **loue** 17.281; ~ **messager** 21.208; **mynistres** 5.60; ~ **mouth** 11.278; ~ **name** B 15.456, A 12.13; ~ **passion** B 18.9; ~ **patrimonye** (= the Church's wealth) B 15.246; ~ **pees** 17.228; ~ **peple** B 14.72, 15.22; ~ **sonde** 16.134; ~ **tresor** (= the Church's doctrine and sacraments) 14.54, B 10.474; ~ **vycary** 14.70; ~ **wordes** 15.274; ~ **writyng** B 12.82

Cristen(e) *a* Christian 13.89, 16.165, 21.351; *in phrr.* ~ **bloed** 21.448; ~ **clerk** B 15.412; ~ **creature(s)** 15.274, 21.375, B 9.80, A 12.110; ~ **kynde** (= Christian people) B 10.424; ~ **kyng(es)** 3.441, B 13.176; ~ **man** 12.61, B 15.398; ~ **men** 19.256, B 10.351, Z 6.62; ~ **peple** 5.193, 11.270, 13.77, 15.230, 21.343, 364, **B** 12.158, 15.90; ~**prouinces** B 15.608, ~ **reumes** B 15.524; ~ **soules** 11.246, 12.152, 20.406, B 15.430

Cristendo(e)m *n* Christianity, the Christian religion 12.80, 110, 14.53, 17.186, 282, 298, 18.209, 19.8, B 15.446, *in phr.* **cart** ~ 21.332; (the) Christian doctrine B 10.447, faith B 14.11, way of life 12.61, 17.251, baptism 7.234, 12.61, 14.205, 17.77, **B** ?11.215*n*, 12.276, 14.320, 15.351, *in phr.* **cote of** ~ (= baptismal regeneration) B 13.274

Cristene *a as n* Christian 17.183, *pl.* 1.89 *et p.*; *in phrr.* **alle** ~ 1.188; **alle kyne** ~ 17.128; **corsede** ~ 17.212; **euen** ~ 6.75; **false** ~ 17.76; **kynde** ~ 22.73; **parfyt** ~ 22.108; **vnkynde** ~ 17.275, 19.256; **we** ~ 17.293; **ȝe** ~ 21.386

crist(e)nen *v* baptize (into the Christian faith) 17.165, **B** 10.348, 11.67, 15.444, 456, A 12.15, *ger.* (the act of) christening B 14.185

croce A 9.86, †B 8.95 = **crose** *n*

crocer *n* cross-bearer 5.113

#crod *n* curd 8.305, 321, Z 7.286

cro(e)s(s) *n* cross [of crucifixion] 11.257, 14.153, *spec.* the cross of Christ 6.318, 10.58, 20.74, 21.14, 41, 50, 63, 200, 323, B 16.164, A 11.28, (*meton.*) Christ's death on the cross 17.203, 20.112; **on ~ wyse** stretched out on a cross, by crucifying 21.142; ornamental cross / crucifix 5.106, 20.474; (bishop's) cross (of office) **B** 5.12, 15.569, A 5.23; (*meton.*) the Christian faith 17.282, B 15.446, 578; (cross stamped on) coin 17.205, 208, B 5.240; cross-shaped seal 19.8, B 17.6

croft *n* (small enclosed) field [for cultivation] 5.17, 8.31, 314, Z 7.108, (*fig.*) 7.218, 219

crois A 11.28 = **cro(e)s** *n*

crok *n*¹ grappling-iron 20.294

crok *n*² (earthen) cooking-pot 21.281

croked(e) *p.p.a* crooked 2.29; crippled, deformed 9.97, *a as n* 12.105, B 16.109

crompe *n* cramp [disease with painful spasms] 6.78 (B 13.335), 22.82,

cronicle *n* chronicle, history 5.178

croos 17.282, 20.112 = **cro(e)s** *n*

crop *n* top 18.75, **B** 16.42, 69, 70, 75, **to þe ~ ward** towards the top 18.108; crop 22.53

crope(n) *p.t.* Pr 200, B Pr 186, 191 *see* **crepen** *v*

croppen *v* eat up **B** 6.32, 15.401

cros 14.153 *etc.*, = **cro(e)s(s)** *n*

crose *n* crosier 10.93

crouch *n* cross-emblem 7.166

croume *n* scrap (of bread) 8.279, 288

croune *n* (royal) crown 4.79, 135, 20.273, 413, 21.468, 469; crown-image (on coin) 17.205 (*with pun on* heavenly crown of glory), A 4.113; **~ of thornes** 21.49, 323; (crown-like) tiara 2.11, 15.163; (*meton.*) messianic sovereignty B 18.109; clerical tonsure 13.112, **B** 13.243, 15.351, (*meton.*) = priestly ordination B 11.299; hair on the top of the head 11.197, 16.352; top of the head 5.177, 22.184

crounen *v* crown (as king) 10.101, 104, 21.41, (as heavenly king) B 18.372, (*fig.*) 21.257, (as pope) 3.318; bedeck with diadem 2.11; tonsure (cleric) 5.56, 59, 63, 13.125, *ger.* Pr 86

crow *n* (*uninfl. gen.*) crow's 15.163

cruwel *a* pitiless B 13.391

cullen (killen, kullen) *v* (*p.t.* **culd(e)** 8.280, **kild(e)** B 5.163, A 3.251, *p.p.* **culd(e)** 17.289, 21.447, **ykuld** Pr 199, **kulled** B 16.152) strike, **~ to dethe** strike mortally 11.270; kill Pr 199, 1.62, 3.232, 8.30, 280, 10.250, 12.243, 21.447, 22.99, 151, B 5.163; slay

10.101, 17.289; put to death 21.142, B 16.137, 152; destroy 16.26

cultour B 6.104 = **kultour** *n*

cumsen Z 3.156, **cumsyng** *ger.* Z 3.172 *see* **com(e)sen** *v*

cunnen A 11.185, †12.32, Z 7.49 = **connen** *v*

cuntre A Pr 95, 2.43 = **contre(y)(e)** *n*

#curato(u)r *n* churchman with 'cure of souls' 17.290, 22.327, B 15.90; priest with spiritual charge of a parish 11.249, 15.16, 16.273, 279, 17.280, 21.413, 454, 22.282, B 1.195; spiritual authority 21.223,

cure *n* spiritual responsibility Pr 86; **~ (of soules)** pastoral responsibility (in a parish) 22.233, 237, 253; benefice B 11.300

curen *v* exercise pastoral responsibility 22.326 (*with pun on* heal); heal (? *with pun on latter*) 14.70

curious *a* artfully cut 21.288

cursen *p.p.* 3.106, 178, B 13.331, A 10.140, 148 *see* **corsen** *v*

curteis(e) *a* B 13.15, 459, A 3.59, 4.105; **curteisie** *n* B 5.89, 10.310, 11.439, 12.77, 14.147, 15.303; **curteisli(che)** *av* B 13.31, 46, 180, 199, A 11.177; *see* **corteys** *a*, **cortesye** *n*, **corteysliche** *av*

†cusen *v* charge with an offence Pr 95

custe *p.p.* 20.466; *see* **kissen** *v*

custume *n* usage, law 3.373; practice, behaviour 3.206, 9.18; traditional practice 14.73, B 12.97

cuueren 3.64 = **keueren** *v*¹

daffe *n* fool, idiot 1.138, 10.179, 13.235

daggen *v* ornament by cutting at the edges 22.143

day(e) *n* day Pr 226, 2.98, 238, 3.182, 303, 6.161, 7.18, 8.277, 10.228, 16.319, 18.283, **B** 1.121, 3.312, 5.489, 10.96, 13.415, A 7.135, 12.66; **thre ~es** 10.113, 15.70, 18.161, 20.31, **in / ar thre ~es aftur** within the space of three days 18.161, 20.41, 22.177; daytime 1.32, B 16.166; daylight 12.154, 20.215, 470, 21.150, (*person.*) 20.60; dawn, daybreak 1.113, 7.65, 20.126; day of the ecclesiastical year **B** 5.2, 11.313; day appointed / agreed upon B 5.241; *in pl.* **daies** = time 1.101, 20.111, 21.101; life 20.53, B 18.53, A 12.94, Z 5.73; *in phrr.* **~ after other** day after day 10.114, B 16.138, A 11.92; **~ bi ~** every day B 15.281; **~ and / ne / or nyghte(s)** at all times 1.32, 9.222, 11.192, 13.190, 17.29, 92, 171, 245, 19.218, (*trs*) 19.270, 21.20, 141, **B** 9.97, 13.369, 18.97; **~ of dome** Judgement Day 9.321, 351, 12.70, 22.294, **B** 7.17, 172, 10.358, 12.91, (*and see* **domes ~**) **~ withouten ende** for ever 2.106, 19.252; **~es doen** days ago 15.70; **~ es iourne** day's stint of work 16.5; **~ sterre** morning star A 6.80; *in time phrr:* **many ~** many a day, often A 5.71; for a long time (now) 5.156, 20.179; **this ~** today 17.223, 20.137, the present time B 16.148, **~ þre ~es** three days from today B 17.110; **a ~ hennes** a day's walk from here 10.128; **prime ~es** prime of the day (= 6–9 A.M) A 12.60; **firste ~** B 5.166; **thridde ~** 7.136,

ferþe ~ A 12.82; *in n. phrr.* **deth** ~ day of one's death 1.130, 9.350, 10.303, **B** 7.114, 12.245, 14.106; **domes** ~ Judgement Day 5.122 *et p.*; **fastyng** ~ day (appointed by Church) for obligatory fasting 2.100, 6.182, 433; **feste** ~ religious feast day 5.30; **haue gode** ~ farewell A 12.75; **haly (holy)** ~ feast-day of (obligatory) religious observance 6.272, 359, 7.25, 9.231, 13.85, A 7.12; **lyf** ~ day of one's life 3.187, B 1. 27; **loue** ~ settlement-day 11.17; *in prep. phrr.* **a** ~ one / a certain day 1.27, daily / ? on the next day 8.331; **be þis** ~ today 7.9, 8.302, 17.223, (*as assev.*) = 'I swear' 4.172, **B** 13.106, 17.63, A 7.170; **a** ~ one / ? in (the course of) one day 20.41, daily B 15.283; **on þe** ~ daily / ? during one day 10.31

dale *n* hollow Pr 17, 1.1, 55; valley, *in phr.* **bi ~s and hulles** = everywhere 10.232

dame *n* mother 2.120, 7.137, 8.81, 9.316, 20, 282, B 5.37; (*as title*) Lady, Madame 6.133, 11.1, B 10.229, Mistress Pr 226, 8.80

dam(o)ysele *n* noble maiden 20.470; young woman B 11.12; handmaiden 10.139

dampnacion *n* damnation B 12.87

dampnen *v* condemn 9.158, 17.213, 215, 19.285; condemn to hell, damn 6.324, 7.146, 12.78, 245, 17.137, 215, 20.308, 427, **B** 2.103, 12.91, 18.293, 379; *p.p.a* damned 19.232, 241, B 10.428

dar *pr. sg.* Pr 218, B 5.101, A Pr 38, Z 6.75, *pr.pl.* B Pr 152 *see* **durren** *v*

date *n* date [of execution of a document], ? name 2.114; year, time B 13.269

dauben *v* daub (with clay), *ger.* 8.198

dauncelen *v* make much of A 11.30

daunger *n* power [of the devil] 18.280; danger / risk (of death) 14.145

daunsen *v* dance 20.182, *ger.* dance 10.180

daunten B 3.288 = **adaunten**, B 15.400 = **endaunten**; cherish B 10.37

dawen *v* dawn 20.470, (*fig.*) arise 20.183

deba(e)t(e) *n* dispute 6.387, **at** ~ in dispute 6.123, B 15.427; strife 21.252, B 5.97

deceite (deseyte) *n* deception 20.376, B 10.19; **in ~ of** to deceive Pr 77; trickery 2.128; false appearance B 12.130

deceyuen *v* play tricks on B 10.214, 217; cheat, defraud 11.16, B Pr 79; lead astray 1.40, 17.184, 18.123, 174

declaren *v* determine [matter of law] 2.148, [verdict] 16.122; plead [legal case] 9.49

declynen *v* decline grammatically A 4.133

*****decourren (of)** *v* depart from B 14.194*c*

decre(e) (degre) *n* law, edict A 11.241; canon law 17.113

decretal *n* papal decree, *pl.* (collection of) decretals B 5.422

#decretistre (of canoen) *n* expert in canon law 15.86

ded 1.182 *etc* = **de(e)d(e)** *a*

ded(e) *p.t.* Pr 123, 12.56 *etc*; *pl.* 12.245, 14.98, Z Pr 54; *see* **don** *v*

dede *n* act(ion), deed 1.30, 3.470, 6.333, 7.3, 146, 150, 10.240, 12.245, 16.191, 20.92, 98, 21.183, **B** 4.68, 5.506, 11.51, **A** 5.254, 10.121; transaction B 5.241; heroic deed 7.140, 21.133, 134; (sexual) act 10.295, 13.155; (virtuous) act(ion) 1.182, B 11.51; sin(ful act) 3.415, 10.232, **B** 12.76, 14.325, 18.334; work, task Pr 225, 3.303, 5.9, 21.279, 331; fact, reality B 13.133, *in phr.* **don in** ~ really do (sth) **B** 5.43, 10.358, A 4.108, Z 4.144; written document (*with pun on* 'effect') A 12.87; charter, legal deed 2.114, 20.191, **B** 2.161, 5.241; *in phrr.* †**wan** ~ evil action Z 5.152; **wel** ~ virtuous action 3.69, 15.305, B 3.70

de(e)d(e) *a* dead 1.182, 12.78, 186, 13.56, 20.64, 66, 72, 158, **B** 3.193, 14.321, 15.593, 18.97; *a as n (sg.)* 20.98, 22.294, (*pl.*) 9.21, 338, 21.53, 197

de(e)dly(ch) *a* destructive B 10.237; mortal (to the soul) 1.142, 5.122, 6.276 (B 13.388), 7.209, 9.238, 10.43, 12.37, 17.203, 291, 20.376, **B** 8.50, 9.207, 13.406, 14.78, 83, 88, 90, 95; *av* grievously, mortally B 5.114, A 10.156, (*of sin*) 9.329

deef *a* (*pl.* **deue**) deaf 11.61, B 10.132, *a as n* the deaf 21.130

deel *n* part B 15.487

deelen B 1.199, 10.215 = **delen** *v*

deen *n* dean [= head of cathedral chapter] B 13.65, [= official in charge of deanery, sub-division of arch-deaconry] B 2.173, A Pr 92, Z 2.146

de(e)p(e) *a* deep Pr 17, 1.55, 126, 20.64, 407, B 1.115, Z Pr 100; profound 20.405; *av* deep(ly) 6.166, 9.145, 11.301, 305, 14.149, 15.99, 21.365, Z 7.245, (*comp.*) **deppore** 11.130, B 15.199

deere *a*[1] B Pr 210 *et p.* = **dere** *a*[1]

deere[2] *a* severe B 14.171 (*or* = *a*[1])

deere B 9.65, 12.42 = **dere** *av*

dees-playere *n* dice-player 8.72

dee† B 3.109 *et p.*, = **de(e)th(e)** *n*

defamen *v* dishonour A 11.64, Z 7.260; speak against B Pr 190, Z 3.121; *and see* **famen** *v*

defaute *n* want [of clothes, food *etc*] 7.305, 8.145, 213, 245, 352, 9.100, 206, 311, 10.203, 11.43, 14.16, 15.273, 294, 298, 17.68, 20.211, **B** 5.7, 9.82, 10.361, 14.165, 15.135; **payn** ~ lack of bread 15.231; defect B 11.214, 391, 12.95, 15.346; mistake 13.121; sin 12.38, B 10.277, **in** ~ guilty (of crime / sin) 2.153; (morally) to blame B 5.144; fault, responsibility 17.89

defenden *v* defend, protect 8.34, 97, 9.9, 16.133, 17.289, 19.268, 21.42, 470, 480, 22.76, 257, B 16.246; speak in defence of 16.36; forbid 3.68, 14.6, 16.168, 20.110, A 6.81, 7.168, 8.40, 12.18, 19

defense *n* prohibition 20.199, Z 6.75

#defyen *v*[1] reject (contemptuously) 22.66

def(f)yen *v*[2] digest 6.429, 16.224, (*fig.*) 6.87; be digested 6.438; help to be digested Pr 231

def(f)oulen *v* trample on 3.191; treat shamefully A 11.60; mortify 17.195; damage 8.31; sully B 14.24

defrauden *v* defraud 9.64

degre(e)¹ *n* level 18.56, 84; stage A 11.90; rank (in society) 5.67, 17.111; respect B 9.145

degre² A 11.241 = **decre** *n*

d(e)yen (d(e)iȝen) *v* die Pr 102, 1.142, 162, 2.221, 3.400, 5.40, 149, 6.318, 7.9, 129, 8.107, 127, 296, 352, 9.238, 10.58, 60, 196, 12.115, 14.211, 15.260, 16.4, 22, 17.192, 19.68, 204, 232, 277, 20.56, 58, 70, 137, 197, 304, 335, 404, 21.175, 22.19, 50, 177, 313, **B** 10.352, 11.283, 12.87, 13.406, 409, 15.138, 16.166, A 8.37, 9.47, 10.177, Z 3.131, 5.144, (*fig.*) 12.183, 20.429; = become subject to death 20.374, 397; be put to death 3.410, 415, 428, 4.5, 7.208, 10.232, 14.146, 17.271, 20.27, 22.62, B 15.518, 521; = give one's life 17.291; be extinguished 6.335

dey(i)ng(e) *ger.* dying, (time of) 9.38, 20.79, (moment of) 17.144; (experience of) 20.222, *in phr.* **deth** ~ hour of death 7.85, 110, state of spiritual death B 11.176; death 17.276 (B 15.525)

dey(e)s *n* dais, raised seat (of judgement) B 7.17; high table 11.40, 15.66

deilen A 11.162 = **delen** *v*

deynen *v*¹ deign 8.331, 11.61

deynen *v*² ?disdain Z 7.312n

deynous *a* disdainful, arrogant 10.81, 16.226

deynte(e) *n* delight 11.316; luxury 15.303; delicacy 15.92

deitee *n* divine nature B 10.56

dekne *n* deacon Z 7.231

delen *v* (*p.t.* **delt** A 12.104) give 1.195; give (as) alms 3.76, 11.69, 71, 13.95, 19.218, 21.379, **B** 10.28, 11.275, 12.245, 13.300, A 11.243; apportion 21.216; share out 8.106, B 15.246; deliver (blow) A 12.104; (have) deal(ings) (with) 8.77, 19.226, 21.352, B 5.245; have sexual intercourse 9.167

delicat *a* luxurious, **~ly(che)** *av* choicely, fastidiously 6.166, 16.91, B 5.375

delys *n* sensual pleasure Z 3.161

delit *n* pleasure B 10.361; sensual delight A 2.65, Z 3.163

delitable *a* pleasurable 1.32

deliten *v* (*refl.*) take pleasure in B 1.29

delyueren *v* free 18.283, B 15.345; discharge 13.40; hand back to 13.13

delt *p.t.* A 12.104 *see* **delen** *v*

deluuye *n* deluge 11.252

deluen *v* (*p.t. pl.* **doluen** B 6.190, *p.p.* **(i)doluen** B 6.180 / A 6.33) dig 21.365, 367, **B** 5.545, 6.141, 247, A 11.187; bury B 6.180, A 7.170

deluer (deluare) *n* digger Pr 225, 8.114, 198, 352

demen *v* (pass) judge(ment on) Pr 94, 4.172, 11.215, 16.185, 21.307, **B** 4.181, 15.551; pronounce (judgement) B 13.306; censure, criticize 6.20, 8.83, 16.226,

B 5.113; adjudicate between 20.36; condemn 3.459, B 15.549; administer 4.175, *ger.* 12.81; judge (at Last Day) 9.21, 21.175, 197; direct B 13.172, Z 5.73; ordain 10.100; think, hold 3.290, 9.319, **B** 3.188, 6.180, Z Pr 54; believe B 19.148; tell 1.82, B 13.306

demme *a* dark 20.362, B 3.193, Z Pr 16; *av*, **loke** ~ have poor eyesight 11.127

dene¹ *n* din, clamour 2.217, 20.64, 126

dene² = **deen** *n*

denyen *v* refuse 11.265

dent A 12.104 = **dount** *n*

#dentiesliche *av* with choice food 8.323

†deol B 18.281 = **doel** *n*

dep 1.55 = **de(e)p(e)** *a*

departable *a* distinguishable 18.215, 19.30, 98

departen *v* part company 17.147; divide B 7.157; dissolve 22.139

depe Pr 17, 1.126 *etc*, Z 7.245 = **de(e)p(e)** *a, av*

deposen *v* remove from office 17.215; put down B 15.551

deppore (deppere) *comp.* 11.130, B 15.199 *see* **de(e)p(e)** *av*

deprauen *v* vilify 3.224, B 5.143

dere *a* excellent, (most) honoured, [of God] Pr 218, 1.83, 13.17, 168, **B** 11.407, 14.325, [of the Church] 7.65, [of a person] 10.127, (*a as n*) B 6.253, [of love] 11.135; (*sup.*) precious B 2.13; expensive B 14.74, [through scarcity] 8.158, 10.199, B 14.171n; dear, beloved 2.33, 8.91, 106, 15.197, 17.291, B 12.12

dere *av* dearly, at a high price 19.267, ~ **abyggen** pay a severe penalty for 8.83, ~ **liken** be well pleasing 8.315, A 6.80

derely *av* in the best manner 21.2

derfly *av* violently 3.415

der(i)en *v* harm 9.38, 19.20, 20.25, 297

derke *n* darkness 12.154, 13.56

derk(e) *a* (*comp.* **derkore**) dark 1.55, 20.62, **B** Pr 16, 1.115; darkened 20.60; black, ? wicked 21.21; hard to understand 11.130; **~nesse** *n* darkness 18.117, 19.200, 20.67, 104, 114, 126, **B** 5.494, 16.251; ~ **liche** *av* obscurely B 10.372

derling *n* dear one, beloved A 12.19

derne *a* secret 3.291; hidden B 2.176; private B 13.54; intimate 10.295, 13.155; *av* **~(ly)** inconspicuously 13.163

derrest *sup.* B 2.13 *see* **dere** *a*

derste *p.t.* Pr 193 *see* **durren** *v*

derthe *n* (period of) scarcity / high price (of food) 8.351, 16.311, B 14.171, 176

derworth(e) *a* (most) excellent 13.17; precious 1.83, 6.89

#desauowen *v* disclaim 3.319

descenden *v* (*pr.t.* **~et**) come down 17.247

deschargen *v* relieve 17.231, ~ **of** relieve (of liability for) B 4.29

descreuen (descryuen) *v* describe 6.196, 20.212, B 5.78; say the names of 22.94; explain B 16.53, 66, Z 3.147

deseyte Pr 77, 2.128, 20.376 = **deceite** *n*

desert *n* reward earned 3.291

deseruen *v* deserve, merit 2.133, 134, 3.294, 4.172, 5.32, 8.40, 204, 14.214, 16.4, 6, 146, **B** 6.87, 14.138, **A** 5.241, 12.92; earn 3.297, 301, 5.42, 45, 8.228, 13.85, B 14.126

desiren *v* wish 22.323, B 9.105, A 12.45; wish (to have) **B** 3.246, 252, 14.188, A 10.125; long for **B** 3.99, 15.468, A 10.47, Z 3.167, (*ger.*) craving B 13.356; desire (sexually) 1.179

#**despeyr(e)** *n* despair (of salvation) 9.38, 22.164, Z 5.144

despen(d)en *v* spend 8.235, 12.237, **B** 5.263, 10.324; employ 14.18, B 12.48; *and see* **spen(d)en** *v*

despicen, despisen 14.64, 6.80 *etc*, *see* **dispisen** *v*

desplesen *v* cause offence to 8.84, B 14.325, (*refl.*) take offence B 13.136

despoilen *v* rob 13.57

desputen 10.20, 12.52 = **disputen** *v*

dessallouwynge *n* refusal of credit 16.7

desseyuen *v* 1.40 = **deceyuen** *v*

destyne *n* destiny, providence 8.296

destrere *n* riding-horse (of noble breed) A 2.137

destruyen (destroyen) *v* destroy B 3.271; wipe out 9.17, 12.236, 16.172, 17.291, 22.383; kill 14.22, 19.182, 258, 266, 276, A 11.288; ruin welfare (of) 3.206, A 7.30, 124; take away 18.43; damage Pr 213; overcome 20.244, **B** 10.329, 16.165, 18.348, A 10.76; neutralise 20.158 B 2.14; drive out 21.313, B 13.250; squander Pr 24

de(e)th(e) *n* death 2.106, 8.187, 9.17, 52, 15.260, 286, 308, 17.203, 19.20, 20.34, 53, 137, 143, 160, 217, 297, 390 (2), 407, 21.51, 175, 308, 22.139, (*person.*) Pr 17, 20.28 *et p.*, 22.89 *et p.*, A 12.63 *et p.*, (death by) execution 3.459, 17.270, 20.424, 427; death-dealing calamity 11.64, 252; (= the plague) 8.351, ? 10.199, 16.311; spiritual death, perdition B 12.87; *in phrr.* ~ **day** day / time of (one's) death 1.130, 9.350, 10.303, **B** 3.109, 7.50, 12.245, 14.106, ~ **deynge** time of dying 7.85, 110, = condition of (spiritual) death B 11.176; ~ **yuel** fatal potion (*fig.*) B 18.53; ~ **of kynde** death (in the course) of nature 20.219; **bale** ~ baleful death B 18.35*n*, **doctour of** ~ death-dealing physician (*fig.*) 20.402; **to** ~ **e** 1.166, 3.476, 11.270, 14.42, 21.10, 141

dette *n* debt, what is owed (by / to sb.) Pr 91, 3.304, 8.107, 13.37, 75, 15.12; obligation (to God / one's fellow man) 9.273, 13.37; debt (to God) incurred through sin 6.299, 22.10, B 5.227; obligation to make satisfaction for sin 21.191, 22.322, *in phrr.* **in** ~ in debt 22.294; into debt B 7.79; **out(e) of** ~ free of debt / obligation 16.4, B 14.107

deuk 21.308 = **duk** *n*

deul[1] 8.127, 19.320 = **doel** *n*

deul[2] Z 2.84, 8.54 = **deuel** *n*

deuren Z 2.72, 3.30 = **du(y)ren** *v*

deue 21.130 *see* **deef** *a*

deuel *n* the Devil [Satan] 8.127, 278, 10.278, 302, 15.260, 18.111, 117, 19.241, 20.161, 297, 325, **B** 1.28, 29, 2.103, 7.114, 9.63, 14.78, 16.165, **A** 2.65, 11.22; (one of the) devil(s) 9.38, 19.20, 20.340, 21.21, **B** 7.50, 16.120, 18.158, 281; *in phrr.* ~**es dysors** 8.52, ~ **power** 18.283, B 10.237, ~ **punfolde** B 5.624; **date of þe** ~ 2.114

deuer (deuoir) *n* duty 17.122, **B** 11.284, 13.213; appointed task 16.5, 17.92, B 14.150, 153; best A 12.2

deuyden *v* divide arithmetically 21.241; distribute 21.216

deuyn *n* divinity, theology A Pr 90

deuinen *v* prophesy 17.312, 21.148, **B** 7.158, 15.598, 603; interpret Pr 218, 9.305; ponder 11.130; find out (about) 21.241; contrive 11.266; expound 15.99; determine 10.102

deuynour (dyuynour) *n* theologian 15.86, 124, **B** 7.136, 10.452

deuisen *v* consider 21.279; plan, specify 7.190, 8.200; fashion 21.331

deuocion *n* devout adoration B 15.295

deuoir B 11.284, 13.213, 14.150, 153 = **deuer** *n*

deuors *n* annulment 22.139, B 2.176

deuouren *v* devour (*fig.*) 2.140; consume 8.139; squander 16.280

deuouteliche *av* fervently 17.245

deuoutours *a pl.* (*or a as n*) adulterous / adulterers 2.184

deuoutrye *n* adultery B 2.176

dewe[1] *n* dew 7.264, 17.21*n*

dewe[2] *a* owed, owing 3.304

dewen A 11.199, 201 = **dowen** *v*

#**dya** *n* pharmaceutical preparation 22.174

***diapen(i)dion** *n* sweet cough-medicine B 5.122

***dyademen** *v* crown, *p.p.* 3.440

diamaund *n* diamond B 2.13

diche (dykke) *n* ditch [defensive] B Pr 16, [drainage] 13.235

dych B 20.19 = **dysch** *n*

dichen (dyken) *v* dig a ditch [defensive] 21.365, [boundary / enclosure / drainage] **B** 5.545, 6.141, 190, 19.239, **A** 6.33, 11.187

dyde *p.t.* 6.9, **dide(n)** B 1.28, 5.540 *et p.*; *see* **do(o)n** *v*

***dido** *n* old wives' tale 15.172*n*

dyen Pr 102, 5.149 = **d(e)yen** *v*

dyeten *v* (*refl.*) regulate diet 8.290

diffoulen 8.31 = **defoulen** *v*

diggen (*p.t.* ~ed) dig 8.114

digneliche *av* honourably B 7.172; worthily Z Pr 54

dignite *n* position of authority A Pr 92

dyhten *v* (*p.t.* **dihte**, *p.p.* **diȝt(e)**) prepare 8.315; get ready 21.2, A 2.137; have sexual intercourse with 1.27

dyk(ke) 13.235, A Pr 16 = **diche** *n*

dyken B 5.545, 6.141, 190, A 11.188 = **dichen** *v*
dyker(e) (dikare) *n* ditcher Pr 225, 6.368, 8.114
dym B 3.193, Z Pr 16 = **demme** *a*
#**dyme** *n* tithe 17.227
dymmen *v* grow dim 6.406
dynen *v* dine, have dinner Pr 228, 7.5, 8.331, 15.27, 16.4, 91, 21.386, B 5.377; eat 6.174, 8.277, 302, A 5.72
dyner *n* dinner 4.38, 8.315, 15.32
dyngen *v* knock (at door) 16.168; ~ **adoun** knock down B 10.329; ~ **vpon (Dauid)** pound away at (reciting) the Psalms B 3.312, (**sheues**) thresh grain B 6.141
dynt B 18.26, 20.105 = **dount** *n*
disalowen *v* refuse credit (*fig.*) B 14.130; *and see* **dessallouwynge** *n*
disceruen 13.85 = **deseruen** *v*
disceuen 17.184 = **deceyuen** *v*
disch(e), dysch *n* bowl [for drink] 20.405, 22.19; dish [for food] 15.92, B 13.54; platter 10.180
disciple *n* disciple 9.118, 18.166, **B** 13.430, 15.88, A 11.295
discomfiten *v* (*p.p.* **disconfit**) defeat Pr 108, 112
discrete *a* discerning, prudent 5.84
discryuen B 5.78, 16.53, 66 = **descreuen** *v*
diseruen 2.133, 134 = **deseruen** *v*
disgisen *v* deck out B Pr 24
dyso(u)r *n* minstrel 8.52, 15.172, A 11.30
dispayr 22.164 = **despeyr(e)** *n*
dispenden 12.237 = **despen(d)en** *v*
#**disperacion** *n* despair (of salvation) 19.291
dispisen (dispicen) *v* look down on 2.84, 21.34; despise 9.190; treat with contempt 6.80, 14.64; regard as worthless 7.118; disregard 17.251; revile 6.122, 20.40, 95; disparage 16.214
dispit *n* spite 8.184
displesen B 13.136, 14.325 = **desplesen** *v*
disputen *v* engage in (formal) debate / controversy 6.122, 10.20, 114, 12.52, **B** 10.447, 11.319; reason about 11.36; argue 6.137, B 10.111, 130; maintain / defend by argument 11.158
disseyuen 11.16 = **deceyuen** *v*
dissh B 13.54 = **disch(e)** *n*
disshere *n* dish-seller 6.371
distru(y)en Pr 213, 9.17, 12.236, 14.22, 19.258, 20.244, 21.313 = **distroyen** *v*
ditten (dutten Z) *v* shut A 7.176
dyuen *v* plunge, dive 13.168, 14.106, B 12.165
dyuer 16.5 = **deuer** *n*
diuerse *a* various, different 2.98, 14.79, **B** Pr 152, 12.67; various kinds of B 15.424; *av* variously, differently 15.81
diuersen *v* differ 17.133
diuinen B 7.158 = **deuynen** *v*
diuinite *n* theology 17.113, B 7.136
dyuynour 15.86 *etc* = **deuynour** *n*

diuors B 2.176 = **deuors** *n*
don Pr 109 *et p.*; *see* **do(o)n** *v*
dobben *v* dub, create (sb.) knight 1.101, (*p.p.*) 20.11
dobelar *n* plate, platter 15.92
Dobest *n* Do-best 10.76 *et p.*
Dobet *n* Do-better 10.76 *et p.*
docto(u)r *n* Doctor of the Church [one of the four great Latin Fathers] 21.317, B 9.73; theological authority Pr 59, B 10.452; learned theologian Pr 85, B 15.73; doctor (of divinity) 15.66 *et p.*; authoritative teacher 11.95, 135, 15.126; doctor (of medicine) 22.177; *in phrr.* ~ **of decre** 17.113, ~ **of lawe** B 15.243 (= doctor of Canon Law); ~ **of deth** (*fig.*) teacher of death 20.402; **Poulynes** ~ expert theologian / canon lawyer of the Pauline order A 2.73*n*
doctrine *n* teaching 11.226; profession, order B 2.109
doel (deol, deul) *n* suffering 8.127, 20.304, †B 18.281; lamentation 19.320, **B** 5.380, 15.146; ~ **ful** *a* miserable, painful B 15.521
do(e)m *n* judgement 2.129, 17.213; judgement at law, (judicial) sentence 3.470, 9.341, 20.27, 195, 427, 12.90, B 2.206, 11.145; (moral) judgement / decision 16.185; = the (Last) Judgement 6.297, 346, 9.321, 338, 351, 12.70, 20.427, 22.294, **B** 7.17, 10.358, 12.91; **domesday** *n* Judgement Day 5.122, 6.324, 9.21, 11.252, 16.36, 21.197; **domesman** *n* judge 21.307
doen 15.229, *pr. pl.* 6.155 *etc*, *p.p.* 15.70 *etc*, **doest** 2 *pr.sg.* 8.83 *see* **do(o)n** *v*
dogge *n* dog 9.261, B 5.117
do3ter B 11.246 = **douhter** *n*
doynge *ger.* (performance of an) act 3.291, 292; action 8.91, 21.130, 433, B 15.476
doysayne (do3eyne) 22.164 = **doseyne** *num.*
doke *n* duck 6.174, B 17.63
dol *n* alms B 3.71
dollen *v* become dazed / stupid Z 4.124
doluen *p.t. pl.* B 6.190, *p.p.* **B** 6.180, 14.321
dombe 21.130 = **do(u)mbe** *a*
dome *n* 6.297 *etc* = **do(e)m** *n*
domen *v* Z 1.31, 5.73 = **demen** *v*
****dompyng** *n* dabchick, moorhen 13.168
do(o)n *v* (*infl. inf.* ~**e** 3.232, 7.229, 8.117, 210, **B** 4.28, 6.203, 11.376, 419, 13.291, 20.371; *p.p.* **(y)do(e)n(e)** Pr 126, 2.128, 7.140, 20.111, **B** 3.263, 18.53, A 6.33; *a as n* (*infl. gen.*) **done** B 18.300; *3 pl pr.* **doon** B Pr 224; *3 sg. and pl. pr.* **do(o)th** 1.24, 6.335, *imp. pl.* **dooþ** B 5.43; *p.t.* **dede(n)** Pr 123 *et p.*, 14.98, Z Pr 54, *p.t. subjv.* 10.189, 17.92, 20.429, **dyde** 6.9, **dide(n)** B 1.28 *et p.*, 5.540 *etc*) do (sth.), perform an act(ion) Pr 126, 3.81, 319, 4.41, 6.53, 276, 7.140, 146, 10.43, 295, 12.90, 245, 15.229, 17.92, 122, 20.161, 376, 21.279, B 1.28, A 4.108; complete [task] 16.5, 21.183, 331; make 19.255; cause (to / to happen) 1.102, 2.221, 3.172, 6.155, 8.296, †11.161, 14.23, 16.91, 226, 17.303,

18.145, 19.299, 20.320, 21.311, 22.380, **B** 3.200, 5.94, 241, 540, 14.83, 15.405, **A** 5.77, 9.90; cause (not to) / prevent (from) 19.306; place 10.138; provide 7.110; (*refl.*) betake oneself 2.221, 10.278, 21.2; put 21.10; give 9.132, B 6.54; act, behave 3.331, 6.324, 9.321, 341, 351, 10.110, 11.226 (1), 12.11, **B** 8.101, 10.422, 12.234, 15.420; fare B 1.34; (*as emph. auxil.*) do 9.328, 19.175, Z 7.268, did B 12.168; (*as subst. for specific v.*) Pr 123, 9.112, 10.179, 16.55, 17.209, 219, 307, 21.44, 101, 212, 22.6, 374, **B** 5.37, 7.123, 10.406, **A** 4.53, 5.132; *in phrr.* ~ **equite** dispense justice 21.310, ~ **hit vpon** appeal to 2.39, ~ **lawe** enforce the law 3.446, 21.308; **what done** what kind of B 18.300

donet *n* elementary grammar (*fig.*) 6.215n

dong(e) *n* dung, manure 4.144, 8.184, 198, 312, 12.226, 231, 233, B 3.310, A 7.176, ~ **hep** *n* dung-heap 16.264, ~ **hill** B 15.111

donge(o)n *n* fortress **B** Pr 15, 1.59, Z Pr 100

doom B 2.206 = **do(e)m** *n*

doon B Pr 206 *et p.*, **doone** B 4.28 = **do(o)n** *v*

dore *n* doorway 6.406; door 67, **A** 11.95, 12.36; ~ **nayl** *n* door-stud 1.182

dorste *p.t.* 20.448, **B** 5.90, 11.86, 16.212, 214 *see* **durren** *v*

doseyne (dosoyne) *num.* dozen 4.38, 6.368, 22.164

doten *v* behave foolishly, *p.p.* foolish 1.138

doth *3 pr. sg., pl.* Pr 225, 1.24 *etc*; *see* **do(o)n** *v*

double *a* twofold [= of amount] **B** 14.148, 153, 156, 15.59, [= of kind] B 2.13; ~ **fold** *a* / *av* double / twice over 9.344

doubler *n* platter B 13.82

do(ug)hter *n* 1.27 [Lot's], 2.33 [Truth's], 2.124, 3.368, 6.134, 8.81 [Piers'], 106, 10.139 [Dowel's], 10.180 [Herod's], 266, 20.472 [Will's], **B** 6.14, 11.246

douhty *a* valiant 11.266, (*comp.*) B 5.101, *sup.* ~ **(ok)est** 7.140, 21.134, = most formidable B 10.452; ~ **lyche** *av* valiantly 20.36

do(u)mb(e) *a* dumb, *as n (pl.)* the dumb 21.130; speechless B 10.139; failing to bark B 10.287; *as n (sg.)* the mute one [*sc.* the Psalter] 2.39, 40

doun *n* hill 4.51; upland A 10.173

doun (down) *av* down 1.4, 18.34, 111, 20.72, 86, 143, 340, 21.340, **B** 1.95, 6.30, 13.21, 14.92, **A** 5.215, 10.217; downward 20.88, ~ **riht** *av* utterly, ? certainly 20.197c

d(o)unt (dynt, dent) *n* blow, stroke 8.187, 20.25, 22.105, A 12.104

doute *n* (state) of uncertainty 6.284,(B 13.398), A 9.60n; doubt 16.32, B 12.32; fear 14.69, B Pr 152, **A** 10.82, 11.299

[**douth**, ~ **in douth** in the world, anywhere ? A 9.60n]

douten *v* doubt 16.230; fear 10.127, 199, 20.312, A 10.80

douue (dowue) *n* dove 17.171, 239, B 15.408

do wel *v. phr. as quasi-n.* 9.289, 21.116, B 13.111; (*person.*) Do-well 9.318 *et p.*

#**dowen** *v* endow 3.319, 17.220, A 11.199, 201

down 18.34, 111 *etc* = **doun** *av*

drad *contr. pr.* B 9.96, *p.p.* 21.21,~**de(n)** *p.t.* 6.276, 15.286, 16.311, 22.65, B 13.406, ~ **dyst** *p.t. 2 sg.* Z 3.131 *see* **dreden** *v*

draf *n* pig-swill 11.9; lees of ale 21.402

dranke *p.t.* 15.66 *see* **drinken** *v*

drap(i)er *n* clothier 6.215, 250

drat *contr. pr.* 7.72, 12.154, 22.380, B 9.93 *see* **dreden** *v*

drauht *n* draught, measure 22.223

drawen *v* (*p.t.* **drow(e)** 6.215 *etc*, *p.p.* **(y)drawe** 8.288, 20.139, B 10.37, A 11.145) pull 2.190; draw 15.57, 21.402; stretch 6.216; bring 11.314, A 11.145, ~ **forþ** advance B 10.37; lead B 5.43; attract 8.52, A 4.108; carry 8.312; remove 8.288, 20.139; ~ **(to)** approach 6.406, 8.190, 9.52, 13.99, 148, 15.286, 22.200; turn 19.63; (*refl.*) betake (oneself) 6.215, 9.145, 13.147, B 18.111

drawere *n* 6.369, 8.287 *see* **lach** ~, **toth** ~

dred(e) *n* fear 7.209, 8.187, 11.64, B 15.413, A 10.82, (*person.*) 2.217, B 2.209; anxiety 12.239, B Pr 152; terror 18.117, 20.60, 22.200, Z Pr 100, †B 7.34; ~ **of dispayr**, ~ **of disperacion** terror arising from (spiritual) despair 22.164, 19.291; awe (of God) 16.306, A 10.79, 118, 122; respect 12.248; = doubt 14.10; = danger, risk Pr 126, 5.121, 7.307, 14.108, 16.7, B 12.168

dreden *v* (*contr. pr.* (= **dredeth**), *sg.* **drad** B 9.96, **dred** B 13.413, **drat** 7.72 *etc*, *pl.* 22.380, *p.t.* **dradde(n)** 6.276 *etc*, *2 sg.* **dreddest** B 3.193, *p.p.* **drad** 21.21) (*refl.*) be afraid 7.9, 72, 85 (B 13.426), 9.238, 12.239, 20.325, **B** 9.89, 18.285, Z 3.131; fear, be afraid (of) 6.276, 9.17, 10.99, 12.154, 13.56, 15.260, 16.311, 22.154, **B** 3.193, 9.96, 10.288, 13.406; stand in awe (of) 9.14, B 9.93, 95, 204, A 10.216; (regard with) respect 8.159, 10.127; shun 1.32, 22.380

dredful *a* dread, terrible 9.338, 22.89, **B** Pr 16, 1.59; ~**ly** *av* fearfully 19.64; **dredles** *av* without doubt A 11.194

#**dregges** *n. pl.* dregs, lees 8.193, 21.402

drem *n* dream 9.305; **loue** ~ B 16.20n

*****dremel(e)s** *n* dream 15.17, **B** 7.155, 13.14

dremen *v* dream †22.378, **B** 8.69, 20.378; (*impers.*) 20.6

drenchen *v* drown B 8.50, A 10.60, (be) drown(ed) B 12.168

dreuelen *v* slobber 11.9, B 10.41, (*fig.*) prate wildly 11.40; *and see* **bidrauelen** *v*

drye (druye) *n* dry weather Z 7.292, **in wete and in** ~ in all weathers 7.175

drye (druie) *a* rainless B 13.269; high and ~ 5.149; *in phr.* **drynken** ~ drain (the pot) dry 9.145; without getting wet 19.304, 20.250

drien *v* feel thirsty B 1.25, (*impers.*) A 1.25

dri3t *n* man, anyone A 9.60n

driȝte *n* lord (*sc.* God) B 13.269, 14.101

drink(e) *n* drink, beverage 8.193, 15.57, 20.403, 404, 407; [= alcoholic] drink 1.24, 10.178, 188, 15.217, 259, 16.63, **B** 1.29, 9.65, Z 7.316; potion 8.296; *in phrr.* **delitable** ~ 1.32, **derworth** ~ 6.89, **likerous** ~ 1.25, 10.178, B 10.166, **swete** ~ 16.150; **breed and** ~ 16.63, B 13.252; **cloth ne** ~ 15.259, **mete (and)** ~ 10.188, 15.217, **B** 5.256, 6.19

drynken *v* (*p.t.* **drank(e)** 15.66, **dronk(e)(n)** 15.113, 267, B 13.404, *p.t. subjv.* 22.19, *p.p.* **dronke(n)** 15.99) drink [water] 6.174, 8.142, 15.267, 22.19, [wine / ale] 1.24, 2.98, 5.9, 6.159, 166, 362, 8.277, 9.145, 13.144 (*ger.*), 155 (*pr. p.*), 15.99, 113, 16.91, 20.409, 22.223, **B** 5.375, 13.404, 14.77, [potion] 20.53, 402, 22.380, (*fig.*) 12.58, 20.405, 412, 22.380

drinkere *n* drinker A 12.85

drynkyng *ger.* drinking [of strong drink] 13.144, 155

drit *n* manure, ? mud A 7.176

driuen *v* (*p.t.* **drof** 18.158, A 12.104, *p.p.* **dryuen** 7.264) drive, chase 6.89, 7.264, 18.158, 19.291, 22.174, **B** 6.190, 14.83; thrust B 14.92; drive [team] 7.295, 8.141, B 9.207; herd 5.19; ~ **forth** pass Pr 226; charge 22.100; strike A 12.104

drof *p.p.* 18.158, A 12.104 *see* **driuen** *v*

#**drogge** *n* drug, medicament 22.174

droghte B 14.171, 176 = **drouthe** *n*

dronke *p.p.a* drunk 20.192, ~**ne** drunken 13.235, ~ **lewe** *a* given to drink 10.81; ~**nesse** *n* drunken state 1.27

drop *n* drop (of) 6.335

droppen *v* drop B 16.79

*****drosenes** *n. pl.* lees 8.193

drouthe *n* dry weather 8.312; lack of water 15.254, B 14.171, 176

druerie *n* treasure, ? love-token 1.83

druie *a* 9.145, 19.304, 20.250; *n* Z 7.292 = **drye** *a, n*

druyen *v* dry 14.22; become dry Z Pr 116

duc A 10.76 = **duk** *n*

ducchesse *n* sovereign duchess 2.33

ducherie *n* sovereign duchy 3.244

duellen A 12.81 = **dwellen** *v*

du(y)ren *v* last 1.106, 5.25 12.224, 20.65, **B** 10.91, A 12.94; *in phr.* **as longe as (my) lyf (may) duyre(th)** 11.90, 15.58, **B** 1.78, 6.56, 10.147; continue 16.11; go on B 15.240; live 3.29, B 10.207; remain (in force) 20.191

duk *n* lord, ruler 10.138, 20.362, **A** 10.76, 12.87; great lord 21.308

dung A 7.176 = **dong** *n*

dunt 8.187, 22.105 = **d(o)unt** *n*

duren 3.29, 20.65, **B** 1.78, 6.56, 10.91, 13.50, 15.240, A 12.94 = **du(y)ren** *v*

durren *v* (*pr. sg.* **dar** Pr 218, *pl.* 3.213, *p.t.* **dorste** 20.448, **durste** 2.250, *subjv.* **derste** Pr 193, **durste** 3.235) dare Pr 218, 2.250, 3.213, 9.261, 10.119, 17.29, 69, 19.64, 211, B 15.382, A 6.81, Z 6.75, *p.t.*

subjv. would have dared Pr 193, 3.258, 6.413, 8.202, (*with pr. sense*) should dare 3.235, 9.257, 21.101; (*as assev.*) venture to 2.36, 4.191, 8.290, 15.115, 289, 20.160, B 10.135

durste *p.t.* 2.250, 3.235 *etc*; *see* **durren** *v*

dust *n* dust, ? small pieces 22.100

dust *p.t. 2 sg.* 20.320 (=**dudest**) *see* **do(o)n** *v*

dutten Z 7.174 = **ditten** *v*

dwale *n* a sleeping draught 22.380

dwellen *v* (*p.t.* **dwelte** 3.15, **dwellede** B 3.14) reside, live Pr 83, 1.130, 5.151, 9.39, 10.13, 17, 27, 75, 111, 128, 303, 11.104, 12.78, 13.88, 19.241, 252, 20.197, **B** 4.34, 5.533, 554, 8.18, **A** 7.182, 12.46, 63, 81; remain 20.304, **B** 1.115, 13.213, 18.192; stay 3.15, 22.345

dwellyng *n* habitation 2.106, 6.115

Ebrew *n* (the) Hebrew (language) 19.4

ech(e) 5.196, B Pr 122, ~ **a** B Pr 51, ~ **one** 1.89 *see* **vch, vch a, vchone** *prn, a, n*

edifien *v* build [*sc.* hermitages] 9.203, [temple] 18.161, 20.42

edwiten *v* reproach 6.420, B 5.364

eefte 20.4 = **eft** *av*

eek A 6.32 = **ek(e)** *av*

eer 1.200 = **er** *av*

eest *n* east 20.121, B Pr 13

eet *contr. pr.* 16.217, *imp.* 15.253, *p.t.* 6.430, 8.319, 15.47, 17.23, 173, B 7.122, 12.232, 13.404 *see* **eten** *v*

eft(e) *av* again, once more 3.475, 7.266, 14.23, 15.146, 17.146, 20.4, 42, 420, **B** 3.348, 14.96, 15.603, 17.112, A 11.82; back (again) 3.331; then, thereupon 4.102, 13.132, 18.24, 128, 20.359, 22.376; likewise, moreover 12.162

eft(e)sone(s) *av* a second time, again 21.5, B 6.170; **ȝut** ~ over and over again 6.327; next time Z 7.152

eg *n* egg [hen's] B 13.63, [wild bird's] 13.163

egge Z 7.33 = **hegge** *n*

eg-toel *n* sharp-edged weapon 3.475

eggen *v*[1] urge A 10.52; incite 1.61, B 18.288

eggen *v*[2] cover over, harrow Z 7.58; *and see* **heggen** *v*

egre *a* fierce, bitter 15.90, ~**lich(e)** *av* bitterly 21.381; sharply B 16.64

eye (eiȝe) (*excl.*) oh! 12.1

eye (eiȝe, eighe) *n* 6.2, 20.383, B 10.125, 263, (*pl.* ~**n** B Pr 74 *etc*) 13.344, **A** 10.52, 12.96 *see* **ye** *n*

ey(e)r 3.431, 5.59, 10.244, A 10.210 *see* **ayr** *n*

eyhte (eighte) *card. num.* eight 8.349 [*in form* **viii**], 22.344, B 6.326, A 10.175; *ord. num.* eighth 16.145 (= **eighteþe** B 14.310)

eylen B 6.128, 256, 15.251 = **aylen** *v*

eir 15.221, **B** Pr 128, 14.4 = **ay(e)r** *n*

eyþer 19.288, B 5.147 *etc*, A 10.179 = **ayther** *prn*

ek(e) *av* likewise 22.274, **B** 2.237, 10.465, 13.165, 15.324, 19.430, **A** 1.2, 166, 3.40, 169, 7.28, 8.71, Z

3.163, 7.245, 8.76; also B 6.†281, 286, **A** 1.79 *etc*, 6.32, †7.266, **Z** 1.7, 23, 7.201

elde *n* (old) age 6.200, 10.268, 12.12, **B** 11.60, 13.354, **old** ~ B 12.8, A 3.89, (*person.*) 11.188, 196, 22.95

eldre[1] *n* ancestor 3.415, 9.214 (*pl.* ~**n**) A 3.242

eldre[2] *a* elder 11.174

eldir A 1.66 *see* **(h)eller(ne)** *n*

eleccio(u)n *n* election by voting [of pope] Pr 137, [of prioress] 6.136

element *n* element [one of the four simple substances earth, air, water, fire] 1.17, 20.245

elynge *a* miserable Pr 204, 22.2; desolate B 10.96; ~**ly(che)** *av* in lonely poverty 22.39; wretchedly B 12.44

el(l)eue(ne) *card. num.* eleven 2.238, 3.226, 6.233, 9.309, 315, 12.176, B 15.437

elle Z 1.121, 2.75 = **helle** *n*

eller B 1.68, 9.149 = **(h)eller(n)e** *n*

elles[1] **(ellis)** *a* besides 6.262, **B** 7.84, 10.400, 12.225, 234, 13.364, 15.6, 18.353, A 10.177, 208; other 3.446, 5.117, 7.230, 268, 9.197, 16.95, 17.61, 21.121, **B** 1.110, 3.306, A 10.211; *a as n* anything else **B** 11.215, 16.143; otherwise, of some other kind 3.291, A 3.59

elles[2] **(ellis)** *av* else 1.49, 3.94, 251, 298, 7.2, 75, 8.238, 9.99, 211, 13.47, 17.16, 19.261, 20.383, 21.464, **B** 5.149, 287, 387, 6.182, 303, 10.376, 433, 20.228, Z Pr 17; otherwise 1.172, 8.335, 10.106, 112, 16.37, 40, 19.151, A 11.260; (*ellip.*, = but that it should be so) 3.148, 9.327, 15.300, B 15.579, A 3.101; elsewhere 21.190; at other times Pr 89; under other circumstances 13.155

elles (ellis) wher(e) *av* elsewhere, in other places 3.234, 10.29; in another place 15.300, 19.163

emcristen(e) 2.99, 7.46, 10.79, 19.217, 228 = **euencristen** *n*

emforth 15.143, 16.221 = **eueneforth** *prep.*

emperesse *n* empress B 13.166

emperour *n* emperor 3.268, 21.430, **B** 11.153, 13.166

#**enbaumen** *v* apply (sacramental) oil (to) 13.106, (*fig.*) 19.88; treat with oil 19.72

#**enblaunchen** *v* make white (*fig.*) 16.268

enchaunten *v* place a spell upon, bewitch (*fig.*) 2.43, 17.176, 286, 22.379

enchesoun *n* cause, reason 6.40

#**encloyen** *v* cripple (by snaring feet) 20.294

enclosen A 10.42 = **closen** *v*

encombren *v* overcome 21.229; *and see* **(a)combren** *v*

encreessen *v* multiply B 11.397

endaunten *v* tame 17.171

ende *n* end 1.93, 128, 3.198, 302, 13.24, 15.284, 18.175, 19.323, 20.207, 21.218, B 2.105; (moment) of death, dying 10.53, B 12.4, 84; conclusion 3.433, 5.97, (of book) A 12.109; last part B 3.248; purpose 21.279; extremity 6.3cf.10.333; edge 3.490, B 5.235; limit

17.105; *in phrr.* ~ **til oþer** 5.111; **good** ~ virtuous death [in state of grace] Pr 29, 2.35, 3.339, 10.60; happy outcome 20.163; **laste** ~ end of (one's) life 12.196, 16.2, 158, 282, ? 19.275n, ? final state B 2.101; **maken** ~ conclude (legal) action 3.198; **worse** ~ worst of it 16.66; **(day) withouten** ~ for ever 2.106, 3.359, 10.171, 18.233, 257, 19.252, 20.235, 21.199, B 18.379

enden *v* (come to an) end 3.303; finish 5.200; die 3.429, 9.291, **B** 1.131, 12.44, A 9.52; *ger.* **endynge** death 16.100

enditen *v* compose poem / letter 17.109; accuse formally 15.120, B 11.315

enemy(e) *n* enemy [one who hates sb.] 6.64, 106, 10.190, 15.143, 166, 17.142, 21.112, 114, **B** 10.199, 11.177, 181, A 11.244; foe in battle 3.242, 250, 440, 5.74, 14.51, 15.174, 17.288; foe (of mankind, = the Devil) 7.105, B 16.105

enfo(u)rmen *v* counsel B 3.241; teach 17.271, 19.97, B 15.519

Eng(e)lisch(e) *n* (the) English (language) 3.342, 4.142, 9.214, 281, 16.118, 186, 21.330, B 5.278, 13.72, 74, 14.277, 278, 15.375, A 11.254; *a* English 16.216, **B** 10.456, 15.414

engendren *v* beget 10.217, 251, **B** 2.119, 9.185, A 10.148; procreate 14.170, *ger.* procreation 13.144

engendrour *n* (pro)creator, beginner (*fig.*) B 6.231

engynen *v* contrive B 18.252

engleymen *v* cloy, constipate 16.217, B 15.64

engreynen *v* dye fast B 2.15, (*fig.*) B 14.20

enhancen *v* increase, advance 11.58

eny (any) *a* any Pr 174 *et p.*; any at all 9.48, 12.122, B 2.136, Z 5.106; any kind of 11.64, 14.182, 15.112, 21.294, A 2.32, *infl. n. phr.* **enys-kynnes** of any kind 2.212, 3.113; *as n* any(one) 6.162, 7.280, 18.111, 20.385; either 19.27; ~ **thyng** *n phr. as av* in any way, at all 20.430

enioynen *v* appoint 16.123; prescribe (for), impose on (sb.) 5.195, 7.71, 22.283, B 5.598; join together [things] 10.131, [persons in marriage] 2.150, B 2.66; *see also* **ioynen** *v*

enleuene 3.226, 12.176 = **el(l)eue(ne)** *card. num.*

enpugnen (inpugnen) *v* call in question validity [of a document] 13.117; find fault with 15.132

enqueste *n* trial by jury 5.57, 13.84; *and see* **queste** *n*

ensa(u)mple (ensaunple) *n* typical instance 4.133, B 10.469; sign, symbolic lesson 5.119, 12.130, 17.264; parabolic comparison / exemplary image 10.246, 11.291, 16.246, **B** 7.128, 10.294, 469, 11.324, 12.236, 15.472, A 10.110; model instance 1.167, 193, 13.26, 200, 16.261, B 15.261, 266, 433, A 11.274

ensense *n* incense 21.†76, 86, B 19.76

#**enspiren** *v* inspire (with zeal) 16.242

entente *n* aim, desire B 8.128

#**ent(i)erely** *av* whole-heartedly 10.190, 17.142

entermetynge *ger.* 13.225 *see* **entremet(t)en** *v*

#entisen *v* incite, tempt 7.90 (B 13.431), 20.316; *ger.* provoking B 13.322, tempting B 18.158

entre(e) *n* entry 12.59

entremet(t)en *v* interfere B 13.291; presume B 11.416; *ger.* intervention 13.225

entren *v* come in, enter 7.266, 20.290, 22.355, B 3.238; take possession [of estate, by entering it] B 15.138; enter, record 11.205

*enuenyme *n* poison B 2.14

enuenymen *v* infect, poison 12.255

enuye *n* enmity, hostility 6.87, 7.261, 10.134, 11.56, 18.164, 20.459, B 10.433, A 5.53; malice, spite 12.41, 20.49, B 13.322; envy 19.256, 21.140, 22.246, (*person.*) 2.88, 6.62, 63, 93, 21.229, 22.273, 295, Z 5.91

epistel 19.319 *see* **pistul** *n*

equite(e) *n* impartial justice, just / fair judgement 19.288, 21.310

er¹ *av* formerly 15.308; previously 1.200, 3.393, B 1.131, 134, *in phr.* **whil ~** some time ago 10.292

er² *prep.* (= **ar, or**) before **B** 5.536, 6.146, 15.539, 17.110

er(e)³ *conj.* before **B** Pr 155, 5.5, 51, 346, 373, 390, 461, 6.65, 11.221, 13.261, 15.2, 17.83, A 12.57, 103

erbe *n* plant 8.321

erber *n* (pleasure)-garden, arbour 18.5, B 16.15

erchebisshop *n* archbishop B 15.244

erchedeken *n* archdeacon [bishop's chief administrator] 5.71, 12.228, B 2.174

erd *n* dwelling-place 8.207

ere¹ *n* ear Pr 76, 4.14, 8.290, 16.143, 17.172, 175, 22.134, 190, **B** 4.146, 12.226, 252, 13.200, 15.401, A 12.23

ere² A 12.57, 103 = **er**³ *conj.*

erede *p.t.* 21.269 *see* **er(y)en** *v*

er(e)mite Pr 30 *etc*; *see* **(h)eremite** *n*

eremore Z 8.4 = **eueremo(o)re** *av*

eren A 7.125 = **eryen** *v*

eretike *n* heretic 19.112

eryen *v* (*p.t.* **er(i)ede**) plough, till 8.2, 66, 113, 123, 9.5, 6, 10.218, 15.236, 21.269, A 7.125

eritage 10.244, 16.127, B 10.341 = **heritage** *n*

erl *n* earl 3.268, 7.11, 10.86, 12.228, **B** 10.320, 13.166; great noble 21.223, **B** 4.189, 11.199, A 11.219

erldom *n* estate(s) of an earl (*fig.*) 2.88

er(e)nde *n* message 3.48, 13.40, A 3.40, †B 3.41

erly *av* early 5.15, 6.373

ermyte 5.4, 9.188 *et p.* = **heremite** *n*

ern *p.t.* 18.164, **ernynge** *pr.p.* 21.381 *see* **rennen** *v*

erraunt *a* arrant, downright 6.306

erren *v* go wrong, err 17.87

ers *n* rear 5.160; buttocks 6.157; anus B 10.125; **~ wynnynge** *n* gains from prostitution 6.305

erst *av sup.* first B 5.461; *and see* **arst(e)** *av*

erthe *n* the (physical) earth [contrasted with heaven and hell] 1.7, 126, 3.165, 14.85, 17.262, 18.99, 19.123, 20.232, 249, 256, **B** 1.17, 18.367, A 11.273; this world [as dwelling of man and other creatures] 1.66, 2.79, 135, 6.287, 7.126, 8.236, 10.160, 231, 11.202, 20.353, 421, 21.73, 261, 22.240, **B** 2.26, 3.303, 4.26, 9.100, 118, 153, A 11.273, 12.44; *in phrr.* **as of ~** (considered) as (an) earth(ly) creature) 18.99; **in / on ~** anywhere 2.10, 20.475, **B** 1.137, 15.211, Z 2.104, (alive) anywhere 10.24, 49; **(vpp)on (this) ~** in this life 3.94, 100, 101, 323, 5.152, 9.185, 332, 13.14, 14.173, 15.94, 16.152, 18.97, **B** 4.26, 8.38, 10.14, A 9.52; the people of this earth / world B 16.211; ground 5.118, 6.3, 407, 15.242, 20.63, 69, **B** 3.230, 12.204, 13.240, [as burial place] A 12.104; (cultivable) land Pr 224, 6.269, 9.2, 12.185, 186, 17.100, **B** 15.458, A 10.126, A 11.184; = flesh [earth as man's material substance] 1.149, 18.92; the primary 'element' earth 10.130, 15.242, 18.92, 20.256, B 17.161

erthely(che) *a* belonging to (this) earth(ly) existence 21.94, 22.151, B 15.175

#eschaunge *n* exchange / conversion of money / or commodities [for profit] 6.280 (B 13.394), B 5.245

eschewen *v* avoid, shun 8.51

ese *n* comfort Pr 55; spiritual comfort / peace 5.152; *in phrr.* **at / in ~** in comfort 5.165, 8.282, 9.143, 152, **B** Pr 157, 10.227, 18.209, **maken / putten at ~** make comfortable 1.19, 3.4, 15.48, **B** 6.150, 13.42; treat hospitably **B** 15.340, 16.227, A 11.174; **with ~** easily 13.53

esy *a* pleasant B 7.124; effortless B 15.207

esily *av* in comfort B 2.98; gently B 20.380

espien B 19.304 = **aspyen** *v*

estward *av* towards the east Pr 14, 1.132, B 16.169

eten *v* (*contr. pr.* **eet** 16.217, *p.t.* **eet** 6.430, **ete(n)** 15.67, 18.244, B 14.77, A 12.74, Z 7.166, *p.p.* **eten** 19.90, B 1.154, *ger.* 13.144, 15.258) eat 6.86, 159, 8.142, 146, 272, 326, 12.40, 41, 15.67, 18.244, 19.90, 20.198, 206, 316, 374, 21.278, 283, 291, 300, 390, 22.3, **B** 5.375, 376, 603, 6.263, 10.98, 101, 11.235, 13.107, **A** 6.93, 7.125, 10.141

#eua(u)ngelie (ewangelie) *n* the Christian Gospel 1.194; the Gospel record 11.204, 12.103, B 11.189; (one of the) Gospel(s) 15.45

euaungelist *n* evangelist B 13.39

eue 3.307, 9.87, B 3.312, **Z** 6.47, 8.76 = **euen** *n*

euel *n* evil B 10.201; wickedness 16.244; harm 3.449, 19.107; disease 3.96, 16.136, 21.46, 22.85

euel (yuel, vuel) *a* wicked, sinful 6.20, 21, **~ wil** *n phr.* ill-will 6.87, 18.164, B 10.433; wrongful 16.259; accursed B 9.121; difficult 6.87 (2), 8.45, 16.224, B 10.209

euel-willed *a phr.* full of ill-will 1.187

euele *av* wickedly 9.290, 291, 10.26, 302, 15.88, 19.290, 21.342; with evil consequences 13.114; badly 5.157, 7.71, 17.196, 22.186, 280, B 5.166; with difficulty 19.324, B 12.8

eue(n) *n* evening 7.225, 8.180, **B** 3.312, **Z** 6.47; *in phrr.* **at** ~ in the evening 5.116, 6.160, 9.87, 142, **B** 5.552, 14.15, **Z** 8.76, **ouer** ~ overnight 3.307, 7.195; eve of a feast-day 6.182, **A** 7.12; **~ynge** *n* evening **B** 11.339; **~song** *n* evensong, vespers 6.395, 7.68, 9.229, 244

euene Z 5.130 = **heuene** *n*

euene *a* equal 18.90; even, definite 22.270; ~ **cristene (emcristene)** *n* fellow-Christian 2.99, 6.75, 7.46, 10.79, 19.217, 228, **B** 2.95, 5.434, 13.105, 390, 17.135, 262

euene *av* directly 20.121, **A** 8.128; squarely 22.103; right, exactly 1.121, 18.6, 19.153, 20.61, 121; evenly (*fig.*), = justly 4.178; steadily 13.67, 16.53; consistently 21.300

eueneforþ *av* equally **B** 13.144, 17.135; ~ **(emforth)** *prep.* to the extent of 15.143, 16.221, 21.310

euer(e) *av* (*selected refs.*) always, at all times Pr 46, 1.102, 3.431, 6.93, 7.245, 8.299, 10.19, 51, 13.206, 15.146, 16.43, 19.218, 20.337, 21.291, 22.205, **B** 1.99, **A** 4.67; perpetually 1.132, 7.269, **A** 11.286; permanently 3.219, 5.96, 6.93, 7.184, 8.207, 9.4, 22.185, **B** 4.192, **A** 2.166; continuously 15.65; progressively 16.140, 18.111; ever, at any time Pr 123, 6.100, 7.12, 9.4, 11.193, 12.143, 20.45, 22.103, **B** 7.97, 8.69, 10.440, 14.304, **A** 2.12, 12.110; for ever 3.197, 4.70, 14.29, 17.93, 18.27, 19.135, 20.197, 21.45; *in phrr.* **for** ~ 2.248, 3.219, 4.124, 7.184 *etc*, **B** 1.115 *etc*, = in perpetuity **B** 2.157, **A** 2.50, = permanently 4.124, **Z** 7.302; **how (so / ...)** ~ in whatever way 12.6, 237; **what** ~ 7.125; **where** ~ **B** 5.89; ~ **after** 5.174

euermo B 7.80 = **eueremo(o)re** *av*

euereche *prn* both 20.76

euer(e)mo(o)re *av* always 3.286, 12.93, 16.3, 64, **B** 17.135; at all times 14.145, **B** 15.179, **Z** 7.38; for good 4.86, **B** 6.239, **A** 12.39; for ever 3.402, 17.66, **B** 15.484; ~ **after** continually, permanently 3.249, 9.170, **B** 7.80, **A** 12.39; in perpetuity **B** 7.4, 18.184

euery *a* every 17.283, **B** 5.246; ~ **creature B** 11.397, **Cristene cr. B** 10.362; ~ **man** 9.229, 10.182, 12.119, **B** 11.435, 15.263, ~ **manere...** 10.286, 19.260; ~ **seg(ge)** 3.67; ~ **wiȝt B** 8.53, **Z** 1.39

euesynges *n. pl.* eaves 19.194

#euidence *n* (piece of) evidence 19.161; authority for belief [from experience] 20.154, [from Scripture] 8.262; example [furnishing proof] 11.286, [of conduct] **B** 15.436

euyl 6.87, **A** 11.155 = **euel** *a*

#ewage *n* sea-coloured sapphire **B** 2.14

ewangelie 1.194 = **eua(u)ngelie** *n*

examenen *v* test for knowledge 17.116

excepte *prep.* except (for) 10.234, 16.213, **B** 11.98; *conj.* except 17.9

#exces(se) *n* surfeit, intemperance 6.416

exciten B 11.189 = **exiten** *v*

excusen (excucen) *v* exonerate 3.218, 9.239; defend, justify 22.6, **B** 12.20, 15.485; pardon **B** 9.183, *in phr.* **haue me / hem excused** forgive me / them 15.130, 19.83; let off, exempt 5.34, 7.297, 13.82

executour B 5.262, 12.257, 20.291 *see* **secatour** *n*

#exiten *v* stir up 6.20, 188; urge **B** 11.189

#experiense *n* (appeal to) practical observation / experience 20.153

experiment *n* feat **B** 10.214

expounen *v* explain the sense **B** 14.278

face *n* face 7.57, 8.241, **B** 1.15; facial appearance 1.10, 10.157, **B** 6.237, **A** 12.77; presence **A** 8.39

fader, fadur *n* (*gen.* **fad(e)res** 18.121, *uninfl. gen.* **fader** 16.27, **Z** 2.97) father Pr 123, 3.162, 5.36, 6.15, 7.213, 9.311, 313, 316, 10.243, 12.157, 16.105, 17.60, **B** 9.115, 147, **A** 10.66, **Z** 2.97, (*fig.*) 2.25, 121; ancestor **B** 16.205; patriarch 13.23; originator 1.14, 60, 10.153, 19.134, **B** 10.105; early Christian Father **B** 15.272; spiritual father, priest Pr 120, 122; (of God) the Father (of Jesus) 18.121, 227, 19.126, 132, 165, 192, 201, **B** 10.241, 16.223, 17.139, 150, 159, 168, 172, 173, **A** 8.39, (*fig.*) Father of Holy Church 2.31, **B** 2.29; (of God as) heavenly Father (of man / all creation) 1.161, 7.143, 10.153, 18.91, 19.210, **B** 7.53, 9.103, 10.105, 15.262, 418, 605, 16.213, **A** 11.64, *in phr.* **þe ~ wille of heuene** the will of the heavenly Father 16.27

faderlese *a* fatherless, orphaned **B** 9.68

fay *a* doomed to die 15.2, 16.195

fayere 22.350 = **fair** *a*

fayful 1.15; **fayfulleche** 8.70; *see* **faythful** *a*; **feiþfulliche** *av*

fail(l)en, fayl(l)en *v* forsake, fail, let down (sb.) 3.56, 11.190, 15.5, 16.317; neglect 12.122; be, prove wanting 2.96, 3.349, 17.144, 18.30, 21.219, **B** 14.88; fail (to do sth.) **B** 4.194; go wrong, err 9.302, 17.96, 103, 22.31; fail to produce (crops) 8.15; fail to grow 8.347; miss one's footing 1.119; leave out (words) 13.120; lack 2.159, 19.136, **B** 9.81, 11.26, 14.33, 15.431; be lacking (to / from) 1.185, 5.148, 6.256, 8.294, 10.168, 11.232, 15.227, 19.156, 214, 22.234, **B** 2.129, 146, 3.347, 7.121, 11.277, 12.7, 14.33, **A** 10.58; be absent, missing 19.139; run out of **B** 4.156, 10.295

fayn *a* happy, delighted 2.171, 8.323, 11.102; willing **B** 11.390; content 8.293, **Z** 6.74; desirous (of) 2.82, 3.154; eager for / to 4.13, 28

fayn *av* gladly, willingly 18.103, **B** 8.127, **A** 12.67

faynen (feynen) *v* fashion **B** Pr 36, (*refl.*) **B** 10.38; (*refl.*) pretend (to be) 8.128

fayre[1] *n* fair 6.211, 13.51; opportunity to sell 4.59; **newe ~** London fair [of low repute], (*fig. use for*) game of barter 6.376*n*

fayr(e)[2] *a* beautiful Pr 19n, 1.10, 11.173, 13.42, 175, 14.158, 177, 16.253, 18.29, **B** 15.333, (*comp.*) 18.55, (*sup.*) 14.170, 18.99; handsome 6.46, B 11.394; attractive 15.8, 18.33, 54, 55, *a as n* = fair side 9.85; pleasant 21.28, 22.350; bright 11.102, 19.173, 206; (deceptively) agreeable [of speech] 2.239, 8.216, 12.13, 18.172, 22.118, B 2.42, 15.350, A 2.130, [of expression] B 16.149; dear 17.143, 18.248; good 3.369; excellent 10.77, 13.201, 14.180, 21.459, B 11.193, (*sup.*) 18.89; splendid 2.163, 12.248, B 16.1 (2); fine 9.268, 10.145, 15.206, (*sup.*) 18.93; seemly (*comp.*) 9. (physically cleanest) B 19.254; ~**nesse** *n* beauty 13.172, B 2.77, 12.46

fayre³ *av* beautifully B 16.66; courteously 1.54, 7.278, 9.129, 322, 13.247, 15.31, 16.170, 17.31, 18.243, 21.73, 483, B 1.4, 6.24, 13.181, 15.9, 16.65, (*comp.*) B 10.227; properly 17.109; nobly 20.70; eloquently 17.83, B 1.74, 16.53 (2); favourably, *in phr.* ~ **hem** / **yow** (**be**)**falle** good luck to them / you 5.199, B 16.1, 53 (1); aptly 10.32; exactly 6.325; well 17.109; moderately (*comp.*) 22.315; clearly 1.2, 10.32

fairye *n* (the land of) supernatural beings B Pr 6

fayten *v* beg under false pretences Pr 43, 5.30, 9.170, 208, B 15.214; *ger.* **faityng** B 10.38

fayth (feiþ) *n* religion 16.251, 17.258; religious faith, belief (in God) 1.14, 17.258, B 15.605, 16.245, 17.133; the Christian faith 1.181, 11.57, 17.271, B 1.76, 13.211, 15.346, 447, 521, 522, 579, A 11.60, 63; Christian doctrine 11.158, 245, 21.272, B 10.233; (*spec.*) (the theological virtue of) Faith B 12.30, 13.129, 14.81, 82, 85, 87, 15.450, (*person.*) B 11.225 (= God), 18.185 *et p.*, 19.23 *et p.*, 20.13 *et p.*, B 17.81 *et p.* (= Abraham); trust 18.255; loyalty, constancy 3.157; honesty, truthfulness 3.194, Z 1.18; *in phr.*: **be my** ~ truly, assuredly 8.293, 12.19; **in** ~ truly 4.13, 50, 5.40, 8.34, 215, 11.229, 277, 14.3, 16.287, 20.128, 22.333, B 5.235; **good** ~ sincerity 4.37, 21.302, 22.28, B 5.264, Z 3.176 (*person.*) 10.148, 22.131; true justice 22.28, B 18.348, 352; (*as assev.*) **in, by good** ~ in all sincerity, 6.287, 340

faythful *a* sincerely religious 6.291; honest B 6.250; trustworthy 17.35, 18.141; loyal 1.15; just, true B 9.103

faythles *a* perfidious 2.143, B 9.119, 10.195, (*person.*) **Fals** ~ 2.42

faythly *av* truly 21.70

faytles Z 2.102 = **feytles** *a*

#**fayto(u)r** *n* deceiver, cheat 2.193, 8.73, 179, 10.299, 11.54, 22.5, B 15.215, A 2.94; false beggar, [esp. one feigning injury or illness] 8.128, 9.64, B 13.243

#**faytrye** *n* deception, imposture 8.138, 12.34

#**fal(l)a(e)s** *n* (*sg. or pl.*) deceptive legal stratagem 11.20, (*pl.*) sophistical argument 16.229

falewen *v* plough 7.294

fallen *v*¹ (*pr. subjv.* **falle** B 16.1; *p.t.* **ful** Pr 106, **fel** B 1.114, A 10.185, **fil** B 14.79, A 1.112, *pl.* **fullen** 1.125, **fellen** B 1.121; *p.t. subjv.* **fulle** 18.128, **felle** B 16.94,

fille B 14.186; *p.p.* (**y**)**falle** 2.102, 7.112, **fallen** B Pr 65; *pr.p.* **fallynge** 10.22, *ger.* 10.41) fall Pr 106, 113, 1.119, 3.102, 107, 6.334, 10.39(2), 13.235, 16.211, 18.48, 107, 19.147, 20.89, 346, 21.5, 22.51, 176, **B** 1.121, 8.32, 14.79, 15.300, A 5.215; *ger.* 18.30, B 16.25; fall (morally / spiritually) 2.102, 10.22, 39(1), 42, 11.305, 15.288, 19.314, *ger.* 10.41, 21.65; *in phr.*: ~ **for** be proper for B 11.99, 394, Z 7.231; ~ **in** fall into 7.112, 9.272, 11.301, 15.288, 21.305, 22.10, 176, B 18.103; come into 19.292; come into contact with B 4.156; ~ **of** become of 6.325; afflict A 10.185; ~ **to** pertain to 1.161; be necessary (to) B 10.233; ~ **to be** become 18.128; be suitable / fitting (for) 18.185, ~ **for** B 11.99, 394, Z 7.231; fall down 15.405; collapse 9.100; be brought low 20.106, 382, 22.228; issue as a consequence B 5.140; descend 3.125, B 10.277; alight upon 2.209; happen Pr 63, 3.90, 477, 17.232, 20.411, 22.32, B 7.158; befall B 16.1; turn out 3.97; turn (out) to (be) B 12.46

fallen² Z 3.90 = **fellen** *v*

fals *n* deceit 22.55; (*person.*) 2.6 *etc*

fals *a* deceitful, treacherous 2.91, 3.91, 114, 300, 9.64, 10.299, 16.274, 17.183, 20.320, 22.64, 285, B 10.195; *a as n* the deceitful 2.4, (*person.*) 3.175; untrustworthy 16.41, 22.285, B 12.257, A 10.210 (2); deceptive A 9.38; dishonest, corrupt 2.55, 6.293, 11.20, 20.27; wicked Pr 106, 3.102, 8.229, 12.199, 240, 21.248, **B** 9.147, 14.24; mendacious 2.83, 85, 6.72, 258, 7.226, 15.79, 18.123, 21.222, 373, 22.118, **B** 3.127, 9.119, 13.401; counterfeit (*fig.*) 17.76; misbelieving 17.258, 20.95, 113; erroneous 21.47; inaccurate 6.258, 13.117, 16.128, B 13.359; *in phr.*: ~ **doem** 20.27; ~ **mesure** B 13.359; ~ **w(e)yhte** 6.258, 16.128; ~ **witnesse** 2.85, 7.226, 16.361, **B** 5.88, 13.359, (*person.*) 2.160

fals(h)ede *n* deceitfulness 1.60, 6.341, B Pr 71, (*person.*) 2.149, 3.41, A 2.50, Z 2.3

falsli(che) *av* treacherously, deceitfully 20.379, B 18.352; wickedly B 17.307; mendaciously 6.427; fraudulently 9.268n

falsnesse *n* deceitfulness 12.34, 22.66, Z 1.18, (*person.*) 2.70, 171, 212, Z 2.165; wrong B 15.262; mendacity Pr 69

fame *n* ill-repute A 5.74

famen *v* slander 3.231

famy(e)n(e) *n* famine, dearth of food 7.305, 8.215, 345, Z 7.326; extreme hunger 12.199

fand *p.t.* A Pr 17 = **fond**; see **fynden** *v*

fangen B 5.558; *see* **fongen** *v*

fantasie *n* fantastic notion A 11.63; extravagant amusement B Pr 36

fare *n* commotion 20.16, 128

faren *v* (*p.t.* **ferde(n)** 10.237, 13.229; *p.p.* **faren** 8.112) go on one's way **B** 2.184, 5.5; betake oneself 8.112; depart, **hennes** ~ depart this life **B** 7.97, 15.145; go by B 12.5; behave, act 12.19, 18.96, 19.114, 22.313, **B** 3.344, 10.94, 15.332; ~ **by / with** behave towards 13.229, 15.119, 22.313, B 13.149; fare, live 5.8, 6.334, 10.237, 11.75, 22.235, **B** 13.51, 15.185, A 11.178; go, happen, turn out 10.41, 11.245, 14.141, 16.110, 20.234; *in phrr.*: **it fareth bi / with** it goes with 10.38, 41, 16.110, 17.76, 18.67, 19.289, 22.290, **B** 12.201, 14.271, 15.350, 455; **fare(th) wel** farewell, goodbye 11.314, B 13.181

fast(e)[1] *a* tight-(fisted) A 2.63.

faste[2] *av* firmly 1.42, 3.176, **B** 13.153, 15.242, 17.133, 157, Z 2.160; securely 1.92, 2.212, B 17.111; soundly B 18.6; stoutly 21.103; closely 2.180; earnestly 7.57, **B** ? 5.382, 14.274; diligently B 15.447, A 7.10, 13; heartily B 6.108; faithfully †6.155(2); eagerly Pr 41, 4.77, 8.214, 11.176, **B** 4.167, 14.331, 16.169, **A** 4.133, 7.192; many times B 10.69, A 5.222; steadily 6.326, 15.66, **Z** 4.62, 5.91; speedily Pr 65, 4.28, 8.343, 17.209, 19.52, 80, 22.325; quickly B 4.30, 33, 42; instantly B 4.24, A 1.113

faste Z 2.95 = **fest** *p.p.*

fasten *v* fast [abstain from food and drink as a religious discipline] 1.99, 6.155, 351, 13.80, ? B 5.382n, A 5.211, ? Z 5.106; *ger.* **fastyng** Pr 69, 9.233, 20.313, ~ **day** 2.100, 6.182, 359, 433, 7.25, 9.94

fastened *p.p.* Z 2.57, **fastnid** A 2.48, 88 = **festned**; *see* **festenen** *v*

fatte *n* fat, grease 21.281

fat(te) *a* plump 9.208, (*comp.*) B 12.263; fertile 12.226

fauchen *n* falchion [broad sword with curved blade] 16.167

faucon *n* falcon 8.30, B 17.63

fauht *p.t.* 3.246, 20.408, 21.103; *see* **fy(g)hten** *v*

faumewarde (vawwarde) *n* vanguard, forefront 5.58, 22.95

faunen *v* fawn, ~ **with þe tayle** show fondness (by wagging the tail) 17.31

faunt *n* child 9.170, **B** 6.282, 16.101, A 10.58, 64, 66

#**faunt(o)kyn** *n* little child 9.35, 10.184, 21.118, B 13.214

***fauntelte(e)** *n* childishness, puerility B 15.150; (*person.*) 11.314

faut *n* reproach (for wrong) B 10.105

fauten *v* be lacking B 9.68; lack 10.184

fauel *n* flattery (*person.*) 2.25 *etc*

#**fauerable** *a* showing favour 3.191

feble *a* (physically) weak Z 5.142; weak (in contest) 16.67; infirm 7.21, B 15.576, (*fig.*) B 17.117; lacking in power B 17.173; impotent (*a as n*) B 9.163; ineffective B Pr 180; thin 6.159; debased B 15.349; (*comp.*) weaker (in faith) B 15.347, worse 1.181; (*sup.*) least powerful 14.171

fec(c)hen *v* (*p.t.* **fet(ten)**) 2.65, 239, A 5.216; *p.p.* **fet** 22.324) fetch 4.7, 8.316, 22.324, B 5.29, 640, A 7.281; bring B 11.56, A 7.33; come for 11.168, A 3.91; carry

away 2.239, 18.286, 20.275, 277, 325, 393, 21.467; carry off 8.154, 21.145, **B** 4.51, 16.49; steal 6.268 (B 13.372), 20.379, B 18.351; carry off to death 8.348; obtain, win 10.279, 18.130, 20.18, 32; draw 7.56; take away B 11.56; collect 20.154; *in phrr.*: ~ **at** seek (from) 3.375; ~ **away** carry off 12.240, 18.49; ~ **forth** bring forward, produce 2.157, 179, **B** 2.163, 11.324, **Z** 2.58, 136; ~ **fro, out of** rescue from 18.281, 286; recover 21.248; ~ **of** obtain from 2.191; *see also* **fetten** *v*

feden (*p.t.* **fedde** 6.433, *p.p.* **fed(d)e**) B 15.471, 16.125, Z 7.316) feed 6.433, 7.133, 17.171, 18.153, 21.126, **B** Pr 190, 15.462, 464, (*fig.*) 7.133, B 15.414; keep supplied with food 8.320, 323, 9.90, 17.11, 15, 57, 68, 21.258, 22.209, **B** 4.119, 14.10, 15.306, 339, A Pr 93; provide with meals 12.106, B 11.192, (*fig.*) B 15.484; sustain, support 7.82, B 6.250; nourish spiritually 17.285, B 14.30

fe(e) *n* estate, **knyhtes ~** 5.77; money 4.128, (*pl.*) 7.227

feeld B Pr 17, 6.235 = **feld** *n*

feele 17.151 = **felen** *v*

feend B 7.67, Z 7.133 = **fend** *n*

feerde *p.t.* 22.313; *see* **faren** *v*

feere B 2.194, 13.163, *see* **fe(e)re** *n*[1,2]; *pl.* B 5.168 = **aferes** *n*

feeste B 15.341; **feestyng** *ger.* †B 5.375 *see* **festen** *v*[1]

feet[1] *n* deed, act (?*with pun on* feet) 1.181

feet[2] 2.193 *etc*; *see* **foet** *n*

feffament *n* document of enfeoffment [investment with an estate] 2.73

feffen *v* enfeoff [put in legal possession of estate] 17.57; endow by way of gift, (*fig.*) 3.369, A 2.37; present with a gift 2.160; affiance, join sb. to another in a marriage contract 2.137, A 2.37, 47, 58

fey(e) 16.195, B 13.2 = **fay** *a*

***feym** Z 7.326 *see* **famy(e)n(e)** *n*

feynen B Pr 36, 10.38 = **faynen** *v*

feynte *a* faint, exhausted B 17.117

fe(y)ntise *n* exhaustion B 5.5, A 12.67, 68

feyr 19.173 = **fayr(e)** *a*

feytles *a* ?perfidious (= **faythles**, ? *with pun on* 'without deeds') A 2.94, Z 2.102

feiture *n* feature, ?creature B 13. 297c; *and see* **feture** *n*

feiþ B 1.76, 10.233, 13.211, 15.450, A 11.60, 63; ~ **ful** B 6.250, 9.103, 15.418; ~ **lees** B 9.119, 10.195; *see* **fayth** *n*, ~ **ful** *a*, ~ **les** *a*

feiþfulliche *av* honestly B 6.69 (= **fayfulleche** 8.70)

fel[1] *n* skin B 1.15

fel[2] *a* treacherous (?destructive) 18.35; terrible †B 3.260 (1); **felle** (*pl.*) severe (? *or* shrewd) 3.492, 6.152; ~**ly** *av* fiercely B 18.92

fel[3] *p.t.* B 3.260 (2), B 7.158 *etc*; *see* **fallen** *v*

felawe *n* companion 15.103, 21.202, 22.341, 350; associate 1.119, 2.183, B 7.12; intimate companion 19.80, 97, 21.88, **B** 17.87, 89 *et p.*, 18.197; fellow-servant 8.254; ~ swimmer B 12.167; ~ fisherman B 15.292; ~ freeman

3.111; accomplice 2.205, 4.27, **B** 9.85, 15.377; *in phr.* **partyng** ~ partner B 13.207

felaws(c)hip(e) *n* company 11.185, B 11.435; partnership (as spouse) 3.154; revelling 2.102; armed crew 4.50; band of associates B 2.208, A 1.112; (heavenly) community B 1.114

feld *n* plain Pr 19, 1.2, 5.111; (arable) field 7.32, 12.194, 21.315, B 6.140, 235; open country 13.175, B 7.129; surrounding country district A 2.39; *in phr.* **a**~ to the field 8.312

felde *p.t.* 3.239, 18.128; *see* **fellen** *v*

fele (vele 6.74) *indef. num. a* many 6.118, 9.95, 11.229, 13.138, 21.222, **B** 9.73, 10.213, 12.5, 15.70, 288; *in phr.*: **bi** ~ **fold** *av phr.* many times over **B** 12.263, 13.320; ~ **tyme(s)** 6.74, 118, 16.228; ~ **ʒer** 16.354; *as n* many 9.91, B 15.332, 519, Z 7.278

felen *v* (*p.t* **felede** 6.114, *ger.* **(v)elynge** 20.131) feel (by touching) 19.146, 21.171, 22.195, *ger.* touch, contact 20.131; feel, experience (emotion) 6.114, 7.130, 20.228, 22.37; perceive 16.187, B 17.179

felicite *n* well-being 22.240

felle *a. pl.* 3.492, 6.152 *see* **fel** *a*

felle *p.t. subjv.* **B** 16.94, 19.244; *see* **fallen** *v*

fellen *p.t. pl* **B** 1.121, 18.311; *see* **fallen** *v*

fellen *v* (*p.t.* **felde** 18.128, **felled** B 3.127) make sth. fall 18.128; bring down B 3.127, A 3.41, Z 3.90; slay 3.239, A 12.66

felly *av* B 18.92 *see* **fel²**, *av*

felo(u)n *n* criminal [*esp.* perpetrator of a felony, *e.g.* treason, theft, murder] 6.325, 10.243, 11.255, 14.141, 20.421, **B** 17.111, 18.383

felonliche *av* feloniously 12.240, B 18.352

felowe 15.103, ~**schipe** 11.185; *see* **felawe** *n*, ~**s(c)hip(e)** *n*

femel(l)e *n* female 13.148, B 11.339

fend(e) *n* (the) Devil 1.38, 118, 2.42, 143, 8.97, 10.48, 14.119, 16.44, 18.43, 120, 130, 137, 20.18, 27, 32, 202, 477, 22.58, **B** 7.67, 11.399, 15.141, 16.48, **A** 7.136, 10.64; fiend, demon 20.315, 343, 21.47, 22.58, 64, B 14.24, A 1.112; *in phrr.*: ~**es biyete** B 2.41; ~ **disciples** B 13.430; ~ **kynne** 2.42; ~ **liknesse** B 1.114; ~ **lymes** 22.77, ~ **procuratours** 7.89

***fendekyn** *n* small/lesser devil 20.415

fenden *v* defend, protect 1.99, 21.46, ?prevent 21.65

fenestre *n* window 20.13; glazed window 16.41

fen(k)elsede *n* fennel-seed 6.359

fentyse A 12.67, 68 = **feyntise** *n*

fer *a* far 9.241, 10.77, 12.239, B 10.473; long ago 16.354; *in phr.*: ~ **(a)way** far and away 16.50; ~ **and fele ʒer** many long years ago 16.354; **be** ~ by a long way 22.23, 315; **(ful)** ~ a long way 11.196, 20.166, 21.483

fer *av* far 14.176, 177, 17.196, B 10.473

ferde(n) *p.t.* 10.237, 13.229 *etc*; *see* **faren** *v*

ferden *v* assemble together 13.148

fe(e)re *n¹* partner 17.19; comrade (in crime) 2.219, **B**

2.6, 194, 4.27, A 4.141; husband 19.302 (1); mate 13.164

fere *n²* fear 2.220, 249, 251, 8.191, 202, 215, 320, 12.199, 19.302 (2), 20.113, 22.169, **B** 2.210, 4.52, 6.183, 11.354, Z 6.74; danger 12.199, B 2.210

feren *v* frighten away 17.285

ferie *n* week day, **heye** ~ holy day [church festival] falling on weekday 4.113, B 13.415

ferly *n* wonder(ful occurrence) Pr 63, 11.229, 18.56, 20.113, B Pr 6, A 12.58, 59; *in phrr.*: **(a)** ~ **me thynketh** I should be astonished 15.119, 16.294, 17.112; **hauen** ~ **(of)** be astonished at 11.229, 20.128

ferme¹ *n* use, **hauen lond to** ~ have use of land (for fixed payment) B 16.16

ferme² *a* steadfast 11.57, B 15.347; firm, steady 14.208, 18.255, **B** 15.579, 17.133; *av* firmly 21.120

fermen *v* strengthen B 10.74

fermerye *n* infirmary B 13.109

fern *av* formerly, ~ **ago** long ago B 15.231

fernyere *n* past year B 12.5; *as av* in past years 7.46

fers (fiers(e)) *a* bold, fierce 6.7; savage B 15.305

ferst A 7.168 = **furst** *n*

ferste A 10.28 = **furst(e)** *a*

ferst(e) A 10.131, 11.135 = **furst(e)** *av*

ferþe (furthe) *ord. num. a.* fourth 21.299, A 12.82; *as n.* 9.56, 16.131

ferþer(e) B 2.202 *etc*, A 7.188 *etc*; *see* **forthere** *av*

ferþest *sup. a.* farthest, most distant B 5.235

ferthyng(e) *n* farthing 4.57, 7.201; ~ **worth** farthing's worth 6.359, 9.94

fesaunt *n* pheasant B 15.462

fest *p.p.* B 2.124 *see* **festen** *v²*

feste *n* religious feast [commemorative church celebration] 17.120 (**heye-festes** 6.182; ~ **day** 5.30); feast, banquet 6.291, 7.97, 115 (*fig.*), 9.95, 11.34, 12.103, 15.207, 21.108, 115, **B** 10.94, 11.216, 15.461, 480, A 11.60

festen *v¹* entertain at a feast B 15.341, (*fig.*) 16.319, B 15.484; *ger.* feasting B †5.375, 11.193; feed abundantly B 15.589

festen *v²* join (in marriage) B 2.124

festenen *v* attach (to), establish (in) 12.8; join (in marriage), *p.p.* A 2.48, 88

#festren *v* fester 19.85

#festu *n* mote B 10.277c

fet *p.p.* 22.324, B 11.324; **feteth** *imp.* Z 7.34; *see* **fec(c)hen** *v*

fet(e) *n pl.* A 11.215, 12.47 *see* **foet** *n*

fet(t)eren *v* fetter, shackle 2.212, 7.21, 16.328, **B** 2.208, 17.111

fether *n* feather 13.138, 14.172, 177, 183, 21.415

fetisli(che) *av* elegantly B 2.11, 166

fette(n) *p.t.* 2.65 *etc*; *see* **fecchen** *v*

fetten *v* (*p.t.* **fette**) fetch 5.131; ~ **forþ** bring forward A 2.49; ~ **of** obtain from A 2.142; *and see* **fecchen** *v*

feture *n* feature 6.46c

feuer(e) *n* fever 3.96, 6.79, 21.46, 22.81, (*person.*) A 12.82

fewe *a* few Pr 63, 8.295, 305, 9.91, 10.259, 13.191, 15.203, 288, 16.130, 142, A 12.58, 66; *as n* 9.244, 18.147, 22.110, **B** 10.437, 11.390, 12.5, 15.4

fy (*excl.*) fie! 2.137, B 15.215

*****fibicches (febicchis)** *n. pl.*? alchemical tricks B 10.213c, A 11.159

fichen *v. refl.* brace (oneself in the saddle) Z 2.160

fierse B 15.305 = **fers** *a*

fifte *ord. num. a.* fifth B 11.47

fiftene *card. num.* fifteen A 3.38

fifty *card. num.* fifty B 3.39

fyge *n* fig 2.29

fight *n* combat B 15.164

fy(g)hten *v* (*p.t.* **fauht** 3.246, *pl.* **foughten** Pr 43, *p.p.* **yfouhte** 8.149) fight 1.96, 99, 3.236, 256, 5.58, 8.34, 150, 14.50, 21.219, 227, 448, 22.141, 166, 168, 302, (*fig.*) 18.137, (*ger.*) B 16.101: quarrel, brawl Pr 43, 1.175, 4.59, 5.154, **B** 4.52, 13.322; struggle spiritually 16.172, 21.65

#figuratyfly *av* in a figurative manner, ? as a hazy or indistinct image 16.294

fykel *a* deceitful 2.25, 3.157, 6.72, 11.20, B 2.79, 130; ~ **tonge** treacherous-tongue 2.6, (*person.*) 2.121, B 2.41

fil (= **ful**) *p.t.* **B** 14.79, 15.300 A 1.112, 5.215; **fille** *p.t. subjv.* B 14.186, 16.107 *see* **fallen** *v*

fyle *n* concubine 6.135

*****filial** *a* filial, as from child to parent 8.216

fille (**fulle**) *n* fill **B** 1.154, 6.263, 16.11

fillen (**fullen**) *v* fill 3.88, 6.389, B 15.337

filosophye 22.296 = **philosophie**

fylosofre 13.27 = **philosophere** *n*

filþe *n* dirt B 14.17

fyn *n*[1] fin 22.45

fyn *n*[2] fine [final agreement relating to alienation of property (rights)] A 2.36, 48

fyn[3] *a* excellent, perfect 19.85, 176; *sup.* Z 7.316; subtle 11.158

fynden *v* (*contr. pr. 2 sg.* **fynst** B 3.266, *3 sg.* **fynd(e)** 5.27, 16.317, **fynt(e)** 4.121, 5.88, 19.314, B 4.131; *p.t.* **fo(e)nd(e)** Pr 19, 1.60, **foond** B 11.293, **fonden** A Pr 36; *p.t. subjv.* **founde** 6.22, 15.220, B 15.311; *p.p.* (y)**founde(n)** 8.138, B 10.255) find Pr 19, 56, 3.492, 4.121, 128, 5.173, 6.76, 7.213, 8.229, 10.77, 13.164, 14.89, 15.104, 16.293; come upon 14.86, 17.161, **B** 3.266, 15.478, **ben founden** be met with 9.343, B 15.230; come across in books, read about 3.59, 494, 11.255, 277, 15.266, 17.84, 165, **B** 3.344, 9.67, 145, 11.154, 225, 277, 12.76, 15.278; discover [by enquiry] 6.22, 7.32, 8.138, 9.288, 12.212, **B** 3.269, 13.318; find out [by experience] 3.477, 11.186, 190, 12.15, 25, 15.185, 220, 16.353, 17.106, 18.172, 19.23, **B** 4.71, 6.58,

9.147, 11.390, 15.153, 230, 311, 424, 17.87, **A** 11.168, 12.59, Z 3.151; discover [by thinking] 1.60, 5.153, 15.138, 19.314; provide, supply Pr 143, 5.21, 27, 49, 88, 7.258, 8.70, 148, 13.71, 15.202, 217, 16.149, 314, 317, 318, **B** 7.30, 129, 130, 9.68, 73, 14.32; devise (for) A Pr 36; provide for, maintain 3.41, 375, 5.76, 9.30, 35, 10.183, 185, 13.108, 15.237, 252, 16.272, 317, 17.34, 21.448, 22.296, **B** 10.93, 15.285, 307, 572; determine and declare [as guilty] 2.153, B 5.144; originate 1.60; ~ **out** think up Pr 37; *pr.p.* explore 3.344; attain to B 13.129; ~ **vp** introduce, formulate 11.54

fyndyng(e) *ger.* (source of) maintenance 6.293, 22.384, B 15.422

fynger *n* finger 2.12, 8.9, 13.106, 14.37, 19.115 *et p.*, 21.171, **B** 10.125, 17.142 *et p.*, Z 7.54

fynt *contr. pr. 3 sg. see* **fynden** *v*

Fyppe *diminutive of* Philip [*name for* sparrow], *in excl.* **farewel** ~ come on, let's be off! 11.314

fir B 7.52 = **fuyr** *n*

firmament *n* air A 8.115

firs *n* (*pl.* ~**es**, ~**en**) furze B 5.345, A 5.194

first 1.23, B 3.244, A 12.59, *av* 1.60, B 1.76; *see* **furst(e)** *a*, *av*

firsen *n pl.* A 5.194 *see* **firs** *n*

fys(c)h *n* fish 5.148, 15.242, 264, 22.45, B 8.54, A 10.174; [*as food*] 6.159, 438, 7.49, 8.333, 9.93, 15.102, 18. 154, 21.126, B 15.431, 590

fischen *v* (catch) fish 17.19

fiscuth *3 sg.* 9.153 *see* **fisken** *v*

fis(c)i(s)cian *n* doctor of medicine 22.176; physician 18.141, 22.316, A 7.168

fysyk(e) *n* medical science 22.178, 342, B 15.383, Z 7.260; medical practice 8.267, 293, 22.315, 379; the medical profession (*person.*) 8.291, 22.169

fisyken *v* treat medically 22.324

#fisken *v* wander idly 9.153

fythele *n* fiddle, viol (*fig.*)7.116, B 9.103

fythelen *v* (play the) fiddle 15.207; recite (to music) 7.106 (B 13.447)

fiþelere *n* fiddle-player B 10.94

fytheren *v* fit with tail-wing (of feathers) 22.118

fyue *card. num. a* five 1.15, 2.12, 10.145, 14.89, 15.82, 18.154, 21.126, B 12.3; *as n* 10.149; ~ **score** B 1.101; ~ **thousand** 18.154, 21.127, B 15.590; ~ **daies** 6.161, B 15.319; ~ **loues** 21.126, B 15.590; ~ **ordres** 8.191, 9.343; ~ **wittes** 1.15, 15.258, 16.232, 21.217, A 11.293; ~ **woundes** A 11.215; ~ **yer** B 6.322; ~ **ȝokes** 7.294

flail *n* flail [for threshing grain] 8.180

flappe *n* stroke B 13.67

flappen (on) *v* beat, thresh 8.180

flatere *n* flatterer 7.82, 89, 21.222, B 13.455

flateren *v* flatter, beguile with pleasing words 8.147, 12.25, 22.110, 235, 384; *pr.p.* 2.43; *ger.* flattering 7.106, 15.79

flaterer(e) flatterer 7.114, 11.6, B 2.166; (*person.*) 17.112, 22.316, 324

flatten *v* (*p.t.* **flatte(d)**) splash 7.57

flaum(b)e *n* flame 19.173, 206, 214

flaumen *v* blaze 19.171, 192; smell B 12.254

fle(e)n *v* (*p.t.* **fley(h)** 2.220, 21.103, **fleiȝ** B 17.89, **fledde** 2.249) flee, run away (from) 2.219, 220, 249, 17.144, 19.302, 22.44, 169, 285, B 17.318; escape 3.175, 21.103; depart 16.195, 20.343, 22.131; *and see* **flyen** *v*

flees *n* fleece 9.268

fley(h)[1] *p.t.* 2.220, 21.103 *see* **fle(e)n** *v*

fley(h)[2] *p.t.* 18.121, 19.59 *see* **flyen** *v*

fleysche 3.59 = **fles(c)h(e)** *n*

#**flekede** *p.pl.* spotted 13.138

Flemmyng *n* Fleming [person of Flemish birth / ancestry] Z 7.278

fles(c)h(e) *n* (human or animal) flesh B 12.242 (1), Z Pr 106; (flesh) meat 6.159, 7.49, 8.154, 333, 9.93, 14.180, 15.102, B 12.242 (2), 263, 13.40, 14.44, 15.431, 464, 16.229; (the human) body 17.195, B 16.101, A 11.215; bodily nature 7.143; man's sensual nature 3.59, 6.7, 16.133, [esp. as enemy of the soul] 1.38, 10.48, 19.312, 20.202, B 11.399, A 7.136, 9.45, (*person.*) 18.35; man's sexual nature 13.152, 18.79; *in phrr.*: ~ **and blode** human nature 1.151; **lost of** ~ lust of the flesh 13.152

flescheliche *a* of flesh 21.171

fleten *v* (*contr. pr.* **flet**) drift B 12.167; swim 22.45

flex *n* flax 8.12

fly *p.t.* 1.118 *see* **flyen** *v*

flicche *n* flitch, side (of bacon) 10.279

flyen (*pr. pl.* **fleeth** 10.233, *p.t. sg.* **fl(e)y(h)** 1.118, 18.121, 19.59, *pl.* **flowe(n)** 2.249, 19.82, *pr.p.* **fleynge** B 8.54) fly 1.118, 10.233, 14.171, 176, B 8.54; hasten 2.249, 8.179, 18.121, 19.59, 82, 20.369, 22.285

flyht *n* power of flight 14.171

flynt *n* hard rock 15.267; flint [for striking fire] 19.211, Z 6.72

flitten *v* change, *pr. p.* **flittyng** changeable, shifty 12.15

*****flobren** *v* dirty B 14.15 *and see* **befloberen** *v*

flo(e)d, flood *n* river 5.148, B 14.43; river-current B 12.167, (*fig.*) 14.119; sea B 15.366; flood 3.91, 8.347, 9.182, 10.228, 15.166, B 10.407; stream (of water) 15.267

flore *n* floor 14.137

flor(e)yn(e) *n* florin 2.157, 160, 3.194, 7.227, B 4.156

florischen *v* adorn, ? cause to prosper 16.131

flour *n*[1] flower 13.175, 14.158, 16.253, B 16.26, 45, (*fig.*) A 10.122

flour *n*[2] flour 8.154, B 14.30

flouren *v* flower 18.35, B 16.94

flowe(n) *p.t. pl.* 2.249, 8.179, 19.82, 20.369 *see* **flyen** *v*

#**flux** *n* morbid discharge (*?fig.*) 6.161*c*; ?dysentery 21.46, 22.81

fobbe *n* cheat 2.193

fobbere *n* cheat, impostor B 2.183

fo(o)d(e) *n* food, sustenance Pr 43, 1.23, 5.27, 49, 6.293, 8.18, 70, 284, 291, 9.76, 15.102, 16.314, 323, 17.19, 22.15, B 7.30, 15.305, 478, 575, A 8.33, 116, 11.185, 186, (*fig.*) 7.258, 18.14 (?*with pun on* offspring) 21.410; *in phrr.*: **angeles** ~ ?= contemplation, ?manna 22.15; **goostly** ~ B 15.572, 575(2)

foe *n* (*pl.* **foes** 3.239, **fo(o)n** B 5.95) enemy 5.58, 6.72, 12.13, B 9.201, 15.262, Z 6.72

fo(e)l, fool *n* fool, stupid person 22.61, 62, 74, 77, B 7.125 (?*with pun on* **foules**), B 11.68; (natural) fool, half-wit 10.184, B 10.6, 15.3, 10, A 10.64; morally / spiritually obtuse person 12.213; (professional) buffoon / jester ? Pr 37, 7.89, 114, ? 11.6; ~ **sage** wise fool 7.82, 103

foend(e) *p.t.* 5.36, 40, 22.296, **foond** B 11.293, **fonden** A Pr 36 *see* **fynden** *v*

foet, fo(o)t(e) *n* (*pl.* **fe(e)t(e)**) foot 1.118, 19.56, B 15.452; **a foote** on foot *n* B 17.106; feet 2.193, 4.82, 18.244, B 12.242, 256, 15.300, A 11.215, 12.47; foot's distance 7.285, 307, B 5.6, 6.2; ~ **lond** foot-wide strip of land 6.268; foundation (*fig.*) B 16.245

fol 9.14 *etc*, 3.159 *etc* = **ful** *a, av*

fold *n* sheepfold (*fig.*) 9.259

fold(e) *n* earth 1.151; world 9.153, B 7.53; ground B 12.254

-fold *suff.* fold, times 12.160, B 11.256, B 13.320

folden *v* close, clench 19.115, 122, 131, 151, 155

fole *n* foal (? *with pun on* fool) 11.251, B 2.163, 11.343

foles 10.184, 22.61, 62, 74, 77 *see* **fo(e)l** *n*

fol(e)wen *v* follow 1.38, 2.196, 3.492, 494, 4.28, 8.349, 15.186, B 3.342, 15.463, 474, 16.162; advance along 6.118, A 12.91; accompany 6.127, 7.307, 10.51*c*, 81, 11.173, 12.74, 144, 13.62, 14.3, 15.307, 16.44, 46, 61, 139, 20.123, 21.272, 418, B 6.2, 11.47, 371, 14.266, 15.224, A 12.67; share, keep 11.185, B 5.641; obey 2.34, 77, 105, 3.246, 375, 7.305, 8.213, 11.311, 12.172, 13.2, 212, 15.9, 16.260, 17.143, 18.79, 19.289, 20.202, 21.33, 59, 22.58, B 3.7, 11.26, 39, 17.124, A 9.45, Z 6.74; observe 10.259; take after 10.247; approve B 11.251; ~ **for,** ~ **after** pursue 19.80; aim for 10.279; search for 3.344, B 15.250; afflict 16.78, B 11.374, A 12.68; consort with 3.363, B 3.39; result 1.182

fol(o)ware *n* 7.188; (farm) servant 17.103

folfillen 16.27 = **fulfillen** *v*

folye *n* (act of criminal) foolishness 10.185, A 10. 70, B 13.149; nonsense 14.82, 22.147; sinfulness, wrong-doing 11.311, 20.234, B 14.186, 15.76, 150; lechery 16.133; madness B 15.10

foliliche *av* sinfully 16.232, 233

folk(e) *n* people Pr 19, 1.2, 5.111, 6.245, 7.258, 8.323, 9.57, 10.3, 259, 11.57, 15.237, 16.187, 232, 17.83, 18.102, 19.176, 201, 22.64, B 5.144, 8.38, 10.217, 11.268, 15.10, 347, 447, 16.245; human beings 15.267; people (of a region), nation 17.258; [*of a group of*] people 7.169, 8.73, 138, 213, 216, 229, 9.95, 11.245, 282, 15.9, 266, 288, 16.328 (1), 17.103, 19.201, 289, 20.234, 21.59, **B** 4.181, 5.140, 150, 406, 6.2, 9.159, 11.99, 13.191, 214, 243, 15.302, 346, 350, 405, 424, 464, 471, 605, 16.246; *in phrr.*: ~ **ywedded** 5.64; **Lordes** ~ **of heuene** (= the blessed) 1.154; ~ **of Holy Chirche** (= the clergy) Pr †116, †118, B 15.384; **fals** ~ 10.299, 12.240, 22.285, **B** 9.119, 10.195; **felde of** ~ Pr 19, 5.111; **Goddes** ~ B 15.135; **good** ~ 3.68; **lewed** ~ 11.251; **lou(h)** ~ 6.227, 13.82, B 3.255; **myseise** ~ B 7.26; **nedy** ~ **B** 12.53, 15.572; **oelde** ~ 20.7; **pore** ~ 8.147, 320, 9.72, 16.328 (2); **trewe** ~ B 7.54, B 9.108; (members of) army 3.246, 21.448

follen *v* baptize 17.285, 21.40, **B** 15.447, 450; *ger.* **fol-lyng** baptism 14.207, 208, 17.76, 21.39

follware 17.103 = **fol(o)ware** *n*

folowen 2.105 *etc* = **folewen** *v*

fond(e) *p.t.* Pr 19 *etc*, B 15.285, **A** 11.168, 12.59 *see* **fynden** *v*

fondement 16.41 = **foundement** *n*

fonden *v* test 18.248; put to trial (by tempting to sin) 14.119, *ger.* **fondyng** temptation 10.42, 16.136, 19.91, B 11.399; try to find 12.106, B 15.333; try (to) 15.145, 16.44, 18.43, 22.166, **B** 6.219, 17.81, Z 2.165

fondlyng *n* bastard, little rogue 10.299

fongen *v* get hold of B 16.96; receive 15.203, 16.7; accept 7.201; partake (of) 9.91

fonk *n* spark 6.334

font(e) *n* baptismal font 12.54, 14.207, A 12.15

foo 12.13, B 9.201 = **foe** *n*

foold B 7.53 = **folde** *n*

for[1] *prep.* because of, on account of Pr 7(2), 28, 1.128, 2.227, 3.447, 4.50, [63], 5.115, 7.303, 8.127, [182, 213, 244, 251,] 9.68, 10.149, 12.34, 13.7, [225,] 14.196, 15.149, 16.261, 17.14, 19.223, 20.64 [, 123, 179, 348,] 21.107, 206, 22.11, [105, 148, 165, 195,] 313, (*with* **to** + *inf.*) 16.262, **B** 1.27, 3.193, [200,] 5.36, [112, 233,] 9.89, [155,] 10.263, [290,] 11.225, 13.333, [405,] 14.177, 15.178, [208, 425,] 18.172, A 2.166, A 10.66; *in phrr.*: **what** ~...**and** both because of .... and 20.113; (*with a*) ~ **bitter** B 5.118, ~ **cold** B 3.191, ~ **wykkid** A 11.263 because of bitterness / coldness / wickedness; by reason of 6.200, 9.249, [312,] 10.268, 11.209, 12.126, 13.10, 15.254, 17.65, 18.289, 22.36, B 5.83, [10.73,] **A** 4.143, 12.73, [76,] Z 2.170; [7.267;] by dint of B 10.140; for the sake of Pr 43, 1.54, 6.173, 8.7, 10.237, 11.177, B 15.146; out of Pr 59, 3.177, 6.47, 8.132, 14.197, 22.251, B 7.115, [16.86,] A 12.111, Z 2.7; [Z 6.74;] *in assevs.*: 1.54, 2.2 [4.137, 7.201]; on behalf of, for the good of 3.53, [99,] 4.93, 8.46, 11.122, 13.122; for use as / on 5.129, 6.359; as, in the capacity of Pr 145, 3.114, [267, 381,] 4.159, [174,] 5.195, 6.40, [387,] 7.103, [107,] 8.223, 9.238, 10.243, [298,] 11.291, [310,]

12.54, [142, 144, 174,] 13.119, [125,] 14.76, 15.126, 16.303, [309,] [371,] 17.159, [201, 297,] 18.99, 19.240 (1), 20.23, [474,] 21.461, **B** Pr 159, 1.151, 2.133, 4.118, 6.195, 11.300, 13.305, 15.5, 16.112, **A** 8.57, 10.81, 111, 11.304; *in phrr.* **as** ~ 2.146, 9.92, 12.197, 15.39, 171, 18.205, 22.20; concerning, with regard to B 11.230, 430, 13.290, **A** 10.65, 11.72; **as** ~ 7.191; ~ **me, mysulf** as far as I am concerned Pr 207, 4.134, B 12.15; (*in excl.*) 12.76, 16.92; for the space of 7.131, †B 1.121; for the purpose of 5.129, B 2.178; (*pleonastically before* **to** + *inf.* Pr 187 [2.221, 6.345] *et p.*, B 11.45; *with* **as** 14.7; in order to get 3.367, 16.63, [17.19, 20.404, 22.239, 326,] B 5.267, A 2.126; in exchange / return for 2.232, 3.42, 5.72, 8.196, 9.276, 12.205, 18.285, 19.205, 22.138, [267,] B 18.343; in payment for 12.17, B 2.105, A 8.43; in reward for 10.180; in punishment for 14.79[, 16.76]; as a remedy for 12.57, Z 5.93; to prevent 2.240, 8.8, 226, 334, B 1.24, A 10.85; to protect against 13.71, B 6.60, Z 7.53; against A 10.73; in spite of 2.211, 216, 3.20, 109, 113, 4.23, 6.35, 437, 7.209, 8.216, 12.13, 14.53, 15.305, 19.240, 244, 20.31, 101, 365, 21.96, 294, 309 (1, 2), 400, 22.342, **B** 5.90, 9.40, ? 10.433n, 17.294, **A** 2.32, 3.249, Z 2.177; in place of 7.103; *with* **to** + *inf.* at the cost of 10.194; ~ **no** in spite of any 7.230, 285, 9.17, 10.253, Z 4.121; ~ **nouhte** in spite of anything 4.57, A 11.258; ~ **hought** Z 4.42; instead of ?7.103, 107, B 15.121; (appropriate) to, (fitting) for 3.264, 5.61 (1), 9.129 [230, 13.108, 17.287, ? 19.144, 21.42, 99] **B** 3.346, [11.99, 15.104], Z 7.231; *in set phrr.*: ~ **pouere or** ~ **riche** A 2.59 (*marriage vows*); ~ (**the**) **beste** 7.125, 16.21, **B** 10.368, 11.197, A 11.154; ~ **þe nones** for the occasion (*or as tag*) A 2.41; ~ **sothe** truly 3.112 *et p.*; ~ **treuthe** in truth 6.386

for[2] *conj.* for (the reason that) Pr 101, 109, 137, 168, 1.36 *et p.*, B 2.25, 123, **A** 2.138, 11.273, 12.109; (+ **that**) since **B** 4.68, 10.352, Z 5.150, Z 7.77; (*introductory*) because 20.78, 183, 347, **B** 5.101, 9.35, 62, 14.77; (*amplifying*) inasmuch as, seeing that Pr 79, 203, 216, 1.14, 2.104 *et p.*, **B** Pr 193, 1.27, 98, A 11.138, Z 5.34; (*pleonastic*) Z 2.4; (*indicating aim*) so that 7.167, 13.164, 21.145

*****forager** *n* (*fig.*) harbinger, forager 22.85, 81 (**forreour**)

forbad *p.t.* B 10.206, 19.252 *see* **forbeden** *v*

forbar *p.t.* 3.426 *see* **forberen** *v*

forbeden *v* (*pr. subj.* **forbede** 3.147, *p.t.* **forbad** B 10.206, *p.p.* **forboden** 3.188) forbid 3.147, 155, 9.327, B 10.206, B 19.252; *p.p.* prohibited B 13.349, *in phr.* **forbodene lawes** laws that forbid (sth.) 3.188; *and see* **forbode** *n*

forberen *v* (*p.t.* **forbar** 3.426) refrain (from killing) 3.426; give up 1.99; do without, spare B 11.209, Z 3.169

forbeten *v* wear out, *p.p.* 22.198

forbis(e)ne *n* model, example 17.277; allegorical parable 10.32

forbiten *v* (*contr. pr.* **forbit**) bite 20.34; eat away 18.39

forbode *n* prohibition, *in phr.* **Goddes (Lordes)** ~ God forbid (that) 3.138, **B** 4.194, 7.177, 15.579

forbrennen *v* (*p.p.* **forbrent**) burn up 3.107, 125

force *n* importance, *in phr.* **#no** ~ it does not matter 14.10

forcer *n* chest, coffer B 10.213

ford *n* crossing-place (in stream) 7.213; (*fig.*) way through (**forth**) 3.194

fordede *p.t.* 20.390, **fordide** B 16.166; *see* **fordo(e)n** *v*

fordo(e)n *v* (*p.t.* **ford(e)de** 20.390, *p.p.* **fordo** 15.231) destroy 5.122, 15.231, 20.28, 41, 154 ('neutralise'), 390; kill 20.67; ruin B 9.65; undo 19.255; defeat, overcome 20.160, 21.51; extinguish 19.263

fore¹ *n* track, footsteps 6.118

fore² (*stressed form of* **for** *prep.*) on account of 9.68, 21.107, 22.195

fore³ *av* in advance Z 2.190; forth Z 5.27*n*

foreyn *n* stranger 9.199

forfader *n* forefather 7.133, 10.237

#forel *n* case, box [esp. for books] 15.104, A 11.159

*foresleue *n* fore-part of sleeve B 5.80

forest *n* forest 9.224; ?(enclosed) wood B 15.332

foretellen *v* mention beforehand A 11.168

fore-teth *n pl.* front teeth 20.383

foreward A 2.50 = **for(o)ward** *n*

forfader *n* forefather 7.133, 10.237

forfaren *v* perish 8.234, B 15.135

forfeten *v* go wrong, transgress 22.25

forfeture *n* loss of property, *in phr.* **vp**~ on pain of losing 4.128

forfreten *v* (*contr. pr.* **forfret**) eat up 18.33

forgen *v* join firmly A 2.23

forget *p.p.* A 11.293 *see* **forʒeten** *v*

forgeuenesse 19.188 = **forʒeuenesse** *n*

forgyuen 3.8, 138, B 4.101, *p.p.* 3.134, 20.186 *see* **forʒeuen** *v*

*forglotten *v* greedily consume 11.66

forgon *v* forfeit 13.48

forgoere *n* leader, guide 2.198; harbinger 2.61 (**vorgoer**)

*forgrynden *v* (*contr. pr.* **forgrynt**) utterly destroy B 10.79

forlyen *v* (*p.p.* **forleyen**) rape 4.46

forlong *n* square furlong of land 7.32; furlong's walk (1/8 mile, = small distance) B 5.5

formallych *av* correctly 17.109

forme *n* figure B 13.297; body 7.130; likeness 1.109, 20.315, 22.52

formen *v* create 1.161, **B** 1.14, 10.105, 11.387, 16.213, Z 1.7; prepare, appoint A 8.39; give instruction B 15.377; teach † B 15.450; make up, form B 17.170

form(e)our *n* creator 10.153, 19.134

formest(e), formost(e) *av* first 1.73; originally 20.161, 162, B 10.217; first of all 17.60; to begin with 17.233; ~ **and furste** first and foremost 6.15, 21.120 (*trs*), A 10.131 (*trs*)

for(o)ward *n* pledge 4.13; agreement **B** 6.35, 11.64; **in** ~ on the understanding A 2.50

forpynen *v* torture, *p.p.* = wretched B 6.155

forren *v* trim with fur, *p.p.* 8.291, 15.203, 22.176

forreour 22.81 *see* **forager** *n*

forsa(e)ken *v* (*p.t.* **forso(e)k(e)**, *p.p.* **forsake**) disown 17.81; reject 20.200; abandon 13.225, **B** 9.66, 15.35; renounce 9.202, 12.156, 168, 16.110, 22.38, 240, **B** 11.274, 16.11; give up 17.195, 18.76; deny (one-self) 12.171; shun 22.231; refuse B 15.84, 311; deny 15.141; repudiate (debt) 7.37, depart from 16.110, 19.290; leave behind 16.104

forschuppen *v* (**forshapen** B) unmake, disfigure (the work of creation) 19.272

forsleuthen *v* spoil through lack of use 7.52; delay Z 7.64

forsothe *av* truly 4.2, 16.284, B 10.185, A 11.291

forst *n* frost 12.190, 194, A 8.116, Z 6.74

forstallen *v* 'forestall' [intercept or buy up goods in advance, to re-sell at profit]

forster *n* forester, officer in charge of a forest (*fig.*) B 17.113

forsweren *v* (*p.p.* **forswore(n)**) swear a falsehood, *p.p.* guilty of breaking an oath 10.280; perjured (in court) 21.372, 374

forth *av* forth Pr 49 *et p.*; forward 11.195; away 12.167; out Pr 4, 67; out of 19.171; after 2.102; ahead 4.34; along 3.107; on, further Pr 226, B 10.437; (in succession) thereafter B 13.210; ~ **with** along with 10.233. **wher** ~ in what direction 16.340; *in phrasal verbs* (*see s.vv*): **beren** ~ 18.115; **blostren** ~ 7.158; **bowen** ~ B 5.566; **bryngen** ~ 1.18, *et p.*; **cairen** ~ B 4.24; **comen** ~ 20.80; **drawen** ~ 11.314; **dryuen** ~ Pr 226; **faren** ~ B 2.184; **fecchen** ~ 2.157; **fynden** ~ A 11.63; **flaumen** ~ B 17.206; **flyen** ~ 10.233; **folowen** ~ 11.196; **fostren** ~ 19.173; **gon** ~ 4.162; **growen** ~ 10.153; **lepen** ~ B Pr 223; **lyuen** ~ B 10.437; **loken** ~ A 7.13; **luppen** ~ 2.69; **passen** ~ 11.263; **plukken** ~ 19.12; **poken** ~ 7.262; **potten** ~ 2.50; **pryken** ~ 2.201; **proferen** ~ 19.117; **rennen** ~ 18.290; **ryden** ~ 2.194; **romben** ~ A 4.30; **springen** ~ 18.231; **standen** ~ 2.72; **strenen** 13.171; **stryken** ~ 7.223; **suen** 2.102; **trollen** 20.332; **walken** ~ 15.2; **wenden** ~ 6.351; **wexen** ~ B 9.32; **yeuen** ~ 12.167

forthenken 20.91 = **forthynken** *v*

forthere *av* further 7.285, 10.11, **B** 2.202, 5.6, 12.35, 39, **A** 10.99, 11.293, 12.30, 68, 76, 89; onwards A 7.188; afterwards, ?more widely 8.76

forthermore *av* in addition 9.232

forthy *conj.* therefore, for that reason Pr 118, 201, 11.232 *et p.*; because B 10.396; ?accordingly B 1.188*n*

forthynken *v* (*impers.*) repent, **hit me ~eth** 10.255, 20.91

forto[1] *part. (with inf.)* = to B 14.7

forto[2] *prep.* till Z 7.250, ? A 7.247

forto[3] *conj.* until 7.213, A 6.54

fortune *n* fortune, *in phr.* **grace of** ~ prosperity due to chance 11.288; (*semi-person.*) 3.239; (*person.*) 11.168, 173, 185, 186, 190, 196, 311, 12.7, 13, 15.5, 22.110, 156, B 6.218; good luck 22.148; state (brought about by chance) 3.477, 16.131; lot 6.127

forwalked *p.p.a* exhausted with walking B 13.205

***forwanyen** *v* weaken morally 5.137

forw(e) *n* furrow 8.65 (B 6.104, A 7.96), furrow's width (of land) 6.268 (B 13.372)

forwhy *conj.* for which reason B 13.281

forwit *n* foresight B 5.164

forȝaf *p.t.* 20.78 *see* **forȝeuen** *v*

forȝat *p.t.* 12.12 *see* **forȝeten** *v*

forȝelden *v* reward, repay; Lord / God **(it) þee for-ȝelde** may God reward you (for it) 8.298, B 13.189

forȝeten, forȝyten *v* (*p.t.* **forȝat**, *p.p.* **forȝete(n)**) forget 7.13, 36, 47, 12.12, 19.209, 315, 22.155, 370; A 11.293

forȝeuen *v* (*p.t.* **forȝaf**, *p.p.* **forȝeue, forgyue(n)**) forgive 19.201, 209, 271, 315, 21.397; pardon 3.8, 134, 138, B 4.101; grant, vouchsafe 20.78, 186

forȝeuenesse *n* forgiveness 6.435, 19.188, 210, 331, 21.185; pardon 5.195; excuse from payment 22.287

fostren *v* produce A 10.122; ~ **forth** generate 19.173, 176

fote 1.118 *etc*; *see* **foet** *n*

fouchensa(e)f *v* undertake 5.49; grant graciously 18.18

fouely 20.95 *see* **foule** *av*

foughten *p.t. pl.* Pr 43 *see* **fy(g)hten** *v*

foul sage 7.103 *see* **foel** *n*

foul, fow(e)l *n* (wild) bird 6.405, 8.30, 10.233, 11.102, 13.137, 164, 14.170, 171, 185, 190, 17.11, 15, 32, 22.44, **B** 7.129, 8.54, 66, 9.140, 15.302, 313, Z 7.59; (domestic) fowl B 15.463, 471, 478

foul *a* dirty B 13.318, B 15.113, (*comp.*) dirtier B 13.320, (*sup.*) dirtiest, ? most menial B 19.254; unpleasant (-tasting) B 12.242; filthy, horrible 6.161, 432, 16.136, 21.46, 22.85, (*comp.*) 3.96; repulsive 18.54; ugly B 11.394; hideous 13.174, 18.110, B 16.77; rough, stormy 8.347; vile, indecent 7.114, 10.276, B 10.40; sinful, wicked Pr 37, 7.54, 63, 114; disgraceful 16.371; low, wretched 21.33; vile, base B 18.94; bad 3.369, (*sup.*) worst, most noxious 12.226, B 18.153; shameful B 11.391

foule *av* filthily **B** 13.401, 14.15; foul 13.243, B 12.254; harshly 20.95, 350, **B** 10.321, 11.214; (*sup.*) in the most repulsive way 14.170; hideously B 5.82; wickedly 2.43; disgracefully 3.231; shamefully 16.15; rudely 22.5; grievously 11.305; basely B 15.352

foulen *v* dirty, soil 9.266; defile (with sin) A 7.136; injure B 3.154; choke 22.315

founde *p.t. subjv.* 6.22, 15.220, B 15.311; **founde(n)** *p.p.* 8.138 *etc*; *see* **fynden** *v*

fo(u)ndement *n* foundation 21.327, (*fig.*) 3.344, 345; basis, motive (for action) 16.41

founden *v* build B 1.64; found B 15.289; provide for, endow 17.57, B 15.324; devise B 10.217

foundo(u)r *n* patron, benefactor A 11.216; originator Z 3.176

foure *num. a* Pr 56 *etc*; ~ **dayes** B 13.65; ~ **doctours** B 9.73; ~ **Euaungelies** 15.45; ~ **fyngres** B 17.158; ~ **ordres** Pr 56, A 8.177; ~ **oxen** 21.263; ~ **sedes** 21.311; ~ **stottes** 21.268; ~ **thynges** 10.129; ~ **vertues** Pr 131, 21.313; ~ **hundred wynter** 19.211; *as n* 9.57, 21.272, B 7.53

fourme 7. 130, 20.315, 22.52 = **forme** *n*; **fourmen** B 15.377, †450, A 8.39 = **formen** *v*

fourty *num. a* forty 3.41 *etc*; ~ **daies** 10.228; ~ **voues** 7.13; ~ **wynter** 3.41 (*perh. as indef. number*), 7.188, 14.3 (**fyue and** ~ B 12.3), 15.266; ~ **wokes** 18.134

fox *n* fox 8.28, 9.224, 22.44

fraynen *v* ask, inquire of 1.54, 7.169, 10.3, 18.291, B 18.18

fraytour *n* refectory 5.173

fram *prep.* from Pr 54, 2.178, 3.127, 132, 5.111, 131, 159, 6.348, 7.88, 255, 8.46, 145, 9.241, 10.185, 15.237, 16.133, 211, 18.188, 19.51, 82, 98, B 15.345; away from B 15.463; out of B 11.417, 16.263

franchise *n* condition of freedom 20.106

#franchisen *v* make (sb.) a freeman, *p.p.* 3.114

frankeleyn *n* franklin [landowner ranking below nobility] 5.64, 10.243; gentleman 21.39

fraternite(e) *n* religious brotherhood, order (of friars) 9.343, 12.8, 22.368

fre(e) *a* free [of rank / condition, not slave / serf] Pr 106, 5.64, 21.33, (*fig.*) 21.39; free of the bondage of sin 1.73, 11.251, 21.59; free, unrestricted in action 19.122 (~ **wil** 10.51, B 16.223, ~ **wit** 10.51); noble 20.106, 22.146; of the gentry / nobility **B** 2.77, 11.383; generous 11.57, B 15.150, 151; freely available 9.57; = as a freeman of a corporation #3.111

freek 15.82 = **freke** *n*

freel 10.48 = **frel(e)** *a*; **freeletee** 19.314 = **frelete** *n*

freet *p.t.* 20.200 *see* **freten** *v*[1]

frek(e) *n* man, person 6.152, 9.153, 11.158, 15.2, 82, 18.185, **B** 4.13, 156, 6.218, 250, 11.26, 13.65, A 12.66

frel(e) *a* weak 3.157; changeable 10.48

frelete *n* frailty, weakness 3.59, 19.314

#freman *n* freeman [member of a town corporation] 3.108, 114

frem(me)de *a as n* stranger 12.157, B 15.141

Frenche *a* French B 11.384, Z 7.278, *as n* 13.203

frend(e) *n* friend 6.72, 10.13, 305, 12.106, 15.197,

17.125, 144, 20.457, **B** 5.100, 9.201, 11.177, 193, 12.257, 15.151, 17.87; intimate 17.143; benefactor 3.56, 9.199, 16.314, 317, 22.286; supporter 16.136, 21.145, Z 3.151; ally 10.87, 11.186, 12.7; relative 5.36, 40, 10.185, 12.157, 16.105, **B** 7.167, 9.115

frendli *av* amicably, *comp.* **frendloker** B 10.227 (**frendliere** A 11.174)

#**freneseye** *n* (bout of) frenzy, delirium 22.85

frenesse *n* gracious generosity B 16.88

Frenssh *n* French (language) B 5.235

#**frentik(e)** *a* crazed, deranged 11.6, 18.179

frere *n* (*uninfl. gen.* **frere** 7.285, 9.208, 15.104, 16.353) friar 2.220, 240, 3.38, 56, 5.173, 6.287, 147, 191, 9.249, 10.8 *et p.*, 11.54, 12.5 *et p.*, 14.89, 15.30, 79, 16.228, 233, 287, 17.35, 52, 60, 22.58, 230, 240, 267, 273, 290, 296, 368, 384, **B** 5.80, (Envye), 135 (Wrathe), 144, 10.94, 11.68, 12.19, 13.199, Z 3.151; **the Freres** the Friars' church 7.27, 16.41; the Friars' convent 2.220, 22.285; ~ **Austynes** the Augustinian Friars 17.15; ~ **Faytour** Friar Deceiver 8.73; ~ **Flatrere** Friar Flatterer 22.316 *et p.*; **faythful** ~ 6.291; **fals** ~ 15.79; **maistres** ~**s** B Pr 62; **mendenaunt** ~**s** Pr 60; **poore** ~**s** B 15.311; **syke** ~**s** 15.119

fresen *v* freeze 12.194, A 8.116

fres(s)h(e) *a* fresh 8.333, B 15.431, Z 7.316; freshly shed 7.133; fresh-flowing **B** 10.295, 15.337

freten *v*[1] (*p.t.* **freet, frete**) eat 2.100, 20.200; chafe 6.74 (**vrete**); *pr.p.* destructive 20.156

freten *v*[2] (*p.p.* **fretted**) adorn B 2.11

Friday *n* Friday 6.351, 438, 7.130, 10.8, 18.167, 21.142, 22.313, *pl.* 5.30, 6.155, 182, 9.94, **B** 13.349, 16.162; **God(e)** ~ Good Friday 7.106, 11.255, 14.131, 141, B 5.489

frien *v* fry, *p.p.* **yfried** 8.333, B 13.63

frith *n* wood(land) 9.224, 14.158, 17.11, **B** 11.364, 17.113

frithen (in) *v* hedge in, enclose 7.227

fro *prep.* from Pr 114, 1.4, 2.47 *et p.*; out of 7.300; against 10.287, 16.132; in distinction from 10.122; away from 7.17, 15.175, 16.335

frokke *n* long gown 16.353, B 5.80

from *prep.* from 7.105, 19.30, B 1.4 *etc*, A 7.128, Z 7.268

#**frounce** *n* wrinkle, crease B 13.318

fruyt *n* produce of crops 8.347, 16.253, 21.315; fruit (of Charity) 18.12 *et p.* (B 16.9 *et p.*) 20.18, (of Eden) 18.123, 20.198, 200, (of Piers) 20.18, 32, B 16.94, (*fig.*) B 5.140, A 10.122; offspring 10.276, 18.79

#**fruyten** *v* (*p.p.* **yfruyted**) come to fruit B 16.39

fuyr(e) *n* fire 6.334, 19.171 *et p.* Z 6.72; destructive fire, conflagration 3.103, 9.182, 11.252, 15.166; flame 21.206; (=) lightning 3.91, 96, 102, 125; the element fire 9.56, 15.243; mystical fire (of the Holy Spirit) 14.208; *in phr.*: **a-fuyre** on fire 7.52

ful[1] *a* full Pr 19, 1.2, 8.182, 10.272; full to capacity 3.88, 18.155, B 15.337, **A** 7.167, 12.71; well-supplied 12.226, 13.58, 19.294, 21.118, **B** 15.333; complete 19.131, **B** 15.153, 17.167, 168, 170, 173; ~ **tyme** fully time B 2.96; ? the moment of completion, noon B 5.489; the (appointed) time of fulfilment 18.137; *as n. in phr.* **to þe fulle** completely, in full measure 17.57; fully 20.410; in full B 13.193; one's fill B 14.178, A 12.72

ful[2] *av* fully, entirely 16.78; most 20.119; very (*with a and av*) Pr 23, 28, 204, 2.12, 19, 154, 164, 3.51, 85, 199, 495, 4.52, 5.123, 7.175, 250, 274, 9.11, 53, 141, 206, 11.2, 196, 317, 14.99, 15.90, 19.50, 52, 22.52, **B** Pr 26, 161, 3.251, 4.74, 6.44, 204, 7.124, 146, 10.186, 211, 11.78, 351, 12.254, 13.204, 15.116, 201, 16.179, 230, 234, 18.119, **A** 6.84, 8.110, 12.78, **Z** 3.157, 168, 5.45, 6.80, 7.298

ful[3] *p.t.* Pr 106, 113, 1.119, 3.107, 6.334, 10.39, 16.211, 20.89, 21.5, 22.51, 176, Z 5.110; **fulle** *p.t. subjv.* 18.128, *p.t.* Z 1.60; **fullen** *p.t. pl.* 1.125; *see* **fallen** *v*

fulfillen (fulfellen, fulfullen) *v* carry out 1.74, 2.127, 3.417, 9.233, 16.27, 17.142; fulfil (prophecy) 21.80; elapse 8.345, 10.228

fullen *see* **ful** *p.t.*

fullen[1] 6.389 = **fillen** *v*

#**fullen**[2] *v* grow full 11.41

#**fullen**[3] *v* full (woollen cloth), *ger.* #**fullyng (stokkes)** B 15.452

fullyche *av* fully, *in phr.* ~ **to his power** to the limits of his capacity B 15.61

fullyng *ger.* 14.208, B 15.450; *see* **follen** *v*

fundement 3.344, 345 *see* **foundement** *v*

furst(e) *ord. num. a* (**first** B 1.76 *et p.*, **ferst** A 1.74, 10.132) first 6.210, 419, 10.145, 15.105, 16.119, 187, 17.316, 18.34, 20.226, 21.70, 277, **B** 3.244, 5.166; original 20.159, B 11.64; primary, ultimate 18.93; *as n* **the** ~ 1.23, 2.65, 109, 12.38, 19.35, 132, 134, B 16.184; the originator 14.164, A 10.28; the chief person(s) 9.250; **at þe** ~ straight away 2.210, 8.168

furst(e) *av* first 3.36, 5.110, 6.210, 7.169, 11.120, 122, 15.5, 39, 18.94, 248, 291, 21.439, **B** 1.76, 5.51, 9.115; beforehand 12.183, 15.211, B 10.283; originally 11.120, 14.160, 19.114, 20.227, 345, B 9.191, A 11.135; in the first place 7.143, 169, 9.221, 20.246, A 12.113; in the beginning 18.123, B 18.158; *in phr.* **formost and** ~ above all, first and foremost 6.15, A 10.131

furst *n* thirst 6.437, 20.410, 22.19, A11.46 (**þrest**), (*person.*) A 7.168 (**Ferst**)

fursten *v* (*impers.*) be thirsty 20.408

furthe 16.131 *see* **ferthe** *ord. num. a*

furwe B 6.104 = **forw** *n*

fust(e) *n* fist 6.66, 19.114, 126 *et p.*, B 17.139 *et p*; **a** ~**wyse** in the manner of a fist 19.151

ga *subjv.* Pr 228 *see* **gon** *v*

gabben *v* lie 3.225, 17.16; *ger.* **gabbyng** lying, deceit 17.129, 21.457, deception 22.125

gable *n* gable (-window) 3.52

gad(e)lyng *n* scoundrel B 4.51; rascal B 9.104; bastard, base fellow 10.298, 22.157

gaderen *v* muster 21.338, 22.113; seek, amass (wealth) 6.259, **B** 12.51, 250, 13.370; gather 18.112; collect (money *etc*) 16.71, 22.369

ga(e)f *p.t.* 21.268, 22.171, **gaf** 2.232 = **ȝaf (yaf)**; *see* **ȝeuen (yeuen)** *v*

gay *a* fine 20.177

gayler *n* gaoler 3.174

gaynesse *n* luxury 11.66

galle *n* bile, ? rancour B 5.118; (*fig.*) malice B 16.155

galoche *n* shoe 20.12n

galon *n* gallon 6.230, 392, 396

galpen *v* open (one's) mouth wide 15.98

game *n* delight, ? pastime B 9.102; pastime A 11.37, †B 10.50; play B 5.407; sport Pr 171

gan *p.t.* 1.168 *etc*; *see* **gynnen** *v*

gangen *v* go 16.14, 18.177, B 2.168; *pr. p.* walking 18.242

gapen *v* stare open-mouthed B 10.41

gardyn *n* garden 20.313, 380, (*fig.*) B 16.13; ~**er** *n* gardener B 5.136

garen *v* (*p.t.* **gart(e), gerte**) cause, make 5.146, 8.324, 11.122, 22.57, 131, **B** 1.123, 5.61, 129, 15.443, A 7.132 (**gere** Z 7.129)

†garisoun *n* deliverance B 6.138

garleek *n* garlic 6.358; ~ **monger** *n* garlic-seller 6.372

garlond *n* wreath, crown 20.48

garnement *n* garment, attire 9.119, 20.177, **B** 13.400, 14.25

gasten *v* frighten Z 7.325; *and see* **agasten** *v*

gat *p.t.* 4.75, B 1.33 *etc*; *see* **geten** *v*

gate *n*[1] gate 2.132, 7.241, 248, 281, 11.42, 12.49, 16.365, 18.242, 20.272; gateway 8.284; *see also* **ȝate, yate** *n*

gate *n*[2] way 19.46, 22.342, **B** 1.205, 17.112, A 12.88, **heiȝe** ~ main road B 4.42; path A 12.88; *in phr.* **letten hym þe** ~ obstruct his progress 3.193, 13.91; going 20.251

gateward *n* gatekeeper 7.242, 13.91

geaunt *n* giant 20.261, 22.215, (*fig.*) B 6.231

gedelyng B 9.104 = **gad(e)lyng** *n*

gederen 22.369 *see* **gaderen** *v*

gees Pr 228, 4.49, 5.19, 15.68, B 6.280 *see* **goos** *n*

gef Z 3.117 *p.t., ?or =* **gyue** *p.p.*; *see* **ȝeuen** *v*

#gendre *n* kind, species B 16.222; (grammatical) gender 3.394

generacion *n* (act of) generation B 16.222

gentel, gentil *a* belonging to the nobility or gentry 5.78, (*fig.*) 12.112, 21.34, 40; noble, gracious 1.180, 11.21, 13.14, 24, 21.48, 266, **B** 10.35, 11.246; gentile, pagan 17.132

genteliche *av* courteously 3.14; pleasantly 15.208

gentrice (gentries) *n* nobility, gracious generosity 20.21, B 14.181

geomesie *n* geomancy [divination from dots and figures on the earth] B 10.210

geometrie *n* geometry (= *geomatria*) B 10.210n

gerl B 1.33 = **gurl** *n*

gerner *n* granary, grain-store B 7.130

gerte Z 5.77 = **garte**

gerþ *n* saddle-girth (*fig.*) B 4.21

gesene *a* scarce B 13.271

gesse *n* consideration, **vp** ~ without thinking B 5.415

gest *n* guest, visitor 10.181, B 15.285; **Goddes** ~ stranger 15.200

geste *n* chivalric tale 15.206; heroic story 7.106; tale B 10.31; writings 11.21

geten *v* (*p.t.* **gat** 4.75, **gete(n)** 20.313, 22.157, B 18.354, *p.p.* **(y)gete(n)** 6.341, 20.101, 322) get, obtain Pr 164, 4.138, 6.340, 7.268, 281, 290, 11.84, 16.278, 18.52, 20.313, 322, 377, B 18.356; win, earn 20.12, 101; beget 10.298, 21.121, 22.157, A 10.160

geterne *n* gittern 15.209

geuen *pr. or p.t. pl.* 6.374; *see* **ȝeuen** *v*

gyde *n* guide 7.306, Z 2.158; leader B 15.435

gyen *v* guide, lead 2.198; (*refl.*) conduct (oneself) 21.228

gif *pr. subjv.* A 12.111 *see* **ȝeuen** *v*

gyft 3.338, 4.138, 7.268, 9.133, 11.288, 14.33, 15.210, **B** 5.53, 12.63, A 3.229 *etc* = **ȝefte** *n*

gyle *n* guile, deceitful behaviour 6.190, 213, 259, 11.268, 16.278, 17.242, 20.162, 313,377, 382, 396, 399, 21.457, 22.67, **B** 13.370, 18.361; deceitfulness, treachery Pr 12, 2.26, 125, 3.130, 211, 286, 12.242, 17.129, 20.322, 392, 21.301, 302, 458, 22.57, B 16.155, A 8.41; (*person.*) 2.70 *et p.*, 3.499, 17.111, A 2.24

gylen *v* deceive 9.65, 16.305, 22.125

gylle *n* gill (= 1/4 pint) 6.396

gylour *n* deceiver 20.162, 164, 382, B 10.194; defrauder 3.100, B 2.121

gilt[1] B 3.108 *etc*, A 3.8 *etc*; = **gult** *n*

gilt[2] **B** 15.221, 17.14, 18.14 = **gult** *a*

gilty *a* B 5.368, 10.258, 12.76, 192, **giltier** *a (comp.)* **B** 5.368, 12.79 *see* **gulty** *a*

gyn *n* device, engine (of war) 20.261

gynful *a* crafty, treacherous B 10.210

gynnen *v* (*p.t. sg.* **gan** 1.168 *etc*, *pl.* **gonne** Pr 145) begin 6.397, 15.98, 19.189, A 10.127; proceed (to) 2.176, 4.90, 5.105, 6.403, 22.110, B 10.111 *etc*; (*as weak auxil. + inf. = simple p.t.*) did / does 1.168, 2.139, 3.11, 4.148, 6.146, 179, 351, 430, 7.200, 8.149, 10.115, 11.87, 314, 12.52, 110, 18.8, 36, 19.63, 20.95, 254, 22.200, 302, 387, A 12.29, (**gonne(n)** Pr 145, **B** 8.116, 13.267, (*2nd pers.*) 7.122); *ger.* **gynnyng(e)** *n* beginning (in time) 10.154, **B** 2.30, 16.187, 194; *and see* **bigynnynge** *n*

gyour *n* (spiritual) guide 21.428, 22.72

gyrdel *n* girdle, belt B 15.123; *in phr.* **styuest vnder ~** most valiant 6.43

girl B 10.79, 177, **A** 10.160 = **gurl** *n*

girte *p.t.* B 5.373; *see* **gurden** *v*

gyse *n* dress, fashion Pr 26

gyuen[1] Pr 74 *et p.*; **gyuere** B 7.68; *see* **ȝeuen** *v*, **ȝeuere** *n*

gyuen[2] *v* shackle (*fig.*) 22.192

gyues *n.pl.* shackles 15.255

glad *a* glad, joyful, merry 3.282, 454, 16.300, *a as n* A 11.193; happy, pleased 16.298, A 10.100, *comp.* **glad(d)er(e)** 11.103, 22.62, B 5.91; cheerful 6.374, B 8.94; pleasant B 16.155

glad(i)en *v* gladden, make joyful 9.300, B 18.255; cheer 19.184, 22.171; comfort 8.126, 21.147; entertain 20.177, B 10.43; please A 10.201

gladliche *av* gladly, willingly 6.105, 16.345

glasen *v* glaze, fit (window) with glass 3.52, 65

glasene *a* (made of) glass, **gyue a ~ howue** delude with an imaginary protection 22.172

glede *n* live coal 19.184, 190, 198, B 2.12; fiery spark B 5.284

glee *n* music(al entertainment) B Pr 34

gleman *n* minstrel 6.403, 11.103, (*fig.*) B 9.102, 104

glenen *v* glean [gather corn left by reapers] 8.67

glyden *v* glide, pass through 20.478

globben *v* gulp, *p.p.* **yglobbed (yglupid** A) 6.396

glorie *n* glory 20.273; splendour 20.342; pride (in worldly renown) B 10.115, Z 2.72; vainglory 22.157

gloriously *av* splendidly 19.16

#**glosar** *n* sycophant 21.222

glose *n* gloss, explanatory comment (on text) 10.245, 15.83, 19.16, **B** 5.275, 12.291, 15.82, (*fig.*) 3.328

glosen *v* gloss, write explanatory comment on (text) 6.301, 11.117, 13.119, 19.13; interpret speciously Pr 58, *ger.* B 13.75; speak deceitfully 22.369, B 10.194, *pr.p. a* flattering 4.138; *ger.* smooth talking 6.259, cajoling words 22.125

gloto(u)n *n* glutton Pr 74, 15.87, **B** 9.61, 13.400, Z 2.92, (*fig.*) intemperate talker B Pr 139; **Goddes ~** 'godly glutton' B 13.78, 400; (*person.*) 6.349 *et p.*, 8.324, **Z** 5.104, 7.275

glotony(e) *n* gluttony [intemperate desire for / indulgence in food and / or drink] Pr 24, 44, 1.29, 2.97, 11.66, 16.73, 76, **B** 1.33, 10.50, Z Pr 82, (*person.*) 16.71, B 14.235, A 7.285, Z 2.72

gloue *n* glove 6.251, 13.47, B 6.153, Z 6.71

glowen *v* glow 19.189, 190, *pr.p.* 19.184; **~ on fuyr** catch fire 3.102

glubbere *n* gulper, **glotons glubberes** gulping gluttons B 9.61; *and see* **globben** *v*

gnawen *v* gnaw, (*fig.*) talk irreverently about 11.41

#**gnedy** *a* stingy 15.87

gobet *n* morsel, small portion 5.100

god *n* deity, divine being 1.86, 20.318, 22.57, B 9.61, Z 7.275

God (*main refs. only*) God Pr 117, 121, 1.26, 103, 177, 2.128, 132, 3.95, 323, 338, 353, 409, 413 *et p.*, 462, 5.67, 105, 6.16, 84, 111, 169, 424, 7.150, 206, 8.217, 236, 9.115, 289, 322, 346, 10.99, 158, 162, 202, 223, 252, 304, 11.27, 41, 46, 52, 61, 149, 212, 230, 309, 12.85, 151, 13.91, 124, 198, 14.37, 133, 194, 217, 15.141, 260, 299, 16.93, 95, 184, 306, 17.59, 80, 90, 131, 141, 152, 18.204, 211, 227, 236, 242, 19.31, 99, 148 *et p.*, 250, 270, 279, 20.186, 195, 216, 220, 226, 230, 246, 250, 258, 318, 323 *et p.*, 21.292, 433, 445, 22.34, 40, 254, 278, **B** 1.122, 2.120, 3.232, 5.53, 72, 6.138, 224, 228, 314, 7.76, 124, 130, 8.51, 9.46, 64, 65, 66, 95, 129, 204, 10.28, 66, 119, 364, 11.242, 272, 279, 395, 12.12, 14.100, 125, 15.66, 260, 263, 285, 16.9; (*with* Christ *as referent*) 1.46, 3.68, 10.208, 246, 12.102, 140, 163, 179, 213, 18.149, 20.446, 21.18, 110, 116, 174, B 10.261, A 12.29; *with standard epithets:* **~ almyhty** 7.217, 15. 281, 18.96, 19.38, **B** 7.80, 9.93, 190, 11.196, 15.295, A 11.32; **dere ~** 1.83, **faythfull** 17.35; **fol** 19.132; **gode ~** 6.435, B 15.250; **grete** 21.209, B 2.29; **grete hye** 17. 256; **grettest** 10.154; **myȝtful** B 11.277; **verray** 6.437; **~ of grace** 21.213; *****God-man** God-made-man B 11.205; **~ sulue** 14.26, 17.179, **hymselue** B 7.55, 9.117, 10.37, 201, 240, 16.13; **~ Fader, Sone, Holy Goost** B 10.241; **Lord ~** 8.135, B 5.563; **o, oon ~** 11.154, 17.134, 18.211, 238, 19.31 *et p.*, **B** 2.30, 15.395; *in phrr.* **~ and good(e) men** 5.67, 6.18; **gifte of ~** 11.288, 14.33; **grace of ~** 6.285, 14.28, 131, 15.228, B 9.59, 178, A 11.300; **wisdom and wit of ~** 13.228; *in assevs:* so me **~** helpe, *etc.* 2.126, 5.22, 6.296, 7.284, 20.240; *in poss. phrr:* **Goddes berthe** 14.93; **body** 20.77, 476, (*sacramental*) 20.240, 21.388, B 12.85; **boys** 9.127; **champion** B 15.216; **chosene** B 11.118; **clerk** 16.190; **derling** A 12.19; **foles** 11.251; **folk** B 15.135; **foweles** B 15.313; **gestes** 15.200; **gloton** B 13.78; **goed(es)** 10.177, 17.67; **grace** 10.168, B 14.20; **herte** 22.226; **heste** 17.142; **hous** B 10.405; **ymages** 20.326; **kynde** 19.254; **knyghtes** 1.107, 13.125; **lawe** 7.118, 9.104, 158, B 15.93; **loue** 6.47, 8.284, 9.66, 10.203, 16.103, B 11.276; **mede** A 3.223; **men** 17.67, B 3.71; **mercy** 11.218, 18.288; **munstrals** 7.99, 9.136; **name** B 13.402; **payne** 7.20; **passion** B 15.255, 16.38; **peple** A 11.198; **resureccioun** 20.473; **salt** B 15.441; **secret seal** 9.138; **seruice** 9.227; **sihte** 11.203; **sone** 18.149, 236, 20 55, 70, 331; **tretor** 19.240; **veniance** 14.69; **werk(es)** 10.290, 12.75; **wille** B 9.154; **word(es)** 6.84, 7.87, 94, 11.235, 21.389,

godchild *n* godchild, *pl.* B 9.75; (*fig.*) B 10.324

godfader *n* godfather B 9.75

godhede *n* the divine nature 18.227, 238, 239, 19.38, 21.158, 198, B 9.46, A 10.36

godmoder *n* godmother B 9.75

go(e)d, good *n* good (*as opp. to* evil) 14.164, 20.318; strength, power B 17.130; good deed(s), right conduct 7.286, 10.94, 16.110, B 10.203, A 4.108, 10.52; (**þe**) ~ good / virtuous people 9.15, 10.311, 11.310, 15.216, 20.301, 21.198, 443; benefit 1.24, 34, B 8.94, 11.381; good thing 3.365; blessing ?21.104, B 14.318; goods, possessions, property 1.177, 2.35, 145, 3.95, 214, 4.158, 6.258, 275, 284, 296, 8.144, 236, 251, 10.45, 168, 177, 257, 264, 300, 11. 57, 66, 12.20, 22, 240, 244, 13.72, 16.86, 282, B 9.164, 14.169, 270, A 3.248; wealth, money 6.340, 9.31, 135, 10.257(3), 11.27, 69, 72, 77, 212, 232, 12.5, 13.4, 16.255, 19.250, 21.104, 22.289, B 5.260, 11.276, 13.357, 370, 15.140, 175, A 11.248; (*fig.*) B 5.296, 9.87; useful knowledge Pr 196

go(e)d, go(o)d(e) *a* good 6.102, 435, 17.90; worthy 5.67, 7.108, 242, 21.271, B 2.30, 10.223; fine, ?strong 6.356, 374, 8.324, 16.73, 22.223, B 6.300; excellent Pr 228, 13.28, 16.120(1), 18.12, 87, 22.34, B 10.292, 12.30, Z 7.49; careful 9.71, 12.46, 14.99, 19.15, B 11.111, 17.104; right 11.307, 18.204; sound 16.120(2), 17.58, 18.84, 20.164, B 5.164, 14.315; valid B 15.349; solid B 5.286; effective B 15.435; honourable 3.302, 13.110, B 15.436; well-bred B 15.216; virtuous Pr 29, 2.35, 3.68, 92, 103, 339, 5.192, 9.50, 10.60, 257 (1,2), 263, 11.62, 14.25, 16.191, 19.260, B 8.61, 9.64, 10.436, 437, 13.73, 15.146, 423, 433, 16.9, A 9.52, 87, 10.53, Z 7.82; pious 17.134; holy 7.174, B 7.74, 10.202; kind 14.194, 19.330(2), 20.220, B 15.147, 169, 250; prosperous 22.111; fortunate 20.163, B 5.96; favourable 6.260; *in phrr.:* ~ **auntur** by good luck 8.79; ~ **day** farewell A 12.75; ~ **fayth** trustworthiness, integrity 4.37, 21.302, 22.28, (*person.*) 131; **by** ~ **fayth** truly 6.340; ~ **Friday** 7.106, 11.255, 14.131, B 12.201; ~ **herte** courage 22.180; ~ **hope** (the virtue of) hope 19.293, 22.167; ~ **is, were** it would be well 20.71, B 15.565; ~ **wille** sincere intention; **with** ~ **wille** willingly 2.168, 7.295, sincerely 6.336, with benign intent 9.111; ~ **woen** in abundance 22.171; **maken** ~ repay 19.77, 205, B 5.272

good *av* well Pr 58, A 7. 131, 11.248 (2)

go(e)dnesse, goodnesse *n* goodness B 16.62; virtue, piety A 10.80; generosity 3.22; merciful kindness 6.61, 7.61, 122, 8.353, 12.85, 20.226, 21.116, B 1.122, 14.170, A 12.111

goodly(che) *av* graciously 11.138; gladly 1.177, B 11.279

goelde 22.171 = **gold** *n*

go(e)n *v* (*imp. pl.* **goth** 7.212, *p.p.* **go** 6.213, *p.t.* (1) **ȝede, yede** Pr 41 *etc*, (2) **wente** (*for refs. see under* **wenden**) walk 22.192, *p.t.* **ȝede** 9.296, 20.3, 22.2, 183, 185, 192, B 17.100; go Pr 44, 2.158, 168, 5.105, 6.213, 349, 7.156, 253, 290, 11.200, 16.73, 19.46, 64, 20.337, 21.147, 395, 22.273, 342, B 7.130, 9.107, *p.t.*

ȝede 6.417, 7.53, 136 (**ȝedest**), 8.108, 13.136, 15.152, 263, 18.169, 19.50, 20.314, 21.4, 153, 22.136,B 1.73; travel 4.124, 7.205, 11.200, 13.52, 14.93, 21.158, B 13.182, †300, 15.435, 443, *p.t.* **ȝede** Pr 41, 6.417, 7.53, 12.124, B 16.170; travel along 10.113, 17.111; go away, depart 2.213, 221, 7.295, B 9.92, 10.61, *p.t.* **ȝede** 4.162, 10.113, B 1.73, 11.339; lead B 1.205; spread 3.194; pass, *p.t.* **ȝede** B 15.304, A 12.60; *in phr.* **Lat** ~ **the coppe** let the cup pass along; move 6.403; engage in (sth.) 8.138, 246, 9.170, *p.t.* **ȝede** 6.267; live 9.117, 10.148, 17.196; *ger.* (way of) living 10.304, B 9.82, A 10.53, *p.t.* B 13.74, A 11.273; live 17.196; dwell 21.214, A 11.273; (*inchoative or semi-expletive*) proceed to, set about (sth.) Pr 228, 5.126, 6.181, 8.28, 67, 151, 227, 9.170, 266, 10.57, 225, 287, 12.50, 165, 18.122, 20.284, 473, 22.369; B 5.640, 6.31, 300, 11.54, 12.16, 13.32, A 12.36; turn to, refer to 1.44, 8.239, (*subjv.*) 18.227, ?B 10.194 (*see note*); be 6.213, 20.328, 22.186, *p.t.* **ȝede** 20.337, = go 11.50, B 10.360; remain free 3.136; (go) dress(ed) 19.247, *p.t.* **ȝede** 12.129, 17.196; be in form of 20.326 (*ger.*), 327; *in phrr:* ~ **agayn** rush to attack 21.362; ~ **gile ayein gile** let guile oppose guile B 18.358; ~ **hennes** die 9.348, B 3.245, (*ger.*) 14.165; ~ **ther God is** = to the next life; ~ **(to)gederes** belong to(gether) 18.238, 3.280

goere (to) *n* frequenter (of) B 9.104

goest 18.75 *etc*; **goestliche** 22.40 *see* **go(e)st-(liche)** *n, av*

goyng(e) *ger.* departure B 14.165; (outward) appearance 20.326, 327; conduct 10.304, A 10.53

#goky *n* fool 13.119, 120

gold *n* gold Pr 178, 4.127, 6.287, 10.168, 21.76, 88, 89, A 2.13; *in phrr.* **brent** ~ B 5.267; **clene** ~ 3.23; **puyre** ~ 4.91; **reed** ~ 21.88, B 2.16; **knappes of** ~ B 6.269; **motoun of** ~ 3.25; **pounde of** ~ 16.297; **rybanes of** ~ Z 2.17; gold money Pr 74, 2.158, 162, 3.174, 227, 9.133, 11.103, 17.205, 22.171, B Pr 34, 5.53, Z 2.167

gold *a* (made of) gold 17.207; ~ **wyr** B 2.11

goliardeis *n* buffoon B Pr 139

gom(e) *n*¹ (*uninfl. gen.* 20.328, *pl.* **gomus** Pr 44) man 7.178, 13.119, 198, 20.226, 328, 21.121, B 2.74, 5.368, 13.182, 357, 15.285, 17.37; man-servant B 17.86; person 13.91, 16.95, 305, B 10.226, †12.60, †14.8, 17.112; *pl.* people Pr 44, 10.238, 16.345, B 13.300, 17.130

gome *n*² heed 19.15; *and see* **ȝeme (yeme)** *n*

gomme *n* aromatic gum 2.236

gongen = **gangen** *v*

gonne *n* cannon 20.291

gonne(n) *p.t. pl.* Pr 145, *sg.* 7.122; *see* **gynnen** *v*

good 1.24, Pr 29, *see* **go(ed)** *n, a*

goos (*pl.* **gees**) goose 8.304; **goose wynge** goose's wing, = thing of small value B 4.37; *pl.* geese Pr 228, 5.19, 15.68, B 6.280

gorge *n* throat 11.41, B 10.66

gospel *n* the (teaching of the) Christian Gospel Pr 58,

1.86, 12.102; = (the text of one of) the Gospel(s) 1.44, 3.74, 10.238, 245, 11.235, 12.31, 213, 13.97, **B** 3.75, 5.54, 6.226, 7.127, 10.112, 261, 275, 475, 12.63, A 12.25; the Gospel (passage) read at Mass 13.120

†**gospellere** *n* evangelist B 10.246

gossip *n* friend 6.47, 356, A 5.154

go(e)st, **goost** *n* devil, demon 20.478; (divine) Spirit B 10.238; spirit (ghost) 12.214, B 15.145; soul (of man) 1.34, 6.175, 11.230, B 9.46; (=thought) 7.150; **Holy ~** the Holy Spirit of God 14.84, 18.52, 75, 196, 19.121, 147, 148, 166, 181, 189, 190, 196, 215, 221, 254, 258, 264, 20.133, **B** 10.238, 241, 12.63, 16.224, 17.156; *see also* (**Seint**) (**E)spirit**; ~**ly** *a* spiritual B 15.572, 575; ~**liche** *av* ?truthfully, really, (*or a*) ?spiritual 22.40*n*

goth(e)l(y)en *n* rumble 6.397, 15.98

gott(e) *n* gut, stomach; *pl.* 6.397, 8.175, 11.41, 15.98, A 12.76, Z 7.163; *sg.* stomach as seat of gluttony 1.34

goudnesse A 12.111 = **go(e)dnesse** *n*

goune *v* gown, robe 15.203, 16.298

gouernen *v* hold sway (over) 3.437; control, have mastery of 22.34; discipline, restrain B 5.51

gowte *n* gout, swelling at joint 22.192

grace *n* God's grace / favour 1.196, 199, 3.339, 5.98, 100, 6.285, 7.156, 268, 281, 290, 9.348, 10.168, 11.227, 14.33, 17.256, 265, 19.250, 20.428, **B** 9.101, 12.68; (*spec.*) grace as divine gift 10.177, 11.212, 15.228; as grace of repentance 3.100, 6.61, 7.120, 10.304, 11.232, 14.23, 28 (2)*n*, 131, 19.279, 291, B 14.20, 170, Z 5.95; as grace of a virtuous life **B** 5.260, 6.227, 8.61, 9.178, 10.188, (*pl.*) **B** 2.29, 15.66, A 10.129, Z 1.128; the state of grace 11.208; (quality of) virtue 14.28(1)*n*, 17.48, 21.321, B 15.423; ~ as special attribute of the Holy Spirit 19.168, 181, 188, 215, 279; ~ as divine power 18.52, 20.163, 392, 396, B 16.51, A 11.300, (*person.*) 7.247, 253, (= the Holy Spirit) 21.121, 209 *et p.*, 389, 428, 22.387; ~ as divine help in secular affairs 2.35, 3.323, 6.84, 8.132, 9.55, 10.211, 11.288, 12.186, 13.22, 17.256, 21.131, B 9.107; God's goodness, *esp.* mercy 1.76, 2.1, 132, 244, 6.319, 7.60, 250, 14.28(2), 57, 132, 197, 20.92, 189, 21.110, 116, 213, 22.140, **B** 10.342, 11.148, Z 5.93; ~ as natural gift 21.216, 228, 234; fortune, luck 6.83, 213, 13.217, 14.2, **B** 5.96, 150, A 10.100; good will / favour 3.330, 6.344, 11.86, 20.428, B 4.73, A 9.95; forgiveness 3.134, 4.138; pardon 5.192; permission 3.217; grace before meals 15.265; *in phr*: ~ **of amendement** 6.102; ~ **of a good ende** 3.339, 9.50, 10.60; ~ **of þe Holy Gost** 18.52, 19.196, 254, 20.133; **withouten ~** out of favour (with the Church) 9.205; **wordes of ~** gracious, blessed words 5.98

gracen *v* thank, *p.p.* B 6.124

gracious(e) *a* merciful 3.353, 14.133; pleasing B 6.226; ~ **liche** *av* by means of grace / beautifully 18.7; by means of grace / mercifully B 18.358

gradde *p.t.* 22.387, B 16.78 *see* **greden** *v*

graes 14.23 = **gras** *n*

graffe *n* graft (*fig.*) 1.199

graffen *v* graft B 5.136

gray *a* drab, unbleached 16.298; *as n* 16.344

grayeth 3.89 = **graiþ** *a*

grayn *n* crop (*esp. of* wheat) 8.126, 132, 12.179, 186, 13.22, B 14.31, (*fig.*) 21.275, 319, seed, (*fig.*) particle, jot 11.84

graiþ *a* ready †B 12.193; direct B 1.205, (*sup.*) 1.199; plain 10.245, Z 8.41; exact, true 3.89, 6.230; ~**(e) li(che)** *av* straightway 7.295, 11.138; quickly B 11.41; properly 22.322

gramarien *n* one who can read Latin B 13.73

gramer *n* Latin (grammar) 11.122, 17.107

grange *n* farm-house 19.73

grape *n* grape B 14.31

gras *n* grass 6.430, 13.176, 15.244, B 11.365; (as cattle-feed) 4.49, Z 7.66; healing herb 14.23

gras 6.84 = **grace** *n*

grat *contr. pr. pl.* 8.284 *see* **greden** *v*

graþest *sup.* 1.199 *see* **graiþ** *a*

graunt mercy *excl.* many thanks! B 10.220, 17.86

graunten *v* grant, give 1.168, 3.100, 134, 330, 6.102, 435, 8.353, 9.184, 19.188, 287, 20.186, 21.104, **B** 3.232, 9.47, 11.148; concede B 12.292; permit, allow 7.253, 12.64, B 11.97, A 12.25; consent, assent (to) 2.168, 18.131, B 4.194, A 2.24; yield (to) 3.365; allot A 8.87; decree **B** 2.120, 18.339, A 10.206; ordain A 11. 196; grant (land, privilege, pardon) 2.70, 2.88, 3.251, 5.192, 9.8, 19, 23, 324, 21.184, B 16.241; promise A 3.233; undertake, offer B 17.86; *in phr.* **God ~** may God grant 2.125, 16.154, B 14.318

graue *n* grave 17.302, 20.64, B 16.113

grauen *v* bury 20.86, Z 2.72; engrave 3.52, *ger.* engraving 3.68, 74; stamp 4.127, 17.75, 207 (B 15. 544)

gre(e) *n* prize (for victory) 20.101

grece *n* fat B 13.63

greden *v* (*contr. pr. 3 pl.* **grat** 8.284, *p.t.* **gradde** 22.387) shriek B 16.78; ~ **after, to** pray fervently for 8.284, 14.133, 22.387, cry for 9.76, call for B 3.71; cry a proclamation B 2.74; go on (noisily) about 21.428

gredyre *n* gridiron 2.130

greet 3.222 *etc*; **greetliche** 20.6; **greetnesse** B 16.59; *see* **gret(e)- ** *a, etc*

gre(e)ut *n* earth, ground 13.22, 176

greyn[1] B 14.31 = **grayn** *n*

greyn[2] *n* colour B 16.59; *and see* **engreynen** *v*

Grek *n* gentile, pagan B 15.604

grene *a* green 15.244, **B** 6.297, 11.365, 16.59; vigorous 16.253, B 15.423, ~ **leued** 17.48; freshly cut 20.48; fresh(ly made) 8.304

gret(e) *a* (*comp.* **gretter(e)**, **grettore**, *sup.* **grettest(e)**) large, big Pr 53, 6.410, 10.45, 18.62, 112, 20.400, **A** 8.44, 12.69; long B 4.46; fat 15.87; pregnant 20.133;

powerful 21.263, 22.215, **B** 13.399, 14.38; abundant 2.162, 19.295, **B** 9.47, 17.313; numerous 21.338; great 3.22, 339, 7.110, 9.50, 10.9, 16.19, 95, 18.56, 19.148, **B** 5.380, 10.304, 12.292, 14.129; of high rank / authority Pr 177, 2.176, 3.282, 8.87, 9.133, 10.148, 15.210, *a as n* B 4.159; good, excellent 6.261, B 17.37; important B 9.59; mighty 6.285, 17.256, 18.149, B 15.66; solemn Pr 137; eminent 5.146, 17.166, 21.128, B 10.66; sublime 1.103, 10.154, 20.125, 21.198, 22.40, B 12.68; holy 21.209, **B** 2.29, 9.28; serious 7.61, 9.258; grievous 3.222, 20.101, (*as comp. av*) 22.28; angry 6.18; vile, wicked Pr 36, 16.76, B 12.79; strong 12.85, 15.186, B 11.262; deep 14.213, B 15.146; bright 20.342; pressing, extreme 9.67, 13.8, 22.20, B 7.82; *as n* much 3.89, B 12.250; *in recurring phrr*. ~ **clerk** 5.146, 11.291, 15.82, 21.271; ~ **lordes** 9.133, 10.148, 15.210, 255; ~ **myhte** 6.285, 19.196; ~ **othes** Pr 36, 2.97, 6.360, **B** 10.50, 13.400; ~ **witte(s)** 10.9, 11.84; ~ **wonder** 18.149, 20.125; ~**ly(che)** *av* seriously 11.313; at length / ? deeply 20.6; ~**nesse** *n* width B 16.59

greten *v*¹ (*p.t.* **grette** 11.116) greet 4.42, 11.116, 138, 18.184, 22.356; pay one's respects to 18.243, B 18.174; bid farewell (to) B 10.220; address 12.208; reward 6.392

greten *v*² weep B 5.380

grette *p.t.* 4.42, *etc*; *see* **greten** *v*¹

greut 13.22 = **gre(e)ut** *n*

greuaunce *n* affliction, disease B 12.59

greuen *v* hurt, injure Pr 171, 3.92, 5.58, 10.306, 11.27, 16.120, 288, 305, 19.147, 167, B 15.257; cause injury 11.133; offend 8.236, 16.207, B 10.28; oppress, harass 4.95, 8.339, 13.59, 15.165, 255, 16.71, 21.220, 22.28, **B** 10.206, 17.112; afflict 15.293; cause discomfort (to) 6.410; anger B 13.73, (*refl.*) get angry **B** Pr 139, 6.314; trouble 6.111, 11.313, 19.20, **B** 10.286, 11.279, Z 7.275; disturb Pr 208; agitate B 5.96

greuous *a* bitter 16.76

grewe *p.t.* 13.176, 18.56 *see* **growen** *v*

grydy *a* ravening 6.397

gri(e)s 8.304 = **grys** *n*¹

grym *a* terrible, monstrous(ly heavy) B 5.354; ~**ly** *av* sternly B 10.261; pitiably A 5.209

grype *n* grasp 19.147

gripen *v* (*p.p.* **grepe, grypen, griped**) grasp 19.128, 168; take 3.89, 227, B 3.250; receive 3.282

grys *n*¹ young pig 4.49; pork of young pig Pr 228, 8.304

grys *n*² grey (squirrel) fur 16.344

grynden *v* grind, *p.p.* **ygrounde** A 7.169; mix by grinding 15.49; sharpen 20.80; *and see* **for-, to-grynden** *vv*

grisly *a* fearsome 20.478

grochen *v* (**ageyn, of, on**) complain, grumble (at) Pr 171, 6.111, 8.227, 337, B 6.314, A 10.116, Z 7.317, 321

grom *n* (low) fellow 8.227

gronen *v* groan (with sickness), ? feel ill 8.269, 22.312, *ger.* A 12.76

gropen *v* feel, touch 19.128, 21.170; play with (sexually) 6.180; examine medically (*fig.*) 22.364

grote *n* groat, silver coin [worth fourpence] 3.174, 5.133, 6.230, 17.207, B 10.47

ground *n* fundamental principle 3.353; source 17.90, 141, B 2.29; basis 17.107, [of a claim] B 5.286; (surface of the) ground 5.120, 13.166, 14.140, 144, 20.44, B 10.140; earth, world 10.45, 60, **B** 5.260, 6.228, 10.226, A 1.88, 11.173; soil (*fig.*) B 16.62

grounde *p.p.* B 13.43 *see* **grynden** *v*

grou(e)n Z 7.59, 106, 108 *see* **growen** *v*

growen *v* (*p.t.* **grewe** 13.176, **growede** 18.7) grow, spring up 8.126, 10.153, 12.179, 13.176, (*fig.*) 14.23, 24, 18.7, 23, 56, 22.57, **B** 14.31, 15.423, 16.9, 12, 13, 56, 58, 62, Z 7.59, 108; thrive 10.209, (*fig.*) 17.48; increase 20.400; grow, be found 12.226, 21.315, (*fig.*) 18.56, 84, B 12.60

growel *n* gruel [soup containing meal] A 7.167

gruc(c)hen 8.227 *etc*; = **grochen** *v*

gult *a* gilded 16.344, 20.12; **with a ~ penne** with a golden pen (= in letters of gold) 19.16

gult *n* sin, transgression 3.8, 103, 134, 138, 6.176, 275, 7.61, 10.55, 236, 11.62, **B** 4.101, 10.280, Z 5.93; fault 15.228, B 19.306; **withouten** ~ undeservedly 4.75

gulty *a* guilty, blameworthy [for sin or crime] 6.175, 424, 21.304, **B** 10.258, 12.76, 192, (*comp.*) 99

gulten *v* offend 7.150

gurden *v* (*imp.* **gurdeth**, *p.t.* **girte**) cut 2.213; vomit B 5.373

gurl *n* child 1.29, 9.76, 11.122, 16.300, 20.6, B 10.79, A 10.160

gut B 1.36 *etc*; *see* **gott(e)** *n*

habben B 14.148, *etc* Z 1.107; *see* **hauen** *v*

haberion *n* coat of mail 20.22

habite B Pr 3 = **abite** *n*

habiten *v* dress, *p.p.* **yhabited** B 13.285

hacche *n* hatch [lower part of divided door] 5.29, 16.336

hachet *n* small battle-axe 3.458; hatchet A 7.59

hackenayman 6.364, 377 *see* **hakeney** ~ *n*

hackyen, hakken (after) *v* keep toiling away (at) 21.404

had *p.t.* 6.146 *etc*; **hadde** Pr 50 *et p.*; **hadden** 10.216 *et p.*; **haddest** 6.320 *et p.*; **haddestow** (= **haddest thow**) B 20.188; **haen** *pr.* 3.269 *et p.*; **haeth** 19.324 *etc*; *see* **hauen** *v*

hayl(l) *n* hail 15.165, B 14.172

hayl *interj.*; **al ~** your health! hello! A 12.62

haylsen *v* greet (respectfully), salute 9.309, 10.10, B 5.100, A 12.79

hayre *n* (penitential garment of) haircloth, hairshirt 6.6

hayward *n* hayward [manorial field-keeper] 5.16, 6.367, 13.44, 46, (*fig.*) 21.334

hakeney *n* hackney-horse [small saddle-horse] 2.175; ~ **man** *n* keeper of hackneys for hire 6.364, 377

halden (holden) *v* (*contr. pr* **halt** 3.386, B 17.106, *p.t.* **he(e)ld(e)** 10.86, 22.145, 298, *pl.* **helden** 9.206, *pr.p.* **haldyng** 3.379, **holdyng** 8.103, *p.p.* **halden** 13.119, **(y)holde(n)** 1.80, 3.267, 6.40) grasp Pr 172, 19.127, 140, 157; hold 5.161, 6.400, 419, **B** 1.44, 17.157, 160, Z 7.58*n*; sustain 18.195; retain possession (of) 10.86, B 12.248, (*ger.* **holdyng**) 12.246, (*ger.* **holdyng** = **holden**), 8.103, 14.196, 19.39, 22.366, B 15.569, A 11.247; preside over 7.33, B 5.421; maintain, keep 3.187, 9.206, B 15.142, A 9.87, Z 2.209; defend 21.359, 22.75, 205, 298; ~ **vp** raise A 12.38; preserve B 6.214; ~ **with** support 1.94, 108, 2.153, 3.379, 8.50, 22.128, 216, 220, B 3.242; observe, keep 5.143, 157, 7.225, 9.24, 166, 221, 22.280, **B** 5.579, 10.291, 13.414; obey 9.166, A 6.97; practise 6.233; follow, keep to 13.67, 16.53, A 12.88; (*refl.*) remain Pr 30, 5.189, 8.207, 9.5, A 7.133, 10.114; hold firm, stand 20.258; ~ **(for)** regard (as), consider 1.80, 3.87, 267, 386, 6.40, 390, 8.74, 223, 9.336, 10.298, 11.311, 13.119, 184, 239, 14.76, 15.126, 127, 128, 16.371, 17.64, 111, 159, 21.373, 463, 22.145, 262, **B** 4.118, 5.257, 413, 11.68, 12.294, 15.10, 16.112, 17.106, **A** 4.136, 8.75, 11.62, Z 7.196; judge, believe 10.290, 11.221; ~ **no tale** have no regard for 1.9

hale Z 2.46 = **halle** *n*

hales 8.60 = **hals** *n*

hal(e)wen *v* consecrate 17.279

half *n* (*pl.* **half** 2.56; *and see* **halue(n)**) half 5.133, 15.181; side (of page = verso) 3.491, **body** ~ front side B 13.317, (*fig.*) 3.226; hand [direction] 2.5, 8; quarter [direction] 18.66; *in phrr.* **bothe** ~ **þe contre** both parts / sides of the country 2.56, **bothe** ~ **the mone** both parts of the lunar cycle 8.350

half *a* half (a / an), ~ **aker** 6.267, 8.2, 3, 113, 123; ~ **a laumpe lyne** B 13.152; ~ **loef** 9.150; ~ **marc** 5.133; ~...**pak of bokes** B 13.202; ~ **peny** 8.328; ~ **a shef of arwes** 3.478; ~ **ȝere** 2.238; *and see* **halue-**

haly, haly- 6.146, 272 see **holy(-)** *a*

halidome *n* (the) sacred relics (*in oath*) B 5.370

halien *v* draw, pull 10.94

halle *n* hall [large (royal or manorial) residence] A 2.38; = large communal room for meals 7.93, 236, 14.139, 15.40, B 10.96, 100; law-court B 4.159, A 4.118, **West-ministre** ~ 22.133; the company (assembled) in the hall B 4.162; *and see* **moet** ~

halpe *p.t.* 21.131, 377, A 11.31 see **helpen** *v*

hals *n* neck Pr 185, 194, 8.60

halsen *v*¹ embrace, *ger.* 6.187

halsen *v*² (**halsenen** Z) adjure 1.70; salute A 12.79 (= **haylsen**)

halt *contr. pr.* 3.386 *et p.*; *see* **halden** *v*

halue-bretherne *n* half-brethren (*fig.*) 20.436

haluendele *n* half-portion, half of it 7.29

hammard Z 3.132 = **homward** *av*

han *pr.pl.*, *3* Pr 63 *et p.*, *1* 3.51 *et p.*, *2* 8.271 *et p.*; *inf.* 9.157, B 20.265, A 3.189 *see* **hauen** *v*

hand (ho(e)nd) *n* 1.84, 3.75, 4.82, 143, 6.109, 8.261, 10.147, 14.59, 63, 16.82, 19.56, 66, 112, 118 *et p.*, 21.170, 22.117, **B** 15.122, 454, 17.138 *et p.*, **A** 7.235, 12.38, Z 7.67; power 3.242; keeping B 10.431; manual work Pr 223, 8.259, 330, 9.58, 198, A 7.232; manual skill B 13.298; action, conduct 6.109, 10.78, 13.110, 19.257, 21.247; *in phrr.* ~ **fedde** fed by hand B 15.471; ~ **mayden** maid-servant 18.132; ~**while** short space of time 21.273; **luft** ~ 7.224, **riȝt** ~ A 3.56; **large handes** liberal hands (for bribery) 3.288; **riche** ~? great wealth, ? money-making abilities 3.118; **two** ~ 1.84, 10.78

*****handy-dandy** *n* as *av* secret bribery 4.68*n*

hand(e)len *v* treat wounds 22.314; deal with, dispense, *p.p.* **yhandlit** A 2.99; *ger.* **handlynge** touching 15.258; caressing 6.187

hangen, hongen *v* (*p.t.* **heng** 8.60, *pl.* 1.169, **hongide** A 1.148, *p.p.* **hanged** Pr 194, **hongen** Pr 185) hang Pr 185, 191, 7.241, 8.60, **B** 15.214, 16.66; fasten B 4.22; be suspended Pr 99, 20.259, *pr.p.* sagging B 5.134; (put to death by) hang(ing) 2.207, 3.177, 6.238, 10.163, 243, 17.138, 20.421, **B** 1.68, 5.232, 279, (*in assev.*) 3.148, *ger.* 3.407; hold to (sb.) 3.226; cling, hold fast (to) B 13.391; depend on 14.214, *pr.p.* B 12.289

#**hangeman** *n* hangman 6.367

hankres Z Pr 29 = **ankeres** *n*

hansull *n* earnest of good fellowship, **to** ~ as a treat 6.374

hap *n* (one's) luck, fortune 3.297; (stroke of) luck 14.51, B 5.96; good fortune 22.386, A 12.111

hapeward 7.283 = **apeward** *n*

hap(pi)liche *av* perhaps, maybe 7.266

happen *v* happen, have the chance to 11.113, 13.46; (*impers. without* it) befall 3.438, 5.95, 9.113, B 6.46; turn out 15.6, 18.120

hapsen *v* fasten; *p.p.* **yhapsed** 1.191

hard *2 sg. pr.* Z 1.29 = **art**; *see* **be(n)** *v*

hard *a* hard 19.12; miserly 12.246, (*comp.*) 1.186; painful, rigorous B 14.322; severe 3.399, 12.200; fierce 22.217, 301; difficult 4.177, 7.280, 16.118, 22.336, **B** 10.209, 17.41, 42

harde *av* tightly 1.191, B 17.157; austerely Pr 28; sternly B 11.85; (*comp.*) more severely Pr 122; (*sup.*) most grievously 14.119; violently 22.185; fiercely 22.216, 302; hard, strenuously Pr 23, B 7.118

hardeliche *av* boldly, strenuously 8.28; (*comp.*) **hardiloker** more boldly 6.305

hardy *a* stouthearted, fearless 3.236, 9.265, 13.61, 21.291, B 14.305, (*comp.*) 21.58; bold (*comp.*) B 17.106; ~ **(to)** so bold as to 3.321, 4.63, 8.181, 13.9, A 12.23; **ouer** ~ rash 3.298; firm 3.351; ~ **nesse** *n* stoutness, courage 21.31; audacity 20.79

hardy *av,* (*comp.*) **hardyore** more boldly 16.101

hardien *v* embolden B 15.436

hare *n* hare 7.32, 8.28

harewen 21.311 = **harwen** *v*

harlote *n* villain, knave 19.258, B 17.109; base fellow B 18.77; low jester 7.93, 8.50, 11.28, B 13.416, Z 7.48; lecher 3.300, 4.113, 22.144, **B** 14.183, 15.134

harlotrie *n* ribald jesting 4.110, 11.28, B 10.45, A 11.31; obscenity 16.258; obscene tale 7.22; lechery 7.75, 7.90, B 13.354

harm *n* harm 3.81, 6.109, 9.47, 15.114, Z 7.245; injury A 5.83; damage(s) B 4.31; calumny 6.117; suffering Z 7.201

harmen *v* injure A 11.252; (do) damage (to) 2.248, B 13.107, A 2.166; do wrong 3.177

harneys *n* armour 16.344; **pyken** ~ plunder (dead men's) armour Z 7.67; **pyke** ~ *n* plunderer of armour 22.263

harow! *excl* a distressed cry for succour 22.88

harpe *n* harp; **in þin** ~ to the (accompaniment of the) harp A 1.137

harpen *v* play the harp 15.207, 20.450

harpour *n* harp-player B 14.25

harwe *n* harrow Z 7.58

harwen *v* (cultivate with a) harrow 5.19, (*fig.*) 21.269, 273, 311

hasche(h)t Z 1.48, 3.155, **hascuht** Z Pr 124 = **asketh**; *see* **asken** *v*

haspen, *p.p.* B 1.197 *see* **hapsen** *v*

hast(e) *2 sg. pr.* 2.137, 3.418 *et p.*; *see* **hauen** *v*

haste *n* haste, **in** ~ in a hurry 8.319; quickly, speedily 8.171, 206, 14.175, 22.136, 144, 332

hast(e)li(che) *av* quickly 12.140, 165, 21.359, 22.167, *sup.* **hastilokest** most promptly 21.472

hasten *v* (*refl.*) go speedily 3.418, A 3.181; come quickly, soon 8.343

#**hastite** *n* haste, **for** ~ through hurrying 17.118

hastow 3.133, 5.26 = **hast thow**; *see* **hauen** *v*

hat *3 pr. sg.* Z 4.133 = **hath**

hat *n* hat 6.202, 7.164, 13.47, B 5.529

hatchet A 7.59 = **hachet** *n*

hater *n* garment 9.157; cloak B 14.1

hateren *v* clothe, *ger.* **haterynge** clothing B 15.78

hath *3 sg. pr.* Pr 62 *et p.*, *pl.* Pr 38 *et p.*; *see* **hauen** *v*

hat(i)en *v* hate 15.215, 16.65, 119, 22.295, **B** 5.99, 114, 13.420; loathe 6.440, B 12.52; despise, scorn 4.110, 6.11c, 7.79, 9.190, 16.258, 17.138, **B** 6.50, 13.226, 239; show enmity towards 3.431, B 11.182

hatrede *n* hatred 3.177

hatte *3 sg. pr.* 3.496 *et p.*, *pl* 7.223 *et p.*; **hatted** Z 6.82,

hatteþ A 6.60 *etc* (= **hatte**); **hattest** *2 sg.pr.* 22.340; *see* **hoten** *v*

haubergeon B 18.23 = **haberion** *n*

hauȝt Z 6.8 = **auht** *av*

hauk *n* hawk 7.44, B 4.125

hauken *v* hunt with a hawk, *ger.* 3.465

haumpelles Z 5.162 *see* **aunpolle** *n*

haunt *n* resort, frequentation 16.92

haunten *v* practise, engage in 15.198, Z 7.134; indulge in Pr 75, 3.57, 63, 11.111

hauthorn 18.183 *see* **hawe-** *n*

hauen *v* (*1 pr.sg.* **habbe** Z 5.137, **haue** Pr 177 *et p.*; *2* **hast** 2.137 *et p.*, *3* **haeth** 19.324 *etc*, **hath** Pr 62 *et p.*, *pl 1, 2, 3* **haen** 3.269, **han** 3.51, 8.271, Pr 63, **an** Z Pr 91, **haue(n)** 2.167, 6.296, 9.174, *2 and 3* **haueth** 1.178, 5.166, **habbeth** Z 1.107; *pr. subj.* **haue** *sg.* 2.50, 6.295, *pl.* 1.8, B 6.11; *imper. sg.* **haue** *pl.* **haue** A 1.149, **haueth** 1.170 *et p.*, **habbeth** Z 1.98; *p.t. 1,3 sg., 1 and 3 pl.* **had(d)e** Pr 50, 128, 6.146, **haued(e)** 3.40, 8.3, 14.150, Z 1.14, *2 sg.* **haddest** 6.320 *et p.*, **hauedest** Z 5.136, *p.t. as conditional* B 5.232; *1 and 3 pl.* **hadden** 10.216 *et p.*, **haueden** Z Pr 52, *p.p.* **(y)had** 7.44, 11.303 *et p*) have, possess Pr 136, 6.259 *et p.*; have (sb.) under one 15.306; have charge of 4.84; enjoy 3.194, 8.314; use, perform B 15.126; hold, keep 5.16, 6.339 *et p.*; remember 8.103; get, obtain Pr 83, 2.35, 3.101, 9.289, 22.328 *et p.*; accept 3.146; receive 6.293, 9.70, 13.169; take (back) 3.331; win 6.77, 17.240, 21.107; experience 6.416, 20.211; bear 6.136; take (pity) 3.86 *et p.*; feel (hate) 7.261, 18.270; have (sth.) to look after Pr 128, 3.51, 8.2; *as auxil., finite with p.p.* Pr 177 *et p.*; *infin. + p.p., with zero meaning:* **to** ~ **be** to be 17.167; **to** ~ **yfouhte** to fight 18.137; *after modal verbs:* **connen** B 15.301, 19.254; **mowen** 16.19, B 11.196; **shullen** 3.259; **willen** 6.418; *after* **durren** Pr 193, 3.258; *as infin. compl.* 3.6, (*with* **to**) 14.214; *as subst. for another (understood) v.* 10.19; *in phrr.:* ~ **a-do, to doone** have business (to do) 5.163, dealings with B 4.28; ~ **(a)down** bring down 18.111, 22.227; ~ **excused** forgive (sb.) 15.130; **to** ~ **and to holde** possess and hold (of sb.) B 2.102; ~ **þe maistry** get the upper hand 20.68; ~ **out** carry away 20.321 (capture), 20.148 (release); bring out 20.287; ~ **at wille** have at one's disposal 13.226; *in assevs.,* **God** ~ **þe, devel** ~ may God / the devil take 6.296, 8.127

hauylon *n* trick(y argument) B 10.131

hawe *n* haw(thorn berry) 11.8, 81; ~**thorn** *n* hawthorn(-blossom) 18.183

he[1] *pers. prn.* (*acc.* **him** 4.64 *et p.*; *gen.* **his(e)** Pr 70 *et p.*, B 7.167 *et p.*, *dat.* **him** 4.64, **hym** Pr 111 *et p.*; *pl.* **he** Z 7.14, **hy** 1.187 *et p.*, A Pr 63 *et p.*, **hij** †B 1.191, *acc.* **hem** Pr 68 *et p.*, *gen.* **here** Pr 30 *et p.*, **hir** B 1.99 *et p.*, *dat.* **hem** Pr 54 *et p* (*qqv*)) he, (him; his; (to) him; they; their; (to) them); *with indef. ref.* a man, (some) one 5.91, 8.143

he² Z Pr 101, 1.14, 16, 2.20 *et p.*, 3.29, 55 *et p.*; *see* **heo** *pers. prn.*

he³ Z 7.14 = **hy** *pers. prn.*

he(e)d (heued) *n* head 2.213, 6.150, 202, 10.175, 180, 12.18, 16.74, 19.72, 20.49, 290, 22.183, 185, 187, **B** 4.22, 6.325, *(fig.)* 13.145, A 10.60, Z Pr 80; *(meton.)* head-gear 5.133; **putten forth** ~ show oneself 4.74, 7.181; ruler, controller 3.379, 17.230, 21.?472, 474, **B** 15.429, 486; origin, source 1.159, 17.140, ?21.472; = life B 2.34; *in assevs*: **by myn** ~ by my life 4.177, 7.280; **hefdes** persons 17.85

heddere 22.334 = **hyddere** *av*

hede *n* heed, note; **nymen / taken** ~ take note (of), observe 9.71, 11.70, 247, 12.46, 221, 14.99, 17.108, 239, 18.19, **B** 6.15, 11.321, 13.316, 319, 15.91, A 8.78, 11.149, Z 5.98

heeld *p.t.* 22.298, B 11.70 *see* **halden** *v*

heele B 14.172, 17.37 = **hele** *n*

heelen B 6.192, 16.112, 17.119 = **helen** *v*¹

he(e)p *n* company 6.235; crowd Pr 51, 6.373, 8.183, **B** 14.305; great pack 5.160; spate 6.384; long list 16.203; *in phr.* **bringen to hepe** bring about 10.191, 193

heer¹ B 14.128 = **her** *av*

heer² *n* hair; **oone heeris ende** = the least little bit B 10.333; *pl.* **heres** hair Z 5.9

heet(e) *p.t.* 18.249, 22.273, 349; *see* **hoten** *v*

heeþ *n* heath, wasteland B 15.458

hef Z 4.96 = **efte** *av*

hefdes *pl.* 17.85 *see* **he(e)d** *n*

hegge *n* hedge 3.168, 8.29

heggen *v* ?harrow, make / cut hedges 5.19

hey! *interj.* used in burden of song 8.123

heigh- B 12.37, **hei3-** B Pr 13 *et p.*; *see* **hey(h)(e)** *a*

hey(h)(e), hy(e) *a (comp.* **herre** A 10.101, **herrore** 2.30, **hyere** B 2.28, *sup.* **hei3est** B 10.453, A 10.45)* high 1.64, 153, 14.176, 15.66, 18.98, **B** Pr 13, 7.17, 18.311, **Z** Pr 99, 2.49, 5.45; divine 1.70, 8.137, 14.84, 17.247, 262, **B** 2.33, 11.81, 12.40, 16.118; heavenly 17.256, A 11.313; exalted 14.135, *(comp.)* A 10.101; great, ~ **dome** Last Judgement 6.297, 346; chief, principal 1.159, ~ **gate** supernal gate 7.248; high road B 4.42, ~ **strete** main road 14.48, ~ **wey** 8.2, 9.32, 188, 203, 11.106, A 7.178, Z 7.6, *(fig.)* 13.67, 16.53, **B** 12.37, 15.434; (of) noble (rank) 2.81, 9.201, 16.33, *comp.* 2.30, B 10.103, 364; solemn 4.113, ~ **festes** solemn (religious) festivals 6.182; deep, lofty 16.234, *sup.* B 10.453; important 14.76; arrogant, haughty 6.8, 22.116; full, ~ **prime** = 9 a.m. 8.119, ~ **tyme** the appointed / fullness of time 18.139; *in phr.*: **an** ~ on high, up above 5.186, 17.222, 18.106, 21.192, B Pr 128, 140; to a high position 12.42; aloud A 12.27

heye *av* high 1.169, 6.238, 14.176, B 11.360; to a great height 3.84; at high cost 3.51; loudly B 2.74; *(sup.)* most highly B 12.144, most intensely A 10.45; *in phr.* ~ **til** right up to 7.225

heyli(che) *av* munificently 3.251; at a high wage 8.335; greatly B 15.525; completely 8.89; strictly A 11.247

heihte 18.4 = **hihte** *pr.*, *see* **hoten** *v*

heynesse (of herte) *n* presumption 22.153

heyr 5.163, 6.255, **B** 2.102, 16.232 *see* **ayr** *n*

held(e)n *p.t.* 1.108, 6.400, 10.86, 17.22, A 4.136 *etc*; *see* **halden** *v*

hele *n*¹ (good) health 5.7, 10, 9.102, 105, 10.182, 16.12, 20.218, 22.153 *(person.)*, 180, 386, *(fig.)* 19.84, **B** 6.258, 14.172, 17.37; healing 21.104; spiritual health 1.86, 19.84, 21.391, A 6.19; comfort 6.85; prosperity, good fortune 9.116; protection 21.474; salvation 17.140, B 5.266

hele *n*² heel A 11.81; crust, **pye** ~ (= thing of little value) 9.345

helen *v*¹ heal [physically] 8.225, 10.309, 21.131, **B** 6.192, 16.112, Z 7.262, *(fig.)* A 7.179; recover *(ger.)* B 17.116; heal [spiritually], free from sin 22.282, 357, B 17.119

hel(i)en (hilen) *v*² cover 7.236, 9.157, 13.163, *ger.* roofing, ?clothing 16.23(1), **B** 5.590, 11.351, 12.230, 232; conceal 22.340; keep secret B 5.166

helle *n* hell 1.120, 126, 183, 3.327, 6.238, 337, 7.88, 133, 9.278, 10.288, 303, 11.200, 221, 12.76, 78, 246, 14.149, 193, 15.302, 304, 309, 18.266, 19.241, 244, 20.127, 148, 150, 173, 180, 193, 232, 258, 270, 349, 364, 375, 407, 414, 420, 439, 21.52, 56, 22.270, *(person.)* 20.274, **B** 1.115, 198, 8.96, 10.109, 369, 11.144, 14.80, 15.75, 16.247, **A** 1.113, 5.242, 10.177, 11.68, Z 1.65; *in phrr*: ~ **pouke** 15.165; ~ **yates** B 11.163, Z 5.39; **heuene and** ~ 3.165, B 17.162; **peyne(s) of** ~ 2.108, 3.101; **to ~ward** towards hell 20.117

(h)eller(ne) *n* elder-tree 1.64, B 9.149

helm *n*¹ helmet 20.22

helm *n*² elm-tree Z 5.45

help *n* help, assistance 6.169, 7.289, 19.58, 83, 20.442, **B** 10.238, 15.196, 16.52; relief 22.169, B Pr 159; favour, good will 11.46; support 3.337, 4.68, 176, 8.256, 15.238, 16.95, 17.185; sustenance B 4.125; source of strength 21.391, B 13.399; supporter 16.95, 21.475, **B** 8.46, 11.218, A 10.47, 49

helples(e) *a* infirm 9.175; useless, lacking (in) B 7.98; unable to act for themselves B 9.70; abandoned, hopeless B 15.457

helpen *v (p.t.* **halp** 21.131, *p.t. subjv.* **halpe** 21.377, **holpe** 20.441, A 11.31, *pl.* **holpe** 8.123, 9.6, *p.p.* **(y)holpe** 11.28, B 5.624)* help, assist 3.208, 4.192, 6.297, 299, 7.275, 8.18, 65, 66, 113, 123, 257, 9.6, 344, 10.278, 14.55, 15.12, 23, 19.62, 221, 21.377, 407, 22.228, 230, **B** 9.37, 10.333, A 11.31; assist (in fight) A 12.65; succour 15.143, 18.13, 21.131, **B** 5.430, 6.20, 142, 7.42, 9.77, 113, 16.124, A 4.60; save, preserve 7.273, 10.43, 14.55, 15.15, 19.57, 20.54, 204, 21.369, 431, B 17.286; rescue B 5.624; relieve 6.84, 8.233, 10.190, 11.30, B

807

7.70; avail, be of use / benefit (to) 1.17, 3.222, 8.137, 12.101, 19.159, 293, **B** 7.54, 13.390, 408, A 8.7; support Pr 74, 3.444, 9.33, 11.187, 12.119, 13.131, 16.44, 19.140, 22.376, **B** 3.242, 243, 15.336 (2), 16.26; provide for 3.251, 260, 8.219, 9.96, 125, 10.84, 186, 14.21, 15.224, 17.60, 62, **B** 7.26, 9.86, 15.336 (1), A 10.69; *in assevs.*: **so ~ me God / Crist ~** so help (preserve) me God / Christ 3.8, 4.11 *et p.*

helthe *n* (bodily) health 16.135, 22.333, Z 7.268; (spiritual) health, salvation 7.174, **B** 10.251, 11.229, 12.39

hem *pers. prn. 3 pl.* them Pr 39, 68 *et p.*; (*refl.*) themselves Pr 22 *et p.*; (*after impers. v. 3 pl. acc., dat.*) to themselves Pr 58; **~ þat** those who Pr 106, 1.169 *etc.*

hemself *emphatic pers. prn.* (**~selue(n)** B 10.83, A 4.107, B 3.216, **~ sylf(e)** Z 1.59, 5.64, **~sylue** Z 5.30, **~ sulue(n)** 9.77, 21.149) themselves Pr 55, B 10.397; (*as refl. obj. of v.*) 10.163 *et p.*, B 4.40, A 5.35; (*without parallel subj.*) (they) themselves **B** 10.313, 18.305

hen *n* hen; **hennes** hen's 21.415, *pl.* Z 7.287

hende *a* well-bred 8.47, 22. 188; courtly 10.146; polite 22.349, 355; well-behaved B 15.216; courteous A 2.52; generous 11.44, B 5.257; **~li(che)** *av* courteously 3.30, 18.184; politely 10.10, B 5.100; meekly 18.132; **~ nesse** *n* nobility 21.31; virtue 2.81, 11.13, 18.13, (*person.*) 22.145

hendret Z 5.162 = **hundred** *num.*

heng(en) *p.t.* 1.169, 8.60; *see* **hangen** *v*

henne(s) *av* from here 4.184, 5.80, 8.301, 10.128, 20.166, 280, 343, 21.322; (away) from this world / life 1.173, 6.312, 9.53, 348, 21.61, 249, 22.203, **B** 3.245, 7.97, A 8.18; from this time B 3.109; ago 5.35; **~ goyng, ~ partyng** *n. phr.* departure from this life **B** 14.165, 10.463

hensong Z 5.123 = **euensong** *n*

henten *v* (*p.t.* **hente(n)** 8.171, 183) take hold of 8.171; grasp 16.80, 19.140, 22.167; take 7.151, 15.249, 22.180; entrap 6.8; get hold of 8.183; overcome B 5.5, A 12.67

heo *pers. prn. 3 sg. fem.* (*acc.* **her** 1.54, **hire** B 1.58, *gen.* **her(e)** 1.10, 2.25, **hire** B 1.10) she 1.68 *et p.*, B 3.29 *etc*, A 1.10 *et p.*

hep Pr 51, **hepe** 10.191; *see* **he(e)p** *n*

her(e)[1] *pers. prn 3 sg. fem. obj.* her 1.54 *et p.*; for her 6.225; **for ~ loue** for love of her 2.37; (*refl.*) herself 4.90, 6.3; for herself 16.149; **by ~ one** alone by herself 20.316; *dat. after impers. v.* **~ were leuer** she would prefer 6.129, **~ were leuest** she would best like 3.6; **~ lef lyketh** it pleases her 7.252; **~ luste** she pleases 3.195

her(e)[2] (**hire** B 2.25 *et p.*) *poss. prn. fem. sg.* her 1.10, 2.25 *et p.*

her(e)[3] (**hire** B 2.150 *et p.*) *poss. prn. pl.* their Pr 30, 2.163 *et p.*, Z Pr 36 *et p.*; *in partitive constrns* of them: **~ either** each of them B 5.163; **~ aytheres / bothe / noyþer wille** the desire of each / both / neither of

them 12.140, 2.67; **~ ayther oþer** each other 22.354; **~ neyther** neither of them 10.275, B 4.33; **~ no(e)n** neither of them 14.105, 16.80, none of them A 7.300; **~ oen** each of them 20.67

her(e)[4] *av* here, in this place 2.69, 3.94, 231, 6.206, 8.126, 133, 15.116, 239, 18.97, 19.4, 18, 24, 92, 20.42, 169, 190, 273, 300, 304, 370, 375, 395, 434, 21.388, 22.88, 318, 351 (2), 358, **B** 5.248, 448, 6.65, 66, 13.191, 276, 14.274, 15.443, 16.24, 17.3, 23, 76, 113; at this point (in book) **B** Pr 38, 13.71, A 12.101; in this fact 1.167; in this matter B 10.111; in this world 1.9, 16, 6.238, 8.43, 9.321, 340, 348, 349, 10.304, 11.202, 272, 12.130, 165, 14.173, 15.300, 305, 16.100, 101, 18.206, 266, 269, 19.163, 20.352, 21.190, **B** 3.72, 233, 254, 8.38, 9.63, 10.123, 465, 11.188, 14.154, 165, 173, 176, 15.106, 486, 16.208, 18.24, **A** 3.63, 7.211, 235, †236 (1), 11.79, 12.92; now, at this time 13.225, B 5.233; *in cpd. avv.* **~ aboute** about this; **ben ~** be active about this 10.193; *and see* **ben aboute** 10.191; **~ aftur** in future 10.19; in the next life B 14.141; later on Pr 221, B 17.78; from now on **B** 7.120, 18.345, Z 7.38; **~ afterward** later on B 10.117; **~ agayn, ~ aȝen** against / opposed to this 10.238, 19.111, B 14.189; **~ beynge** *n. phr.* life in this world 16.9; **~ by** by this means 6.121; **~ fore** on this account 11.34, 22.295; **~ ynne** in here 17.39, 40, 22.343; **~ of** about / concerning this 9.1, 11.146, 148, 154, 16.35, 18.213, 19.249, 20.141, 279, 22.325, B 5.114, 6.183; **~ on** about this matter B 13.131; on this matter 12.97, B 10.283; **~ to** to this 2.15, to this point 4.177; for this B 9.36; **~ with** with this 12.162, B 13.157, by means of this 18.28

herayein B 14.189 = **heragayn** *av*; *see* **her(e)**[4]

heraud (of armes) *n* herald [at tournament, announcing knights] 18.186, 266, 20.14, 22.94, **B** 14.25, 16.177, 17.20, 53, 132

herber B 16.15 = **erber** *n*

herberwen 6.235 = **herborw(en)** *v*

herborw *n* place of refuge 11.248

herborwen *v* lodge 6.235, B 17.74, A 2.38, (*fig.*) 7.257; store 21.320

herd *p.p.* 13.128; **herde** *p.t.* Pr 95 *et p.*; *see* **heren** *v*

here A 6.37 = **huyre** *n*; Z 4.14 = **ere** *n*

hereaboute; hereaftur; hereagayn; hereayein; herby; her(e)ynne; herfore; her(e)of; heron; herto; *see* **her(e)**[4] *av*

hered *p.p.* Z 7.5 = **(y)ered**; *see* **eren** *v*

(h)er(e)mite *n* hermit [religious solitary] Pr 3, 30, 51, 55, 5.4, 6.367, 8.146, 183, 9.140, 187, 188, 190, 192, 195, 203, 217. 240, 17.6, **B** 13.30, 285, 15.213, 276, 416

heren *v* (*imper.* **yheer** B 17.138, *p.t.* **herde(n)** Pr 95, B 15.558, A 12.27, *p.p.* **(y)herd** 7.68) hear 4.157, 20.269, 21.21, 22.190, *ger.* (the act of) hearing A 10.52; understand 10.146, 11.221, 16.216, Z Pr 94; listen (to) 4.8, 110, 6.116, 434, 7.22, 77, 111, 8.48, 50, 16.16, B 12.243;

hear, attend 6.354, 7.66, 9.227, 229, 231, 242, 21.3, B 5.2; answer (prayer) 11.61, 19.221; hear (accounts read) 7.40; hear about (sth.) 7.74, 79, 10.109, 11.76, **B** Pr 164, 11.390, 15.58

her(e)of 9.1, 18.213 *etc*; *see* **her(e)**[4]

heres Z 5.9 *see* **heer**[2] *n*

herien *v* honour A 11.247

heryen Z 7.93, 8.5 = **eryen** *v*

herynne 17.39, 40, 22.343 *see* **her(e)**[4]

heritage *n* (sovereign) inheritance 3.242; (legal) inheritance 16.127, (*fig.*) spiritual inheritance (= place in heaven) B 10.341, 350

heresulue (~ **self** A, ~ **selue** B, ~ **silf** Z) *emphatic prn. fem. sg.* herself 20.254; she herself 3.180, 207; **by** ~ all by herself, all alone B 18.288

herken(en) *v* listen carefully 8.223, Z 7.20

herne *n* corner, secret hiding place 2.249 20.447

heron B 13.131 *see* **her(e)**[4]

heroudes 22.94 *see* **heraud** *n*

herre A 10.101, **herrore** 2.30 *comp.*; *see* **hey(h)(e)** *a*

herrys Z 2.74, *see* **ayr** *n*

herte *n* [physical] heart 1.169, 10.175, 12.51, 17.268, 20.87, 21.58, 171, 22.226, **B** 9.57, 16.15, **A** 6.50, 12.48; = stomach 6.214; (true, inner) self, soul 1.39, 6.331, 7.17, 254, 9.183, 11.53, B 10.433, A 10.78; heart [feeling(s)] 2.16, 3.489, 4.36, 6.11, 63, 89, 146, 7.261, 16.140, 19.329, 22.2, B 15.218, A 12.114; mood, spirits 22.171, B 5.111, A 5.97; mind, understanding 1.140, 159, 160, 6.289, 16.209, **B** 3.304, 6.49, A 11.259, Z 1.131; courage B 3.199; character, disposition 3.224, 351; desire 11.231; *in phrr.* **at, in** ~ to heart, seriously **B** 10.290, 15.259; **fre** ~ generosity B 15.151; **gode** ~ sincerity 17.134; courage 22.180; **hardy** ~, **hardinesse of** ~ valour 9.265, 21.31; **heyh** ~ 6.8, **heynesse of** ~ arrogance 22.153; **(with) heuy** ~ grudgingly 6.63; **hol(e)** ~ true, upright heart / disposition 3.351, 7.257; **louherted** humble 22.37; **lowe** ~, **lowenesse of** ~ humility 9.184, B 7.62; **milde** ~**s** kind, gracious hearts 19.201; **poore (of)** ~ humble B 14.195, 16.8, humility B 14.99; **rewful** ~**s** merciful hearts B 14.148; **sorowe of** ~ heartfelt sorrow (for sin) 16.29, 18.260; **wil of** ~ heartfelt intention **B** 13.141, 14.14; **wikkede** ~**s** evil hearts 14.25; **with** ~ inwardly, in truth B 13.279; **with mouthe and** ~ in words and sincere intention 12.72, 18.260

herten *v* hurt, injure (*p.p.* **hert(e)**) 19.153, 20.384, 22.318, 336

herthe Z 1.62 = **erthe** *n*

herto 2.155, 4.177, B 9.36 *see* **her(e)**[4]

heruest *n* harvest-time [early autumn, ?August] 5.7, 6.112, 8.121, 322, B 6.66; = the ripened crops 8.314, 12.201

herwith 12.162, 18.28, B 13.157 *see* **her(e)**[4]

hest(e) *n* command, bidding 3.148, 17.142, 18.250, A

10.142, 160; instruction 8.213; Commandment 2.87, 9.334, 13.67, A 11.253

hete *n* heat 9.109, 16.179; warmth 18.75, 19.194; drought 15.165, 261, **B** 14.172, 15.271; hot weather 1.123; *in phr.* **in chele and in** ~ = in all circumstances 8.249

hete *p.t.* A 12.74; *see* **hoten** *v*

heten *p.t.* Z 6.89, 7.307 = **eten** *v*

hethen(e) (**heþen(e)**) *a* heathen, pagan 21.351, B 15.457, 458; *as n* a pagan B 10.348, (*collective*) heathens A 11.251, B 10.363; ~**esse** *n* a pagan country B 15.442

†**hetyn** *v*[3] Z 4.108 = **hat(i)en** *v*

hette *p.t.* 1.17, *pr.* Z 7.44 *see* **hoten** *v*

heued 3.379 *et p.*, B 14.233, A 4.64, 6.25, 10.49, Z 2.181 *et p.*; *see* **he(e)d** *n*

heuen(e) *n* heaven Pr 133, 150, 1.103, 132, 148, 2.38, 132, 3.98, 5.186, 6.307, 330, 8.43, 11.200, 222, 12.99, 14.84, 135, 206, 16.51, 211, 17.149, 247, 20.247, 346, 440, 21.74, 81, 192, 22.270, **B** Pr 128, 1.111, 120, 123, 151, 3.50, 9.100, 10.335, 351, 14.141 (2), 165, 15.479, 16.208; **A** 1.113, 8.38, 10.46, 11.173, Z 5.130, 6.63; (*fig.*) = (place of) supreme happiness 1.9, 5.152, **B** 3.72, 9.118, 14.128, 141 (1); (*euphem.*) **in** ~ dead 22.194; the (natural) heaven, sky 15.268, 22.276; *in phrr.* ~ **blisse** B Pr 106, 14.154; ~ **dore** 16.168; ~ **gate(s)** 2.132, 7.248; **hey** ~ 18.98, **B** 2.33, 12.40, 16.118; **as in** ~ from the stand-point of ~ 18.88, 89; **while God is in** ~ for ever B 2.107; **to** ~**ward** toward heaven 16.53, B 10.333; **as to** ~ **ward** in respect of heaven B 15.457; ~ **and erthe** 20.232; ~ **and helle** 3.165, B 17.162; **helle or** ~ 14.193; **archangel of** ~ 1.107; **blisse of** ~ 7.135; **court of** ~ 3.455; **ducchesse of** ~ 2.33; **eyres of** ~ 5.59; **eritage in** ~ B 10.341, 350; **fader of** ~ 18.91, 227, 19.210, **B** 7.53, 16.213; **game of** ~ B 9.102; **God of** ~ 15.406; ~ **godhede of** ~ B 9.46; **Holy Goest of** ~ 19.121, 166; **(Iesu) Crist in / of** ~ B 11.184, 12.126, 16.222; **Kyng of** ~ 13.66, 17.262; **konnynge of** ~ B 12.66; **Oure Lord in / of** 12.161, **B** 17.164, 18.357; **loweste of** ~ 14.151; **messager of** ~ 17.178; **munstrals of** ~, **munstracie of** ~ 9.126, 16.310; **paleys of** ~ B 10.462; **paradys oþer** ~ 11.299; **prince of** ~ 17.248; **reume of** ~ 5.125; **Registre of** ~ B 5.271; **Oure Saueour of** ~ B 9.127; **Seintes in** ~ **B** 5.509, 10.425, **A** 3.223, 8.33; **sire of** ~ 20.302; **sonne of** ~ 18.72; **souereynes in** ~ 11.271; **thef in** ~ 14.150; **triacle of** ~ 1.148; **Trinite of** ~ 18.26; **way(es) to** ~ 1.199, 13.29, B 12.37; *in genitival phrr.* **þe Fader wille of** ~ the will of the heavenly Father 16.27; ~ **riche blisse** the blessedness of the kingdom of heaven Pr 29, 16.100, B 15.175; **the Kynges marke / sone of** ~ mark / son of the King of Heaven 17.77, 20.363; ~ **the Lordes / Cristes loue of** ~ the love of the Lord / Christ in heaven 8.16, 15.35, **B** 6.220, 13.143; **Mary loue of heuene** the love of Mary in heaven 2.2; *in other assevs.* **by deere God in** ~ B Pr 210; **by Marie of** ~ 4.139, 173, 11.189, B 3.201

heuegore (*comp.*)14.105; **heuegeste** (*sup.*) 6.242 *see* **heuy** *a*

heuy *a* heavy 1.148, B 4.22; *comp.* **heuegore** heavier 14.105; **heuegeste** heaviest 6.242; sorrowful, dejected 6.63, 11.188; ~ **chere** mournful face 4.160; ~ **chered** with a gloomy expression 22.2; ~ **nesse** *n* grief 20.256

hew *n* colour 13.176, 14.158

hewe *n* (*pl.* **hewes** 1.123, **hewen** 16.3, B 14.3) servant 3.307, 4.58, 102, 7.195, 8.195, 10.218

hewen *v* chop (wood) A 7.59; strike 19.211

hexte *sup.* B 12.144 *see* **hey(e)** *av*

hy[1] *pers. prn. 3 pl.* they 1.187, †3.321, 6.56, 9.63, 14.191, †19.138, 20.422, 22.261, †301, **A** 1.165, 2.25, 126, †185, 3.24, 74, †155, 4.25, 5.†95, 256, †6.52, 7.125, 131, 190, 192, 277, 8.73, 10.16, 213

hy[2] 17.247, 18.106, 139 = **hey(h)(e)** *a*

hidde(n) *p.t.* 20.447, B 11.351, 17.109 *see* **h(u)yden** *v*

hyd(d)er(e) *av* hither, to this place 15.238, 18.17, 20.321, 336, 346, 22.334 ~**ward(es)** in this direction 8.343, 20.341

hyden 22.124 = **h(u)yden** *v*

hye 1.169, 17.222, B 3.48 = **heye** *av*; 7.248, 14.48, 17.256, 262 = **hey(h)(e)** *a*

hyen *v* hurry 22.325, **B** 3.194, 5.378, (*refl.*) 8.206

hyere B 2.28 = **herrore** *comp.*; *see* **hey(h)e** *a*

hif Z 6.91 = **(ȝ)yf** *conj.*

highte *3 pr. sg.* B 16.15, 61, 188, 17.108, Z 6.21 = **hatte;** *p.t.* B 17.134 *etc,* **hiȝte** B Pr 102 *et p.,* A 1.17 *et p.,* **hyȝt(h)e** A 12.49, 53; *p.p.* B 18.79; **hihte** *p.t.* 3.9 *et p.,* *p.p.* 6.309, 7.298, 20.81, 21.332 *see* **hoten** *v*

hij B Pr 66, 1.191, 5.565, †20.261, †301, †380 = **hy** *pers. prn.*

hilen B 12.232 *see* **helen** *v*[2]

hil(le) B Pr 5 *etc,* Z Pr 99 = **hul(le)** *n*

hym, him *pers. prn. 3 sg. masc. as dir. obj.*: him Pr 70 *et p.*; *as ind. obj.*: to him 3.193, 4.15, 11.115, 13.90, 14.18, 125, 18.97; for him 9.3, 16.314, 318, B 13.248; from him 8.254, 258, 19.208; *after impers. vv.* Pr 187, 189, 2.241, 5.95, 9.87, 10.176, 16.68, 18.204, 19.144, 20.438 *etc,* **B** 8.34, 9.38, 16.201, 17.140; (*refl.*) himself 2.221, 6.390, 421, 7.62, †247, 8.194, 207, 9.5 (2), 90, 144, 237, 10.87, 11.257, 12.159, 13.89, 244, 246, 14.132, 153, 16.75, 111, 17.154, 284, 18.206, 20.39, 103, 21.102, 297, 440, 22.116, 123, 144, 22.167, **B** Pr 190, 1.29, 5.11, 89, 7.78, 9.97, 12.192, 13.291, 16.201, 17.82, 109; for himself 10.87, 21.338, 22.152, **B** 13.60, 18.14; to himself B 1.30; *semi-refl., dat. of interest, usu. not translated*: 2.116, 6.197, 7.72, 8.68, 149, 156, 166, 9.151, 10.218, 15.286, 19.79, 20.298, 22.289, **B** Pr 139, 10.90, 13.136; (*with v. of motion*) 6.350, 8.206, 343, 9.145, 11.64, 15.286, 18.118, 19.63, 22.175, 353; *in absolute constr.* ~ **wilnyng** while he desires B 13.280

hymsulue(n) (**himself** A 6.96, **himselue(n)** A 10.35, 1.44, **hymsylf** Z Pr 76, **hymsulf** 7.100, 13.77, 91, 15.236) *emph. pers. prn.*: himself, *appositive* 3.416 *et*

p., Z 1.7; (*refl.*) 8.117, 10.183, 13.208, B 3.310; *with prep.* 3.132, 4.43 *etc*; **by** ~ by itself, separately 6.227; on his own 10.241, 14.144; on its own, in itself 19.141; in himself B 13.283; **of** ~ of its own accord 17.49; (of) its own 20.159; in itself B 14.283; **with** ~ himself with 21.228; *as subj.* he himself Pr 68, 5.187, 7.112, 17.193, 240, 18.256, 20.302, 21.334, 450, **B** Pr 206, 9.118, 16.145, A 10.167; *as obj.* 10.133, 18.203

hynde Z 3.97 = **ende** *n*

hynde *n* hind, female deer 17.9

hyne *n* servant 6.262, **B** 6.131, 14.149, A Pr 39; (*fig.*) thing of little worth B 4.118

hippynge B 17.60 *see* **huppen** *v*

hire B 2.123, 3.72, 256, 6.139, 195, 14.128, 143, 149 = **huyre** *n*

hir(e)[1] *pers. prn. fem. obj.* **B** 1.58 *et p.,* A 2.24 *etc*; *see* **her(e)**[1]

hir(e)[2] *poss. prn. fem.* **B** 4.50, 9.56, 10.152, 12.46, 226, 14.266, 16.101, 17.320 (1,3), **hire** A 1.10 *et p.*; *see* **her(e)**[2]

hir(e)[3] *poss. prn. pl.* **B** Pr 28, 1.99 *et p.,* **hire** A 3.137, 252 *et p*; *see* **here**[3]

hireself A 3.133, **hirselue** B 3.148 *see* **heresulue** *emph. prn.*

his *poss. prn. masc. sg.* his Pr 70 *et p.,* (*with pl. n, infl. as a*) **hise** B 7.168 *et p.*; *as n* his people / dependants 19.251; his followers 21.220, 22.61; his possessions / wealth A 4.61

hit (**it**) *prn. neut. sg.* it Pr 11, 39, Z 1.79 *et p.*; *as subj. with pl. antecedent* 16.92, A 7.46, *as obj.* 9.57, 16.309, 18.11; *as subj. of pl. v with following pl. n.,* = there 15.288, = they 5.59, 8.52, 217, 9.118, 126, 194, 12.98, 15.309, Z 7.49, 263; = he 13.120, 19.271; *as anticipatory compl.* 15.237; *in ref. to understood subj.* 14.87, 165, *or obj.* 22.363, Z 7.58; *as grammatical obj. emphasising real obj.* [things] 4.177, [the consequences] 6.276; *or a foll. clause*: 3.147, 6.289, 7.4, 144, 8.212, 10.191, 12.100, 20.302, *or prec. clause*: 9.331, 13.239, 15.126, 16.280; *as subj. of imper. v.* 6.100, 7.50, 9.163, 19.34; *in pleonastic uses*: 14.58, 16.53, 131, 17.130, 18.80, 215, 20.147, 150, 337 (2), 21.476, 22.28, 54, 147, 275, B 10.441; *in phr.* **don** ~ **vppon** appeal to 1.82, 2.39

hitsilue *emph. refl. prn.* itself 1.149

hitten *v* (*contr. pr.* **hit** 20.383, *p.t.* **hit(te)** 6.377, 22.103) hit, strike 14.51, 22.103, 175, 190, B 5.162, A 7.166; knock 20.383; ~ **aftur** strike at 18.120, throw 6.377, ? B 16.87n; ~ **on** encounter 11.113

†**hywe** A 6.39 = **hewe** *n*

ho *prn* (*see also* **hoso, wham, who(m), whos**): *interrog. prn* who 3.66, 72, 6.419, 9.70, 10.72, 110, 11.149, 155, 217, 264, 274, 12.215, 13.198, 16.34, 314, 17.63, 18.130, 20.17, 26, 68, 212, 21.11, 58, 351, **B** 3.235, 7.129, 132, 10.245, 310, 422, 436, 11.360, 15.120, 325, 17.105; *rel. indef. prn* whoever, any(one) who 1.84

(**who**), 3.61, 7.277, 279, 11.16, 17.4, 19.153, 20.383, 21.58; *with understood conditional conj.* (if) 3.235, 14.10, 17.108, 254, 19.120, B 1.145, ~ **þat** B 19.257; those who B 15.485; *in phrr.* **as** ~ as if one B 9.36; as if to B 15.307; **maugre(y)** ~ in spite of any who, whoever may 8.68, 155; **~es** whose, of whom 1.46

hobelen *v* hobble, limp A 1.113

ho(e)d *n* hood 5.133, 6.202, 377, 380, 390, 13.47, Z 7.48; [distinctive] academic hood [of physicians] 8.291, 22.176 (*and see* **houe** *n*)

hoem 5.131 *etc* = **hom** *n*

hoen (on) *v* shout at B 10.61

hoend 19.112 *etc* = **hand** *n*

hoer 8.92, 18.183 = **hoor** *a*

hoerd *n* hoard, collection 18.116

hoes 1 46 *see* **ho** *prn*

hoet 20.211, 290 = **hot(e)** *a*

hoet *imper.* 20.287 *see* **houten** *v*

hogge *n* pig 11.8, B 6.181

hoke *n* crook (fixed part of hinge on which gate hangs) 7.241

hoken *v* bend like hook, *p.p.* hooked Pr 51, 10.94, Z 7.67; barbed 22.226

#**hokkerye** *n* retail trade 6.233

hold(e)[1] Z 7.48, 69, 8.86; = **old(e)** *a*

holde[2] *a* loyal 8.195, A 7.123

holden *v* 1.148 *etc*, A 10.114 = **halden** *v*

holdyng[1] *pr. p.* 8.103 *see* **halden** *v*

holdyng[2] *ger* grasping 12.246

hole *n* hole (in cask) 21.402; lair, den 22.44

hol(e) *a* entire, untorn B 6.59; whole, sincere 3.351, 7.257; full 20.419; **~ly** *av* together 19.29; completely 3.148, 9.231, 21.3

holy (haly) *a* (*of God*) holy 14.84, B 15.504; consecrated, hallowed (*of festivals, etc*) 1.123; (*of saints*) blessed 12.134, 173, B 3.235; pious, devout 6.40, 48, 9.187, 190, 201, 17.34, 185, 194, 18.116, 22.65, 252, **B** 12.23, 13.296, 15.429, 437; *in phrr*: ~ **bred** blessed bread 6.146, Z 8.75; ~ **chirche** the / a church 6.272, 354, 17.275, B 12.27; ~ **Chirche, Kirke** (*see below*); ~ **clergie** sacred learning, = scripture 16.238; ~ **comune** sacred community, society 5.186; ~ **day** holy day [church festival incl. Sundays] 1.123, 6.272, 7.18, 225, 9.24, 231, 13.85, B 13.415, A 7.12; ~ **eremytes** devout hermits 9.187; ~ **euene** eve of a holy day 13.85, A 7.12; ~ **fadres** (Desert) Fathers B 15.272; ~ **God** B 15.504; ~ **Go(o)st** the Holy Spirit 14.84 *et p.* (*see* **go(e)st**); ~ **hilles** (*fig.*) = heaven B 3.236; ~ **let(t)rure** holy scripture 11.26, 15.74; ~ **lore** (the) religious teaching (of the Church) 11.36; ~ **men** men of virtuous and pious life 17.34 *etc*; ~ **name** sacred name A 12.13; ~ **Scripture** 21.273; ~ **seintes** B 14.155, 15.269; ~ **water** blessed water (in church) Z 8.75; ~ **wordes** divine teaching B 15.449; ~ **writ** (*a*) sacred scripture, the Holy Bible Pr

104, 205, 1.69, 2.142, 3.486, 5.37, 8.86, 10.240, 248, 296, 11.31, 80, 209, 235, 253, 13.27, 15.78, 265, 17.4, 37, 190, 19.127, 247, 296, 300, 21.109, 329, **B** 1.130, 10.381, 395, 11.396, 13.132, 432, **A** 8.56, 12.97, Z 5.35; (*b*) authoritative (patristic) writings, Church tradition 1.125, 15.158, 16.240, 17.6, 19.288, 20.432, A 10.94; **lyf** ~ 9.195 *see* **lyf** *n*; **pop** ~ pope-holy, affectedly pious 6.37

Holy Chirche *n* the (institutional) Christian Church Pr 64, 87, 116, 118, 1.186, 2.140, 248, 3.163, 397, 5.191, 6.19, 119, 7.81, 8.78, 9.24, 104, 218, 219, 10.186, 198, 11.146, 221, 248, 253, 12.120, 156, 14.9, 21, 152, 16.35, 241, 243, 244, 250, 279, 296, 337, 17.5, 41, 50, 71, 124, 125, 167, 202, 230, 286, 18.74, 207, 209, 19.274, 21.224, 330, 336, 369, 383, 445, 22.75, 229, 245, 298, (*uninfl. gen.* Holy Church's 17.231, 21.475, **B** 10.252, 17.119) A 2.166, 12.17; (*person.*) 1.72, 12.53; **B** 6.242, 10.121, 232, 11.98, 159, 14.86, 15.244, 429, 486, 16.6; ~ **Kirke** Pr 138, 3.356, 5.179, 8.26, 53, 159, 9.9, 11.246, 250, 306, 13.89, 14.39, 17.77, 220, 276, 21.413, 470, †22.120 (Holy Church's 8.53, 13.89, 16.255), **B** 10.411, 12.82, 13.274, 15.136, 384, 545, Z 8.9

holynesse *n* (Christian) holiness (of life) 16.241, 18.5, 21.366, 377, 383, 404, 424, 22.145, 227, B 19.111; devotion, piety 4.113, 11.13, 18.159; virtue 2.81, 18.13, B 10.290; (*person.*) 12.1, 22.145; **lyf** ~ 5.80, 21.111 *see* **lyf** *n*

holiwrit A 10.94 *see* **holy** ~ *a*

holpe *p.t. subjv.* 20.441; **~(n)** *p.t. pl.* 8.113, 123, 9.6; *p.p.* 11.28, B 5.624, 7.70, 15.134, 16.124 *see* **helpen** *v*

holwe *a or av* hollow(ly) B 5.187

hom *n* dwelling 3.126, (*fig.*) B 9.56; *in phrr*: **at** ~ in (his) dwelling-place 9.5; present 10.28; **fro** ~ away from home 12.65; **~liche** *a* (making oneself) at home; **~ward** *av* homewards B 3.194

hom *av* (back) home 4.56, 5.131, 8.108, 207, 9.151, 21.332, A 7.33; *in phr*: **fer** ~ a long way to go home 21.483

homage *n* homage, **don** ~ acknowledge allegiance 14.98

hond 16.82, B 5.287, *etc*, A 3.55 *etc*; ~ **mayden** 18.132 *see* **hand** *n*

hondred 22.69 *see* **hundred** *num.*

honerably *av* reverently 14.98

honeste *a* virtuous 17.34; worthy, honourable 21.94

honeste(e) *n* virtue 16.241

hony *n* honey 16.217, 224

honouren *v* honour, show respect to 6.40, 7.213; respect 14.43, A 11.247; worship 5.105, 17.134, 153, 18.93, 19.39, B 15.605; show reverence for 17.206, 210, 282, 18.249, 20.267, B 15.446; venerate 14.93; celebrate 2.174; enrich 3.266, admire 14.179; bless 17.276; adorn 8.11

honten 9.223 = **hunten** *v*

hood 6.202 *etc* = **ho(ed)** *n*

hoolden 8.50, B 6.214 *see* **halden** *v*

hoom B 9.56 = **hom** *n*

hoor *a* hoary-headed, grey 6.193, 8.92; white (-haired) 9.175, 18.183, *a as n* 22.95, 202

ho(o)re *n* (*pl.* **hores** 16.259, **horen** 14.21) prostitute 3.300, 6.305, 14.21, 16.259, **B** 14.183, 15.85, 134; whore 4.161, 6.149; ~ **dom** *n* lechery 7.75, B 13.354

hoost B 20.113 = **oest** *n*

hoot B 18.206 = **hot(e)** *a*

hope *n* hope 3.135, 7.289, 9.142; expectation 1.100, 7.83, 22.180, **B** 3.200, 10.363; trust Pr 29; (the theological virtue of) hope in God 3.351, 14.214, B 12.30, A 5.242, (*person.*) (*a*) 7.151 (*b*) 19.61, 85, 100, **B** 17.53, 116, 118, 134; *in phr.* **gode** ~, **wel** ~ positive (attitude of) hope (in God) 7.113, 19.293, 22.167

hopen *v* hope 5.94, 14.194, 17.118, 146; trust 5.99, 12.200, B 15.479; think, believe 20.153, 21.385, *in phr.* **as I** ~ I believe 6.255, 8.103, 137, 9.273, 10.19, 16.21, 17.185, 18.1, B 10.153, Z 7.268; expect 8.314, 9.290, 14.11, 18.250, 254, 19.251

hoppen *v* leap, dance B 3.200

hopur *n* seed basket 8.60

hor Z 1.16 = **or²** *prep.*

hore 4.161 = **ho(o)re** *n*

hore 9.175, 22.95 = **hoor** *a*

horen *pl* 14.21 *see* **ho(o)re** *n*

horn *n* horn 5.16, (*fig.*) 7.151; horn-blast (*fig.*) 6.400

hors *n* (*pl.* **hors**) Z 4.124, *pl.* 2.176, 13.61, B 11.342; horses' 8.225; **on** ~**e** on horseback **B** 17.105, 18.83

hos(e)bande *n* husbandman, farmer 7.298 (*with pun*), 12.200, A 11.183; husband 10.270

hosbondrye *n* thrift 1.53

hosel *n* Holy Communion; ~ **en** *v* give Communion, **ben hoseled** receive Communion 21.3, 398, 478

hosewyf *n* wife 13.9, B 14.3

hoso (whoso) *indef. prn.* whoever, anyone who 1.57, 98, 3.406, 445, 494, 5.138, 6.380, 391, 8.120, 9.236, 321, 10.25, 78, 11.72, 226, 12.58, 156, 170, 212, 18.155, 19.5, 19, 120, 162, 167, 262, 20.383, 21.66, 278, 291, **B** Pr 144, 1.88, 3.283, 4.70, 5.54, 6.65, 67, 7.83, 10.211, 353, 13.376, 15.91, A 12.3; anyone (*with implied conditional conj.* if) Pr 205, 1.143, 4.128, 7.197, 204, 10.202, 16.368, 17.204, 254, 18.155, B 5.116, 275, **A** 5.97, 10.133; one **B** 6.1, 10.197, A 8.78; (some) one 3.362, 6.90, 405, 7.306, **as** ~ as if someone B 15.337; someone who 10.39

hostelen *v* provide lodging for (*fig.*) B 17.119

hostiele *n* lodging-house 13.63

hostiler *n* innkeeper 19.76, B 17.116; ostler, stableman 6.388, 390

hostrie *n* inn B 17.74

hot(e) *a* hot Pr 227, 5.7, 9.142, 15.144; peppery-hot 6.357, A 5.154; biting, burning 20.211

hoten *v* (*1 pr sg.* **hote**, 2.211, *p.t.* **hi(g)hte** 7.14, B 17.134, *p.p.* **yhote(n)** 8.78, 2.20, B 1.63, *passive pr. 1 sg.* **hatte** 3.496, **hote** 16.196, *2 sg.* **hattest** 22.340, *3 sg.* **hatte** 7.219, **hette** Z 7.44, **hoteth** 2.31, **hattiþ** A 6.60, **highte** B 16.15, **hyȝthe** A 12.53, *3 pl.* **hatte** 7.223, *p.t.* **he(e) t(e)** 18.249, 22.273, 349, **hi(g)hte** 7.14, **hyȝte** A 12.49, *p.p.* **hi(g)hte** 7.298, B 19.333) name, call 2.20, 7.298, 11.1, **B** 1.63, 10.150, Z 3.10, 174; be named, called 3.496, 7.219 *et p.*, 8.80, 10.134, 144, 11.170, 188, 308, 16.156, 196, 182, 184, 17.159, 18.9, 18, 183, 292, 20.81, 118, 122, 131, 239, 21.270, 277, 282, 326, 332, 22.340, **B** 6.44, 9.49, 10.163, 16.8, 61, 62, 188, 17.108, A 11.183; command, order 1.17, 2.211, 3.416, 4.3, 7.14, 246, 8.78, 89 (1), 9.219, 10.99, 13.44, 14.41, 18.249, 22.273, 349, **B** 5.545, 6.258, 8.94, 10.201, 364, A 12.74; bid 8.85, 89 (2), 272, 11.44, 67, 18.106, **B** 16.134, 17.134

hou Pr 130, 1.6, 12.106 *see* **how**[1,2]

hound *n* dog 6.412, 430, 8.225, **B** 5.257, 10.61, 11.342; (hunting) hound 5.160, **B** 4.125, 10.308; herdsman's (watch)dog 9.265, B 10.287

#houpen *v* shout out 8.168

houre *n* hour B 14.12; *pl.* (Divine Office for) the canonical hours **B** Pr 97, 1.183, 15.385

hous *n* (*pl.* **houses** 3.96 *et p.*, **hous** Z 6.64) house 3.96, 102, 126, 6.352, 7.52, 19.303, 21.167, B 10.95, A 12.53, (*fig.*) 7.236; shelter, lodging A 2.38; shed (for corn) A 6.32, (*fig.*) 21.320, 330; building B 14.253; (consecrated) place 18.159; religious community **B** 3.63, 5.264, 267; buildings (of a religious house) **B** 11.65, 15.422; family B 16.177; household (*fig.*) B 10.229, A 12.84; establishment 9.206, B 15.142; ~ **hyre** rent for housing 9.74; *in phrr:* **burgeis** ~ 14.91; **caytyfs** ~ 14.90; **Goddes** ~ the Church B 10.405; **hungry** ~ = establishment with little to eat 9.206, **(in)to** ~ indoors 2.229, 9.125

housen *v* house, *ger.* **housynge** building (houses) 16.234

houswif B 14.3 = **hosewyf** *n*

houten *v* shout at; ~ **out** shout out 20.287; *p.p.* **yhouted** 2.228; ~ **out** shout out 20.287

houe *n* lawyer's coif Pr 159 (B Pr 211, A Pr 84), 3.447; **glasene** ~ glass hood (= a delusive protection) 22.172

houen *v* hang suspended Z 3.146n; wait about in readiness Pr 159, 20.82

how[1] *interrog. av* how 1.80 *et p.*

how[2] *conjv. av* how 1.6, 125 *et p.*; the manner in which Pr 130, 11.71, B 10.137, A 6.82; that B 5.109; (as to) how 6.264, 19.236, 20.333, B 16.147; (saying) how / that 8.130, B 5.364; (to hear) how 11.77; ~ **euere** all the ways in which B 12.223; ~ **so, so euere**, ~ **... euere** in whatever way 12.6, 237, 18.120, 19.152, A 11.260; ~ **þat** how 11.139, 13.142, 15.9, 73, 16.232, 18.162, B 13.353, A 8.17; **Lo / loke** ~ see the way in which 12.248, 13.20, 14.130, 22.202

how[3] B 6.116 *see* **hey** *interj.*

hucche B 4.116 = **whicche** *n*

hudde(n) *p.t.* 13.163, 21.102 *see* **h(u)yden** *v*

huge *a* severe, grave 19.286; vehement 12.137

h(u)yden *v* (*p.t.* **hudde** 21.102, **hidde** B 17.109, *p.p.* **yhudde** B 10.430) hide 13.163, 21.460, **B** 10.430, 11.353; (*refl.*) 21.102, B 17.109; keep secretly 22.124; wrap round 19.127; state in a cryptic manner 10.245

h(u)yre *n* payment for service 3.301, 14.215, B 3.72; wages 3.307, 7.193, 195, 8.115, 9.273, 16.3, **B** 2.123, 3.256; rent 9.74; hire, **to** ~ for hire 2.175

h(u)yren *v* pay, *p.p.* 8.121, 335

hul(le), (hille) *n* hill 7.158, 10.232, Z Pr 94, 99; þe ~ Cornhill 12.220; **Maluerne Hulles** Pr 6, 163, 5.110, 9.295

Humylite A 6.109 = **Vmbletee** *n*

hundred *card. num.* hundred B 13.270; †**seuenty** ~ B 18.283; (*as indef. large number*) 7.164, 266, 12.176, 21.212, 22.218, **B** 15.374, 18.408, A 12.27, *pl.* 22.69; **enleuene** ~ 12.176, **foure** ~ 19.211, **seuene** ~ B 14.68, **ten** ~ 7.38, **þre** ~ B 13.270, **twenty** ~ B 16.10, ~ **fold** a hundred times over 12.160

hunger *n* (feelings of) hunger 6.437, 8.246, 272, 20.211, **B** 3.194, 15.281, A 11.46; lack of food 9.77, **B** 6.328, 15.271, Z 7.201; starvation 15.237, 261, (*person.*) 8.168 *et p.*, A 12.63, 74

***hungirly** *a* hungry-looking A 5.108*n* (*or* = **hungrily-(che)** *av*)

hungren *v* be hungry 8.225, (*impers.*) 15.253

hungry *a* hungry 6.412, B 18.395; (*as n*) hungry person(s) 8.192, B 5.374; meanly provided with food 9.206; greedy, avaricious 15.190, (*comp.*) **hungriore** 1.186; ~ **li(che)** *av* (*or a*) greedily 22.123, ?hungry-looking, emaciated(ly) 6.197

hunsen *v* abuse, insult A 11.48

hunten *v* hunt, ~ **to** hunt after 8.28, *ger.* hunting 3.465, (*fig.*) B 3.311

huppen *v* leap, gad (about) 17.279; *pr.p.* dashing, hurrying 19.61

hure A 12.41 = **her(e)**², A 12.48 = **her(e)**¹

hurten *v* injure B 10.364

husbond A 11.183 = **hos(e)bande** *n*

huserye Z 8.40 = **vsurye** *n*

hutten 14.51 = **hitten** *v*

huxterie A 5.141 = **hokkerye** *n*

Y, I (**Ich** *before vowels, emph.* A 9.65, Z 8.62, *dial.* **Ik** B 5.224n, **Yc** Z 3.35) 2.216, 8.2, 3, 11.311, 13.128, 14.138, 15.89, 218, 16.286, 343, 348, 20.330, 342, 22.190, **B** 5.258, 7.143, 11.75, 12.28, 13.226, 248, 369, 370, 379, 384, 15.24, 36, *pers. pr. 1 sg.* I Pr 2, 56 *et p.*

y Z 3.149, 5.110 = **yn** *prep.*

i-, y- *prefix marking p.p.* Pr 42, A 2.9 *et p., inf.*, 1.71, 4.187, 6.200, B 17.138, *av* 6.183, 10.116, 14.148, 21.442; *see under root-form entries*

y-armed *p.p.* 21.144 *see* **armen** *v*

ybake *p.p.* 8.333, **B** 6.182, 282, 15.432, 462 *see* **baken** *v*

ybaptised *p.p.* 19.88 *see* **baptisen** *v*

ybarred *p.p.* 21.167 *see* **barren** *v*

ybe *p.p.* 6.17, 7.54, 188, B 14.95 *see* **ben** *v*

ybedded *p.p.* 17.197 *see* **bedden** *v*

yberied *p.p.* 12.22 *see* **burien** *v*

ybete *p.p.* 4.89 *see* **beten** *v*¹

ybetered *p.p.* 5.21 *see* **beteren** *v*

yblamed *p.p.* 3.435, 439 *see* **blamen** *v*

yblessed (yblissed) *p.p.* Pr 76, 7.135, 8.260, 9.13, 11.248, 16.201, 21.179, 180, 388, 440, B 11.163, Z 7.238 *see* **blessed** *p.p.a and* **blessen** *v*

yblowen *p.p.* 19.179 *see* **blowen** *v*

ybore *p.p.* 2.144, 14.90, 20.136, 241, 243 *see* **beren** *v*

yborwed *p.p.* B 15.312 *see* **borwen** *v*

ybosted *p.p.* 19.61 *see* **bosten** *v*

ybotresed *p.p.* 7.235 *see* **botresen** *v*

ybought *p.p.* Pr 191, B 11.207 *see* **byggen** *v*

ybounde *p.p.* Pr 97, 193, 1.120, 7.161, 13.79, 19.54, 20.100, **B** 13.153, 18.95 *see* **bynden** *v*

ybrent *p.p.* 3.105 *see* **brennen** *v*

ybroke(n)(e) *p.p.* Pr 69, B 19.347 *see* **breken** *v*

ybrouhte *p.p.* 3.2 *see* **bryngen** *v*

ycald *p.p.* 9.213, 11.175, 14.14, 15.82, 16.181, 183, 190, A 4.140 *see* **callen** *v*

ycalled *a* wearing a cap 16.352

ycaryed *p.p.* Z 6.20 *see* **caryen** *v*

ycarped *p.p.* B 15.301 *see* **carpen** *v*

ychaffared *p.p.* 5.94 *see* **chaffaren** *v*

ychaunged *p.p.* 5.81 *see* **cha(u)ngen** *v*

***ycheuelen** *v* tremble 6.200; = **chyuelen** B 5.190

iche A 2.39, 7.135, 10.71, 207, 11.61, 250, **ichone** A 3.37, 249 *see* **vch** *a*, **vchon(e)** *prn*

ychose *p.p.* 6.379 *see* **chesen** *v*

yclansed *p.p.* 3.358 *see* **clansen** *v*

yclyketed *p.p.* 7.265 *see* **clyketen** *v*

yclosed *p.p.* 7.264, †10.172, 15.268 *see* **closen** *v*

yclothed *p.p.* 1.3, 2.9, 5.2, 17.196, 20.170, 174, B 13.273 *see* **clothen** *v*

yclouted *p.p.* B 6.59 *see* **clouten** *v*

ycome *p.p.* 3.455, 12.49, 18.127 *see* **comen** *v*

ycongeyed *p.p.* 16.367 *see* **conieyen** *v*

ycoped *p.p.* 3.38, 22.345 *see* **copen** *v*

ycouped *p.p.* 20.12 *see* **coupen** *v*

ycoupled *p.p.* B 9.126 *see* **couplen** *v*

ycrammed *p.p.* Pr 42 *see* **crammen** *v*

ycrimyled *p.p.* 16.352 *see* **crimylen** *v*

ycrouned *p.p.* 5.56, 59, 21.41 *see* **crounen** *v*

ycursed *p.p.* B 20.263 *see* **(a)corsen** *v*

ydampned *p.p.* 12.245 *see* **dampnen** *v*

ydel *n* vanity, **an** ~ in vain 7.217, B 13.402; to no purpose 14.7, 16.37, 21.405, 22.300

ydel(e) *a* worthless 7.19; sinful 2.95, B 14.13; idle, without work 5.27; *a as n* idle people B 13.226 (? *or n* **ydel**); ~ **nesse** *n* vanity 21.287; idle / worthless words 2.101; idleness, indolence 9.152, 15.215, 22.116, (*person.*) 21.229

ydyademed *p.p.* 3.440 *see* **dyademen** *v*

idyked *p.p.* A 6.33 *see* **dichen** *v*

ydyned *p.p.* 8.302 *see* **dynen** *v*

ydiot *n* ignoramus, simpleton B 16.170; #~**es** *pl. a* unlearned B 11.316

ydo(e)(ne) *p.p.* 2.128 *et p.*, 20.111, B 18.53, A 6.33; *see* **do(o)n** *v*

idoluen *p.p.* A 6.33 *see* **deluen** *v*

ydrawe *p.p.* 18.217, 229, 20.139 *see* **drawen** *v*

ydremed *p.p.* 21.1 *see* **dremen** *v*

ydronke *p.p.* 6.418, 8.302, 17.223, Z 7.245 *see* **drynken** *v*

ye (**eye** 6.2, **ei3e** B 10.125) *n* eye 6.2, 236, 406, 7.1, 8.172, 16.333, 18.49, 147, 19.305, 325, 20.50, 88, 238, 21.381, B 10.125; sight Pr 72, 14.44; ~ **syhte** eye-sight, (good) vision 9.102; *in phrr.* **blered here** ~**s** hoodwinked them Pr 72; **Coueytise of** ~**s** Lust of the Eyes 11.175, 193, 312, 12.3; **lokyng of an** ~ instant, twinkling of an eye A 12.96; **waitynges of** ~**s** watchings-out, observations 2.94

yentred *p.p.* 11.205 *see* **entren** *v*

yf, if[1] (**3if** 6.343 *et p.*, A Pr 37 *et p.*, B 9.77, **3ef** 7.259; **yif** B 5.424, †**yyf** Z 5.124) *conj.* if Pr 171 *et p.*; provided that 4.171, 7.147, 9.13; assuming that 2.129, 9.212; if only, supposing that Pr 38, 80, 12.55, 18.216; that 22.336; whether 2.169, 9.298, 10.4, 15.107, 16.164; (to learn) whether 22.311, B 2.136; *in phrr.* **þat** whether B 2.156; **but if** unless 1.176, 3.459, 5.161 *etc*, Z 4.130; **parauntur** ~ if perchance 7.296

yf[2] *3 pr. subjv.* Z 3.101, *imper.* Z 7.48, *p.p.* Z 5.108 *see* **3euen** *v*

yfalle(n) *p.p.* 7.112, 9.179, 182, 13.70, 20.106 *see* **fallen** *v*

yfed *p.p.* B 15.302 *see* **feden** *v*

yfere *av* together Z 5.63

yfet *p.p.* Z 7.165 *see* **fecchen** *v*

yfolde *p.p.* 19.115, 131 *see* **folden** *v*

yfolled *p.p.* 21.40 *see* **follen** *v*

yfolwed *p.p.* B 3.39 *see* **fol(e)wen** *v*

yfouhte *p.p.* 8.149, 18.137 *see* **fy(g)hten** *v*

yfo(u)nde(n) *p.p.* 3.41, 492, 16.285, 19.23, B 10.255, 15.230, Z 3.148 *see* **fynden** *v*

yfranchised *p.p.* 3.114 *see* **franchisen** *v*

yfried *p.p.* 8.333, B 13.63 *see* **frien** *v*

yfruyted *p.p.* B 16.39 *see* **fruyten** *v*

yftus Z 1.49 *etc*; *see* **3ift** *n*

ygadered *p.p. see* **gaderen** *v*

ygete *p.p.* 20.322 *see* **geten** *v*

ygyue *p.p.* 2.162 *see* **3euen** *v*

yglobbed *p.p.* 6.396 *see* **globben** *v*

yglosed *p.p.* 11.117, 19.13 *see* **glosen** *v*

ygon *v* pass, **longe ygo** a long time ago 20.296; **fern ago** in the distant past B 15.231

ygraced *p.p.* B 6.124 *see* **gracen** *v*

ygraunted *p.p.* 9.184, B 7.8, A 10.206 *see* **graunten** *v*

ygraue *p.p.* 4.127, 17.75, B 15.544, Z 2.72 *see* **grauen** *v*

ygreued *p.p.* 16.207 *see* **greuen** *v*

ygrounde *p.p.*, 15.49, 20.80, A 7.169 *see* **grynden** *v*

yhabited *p.p.* B 13.285 *see* **habiten** *v*

yhad *p.p.* 7.44 *see* **hauen** *v*

yhandlit *p.p.* A 2.99 *see* **hand(e)len** *v*

yhapsed (**yhasped** B 1.197) *p.p.* 1.191 *see* **hapsen** *v*

yhated *p.p.* B 9.100 *see* **hat(i)en** *v*

yheeled *p.p.* B 14.96 *see* **helen** *v*[1]

yheer *imper.* B 17.138 *see* **heren** *v*

yheled *p.p.* 7.236 see **hel(i)en** *v*[2]

yherd(e) *p.p.* 7.68, 16.51, B 10.103 *see* **heren** *v*

yheren *v* hear Z 2.86; hear (legal argument) 4.187

yhoked *p.p.* Z 7.67 *see* **hoken** *v*

yholde *p.p.* 1.80, 3.267, 5.157, 14.196, *see* **halden** *v*

yholpe *p.p.* 19.62 *see* **helpen** *v*

yhote *p.p.* 2.228, B 1.63, Z 3.10, 174 *see* **hoten** *v*

yhouted *p.p.* 2.228 *see* **houten** *v*

yhudde *p.p.* B 10.430 *see* **h(u)yden** *v*

yhuyred *p.p.* 8.335 *see* **h(u)yren** *v*

Ik (**Yk** Z) B 5.224 = **Ych** *pers. prn.*

ykald *p.p.* 9.249, 18.14 *see* **callen** *v*

ykeyed *p.p.* 7.265 *see* **keyen** *v*

ykept *p.p.* Z 6.20 *see* **kepen** *v*

ykyuered *p.p.* 21.86 *see* **keueren** *v*[1]

yknyt *p.p.* B 15.242 *see* **knytten** *v*

yknowen *v* recognise 4.71, 7.206, 12.123, 16.166, 20.23; admit Z 3.35; find out 13.223, B 11.405; *p.p. a* familiar 16.169, Z 2.70

ykud *p.p.* 12.198 *see* **kithen** *v*

ykuld *p.p.* Pr 199, 10.250

ylabored *p.p.* 8.255 *see* **labouren** *v*

ylasted *p.p.* B 3.192 *see* **lasten** *v*

ile *n* island, domain A 2.63

ylefte *p.p.* 17.162 *see* **leuen** *v*

yley(e) *p.p.* 11.260, **B** 5.81, 16.113 *see* **li(gg)en** *v*

yleyd *p.p.* 3.258 *see* **leggen** *v*

yleke Z 1.36 = **lyk** *av*

ylered *p.p.* 10.10, 11.127, *as a* B 13.214 *see* **leren** *v*

ylet[1] *p.p.* 3.204, 5.3 *see* **leten** *v*

ylet(te)[2] *p.p.* 13.36, 49, 21.385 *see* **letten** *v*

ylettred *a* educated 11.236

yleued *p.p.*[1] 16.248 *see* **leuen** *v*[3]

yleued *p.p.*[2] 16.286 (= **ylyued**) *see* **lyuen** *v*

ilych(e), ylyk(e) (to) *a* like, resembling 7.128, 10.68, 116, 13.192, 18.70, 20.3, **B** 1.91, 18.338

iliche, ylik(e) *av* likewise 15.34, B 1.50; alike, equally 14.148, 16.20, 18.22, 62, 21.442, B 13.350; as, equally with 10.133, 19.332

ylikned *p.p.* 16.264, 17.82 *see* **liknen** *v*

ylyued *p.p.* 11.256 *see* **lyuen** *v*

ilke *a* very, same 7.244, 10.142, 18.265, **B** 6.162,

9.189, 17.112; *prn* same (thing) 1.79; very person
16.312

ille *n* evil 20.318; wrong Pr 109, 1.49, 20.432, **B** 5.113,
10.26, A 9.93; sin 1.61; harm 1.85, A 10.68

ille *a* wicked 10.94, 16.191, 20.301

ille *av* wickedly 6.324, 20.429, B 2.195; badly Pr 225,
8.211

ylore *p.p.* 6.193, 12.185, **ylorn** B 18.313 *see* **lesen** *v*

ylost *p.p.* Pr 195, 12.96, 20.268, 349, 21.412 *see* **losen** *v²*

ylow *p.p.* 2.20 *see* **lyen** *v*

ima(e)d(e) *p.p.* 5.77, 6.250, 295, 7.139, 11.205, 16.19,
A 2.26, **ymaked** 2.73, 8.289, 10.87, B Pr 14 *etc*; *see*
maken *v*

ymage *n* image, representation B 1.50; likeness 20.326,
A 10.35

Ymagenatyf *n* the imaginative faculty of the mind, *person.* 14.1, 202, 15.17

ymagenyen *v* think ahead 21.278; brood over B 13.289;
form a plan B 13.358

ymaginacioun *n* forethought 22.33

ymaymed *p.p.* 5.34, 9.216, B 17.190 *see* **maymen** *v*

ymaked 2.73 *etc*; *see* **ima(e)d(e)** *p.p.*

ymanered *p.p. as a* 10.263 *see* **maneren** *v*

ymaried *p.p.* 2.41, 46 *see* **marien** *v*

ymartired *p.p.* B 15.522 *see* **martiren** *v*

ymedled *p.p.* 10.130 *see* **medlen** *v*

ymorthred *p.p.* 12.244 *see* **mortheren** *v*

impe, ympe *n* scion, graft B 5.136; sapling 18.6; **~n** *v*
graft B 9.149, (*fig.*) B 5.137

impugnen *v* call in (question the validity of sth.) 9.301,
15.132, **B** 11.304, 13.124; find fault (with) Pr 136

yn *n* dwelling, **at ynne** at home, living 10.4

in (**yn** 5.44, 11.44, 13.70, **ynne** 1.133 *etc*) *prep.* in Pr 3,
1.133 *et p.*; inside 1.184, 12.219, 21.346; within 18.164,
20.254, 271, 21.82; on 1.112, 123, 2.172, 3.491, 6.284,
285, 9.75, 10.24, 11.202, 231, 12.151, 15.186, 16.234,
322, 17.207, 18.64, 19.48, 194, 21.356, **B** 12.48, 15.76,
328, 16.160; at 2.153, 8.284, 10.123, 11.71, 232,
17.120, **B** 6.66, 9.121, A 10.202; at the time (of) 7.85,
110, 9.38, 14.58, 17.124, 144, 20.79; to Pr 27, 8.198,
13.8, 84, 15.189, 16.360, 17.173, B 10.255 (1); toward
Z Pr 14; in a state of 21.249; amongst 11.59, 16.47;
into 2.102, 3.201, 6.337, 7.4, 113, 8.163, 9.253, 10.33,
11.167, 12.52, 65, 13.70, 14.104, 17.181, 19.292,
20.420, 21.289, 305, 420, 22.10, 176, **B** 5.279, 7.79,
10.278, 15.396, 18.103, **A** 3.144, 5.74, Z 4.35; within
(the course of) Pr 63, 5.50, 6.398, 7.29, 12.219, 17.23,
36, 237, 20.41, 21.273, 357, 22.284, B 1.101, **A** 12.58,
66; during 1.25, 101, 6.183, 19.185, **B** 10.122, 14.24;
under, subject to 14.9, 31, 17.295, B 7.62 (2), A 10.51,
146, Z 7.77; in (with) respect of / to 6.30, 13.144, 188,
16.102, 21.8, **B** 7.149, 15.497; according to B 11.397;
of 20.108, B 17.181, A 2.66; against 9.16, 19.162; by
22.254, **B** 10.288, 15.304; by means of, through 3.159,

6.177, 7.190, 14.207, 20.110, 326, 382, 418, 21.433, A
9.28, Z 6.101; with 1.58, 14.211, 19.66, 204, 20.469,
21.181, 22.116, 144, **B** 9.125, 13.21, 15.174, 521, Z
2.14; as (a / an) Pr 86, 2.109, 4.149, 5.119, 13.200,
16.325, 17.264, B 10.294; *in phrr.* ~ **amendement /
confort / deseyte / helpe / sauacioun of** to amend /
support / deceive / give strength for / save Pr 3, 3.122,
5.75, 21.391, 5.198, 17.274; ~ **his bileue** in belief in him
18.255; ~ **couenant (foreward)** on condition 6.389,
8.26, 21.187, A 2.50; ~ **hope to** in the hope of (getting)
Pr 29, B 10.363; ~ **lenghe and ~ brede** in every direction 2.93; ~ **menynge (signe, tokenynge) of / þat** as a
sign / signifying that Pr 99, 5.121, 15.245, 17.33, 18.93,
20.139, B 10.143; ~ **point** ready B 13.111; ~ **my power**
as far as I'm able 4.137; ~ **werke (dede)** actually 4.143,
B 7.158, A 4.108; ~ **wete and in drye (chele and in
hete, somur or ~ wynter)** at all times 7.175, 8.249,
16.146; ~ **wille** willing, desirous **B** 10. 168, 11. 278,
12.194, A 12.21; ~ **witnesse of** as a witness to 2.109,
9.285; ~ **þat** in as much as 13.93, 15.117; ~ **as moche
as** as far as 19.203, B 7.15; **as ~** with regard to, in the
case / matter of 2.94, 6.176, 11.265, 12.81, 13.155,
17.149, **B** 10.259, 13.278, 14.157, from the standpoint
of 18.88, 89, 20.25, (as it were) in 19.164

in (**yn(ne)**) *av* (*with phrasal vv.*) within, inside 6.231,
360, 7.252, 11.44, 12.50, 20.286, 21.320, 22.345

incurable *a* beyond cure 5.177; irrevocable 15.16

#**indepartable** *a* indivisible 18.27

indirect *a* not direct (*grammar*); **relacioun =** ~ syntactic
relationship between words not indicated by inflexional
agreement 3.333, 341, (*fig.*) 3.362, 370, 382; **relatif** ~
relative (pronoun *etc*) not agreeing with its antecedent
3.387

#**indulgence** *n* divine mercy / forgiveness for sin granted
to the penitent 9.52; formal remission of punishment
for sin [obtained by penitential act] 9.319, 344, 19.220,
22.322

ynempned *p.p.* B 9.54, 16.203, A 10.43 *see* **nem(p)nen** *v*

infinite *n* (*? or a as n*) unlimited (thing) B 13.128, 129

ingang (ingong B) *n* entry 7.281

inhabiten *v* dwell 9.188

inliche *av* deeply, earnestly 3.370; inwardly B 14.89

†**inmiddes** *prep.* in the middle of B 5.284; in between
1.155 (B 1.160)n; *and see* **amydde(s)** *prep.*

ynne 1.133, 184, 12.219, 17.198, 21.420, 22.193 = **in**
prep., 22.345 = **in** *av*

ynne *n* 10.4 *see* **yn** *n*

innocence *n* innocence, = (people of) guileless simplicity
3.98, 19.270

innocent *a* unoffending, guiltless 9.47, *a as n* **B** 3.242,
7.41

inobedient *a* disobedient 6.19; ~ **to ben** resentful at being
B 13.282

ynoʒ B 14.33, 15.315, 317 = **ynow** *n*

ynome *p.p.* 22.46, B 11.212 *see* **nymen** *v*

ynow (yno(u)ʒ B) *n* enough 20.225, **B** 7.84 (1), 15.317; ~(e) *a* plenty of 2.157, 160, 11.179, 19.220, 20.292, **B** 2.163, 12.17; enough 2.35, 9.43, 10.183, 14.138, 15.239, 18.257, 22.249, **B** 7.84 (2), 9.178, 13.262, 15.315; *in phrr.* **moore þan** ~ B 12.198; **tyme** ~ soon enough B 11.36; ~ **þat** enough for one who A 7.137; **þat** ~ that in abundance / sufficiency B 14.33

inpacient *a* incapable of bearing suffering 6.110, 19.321

inparfit *a* morally faulty, sinful 3.385, 6.119, 11.208, 16.210, 245, 276, 17.229, 19.105, 21.431, 22.229; imperfectly formed (*fig.*) 18.103; defective, wanting in virtue 15.137

inparfitly *av* imperfectly B 10.465

inposible *a* impossible 20.465, B 10.335

inpugnen *see* **impugnen** *v*

#insolible *n* insoluble (logical) problem, logical paradox 16.229

intestate *a* without making a will B 15.138

intil *prep.* into B 13.211

into *prep.* into Pr 2 *et p.*; onto 14.85, B 3.303; (down) onto 20.249; to 7.206, 8.207, 11.18, 21.79, 147, B 1.205; toward B Pr 13; *in phrr:* ~ **þe bodyward** into the body A 7.167; ~ **pursward** for the making of money Pr 101

inwit *n* mind, understanding [esp. the moral reason] 6.420, (*person.*) 10.144, 174 *et p.*, 184, B 9.59, 60, 71, A 10.47, 56, 60; *in phrr.* **to / bi myn** ~ to my mind 9.117, 19.262, **þurgh** ~ through reflection A 12.99; **in** ~ in sound mind 5.10; will, soul 17.269; the inner faculties 18.180, B 13.289

ypay(e)d *p.p.* 3.305, 389, 22.309 B 19.393 *see* **paien** *v*

yparayled *p.p.* 7.160 *see* **(ap)paraillen** *v*

yparroked(e) *p.p.* 6.144, 17.13 *see* **parroken** *v*

ypassed *p.p.*Pr 203, 15.154, 16.369, 20.136, B 13.265 *see* **passen** *v*

ypersed *p.p.* B 17.190 *see* **persen** *v*

yplyht *p.p.* 6.208 *see* **pli(g)hten** *v*

ypocrisye *n* religious hypocrisy [pretence of virtue] 16.262, 263, (*person.*) 22.301 *et p.*

ypolsched B 15.111, Z 6.80 = **polishid** *p.p.*; *see* **poleschen** *v*

ypot *p.p.* 16.125 *see* **potten** *v*

ypresed *p.p.* 10.311, 12.197 *see* **pre(i)sen** *v*

ypreued *p.p.* 11.159 *see* **preuen** *v*

ypriked *p.p.* 22.86 *see* **priken** *v*

ypurchased *p.p.* 5.77, 158 *see* **purchacen** *v*

yquited *p.p.* 8.107 *see* **quyten** *v*

yrad *p.p.* 11.276 *see* **reden** *v*

yraueschid *p.p.* 11.294 *see* **raueschen** *v*

yraunsomed *p.p.* 11.261, 19.285 *see* **raunsomen** *v*

ire *n* anger 2.88, 11.110, 20.435, (*person.*) Z 5.91

yre(n) *n* iron 21.57; iron bands Pr 97, 16.87; ~s shackle(s), iron chain(s) 4.81, 8.143

yrented *p.p.* 10.268 *see* **renten** *v*

yreuestede *p.p. see* **reuesten** *v*

yrynged *p.p.* 2.12 *see* **ringen** *v*

yrobbed *p.p.* 9.180, 12.154, 21.447 *see* **robben** *v*

yrobed *p.p.* 10.1, 11.19, Z 2.17 *see* **roben** *v*

yron 4.81 = **yre(n)** *n*

yr(u)yfled *p.p.* 19.92 *see* **ruyflen** *v*

yruled *p.p.* 21.399 *see* **reulen** *v*

is, ys *3 sg. pr.* Pr 40 *et p.*, 1.145 *et p.*; *see* **be(n)** *v*

ys Z Pr 78 *etc* = **his** *poss. prn.*

ysaide *p.p.* 15.24 *see* **seyen** *v*

ysaye 18.140 = **ysey(e)n** *p.p.*

ysaued*p.p.*7.235, 10.235, 11.241, 244, 255, 258, 296, 12.84, 14.77, 101, 201, 18.152, 19.32, 86, 21.409 *see* **sauen** *v*

yschape *p.p.* 15.301 *see* **shapen** *v*

ysey *p.t.* 12.85 *see* **ysen** *v*

yseide *p.p.* 15.125 *see* **seyen** *v*

ysey(e)(n) *p.p.* 16.343, 348, 18.240, 19.283, B 5.4 *see* **ysen** *v*

iseised *p.p.* B 18.283 *see* **sesen** *v²*

isekel *n* icicle 19.194

ysen *v* (*p.t.* **ysey** 2.67, 12.85, *p.p.* **ysey(ʒ)e(n)** 16.348 *etc*) *see* 18.240, B 5.4, Z 4.75, 6.92; observe 14.103, 16.343, 348, 19.283; discover 2.67; witness B 16.216; look at 19.6; find (in books) B 14.155; take cognisance of 12.85; see to it Z 7.198; *and see* **sen** *v*

ysent(e) *p.p.* Pr 77, 7.126, 20.172, A 10.100 *see* **senden** *v*

yserued *p.p.* 3.309, 6.390, 7.189, 14.144, 21.439, B 5.413 *see* **seruen** *v*

yset *p.p.* Pr 97, 7.52, B 15.224, A 10.22 *see* **setten** *v*

yshaue *p.p.* 6.201, 16.352 *see* **shauen** *v*

ysherewen B 13.331 = **shrewen** *v*

ysheued, yshewed *p.p.* A 12.34, B 2.135 *see* **shewen** *v*

yshryue *p.p.* B 5.90 *see* **shryuen** *v*

ysyne(g)ed *p.p.* 10.216, A 8.163 *see* **synegen** *v*

yslepe *p.p.* A 5.4 *see* **slepen** *v*

ysoden *p.p.* B 15.432 *see* **sethen** *v*

ysoffred *p.p.* 3.449, 13.114, 20.216 *see* **soffren** *v*

ysoiled *p.p.* B 13.458 *see* **soilen** *v*

ysouʒt, ysougwth *p.p.* B Pr 50, Z 6.3 *see* **sechen** *v*

ysowed, ysowen *p.p.* 8.3, B 5.543 *see* **sowen** *v*

yspended, yspened *p.p.* B 14.102, 16.278 *see* **spenen** *v*

yspilde, yspilt *p.p.* 7.48, **B** 5.374, 436 *see* **spillen** *v*

yspoused *p.p.* B 9.126 *see* **spousen** *v*

yspronge *p.p.* 10.263, B 16.209 *see* **spryngen** *v*

issue *n* progeny, offspring 10.246, 12.115, 18.206 (*fig.*), 220, 235, 246, 256, 258, 20.196, 303, **B** 9.125, 16.206, 18.345; (*fig.*) = successors in office B 10.325

it Pr 34 *et p.*, **yt** Z 2.162 *et p.*, B Pr 10 *et p.*, A Pr 10 *et p.*, Z 3.176, 6.57 = **hit** *prn*

ytayled *p.p.* 7.35 *see* **taylen** *v*

ytake *p.p.* 9.92, 12.150, 16.326 *see* **taken** *v*

ytauhte, ytauʒt *p.p.* 8.20, 300, 22.186, A 11.172 *see* **techen** *v* yteynted *p.p.* B 15.454 *see* **teynten** *v*

ytempted *p.p.* 21.64 *see* **tempten** *v*

ythryuen *v* prosper Pr 34; *and see* **þryuen** *v*

ytilied *p.p.* B 15.107 *see* **tylien** *v*

ytynt *p.p.* 5.93 *see* **tynen** *v*

ytolde *p.p.* 3.132, 7.202 *see* **tellen** *v*

ytouked *p.p.* B 15.454 *see* **touken** *v*

yuel(e) 9.290, 10.302, **B** 7.41 *et p.*; *see* **euel(e)** *n, a*

yvsed *p.p.* B 16.148 *see* **vsen** *v*

yvenkused 20.104 *p.p. see* **venkusen** *v*

ywa(e)r *a* aware 10.115, 11.83; careful 1.40, 2.151, 9.51, 19.226, 20.354; warned 7.80, 11.63; on guard (against) A 10.85, Z 6.94

ywaged *p.p.* 22.261 *see* **wagen** *v*

ywalked *p.p.* 7.175 *see* **walken** *v*

ywasche *p.p.* 9.268, 10.228, B 13.315 *see* **waschen** *v*

ywedded *p.p.* 2.44, 5.64, 12.136 *see* **wedden** *v*

yweten (ywiten) *v* know Pr 181, 3.76, 18.275, 20.215, 219; learn 10.125; *and see* **witen** *v*[1]

ywhitlymed *p.p.a* lime-washed 16.266

ywis *av* certainly 13.220

ywitted *a*, wel ~ provided with good sense 11.236

ywoned *p.p.* 17.89 *see* **won(y)en** *v*

ywonne *p.p.* 3.247, 6.258, 12.111, 237, 19.245, 20.396, B 5.92 *see* **wynnen** *v*

yworded *p.p.* 15.150 *see* **worden** *v*

yworthen *v* be (left alone) Pr 201, 8.86, 10.164, B 6.225

ywounded *p.p.* 19.82, 22.306, 358 *see* **wounden** *v*

ywounden *p.p.* B 5.518 *see* **wynden** *v*

ywrye *p.p.* 16.74 *see* **wryen** *v*

ywrite(n) *p.p.* 1.194, 9.285, 17.84, B 10.412 *see* **writen** *v*

ywrithe *p.p.* 7.162 *see* **writhen** *v*

ywrouht(e), ywroȝt *p.p.* 1.131, 8.336, **B** 3.239, 4.68, 9.114, 117 *see* **worchen** *v*

yȝoten *p.p.* 1.149 *see* **ȝeten** *v*

*iacen *v* hurry 19.52

iang(e)len *v* chatter idly 2.99, *ger.* spiteful gossip 6.133; grumble B 6.313; dispute, argue 9.292, 10.119, (~ to) ~ with 15.93, **B** Pr 130, 4.155, *ger.* 180; *ger.* 10.273, 21.400; object B 16.119; protest B 16.144; cry out *pr.p.* B 9.82

iangelere *n* teller of (ribald) tales **B** Pr 35, 10.31

iangle *n* disputing 4.174

iape *n* trifle 22.145

iapen *v* deceive B 1.67; ~ mock (at) 20.40; tell jokes 2.99, 15.208, B 13.353

iapare, iaper *n* trickster 17.308; scoffer B 15.237; professional jester **B** Pr 35, 9.91, 10.31

ielosye *n* jealousy 10.273

ientel 21.40, A 1.159 = **gentel** *a*

ieroures Z Pr 70 *see* **iurour** *n*

Iesu(s) Jesus, *in oaths* **by** ~ Pr 180, 3.192, 20.462, 21.400, Z 5.130

Iew *n* (*gen. pl.* **Iewen(e)**) Jew [person of Jewish race / religion] 3.454, 479, 4.194, 6.241, 12.56, 14.200, 17.156, 252, 295, 315, 21.425, **B** 9.82, 85, 10.346, 13.210, 15.583; (Palestinian) Jew(s) [of the Old or New Testament, esp. their leaders] 1.63, 14.40, 17.304, 18.150 *et p.*, 20.15, 37, 40, 95, 113, 266, 21.10 *et p.*, 108, 139 *et p.*, **B** 10.35, 11.246, 12.42, 73, 78, 91, 15.264, 594, 16.127, 18.301; **Iewene** of the Jews 1.63, 20.266, (*as a*) Jewish 20.40, 21.108, **B** 15.583, 18.41)

iewel *n* jewel, treasure 3.192, 20.474, (*fig.*) †B 11.184

i(e)wyse *n* judicial sentence, (death) penalty 20.424n

#iogelen *v* entertain [with jesting, conjuring *etc*] 15.208

iogelour *n* jester, clown 8.71, B 10.31; illusionist 17.308

ioggen (iuggen B) *v* hurry, dash off 22.134

ioy(e) *n* happiness 13.14, 19, 15.299, 301, **B** 2.157, 12.42; pleasure 6.255, 15.295; satisfaction 20.266; joy 9.41, 18.16, 20.15; (spiritual) joy / happiness (*esp.* of heaven) 3.339, 9.50, 325, 10.22, 13.24, 14.78, 15.72, 291, 16.17, 56, 17.145, 20.183, 233, 345, 21.25, 66, 198, 22.40, 47, **B** 7.36, 11.167, 184, 14.285, 16.207; rejoicing 3.14, B 3.103, (cause of) rejoicing B 16.163; *in phr*: **bely** ~ pleasure(s) of eating B 7.119; ~**les** *a* joyless, unhappy 10.273

ioynen *v* hitch (*fig.*) 21.266; join (in marriage) 2.66

ioynte *n* joint (of leg), **out of** ~ dislocated 9.215; finger 19.143

ioyntly *av* together (in marriage) B 2.157

iolyf *a* joyful, happy 13.19

ionette *n* early ripening tree 12.223; *see* **pere** ~

*iot A 11.311 = **iut(te)** *n*

iouken *v* rest 18.126

iourne *n* (day's) stint of work 16.5

ioustare *n* jouster 21.10

iousten *v* joust (*fig.*) 18.129, 19.52, 20.17, 21, 26, 84, 183, 22.134, B 16.163;

ioustes *n pl.* jousting [single combats of mounted knights] (*fig.*) 20.14, B 17.52, 75

ioute *n* broth (*fig.*) 6.133

†iuele *n* B 11.184 = **iewel** *n*

iuge *n* judge 9.335, [of Christ] 15.291

iugement *n* judgement, **of** ~ **armes** trial by combat 18.129

iug(g)en *v* try in a court of law 16.123, Z Pr 70; pass (moral) judgement on 2.99; decide (concerning sth.) 2.169, 22.29, B 16.119; adjudge, assign B 2.137, 157; deem B 9.85; form the opinion, judge (that) 1.180, 17.132; express the opinion (that) B Pr 130; interpret 9.310; rule, act a final judge (over) 21.477

iu(y)ste *n* vessel with long neck and large bottom, *in phr.* ~ **womb** bottle-belly 15.93

#iurdan *n* chamber pot (*with pun on name* Jordan) 15.93n

iurour *n* juror [sworn witness in court of law] 2.150, B 7.44, Z Pr 70

iusten B 16.163; **iustes** B 17.52, 75 *see* **iousten** *v*, **ioustes** *n pl.*

iustice *n* judge, justice 2.49, (= Chief Justice) 150, 3.14, 192, 473, 16.123, 22.134, B 7.44, Z Pr 70, (*fig.*) 8.351; (= God) 18.126, (= the Roman procurator), 162, 178, 20.37; *in phrr*: **chef** ~ presiding judge (at Courts of Common Pleas or King's Bench) 13.116; **kynges** ~ presiding itinerant judge 4.186, 8.338, 19.284; ruler 9.314

iustifien *v* judge matters (for sb.) 21.44; ?govern, ?vindicate B Pr 130*n*

***iut(te)** *n* person of little consequence, nobody B 10.461

#**iuventee** *n* (time of) youth 21.108

kaes 3.432 = **caes** *n*

kaye 7.166 = **keye** *n*

#**kaylewey** *n* dessert pear B 16.69n

kayren 6.350 = **cayren** *v*

kayser 3.322, B 9.111 = **cayser** *n*

kaytif 6.206, *pl.* **kaytyues** Z 7.261 *see* **caytif** *n*

kalculen *v* learn by calculations 17.106

kald *p.p.* 3.401; **kalde** *p.t.* 4.17; *see* **callen** *v*

kalender *n* the ecclesiastical year B 13.154

kalketrappe *n* caltrop [spiked iron ball placed on ground to impede enemy] 20.294

kam *p.t.* 2.202, 22.327 = **cam**; *see* **comen** *v*

kan Pr 205, B Pr 111 *et p.* = **can**; **kannen** Z 7.261 = **konnen**; **kanst** 2.47 = **canst**; *see* **connen** *v*

kattes Pr 193 *see* **cat** *n*

kauȝte *p.t.* B 13.405 = **cauhte**; *see* **cacchen** *v*

***kaurymaury** *n* rough cloth B 5.78

keye (kaye) *n* key 7.166, 251, 14.54, **B** 10.322, 15.247

keyen *v* lock with a key, *p.p.* **ykeyed** 7.265

#**kelen** *v* keel [cool liquid by stirring and skimming to prevent boiling] 21.281

kemben *v* comb [disentangle threads from] 9.80, 11.15

ken *imper.* A 12.53; **kende** *p.t.* 18.17, 21.235, A 11.135; **kenet** *3 pr. sg.* 1.140; *see* **kennen** *v*

kene *a* bold 22.129, 141; fierce 16.81, 22.375, B 18.415; sharp 2.29, 6.140, 20.47, 80, B 9.182, (*fig.*) 10.289; bitter, acrimonious 6.65; painful 18.173, 22.97; strong 20.435, B 13.348; earnest B 12.251

kenis A 10.2, 26, 27, **kenne** A 12.110, = **ky(n)ne(s)**; *see* **kyn** *n*

kennen *v* make known 1.88, †B 11.439; teach, instruct 1.136, 140, 2.4, 3.276, 4.41, 7.91, 11.91, 21.9, B 6.14, 23, 7.71, 10.112, 198, 337, 14.16, A 11.135, 222, *ger.* teaching B 10.†190, 196; explain 9.281, **B** 5.420, 14.277; direct 7.183, 11.93; guide B 17.114; come to know, learn 11.140, 21.241

kepar(e) *n* guardian 16.273; protector 21.446, 22.72; governor B 12.126; (~ **of bestes**) herdsman 14.88, B 15.460

kepe *n* heed, attention, notice 13.145, 165, 170, 15.177, B 13.272, A 10.97; care, concern 19.76, 22.359

kep(i)en *v* (*p.t.* **kept(e)** 3.411; *p.p.* **(y)kept** Z 6.20, A 10.50, **kepide** A 6.32; *ger.* **kepynge** 21.356) want B 4.193, A 1.8; wish, care (to) 3.432, 13.233; hold Pr 128, 1.42, 12.216, 14.54; ~ **wiþouten** prevent from entering B 5.614; restrain B 10.165; possess 12.238, 243, B 10.359; keep 8.274, **B** 1.195, 15.247; preserve 5.129, 8.100, 145, 11.306, 19.258, **B** 14.11, 15.580, A 10.158; guard 10.137, 143, 21.144, 149, 22.257; defend 22.377, B 7.9; protect Pr 148, 2.47, 8.26, 157, 18.28, 21.144, †B 8.100, Z 7.65, 200; take care of, look after 1.51, 3.264, 411, 4.135, 5.17, 10.150, 19.7, 21.426, 22.92, **B** 15.346, 17.75, A 6.32, 7.181, Z 2.189; (keep) watch over **B** 10.471, 474, 19.282; administer 2.21, 3.78, 12.91, 16.337, **B** 5.52, 15.465; govern 3.441, A 8.149; obey, observe 11.142(1); abide by 1.90, 7.73, 9.340, Z 8.74; *ger.* behaviour 21.356

kerke 8.26 = **kirke** *n*

kernel[1] †B 5.588, **kirnel** A 6.75 = **carnel** *n*

kernel[2] B 11.260, 264 = **cornel** *n*

kernen *v* form grains 12.182

kerse B 10.17 = **carse** *n*

keruen *v* (*p.t. pl.* **coruen** 8.185) cut 8.185, Z 3.153; cut (furrows in) soil 8.65; *ger.* **keruynge** carving B 17.171

keruer *n* carver, sculptor 11.125

kete *a* distinguished A 11.56, 308

keueren *v*[1] cover 9.249, B 14.331; build / repair roof 3.64; protect 21.297; hide 9.138; conceal by disguise 21.349; mystically represent 21.86

keueren *v*[2] recover 22.336; deliver 14.118

kychene *n* kitchen 6.130, B 5.257

kidde *p.t.* B 5.434 *see* **kithen** *v*

kyen *n. pl.* cows ('kine') B 6.140 *and see* **cow** *n*[1]

#**kyken** *v* kick 4.22

killen (*p.t.* **killed** B 3.187, **kilde** 20.99, A 3.251; *pl.* **killeden** 19.142; *p.p.* **kild** B 5.163) = **cullen** *v*

kyn *n* kindred, family 1.188, 2.42, 57, 3.260, 5.66, 77, 6.58, 10.261, 13.112, 14.182, 16.166, 17.62, 196, 20.265, 441, **B** 12.93, 13.379; race A 10.156; kinsman, relative 7.282, B 11.190; parentage, stock 9.201, 10.261, B 2.131; kind, sort 3.279, 363, 5.183, 20.288; **kyn(n)e** kind(s) of 3.458, 8.69, 10.15, 11.124 *et p.*, **B** 2.201, 8.15 *et p.*, **(s)kenne(s)**, **skynes** A 2.162, 8.34, 10.2, 26, 27, 84, 12.110

kynde *n* (essential) nature 3.401, 18.57, 19.254, 20.188, 230, 417, 435, B 15.14; natural disposition Pr 147, 9.168, 13.212, 19.313; character 21.403; physical nature 6.429, 10.47, 12.149, 20.219, B 15.14; natural power / force 15.243, 19.214, B 14.44; natural form 13.178, 18.21; way, manner 20.11, B 12.228; natural instinct(s) 6.193, 17.161, 18.78; instinctive behaviour 17.164; the innate moral sense 8.231; habitual / proper / customary action / occupation 3.250, 16.368, 17.287, 21.106; the natural / proper order (of things) 2.247,

3.397, B 11.67; the nature of things 16.212, B 14.119; nature [as source of created things] 3.60, 19.255; (*person.*) God as ~ 10.129 *et p.*, 13.131, 14.160, 15.18, ? 19.255, 20.78, 22.76 *et p.*; kind / class (of thing) 7.234, B 15.316; species 10.234, 13.151, 14.163, 18.62, B 11.397; race Pr 200, 18.67; people B 10.424; one's fellow man 19.220; stock 2.27, 81, 10.206, 21.123, B 9.128; parentage 10.247 (2); station / rank (by birth) 3.129, 21.479; progeny 10.247 (1), 13.151, 171, 18.223; gender 3.336, 371; grammatical aspect 3.361; *in phrr*: a3eyns ~ 16.212; by ~ of owing to the nature of 19.322; cours of ~ 3.60; deth of ~ 20.219; lawe of ~ 8.231, 17.152, 160, 22.18

kynde *a* natural 20.132; innate, instinctive 3.71; proper, suitable by nature 2.29; correct, own 10.69; right A 11.254; (its) own B 15.466; genuine, real 15.183, 16.109, 22.73; kind, loving 15.144, B 11.187, A 11.250; generous 16.255; gracious, noble 13.12, A 12.15; ?excellent B 16.70n; *in phrr*.: ~ knowynge natural knowledge [instinctive not learned] 1.136, 140, 160, 10.56, 109, 14.79, *pl.* B 12.136; ~ loue 3.451, 16.109, B 13.151; ~ vnderstondynge intuitive grasp 5.56, 14.102; ~ wille inward intent 3.71; ~ wit natural reason [practical understanding based on experience not education] 11.228, 14.17 *et p.*, 163, 17.216, 21.317, B 12.45, 14.125, (*person.*) Pr 141 *et p.* 1.51, 3.436, 4.152, 7.183, 8.59, 13.238, 19.111, A 12. 41, 53; ~ witted endowed with ~ wit 14.52

kyndeli(che) *av* correctly 4.147, 17.110; properly 9.213; truly 20.212, 229, B 14.87, 15.2; rightly 1.78, 11.91, 101; thoroughly, completely 16.209; ?familiarly 7.182n; kindly, pleasantly B 3.15

kyndenesse *n* (acts of) kindness 7.46, B 13.390; kind feeling, benevolence A 3.274

kyndly *a* in accordance with (the law of) man's nature 17.153

kyne 22.97 = kene *a*

kyn(e)dom, kyngdoem *n* kingdom 2.247, 3.243, 411, 20.112, 423, 21.49, 138, B 7.156, (of heaven) Pr 133, (of Coueitise) A 2.62

kyneriche *n* kingdom Pr 148, 10.112, B 7.156, (of heaven) 12.170

king *n* (*gen. pl.* kyngene of (the) kings 21.79, B 1.105) king Pr 90, 1.155, 3.246, 250, 255, 260, 264, 314, 318, 322, 374, 377, 379, 412, 441, 467, 4.126, 135, 5.193, 194, 9.9, 305, 10.101, 11.281, 13.107, 109, 15.170, 16.124, 17.287, 19.287, 20.423, 441, 21.27, 29, 42, 97, 223, 257, 305, 306, 468, 22.67, 101, B 4.150, 151, 10.46, 13.166, 170, [= the Messianic king] 3.441, 5.168, 178, B 10.326, [= the Jewish Messiah] 3.455, [= Christ] 20.273, 277, 413, 426, B 1.105, ~ of Iewes / Iuda 21.41, 49, 138, (of Heuene) [= God] 7.251, 13.66, 17.262, 20.78, 363; *particular kings*: [Abimelech] 13.12, [Agag] 3.408, [Caesar] B 1.48, [David] B 2.36, [Magi] 21.72 *et*

p., [Nebuchadnezzar] B 7.154, [Saul] 3.430, = the King of England Pr 90, 139 *et p.*, 2.11, 146 *et p.*, 3.3 *et p.*, 4.3 *et p.*, 5.113 *et p.*, 8.338, 21.446, 468 *et p.*, B 15.444, Z 4.125, A Pr 91, [Richard] A 12.113; *in phrr.* ~es bench A Pr 95, ~es consayl 4.119, 22.30, 129, B Pr 144; ~ court 2.202, 3.472, 16.358, 18.95, 21.427; ~ iustice 4.186, 8.338, 19.284; ~ munstral 7.96, ~ sone 20.78, ~ tresor 5.181, ~es wille 2.218, 3.246, 10.244; ~es and knyhtes 1.90, 3.44, 9.9, 22.101, 257, B 7.9, 9.111, A 10.137

kinghed *n* kingship A 11.219, (kynghod) B 10.332

kyngryche B Pr 125 = kyneriche *n*

kynnesman *n* kinsman, relative B 15.247

kynneswomman *n* kinswoman 2.146

kynrede *n* family, kindred 10.261, B 9.174; progeny A 10.158

kirk(e), kyrk(e) *n* church Pr 138, 3.64, 5.60, 104, 179, 6.288, 8.26, 100, 11.246, 250, 306, 13.89, 14.39, 17.220, 276, 21.413, 470, †22.120, B 5.1, 103, 10.409, 411, 12.82, 13.9, 274, 15.136, 197, 384, 545, 19.446; Holy ~ 3.356, 397, 5.179, 8.26, 53, 159, 9.9, 11.246, 250, 306, 13.89, 14.39, 16.255, 17.77, 220, 276, 21.413, 470, 22.120, B 12.82, 13.274, 15.384

kyrkeward, to, *n. phr.* towards church 6.350

kyrke3erde *n* churchyard 15.11

kirtel *n* (man's) outer garment, tunic B 5.79, 11.283

kissen (cussen, kussen) *v* (*p.t.* kiste, kuste (custe)) kiss 2.146, 4.3, 18.170, 20.463, 474, 22.354, B 16.152, 18.430, A 11.177, 12.47, *ger.* kissing 6.187, 18.173, B 16.149

kithen *v* (*p.t.* kud, kidde *p.p.* ykud) show (towards) 7.46, B 13.390, B 15.303; *p.p.* illustrious 12.198

kyto(u)n *n* kitten Pr 204, 208, 215

kitten (*p.t.* kitten B 6.188; *imp.* kitte A 4.140) = kutten *v*

kix *n* hollow stem [of hemlock *etc,* used for lighting] 19.186

knappe *n* button B 6.269

knaue *n* fellow A 12.77; servant, serving-man Pr 40, 227, 3.411, 4.17, 5.161, 6.363, 370, 9.205, 20.287, B 5.115; common labourer 1.124, 5.54, 62, 8.46, 9.209, A 7.181; wastrel, rogue Pr 45, 3.167

kne(e) *n* knee 1.76, 2.1, 3.93, 5.106, 6.409, 20.89, 474, A 12.47

knelen *v* (*p.t.* kneled 2.1, *pl.* knelede Pr 71; *pr.p.* knelend 21.74, knelyng 3.151) kneel 1.76, 3.45, 5.161, 7.3, 119, 17.177, 21.12, 17, 28, 81, 91, 95, 201, 208, 210, B 5.103, A 12.47

knet *p.p.* 3.210 *see* knytten *v*

kneu3 *p.t.* A 2.188, 4.48, 66 = knew

knew(e) *p.t.* 4.64 *et p.*; *see* knowen *v*

knew(e)lichen B 12.192, 19.187, = kno(we)lechen *v*

knyf *n* (*pl.* knyues) knife 20.219, B 5.79, 163

kny(g)ht(e) (kni3t) *n* knight Pr 179, 190, 1.90, 97, 101, 2.58, 467, 3.44, 49, 5.72, 77, 6.250, 8.21 *et p.*, 46, 9.9,

11.52, 12.104, 13.107, 16.210, 17.287, 20.11, 21.27 *et p.*, 149, 22.101, 104, **B** 7.156, 10.146, 12.107, 15.331, A 4.105; *with spec. ref.* (= Conscience) 3.145, (= Inwit) 10.144, (= Trajan) 14.149, 205, (= Longeus) 20.80 *et p.*, (= Confort) 22.91, (*fig.*) (= angels) 1.104, 107, (= clergy) 13.125 (= Christ) 20.78; *in phrr.* ~es court 7.33, ~es douhter 6.124, ~es fees 5.77, ~es of cuntres knights of the shire A 2.43

kny3ten *v* to make (sb.) a knight B 1.105

knyghthed(e), knyhtho(e)d(e) *n* the knightly class Pr 139, 142, 17.216, B 10.330, 332, A 11.219; the order of knighthood 1.98; (ideal) knightly conduct 20.99

knytten *v (p.p.* **knet)** fasten Pr 184, 3.210; bind, unite, *p.p.* B 15.242

knok *n* blow (*fig.*) 5.177 (B 10.326)

knokken *v* knock (at gate) 8.287, 22.330; beat (breast) 5.106, 7.6, Z 5.97; strike a blow (against) B 16.128, (*fig.*) 22.130

knoppe A 7.254 = **knappe** *n*

knotte 17.127 *see* **loue** ~ *n*

kno(we)lechen *v* acknowledge 21.77; confess 6.327, 7.147, 13.89, B 12.192; agree 21.187n; *ger.* B 14.187

knowen *v (contr. pr. 2 sg.* **knowestou** 3.223, *p.t.* **knew(e)** 4.64, *pl.* **knewe(n)** 16.366, *p.p.* **(y)knowe** Pr 54, 20.209) know (as true) 3.436, 5.83; perceive [with senses] 14.97, [with mind] B 16.229; grasp, understand 1.158, 7.167, 11.40, 14.74, 76, 16.183, 17.54, **B** 10.209, 12.133, *p.p.* 13.223, 20.209; get to know, find out 10.75, 13.133; be skilled in 6.322, 19.119, *pr.p.* 11.295; be familiar / acquainted with 2.129, 7.182, 15.31, 16.166, 17.292, 298; know about B 10.466, *pr.p.* 22.67; (know by) experience 15.292, B 16.215, Z 2.70; encounter 12.123; recognise 1.72, 2.4, 4.32, 71, 8.45, 12.125, 20.23, 21.350, *p.p.* Pr 54, 4.159; make (sth.) known B 16.192; acknowledge 7.206, 11.95, B 4.41; acknowledge (with honour), observe 9.232; have consideration for 22.282, B 6.219; have sexual intercourse with A 10.146

knowyng(e) *ger.* knowledge, acquaintance, **kynde** ~ direct natural knowledge, intuitive understanding 1.136, 140, 160, 10.56, 109, 14.79; recognition, **for** ~ to prevent recognition 2.240; ability 21.310

koes Z 7.125 *see* **cow** *n*²

koyne 1.46 = **coyne** *n*

koke 5.13 = **coken** *v*²

konne 21.204, B 6.149 *et p.,* A 12.7, Z 1.119 *see* **connen** *v*

konnyng 11.295, 21.235, **B** 11.165, 211, 300, 12.66, 13.293 = **connyng** *n*

konnynge B 10.458, 11.70 = **connynge** *a*

konstable Z 2.188 = **constable** *n*

koude B Pr 129 *et p.* = **coude; koudest** B 8.76, **koudestow** B 5.533 = **coudest(ow);** *see* **connen** *v*

kounten Z 4.11 *see* **acounten** *v*

kouþe B 1.116 *et p.* = **couthe; kouthest** 7.177 = **couthest (thow);** *see* **connen** *v*

kud *p.t.* 7.46 *see* **kithen** *v*

kullen (*p.t.* **kulde** 3.232, 22.99, *p.p.* **kulled** 10.101, 16.26, B 16.152, 232 = **cullen**

kultour *n* coulter **B** 3.308, 6.104

kunne 11.101, 21.26, A 8.13 *see* **connen** *v*

kunnyng 11.228, B 10.472, (*pl.*) 11.94 = **connyng** *ger.*

kussen (*p.t.* **kuste** 18.170) 2.146 etc = **kissen** *v*

kuth (**kiþ, couthe**) *n* people 3.260, **here kingene** ~ the land over which they ruled 21.79; *in phr.* ~ **and kin** country and kinsfolk 17.196, B 13.379

kutten *v* (*imper.* **kut** 4.159) cut 5.134, 22.56

labben *v* blurt 12.41

laberen 11.254 = **labour(i)en** *v*

labo(u)r *n* (hard) work 5.42, 85, 16.145, 21.233; (physical) work 8.196, 9.207, 21.238, B 8.81; (piece of) work, task B 6.26; activity 14.107; type of work 5.43; effort Pr 195, 15.201, 16.40, 19.213; *in phrr.* ~ **of body** B 14.129; ~ **of handes** 9.198; ~ **of tonge** 21.233; **feiþful** ~ B 6.250; **lel(e)** ~ honest work Pr 146, 8.261, 10.79, 16.145

labo(u)r(i)en *v* (do) work 5.8, 45, 66, 8.25, 135, 214, 222, 250, 294, 9.103, 223, 245, 11.254, 21.237, A 7.13, Z 7.77, (*fig.*) 21.387, 22.239, B 15.187 *ger.* **laboryng** (hard) work (done) 8.251

labo(u)rer *n* manual worker, (*esp.* agricultural) labourer [of lowest social class] 3.309, 347, 452, 4.144, 6.227, 8.330, 339, 9.58, 11.254, **B** 3.255, 10.460, **A** 2.45, 6.35; servant 5.73, B 15.329; *in phrr.* **leel** ~ 3.347; **lewede ~s** 11.298, 304; **libbynge ~s** 9.58, B Pr 223

lac(c)hen *v* (*p.t.* **lauhte, laghte**) ensnare Pr 169, 6.405; catch 2.215; seize 18.119, B 16.50; take 22.152, B 1.30, Z 2.165; assume 19.125; get, obtain 1.100, 2.138, 3.390, 9.141, 15.204, 16.363, **B** 6.227, 11.222, 299, Z Pr 63; catch up, remove B 18.327, A 12.96; take (leave) 1.203, 3.26, A 12.55; *ger.* **lacchynge** receiving B 1.103

lach(e)-drawer *n* beggar from door to door 8.287, 9.192

lac(c)hesse *n* laziness, remissness 8.253, 9.267, 277, B 8.37

la(c)k(i)en *v* lack B 9.71, 13.265, 17.293; be lacking / wanting 6.311, 21.112, 22.249, B 10.188; (*impers.*) lack 3.386, 13.102, 21.471, 22.210, 249, **B** 9.38, 10.188, *ger.* lack, want 22.36; disparage 2.21, 13.25, 15.80, B 10.205; find fault (with) 6.98, 7.23, 13.207, 14.6, 17.310, 19.103, 21.255, **B** 10.262, 11.394, 13.323 (*ger.*), 15.249, 253; criticise 1.115, 2.49, 3.58, 11.164, 12.41, **B** 6.224, 11.2, 213, 419, 12.97, 13.287, 15.4, 204, Z Pr 72

lacles *a* without fault 13.210

lad *p.p.* 10.142, 15.15; **ladde** *p.t.* Pr 139, 3.128, 9.340, 18.3, 178, 19.66, 73, B 5.247, 491, Z 3.10, *2 sg.* **laddest** B 7.190 *see* **leden** *v*

ladde *n* male servant, attendant 3.247; low fellow, churl 8.194, 21.32

laddere *n* ladder 18.44

ladel *n* ladle 21.280

lady *n* mistress of household B 10.97; (*in ref. to*) nun 6.132, 142; woman of high birth or rank 3.488, 8.5, 7, B 6.10, A 11.203; (knight's) lady-love 22.104; nobleman's wife B 10.97, (*in title*) **my** ~ 22.346, 367; (*of allegorical figures*) (Holy Church) 1.3, 115 *et p.*, 2.53, (Mede) 2.44, 3.26 *et p.*, (Largenesse) 7.274, (*Anima*) 10.140, (Scripture) A 12.42; (*as title of Virgin Mary*) **Oure** ~ 3.99, 141, 4.39, 6.170, 7.12, 250, (*in assev.*) B 4.188; *in phr.* **lord(es) and / or lady(es)** 4.109, 6.249, 9.130, 11.202, 15.306, 17.44, 56, **B** Pr 95, 15.6, 309; woman 11.180, (*uninfl. gen.*) woman's B 18.338

lafte *p.t.* **B** 3.197, 20.251, 372 *see* **leuen** *v*¹

laghynge *pr.p.* 3.55 *see* **lauhen** *v*

laghte *p.t.* Pr 169 *see* **lacchen** *v*

lay *n*¹ song 10.65, (*fig.*) 7.116

lay *n*² law 21.43

lay *p.t.* Pr 8, 1.28, 2.130, 6.192, 227, 228, 261, 9.284, 18.144, 20.127, 22.312, B Pr 9 *et p.*; *see* **liggen** *v*

layd(e) *p.p.* 12.185, 17.302; **layth** *pr. sg.* 6.405 *see* **leggen** *v*

lay3e *p.p.* 6.329 (= **layn**) *see* **liggen** *v*

lai3es *pl.* A 8.5 *see* **leye** *n*²

layk *n* sport 16.84; ~ **en** *v* play, sport Pr 187, 16.174

layn *p.p.* 3.40 *see* **liggen** *v*

laynen *v* conceal 2.18

layth *3 sg.* 6.405 *see* **leggen** *v*

lak *n* fault, failing B 10.262; *and see* **lacles** *a*

lakken *v* 6.98 *etc*; *see* **la(c)k(i)en** *v*

Lammasse tyme *n. phr.* the time around Aug. 1, the feast of St Peter ad Vincula [harvest time] 8.313

lamb(e), lomb *n* (*pl.* ~**es** 16.269, ~**ren** 3.411, 9.260, B 15.206) lamb 17.38; *in phr:* **as louh as a** ~ as meek / humble as a lamb 7.196, 10.83, 22.36

lame *a* lame, crippled in the feet 8.189, 9.215, *a as n* lame people 21.125

land (lond) *n* land, country, kingdom Pr 149, 3.209, 212, 234, 247, 259, 376, 419, 4.145, 10.192, 16.163, 17.237, 20.108, **B** 3.221, 7.157, 10.25, 13.209, A 11.203, Z 6.78; territory 3.419, 20.314, 21.32; land(ed property) 3.172, 315, 5.26, 158, 163, 167, 9.202, 10.194, 285, 11.184, 13.110, 15.168, 17.218, 221, 227, 20.93, 22.251, **B** 4.73, 10.86, 306, **Z** 2.42, 3.96; (farming) land 8.15, 294, 330, 12.226, 233, 20.108, **B** 6.271, 8.81, (*fig.*) 16.16; field 6.67; strip of ploughland 6.268, 19.60; the earth 17.102, 20.349, (*fig.*) = life B 5.476; the world, **in / on** ~ in this world Pr 146, 10.124, B 15.152; land [in contrast with water] 15.19 *etc*; *in cpds,* ~ **lepere** *n* as *a* vagabond B 15.213; ***~**tilynge** *a* engaged in husbandry 8.140, 11.298; **foet** ~ 6.268, **leye** ~ 10.219, **ouer** ~

9.159; *in phrr.* ~ **of bileue** the kingdom of faith 21.336; ~ **of longyng** domain of desire 11.169; **a** ~ **and a watre** on land and sea, everywhere 15.19, 20.29, 21.237, **B** 16.189, 18.314; ~ **and / or lordschipe** estates and rank 3.315, 9.202, 11.12, 16.102, 158, 18.257, B 14.327

lane *n* lane, alley 2.226

lang 2.192 = **long** *a*

langage *n* language 18.80, 21.204, B 15.375

langour *n* sickness 18.142; suffering 15.298, B 18.226

lankart Z 2.152 = **lang cart** *n*

lanterne *n* lantern B 6.177

lapen *v* lap (up) 6.413; take a drink 22.18

lappe *n* lap 6.411; folded skirt / loose sleeve 8.317; bosom B 17.71, (*fig.*), (**Abrahames**) ~ 'Abraham's bosom', = the Limbo of the Fathers 8.282, 18.272, 275, 19.24, 33

large *n* munificence 21.43; freedom, **at** ~ freely 22.192

large *a* munificent 11.73; generous 3.248, 14.215, B 13.299; prodigal 3.288; lavish 3.315, 450; large, big 18.70, 21.264; wide, broad 18.22, 20.44, (*fig.*) 13.29; ~ **myle** a full / good mile B 10.164; *av* fully, *comp.* (**more**) **largere** (more) fully B 11.160; ~**liche** *av* munificently 12.109, 21.60; copiously 2.138, 4.67; fully 22.87; ~**nesse** *n* munificence 17.65, generosity (*person.*) 7.274

largesse *n* generous gift, **crien a** ~ call out thanks (*sc.* for a generous gift) 7.108

larke *n* lark 14.185, 187

lasar, lazar *n* leper 18.142, 272

lasse *n* a smaller amount 8.286, 16.71, 140, B 5.248; **at** ~ at even less 9.303; **no** ~ (at) no lesser price B 5.220; *a* smaller 14.185, 16.88, B 16.57; less 3.136, 289, 11.69, 13.4; less (in importance) 2.48, 3.258, 19.148 (**lassore**); *av* less 4.156, 7.203, 8.165, 12.44, 154, B 11.69; þe ~ the less 7.204, B 11.69, 14.1; *in phrr.* **more oþer** ~ more or less (in quantity) 3.289; to a greater or less extent 9.108; of whatever rank / status 10.7, A 4.135; all of them 15.201; more or less (in number) 22.272; of whatever kind B 14.327; ~ **other / ne more** the greater or the less(er) 2.48; the smaller or the bigger B 10.265; less or more B 13.17

lassore 19.148 = **lasse** *a*

last(e) *conj.* lest 5.144, 7.86, 11.254, 14.68, 20.325, 334, Z 7.133

last *a* latest B 18.313; final 2.76, B 2.101; *in phrr.* **at þe laste** finally, in the end 4.155, 7.7, 22.157, **B** 12.26, 52, 14.143, 15.14, 16.20, A 3.87; eventually 5.95, 9.207, 12.187, 13.22, 15.272, 17.138, 20.208, 321, 22.175, 347, B 13.21; as a last resort 6.265; at the last day Pr 126, 2.154, 12.67, 17.137, 146, 20.352, 355, 21.193, B 14.147; at the end of time 20.392, 22.150; at death 20.321; **at þe** ~ **ende** at the end of the day 5.97; at the time of death 12.196, 210, 16.2, 158, 282, 19.95; at the last judgement 19.275

lasten *v* (*contr. pr.* **last(e)** 10.171, 16.11, Z 3.124, *p.p.*

ylastede B 3.192, **last** A 3.179) last Pr 146, 10.171, 21.45, 22.211, **B** 4.195, 13.332, **A** 3.27, 10.37, **Z** 1.22, 5.73; continue 8.312, 16.11, A 12.93; endure 3.204, 12.161, 17.66, 21.89, B 9.45, A 2.60; keep 12.222; live 21.176, B 3.28; hold out 3.32, 11.73, 22.142, Z 3.33; persist **B** 15.258, 17.8; extend B 20.382

lat(e)[1] *contr. pr.* 3.173, 19.147, 22.361, 362, A 11.142; *p.t. sg.* 6.261; *imper. sg.* Pr 201, 2.49, 3.75, 4.21, 5.137, 6.393, 7.274, 8.37, 10.33, 11.309, 13.235, 15.95, 17.227, 18.105, 20.464, 22.241, Z 7.67 *etc*; *imper. pl.* **late** 4.174, 5.137, B 2.171 *etc*; *inf.* **lat(e)** Pr 201, 20.56; *pr. indic.* 3.136, B 5.410, *pr. subj.* B Pr 155 *see* **leten** v

lat(te)[2] *contr. pr.* 13.55, 15.278, B 9.58, A 11.142, Z 3.99 *see* **leden** v

late *a* tedious, protracted 7.159; *comp.* **lattere** subsequent 20.348

late *av* (at a) late (hour) 4.48, 10.140, 16.168; late in the day, only slowly B 10.211; recently 3.145, B 16.249; ~ (...) **longe** a long time later 6.160; ~ **and rathe** late and early (= at any time) 10.140, 11.89, B 3.73 *comp.* **latter** less readily, more tardily B 1.199

Latyn *n* (the) Latin (language) 1.139, 14.204, 15.80, 16.194, **B** Pr 129, 143, 3.332, 11.213, 13.152, 15.375; **a** ~ in Latin 11.164, 19.4; **fals** ~ incorrect Latin 13.117; piece of (writing in) Latin 3.124, 487, 9.164, 212, 10.92, 16.194, 17.54

laton (= **laten**) 10.202 *see* **leten** v

lauchen Z Pr 63 = **lacchen** v

lauden *v* praise, commend B 11.106

lauȝen, laughen B 5.111, 11.208, 13.353, 14.35, 15.172, **laughyng** B 16.155, 18.416 *see* **lauhen** v

lauȝte, laughte, lauȝþe *p.t.* **B** 1.30, 18.327, A 12.42, 55 = **lauhte**; **lauȝth** *p.p.* A 12.96 *see* **lacchen** v

lauhen, lawhen *v* (*p.t.* **lauhede** 2.32, **louh(e)** 12.23, 18.3, **lowh** 21.462, 22.143, **louȝ** A 4.137, **low** A 12.42) laugh 2.32, 4.101, 7.83, 15.204, 18.3, 21.462, B 13.353, A 4.137, Z 7.68; ~ **of** laugh at 4.19, 7.22, B 5.111, ~ **on** / **vp** rejoice with 15.148, B 11.208, smile at 12.23, A 12.42; *pr.p.* laughing 6.23; merry 22.114; smile 22.242; be happy 7.109; express pleasure (at) 15.201; *ger.* (**leyhing**) laughing 6.393; cheerful manner B 16.155; (**louhynge**) amity 20.460

lauhfollyche *a, av see* **laweful** ~ 9.59

laumpe *n* lamp 1.184; ~ **lyne** inscription on a lamp B 13.152

launce *n* lance 3.457

launcen, launsen (**vp**) *v* spring up 12.187, 224; bring forth 18.10

launde *n* glade, clearing Pr 8, 10.64, B 15.298, 304; (tract of) ground Z 2.47; plain (*fig.*) B 10.163

lauen *v* wash (*fig.*) 16.331, B 14.5

#lauendrie *n* laundry 16.331

lawe *n* the law [*generally* = the (body of) rule(s) governing human conduct] **B** Pr 122, 12.97, 18.284; specific law(s), statute(s) 21.33, **B** 5.52, 15.465, 16.119, Z Pr 72; [*with ref. to* the Mosaic law] divine (positive) law 10.197, 221, 17.295, 297, 18.186, 19.11, 36, 47, 21.112, **B** 15.583, 585; the (Christian) law (esp. the moral law taught by the Church) 6.45, 7.73, 259, 9.276, 277, 10.305, 11.99, 12.33, 13.86, 90, 92, 17.126, 136, 137, 139, 162, 292, 293, 20.110, 393, 22.266, **B** 10.352, 354, 12.34, 14.146; (divine) command(ment) or prohibition 20.306, 22.278, B 17.15; moral law (of reason) 12.88, 14.209, 210, B 9.78; the law (of the land) 3.293, 376, 378, 4.174, 175, 8.85, 165, 9.425, 12.64, 91, 94, 13.49, 117, 14.146, 20.425, 428, 443, 21.472; = prerogative, right 3.271, 21.471, 482; the (system / process of civil) law (as administered / executed) Pr 161, 2.21, 137, 148, 169, 209, 3.78, 195, 4.169, 12.81, (*person.*) 3.198, B 4.174; *in phrr.* **declaren** ~ practise the law 9.49; **don** (**þe**) ~ administer / execute legal justice 3.446, 21.308; (the process of ecclesiastical) law 16.363; law [as body of knowledge] 11.118, 22.274, B 11.218 *et p.*; the law [as a profession] 3.452, **B** 11.222, (*person.*) 4.144, B 4.174; **Wryng-lawe** the abuse of legal process (*person.*) 4.31; faith, religion 10.192, 17.133, = (Mahomet's) doctrine B 15.410; way of life / behaviour 10.126; *in phrr.* **aȝeyne þe** ~ in breach of the law (of land / Church) 3.120, 193, 9.212, 17.280, 20.393; **by goed** ~ with justice / with a sound legal claim 17.58; **by puyre** ~ by sheer right 15.290; **by þe** ~ in accordance with the law 8.165, 10.212, 17.283, B 14.109; **for** ~ as legally required 3.88; **bothe** ~**s** canon and civil law 13.79, B 7.14, A 8.13; **konnyng of** ~ expertise in law B 11.165; **men of** ~ lawyers (barristers and judges) 4.67, 148, 168, 9.44, 51, 17.46, 20.354; **clerkes of þe** ~ those learned in the law 11.281; **doctours of** ~ experts in canon law B 15.243; **þe comune** ~ the custom of the state 20.74; **Cristes** ~ the law / commandments of Christ, Christian moral teaching 9.340, 17.251; **Goddes** ~ the law of God 7.118, 9.104, 158, 166, B 15.93; **Newe** ~ the doctrine / moral law of the New Testament 18.265, 19.34, 20.268, 339, 21.35, 59, 111, 312, 449; **þe olde** ~ the (Mosaic moral) law of the Old Testament 12.114, 14.58, 17.71, 18.222, 20.381, 387, 21.312, 449; **Treuþe** ~**s** the laws of divine Justice A 6.97; **Westminstre** ~ the (common) law (of England administered in the king's courts) at Westminster 10.242; **wickede** ~**s** unjust ordinances 3.205; ~ **of Holy Churche** the moral teaching and / or discipline of the Church 9.218, 220, 326, 10.96, 13.82, 86, 14.9, 152, 21.336, B 16.6; ~ **of kynde** natural law (of reason) 8.231, 17.152, 160, 22.18, B 9.78; ~ **of Levyticy** Mosaic law in Leviticus 5.55; ~ **of lyf** teaching leading to (eternal) life 21.45; (**the**) ~ **of loue** the divine doctrine of love 12.121, 14.38

laweday *n* day for meeting of law-court 5.158

laweful *a* just B 11.145; upright B 15.308; ~**lyche** *av* in accordance with law 9.59

lawiere *n* lawyer B 7.59

lawnde Z 2.47 = **launde** *n*

lazar, laȝar 18.272 (B 16.255) = **lasar** *n*

le(a)ute(e) (lew(e)te(e)) *n* uprightness, honesty 17.127, 162, B 15.467; faithfulness, honour 6.195; (*person.*) Loyal Faithfulness Pr 149, 2.20, 4.156, 12.23 *et p.*, 22.63, 146; lawfulness, respect for law 17.130, 138; legal justice B Pr 122, (*person.*) A 2.100; right, justice 3.378, 4.174, 12.90, 94, 21.89, B 14.146, (*person.*) 2.20, 49, 3.196, 446; trust 11.160n. *in phr.* **loue and** ~ love and uprightness / integrity 3.443, 4.36, 7.259, 12.81, 96, 98, 15.134, 17.126, **B** 11.166, 15.467

lecche 1.198 = **leche** *n*

lec(c)herye *n* lechery, lust(fulness) Pr 75, 2.188, 3.161, 6.194, 9.18, 10.161, 288, 17.79, 18.36, 21.421, 22.312, **B** 1.30, 6.143, 10.49, **Z** 3.161, 163; (*as allegorical domain*) 2.93, B 10.163; (*person.*) 6.170, 16.90, 22.111, 114; *in phr.* **likyng of** ~ lustful pleasure(s) 6.176, 11.265, B 13.344; extravagance 16.254;

lec(c)herous *a* lustful **B** 2.125, 6.265

lec(c)hour *n* lecher, lustful person 6.195, 17.137, B 13.353, A 7.250, (*person.*) = Lust B 5.71

leche *n* physician 2.233, 3.300, 8.295, (*fig.*) 16.136, 22.305, 310, 319, 346, ~ **of lyf** 1.198, B 16.118; medicine B 14.315

lechecra(e)ft *n* medical art 18.138, 22.173, B 6.253, (*fig.*) 6.81

lechen *v* cure 15.221, 18.142, **B** 13.254, 16.113, (*fig.*) 8.189, 19.95; *ger. phr.* **a-lechynge** to be cured 19.75

lecuth Z Pr 130 = **lyketh** *see* **lyken** *v*

ledare *n* ruler 21.100; principal, chief 1.154, 156, 15.171, B 10.188; person in charge 8.251; guide 16.156, B 12.96; *in phr.* ~ **of lawedays / louedaies** one who presides at court sessions / settlement days 5.158 (B 10.306)

ledden *p.t. subjv.* B 9.190 *see* **leden** *v*

lede *n* man 3.281, 6.301, 7.159, 10.178, 13.59, 17.40, 19.78, **B** 1.141, 3.97, 5.174, 8.7, 17.64, 18.357, A 3.31; person 11.73, 13.210, 20.444, 21.412, **B** †15.393, 16.181, 201; retainer 17.221; subject 4.178; (*pl.*) = landed property 11.69, 17.221

leden *v* (*contr. pr.* **lat** 7.274, 15.278, **latte** 13.55, **leet** 3.195, *p.t.* **ladde** Pr 139 *et p.*, 2 *p.* **laddest** B 7.190, 3 *p. pl. subjv.* **ledden** B 9.190) conduct Pr 139, 2.148, 3.128, 7.274, 11.182, 15.278, 21.225, Z 3.10; guide **B** 10.22, 17.118; bring 7.115, 252, 15.15, 18.3, 178, 19.73; direct 4.12, 12.96; lead 19.66; rule, govern Pr 149, 4.145; manage 3.195, *ger.* **ledynge** management, plan 2.44; ~ **forþ** preside over B 10.20; bear, carry 2.192, 4.144, 13.55, 16.140, 20.278, 280, 443, 449, **B** 5.247, 15.83; carry away (captive) B 5.491; ~ **lyf** pass / live one's life 9.340, 16.18, 18.77, Z 8.84

ledene *n* cry (of a bird) 13.172, 14.178, 185, B 12.252

leed *n* lead [for seal] B 13.83, [for roofing] 7.237, B 13.247

le(e)f (leue) *n*¹ (**leues** *gen. sg.* 3.490, *pl.* 16.247, 18.48, B 5.267 *etc*) leaf 1.150, 16.247, 253, 17.14, B 12.230, (*fig.*) **B** 5.138, 16.6, 28, 35; page 3.491, 15.105, B 5.267; (*fig.*)= a small amount 6.209, B 6.253, A 8.160, *in phr.* **setten at a** ~ regard as worthless 5.97; *and see* **leuen** *v*³

leef (leue) *n*² beloved B 2.33; pleasure (**leue**) 9.146

le(e)f³ *imper. sg.* 1.36, 193, 5.24, 6.158, 275, 10.307, 13.210, 19.18, 22.208, Z 7.253 *see* **leuen** *v*²; Z 6.53 = **leuen** *v*¹

le(e)f (leue)⁴ *a* (*comp.* **leuer** 6.129 *etc, sup.* **leuest(e)** B 1.151 *etc*) dear 2.18, 17.148, 20.57 (2); beloved 6.171, 11.74, B 5.38; good 3.73, 7.199, 12.24, 18.1, 105; pleasing 1.35, B 9.58; precious, valued 20.457 (1), **B** 1.151, 17.281, A 1.136; agreeable, acceptable 3.6, 5.85, B 10.14; willing, eager, glad 6.116, 22.195, 312 (**Lyf**), B 13.323n; affectionate 12.118; *in impers. constr.* **me / þe / h(e)m is / were leuere / leuest** I / you / (t)he(y) (would) rather (most) prefer 6.129, 292, 313, 11.9, 227, 15.180, B 10.14, Z 3.123; *in pers. constr. (with* **hauen**) would prefer 7.22, B 5.140

le(e)f⁵ *av* willingly 6.183; *in impers. constr.* **the / here leef li(c)keth** it well pleases you / her 3.19, 4.145, 7.252, *comp.* **leuere** more dearly B 1.143, A 6.50; more willingly **B** 15.195; *sup.* most dearly 1.141, **B** 5.563, 10.355

le(e)ge *a* (true) subject [of a sovereign] 3.414; ~ **ledes** loyal subjects 4.178; *as n pl.* 3.316, 317, 20.395

le(e)k *n* leek B 5.81; ~ **sed** leek seed 12.192

le(e)l(e) *a* loyal, faithful 12.131, 16.24, 21.60, †B 9.188, (*a as n*) 3.316, 317; true 7.196, 8.140, 10.212, 12.90, **B** 15.581, 16.6; honest 8.74, 295, †11.17, 21.238; just 17.131, 20.307, (*a as n*) 13.68, 19.45; virtuous, upright 9.14, 14.188, 17.139, 20.338, 21.251, **B** 10.432, 15.422, 467; trustworthy 19.28, **B** 11.166, 218; lawful 10.294, 22.138; worthy 7.250; sound, good 5.103, 19.183; excellent B 13.295; *in phrr.* ~ **bileue** true faith 12.88, 15.246, 17.22, 127, 158, **B** 10.349, 15.438; ~ **labour** honest toil Pr 146, 8.261, 10.79, 16.145; ~ **laborer(es)** honest workm(a)n 3.347, 11.298; ~ **lif** virtuous life 21.238, B 13.288, A 11.182; ~ **lyuynge (men)** men of virtuous life 3.338, **B** 12.62, 15.93; ~ **loue** true / faithful love Pr 88, 15.138, 16.194, **B** 11.161, 17.217; ~ **speche** truthful speech 7.237, B 11.69

le(e)l(l)y(che) *av* wholeheartedly 7.207, 11.143, 147, 15.155, 17.217, 18.200, 19.94, 21.182, 22.210, **B** 7.124, 10.121, 13.142, A 11.144; sincerely 9.327, 11.268, 19.191, B 13.150, A 12.114; faithfully 3.31, 8.255, 10.140, 21.387, **B** 1.78, 2.32, 15.155; honourably 3.309, 8.140, 9.59, 21.233; virtuously 16.357; assuredly 2.76, B 12.173; in fact 10.275; rightly 16.193, 17.133; accurately 8.298, 17.117

le(e)me *n* radiance 20.127, B 18.137

leene B Pr 123 = **lene** *a*

leep *p.t.* B 2.69, 216 *see* **lepen** *v*

lees *p.t.* 7.131, 10.197, 13.152, 22.87, B 7.159 *see* **lesen** *v*¹

leest(e) *sup.* 3.209 *etc*, B 13.187 *see* **leste** *a*

leet¹ *p.t.* 3.195 *etc*, B 1.167 *etc,* **leete** *inf.* 8.293 *see* **leten** *v*

leet² *contr. pr.* 3.195 *see* **leden** *v*

leeue *v* B Pr 34 *etc*, *a* B 4.39 *see* **leuen** *v*², **le(e)f**⁴ *a*

lef *imper. sg.* 5.24, 6.158 *see* **leuen** *v*²

left(e)¹ *a* †1.112, 2.5, B 2.7 *etc* = **luft** *a*

lefte² *p.t.* Pr 130 *etc*, B 4.153 *etc*, A 3.184; *see* **leuen** *v*¹

leg *n* leg 8.129, 9.143, 215, 20.75, A 12.78

legate *n* (papal) legate 7.81

lege 20.395 = **le(e)ge** *a*

legende *n* written account (of lives), ~ **of lyf** the list of those predestined to eternal life 11.206; ~ *Sanctorum* the *Lives of the Saints* 17.157, B 11.160

leggen, leyen *v* (*3 sg. pr.* **layth** 6.405, *p.t.* **leyde** 5.73, *p.p.* **layd** 12.185, **yleyd** 3.258) lay, set 6.405, 409, 8.129, 14.59, 63, 17.302, 20.33, B 17.71, 18.77; lay (eggs) B 11.347; *in phrr.* ~ **eyes togederes** close eyes 20.59, ~ **ere to** listen to 16.143; place (in position) 6.405, 13.159, B 16.44; ~ **on** beat upon (*fig.*) 15.148, 22.114, 189, B 15.191; give as security, ~ **(to) wed(de)** 5.73, 20.30, 22.13, B 5.240, 16.267; pawn 8.292; wager 8.290, 12.94; ~ **lyf** stake one's life 3.258, 4.191, 20.160, ~ **heed** B 2.34; ~ **fautes on** ascribe blame to B 10.105

legion *n* legion, great company B 1.111; myriad, throng 22.87

legistre *n* expert in law B 7.14, 59

legityme *a as n* legitimate (people) 10.212

ley¹ *imper.* 12.94; **leid(e)** *p.p.* 20.30, B 15.592, *p.t.* 14.63 *etc*; *see* **leggen** *v*

ley² *p.t.* 13.159 *see* **liggen** *v*

l(e)ye *n*¹ flame 19.173, 180, (*fig.*) 259

leye *n*² field 9.5; ~ **land** fallow ground 10.219

leye(n) *p.p.* 21.55, B 3.38, *pr. pl.* Pr 89, **leyȝe(n)** *p.t. pl.* A 7.178, 10.180 *see* **liggen** *v*

leighe *p.t.* B 18.403 (= **low**); *see* **lyen** *v*

leyhing *ger.* 6.393 *see* **lauhen** *v*

leiþ A 3.146 (= **lyth**); *see* **lyen**; **leyth** 18.44, B 16.44 *see* **leggen** *v*

lek-sed 12.192 *see* **le(e)k** *n*

lel 16.145, **lele** Pr 88 *etc*, **lelest** B 13.295; **le(le)lyche** 16.357, 17.217, 19.191, **lely** 9.327 *etc*, **lelly** 2.76 *etc*; *see* **le(e)l(e)** *a*, **le(e)l(l)y(che)** *av*

leme B 18.137 = **le(e)m(e)** *n*

lemman *n* lover, ~**es knyhtes** lover-knights 22.104; mistress, paramour 7.26, 16.277, 22.152, 156; concubine 3.187; (spiritual) beloved 2.20 (*Leaute*), 10.133, A 10.46 (*Anima*), 20.184, B 13.140 (*Loue*), B 14.300 (*Poverte*)

lene *a* lean 10.116, B Pr 123; spare 11.2; emaciated 8.279; lank B 5.82; skinny A 12.78; scanty 8.263

lenedestow *p.t. 2 sg.* 6.248 (= **lenedest þow**) *see* **lenen** *v*²

lenen *v*¹ support oneself B 16.246; recline Pr 8, 10.64, (*refl.*) lie down (to rest) 20.5

lenen *v*² (*contr. pr.* **lent(e)** 11.47, B 9.106, *p.t.* **lened(e)** 6.244, 16.312, **lente** 6.243, *p.p.* **lent(e)** 6.249, 15.240) give Pr 75, 8.286, 10.92, 11.47, 15.240, 17.129, 155, 19.329, B 5.296, 7.75, 9.106, 10.42, 11.179, 13.17, 299, 15.86, 155; grant B Pr 126, 5.259, 10.404; give (as alms) 11.307, 12.118, 13.80, 22.239; afford 8.15, Z 7.107; lend (to) 4.191, 6.243 *et p.*, 277, 8.247, 16.130, 312, B 13.360; *in phr.* **lou(y)en...and** ~ 1.176, 8.231, 10.307, 12.109, 13.68, 14.13, 19.40, B 10.200, 354, 11.178, 15.170, 17.45, A 3.223

lengen *v* reside, dwell 6.158, 21.421, B 8.7; remain B 1.209

lenger, lengur *comp.a* longer 3.490, 6.216, 22.287; taller B 16.181

lenger(e), lengore, lengur *comp. av* (for a) longer (time) 1.202, 3.136, 4.1, 13.4, 36, 19.333, 22.63, B 17.8

lenghe (lengþe) *n* length 2.93, 3.259, 16.82 (**lenthe**), 18.20, 19.60, B 16.182; (time taken to walk) the distance (of) 13.38, B 15.187

lenghen *v* prolong 20.53, 335

lent(e) *contr. pr.* B 9.106, *p.p.* 6.249, 15.240, *p.t.* 6.243 *etc*; *see* **lenen** *v*²

lente(n) (lenton) *n* spring; ~ **sedes** seeds sown in springtime 12.192; (the liturgical season of) Lent Pr 89, 6.183, 7.26, 13.80, 14.120, 20.5, 21.385, 387, 22.362, *pl.* 13.80 *in phr.* **mydde-Lentones Sonenday** mid-Lent Sunday 18.182

lenterne *n* lantern 8.174

lenthe 16.82 *see* **lenghe** *n*

leode †10.7, B 1.141 *etc*; *see* **lede** *n*

leon B 15.277 *see* **lyoun** *n*

leopard *n* leopard B 15.277, 298

lep *p.t.* 2.225, *inf.* 2.241 *see* **lepen** *v*

lepare, lepere *n* hopper; ~ **aboute** vagabond 9.107, 137; ~ **ouer lond** wandering (mendicant-) confessor A 11.203

lepen (lyppen, luppen) *v* (*p.t.* **lep** 2.225, *pl.* **lepen** 1.109, **lope** B 4.153, *pl.*, **lopen** B 1.117, *pl.*; **lup** 2.69, 7.134, **lepte** 22.152) hop 6.204; rush forward 2.69, B Pr 223, 4.153; travel B 5.476; run 7.215, 21.125; *in phrr.* ~ **alofte** leap on high (= aspire upwards) 1.112; ~ **asyde** dart away 22.152; ~ **from** digress from B 11.317; ~ **in** shine in, penetrate 20.286; ~ **out** leap out 1.109, 14.85, B 5.161, 18.312, radiate 7.134, roam abroad 2.241; ~ **vp** mount 2.186

lere *n* face 1.3, B 10.2

leren *v* teach 1.203, 3.212, 5.142, 6.348, 9.164, 11.146, 237, 15.95, 118, 16.33, 151, 19.101, 20.235, 338, 21.237, 249, 251, 280, B 7.125, 10.196, †304, 13.187, 15.390, 16.104; teach (to) 1.134, B 6.253, A 8.14; instruct 4.118 (2), 9.19, 11.127, 14.122, 124, 17.318, B 5.44, 11.169; *ger.* **leryng** instruction 10.142, 174,

17.160; [by example] A 1.173; *p.p. as a* **lered** learned, educated 16.226, instructed B 13.214; ~ **man** cleric 7.104, wise man 16.151; ~ **men** the clergy, clerics 3.40, 4.118, scholars 16.192, 18.82; bid 11.132, 17.131, 19.45; advise B 3.69; relate 7.104; inform 9.326, B 11.160; tell 8.222, 14.6, **B** 9.74, 11.420; learn 6.215, 10.10, 22.207, B 1.146, **A** 1.109, 9.103, 11.278, Z 7.25, *refl.* ~ **hym**, **þe** learn **B** 13.121, 143; *in phrr.* **lered (and) lewed** educated and uneducated (= all men) Pr 88, 3.169, 4.12, 9.230, 14.55, 15.14, 17.182, 21.114, 22.102, 247, **B** 10.234, 274, 15.394, A 2.45; **lewed... (and)** ~ 6.116, 11.36, 14.71, 16.33, 230, 281, 19.43, 22.266

lernen *v* learn, receive instruction 11.123, 13.80, B 10.303, A 10.84, 12.6; acquire knowledge of 1.139, 144, 6.241, 11.107, 12.121, 19.47, **B** 1.111, 5.205, 17.41; learn (how to do sth.) 5.43, 6.209, 7.191, 8.294, 11.134, 13.159, 14.107, 22.208, 250; study 22.274, **B** 5.234, 440, 10.302, 11.172; find out 10.57, 11.77, **B** 8.110, 10.231, 12.256, *ger.* **lernyng** B 11.151; teach 11.118, **B** 4.12, 5.295, 7.132, 10.181, 373, *ger.* example **B** 1.199, instruction, guidance B 15.472; prescribe 8.339; *in phr.* **lykyng to** ~ pleasure in receiving instruction 5.155, 7.74

lesen *v*[1] (*p.t.* **le(e)s** 7.131, *pl.* **loren** 14.63, *p.t. subjv.* **lore** 16.312, *p.p.* **(y)lore** 6.193, 20.81 **(y)lorn** Pr 112, B 18.313) lose Pr 112, 10.197, 14.63, 22.87, B 12.40; be dispossessed of 17.218, **B** 7.159, 18.109; forfeit 2.37, 3.466, 7.267, B 5.240; suffer the loss of 3.172, 4.169, 6.245, 314, 9.267, 10.194, 16.312, 20.81, **B** 3.159, 5.94, 12.54, A 10.102, *ger.* **lesynge** loss(es) B 5.111; give up 13.152; waste 16.272; destroy 10.178; *and see* **losen** *v*[2]

lesen *v*[2] glean B 6.66

lesewe *n* grassy place Z 2.47

lesynge *ger.*[1]; *see* **lesen** *v*[1]

lesyng *ger.*[2] lie B 10.414; falsehood 2.138, 17.310, 18.44, 20.345 *et p.*, 21.293, **B** 5.137, 10.22; fiction 15.105; idle tale 4.19, 7.22, B 10.166

lesse *a, a as n* B 5.220, 10.456, A 4.135, 8.143 *see* **lasse** *a, n*

lesso(u)n *n* scriptural text 3.488, B 11.221, Z 1.36; sermon **B** 10.36, 371; lesson [to be learned] B 17.40, (*fig.*) 6.217; lesson [for guidance in action] 12.91, **B** 6.275, 10.92; piece of instruction 6.210, 241

lest *conj.* lest, so that (not), for fear that Pr 127, 8.294, **B** 11.430, 12.7, 13.427, 15.385, A 7.136; *and see* **last(e)** *conj.*

lest *contr. pr.* **B** 11.97, 12.173 (= **lust**) *see* **lusten** *v*

lest(e) *sup. a* smallest 14.190; (very) least, slightest B 13.187, Z 6.49; lowest A 11.90; lowest (in rank), least important 3.25, 247, 261; *a as n* least (= smallest amount); smallest (one) 13.157; briefest poem 7.12; least important (one) 2.208, 20.448, B 11.49

leste *av* least 3.209; the least bit (of all) B 17.41, 18.284, Z 7.64

lesten A 12.93 = **lasten** *v*

let *contr. pr.* 10.161; *see* **letten** *v*

leten *v* (*contr. pr.* **lat** 3.173, A 11.142 *etc; imper. sg.* 3.75 *et p., pl.* **late** 4.174, *p.t.* **lat** 6.261, **le(e)t** 1.162, 8.119 *etc*, **lette** 4.156 *etc*, *pl.* **leten** 2.172) give up 2.104, 3.263, 6.101, 8.293, 11.22, 12.217, 19.290, 20.386, **B** 5.224, 10.393, A 12.21, **Z** 3.154, 5.95, *ger.* **letynge (of lyf)** moment of death 17.124; leave 3.241; leave behind B 18.407; forsake, desert 11.184, B 4.191; cause (sb. to do sth.) 2.172, 209, 213, 215, 4.84, 142, 17.227; cause (sth. to be done) 2.172, 190, 22.143, **B** 2.171, 4.21, A 7.210; allow Pr 173, 1.162, 3.75, 173, 5.137, 6.393, 8.119, ?276, 12.50, 18.276; consider Pr 195, 4.156, 17.297, (*refl.*) conduct oneself, behave ? Z 2.160*n; in phr.* ~ **bi** esteem 3.204, 5.3, 7.267, B 10.187; let, may 20.205, 464; (*in supposition*) let (us suppose that), ~ **bryng a man** suppose a man were to be brought 10.33; cease, ~**...that** (not) cease until 6.311

letherne *a* of leather 6.199

leþi *a* empty, vain B 10.186

#**letynge** *ger.* 17.124 *see* **leten** *v*

letten *v* (*p.t.* **lette** 3.238, *p.p.* **(y)lette(d)** 21.385 (B 19.386)) hinder **B** 15.562, 16.46; prevent 17.168, 18.115, B 10.370, ~ **that** prevent (from) 3.35, 238, 10.161, 12.73, ~ **to** 14.177, 15.167, B 10.265; impede 4.170; obstruct 2.38, 3.450, 11.17, 13.90, 18.287, 20.283, 21.385, **B** 10.288, 14.212, 15.66; put a stop to B 3.198; stop 11.60, 13.9, 49, 15.221, 20.334, 22.173, 322, ?Z 2.166*n*, (from piercing) 1.153; delay 1.202, 13.36, 38, 19.78, 333, 20.53, B 9.131, *ger.* **lettyng** delay 8.5, 11.136

lettere *n*[1] obstructor 1.65

lettere *n*[2], 22.310, A 12.86, Z 7.261 *see* **lettre** *n*

let(te)red(e) 14.198, 16.254, Z 3.164, A 8.45 *see* **lettred** *a*

lettre *n* character (of the alphabet), letter 9.284, Z 7.261; letter (private) 2.233, 4.129, 13.59, 22.310, **B** 9.38, 40, 15.375; official document [recording agreement, granting rights or privileges] 2.83, 107; = charter 13.117; = licence 22.326, 327; = privy letter 9.27, 20.172, 184; letter patent 19.4 *et p.*, B 17.34, 118; written orders 11.268; authorisation, credentials 13.40, 88; (written) authority 20.81; scriptural text 12.114; inscription B 1.49; *in phrr:* **bisshopes** ~**s** licences for preaching of indulgences 9.320, B 5.640; **Lumbardus** ~**s** bills of exchange 6.246; **prinses** ~**s** letters of intercession or pardon 21.309; **priue** ~**s** letters sent under king's privy seal 4.189; **prouinciales** ~**s** letters of fraternity 9.342; ~**(s) of (oure) lif** written assurance of (length of) life B 10.91; communication concerning Life A 12.86*n*

lettred *a* educated (*esp.* in Latin) B 7.132, 12.96, 144, A 8.45, *a as n* 1.134; *in phrr:* ~ **leodes** learned men B 3.97; ~ **lordes** educated noblemen 3.124; ~ **men**

learned men, the clergy 9.326, 11.76, 12.45, 17.73, 87, 210, 18.80, 21.85, **B** 11.83, 12.157, 15.476; ~ **(men) (and) lewed (men)** 14.198, **B** 13.287, 15.353

lettrure *n* learning Pr 137, 9.195, 198, 11.99, 14.49, 127, 15.182; authority 11.210; **holy** ~ Holy Writ 11.26, 15.74

leute(e) 4.36, 7.259 *etc.*, *(person.)* 2.20 *see* **le(a)ute(e)** *n*

leue¹*n* leave, permission 2.241, 3.16, 131, 6.439, 12.64, 13.82, 22.188, 189, B 3.231, A Pr 94; right Pr 50, 8.67, 9.146, 14.59; authorisation 2.115, 22.326, B 16.47; *in phrr:* **aȝenes** ~ in defiance of authority 20.275, 314, 381; **lengore ȝeres** ~ longer period of grace 22.287; **licence and** ~ formal permission Pr 83, 6.121, Z Pr 63; leave (to go), farewell 3.46, 4.15, 7.292, 21.483, A 12.55

leue² 2.18, 3.73, *etc; see* **le(e)f (leue)**³ *a*

leuele (lyuel A) *n* mason's level [T-square and plumb line] 11.126

leuen *v*¹ (*p.t.* **lefte** 2.53 (**lafte** B 3.197), *p.p.* **ylefte** 17.162) cease (from) 9.209, 22.372, ~ **to** desist from B 7.150; leave off 16.174, A 3.185; abandon 15.7, 16.195, 17.162, 22.40, B 4.153; renounce 3.73, 5.128, 16.103, B 14.264; give up 6.339, 12.217, 16.254, 256, 22.108, 250, 251, 352, B 3.207; leave behind 18.155, 19.75, 20.449; *ger.* **lyuynge** vomit 6.413; allow 22.102, grant, **God / Lord / Crist** ~ may God / the Lord / Christ grant 7.156, 11.245, 17.40, 117, Pr 149; leave 2.53; pass by 7.224; put by 17.102; bequeath Pr 130, 6.254, 16.280, B 15.322; remain B 3.197

leuen *v*² (*imp. sg.* **leef** 1.36 *etc*) believe, have faith 14.199, 15.225, 17.124, 158, 182, 297, 19.94, 20.444, B 17.25, A 11.144; believe (sb. or sth.) 2.76, 3.220, 487, 5.3, 6.55, 275, 9.173, 267, 11.210, 13.193*n*, 210, 15.105, 17.217, 18.58, 198, 200, 19.18, 20.260, **B** 9.201, 11.49, 176, 12.94, 14.36 (1), Z 8.74; believe (that) 9.327, 11.202, 226, 14.150, 18.265, 19.103, 275, 20.56, 214, Z Pr 56; ~ **be** that he / there / it is 2.104, 14.210, B 5.275; trust (in) Pr 70, 1.36, 75, 2.105, 5.142, 6.81, 8.99, 19.24, 20.347, **B** 1.118, 6.265; think that, be sure Pr 103, 3.46, 4.169, 6.82, 253, 8.214, 298, 10.202, 16.281, 18.1, 19.137, 20.351, 21.411, 22.363, **B** 3.337, 9.40, 10.437, 12.252, 254, 13.264, 14.36 (2), 15.155, 18.314; suppose, think 1.139, 3.327, 5.187, 6.204, 301, 9.173, 12.44, 13.25, 38, 14.166, 17.168, 20.147, 171, 193, 307, 335, 393, 22.173, B 5.295; *(subjv.)* **no man** ~ let no one suppose 1.117; *in phr:* **as Y leue** in my opinion, as I think Pr 17 *et p.*

leuen *v*³ (come into) leaf, *p.p.* **leued** in leaf, leafy B 15.97; **grene yleued** covered with green leaves 16.248

leuen *v*⁴ 3.281, 419, 4.194, 5.44, 8.16, 12.230, ? 13.193*n*, 14.9, 15.180, 246, 17.182, Z Pr 36, 7.88 *see* **lyuen** *v*

leuer *comp.* 6.129 *etc*; **leuere** *comp.* B 1.143; *see* **le(e)f**⁴ *a*; **leef**⁵ *av*

leues *gen. sg.* 3.490; *pl.* 16.247, B 5.138 *etc; see* **le(e)f** *n*¹

leuest(e) *sup.* 5.85, B 1.151, A 1.178; **leuest** *sup.* **B** 5.563, 10.355; *see* **leef**⁴ *a*, **leef**⁵ *av*

leuestow B 18.188 = **leuest thow**; *see* **leuen** *v*²

lewdeliche Z 3.164 *see* **lewed** ~ *av*

lewed *a* uneducated, ignorant Pr 70, 102, 1.134, 3.185, 6.23, 9.164, 14.20, 49, 101, 113, 120, 124, 125, 130, 198, 16.260, 272, 17.87, 21.412, **B** Pr 129, 7.137, 10.472, 12.96, 144; *a as n* uneducated / ignorant person 15.14, 17.182, *pl* 17.292, B 3.255; untrained 14.123, Z 7.274; ~ **of** ignorant of 14.107; unable to read Latin 11.293; lay (= non-clerical) 1.193, 11.307, 12.43, 13.25, 15.15, 17.54, 19.43, 20.355, **B** 12.231, 15.70, 119; *a as n* layman 14.59, 63, 113, 16.290, **B** 10.276, 11.96, 108, 302, 15.144, 391; laymen **B** 12.233, 15.353; lay people B 10.248; ordinary, common 9.223, 11.251, 298, A 10.103; useless, idle 1.184, A 11.141; *in phrr.* ~ **counsayle** worthless advice 17.56; ~ **ermytes** idle hermits 5.4, 9.140, 240; ~ **iuttes** uncouth nobodies B 10.461; ~ **knaues**, ~ **laboreres** ignorant workmen 9.209, 11.304; ~ **(men) and lered (men)** educated and uneducated / people of all kinds 3.40, 6.116 *etc*, **B** 3.38, 12.96 *etc* (*see also under* **lered**); ~ **peple** ordinary lay people 1.193, 17.121; ~ **preestes** ignorant / incompetent priests B 11.317; ~ **vnderstondynge** poor understanding 13.115; ~ **wit** untrained mind B 15.83; **clerk and / n(oþer)** ~ cleric and / (n)or layman 16.290, 22.68, B 10.51, A 11.38; **~liche** *av* ignorantly, foolishly Z 3.164; **~nesse** *n* lack of learning 3.35

lew(e)te(e) Pr 149, 3.378, 443, 446, 6.195, 21.89, B 12.32, Z 2.107 = **le(a)ute(e)** *n*

lyard *n* [name for] horse (spotted with grey) 19.66, 78, 333, B 17.72

lyare *n* liar, deceiver 1.36, 5.187, 7.82, 10.299, 21.293, **B** 9.119, 13.288, Z 7.253, *(person.)* 2.6, 69, 77, 192, 205, 215, 225, 234, 237, 22.146; charlatan A 7.257

libben 6.125, 8.70, 9.193, 17.249, 20.109, B 2.187, **A** 4.158, 10.144, *pr. p.* **libbyng(e)** 9.58, **B** Pr 223, 9.108, 10.430, 15.93 = **lyuen** *v*

liberal *a* magnanimous, bountiful B 15.150

lycame *n* body 6.52, 10.221, 19.95, 237, 20.93, B 12.233; flesh [as seat of sinful passions] Pr 32, 1.35, 36, B 15.67, Z Pr 36, 3.161; *in phrr:* **~es gultes** sins of the flesh 6.176, 275; sins of (one's) life 10.55; ~ **and lyf** body and life 6.52, 15.58, 19.183, A 12.93; *see also* **lich**

licence *n* authorisation, *in phr:* ~ **and leue** formal permission Pr 83, 6.121

lich *n* body B 10.2, †19.28

liche 7.123, B 9.63, A 11.246 = **lyk(e)** *a*

licketh 3.19 = **lyketh**; *see* **lyken** *v*

lycour *n* juice 12.222

licud Z 8.26 = **likede**; **licuth** Z 3.150 *etc* = **lyketh**; *see* **lyken** *v*

lye 19.173 = **l(e)ye** *n*¹

lief 17.126 = **lyf** *n*

lyen (**liȝen**) *v* (*p.t. 2 sg.* **low(e)** 20.348, 445 (**leighe** B 18.403), *p.p.* (**y**)**low(en)** 2.20, B 5.94) (tell a) lie 2.32, ? 3.193*n*, 6.55, 98, 138, 20.348, 445, 22.238; speak falsely Pr 50, 1.65, 6.52, 14.6, 16.304, 18.185, 22.277, 20.30, B 13.179, *ger.* B 13.323; make a false claim 10.275, 16.236, 19.224, 227, B 1.118, A 8.61; ~ **on** slander 2.20, **B** 5.94, 10.42, 200; tell lies about **B** 10.39, 205, 15.172; misinform, mislead 8.238, 17.27, **B** 3.251, 7.125, 9.74, 10.331, 11.83, ~ **on** B 15.83; be false to, deceive **B** 1.69, 14.144; speak untruthfully 2.39, ? 5.89n, 6.301, 15.179, B 11.223; tell tall stories 15.204, Z 7.68; be mistaken B 10.111

lieutenaunt *n* deputy B 16.47

lyf *n* (*gen. sg.* **lyues** 19.323, 21.218, *dat.* **lyue** 1.25) life, animate existence Pr 146, 173, 2.104, 3.172, 466, 6.101, 10.55, 174, 194, 197, 11.22, 90, 14.63, 15.58, 240, 17.124, 155, 18.285, 19.183, 259, 20.387, 425, 21.105, 22.11, 87, **B** 1.78 3.197, 4.73, 195, 5.98, 6.56, 8.37, 9.45, 54, 10.349, 393, 16.189, 17.308, 18.344, **A** 2.14, 10.46, 12.86, 93, 112; vital spirit A 6.50; *in phr.* ~ **and (of / for) soule** 6.314, 14.127, 17.22, 20.268, 370, 21.411, **B** 9.188, 17.25; (*person.*) = (principle of) earthly life A 12.44, 64, 86; = Pride of Life 20.30, 22.143 *et p.*, 312, 352; = (principle of) divine life, God 20.56, 67, 105; (span of) life 1.25, 9.340, 12.201, 15.262, 298, 16.18, 18.77 (1), 19.323, 21.218, 22.111, **B** Pr 49, 1.27, 5.366, 10.414, 14.24, 97, 124, 15.234, 17.307, A 10.145 *in phrr.* **o lyue** alive A 2.14; duration of (one's) life 7.111, 8.110, 174, 9.173, 12.92, 20.335, B 10.91; (the present) life 2.105, 6.313, 12.71, B 10.122; (the future) life (in heaven) 12.161, 18.257, *in phr.* **lawe of** ~ 21.45; divine life 10.171, B 9.48; state / way of life Pr 88, 5.31, 9.103, 140, 12.164, 13.98, 16.153, 18.77 (2) 20.110, 339, 21.238, **B** Pr 120, 10.134, 232, 11.255, 272, 13.288, A 11.182, 12.4, 90; (moral) conduct of life 6.45, 436, 10.294, 19.332, **B** 9.63, 64, 13.296, **A** 9.87, 11.217; manner / way of life 5.103, 8.278, 10.50, 126, 13.29, 18.81, **B** 3.166, 9.190, 11.386, 15.4, A 9.52, *in phr.* ~ **of usurie** B 3.240; living creature 15.19, B 13.17; human being, one 3.233, 446, 6.67, 423, 7.50, 9.197, 11.265, 12.33, 13.73, 207, 17.131, 18.105, 19.276, 20.386, 22.92, **B** 10.262, 11.213, 389, 13.282, 332, 15.6, 249, 354; (written) life (= biography) 7.31, B 7.85, 15.269; *in assevs.* ~ ...(to) **wedde** 2.36, 3.258, 20.30, **legge** ~ 4.191, 20.160, **by thy lyue** on your life! 8.234, 11.74; *in phrr.* **Actiua** ~ 18.80; **Contemplatif** ~ B 6.248, ~ **of contemplacioun** 18.77; **lec(c)he of** ~ 1.198, B 16.118; **legende of** ~ 11.206; **lord of** ~ 10.155, 20.59, 403, B 13.121; *in cpds.* ~ **dayes** (days of one's) life 3.187, B 1.27; ~ **holy** of holy life 4.175, 9.195, 11.2, 14.188, **B** 12.62, 15.206, 308, ~ **holiest** 10.50, ~ **holynesse** holiness of life 5.80, 21.111; ~ **tyme** lifetime, course / duration of (one's) life Pr 50, 1.75, 2.32,

6.239, 436, 440, 7.215, 8.25, 10.169, 11.182, 256, 15.198, 17.36, 18.200, 19.110, 20.3, 22.366, **B** 5.236, 476, 13.142, 15.142

liflode *n* sustenance, living 1.35, 3.466, 4.115, 5.42, 45, 6.311, 8.15, 222, 242, 9.245, 17.36, 22.239, **B** 8.81, 9.107, 14.34, 15.255, 19.231, 240, **A** 7.236, 8.110; food 8.15, 196, 263, 313, 9.100, 197, 13.102, 15.239, 272, 22.238, **B** 1.18, 11.280, 14.32, 15.184, 277, 308, 17.77, Z 7.107; the necessities of life 8.294, 17.155; means of living / to a livelihood 6.68, 13.113, 15.240, B 7.124; way of life Z 1.127

lyft[1] *n* sky, **byleue to þe** ~ trust in weather-lore 17.95

lyft[2] 3.75, B 5.578 = **luft** *a*

lyften *v* (*p.t.* **luft** 17.302 (**lifte** B 15.592), *ger.* **luftynge** 6.410) lift 6.409, 410, B 12.120; raise (from the dead) 17.302, 18.144

liges B 18.350 *see* **le(e)ge** *a*

ligge ? *a* flattened 12.234n; *see next*

li(gg)en *v* (*contr. pr.* **lith, lyth** 1.127, 4.62, *p.t.* **lay** Pr 8 *et p.*, **ley(ȝe)** 13.159, A 7.178, *p.p.* **layȝe** 6.329, **layn** 3.40, (**y**)**ley(e)** 11.260, 21.55, **B** 5.81, (**y**)**ley(e)n** B 16.113, A 11.284) lie (down) 5.149, 7.26, 22.378, **B** 13.21, 16.20, *pr.p.* **lyggynge** 2.53; recline, lie at ease 9.143; lie (fallen) 12.234n, 13.236, (sick) 22.312, A 7.130, 178, (buried) 13.22, 15.11, 18.144, B 12.255, (prostrate) B 5.63, (in torment) 1.127, 2.130, 20.146, Z 3.123; stay 14.120, 18.285; remain 19.180; remain in place 22.361; rest idle 8.160; be found 3.221, 6.227, 261; reside, lodge Pr 89, 4.122, 21.421, **B** 6.15, 17.116; spend (night) 5.16; lie hidden 7.45; *in phrr.* ~ **aȝeyn** ? obstruct 3.193*n*; ~ **by, togideres** sleep with, have sexual intercourse with 1.28, 3.40, 169, 4.62, 6.192, 329, B 2.136, A 2.25 (*subjv.*); ~ **in** depend on Pr 137, 20.428, B 4.73; ~ **on** bend forward above B 17.225; exist A 11.141; be 18.272; stand 20.127; consist 9.284, A 10.188; ? be relevant 5.89n

liȝt, light B 1.189 *et p.*; *see* **lyht(e)** *n*

lyht(e) *n* light 7.132, 134, 10.155, 20.59, 127, 140, 147, 172, 193, 271, 275, 280, 283, 286, 296, 306, 342, 359, 368, 369; radiance [of comet] 20.249, [of sun] 20.254, [of spiritual substance] Z 1.58, [of Paraclete] 21.206; flame [of lamp / torch] 1.184, 19.180; (the realm of) light (= heaven) A 12.96; sight 21.125, *in oath* **bi this** ~ 21.462; (*fig.*) = human life 19.263; (divine) source of life

lyht *a* light (in weight), *comp.* ~**ere** 1.150; easy 19.43, *comp.* ~**er** B 17.40, 44; cheerful, *comp.* ~**ere** 16.140

lyhte *av* lightly, *in phrr.* **acounten** ~, B 11.16, **leten** ~ **of** 8.165, **setten** ~ **by** 11.164 set small store by, hold in low regard; easily, quickly 20.260

lyhtli(che) *av* (*comp.* **lyhtloker** 7.215, B 15.438 etc) mildly B 14.35; easily Pr 169, 4.101, 14.101, 17.253, 19.315, 323, 20.278, B 15.438, 501; nimbly 7.215; quickly 9.11, 12.224, 16.280; smartly 2.225; readily

16.130; promptly 4.168; immediately B 15.137; without good reason 7.301

lihtnynge *n* flash of flame 21.203

lyk(e) (liche 7.123, B 9.63) *a* like, similar (to) 1.87, 110, 2.224, 3.488, 6.75, 7.123, 10.45, 157, 21.8, **B** 5.117, 8.117, 9.63, 12.252; *and see* **ilych(e), ylyk(e)** *a*

lyke(y)liche 19.332, **ylike** 20.3) *av* like, in the same way (as) 2.224, 6.75, 403, 8.174, 9.158, 12.19, 19.332, 20.3, 332, **B** 15.348, 17.131

lyken *v* please 1.41, 22.156, **B** 1.28, 14.78; (*as impers. constr. with subj.*) 4.36, 22.156, B 11.24, (*without subj.*) Pr 168, 170, 188, 1.41, 2.241, 3.19, 175, 180, 227, 5.41, 8.154, 9.28, 20.33, 449, **B** 8.51, 11.97, 14.167, 16.230, 18.375, **A** 10.149, 12.37, 51, Z 3.150; (*subjv.*) 3.44, 11.134, 185, 19.329, **B** 9.190, 13.187, **A** 8.122, 12.1; like Pr 70, 3.330, 10.275, 22.30, 310, **B** 10.97, 13.264; (be) please(d) 14.146, 15.260, 19.120, **B** 12.166, 167, 15.91, **A** 8.58, 12.112; wish, desire 6.45, 12.164; *in phrr:* **lyketh and luste** pleases and wishes 9.146, 19.116, **B** 11.97, 12.173; **dere lyketh** best pleases 8.315, **lef lyketh** pleases well 4.145, 7.252, **B** Pr 163, 206; **good / best lykede** pleased well / best Pr 58, 9.28

lykene 16.308 *etc*; *see* **ly(e)knen** *v*

likerous(e) *a* lascivious B 10.163; luxurious(ly self-indulgent) Pr 32, B 6.265; delicious 1.25, 10.178, B 10.166

lykhame A 12.93 = **lycame** *n*

lykynde *pr.p.a* 18.78 = **lykyng** *a*

lykyng(e) *ger.* pleasure (in), enjoyment (of) 2.75, 11.12, 16.102, **B** 1.27, 14.129; sensual pleasure 11.182, **B** 9.181, 16.32; wish, desire 5.155, 6.194, 7.74, 83, 13.152, 16.308, **B** 5.174, 11.45, 49, 420, 12.219, 15.67, **in ~ of** affecting a desire for B 13.288; affection B 10.304; *in phrr:* **at...~** as one likes 14.55, 15.168, 16.174, 20.93, B Pr 62; **lust and ~** 16.211; **~ and lust** 11.82; **~(s) of body** 9.202, 11.12, 16.102, 22.71; **~ of lecherye** lustful pleasures 6.176, 11.265, B 13.344

lykyng *a* pleasing 11.133, 18.78, B 11.272; sexually stimulating 10.288, *sup.* 6.44

#lykyngliche *av* attractively 19.243

likken *v* lick, *ger.* licking B 15.304

lyk(e)nen *v* liken, compare 14.168, 190, 16.264, 17.73, *p.p.* **likned** analogous to 10.44, 47, 19.169, 260, 21.89, 111, Z 1.116; make derogatory comparisons (of) B 10. 276; mimic (satirically) 7.23, 16.308, B 10.42

lik(e)nesse *n* guise, shape 12.123, 133, 17.179, 20.328, 21.203, 206, **B** 1.114, 121, 11.186, 231, 241, 18.355, 357; likeness, image **B** 9.66, 10.365

lyme *n* limb 8.261, A 7.180; member 22.195; *in phrr:* **in alle ~es** in every part 21.8; **fendes ~es** instruments of the devil 22.77; **lif and ~** 21.105, B 5.98; **~es to labory with** 5.8, 8.135, 9.103

lymytour *n* licensed mendicant friar 22.347, 363, B 5.137

lym3erd *n* stick smeared with birdlime (*fig.*) 10.288

lyn *n* flax, **~sed** seed of flax, linseed 12.192

lynage *n* good birth 9.195; descendants B 9.48; family 9.197; **~ riche** well-to-do relatives 5.26, 13.110

lynde *n* linden (lime) tree 1.150, 10.64

lyne *n* cord (set as snare for birds) 6.405; (mason's) line 11.126, B 10.181; line (of writing) 9.284, **B** 3.340, 5.422; *in phr.* **laumpe ~** inscription on lamp B 13.152

lyn(n)en *n* linen cloth 1.3, 18, 13.102, **B** Pr 220, 11.280, 14.56; linen yarn A 7.13

lyo(u)n *n* lion 9.196, **B** 13.302, 15.204, 277

lippe *n*[1] lip, *pl.* Pr 162, 6.104, 245, 8.273, 11.227, 17.253, 20.52, **B** Pr 214, 5.83, A 7.166

lippe *n*[2] little bit (*lit.* mouthful) 2.37, 17.251

lyser *n* selvage 6.216

lysse *n* comfort 6.314; joy 10.155, 20.235; relief 1.198

list *n* strip of cloth 7.161

listen (*cont. pr.* **list** B 3.158, *subjv.* A Pr 37, *p.t.* **liste** B 1.150) = **lusten** *v*

lyst(e)nen *v* listen 15.251, 20.295, B 14.308

listre *n* lector, ? preaching friar B 5.137c

lite *n* little B 13.150, Z 2.159

lyte (litte) *a* little 1.139, 8.263, 9.207

lytel *n* little 2.200, 5.163, 11.74, 14.121, **B** 10.90, 12.250, A 10.116; (*as semi-av*) **a ~** a little, somewhat 16.120, 17.54, 20.357, **B** 13.268, 14.35, 15.422, a short time 18.167

litel *a* little 3.130, 263, 390, 11.229, 304, 12.26, 15.10, 155, 16.85, 90, 17.237, 19.94, 22.148, 368, **B** 10.472, 11.220, 15.475; small 17.24, 18.70, **B** Pr 191, 9.78; short 1.106, 12.224, 16.369, 17.237, 19.47

litel *av* 4.69, 5.31, 6.145, 11.34, 47, 16.143, 22.27, **B** 7.137, 10.371, 441, 17.91; *in phr.* **(a)counten ~** make small account (of), care little (for) 3.392, 10.261, 11.317, 21.454; **leten ~ by** have small respect for 5.3; **~ um** a little at a time 17.318

lyþ *n* body (*lit.* limb) B 16.181

lith *contr. pr.* Pr 137 *et p.*; *see* **liggen** *v*

lithen *v*[1] ease (pain of) 19.71, A 7.180

lythen *v*[2] listen to 6.194, 7.83, 97, 115, 10.65, 11.77

liþer B 10.166, 437, **lyther** 10.167 *see* **lu(y)ther** *a, av*

litheren (to) *v* attack (with sling) 18.48c

litte 9. 207 *see* **lyte** *a*

lyue (*dat*) 1.25, 6.313, B 5.366, A 2.14 *see* **lyf** *n*

lyuen (leuen 3.281 *etc*, **lybben** 3.202 *etc*) *v* live, be alive Pr 102, 1.16, 3.281, 8.194, 15.171, 17.115, 248, 18.198, 20.29, **B** 2.187, 14.32, A 12.112; (continue to) live 3.296, 6.67, 10.50, 57, 11.180, 202, 13.4, 14.146, 15.180, 264, 266, 270, 272, 19.44, 75, 20.30, 264, 21.161, 22.63, **B** 6.181, 14.322, **Z** 5.123, 6.44; live eternally 3.359, 20.398; dwell 5.44, 16.286, 17.7, 292, 20.29, **B** 4.195, 8.93, 10.298, 14.43, A 10.144; live (in some state / condition) 6.314, 9.158, 159, 166, 173, 212, 15.298, 16.103, **B** 10.437, 11.176; live (in some manner) Pr

28, 175, 3.249, 288, 324, 4.118, 5.142, 7.73, 8.57, 70, 9.43, 159, 173, 193, 10.96, 126, 11.237, 256, 12.230, 14.9, 210, 15.273, 298, 303, 16.20, 269, 357, 17.158, 182, 19.237, 243, 290, 20.218, 21.355, 22.71, 90, 123, 312, **B** 3.227, 5.117, 10.134, 434, 14.152, Z Pr 36, 83; conduct oneself [according to / against a law / religion / rule] 3.202, 7.73, 8.69, 9.104, 291, 10.204, 15.95, 246, 262, 16.103, 17.139, 160, 258, 295, 18.73, 78, 21.249, 408, 22.247, **B** 3.164, 5.381, 10.25, 38, 12.34, 15.390, Z Pr 56; live (by feeding on) 5.174, 6.121, 292, 8.313, 9.200, 10.79, 173, 174, 12.187, 13.78, 15.241, 246, 17.21, 102, 18.10, 22.7, **B** 6.19, 15.255, 314, 422, (*fig.*) 15.246, 22.241; get a living [from benefice, interest *etc*] 4.194, 5.26, 6.125, 342, 17.219, 227, 20.109, 21.218, B 2.125; earn living [from work] Pr 146, 8.330, 9.58, 198, 17.20, 21.233, 238; *in assev.* **as longe as I ~** 4.104, 8.16, 11.89, B 4.191, 6.36, Z 7.88

lyuere *n* living person, †**olde ~ is** people who lived in the past B 12.131

lyues *a* alive 21.159

lyuyng *n* living, life 14.127, B 11.151, 161; way of life, conduct 2.55, 6.33, 286, 12.97, 115, 231, 461, 14.168, 15.104, 16.37, 21.382, 461, B 13.95, 15.391, 417, 423; (*person.*) **Pruyde of Parfit ~** the Pride of Life 11.176, 194

lyuynge (libbyng) *a* living, alive 9.58, 21.176, **B** 9.108, 13.282; *in phrr:* **lele ~** righteously living **B** 12.62, 15.93, *as n* 3.338; **lyther ~** evil-living 10.167; **lowe ~** humbly living B 12.264, 14.187, *as n* 16.152; *as n* **wel ~** B 10.430

lixt *2 pr. sg.* (= **liest**) *see* **lyen** *v*

lo *interj.* behold, look 2.5, 69, 6.55, 8.259, 11.26, 12.90, 221, 248, 13.20, 15.239, 292, 16.40, 236, 240, 17.65, 18.132, 239, 276, 19.4, 24, 20.254, 370, 22.202; see how 1.25, 5.186, 20.256, 258; *in phrr:* **~ here** look, here is 20.190, **B** 17.76, 18.328; **~ me here** here I am 20.370

lobi *n* lubber, lazy lout Pr 53

locud *p.t.* (= **lokede**), **locun** *pr.* (= **loken**) *see* **loken** *v*

lode-sterre *n* guiding-star 17.95

loef, loof *n* (*pl.* **loues**) loaf of bread 8.286, 9.150, 15.56, 17.24, 18.154, 21.126, **B** 14.222, 15.590, Z 7.107; **~ of benes** loaf of bean-flour B 6.282; **pese ~** loaf of pea-flour 8.176

loerd 20.283 = **lord** *n*

lo(e)s(se), loos *n* loss 6.275, 16.147, 21.293, **B** Pr 191, 13.387, 14.7

loest *p.p.* 16.40 (= **lost**) *see* **lesen** *v*

lo(e)th *a* hateful, unpleasant 15.80, 20.260, B 9.58, 12.243; spiteful 15.80; unwilling, reluctant Pr 53, 3.198, 8.48, 265, 9.44, 11.133, 12.217, 16.145, 260, 17.44, 22.361, **B** 11.222, 13.260, 15.5, 144, 309, A 12.6; *comp.* B 15.391; **me was ~** I was unwilling **B** 14.7; difficult 15.138

lo(e)thli(che) *a* fearsome 1.109, 21.56; disgusting 14.178, 16.264

l(o)oft *n* upper chamber Z 3.10; *in phrr:* **a ~e** on high Pr 175; **a ~ and o grounde** high and low, in every direction 20.44; **agrounde and o ~** on earth and in heaven B 1.90; *and see* **alofte** *av*

logge *n* encampment, shelter Z 2.47

loggyng *n* lodging A 12.44

logh 10.83 = **lowe** *a*

loghen 12.159 = **lowen** *v*

logyk *n* logic [the liberal art of reasoning] 11.118, 22.250, 274, **B** 11.218 *et p.*, 12.97; treatise on logic 14.190

lok *n*[1] lock [on chest or door] 6.266, *fig.* (*or* river-barrier) 1.196c; *and see* **louken** *v*

lok *n*[2] expression (of face) 11.268

loken *v* look Pr 187, 2.5, 8, 131, 6.4, 44, 7.50, 8.181, 11.170, 13.132, 15.251, 18.54, 272, 20.117, 368, **B** Pr 123, 18.118; gaze 13.173; glance 15.111; peer 11.127; stare 8.341, B 11.85; glare B 15.204; look about 4.63, B Pr 152; look up **B** 5.63, 10.138; *in phrr:* **~ on** look at 1.162, 4.67, 106, 167, 6.44, 315, 10.262, 11.85, 18.54, 20.425, 428, 448, **B** Pr 9, 4.173, 11.408, 186, 13.302, 16.64; **~ þerafter** look towards (it) 7.224; **~ vp** stare B 15.253; (be able to) see B 10.265, Z 3.28, *in idiom* **lyuen and ~** live and have the use of one's faculties 10.57, 20.29, 21.159, 176, B 14.32; appear, look 5.162, 8.174, 9.141, 11.2, 16.69, 269, 20.10, **B** 5.82, 15.206, 348, (*with ethic dat.*) 6.197; see, find out 2.169, 7.292, 15.251; look at, read 6.301, **B** 3.345, 7.137, consult A 8.14; examine 2.234; **~ forþ** search out A 7.13; see, consider 9.240, 277, 13.207, 14.130, B 11.83; be concerned (about), take heed (of) 8.234, 11.74, ?**B** 5.394, 15.185, 318; pay attention to 13.236, B 9.57; watch over 8.85, **B** 1.209, 7.166, 15.9, 16.47, Z 1.100; protect 20.379; see to it / take care (that) 1.144, 7.221, 228, 8.36, 277, 10.285, 11.147, 19.110, 21.255, 22.206, **B** 3.271, 5.575, 10.189, 207, 254, **A** 3.248, 10.92, 116; (*refl.*) conduct oneself †B 10.90; decree, decide 2.209, B 6.316; **~ after** wait for 14.120, 18.267; expect 3.248, 9.269, 13.73, 19.263

lokynge *a* fully conscious 21.159 (*and see* **loken** *v*)

lokyng(e) *ger.* looking, gazing (at) B 13.344, Z 6.101, *in phr.* **~ of an eye** twinkling of an eye A 12.96; expression 18.10, B 16.7; judgement 2.122; glancing at, referring to B 11.317

#lollare *n* idle vagabond 5.2, 4, 8.74, 287, 9.103, 107, 137, 158, 159, 192, 240, B 15.213, *gen. pl.* (*or a*) **lollarne** of a loller (idler) 5.31, 9.140

lollen *v* hang loosely 6.199; dangle (sb. from noose) 14.130; rest 14.152, 18.286; limp / ? act as a Lollard 9.215, 218*n*

lolly B 6.116 *see* **trollilolly** *excl.*

lomb(e) 7.196, 10.83, *pl.* **lombren** 9.260 *see* **lamb(e)** *n*

lome[1] *n* tool 5.45

lome[2] *av* frequently 10.167, 12.123, *comp.* 22.238

lompe *n* lump, piece 9.150

lond 3.172 *etc*, B 4.73; #**londleperis** B 15.213 *see* **land ~ n**

lone *n* (money-)lending 4.194; gift (of food from employer) 8.196

long *a* long (*spatially*) 20.44, 21.280, B 16.57; extensive A 11.118; *in phrr.* ~ **clothes** (= cleric's garb) 5.41; ~ **day** the whole / livelong day B Pr 225; ~ **lenthe** extensive reach 16.82; tall Pr 53, 5.24, 10.116, (*in name*) 15.152, (*a as n*) 16.84; long (*temporally*) long-lasting 7.203, 8.5; *in phrr.* ~ **labour** 9.207, ~ **lesson** B 10.371, ~ **lyf** 22.111, ~ **sorwe** B Pr 191, ~ **study** Pr 195, ~ **tale** B 9.72, ~ **tyme** 7.203, 20.5, 65, Z 6.44; ~ **trauayle** 19.213, ~ **while** 4.44, ~ **ȝeres** 11.260, 16.286, 17.26, **ouer** ~ of excessive duration 16.363, 22.363; **woke** ~ all week long 9.253; late, delayed 6.277, 7.159

long(e) *av* long, (for) a long time 3.296, 5.80, 123, 8.274, 11.180, 206, 12.194, 222, 13.178, 14.38, 15.7, 58, 16.60, 17.187, 18.287, 20.81, 171, 20.279, 339, 21.55, **B** 4.191, 195, 5.63, 81, 376, 6.36, 10.207, 13.21, 265, 268, 15.1, 191, 16.20; *in phrr.* ~ **ygo** a long time ago 20.296; ~ **lybbynge** long-lived 14.168; **as ~ as** as long as 4.104, 6.342, 8.16, 11.89, 15.58; **or ~ or** for a long time before 6.277; **ar come auht** ~ before long 17.214; **late and** ~ a long time later 7.159; **ouer** ~ for too long 22.361

longe *n* lung 8.189

longen *v*[1] be fitting (*?or* obligatory) B 11.419; appertain B 10.134; be characteristic (of) B 10.212; be appropriate (to) Z 6.65; belong (to) 7.270, B 2.46, A 12.64; live, dwell 10.7, (as part of retinue) 3.247, 9.130

longen *v*[2] (**after**) long (for) 8.279

longynge *ger.* yearning, desire 11.169, 21.249

loo 2.5 *etc* = **lo** *interj.*

loof 8.176 = **loef** *n*

loofte *n* height; *in phr.* **on ~** 20.44 = **alofte** *av*

loore B 5.38, 9.71, 10.121, 14.86, 15.357, 19.240, ~**sman** B 15.390 *see* **lore(sman)** *n*

lo(o)s *n*[1] reputation 7.108, 13.110, B 13.299

loos *n*[2] 6.275 *see* **lo(e)s(se)** *n*

looþ B 9.58, 11.222, 13.360, 14.7, 15.5, 144, 309, 472 *see* **lo(e)th** *a*

lope *p. t. subjv.* 4.101, **lope(n)** *pt. pl.* **B** Pr 223, 1.117, 4.153, 5.161, 18.312 *see* **lepen** *v*

lord *n* (*infl. gen. pl.* **lordene** 1.95) head of household, lord of manor B 10.97; (*as title*) **my ~** 22.346, 347; master Pr 175, 19.18; employer 7.97, 8.251 *et p.*, 9.269, 13.88, (*fig.*) 14.215; owner of property 13.87, 14.20, B 3.297; rich man 3.31, 11.26, A 3.273; ruler 3.259, 378, 4.69, 18.201, 21.56, **B** 10.25, 334, A 12.44, Z 7.270; governor 16.281; lord justice 2.21, **B** 3.25, 5.94; sovereign 7.207, 15.168, 171, 290, 21.174 (1), B 3.298; (*fig.*) **~ of lyf** B 13.121, (*as title of king*) 3.147, 220, 4.69,

B 3.197, 231, 244, A 3.222; feudal lord 1.95, 3.309, 5.167, 9.73, 10.219, 11.184, 12.64, 15.14, B 10.92, 470; (ecclesiastical) authority, bishop 22.326, **lettred ~** (senior) churchman 3.124; priest A 11.217; nobleman, man of rank Pr 62, 93, 3.57, 73, 268, 282, 381, 5.160, 163, 7.91, 95, 9.14, 18, 223, 230, 10.96, 148, 11.34, 76, 78, 202, 12.90, 117, 14.87, 15.210, 211, 16.143, 236, 17.227, 21.32, 355, **B** 3.346, 5.138, 7.157, 9.38, 10.22, 111, 11.188 (1), 12.144, 13.227, 15.86, 202, A 12.114; leader A 11.143; *in phrr.* ~**es kyn** 5.66; ~**es munstrals** 15.205; ~**es sones** 5.73; **~ of lust** 21.385; **grete ~es** 9.133, 10.148, 15.255, 17.67; **ryche ~es** 14.87; **~ and ladies** 4.109, 6.249, 7.81, 12.221, 15.306, 17.44, 56, **B** Pr 95, 5.243, 15.6, 309; ~**es and lorelles** high and low 15.216; noble warrior 18.286, 22.94; (*as general honorific title*) 20.280, 295, 297, 307, 360, 21.462, 22.71, 90, 92, B 18.88; (*as polite term of address*) B 6.124, 15.9; (*as title for God*) 1.110, 141, 11.47, 17.155, 157, 18.265, 19.44, 20.249, **A** 2.31, 12.112; **oure ~** Pr 28, 130, 162, 1.87, 154, 2.131, 3.240, 419, 5.55, 85, 7.108, 9.49, 184, 10.221, 12.93, 98, 196, 13.11, 29, 73, 14.38, 150, 15.15, 74, 118, 278, 16.2, 151, 193, 17.26, 136, 168, 219, 235, 295, 18.78, 82, 198, 19.183, 263, 275, 323, 20.110, 201, 352, **B** Pr 214, 1.204, 209, 6.233, 9.106, 10.39, 205, 11.174, 188 (2) 15.170, 185, 354, 17.131, **A** 1.110, 10.129, 180; (*address to God*) 6.101, 195, 423, 16.17, **B** 3.235, 10.129, 14.174; *in phrr.* ~**es ere** B 12.252, ~**es good** (= grace) B 5.296; ~**es loue** love of our Lord (God) 3.400, 4.39, 12.93, 15.74, 16.151, 17.26, 18.254, B 11.172; **(the) ~es loue of heuene** the love of Heaven's Lord 8.16, B 13.143, **A** 3.223, 8.33; **~ (....) almyhty** 17.135, 152, 19.42; **~ God** 8.135, 10.55, **B** 5.563, 10.355; **~ Treuthe** 9.19, 59; **~ (...) of heuene** **B** 16.118, 17.164, 18.357; **~ of lyf** 10.155, 20.59, 403; **~ of liht** 20.306; **~ of myhte** 20.361; *in oaths:* **by oure ~** Pr 103, 6.292, 8.67, 11.210, 227, 15.180, B 6.66, 14.36, Z 3.123; *in excls:* 1.111, 6.4, 18.276, B 15.249, 16.12; *in prayers and wishes:* **B** 1.209, 10.129; *in assevs:* 3.147, 8.298, 9.327, 17.40, 117, **B** 6.272, 11.179; *in execrations:* 3.212, B 3.166; Christ 3.400, **oure ~** 3.75, 99, 4.39, 6.81, 7.12, 74, 104, 12.45, 121, 123, 159, 161, 15.246, 20.369, 370, 443, 448, B 12.54, 94, Z 6.2, 46; **~ Iesu** 21.8, 96, 174 (2)

lordeyne *n* evil-doer 18.48; rascal 5.162, 22.189; villain 20.105

lorden *v* govern †B 3.298; **~ in** act as lord in / be owner of 11.69

lordene *gen. pl.* 1.95 *see* **lord** *n*

lordliche *a* haughty 3.198, B 13.302; *av* luxuriously 19.237, 243

lords(c)hip(e) *n* retinue B 2.46, A 6.35; ownership 17.218, 20.108; kingdom 3.263, (*fig.*) A 12.64; sovereignty B 7.159; dominion 2.107, 19.10, 22.251; *in phr.* **lond (and) ~** territory and dominion 3.315, 9.202, 11.12,

16.102, 158, 18.257, B 14.327; authority B 16.191; (feudal) estate 3.248, 17.221, (*fig.*) 2.93; favour 2.48; power 20.349, B 9.40

lore *n* instruction 11.127, 15.262, 22.352, **B** 5.38, 9.71; teaching(s) 1.67, 9.104, 11.36, 177, 13.193, 16.260, 283, 17.235, 310, 20.201, 21.35, 408, **B** 10.111, 121, 14.86, A 2.17; learning, knowledge 11.99, 14.198, B 15.357; wisdom 11.76; guidance B 19.240; religion 17.182; narrative 17.65

lore *p.t. subjv.* 16.312, *p.p.* 20.81; **loren** *p.t. pl.* 14.63; **lorn** *p.p.* Pr 112 *see* **lesen** *v*

lorel *n* scoundrel Pr 75, 8.129, 9.101, 14.20, B 17.45; wastrel B 15.5; beggar 6.313, 15.216; fool 20.3

loresman *n* instructor 14.122, **B** 9.88, 15.390

lorken *v* lurk, creep stealthily, *pr.p.* 2.226

los 13.110 = **lo(o)s** *n* B Pr 191; = **lo(e)s(s)e** *n*

Loscheborw *n* (counterfeit) light coin from Luxemburg 17.73, 168, B 15.348; *as a* ~**es sterlynges** (counterfeit) silver pennies from Luxemburg 17.82

losel *n* scoundrel 8.74, **B** Pr 77, 6.122, 10.49; wastrel 16.280

losen *v*¹ praise **B** 11.419, 15.253

losen *v*² (*p.t. pl.* **losten** Pr 108, 20.345, *p.p.* **(y)lost** Pr 195, 2.104 *etc*) lose (possession of) Pr 108, 195, 3.196, 5.95, 6.277, 9.181, 20.345, 347, **B** 5.98, 8.37, 13.389; let slip B 18.310; forfeit 3.196, 20.349; waste Pr 195, 12.96, 16.40, 19.213, B 10.271; destroy 11.254; damn [of soul] 2.104, 14.71, 134, 20.268, 21.411, 412; fail to gain 5.95; lose (fight) 20.105; *and see* **lesen** *v*

losengerie *n* deceitful flattery, ? idleness **B** 6.143, 10.49

losliche *av* at ease (*lit.* loosely) 14.152

losse 21.293, **B** 13.387, 14.7 = **lo(e)s(s)e** *n*

Lossheborw 17.82, 168 = **Loscheborw** *n*

lossum *a* delightful (= 'lovesome') 10.262

lost¹ *n* loss 5.97

lost² *n* 13.152, ? Z 3.163n,c *see* **lust** *n*

lost *p.t.* 9.181, *p.p.* 2.104 *etc.*, *see* **losen** *v*

lote *n*, (*pl* ~**s**) manners, bearing 15.8

loteby *n* concubine 3.187

loth, loþ Pr 53 *etc*, A 12.6, *comp.* ~**er** B 15.391; *see* **lo(e)th** *a*

lothen *v* (*impers.*) be hateful to, **vs lotheth** we hate Pr 173, **eche lyf hit lothed** everyone felt disgust 7.50; hate 6.142, B 7.96

lotien *v* lurk B 17.103

louable *a* praiseworthy 5.103

loud(e) *a* loud 20.469; *av* loudly 18.36, 20.271, A 4.138, 12.16; with a loud noise 20.38; aloud B 13.180; *in phr*: ~ **ouþer stille** at all times B 9.106

loueliche 16.69 *see* **lou(h)liche** *av*

louȝ *p.t.* A 4.137, †B 11.84, **louh(e)** 12.23, 18.3 *see* **lauhen** *v*

louȝ A 11.2, **louh(e)** 6.227, 7.196, 12.185, 16.152, 22.36 *see* **lowe** *a*

lou(h) 21.264, 22.37 = **lowe** *av*

lou(h)liche *av* humbly 9.141, 16.69

louhynge *ger.* 20.460 *see* **lauhen** *v*

louhnesse 5.155, **louȝnesse** A 6.78, 10.102, 129 *etc, see* **low(e)nesse** *n*

louken *v* lock up, hide 20.254

lound Z 6.78 = **land** *n*

#**loupe** *n* loophole, ?louver 20.286c

louren *v* scowl 2.233, 6.98, *pr.p.* **lourynge** 5.162, B 5.82 (**lourande** A), *ger.* 6.393; frown 14.202; ~ **on** scowl, lower at 12.23, 24, B 10.310; look angrily 4.168, 7.301, B 13.265; look sad 16.302

lous *n* (head-)louse 6.204

#**lousy** *a* lice-infested B 5.192

louten *v* bow 11.85, 87, **B** 13.26, 15.9, *pr.p.* A 12.55; make obeisance 3.151, 5.171, B 15.86, A 3.35; intercede 3.99, 6.171

loue *n* love Pr 130, 3.316, 376, 378, 443, 4.191, 11.75, 12.88, 14.215, 17.136, B 13.357, A 4.96; friendship 4.69, 7.267, 11.75, 15.145, 20.201, 457; amity, concord 3.452, 8.214, 17.237, (*person.*) 4.145, 156; the (Christian) virtue (of) love, charity Pr 137, 1.65, 145, 162, 198, 203, 5.80, 7.45, 237, 9.14, 166, 10.197, 204, 11.133, 14.27, 85, 15.148, 278, 17.22, 24, 139, 19.191, 276, 20.20, 235, 403, 458, **B** 1.150, 9.95, 10.186, 187, 188, 190, 432, 11.170, 12.68, 13.125, 14.47, 15.218, 255, 17.118, A 1.136, 178, Z 1.116, (*person.*) 1.154, 156, 20.171, 172, 184, 460, 469, B 13.140; love [between the sexes] 10.285, 11.169, 16.104, A 10.204; a loved one B 4.49; partiality 1.100, 12.41; sake (*in* **for** + *gen. or* **of** *-phrases*), = for the sake of / on account of Pr 28, 103, 162, 3.400, 6.101, 173, 243, 248, 7.97, 9.49, 184, 12.159, 167, **B** 3.159, 5.240, 377, 6.26, 7.75, 9.54, A 10.129, **no lordene** ~ no lords' sake 1.95; **for a mannes** ~ 16.104; **for Haukyns** ~ for the sake of Haukyn; **for Piers** ~ **þe palmare / plouhman** for P. the p.'s sake 15.132, 22.77, A 8.132; *in set phrr.* **for Cristes** ~ **(in heuene)** for the sake of Christ (in heaven) 14.35, 15.35, 16.164, 17.281, 290, **B** 6.220, 15.15, 523; **for Goddes** ~ for the sake / love of God 6.47, 8.284, 9.35, 66, 13.202, 16.103, **B** 10.203, 11.276; **for (oure / the) Lordes** ~ **(of heuene)** for the sake / love of our / the Lord (in heaven) 3.400, 4.39, 8.16, 9.130, 12.93, 15.74, 16.151, 17.26, 18.254; B 13.143, A 3.223, 8.33; **for Marie** ~ **Thi Moder / ** ~ **of heuene** for the sake of your mother Mary 7.148 / Mary in heaven 2.2, 8.16; *in cpds*: ~ **drem** love-dream B 16.20; ~ **knotte** love-knot 17.127; ~ **lawe** law of love 17.130, Z 1.100; *in phrr*: **dere** ~ 11.135; **filial** ~ 8.216; **fyn** ~ 19.176; **good** ~ pure, virtuous love 5.192, 10.300; **kynde** ~ true love 3.451, 14.14, 16.109; **lele** ~ faithful love Pr 88, 15.138, 16.194, **B** 11.161, 17.217, 225; **parfyt** ~ 15.219; **trewe** ~ 1.135, 18.9; **and leue** permission and leave 20.314, 381; ~ **and lewetee** love and faithfulness / loyalty

3.378, 443, 4.36, 7.259, 10.173, 11.160, 12.81, 96, 98, 15.134, 17.126, **B** 11.166, 15.467; ~ ~ **and lyf** 10.171, 19.259; ~ **and lownesse** 3.443, 5.155; ~ **of charite** 16.283; ~ **of soule** spiritual love 10.294; ~ **of þe worlde** love of worldly things 11.82; **lawe of** ~ 12.121, 14.38; **lok of** ~ 1.196

loueday *n* (meeting on) day for settlement of dispute out of court 3.195, 196, 11.17, **B** 5.421, 10.306

louelees *a* without love, unloved B 5.117

loueli(che) *a* friendly, kind 12.131, 18.10, **B** 11.186; agreeable 10.83, **B** 5.553, 11.239; lovely, beautiful 1.3, 10.65, 262, 22.104, **B** 6.10, 8.66, 12.261, *comp.* **louelokere** pleasanter 14.185, *sup.* **louelokest** most beautiful 1.106, 6.44, 192, **B** 1.112; excellent 16.84, **B** 6.275, 17.44, *av* kindly 16.69*n*; graciously 3.55, **B** 13.26

lou(y)en *v* love [feel affection / friendship / warm esteem (for)] 3.35, 209, 4.153, 196, 6.145, 249, 7.203, 252, 8.25, 10.133, 11.279, 12.163, 16.106, 17.131, 19.93, 276, 329, 332, 20.56, 334, 338, 369, 444, **B** 9.106, 11.88, 13.140, 15.464, 16.2, 231, 17.281, 18.337, 356, **A** 3.199, 6.23, 12.114; show love (friendship, kindness) to 2.75, 3.57, 119, 5.180, 196, 8.218, 221, 231, 10.79, 92, 189, 192, 201, 202, 306, 307, 11.34, 132, 134, 12.7, 93, 109, 118, 13.68, 86, 14.13, 15.118, 16.90, 357, 17.138, 142, 143, 19.40, 45, 101, 21.112, 114, 251, 255, 22.208, 210, 250, **B** 9.201, 10.200, 205, 207, 357, 11.176, 178, 180, 182, 195, 222, 12.54, 13.143, 15.170, 185, 354, 472, 476, **Z** 5.96; *pr.p.* kind, generous 15.19, 16.24; love [God / Christ] (= worship, obey) 1.141, 11.47, 13.133, 16.170, 17.135, 141, 152, 157, 19.42, **B** 7.124, 10.355, 12.13, 15.393, 17.129; serve loyally [Church, king] Pr 149, 1.75, 2.34, **B** 9.94; love (sth.) 3.161, 7.118, 11.12, 13.29, 21.66, **B** 10.50, 336; desire 19.140, **Z** Pr 36; love, esteem, care for [quality] 1.202, 2.36, 48, 188, 3.58, 130, 144, 281, 4.19, 109, 6.142, 12.44, 13.193, 14.188, 17.52, 21.66, **B** 4.32, 10.187, 202, 12.92, 94; love / enjoy doing (sth.) 5.8, 7.111, 11.78, **B** 10.92, 11.223; love [person of opposite sex] 6.192, 7.301, 10.274, 11.180, 16.106, 22.195, **B** 12.33; make love 17.137, 18.225, **B** 13.353; *impers. use:* **hym louede** it pleased him B 16.201, 17.140; *in phrr.* ~ **and byleuen** 10.169, 19.42, 110, **B** 15.476, 17.35; ~ **lelly** 1.176, 3.31, 7.207, 15.155, 16.193, 17.217, **B** 1.78, 7.124, 10.189, 13.142, **togideres** ~ **lelly** love each other mutually B 15.553

#**louer** *n* louver [smoke-turret] 20.286c

loues *pl.* 17.24 *etc, see* **loef** *n*

low *p.t.* A12.42 *see* **lauhen** *v*

low(e) *p.t. 2. sg.* 20.348, 445, **lowen** *p.p.* B 5.94 *see* **lyen** *v*

lowe[1] *n* flame 20.140

lowe[2] *a* low, *sup.* (*a as n*) lowest part 14.151; (*as av*) (down) below 14.85, 20.249; (of), low (social rank) 21.35, (*comp.*) B 7.157, 159; *a as n* 16.33, **B** 6.227, 10.364; ~ **folk** simple common people 13.82, **B** 3.255,

6.227; humble, meek 7.196, 9.184, 10.83, 12.131, 16.69, 17.30, **B** 5.138, 591, 7.62, 11.239, 12.60; **lowliche** *av* humbly B 14.228

lowe[3] *av* low 5.24, **B** 13.26, *sup.* 1.127; down B 4.22; *in phrr:* ~ **chered** of humble countenance 21.264; ~ **herted** humble-hearted 22.37; ~ **lyuynge** of humble life 14.187; **lyggen** ~ lie in ruins 19.10; **potten...lowe** humble, bring down low 12.14; humbly 6.8, A 7.26

lowen *v* descend B Pr 129; humble 10.306, 12.159; make obedient to 8.194, *ger.* submitting (oneself) B 15.304

low(e)nesse *n* humility, meekness 3.443, 15.134, B 4.109, Z 8.91; lowly state 16.18

lower *n* recompense Z 7.270

low(h) *p.t.* 21.462, 22.143, A 12.42 *see* **lauhen** *v*

lowten A 12.55 = **louten** *v*

luft[1] (**left, lyft**) *a* left †1.112, 3.75; ~ **half / hand** left-hand side 2.5, 8, 7.224, **B** 10.164, verso side (of page) 3.491; *as n* villain B 4.62

luft[2] *p.t.* 17.302, 18.144, **luftynge** *ger.* 6.410 *see* **lyften** *v*

lu(y)ren *v* lure (*fig.*) 7.45

lu(y)ther *a* wicked, evil †1.109, 193, 4.104, 10.161, 14.101, B 10.437; sinful 6.436, 8.253, 9.18, 13.115, *a as n* wicked men 15.216, 17.82, the bad B 10.434; wrongful 17.36; deceitful 8.295, 9.181, **B** 10.166, 18.355; treacherous 3.317; false 19.246; foul, ~ **eir** = pestilential air 15.221; vicious B 5.117; *av* wickedly, ~ **lyuyng** evil-living 10.167

lunatik *n* madman B Pr 123; *a* suffering from recurrent madness [believed due to varying lunar phases] 9.107, 137

lup(pen) *p.t. pl.*, *sg.* 1.112, 2.69, 7.134 *see* **lepen** *v*

lusard *n* serpent B 18.338

lust(e), (lost) *n* desire 1.110, 6.158, 11.82, 16.211; bodily appetite 21.355, 385, 22.90; ~**es of synne** sinful sexual desires 17.79; sexual pleasure 13.152, Z 3.163; sexual gratification 18.36, A 2.65

lusten (lesten, listen) *v* (*contr. pr. i*(*ndic. and subjv.*)) **lust(e)** Pr 175, 187, 3.169, 9.146, *p.t.* 15.25, 19.116, B Pr 130) *impers. without subj.* **me / us / hym / hem / here luste** it please(s) me *etc*, I *etc.* wish(ed) Pr 175, 187, 3.169, 195, 10.96, 13.236, 15.25, 20.449, 460, 22.18, B 1.150, A Pr 37, *in phr.* **liketh and** ~ please(s) and wish(es) 9.146, 14.113, 19.116, B 11.97; (*pers.*) wish, like 11.76

lustnen 20.295 = **lystenen** *v*

#**luten** *v* sing to the lute 20.469

luther 1.193 *etc* = **lu(y)ther** *a*

ma 2.250 = **mo** *n*

maad B 5.95, 398, 8.89, 9.44, 113, 10.101, 11.196, 220 = (**y**)**ma(e)d(e)** *p.p.*; *see* **maken** *v*

macchen (togideres) *v* marry (each other) B 9.175

macere *n* mace-bearer, ? sheriff B 3.76

#**mache** *n* wick 19.180

macuht Z 7.276, **macuth** Z 7.262 = **maketh** *see* **maken** *v*

mad¹ *p.p.* 3.208, A 2.22, 11.174 *see* **maken** *v*

mad² *a* (*pl.* **madde**) mad, insane B 9.70; furious A 5.106

madame *n. phr.* my lady (*polite term of address*) 1.11, 41, 56, 2.2 (*Holy Church*), 11.88, B 10.220 (*Studie*), B 3.344 (*Mede*)

madden *v* suffer fits of madness 9.108

made *p.t.* Pr 55 *etc*, *pl.* **maden** 7.184, *2 sg.* **madest** 6.234 *etc*, *p.p.* 4.97, 5.70; **maed** *p.p.* 10.130, 15.39 = **made**; *see* **maken** *v*

mageste B 9.52, 15.480 = **maiestee** *n*

may *n*¹ maiden, virgin A 12.116

May *n*² (the month of) May Pr 6, 16.10

may *pr. sg* Pr 9 *et p. see* **mowen** *v*

mayde(n) *n* maiden [(young) unmarried woman] 2.19, 145, 250, 3.1, 4, 39, 115, 4.163, 9.33, 12.136, 16.104, 106, 107, 18.92, 20.118, 124, B 2.44, 57, 3.105, 6.326, 9.70, 14.268, A 2.196, 3.35, 10.15, Z 2.104; unmarried person [of either sex] 10.283; girl 6.178, 11.174; virgin 7.127, 10.263, 11.144, 145, 17.267, 18.125, 131, 135, 19.87, 125, 20.131, B 12.38, 18.128, 139; consecrated virgin 10.207, 14.143, 18.71, 97, B 9.112, 15.468; lady-in-waiting 7.287; waiting-woman 11.173; maidservant 4.62, 7.272, A 4.46

maydenhe(e)d, ~hod(e) *n* virginity 1.179, 4.48; (consecrated) virginity B 16.71

maymen *v* maim, injure 5.34, 9.216, 20.384, B 17.190

mayne *n*¹ power 20.361

mayné *n*² household 18.253, B 10.93; retinue 3.25, B 5.97; company, troop B 1.108

maynpernour *n* (one standing) surety [for sb. to appear in court] 4.107, (*fig.*) B 18.184

maynprise *n* (*lit.*) release of a prisoner to a maynpernour, *here* = bail (*fig.*) 18.281, (*person.*) 4.84; *in phr.* **nymen vnder ~** act as surety for 22.17

maynprisen *v* arrange release (of prisoner), stand surety for 2.208, 4.173, (*fig.*) 20.187

mayntenaunce *n* support, backing [*esp.* at law] 6.248

maynte(y)nen *v* uphold 3.230, 271, B 2.37; support B 3.90; help 3.186; aid and abet 2.207, 4.58, B 3.167, 247; pay for 17.234; defend B 6.36, 13.126, Z 7.31

mayntenour *n* aider and abettor 3.286

mayr(e) *n* mayor (of a town) 1.155, 3.77, 108, 115, 122, 467, 8.87, 9.122, 335

maister *n* governor, ruler 3.442, 444, 8.340, 12.219, 15.169, 17.100, 296, 18.117, 20.458; leading civic official 2.176, 8.87; magistrate 9.335, B 3.246; important person 3.214, 4.26, B 10.115; master (= superior) 4.155, 5.188, 7.247, 8.38, (= employer) 3.273, 6.212, 11.303, 16.58, B 3.255, 6.239; teacher, instructor 3.276, 14.46, 17.111, B 11.359, 14.255, 15.439, A 10.82; learned man, theologian Pr 60, 10.9, 11.218, 15.30, 39, 46, 91, 16.285, 17.312, 21.85, B 10.66, 11.80, 12.231, 15.70; master of arts / divinity Pr 85,

17.113, B 11.173; (*as title of master craftsman*) 21.289; expert (practitioner) Z 7.262, 263, 276

maistrie *n* control 4.132, B 6.326, 14.328; victory 3.284, 11.287, 18.52, 20.105; upper hand 6.77, 20.68; force 20.299, 394; remarkable feat B 4.26, 16.112; miracle B 16.115; skill 21.256; cunning 6.191; power, ability B 5.102, A 9.47, Z 3. 174

maiestee *n* sovereign majesty, sovereignty B 1.107, 16.184; þe **~** the divine majesty (*as title of God*) B 9.52, 15.480

make *n* spouse, wife 3.154, B 12.33, 14.124, 266; mate 13.139, 153, 18.224, 225, 235, B 11.343, 355, 374

mak(y)en *v* (*p.t.* **made** Pr 55 *et p.*, *pl.* **maden** 8.130, 17.30, B 10.407, A 9.57, *2 p. sg.* **madest** 6.234, 7.123, 128, 20.402, (*uncontr.*) **makede** B 9.130, *p.p.* **maad** B 4.103 *etc*, **mad** 3.208, A 2.22, 11.174, **ymad** 6.295, **maed** 10.130, 15.39, (*uncontr.*) (**y**)**maked** 7.12, 9.297, 10.87, B 6.186, 13.215) create 3.164, 6.5, 7.122, 123, 8.96, 239, 10.256, 13.208, 211, 17.314, 18.211, 19.279, 20.255, 361, 22.254, B 9.27, 33, 130, 10.226, 12.22, 15.170, 16.13, A 10.35, 142, 11.64, Z 5.37, 40; *in assevs*: **by / for Hym / God þat me / her made** 1.54, 3.164, 6.307, 15.159, B 2.128; establish 14.39, 18.265, 22.278, 367, B 7.53, 9.117, 191, A 8.28; construct, produce Pr 145, 3.64, 452, 7.256, 8.185, 10.129, 11.250, 13.156, 161, 17.17, 18.116, 19.206, 21.326, 329, 22.163, B 3.297, 9.72, 14.72, 73, A 10.79; make 2.192, 3.452, 5.14, 6.221, 263, 8.13, 13.121, 18.116, 20.48, 21.32, 242, 390, 22.337, B 6.142, 9.122, 13.251 14.16, 16.166, Z 7.262; cook 6.133, 182, 8.308, 9.75, B 6.186; draw up 8.95, 12.63, 16.35; write 7.12, 24, 11.148, 154, 14.46, 17.110, B 3.343, 9.38, 10.284, 15.89, A 11.274, 12.109; compose (poetry) B 12.22, ?5.5c; produce (sound) 18.110, B 4.23; make (look, gesture) 6.178, 11.163, 15.121; bring about 13.75, 15.230, 17.86, 202, 238, 248, 20.163, B 3.221, 4.64; arrange 10.249, B 15.241; hold 3.195, 7.101; obtain B 5.72; give 12.103, B 15.461, 480, 16.140; make (vow) 7.63, B 5.398; utter (threat) B 18.281; decree (law) 20.306; provide 16.88; cause 2.86, 7.4, 28, 64, 109, 9.317, 10.119, 19.297, 20.324, 21.284, B 4.70, 142, 5.97; inflict (wound) upon 20.90; cause (to be) 1.19, 3.4, 31, 267, 6.94, 7.128, 263, 8.158, 212, 271, 9.317, 11.214, 12.113, 241, 13.209, 15.294, 16.23, 17.229, 21.59, 294, 22.184, 197, B 2.148, 3.198, 5.95, 7.29, 10.116, 12.127, 13.215, 15.218, 16.133, A 10.83, 12.59; cause to be otherwise 9.233, 10.158, 20.324, B 4.72; turn (into) Pr 37, 1.73, 6.72, 15.233, B 14.81; cause to do 3.158, 479, 6.2, 7.109, 8.117, 221, 271, 9.297, 317, 10.35, 63, 66, 11.119, 170, 12.151, 16.94, 20.83, 346, 376, 21.125, 204, 383, 22.37, 127, 138, 307, B 3.278, 12.40; **~ of** regard 5.5n, **~lytel tale of** have little regard (for sth.) 3.390; form 19.155; compose 10.130; win 10.87; *in phrr*: **~ amendes** make reparation 4.97;

~ **at ese** entertain 3.4, 15.48, **B** 15.340, 16.227; ~ **deul** lament 19.320; ~ **ende** conclude 3.198, 433; ~ **fayere chiere** give pleasant reception (to) 22.350; ~ **good** pay, compensate 19.77, 206, B 5.272; ~ **heuy chere** lament 4.160; ~ **mencioun** mention, speak of 8.247, 11.284; ~ **merye, murþe** enjoy (oneself), have a good time 8.68, 22.289, B 15.139; entertain 15.199; ~ **mynde** mention 15.310, B 9.122; ~ **mone** complain 8.130; pray 16.184, 17.257; ~ **pleinte** make (a) complaint; ~ **restitucion** make restitution 6.295, 19.202, B 5.270; ~ **sacrefice** offer sacrifice 18.249; ~ **sawt** make an assault 22.217; ~ **sorwe** lament 3.17, B 13.411

maker(e) *n* creator **B** 10.242, 16.184

makyng(e) *ger.* creating B 17.169; making, construction 3.66; devising B 10.213, A 11.160; contracting 10.249; preparing B 13.52; writing, composing 3.493; (writing of) poetry B 12.16, **A** 11.32, 12.109; dubbing 13.109

male *n*¹ male (animal) 13.147, B 11.339

male *a* male 18.253

male *n*² bag 6.236, 13.55

male(n)colie *n* melancholic rage 6.77 (B 13.334)

mal(e)ese *n* hardship 8.233; suffering 15.85; pain 19.158

malt *n* malt(ed barley) Pr 213

mamelen *v* babble 5.123, 13.227

man *n* (*gen. sg.* **mannes** 6.73, 7.88 *etc, gen. pl.* **men(ne)** 3.7, 102, 5.29, 13.45, 14.168, 15.277, **mennes** 3.103, 9.214, 12.114, 199, 20.414, *dat. sg.* **manne** †B 1.82) (human) person Pr 212, 3.197, 294, 6.86, 7.70, 80, 95, 109, 243, 10.33, 310, 11.187, 13.19, 14.15, 44, 52, 15.305, 16.217, 327, 17.154, 165, 281, 19.316, **B** 8.18, 127 (1, 2), 10.350, 351, 432, 11.67, 80, 277, 423, 12.99, 13.409, 14.84, 89, 15.58, 158, (*collective*) 3.421; *in phrr.* **eny** ~ anybody 6.117, 7.36, 42, 8.37, 21.18, **B** 14.328, 17.42; **euery** ~ everybody 9.229, 10.182, 12.119, B 15.263; **Y** ~ I, this person 2.133, I man 20.389; **many** ~ many people / a person 10.5 (B 8.5); **many oþere** ~ many another group of people 9.172; **no** ~ nobody 1.85, 117, 2.136, 4.40, 5.154, 8.246, 257, 9.47, 70, 121, 10.186, 295, 15.150, 16.207, 17.14, 20.214, 21.137, 22.102, **B** 4.127, 5.439, 10.364, 11.212, 13.136, 333, 15.257, 17.163; **sum** ~ somebody 14.137; **vche (eche)** ~ everybody 3.461, 5.196, 6.312, 8.117, 12.131, 13.244, 14.68, 20.338, 21.228, 397, 419, 460, **B** 5.272, 10.356, 370, 11.208, 209, 17.104; **what** ~ whoever 2.34, 36, 4.10; who B 13.25; what kind of person 4.10, 10.5; *pl.* **men** people Pr 34, 119, 214, 217, 1.42, 67, 2.64, 78, 189, 195, 3.63, 81, 158, 168, 170, 172, 265, 266, 289, 435, 456, 4.105, 170, 181, 5.5, 29, 6.69, 244, 295, 7.23, 69, 90, 92, 154, 167, 8.52, 296, 9.19, 30, 68, 84, 97, 126, 179, 180, 10.5, 84, 94, 97, 201, 249, 261, 11.127, 132, 161, 198, 217, 218, 236, 293, 12.28, 241, 13.65, 142, 14.46, 47, 56, 181, 15.48, 78, 199, 204, 227, 245, 270, 273, 277, 16.19, 40, 45, 70, 91, 123, 124, 130 (2), 155, 301, 302, 308, 17.97, 170, 178, 187, 222, 265, 273,

300, 18.95, 174, 19.62, 207, 208, 232, 264, 320, 324, 20.338, 21.4, 28, 112, 186, 191, 247, 280, 390, 430, 22.12, 27, 28, 264, 275, 278, 307, 380, **B** 2.36, 3.159, 219, 5.113; human being 7.127, 130, 11.145, 205, 15.264, 17.267, 18.135, 216, 19.39, 20.221, 21.153, **B** 8.127 (1, 2), 16.217; **to** ~ as a human being B 1.82; anyone 8.200, 11.213, 290, 15.160, 19.92, **B** 1.116, 5.283, 10.451, 14.98, 188; man(kind) 1.157, 2.38, 134, 3.354, 7.123, 10.51, 157, 256, 11.159, 12.151, 13.181, 192, 211, 14.119, 15.85, 17.263, 18.123, 211, 20.139, 162, 389, 417, **B** 8.47, 55, 9.33, 44, 52, 130, 11.398, 16.200, A 12.116; man (= adult male) 1.179, 3.45, 271, 420, 469, 475, 4.95, 140, 6.320, 347, 7.21, 95, 8.51, 69, 247, 9.132, 10.35, 68, 147, 11.197, 13.6, 15.30, 195, 16.106, 17.31, 159, 210, 18.92, 182, 237, 19.55, 82, 84, 287, 299, 20.239, 21.98, 22.93, **B** 3.24, 94, 8.127 (3), 9.21, 112, 12.33, 15.280, 415, 480, 574, 16.204, 17.75, 116; (*collective sense*) 13.139, 153, 18.224, 235, B 11.370, 374; *in phr.* **m(e)n and wom(e)n** 2.7, 7.205, 9.106, 17.181, 19.22, B 9.186; soldier 3.236, 252, 256, 257, 475, 17.234, 22.259, B 3.198, 221; man of rank / means 3.249, 267; vassal 11.88; retainer 4.58, B 3.167; (man-)servant 3.25, 4.129, 7.243, 15.215, 16.58, **B** 4.155, 13.40, 17.116; *in phrr.* **actif** ~ **B** 13.273, 458, 14.26, 320, 16.2; **badde** ~ 9.16; **beste** 21.436; **blynd(e)** ~ 7.107, 14.50; **crafty** ~ 3.279, 8.69; **Cristene** ~ 12.61, B 15.398, **cursed** ~ 21.470; **dede** ~ 20.64; **Englische** ~ 16.216; **fals** ~ 3.102, 8.229, 21.248, B 14.24; **fre** ~ 1.73, 5.64, 21.33, 39, 40; **Frenche** ~ B 11.384, Z 7.278; **gentel** ~ 12.112, 21.34; **God-Man** 12.115; **good(e)** ~ 3.92, 302, 5.67, 7.242, 10.263, 11.62, 19.260, 262, **B** 3.75, 7.74, 10.223, 436; **hardy** ~ 13.61, B 14.305; **holy** ~ 17.34, 185, 194, 18.116; **honest** ~ 17.34; **ydel** ~ 5.27; **ille** ~ 10.94; **kynde-wittede** ~ 14.52, 72; **lame** ~ 8.189; **lele** ~ 8.74, 140, 17.139; **lered** ~ 3.40, 4.118, 7.104, 16.151, 192, 18.82; **lettred** ~ 9.326, 11.76, 12.45, 14.198, 17.73, 87, 210, 18.80, 21.85; **lewede** ~ Pr 70, 102, 1.134, 3.40, 6.23, 9.164, 223, 11.307, 12.43, 13.25, 14.20, 49, 101, 124, 198, 15.15, 16.260, 272, 17.54, 87, 20.355, **B** Pr 129, 1.199; **longe-lybbynge** ~ 14.168; **lowe-lyuynge** ~ 14.187; **luyther** ~ 3.317, 9.181; ~ **lyuyng** ~ 10.167; **mene** ~ 9.54, 11.49, 53; **mylde** ~ 22.65; **myseyse** ~ 9.30; **northerne** ~ 1.114; **olde** ~ 9.175; **parfit** ~ 5.84; **pore** ~ 3.213, 7.78, 84, 194, 8.39, 12.136, 15.36, 16.126, 323, **B** 3.195, 241, 5.253, 254, 6.195, 11.241; **riche** ~ 2.184, 7.98, 12.107, 13.57, 97, 14.87, 95, 173, 184, 16.12, 356, 19.227, 229, 20.218; **rihtfole** ~ 17.259; **sad** ~ 10.31, 49; **seculer** ~ 10.286; **synnefol** ~ 7.145, 10.162; **tidy** ~ 3.474, 20.332, 21.442; **trewe** ~ 3.444, 7.38, 17.33; **wedded** ~ 10.205, 296, 18.71; **wiȝt** ~ B 9.21; **wykked** ~ 4.65, 8.27, 14.134, 16.275, B 16.146; **wys** ~ 3.7, 7.94, 8.240, 9.51, 336, 13.64, 19.226, 21.84; **world-riche** ~ 16.216; ~ **of gode** men of wealth 3.214; ~ **of lawe** lawyer 4.67,

148, 168, 9.44, 17.46, 20.354; ~ **on (þis) molde / of (this) worlde** (any) living person 2.208, 3.6, 10.14, 11.231, **B** 2.37, 3.80; *in vocative uses*: 4.92, 11.7, 92, 189, B 10.253

mana(s)c(h)en *v* threaten (sb.) 4.62, 15.6, B 6.170; threaten (to) B 16.49, 127

maner(e) *n*[1] manorial estate 5.159, B 5.242, Z 5.101; manor-house 7.232, (*fig.*) A 10.15

maner(e) *n*[2] kind / sort (of) 3.110, 332, 304, 6.282, 8.282, 9.7, 33, 10.286, 17.151, 19.260, 20.384, 21.326, **B** 2.13, 3.256, 5.25, 6.219, 266, 7.95, 13.40, 14.164; **al(le)** ~ every kind of 20.43, 22.254, **B** 14.224, 18.319, Z 7.31, **al(le)** ~ **men** Pr 20, 3.396, 4.121, 5.196, 8.17, 232, 9.219, 13.70, 17.249, 19. 41, 331, 21.185, 22.112, **B** 10.268, 278, 11.177, 15.439, Z 3.167; type 8.248; kinds / sorts (of) 3.268, 21.186, **many ~ men** 2.57, 197, 6.26 (1), 212, 7.86, 109; 9. 128, 17. 156, **suche ~** 9.124, 10.246, 16.249; 16. 310, 106, B 3.244, A 10.63; **B** 3.231, 256, 6.266, 14.38, 183, 15.259, manner 3.403; form 21.98; nature, habit 7.44; character 2.7; fashion 15.3, B 13.459; way, manner (of doing sth.) 6.26 (2), 7.23, 230, 8.117, 9.162, 11.178, 14.74, 103, 17.170, 22.197, **B** 1.118, 5.280, 9.44, 10.275, 15.207, 397, A 2.47, Z 2.166; measure, degree B 1.19

maneren *v* have certain manners, *p.p. in phrr.* **is manered after** takes after 2.27, B 15.415; **wel ymanered** with good breeding 10.263

*****mangen** *v* eat 8.271, A 12.72

mangerye *n* feast 12.48; meal B 15.591

mangonel *n* siege-catapult 20.293

manhede, manhode *n* human nature 18.220, 239, 21.158; humanity, the human race B 16.202, 209, 220; human value / excellence B 12.295; dignity, honour 3.230, 17.66

many(e) (mon(e)y(e)) *a and n* many Pr 5, 60 *et p.*; (*with uninfl. pl. n. foll.*) 6.151, 9.297, 15.3; (*following n.*) Pr 96, 2.112, 7.227, 11.181, 14.189, 15.44, 16.133, 17.12, **B** Pr 219, 2.6, 3.23, 102, 6.293, 7.123, †13.44, 15.268; *in phrr*: ~ **kyne** many kinds of Pr 26, 10.15, 13.55, 19.159, 22.97; ~ **manere** many kinds of 2.57, 197, 6.212, 17.156; many a Pr 212, 3.236, 310, 5.156, 7.243, 12.219, 244, 13.50, 15.305, 17.270, 281, 18.61, 20.179, 21.412, 22.318, **B** 2.57, 6.266, 8.5, 9.206, 13.134, 15.121, 200, A 4.21; (= many, *with ref. to antecedent or understood n.*) 9.41, 11.239, B 4.64, A 12.8; *as n* (= many people) Pr 27, 127, 2.226, 3.13, 159, 7.274, 8.113, 14.17, 15.182, 18.174, **B** 14.169, 16.116, A 5.104; ~ **of** many of 13.162, 19.229, 20.436

manyfold *n* abundance, **by** ~ by much, many times over 12.145

mankynde *n* (*uninfl. gen.* 11.144, B 16.162) mankind, the human race 3.403, 7.127, 13.181, 187, 16.98, 18.135, 215, 19.101, 20.185, 186, 221, 277, 21.324, **B** 10.236, 242, 16.209, 17.108, 18.398; human nature 18.234, 19.125, 20.440, 21.72, 22.41; the male sex 11.145

manlich *a* generous B 5.256

manliche *av* boldly B 10.284, 16.127; generously B 10.89, 93

manoir B 5.242, 586 = **manere** *n*[1]

manschipe *n* act of courtesy 12.107

mansen *v* curse, *p.p. a* **mansed(e)** accursed, damned 2.41, B 4.160; ? excommunicated, ?vicious 22.221, **B** 10.278, 12.84, †A 10.154

mansion *n* abode 16.58

manslauht *n* killing of men in battle 4.182, 17.241

mantel *n* mantle [sleeveless outer robe], cloak 15.205, 22.138

marbil *n* marble A 10.104

marc[1] mark [money of account worth 13s 4d], **half ~** 5.133

marc[2] B 9.31 *see* **mark(e)** *n*

marcat (market) *n* market 19.74, B Pr 221; market-place B 5.99

march *n* province 22.221; territory, region 10.138, B 15.445

marchal B 3.201 = **marschal** *n*

marchaunden *v* trade, do business 6.280 (B 13.394)

marcha(u)n(t)dise *n* trading, commerce, buying and selling 3.110, 280, 312, 6.339; merchandise, wares Pr 61, 6.212, 260, 13.50, 52

marcha(u)nt *n* merchant, wholesale trader 2.222, 4.129, 193, 6.96, 9.22, 41, 13.32 *et p.*, 17.46, 21.352, Z 3.169

marchel 3.257 *see* **marschal** *n*

marchen (togyderes) *v* go reciprocally Pr 61

mare[1] *n* mare, **cart ~** mare for drawing a cart 8.311

mare[2] 4.93 = **more** *comp. av.*

mareys *n. pl.* marsh(es) 13.167

margerie perle *n* pearl 11.7

margine *n* margin 9.22

mariage *n* marriage 10.249, B 9.155, 158; ~ **of wedlake** bond of matrimony A 10.207; marriage ceremony, wedding A 2.22, 26; woman's dowry, **feffen in ~** endow with marriage portion A 2.37, 47; **lachen to ~** take in marriage Z 2.165; **loue of þe ~** marital affection, ? desire to marry 16.109

marien *v* give in marriage 16.107, B 9.155, A 10.181, 183; marry 2.54, 80, 170, **to ~** able to marry; *p.p.* **maried** B 12.33, A 10.113; ~ **togyderes** marry each other 10.283; ~ **wiþ** get married to B 2.31, A 10.154; witness / attend wedding (of) B 2.57; provide for marriage (of) B 7.29

mark(e) *n* boundary-post 3.381; stamp (on coin) B 15.349; sign, **the kynges ~ of heuene** the token of heaven's king 17.77 (B 15.351); feature B 9.31; note B 17.104

marken *v* note, observe 14.74 (B 12.131), †B 6.325; note down (= predestine) A 11.261; allot, ordain 14.125

market B Pr 221, 5.99 = **marcat** *n*

marl *n* marl [clay mixed with calcium carbonate] 12.233

marschal *n* commander-in-chief 3.256, 257

martir *n* martyr [witness by death for the Christian faith] 10.206, 12.197, 14.143, 18.97

mart(i)ren *n* (put to death as a) martyr 17.281, 20.334, B 15.265

mas-pens 3.278 *see* **masse** *n*

masager A 12.83 = **messager** *n*

maȝe B Pr 192 = **mase** *n*

mase (maȝe) *n* confusion 3.197, B Pr 192; vain activity 1.6

maso(u)n *n* mason [builder / worker in stone] 13.161, **B** Pr 222, 10.180, **Z** Pr 89, 6.78

masse *n* Mass, the Eucharist(ic celebration) Pr 125, 1.178, 3.310, 5.68, 6.272, 354, 8.103, 9.243, 12.87, 13.104, 114, 17.117, 21.3, 4, Z 5.37; *in phrr*: ~ **and / or matynes** mass and / or morning service Pr 125, 3.53, 6.282, 7.27, 66, 9.228, 13.121, 22.367, **B** 5.2, 11.282; ~ **of þe day** mass of (a specific) day (in the church calendar) 13.126; ~ **pens** pence offered by the faithful at mass 3.278; **mannes** ~ mass said by a man B 13.259

mataynes 3.53, 7.66 = **matynes** *n*

matere *n* physical substance 13.211; business, event(s) 5.110, 15.25; subject 5.123, 19.48, **B** 9.72, 11.159, 15.89, Z 7.230; subject-matter, **good** ~ edifying matter B 15.58; *in phr*: **meuen** ~ discuss subject / question 1.122, 10.119, 12.43; broach topic **B** 11.230, 15.71

matynes *n* matins, morning service [before mass of the day] Pr 125, 3.53, 6.282, 7.27, 66, 9.228, 13.121, 22.367, **B** 5.2, 11.282

matrimonye *n* (the state of) marriage 10.211, 18.86, 110, 221, 237, 22.138, B 16.209, 211; (a) marriage, matrimonial union 2.149, 10.256, B 15.241

maugre(e) *n* blame, reproach **B** 6.239, 9.155

maugre(y) *prep.* in spite of 2.214; ~ **my / his / hire chekes / teth** in spite of all I / he / she could do 8.38, 20.83, **B** 4.50, 14.4 ~ **ho** no matter who 8.68, 155

maumet *n* idol Pr 119

maundement *n* writ, law (= the Commandments) 19.2, 62

maungen A 12.72 = **mangen** *v*

mawe *n* stomach 6.90, 432, 8.334, 15.91, 16.217, **B** 6.266, 15.64; belly 8.171

me[1] *impers. prn (reduced form of* **men** *prn)* one, people 3.406, 412, 477, 4.121, 5.54, 7.76, 9.128, 132, 133, 302, 11.29, 12.114, 13.5, 16.123, 130, 288, 293, 295, 17.73, 18.61

me[2] *1 p. prn (as dir. obj.)* me 1.4, 71 *et p.*; (*as indir. obj.*) to me Pr 182, 207, 1.43, 74, 3.147, 156, 4.61, 5.36, 49, 6.292, 313, 7.42, 11.137, 227, 16.168, 18.251, 258, 261, 19.2, 107, 20.281, 379, 408, 21.471, **B** 6.253, 7.121, 10.225, 11.148, 13.85, 190; for me B 5.278; from me 4.180; on me B 5.598; (*as refl.*) myself Pr 2, 4.16, 6.8, 10, 28, 74, 94, 175, 215, 288, 424, 433, 7.53, 65, 8.56, 19.279, 20.5, 92, 21.2, **B** Pr 7, 12.20, 17.84, A 12.75; (*as dat. of interest*) for me / myself, on my behalf 6.32,

7.9, 46, 85, 9.238, 20.312, B 10.386; (*in impers. constr. after impers. v* Pr 7, 9, 180, 196, 5.41, 6.27, 7.292, 294, 11.187, 13.153, 162, 15.25, 18.185, 20.6, B 16.230, A 12.37, Z 3.123; *after* **ben** 13.215, B 14.7; (*with prep.*) Pr 207, 1.75, 203, 2.214, 4.56, 11.164, 15.131, 22.200, 372, B 13.333, A 5.241, Z 7.231; **as for** ~ as far as I am concerned B 12.15

meble *n* (movable) wealth (*pl.* personal possessions or property) 9.270, 10.97, 13.6, 14.181, 15.169, 16.12, 19.257, B 9.83; *in phr.* ~ **and / ne vnmeble(s)** movable and immovable wealth / possessions 3.421, 10.188

mechel 6.332, A 12.102 = **muche(l)** *a*

meddeled *p.p.* 6.260 *see* **medlen** *v*

mede *n* reward, payment B 3.331; material reward / payment [in money or kind, for services] 2.52, 3.248, 265, 281, 294, 297, 310, 423, 7.84, 199, 202, 9.54, 274, 276, Z 3.96; fee, ? bribe 2.138, 3.123, 287, 289, 290, 292, 304, 312, 332, 390, 495, 498, **B** 3.245, 247, 352, 7.58; (*person.*) 2.19 *et p.*, 3.1 *et p.*; material wealth 3.408, 430; (final) spiritual reward [for life of vice or virtue] 2.76, 133, 134, 13.96, 17.66, B 12.289, 292; retribution 20.356

meden *v* reward B 3.216

medicyne *n* healing substance 19.84; medicine, medicament 20.157, Z 7.276, (*fig.*) remedy 1.33, 17.225; healing, treatment 19.77

medlen *v* mix, commingle 10.130; blend together (illicitly) 6.260; have to do 14.67; engage in A 12.109, (*refl.*) involve (oneself) B 12.16; fight 22.179; couple (sexually) with B 11.343

meekliche 3.265 = **mekeliche** *av*

meel B 1.24 = **mel(e)** *n*[1]

meene B 1.108, 10.67 = **mene** *a*[1]

mees *n*[1] (*pl.*) B Pr 147, 198 (= **muys**) *see* **mous** *n*

mees *n*[2] course, dish (of food) **B** 13.53, 15.316; (**messe**) ?meal, ? Host Z 5.37n

meeten B Pr 215 = **meten** *v*[1]; B 15.251 *see* **meten** *v*[3]

#**megre** *a* emaciated 6.94

meynee B 1.108, 10.93 = **mayné** *n*[2]

meynpernour B 18.184 = **maynpernour** *n*

meynte(y)nen 3.271, 4.58, Z 7.31 = **maynte(y)nen** *v*

meke *a* kind 1.171; gentle B 18.115, **A** 9.71, 10.83, 128; merciful 1.168; humble, meek 16.23, 18.125, B 15.306; *a as n* the humble 9.15; submissive 8.212; tame 15.294

mekeliche *av* humbly 1.163, 237; obediently 3.265; uncomplainingly 9.183, 12.180; courteously A 3.35; mercifully 1.165

meken *v* humble 6.10, 17.154; become humble 22.35; submit, incline 4.90, 7.247

mekenesse *n* humility, meekness 7.205, (*person.*) 4.155, B 4.160; contrition 12.74, 19.205, B 4.142; kindness, generosity 8.38; courtesy 11.92

mekil A 6.111 = **muche(l)** *a*

mel(e) (meel) *n*[1] meal 12.107, **B** 1.24, 10.101; *in phrr*: **a**

~s **mete** food at a meal 6.289, 15.36; ~ **tyme** meal-time 7.132, 9.246

mele n^2 ground wheat, meal 9.75, B 13.261

mel(l)en v speak B 3.36, A 11.94

melten v (*p.p.* **molten** B 13.83) *intr.* melt 19.195, *tr.* (*fig.*) melt, soften 19.193, 197, *p.p.* molten B 13.83

membre n limb 5.33, 9.177, 216, 10.157; part (of the body) 20.384, B 12.229; (subsidiary) part 21.473; *in phr:* ~ **for** ~ 'an eye for an eye', limb for limb B 18.343

memorie n memory, recollection (*esp.* in prayers) A 11.216; commemorative mention (in bidding prayers at mass) 7.27, 8.104

memprysen Z 2.175 = **maynprisen** v

men *impers. prn* one, people Pr 181, 214, 2.27, 3.165, 7.167, 176, 9.302, 11.174, 15.269, 284, 16.6, 81, 130, 17.222, 18.12, 19.6, 51, 20.471, 21.18, 28, **B** 3.325, 5.424, 12.75, 13.318, 14.150, 278, 445, 17.227, 263, **A** 1.138, 10.96; *and see* **me** *impers. prn*

men *pl.* Pr 20 *et p.*; *see* **man** n

mencioun n account, **maken** ~ give an account, tell 8.247, 11.284

mende (*pl.* **mendis**) n reparation, amends A 4.90, (*person.*) satisfaction A 2.83

menden v put right 3.61; cure, redeem Z 1.91; repair 6.288, A 3.51

mendena(u)nt n (*pl.*) orders of mendicant friars 13.78, 15.82; beggar 5.76, 9.179, 11.50, 15.3, **B** 10.65, 15.154, A 11.201; *n as a* mendicant Pr 60

mene n means 18.202, state (causing sth.) 16.94; intermediary 1.155, 9.347, 10.120, B 3.76; intermediary means B 9.34; mediator 17.158, 258

mene a^1 poor, of low rank Pr 20, 219, 3.81, 197, 9.54, 11.49, 53, B 10.67; (*comp.*) poorer B 14.166; lesser B 1.108

mene a^2 intervening, mean 6.281; intermediary B 9.114

men(e)gen v commemorate 8.104; ~ **of** remember †B 5.412

menen v^1 mean, signify 4.147, 5.37, 9.164, 11.83, **B** 10.89, 275, 13.212, 15.119, **Z** Pr 94, 1.3, 5.43, 7.232, *in phr.* **be to** ~ mean, signify 1.11, 3.124, 395, 6.303, 10.92, 210, 11.72, 247, 249, 293, 13.64, 65, 14.4, 16.155, 216, 17.41, 20.129, 215, 225, 21.62, 93, **B** 9.50, 11.273, 14.275, 319, 15.450, 458, **A** 8.139, 11.297; symbolise B 16.63; intend 11.114, *pr. p.* 8.248; aim for, seek, *pr.p.* 17.176; assert B 5.276; be caused by 20.129; *ger.* **menynge** understanding (*pl.*) 1.137; *in phrr:* **(in)** ~ **(as) after** in desire / search for 17.176, B 15.474; **in** ~ **of** in commemoration of Pr 99; **in** ~ þat in token that 15.245, 18.93, 20.139, **B** 15.306, 16.200

menen v^2 (*refl.*) complain 3.215, B 6.2

meneuer n fur (of grey squirrel) 22.138

mengen v^1 **B** †5.412, 6.95 = **men(e)gen** v

mengen v^2 mix (= adulterate) B 13.362

meny 19.22 = **many(e)** a

menyng *pr.p.* 8.248 *etc*, *ger.* Pr 99 *etc*; *see* **menen** v^1

menyson (blody) n ? dysentery, ? morbid menstrual flow B 16.111c

menne (*uninfl. gen. pl.*) men's 2.122, 4.115, 6.95, 293, 7.219, 9.191, 10.16, 13.45, 75, 78, 14.168, 15.173, 16.336, 21.381, 22.55, 187, 289, Z 7.179

mennes (*infl. gen. pl.*) men's 3.103, 9.214, 12.114, 199, 20.414, **B** Pr 198, 6.102, 10.95, 131, 213, 11.245, 15.422, 473, 476

Meno(u)r n Minorite, Franciscan friar 10.9, B 8.18

mensioun 11.284 = **mencioun** n

menthynen Z 2.174 = **maynte(y)nen** v

*mercede n wages [(due) payment for work] 3.290, 304, 332

mercement n fine, penalty 1.157, 4.182

mercer n mercer, dealer in textiles 6.250

mercy n forgiveness 1.165, 168, 6.16, 92, 274, 337, 7.147, 232, 9.237, 346, 12.72, 13.12, 14.56, 19.208, 268n, 292, 316, B 11.263, 14.187, 331, 16.5; *in phr.* ~ **for mysdedes** forgiveness for wrongdoing 6.274, 7.232, 12.72, 14.56, 18.259, B 5.72; pardon 19.287, 20.89, 21.185, Z 4.78; mercy 6.339, 17.265, 19.181 *et p.*, 324, 331, 20.431, 440, 21.93, 185, 326; (*person.*) 7.287, 12.74, 20.118, 124 *et p.*, B 2.31; clemency 3.471, 4.73, 90, 95, 139, 6.323, 332, 8.37, 9.274, 276, B 10.370; favour 2.133, 6.323, 21.76; charity, kindness 11.49, 13.142, 16.23, **B** 10.67, 15.468, 439; grace B 10.123, 13.409, A 11.261; *as excl.* pardon! 1.11, 2.2; have mercy! 6.4; *of thanks* 1.41; *of surprise* 18.276; *in phrr:* **do** ~ grant forgiveness 7.121; exercise clemency 4.139, 20.431, 440, **Goddis** ~ 11.218, 18.288, 19.326, ~ **of God** B 5.284; *excl.* **for** ~**s sake** to gain (oneself) mercy, at all costs B 10.253; **graunt** ~ many thanks B 10.220, 17.86

merciable a merciful, forgiving 9.15, 20.417, 436, *a as n* the merciful 19.197; compassionate B 5.504; generous, charitable 17.46, B 15.154

#**mercyen** v thank 3.21

merciful a forgiving, compassionate B 2.32

mercymonye n reward B 14.126

mere n ? lake, ? boundary 3.380n

mery(e) 2.167 *etc*; *see* **mury(e), (mery(e))** a

meryte n merit, spiritual credit 1.178, 11.159; (cause of) spiritual reward 16.327, **B** 5.379, 11.182

meritorie a suitable [in terms of desert] 9.68; spiritually profitable B 11.79

merk n stamp, imprint B 15.349

merke ^{1} n darkness 19.207

merke (myrke) ^{2} a dark 1.1; obscure, mysterious 18.197, B 11.159; n ~**nesse** n darkness (of hell) 20.139; (*fig.*) darkness of sin 20.179

†**merken** B 6.325 = **marken** v

mersyen v levy fine (on) 8.37; *and see* **amercyen** v

merthe 20.227, A 12.92 = **murthe** n

merueil *a*, (*sup.*) **merueilleste** A 9.59 = **merueillouseste**; *see* **merueillous** *a*

merueyl(l)e *n* wonderful work B 15.589; wonderment, astonishment, **hauen** ~ be astonished 20.130, B 11.75; cause of astonishment, ~ **me þynkeþ** I find it astonishing B 9.150

merueyl(l)en *v* (feel) wonder 15.21; (*impers.*) **me ~ed** I marvelled 13.162, 18.23, I wondered B 11.359, **me ~eth** I am astonished 13.192

merueillous *a* wonderful, astonishing B Pr 11, 11.6, (*sup.*) B 8.68

merueylousli(che) *av* wonderfully, **mette** ~ had an astonishing dream Pr 9, 9.308, 10.67, 22.52

mesager 2.237, 9.136, 13.32 *see* **mes(s)ager(e)** *n*

meschaunce *n* calamity 6.69; evil fate 19.231; adversity, misfortune Pr 105, 3.97; ill-luck **B** 3.167, 5.91; wrong-doing, sin 10.59, B 14.75, Z 5.74

mesch(i)ef *n* misfortune, calamity Pr 65, B 12.84; trouble 3.222, B 4.72*n*; affliction Pr 212, 9.183, 12.180, 203, 16.310; misery 15.160, 16.78, B 14.238; harm 22.65, *in phr.* ~ **and / or male(e)se** misery and suffering 8.233, 15.85; penury, distress 9.179, 10.203, 13.70, 16.94, B 14.174; want (of food) 8.212, 21.284; (spiritual) need 11.233, *in phr.* **at** ~ in need B 9.76, 10.451, 11.298, A 11.201; wickedness, sin ? **B** 3.278, 14.75, *in phr.* **at** ~ wrongfully A 10.181; infirmity 9.216; disease 16.249

mese(y)se *n* suffering, illness 15.160, B 9.76; starvation B 1.24; ~ *and see* **myseise** *a*

mesel (**musel**) *n* leper 3.168, 9.179, **B** 7.101, 16.111

meson-dew *n* hospital (for the poor) 9.30

mesour A 12.73 = **mesure** *n*

message *n* communication (*sc.* to God), prayer 17.257

mes(s)ager(e) *n* messenger, courier 2.237, 4.129, 13.32, 36, 39, 42, 53, 58, 63, 78, 87, *in phr.* **mynstrals and ~s** 2.237, 9.136, Z 7.49; (divine) envoy 9.136, 17.178, 18.131, 21.208, B 15.407

messe[1] B Pr 97, A 3.211 = **masse** *n*

messe[2] Z 5.37 *see* **mees** *n*[2]

Messie *n* Messiah 3.456, 17.159, 296, 301, B 15.603

mester 9.7 = **muster** *n*

mesurable *a* moderate B 1.19; appropriate B 3.256

mesure *n* measure [instrument / vessel for measuring quantity] 6.230, 16.128, B 13.359, (*fig.*) = amount 1.172; size B 16.182; proper quantity 22.254; what is appropriate / in proportion 22.26; moderation, temperance 1.19, 33, 15.273, 17.52, B 14.74, A 12.73; *in phr.* **out of** ~ immoderately 13.188

mesurelees *a* immoderate, without (proper) limit B 3.246

mesuren *v* (*refl.*) moderate, control (oneself) B 14.77, 81

met *n* (instrument / vessel for) measurement B 13.359

met *p.p.* 13.216 *see* **meten** *v*[2], B 11.242 *see* **meten** *v*[3]

metal *n* metal (of coin) 17.74, (*fig.*) 17.78 (B 15.349, 352)

mete *a* ? pleasant, ? sufficient A 8.110n

mete *n* food 3.278, 6.289, 7.84, 9.251, 10.188, 203, 13.85, 188, 227, 14.137, 15.33 *et p.*, 217, 233, 247, 16.72, 17.32, 176, 18.155, 21.284, 289, **B** 1.24, 5.256, 6.19, 266, 7.129, 11.277, 282, 13.53, 404, 14.157, 15.207, 474; *in phr.* ~ **tilien** get one's food (by tilling) 15.270, B 6.232; ~ **and / or moneye** 8.204, 16.70, 19.232, B 11.195, A 7.210; sustenance 22.211; dish 15.44, 67, 91, B 13.108; meat ? 9.149, Z 7.316; meal, *in phr.* **at (þe)** ~ at table 8.51, 11.35, 16.341; dinner 6.147, 7.67, 9.228; banquet 21.418

#meteȝyuere *n* provider of hospitality B 15.147

metele(e)s *a* without food 9.295, B 10.65

metel(e)s *n* dream Pr 217, 9.296, 297, (*pl.*) 317, 15.4, **B** 2.53, 8.68, 11.6, 86, 405

meten *v*[1] measure Pr 163 (B Pr 215); measure out 1.172

meten *v*[2] (*p.t.* **mette** Pr 9 *etc*) dream 9.308, 22.52; (*impers.*) dream Pr 9, 219, 5.109, 110, 10.67, 11.167, 21.5, 484, B 11.6, †B Pr 11 (A Pr 11, Z Pr 12); **metyng(e)** *pr.p.* dreaming 2.54, *ger.* dream **B** 11.319, 13.4, A 9.59

meten *v*[3] (*p.t.* **mette** 2.237 *etc*) come across 4.48, 6.178, 7.159, 296, 10.3, 8; meet, encounter 15.30, 17.30, 18.247, 19.53, 20.124, 21.157, **B** 5.99, 13.6; come upon 18.168; come together 20.124; meet (in battle) 22.93; enter the presence of 4.41; keep a rendezvous with B 16.146; catch up with B 17.81; ~ **togidere** meet one another 13.32, join, run (together) A Pr 60; ~ **with** meet, encounter 2.237, 4.140, 5.6, 9.122, 10.115, 11.189, 13.56, 61, 15.30, 192, 16.141, 18.182, 20.224, 22.4, B 15.251

methet Z 1.101 *see* **meten** *v*[1]

mette *n* table-companion 15.41, 55

meuen *v* (*tr.*) move 19.160, shake 18.110; (*intr.*) move **B** 8.33, 17.166, *pr.p. a* **meuynge** shifting, changeable 9.110; arouse, stir up 13.179, 14.67, 21.287, **B** 10.263, 13.192, (*refl.*) 18.118; raise, *in phr.* ~ **matere** raise topic, question 1.122, 10.119, 12.43, **B** 11.230, 15.271, ~ **motif** advance a proposition 15.131, 16.229, B 10.115; urge B 12.4

myche Z 2.3, 8.89 = **muche** *a*

my(n)(e) *poss. prn* (**mi** A 12.82, **myen** 18.255, **myn** 20.431, A 3.51, 11.261, *and before vowels and mute* **h** 4.58, 6.75 *et p.*, *pl.* **myne** 4.97, 6.152) my Pr 203, B Pr 203, A 1.69, Z Pr 93, *et p.*; mine *sg.* 6.263, *pl.* (**myn**) 8.148, 16.206, B 5.110, (**myne**) 20.301, 372, B 6.148, 18.351

myd (**myt**) *prep.* with 4.73, †6.336, **B** 5.74, †12.203, †15.352, Z 5.90, 6.11, 7.58, 139, 177, 304, 8.18; at the same time as, **riȝt** ~ **þat** at that very moment B 12.295; accompanied by 16.180; in (the keeping of) B 17.169; ~ **fole** in foal †B 11.343

myd *av* by means of it Z 7.299

mydday *n* mid-day, noon 16.169; *in phr.* **aboute** ~ round about noon 7.132, 9.246, 20.137

mydde-Lentones (Sonenday) Mid-Lent Sunday *n. phr.* [4th Sunday of Lent] 18.182

myddel(l) *n* middle 19.158; waist 3.10, 6.408; full (of moon) 3.479

myddel *a* middle 18.119, **B** 12.7, 16.5

myd(d)elerd (~erthe) *n* the earth 11.170, 13.132

myddes *n* middle 2.195, 7.232, 21.4, A 2.40, *in phr.* **euene in þe ~** right in the middle 18.6, 19.153

mydmorewe *n* mid-morning A 2.40

mydnyht *n* midnight 16.169, A 8.151

myen 18.255; *see* **my(n)(e)** *poss. prn*

myght Pr 140, 18.30, **B** 9.52, 16.182, **miȝte** 18.202, A 10.63, 64, 77, = **myht** *n*

myghte *p.t.* Pr 100, (*2 sg.* **myghtest** Pr 163), 174, 181, 1.148, **B** 1.82, 17.191, A 3.224, 8.123, 10.59, 86, 119, Z 3.169 = **myhte**; *see* **mowen** *v*

myghtful **B** 11.277, 17.312 = **myhtfull** *a*

miȝtiest *sup.* A 10.54 *see* **myhty** *a*

Mihelmasse *n* Michaelmas day [Sept 29] 15.217

myht(e) *n* (supernatural) power [of God] 1.158, 6.285, 9.115, 17.314, 18.288, 19.135, 149, 193, 196, 294, 20.477, 21.24, 186, 390, **B** 1.107, 5.132, 9.37, 44, 52, 10.104, 16.54, 184, 18.255; *in phrr.*: **~ and mayne** power and might 20.361; **~ of miracle** power to perform miracles 15.227; power [of devil] 18.151, **B** 10.329, 16.120, 165; potency B 13.156, 168; dominion 16.59; control 7.287; authority, warrant Pr 140; force 6.73, 8.208; firm severity B 4.173; capacity 16.85, 19.119, **B** 5.102, 12.7, 18.255; ability 18.202, *in phrr.* **by ~..., emforth ~...** according to (one's) capacity 6.295, 15.143, B 10.253; faculty 1.160; vigour 16.135; (physical) strength 18.30, B 16.182

myht(e) *2 sg. pr.* 1.144, 3.29, 423 *etc* (**myhtow** = **myht þow** 1.167); *1 and 3 sg. p.t.* Pr 68, 3.128, 229 *et p.*, *pl.* Pr 175, 4.78 *etc*, *2 p.* **myhtest** 16.19; *as cond.* Pr 39, 2.118, 146, 3.294; *2 p.* **myhtest(e)** 16.206, 19.281 *see* **mowen** *v*

myhtfull *a* possessed of (supernatural) power 1.168, B 17.312; mighty B 11.277

myhty *a* powerful 21.265, (*sup.*) A 10.54; capable of possessing power (to) 1.171

mylde *a* kind, gracious 9.15, 19.201, B 15.306; humble 14.143, 20.118, 22.65, (*sup.*) 21.256, B 15.468; **~ speche** humble / diffident language / address 11.92, 15.277, 21.93, A 9.71, 10.83; gentle 17.239, B 15.280; tame 15.294; **~liche** *av* kindly 3.10, 39; graciously 3.21, 77, 20.152; humbly 18.131, 19.280, Z 1.91; obediently 9.183; gently 17.30; **~nesse** *n* humility B 15.174, 258

myle *n* (*pl.* **myle**) mile 7.17, 19.74, 22.164, **B** 5.373, 402, 16.10; *in phrr.* **~ way** distance of a mile 9.296; **large ~** full mile B 10.164; **lenghe of a ~** time taken to walk a mile 13.38, B 15.187; **arst...be a ~** a mile ahead A 4.29

myleliche Z 1.91 = **myldeliche** *av*

mylion *n* million A 3.249, 10.152

mylk *n* milk 7.51, 9.75, B 15.280, 466, 469; **~en** *v* milk 17.10

myllares Z Pr 89; **millere** B 2.112 = **mullere** *n*

myn(e) 4.28, 62 *et p.*; *see* **my(n)(e)** *poss. prn*

mynde *n* mind 6.339, 12.91, 16.180; thought(s) 6.284, 19.292, **B** 11.50, A 11.216; memory, remembrance, **hauen ~ in** remember, think about 12.151, B 15.147; meditation B 15.295, 16.38; mention 15.310, B 9.122; reason 17.154; understanding B 16.58, **ryhte ~** sound judgement 3.326

mynistre *n* minister B 15.418; (**Cristes**) **~** priest 5.60, B 15.418; official 16.124

ministren *v* render service / minister (to) 18.97; serve 19.119; administer (estate) B 12.52

mynne *a* *as n* less, *in phr.* **more ne ~** no more or less, nothing else 3.395

minnen *v* (re)call to mind 17.210, **B** 15.461, †15.547; reflect †B 12.4

mynour *n* miner B Pr 222

mynstra(l)cie *n* music(al entertainment), minstrelsy [the minstrel's art] 3.12, 275, 15.197, 199, (*fig.*) 16.310, B 10.48; ? singing, ? story-telling B 10.43

mynstre *n* monastery 5.91

mynstrel (munstral) *n* minstrel (instrumental / vocal) musician, musical entertainer Pr 35, 2.237, 3.275, 9.128, 11.35, 15.195, **B** 3.133, 14.27, Z Pr 89, 7.49; **kynges ~** 7.96, **lordes ~** 15.205 minstrel retained by a king / lord; trumpeter 22.93; (*fig.*) **Goddes ~** = the poor 7.99, 102, 109; the half-witted 9.136; **~s of heuene** 9.126

myn(u)t(e)-while *n* space of a minute (= a very short time) 12.219, 13.199, 19.195

myracle *n* miracle Pr 99, 9.113, 15.227, 17.263, 301, 18.146, B 15.445, 448, 589

myre *n* bog, swamp 13.167

myrke 18.197 = **merke** *a*

mirre *n* (ointment of) myrrh 21.76, 92, 93

myr(r)our *n* mirror B 15.162, (*fig.*) 11.181, B 12.95, **~ of Myddelerd** mirror of the world 11.170, 13.132; = example 17.277, 18.174

myrthe 3.12, B 3.220 = **murthe** *v*

misbeden *v* insult, maltreat 8.42

mysbileue *n* false (religious) belief 3.327, 17.273, 18.151; superstition Pr 102; *in phr.* **bryngen / maken in ~** lead into false belief / heresy 17.181, **B** 10.116, 15.396

myschaunce 19.231 = **meschaunce** *n*

myschief B 9.76 = **mesch(i)ef** *n*

mischeuen *v* come to grief B 12.117

mysdede¹ *n* misdeed, transgression 1.157, 163, 3.45, 6.274, 7.70, 121, 12.72, 14.56, 16.261, 18.259, 22.308, **B** 5.72, 10.370, Z 5.136

mysdede² *p.t. see* **mysdon** *v*

mysdoer(e) *n* wrongdoer B 3.247, 297

mysdon *v* (*p.t.* **mysdede** 20.389, B 4.99, A 4.77, *p.p.*

mysdo 4.86) do wrong, transgress 3.158; do (sth.) wrongfully 4.86, 20.389, **B** 15.109, 18.342, A 4.77; wrong, injure **B** 4.99, 15.257, 18.97; beat up Z 7.152

myseise *a* infirm 9.30, *a as n* A 8.28; *see* **mese(y)se** *n*

myself 6.74 *etc*, **myselue** 3.233 *etc*; *see* **mysulue** *prn*

mysfaren *v* come to grief 10.162

***mysfeet** *n* misdeed B 11.374

myshap(pe) *n* accident 5.34, 12.203

myshappen *v* meet with bad luck, come to grief 3.481, 11.187, B 10.282

mysylfe Z 7.61, 198 *see* **mysulue** *prn*

mysliken *v* be displeased 16.312

myspenden *v* waste 10.187; misuse B 15.76

myspenen *v* misuse 5.93, 10.176, 16.232

mysproud *a* arrogant 7.95 (B 13.436)

mysrulen *v* misuse, abuse B 9.60

misseyen *v* insult, disparage 6.9; revile, rebuke 20.350, B 16.127

missen *v* be deprived of 14.44; be free of B Pr 192; *ger.* lack 10.203, A 12.73

mysshape(n) *p.p.a* deformed 9.171

myssomur *n* midsummer 16.13

***mysstanden** *v* be amiss B 11.380

myst *n* mist Pr 163; vapour 19.195

myst(y)(li) *a* obscure, hard to grasp, *comp.* **mysti(lok)er** 11.129

mysulue (mysulf 4.134 *etc*, **myself** 6.74 *etc*, **myselue(n)** 3.233 *etc*, A 11.163, **mysilfe** Z 7.61, 198) *emphatic prn* (*as appositive to subj.*) myself 2.183, 3.5 *etc*; (*as refl. obj.*) 6.74, 8.26, 19.159; (*as obj. of prep.*) 10.68, 12.52, 13.217, 14.140, 15.213, 19.93; (*indep., as subj.*) I myself 8.268, 18.253, B 10.228, (*as v. obj.*) (me) myself **B** 2.179, 13.122, 15.162, (*as obj. of prep.*) 20.373, **B** 6.137, 16.47; *in phr.* **for** ~ for my part 4.134

mysturnynge *ger.* going astray 7.307

***myswynnen** *v* (*p.t. pl.* **myswonne**) gain wrongfully 15.48

myt Z 5.50, 90 *etc* = **myd** *prep.*

myte *n*¹ mite [insect] †B 14.23

myte *n*² mite [coin] = (1/2 farthing) 13.96; (*fig.*) jot, whit 9.274, 22.179, **B** 7.50, 13.197

#mitigacioun *n* mitigation, lessening of punishment [i.e. for sin after death] 6.323

mytren *v* (invest with) mitre, *p.p.a* **mytrede** 4.193

mywen *v* stack (hay, grain) 5.14

***mnam** *n* mina [Greek coin = 100 drachmas] B 6.238, 240, 241, †Z 5.124

mo *n* other(s) 2.250, 3.1, 6.347, 15.153, 19.26, 22.272, B 15.334

mo *a* more (in number) Pr 166, 9.171, 14.3, 21.127, **B** 1.116, 5.242, A 7.257; additional, further 19.37, 264; *in phrr.* ~ **othere** others besides 4.10, B 12.118, **other** ~ 20.180, 21.54, B 10.176; **withouten** ~ without further 12.86

mo *av* to a greater degree B 14.328; besides, in addition 2.7, 113, 20.181, 21.165, B 17.282, A 10.152

moche 6.309 *etc*, Pr 196 *etc*; *see* **much(e)(l)** *n, a*

mochel 6.323 = **muche(l)** *a*

moder *n* (*uninfl. gen.* 21.124) mother 6.15, 16.104, 20.131, B 16.217, (*Amendes, mother of Mede*) 2.122, 123, (*Mary, mother of Christ*) 2.51, 4.39, 7.148, 155, 8.21, 9.347, 12.135, 21.119, 21.124, 148, B 18.255, A 12.116, (*fig.*) 16.135, (*the Church*) 18.207

mody *a* proud, *as n* (**þe**) ~ the proud one [= the Devil] B 9.205 (A 10.217)

modiliche *av* angrily 4.167

moebles B 3.269, 17.275 = **meble** *n*

moed (mood) *n* spirits, attitude 13.179; heart, feelings, **meuen** ~ stir up (one's) feelings , prompt (one's) heart B 13.192; anger, **meuede hym** ~ wrath (be)stirred (itself) 18.118, **meuen** ~ get angry B 10.263

moes *n* moss 17.14

moest (*sup.*) *a* 17.63, 19.237, 21.256, 421, *av* 16.119, 19.105 = **most(e)** *a, av*

moet 21.368 = **mote** *n*²

moet-halle 4.163 = **mot-halle** *n*

moet *pr. sg., pl.* 11.234, 302, 12.171, 16.70, 20.207, 208, 21.321, 368, 22.46, 238 *see* **moten** *v*

moeuen B 15.71, 19.288 = **meuen** *v*

#moilere (moylo(u)re) *a* born in wedlock 2.120, 145, 10.211; *as n* (legitimate) offspring 18.221, 235

moist *a* juicy 18.86

moisten *v* refresh 20.410

mok (muk) *n* dung B 6.142; (*fig.*) (landed) property 10.97

mold(e) *n*¹ earth 8.17, 19.84; world Pr 65, 1.42, 3.444, 12.180, 19.84, **B** 9.83, 11.273, A 3.233, Z 2.18, *in phr.* **man (...) (vp)on** ~ (mortal) human being 2.208, 9.172, 10.14, 11.231, 14.167, 17.249, **B** 2.187, 3.80, A 10.128

molde *n*² pattern, model 13.161

#mol *n* stain, mark B 13.315; *a* ***moled** spotted B 13.275

molten *p.p.* B 13.83 *see* **melten** *v*

mom B Pr 216 (A Pr 89, Z Pr 69) = **mum** *n*

mone *n*¹ complaint 8.130; prayer 16.184, 17.257

mone *n*² moon 9.108, 110, 308, 17.91, Z 6.68; *in phrr*: **on bothe half þe** ~ ? both before and after the full moon 8.350n; **myddel of a** ~ full (of a) moon 3.479, B 13.156

mone (moneye) *n*³ money Pr 61, 164, 2.170, 3.263, 423, 6.244, 280, 9.270, 12.244, 13.48, 60, 97, 15.36, 169, 205, 17.234, 19.233, 21.352, 22.12, B 16.129, A 3.249, Z 3.95, 5.101; coinage 17.74, B 15.349; wealth 1.42, **Mammonaes** ~ ill-gotten gains 10.87; payment, ? bribe B 15.241, *in phrr.* **mede and / ne** ~ reward and / nor payment B 3.253, 271, **mete and / or** ~ food and / or money 8.204, 15.36, 16.70, B 11.195

moneye *pl.* 2.226 = **many(e)** *a, as n*

#moneyeles *a* moneyless 9.110, 295

monek 3.168, Z 3.69 = **monk** *n*

monewen A 7.87 = **men(e)gen** *v*

mony(e) Pr 27, 60, 2.113 *etc*; *see* **many(e)** *n and a*

moniale *n* nun 5.76, 170, 18.74, 22.264

monk *n* monk 3.168, 6.131, 151, 158, 7.66, 17.35, 52, 60, 18.74, **B** 6.325 (~**es heddes**), 15.274, A 10.113, 136; *in phrr.* ~**es and / or chano(u)ns** 5.156, 170, (B 10.318), 17.55, **and freres** 17.52, **B** 15.416, **and moniales** 5.76 *etc*

mont (mount) *n* mount(ain) 19.2, B 11.169

montai(g)ne *n* mountain 1.1, B 11.323, A 2.40

month *n* month 3.181, 5.50, 6.131, 21.391, B 10.151 *and see* **twel~**

mood B 10.263, 13.192 = **moed** *n*

moolde B 2.37, 9.83, 11.273 = **molde** *n*[1]

moone B 13.156 = **mone** *n*[2]

moore B Pr 52, 111, 2.76 *et p.*; **moost** B 1.151, 3.80 *etc*; *see* **more, most(e)** *n, a, av*

moornen B 13.192, 386, 411 = **mournen** *v*

moot *sg. pr.* **B** †3.319, 9.15 *etc*; *see* **moten** *v*[1]

moot-halle B 4.135, 152 = **mot-halle** *n*

mor *n*[1] marshland 13.167

mor *n*[2] 13.223, A 12.92 = **more** *n*[2]

more *n*[1] root 16.249, 17.21, 21.340, B 16.5, 14, 58

more *n*[2] (*comp. of* **muchel** *n*) more (= greater amount) Pr 219, 232, 1.122, 4.97, 100, 7.193, *in phr.* **lasse ne** ~ less or more B 13.17, the smaller or larger B 10.265; (= an additional amount) 1.189, 3.218, 5.109; something further B 9.36; **þat ~** what further amount 19.77 (**what...moore** B 17.78); [*ref. to social rank*] *in phrr*: **lasse other / ne** ~lower or higher / greater 2.48, 10.7, 15.201; [*ref. to quantity*] ~ **or lesse** greater or smaller amount; **a poynt of** ~ one thing further 8.35; **no** ~ nothing else 13.39; ~ **ne lesse** nothing else but B 10.456; **is no ~ to mene** signifies nothing else 10.210, 11.72, 247, 293, 13.65, 17.41; **withouten ~** forthwith 19.198; without any further action B 10.351

more *comp. a* bigger 21.124; more (in quantity) 1.178 *et p.*; greater 7.61, 281, 13.97, 14.216, 15.47, 17.232, 21.24, **B** 5.282, 284, 6.47, 7.81, 9.150, 16.133; longer 11.136

more *comp. av* more (= to a greater extent / degree) 2.80, 3.230, 7.98, 9.108, 11.49, 17.211; further 13.162, 21.69, **B** Pr 111, 11.47; **eny ~** any further 3.138, **ȝut ~** still further 12.241, 13.75, 16.132; **no ~** not again Z 8.32; rather 16.261, B 15.448; longer B 3.290; (*comp. degree, with positive a*) 10.109, **B** 12.261, 14.27, 89, 101, (*as intensifier with comp. a.*) 18.65, 88, 21.24, B 7.70, (*with comp. av*) **B** 11.160, 15.199

moreouer *av* besides, in addition 5.53, 18.225

moreyne *n* death, mortality 20.224; plague 3.97

#**morgagen** *v* mortgage **Z** 3.96 [= pledge in return for loan], 5.101 [= accept as pledge in return for loan]

mornen 4.160 = **mournen** *v*

mornyng[1] Pr 6 = **morwenyng** *n*

mornyng(e)[2] 12.205, 21.294 = **mournynge** *ger.*; *see* **mournen** *v*

morreyne 3.97 = **moreyne** *n*

morsel *n* mouthful B 13.108

mortel *a* deadly 17.288

morter *n*[1] mortar [grinding / mixing bowl]

morter *n*[2] mortar, cement B 6.142, (*fig.*) 21.326

mortheren *v* murder 4.58, 19.262, A 5.84; slaughter A 3.249

morthrar *n* murderer Z 7.263

mortrew(e)s *n* stew(s) of pounded meat 15.47, 67, 101, B 13.108

morwe(n) *n* morning 6.352, 373, 8.180, 9.243, 11.102, B 14.15, Z Pr 6, 2.49; the next day 10.271, B 6.146; **a-~** on the next day 7.13

mor(we)nyng *n* Pr 6, B 13.262; **a-~** in the morning(s) 13.147

moskele *n* mussel 9.94

mosse *n* moss B 15.287

mossen *v* become mossy A 10.104

most(e) (**moest** 16.119 *etc*, **moost** B 3.80 *et p.*) *sup. a* most (= greatest, largest in size) 1.7, 3.382, B 10.93, (= largest in number) B 4.159, 181, (= largest in quantity) 7.132, 11.27 (1), 21.421, B 10.29 (2); *a as n* 11.289, B 8.55 (1); greatest Pr 65, 3.81, 11.190, 233, 14.108, 15.5, 17.63, 19.238, B 11.398, A 10.54; chief **B** 9.56, 15.255

most(e) (**moest** 16.119, 19.105, **moost** B Pr 158 *et p.*) *sup. av* most (= to the greatest degree) 2.38, 9.71, 11.27, 13.179, 16.119, **B** 5.99, 8.55 (2), 9.100, 10.28 (2), 12.52; (*with a*) Pr 131, 145, 176, 2.64, 3.471, 9.68, 10.157, 11.295, 13.192, 15.39, 21.266, **B** 4.166, †9.33, 10.29 (1), 11.272, 13.298, 15.156; (*intensifying sup. a*) 12.225, B 14.44; (*with av*) 10.14, 16.338, 19.237, (*with sup. av* 12.225); principally 13.179, **B** 11.230, 15.295

moste *p.t.* 3.256, 15.11, 16.161, 18.126, B 4.112, A 12.39, Z Pr 71, (*with pr. sense*) 7.2, 291, 9.280, 17.225, 243, **B** 5.150, 7.21, 13.315, 14.192, 277, 16.200, 19.67 *see* **moten** *v*[1]

#**mo(u)stre** *n* show, display 6.260 (B 13.362)

mote *n*[1] mote, speck B 10.263

mote *n*[2] moat 7.232, 21.368

mote *n*[3] assembly Z 4.150

moten *v*[1] (*pr.* **mot(e)** 1.136 *etc, pl.* **mot(e)(n)** 3.86, 7.205, *p.t.* **most(e)** 3.256, B 4.112 *etc*, (*with pr. sense*) 7.2, **B** 5.150, 7.21) be allowed, may 7.156, 20.207, 208, (*p.t.*) might 13.33, 16.161, **B** 4.112, 15.398, A 12.39; must 1.136, 7.2, 205, 291, 8.313, 9.280, 12.171, 13.48, 67, 21.67, 321, **B** 9.15, 37, 43, 109, 12.185, 14.192, 16.200; be compelled to †B 3.319; have to 6.127, 11.302, 16.70, B 13.261, will have to B 14.277, 21.321, would have to 18.126, B 13.179, should have to 3.256; (*absolute*) is necessary 17.225, B 9.36; ought 17.243,

B 13.315; *in phr.* ~ **nede(s)** must needs / of necessity 3.280, 11.234, 13.36, 19.87, 22.46, B 5.253; insist on 5.28; (*in asseverations, blessings, curses*): may 2.117, 7.156, 9.25, 15.149, 21.179, 180, B 10.132

moten v^2 go to law, plead a case 1.171, 3.197, A 4.118; *ger.* **motyng(e)** legal pleading, advocacy 4.132, 9.54

mo(o)t-halle *n* court-room, court of law 4.148, 163, B 4.135

mothe *n* (clothes)-moth 12.219, B 14.23, ~ **eten** moth-eaten B 10.360

#**moty(e)f** (*pl.* **motyues**) *n* proposition, argument, **meuen** ~ formally propose an argument for discussion 15.131, 16.229, B 10.115,

motyng(e) 4.132, 9.54 *see* **moten** v^2

motoun *n* gold coin [stamped with image of Lamb of God] 3.25

mouhte *p.t.* 11.159, 267 = **myhte**; *see* **mowen** v^2

mount B 11.169 = **mont** *n*

mountai(g)ne B 11.323, A 2.40 = **montai(g)ne** *n*

mounten (vp) *v* increase, ? spring up Pr 65

mo(u)rnen *v* grieve 6.274; sorrow 7.70; be troubled, anxious 3.17, 215; lament, complain 4.160, 15.65; *ger.* **mournynge** sorrow, grief 12.205, 17.147, 21.294, B 14.238

mous *n* (*pl.* **muys** Pr 166 (**mees** B)) mouse Pr 196, 207, 213

mouth *n* 6.180, 22.191, [*as organ of eating*] 6.432, 21.289, B 12.232 [*as organ of speech*] Pr 164, 1.165, 3.395, ? 6.161, 10.66, 11.31, 53, 278, 13.39, 58, 15.223, 16.30, 18.124, **B** 4.155, 5.281, 367, 10.445, 14.88, 90, **A** 3.240, 4.105, 11.306; speech, words 6.73, 16.341, B 15.257, A 9.71, *in phrr.* **with ~e and herte** with word and will 12.72, 18.260, **with ~e or with handes** by speech or action 19.257

mouthed *a* mouthed, **merye** ~ 9.126 *see* **mery(e)** *a*

mouthen *v* utter, speak 4.110, 20.152, B 6.237

moued *p.t.* 18.118 *see* **meuen** *v*

mowen v^1 mow 5.14, *ger.* 8.186

mowen v^2 (1, 3 *sg. pr.* **may** Pr 9, 1.11 *et p.*, 2 **miht** 1.144 *etc*, *subjv.* **mowe** 8.233, *pl.* **mowe(n)** Pr 185, 10.211 *et p.*, **may** 7.173, 8.130, 134 *etc*; *p.t.* 1, 3 **myhte**, (*with pr. sense*) Pr 39 *etc*, **mouhte** 11.159, 267, 2 **my(g)htest** Pr 163, 16.19, 206, 19.281, *pl.* **my(g)hte** Pr 174, 4.78 *etc*): **may, myhte(e)** have power (to) Pr 68, 1.80, 148, 3.222, 229 (1, 2), 7.252, 10.258, 12.16, 74, 101, 15.229, 16.60, 19.83, 287, 20.157, 297, 431, 478, 21.29, 51, 22.179, 197, 322, **B** 5.57, 10.439, 17.166, A 6.80; can, be able (to) 1.80, 153, 167, 2.161, 3.61, 181, 194, 252, 319, 329, 390, 406, 4.84, 97, 133, 5.34, 6.77, 88, 94, 305, 7.3, 173, 267, 275, 303, 8.130, 134, 232, 332, 9.74, 148, 10.27, 57, 84, 160, 212, 238, 286, 310, 12.65, 87, 108, 195, 13.1, 52, 53, 92, 95, 14.44, 126, 176, 15.58, 16.65, 79, 80, 99, 101, 121, 147, 285, 327, 17.73, 86, 123, 18.61, 85, 19.78, 154, 193, 214, 260, 292, 298,

324, 329, 333, 20.204, 224, 372, 437, 438, 21.27, 303, 472, 478, 22.44, 190, 192, **B** Pr 196, 1.149, 3.227, 269, 5.132, 272, 10.276, 11.80, 82, 209, 361, 377, 12.49, 240, 13.171, 408, 14.74, 171, 15.389, 16.218, 17.92, 104, 117, 255, **A** 5.112, 7.37, 12.68, **Z** 6.68, 7.266; may be able (to) 6.332, 7.290, 11.171, 181; will be able 1.144, 3.249, 7.290, 8.178, 315, 9.274, 11.197, 15.159, 16.6, 340, 20.409, **B** 2.45, 15.561; (*sg. sbj.*) **mowe** (should) be able 3.139, 8.40, 233, **B** 14.312, 18.203, (*pl. sbj.*) 7.141, B 4.88 **mowe(n)** (*pl.*) can, be able 3.273, 8.342, 9.176, 10.211, 301, 12.188, 190, 16.216, 19.200, **B** 1.132, 6.39, 7.15, 10.347, 14.61, 15.86, will be able B 10.284; (*p.t. with pr. or fut. sense*) **myht(e)** could, might / should (be able to) Pr 39, 174, 181, 2.204, 3.61, 4.136, 5.123, 6.151, 7.220, 307, 8.137, 221, 11.77, 159, 12.73, 13.199, 15.159, 220, 245, 16.101, 138, 206, 17.225, 18.198, 224, 288, 19.11, 159, 265, 268, 280, 281, 282, 22.383, **B** 1.82, 6.139, 7.135, 9.72, 10.93, 272, 11.388, 12.16, 14.84, 15.89; (*p.t.*) could, was / might (be) able (to) 3.128, 196, 216, 4.150, 6.39, 86, 264, 281, 402, 429, 431, 7.185, 9.7, 11.84, 159, 285, 12.16, 80, 13.60, 14.167, 15.46, 16.19, 17.14, 169, 265, 18.55, 198, 224, 288, 19.56, 106, 236, 242, 20.179, 258, 333, 368, 21.293, 312, 22.93, 121, 197, **B** 1.120, 5.6, 255, 283, 439, 9.83, 116, 10.141, 11.196, 405, 13.313, 15.140, 334, 591, 16.137, 217, A 12.103; could have B 5.374; may, be allowed to 1.202, 2.123, 134, 136, 149, 3.245, 12.63, 15.297, 16.198, 18.281, 20.363, 22.20, B 10.30; may possibly 22.351; *p.t. with pr. sense* **myht(e)** might (be allowed) to 2.146, 3.61, 8.237, 16.206; be entitled 12.59, 16.99, 17.58, 70, B 10.342; must []; shall, will Pr 9, 1.58, 2.148, 3.29, 4.133, 8.42, 11.187, 12.212, B 7.96; (*p.t. with pr. sense*) **myhte** should Pr 175, 2.118, 6.167, B 15.251; *p.t.* should 3.294, 4.107, 8.204, 11.267, 18.120, 21.368, B 13.6; would 11.50, 12.58, **B** 1.120 (1), 15.140; ?ought 17.101; (*neutral use* = do) 4.157, 8.204, 13.139, 16.146, 22.93; (*with implied inf.*) 3.423, 4.78, 10.136, 16.292, 17.317, 19.75, **B** 11.152, 16.137, 17.82, A 10.212; (*absolute uses,* = be capable of) 6.185, 15.96; *in phrr.* **may ...be (to)** can possibly 1.11; ~ **be so, so ~ be** possibly 5.34, 8.41, 17.151, B 16.202; ~**...wel** can easily / readily 3.312, 13.211, 14.126, 16.129, 20.224, 21.62, 162, 22.323, **B** 6.46, 12.38, 14.311, 15.263, 591, ~ **þe bet** might more easily Pr 163, 20.372; ~ **nat be** is impossible 14.29, **be ne** ~ could not exist 19.139, B 12.85, **if hit ben** ~ if it were possible 9.298

much(e)(l) *n* much, a great deal Pr 207, 1.19, 33, 3.181, 6.309, 11.213, 13.94, 15.199, 16.52, 272, 21.405, 22.133, **B** 5.456, 10.89, 14.74; size B 16.182; *in phr.* **as ~ to mene** = signifying B 9.50, A 10.39, 11.296; **by so ~** to that extent 7.141, B 3.353; **in as ~ as** to the extent that 19.203, B 7.15; **ouer ~** too much 8.271

muche(l) *a* much, a great deal (of sth.) Pr 99, 3.486, 4.65, 170, 5.109, 7.86, 9.77, 206, 13.53, 96, 14.138,

15.4, 16.217, 17.74, 19.320, 21.68, 76, 22.158, **B** 5.254, 7.134, 8.84, 14.74, 15.448, **Z** 2.3, 8.89; many, ~ **peple** (**folk**) 7.273, 8.348, 17.299, 20.35, 22.98, 290, A 12.102, *a as n* = so many things B Pr 202; tall 10.68; large 21.368, B 15.89; great 6.323, 7.148, 9.84, 10.176, 11.72, 194, 12.205, 13.7, 161, 14.125, 16.10, 12, 327, 18.179, 277, 19.55, 20.43, 21.98, **B** 9.150, 10.123, 11.75, 12.295, 13.263, 14.157, 175, 15.120, 378, A 10.147; utter A 4.136

muche *av* much, greatly 14.67, 15.199, 16.106, 285, 18.23, 199, 19.41; (*with comp. a*) 16.101, (*with comp. av*) 7.98, **B** 11.79, 11.319, 13.383, Z 5.35; (*with inf.*) 18.221; utterly 19.328; frequently 11.53, B 10.66; *in phrr.* **as ~ worthe** worth as much 13.94; **to ~** B 16.148

mu(y)le *n* mule 19.49

muynde 6.284 = **mynde** *n*

muys *pl.* Pr 166, 213 *see* **mous** *n*

muk B 6.142 = **mok** *n*

mulere A 2.96, **mul(l)iere B** 2.119, 132, 16.219, 221 = **moilere** *a, n*

mullere *n* miller 2.113

mulleston *n* mill-stone 20.293

multiplien *v* multiply, *p.p.* B 6.326; cause to prosper / augment Z 3.120*n*; increase 8.132, 18.86; produce (offspring) 18.225; populate B 16.211

#**mum** *n* 'mmm' [murmured or mumbled sound] Pr 164

munstracye 15.197, 16.310, **munstral** 3.275 *etc; see* **mynstra(l)cie** *n,* **mynstrel** *n*

muracle 9.113 *see* **myracle** *n*

murgust *sup.* Z 2.104; **mury(e)** 8.155, 9.41 *etc,* 13.216, **murie** B 2.154 *etc,* **murier** B 1.107, **murieste** 16.341 *see* **mury(e)**

mury(e), (mery(e)) *a* cheerful, in good spirits 2.167, 13.58, A 1.138, (*sup.*) 16.341; mirthful 9.136; glad, happy 9.41, 16.78, 21.294; festive 22.181; pleasant, agreeable 2.161, 167, 14.180, (*comp.*) B 1.107, (*sup.*) Z 2.104; cheering 14.128, B 13.58; bawdy 6.185 (B 13.352); ? lively, ? keen Pr 217; **maken ~** cheer up (sb.) 15.199, B 3.198, (*refl.*) enjoy (oneself) 8.68, 155, 15.65, 22.289; **~ mouthed** of cheerful speech 9.126; (*av*) pleasantly 13.216, 22.292; sweetly B Pr 10

murthe (**merthe, myrthe**) *n* joy 20.130; enjoyment 16.10, 12, B 15.143, **maken ~** enjoy (oneself) **B** 13.60, 15.139; pleasure 11.181, **B** 12.295, 14.124, 157; (spiritual) happiness 12.205, 17.147, 20.227, A 12.92; delightful sound 10.66; feasting B 10.52; entertainment Pr 35, 3.12, 7.77, **B** 3.220, 10.48, Z 7.49

murthen *v* cheer 19.207; afford pleasure to B 11.398

musel 3.168 *see* **mesel** *n*

musen *v* ponder, reflect upon 11.129, 13.227, 14.74, 15.25, *pr.p.* 9.296, B 10.116

musyk *n* (the art of) music 11.119, B 10.43, A 11.32

muson *n* measure 11.119

must *n* new wine 20.412

muste A 4.99, 8.23, 89 = **moste** *p.t.*

muster (**mester**) *n* craft, trade 3.110, 9.7

mute *a as n* dumb (people) B 16.111

na *av* (= **ne**) not 1.178 (1), (= **no**) 1.178 (2) no, (*with a as n*) ~ **mo** 3.1, B 2.235, (*with comp. a*) ~ **more** 1.178 (2), **B** 10.43, 12.279, (*with comp. a as n*) ~ **moore** B 3.344, 4.103, 5.284, 6.146, 13.352, 20.9, (*with comp. av*) ~ **moore** B 3.290, (4.97) 5.302, 12.100, 107, 16.217, (20.222)

nacion *n* (*sg. for pl.*) nations, groups (of people) 18.102

na3t B 5.186 = **nauht** *av*

nay *interj.* no 3.220, 285, 4.4, 99, 6.240, 7.178, 200, 16.177, 19.7, 20.27, B 13.189, A 12.89, Z 4.132; *in phr.* **construen ~** judge in the negative / 'no' A 8.134

nayl *n* (finger)nail 6.140, **B** 3.191, 6.60; (metal) nail 20.51, 22.226

naylen *v* nail, ~ **vpon a rode** crucify 20.51

naked *a* naked 20.51, 22.196; scantily clad, destitute 13.83, **B** 6.15, 10.360 *in phr.* ~ **as a nedle** stark naked 14.105, 19.58

nale *n. phr.* **atte / at þe ~** = **atten / at þe ale** over the ale, at their drink(ing) B 6.115, A 10.59

nam 11.205 = **name** *n*

nam A 7.223, 225 *see* **mnam** *n*

nam *p.t.* B 5.456 *see* **nymen** *v*

nam Z 4.48 = **ne am**; *see* **be(n)** *v*

name *n* name 1.4, 59, 2.17, 3.3, 34, 52, 143, 10.70, 11.205, 12.177, 13.248, 15.195, 17.25, 19.26, 22.158, 256, 340, **B** 9.79, 10.152, 11.321, 13.140, 226, 290, 15.152, 16.19, 250, **A** 3.51, 12.82, **Z** 2.40, 3.148; title, appellation Pr 134, 12.116, 16.187, 194, 199, 201, 203, 205, 17.190, 261, 278, 18.192, 21.24, 69, 128, 276, B 15.26; name of God B 13.402, (Jesus / Christ) 7.217, 18.282, 21.18, 19, 21.70, **B** 15.456, 16.161, A 12.13, (Holy Ghost / grace) 18.196, 21.209, **the hey ~** the divine name 1.70; *in phrr.* **to ~** as title / name 12.213, by name 16.198; **kynde ~, ryhte ~** actual name 6.232, 10.69, 16.186; **propre ~** own / specific name B 16.185; **singuler ~** sole / single name B 16.208; reputation 6.26, B 5.258, **fals ~** reputation for dishonesty 3.114

nam(e)li(che) *av* especially, particularly 2.159, 6.96, 7.217, 8.51, 275, 9.335, 12.101, 16.80, 17.292, 20.442, 22.196, **B** 7.41, 10.204, 12.71

namoore (= **no more**) *n* nothing further B 3.173, 6.96; *av* no more 17.221; any more **B** 7.117, 17.166

nappen *v* doze off 7.2

nar *pr. pl.* Z 3.35 = **ne ar**; *see* **be(n)** *v*

naroos *p.t.* B 19.52 = **ne aroos**; *see* **arysen** *v*

narwe *av* straitly, **pynchen ~** encroach closely B 13.371

nas *p.t.* B 19.295, 376, A 2.38, 39, 4.135, Z 3.127, †5.155 = **ne was**; *see* **be(n)** *v*

nat *av* not Pr 162 *et p.,* Z 3.155 *et p.*

nat Z 1.56, ? 8.74n = **nauht** *prn*

naught 16.288, 17.241, B 10.337 *etc* = **nauht**¹·³

nauht¹ (no3t) *prn* nothing Pr 115, 1.181, 7.123, 8.257, 11.30, 13.11, 16.288, 17.306, **B** 5.608, 7.84, 13.131, 303, A 7.209; *in phrr*: **at** ~ of no value 9.303; **by** ~ for nothing (= as far as) B 10.332; **bryngen to** ~ ruin 2.139, 3.200; **for** ~ however much 4.57, A 11.258; **ryht** ~ nothing at all 17.42, 19.154, **B** 6.151, 17.191

nauhte² *a* worthless 17.74

nauht (no(u)3t, nouht)³ *av* not Pr 31, 77, 78, 100, 110, 115, 1.190, 2.18, 62, 3.74, 8.40, 257, 15.116, 16.292, 17.241, 18.221, **B** Pr 111, 10.37 *etc*; *in phr*. **ryht(e)** ~ not at all 5.82, 9.123, 14.87, 21.451, B 10.334

nautht 1.181 = **nauht** *prn*

nawher *av* nowhere 2.227, Z Pr 17

ne¹ *av* (*preverbal*) not Pr 80, 3.293, 366 *et p.*, B Pr 129 *et p.*; ~ **were** it not for Pr 215, A 11.141; were not 11.49; (*in double / multiple neg. constr.*) **B** 12.224, 17.55; (*in contractions*) **nam, nar** (= ne am, ne ar) am / are not Z 4.48, 3.35; **nas** (= ne was) was not B 19.275, 295, **A** 2.38, 39, 4.135, †Z 5.155; **nelle** Pr 136 *etc* (= **ne wille**) do not wish to; **nere** (= ne were) were not 1.114, 3.171, 15.212, **B** Pr 200, 10.186, 11.104; **nis** (= ne is) is not 15.167, **B** 5.284, 13.166, 194, 208, 14.155, 243, 15.213, 17.346, **nyste** (= ne wiste) B 13.25; **nolde** (= ne wolde) Pr 110, 7.201, 9.23, **B** Pr 205, 11.64, 15.463, A 7.223, Z 3.165; **null** (= ne wille) 21.467

ne² *conj.* nor Pr 194 *et p.*, B 3.271 *et p.*; or 1.153, 178 *et p.*, B 3.73 *et p.*, A 2.38; and 3.17 *etc*, B 5.422, A 4.141; ~...~, **neither...nor** 14.200, B 12.208, Z 5.144; nor...or 10.187; either...or 15.102; ~ **neuere** and never 6.322; ~ **no**; **non(e)** nor any 1.153, 3.448, 9.113, 254, B 5.36, Z Pr 100; ~ **noþer** nor either, and neither 6.90, 8.304, 15.165; ~...**nother** nor 6.90, 10.187, nor...either 6.166; **noþer...**~ neither...nor 3.293 *etc*, A 3.58; (*emph. double neg.*) 1.178, 13.233 *etc*, Z 7.107

#**necessarie** *n* necessary thing, necessity (of life) 22.249

neddre *n* adder, viper (*fig.*) B 5.86

nede *n* need 11.30, **B** 7.76, 82, 15.336, (*person.*) 13.240, 22.4 *et p.*, 232; want 16.20; necessity 22.9, 10, Z 3.155; compelling reason 6.427, 7.216, 9.67; ? affliction 22.46; affair(s) 22.55; *in phrr*: **at** ~ when needed 1.52, 5.129, 7.42, **B** 1.18, 10.337, in (time of) need 8.126, 10.190, 11.307, 15.146, 16.315, 20.442, 22.20, **B** 3.245, 5.49, 15.178, 17.87, A 11.152; **for** ~ out of necessity 9.312, 315, 22.384; **hauen** ~ need, must 7.293, 9.63, 161, 18.85, 21.392, 22.319, Z 7.193; **moste** ~ (time of) greatest need 11.190, 15.5, 17.63

nede(s) *av* of necessity, necessarily 12.217, 20.442, 22.37, *in phr*: **mot(e)** ~(s) must needs 3.280, 11.234, 13.36, 19.87, 20.442

neden *v* be necessary 5.20, 9.163, 19.34, **B** 6.243, 11.209, 15.575; need 13.104, 16.345, 19.232, B 17.163; be in need 9.71, 12.118, 18.13; (*with obj.*) **hem / yow / hym nedeth (nedede)** they / you / he need(s) / needed 8.148,

219, 9.87, 11.48, 16.292, 17.18, 22.36, **B** 6.209, 8.86, 9.86, 10.200, 11.289, 14.33

nedfol (nidefole) *a* necessary 1.21; beneficial 21.20; in want 4.121, 19.239; *a as n* people in need 13.76

nedy *a* needy, in want 8.289, 9.47, 175, 11.28, 73, *et p.*, **B** 6.223, (*comp.*) ~**er** 7.69, (*sup.*) ~**este** 7.70, 11.242, 12.53, 14.134, 15.572; *a as n* the needy 9.64, 22.38, B 6.15

nedlare *n* needle-maker 6.364

nedle (nelde) *n* needle (for sewing) 1.152, 14.105, 19.58, B 1.157; **bat** ~ packing needle 6.218

neede 22.37 = **nedy** *a*

neen Z Pr 54 = **no(e)n(e)** *a*

neer *prep.* near B 6.298, 16.69

neet *n* ox 21.267

neghe-, ne3ebore B 5.93, 131, 256, 258, 408, 13.364, 373, 16.42 = **neyh(e)bore** *n*

nei3(e)¹ *a* near B 5.93; near (in time) B 11.212; near, close(ly allied) **B** 12.93, 14.273

nei3² B 16.29 *see* **ny** *av*

ne3en B 6.298 = **n(e)yhen** *v*; **neghen** B 17.59, **neyghlen** Z 7.303, *see* **neyhlen** *v*

ney(h) *prep.* near (to) 8.297, 20.290, 22.4, 200

neyh(e)bore *n* neighbour 6.262, 269, 7.210, 8.289, 9.87, B 5.93, 256, 258, (*fig.*) 9.71; fellow-citizen 6.98, B 5.131, 408; fellow-Christian 15.114, 16.129, B 16.42

neyhelen *v* approach 19.60, Z 7.303

n(e)yhen (neyh / ner) *v* approach (close to) 8.322, 22.4, 232

neyther Pr 36, 6.166, 10.275, 14.176, B 3.315 *et p.*, **A** 3.58, 4.113 *see* **no(y)ther** *prn, conj.*

nekke *n* neck Pr 114, 178, 193, 16.80, **B** 10.282, 11.17, (skin of the) neck B 5.134

nelde 1.152, 6.218 = **nedle** *n*

nel(le), nile (= ne wille) Pr 136, 1.122, 6.311, 11.184, 22.29, **B** 4.191, 9.87, 10.331, A 7.262, Z 7.140; **neltow** (= ne wil(le) thow) B 6.156; *see* **willen** *v*

nem(p)n(i)en *v* mention (by name) 1.21, 22.261; speak aloud (the name) 21.18, 20; call, name 21.137, **B** 2.179, 7.154, 9.110, 11.321, A 11.107, *ger.* B 9.79, ~ **to name** give as a name 16.198; assign 22.256; nominate 6.387; offer 6.376

neodfole 4.121 = **nedfol** *a*

ner¹ *a* near, *contr. comp.* (= **nerre**) *in phr*. **neuere þe** ~ never any nearer (to) A 11.258

ner² *av* near 22.232; nearly, almost 8.175, 9.264, 18.179; (*comp.*) **nerre** nearer (to) 19.64

nere¹ *av* never 5.40, 15.235, B 14.119, **Z** 3.122, 4.130, 5.94, 7.68

nere² *p.t. subjv.* (= ne were) were not, did not exist 3.171, **B** 10.186, 11.104, A 5.242, Z 5.140; ~ **hit** were it not 1.114, 15.212

nerhande *av* almost 15.1

nerre *comp.* 19.64 *see* **ner**² *av*

nese *n* niece, kinswoman (*fig.*) 5.176

nest *n* nest 13.156, 159, 160

neste *p.t.* (= ne wiste) 13.219; *see* **witen** *v*¹

neuer(e) *av* never Pr 202 *et p.*; *as emph. neg.*) certainly not, not at all Pr 209, 2.144, 3.342, 4.136, 10.6, 11.202, 241, 14.59, 15.285, 16.275, 17.35, 18.204, 19.275, 20.99, 147, 194, **B** Pr 12, 10.222; *with* **recchen** care not at all 3.387 *etc*, *with* **witen** not know at all 3.296, 6.343; *in phrr*: ~ **eft** never again 3.475; ~ **more** no longer 3.320; never again †15.273, 17.147, ever again 3.442; at no time 12.38, 16.78; ~ **so** however 3.422, 10.36, 16.168, 20.429, 22.260; ~ **þe betere** no better 4.89; ~ **þe ner** no nearer A 11.258

newe *a* new 19.74, 21.429, *a as n* new one 21.274; fresh(ly reaped) 8.322; renewed 13.19; hitherto unknown B 20.256; modern B 15.372; *in phrr*. ~ **fayre** = barter 6.376 *n*; ~ **lawe** Law of the New Covenant 18.265, 19.34, 20.268, 21.312

newe *av* again, anew 5.179, 6.328, 18.161, 20.42, *in phr*. **al** ~ entirely anew B 2.164

nex(s)t *a* next [immediately following] B 13.155; closest 6.269, 7.210; *av* next (time) A 7.155; *prep.* (spiritually) closest (to) 18.98, 19.270, 22.35, B 1.204

ny *av* almost, nearly 3.181, 185, B 16.29

nidefole 1.21 = **nedfol** *a*

nygard *n* miser 19.239, B 15.140

nigromancie *n* necromancy A 11.16

nyhed *p.t.* 8.322 *see* **n(e)yhen** *v*

nyht *n* night 18.179, 20.62, 214; *in phrr*: **a** / **on** ~ / ~**es** at night 9.78, 19.174, 22.196, **by** ~**(es)** by night 4.47, B Pr 197; **forboden** ~**es** penitential nights before feast-days B 13.349; **on** ~**es tyme** at night-time 16.141; **seuen** ~ **week** 7.300; **wynteres** ~**es** winter nights 19.185; ~ *****comare** nocturnal thief 21.144; ~ **olde** last night's 8.331; **(by) day and / ne (by)** ~ 1.32, 13.190, 17.29, 92, 171, 245, 19.218, 21.141, **B** 9.97, 18.97, **(by)** ~ **and** / **ne (by) daye** 19.270, 21.20, B 13.369 = at all / any time(s)

nyhtes *av* at night 5.16, *in phrr*. **a**-~ 19.174, 22.196; **o(n)** ~ 9.78, B 14.2; *av. phr*. **(by) dayes and (by)** ~ at all times 9.222, 11.192, A 12.81

niyed *p.t.* 2.19 *see* **n(o)ien** *v*

nymen *v* (*p.t. 1 sg.* **nam** B 5.456, **noem** Z 5.98, *2 sg.* **nome** 22.9, *3 sg. subjv.* **nyme** 3.391, *3 pl.* **nomen** A 4.63, *p.p.* **ynome** 22.46, B 11.212) take 2.139, 3.391, 8.40, 16.92, 22.20, **B** 5.456, 10.60, A 4.63; carry off B 11.212; pick 18.85; pick (up) 13.240; seize 22.46; misappropriate 6.269; receive 13.104, Z 5.98, ~ **vnder maynprise** agree to stand surety for 22.17; take (heed) 9.71, 11.247, 17.108, **B** 6.15, 11.321, Z 5.98; (*refl.*) betake (oneself) 3.402

nyne *card. num.* nine 19.60, B 1.121, ~ **hundred** B 5.371

nynthe *ord. num.* ninth B 14.313

*****nype** *n* ? extremity, ? biting cold 20.166c

nyppen *v* bite, *pr. p.* 6.104

nis, nys = *ne is 3 sg. pr.* 15.167, **B** 5.284, 13.166, 194, 208, 14.155, 243, 15.213, 17.346 **A** 3.50, 5.221; *see* **be(n)** *v*

nise *a* lascivious 18.37

nysot *n* (*? as a*) fool(ish) Z 2.99c

nyste *p.t.* (= ne wiste) B 13.25; *see* **witen** *v*¹

nythe *ord. num.* ninth 16.148

nythynge *n* miserly wretch 19.239

niuilen *v* snivel, run at the nose, *pr.p.* 6.104

no¹ *a* no Pr 32 *et p.*; not any 8.244, 9.318, 10.119, 11.265 *etc*; (*in double neg. constr. after / before* **nat, ne, neuere**) 3.17, 87, 209, 213, 4.108 *etc*: **nat...no** not...any 4.108; **ne no** nor any 3.293, 448, 4.57, 190, 6.282, 427, 7.95, 8.308, 326, 332 *etc*; **ne...no** nor...any 5.58, 8.275; **no...no** no...any 5.54; *see also* **no(e)ne** *a*

no² *av* no 1.8, 122 *et p.*; = **ne** 6.166

noble *n* noble [English gold coin worth £1/3] 3.47, 391, 6.245, 10.272, 285, 17.200, 207, 22.132, **B** 10.289, 12.247, 15.86

noble *a* noble, illustrious 21.50

nobody *n* no one 3.306, 18.115

noem *p.t.* Z 5.98 *see* **nymen** *v*

no(e)n(e), noon¹ *n* noon, midday 2.100, 6.433, A 7.135; (the) midday meal 6.428, 8.146, 196, 275, 9.87, 22.4, **maken** ~ **dine** 8.289

no(e)n(e), noon² *prn* no one 4.124, 6.37, 49, 10.112, 11.44, 17.108, 21.255, B 11.214 *et p.*; no creature 13.187; not one 2.159, 7.275, 8.340, 11.63, 244, 20.475; none 1.21, 186, 2.10, 11, 3.62, 11.294, 296, 12.166, 13.145, 16.42, 247, 18.55, 21.20, 36, **B** 2.146, 167, 12.31, 16.57, A 11.231, 291; *in phr.* **here** ~ none of them A 7.300, neither of them 14.105, 16.80; *in double neg. constr.* **ne** ~ nor any 16.60, **ne neuere** ~ nor ever any 22.50

no(e)n(e), noon *a* no Pr 192, 1.128, 153, 2.10, 3.433, 6.49, 127, 412, 7.67, 72, 93, 157, 195, 8.50, 10.116, 13.24, 62, 14.51, 15.114, 18.141, †22.13, B 1.120 *et p.*, (*in double neg. constr.*) **ne** ~ nor any 1.153, 3.203, 13.44, 18.141, 19.328, B 13.162 *etc*, **ne...non** 9.109; *in phr.* ~ **oþer** no other(s), no one else 10.116, 19.197, B 17.163; nothing else 6.298, 7.289, 9.173, 290, 13.210, 19.251; anything else B 1.88, 5.101, 295, 7.45, B 17.163; no otherwise B 6.180, Z Pr 54

no3t Pr 31, 2.39, 8.331, B Pr 29 *et p.*, **noght** Pr 110, 115, 138, B 17.312 = **nauht** *av*

noy *n* distress, suffering B 10.60, †11.430n

n(o)ien *v* (do) harm (to), injure 2.19, 3.433, B 2.127, Z 2.99; distress 7.220; trouble B 3.189

noyse *n* outcry 18.110; commotion 18.179

no(y)ther *prn* neither, *in phr.* **her(e)** ~ neither of them 3.365, 10.275, B 4.33; *with double neg. constr.* **neuere...~** in no way is either 13.127

no(y)ther (**neyther** Pr 36 *etc*, B 5.397 *etc*, A 3.58) *conj.* neither, *in constr.* ~ **(...) ne** neither...nor 1.99, 175 *et p*,

B 11.283, A 3.58; (n)or 10.188, 16.290; *in emph. double neg. constr.* **ne...noyther(e)** nor...(either) 10.117, 187, 11.46, 14.176, 15.114; **ne** ~ (and) neither, nor either 6.90, 8.304

noke, þe A 5.115 = **þe oke**

nolde (= **ne** + **wolde**) *vp.t.* Pr 110 *etc; see* **willen** *v*

nombre (**noumbre**) *n* number 21.241, 22.270, 272, **certeyne** ~ fixed, definite number 22.255, 265; *in phr.* **out of** ~ to excess, beyond counting 13.6, 22.269; large number 3.391; company 3.402; order(ed list) 22.259, 261; (grammatical) number 3.336, 346, 357, 364, 371, 394, B 10.239

nombren *v* count B 1.116; fix the number of 22.256

nome(n) *p.t.* 22.9, A 4.63 *see* **nymen** *v*

non *prn* 1.21 *etc, a* 1.128 *etc,* **none** *prn* 1.186 *etc, a* 3.85 *etc; see* **no(e)n(e)** *prn, a*

nones *n*[1] *pl.* 6.428, 8.146, 196 *see* **no(e)n(e)** *n*

nones *n*[2]*, in phr.* **for þe** ~ for the time being, occasion, ? suitably A 2.41

nonne *n* nun B 7.29, **to** ~ who is a nun 6.128

noon(e) 2.100, 8.275 = **no(e)n(e)** *n*

noon *prn* 2.159 *etc, a* 3.203 *etc; see* **no(e)n(e)** *prn, a*

noot *pr. sg.* (= **ne woot**) B 11.212; *see* **witen** *v*

nor *conj.* nor B 10.60

noris(ch)en *v* suckle B 15.466; sustain, support †B 6.223n; foster 12.236, 18.37

north *n* north 1.117, 20.166, *a,* ~ **half** north side 18.66

northerne *a* living in the north (of Britain) 1.114

nose *n* nose 6.104, Z 5.98, *sg. for pl.* 6.400; *in phr.* **han pepir in þe** ~ treat with disdain B 15.203; (*assev.*) **kut of my** ~ 4.159

noskines *a* no kind of Z 7.108

not *av* not 12.193, 13.9, 20.315, 21.117, A Pr 29 *et p.*

notarie *a* (*uninfl. gen* 22.272) notary [scribe authorised to draw up and authenticate documents and legal instruments] 2.139, 156, 159, 185, 22.272, B 2.167, Z 2.99, (*fig.*) 16.190

note *n* song 10.65, 14.180, 20.452; melody 20.469; point, degree 1.117

nother 1.99 *et p.; see* **no(y)ther** *conj.*

nothyng *n* nothing 3.328

nouȝt *prn* Pr 211, *av* Pr 77, 78, 100, 211, 1.190, 2.62, 3.74, B 1.36 *et p.,* A Pr 87 *et p.,* **nou(g)ht(e)** *prn* 4.57, *av* 2.18, 14.87, 15.116 *see* **nauht** *prn, av*

nouȝty *a* destitute B 6.223

noumbre 3.391, 394, 402 = **nombre** *n*

noumper *n* umpire 6.387

nouthe *av* at the present (time) 2.15, 8.212, 9.163, 13.174, 17.107, 108, 21.181, B 3.290, 10.48; in a while 21.384; now 6.171, 19.277; then (*non-temporal*) 8.299, 19.244, B 13.184

now[1] *n* now, the present time 7.180

now[2] *a* of the present time 17.69

now[3] *conj* now that 8.92, 15.99, B 5.142

now[4] *av* now, at (the) present (time), 3.382 *et p.,* Z 3.156; (*in historic pr.*) now, then 3.1, 6.349, 8.112, 21.337, B 5.133; (*in antithetical phrr.*) ~...~ at one time...at another 5.51; *as emph. part.* (*in exhortations and commands*) 6.164, 8.222, 9.240 *etc,* (*in assevs.*) 2.117, 126, B 10.132, (*in oaths*) 2.204 *etc,* (*in prayers*) 6.195, 22.385; (*as phrasal intensifier*) ~ **certes** 18.16; (*introducing clause*) 18.227, B 2.50, 7.174, (*non-temporal*) then 8.223, B 6.276, 16.67, 17.138

nowadayes *av* nowadays, at the present time 11.61, A 11.37

#nownpower *n* powerlessness 19.294

nowthe 21.181 = **nouthe** *av*

nuyen 3.433, 7.220, Z 2.99 *see* **n(o)ien** *v*

null (nel) = **ne wille** 21.467; *see* **willen** *v*

o[1] *num* one B 13.68, 17.37, 40, 139, 18.42, **A** 8.93, 9.91; = first B 19.86; (only) one, a single 3.441, 473, 7.238, 12.111, 13.33, 51, 17.126, 18.21, 28, 57, 188, 189, 234, 237, 19.38, 109, 20.418, 22.245, **B** 2.30, 3.238, 9.145, 15.316, 16.58, A 2.69; ~ **kynde** 3.397, 18.57, 59, 62, 70; ~ **man** 18.237, **B** 9.112, 16.204; ~ **wille** 15.277, 16.179, 17.128; ~ **wit** 20.242, ~ **wit and wil** 5.185, 18.28, 190; *in phr.* ~...**the / (an)other** one...the / (an)other 6.38, A 8.14; one [of God] 11.154, 17.134, 18.211, 216, 238, 240, 19.31, 150, **B** 16.224, 17.128, 130, 182; one (Lord) 17.135, 18.198, 19.42, 44, 100, 109, one (**Lede**) †B 15.393; one and the same 18.20, 21, 28, B 11.195, 16.59; *see also* **a**[1] *num.*

o[2] *prep.* (up)on 20.44; in 2.55, 15.19, 18.198; by 6.52; *in avl phrr.* ~ **lyue** alive A 2.14; ~ **nyghtes** at night B 14.2; *and see* **a**[2] *prep.*

obedience *n* (obligation of) obedience [to law / authority / commandments of the Church] 9.220, 235, 241; religious (vow of) obedience 9.222, **B** 12.37, 13.286

obediencer *n* obedientiary [holder of subordinate office in monastery] 5.91

obedient *a* subject, obedient (to rule) 5.147; willing to serve A 11.191

oc(c)u(e)pien *v* be busy (with) 7.18; (*refl.*) be active 18.206

oelde 11.290, 20.7, 21.274 = **olde** *a*

oen (**o(o)n**) *prn* someone 5.10, 7.291, 298, 10.125, 11.188, 12.76, 20.8, 22.158, **B** 11.319, 15.13, A 12.62; **such** ~ someone like that 16.106, 22.344; man 10.101, 104; one (person) 19.129, 21.270, B 16.183; anyone 16.140; **bond** ~ person of servile status 10.266; **souerayn** ~ person of importance 6.27; member 9.211; one [of a class] 12.54, 16.210, B 1.107; the one 13.35; [numbered set] 7.271, **B** 1.23, 15.374; one of the two 6.384; **that** ~ one 19.301, 21.264, B 3.232; that one 16.140; the one 14.153, B 8.96, A 12.84; **that** ~...**that oþer** the one...the other 14.106, 107; (*with partitive gen.*) **here** ~ the one of them 20.67; *in phrr.* **myn one**

alone 11.200, by myself 10.61; **by here** ~ on her own, while alone 20.316; **by his** ~ by himself B 16.183

o(e)n (oon) *num.* one 14.116, 18.220; (only) one, a single 10.192, 19.38, 152, **B** 3.289, 318, 321, 4.37, 11.168, 13.211, 14.1, 16.181, A 8.179; one particular 14.153; at one, united 6.181, **of** ~ **wille** in singleness / integrity of heart B 3.238; *in phrr.* (*esp. after* **but, except, saue**) alone, only 3.142, 5.52, 13.112, 15.213, 16.213, 372, 17.8, 21.122, 191, 301, 371, 376, B 9.36, 13.125, 14.330, 15.210, **in hymself** ~ solely in himself 1.167, **to hymself** ~ to his own self / himself alone B 9.33; one and the same 21.402, **B** 15.394, 395, 605, 16.182; a certain (person) / someone called 2.25, 42, 4.27, 16.318, 18.126, 21.202, 266, 342, 22.160, 162, 316, **B** 13.124, 15.396; *see also* o¹ *num.,* a¹ *num.*

oenliche 22.267 = **onli(che)** *av*

oest(e) 21.338, 22.113 = **oste** *n*

of¹ *av* off, *in phrasal vv.* **casten** ~ 6.375, **gurden** ~ 2.213, **kutten** ~ 4.159, **potten** ~ 16.121, B 14.191 *etc*

of² *prep.* (*sel. exx.*) out of 1.20, 2.192, 3.314, 6.344, 17.220, 19.250, 20.21, 405, 21.32(1), 110, 325, **B** 3.297, 11.209; from (out of) Pr 164, 230, 12.110, 232, 14.45, 18.216, 230, 19.329, 20.431n, 21.146, **B** 5.3, 12.85, 13.261, 15.337; from among 3.246, 9.172, **B** 3.245, 12.19, 158; (proceeding) from Pr 98, 2.134, 6.255, **B** Pr 128, 5.86, **B** 9.46, 110, 10.238, 13.226, 15.107; (born) from 2.30, 5.64; from Pr 69 (1, 3), 214, 6.161, 305, 13.73, 15.290, 16.70, 17.36, 300, 18.184, 19.66, 171, 250, 20.55, 21.25, 463, 22.221, 266, **B** 10.326, 12.67, 14.194, 15.472, 17.108, 18.84; of (= belonging to) Pr 10, 105, 116, 168, 2.61 *et p.*, **B** 4.193, 5.235, 10.190, 229 *et p.*; inherent in 14.213; made of Pr 159, 6.65, 7.232, 8.292, 18.92, **B** 2.15, 5.80, 14.192; (consisting) of Pr 20 (1), 6.369, 14.38, 18.288, **B** 5.87, 7.120, (=*objective gen.*) Pr 59, 1.200, 2.109, 6.176, 14.107, **B** 1.27, 11.110 *etc*; *in phrr:* **in deseyte** ~ to deceive Pr 77; **for loue** ~ Pr 28, 103; **in menynge** ~ signifying Pr 99; *with phrasal vv.* **acounten** ~ 8.159, 103; **amenden** ~ 7.121, 16.261; **borwen** ~ 4.56; **cessen** ~ B 7.118; **douten** ~ 16.230; **dreden** ~ 16.311; **faylen** ~ 18.30; **leten** ~ 4.156; **parceyuen** ~ Pr 128; **recchen** ~ 3.387; **sen** ~ 19.59; **witen** ~ 20.220; (= *partitive gen.*) 2.7 (2, 3), (*with numbers*) 7.154, 164, 12.160, (some) of 6.269 (2), 296, 8.92, 273, 285, 16.356, 20.47, 22.170 (2), **B** 10.30, 13.52 *etc*; (any) of 13.233, 15.46; (possessed) of, having 2.7 (1), 145, 3.214, 5.56, 6.203, 9.195, 11.268, 16.81, 18.28, 190, 19.149, 20.418, 21.361, **B** 3.238, 10.472, 11.199, 14.125, 300; *in phrr:* (= *descriptive gen.*) **more** further 8.35; ~ **pouer** able 8.283, **as** ~ from among 3.62, 18.99, B 2.58; **conqueror** ~ **Cristene** Christian(s') conqueror 21.14; **deth** ~ **kynde** death in the course of nature 20.219; **drede** ~ **disper(acion)** despairing fear 19.291, 22.164; **lecherye** ~ **clothing** luxurious dress 16.254; **loue** ~ **charite** charitable love

16.283; **shrift** ~ **mouþe** oral confession B 14.88; **tale** ~ **nauht** worthless title 13.113; **tokenynge** ~ **drede** fearful portent 5.121; **vers** ~ **Latyn** Latin verse B Pr 143; **renable** ~ **tonge** eloquent B Pr 158; because / on account of 1.20, 19.294 (1), 20.220; for 3.22, 5.196, 6.16, 319, 369, 420, 7.245, 8.58, 133, 269, 9.255, 269, 11.124, 16.73, 127, 325, 20.92, 21.131, 22.170 (1), 287, **B** 5.125, 325, 10.122, 323, 14.169; through 7.250, 9.55, 11.145, 13.92, 110, 16.23, 17.267, 18.135, 20.21, 189, 299, 21.30, 254, B Pr 118; at the hands of 18.166, **B** 11.282; by 2.226, 9.168, 10.311, 12.196, 16.16, 106, 17.49, 18.170, 224, 21.48, 121, **B** 2.119, 3.275, 9.100, 13.94, 14.9, 15.456; with 4.13, 8.210, 9.178, 10.84, 87, 11.57, 15.44, 16.255, 19.233, **B** 1.18, 5.191, 256, 9.86 (2), 87, 11.211, 13.355; by means of 12.111, 14.30, 20.32(2), 216, **B** 10.342, 11.198; in accordance with 20.431; between 15.174; concerning, about Pr 12, 39, 171, 209, 1.45, 2.15, 3.69, 5.5, 6.117, 10.246, 14.192, 15.104, 16.240, 20.46, 125, 21.80, 241, 22.32, **B** 5.10, 7.85, 9.74, 15.384, 16.55; as for Pr 134; at 6.286, 11.56, 166, 13.172, 15.201, 18.270, 22.242, B Pr 204 *et p.*; (up)on 8.158, 331, 20.432, 434, 22.300, **B** 5.254, 15.82, 262; towards 11.56; in respect of Pr 3, 92, 1.98, 3.157, 4.17, 7.143, 8.219, 10.157, 11.99, 13.192, 231, 14.171, 15.257, 16.159, 21.24, 22.163, **B** 1.195, 7.98, 9.150, 10.384, 12.91, 14.77, Z 1.58; in relation to **B** 10.112, 429, 14.195, 328, 15.362; in 4.173, 12.100, **B** 1.153, 14.283

offecer 4.195 = **officer** *n*

offenden *v* sin against 19.264

office *n* official position B 3.100; (high) ecclesiastical office A 11.195; employment, **putten in** ~ set to work A 7.184; *pl.* duties Z Pr 54; (church) services (*esp.* mass) B 15.385

officer *n* (high) official 4.195; military retainer 22.258

official *n* bishop's officer [*esp.* his representative presiding in the consistory court] 22.137, B 2.174, (*n as a*) Z 2.148

offren *v* present as a gift 21.75, 83, 87, 94; make (as) an offering B 13.198, †A 4.61; *ger.* **offrynge** offering (at mass) 21.4; offering (of money to the Church) 6.300, 17.43

ofgon *v* obtain B 9.107

ofrechen *v* (*p.t.* **ofrauȝte**) reach to B 18.9

ofsenden *v* send for B 3.102, *p.p.* A 2.35

ofte(n) *av* (*comp.* **ofter** 6.274, 20.422, B 11.50) repeatedly, again and again 2.185, 242, 5.94, 6.274, 7.62, 11.52, 13.242, 14.112, 16.332, 18.271, 21.372, **B** 5.97, 10.327, 11.50, 12.10, **A** 10.104, 12.22; often, frequently 2.241, 3.173, 6.123, 9.302, 13.187, 15.76, 16.91, 367, **B** 3.82, 154, 190, 4.70, 156, 169, 5.93, 7.149, 11.52, 231, 13.72, 405, 15.235, 303, 362, A 7.138, 242, Z 7.245; many times 6.425, 9.246, 18.152, 20.141, 21.392, B 4.99, 13.261; time and again 3.90, 133, 200;

in phrr. **fol ~ (ryght ~** Z 3.90, **swiþe ~** B 13.403, **wel ~** 22.25, **A** 5.75, 12.106) very often / many times 2.19, 10.3, 12.239, 14.4, 16.362, 17.300, 20.422, 22.119, **B** 14.326, 16.112, 17.20, Z 7.275; **fele (mony) tyme(s) and ~** many a time and oft 6.118, 12.241, 18.61, 22.26, B 11.370

oftetymes *av* frequently B 15.72

***ofwandrit** *p.p., in phr.* **wery ~** worn out with wandering A Pr 7 (†B Pr 7); **for werynesse ~** worn out with fatigue from wandering †Pr 7

oyle *n* oil 19.71

oke¹ *n* oak(-tree) 5.120, A 5.115 (**noke**) Z 5.45

oke² *p.t. subjv.* 19.160 *see* **aken** *v*

o(e)ld(e) *a* old, aged 6.189, B 9.163; older 20.7; *in phrr*: **~ age** 18.246, **~ elde** B 12.8 old age; **~ and hoor** old and grey(-haired) 6.193, 8.92, 9.175; *a as n* 10.308; long-standing B 6.131; ancient 17.232; *in phr.* **~ the lawe** the Law of the Old Covenant 12.114, 14.58, 17.71, 18.222, 20.381, 387, 21.312, 449, **B** 12.73, 13.186, 18.343; belonging to antiquity 9.214, 20.15, *a as n* 21.274; **þe ~** the early Father 11.148, 290, A 11.72, the old patriarch 19.109; earlier, former 6.188, 21.429, B 12.235, *in phr.* **nyhte ~** last night's 8.331

olofte B Pr 157, 1.90, 5.353 = **alofte** *av*

on¹ *av* (*with phrasal vv*) on, upon 8.180, Z 2.41; near B 7.56; at B 13.295, 302; *in phr.* **taken ~** behave, act 3.84, 13.154

on² *prep.* on Pr 6, 49, 106, 121 *et p.*, ? 5.116 (*or* one), B Pr 14 *et p.*; down on 3.95; upon Pr 123, 1.162, 2.137, 201, 209, 6.267, 11.144, 13.173, 15.148, 18.23, 19.72, 192, 21.203, 288, 22.127, **B** 3.260, 5.131, 11.246, 12.4, 204, A 2.80; over B 17.225; in (*place*) 2.216, 3.419, 12.186, 13.159, 15.269, **B** 9.166, 15.298, 16.255; (*dress, manner*) 5.51, 10.117, 12.208, 17.170, 19.14, 21.356, **B** 5.278, 571, 7.106, 13.74, 15.207, **A** 4.129, 12.13 (2), Z 2.166; (*thing*) **B** 1.70, 5.234; (*person*) **B** 1.149, 4.122, 5.42; (*time*) within 20.41; *in phrr*: **~ þe / a daye** daily 10.31, B 15.283; **~ a hep** in a crowd Pr 51; **~ heiȝ** up above B Pr 128, Z Pr 99, aloud A 12.27; **~ (þis) erthe / folde / grounde / molde** in this world Pr 65, 3.94, 9.153, 10.160, *etc*, **B** 2.187, 3.80, 4.26, 9.83, Z 2.18, 104; in this life 3.100, **B** 5.260, 8.38; **(bi)leuen ~** believe in 1.75, 2.105 *etc*, **B** 10.235, 15.395 *etc*; about 2.20, 236, 6.120, **B** 5.94, 10.39, 42, 200, 11.117, 14.144; at 4.148, 6.148, 7.57, 301, 9.78, 10.262, 12.23, 13.236, 15.148, 16.141, 20.19, 425, 448, **B** Pr 9, 3.345, 7.137, 8.96, 10.61, 310, 11.84, 186, 317, 408, 13.86, 16.22, 128, 18.21, 39, A 8.14, Z 1.100; against 3.250, 4.31, 6.111, 12.137, 20.399, 22.175; to 17.128, 19.313, 22.78, B 5.71, 11.70, 15.83, **don...~** appeal to **B** 1.86, 3.188, **A** 4.60, 12.13 (1); towards 11.163, B 10.136; with 8.10, 13.175, 20.337; by B 9.121; through 10.290; *in phrr.* **~ cros-wyse** by crucifixion 21.142; **~ the hey name** by the divine name 1.70; **lernen ~ boke** educate

B 7.132; by way of 22.135; in regard to B 15.128; for the sake of 19.235; *in conjv. phr.* **~ auenture** lest, in case **B** 3.72, 13.72

one *a* 1.167 *et p.*, *prn* 10.61 *et p. see* **o(e)n, o(o)n** *num., prn*

onelich(e) 16.153, 22.61 = **onli(che)** *av*

ones *av* once, on one occasion (only) 2.237, 3.181, 6.174, 235, 15.132, 21.391, **B** 3.338, 5.601, 15.8; ever, at all Pr 162, 13.9, 14.145, 20.150, 420, B 4.86; at one time (in the past) 8.76, 16.353, 22.344, **B** 10.454, 11.66, 13.139, 16.178; *as n in phr.* **at ~** at one and the same time (together) 11.252, 13.31, 141, 18.154, 263, 19.53, 21.94, 434, **B** Pr 146, 5.161, 376, 509, 15.484, A 12.71

onli(che) *av* only, solely 10.234, 12.29, 81, 16.153, 17.32, 21.117, 22.61, 267

onswerien *v* be answerable 6.346

oo B 2.30 = **o**¹ *num.*

ooen 4.27, **oon** 2.25, 42 = **o(e)n** *num.*, **oon(e)** B 1.23 *et p.*: *see* **oen** *prn*, **o(e)n** *num.*

oones B 15.484 = **ones** *av*

ope 12.232 *see* **vp(p)on** *prep*

opelond *av* out in the country 5.44

open *a* open 20.365

openen *v* open 2.132, 7.248, 20.258, B Pr 106

or¹ *av* first 21.397

or² *prep* before 11.259, 17.61

or³*conj.* (a) or Pr 186 *et p.*; or (else) 8.142, 9.63, 278, 13.106, 21.11, B 3.251; nor 16.123; **or...or** either... or 6.125-6, 9.169, 15.205, 16.58, **B** 6.247, 14.14, ? A 7.211; whether..or B 14.58; *in phr.* **~ ellys** or else 1.49, 3.94, 251, 298, 7.2, 75, 17.16, 19.261, 21.464, **B** 5.149, 10.376, 433, 20.228; or anything else **B** 11.215, 16.143; **~ any...elles** or any other 6.262

or⁴ (**ar**) *conj.* (b) before Pr 164, 1.70, 6.277 (2), 8.345, 17.282 (1), 21.226, 22.228, **~ þat** 21.395

ordeynen *v* build, construct 21.320, 322; set, apply B 10.244; devise B 10.216; decree 5.55, 10.221; foreordain 3.240; establish 17.16, B Pr 119; arrange B 8.99; allot A 12.90

ordre *n* ordination (as priest), holy orders 13.103; order (of knighthood) **B** 1.104, 6.166; manner of life 1.97; (religious) order 8.73, 9.211, 17.16, 22.265, B 13.285, **Austynes ~** the order of Augustinian friars B 15.289, **(þe) foure / fyue ~s** (the) four / five orders (of mendicant friars) Pr 56, 8.191, 9.343; (house of) a religious order 3.54, 67

orgene *n* organ, **by ~** to the organ 20.7n, c

***oriental** *n* oriental, [kind of] sapphire B 2.14

oryson *n* prayer 18.159

oste *n* army 3.251, 418; crowd of armed men 21.338, 22.113

ote *n* oat, *pl.* 4.61, 8.305; **~ cake** oat(en) cake A 7.179

oth *n* oath B 13.383, (in law court) 2.150; curse, swearing 6.384, 7.37, 22.225, A 8.40; **bold ~** profane oath

6.34 (B13.281); **gret** ~ violent profanity Pr 36, 6.360, **B** 2.70, 10.50, 13.400

other (oþer)[1] *prn (pl.* **oþer** 1.108, **othere** 4.133) second, other 11.175, 14.107, 154, B 3.341, **A** 1.24, 8.14, 12.85 (= either of two); each other 19.98; *in phrr*: **ayþer...**~ either...the other 6.149, 16.65, 20.125; **here ayþer** ~ both the others 20.174, each one the other 22.354; **ayther...~es** either...the other's 3.337, 16.179, (each of) the others' B 16.207; **either** ~ one another 6.188, 10.284, B 7.139, A 10.179; **here oen...her** ~ either of them... the other of them 20.67; **here neyther / noen...othere** neither of them...the other 10.275, 14.105; **som** ~ something else / other than 20.216; **vch (on)...**~ each (one)...the other 6.122, 12.106, 107, 131, 14.68, 20.338, 21.397, 419; **vch (man)** ~ each (man) the other B 12.125; (an)other 9.89, 11.63, B 10.469; *in phr.* **day aftur** ~ one day after another 10.114; any other 13.145; **noon** ~ no other 10.116; **noen...**~ none... any other(s) 21.255; others 3.150, 496, 4.133, 6.20, 22, 11.121, 15.127, 16.302, 305, 17.12, 21.234, 267, 22.6, B 5.314, A 12.108, Z 7.266; others' 9.152; the others 18.188, 20.447, 463, 21.251, *in phrr*: **alle** ~ all others 22.262, all other things 22.208; **alle þe** ~ all other creatures B 12.255; suchlike B 7.101; **many** ~, ~ **many** many others 22.335, 378, B 7.123; ~ **mo** others besides 2.113, 4.10, 20.180, 21.54, B 10.176; **this** ~ these others 2.192, 8.93

other (oþer)[2] *a* other Pr 93, 2.58, 91, 3.97, 5.20, 6.42, 138, 8.116, 190, 321, 9.84, 105, 234, 10.168, 12.184, 13.37, 14.32, 136, 15.55, 256, 16.238, 17.34, **B** 5.282, 528, 12.118, 15.244; any other 1.9, 6.265; *a as n* other (days) 7.18, other (people) 16.193; another kind of B 10.191; **al** ~ every other (kind of) B 16.11; **non** ~ of no different kind 6.127

other[3] *av* otherwise 1.117, 5.189; **non** ~ not otherwise, nothing else 6.298, 7.289, 9.173, 290, 13.210, 16.275, 19.251, 20.171, 351, B 1.88, Z Pr 54

other(e), (o(o)þer)[4] *conj.* or Pr 183, 186, 2.48, 81, 3.96, 110, 113, 5.81, 6.42 (1), 74, 220, 9.150, 12.66, 14.123, 17.312, 20.10, 424, **B** 5.53, †6.219, 9.106, 10.265, 12.223, 13.230, 15.431, 16.133, 17.217, **A** 4.116, 10.65, 75, 108; ~**...or** either...or 13.47, 15.300, B 13.230, A 7.232; *in phrr.* ~ **elles** or otherwise 1.172, A 11.260, or of some other kind 3.291; **more** ~ **lasse, lasse** ~ **more** more or less, less or more 2.48, 3.289, 9.108

oþergatus *av* in a different way 10.298

oþerwhile(s) *av* sometimes 7.19, 193, 10.29, 16.365; occasionally 16.291, 17.9; at times 21.302, B 12.23; at one time or another 5.50; at various times 18.42, B 5.404; from time to time 10.163, 17.3, A 7.239; at other times 6.160, 21.103; at another time 16.322

oþer(e)wyse *av* in a / some other / different way than 5.81, 12.230, 19.142, (*emphatic*) ~ **ne elles** otherwise 10.106; contrarily / in opposition to what 3.427, 7.211

ouet 11.126 = **oute** *av*

ouht (ouȝt) 7.35, 45, B 11.49, 13.300 = **auht** *prn,* A 8.61 = **auht** *av*

oughtest 1.72, **ouhte(n)** 2.30, 3.72, 108, 5.69, 6.86, 7.98, 9.229, 12.91, 19.318, 22.276 *see* **owen** *v*

oune *a* Pr 124, 10.177, 12.99, 16.134, 17.81, 18.14, 166, 19.300, **Z** 6.38, 7.65 = **owen(e)** *a*

oure *n* hour B14.12; Divine Office of the canonical hours Pr 125, 1.178, B 15.385

oure Z 7.116 = **ȝoure** *prn*

oure *poss. prn* our Pr 34 *et p.*, [*with ref. to humanity in general*] 1.163, 3.401, 8.239, 18.67 *etc*, [*with ref. to Christians*] 3.358 *etc*, *in phrr:* [*with Christian ref.*] ~ **Lady** 3.99 *etc*, ~ **Driȝte** B 13.269, ~ **Lord** Pr 28 *et p.*, B 5.563, A 1.110, Z 6.46 *etc*, *in oaths* Pr 103, Z 3.123; ~ **Lordes loue** for love of our Lord 16.151, 17.26, B 11.172, ~ **prince Iesu** 13.3, B 16.37, ~ **Sauiour** 7.120, B 9.127*etc*; *in phrr:* (= of us) ~ **aller** of all of us B 16.205, ~ **Iewene** of us Jews 20.40; **bothe** ~ of both of us 6.181

ouresulue (~seluen, ~ sylue) *emphatic pers. prn* ourselves 19.41, A 11.248, Z 3.171; *in phr.* **bi** ~ by ourselves 15.42

ourf *n* cattle Z 7.64

out(e)[1] *av* out 6.222, 20.420; away, absent 22.347; (*with various phrasal vv.*) Pr 37, 1.109, 2.241, *etc*, **B** 1.121, 4.186, *etc*; + **of** *in in phr.* **out of** out (of) 2.65, 4.163, 5.151, 6.183, 184, 10.211, 11.208, 12.76, 211, 13.176, 228, 14.112, 15.249, 16.241, 17.247, 18.217, 20.64, 21.74, 285, **A** 2.20, 10.124, 126, 127; out / away from 2.247, 5.151, 8.206, 10.42; from 18.283, from the direction (of) 20.116, 166; from out of 21.381, Z 3.148; down from 22.80

out(e) of *cpd. prep., in phrr.* ~ **aray** in disorderly manner 5.157; ~ **dette** free of debt 16.4; ~ **my menynges** beyond my comprehension 1.137; ~ **lawe** beyond / outside of the law B 10.25; ~ **lele byleue** cut off from the true faith 17.158; ~ **mesure** to excess, immoderately 13.188; ~ **nombre** in excessive quantity 13.6; too numerous 22.269; ~ **resoun** immoderately 2.89, 6.434, 13.154, B 1.25; ~ **reule** outside of the rule 3.202; ~ **tyme** except at the proper time 1.24, 10.291

oute(n)[2] *a* alive, in the world 14.190, B 12.144

ouþer *pl.* **B** 4.136 = **other**[1] *prn; conj.* either **B** 5.53, 9.106, 10.265, 12.223, 13.230, 15.431, 16.133

ouþerwhile B 12.23 = **oþerwhile(s)** *av*

outlawe *n* outlaw, robber (*as name*) B 17.103

#outrydere *n* 'rider out' [agent riding out to administer affairs of a monastery] 4.116

outtaken *v* exempt, *p.p. as prep.* with the exception of A 10.175

outward *av* outwards 9.85

outwit *n* external sense(s) B 13.289

ouer[1] *av* across, **passen** ~ leave (subject) B 13.133; too, excessively 8.271, 15.49, 22.27, B 11.240; *and see* **ouer-**

ouer[2] *prep.* over 7.158, 287, 22.183, 187, A 5.178; Z 3.146; across 13.45, B 5.476, A 11.203; in charge of 7.270, 8.251; (victorious) over 4.155; more than, above 19.39, Z 1.22; above (= in authority over) 3.256, 11.96, 16.124, 17.170, 242, 20.426, 21.139, 223, 446, 22.73, 321, **B** 1.108, 15.90, (= ruling over) 5.193, 6.138, 22.64, **B** 3.298, 14.328, **A** 10.72, 11.198, (= in control of) A 10.63; *in phrr*: ~ **eue(n)** overnight 3.307, 7.195; ~ **see** overseas, abroad 4.126, 6.278

oueral *av* in every place 2.228, B 9.55; especially B 13.291

ouercam *p.t.* 20.112, B 15.440 *see* **ouercomen** *v*

#**ouerclosen** *v* blot out 20.138

ouercomen *v* (*p.t.* ~**cam** 20.112, ~ **kam** 21.161, ~**come** 15.13, *p.p.* ~**come** 3.430, 17.289) surpass 11.285; overcome 3.430; dominate 15.13, Z 5.94; win over 4.78; vanquish, conquer 17.203, 289, 20.112, 21.161; be victorious over 22.122

ouer-delycaty *av* too choicely 6.166, B 5.375

ouerdoen *v* do (sth.) / act to excess 13.190

ouergilden *v* overlay with gold, *p.p.* **ouergilte** B 15.124 gilded

ouer-hardy *a* too presumptuous 3.298

ouerhippen (~**huppen** B) *v* skip over (parts of text) 17.118, **B** 13.68, 15.385

ouerhouen *v* hover over 20.173, B 3.208

ouerkarken *v* overburden 3.468

ouer-land *av* across the country, *as a in phr.* ~ **strikares** 9.159

ouerleyen *v* cover over, *p.p.* 12.233

ouerlepen *v* (*p.t.* ~ **le(e)p** Pr 169, 20.357) overtake, pounce upon Pr 169, B Pr 200; digress 20.357

#**ouerlong(e)** *a* too long 22.363, B 11.221; too protracted 16.363

ouerlonge *av* (for) too long (a time) 22.361

ouermaistren *v* gain mastery over B 4.176

ouer-moche *n* too much 8.271

#**ouer-more** *av* in addition 9.157

****ouer-plente(e)** *n* over-abundance, excess 12.236, B 14.73

ouer-rechen *v* reach over, encroach 6.270

ouersen *v* (*p.t.* ~ **sey(e)** *p.p.* ~ **seyen**) peruse 11.115, B 10.327; oversee 8.120, B 6.113; forget (oneself) (= over-eat) B 5.372

ouerskippen *v* leave out 13.118

****ouerskippere** *n* priest who leaves out parts (of the Offices) 13.122

****ouer-soppen** *v* eat to excess 6.428

ouerspreden *v, p.t.* ~**spradde** cover, envelope 21.207

ouertaken *v* catch up with B 17.83; catch B 12.241

ouerthrowen *v* demolish 18.160; overturn B 8.36

#**ouertulden** *v* (*p.t.* ~ **tulde** / ~**tilte**) upturn, overturn 22.54, 135

ouerturnen *v* throw down B 16.131, *ger.* destruction 18.163; come to ruin 17.209; overturn 18.157

ouerward *av* about to cross over 4.128

oure Z 1.22 = **ouer** *prep.*

owen(e)[1] *a* own Pr 124, 8.207, 10.177, 12.99, 14.175, 16.134, 17.81, 195, 18.14, 166, 19.254, 289, 300, **B** 5.214, 10.365, 409, 16.192, 18.76, A 10.75, Z 6.38; *a as n* 3.209 [land], 7.221, 8.92, 22.20, 92 [property]; **ownere** *gen. pl., in phr.* **here** ~ **wil** their own (individual) wills 18.76; *in phr.* **ben thyn** ~ are your servants 3.28

owen[2] *v* (*p.t.* **o(u)(g)ht(e)(n)** *with pres. sense* 1.72, 3.72, *etc*) own 3.72; owe 21.395; (*modal*) ought (to), should 1.72, 2.30, 5.69, 6.86, 7.98, 22.276; be obliged to 3.108, 9.229, 19.318, A 7.123; have a duty (to) 12.91

oxe *n* ox B 15.466; (*pl.*) ~**n** oxen 21.263, 269

paast *n* pastry B 13.251; dough B 14.29

pacience *n* (the moral virtue of) patience [calm endurance of suffering and adversity] 2.201, 12.197, 13.2, 14.16, 15.161, 181, 183, 276, 16.56, 149, 152, 17.236, 242, 306, 19.91, 20.170, 174, 461, 21.250, 296, A 11.230, (*person.*) (a) 7.273, (b) 15.33 *et p.*, 283, 16.114 *et p.*, 161, **B** 13.29 *et p.*, 14.29 *et p.*, (c) (*tree*) B 16.8; *in phr.* **pouerte and (...)** ~, ~ **and (...) pouerte** 12.144, 13.20, 15.281, 16.59, 61, 152, 21.250, **B** 10.340, 11.317–18, 12.61, 14.192–3; forbearance B 14.10, 99

pacient *a* patient [able to endure suffering *etc* calmly] 12.132, 16.111; *a as n, in phr.* **pore (and)** ~ 9.178, 13.30, 98, 15.280, 287, 16.99; *in phr.* ~ **pouerte** (condition of) poverty that calmly endures 12.178, B 14.101; forbearing, self-restrained B 15.201

paciently(che) *av* with steadfast endurance 11.263, 12.150, 202, 16.326, 19.105; with forbearance / self-restraint 17.284; humbly 6.14

pay *n* satisfaction, *in phr.* **to** ~**e** satisfactorily 7.189, 192, 13.160, 16.93, 21.187; reward 9.278; pay, wages (*or* favour) 3.299, 348

payement *n* payment 22.365

payen *v* please 8.332, **A** 7.100, 10.130, Z 7.279; content A 10.117; make payment (of) 6.251; pay (money) 3.66, 389, 4.68, 9.45, B 13.377; pay (wages / fees 3.299, 305, 349, 7.41, 8.115, 9.45, B 7.43; pay (for purchase) 16.323, 21.417, B 13.381; pay (tithe) 8.102; pay (ransom for) 3.173, 7.276; recompense 12.108, B 15.155; return 16.129; repay 4.55, 6.277, 16.313; atone 16.31; make satisfaction for 19.203, 298, 21.195, 196; fulfil (conditions of) 21.189, 392, 22.309

payere *n* payer of wages 3.305, (*fig.*) 7.194

#**payn(e)** *n*[1] bread 8.285, 9.92, 15.202, 218, 232, 235, 16.149, **B** 6.150, 7.122, 9.81, 14.76, 15.315; *in phr.* ~ **defaute** lack of bread 15.231

payne (peyne) *n*[2] punishment 15.256; torture 7.276, Z 3.123; suffering 1.198, 10.155, B 1.169; agony [of Christ] 7.20, 21.328; punishment / suffering [in hell or purgatory] 1.128, 7.117, 255, 11.223, 262, 20.146, 197, 204, 207, 416, **B** 2.106, 11.162, **bittere** ~(s) 12.44, 15.50, **B** 11.152, **incurable** ~s 15.16, ~ **of helle** 2.108, 3.101, ~ **of purgatorie** 11.33; (physical) pain 19.156; physical discomfort 6.129; source of woe **B** 12.247

paynen (peynen) *v* torture (= crucify) 1.166; suffer (crucifixion) 21.324; encumber **B** 12.246; strive **Z** 7.98, (*refl.*) exert (oneself) 21.437, 440, (*with prn om.*) **Z** 7.98; endeavour **B** 7.42

payny(e)m *n* pagan **B** 11.162; Saracen, Moslem 7.160, 17.255

paynten (peynten) *v* paint 3.66, 70, 19.137; inscribe 13.118; stain 21.11; (*fig.*) pick out in colour 16.321; *p.p.* smeared 21.6; colourful, decorated (*fig.*) 4.23; brightly coloured 14.179; specious 22.115

payre *n* pair (of) 6.251, **B** 12.19; (sexual) pair 10.234; couple **B** 13.197; (married) couple 10.274

pays 18.177, **Z** 4.52 = **pe(e)s** *n*

pak *n* load 16.54; bag, pack 15.181

pakken *v* pack, bundle 16.330

palays (paleis) *n*¹ palace 2.23, ~ (*pl.*) 10.16

palays (paleys) *n*² (= **palis**) palisade **B** 10.462; enclosed garden 20.378; enclosed courtyard **B** 13.29

pale *a* pallid 20.58; pale [grey] **B** 5.77

pal(e)sy(e) *n* (attack of) palsy, paralysis 22.176, **B** 5.77

palfray *n* palfrey [light riding-horse] 4.115, 5.159, 21.418, **B** 2.190, 13.244, **in** ~**es wise** like riding-horses **B** 2.171

#**pallen** *v* strike 18.34, 50, **B** 16.51

palmer(e) *n* pilgrim [*esp.* to Holy Land] Pr 47, 7.179, 8.63, 15.34, 132, **B** 5.105, **Z** 5.158

#**palpable** *a* tangible, evident 18.234

paltok *n* jacket 22.219, **B** 18.25

panele *n* jury(-list) 3.469

pan(e)s *pl.* 2.232, 3.32, 117, 199, 6.242, 9.91, 12.166, 248, 18.165, 19.76, 21.379, **A** 4.50, **Z** 3.33 *see* **peny** *n*, **mas** ~ 3.278

paniar *n* basket 17.17

paniter *n* dispenser of bread (*fig.*) 16.149

panne *n* skull 4.74

#**papelote** *n* mess of porridge 9.75

paper *n* written document(s), account(s) 13.37

paradys *n* paradise [the Garden of Eden] 13.226, 20.378; the earthly paradise (? Eden) **B** 10.12; heaven 9.12, 11.299, 16.223, 21.61, **B** 10.464, **A** 8.12, 11.286; *in phr.* **Prince of** ~ (= God) **A** 7.109

parail 10.117 *etc*, ~**en** Pr 25 *etc* (*aphetic forms of* **aparayle** *n*, **-en** *v*, *qq.v.*)

paramour *n* lover, beloved 16.105; ~**s** *n* sexual love 6.186

parau(e)nture *av* perhaps, perchance, maybe 3.466, 7.296, 8.43, 9.180, 11.172, 12.246, 14.123, 16.49, 22.234, **B** 11.421, **A** 12.8

parceyuen B Pr 100 *etc* = **pars(c)eyuen** *v*

parcel 13.37, 22.292, **B** 17.27 = **parsel** *n*

parchemyn *n* sheet of parchment **B** 9.38, 14.192; document (written on parchment) **B** 14.194

pardo(u)n *n* forgiveness (from God) **B** 10.122; pardon [remission of (*esp.*) temporal punishment for sins already] forgiven 2.232, 8.63, 9.8, 11, 43, 53, 60, 288, 300, 318, 323, 324, 328, 337, 345, 12.9, 21.184, 188, 189, 22.309, **B** 7.16, 102, 13.253, **A** 8.18, **Z** 8.89; formal document of pardon 9.279, 280, 282, 292, **B** 13.253; *in phrr.* ~ **a pena et a culpa** absolute pardon, pardon from both punishment and guilt 9.3, 186; ~ **of Pampilon** 19.219c; ?release **B** 15.183c

pardoner *n* pardoner [purveyor of pardons / indulgences] Pr 66, 79, 2.229, 17.61, **B** 5.639, **Peres þe** ~ 2.110

paren *v* clip (coins) 6.242

*****parentrelynarie** *av* between the lines 13.118

parfay *interj.* by my faith, certainly 16.117

parfit *a* perfect 3.453, 11.300; complete, whole **B** 15.583; (spiritually) ideal / perfect 12.164, 13.99, 17.51, 20.151, **B** 11.274; (*comp.* **B** 12.24, *sup.* 13.98); thoroughly good / virtuous 5.84, 8.136, 17.299, 18.103, **B** 11.318, 13.215, **A** 1.120; true, ideal *in phrr.* ~ **byleue** 11.300, 17.266, **B** 14.193; ~ **charitee B** 15.148; ~ **Cristene** 22.108; ~ **lyuynge** thoroughly virtuous way of life **B** 15.417; perfection of (worldly) existence 11.176, 194, 13.231; ~ **loue** 15.219; ~ **pacience** 15.276; ~ **pouerte B** 11.271; ~ **preesthoed** truly virtuous clergy 16.243, 17.233, 250; ~ **treuthe** 3.453, **B** 14.99; perfectly skilled **B** 16.107; ~ **ly(che)** *av* flawlessly 17.75; completely 16.338, 21.195; thoroughly 7.10, 15.181; fully 17.255; in (its) entirety **B** 16.220; virtuously 9.43; properly 19.137; ~ **nesse** *n* perfect goodness 18.41; a perfectly virtuous way of life 5.90, 15.185; spiritual perfection **B** 10.202, 15.208; holiness **B** 16.135

parformen (parfournen) *v* finish (task) 3.349; carry out, perform 6.283, 7.14, 17, 246, 15.88, **B** 15.490; fulfil 13.92, 16.126, **B** 15.325, 327; bring about 15.174

par(is)sch(e) (*pl.* **parissh A** Pr 81) *n* parish [ecclesiastical and administrative division of England] Pr 80, 82, 22.263, 280; people of a parish 15.212; ~ **chirche** principal church of a parish **B** 11.65; ~ **prest** priest in charge of a parish Pr 79, *in phr.* **persone(s) and** ~ ~(s) Pr 81, 14.123, 22.281, 320, **B** 10.267

par(is)sch(i)en *n* parishioner 6.120, 22.283, **B** Pr 89, 5.420

parlement *n* the king's council [sitting as court of law] 4.45; ? the parliament of England 4.185

#**parlen** *v* speak, talk 20.279

parlour *n* separate chamber [off main hall] **B** 10.99

#**parroken** *v* enclose, *p.p.* 6.144, 17.13

pars(c)eyuen *v* perceive, (take) notice (of) Pr 128, 20.251, **B** 5.142, 13.355, 16.23, 103; sense, understand **B** 13.86, 17.151; hear 21.163; apprehend 19.68; discern **B** 15.199

parsch(e) Pr 79 *etc* = **par(is)sch(e)** *n*

parsel *n* portion 22.292; section 13.118; small amount 11.48; *in phrr.* **a~ / in ~es** separately 19.98, B 17.27; **~ of paper** itemised list (= ? account roll) 13.37

parselmele *av* in small portions (= by retail sale) 3.86; bit by bit B 15.246; separately 19.30

parsilie *n* parsley 8.309

parsonage Z Pr 58 = **personage** *n*

part *n* share 3.245, **~ of / in pardon** 9.174, A 8.8

part(e)y(ȝ)(e) *n* part, *in phr.* **most ~** majority 1.7, 3.382; member 16.166*n* (*or* **a ~** = in part, partly); side 3.379, 15.175; party / person involved [in lawsuit] 1.95, 3.389, 19.286, 288, [betrothal] B 14.269

parten *v* cause a division between 5.184; share Pr 79, 8.285, *ger. in phr.* **~ felawe** partner B 13.207; **~ with** share with 16.256, share in 8.144, endure along with 6.299, **~ with / (a parsel)** grant a part (to) 11.48, 65, 15.117; depart, *ger. in phr.* **(~ hennes)** departure from this life, (= death) 9.53, 16.159, 21.61, (A 11.313); give, distribute 1.177, A 3.57

Pasche (Paske, Pasque) *n* (the feast of) Passover 18.167; **~ woke** Easter week 12.124

paschen *v* dash, strike violently 22.100

pase *n* road, passageway 16.137

Paske *n* 12.124 = **Pasche** *n*

passen *v* travel 16.139, B 15.570; go 22.339; leave 8.93, 9.132, 10.11, 15.154, 185, B 13.179; pass (through) 9.11, 325, 11.300, 13.30, 16.138; go past 2.201; pass by 22.199; *in phr.* **leten ~** allow to get out Pr 173, 3.173; (*of time*) pass, *p.p.* 20.136, (= ago) Pr 203, 16.369, 22.344; leave (this life,) die, *in phrr.* **~ forth** 11.263, **~ hennes** A 8.18; vanish 15.154, B 13.20; persist, *in phr.* **~ ouer til** hold on until B 13.133; ignore B 5.416; surpass 15.117, 21.267, A 12.4; exceed 9.319, 323; *pr. p. as prep.* more than 7.30, 22.218; go beyond / against 1.98, 17.5; sojourn 1.7

passio(u)n *n* penitential suffering 11.262, 17.266; grievous hardship B 15.270; passion [suffering and death] of Christ 7.20, 11.33, 17.192, 18.41, 21.63, 328, **B** 15.255, 17.96, 18.9, [of saint or martyr] 7.78; narrative of passion [of Christ] A 12.26, [of martyr] 15.100

pastour *n* shepherd 11.297, 14.92; herdsman A 11.310; shepherd of souls, pastor B 15.495

patente *n* document of proclamation [of a statute issued by a sovereign](= **lettre patent**) (*fig.*) 19.12, of grant [of a privilege] (*fig.*) 20.190, [of a release] (*fig.*) B 14.192, [of a pardon / indulgence] B 7.195

Paternoster *n* Our Father [the Lord's Prayer] 5.46, 87, 107, 6.283, 7.10, 11.299, 15.250, 16.321, 21.397, **B** 10.468, 13.237, 14.197, **~ while** time taken to say an 'Our Father' 6.398

path *n* path, **~ of pees** unmolested passage 16.137

patriarch (patriark) *n* Old Testament patriarch 13.20, 14.60, 17.51, 20.151, *in phr:* **~s and prophetes** 7.87,

9.12, 10.207, 11.150, 14.81, 18.208, 273, 20.141, 146, 279, 366, 21.16, **B** 10.338, 16.251; patriarch of the Christian church [bishop ranking after Pope] B 13.167

patrimonye *n* endowment(s) 22.234, *in phr.* **Cristes ~** = the wealth of the Church B 15.246

patron *n* mentor B 12.226; patron [layman or cleric with right of patronage over benefice] 5.78

Paulines *n* ? the order of Paulines (the Crutched Friars), ? jurors at the consistory court held at St Paul's B 2.178c; **~ doctour** A 2.73; **~ doctrine** B 2.109; **~ peple** A 2.139; **~ queste** 2.110c

paume *n* palm (of the hand) 19.117, 118, 121, 124, 126, 128, 130, 141, 143, 156, 164, 166, B 17.151, 183

paunche *n* stomach 15.97

paueloun *n* large tent, pavilion A 2.41; lawyer's cape 3.448

#peccunie *n* money 3.389

pece *n* piece 20.61, (*fig.*) 15.250; slab 8.332, 19.12; drinking vessel B 3.89

pecok 14.179, 183, B 12.228, 239, 240 262 = **pocok**; *see* **po** *n*

pedlere *n* pedlar B 5.254

peel B 17.304 = **ap(p)e(e)l** *n*

peeren *v*[1] B Pr 173 = **ap(p)eren** *v*

pe(e)ren *v*[2] be the equal of B 15.417, A 12.4

pe(e)s *n* peace / concord between people 14.16, 15.219, 230, 17.93, 199, 226, 20.236, 458 (*person.*) 4.45 *et p.*; amity, peaceableness (*person.*) 22.299 *et p.*; *in phr.* **maken ~** (for sb.) obtain pardon 13.75, ? *or* settle out of court B 4.64, 75; reconciliation [between God and man] 17.248; (*person.*) = daughter of God 20.170 *et p.*; the peace of heaven [*meton. for* God's presence] 15.140; *in phrr.* **Cristes ~** 17.228; = the Christian virtue of peace 1.147, (*person.*) 7.273; freedom from molestation / disturbance 13.2, 16.137, 139, 18.177; state of peace 21.360; peaceful relations (between nations *etc*) 5.195, 13.140, 15.174, 17.86, 236, B 13.176, 209, 15.426; peace within the country, civil order B 3.221, (*person.*) = the King's peace 4.45 *et p.*; silence, quiet 21.154

pehen B 12.239 = **pohen**; *see* **po** *n*

peyne 2.108 *etc* = **payne** *n*

peynd *p.t.* Z 7.98, **peyned** *p.t.* 21.324, **peyneth** *pr.* 21.440 *see* **paynen** *v*

peynten 3.66, 16.321, 19.137, **peynted** *p.p.* 4.23 *etc see* **paynten** *v*

peire B 12.19, 13.197 = **payre** *n*

peyse *n* weight; **~ of led** = lead seal B 13.247; balance, scales 6.242

peysen *v*[1] weigh 6.223

peysen *v*[2] appease, satisfy Z 7.302

#peytrelen *v* put *peytrel* [ornamental harness] upon 4.23

pelet *n* gunstone, cannon-ball B 5.77

pelour[1] *n* accuser (in law-court) 20.39, (*fig.*) Z 1.65

pelour[2] 21.418 = **pilour** *n*

pelure *n* fur (trimming) 2.10, 3.448; fur-trimmed gown 4.115, 21.418, B 15.7

pena(u)nce *n* (sacramental) penance 6.328, 7.240; act(s) of penitential satisfaction 5.171, 195, 6.283, 7.14, 71, 246, 13.81, 21.379, 22.307; punishment 16.76, B 10.34, A 9.95; (penitential) punishment 3.101, 6.14, 304; (purgatorial) punishment 9.185, 325, 11.262, B 10.122, A 11.313; (act(s) of) penitential self-mortification Pr 27, 3.399, 5.84, 7.78, 8.93, 9.174, 234, 328, 15.84, 94, 107, 112, 16.38, 19.218, 21.67; suffering 6.110, 15.71, 73; 17.266, 18.41, 19.321, B 17.96, 18.9; hardship 16.326, B 11.279, 12.9, 13.66; affliction 12.150, 195, A 11.230; pain 15.97

*****pena(u)nceles** *a* without suffering purgatorial penance 11.300

penaunt *n* penitent, person doing penance 4.130, 15.102

pencyf *a* thoughtful, pensive 9.299

pencyoun *n* payment A 8.47, Z 7.272

#pendaunt *n* pendant [ornamened hanging end of girdle] B 15.7

peneworth *n* (small) quantity (of goods worth a penny) 3.313, 6.383; ~ **gode** penny's worth of goods Z 7.273

peny *n* (*pl.* **pan(e)s** 2.232, 3.32 *etc*, **penyes** Pr 161, **pens** B 12.247) (English silver) penny Pr 161, 6.242, 9.91, 16.297, B 12.247, 13.381; = Biblical denarius 1.45, 19.76, argentarius 18.165; money, cash 2.231, 3.32, 117, 199, 8.303, 12.122, 166, 248, 16.313, B 4.64, 75; *in phrr.* ~ **ale** light ale costing a penny a gallon 6.226, 8.332, 9.92, B 15.315; ~ **delyng** alms-giving 21.379; **mas ~s money** offered at mass by the faithful 3.278

penyles *a* destitute 12.26

penne *n* feather 14.179, B 12.246; pen B 9.39; (*meton. for*) lettering 19.16

pensel *n* pennon, banner 18.188

pen(y)tauncer *n* penitentiary [priest with authority from pope / bishop to administer penance *esp.* in reserved cases] 6.256, 22.320

pe(o)ple *n* people, persons 1.5, 7, 2.198, 3.382, 7.273, 8.190, 348, 9.43, 118, 219, 325, 10.300, 11.6, 15.196, 16.125, 17.61, 20.82, 22.86, B 12.67, 14.183, 195, 15.590, 16.251, 17.36, = the public, people at large Pr 57, 145, 2.224, 9.300, 10.29, 11.19, 16.235, 21.458, B 3.82, 8.111, 10.214, 11.158, 174, 13.251; mankind 3.453, 9.20, 18.86; = people of a region 6.30, 36, 60, 9.114, 15.232, 16.242, 251, 17.84, 17.174, 177, 180, B 5.23, 6.163; people (in a place) B 4.159, A 2.38; = *spec.* the Christian community Pr 77, 3.277, 5.141, 10.89, 15.76, 214, 17.250, 284, 21.431, 22.109, 125, 281, B 5.104, 145, 10.202, 13.237, 17.337, A Pr 93, Z 7.232; chosen people [in *OT*] B 12.72; = (some specific) group of people 1.45, 166, 12.49, B 15.325, 327, A 2.139; *in phr.* **moche** ~ large number of people, crowd 8.348, 17.299, 20.35, 22.98; many (other) characters A 12.102; the common people, the labour-

ing classes 3.86, B 7.10; *in collocations*: **comune ~** ordinary folk 2.58, 21.7, 132, 423; **poore comune ~** 11.297; **Cristene ~** 5.193, 11.270, 13.77, 21.343, 364, B 12.158, 15.90; **Cristes ~** B 14.72, 15.22; **fals ~** 3.91; **Godis ~** A 11.198; **inparfit ~** 3.385; **land-tylyng ~** 11.298; **lewed ~** (uneducated) lay people 1.193, 17.121, B 12.110, 15.72, A 11.182; **mene ~** people of modest means 3.81; **nedy ~** B 11.242; **poore ~** Pr 80, 3.83, 8.205, 316, 9.34, 12.101, 122, 166, 15.10, 17.70, B 11.183, 14.174, 15.203, A 8.48; **rihtfole ~** 17.34; **witty ~** 17.94

pepur *n* pepper-corn 6.358; **han ~ in the nose (to)** treat superciliously B 15.203

percile B 6.285 = **parsilie** *n*

pere *n*[1] match 9.306; equal in rank [social] 3.261, 9.20, 10.141, A 11.197, [spiritual] 18.90, B 16.71

pere *n*[2] pear (*with pun on* **pere**[1]) B 16.71, **~ionette** an early-ripening pear 12.223

perel *n* peril, danger 16.138, 19.68, 20.298; perilous situation B 16.107; tribulation 15.280, 20.461; spiritual danger, risk 11.194, 17.232, 260, A 8.16 *in assev.* **be / for ~ of...soule** at the risk of (one's) soul 4.137, 7.200, 228, 8.102, B 6.117, 171

#peren *v* be the equal of B 15.417, A 12.4

perfite A 1.120 = **parfit** *a*

perye (perrei3e) *n* precious stones 11.10, A 2.12

perilous *a* terrible B 6.44

perilously *av* dangerously Pr 170

#perimansie *n* pyromancy [divination by fire] A 11.161

perle *n* pearl, *in cpd.* **margerie ~s** 11.7

#permutacioun *n* exchange of one thing for another [of proportionally equivalent value] 3.313

#permuten *v* exchange (benefice / church) 2.185; ~ **with** exchange...for B 13.111

perpetuel *a* everlasting, (**peyne**) 7.117, 20.204, (**pardon**) 9.60, (**helle**) 9.278, (**blisse**) 11.263, (**pees**) 15.140, (**ioye**) 16.56; unceasing 5.195, 17.248; lasting 17.93; ? = eternal 18.27

perpetuelly *av* for ever 9.8

persaunt *a* 1.152 *see* **persen** *v*

persecucioun *n*, ~ **of body** physical torture 12.207

persen *v* pierce, *p.p.* B 17.190, *pr.p. a* piercing, sharp 1.152; (*fig.*) = get through to 11.299

perseuen 19.68 = **pars(c)eyuen** *v*

#personage *n* benefice B 13.246, Z Pr 58

persone *n*[1] person, individual 16.108, 110, 21.27, 196, 19.105, **mene ~** person acting as intermediary B 9.114; (bodily) person 15.196; self 3.224; divine person [of the Trinity] 18.27, 188, 215, 236, 19.30, 37, 44, B 10.239, 16.185, 188; human persons [conceived analogously to the persons of the Trinity] 18.234, B 16.207; form 20.378

perso(u)n(e) *n*[2] parson [priest entitled to parish tithes] 2.185, 5.165, 6.144, 16.250, 22.360, B 5.141, 142; *in phrr:* **~(s)** B 10.468, **and / or (parissh) prestes(s)**

Pr 81, 3.186, 14.123, 16.250, 22.281, 320, **B** 10.267, 11.98, 15.485; **prestes and ~(s)** 3.463, 7.30, B 3.252

pertliche 5.117, B 5.23 = **apertly(che)** *av*

pes(e) *n* (*pl.* **peses** 8.306, B 6.186, **pesen** B 6.195, 297) pea 8.306 *etc; in phrr:* **setten (counten) at a ~** care nothing for 8.166 (A 7.154), 9.345; **~ cod** pea-pod 8.316, 12.223; **~ loof** loaf of pea-flour 8.176

pestelence *n* plague (*esp.* bubonic) 5.115, 8.348, 10.274, 11.60, 15.219, 22.98, **B** 5.36, 12.11, 13.249, *in phr.* **~ tyme** time of the (Great) Plague Pr 82, B 10.72

pethe *n* strength, essential part 19.118

#pety(t) *a* small, little 9.53, 16.83

pharisee *n* Pharisee B 15.604

philosofer, philosopher *n* learned man, scholar 17.115; natural philosopher 21.245, B 15.357; philosopher (of antiquity) 13.27, 22.38

philosophie *n* learning, scholarly knowledge 17.115; philosophy 22.296

Phippe B 11.42 *see* **Fyppe**

phisik B 15.383 = **fysyk(e)** *n*

pyc(c)hen *v* (*p.p.* **py3t** A 2.41) thrust, **~ ato** thrust apart 8.64; erect A 2.41; pitch (hay) 5.13

pye *n*[1] magpie 13.158, B 12.226, 252

pye *n*[2] pie Pr 227, **~ hele** pie-crust (= thing of little value 9.345

piece B 3.89 = **pece** *n*

pyement *n* sweetened, spiced wine 20.409

py3t *p.p.* A 2.41 *see* **pyc(c)hen** *v*

pyk *n* pointed tip, spike 10.95, B 8.97; (= **~ staf**) 7.179, B 5.475, Z 7.90; **~ staf** spiked (pilgrim's) staff 6.328, B 6.103

pykare *n* (corn)-stealer 5.17

pikede *a* with long pointed toe 22.219

#pikeharneys *n* despoiler of armour [of men slain in battle] 22.263

pyken (aweye, vp) *v* dig up 8.118, B 16.17

pikepors *n* stealer of / from purses 6.369

pikois *n* pick-axe 3.461

pil *n* prop B 16.23, 24, 26, 30, 36, 86

pile *n* fort, stronghold 21.366

pilede *p.p.* 6.369 *see* **pil(i)en** *v*

piler *n* pillar 7.240

*pilewhey *n* ? drained whey, ? spring water A 5.134

pilgrym *n* pilgrim [traveller to holy place] Pr 47, 7.199, 9.180, 12.132 (1), 15.187, **B** 5.105, 13.179, 216, (*fig.*) 8.112, 12.132 (2), 22.381; wayfarer 12.126, 133, **B** 11.241, 13.183, 188; *in phr.* **in ~es clothes / wyse** 7.160, B 13.29, (*fig.*) 8.56

pilgrimage *n* pilgrimage [journey to a holy place] 9.234, 323, 16.38, 21.378, (*fig.*) 8.63, 93, 16.322

pil(i)en *v* rob [by heavy taxation] 21.445; peel 9.81; remove hair from, *p.p.* (*as term of abuse*) hairless, bald 6.369, A 7.142

pylorye *n* pillory 2.216, 3.79

pilour *n* despoiler [of the slain in battle] 22.263; robber 13.2; thief B 3.195; extortioner 21.418

pyn *n* wooden peg 8.199

pynchen *v* encroach 6.267 (B 13.371)

pyne *n* punishment, *in phr.* **wyuene ~** punishment for wayward wives or scolds 5.131*n*; torture A 1.143; punishment in hell **B** 2.104, 10.387, 11.142, A 2.70, **wykkede ~** punishment of the / meted out to the wicked in hell 11.275

pynen *v* torture, crucify A 1.145, (*with pun on* **pynnen**) B 5.209 (A 5.127); endure pain B 19.325; **pynyng** *ger.* punishment, **~ stol** seat of punishment, cucking stool 3.79

pynnen *v* fasten tightly 6.219, 22.299

pyonie *n* peony-seed 6.358

pipen *v* play on a pipe 15.208; blow a horn 22.93; sing out in a shrill voice 20.452

pirie *n* pear-tree 5.118

#pissare *n* pisser, (*cant for*) soldier, ruffian 22.219*n*

pissen *v* piss, urinate 6.67, 398, 8.151

pistul *n* epistle 16.289, 19.319, **B** 12.29, 13.69, **A** 10.109, 11.233

pytaunce *n* donation to a religious house [for providing additional food on special occasions] B 5.266; (the) allowance of food (so provided) 9.92; (small) portion 15.61, B 13.55

pite(e) *n* mercy 1.166, 6.172, 20.189, 21.92, B 17.294, **A** 5.12, 9.95, **hauen ~ on** be compassionate towards 3.86, 349, 5.166, 191, 15.88, B 5.253, 254; kindness 3.348; (feeling of) pity 2.229, 8.205, **withouten ~** pitilessly B 3.195, **hauen no ~ to killen** have no compunction about killing 11.269

pitous *a* piteous, doleful A 7.115

pitousli(che) *av* mercifully, forgivingly 4.94; pitiably, miserably 1.77, (*as a*) wretched(ly) 20.58

#pyuische *a* ? ill-tempered, ? foolish 8.151*n*

place *n* place, location Pr 96, 3.106, 5.165, 7.180, 9.225, 10.15, 13.50, 15.189, 16.121, 165, 17.86, 20.19, 176, 231, 272, 362, 22.3, 42, **B** 5.528, 6.44, 12.24, 61, 13.134, 16.21, 135, 171, Z 1.65; square 20.82; spot 20.157, B 13.275; position 21.61; house B 12.147; manor-house 5.159, 7.270, 12.248, 22.181, Z 6.65; dwelling-place 7.183, 198, 15.278; ? place of custody (in castle) 7.276*n*; *in phrr.* **in ~s** to (any) place 17.173, **in ~s þer** wherever 16.313; **in alle ~s** everywhere B 15.161; **in no ~** nowhere 17.86; **to what ~** in whichever direction 19.117

play *n* joy A 12.95

playen *v* enjoy oneself, relax Pr 22, 186, 188, B 12.24; (*refl.*) disport oneself †22.292; play, sport Pr 170; be joyful A 8.12; rejoice 18.273, 20.170; jest, joke 9.114; **~ with** use (tool) 3.461

playere *n* player, *in cpd.* **dees ~** 8.72

playnen 4.30, 8.166 *see* **pleynen** *v*

playten *v* fold, ? fasten B 5.208

planete *n* planet 22.80

planke *n* plank (= prop) 18.34, 40, B 16.50

plante B 1.152, 5.582 = **plonte** *n*

planten *v* plant (out), *p.p.* A 7.270 (Z 7.290)

plase 10.15, Z 6.4 = **place** *n*

plast(e)re *n* medicinal plaster, poultice [of herbs *etc*] (*fig.*) 22.360, 362, 364

plasteren *v* cover with a plaster (*fig.*) 19.91, 22.311, 315, **B** 17.96, 20.380

plate(s) *n* (set of) plate-armour (*fig.*) 20.24

platten *v* (*refl.*) prostrate oneself 6.3

pleden *v* argue (a case) 15.289, 21.296, (legal case) Pr 161, **for nouhte Y couthe** ~ in spite of any legal case I could make 4.57; plead in court B 7.42; dispute B 14.189; *ger.* pleading, arguing cases 3.448, 9.45

pledour *n* advocate B 7.42

pleyen Pr 186 *etc* (**pleyden** *p.t.* B 12.24) *see* **playen** *v*

pleyn *a* full, plenary B 7.102

pleynen *v* complain Pr 81, 6.110, (*ref.*) A 7.115; make a (legal) complaint / accusation (against) 3.213, 4.30, 70, 6.120, 16.67, (*refl.*) lodge complaint 8.156, make a legal complaint 8.166, B 4.66; *in phr.* **preiere** ~ utter petition B 17.294

pleynt *n* lament †B 6.123; complaint 12.137; legal complaint, lawsuit 3.213, B 2.172

plener *a* full B 16.103; **~e** *av* fully 12.49

plente(e) *n* plenty, abundance 8.160, 12.205, 13.140, 15.232; prosperity, *in phrr.* **pees and** ~ 17.93, 199, ~ **of pes** Z 1.86

plentevous *a* abundant A 12.95; generous B 10.82

plesaunce *n* pleasure 8.14

plesa(u)nt *a* pleasing, acceptable (to God) **B** 14.101, 15.156; gratifying 16.47

plesen *v* please, be acceptable to 5.85, 8.118, (*esp.* God) 11.230, 15.281, B 5.53; satisfy 3.199, 8.318, 15.202, Z 7.313; treat kindly B 11.183; gratify Pr 32, 3.489, 11.55; ingratiate (oneself) with 16.62, 236; flatter B 5.138; indulge B 5.36; attract B 13.313; entertain 3.12; serve A 10.213

plesinge *ger.* pleasure, ? offering B 3.252

pleten B 19.297, *p.t.* **B** Pr 213, 7.39 *see* **pleden** *v*

plicchen (plucchen) *v* (*p.t.* **plihte, pluhte**) pluck, pull 12.50, 19.12

pli(g)hten *v* (*p.t.* **pli(g)hte(n)**) promise, pledge, *in phrr.* (*refl.*) ~ **togyderes** unite by oath (in fellowship) Pr 47, (in marriage) B 9.167; bind (as apprentice) 6.208; ~ **treuthe** make a promise 2.124n, swear an oath (as juror) 3.469, pledge (one's) faith 8.33, make (marriage) vows 10.274

plihte *p.t.* 12.50 *see* **plicchen** *v*

plogh Pr 22, 145, 3.461, 8.151; ~ **man** 15.34, 139, 151 **plough (plouȝ)** 6.267, 15.236, **B** 6.169, 7.120, ~ **men** 11.297 *see* **plo(u)(g)h** *n*, ~ **man** *n*

plokken *v* pluck 7.228, B 12.248; pull **B** 11.114, 17.10

plomme *n* plum 12.223; ~ **tree** 5.118

plonte *n* plant 1.147, 7.228; sapling 18.25, 101

plot *n* stain B 13.275, 276, 318

plough (plouȝ) *n* 6.267, 15.236, **B** 6.169, 7.120, ~ **men** 11.297 *see* **plou(g)h**, ~ **man**

plo(u)(g)h (plouȝ, plow) plough Pr 145, 3.461, 8.111, 119, 160, 15.236; (*fig.*) 21.429; ploughing 8.131, 15.235, B 6.169, (*fig.*) B 7.120; **to / for þe** ~ to / plough(ing) Pr 22, 6.267, 7.191, 8.112, 21.337; = tool for earning a living B 15.125; team (of oxen) for ploughing (*fig.*) 21.267

plouhman (plowman) *n* ploughman 7.181, 9.186, 21.261 (= Piers) B Pr 119; (= as type of) person of low social rank 11.297; *see also under* **Peres, Perkyn**; *in phr.* **Peres...þe** ~ Piers the Ploughman's 15.196, 20.18, 24, 21.360, 393, 22.77

plowpote *n* plough-pusher B 6.103

pluhte *p.t.* 19.12 *see* **plicchen** *v*

plukke(de) *pr., p.t.* **B** 5.582, 11.114, 12.248, 17.10 *see* **plokken** *v*

plum-tree *n* plum-tree 5.118

pluralite *n* plurality [concurrent tenure of more than one benefice by a single cleric] 3.33, A 11.200

plurel *a* plural B 10.239

pnam Z 7.222, 224 = **mnam** *n*

po *n* (*uninfl. gen*) peacock's B 12.256; ~ **cok (pecok** 14.179 *etc*) *n* peacock 13.170, 14.161, 172, 174, 179, 183, B 12.228, 239, 240, 246; ~ **hen** pea-hen 14.174, B 12.239

poddyng *n* (kind of) sausage [stuffed lining of stomach] 15.67, B 13.107; ~ **ale** *n* thick ale 6.226

#poesie *n* (Latin) poetry, **of ~ a note** a song in Latin verse B 18.410

#poete *n* (Latin) poet 17.110, 20.452; = ancient learned authority 14. 183, **B** 10.338, 12.236; sage 14.92c; **Plato þe** ~ 11.120, (*with ref. to* Plato) 11.308, 12.175, 14.189

pohen 14.174 *see* **po ~** *n*

poffen *v* blow 5.118; pant, breathe heavily 15.97

poynt(e) *n* speck of dirt B 13.255; moment of action, *in phr.* **in ~ to** ready to B 13.111; teaching Z 7.232; thing 8.35; reason 5.117; part, detail 20.43, 22.31, **B** 13.187, 16.133; bit Z 8.90; principle, stipulation 1.98; virtue 16.119; point 1.152

poynten *v* aim (one's words) 8.297

poysen *n* (*fig.*) (source of) spiritual evil 17.229, 232; lethal drugged potion 20.52

poysenen Z 3.64, B 3.82 *see* **(a)poisenen** *v*

pok *n* pustule, *pl.* (small) pox 22.98

poke *n* bag, pouch 15.187, 249, 16.86, ~ **ful (pouheful)** *n* bag-ful 9.342

poken *v* incite 1.128; ~ **forth** stir up 7.262; ~ **to god** urge to good works 7.286

pol *n* head 22.86, B 13.247; person, *in phr.* ~ **by** ~ individually 12.10

pole *n* pole, staff 20.52

polen *v* restrain [head of horse, ? by means of a martingale] 4.23

poleschen *v* polish 6.328 (B 5.475), A 6.84

polet *n* pullet, young chicken 8.303

pollen *v* drag 2.229; ~ **adoun** pick B 16.73; ~ **atweyne** tear apart B 7.115

pomade *n* apple drink, ? cider 20.409

pomp(e) *n* show, ~ **and pruyde** ostentation and display 16.235, B 14.194, ~ **of the worlde** worldly vaingloriousness 3.70

pondefold *n* (*fig.*) pound, **þe poukes** ~ the devil's enclosure (= Limbo) 18.281; **þe deueles** ~ = the state of mortal sin B 5.624c

poore *a, n* Pr 80, 8.144, B 11.244 *etc*; *see* **pore** *a, n*

pop-holy *a* hypocritically holy 6.37

pope *n* pope Pr 135, 3.163, 314, 318, 329, 5.78, 112, 10.207, 12.77, 17.167, 21.224, 431, 22.101, **B** 5.600, 10.292, 11.155, 13.167, 15.490; the [actual] Pope 3.183, 270, 5.191, 9.324, 337, 15.174, 218, 15.228, 17.188, 233, 243, 260, 21.445, 22.127, B 7.19; *in phrr*: ~**s bulles** 9.337, ~**s grace** 2.244, ~ **palays** 2.23, ~**s ȝifte** B 13.246,

popeiay *n* parrot 14.172

*****poperen** *v* ride rapidly A 11.213c

porche *n* porch (of house) 18.241

porcio(u)n *n* allotted share B 8.53, A 10.117

pore *a* (**pouere** A 2.59, 3.155, B Pr 82 *et p.*, *comp.* **porore** 22.50, *sup.* **porest** 16.159) poor [lacking wealth] 4.122, 6.60, 12.26, 136, 153, 15.10, 16.3, 22.50, B 11.197, **A** 3.273, 11.244, *in phrr*: ~ **clerkus** Z Pr 58, ~ **comune** 15.11, ~ **folk** 8.147, 320, 9.72, 12.167, 16.328, ~ **heremyte** B 13.30, ~ **man / men** 3.213, 4.115, 7.78, 84, 194, 8.39, 10.16, 15.36, 16.126, 323, **B** 3.241, 5.253, A Pr 93, ~ **in pacience** A 11.230, ~ **peple** Pr 80, 3.83, 8.205, 316, 9.34, 11.297, 12.101, 122, 166, 17.70, **B** 3.81, 84, 11.181, 183, 185, 14.174, 15.203, A 8.48, 11.310, ~ **pilgrymes** B 11.245, ~ **prouisores** 2.186, ~ **thyng(es)** 15.33, 309, A 12.50, **wydewe(s)** B 13.197, A 8.32; *a as n* (**þe**) ~ the poor, poor people 1.170, 176, 4.114, 5.166, 7.103, 8.14, 144, 9.178, 11.28, 48, 65, 12.102, 105, 108, 14.16, 15.88, 117, 16.92, 256, 19.239, **B** 11.230, 14.145, 15.154, 246; poor man 3.282, 9.46, 11.67, 15.289, 16.49, 54, 62, 66, 67, 79, 90, 123, 125, 127, poor man's 12.133, *in phr*. ~ **pacient** 9.178, 13.30, 98, 15.280, 287, 16.99; poverty-stricken Pr 82, 4.123; impoverished 5.78; (of clothes) mean, shabby 12.126, B 11.234, 244; (voluntarily) poor 12.159, 22.234, ~ **freres** B 15.327, ~ **ladies** 6.132, ~ **religious** B 4.125; (spiritually) poor, humble, ~ **(of) herte** 16.24, **B** 14.99, 195, 16.8; ~ **of** deficient in 16.159, B 13.301; *in stock phr*. ~ **and / or riche** 15.202, 16.21, 47, 17.199, B 14.27, 73, **A** 2.59, 10.117, Z 2.67, **riche and / ne / or** ~ 11.59, 13.182, 17.2, **B** 12.74, 14.182

porest *sup.* 16.159 *see* **pore** *a*

poret *n* leek, ~ **ployntes** leek-plants 8.309, B 6.297

porfiel *n* fur trimming 4.111, 5.128

porore *comp.* 22.50 *see* **pore** *a*

pors *n* purse, money-bag 6.199, 266, 13.48, B 13.301, *in phr*. **into ~ward** in respect of (your) purses, monetarily Pr 101

porsen *v* put in (one's) purse 12.166

port *n* bearing, demeanour 6.30 (B 13.278)

#**portatif** *a* light, portable 1.152

porter *n* gate- / door-keeper 12.49, 22.299, 331; keeper of gate of heaven 7.270, **Peter the** ~ 16.167

porthors *n* portable breviary B 15.125

portour *n* porter, carrier 6.369

portrayen 19.137, B 3.62 = **purtrayen** *v*

#**posen** *v* put it (that) 19.277

possen *v* push, toss B Pr 151, *p.p.* Z 5.44

possession *n* possession B 12.247, possession of property 16.110, 17.226, 229; (material) possessions, property **B** 11.271, 274, 13.301, A 11.200

possessioner *n* beneficed cleric B 5.143

post *n* (wooden) prop B 16.54

poste *p.p.* Z 5.44 *see* **possen** *v*

postern *n* side door 7.270

postle 9.118, 18.177, B 6.149 *see* **apostel** *n*

pot *imp.* 2.50, *p.p.* 13.228, 15.41 *see* **potten** *v*

pot(te) *n* jar B 13.255, (*fig.*) 15.226; ~ **ful** *n* (cooking)-pot full 8.182, Z 7.286

potage *n* (thick) soup 8.182; stew 15.47; *in phr*. **payn(e) and / ne (...)** soup and bread 8.285, 15.235, **B** 6.150, 9.81, 15.315

potager *n* soup-maker 6.132

pote 8.64 *see* **plouh** ~ *n*

potel *n* half-gallon 6.398

potente *n* staff, (= bishop's crosier) B 8.97

potten (putten) *v* (*imp.* **pot** 2.50, *contr. pr.* **potte** 16.111, **(put(te))** **B** 3.234, 14.272, 17.154, *p.t.* **potte(n)** Pr 27, **put** 4.74, **put(te)** 4.74, 111, *p.p.* **pot** 13.228, **ypot** 16.125, **put** 2.216) push Pr 170, 15.175, ~**...lowe** bring low 12.14, ~ **in pouerte** reduced to poverty 13.8, ~ **of** repel 16.121, B 14.191, ~ **out (of) / fram** expel (from) 13.228 (B 11.417), 16.223; put 3.83, 469, 6.219, A 9.95, ~ **in ere** suggest B 12.226; place 2.216; direct 15.41; (*refl.*) subject (oneself) 2.244, make (oneself) †B 6.150; ~ **forth** stretch out / forth 4.74, 7.181, extend B 17.154, (*refl.*) appear 15.236, 20.39; ~ **vp** reach up 20.52; ~ **to** set (sb.) (to) 5.171, 7.191, 8.197, 203, 11.120, B 19.254, appoint 3.469, 16.125, A 7.184; (*refl.*) set (oneself) to Pr 22, 25, 27, 16.111, 21.67; ~ **in** store (away) in 4.111, 16.86; ~ **forth** propound 2.50, 10.121, 11.39; declare B 3.234; ~ **byfore** put first, prefer 12.142, ~ **byhynde** push to the back (= value at little) 16.49

poudre *n* medicinal powder 22.360

pouer 8.283, Z 3.103 *etc* = **power** *n*

poues *n* pulse 19.68

pouheful = **pokeful**; *see* **poke** *n*

pouk(e) *n* (the) Devil 18.50, 278, 281, B 14.189, 191, **A** 10.62, 11.161; **helle** ~ *n* fiend from hell 15.165

pound *n* pound-weight [for measuring] 6.223; pound [measured weight] 6.358; Troy pound [for measuring gold, = 12 oz.] 16.297; pound sterling [monetary pound] Pr 161n, ~ **of nobles** (value of) a pound sterling in nobles B 10.289

poundmele *av* by pounds at a time 2.232

pouren *v* (**togederes**) (mix by) pour(ing) together 6.226

poustee *n* power, ~ **of pestilence(s)** violent attack of the plague **B** 5.36, 12.11

pouere *a* B Pr 82 *et p.*, A 2.59 *see* **pore** *a*

pouerte *n* (state of) poverty 2.84, 12.150, 236, 13.3, 26, 99, 15.281, 16.57, 59, 61, 71, 97, 114, 119, 120, 155, **B** 11.317, 14.274, (*person.*) 13.1, 16.83, 85, 86, 93, 122, 126, 138, 139, 149; destitution 9.182, 12.14, 13.8, 140, 15.159, 16.18, 32, **B** 12.11, 14.284, 15.208, *in phrr*: **penaunce and ~, ~ and penaunce(s)** (a state of) hardship and penitential suffering(s) 12.150, 21.67, **B** 15.270; 9.234, 16.326, B 12.9; poverty (voluntarily adopted) 16.111, 22.236, **B** 14.273; (the virtue of) poverty 12.144, B 11.271, *in phrr*: **pacient ~** 12.178, B 14.101, **pacience and ~, ~ and pacience** 13.20, B 12.61; 16.56, 152, 21.250, B 10.340; poverty of spirit, humility 12.142, B 14.192; shabbiness of clothing 10.117

power *n* power, ability (to do sth.) 6.256, 11.60, 16.159, 221, 19.141, 143, 156, **B** 3.168, 16.37, 54, *in phrr*. **of ~ able** 8.283, **in (by) my / þi / here ~** as far as I / you / they am / are able 4.137, 8.33, 9.17, 13.69, B 13.105, A 5.75; spiritual power Pr 128, 136, 15.226, 21.184, 189, 389; spiritual authority 22.321; control, dominion (over) 3.434, 16.61, 17.306, 18.283, **B** 10.237, 11.164, A 10.62; legal power / authority Pr 135, 2.50, 9.324, 17.224; authorisation B 6.149; force of supporters 4.70

praye *n* quarry, captives B 18.310

prayen 5.82, 7.296, 8.131, 266, 22.340, B Pr 90 *see* **preyen** *v²*

prayere 15.230 = **prey(e)re** *n*

praisen 14.183 = **preysen** *v*

praktisour *n* (medical) practitioner B 16.107

prechare 16.245 = **prech(e)our** *n*

prechen *v* preach (sermon) (to) Pr 57, 66, 78, 3.277, 5.114, 9.112, 11.56, 207, †218, 16.262, 17.83, 174, 188, 20.329, **B** Pr 90, 3.223, 5.145, 6.149, 7.14, 135, 10.267, 15.443, 20.127, A Pr 93, 5.11, 23; *ger.* preaching 7.285, 17.17, **B** 4.122, 15.405, 448, A 4.107; declare religious doctrine 12.42; proclaim 5.141, 10.89, 15.70, 75, 76, 84, 89, 16.287, 17.191, B 13.118; exhort B 10.202, **A** 11.198, 12.22, ~ **to** exhort to do B 3.223; teach 22.275, 277, B 10.388, A 8.16; declare Pr 39, **A** 1.137, 3.64; ~ **of** recount, speak about 16.324, **B** 3.234, 10.34, 13.85, A 11.72; speak out B 5.143

prech(e)our *n* (authorised) preacher [of Christian faith] 7.87, 11.207, 16.245, 250, 267, 276, 21.232, **B** 12.19, 15.440, 498; ~**s** preachers' B 4.122

precious(e) *a* precious 1.147, 11.10; of great worth B 16.261; costly 20.409

#predestinaeten *v* predestine (to salvation) *p.p.* **predestinaet** 11.207c

preest 4.130, 14.123, B Pr 60, ~ **hoed** 16.243, 245; *see* **pre(e)st** *n*, ~ **hoed** *n*

preyen *v¹* prey upon, ravage 22.86

preyen *v²* (*p.t.* **prey(e)de** 1.77, 5.128 *etc*) entreat, beg (of) 1.77, 2.71, 4.94, 5.128, 140, 191, 7.302, 8.7, 35, 169, 176, 10.11, 15.122, 218, 234, 16.114, 20.207, 21.154, 22.245, 339, **B** 6.199, 16.24, ~ **to** make entreaty to 9.279, B 4.98, ~ **of** beg (to) 21.154, for **B** 6.123, 10.122; ask for 15.33, **B** 11.245, 13.30, 16.73; ask (that) 15.193, 20.176, B 6.196; (say) pray(er) 3.464 (pray psalter), 9.42, 17.244, 250, 255, Z 5.92; pray (for) 1.77 (2), 8.131, 9.42, 12.10, 15.212, 214, 17.226, 21.250, 22.292, 365, B 5.104

prey(e)r(e) *n* entreaty, plea 2.68, 7.209, 20.204, B 10.289, *in phr*. **for eny / no ~** in spite of any entreaty 2.216, 21.309, B 17.294; request 9.282, B 13.136; prayer (to God), *esp.* of intercession 3.274, 5.84, 8.136, 11.60, 12.101, 17.86, 236, **B** 11.155, 15.345, 16.135; action / practice of (saying) prayer(s) Pr 27, B 6.247, A 12.98, *in phr.* ~**(s) and / ne / or penaunce(s) / penaunce(s) and ~(s)** 7.240, 9.174, 328, 16.38, **B** 7.120, 178, 12.9, 15.148, 426, 16.38

preynte *p.t.* 15.122, 20.19, †B 13.86 *see* **prinken** *v*

pre(i)sen *v* praise, commend 6.60, 7.262, (*p.p.*) 10.311, 12.197, 13.26, **B** 6.108, 7.38, 10.340, 11.318, 13.313, 14.48, 274, 15.156, 252, **to ~** to be commended 13.207, 18.221; value, esteem 5.31, 6.45, 12.144, 17.164, 22.149, B 11.253; assess the value (of) 6.379, 383

prelat *n* prelate [churchman of episcopal or abbatial rank] Pr 101, 2.182, 3.270, 5.140, 6.120, 16.267, 17.188, 192, 225, 260, 22.127, **B** 9.81, 15.490, 608; *in phrr.* ~**es and prestes** 10.198, 17.244, 317, ~**es of Holy Churche** 6.119, 16.243, 22.229, **B** 11.98, 15.244, **princes and** ~**es** B 7.43, Z 7.271

prenti(e)s *n* (*pl.* **prentis** 3.279, 6.279, ~**es** 21.232) apprentice 2.224, 6.208, 279; ~**es of lawe** law-students, ?novice barristers 21.232; *in phr.* **Peres ~ þe Plouhman** P. the P's apprentice 15.196, **#prentished (~hode B)** apprenticeship (*fig.*) 6.251

#prescite *a* foreknown (to be damned) 11.208c

presence *n* presence Pr 188

present *n* gift 3.270, 8.39, 318, 14.97, 18.277, 278, 21.96; offering (made as a bribe) 3.117, 199, 4.91, B 13.377, *in phr.* **for ~** in spite of bribes 21.309

presenten (with) *v* offer as a present (to) 21.92

pre(e)s(s)en *v* push on 16.54; bring pressure upon, ? importune 22.127

presompcion 13.231 = **presumpcioun** *n*

pressour *n* press (for stretching cloth) 6.219

prest *a* eager, willing 16.62; prompt, quick 7.194 (*sup.*), **B** 6.196, 13.251, (*comp.*) B 10.289, A 12.98; (*as av*) at once 20.272; **~ly** *av* promptly 3.305, 8.102

pre(e)st *n* (*sg. as pl.* 3.310, B 15.121) priest (= parish priest) Pr 118, 121, 2.182, 3.186, 277, 4.130, 6.298, 304, 7.10, 14, 30, 71, 246, 8.190, 9.280, 288, 292, 301, 318, 12.29, 13.81, 100, 111, 15.214, 16.250, 267, 276, 17.61, 72, 117, 122, 238, 244, 21.232, **B** 5.104, 165, 7.131, 135, 11.98, 281, 302, 13.11, 237, 14.9, 91, 15.117, 121, 128, 440, 485, A 12.22; Jewish priest [of the Old Testament] Pr 116, 14.60; *in phrr.* **badde ~es** B 10.280; **fals ~es** Pr 106; **ydiotes ~es** B 11.316; **inparfit ~es** 16.276, 22.229, B 15.131; **lewed ~es** B 11.317; **mansed ~es** 22.221, B 10.278; **parsche ~es** Pr 79, 81, 14.123, 22.281, 320, B 10.267; **proute ~es** 22.218; **~es and persones** 3.463, B 3.252 (for **persones / prelates** and **~es** *see svv*); **~is fyle** 6.135, **~is sone** 14.60

pr(e)est(e)ho(e)d *n* (the order of Christian) priesthood (*person.*) 21.334; the body of (Christian) priests [collectively] 16.243, 245, 17.233, 250

presumen *v* presume, *in phr.* **power ~ in hemself** presume the power resides in themselves Pr 135

presumpcio(u)n *n* presumption B 11.421, **~ of** arrogance in regard to 13.231; a supposition 11.39

presumptuously *av* arrogantly A 12.8

preuen *v* put to the test 10.121, 11.39; try, assay B 13.215; discover †B 7.45; prove (by argument / authority) 12.31, 175, 13.26, 15.100, 135, 137, 140, 287, 289, 215, 22.275, **B** 10.344, 14.191, 17.156, 18.152, (? *or* manifest), A 11.233; demonstrate 11.159; show 5.115, 18.59, 19.224, B 12.259; explain **B** 12.19, 29, 13.†85, 123; spell out Pr 39; declare 6.119, 9.318, 12.142, 178, 17.4; demonstrate in practice 12.202, 15.89, B 13.133; illustrate 6.186; endeavour 17.317; put into practice 5.141, 16.262, B 13.80, A 4.107

preuete 13.230 = **pryuatee** *n*

preuyli(che) A 3.57, 71 *see* **pryue(y)ly(che)** *av*

pryde 20.346, (*person.*) 21.224 *et p.*, 22.70, **B** 13.276, 14.73, 194, 281, 15.67, A 3.57 *see* **pr(u)yde** *n*

prien *v* peer, **~ after** peer in search of B 16.168

prike(a)re *n* horseman, mounted warrior 10.135, 20.24; rider B 10.307

prik(i)en *v* pierce 19.164; wound 22.86; spur 19.333, B 2.190; gallop 2.201, 4.24, 5.159, 22.149, *in phr.* **cam ~** came galloping 20.9; incite, stir up 19.91

prime *n* prime [period from 6 to 9 a.m.] *in phrr.* **aȝen ~ daies** before prime A 12.60, **hey ~** high prime (= towards 9 a.m.) 8.119

prymer *n* primer [layman's devotional manual] 5.46

prince *n* sovereign 9.279, 11.10, 18.277, **~s lettres** 21.309, **~s paleises** 10.16; ruler 13.8, **B** 7.43, 13.51, 18.263,

A 2.12, 11.298, Z 7.272, (*in ref. to* God) **~ of heuene** 17.248, **~ of Paradis** A 7.109; (*to* Christ) **~ Iesu** 13.3, 21.96, B 16.37; spiritual ruler (= pope) 17.167, 21.224, (= bishop) 10.198, A 11.198; chief 12.178; leader 2.84

principalli(che) *av* chiefly B 10.468; above all B 14.195

prinken *v* (*p.t.* **preynte**) wink, signal by a look 15.122, 20.19, †B 13.86

printe *n* imprint 17.75

printen *v* stamp (*fig.*) 17.80

prio(u)r *n* prior [deputy head of monastic / mendicant house] 5.91, 6.153, **~ prouincial** = head of all houses of religious order in a province 12.9

prioresse *n* prioress [head of convent of nuns] 6.135, B 5.165, (*uninfl. gen.*) prioress's 6.132

pris[1] *n* (monetary) value, cost B 2.13; value 18.277; esteem, **setten at litel ~** care little about, think little of 12.26, 15.10

pris[2] *a* most excellent 21.267

priso(u)n *n* imprisonment 15.256; prison, gaol 4.123, 7.21, 9.34, 72, 180, **B** 8.102, 15.265, (*fig.*) = (captivity in) purgatory ? 7.276, 12.69, B 18.393; prisoner 3.173, 9.34, 72, 180, 16.323, 20.58, (*fig.*) captive of purgatory B 15.345, poor / sick person as 'God's prisoner' B 14.168c

prisoner *n* prisoner B 3.137, (*fig.*) poor person as 'God's prisoner' B 14.174

pryuatee (preuetee) *n* secret(s) 13.230; (divine) mystery 18.5

priue(e) *a* secret 4.189, **~ ȝeft** 3.117, **paiement** 22.365 (= bribe); confidential (*pl.*) B 2.178; concealed 17.242; treacherous 22.115; intimate, familiar 2.23, 64, 3.183, 9.118, (*sup.*) 18.98, B 13.207; private 12.40, 13.37, B 10.99, **~ membres** sexual organs B 12.229; personal, individual 13.81, 21.379

pryue(y)ly(che) *av* secretly, on the side B 13.377, A 3.57; (hidden) secretly 17.172; stealthily 21.302; furtively 6.266, B 3.82; treacherously 18.165; alone, *Pauci ~* only a few by themselves 12.50; quietly 15.151, 22.108, B 13.55; ? mysteriously 18.101

priueoste *sup.* 18.98 *see* **priue(e)** *a*

procuratour *n* agent 7.89; steward, manager 21.259

profecyen *v* speak as if inspired B 18.108, **~ of** prophesy about 9.114, **~ bifore** foretell 21.16

proferen (forth) *v* extend 19.117, 118

professioun *n* solemn pledge (of duty) 1.97

profete (prophete) *n* prophet (*with ref. to* Christ) 17.299, 21.48; prophet of the Old Testament 3.427, 11.259, 12.202, 21.145, (**Dauid) þe ~** B 3.234, 7.122, 11.94, **Ysaye þe ~** 18.113, **Samuel þe ~** 3.413; **~s and patriarkes** 10.207, **patriarke(s) and / or ~(s)** 7.87, 9.12, 11.150, 14.60, 81, 18.208, 273, 20. 141, 146, 279, 366, 21.16, **B** 10.338, 16.251; 'holy fool' [insane person believed divinely inspired] 9.211; **false ~s** 21.222

profyt *n* benefit 8.7, 14, 111, 22.333, **B** Pr 119, 4.150;

interest(s) 6.208, 279, B 13.238; *in phrr.* ~ **of the wombe** so as to fill the(ir) belly Pr 57, **comune** ~ Pr 167, 184, 4.119; (spiritual) benefit 5.101, 13.201

profitable *a* beneficial Pr 145; spiritually beneficial 15.84; to the satisfaction (of) 15.175; useful 6.263, 7.191; worthwhile **B** 6.274, 17.151

profiten *v* be of advantage / profit Pr 101

profren *v* offer, present 4.91, 7.199, 8.39, 318, 15.250, **B** 4.64, 13.190, 381; offer a bribe 4.67; (*refl.*) offer one-self (in service) B 6.24; offer battle, challenge (to fight) 8.150

properliche 15.154 = **propreliche** *av*

prophecie *n* prophetic utterance B 15.325

prophete 3.413 *etc* = **profete** *n*

propre *a* individual, distinct **B** 10.239, 16.54; proper, particular B 16.185; appropriate, ? fine 9.301; goodly 15.64, 18.101, B 13.51

propreliche *av* strictly B 14.284; exactly 16.117, B 14.275; fittingly 15.154

proud *a* proud, haughty 10.135, 22.218, B 12.239, ~ **herte** 3.224, (*as name*) 6.3, ~ **herted** B 15.201; ~ **for** proud on account of B 13.190; ~ **of** greatly pleased with, elated about 6.46, 304, 8.203, 16.297, *in phr.* ~ **of aparayle** splendidly dressed 6.30, B 13.278, stately A 2.41; splendid 14.172

proudly *av* splendidly B 11.240

prout(e) 6.46, 22.218 = **proud** *a*

proue(n) A 9.115, 11.229, 233 *etc* = **preuen** *v*

prouendre *n* fodder B 13.244; prebend, stipend of a canon 3.32, B 13.246, Z 3.33

prouendren *v* provide with a prebend 3.186

prouerbe *n* (Biblical) maxim, proverb 8.264, 12.173, 17.51

prouince *n* province [area under a bishop's jursdiction] 17.284, B 15.608

#prouincial *n* head of a province (= district) of an order of friars, *gen. sg. or pl.* 9.342; *a in phr.* **Priour** ~ = head of a province of friars 12.9

prouisour *n* provisor [cleric granted right by the pope to assume a benefice on one becoming vacant] 2.182, 186, 3.183, 4.130, B 2.171

prowour *n* purveyor [provider / overseer] 21.261

pr(u)yde *n* (the sin of) pride [excessive self-love / self-esteem] 1.128, 2.84, 5.117, 6.13, 8.348, 11.58, 64, 12.236, 15.231, 236, 16.121, 227, 263, 330, 17.215, 20.346, **B** 14.73, 15.67, A 10.102, (*fig.*) B 13.276, (*person.*) (the deadly sin of) Pride 6.14, 16.47, 57, 59, 119, 210, 21.224, 229, 337, 354, 357, 362, 384, 22.70, 108, 149, 353, 374, 383; ~ **of Parfit Lyuynge** the Pride of Life, Vainglory 11.176, 194; love of praise, vanity 3.70, 6.59, 7.262, 16.235, A 3.57; over-confidence (in) 13.231; love of display, ostentation Pr 25, 10.117, 16.235, 256, B 14.194, 281

pruynses *pl.* 2.84 *see* **prince** *n*

psalm *n* Psalm 14.116, **B** 3.248, 6.249, 11.313; **seuene ~s** the seven Penitential Psalms 3.464, 5.47

publischen *v* make public 12.40

puddyng B 13.107 = **poddyng** *n*

#pue *n* pew [enclosed seat in church] 6.144

pu(y)r *a* pure 4.91; fine 2.10, A 2.12; strict 5.166; total **B** 14.193, 285, 16.220; simple, sheer, *in phrr.* ~ **bileue** B 10.464; ~ **charite** 11.65, **B** 10.314, 15.79; ~ **enuye** 11.56, ~ **grace** 20.189, ~ **ioye** B 16.18, ~ **lawe** 15.290, ~ **mercy** 6.172, ~ **nauht** 17.306, ~ **pacience** B 14.193, ~ **pouerte** 16.152, ~ **resoun** 15.289, 19.321, **B** 13.167, 14.108, A 8.153; ~ **reuthe** 13.92, ~ **riht(e)** 16.99, 17.70, ~ **synne** 5.115, B 11.429, ~ **skile** 15.137, ~ **sleuþe** B 14.76, ~ **tene** 8.124, B 16.86, ~ **treuthe** 3.348, 21.195, B 11.155; true 12.197; very 1.97, *in phrr.* **on...~ erthe** 3.101, 9.185; ~ **tree** the tree itself B 16.8

pu(y)re *av* absolutely, completely B 11.274; very 7.20, 12.136, 18.103, **B** †5.405, 11.194; thoroughly 3.382, 15.309, B 11.194

pu(y)rli(che) *av* completely 15.231; integrally, essentially 19.141; solely B 16.51; simply 18.234

puken A 6.122 = **poken** *v*

pullen B 7.115, 16.73 = **pollen** *v*

pulsshen A 5.250 = **poleschen** *v*

pulten *v* (*p.t.* **pulte** B 1.127, 11.62, *p.p.* **pult** 11.208) thrust, ~ **adoun** 10.95, ~ **out** put forth 19.143, ~ **oute (of)** remove from 11.208; expel B 1.127, release by force B 11.162; put, place Z 7.182

punfolde B 5.624 = **pondefold** *n*

pungen *v* thrust A 9.88

punys(c)hen *v* (inflict legal) punish(ment upon) 2.50, 3.79, 16.125; torment B 14.189; (inflict divine) punish(ment on) 21.196, B 10.369

puple Pr 145, A 12.102 = **pe(o)ple** *n*

purchacen *v* obtain (a pardon) 3.32, 9.3, 42, 337, 19.219; acquire [by gift or purchase] 5.77, 158, 12.248

pure B 4.95 *et p.*, A 8.101, 153, **pureste** A 2.9, 12, **B** †5.405, 11.194, 247; **pureliche** B 16.51 *see* **pu(y)r** *a*, **pu(y)re** *av*, **pu(y)rli(che)** *av*

purfil B 4.116, 5.26 = **porfiel** *n*

purfiled *p.p.a.* wearing apparel richly trimmed 2.10; *and see* **porfiel** *n*

purgatory(e) *n* purgatory 2.108, 6.299, 7.117, 9.11, 11.33, 300, 12.69, 13.30, 15.309, 18.15, **B** 6.44, 10.369, 15.345, 18.393, *in phrr.* **appurtinaunces of** ~ subsidiary rights (*iron.*) of p. 2.108, **pardon in** ~ remission of panishment in p. A 8.59, **penaunce in / of** ~ punishment in ~ **B** 9.77, 10.420; (*fig.*) = cleansing from sin through earthly suffering 9.185, ~ **on erthe** 15.94

purgen *v* purge 17.232

purpos *n* proposition 10.121, B 10.117

pursuen *v* follow after 21.163; follow, attend 11.176, B 11.185; follow (example of) 21.433; pursue (with hostile intent) 12.14, 18.165; chase B 12.240; strive after

B 3.241; strive / seek (to) 14.174, 17.167, A 5.75; bring a suit, prosecute 19.286

pursward Pr 101 *see* **pors** *n*

purtinaunce 16.330, A 2.68 = **appurtinaunce** *n*

purtrayen *v* draw 3.66, 19.137, (*fig.*), ? (*with pun on* 'form mental image(s) of') 16.321

purueien *v* provide B 14.29; make provision (for) †B 5.165

put *n* (*pl.* **puttes**) dungeon, (underground chamber in) prison 9.72, B 5.406, ~ **of helle** B 10.369, (*fig.*) ~ **of meschief** B 14.174

put(te) *p.t.* Pr 25, 4.74 *etc*, *p.p.* 2.216, 13.8, *contr. pr.* **B** 3.234, 14.272, 17.154 *see* **potten** *v*

#**putour** *n* pimp 6.172

putrie *n* prostitution, ?lecherous living 6.186

quad *p.t.* Z Pr 130 *et p.* = **quod** *see* **quethen** *v*

quaken *v* (*p.t.* **quakid** 20.257, **quoek** 20.63) shiver, shake [with cold] 11.42, [with fear] 22.200, [with grief] 20.63, 257

quantite *n* mesure, (*as av*) **a** ~ to some degree 21.377

quarter *n* (*pl.* ~ Z 4.46, ~**es** 4.61) [as measure of weight] quarter (of a pound) 6.223; [measure of capacity, = 8 bushels] quarter (of) 4.61

quath Pr 182, **quaþ** A 1.12 *et p.* = **quod** *see* **quethen** *v*

quauen *v* tremble, quake B 18.61

queed *n* evil one [= the Devil] B 14.190

queene *n* queen 8.46, B 13.170, A 2.14c

queynte *n* cunt (*with pun on* 'clever device'), *in phr.* ~ **comune** (? = sexually promiscuous) 4.161

queynte *a* cunning 19.234, *comp.* elegant A 2.14c

queyntly *av* artfully, speciously 21.349

que(y)ntise *n* stratagem 20.297, (*with pun on* 'elaborate trappings') 21.354

quellen *v* (*p.p.* **quelt** B 16.114) kill Z 7.263; *p.p.* dead B 16.114

quen A 2.14 = **quene** *n*[1]

quenchen *v* (*p.p.* **queynte** 20.391) quench, stifle (*fig.*) 19.168, 222, 253, 326

quene[1] *n* low-born woman 8.46

quene[2] B 13.170 = **queene** *n*

†**querelen** *v* quarrel 5.154 (†B 10.301)

queste *n* judicial inquest, trial by jury (= **enqueste**) 22.162, **fals** ~ inquest inititated invalidly / resulting in unjust verdict 11.20; **of Paulines** ~ belonging to the inquest (*or* ? collecting-mission) of Paulines 2.110c

question *n* (theological) problem 11.54

quethen *v* (*p.t.* **quath** Pr 182, A 1.12 *et p.*, **quod** Pr 138 *et p.*) say (*with direc, declarative imperative or exclamatory quotation following*) 3.155, 283, 340, 4.176, 5.89, 7.304, 8.1, 124, 15.139, 21.12, 208, 21.358, 22.317, (*with quotn. preceding*) 6.62, 7.181, 199, 286, 11.314, 12.24, 14.202, 15.95, 18.156, 169, 19.78, 333, 20.47, 50, 57, 360, 21.357, 22.140, 189; (*after first and before*

second part of quotn.) Pr 138 *et p.*, B Pr 160 *et p.*, A 3.162, 12.1 *et p.* (**quod**), A 1.12 *et p.* (**quaþ**), Z Pr 103 *et p.* (**quad**); ask (*with quotn. preceding*) 7.55, 10.151, 12.24, 13.220, 15.112, 113, 276, 283, 16.114, 314, 17.125, 18.184, 274, 19.18, 20.19, 192, 360, 21.394, **B** 14.37, 97, 15.149, (*between first and second part of quotn.*) 5.26, 6.234, 357, 7.176, 10.70, 72, 74, 151, 13.198, 15.247, 16.163, 177, 337, 18.274, 20.26, 21.10, 22.207, **B** 10.330, 15.22, 16.24, 180; speak 16.113; answer A 12.88

quyete *n* repose, **in** ~ in peace 17.240, at rest B 1.123

quyk[1] *a* living 20.257; alive 17.303, 18.145, (when) alive, during life 15.12; ~**...o lyue,** ~ **on molde** anywhere alive A 2.14, Z 2.18; *a as n, in phr.* ~ **and dede** the living and the dead 9.21, 21.53, 197

quyk[2] *av* at once 15.283, **as** ~ at once, as quickly as possible B 14.190

quyk(i)en *v* cause to revive 20.391; animate 16.181

quyten *v* (*p.p.* **quyt** 4.98, **yquited** 8.107, *contr. pr.* B 11.193) repay (in full) 8.107, 9.273, 13.75, 15.12, B 18.358; give recompense for 20.387, 388; make satisfaction for 16.31, 20.391; requite, pay back 12.106, 109, B 11.192, 193

quoek *p.t.* 20.63 *see* **quaken** *v*

quoer *n* choir (of a church) 5.60

raap *p.t.* 6.270 *see* **repen** *v*

rad *p.p.* 3.496, **radde(n)** *p.t.* 3.488, 4.105, 5.125, 143, 15.52, B 5.124, Z 4.5 *see* **reden** *v*

#**radegounde** *n* skin-infection of face 22.83

rage *n* fit of anger 13.129

#**rag(e)man** *n*[1] (name for the) devil 18.122

rag(e)man *n*[2] bull, document with seals attached Pr 73

ragged *a* tattered 11.195, 16.349; gnarled A 10.124

ray *n* fine striped cloth 6.217

ray *a* made of striped cloth (**ray**) A 3.271

raymen *v* acquire 13.95

rayne (**reyn(e)**) *n* rain 14.24, 15.269, 19.303, 317, B 3.208

r(a)ynen *v* (*p.t.* **roen** 15.269) rain 5.164; fall 15.269, 19.317

rakeare *n* scavenger, street-cleaner 6.370

ran *p.t.* Pr 165, 2.62, 6.1, 15.152 *see* **rennen** *v*

rang *p.t.* 20.471 *see* **ringen** *v*

ransaken *v* despoil 18.122

rape *n* haste, **in** ~ quickly B 5.326

rap(p)(e)ly(che) *av* hastily 6.382; swiftly 18.290, 19.50

rapen *v. refl.* hurry 5.102, 7.8, 8.125, 19.79

rappen *v* strike 1.91

rat *contr. pr.* (= **redeth**) 3.406, 12.212, 15.269, 19.234 *see* **reden** *v*

rathe *av* early, *in phr.* **late and / ne** ~ = at all times 10.140, 11.89, B 3.73; (*comp.*) **rather** sooner, earlier 8.44, 9.123, 10.73, 11.261, 294, 13.31, 16.51, 57, B

12.233, ~**...til** before 10.54; at an earlier time B 13.85; more readily 4.5, 9.134, 11.29; on the contrary 4.4; rather 1.142, 6.290, 7.208, 13.186, 14.154, **B** 11.77, 14.107, 15.341, *in phr.* þe ~ the more swiftly Pr 117; the more readily 16.237, B 13.24; at once 8.125, 19.69, **B** 5.259, 280, 8.35; (*sup.*) **rathest** earliest 12.225; first 6.391, B 16.71; most readily 9.148, 16.45, 351

rato(u)n *n* rat Pr 165, 176, 182, 190, 192, 198, 214, 216

ratoner *n* rat-catcher 6.370

rau(g)hte *p.t.* Pr 73, 4.179, **B** 8.35, †11.438, Z 4.129 *see* **rechen** *v*

raunsomen *v* ransom 19.285, (*fig.*) redeem, deliver from damnation 11.261

raunsoun *n* release of prisoner by payment, (*fig.*) redemption B 18.353

rauen *v* be mad 20.192; behave like a madman B 15.10

rauener, -our *n* plunderer [one who takes goods by force] 17.43, 47

raueschen, -yschen *v* plunder 21.52; rape 4.47; transport (into vision) 11.168; enrapture 2.16; seduce, lead astray 11.294

raxen B 5.392 = **roxlen** *v*

realte A 11.228 *see* **ryalte** *n*

re(a)(u)m(e) Pr 192, **B** 3.208, 298, 5.11, A 10.134 *see* **reume** *n*[^1]

reautee B 10.334, 14.210 *see* **ryalte** *n*

rebaude 15.233 = **rybaud** *n*

rebuken *v* reprimand Pr 110, 12.67, 13.237, **B** 5.365; upbraid 16.15; reprove 5.82, 20.352; reproach **B** 11.372, 436, *ger.* **B** 12.217; repulse 22.63

rec(c)heles *a* heedless, reckless 12.66; imprudent A 10.106, *a as n* reckless behaviour A 10.51; indifferent to / ? undisturbed by care 20.2; ~**li(che)** *av* rashly 13.154; heedlessly B 11.130; ~**nes(se)** *n* heedless rashness 10.217, 12.70, (*person.*) 11.195, 199, 276, 286, 13.129

rec(c)hen *v* (*p.t. subjv.* **rouhte** 12.21) care 8.127, ~ **of** care about 4.34, 16.316, 20.2, 21.451; care / be concerned (that) 3.387, 4.69, 9.101, 12.21, 13.237; (*refl.*) concern oneself 11.195, 12.4

rece(y)uen 4.196, 19.145, **B** †6.148, 17.191 *see* **resceyuen** *v*

rechen *v* (*p.t.* **rau(g)hte** Pr 73, 4.179, **B** 8.35, †11.438) reach to B 8.35; catch hold of, reach B 11.361; lay hold of 3.499; extend, suffice 16.72; be stretched 4.179; come into contact with 19.145, B 17.191; †~ **after** go / proceed after B 11.438

reclusen *v* enclose 4.116

recomenden *v* commend, praise 16.356

reconforten *v* give fresh heart to B 5.280

record *n* record, agreement (*with pun on sense* 'testimony') 3.343; witness, **take** ~ **at** call to witness B 15.87

recorden *v* pronounce, set down 3.470; declare 4.151, B

4.172; testify [esp. in recollection of what has passed] 4.29, 20.203, 373; repeat (from memory) 17.320

recoueren B 18.353 *see* **rekeueren** *v*

recouerer *n* treatment, remedy 19.69

recrayen *v* be cowardly (in battle), *p.p.a* **recrayed** (*as term of abuse*) recreant, cowardly B 3.259

recreaunt *a* admitting defeat, overcome 20.103

***rect** *a* right 3.366; direct [of grammatical relationships] 3.333, **relacion** ~ inflexional agreement 3.343, 360, (*fig.*) 373, **relatif** ~ relative pronoun agreeing with its antecedent (*fig.*) 3.354

red *p.p.* A 5.180, 11.221 *see* **reden** *v*

re(e)d *n*[^1] advice, counsel 4.29, A 9.99; command 6.270 (B 13.374)

re(e)d *n*[^2] reed 20.50

re(e)d(e) *a* red 21.11, A 10.123, Z 2.16, ~ **rubies** 2.13, ~ **scarlet** B 2.15; (= reddish-hued) ~ **gold** 21.88, B 2.16, ~ **noble** 17.200; **sam** ~ half-red 8.310

redels *n* riddle **B** 13.168, *pl.* ~ 13.185

reden *v* (**redon** 5.69; *contr. pr.* **rat** 3.406 *etc,* **ret** 3.412, 13.5, **B** 14.66, *p.t.* **radde** 3.488 *etc,* Z 4.5, **redde** 7.119, A 4.97, *2 pers.* **reddest(ow)** B 3.259, *p.p.* **(y)rad** 3.496, 11.276, **red** A 5.180, 11.221) read Pr 205, 3.406 (1), 488, 496 (2), 7.31, 9.280, **B** 3.259, 5.234, 10.302, 12.65, 13.73, **A** 10.86, 12.22, Z 7.261, 265, *ger.* B 7.85; (read with) understand(ing) 7.34, **B** 5.422, 15.375; read out [official document] 2.71; read aloud, chant 13.126, 16.348, 17.120; (learn by) read(ing) 3.406 (2), 412, 496 (1), 10.238, 13.5, 15.269, 284, 17.194, 19.234, **B** 12.49, 15.445, A 11.221; instruct A 12.30 (2); interpret B 13.185; express 2.14, 9.82; declare (*or* ? perceive) 17.200 (1)), B 11.102; reckon 5.69, 7.40; advise 4.5, 13.206, 19.108, **B** 4.30, 7.182, 12.94; counsel 5.102, 6.291, 7.101, 9.332, 19.249, B 5.124, A 2.32; urge 1.170, 4.105, 5.125, 143, 8.283, B 10.266, A 12.30 (1); order, bid 7.119, 15.52, A 5.180

redy *a* ready 18.111; *and see* **aredy** *a*

redyly *av* quickly 4.184; clearly B 17.155; to be sure, indeed 6.91, 253, 286, Z 4.132

***redyng-kyng** *n* ? reed-thatcher, ? retainer who rides on errands 2.112c, 6.371

redon 5.69 = **reden** *v*

refte *p.t.* 3.326 *see* **reuen** *v*

refusen *v* reject 5.78; forsake 13.232; spurn 7.84; decline 16.189, 19.145; renounce 3.366, 21.371; refuse to accept 17.43, 47; refuse 13.142

registre *n* official record book (of accounts) 22.271, (*fig.*) B 5.271; historical account 11.276

registrer *n* registrar, book-keeper B 2.174, (*fig.*) 21.260

regnen *v* reign Pr 140, 4.171; hold sway 3.439, 16.57, 21.52, 22.64; prevail 9.256; predominate 1.116, 20.437; live, exist 10.24, 13.185, 16.46, 121, 20.236, B 2.54; flourish 14.173; be rife 21.421; extend 22.382

[^1]: *n*[^1] and *n*[^2] markers appear as superscript in source.

#**regrater** *n* retailer 3.113, 118, 6.232, B 3.90

#**regraterye** *n* retail-selling 3.82

rehercen, -sen *v* enumerate 17.25; explain (to) 13.224, B 10.293; set out 6.1; repeat 1.22, 6.164, **B** 11.391, 13.72; utter Pr 198; declare 4.150, 9.341, A 4.145; express 12.37

reygnen 14.173 = **regnen** *v*

reik *n* way Pr 216n

reyken *v* (*3 pl.* **reykes**) proceed Z 4.158

reyne 14.24, 15.269, 19.303, B 3.208 = **rayne** *n*

reisen *v* raise, conjure up A 11.161

reioysen *v* (*refl.*) find one's joy (in) 17.198

rek(e)nen (**rykenen**) *v* enumerate 1.22; name A 12.113; number 2.62, 17.25; give account (of) 11.302, 13.34, 16.52; ~ **wiþ** call to account 4.171, 12.67; settle accounts (*fig.*) 15.285, B 5.270

rekenyng(e) (**rykenynge**) *n* statement of account B 5.421; reckoning of what is due 7.40; (*fig.*) account (of conduct) 6.347, B 14.107

rekeueren *v* come back to life 21.161; win back (by force) 21.246, (by law) B 18.353

rekken 21.451, B 15.177 = **recchen** *v*

relacio(u)n *n* (grammatical) relationship 3.332, (*fig.*) 351; ~ **rect** direct / right relation(ship) 3.341, 343, 360, (*fig.*) 373

relatif *n* relative pronoun, ~ **rect** 3.354, ~ **indirect** 3.387

#**relen** *v* wind yarn (on a reel) 9.81

relees *n* release (from an obligation), (*fig.*) forgiveness of sin 8.99

relesen *v* remit (debt / obligation), (*fig.*) forgive (sin) 3.62

releuen *v* bring relief (to) 13.20; support 9.36; provide for (with alms) 13.69, 16.315; deliver 17.311; raise up again 20.143; restore 20.390

#**relyen** *v* rally 22.148

religio(u)n *n* (the) religious order(s) 3.202, 5.143, 9.36, 11.59, A 10.106; the way of life of a religious order 9.221, 10.88, 22.264, A 11.202, **B** 10.293, 13.286, 15.87, (*person.*) 5.150, **B** 6.151, 10.305; member(s) of (a) religious order(s) 5.143

religious *n* (*pl.*) members of (a) religious order(s) 5.147, 164, 9.221, 17.47, 206, 213, 22.59, **B** 4.125, 10.291, 15.307, 317, 341, Z Pr 57; (*sg., pl.* ~**es**) **B** 10.316, 12.35

religious *a* bound by rule [of a religious order] 4.116, B 4.120

relyk *n* relic 20.475, 21.426

reme B 8.106, 10.76 = **reume** *n*[1]

remembraunce *n* recollection [of past experience] 5.11

remen *v* cry out with grief, *pr.p.* 20.103

remenaunt *n* remaining portion 22.293, *in phr.* **residue and** ~ 8.109, B 5.460; rest, remaining group 12.50; remainder, difference 19.205; *in phr.* **al þe** ~ every other matter / everyone else 21.451

remyng *pr.p.* 20.103 *see* **remen** *v*

remissioun *n* release from debt, (*fig.*) forgiveness of sin 3.357, 8.99, A 11.285

ren *imper.* B 12.35 *see* **rennen** *v*

renable *a* eloquent B Pr 158

renaboute *a* run-about (*as nickname*) B 6.148; *and see* **rennare** *n*

renden *v* tear B 4.186; rip B Pr 199

rendren *v* recite 6.217, ? 17.320; read aloud, recite, ? expound 10.88c

reneyen (*p.p.*) 12.66, B 11.125, 126 *see* **renoyen** *v*

reng 10.24 = **renk** *n*

reninde *pr.p.* 3.333 *see* **rennen** *v*

renk *n* man 14.110, 20.2, 22.293, **B** 12.51, 14.105, A 4.134; person 10.24, *pl.* people 9.332, 20.300, = human beings 13.186, 191; *in phr.*, **no** ~ nobody B Pr 197

rennare *n* roamer, ~**aboute** A 11.202; **Rome** ~ pilgrim / one taking papal revenues to Rome 4.125

rennen *v* (*p.t. sg.* **ran** Pr 165 *etc*, **ern** 18.164, †**arne** B 16.136), *pl.* **ronne** Z Pr 57, *p.p.* **ronne** 10.88, *pr.p.* **reninde** 3.333, **rennynge** 20.167, **ernynge** 21.381) run (forth) Pr 165, ~ **awey** B Pr 166; run a course (of joust) (*fig.*) B 18.100; run free B 15.460; wander A 10.105, 110; enter, find refuge in 10.88; travel 2.62, 193, 16.349, Z Pr 57, ~ **at ones** travel along together 13.31; hasten (along) 6.1, 15.152, 18.290, 20.167, B 17.84; well up 18.164, 21.381; proceed 3.333

renoyen (**reneyen**) *v* abjure, forsake 12.61, 62; *p.p.a* disloyal, forsworn 12.66

renown *n* renown, **of** ~ of good repute Pr 176

rental *n* register of rent due, (*fig.*) record of sins [spiritual 'debts'] 8.99

rente *n* revenue from property 17.221, B 10.15, A 11.228, Z 2.100; income 16.72; property (yielding income) 3.82, 5.73, 14.184, 16.315, 316, B 15.320; rent (= payment) 9.73

renten *v* (*p.p.* **yrented**) endow with income-yielding property 9.36, 10.368

#**repaest** *n* meal 9.148

repen *v* (*p.t. sg.* **raap / rope**, *pl.* **repe / ropen**) reap 5.15, 6.270 (B 13.374)

repentaunce *n* repentance, sorrow for sin 19.282, 285, (*person.*) 6.1 *et p.*, ~ **of** repenting for 10.217

repenten *v* feel regret B 12.249; be (feel) sorry for / repent (of sin) 9.236, 19.202, 281, 21.444, 371, B 12.83, (*refl.*) 6.164, 7.149, B 5.259, **to** ~ to enable (him) to repent 10.52; have second thoughts 6.391

repreuen *v* reprove, censure 5.172; rebuke B 10.261; condemn 14.81; disapprove of 3.385; disprove 20.151; refute B 10.343

rerage B 5.242 = **(a)r(r)erage** *n*

re(s)ce(y)uen *v* receive, take 3.499, 5.69, 21.260, †B 6.148, A 8.60; accept 6.300; (be able to) hold 19.145, 154, B 17.191; regard (as) 17.201; admit 8.44; appoint 4.196

rescetour *n* harbourer [of criminals] 3.497

resemblen *v* be like B 16.214; compare 14.187

residue (resudue) *n* remains of dead man's estate (after discharge of dues) 12.218, *in phr.* ~ **and þe remenant** 8.109, B 20.293

resoen 17.264 = **reso(u)n** *n*

reso(u)n *n* the intellect B 15.65; (faculty of) reason [*esp.* as grasping the natural moral law] 3.144, 16.175, 186, A 10.57; **knowen / konnen** ~ possess understanding 19.227, 21.26, B 15.475; (common) logic / sense 12.155, 15.287, 16.252, 19.154, **B** 14.123, 17.39, 155, 18.152, A 8.153; **puyr** ~ sheer common sense 19.321, B 13.167; wisdom 3.324, 14.49; good / right judgement 5.5, 69, **aȝeynes** ~ in defiance of right reason 20.203; measure, moderation, **by** ~ moderately 13.191; **out(e) of** ~ immoderately, to excess 2.89, 6.434, 13.154, **B** 1.25, 5.36; means, action B 18.353; justice 3.385, 11.99, 17.213, 19.285, 21.83, 86, 90, 481, B 10.114 ~ **and / ne riht** 3.293, 14.148; *in phrr.* **aȝeynes alle** ~ 20.377; law, **ayeins** ~ against the law B 3.92; (principle of) equity, **puyr** ~ 15.289; (principle of) law B 18.340; right order 12.62, 16.212, 19.327, A 10.51; **by** ~ rightly, properly 1.90, B 17.255; order, **by** ~ in order 18.98, B 1.22; cause, **by** ~ **of** on account of 16.48, B 12.260; argument Pr 190, 11.38, 16.143, 17.264; case 2.50; (*person.*) [as reeve] 13.34, [as bishop] B 5.11, [as pope] 5.112, [as moral teacher] 1.50 *et p.*, [= (divine) principle of moderation (in nature)] 13.143 *et p.*

resonable *a* orderly and accurate 13.34; right 3.366; equitable 6.33; lawful, ~ **obedience** subjection to a religious rule B 13.286; eloquent Pr 176

resonabl(el)yche *av* in the right way, in accord with right reason 12.17, 15.282

resseyuen 6.300 = **re(s)ce(y)uen** *v*

rest *n* sleep Pr 214, 14.95, B Pr 197, *in phrr.* **a** ~ asleep 6.236; **bryngen to** ~ bring to a place of rest A 2.138; **gon to** ~ set 6.417; leisure, comfort 20.218, B 10.15; idleness 15.233; (eternal) rest (in heaven) 14.197, 16.154, **B** 7.78, 14.156; spiritual tranquillity 10.54, 20.223

resten *v* (*contr. pr.* **reste**) Pr 186, *p.t.* **reste** 13.146, B 18.6) rest, repose 4.16, 13.146, B 3.236; sleep Pr 186, 19.317; (*refl.*) lay (oneself) down 9.144, **B** Pr 7, 18.6; stop 11.108, 13.33, 20.167; cease 6.126; remain 4.103, 13.232, B 4.192; settle A 10.78

restitucio(u)n *n* reparation, amends [*esp.* by restoration of ill-gotten goods to rightful owner] 6.234, 237, 295, 19.202, 297

restituen *v* restore property (to its proper owner) 6.297, 343, 12.17; give back 10.54

restoren *v* refresh, reinvigorate 12.149

resudue 8.109 = **residue** *n*

resureccioun (resurexioun) *n* resurrection 12.116, 18.163,

20.267, 473; (feast of the) resurrection (of Christ) 20.471

ret *contr. pr.* 3.412, 13.5 *see* **reden** *v*

retenaunce *n* retinue 2.55

retoryk *n* poetic language 12.37

retribucioun *n* repayment, reward 3.337

returnen *v* come back B 17.120

reufulliche *av* sorrowfully 19.202; compasssionately B 14.152; pitiably B 12.47; piteously B 16.78; *and see* **rufol** *a*

*****reule** *n*¹ space between bed and wall 9.79

reule *n*² Rule [of a religious order] 5.143, 147, 157, 169, 9.221, 21.426, 22.247, 265, **B** 10.291, 12.36, 13.286, 15.87, 317, *in phrr.* **in** ~ in orderly condition A 10.51; **oute of** ~ in disregard of one's Rule 3.202; habitual practice B 10.98

re(u)len *v* (*p.t. 2 sg.* **reuledest** 13.186, *p.p.* **(y)ruled** 21.399) govern, rule Pr 216, 9.10, 20, B 18.397, ~ **alle / my / thy reumes(s)** 4.9, 180, 10.105, 11.214, 19.3, 21.481, *ger.* **ruylynge** government Pr 150; direct, guide 1.50, 13.182, 186, 14.36, 19.226; restrain 13.206, (*refl.*) control 13.191, 21.399

reume *n*¹ kingdom, realm Pr 192, 3.190, 203, 264, 293, 437, 4.9, 135, 180, 182, 5.74, 114, 125, 190, 11.59, 21.481, **B** 3.208, 298, 15.524, A 12.113, Z 4.130, 152; region 1.91, 3.254, 4.180, 182, 9.10, 10.105, 11.214, 17.259, 19.3

reume *n*² cold, catarrh 22.83

reuth *n* pity 1.170, 4.103, 7.149, 13.69, 16.22, **B** 5.478, 16.5, 18.91; a piteous thing 7.40, 9.82, 15.300, 16.16, 17.194; a pity B 14.127; a sad / regrettable thing 17.200, 259; compassion B 14.145, **of puyr** ~ simply through compassion 13.92; mercy 4.105, 108, 131, 6.422, 19.282, **B** 10.342, 14.168; sympathy 3.118; sorrow 6.286, **hauen** ~ feel sorry 22.193, **B** 15.11, 16.78

reuare *n* plunderer 13.57, B 14.182

reue *n* (manorial) reeve, bailiff 2.112, 180, 7.33, 11.302, 12.218, 21.463, 466, **B** 5.421, 10.471; (*fig.*) = (God's) agent 3.308, 21.259

reuel *n* festivity 7.101 (B 13.442), (a place of) revelry 22.181

reuelen *v* become wrinkled 10.268

reuen *v* (*p.t.* **refte** 3.326) seize by force (from) 18.122, B 16.89; take away 16.1; deprive (of) 3.226, 4.180, 20.299, 308; *and see* **to-** ~ *v*

reuerence *n* veneration B 12.119; sign of honour, obeisance 9.191, 16.46, 17.43

reuerencen (-sen) *v* (treat with) respect, honour 11.19, 16.48, 237, 17.201, 22.59; do reverence to 19.261, 20.248, 267, 473; regard highly B 12.259; pay homage to 21.73; reverently salute 18.243; courteously greet 13.247, 15.29, 20.175; bow / pay obeisance to 9.123, B 15.5

reuerentlich(e) *av* reverently 5.114; courteously 20.466; (*comp.*) ~**loker** with greater honour 8.44

reuers *n* opposite 12.212

reuesten *v* dress in ceremonial vestments, *p.p.* **yreuestede** 5.112

reward *n* regard, heed, **hauen / taken ~ at / of** take heed of 4.40, 19.249

rewarden *v* reward Pr 150, 14.148, 21.194; (*pr. p.*) pay 3.308; requite 5.32, 12.70; grant 14.148, B 3.318, 156; care for B 14.145, 168; watch over B 11.369

rewe *n* row (of houses) 3.107; *in phr.* **by ~** in order 1.22

rewele A 10.51, 11.205 = **reule** *n*

rewen *v* regret, rue B 16.142; have pity 6.321; (*in impers. constr.*) **bote hym rewe** without his feeling pity 20.438

rewful *a* compassionate B 14.148

rewfulliche B 14.152 = **reufulliche** *av*

rewlen 21.481, Z 4.130 = **reulen** *v*

rewlyche *a* wretched, miserable A 12.78

rewme 3.190, 293, 4.9, 21.481, A 12.113, Z 4.130, 152 = **reume** *n*[1]

ryalte (realte, reautee) *n* royal status, ? lordship 16.51; possession (of land) B 10.334 (A 11.228)

ryb *n* rib B 9.34, A 4.149

ryban *n* ribbon, border B 2.16, Z 2.17

rybande *p.p. a.* bordered A 2.13

rybaud *n* villain 10.217, 16.45, 18.169, 20.50; sinful wretch 7.149; foul-mouthed rascal 6.434

*rybauder *n* lewd jester 8.75

rybaud(r)(y)e *n* scurrility 6.434; obscenities, debauchery Pr 45; foolish jesting 11.199

#rybben *v* clean flax 9.81

rybibour *n* fiddle-player 6.370

riche[1] *n* kingdom B 14.179, **heuene ~ blisse** 12.160, 16.100

riche[2] *a* rich, wealthy 2.55, 82, 184, 4.47, 5.26, 6.33, 126, 7.98, 9.332, 10.167, 268, 11.109, 12.4, 25, 107, 228, 13.5, 57, 65, 97, 13.110, 182, 14.87, 95, 184, 15.9, 285, 308, 16.12, 21, 42, 356, 19.227, 229, 231, 22.39, 235, **B** 2.56, 9.174, 10.335, 342, 345, 11.196, 197, 198, 12.51, 74, 239, 14.105, 123, 127, 144, 145, 152, 156, 157, 163, 168, 15.176, 323, 331, 335 (2), 341, 342, **A** 3.272, 11.61, 231 *in phrr.* **riche ~** (the) very wealthy 11.49, 12.155, 14.173, 16.127, 20.218; precious, costly 15.233, 16.72, 351, 20.175, B 2.15, A 3.271, Z 2.16; luxurious 22.181; (*comp.*) potent, powerful 20.475; splendid 2.14, 22.181; prosperous 3.203, 11.214; fertile B 3.208, A 10.134; *a as n* rich man 10.264, 13.31, 95, 16.48, 52, 62, 19.249, **B** 10.98, 12.244, 249; the rich Pr 219, 9.129, 12.212, 13.79, 14.181, 16.237; rich people 5.182, 7.101, 9.101, 134, 191, 11.23, 70, 12.104, 134, 15.288, 16.8, 17.206, 19.244, B 4.40, 14.212, 15.335 (1), 339; *a. phr.* **pore and / or ~, ~ and / ne / or pore** = all people 4.26, 153, 8.111, 11.59, 13.182, 15.202,

16.47, 17.2, 199, **B** 11.207, 14.27, 73, 182, 212, A 10.117; *in phrr.* **for ~ or for ~** for poorer for richer A 2.59, **in ~ ant in ~** ? under all circumstances Z 2.67; **~ handes** capacity to give large bribes 3.118; **(þe) mene (and) (þe) ~** Pr 20, 219, **B** 2.56, 10.64

†richeles *n* incense 21.90

richeliche *av* splendidly 2.12

richen *v* become rich 3.82

richesse *n* riches, wealth 2.80, 3.324, 326, 12.145, 13.25, 69, 15.282, 16.1, 45, 46, 48, 51, 16.316, 17.198, 212, 19.235, 21.286, **B** 2.17, 10.15, 85, 334, 339, 11.318, 12.58, 244, A 11.266, *in phr.* **~ ope ~** wealth heaped upon wealth 12.232; opulence 2.16; (state of) affluence 16.57; (store of) valuable goods 14.184; (*pl.*) precious things, treasures 9.191, 12.249, 21.73, **B** 3.23, 90 (*sg. for pl.*), (*fig.*) treasure / wealth in heaven B 14.148

ryden *v* (*contr. pr.* **riht** Pr 186, **ryt** 4.25, B 4.14, *p.t.* **roed** 22.181, **rood** 4.14, 40, B 17.100, *pl.* **ryde(n)** 4.28, 13.154, B 4.30, *p.p.* **ryde** 5.157, B 11.337) ride (on horseback, mule) 6.126, 16.349, 19.79, 22.181, **B** 4.14, 30, 17.100, *in phrr.* **~ ful rapely** gallop 19.50, **~ softe** amble 4.54; ride along (road) 19.79, B 4.42; ride forth (on errand / expedition, to joust *etc*) 1.91, 3.269, 4.16, 34, 20.24, 21.246; ride to battle 5.74; (*fig.*) = use, be supported by 2.180, 184, 188, 194, 4.40, 54, B 4.33, 40, Z 4.131; move about Pr 186; copulate 13.154, B 11.337; *in phr.* **~ out of aray** go astray [= observe rule negligently] 5.157

rydere *n* rider on horseback B 10.305

ryflen 6.236, *ger.* B 5.234 = **ru(y)flen** *v*

rygebone 6.399 *see* **rug-** *n*

right B 3.239, Z 4.132, **~ (e)** 2.180, B 9.38 *etc*, Z 3.90, 4.24 *see* **riht(e)** *n, av*

riȝht(e) *n* 19.3, B 10.342, **riȝt** *a* 18.290 *see* **riht** *n, a*

riht 3 *pr. sg.* Pr 186 *see* **ryden** *v*

riht(e) (riȝt, right) *n* justice 11.27, 20.373, 439, 21.90, 353, *in phr.* **~ and / ne resoun** true justice 11.29, 19.3, 20.300, 395, 21.463, B 3.239, **resoun ne ~** 3.293, 14.158 (*and see* **resonable ne rect** 3.366); law 8.53, 17.42; judgement Z 4.132; rightful ownership 20.299, 308; just claim / (en)title(ment), right 3.367, 5.74, 16.99, 22.96; title B 10.342; claim, *in phr.* **þer beyre / oure bothe ~** the claim(s) of both of them / us 20.36, 371

riht *a* direct 19.79, B 4.42; right-(hand) 3.76; **~[name]** actual 6.232, proper 16.186; sound 3.326; very (same) 18.290, 19.50; true 11.294, 16.251

riht(e) *av* exactly, just, *in phrr.* **~as** just as 2.209 *et p.*, B 9.38; just like 5.112; **~ so** just so, exactly in that way 1.156 *et p.*; **~ thus** exactly as follows 6.422, 9.285; **~ with þat** immediately thereupon 4.196, 6.1, 62, 7.55, 13.247, 20.94, 471; right 11.168; very, extremely 2.180, 11.49, 12.141, 155, 14.173, 16.52, 21.8, 73, 194, Z 3.90; to any great degree 16.127, *in phrr:* **~**

nauht 5.82, 9.123, 14.87, 19.154, 21.451, ~ **saue** just except †21.371; thoroughly 3.354, 21.481; truly 6.91, 7.15, 17.194, 18.71; righteously 3. 324; completely 20.62, 103, 192, 412; straight, directly 7.198, B 4.14, *in phrr.* ~ **til / to** right (up) to 12.70, 15.284, 18.169, Z 4.24, straight (out) to 13.183, right (down) to 18.39, ~ **with** straight along with 15.152; *in cpd.* **anon** ~ immediately 4.150, 15.52

riht *contr. pr.* Pr 186 = **ryt**; *see* **ryden** *v*

rihtfo(e)l, **~ful(l)** *a* even-handed 15.291; just Pr 150, 17.213, 20.94; righteous, virtuous 4.153, 5.147, 6.33, 10.24 (*sup.*), 10.41, 17.34, 259; *a as n* the just man 10.38, 11.16; right-thinking people 4.151; in accordance with reason 3.373; proper 12.88n; authentic A 11.202

rihtful(l)ly(che) *av* justly 9.10; rightly B 4.172, Z 4.126; legitimately 12.62; virtuously 13.95; honestly 19.235, B 14.102; in the proper manner 1.50, 15.282

rihtfulnesse *n* (the cardinal virtue of) justice 21.83; divine justice 5.32

rihtwisnesse *n* justice 19.282, 297, (*person.*) 20.167, 175, 192, 203

rykenen 2.62, 4.171, 11.302, 13.34, (**rykenynge** *ger.* 6.347) *see* **rekenen** *v*, **rekenyng(e)** *ger.*

ryme *n* rhymed [*sc.* alliterative] verse 9.82; (*pl.*) verses, ballads 7.11

rynen 17.99, *p.t. subjv.* 5.164 *see* **r(a)ynen** *v*

ryng *n* (gold finger) ring Pr 73, 3.24, B 3.90, A 2.11

ryngen *v*[1] adorn with finger ring(s), *p.p.* **yrynged** 2.12

ryngen *v*[2] (*p.t. pl.* **rang**, **rongen**) ring bells 20.471, (B 18.427), 22.59, *ger.* ringing of bells 7.5

rype *a* ripe 18.42, 64, 128, 20.412n, B 6.293; *a as n* the ripe ones 18.107; ready 7.5

ripen *v* grow ripe 12.225, 234, 21.319

ripereue *n* guardian of crops [against thieves at harvest time] 5.15

rysen *v* (*p.t.* **ro(e)s** 6.236, 18.243, *pl.* **rysen** 6.382, *p.p.* **rysen** 9.147) get up 13.236, 15.27; get to one's feet 18.243; survive 19.69; rise (from bed) Pr 45, 6.235, 7.5, 9.79, 146, 147; rise (from dead) 9.338, B 15.594, 20.264, 21.146

risshe B 4.170, A 11.17 = **ru(s)che** *n*

ryt *contr. pr* 4.25, **B** Pr 171, 4.14 *see* **ryden** *v*

ryuer *n* river B 15.337

Robardus knaues *n* Robert's boys [*punning name for* marauding thieves] Pr 45; *and see* **Robert** (*Index*)

robbare *n* robber 11.261, 12.249, 13.57, **B** 4.128, 5.231, 462, 14.182

robben *v* rob 4.54, 9.180, 12.154, 20.299, 21.447, **B** 3.195, 17.90, 100, 18.339, *ger.* being robbed 16.138; despoil 10.196, B 16.89; steal from (by deceit) 11.19; alienate 16.1

robe *n* robe [long, loose outer garment] 15.203, 16.351, 356, B 2.15, A 3.271

roben *v* (provide with) clothe(s) 11.19, B 15.335, 339, A 2.13, Z 3.170, *ger.* clothing, dress 2.14; dress 10.1

roch(e) *n* rock 19.12, 20.62, 257

rodden *v* grow red, flush 15.109

rod(e) *n* cross [of Christ] 2.3, 10.116, 16.22, 17.198, 201, 20.51, 55, 259, 21.325, 22.43, B 18.84; crucifix [in church] 7.68, 20.267, B 5.103, ~ **of Bromholm** B 5.227, ~ **of Chestre** B 5.460, A 7.92, ~ **of Lukes** 8.109; cross-symbol [on coin] 17.206

rody *a* red 15.109

roen *p.t.* 15.269 *see* **r(a)ynen** *v*

roep *n* cord 18.156

roes *p.t.* 6.236 *see* **rysen** *v*

roggen *v* shake B 16.78

roilen *v* stray about idly A 11.209, †B 10.297

#roynous *a* rough, scaly 22.83

rokken *v* rock 9.79, B 15.11

rolle *n* roll, list [of burgesses] 3.111; account roll 21.466

rollen *v* record B 5.271

Romaynes *n.pl.* the Romans 17.281 (B 15.530)

romber A 10.105 = **romere** *n*

rombide *p.t.* A 4.30 *see* **romen** *v*

Rome-rennare *n* traveller to the papal court 4.125

romede *p.t.* 7.7 *see* **romien** *v*

romen *v* walk 9.147, 15.27, 28, 29, 18.145, B 15.594; go forth Pr 186, A 4.30; travel, journey (*fig.*) 5.11, 6.330, 22.212; wander about 10.1; wander off 12.65; go away 12.50

#romere *n* wanderer **B** 4.120, 10.305, A 10.105

romien *v* (*p.t.* **romede**) roar 7.7

ronde *n* round slice 9.148

rong *n* rung (*fig.*) 18.44

rongen *p.t.pl.* 22.59, B 18.427 *see* **ryngen** *v*[2]

ronne *p.t. pl.* Z Pr 57, *p.p.* 10.88 *see* **rennen** *v*

rood *p.t.* 4.14, B 17.100 *see* **ryden** *v*

roode B 5.103 *et p.* = **rod(e)** *n*

roof *n* roof (*fig.*) 21.329

roon *p.t.* B 14.66 *see* **r(a)ynen** *v*

roos *p.t.* 18.243, B 5.230 *see* **rysen** *v*

roost *n* roast-meat Pr 231

roote B 12.58, 71, 14.94, 15.65, 16.22 *see* **rote** *n*

rope(n) *p.t. sg.*, *pl.* B 13.374 *see* **repen** *v*

ropere *n* rope-maker / seller 6.371, 386

rose *n* rose 15.109, A 10.123

rosten *v refl.* toast oneself 9.144

rote *n* root 8.64, A 10.124; (edible) root 15.244; (*fig.*) 16.251, 22.54, B 14.94; basis, origin 20.322, B 12.58, 71, A 10.134; essential nature B 15.65

*rotey *n* rutting, *in cpd.* ~ **tyme** time of rutting B 11.337

*roteyen *v* rut 13.146

roten[1] A 10.78 *see* **rot(h)en** *v*

roten[2] 13.21 = **rot(y)en** *v*

roten, **roton** *a* rotted, decayed **B** 15.101, 16.252

rot(h)en *v* (*refl.*) root, settle oneself firmly in (*fig.*) 2.55; take root in (*fig.*) A 10.78

rot(y)en *v* (become) rot(ten) 12.225, 18.60; decay 5.150; languish 13.21; perish 3.357, B 10.114

rotten *v* (*p.t.* **rotte, rutte**) snore 7.7; sleep 14.95, B 18.6

rouen 20.126 *see* **rowen** *v*[2]

rouȝ *a* rough, thorny A 10.124

roumen *v* leave clear Pr 181, 189

rounen *v* whisper 4.14; consult, 4.25, 6.382

rousty *a* filthy 8.75

route *n* pack Pr 165, 192, 198, 214; retinue 2.62; body Z Pr 57; crew B 18.405

routen *v* settle in A 10.78

rowen *v*[1] row (*fig.*) 10.52

rowen *v*[2] dawn 1.113, 20.126

rownd *a* sonorous (*?with pun on* 'round-shaped') 6.399

roxlen *v* stretch 7.7, B 5.392 (**raxed**)

rubben *v* rub (*p.t. or p.p.*) B 13.100

rub(i)e *n* ruby 2.13, 3.24

ruche 12.198 = **ru(s)che** *n*

rude *a* ignorant, uneducated B 15.475; untrained B 15.460; foolish 13.229

ruet *n* horn 6.399

rufol *a* wretched 6.237; compassionate B 14.148

rufulliche B 16.78 = **reufulliche** *av*

rug(ge) (ryge) *n* back 9.144, 16.54, 21.288; ~ **bone** backbone 6.399

#ruyflare *n* robber 4.125, 6.315

#r(u)yflen *v* rob, plunder 4.54; despoil (of) 10.196, 19.92; rifle 6.236, *ger.* B 5.234

ruylen 9.10, *ger.* Pr 150 = **reulen** *v*

rule B 10.98, 291, 12.36, 13.286, 15.87, 317, **rulen** B 11.369, 18.397 *see* **reule** *n*, **reulen** *v*

ru(s)che *n* rush-stalk 9.81; (*fig.*) = worthless object, *in phrr.* **counten nat a** ~ **(of)** consider of no value at all 3.178, 12.198, 13.238, **worþ (of) a** ~ worth (of) anything B 4.170, A 11.17

russet *n* coarse woollen cloth 10.1, 16.298, 343

ruþe B 5.478, 10.342, 14.127, 145, 15.11, 16.5, 78, 18.91 *see* **reuth** *n*

rutte *p.t.* B 18.6 *see* **rotten** *v*

saaf B 7.51, 8.49, 10.345, 12.166 = **sa(e)f** *a*

sacrefice *n* sacrifice 18.249, 264; devotional offering Pr 98, 119

sacreficen *v* offer sacrifice 14.61

sad(de) *a as n* fixed, firm base 3.334; constant (*comp.*) 11.296; steadfast (in virtue) 5.90, 10.31, (*sup.*) 10.49; grave 10.118; serious 17.264; *n* ~**nesse** firm trust B 7.151

sad *av*, (*comp.*) **saddere** more soundly B 5.4

sadel *n* saddle 4.20

sadelen *v* (put a) saddle (on) B 2.170, **lat** ~ **hem** let them be saddled B 2.175

saet *p.t.* 6.361, 15.108, 18.241, 22.199 *see* **sitten** *v*

sa(e)f *a* safe / free from danger 10.38, 40, 14.112, **B** 7.51, 8.49, 12.166, A 8.38; saved (from damnation) 14.191, 206, 17.313, B 10.345

safly *av* safely 17.63

sage *a* wise 3.121, 8.243, 11.211; *in phr.* **fo(e)l** ~ wise fool [= licensed jester] 7.82, 103

say *1 pr. sg.* 8.307, A 11.13, *imper.* 7.229, 12.39 *see* **seggen** *v*

say(h) *p.t.* Pr 5, 13, 15, 221, 232, 2.9, 5.124, 8.281, 11.51, 22.199, **saiȝ** A 5.22 *see* **sen** *v*

said *p.t.* 10.18, 12.206, 14.47, 20.302, **~e** Pr 68 *et p.*, **sayede** 10.223, *pl.* **sayden** 3.17, **saidest** 14.103, **saye** *inf.* 21.243, **sayn** *inf.* Pr 203, **sayen** *pr.pl.* 9.131 *see* **seggen** *v*

saylen *v* dance 15.209

sayn Pr 203 = **seggen** *v*

saynt (seynt) *n* the just [of the OT] 7.132; saint [canonised Christian in heaven] Pr 48, 3.98, 7.31, 78, 113, 153, 240, 11.13, 271, 12.134, 173, 14.136, 16.346, 17.270, **B** 3.235, 4.39, 7.36, 85, 11.244, 14.155, 15.269; (*as title*) ~ **Austin** 16.151, ~ **Aueroy** 15.100, ~ **Beneyt** B 4.121, ~ **Bernard** 16.220, ~ **Fraunceis** B 15.231, ~ **Gregori** 12.79, **B** 5.164, 11.156, 228, ~ **Iame(s)** 1.180, ~ **Io(ha)n** [the Evangelist] 7.100, 12.100, 14.136, **B** 11.226, [the Baptist] 11.258, 18.114, 268, 20.367, ~ **Luke** 1.87, 17.235, ~ **Marie** [the Blessed Virgin] 7.137, 12.135, 19.125, ~ **Mihel** [the Archangel] 9.37, ~ **Paul** 10.89, 11.56, ~ **Peter** B 10.442, ~ **Thomas** 7.201, ~ **Treuthe** 5.198; (= *place*) ~ **Marye** [church] Z 2.100, ~ **Petres churche** B 7.173, ~ **Poules** [cathedral] 11.56, B 10.46, Z 2.80; [*meton. for* shrine of saint] 7.174, **B** Pr 50, 12.39, ~ **Iame(s)** Pr 48, 5.197, 4.122, 5.197, **~es of Rome** Pr 48, 5.197; (*in assev.*) 3.141, 8.1, 54, 297, **B** 6.3, 24, 55, 4.188, A 7.3, Z 4.152

saynt *a* holy 1.80, 11.204, (*as title*) ~ **Spirit** the Holy Spirit of God 11.153, 14.27, 47, 18.72, 232, 19.162, 167, 175, 187

sayst(e) *2 sg. pr.* 6.290, 8.237, 298, 20.466 *see* **seggen** *v*

sayth *3 sg. pr.* 1.39 *et p.*; *see* **seggen** *v*

sak *n* sack (for grain) 8.8

sake *n* sake, *in phr.* **for the** ~ **of, for** ~**(s)** ~ for the good / benefit of 2.197, 11.144, 16.364, 17.231, 20.408, **B** 5.489, 6.102, 16.162; out of regard / consideration for Pr 138, 4.99, 9.133, **B** 9.90, 15.91; out of love for 12.206, 14.5, 18.252, **B** 10.253, 11.195, 12.92, 14.321; because / on account of 6.320, 20.357, **B** 3.189, 15.521, ? Z 4.100

#salarie, salerie *n* salary †3.272, 7.39; wage B 14.142

salme B 3.248 = **psalm** *n*

salt *n* salt B 15.428, 431, (*fig.*) 430, 441

salt(e) *a* salt 15.51; salted 8.307

saluacio(u)n B 15.497, A 11.282 = **sauacio(u)n** *n*

salue *n* medicinal ointment **B** 13.195, 249, 17.76; healing remedy 22.170, *(fig.)* 1.146, 9.263, 12.57, 15.226, 22.307, 337, 373, B 17.120; *and see* **saue** *n*

saluen *v* apply medicinal ointment to, *(fig.)* 22.306; treat 22.348; heal spiritually **B** 10.270, 11.217, 16.109

Samarita(e)n *n* Samaritan 19.49 *et p.*, 20.8

same *prn* the same one, he 10.59; him B 9.198; it 3.58; that 8.243; the same thing Pr 229, 3.30, 4.87, 9.187; the same (text) B 10.194; *(with avl. sense)* the ~ likewise 3.27, 11.24, 183, 13.111, 15.245, **B** 5.39, 6.234, 9.176, Z Pr 56

same *a* same, identical 1.172, 12.184, 19.149, 20.385, 22.224, **B** 7.63, 10.110, A 11.69

#**sam-rede** *a* half-red 8.310

sand 21.78 = **so(e)nd** *n*

sandel B 6.11 = **sendel** *n*

sang *p.t.* 21.212 *see* **singen** *v*

sank *p.t.* 20.69 *see* **sinken** *v*

sannure *comp.* Z 7.165 = **sonner**; *see* **sone** *av*

saphire *n* sapphire B 2.13

#**Sapience** *n* the OT wisdom writings [the book(s) of Proverbs, Wisdom *etc*] 3.484, 494, 11.117, 211, B 3.345, 6.234, A 8.46; (the) wisdom [*sc.* in these books] B 9.94; spiritual wisdom, knowledge B 12.57

sarmon *n* discourse 3.121, 11.291, 14.200; sermon 12.47, A 11.274; preaching 5.200, 7.88 (B 13.429); sermon-text A 11.245

Sar(e)sin(e), Sarrasyn *n* non-believer [in Christianity], Moslem 3.480, 14.200, 17.132, 150, 151, 156, 184, 240, 252, 307, 313, 315, **B** 13.210, 15.389, 392, 397, 497; pagan 12.56, 89, 17.123, **B** 10.346, 11.156, 164

sarrore *comp. av* more sorely 15.286 *(and see* **sore** *av)*

sat *p.t.* Pr 114 *etc; see* **sitten** *v*

satisfaccio(u)n *n* satisfaction [penitential reparation enjoined after confession] 16.27, 19.298, B 14.21, 94

Saturday *n* Saturday 5.116, 6.173, 417, B 13.154, þe ~ on Saturdays B 5.73

sauce *n* sauce *(fig.)* 8.273, 15.49

saufte *n* (spiritual) safety B 7.36

sauȝ *p.t.* **B** 2.17, 5.9, A Pr 90 = **say(h)**; *see* **seen** *v*

sauhtenen *v* be reconciled 4.2

#**saulee** *n* food, (satisfying) meal B 16.11

saumplare *n* exemplar, *(fig.)* = instructor 14.47

*****saunbure** *n* saddle, ? litter 2.178

saunȝ *prep.* without B 13.286

saut B 20.217, 301 = **sawt** *n*

sauten *v* leap B 13.234

sauter *n* Psalter, Book of Psalms 3.287, 7.92, 8.259, 10.165, 213, 11.23, 51, 12.28, 13.122, 14.116, 15.310, **B** 2.38, 3.234, 237, 248, 7.40, 51, 123, 10.26, 284, 11.94, 278, 284, 12.13, 14.93, **A** 3.221, 8.46, 10.86, 11.192; (copy of) psalter 3.464, 5.47, B 12.16, ~ **yglosed** glossed (copy of the) Psalter 6.301, 11.117

sautrien *v* play the psaltery 15.209

sauacioun *n* salvation 3.352, 12.83, 17.119, **B** 5.125,

17.32, *in phr.* **in** ~ **of** for the salvation of 5.198, 17.274, for the protection of B 15.522

saue[1] 12.57 = **salue** *n*

saue[2] *prep.* except 6.240, 13.181, 21.191, 376, 22.61, 151, 267, B 13.125, Z 2.214; except (...) for 2.250, 8.71, 12.29, 13.153, 15.134, 153, 19.93, 21.370, 371, 22.321, **B** 13.236, 247, 14.330, 17.101, A 10.35; *(as conj.)* except B 16.113; except that 9.112, 21.439; unless †21.408n, B 15.127

sauen *v* save (= bring safety to) 3.233; deliver, rescue 7.255, 10.235, 11.241, 244, 12.84, 87, 89, 14.127, 130, 18.269, 20.153, **B** 4.31, 5.57, 10.236, 11.156, 164, 12.77, 82, 13.446; save (from damnation), redeem 1.80, 6.332, 7.235, 9.328, 11.255, 258, 296, 14.12, 53, 77, 101, 141, 195, 201, 16.98, 17.123, 265, 18.135, 19.32, 35, 280, 20.194, 221, 244, 21.409, **B** 2.38, 10.347, 357, 475, 11.217, 12.31, 82, 13.130, 407, 15.389, 17.123, 18.139, 305, 329, A 5.104; redeem (by mainprise / ransom) 20.185; *in phr.* ~ **with** save ...with 17.121; *(in assev.)* 21.452, B 4.144; promise salvation to **B** 7.40, 11.226; spare 3.408; protect 7.234, 9.314, 10.59, 149, 11.306, 14.163, 19.21, 21.22, **B** 1.23, 3.197, 16.39, 245, A 7.127; defend 20.288, 21.432, 22.214; preserve 7.88, 15.237, 21.435, 22.11, 22, **B** 15.428, 441, 16.104; maintain 22.128; safeguard 20.371; keep safe 9.270, **B** Pr 115, 3.292, 10.405, **A** 10.77, 12.115; save (= reserve) 21.281; [money] 9.29; heal, cure 17.299, 300, 18.152, 153, 19.86

saueour, sauyour *n* deliverer 18.152; saviour from (the penalty of) sin 7.120, 144, 12.138, B 16.143; *(as title of Christ)* **Oure** ~ 12.138, 16.98, A 3.64, *(as title of God)* 17.183, **B** 9.127, 10.107, 15.156

sauer(y)en *v* be to one's taste 10.108, ~ **with** please... with 8.273

saw *p.t.* 5.111, 7.179, 10.73, 18.289, A 12.20, 107 *see* **sen** *v*

sawe *n* speech, words 10.108, 213, A 12.107; assertion, ? opinion 20.151, A 4.144; saying, proverb B 7.138, 9.94, 10.16, A 11.274

sawt *n* assault 22.217, 301

scabbe *n* blister (on scalp) 22.83

scalle *n* scabby disease (of scalp) B 20.83

scapen B 3.57 = **askapen** *v*

scarlet *n* rich cloth [*usu.* dyed scarlet] 16.299, **B** 2.15, 14.19

sc(h)athe *n* injury 4.75, 92; wrong 3.61; harm B 15.59, A 12.17

schaef 8.349 = **sh(e)ef** *n*

schal *1 pr. sg. 1* 11.183, 15.93, 22.363, **Z** Pr 60, 3.152, 4.130, 134, 5.41, 7.198, 272, 8.49, 70 = **shal**; *see* **shollen** *v*

schalke *n* man 10.160

schalt *2 pr. sg.* **Z** 2.97, 3.122, 4.131, 132 = **shalt**; *see* **shollen** *v*

schapen Z 3.166, 7.276 = **shapen** *v*

scharp 22.307 = **sharp** *a*
schast Z 1.104 = **chast** *a*
schat *2 pr. sg.* **Z** 6.48, 7.238 = **shalt**; *see* **shollen** *v*
schathe 4.75 = **sc(h)athe** *n*
sche 6.222, 233, Z Pr 103 *etc* = **she** *prn*
schent *p.t.* Z 4.152 *see* **shenden** *v*
scheryue Z 2.189 *etc* = **shyreue** *n*
schewen Z Pr 70 *etc* = **shewen** *v*
*****schingled** *a* clinker-built [with over-lapping oak tiles] 10.235
Schyr Thorsday *n. phr.* Thursday of Holy Week Z 8.76
schyres Z 2.189 *see* **shire** *n*
s(c)holde *p.t.* 15.204, 19.293, **B** 2.170, **Z** 5.99, 7.270, 8.26 *see* **shollen** *v*[1]
schop *p.t.* 22.307 = **shop**; *see* **shapen** *v*
schoppen 14.68 *see* **choppen** *v*
#**schoriar** *n* prop, support 18.20
schrewe 11.26, **Z** 7.31, 8.76 = **sh(e)rewe** *n*
schryuen Z 3.152, A 12.14 = **shryuen** *v*
schullen **Z** 2.146, 8.37 = **shollen** *v*
schupestare *n* dressmaker 6.75
schutten Z 6.88 = **shetten** *v*
science *n* knowledge B 15.62; wisdom B 17.172; learning 14.65; branch of knowledge / learning 11.131, 12.95, 14.77, 81, 16.208, **B** 10.191, 208, 212, 216, Z 7.260; knowledge (of different kinds of learning) 16.225; kind of knowledge 14.76, 16.222, **B** 11.166, 13.125; skill 10.209
sclayre *n* veil 8.5
sclaundre, sklaundre *n* slander, calumny 2.86; harm to (one's) reputation 3.61, **fel... to** ~ became only a source of disgrace (for) B 12.46; disgrace, scandal A 12.17
scoffen *v* scoff, deride, *ger.* derision B 13.277
scolden *v* be abusive B 2.82
scole *n* school B 7.31, A 10.84; university 5.153, 155, 15.130, 22.273; *in phr.* **to** ~ at school 9.35, at university 5.36, 22.296, to learn B 10.170; place of learning 13.169, 22.251, *(fig.)* A 11.145
scolere *n* schoolboy A 10.84; student B 7.31
scollen Z 1.66 = **shollen** *v*
score *n* twenty 3.158; *in cpds.* (= a considerable number (of)), **fyue** ~ B 1.101, **sixe** ~ 3.182, **ten** ~ 11.128, **many** ~ **thousand** 19.22
scorn *n* scorn, contempt B 10.303, *in phrr.* **laughe to** ~ B 15.172, A 4.137, **likene to** mock / mimic derisively 16.308
scornare *n* contemptuous mocker 6.25, 21.285
scornen *v* speak scornfully B 10.331; mock 2.86, *ger.* mockery B 13.277; deride 6.22, 11.162, 13.130
scorpioun *n* scorpion 20.156
scourge *n* whip B 13.67
screueyn *n* scribe, copyist 11.96, B 10.331
scribe *n (pl.* **scribz**) interpreter of the Jewish Law 17.252, 20.26, B 15.389, 604

scrippe *n* bag [for seed] 8.60; pilgrim's satchel 7.179
scripture *n* sacred scripture, the Bible *(person.)* 11.100 *et p.*; written authority 14.192
scryueyn B 10.331 = **screueyn** *n*
se(e) *n* sea 13.135, 173, 17.91, 20.255, 21.78, B 5.284, A 12.115; *in phr.* **ouer** ~ across the sea 4.126 (B 13.392), 6.278
se Pr 207 *et p.*; *see* **sen** *v*
seal 9.27, 138 = **sel** *n*
secatour (secu-, seke-, execu-) *n* executor [of a will] 2.189, 6.254, 16.277, 22.291, **B** 5.262, 12.257, 15.248
seche Z Pr 33 = **suche** *a*
sechen, seken *v* (*p.t.* **sou(g)hte** 3.165, *p.p.* **souht(e)** 4.66, **(y)sou3t** B Pr 50, 5.531) look for 3.352, 9.312, 10.2, 18.268c, 19.7, 21.164, 22.383, B 16.249, ~ **after** 14.156, B 16.178; look, seek **B** 12.39, 16.171, A 10.99, ~ **and** ~ keep looking 19.304; search 3.165, 16.293; reach, penetrate B 14.6; look up [text] 3.494, B 10.327, A 11.55; appeal to 4.66; try to find A 9.53; seek / find out 16.329, **B** 14.94, 16.108, A 11.190; go to see 9.315; go on pilgrimage to Pr 48, 4.122, 5.197, 198, 7.168, 174, B Pr 50, Z 6.3; travel 17.169
seco(u)nd(e) *num. a* second 18.40, 21.87, 282, ~ **table** lower table [in hall] 9.252; *as n* 1.23, 11.183, 18.194
secret(e) *a* private, personal, ~ **seal** privy seal 3.182, *(fig.)* 9.27, 138
secte *n* class 12.134; class of people 15.13, 80, **in that** ~ as one of that class of people 16.98; bodily form, **in oure** ~ in our likeness 7.129, 136, 140; in human flesh B 5.491; (religious) order 6.38, 16.293, 355
seculer *a* lay 10.286, *a as n* lay person B 9.179
secutour 22.291, B 15.132 = **secatour** *n*
sed 12.190, 21.311, 345, A 10.159, Z 7.59 *see* **seed** *n*
seden *v* beget offspring 10.254
see 4.126, 6.278, 13.173, B 5.284 = **se(e)** *n*
see 2.45, 4.133, 18.276, 22.178, B 2.71 *etc*; *see* **sen** *v*
seed *n* seed, grain 7.186, 12.181, 184, 188, 190, 17.88, 91, 101, Z 7.59, *in cpds.* **fenkel** ~ 6.359, **lek-, lente** ~, **lyn** ~ 12.192; *(fig.)* (spiritual) seed [virtue] 21.277, 282, 283, 290, 291, 299, 300, 311, 345, 409; offspring †3.429, 18.226, **B** 3.277, 10.110, (= creature made in God's image) B 10.120, 127, *in phrr.* **Caymes** ~ 10.223, ~ ~ **his brother** his brother Cain's progeny 10.254, **suster** ~ sister's children A 10.159
seeknesse 19.318, 21.292 = **sykenesse** *n*
seel Pr 77 *etc*; *see* **sel** *n*
seem *n* horse-load (of) 3.42
seemely 3.112 = **semely(che)** *a*
seen *pr. pl.* 12.29, 14.116, 18.226, B 1.51, *inf.* B 18.250; **seest** *2 pr.sg.* 10.159, 16.301, 19.178, **B** 10. 259, 12.176, ~**ow** 1.5; *see* **sen** *v*
seende *imp.* 22.386 *see* **senden** *v*
seene B 1.149 = **sene** *a*
seet(e) *p.t.* 8.122, B 20.199, *p.t.subjv.* 6.99; *see* **sitt(i)en** *v*

seeth *3 pr. sg.* 1.39 *see* **sen** *v*

seg *pr. sg.* Z 4.59 *see* **seggen** *v*

sege *n* ? company of besiegers, ? town 22.311c, 314

seg(g)(e) *n* man 12.153, 163, 13.196, 15.125, **B** 5.387, 16.178, 17.62, †90, A 12.54, *pl.* men B Pr 160; person 3.67, *pl.* people 2.172, 5.119; anyone B 11.243

seggen, sey(e)n, seiȝen, siggen *v* (*1 pr.sg.* **segge** 5.48, **sey(e)** Pr 118, 207, **seiȝe** A 1.180, **syg(ge)** 6.54, 11.11, *2* **sayst** 6.290, **seist** B 6.229, *3* **sayth** 1.39, **seyt** Z 7.267, **seyth** 19.23, B 1.41, **seiþ** B 3.248, A 10.86, *pl. 1 & 2* **seggeth** 15.265, 13.242, *2* **seyn** 11.201; *pr.p.* **segg-yng** 5.107, *ger.* B 8.109, A 9.102, *p.t. sg. 1, 3* **say(e)d(e)** Pr 68, 1.11, 10.18, 223, *2* **saidest** 14.103, **seydest** 7.144, Z 3.122, *pl.* **sayden** 3.17, **seyden** 2.181, *p.p.* **ysaide** 15.24, 125, **seid** B 13.20) (*selected refs.*) say Pr 96, 147 *et p.*; express, utter (aloud) Pr 211, 9.131, 12.27, 13.11, **B** 5.608, 16.214; state, declare Pr 68, 3.428, 6.54, 7.192, 301, 9.257, 313, 12.47, 206, 13.224, 15.140, 19.21, 20.42, 358, 21.243, **B** Pr 50, 13.307, 15.382; maintain, express (the belief that), **men saith** people say 11.271; assert, affirm Pr 118, 207, 3.287, 4.15 (2), 134, 6.290, 7.92, 8.237, 241, 346, 10.23, 204, 11.11, 279, 12.16, 100, 14.82, 165, 15.21, 16.8, 17.304, 18.148, 256, 19.5, 20.28, 70, 22.224, **B** 10.365, 13.339, 15.267, 428, 598, 16.98, 130; say, recite 19.26, [prayer, service] 5.107, 6.283, 13.126, 15.265, 17.117, **B** 5.7, 12.16, 15.125, 127, 193; speak 1.144, 2.200, 3.435, 8.298, 11.4, 14.204, 15.24, 125, 18.162, 20.49, B 14.181, A 12.16; reply 1.44, 20.66, 360; tell 1.39, 4.15 (1), 5.124, 9.307, 10.30, 11.115, 18.18, 19.81, Z 2.183; ~ **so(e)th** speak truly 2.26, 4.64, 12.42, 14.103, 19.108, 20.466, B Pr 52, ~ **treuthe** 4.151; speak about, give (exact) account of 4.133, **B** 5.10, 15.296, 17.30, Z Pr 5; **heren** ~ hear tell / reported B 16.249; explain 10.30; teach (authoritatively) 14.200, **B** 10.397, 13.118, *with cited source*: **saith the Boek** 10.23, B 11.275; ~ **Dauid** 13.122; ~ **Piers þe Plowman** B 13.130; ~ **þe Sauter** 11.51, B 3.248; ~ **Seynt Bernard** 16.220; **Seneca** B 14.306; **þe Gospel saith** 12.102; **Salamon sayth** 3.484; direct 11.137; command 12.34, 17.192, 18.261 (1, 2), B 15.497; inform (us) 11.152, B 10.191; write 3.484, 11.289, 291, 16.227, 20.358; (*in cpd. names*) **Say-soth...** speak truly 7.229; **Sey-wel** speak virtuously 10.146; *in phrr.* **as who seiþ** as if to say B 15.307; **to** ~ to speak of (= be mentioned) 13.174, B 17.23

seying *ger.* words, speech B 8.109

sey *p.t. sg.* Pr 109 *etc* [7.137, 11.152, 12.83, 13.141, 143, 14.165] Z Pr 5, *pl.* 12.134 *etc* [18.148, 19.49, Z 2.45], **ysey** 2.67, *p.p.* 13.242, (**ysey**) 16.343; **seye** *p.t.* B 8.75, A 12.5, **seyen** *p.p.* Pr 177, 4.133, 11.237, B 11.244, 15.220; **seigh** *p.t.* Pr 17, B 17.107; **seyȝe** *p.t. (subj.)* B 5.85; **seiȝe** *p.p.* A 3.57, 11.221; **seiȝen** *p.t. pl.* B 12.132, 15.588, 16.116, *p.p.* B 10.68; **seyh** *p.t.* 2.200 *etc* (**seyhe** 13.135); **(y)sey(e)n** *p.p.* 3.104, B 14.155 *see* **sen** *v*

seide *p.t.* (= **say(e)d(e)**) Pr 96 *et p.*; **seyen** *inf.* 4.133, 12.27, B 14.279, *pr. pl* 17.117, 307, B 15.140 *see* **seggen** *v*

sey(h)(e) *p.t.* 2.200, 13.135 *et p.*; *see* **sen** *v*

seillen *v* glide (*lit.* sail), *ger.* B 18.306

seyn[1] *pr. pl.* 4.154, *p.p.* 3.104, *see* **sen** *v*

seyn[2] *inf.* 18.261, 19.26, *pr. pl.* 11.201, **B** 6.129, 15.173, 16.249 *see* **seggen** *v*

seynien *v* (*refl.*) bless oneself (with sign of cross) 7.62

seynewrye Z 2.73 = **signiure** *n*

seynt Pr 48 *et p.*; 11.204, B 1.84 *see* **saynt** *n, a*

seyntwarie *n* sanctuary, (*meton.*) the church 5.79

seke 22.324, A 7.239, 11.190 = **syk(e)** *a*

seken *v* Pr 48, 10.2, 18.268, 19.7, 21.164, 22.383, **B** 10.94, 327, 12.39, 14.6, 94, 16.178, A 11.55, 190 *see* **sechen, seken** *v*

sek(e)nes(se) 7.28, 64, 8.134, 270, 16.309, 19.322 = **syk(e)nes(se)** *n*

sekte 6.38, 7.136, 140, 16.355, 293 = **secte** *n*

sel *n* seal [authenticating device impressed on wax]: [bishop's] Pr 67, 77, 2.231, [pope's] **B** 13.249, [king's privy] 3.182, (*fig.*) [God's] 9.27, 138, [Christ's] 19.7, [merchant's] 13.88, [official] 2.156

selcouth(e) *a* wonderful, extraordinary Pr 5, 12.47, 13.177; strange 17.300; *as n* marvel 13.174; strange occurrence / thing 14.75

selde(n), seldom *av* seldom, rarely Pr 22, 2.26, 127, 6.93, 252, 7.20, 11.237, 301, 305, 16.4, 122, 125, 127, 355, 360, 18.66, 19.283, **B** 7.138, 9.152, 10.397, 14.2, 155, 178, 15.275, 282, A 10.104, 108; at infrequent intervals 17.10

selen *v* (set a) seal (on) 3.184, Z 2.39; certify as accurate (with a mark) 3.88; close up with a seal (*fig.*) 4.189

self B 11.249 = **sulue(n)** *a*

selk(e) *n* silken cloth Pr 159, 8.10, B 15.220; *a* silken 3.447, (~**en**) Z Pr 65

selle *n* (hermit's) cell, hut Pr 30, 17.7, 10, A 7.133

sellen 3.120, **B** 3.196, 7.22, 11.275, Z 3.149 *see* **sullen** *v*

seller B 3.88, A 2.44, 3.77 *see* **suller** *n*

selli *n* remarkable thing Pr 5

selue B 1.204, 5.488, 7.128; ~**n** A 1.110, 10.86 *see* **sulue(n)** *a*

seluer (syluer, suluer) *n* silver Pr 183, 3.23, **B** 2.175, 15.7, 123; (silver) money Pr 79, 84, 90, 1.63, 100, 2.156, 3.116, 4.51, 52, 126, 127, 191, 6.254, 13.100, 104, 16.90, 108, 363, 21.374, 22.222, 368, **B** 2.68, 3.207, 4.31, 35, 5.94, 6.192, 9.91, 10.336, 359, 11.74, 173, 222, 275, 281, 15.127, 131, 16.143 17.76, Z 3.171; wealth 16.237; *in phr.* **at** ~**es preyere** as a bribe 2.68

seluerles *a* without money 9.119

semblable *a* like, similar to 3.334, 10.158, 16.112, 18.212, B 10.365; resembling 20.8

semblant *n* countenance 10.118

semblaunce *n* form, likeness B 18.287

semble A Pr 97 = **assemblee** *n*

semely(che) *a* excellent 15.59; fitting, proper 3.112; *av* suitably (dressed) 19.247

semen *v* seem Pr 33, 1.148, 2.135, 6.216, 7.141, 11.2, 45, 273, 14.109, 16.8, 262, 19.57, 167, 21.450, 459, **B** Pr 52, 5.77, 9.41, 10.273, 12.169, 13.320, 17.37, (*in parenth. impers. constr.*) **(as) it semeth / semed(e)** Pr 34, 160, 7.129, 9.105, 115, 117, 12.66, 72, 11.163, 17.86, 19.272, 20.120, 404; appear to be 3.382, 5.27, 90, 6.27, 7.298, 11.129, 15.116, 307, 16.262, 17.86, 301, 20.62, B 10.255, 257; indicate, *pr.p.* 6.179, 11.86; ~ **to** resemble *pr.p.* B 15.392

#semyui(e)f *a* half-alive 19.57c

sen *v* (**see** 4.82, **seen** B 4.86, *assim. pr. 2* **seestow** 1.5, *p.t.* **say** Pr 5, **sayh** 5.124, **sau3** A 5.9, **saw** 5.111, **sey(h) (e)** Pr 109, 2.200, A 12.5, **sye** 14.75, 20.255, **sigh** Pr 11, **sihe** 19.59, 20.358, *pl.* **seye(n)** Pr 177, 17.304, *p.p.* **ysaye** 18.140, **(y)seyen** 16.343, **sei3e** A 11.221); see Pr 11, 109, 1.5, 9.294, 10.73, 146, 11.152, 13.135, 141, 143, 174, **B** 1.51, 4.152, 11.320, 364, 15.162, 17.84, Z 2.45; catch sight of Pr 177, 4.82, 18.240, 289, 19.49, **B** Pr 50, 16.178, 17.107, ~ **of** 19.59, **B** 2.189, **to ~ vpon** to look at 18.191; view Pr 5; observe 10.159, 12.134, 13.143, 14.75, 16.301, 343, 18.226, 19.178, 22.374, A 12.20; witness 6.51, 12.29, 17.304, 18.148, 20.255, 259, **B** 15.588, 16.117; encounter 7.179, 16.343, 18.241, 269, 19.29, **B** 9.152, 11.104, 244, 13.25, 305, 15.158, 196, A 11.221; meet 7.137, 12.134, B 15.196; read 11.51, 204, 14.116, **B** 6.234, 10.191, 412, 454; see (in vision) Pr 221, 232, 5.111, 124, 9.298, 11.153, 20.358, **B** 11.320, 15.12; foresee B Pr 202; know 3.325; perceive 1.39, 4.154, 12.83, 20.333, **B** 5.85, 10.259, 12.20, A 12.5; find 7.15, 11.237, A 3.57; realise 7.168; understand 4.154, 11.289, **B** 2.67, 9.156; experience 3.104, 6.57, 20.222

senatour *n* member of governing body, alderman 8.87

sendel *n* sendal [thin rich silk] 8.10

senden *v* (*contr. pr.* **sent(e)** 1.177, 8.346, 14.27, 17.155, 21.435, *p.t.* **sent(e)(n)** 2.231, 3.128 *etc*, *subjv.* B 13.249, *p.p.* **sende** 2.197, **(y)sent** Pr 77, 9.55) dispatch (messenger / message) 2.197, 231, 6.189, 278, 7.126, 9.37, 119, 11.267, 15.238, 17.246, 262, 18.205, 19.123, 20.172, 21.341, 22.81, 111, **B** 10.230, 14.21, A 12.54; send 7.126, 8.273, B 13.249; cause to be brought 9.39; circulate Pr 77; issue 4.190; send (word) 2.233, 243, 3.128, 413, 8.346, 9.1, 27, 10.252, 13.11, 18.261, 20.172, 184, 22.310, **B** 3.261, 9.124, 10.366, **A** 3.244, 251, 4.15; grant 1.177, 9.55, 15.295, 299, 16.17, 25, 21.435, 22.386, **B** 6.138, 7.63, A 10.201; provide 9.199, 17.155, B 15.305; send down upon 3.95, 21.292; send forth 14.27; send (for), summon 10.150, 22.205

sene *a* visible 22.185, **B** 1.149, 14.96

sen(n)es 4.15, 6.355, 11.171, 21.78, 311, 398, **Z** 6.16, 7.266 *see* **seth(e)(n)**[1] *av* 21.15, 22.323 *see* **seth(e)**[3] *conj.*; 11.55, 22.187 *see* **seth(e)**[2] *prep.*

#seneschal *n* seneschal [chief administrative officer of lord's household] Pr 93

sense *n* incense 21.86

sent Z 2.80 = **saynt** *n*

sent(e) *contr. pr.* 1.177, 14.27, 21.435, *p.t.* 2.233, 9.119, *p.p.* 9.55, 19.123, B 7.63 *see* **senden** *v*

sepulcre *n* tomb (of Christ at Jerusalem) 7.170

seraphyn *n.pl.* seraphim 1.105

serelepes B 17.165 *see* **suyrelepes** *a, av*

seria(u)nt(e) (sergeaunt) *n* sergeant-at-arms [royal officer], (*fig.*) 21.341; officer of law court **B** 2.207, 3.102, Z 2.189; sergeant-at-law [senior barrister, justice] Pr 160 (B Pr 212), 3.78, 447, B 15.8, Z Pr 65

serk *n* undergarment 1.99, 6.6

sermoun A 11.245 = **sarmon** *n*

serpent *n* serpent B 18.287

sertayn(e) 3.85, 22.255 = **certeyn(e)** *a*

sertes 5.22, 18.58, A 9.18 = **certes** *av*

seruaunt *n* servant [one owing service to a lord / master] 11.301, 16.96, **B** 10.470; hired labourer 3.272, 7.39, 220, 8.268, 21.439, **B** 14.142; administrative officer B Pr 95; factor 6.278, **B** 15.248; agent 18.203, 205; servant of God (= disciple) A 7.227

seruen *v* be in the service of, work for Pr 90, 93, 3.265, 5.66, 6.130, 7.189, 192, B 10.470, A Pr 91; work Pr 160; attend upon (as servant) 7.269, 10.140; serve (as apprentice) 6.207; wait upon 2.224, A 11.22 (1); serve (as knight / retainer) 1.102, 4.2, 18.96, B 13.120; obey B Pr 131; serve (as priest) 5.61, 6.19; assist at mass 5.12; serve (God by obedience to his will) 7.184, 189, 192, 16.93, **B** 11.277, 279, A 11.300; follow (the devil, sin) 4.33, 10. 302, **B** 9.62, **A** 2.65, 11.22 (2); serve (food) 14.144, 15.44, 21.439; minister to 2.182, **B** 2.179, 13.227; serve purpose, perform function 16.171, (*impers.*) be useful to 19.174, B 5.439; be of service B 17.146; ~ **of** be of use 12.33, 14.48; satisfy 6.390, B 5.413; treat 3.309, 14.147

seruyse, seruyc(i)e *n* labour 3.272; task, duty 3.447; religious service [mass and matins] 9.227, 231, 242, **his ~** the mass he is obliged to celebrate B 15.126; serving / service [at table] 15.59, 64; use, care, **in my ~** in my care 7.52

sesen[1] 2.165, 14.41, 22.107, 109 *see* **cessen** *v*

sesen[2] *v* take possession of 6.271, Z 2.42, ~ **in / with** enfeoff, put in legal possession of A 2.66, Z 2.56, 73, *p.p.* **(i)se(i)sid** put in possession 20.309

seso(u)n *n* season, time, **somur ~** Pr 1, 10.2; period of time, *in phr.* **out of ~** = untimely 6.184 (B 13.351)

se(e)st 2 *p. sg.*, (*assim. form*) **~ow** (= **se(e)st þow**) 1.5, **B** 9.152, 15.196 *see* **sen** *v*

set *imp.* 20.293, *p.p.* **B** 6.47, 13.125 *see* **setten** *v*

sete *n* seat, place (in heaven) A 8.39

sete *p.t.* B 18.287, (*subjv.*) 14.2, **~n** *p.t. pl.* 6.395, 7.164, 15.42, B 6.115, 192 *see* **sitt(i)en** *v*

seth¹ *3 pr. sg.* 14.41, 16.301, *pl.* 9.302, Z 8.63 *see* **sen** *v*

seth² *3 pr. sg.* Z 7.218 = **seith**; *see* **seggen** *v*

seth(e)(n)¹ (**sen(n)es, syn, sithe(n)(es)**) *av* afterward, after that, then 3.408, 4.15, 5.40, 140, 143, 180, 191, 6.355, 7.124, 129, 144, 184, 8.62, 281, 9.29, 39, 307, 10.226, 251, 11.171, 12.100, 13.88, 173, 15.57, 178, 18.18, 261, 19.40, 20.49, 228, 21.78, 87, 143, 268, 276, 311, 398, 22.137, 387, **B** Pr 128, 1.68, 146, 5.139, 9.101, 116, 11.320, 13.19, 200, 14.142, 16.235, 17.36, 88, 18.283, **A** 7.227, 10.153, 159, 11.181, 221, 251, **Z** 2.118, 6.16, 7.266, 288; next †B 10.251; since then 7.47, 54, 16.355, 17.270, 18.140, †B 5.400

seth(e) *etc*² *prep.* (in the time) since Pr 82, 10.274, 11.55 **~ whanne** since when 22.187

seth(e) *etc*³ *conj.* since (the time when), after Pr 62, 5.40, 70, 6.310, 20.136, **B** 2.26, 6.63, 10.226, A 11.273; (during the time) since Pr 62, 6.310; because, since, seeing that 2.134, 3.367, 9.115, 10.197, 14.194, 15.226, 17.183, 190, 315, 18.81, 176, 192, 19.35, 242, 247, 274, 20.307, 308, 21.15, 60, 474, 22.49, 63, 236, 323, **B** 9.85, 10.133, 259, 264, **A** 8.62, 10.206, 11.89, 12.18; **~ þat** since 17.252, 315, 20.350

sethen *v* stew, *p.t. pl.* **sode** 9.149, 17.20, *p.p.* **ysode** B 15.432

setten *v* (*p.t.* **sette** 4.43 *etc, contr. pr.* 12.26) make sit 4.43, 14.137; place, set 1.118, 4.20, 43, 6.6, 7.52, 15.56, 19.72, 20.49, 227, B 2.164, A 4.18; set [heart] 11.231; put in position 20.291; **~ forth** put out Pr 97; fix B 17.133; plant 7.185, 9.6, 15.213, 18.9, B 15.334, *ger.* Pr 23; *in phr.* **~ by, ~ in, ~ on** attach 9.302, B 7.151, Z 2.41; proceed B 16.36; consider B 15.224; value, esteem 5.97, 8.166, 9.345, 12.26, 15.10, *in phrr.* **~ lihte, ~ short (by)** think little of 11.164, 14.65; determine, establish 22.255, B 13.154; appoint 10.149; put [to learning] 11.117, 14.126, **B** 7.31, 10.170; make ready, ? use 18.40

s(e)ute *n* retinue 16.96; clothing, (*fig.*) = flesh B 5.488, 497 (*with pun on* 'legal cause')

seuth *3 sg.pr.* Z Pr 129 = **seeth** *see* **sen** *v*

seue(ne) *num.* seven, *also as indef. number* Pr 203, 232, 6.108, 214; *in phrr.* **~ ars** 11.97, 12.95, 17.114; **~ daies** B 15.296; **~...geauntes** 22.215; **~ 3er** 4.82, 7.64, 10.73; **~ nyhte** 7.300; **~ psalmes** 3.464, 5.47; **~ synnes** 16.43, 60, B 15.74; **~ sithe(s)** 10.23, 31, 49; **~ sones** B 13.120; **~ sterres** 17.98; **~ susteres** 7.269; *a as n* 7.37, 277, 279, 15.271, 19.74, B 3.63, 13.122, *in phr.* **suche ~** seven like these 1.105; *in cpd. num.* **~ hundred (wynter)** B 14.68, **~ thousand (wynter)** 20.309

seue(n)the *a as n* seventh 16.142

seuenty (hundred) *num.* = seven thousand †B 18.283

sew(e) *p.t.* 6.271 (B 13.375), 17.101, 21.276, 290, 299, 311, 345, 409 *see* **sowen** *v*¹

sewen¹ (**su(e)(w)en**) *v* follow B 17.107, A 11.245; walk behind [as ploughman], drive 7.186, Z 7.64; accompany Pr 46, 3.352, 10.73, 13.143, 180, 17.145, 19.81, 22.126, **B** 4.167, 11.374; support 18.72; associate with 2.102, B 11.422; (be a) follow(er) [disciple] (of) 12.168, B 10.204, A 11.249; strive for 22.22; correspond, *pr. p.* correspondingly, accordingly 18.63; follow through with, *pr.p.* **suynde** 20.358; pursue B 14.323, A 2.53, **~ to** A 8.62, Z 8.63; obey 3.325, 5.200, 11.183, A 2.53; act in accordance with B 17.102; come after [as descendant] B 18.191; sue at law 3.367

sewen² A 7.9, 19 = **sowen** *v*²

sewere *n* cobbler A 11.311

shabbede *a* afflicted with scab [skin-disease of sheep] (*fig.*) 9.264, A 8.17

shadde *p.t.* B 19.58 *see* **sheden** *v*

shaddewen *v* cast a shadow 20.478

shaft *n* form, figure **B** 9.31, 11.395, 13.297

shaken *v* (*p.t.* **sho(o)k(e)** 6.13, 266) shake 18.47, 105, 107; = empty out 6.266; **~ of** get rid of 6.13

shal(l) *pr.sg.* Pr 13 *et p., pl.* Pr 221 *et p.*; **shalt** *2 sg.* 2.46 *et p*; **shaltow** 7.226 *etc* (= **shalt thow**) *see* **shollen**

shale *n* shell 12.148

shame *n* (sense of) shame 6.90, 13.234, B 11.431, (*person.*) 13.244; fear of shame 22.284; *in phr.* **for ~** for decency's sake 6.431, B 14.330, out of shame B 12.80, despite fear of shame B 5.90, for sheer embarrassment B 15.382; ignominy B 4.31; disgrace B 9.88; a disgraceful thing A 12.16; **~les** *a* without any sense of shame 3.46

shamen *v* be ashamed B 5.367; shame, disgrace B 3.190

shap *n* looks, appearance B 11.395

shapen *v* (*p.t.* **shupte** 19.183, **shapte** B 20.139, **sho(o)p(e)** Pr 2, 2.177, 22.307, A 5.102 (*subj.*), *pl.* **shopen** B Pr 57, *p.p.* **(y)shape(n)** 15.240, 301) create 6.423, 15.301, 19.183, **B** 9.66, 11.395; make 22.307, Z 7.276; fashion 5.18; build 10.225, 11.240; (*refl.*) turn oneself into B Pr 57; institute, establish 1.156, B Pr 122; arrange 2.177; bring about 22.139, A 5.102; provide 15.240; cause 9.62, B 11.424; prepare 3.18, (*refl.*) get ready 13.246; direct Z 3.166; set about B 17.84, **~ into** dress in Pr 2

shar *n* plough-share 3.460

sharp *a* strong, stinging 22.307; violent 20.455

sharpe *av* loudly B 18.39; **~liche** *av* vigorously 18.107; severely energetically, promptly 6.13*c*.

sharre (shere) *n* scissors 6.75 (B 13.331)

shauen *v* shave, *p.p.* 6.201; tonsure 16.352

she *prn. fem. sg.* she 1.12 *et p.*; *and see* **heo** *prn*

sheden *v* (*p.t.* **shedde**) shed 19.272, 21.58, *ger.* **bloed ~** 14.207, 15.157; spill, *ger.* **for ~** to prevent spilling 8.8

she(e)f *n* (*pl.* **sheues**) sheaf of grain 5.14, B 6.141, (*fig.*) 21.332; quiverful 3.478, 8.349, (*fig.*) 22.225

she(e)p *n* sheep (*sg.*) Pr 2, B 15.360, (*pl.*) 3.411, 5.18, (*fig.*) 9.262, 264, A 8.17

she(e)pherde *n* shepherd 14.96, 17.98, **B** 10.461, 15.367

shelle B 11.259 *see* **shale** *n*; ~ **of Galys** souvenir scallop-shell from Compostella 7.165

sheltrom *n* battle-formation 20.292, (*fig.*) = spiritual defence B 14.81

shenden *v* (*p.t.* **shent(e)** 19.272 *etc*, **shent** 3.171) do harm to A 7.148; ruin 3.171, B 9.206, A Pr 95; bring to destruction **B** 2.126, 4.174, 6.173; destroy 20.336; damage 13.114*n*; spoil B 9.206; corrupt 3.192; mortify B 11.424; bring about the death of 19.272, 22.98

shene *a* bright 20.455

shent(e) *p.t.* 19.272, 22.98, *p.p.* 3.171 *see* **shenden** *v*

shentfolyche *av* ignominiously 3.429

sheo A 5.141 = **she** *prn*

shep Pr 2 *etc*, = **she(e)p** *n*

shepherde B 10.461, 15.360 = **she(e)pherde** *n*

shepstere B 13.331 = **schupestare** *n*

shere B 13.331 = **sharre** *n*

shereue 2.177 = **shyryue** *n*

sherewe B Pr 192, 1.129, 2.40, 5.90, 279, 6.160, 9.122, 147, 150, 10.436, 17.43, 19.377 = **shrewe** *n*

sherewednesse B 3.44 *see* **shrewed** *a*

sherte *n* shirt B 14.330

shete *n* bed-sheet 16.75; ? cloth bag B 5.107

sheten *v* (*p.t.* **shet** A 12.12, *pl.* **shot(t)e(n)** 20.50, 22.225) shoot 20.292, 22.225; ~ **vp** raise A 12.12, thrust towards 20.50

shetten *v* (*p.t.* **shette**) shut, close 7.249, B Pr 105

sheues *pl.* 5.14 *etc*; *see* **sh(e)ef** *n*

sheware *n* revealer, (*with play on sense* mirror) 14.96

shewen *v* view with favour 10.162n; be visible (to) 10.160; present Pr 202, B 14.190; (*refl.*) present oneself 13.244, 17.284; appear B 5.89; display 4.126, *ger.* B 15.78, (for sale) 2.223; show 11.11, 19.112, **B** 12.88, 16.21, 201, 18.394; manifest **B** 9.43, *ger.* B 17.153; make known 6.21, 7.108, 13.88, 17.257, 18.202n, **B** 10.168, 14.125; make clear 14.110, 19.154, B 14.123; explain 3.432, 10.32, 21.230, B 10.372, A 12.14, 54, *ger.* 16.1; declare 1.69, 2.107, 11.209, 19.300, **B** 2.135, 7.16, 49, 10.254, 12.50, 13.449; tell Pr 182, 6.325, 8.264, 9.82, 11.5, B Pr 167, 11.54, A 11.73; describe A 10.185; speak 16.142, B 17.39; assert 2.40; expound 11.207, B 4.172; teach **B** 7.128, 10.36, A 11.154, 245, ~ **of** instruct about 13.233; bring forward 11.162, 13.130, B 4.136, A 12.34; produce Pr 164, 13.40; cite B 3.351; disclose 11.80; reveal B Pr 106; confess 6.350, B 5.233, 367, ~ **shrift** make one's confesion B 5.141, *ger.* 5.379; lay (complaint) 3.213; put (case) 12.174; stretch out 19.133; perform B 13.213

shewynge *ger.* representation B 17.153

shide *n* plank 10.225, 11.240, 18.20

shiften *v* (*p.t.* **shifte**) (*refl.*) bestir oneself B 20.167

shilden *v* protect B 10.406

shille *av* with a clear voice 6.46

shille A 6.9 = **shelle** *n*

shillyng *n* shilling 3.391, 14.89

shyne *n* shin B 11.431

shynen *v* (*p.t.* **schoen** 14.96) give light 19.222; shine 14.96

ship *n* ship 3.478, 8.349, B 15.360, = (Noah's) ark 10.225, 235, 11.240, B 10.406

shipman *n* sailor, seaman 17.94, 98, 103, B 15.360

shyre *n* shire, county 3.171, B 2.159

shyreue, shyryue *n* sheriff [king's chief legal and administrative officer in the shire] 2.59, 177, 3.171, ~**es clerk** clerk of the sheriff's court 4.164

shyten *v* (*contr. pr.* **shyt**) ?befoul 9.264n, c

sho *n* (*pl.* ~**es**, ~ **(o)n**) shoe 5.18, 22.219, B 14.32, 330

shoen[1] *v* provide with shoes, *p.p.* **sho(e)d** shod B 2.164

shoen[2] *p.t.* 14.96 *see* **shynen** *v*

shoke *p.t.* 6.266 *see* **shaken** *v*

sholde *p.t.* Pr 77 *et p.*, ~**n** *pl.* 2.182 *etc*, ~**est** *2 sg.* 13.223 *etc*; *see* **shollen** *v*

shollen *v* (*pr.* **shal** Pr 13 *et p.*, *pl.* 2.165, *2 sg.* **shalt** 2.45, *assim. form* **shaltow** 7.226, B 5.570, *pl.* **sholle(n)** 1.131 *etc*, **shul** B 2.38 *et p.*, **shull(e)(n)** 9.311, 338, B 1.178, A 2.138 *etc*, *p.t.* **sholde** Pr 77 *et p.*, *2 p. assim. forms* **sholdestow** B 11.101, **shost** 3.135; **shulde** Pr 120 *etc*, B 14.188) *modal auxil.* [selected refs.] **shal** should Pr 208; ought to 6.346, 16.8, B 1.26, 48, A 10.66; have (duty) to 5.161; must, will [command] 4.184, 7.226, **B** 5.642, 6.232, A 12.51; (will) have to 8.83, 142, 9.311, 11.197, 20.415, 446, 21.347, B 6.166, A 12.86; shall, intend to 6.173, 8.15, 18.59, B 10.369; will assuredly 11.282, 12.109, 15.164, **B** 5.555, 10.155, 11.194, A 10.176; will [prediction / prophecy] 2.35, 3.437, 5.142, 8.67, 12.160, 21.220, B 16.131, 156; must, have to [necessity] 7.40, 14.125, **B** 9.148, (*after* **allas**) should (have to) / be able to 12.2, 16.1, 18.287, B 9.65, 84; be required to 3.264, 4.2; will / be going to Pr 13 *et p.*, B 10.117, A 10.177; be to 4.10, 8.96, 12.214, 15.131, 18.277, 19.96, 20.68, B 17.125; were to A 11.276; be wont / apt (to) 22.291; will be able to, can 2.28, 208, 3.35, 10.208, 13.234, 19.95, 20.25, 153, 173, **B** 7.50, 106, 9.165, 14.17, 17.8; (*with implied inf.*) 7.64 [come], 245 [be], 12.119, B 15.13 [go], Z 8.37 [die]; *with Ø-sense* (=do) B 11.208, 12.253; **sholde** would Pr 77, 3.259, 4.82, 7.146, 10.186, 15.27, 17.93, 18.129, 269, 20.17, B 8.102, A 3.51; ought to 1.50, 3.152, 5.43, 19.310; have duty to 4.29, 5.76, 11.246, 21.431; must 2.234, 3.415, 5.119, 7.2, 8.77; had to 20.424; should have to 5.42, 8.34, 15.285, 16.336; would have to 6.384, 20.374; be required to 5.57; have to 19.317; should Pr 143, 4.149, 6.23, 17.264, (so that)...should 18.107; were to 11.222, 14.47, 15.180, B 9.38; are to 8.6; might be able to 21.145, B 15.314; should wish

6.290; might wish 19.117; could 6.108, B 15.151; should be able to 16.213; would be able to Pr 80, 6.205, 7.5, 12.183, 13.160, 15.252, 19.138, 22.173, B 14.188; be allowed to 6.67; (*with implied inf.*) ought to [be] 9.13; should [be able to] **B** 13.254, 15.439, would [go] B 15.13

shon(y)en *v* avoid 13.244, B 5.167; keep out of B Pr 174

shoon *pl.* B 14.330 *see* **sho** *n*

sho(o)p *p.t.* 2.177, 6.423, 11.240, 13.246, **B** 9.66, 11.395, 17.84, A 5.102, **shopen** *p.t.pl.* B Pr 57, 122 *see* **shapen** *v*

shoppe *n* shop 2.223, 14.184

shor(r)iare prop 18.25, 50, 119

short *a*, ~**e** *a as n* short (person) 16.84; brief (*comp.*) 15.261; curt 20.331

shorte *av* at low esteem, *in phr.* **sette** ~ **by** have a low opinion of 14.65

shost *assim. 2 sg. pr.* = **sholdest** *see* **shollen** *v*

shot *n. pl. (coll.)* missiles, ? bows 20.292, 22.225

shoten *p.t. pl.* 22.225 *see* **sheten** *v*

shour *n* rainstorm 20.455

shouele *n* shovel B 6.189

shrapen *v* scrape 6.90, B 11.431; scratch A 5.208

shrewe *n* scoundrel 4.105, 6.317, 7.260, 11.26, **B** 5.90, 279, 6.160, 9.122, 147, 150, 10.436, A 4.67, Z 7.31; evil person **B** 17.43, 19.377; wretch 6.173, 6.421, 8.151, 13.234, **B** 2.40, 4.160, A 5.208, Z 8.76; villain B Pr 192; fiend B 1.129

shrewed *a* depraved, accursed Pr 122, 124; ~**nesse** *n* wickedness B 3.44

shrewen *v* curse 6.75 (B 13.331), B 5.76

shryft *n* (sacramental) confession 6.63, 90, 349, 7.8, 14.121, B 3.37, A 5.102, (*person.*) 22.307; (act of) confession 22.284, **B** 5.139, 13.54, *in phrr.* ~ **of mouthe** oral confession 16.30, B 14.88, 89, 90, **shewen** ~ make one's confession B 5.141, 379

shryne *n* shrine 7.201

shryuar *n* confessor Pr 64

shryuen *v* (*p.t.* **shro(e)f(e)**, *p.p.* **(y)shryue(n)**) make one's confession 22.290, (*refl.*) 6.13, 175, 421, 9.237, 11.257, 22.167, B 5.141, 367, **be shryue** confess, be absolved 6.355, 7.2, 28, **B** 5.90, 14.9, A 12.14; hear the confession (of) Pr 62, 5.194, 22.281, B Pr 89, A 11.203, Z 3.152; hear confessions, administer penance 22.305, 369; absolve 3.46

shroud *n* garment, *pl.* clothes Pr 2

shuyuen (vp) *v* support, prop 18.20

shul B 1.132 *etc*, A 8.17, 141, **shulde** Pr 120, A Pr 76, **shull(e)(n)** 3.481, 9.311, B 10.154, A Pr 97 *etc*; *see* **shollen** *v*

shupte *p.t.* 19.183, 22.139 *see* **shapen**

si (*Lat.*) 'if' [word indicating a condition] 3.328n

sib *a* kin to, related to (*fig.*) 7.277, 279, 288, 11.97, 198, 16.112

sybbe *n* kindred 12.157

sycurly 10.26, Z 8.55 = **sikerliche** *av*

syde *n* side [direction] 1.112, 113, 7.163, [of body] 5.79, 6.163, 426, **B** 2.99, 13.317, A 11.214, Z 4.131, (= hand) 3.76; [in bargaining / negotiation] 6.378, B 2.55; edge 10.62; district 2.172; (*in cpds.*) ~ **benche** 9.252, ~ **borde** B 13.6, ~ **table** 14.139, 15.42; **sonne** ~ sunny side 1.113, 18.64; *in phr.* **by** ~**s** nearby Z 2.51

syde *av* low, (*comp.*) **syddore** 6.200

sye *p.t.* 14.75, 20.255 *see* **sen** *v*

syg(g)(e)n 6.54, 7.301, 9.257, 11.11, 20.358, **B** 13.307, 15.125, 296, 382, 428, 17.30 *see* **seggen** *v*

si(g)hen, syȝen (syken) *v* moan 7.300, 20.91, B 14.326; groan 20.274; lament 3.399, 5.107, A 11.193

si(g)ht *n* (power of) sight 7.131, 14.48, 20.81, **ye** ~ 9.102; eyes 4.180, 19.307, B 17.323, *in phrr.* **in** ~, **to** ~ before his / the(ir) eyes (of) 21.181, **B** 10.273, 16.130, 18.303; looking 15.257; visual observation 14.30, 79; view 7.300, 20.344; presence 11.203; witness, *in phrr.* **by** ~ **of** with the witness of 1.200, 2.115; **as by** ~ as it would appear 21.456; discernment 21.235; judgement, *in phrr.* **to my / oure, to** ~ **of** in my / our / the eyes (of) Pr 34, 6.36, 9.115, 11.45, B 17.38; appearance, **in / of** ~ in appearance B 10.255, A 3.58; sight 19.63, 65, B 16.117, 17.90; spectacle, attraction (to the eye) 3.480, 6.282, 18.33, 37; aspect B 17.153

signe *n* sign, token Pr 89; tokening, symbol B 13.154; *in phr.* **in** ~ **þat** indicating that 4.149, B 10.143; gesture 6.178 (B 13.345); stamp 4.126; identifying mark(s) 16.97; (pilgrim) badge 7.165, 168, 173; (impression of) seal 2.156, 22.272, Z 2.41; message in symbols [written] 14.40, [spoken] B 10.170

signiure *n* domain A 2.66

sihe *p.t.* 19.59, 20.358 *see* **sen** *v*

syhen 20.91, 274 *see* **si(g)hen** *v*

siht 1.200 *etc*; *see* **si(g)ht** *n*

syk(e) *a* sick 8.147, 271, 9.99, 15.119, B 16.106, 108, 109, A 7.239, 11.190, Z 7.198; infirm B 15.576; *a as n* the sick 15.221, sick person(s) 4.122, 19.63, 328, 22.324; injured man 19.63; (*fig.*) (spiritually) sick (from sin) 22.335, *a as n* 22.357, B 17.120, 121; ~**nes(se) (seke-nesse)** *n* sickness 7.28, 64, 8.134, 270, 16.309, 19.318, 322, 21.292; spiritual malady 7.124

sykel *n* sickle 3.460, 5.23, 6.271 (B 13.375)

syken 3.399, B 14.326, A 11.193 *see* **si(g)hen** *v*

syker *a* safe, reliable 9.331; free from trouble 1.116; *a as n* sound, stable (base) 3.334; strong (*comp.*) B 12.161; beneficial (*sup.*) 5.39; certain 14.29, **B** 1.132, 3.50, 16.234; definite 22.255; *av* securely 12.153; to be sure A 11.163; (*comp.*) confidently B 5.502; ~**ly(che)** *av* assuredly 10.26, A 8.54; without fail B 5.540; truly 8.23; (*comp.* ~**loker**) confidently 7.141; safely 4.51

sykeren *v* promise faithfully 7.184

sikorere 12.153 *comp.*; *see* **syker** *av*

#**sylen** *v* drop down, proceed 20.341

silk B 15.220 *see* **selk(e)** *n*

syllare Z 2.53, **sylle(n)** Z 3.134 *etc*; *see* **sullere** *n*, **sullen** *v*

siluer Pr 90 *etc* = **seluer** *n*

***simile** (*Lat.*) *n* analogy 19.161, **in a** ~ by way of analogy 18.228

symonye *n* simony [the sin of buying or selling church office, service or property] Pr 84, 9.55, (*person.*) 2.63 *et p.*, 3.184, 22.126, 137

symple *a* humble, modest 15.188; *a as n* the humble B 16.8

sympletee-of-speche *n* (*person.*) humility, modesty of address B 10.167

syn B 9.85 *see* **seth(e)**³ *conj.*

syne(ge)n *v* (commit) sin Pr 109, 6.7, 355, 7.124, 9.329, 10.25, 31, 49, 12.242, 14.112, 19.266, 277, 20.228, 22.15, ~ **aʒe(y)n / in** sin against 19.162, 167, 266

synfol(e), synful(le) *a* sinful 7.137, 145, 10.162, 20.371, 394, **B** 9.63, 122, 11.226, *a as n* (the) sinful (people), sinners 3.464, 7.120, 138, 153, 12.130, 21.22, 444, **B** 5.487, 7.15, 16.108, 109, A 12.20, 24; wicked 6.317, 10.165, Z Pr 73

syngen *v* (*p.t.* **sang** 21.212, **song** 6.46, *pl.* **songe(n)** 6.395, *etc*) sing (song) 6.46, 395, 8.122, 21.135, A 11.193, [to instrument] 15.209; chant (religious service) 3.53, 480, 5.122, 7.10, 31, 13.16, 126, 14.94, 16.334, 348, 17.120, 20.7, 21.74, 210, 212; sing in praise (of God) 7.153, 20.15, 181, 367, 450, 468, 21.71, 151; celebrate mass Pr 84, 3.310, 5.68, 13.104, *ger.* 12.87, [requiem] 15.51

synguler *a* quite alone B 9.35; sole B 16.208; special, extraordinary 6.36 (B 13.283)

synken *v* (*p.t.* **sank,** *pl.* **sonken**) sink (into) A 2.70, B 14.80; (down into) 20.69

synne *n* sin(fulness) Pr 124, 1.145, 192, 197, 10.158, 223, 11.142, 305, 12.57, 113, 13.239, 14.114, 16.76, 17.3, 81, 245, 285, 18.287, 19.177, 290, 20.234, 244, 330, 391, 430, 21.65, 371, 460, 22.306, 380, **B** 8.46, 12.79, 14.323, 15.352, 18.305, **A** 5.207, 10.74, 77, 12.21, Z 2.100, 5.95, 118; (the state of) sin 10.52, 215, 14.112, 20.388, 22.155; = original sin 7.126, 18.212, B 10.110, A 11.69; (acts of) sin, sin(s) Pr 107, 3.46, 62, 358, 399, 410, 429, 4.130, 5.107, 6.92, 257, 335, 420, 7.15, 59, 245, 9.138, 11.58, 12.27, 14.62, 19.32, 177, 20.430, 21.186, 191, **B** 1.80, 5.296, 10.473, 11.54, 100, 217, 13.192, 14.237, 18.392; ((any) kind(s) of) sin 7.72, 10.161, 101, 12.28, 73, 16.227, 17.79, **B** 5.224, 14.185, 322, 18.303, *in phr.* **alle kynne / manere** ~ 16.26, 21.186, 22.373; = sexual sin 6.188, 276, 7.90, 8.52, 10.287, 18.133, 143; vice 9.256, B 2.175; *in phrr.* **dedly(che)** ~ mortal sin 1.142, 5.122, 6.276, 7.209, 9.238, 10.43, 12.37, 17.203, 291, 20.376, **B** 8.50, 9.207, 13.406, 14.78, 83, 88, 90, 95, 15.540; **forgeuenesse of**

(...) ~ 19.188, B 14.154; **merkeness** 16; **puyre** ~ sheer sin 5.115, B 11.429; **sevene** ~**s** the seven deadly sins B 15.74; **sorwe of** ~ B 5.125; **venial** ~ B 14.92; **wormes of** ~ 18.38; **to** ~**ward** toward (sexual) sin 6.179

synnele(e)s *a* without sin 14.41; *a as* av without blame / reproach 8.237, B Pr 34

sir(e) *n* sir [*title for knight* 8.23, *for priest or cleric*] ~ **Iohan, Geffrey** 15.123, ~ **Peres of Prydie** 6.366, ~ **doctour** 15.112; ~ **Peres [Plowman]** 21.345; *before king* 2.246, 4.142, B Pr 125, 7.155; *for allegorical fig.* ~ **Actyf** 15.234, **Covetyse (Heruy)** 6.197, **Dowel** 10.128, 138, **Elde** 22.186, **Furst** Z 7.165, **Gloton** 6.392, **Go-wel** 10.148, **Hunger** 8.169 *et p.*, **Inwit** 10.144, *Liberum Arbitrium* 16.171, *Penetrans-domos* 22.341, **Resoun** 4.34 *etc*, 5.53, **Simonye** 2.115, A 2.35 *etc*, **Se-wel** *etc* 10.146, **Sorfeet** 8.276, **Waryn Witty** B 4.67, **Worch-wel** 10.147; lord 8.281, 20.302; **grete** ~ important person, lord Pr 177, A 11.22; [*as respectful term of address*] 13.220, 16.207, 18.81, 19.96, (*pl.*) 22.244, **dere** ~ 10.127, **leue** ~ 12.24, **swete** ~ B 17.125; father Pr 109, 203, 2.143, 6.134, 10.241, 22.161, **B** 5.37, 608, 9.148, 152, A 2.19, = God the Father 11.153, 18.193, 232, 19.139 *et p.*, B 17.156

sirename *n* father's family name, surname 3.366

syse *n* (session of) assise court 2.178

sismatik *n* schismatic 12.56

syso(u)r *n* juryman, sworn witness at assise court 2.59, 63, 179, 3.170, 4.162, 21.372, 22.161, 291, B 2.165

sister *n* A 10.153, (*uninfl. gen.*) 159, 179, *pl.* A 6.113 = **suster** *n*

sit *contr. pr.* 9.108, 14.142, 16.122 *see* **sitt(i)en** *v*

sithe *n* (*pl.* ~ 6.427 *etc*, ~**s** Pr 232 *etc*) time 6.427, 7.37, 9.329, 10.23, 31, 49, 18. 17, **B** 8.44, 14.188, A 12.48; times [*in multiplication*] Pr 232

sith(en) Pr 62, 5.70, 6.310 *see* **seth(e)**³ *conj.*; **sithe** Pr 82 *see* **seth(e)**² *prep.*, B 10.251 *see* **seth(e)(n)**¹ av

sitt(i)en (setten) *v* (*contr. pr.* **sit** 9.108 *etc*, *p.t.* **saet** 6.361 *etc*, **sat** B 2.165, **sete** B 18.287, *subjv.* 6.99, 14.2, *pl.* **seet** 8.122, **seten** 6.395, 7.164, 15.42, B 6.192) sit Pr 114, 6.99, 361, 7.103, 8.122, 9.108, 250, 252, 16.341, 18.241, 19.49, 200, **B** 2.165, 3.345, 5.376, 6.192, 16.141, ~ **adoun** B 5.7, ~ **vp** 7.62; sit enthroned 1.121, 133; lie B 18.287; be placed 7.164, 261; judge 21.306; have place (in heaven) 9.12, 11.203, 14.142, B 7.17; sit as juryman 16.122; ~ **stille** remain silent 15.108; afflict 2.154

Syuile *n* Civil (Roman) law (*person.*) 2.63 *et p.*, 22.137

sixe *num.* six, ~ **myle** 19.74, ~ **monthes** B 10.151, ~ **sithe** 7.37, ~ **sonnes** 3.478, *in cpds.* ~ **score** 3.182, ~ **thousand** 19.26

sixte *num.ord.* (*as n.*) sixth 16.137

sixty *num.* sixty, ~ **wynter** 15.271; (*as indef. large number*) ~ **sythes** 7.47, *a as n* 22.224, *in cpd.* ~ **thousand** B 17.23

skalon *n* shallot 8.309

skathe 3.61, A 12.71 = **sc(h)athe** *n*

skele A 12.34 = **skil** *n*

skenis *suffix in phr.* **alle skenis** A 10.84 = **alles kynnes**; *see* **kyn** *n*

skil(l) *n* reasonableness 6.25, *in phr.* **bryngen out of** ~ cause to lose self-control 21.285; reason, cause 5.153, B 12.215, *in phr.* **(by) goed** ~ for a good reason 16.120, 18.84; argument 11.162, 13.130, A 12.34, **by puyre** ~ by simple reasoning 15.137, **bi this** ~ from this line of argument B 17.196; excuse 6.22, 19.314; (rational) knowledge B 10.303

skilfole *a* knowledgeable 11.96

skynes *suff. in phrr.* **any** ~ (= **enys-kynes**) A 2.162, **summe** ~ some kind of A 8.34 *see* **kyn** *n*

skyppen *v* leap, **skypte an heyh** briskly mounted a pulpit 12.42

sklaundre 2.86, A 12.17 = **sclaundre** *n*

skolde *n* scold, railer A 12.34

skolden *v* rail, quarrel 2.86

skornen 2.86 = **scornen** *v*

skornfully *av* disdainfully A 12.12

slaken *v* slake, quench **B** 15.281, 18.369; *and see* **slokken** *v*

slawe *p.p.* Pr 113, 11.267, 17.275 *see* **slen** *v*

sleep B 2.97 = **slep** *n*; *p.t.* 6.417, B 5.376 *see* **slepen** *v*

sley *a* deft (*sup.*) B 13.298; ~ **of** cunning in 22.163

slei3te B 13.365, 408 = **sleythe** *n*

sleyliche *av* treacherously 6.107, (*sup.*) **sleylokeste** 11.267

sleythe *n* practical wisdom, resourcefulness 21.98; expert skill B 13.408; art 21.99; stratagem 20.164, 21.460; cunning 6.73, 22.14; crafty scheme, wile 2.91, 6.107, 16.274, 19.234; trick B 13.365

slen *v* (*p.t.* **slowh** 22.150, *pl.* **slowe** 11.37, *p.p.* **slawe** Pr 113, 11.267, 17.275) slay, kill Pr 113, 3.419, 439, 7.223, 21.432, 22.150, **B** 10.365, 367, A 11.252; murder 6.107, 11.37, 17.275, 19.257; destroy B 14.90, 94

slep *n* sleep Pr 46, B 2.97, 99, Z Pr 11, **a** ~ to sleep A 9.58, Z 5.26; sleep(iness) Z 5.24; dream Z Pr 93

slepen *v* (*p.t.* **sleep** 6.417, B 5.376, *pl.* **slepen** 15.271, **slepte** Pr 8 *etc*, *p.p.* **slept** B 5.4, **(y)slepe** A 5.4, Z 5.22, *assim. 2 pr. sg.* **slepestow** 1.5) sleep 5.9, 7.251, 12.153, 15.25, 20.4, **B** 7.121, 12.28, ~ **druye** sleep in a dry place 19.304, (*fig.*) 15.307; be asleep 1.5, A 8.151; fall asleep Pr 7, 8.324, 10.66; *pr.p.* **slepynge** while asleep and dreaming Pr 13, 221, 232, 5.124, 9.298, 13.217, 222, B 11.320; in her sleep B 18.299*n*; *ger.* sleep B 5.6; *in phr.* **don...to slepe** prevent from sleeping 19.306

sleuthe, slewthe *n* (the deadly sin of) sloth Pr 46, 2.102, 7.54, 63, 69, 11.110, 16.93, **B** 3.310, 6.143, A 2.66, (*person.*) 7.1, 47, 62, 16.93, 22.158 *et p.*; spiritual torpor B 8.51; idleness 8.245, 9.159, **B** 2.99, 14.76, 235; negligence 8.253

sliken *v* make smooth / fat B 2.99

slymed *a* slimy 7.1

slynge *n* sling (for hurling missiles) 22.163, 217

slokken *v* quench 20.410; *see* **slaken** *v*

slombren *v* doze off B Pr 10

sloo *n* mud, earth 12.181

slouþe A 2.66 = **sleuthe** *n*

slow(e) *a* sluggish, lazy 8.244, B 13.408

slow(e), slowh *p.t.* 11.37, 22.150; *see* **slen** *v*

smacchen *v* (*p.t.* **smauhte**) smell 6.413

smal *a* little Pr 166; small 18.63, 112; skinny A 12.78

smauhte *p.t.* 6.413 *see* **smacchen** *v*

smellen *v* smell (*intr.*) 13.243; (*tr.*) 7.50

smerte *av* sharply, painfully 13.243

smerten *v* sting, cause to smart 19.307; suffer pain, hardship B 3.168

smethe *a* smooth Z 6.80

smethen 3.476 = **smyth(y)en** *v*

smyllen 7.50 = **smellen** *v*

smyten *v* (*contr. pr.* **smyt** 13.243, *pl.* 19.305, *p.t.* **smoet** 18.156, *p.p.* **smyte** 3.476) strike 3.476, 6.105, 18.156, 20.385; sting 13.243; ~ **in** penetrate 19.305, 325

smyth *n* blacksmith 3.476

smyth(y)en (smethen) *v* forge (on anvil) 3.476, **don it** ~ have it beaten 3.459

smoke *n* smoke 19.305, 307, (*fig.*) 325

#smolder *n* choking fumes 19.305, 325

snake *n* snake 16.265

snowe *n* snow 16.265

so[1] *av* thus, in this way 1.71, 2.68, 3.95, 4.100, 5.92, 6.395, 7.235, 264, 9.117, 10.38, 220, 12.202, 206, 216, 13.119, 216, 15.24, 17.20, 76, 123, 184, 192, 18.67, 96, 19.277, 20.234, 321, 21.101, 22.99, 209, 290, **B** 1.120, 5.37, 6.14, 233, 7.70, 9.41, 155, 10.89, 11.193, 381, 12.55, †A 5.130, 7.212, 236, 10.94, 11.124, 240, **Z** Pr 145, 5.34; in such a manner 19.181, 215, 20.160, 434, 21.44, 316, 22.15, 63, 277, 348, **B** †Pr 206, 2.100, 10.347, 11.82, 163, 13.409, 15.389, **A** 9.47, 10.127, 11.291*n*, 12.106, **Z** Pr 56, 1.121, 6.47; *in phrr.* ~ **forth** thus continually 13.173, 16.11, B 14.159; thus likewise B 13.210; ~ **may be** perhaps 5.33, 8.41, ~ **myhte happe** should it so happen 15.6; ~ **may befalle** it may happen 22.351, B 16.60; (*as quasi-prn*) such, that Pr 211, 2.24, 3.232, 6.9, 8.97, 231, 12.168, 13.190, 16.180, 334, 17.92, 290, 19.32, 20.74, **B** 2.122, 10.197, 246, **A** 2.19, 11.236 (2); (so) likewise 3.377, 6.321, 12.56, 13.17, 14.120, 150, 16.8, 18.232, 236, 19.108, 132, 20.163, 182, 327, 22.224, **B** 10.469, 11.75, 12.247, 14.284, 15.261, 16.150, 194, 17.36, A 4.53; correspondingly †B 14.311; *in phr.* **ry3t** ~ in just this manner, exactly thus Pr 182, 1.156, 2.135, 5.150, 7.89, 8.81, 9.134, 217, 12.21, 13.229, 14.49, 110, 181, 16.225, 244, 267, 295, 17.214, 19.139, 21.437, **B** 10.434, 472, 12.35, 47, 51, 58, 90, 260, 13.118, 14.123, 127, 151, 15.335, 339, 475, 17.39, 155, **A** 10.105, 12.30; **ry3t** ~ **sothly** 3.329, 12.195, 227, 235, 16.225, ~ **aftur** in that way accordingly 12.150; then 7.212, 231, 20.396, 22.181, **B**

9.205, 13.143 *in phr.* **ri3t** ~ at once B 5.365; therefore, accordingly 3.328, 494, 5.44, 99, 6.321, 9.323, 327, 10.43, 12.244, 20.220, 393, 21.115, 440, 478, 22.50, B 14.79, A 11.195; so (*with a or av or alone,* = to such an extent) Pr 84, 6.205, 7.303, 8.175, 10.161, 11.58, 16.78, 17.87, 18.48, 19.61, 20.368, 408, 21.428, 22.42, 198, ~...**to** so...as to Pr 202; so that 15.69; ~...**as** in the way that 11.237; ~..**that** in such a way that Pr 149, 3.434–5, 8.172, 10.186, 15.25; the case that 4.134 –5, 17.151; so well...that 16.169–70, 19.281–2, B Pr 126, A 2.24; ~ **þat** with the result that 19.190, provided that 22.22; so very 1.191, 3.198, 4.101, 5.167, 16.306, B 14.322; that 3.296, **B** 3.353, 14.273; so greatly 8.269; as 9.95, 331, 12.193, 13.187, 202, 14.138, **B** 10.228, 12.281; as 13.202, ~...**as** as...as 10.252; exceedingly 3.454; *in correl. constr.* **so...as** = as...as 6.276, 13.52–3; **as...so** like 6.430; **so...so** as...as 19.65; **so muche... as** as much ...as 14.138–9; *in oaths / assevs., blessing,* ~ **me God (Crist) helpe / spede** so help / prosper me God (Christ) 3.8, 4.11, 5.22, 10.108, **B** 3.250, 13.206, 15.158, 16.180, **A** 4.91, 7.131, Z 7.200, ~ **thee Ik** so may I prosper B 5.224; *in misc. phrr.* ~ **muche after** such grave consequences Pr 207; **by** ~ **muche** to that extent 7.141; **neuer** ~ however 3.422, 10.36, 16.168, **B** 9.39, 14.90; **none** ~ ... no...so 6.412, 7.157, 18.141; **what** ~ whatever 14.216, B 4.155; ~... **with** with such (a) 7.41, B 5.82

so² *conj.* as, while B 5.8; so / with the result that 4.124, 6.247, B 16.130; provided (that) 2.125 (2), 3.388, 7.229, 290, 13.202, 16.207, 21.440, 22.22, 222, **B** 4.193, 12.166, A 12.97; *in phr.* **by** ~ **(þat)** provided that 4.98, 187, 5.39, 6.331, 10.310, 12.4, 22, 15.123, 257, **B** 13.136, 14.85, 279

sobben *v* sob B 14.326

sobre *a* temperate, restrained 15.256

sobreliche *av* gravely B 13.204

sobrete(e) *n* moderation, temperance [*esp.* in food and drink] 15.188, 16.132, B 10.167; sobriety 16.150

socour *n* succour, aid 22.170

sode *p.t. pl.* 17.20, *p.p.* 9.149 *see* **sethen** *v*

sodeynliche *av* suddenly 15.24, 19.178; right away 21.5

*****soden** *n* sub-dean 2.187, 16.277, B 2.173

so(e)nd *n* sand 13.135, 14.40; land 17.88, 21.78

soercerye *n* sorcery, witchcraft 17.304, 309, 18.150, 20.71, B 10.212; magic B 15.12; enchantment(s) 6.191

soeth *a* 19.5, 20.312; *n* 19.108, 20.462, ~ **faste** *a* 17.119, 18.69; ~**ly(che)** *av* 19.93, 123, 21.87, 22.215, 244; ~**nesse** *n* 12.83 see **soth(-)** *a, n*

soffisen (sufficen) *v* be sufficient 14.12, 17.119, 19.35, 204, B 15.386

soffra(u)nce *n* patience (in suffering hardship / affliction) 13.202, B 11.378, A 10.119; (the) long-suffering (of God) B 6.144; (improper) tolerance of wrongdoing, *in phr.* **vnsittyng** ~ 3.207, 4.189

soffr(y)en *v* suffer (distress, affliction) 7.104, 9.84, 12.180, 202, 15.71, 16.325, 20.255, 256, 21.68, 102, 22.47, **B** 2.106, 13.66, 14.175, 15.200, 260, 266, 267, 270; undergo, experience 3.399, 449, 6.57 (B 13.310), 129, 7.304, 9.77, 11.107, 12.146, 16.173, 17.270, 20.210, 216*n*, 231, B 10.110; be subject (to) 12.188, ? 18.203*n*, **B** Pr 131, 5.608, 11.382; endure patiently 12.195, 15.280, 16.327, 19.318, 21.292, 295, **B** 9.204, 12.8, A 10.99, 118, 216, Z 5.95; be long-suffering 4.20, 13.200, B 11.381; forbear for a while 20.165, 269, 22.107; wait patiently 2.45, 13.222; put up with (sth.) Pr 211, 6.9, 13.11, 195, 198, 221, 21.444, B 18.395, ~ **(wel)** willingly put up with 8.89, 10.91, 19.105, 324, 22.323, B 10.367; accept **B** 10.251, 15.174; allow Pr 109, 119, 1.144, 3.120, 4.1, 7.124, 138, 8.82, 9.117, 256, 10.162, 254, 255, 256, 14.165, 16.162, 17.183, 18.177, 20.228, **B** Pr 206, †4.86, 6.181, 8.93, 10.120, 16.74, A 9.47; countenance Pr 96, 3.449, 13.114, B 2.175; tolerate Pr 101, 9.131, **B** 10.107 (A 11.66), 12 53, 18.303; leave 22.294; consent 20.222, B 15.518; submit 17.10

sofistre *n* clever deceiver, ~ **of soercerie** cunning magician 17.309; *and see* **sophistrie** *n*

softe *a* mild Pr 1; quiet, gentle 10.118; *av* gently 22.314, (*comp.*) 311; quietly Z 6.70; gingerly 16.52; ~ **ly(che)** in quiet tones 2.165, 3.54, **B** 3.37, 5.7; unobtrusively 4.162; at an easy pace 2.178, 189, 4.54, B 2.165; slowly 15.29, 20.120

soilen¹ *v* dirty **B** 13.343, 400, 458, 14.2, 13

soylen² Z Pr 76, 3.171= **assoylen** *v*

soiournen *v* reside 10.18; linger B 17.84

sokene *n* district, soke 2.111

solace, solas *n* joy, happiness 12.210, 13.18, 14.94, 16.17, 20.227; pleasure 16.11, 309; enjoyment('s sake) 8.22; *in phr.* **in** ~ in good part, as a joke 9.131; comfort B 7.85

solacen *v* entertain (*fig.*) 7.102, 112, B 12.22; cheer 7.255, 19.200; comfort 7.138, 16.150, 18.15, 21.22, **B** 7.85, 14.283

sold *p.p.* 3.245, 20.222, B 16.142; **solde** *p.t.* 6.97, 17.20, 18.158, B 16.143 *see* **sullen** *v*

soleyn *n* solitary person, ~ **by hymsulue** all by himself alone 14.144

solempneliche *av* reverently 3.54

solfen *v* sing a scale 7.31

solitarie *a* in solitude 17.7

som B 13.377 = **som(m)e** *n*

som(m)(e), summe¹ *prn sg. & pl.* some, certain (ones) Pr 22, 25, 33, 35, 59, 90, 93, 1.126, 6.179, 8.8, 118, 9.197, 13.165, 177, 16.247, 18.69, 70, 21.241, 243, 22.348, **B** 5.627, 9.127, 156, A 6.115; (*in apposition*) 3.14*n*; **somme...somme** some...others 21.253; some part, a portion 8.274, 286, 17.20, B 15.248, 329

som(m)(e), sum² *a* one 18.283, B 16.142; a 14.137, 20.172, **B** 5.374, 10.436, 13.55, 377; some (kind of)

2.4, 128, 3.291 *et p.*, **B** 7.31, 17.315; some...or other 9.169, 211, 216, 11.209, 12.5, 18.105; some, certain 3.14n (*or*, together), 4.105, 11.198, 16.247, 18.150, 21.230, 237, B 15.350; *in phrr.* ~ **body** *n* someone 22.27; ~ **de(e)l** *av* partly 20.8, B 16.39; to some extent 16.118, B 3.92; somewhat 7.44, ? very much 7.189; ~ **manere** some kind of 9.33, 15.299, **B** 5.25, 14.164; ~ **tyme** *av* sometimes, occasionally 3.104, 5.47, 6.57, 79, 112, 137, 428, 7.28, 39, 9.149, 10.159, 12.39, 16.334, 343, 18.37, 49, 19.178, **B** 5.376, 14.237, 15.186, 16.46; some time 8.22; from time to time B 12.22; (at) some time (or other) 6.115, 13.212, 15.299, 17.1, B 11.401; ~...~ at one time ... at another time 6.38, 191, 404, 21.102, 103, 104, B 5.546; on one occasion 20.330; at one time [past] 6.207, 15.302, 16.366, 22.182, **B** 5.135, 12.293, 15.245, 442; ~ ~ þat such time as 21.444

som(me)³ *n* number, quantity 19.33; sum B 13.377

somer 8.245 *etc*; *see* **somur** *n*

som(p)nen *v* invite 12.48; summon 21.215, **leten** ~ have summoned 2.172; call for Z 2.42; order to appear 3.468

som(p)nour *n* summoner, apparitor 2.59, 187, 3.170, 4.162, 9.263, 16.277, 21.372, B 2.170

somur (somer) *n* summer 6.112, 8.245, 9.119, 15.295, 16.11, 146, 18.241; ~ **game** B 5.407, ~ **sesoun** Pr 1, 10.2, ~ **tyme** 16.246, B 14.178 (*fig*) 15.307, 16.17,

somwhat *prn* something 8.277, 18.264, **B** 6.259, 15.392, A 11.181; some (good) reason 12.34; *av* to some extent 21.456, B 12.20

sond 13.135 = **so(e)nd** *n*

Son(e)day 7.64, 20.69, B 13.236 = **Sonenday**

sonde *n* sending, **Goddes** ~ what God sends 6.111, 9.178; command [sent by God] B 9.127; gift [sent by Christ] 16.134

sondry *a* separate 18.192; different Pr 96, 3.90, 20.231, 22.42, B 13.275; distinct 18.191, **B** 16.207, 17.153; various 15.44, 67, 16.108; several, ~ **tymes** 18.153, B 12.31, ~ **tyme** from time to time B 15.282

sone¹ *n* son 3.367, 5.72, 73, 10.241, 14.60, 75, 18.67, B 9.148, [Abraham's] 18.248, 252, B 16.234, [Adam's] 10.251, [Cato's] B 12.21, [Clergy's] B 13.120, [Heli's] Pr 113, [Inwit's] 10.145, [the Jews'] B 16.123, [Joseph's] 9.312, [the King's] 4.43, [men's] 12.114, [Nebuchadnezzar's] 9.307, [Noah's] 10.226, 11.243, [Piers's] 8.82, 92, [Saul's] 3.410, 14.62, [Simon Magus's] = simoniac 5.79, [Symeon's] 20.259, [Tobias's] 11.71, 74; God's son (= Christ) 1.162, 6.171, 7.126, 128, 288, 11.143, 17.262, [justice's 18.126], 18.149, 194, 205, 20.255, 70, [king's] 20.78, 331, (**kynges** ~ **of Heuene**) son of heaven's king 20.363 (= the Second Person of the Trinity) 11.153, 18.228 *et p.*, 19.123 *et p.*, **B** 10.236, 241, 16.214, 223, 17.147 *et p.*; [10.30, 18.67, **B** 1.5, 5.490, 491

sone² *av* straightaway 3.50, 18.8, B 18.317, **A** 11.245, 12.47, **thus** ~ at once 12.6, 15.44; before long 15.96, 108, 22.69; soon B 6.129; presently 15.99, 22.159, B 13.32; quickly 3.61, 180, 13.63, 15.177, 22.87, **B** 6.192, 11.423, 12.31, 241, 16.23, **A** 4.57, 8.11, Z 1.13; *in conjv. phr.* **as** ~ **as** 3.325, **so** ~ (**so**) 10.252, 19.65, B 10.228, **thus** ~ (**as**) as soon as 3.180; (*comp.*) **son(n) er(e)** more quickly 2.141, 3.62, 11.258, 296, 14.111, 18.60, 64; (*sup.*) **son(n)est** most quickly 1.66, 3.435, B 3.58, (+ **most**) 12.225

Son(en)day *n* Sunday 2.231, 6.417, 7.64, 9.227, 242, 244, 15.212, 20.69, B 13.236, **mydde-Lentones** ~ mid-Lent Sunday (4th in Lent) 18.182

song *n* song 13.58; (love) song 6.189; hymn of praise 14.94 (2), 21.212; acclamation B 18.325; singing, **sotil of** ~ B 13.298

song *p.t.* 6.46, 13.16, 20.468, **song(e)(n)** *pl.* 6.395, 7.153, 8.122, 14.94, 20.7, 367, 450, 21.74, 135, 151 *see* **syngen** *v*

songewarie B 7.149, 151 = **sowngewarie** *n*

sonken *p.t. pl.* B 14.80 *see* **sinken** *v*

sonne *n* sun Pr 14, 1.116, 3.478, 6.417, 7.131, 9.294, 308, 10.159, 13.135, 17.91, 20.60, 138, 254, 255, 455, 21.78, B 6.325, A 6.79, (*fig.*) 18.72; sun's rays Pr 1; sunshine 18.66, 19.194, 21.435, B 5.81; sun's heat 18.75; *in cpds.* ~ **rysynge** sunrise 20.69; ~ **syde** sunny side 1.113, 18.64; *in phr.* **vnder** ~ anywhere 3.203, 10.50, 12.95, 16.208, B 10.208

sonnen *v* dry in the sun B 14.21

sonner(e) *comp.* 2.141, 3.62, 11.296, 14.111, 18.60, B 10.416; **sonnest** *sup.* 3.435, 12.225, B 1.70; **soone** B 6.129, 192, 11.423, 12.31, 241, 13.32 = **sone**; *see* **sone** *av*

soor B 14.96, ~**e** B 5.96, 116, 14.96, 106, 18.88 *see* **sore** *a, av*

sooth 16.303, B Pr 52 *etc*, B 10.16 *etc*; *see* **soth** *n, a*; ~**ly** B 15.433 = **sothly(che)** *av*

sop *n* mouthful (*fig.*) B 15.180, *in phr.* **at a** ~ at a morsel's worth B 13.125

sopare *n* soap-maker / seller 5.72

sope *n* soap (*fig.*) B 14.6

soper(e) *n* supper, evening-meal 6.428, 8.275, B 16.141 ~ **tyme** 8.274

sophistrie *n* sophistry 21.349

sorcerie B 10.212, 15.12 = **soercerye** *n*

sore *n* ailment, disease 17.300, 22.97; wound 22.359; hurt 20.385; *a* harsh, painful 22.360; (spiritually) sore B 14.96; *av* sharply, painfully 20.49; strongly 19.274; bitterly 6.316, 20.91; earnestly 7.149; hard 21.441, 22.260; grievously 21.127, **B** 14.162, 18.88, (*comp.*), **sorre** the more grievously Pr 171, **sarrore** more keenly 15.286; intensely B 5.116; closely B 11.224; greatly 6.276 (B 13.388), 7.9, 85 (B 13.426), 20.312, **B** 5.96, 14.106

sorewe A 3.144, 5.215 = **sorwe** *n*

sorfeet (surfete) *n* over-indulgence (in food) B 13.405, A 5.203, (*person.*) 8.276

sorfeten *v* indulge to excess 13.187

sorowe 16.29 = **sorwe** *n*

sorserie 6.191, 18.150 = **soercerie** *n*

sory *a* sad, sorrowful 16.301; upset B 14.323; angry 6.93, 15.213; sorry, repentant, ~ **for synnes** 6.91, 7.59, 145, 245, 11.58, 19.278; remorseful 6.308, 7.15; regretful B 11.104; miserable 19.328, A 11.193, Z 7.198; wicked 3.358, B Pr 45

sorwe *n* sorrow, grief Pr 113, 7.130; distress (of heart) 7.131, 12.210; lamentation 3.17, Z 5.104; contrition 16.29, 19.298; harm, evil B 4.62, Z Pr 73; wretchedness 13.16, 18, 14.80, 16.173, 20.2, 228; misery 22.199; suffering 16.309, 19.318, 21.66, 22.43, 47; pain 22.105, B 14.283; anguish 20.222, A 5.215; misfortune 3.90, 14.61, 62, B 12.245; trouble B Pr 191, A 3.144; torment, *in curses* ~ **mot thow haue** 2.117, **God / Crist ʒeue þe / hym** ~ 2.126, 3.212, 19.309, B 5.106 ~ **on** A 2.80; = torment [in hell] 7.86, 116, 17.145

sorw(e)ful *a* wretched B 17.90; suffering 18.15

sot *n* (*pl.* **sottes**) fool B 10.8; scoundrel 9.256; wretch A 10.59

soth, soþ[1] *n* (the) truth 1.82, 2.26, *in phrr.* **sayen / seggen** ~ speak the truth 2.26, 4.64, 7.229, 12.42, 13.242, 14.103, 19.23, 108, 20.466, **B** Pr 52, 6.129, 12.20, **tellen** ~ 17.211, 20.462, B 9.156, Z 4.50; the truth of the matter 1.121, 3.285, 4.37, 16.122, 17.211, 21.9, **B** 4.80, 5.275, 10.55, Z 4.157; *in phrr.* **witen the** ~ 1.121, 3.285, 4.37, 7.244, 9.128, 10.22, 12.79, 162, 14.191, 16.252, 19.9, 20.149, **B** 2.122, 5.562, A 8.56, Z 3.175, **for** ~ as / to be the truth 7.284, 13.111, 16.303, *as emph. parenth. phr.* truly, indeed 3.112, 4.2, 5.3, 86, 6.237, 7.242, B 11.238, Z 3.122

soth, soþ[2] *a* true 5.92, 10.213, 12.73, 13.246, 16.204, 19.5, 20.312, **B** 10.16, 327, 429, 13.206, 212, 15.173, 16.60, (*sup.*) 10.440, A 10.81, 12.5; genuine 9.62; (indeed) the case 16.204, 18.193, 20.169

sothe *av* tru(thful)ly (*sup.*) 3.435

sothewoste Z 5.32 = **south-weste** *a*

sothfaste *a* true 11.289, B 10.236; real, steadfast 11.131, 15.188, 17.119, 18.51, 69; **~nesse** *n* Divine Truth (= the Son) B 16.186

sothly(che) *av* truly 2.135, 3.5, 7.279, 9.217, 11.131, 286, 13.143, 22.215, 244, **B** 10.228, 15.433; *as emph. parenth. phr.* 2.135 *et p.*; in truth 14.77, 17.179, 19.123, 20.115; with truth, justly 1.115; indeed 3.235, 6.240, 19.93, 21.374; certainly 3.329, 10.18, B 3.190; actually 16.146, 19.57, B 10.273; in fact 7.208, 10.21, B 10.230; for a fact 18.58, B 15.162; assuredly 1.47, 3.245, 12.83, 17.184; for his part 21.87

sothnesse *n* truth(fulness) 19.283; righteousness 12.83, (*person.*) (*a*) 2.24, 200, A 4.138, Z 2.45, 4.50, (*b*) Divine Truth B 18.282

sotil *a* ingenious 10.209, 20.54; subtle, sophisticated 16.208; clever B 15.399; graceful, skilful B 13.298; insidious 4.149; fine-drawn, ethereal B 15.12

sotilen *v*, **(inne)** speculate subtly (upon) B 10.185; scheme, contrive 17.169, 19.236, 20.333, 21.460; cleverly devise 6.189, B 10.216

sotiltee *n* cunning stratagem 12.242; intricacy 14.76

souchen *v* devise 2.26, 12.242

soude *n* payment B 3.353

souden *v* hire (as mercenaries) 21.432

souel (sowl) *n* relish [eaten with bread] 8.285, 17.24

sou(g)ht(e) *p.t.* 3.165, 4.66, 9.315, 16.293, 17.169; *p.p.* 4.122, 7.168, 174 *see* **sechen** *v*

souhteres *n* female shoemaker 6.361

souken *v* suck 12.57

soule *n* (*uninfl. gen.* **soule** 7.174, 20.408, **B** 5.531, 11.228) (the human) soul 1.35, 39, 5.39, 152, 7.76, 88, 112, 8.96 (2), 9.329, 331, 10.158, 14.77, 115, 197, 15.51, 84, 16.31, 131, 148, 153, 17.81, 18.15, 19.313, 20.371, 406, 21.453, 22.233, **B** 11.264, 14.30, 283, 285, 15.344, A 10.77; (= individual) soul 1.80, 2.154, 5.48, 103, 198, 6.345, 7.102, 105, 174, 255, 258, 8.96 (1), 9.39, 289, 12.82, 14.206, 16.25, 154, 273, 17.22, 143, 145, 19.228, 20.336, 341, 388, 394, **B** 1.132, 2.106, 3.50, 4.151, 5.72, 531, 7.51, 8.49, 10.208, 251, 257, 12.15, 54, 13.142, 14.85, **A** 7.136, 10.63, 72, Z 7.76; (living) soul [= animating principle] B 9.50; person B 3.353, A 10.175; heart 19.20, 21.294, B 16.234; *in phrr.* **body and (...)** ~ 1.58, 9.40, (19.28), 20.301, 21.180, **B** 6.251, 15.425, ~ **and (...) body** 1.146, 7.128, 12.89; **Cristene ~s** 11.246, 12.152; **dampned ~s** B 10.428; **gode ~s** Z 7.82; **in** ~ spiritually, inwardly **B** 10.259, 13.288, 15.412, A 3.58; **lyf and** ~ = utterly, absolutely 6.314, 14.127, 20.268, 370, 21.411, **B** 9.188, 17.25; **loue of** ~ heartfelt affection 10.294; **(a) m(a)nnes** ~ 7.88, 16.1, 225, 17.78, 274, 20.194, 244, 408, 414, 21.276, **B** 8.47, 10.475, 11.228, 12.57, 13.130, 15.352, 433; **sauacion of** ~ B 5.125; **synfole ~s** 20.371; **to the** ~ with respect to the soul B 14.285; *in oaths and assevs.* **be (my)...** ~ 8.307, 9.25, 13.242, 19.229, B 5.266, Z 2.97; **bi / for perel of (...)** ~ upon danger of losing (one's) soul 4.137, 7.200, 228; **Godes** ~ 6.426; *in imprecations* **B** 12.39, 13.165, 15.141, A 12.105

sound *a* unharmed A 12.115, *in phr.* **saef and** ~ 10.38, 40

sounen *v*, ~ **of** concern 11.79, ~ **to** have to do with 9.216, 21.456; lead to, foster 6.59

soupen *v* (eat) sup(per) 8.228, 16.13, **B** 2.97, 14.178, 15.180

sour *a* sour 15.49, 18.100, ~ **loef** leavened bread 15.56; bitter (*fig.*) 12.146, 20.217; harsh 22.47; **~e** *av* severely 2.154, B 10.359

souter(e) *n* shoemaker 6.83, **B** 5.407, 10.461, A 11.184

south *n* south, *in phr.* **bi ~e** in the south(ern quarter) 1.116, 20.169; southern sky 9.294; *av, in phr.* **euene**

~ directly to the south A 8.128; ~ **weste** *a* from the south-west 5.116

souþden B 2.173 = **soden** *n*

#soueraynes *n* (elevation to) high rank A 10.119

souereyn *n* lord, master A 10.72; superior 8.82; sovereign ruler 21.77; ruler 11.271; principal guest 14.139

souereyn(e) *a* chief, principal 15.295, B 10.212, ~ **oen** leading person 6.27; supreme 20.227; excellent 1.146, 22.373, B Pr 159, 11.378; efficacious B 10.208

souereynly(che) *av* above all 6.92, 13.202; most especially 17.278, A 11.249; like a conqueror 20.394

soware *n* sower (*fig.* = progenitor) 18.226

sowe *n* sow 6.397, 13.150

sowen *v*¹ (*p.t.* **sew(e)** 6.271 *etc, p.p.* **(y)sowe(n)** 8.3, 12.190, B 5.543) sow (seed) 7.185, 186, 8.3, 24, 62, 9.6, 10.218, 12.181, 188, 190, 15.213, 17.101, B 5.546, *ger.* Pr 23, B 7.118, (*fig.*) 21.276, 290, 299, 311, 345, 409

sowen *v*² sew 8.8, 10

sowestre *n* seamstress A 5.158

sowl 8.285 = **souel** *n*

sowle Z 2.97, 7.76, 82 = **soule** *n*

sownen 21.456 = **sounen** *v*

so(w)ngewarie *n* dream-interpretation 9.302, B 7.151

sowsen *v* steep (*fig.*) Z 2.100

space *n* period B 9.98; time, opportunity 3.216

spade *n* spade 3.461, 8.183, B 6.189

spak(e) *p.t.* 6.222, 419, 11.284, 13.226, 15.154, 16.36, 18.124, 231, 21.376, B 9.32, 13.24, 181 *see* **speken** *v*

spanne *n* hand's breadth [of masonry] Z 6.78

sparen *v* spare [= hold back from destroying] 3.424, 425; ~ (...) **to** refrain from 12.36, 21.304, B 3.51, 10.102, 16.64, ~ **fingeres** work slowly with fingers A 7 *ger.* **sparynge (of)** refraining / ceasing from 7.48; save 9.74, 13.76; hoard B 12.51, 15.143; put aside (to give away) 10.84, B 5.374; keep away 6.151, ~ **to** avoid B 10.102

speche *n* power of speech B 4.156, 9.101; (manner of) speech / speaking 4.17, 10.83, 118, 11.92, 13.229, 15.188, 277, 16.69, 20.119, 239, 21.93, B 5.553, 566, 10.210, 11.239, 13.276, 302, 15.218, 350, A 9.71; speaking, eloquence 11.285; speech, words 2.43, 83, 161, 239, 3.157, 4.138, 149, 153, 6.165, 186, 7.48, 237, 8.216, 9.46, 10.187, 11.20, 92, 14.7, 15.144, 147, 16.206, 18.172, 21.287, 22.115, B Pr 52, 2.42, 5.98, 138, 9.98, 10.166, 11.4, 69, 13.322, 401, 14.13, 16.154, A 10.53, 11.104; word 18.189; utterance 20.132, B 9.37, A 10.34; maxim A 11.241; discourse 10.56, A 12.100; conversation B 13.151; language (*fig.*) 3.109; (*in cpds., person.*) **Benigne** ~ kindly words 18.11, **buxom** ~ mild words B 16.7, **Fair** ~ A 2.130, **Hende** ~ courteous address 22.349, 355, **Sympletee of** ~ humility in speech B 10.167

spechelees *a* without the power of speech 16.196

special *a* exceptional 21.30

sped(de) *p.t.* 13.23, B 17.82, A 12.100 *see* **speden** *v*

spedelich *a* profitable A 12.100

spedily *av* quickly, ? profitably A 7.11

speden *v* achieve one's purpose 3.216; succeed B 17.82 (2); prosper 3.424, 7.239, 8.42, 13.23; help 10.108; satisfy 22.55; (*refl.*) set oneself (to a task) A 12.100, hurry B 17.82 (1)

*speke *n* cave B 15.275

speken *v* (*p.t. sg.* **spak** 6.222 *etc, 2 p.* **speke** 21.80, B 12.191, *3 pl.* **speke(n)** 2.235, 21.130, B 15.275) have power of speech 16.216, 21.130, B 14.84; speak 2.101, 4.44, 21.80, B Pr 129; say, tell 21.70, B 12.191; utter 2.101, 17.319, B 10.40; express 6.431; speak up 20.270, B 17.33; talk 14.7, 21.405; answer 3.216; argue 6.122, B 13.132; converse B 15.275; preach 3.462; ask 2.235, 6.222; plead (for) 9.46; mention 13.100, 14.87, B 1.49; write (about) B 15.117, 573, (against) 16.214; (*person.*) ~ **euele** 21.342

spelen *v*¹ save up 13.76

spelen *v*² recite, ? make out 17.319

*spelonke *n* cavern, den B 15.275

spenden *v* (*p.p.* **yspended** B 14.102) spend (money), expend (wealth) 16.233, *ger.* spending 16.39, *in cpd.* ~ **suluer** spending money 13.100; spend B 5.374, 14.102, A 7.209; expend B 11.292; consume B 10.102; use A 8.49

spendour *n* spendthrift 5.28

spenen *v* (*p.p.* **yspened** 16.278) spend money 2.101, 5.28, B 15.77, 144; spend 9.74, 11.77, 15.282, B 15.144, 328; incur expense B 17.78; expend, lay out 5.69, 13.76, 107, 17.72; use, employ 9.46 (Z 8.50)

spense *n* charge, expense 16.39

spere *n* spear, lance 20.10, 80, 88

speren 19.1 = **spyren** *v*

sperhauk *n* sparrow-hawk B 6.196

spice *n* spice 6.357; medicine, ? species (of remedy) B 1.149c

spicen *v* flavour with spices 21.289

spicer (spysour) *n* spice-dealer, apothecary 2.235, A 10.125

spie *n* spy, scout 21.342; seeker 19.1c

#spiek *n* ear of grain 12.182

spien *v* examine closely B 2.226

spyer 18.231 = **spir(e)** *n*

spilde *p.t.* 6.431 *see* **spillen** *v*

spillen *v* put to death 21.304; lay waste, destroy 3.424; perish 11.43, B 15.135; ruin B 3.310; spoil 5.138; waste 3.462, 5.127, 7.48, 10.187, 14.7, B 10.102; expend in vain B 9.101; vomit up 6.431; shed 21.448; *in cpds.* ~ **tyme** *n* time-waster 5.28; ~ **loue** (*person.*) Destroy-Love 21.342

spynnen *v* spin [fibre into thread] 3.462, A 7.11, *ger.* spinning thread 9.74; spin [thread] 6.222, 8.12

spynnestere *n* [female] spinner of thread 6.222

stille *av* motionlessly (= inactive) 14.120; quietly, privately, *in phr.* **loude ouþer** ~ (= at all times) B 9.106; continually, always 21.424, †B 15.224

styngen *v* sting 20.157

stynken *v* stink, *p.t.* B 15.593

stynten *v* stop, halt 7.222, B 10.222; desist, give up 2.166; bring to a stop [commotion in heaven] B 1.122

stiren B 20.103 = **steren** *v*

styuest *sup.* 6.43; *see* **stif** *a*

styward 3.122, 15.40, 21.464 = **steward** *n*

stywen Z 5.68 = **stewen** *v*

stod(e)(n) *p.t.* Pr 197 *etc*, 20.85, A 4.143, Z 4.124 *see* **standen** *v*

stodie A 12.61, (*person.*) A 11.176 *see* **studie** *n*

stodien A 8.131, 12.6, *ger.* **stodyenge** A 4.143 *see* **studien** *v*

stoed *p.t.* 15.40, (*subjv.*) 16.92, 21.366

stoel *n* (kneeling) stool 7.3, **pynyng** ~ punishment seat 3.79

stoen 14.42 = **ston** *n*

stok *n* tree-trunk 18.30, B 16.5; tree 16.249, B 16.14; grafting-stock 10.209; tree-stump 7.222; frame, **full-yng** ~ frame for cleansing wool B 15.452; *pl.* stocks [frame for punishment] 4.103, 8.163, 9.34

stole *p.p. a* stolen 17.40

stolen *p.t.pl.* B 19.156 *see* **stelen** *v*

stomblen *v* lose one's footing 10.35, B 8.33

ston, stoon *n* stone 6.106, 14.42, **B** 12.75, 15.282; boulder Z 5.3; rock B 12.222; tomb-stone B 15.593; gem-stone 2.13

stonden 7.222, 10.36, **B** 1.50, 8.47, 15.582, 16.24, A 6.82 = **standen** *v*

stonen *v* pelt with stones B 12.75

stop(p)en *v* block out 20.283; stop up 20.285; make an end of 20.461; cause to desist 4.150

storye *n* narrative B 13.447; (*pl.*) sacred histories B 7.71, 73

stot *n* plough-horse 21.268

stoue *n* place, *as surname* 5.130

stounde *n* while 10.64

stoupen *v* bend down 5.24, 7.3; stoop 11.197

stowlyche *av* haughtily Z 3.158

strayf *n* (*pl.* **strayues**) *in phr.* **wayues and** ~ strayed domestic animal Pr 92

strayues *pl.* Pr 92 *see* **strayf** *n*

straunge *a* unfamiliar, unrelated, ~ **men** strangers 16.70

straw(e) *n* cornstalk 12.182; (bed) straw 16.75; = thing of no worth, *in imprec.* **a** ~ **for** fie upon! 16.92

strecchen *v* stretch 16.75

streynen *v* (*refl.*) exert (oneself) 16.75

streyte *av* strictly, ascetically B Pr 26

strenen *v*, ~ **forth** procreate 13.171

strengest *sup.* 6.43 *see* **strong** *a*

stren(g)(t)(h)e *n* strength 10.147, 15.173, B 12.41, *in phrr.* **of** ~ strong enough 21.361, **helplees of** ~ lacking in physical capacity B 7.98; **don by** ~ force B 17.317; **mannes** ~ physical force 17.241, B 13.329; stronghold 3.237, 344, 21.368; prowess in arms 13.108

streng(þ)hen *v* strengthen 3.345; give strength to B 8.47, (*refl.*) A 10.114

strete *n* road B 10.305, **hye** ~ highway 14.48; street 6.50, 9.122

#**strikare** *n* wanderer 9.159

striken *v* (*p.t.* **strok** Pr 197) strike, beat 14.42, B 12.14, 75; go, ~ **forth** proceed 7.223, come forward Pr 197

stryuen *v* contend 8.341

strok *p.t.* Pr 197 *see* **striken** *v*

strompet *n* harlot, adulteress 14.42

stronge *a* sturdy 14.104, Z 7.196, *sup.* 6.43; fit 19.89; tough Z 4.20; confirmed, bold 14.129

struyen *v* kill 17.305 (1); ruin 8.27, 17.305 (2)

struyore *n* destroyer Z 7.196

studeden *p.t.pl.* 17.305 *see* **studien** *v*

study *n* effort Pr 195; study 15.182; (*person.*) 11.1 *et p.*; study [room] B 3.345

studien *v* strive 17.305; (apply oneself to) study A 12.6; reflect 9.297; deliberate B 15.596; brood (about) B 13.289; wonder, *ger.* perplexity A 4.143; seek to understand B 12.222

stuyues *n.pl.* brothel 13.74, 16.92, 21.438, 22.160; the Stews [brothel-area at Southwark] 8.71

stumblen B 8.33, A 9.28 = **stomblen** *v*

stunten 2.166 = **stynten** *v*

sturen 22.103 = **steren** *v*

sturne(ly)(che) *av* sternly, severely Pr 197, 8.341, 11.4, **B** 6.318, 15.253

*****stuty** *a* stumbling Z 4.124

such(e), (swich) *prn* such a person 6.290, 300, **non** ~ no such person 6.37, 13.62; **eny** ~ any such thing 14.15; that (is what) A 11.245; (*pl.*) such people Pr 46, 7.84, 9.19, 13.114, 15.310, 16.214, 17.57, **B** 6.219, 7.42, 15.8, 382, 16.112, **A** 8.33, 10.110, 11.72, ~ **as** those who(m), (the kind of people who(m) 2.45, 3.78, 5.48, 19.93, 21.432, B 15.329; ~ **that** those who 3.287, 6.54, 12.227, 13.111, 17.278, 19.298, **B** 7.40, 10.26, 204, 11.278, 12.13, 15.267, A 11.249; someone who 19.298 (†B 17.316); those [birds] B 6.32

such(e) *a* (of) such (a kind) Pr 34, 64, 134, 2.102, 13.211, *etc*, 20.184, B 19.277; ~ **a** ~ a ~ like this **B** 4.69, 9.129; like these A 7.115; ~ **an othur** another like it Z 6.77; ~**...as** whatever ~ 1.177 *etc*, B 10.36; ~ **oen** someone like that 16.106, 22.344; ~ **...that** of such a kind that 3.409, A 12.33; (*as intensive*) such (a) great / so great (a) 3.452, 5.98, 6.77, 8.187, 20.442, **B** 3.278, 6.322, 14.165, **A** 5.72, 10.82; such hard 8.339, 11.54; so good (a) 5.96, 14.2, 18.140, **B** 15.151; such evil 6.141; *in phrr.* ~ **seuene** seven of such a kind 1.105; ~ **tyme** at (such) a time (when) 20.426

sucre 16.148 = **sugre** *n*

suen 2.102, 10.73, 12.168, 22.126, B 4.167, **suewen** 7.186 = **sewen** v¹

sufficen 17.119, 19.35, 204 = **soffisen** v

suffraunce 4.189, **B** 6.144, 11.378, A 10.119 = **soffra(u)nce** n

suffren A 9.47 etc, B 2.106 etc; see **soffr(y)en** v

sugestioun n motive, reason 9.62

sugre n sugar 6.88, 16.148

suynde pr.p. 20.358, **suynge** 18.63 see **sewen** v

suyred pt. Z 6.16 see **suren** v

suyrelepes a separate, distinct 18.192; av separately B 17.165

sullen (sellen) v (p.t. **solde** 6.97 etc, B 16.143, p.p. **sold** 3.245 etc) sell 3.120, 243, 6.225, 8.329, 9.29, 12.63, 165, 220, 17.20, 101, 129, 18.158, 21.401, **B** 3.196, 7.22, 11.275, Z 3.149, ger. 21.236; succeed in selling 6.97; give away for payment 3.245; give in exchange 6.376, 8.291; betray for money 20.222, B 16.142

suller n merchant, vendor 3.116, A 2.44

sulue(n) a (as intensifier with prec. n. / prn.) himself 7.206, 12.138, 14.26, 16.112, 17.179, 18.96, 130, B 1.204, A 1.110, (post-positive with prn.) **þi** ~ you yourself A 10.86, **vs** ~ (us) ourselves B 7.128; (with foll. n.) own 7.254, B 5.488

suluer 1.63 etc; see **seluer** n

sum(me) prn. a Pr 25 etc, 2.4 etc; see **som(m)(e)** prn, a

sumnour 9.263 = **som(p)nour** n

sumtyme 10.159; see **som-**

sumwhat 12.34, 8.277 see **somwhat** prn.

sundry 20.231 = **sondry** a

sunnere comp. 11.258 = **sonner(e)**; see **sone** av

suppriour n sub-prior 6.153

suren v give one's word (to) B 5.540

surgerie n surgery 22.178; surgical skill (fig.) B 16.106

surgien n surgeon 22.311, 314, 316, 337; healer 18.140, (fig.) B 14.88

surquidours, (surquidous) a as n arrogant (person.) 21.341n

suspectioun n expectation 17.313

#sustantif n substantive, noun 3.335, 342, 352, 360, 393, 403

suste(y)nen v provide for, feed 8.17, **B** 15.280, (fig.) B 15.467; perpetuate 10.205, B 9.109

suster (sister) n (pl. **susteres** 7.269, **sust(u)r(e)ne** A 11.191, uninfl. gen. A10.159) sister 12.171, B 5.642, A 10.153, 159, 179, (fig.) 3.207, 7.269, 11.97, 20.120, 187, 194, A 6.113; nun, female member of religious order 3.54, 6.137, 16.293; honorary sister B 3.63

sustinaunce n livelihood 5.126; food 22.7

sute n apparel, guise [sc. human flesh, with play on 'cause'] B 5.488, 497; retinue, company of followers B 14.257

suthe 18.192 = **sethe**³ conj.

suwen B 10.204, 17.102, 107, 18.191 = **sewen** v¹

swaer p.t. 17.178 see **swer(i)en** v

swagen A 5.100 = **aswagen** v

swan-whit a as white as a swan 20.213

sweyen v sound, ? move along B Pr 10

swellen v (p.t. pl. **swolle** Z 7.163) become swollen 21.284, A 12.74, Z 7.163; cause to swell [sc. with pride], become puffed up 16.225; ger. swelling [as if pregnant] 18.100; flatulence 6.88

swelten v (p.t. **swelte(d)**) lose consciousness, faint 6.129, 22.105

swerd n sword 1.102, 3.457

swer(i)en v (p.t. **swaer** 17.178, **swoer** 22.161, **swo(o)r(e)(n)** 2.181, 4.79, Z 8.23, p.p. **sworn** 6.426) swear (an oath) 1.102, 16.304, 17.178, B 13.382, 383; swear [by God's name, etc] 4.79, 6.426, 7.200, 216, 9.25, **B** 5.224, 13.403, 14.35, Z 7.288, (person.) ~ **nat...** 7.216; ~ **for soþe** swear to be true 16.303; ~ **gret othes** curse Pr 36; testify (in court) 5.57, ~ **treuth** testify truthfully 22.161; solemnly declare B 15.405, Z 4.50; emphatically affirm 6.51, **B** 2.169, in phr. **seien and** ~ 2.181, B 15.595

swete n something pleasant 12.146

swete a (comp. **swettore** 14.186, 16.148, 18.60) sweet (-tasting) 6.88, 12.222, 18.60, 63, 65, 100, **B** 9.149, 12.263, 15.469, (fig.) 16.148, 150, 20.217; sweet-smelling 13.177, A 10.123; agreeable, pleasant Pr 84, 12.11, 14.186, Z 7.259; satisfying B 15.184; dear B 17.125; av (comp.) **swettere** more pleasantly 8.228; ~**nesse** n sweetness 18.63

sweten v sweat 8.241; toil hard B 13.261; in phr. **swynke and** ~ Pr 36, 5.57, 8.24, 134

sweue(n)(e) n dream 9.310, B Pr 11, A 8.139

swich B 1.194, 2.17, etc; see **such(e)** a

swiȝen A Pr 10 = **sweyen** v

swift a rapid, comp. ~**ore** 14.186, B 12.262; timely, without delay B 11.378

swymmen v swim 14.106, 107, 109, 171, B 12.168; ger. swimming B 12.166

swymmere n swimmer B 12.166

swyn n (pl. ~) pig 5.19, B 2.98

swynk(e) n toil 8.203, 241, B 6.232

swynkare n workman 8.259, 19.174

swynken v (p.t. **swonken** Pr 23) work hard, labour Pr 53, B 6.194, in phr. ~ **and swete** Pr 36, 5.57, 8.24, 134; work Pr 23, 7.185, 8.227, 262, B 7.118

swythe av actively A 4.23; very 6.316, B 13.403; frequently B 5.449; quickly 13.52, B 9.132; promptly, **as** ~ at once 6.421, B 3.102

swoenen 20.57 see **swowenen** v

swoer p.t. 22.161 see **swer(i)en** v

swoet n sweat 8.241

swonken p.t. pl. Pr 23 see **swynken** v

swolle p.t. pl. Z 7.163 see **swellen** v

swo(o)r p.t. 4.79, 6.51, B 2.169 etc, **sworen** pl. 2.181, B 5.370, Z 4.152, **sworn** p.p. 6.426 see **swer(i)en** v

swounen B 14.326, 18.57 *see* **swowenen** *v*

swowe *n* faint, **a ~, y~** in a faint A 5.215 (Z 5.110)

swowen *v* (fall in a) faint 6.129, B 16.19; fall unconscious 22.105

swowenen *v* faint 7.55, 20.57, 22.105, **B** 14.326, 16.19

tabard *n* (sleeveless) short coat 6.203

table *n* (moneychanger's) table 18.157; (dining) table 7.103, **B** 10.103, 13.177, **seconde ~** 9.252, **syde ~** [for inferiors in hall] 14.139, 15.42

tab(o)ren *v* play the drum 15.206

tacche *n* vice, fault B 9.148

tache B 17.246 = **tasch** *n*

taek *imper.* 22.135, 359 *see* **taken** *v*

taȝte B 6.300 = **tauhte** *p. t.*

tayl *n* (*pl.* **~** 5.121, **~es** 17.31) tail 17.31; tail feathers B 12.241, 248, (? *with pun on* **tayle**) 245; (*meton.*) 'tail' [sexual organs] 3.166, 10.80, 16.257; roots 5.121; train (of followers) 2.196; end, conclusion B 3.351

tayl(l)e *n* tally-stick, **taken ~** offer promise to pay later 4.61, **taken bi ~** ? receive on credit B 5.248 (*see note*); reckoning, account (*with pun on* **tay(l)** 'end') B 12.245

taylen *v* record (on a tally-stick), *p.p.* 7.35

taylende *n*[1] backside 7.4

taylende *n*[2] reckoning of accounts B 8.82 (*with pun on ~ n*[1]); income, revenue (*with pun on meton. sense of ~ =* 'genitals') 3.369

tayler *n* tailor, clothes-maker Pr 224, 4.120, 9.204, A 11.184, **~s** tailor's (**craft, hand**) B 5.547, 15.454

taken *v* (*imper.* **ta(e)k** 22.135, A 3.222, 10.97, *p.t.* **toek** 4.166 *et p.,* **tok** 3.84 *et p.,* **toke** 3.47 *et p.,* **took** 4.15, 40, 12.46, B 5.248 *etc, pl.* **token** 4.73 *etc,* Z 8.65, *p.p.* **take** 17.287, **ytake** 9.92) take (hold of) 5.130, 8.272, 9.2n, 14.104, 15.161, 20.47, 21.170, B 14.190; take (aside) 4.166, 15.176; carry 4.52, B 13.164; seize (by force) 1.92, 3.176, 4.49, 17.227, B 4.48; arrest 18.176, 21.56, B 16.160; apprehend, catch 19.212, B 12.74; take hold 6.80; steal 22.11; get, obtain 3.445, 9.91, 13.43, 44, 17.45, 21.463, 471, 476, Z Pr 64; take (leave) 7.292, 21.483; strike down B 6.144, 17.54; defeat (in battle) 17.287; lead, bring 3.4, 4.73; deliver 14.129; receive 3.144, 273, 4.29, 9.54, 65, 92, 13.103, 14.205, 16.145, 21.466, **B** 3.254, 255, 6.139, 7.61, 77, 12.90, 14.142, 184, Z 1.131; accept 1.96, 3.116, 123, 126, 310, 495, 6.289, 9.54, 16.309, 356, 17.186, **B** 2.34, 3.247, 253, 353, 7.40, 61, 8.82, 11.281, A 3.222, Z 7.273; put on, assume 1.151, 20.230, 21.72, 22.41, B 15.208; choose 5.79, 15.83, (as wife) 16.106; undergo, endure 6.77, 9.183, 12.150, 16.326, B 7.101; feel 6.77; react to, take 9.131, 14.66; pay heed, take note, *in phrr.* **~ gome (ȝeme)** 3.485, 19.15, B 10.197, **~ hede** 11.70, 12.221, 14.99, 17.239, 18.19, B 15.91, A 8.78; **~ kepe** pay attention (to) 13.145, A 10.97, observe 15.177,

look after 19.76, 22.359, **~ mark** take note B 17.104, **~ reward** take heed19.249; **~ record at** call to witness B 15.87; **~ witness (at / of)** call to witness 6.53, 12.77, **~ to witnesse** 11.38, 15.103, 20.135, **B** 11.87, 15.488; review 21.466; draw (out from) B 16.204; take (down from) 20.72, 86; pick 20.305; give, grant 1.52, 3.350, 4.61, 9.275, 13.105, 19.2, 76, 22.260; attribute 19.37; bribe 22.137; sell 3.87, bid (farewell) B 13.203; (make) use (of) 20.93; speak to 15.106; **~ togyderes** confer together 6.154; invoke,**~ on** act, behave 3.84, 13.154; execute (vengeance) Pr 117, 121, 20.135, **B** 6.224 15.261; take out (writ) 2.187

talage (taillage) *n* tax, levy 21.37

tale *n* story Pr 49, 8.48, 50, 20.135, B Pr 51; exemplum B 12.265; lesson A 11.222; sermon B 9.72, Z 7.230; discourse 12.46, B 10.373; idle fable, **disours ~** B 10.49, **~ of Walterot** = absurd nonsense 20.144; gossip 7.19, B 5.377; lying gossip 6.50, 154, B 13.333; lie 2.227, 4.18, 34; dishonest confession 3.47; speech 2.116, B 4.69; **soþ ~** true principle A 10.81; remark(s) B 11.99, 100; words 7.90; talk, conversation 6.28, 185, 194, 18.3, 22.119, B 13.58; argument B 10.373; case 12.174; account 13.87; esteem, regard, *in phrr.* **~ of nauht** thing of no worth 13.113; **gyuen neuer ~, holden no ~, maken litel ~** regard / treat as of little importance / value 1.9, 3.390, 21.457,

#**tale-tellare** *n* tale-bearer 22.300; maker of (religious) controversy A 11.73

talewys *a* garrulous 3.166

talken *v* talk B 17.83

tame *a* domesticated 15.296

tanner *n* tanner of hides Pr 224

taper *n* wax candle 19.169, 261

tarre *n* tar [for sheep-salve] 9.262

Tarse *n* costly (?silk) fabric [from Tharsia] B 15.168

***tasch** *n* touchwood, tinder 19.212

tasel *n* fuller's teasel B 15.453

taste *n* (tangible) experience B 12.130

tasten *v* feel (by touching) 19.124, B 18.84, (? *with pun on* 'taste') 6.179

tauhte *p.t.* 1.71 *et p.,* **tauȝte** B 1.76 *et p.* (**tauȝtest** B 14.154), **taughte** Z 1.121, *p.p.* **ytauhte** 8.20, **tauȝt** B 10.223; *see* **techen** *v*

taxen *v* impose (fine) 1.157

***taxour** *n* assessor 8.37

tecchen 1.143 = **teche** *v*

tauerne *n* tavern 2.98, 6.50, **B** 5.377, 9.104, 13.304

tauerner *n* tavern-keeper Pr 229

techare *n* (moral / religious) teacher 14.20, 16.240, 245, 17.78, 22.120, 303

techen *v* (*p.t.* **tauhte** 2.8 *et p.,* **tauȝte** B 1.76 *et p.*) *p.p.* (**y)tauht(e)** 8.20, 22.186, B 10.222) preach 4.118, ?Z 7.234; deliver a sermon B 5.12; say, tell, inform 3.436, 8.86, 9.124, 10.107, 125, 296, 18.82, 19.99, 21.363, **B**

3.254, 15.282, **A** 7.81, 11.28, 165, 268, Z 7.266; teach (about), explain 11.218, 14.12, 75, 16.231, 17.51, 83, 19.109, 319, 21.272, **B** 15.93, 584, 17.41, A 12.2; proclaim (to), propound 3.75, 11.245, 12.60, 99, 15.128, 17.51, 294, 298, B 15.93, 584, **A** 11.196, 12.97; reveal 17.295, 21.44, 22.278; instruct (in, about) 1.71, 143, 3.277, 8.20, 11.3, 149, 217, 14.52, 15.127, 17.174, 180 (2), 254, 18.138, **B** 7.176, 10.225, 12.107, 132, 13.117, 15.571, 17.117; show, indicate 8.4, 9.88, 21.170, B 15.434; direct 1.79, 2.8, 5.5, 17.180 (1), 18.2; teach (how to) 8.59, 10.201, 11.121, 14.161, 21.239, B 8.56; bring up, *p.p.* bred, mannered 22.186; urge (to vice), suggest (sin) to 1.36, 3.160, 20.202, Z 3.164; counsel, advise 4.96, 13.196, **B** 7.73, 15.342; prescribe, enjoin 1.13, 2.126, 5.130, 6.12, 8.218, 9.24, 351, 10.102, 305, 11.70, 71, 13.193, 14.69, 210, 15.126, 16.185, 306, 342, 17.59, 139, 219, 21.170, 22.9, **B** 6.82, 226, 10.84, 197, 205, 267, 12.32, 36; discipline, teach (through chastisement) to 8.141, 20.237

techyng *ger.* teaching, instruction 11.224, 14.34, **B** 12.64, 15.73, 17.124, **A** 7.232, 11.293; teaching 12.100, *in phrr.* **Beatus virres** ~ B 10.320, **Catons** ~ B 7.72, **clerkis** ~ B 15.68, **fyue wittis** ~ A 11.293, **Holy Cherche** ~ B 10.252, **kynde wittes** ~ 14.34, **olde mennes** 9.214; counsel 2.22, 21.318, A 10.97; guidance 22.8; direction 19.124, 21.476, **B** 10.153, 14.26

teeme B 19.263, A 3.84 = **teme** n^1, n^2

†**teen** *v* go, †**teeth** B 17.38

teeþ *pl.* B 15.13 = **teth** *see* **to(e)th** *n*

teyen *v* bind 1.92, 3.176

teynten *v* stretch, *p.p.* **yteynted** B 15.454

tel *imper.* 7.244, **B** 1.83, 10.158, A 12.28 *see* **tellen** *v*

telden *v* (*p.t.* **telde, tilde,** *p.p.* **telid**) pitch (tent) A 2.42; dwell 14.149

telye(n) Z 7.216, 8.2 = **tilien** *v*

telþe A 7.127 = **tulthe** *n*

tellen *v* (*pr. subjv.* **telle** 7.125, 19.120, *p.t.* **tolde** Pr 229 *et p.*, *p.p.* **told(e)** Pr 111, B 1.208 *etc*) speak 19.311, **B** 1.88, 3.104, 4.157, 10.137, **here** ~ hear said B Pr 164; (make) mention (of) 19.37, **B** 13.420, 15.413; *in phrr*: **soth(ly) (for) to** ~ 7.279, B 9.156; ~ **(þe) sothe** 17.211, 20.462, **to** ~ **treuthe** 17.211, **treuliche to** ~ 2.251, B 16.4; say (to) Pr 229, 5.156, 7.125, 297, 14.131, 15.89, 16.187, 295, 19.163, 20.111, 144, **B** 5.268, 17.263, A 2.26, Z 4.50; talk (of) 15.111, 20.149, B 13.354, A 11.62; declare **B** 5.54, 11.66, *in phr.* ~ **with tonge** declare outright / clearly 7.17, 16.369, A 12.24; state 1.145, 16.192, B 1.130; tell, recount Pr 9, 1.125, 6.108, 11.32, 37, 15.206, 21.115, **B** Pr 51, 11.160, 12.236, 17.88, (*in writing*) 5.109, A 5.10, Z 5.27, *in phrr.* **as (þe) Bible** (*etc*) ~**eth**: Bible 5.169, B 9.41, **Boke** Pr 129, 1.28, 5.38, 9.120, 127, 12.75, 13.15, 14.169, 21.71, A 12.3, **crede** 8.98, **Gospelle** 12.213, B 12.63, **lettre** 12.114, 20.81, **B** 12.73, 17.118, **holy lettrure** 15.74, **holy lore** 17.65,

Sauter 7.92, B 3.237, **Holy Writ** ~ Pr 104, 2.142, 3.486, 10.248, 19.127, 296, 21.109, **B** 10.381, 17.306; explain (to) 1.79, 114, 3.393, 10.125, 151, 11.71, 14.99, 15.17, 16.114, 117, 118, 19.100, 20.173, 22.253, **B** 2.122, 11.80, 12.18, 25, 15.71, 74, 571, A 11.86; teach, instruct 18.2, 21.414, B 11.80, Z 7.234, *ger.* 22.8, A 7.232; tell (to), inform 1.43, 2.202, 4.18, 6.56, 7.297, 302, 8.76 (1), 10.13, 11.198, 14.192, 15.193, 17.100, 18.8, 21.23, 22.232, 268, **B** 15.317, 16.144; disclose, make known 6.70, 71, 8.76, 13.248, 15.193, 16.164, 18.245, 292, 19.120, 20.65, 21.276, **B** 10.5, 225, 13.14, 15.13, 16.61, 63, 147, 230, **A** 11.218, 12.18; proclaim 13.103, **B** 13.300, 15.91; describe 2.15, 196, 19.311, A 6.82; utter **B** 10.373, 11.1, 16.212; (say in) confess(ion) 3.47, 7.29, 14.121; direct 17.180; preach (about) 15.83, B 13.69; cite **B** 3.346, 10.269, 12.265; prophesy, foretell 5.178, 17.99, 21.145, **B** 7.167, 19. 244; report (to) Pr 111, 6.47, 7.244, 11.138, 13.39, 87, 18.162, 21.155, 344, *in phrr.* **tales to** ~ spread gossip 4.18, 6.50, 154, **B** 11.99, 13.304, 333, ~ **tale** engage in conversation 6.28, tell a lie B 18.289; count Pr 90, 6.425, 12.177, 19.33, B 5.248; reckon 11.213; judge, regard 19.240

tellere A 11.73 *see* **tale-** ~ *n*

tellyng *ger.* instruction 22.8, A 7.232

teme n^1 team [of draught animals] 8.20 (*with pun on* 'theme'), 141, 9.2*n*, (*fig.*) 21.262, 263, 272

teme n^2 topic, subject 12.46, B 10.118; theme (of sermon) 6.1, 15.83, 20.358, **B** 3.95, 7.136

#**temperaltee** *n* temporality [lay income and property belonging to prelate's office] 22.128

tempest *n* storm 20.65

temple *n* temple [of Jerusalem] 1.45, 18.157, 163, 20.61, B 16.131, **oure Iewene** ~ our Jewish temple 20.40

Templers *n* the Knights Templar 17.209

tempren *v* tune (*fig.*), ~ **þe tonge** direct (one's) speech 16.144, B Pr 51

tempten *v* tempt (to sin), *p.p.* 21.64

ten(e) *num. a* 1.104, 4.61, 6.220, 7.17, 29, 16.231, 21.165, **B** 6.241, 13.270, ~ **hestes (comaundementis)** 2.87, 9.334, 11.142, 13.67, 16.231, A 11.253; (*qualifying other nums.*) ~ **hundrit** 7.38, ~ **score** 11.128, ~ **thousand** A 2.42; *as n* A 1.103, 7.226

tenaunt *n* tenant [one holding land by service or rent] 8.36, 17.45

tenden *v* (*p.t. pl.* **tend(ed)en**) kindle 20.248

tender (**tonder**) *n* tinder 19.212

tene *n* injury, pain 1.164; suffering, distress 12.51, 13.7, 16.173; anger, **pu(y)re** ~ sheer rage 8.124, **B** 7.115, 16.86, **turne to** ~ make angry A 12.9; **trauail and** ~ painful effort B 6.133, A 10.145

teneful *a* painful, troubling 3.495

tenen *v* harm 7.38, **B** 8.98, 15.419; oppress Z 2.170; hurt 3.159, 22.119; trouble 3.139, 474, 8.36, 11.128, 14.8, 15.161; (*refl.*) get angry 2.116, Z 2.169

tente *n* tent, pavilion A 2.42

teologie (theologie) *n* (the discipline / study of) theology 11.128, B 10.373; (*person.*) 2.116, 129, B 10.197, A 12.9, 18, Z 2.169

#tercian *n* tertian fever, (*person.*) A 12.85

tere *n* tear 15.51

teren *v* (*p.p.* **tore**) tear 6.203

terme *n* saying, expression B 12.236

terminen *v* pronounce judgement (on) 1.93

***termison** *n* termination, (inflexional) ending [of a word] 3.405

testifien *v* attest, ~ **for gode** vouch for (as) 11.310; ~ **for treuthe** certify as true 12.174; ~ **of** (make) affirm(ation) concerning B 13.94

teth *pl.* 20.83 *see* **to(e)th** *n*

tetheren *v* tie, fasten Z 3.76

text 1.200, B 2.122 *etc; see* **tix(s)t** *n*

thay 13.101, 20.209 = **thei** *prn*

than Pr 165, 187, A 12.72 = **thanne** *av*

than *conj. of comparison* than Pr 123, 164, 7.24, 9.123, 14.154, 18.88, 19.104, 20.456, B 1.143, 184 *etc*, **þanne** A Pr 89; *and see* **then** *conj.*

thank *n* thought, regard, *gen. in avl. phr.* **his ~es** willingly 9.66

þanked *p.t.* A 12.48 *see* **thonken** *v*

thanne, þanne Pr 185, 19.34, B 1.58 *et p.*, A 1.112 *etc* = **thenne** *av*[1]

thar *impers. 3 sg. pr.* 15.259, **tharstow** *2 sg.* = **tharst þow** B 14.56; *see* **thuruen** *v*

thare Pr 133 = **ther** *av*

that (þat)[1]*dem. prn* that Pr 39, 1.57, 161 (1), 196 (1), 3.338, 353, 474, 8.271, 334, 19.315, 21.10, B 9.61, 10.343, ? 11.368, Z 7.245

that[2] *rel. prn* who Pr 86, 119, 160, 2.3, 32 *et p.*, B 1.130 *et p.*, whom Z 3.151; **hem alle** ~ all those who 2.47–8, 20.178–8; which, that Pr 132 *et p.*, Z Pr 58, *in prnl. phrr.* ~ **(you)** who 1.80, 2.79, 20.402, B 11.223, for whom 15.301; of which 17.69; ~ **he** who 16.291, 21.377, ~...**hit** which 18.80, ~...**his** whose 1.59; ~...**hit** which 18.80; **hem...** ~ those...who 1.164; **here...** ~ of those who 2.76–7, 16.283, 17.25–6; **his...** ~ of him who 9.53–4, B 1.82; **ȝe...** ~ you...who 17.82–3; against whom A 5.53; on which, when 7.65; *in phr.* **the whiche** ~ who 3.93, **þe which...** ~ (for) which 13.82; *indep. rel.* the one who 1.66, 8.127, 12.185, 14.126, 15.155; for one who B 10.357, A 7.137; he who 1.110, 3.485, 9.48, 208, 14.41, 15.127, **B** 7.124, 10.345, A 11.157, Z 8.50; those who 1.66, 3.13, 288, 4.33, 6.252, 9.183, 208, 10.102, 11.18, 12.109, 195, 21.444, **B** 6.192, 9.63; (on) those who 3.95; that which, what Pr 39, 1.97, 2.38, 128, 139, 3.83, 319, 322, 4.86, 150, 5.141, 7.17, 8.105, 108, 140, 9.74, 260, 12.217, 224, 15.89, 19.5 (2), 248, 258, 267, 20.142, 391, 21.246, 22.7, **B** 1.28, 3.255, 5.545, 6.129, 133, 9.15, 10.321, 13.135, 15.159, 16.183, **Z** Pr 70, 3.122, 6.67

that[3] *dem. a.* that 2.53, 3.490, 4.13, 128, 5.43, 17.276, 19.78, 116, 20.200, **Z** 1.65, 3.8, 7.253, ~ **ilke** B 9.189; *as def. art.* = the 20.150; *in phrr.* ~ **ilke** the (same) one 16.312; ~ **on** (the) (first) one 7.271, 19, 301, 21.264, **B** 1.23, 3.232; ~ **on...**~ **oþer** the first...the second 14.106–7, A 8.14, 12.84

that[4] *particle, in phrr.* **by** ~ by that time 8.314, 322; according to what 11.271, 273, 16.295; **for** ~ because B 4.68, **Z** 5.150, 7.77; **how** ~ how, in what way 16.232, A 8.17; **yf** ~ if 20.198; whether B 2.156; **manere** ~ way that A 2.47; **so** ~ provided that B 4.102; **ther** ~ where 3.222; **tho** ~ when 20.241; **thogh** ~ even if 19.320; **tyl** ~ until Z 2.72; **why** ~ why B 10.119; **where** ~ wher(ever) A 8.58; **with** ~ at that, thereupon 13.247, provided that 6.173

that[5] *conj.* that Pr 34, 82, 102, 104 *et p.*; = than that B 7.114; **so** / **with the result that** Pr 173, 2.32, 168, 3.67, 142, 194, 211, 431, 6.268, 400, 7.153, 8.174, 181, 9.82, 10.48, 11.57, 13.12, 15.269, 16.230, 17.80, 18.140, 19.292, 20.242, 358, 21.278, 350, 22.176, **B** 1.26, 158, 5.6, 118, 145, 361, 373, 10.79, 11.48, 422, 13.407, 14.96, 15.10, 72, 354, 410, 16.78; (+ **ne**) = but that, who / which...not 6.284, 312, 7.61, 11.185, 14.150, 16.291, 19.92, 329, 21.52, **B** 5.552, 7.51, 114, 8.101, 14.13, 15, **A** 2.39, 4.136, 8.38, 10.161, **Z** 3.176, 7.163; lest 5.122, 19.310; **so** / **in order that** 3.309, 376, 5.185, 6.167, 7.207, 9.38, 15.79, 17.14, 19.288, 332, 20.23, 286, 363, 21.120, 229, 312, 366, B 6.242, A 12.95, Z 5.94; (*with inf.*) 20.31, B 12.227; when 6.259, 18.128, 168, 20.471, B 16.94, A 7.283; because, since 14.127, 18.17, **B** 5.31, 113, 16.19, (implying wish / entreaty) 4.7, 5.199, 8.10, 21.482, **B** 4.127, = (saying) that / (to the effect) that 2.130 (1), 234, 3.414, 6.172, 328, 9.348, 10.253, 13.101, 18.126, 20.196, **B** 5.165, 10.353, = from, *in phrr* **letten ...**~ prevent from 3.36, 6.312, 10.162, 15.183; **reste** ~ desist from 6.127

thauh 9.122 = **thogh** *conj.*

the(e), þe(e)[1] *prn 2 sg., pers. as dir. obj.* thee, you (*addressed variously to inferior, equal, superior*) Pr 148, 1.24 *et p.*, (*Mede*) 3.19, (*King*) Pr 149, 3.208, (*Christ*) 7.137, (*God*) 7.150; *as indir. obj.* (to) thee / you 7.253, 8.33, 298, 9.281, **B** 10.168, 11.419, A 3.244, Z 4.143; *for you* 7.106; *as dat.of interest* Z 3.131, (*after prep.*) 3.135 *et p.*; *as refl.* thyself, yourself 3.418, 4.16, 5.102, 6.12, 13, 164, 338, 7.8, 260, 8.290, 10.287, 290, 306, 11.142, 195, 12.4, 194, 13.194, 14.9, 22.205, B 13.143, **A** 7.26, 10.114; for yourself 6.340, 11.75, 21.320; *as obj. of impers. v.* 3.44, 7.55, 15.253, 22.210, A 1.25, **Z** Pr 117, 3.150

the (þe)[2] *def. art.* the Pr 10 *et p.*; *with rel. prn* ~ **which(e)** who 3.93, 191, 9.107, 10.154, 171, whom 18.72, 19.39, which 3.496, 6.243, 9.140, 11.82, 12.152, 14.54, 16.112, 17.140, 247, 18.41, 51, 207, 235, 19.8, 259, 20.110, 223, 21.129, **B** 13.408, 15.131, *with rel.*

a. ~ **which(e)** ~ 15.278, 18.11, 19.87, 20.339, 22.62; *in unique ref. with name / title* 1.38, 1.70, 2.19, 146, 3.175, 270, 5.38, 6.317, **B** 4.179, 11.160, Z 2.88; *with occupational names* 6.352, 7.302; *in generic ref.* Pr 231, 1.99, 2.224, 3.176, 6.144, 438, 8.122, 9.264 *etc*, B 5.2, A 7.21; *with a. forming n. phr.* 2.39, 153, 3.317, 477, 5.139, 6.261, 7.103, 9.64, 10.76, 11.36, 12.105, 18.107, 20.98, 21.198 *etc*, B 2.46, Z 2.118; *in avl. phrr.* **at** ~ **furste / laste** 8.168, 9.207, Z 3.173; ~ **nones** A 2.41, ~ **same** likewise 3.27, ~ **while(s)** while 3.29, 57, 324, 5.137, 9.349, 20.140, 21.334, Z 4.16, meanwhile 8.6

the (þe)³ *av* (so much) the (*with comp. a / av*) Pr 104, 3.424, 4.102, 6.216, 7.141, 239, 8.42, 125, 10.311, 11.129, 12.44, 17.253, 21.420, **B** 1.107, 15.425, **Z** 6.44, 7.165, *in correl. constr.* ~...~ 3.136, 15.262, 16.118, 19.69

thec(c)hen *v* (cover roof with) thatch 21.239, *ger.* 8.199

thechen Z Pr 126 *etc.,* = **techen** *v*

thed(de)r(e) *av* thither, to that place 1.118, 7.157, 204, 291, 22.286, B 2.162, A 3.246

thedom *n* activity, industry 7.53; prosperity A 10.108

theen *v* prosper, *in assev.* **so thee Ik** so may I prosper B 5.224

the(e)f *n* (*pl.* **theues** 5.17 *etc*) thief 5.17, 13.61, 14.129, 130, 135, 145, 147, 150, 153, 17.138, 19.54, 255, 20.73, 76, 424, **B** 9.119, 13.161, 14.305, 17.90

thefliche *av* by stealth B 18.339

thefte *n* theft, stealing 2.92, 6.348; act of theft B 5.231

thei, they *pers. prn 3 pl.* they Pr 108 *et p.* 2.102 *et p.*; (*with indef. a. or num.*) of them 9.201, 10.106, 11.261, 12.75, 19.81, B 10.153; them 21.371; *see also* **hy, hem** *pers. prn.*

they Z 3.103 = **thogh** *conj.*

theyr Z 3.21 = **her(e)**³ *poss. prn.*

thekynge 8.199 = **thechynge** *ger.; see* **thec(c)hen** *v*

then¹ *conj. of comparison* than Pr 166 *et p.*; *and see* **than, þanne, thenne** *conj.*

then² 4.90, 6.418, 15.286, 309, 16.196, Z 1.14 = **thenne** *av*¹

thenken (þynken¹**)** *v (p.t.* **thouhte** 12.53, **þoȝt** B 6.297, *p.p.* **thouhte** 6.51, **þouȝt** B 13.268) think 18.245, B 13.86, Z 6.68; realise 16.94; imagine B 5.283; recall 8.278; remember **B** 13.268, 19.255; consider 10.97; ponder 12.53, 92; reflect upon **B** 5.600, 7.168; intend, purpose 1.21, 18.265, 19.316, 21.183, 196, 338, **B** 3.95, 5.84, 6.297; plan B 12.89; intend to go 20.121, 232, B 16.175

thenne (þanne)¹ *av* then, at that time 2.50, 7.260, 8.315, 16.6, 20.413 *etc*; at that (very) moment 11.188, 13.219, 241, 15.286, 19.293; after that, next Pr 141, 3.9, 342, 5.109, 7.298, 18.87 *etc*; next in turn 6.62, 308 *etc*; thereupon Pr 139, 147, 1.68, 8.255, 10.72 *etc*, Z 8.81; now 11.1, 173, 6.308, 15.187, 252, 16.156, 20.13, 238,

Z 7.284; *as conj. av* therefore 19.126; in consequence 3.102, 13.183, 15.204, 17.44, 19.291, A 1.112; in that case 10.189, 11.45, 224, 14.10, 15.115, 16.177, 20.56, 311; in those circumstances / that situation 16.178, 186 *etc*, 20.158, Z 4.119, 7.43

thenne² 2.225, 3.262 = **thennes** *av*

thenne³ 1.113, 7.209, 11.228, 17.203, 19.296, Z 8.83 = **then**¹ *conj.*

thenne(s) *av* thence, from there / that place 1.70, 2.239, 3.262, 7.67, 135, 21.427, 22.205, B 10.61

theologie *see* **teologie** *n*

þer *poss. prn* (= **her(e)**³) their, ~ **beyre rihte** the right of each of them 20.36

ther(e) (þer(e)) *av* there Pr 66 *et p.*; in that place Pr 99, 6.19, 61, 11.168, 12.111, Z Pr 17, 6.78; from there 7.221, 20.154, 379; at that time, then 8.340, B 2.45, A 12.75; on that 10.245; for that reason A 9.32; where Pr 170, 204, 1.113, 116, 120, 130, 2.148, 3.15, 190, 204, 5.164, 13.244, 16.121, 252, 313, 341, 17.11, 18.117, 213, 19.252, 20.157, 21.315, 22.56, 329, 345, 284, **B** 5.264, 11.209, 12.61, 255, 15.94, 97, 304, 336, **A** 6.79, 9.78, 11.60; in which Pr 114, 3.238, 7.94, 15.190, 16.59, 21.136, 160, **B** 10.97, 13.121, 18.400; on which 16.247; (in / to a / the place) where 1.120, 133, 3.37, 4.82, 122, 132, 5.32, 7.204, 9.39, 67, 11.44, 13.91, 16.323, 19.317, 20.278, 386, 478, 21.421, 22.330, 369, **B** 11.67, 12.227, 13.157, 15.183, 312, 17.116, Z 6.9; (in circumstances) where 3.256, 4.35 (1), 36, 16.245, 302, 19. 283, 285, 286, 20.322, **B** Pr 194, 11.152, 165, 318, 13.291; to whomever 3.330; when 6.427, 8.256, 16.228, **B** 5.490, 6.243, 15.155, 204, 16.140, A 1.138; near whom B 15.214; whereas 7.114, 12.236, 13.39, 55, 58, 14.120, 130, 15.289, 16.49, 54, 87, 22.46, **B** 3.197, 5.113, 10.342, 11.243, 12.167, 14.92, *in phrr.* ~ **as** in a place / situation where / in which 9.274, 16.139, 20.236, ~ **before** previously A 7.226, ~ **bytwene** between those (two) places Pr 19, ~ **þat** wher(ever) 3.222, 16.46, 17.292, B 10.188, where 7.94, when 2.96, 20.427, A 5.95; *pleonastic* 1.31, 4.71, 6.379, 8.340, 21.462, **B** 14.40, 16.116, Z 2.119; *in correl. constr.* ~...~ where B 14.99–100

þeraftur *av* after that 1.150, 6.229c, 7.136, **B** 3.342, 5.73, 11.337, A 11.180; in the next life A 8.12; in response 3.483, 11.186; towards (them), in that direction 7.224; for it B 17.122; accordingly Pr 25, ?6.229c, 8.90, 121, 11.147, 16.218, **B** 1.147, 3.187, 10.90, 294, 397, A 12.10, Z Pr 36, 1.145

þeran 19.8 = **þer(e)on** *av*

þeraȝeyn(e) *av* in opposition to that 20.310, **B** 16.119, 17.136

þerby *av* by means of that 10.173, 18.170, **B** 11.173, 13.299; by it B 13.403

þerfore (therfore) *av* for it 3.246, 14.23, 18.129; (in payment) for it 3.89, 276, 4.57; because / in consequence (of that / those things) 7.147, B 5.232; on that account 10.194, 12.245, 13.56, **B** 6.236, 9.96; for that reason 13.192, **B** 1.17, 16.64, A 12.94, Z 7.269; and so A 12.20, Z 7.71; that is why 22.334

þerfro *av* away from it 12.239; away from there B 11.353

ther(e)ynne (þerinne) *av* in there / that place Pr 15, 1.12, 59, 10.172, 11.108, 18.272, **B** Pr 15, 10.412, 15.334; inside 3.105, 10.227, B 10.406; therein, in that 8.61, **B** †10.186, 13.153, 158; in it B 14.2, A 11.141, Z 3.160; within them 6.219; within it B 15.580; into it / that place 1.57, 6.415, 7.218, 16.359; upon it / theron **B** 1.50, 10.183, 12.289

þermyd(e) *av* by means of it 8.68, 155, A 7.212; with it 3.252, **A** 2.37, 7.166, **Z** 5.60, 8.28; in addition 9.270, B 15.316

þerof, thereof *av* for that Pr 110, B 5.367, A 3.63; about them 7.79; about it 14.75, **B** 3.234, 16.65; concerning that **B** 3.248, 16.234, A 10.86; of that 6.229, 13.170, **B** 5.183, 13.459; out of it / that 14.32, 17.139; out of them 18.12, B 16.34; from it 20.305, B 5.140; of it 12.166, 17.296, **B** 8.55, 12.250, 15.135, 16.5, 17.213, Z 6.50; of them 10.196; with it 11.73; because of that 8.203; on that account 11.159; at that 7.131, 13.153, 20.60, 130

þer(e)on, ther(e)on *av* on it 2.13, 12.234, A 7.13; on them B 5.405; upon it 11.129, 241, 14.63, 74, 214, 18.199, 19.8; at it 7.50; in it 11.132; over it 11.9; to it B 11.224

þeroute *av* out in the open 5.16; out(side) A 6.74

ther-thorw *av* by that means 20.229

þertyl *av* to (do) that 4.5 (Z 4.5)

þerto, therto *av* to it 18.44, 20.158 182; *in phr.* **comen** ~ attain 11.172, 22.14; to them 12.104, 105; into it 12.59; to (do) that 16.123, B 4.5; for it / that 9.91, 13.161, 17.225; before it 21.201; against it 18.48; in addition, as well 16.257, **B** 4.59, 15.127, **Z** Pr 64, 3.33; *in phr.* ~ **to** compared to B 13.194

þervnder *av* under (cover of) them B 15.116; under (the form of) it 21.388

þervppon *av* in (the truth of) that A 11.144

þerwiþ, therwith *av* with it 1.173, 3.319, 476, 5.135, 10.290, 18.279, **B** 8.56, 15.139; with that 8.115, 18.42, 19.9, B 10.162; with them 1.16, B 10.215; (in) that with which 19.168; by means of it / that / them 3.486, 5.43, 6.342, 8.110, 9.30, 11.75, 14.195, 19.3, 21.64, 327, **B** 1.48, 7.14, A 3.224, Z 5.129; in that way B 13.73; in addition, moreover 1.85; at that, thereupon 13.215, 15.1, 19.334, 21.484, **B** 14.332, 16.167; as a consequence ? Z 1.102n; *in phr.* **acorden** ~ agree with that (statement) 4.87, 9.69, 13.213

thes(e) 7.149, 16.36, 20.470, Z 2.147; *see* **this(e)** *a*

these 9.96, 16.28, 18.75 *see* **this** *prn*

þesternesse *n* darkness B 16.160

theues *pl.* 5.17, B 9.119 *etc*; *see* **the(e)f** *n*

thew *n* manners, behaviour, *pl.* 6.141

thy, thi, þi, þy (~n(e) *before vowels* 1.140, 3.28 *etc*, *before consonant* 8.289, B 5.501) *poss. a* 2 *sg.* thy, thine, your Pr 148 *et p.*, B Pr 125 *et p.*; **thien** 19.112

thider 7.157 = **thed(de)r(e)** *av*

thief 20.424 *see* **the(e)f** *n*

thykke *a* thick, undiluted 21.403; (*sup.*) most dense B 12.227

thykke *av* thickly(-strewn) 3.194

thyl Z 8.76 = **til** *prep.*

thilke *prn* those B 10.28

thyn, þyn *poss. prn.* 2 *sg.* yours 6.289 = your people 3.135, 4.192

thyng, þyng *n* (*pl.* ~es 1.20 *et p.*, ~ 8.219, 10.156)) thing (=substance, being) 10.151, 152, 156, 170, 18.93 (2), 195, 19.134, **B** 15.12, 17.169, A 10.28, = (inanimate) object 3.87, 18.271, 21.94, **swete** ~ 6.88; material substance 10.129; = property, goods 16.274, 292, 17.40, 22.276, B 15.107, **litel** ~ 15.155; = commodity 13.55; = necessity 1.20, 5.88, 16.318, B 14.33; = attribute, quality (virtue, vice) 3.377, 16.284, 296, B 1.151, **lykyng** ~ 10.288, 11.133; = living being / creature 3.421, 15.137, 18.93 (1), 20.150, 257, **B** Pr 123, 18.356; (*as affectionate term*) **meke** ~ 18.125, **B** 15.306, 18.115, **mylde** ~ 20.118, B 15.306; **pety** ~ 16.83, **pore** ~ 15.33, A 12.50; **trewe** ~ 14.8; (*as a pejorative term*) **pore** ~**s** 15.309; action A 6.81; way of behaving 17.153, A 6.81; event, happening Pr 5, 6.51; (thing) request(ed) 22.245; (state of) affair(s) 12.36, 40; circumstance, condition (of things) 3.362, 19.299; matter (for consideration), point 18.197, B 10.169; subject, discipline B 10.209; skill 14.73; item(s) of a craft Z 2.206; (legal) agreement, contract 2.109, **B** 2.105, 4.29; (*as vague general subst. for more precise term*) 10.155, B 11.409, 419; **confortable** ~ B 14.282; **leþi** ~ B 10.186; **thre** (...) ~**es** 1.20, 3.377, 19.299, 22.11; **wykked** ~ 12.238; *in phrr.* **al(le)** (...) ~(**s**) everything, all things 5.88, 8.219, 10.152, 170, 19.39, 20.213, 361, 22.254, **B** 5.563, 10.435, 16.184, 17.157, A 10.34; **eny (kyne)** ~ anything (whatever) 8.267, 19.267; *as av* **eny** ~ to any degree B 18.389; **no** ~ nothing 13.243, 20.465, 22.249, A 12.20

thynken, þynken[1] *v* (*pr. subjv.* thynke 20.260, *p.t.* **tho(u) (g)hte** Pr 196, 11.316 *etc*, **þo(u)ȝte** B Pr 6, 1.107), *impers. generally with* ∅-*subject* + *indir. prn. obj.*) seem, **hem / hym thouhte** it seemed to them / him 21.139, B 1.107; **me ~eth** it seems to me 3.283, 284, 7.98, 13.161, 15.80, 16.206, 17.184, 243, 253, 19.262, 20.165, A 12.5; **me thouhte** it seemed to me, I thought Pr 196, 10.68, 15.192, 18.21, 204, 19.55, 20.116, 21.201, **B** Pr 6, 11.323, 16.20, Z Pr 17, I imagined B 2.53; *with compl.* 11.130, 316, 13.177, 181, 18.204, A 12.5, 16; *in set phrr.* **ferly me thynketh / thouhte** 15.119, 16.294, 17.112, (**thouhte**) 18.56, **wonder me thynketh** 3.228, 13.161, 17.116

thynken, þynken[2] B 5.283 *etc.*; *see* **thenken** *v*

thynne *a* thin, weak 21.403

þirled *p.t.* B 1.174 *see* **thorlen** *v*

this, þis[1] *dem. prn (sg.)* this 1.11, 143 *et p.*, B 3.236 *etc*, *in phr.* ~ **for þat** (= *quid pro quo*) recompense for something done 9.275, *(with generic ref.)* 15.221; *(pl.)* these 1.194, 5.48, 7.80, 8.262, 21.12, A 11.192n; **~e** 5.66, 7.112, **B** 3.292, 7.54

this, þis[2] *dem. a (sg.)* (**thise** Pr 190) this 1.5, 7, 8, 2.198 *et p.*, *in set phrr.* **on ~ folde / molde, in / of ~ worlde** anywhere 9.153, 172, 3.6, 4.136, Z 6.71; ~ **erthe / grounde / lyue / world** this world / this present life 1.8, 3.94, 10.45, 6.313*etc*: ~, **~e** *(pl.)* these Pr 198, 3.81, 1.200, 2.192, 3.41, 5.41, 10.123, 138, Z 1.72 *(with unique ref.)* 3.119, 19.36, 20.21, 84, 240, 21.108, 22.114, 163, B 15.398 *(with generic ref.)* 3.58, 118, 185, 8.158, 9.83, 164, 240, 330, 10.205 (1), 11.26, 63 (1), 271, 12.202, 13.78, 15.210, 16.16, 17.78, 117, 252, 315, 19.174, 184, 255, 20.355, B 5.143, A 11.192, **Z** Pr 82, 7.278; *(in temporal ref.* ~ **pestilences** the recent plagues 5.115, 10.274, 11.60; **~...ȝer / wynter** the last...years 6.214, 233, 7.188, 10.73, 20.329; ~ **seuene ȝer** for the next seven years 6.108, 7.64, B4.86

thysulue(n) (**thiself** B 5.487, ~ **selue** Z 1.80, **~sylf** Z 3.128, **~sylue** 2.127) *emph. prn (used appositively)* thy-, yourself 3.235, 20.401, B 13.169, A 9.44; *(as emph. refl.)* yourself 7.60, 128, 262, 15.114, **B** 1.143, 8.50, 10.259, 18.54, A 10.93, 114; *(as obj. of prep.)* 6.101, 7.59, 267, 18.173, **B** 1.24, 4.71, 5.482, 565, 606, 13.144; *(indep. / absol.)* = (you) yourself 2.127, 7.123, 10.226, 11.115, **B** 2.126, 5.490, 8.49, 10.264, 11.376, 16.157, 17.102, A 10.88, Z 3.152, 153

tho (þo)[1] *prn* those 3.444, 4.196, 5.49, 6.382, 7.115, 8.25, 57, 260, 9.173, 11.27, 30, 272, 12.245, 14.139, 16.357, 17.230, 18.64, 66, 148, 175, 19.47, 20.247, 369, 21.38, 392, 22.306, **B** 3.233, 238, 10.131, 427, 471, 13.198, 18.329, A 11.13, 192, Z 7.196; they 6.382, B 6.162; them A 10.108

tho (þo)[2] *def. art. and a.* Pr 18, 140, 1.21, 2.206, 211, 5.5, 7.86, 9.233, 13.6, 14.198, 15.51, 16.45, 248, 17.31, 170, 210, 212, 213, 259, 19.258, 20.444, 21.154, 459, 22.110, **B** 4.40, 5.174, 12.59, 14.123, 175, 15.478, 600, **A** 11.201, 224, 12.21, **Z** Pr 72, 3.158, 4.149, 7.206; *(with unique ref.)* the Z Pr 55; *in phrr.* ~ **seuene** B 13.122; ~ **thre** 10.111, 21.82, B 13.427; ~ **two** 14.108, 13.41, B 10.211

tho[3] *av* then 1.54, **B** 2.167, 5.364, A 4.49, 141; at that time Pr 146, 196, 1.106, 111, 2.220, 6.319, 7.133, 14.95, 15.55, 192, 17.199, 19.55, 20.73, 21.112, **B** 10.441, 11.323, 13.179, 16.150, Z 4.123; thereupon 1.152, 2.18, 157, 3.129, 4.13, 43, 66, 21.53, B 11.63, 84, A 12.12; when Pr 191, 2.162, 3.137

tho[4] Z 5.20, 92, 6.95 = **to** *prep.*

thogh (**thauh** 9.122, **though** 14.29, **thouȝ** B 1.176 *et p.*, **thouh** 8.107 *etc*, **thow** Pr 210 *etc*, **þeiȝ** B Pr 192 *etc*,

A 1.10 *et p.* (**þei** A 12.65)) *conj.* though, in spite of the fact that 8.39, 43 *etc*, B 15.260; if 10.243; even if Pr 200, 1.33, 2.150, 3.165, 9.100, 10.257, 12.61, 13.237, 15.284, 16.79, 284, 20.422, **B** Pr 192, 1.144, 3.352, 5.267, 600, 9.39, 11.100, 15.184, 386; if, whether 1.124; that 11.230, B 14.2

thoght *n* 10.107 *see* **thouht(e)** *n*

thoghte *p.t.* 2.64, 10.68, 18.21 *see* **thynken** *v*

thol(y)en *v* undergo (penalty) 4.80, (penalty of death) 20.73, 137, 424; suffer 12.206, 15.73, 85; suffer (death) 20.258, 21.175; endure, put up with 16.32, 19.107, B 11.398

thombe 19.136 = **thumbe** *n*

thondren *v* thunder Z Pr 17

thone Z Pr 12 = **thenne**[1] *av*

thonken *v* thank 4.152, 8.135, 10.107, 18.17, 19, 19.107, A 12.48, *ger.* **~ynge** (expression of) thanks 2.162

thorgh B 9.52 = **thorw(e)** *prep.*

thorlen *v* pierce 1.169

thorn *n* thorn 20.47, 21.323; (haw)thorn tree 2.29, 20.48, B 12.227

thorp *n* village Pr 220, A 2.45

Thorsday Z 8.76 = **Þursday** *n*

thorw(e) (**thoruȝ** B) *prep.* through 2.226, 16.137, 20.287; through(out), over 7.205, 9.11, 17.284, 22.213, B 17.99; = from beginning to end (of) 9.253; on account of / because of 10.36; = as a consequence / result of Pr 106, 2.247, 3.91, 106, 430, 4.139, 5.34, 7.126, 8.296, 347, 9.182, 293, 10.42, 178, 13.115, 15.16, 231, 16.340, 17.85, 276, 19.282, 194, 20.284, 391, 21.39, 130, 22.229, 352, **B** 5.242, 6.144, 10.278, 12.255, 14.14, 76, 176, 186, A 1.111; by / through the agency of 1.31, 2.248, 3.104, 449, 4.71, 7.268, 9.181, 10.48, 13.223, 15.263, 16.243, 367, 314, 21.121, 389, 22.355, **B** 9.153, 14.18, 15.210, 16.9, A 1.107; by virtue of B 15.417, 423; with the help of 17.239; by 3.2, 20.392, 396, 21.95, 303, 22.306, 318, **B** 11.207, 16.142, 161; by means of 2.150, 167, 239, 244, 3.82, 196, 269, 450, 4.78, 139, 5.98, 127, 6.21, 72, 73, 85, 186–7, 7.88, 90, 289, 8.208, 261, 344, 9.156, 301, 10.79, 209, 11.20, 127, 12.186, 13.18, 22, 60, 14.18, 25, 23, 77, 208, 15.79, 145, 238, 246, 17.185, 241–2, 265–66, 306, 18.10, 33, 36, 46, 123, 151, 20.112, 132, 142, 159, 162, 320, 395, 397–8, 461, 21.122, 245, 247, 357, 378, 22.99, **B** 2.153, 3.127, 5.132, 6.19, 9.44, 207, 10.109, 238, 320, 11.81, 124, 155, 299, 322, 357, 12.77, 78, 100, 13.168–9, 361, 370, 14.82, 185, 15.65, 210, 280, 295, 345, 445, 448, 466, 479, 16.51, 101, 120, 17.119, 18.139, 353, 390

thou, þou *prn* B 14.184, A Pr 88, Z Pr 122 *see* **thow**[1]

though 14.29, **thouȝ** B 1.176 *etc*, **thouh** 8.107 *etc* = **thogh** *conj.*

thouht(e) *n* idea, notion 19.111; opinion 6.100; (object of) reflexion B 13.21; (sinful) fancy 2.95; thought,

meditation 15.4; (faculty of) thought (*person.*) 10.74
et p., 16.183; mind 7.20

thouhte[1] *p.t.* 12.53, 18.245 *etc, p.p.* 6.51 *see* **thenken** *v*

thouhte[2] (**thoughte**) Pr 196, *p.t.* 11.316, 13.177 *see*
thynken *v*

thousand *a* thousand 20.309 (**seuene** ~); (*as indef. large
number*) 18.17, A 12.48; *as n* **B** 1.116, 5.624, 13.270
[date], *in phr.* **fyue** ~ 18.154, 21.127; *as n = indef.
large number* Pr 166, 7.154, 8.188, *in combs.* **fyue** ~
B 15.590, **meny score** ~ 19.22, **six** ~ 19.26, **sixty** ~
3.233, B 17.23, **ten** ~ A 2.42

thow[1] (**thou** B 14.184, A Pr 88, Z Pr 122, **þou, thowe**
12.39, 20.326, A 1.138, **þow** 1.144, *enclitic form* **-ou,
-ow** 1.5 *etc*) *pers. prn 2 sg.* thou, you Pr 163 *et p.*, B
1.21 *et p.*, A 1.26 *et p.*, Z 3.149 *et p.*; *used variously in
address* to (God) 6.423, (Christ) 7.136, (King) 21.480,
(knight) 8.25, (lady) 3.488, (pupil) 11.109, (servant) B
1.77, (reader) B Pr 215

thow[2] Pr 210, 1.10, 19, 124, 171, 174, 2.150, 3.87, 185,
197, 314, 389, 4.70, 5.164, 6.60, 108, 290, 311, 7.192,
267, 304, 8.34, 127, 195, 9.343, 10.39, 42, 11.311,
13.51, 16.93, 288, 21.447, 22.16, Z 1.100, 7.316 *see*
thogh *conj.*

thowne Z 2.54 *see* **toun** *n*

thral *n* bond-servant, serf 21.33, (*fig.*) A 8.57; ~**doem** *n*
servitude 20.106

thre *num. a* three 3.405, 7.109, 8.248, 16.32, 18.20, 25,
(*postpositively*) 10.106, 111, 226, *in phrr.* ~ **clothes**
10.195, ~ **dayes** 10.113, 15.70, 18.161, 20.31, 41,
22.177, B 17.110, ~ **degrees** 18.56, 84, ~ **kynges** 21.82,
95, ~ **loues** 17.24, ~ †**leodes** B 16.201, ~ **maner men**
8.248, **B** 13.427, 16.227, ~ **maner minstrales** 7.109, ~
nayles 20.51, ~ **persones** 18.27, 215, 234, 19.30, 44,
98, **B** 10.239, 16.207, 17.44, ~ **places** 20.231, ~ **shypes**
8.349, ~ **siʒtes** B 17.153, ~ **sones** 10.226, ~ **thynges**
1.20, 3.77, 19.299, 22.11, B 17.164, ~ **vertues** 10.77, ~
wyndes 18.29; ~ **wittes** 10.105, *as n* three 10.106, 111,
16.32, 18.201, 219, 238, 19.311, B 17.160, A 10.167,
in phrr. **a / o** ~ in three 18.198, 213, 242, **alle** ~ 11.154,
18.22, 218, 237, 240, 19.31, 99, 150, **thise** ~ 16.32,
36

thredbare *a* threadbare, worn-out 6.205

þresschen *v* thresh (grain) B 5.546, *ger.* **threschynge**
8.199

thres(sh)fold *n* threshold 6.407

þrest A 11.46 = **furst** *n*

þretynge *ger.* dire threat B 18.281

threttene *num. a as n.* thirteen 6.220

þreve *n* bundle (*fig.*) = large number B 16.55

threw *p.t.* 6.407, 22.164 *see* **throwen** *v*

thridde *num. a* third 7.136, 18.50, 21.91, 290, *as n* 10.76,
103, 11.37, 160, 18.195, 21.265, B Pr 121, A 8.55

thrift *n* wealth A 10.108

thringen *v* throng, crowd *p.t.* **throngen** 7.154

thritty *num. a* thirty, ~ **wyntur** 7.30, 17.23, 20.136, 329;
in phr. **twies** ~ B 13.270, **two and** ~ 20.332

þriuen *v* prosper B Pr 32, 5.277, 10.211; *and see* **y~** Pr
34

þrobben *v* throb, beat strongly, *pr. p.* **þrobbant** A 12.48

#**thromblen** *v* bump against 6.407

throngen *p.t. pl.* 7.154 *see* **thringen** *v*

þrop A 2.45 *see* **thorp** *n*

throte *n* throat 19.308

throute Z 6.61 = **þeroute** *av*

þrowe *n* time B 18.76

throwen *v* (*p.t.* **threw**, *p.p.* **þrowe**) hurl 20.293, cast, hur-
tle 6.407

thumbe *n* thumb 7.45, 19.136

thurgh A 12.60 = **thorw(e)** *prep.*

Þursday *n* Thursday B 16.140, 160; **Schyr** ~ = Maundy
Thursday Z 8.76

þurst *n* thirst B 18.369 (= **furst** *n*)

thuruen *v* be necessary, *pr. sg. 2 pers.* **tharstow** B 14.56,
3 (*impers.*) **thar þe** you need 15.259

thus *av* thus, in such a way (as aforesaid) 3.212, 4.180,
5.200 *et p.*, **B** 13.458, 15.145, 17.163, *in phr.* ~ **sone**
just as quickly 3.180, straightaway 12.6, 15.44, 96,
108, 22.69; *in phr.* ~**..þat** in such a way ... / with the
result that 3.430; so 4.178, 20.350; as follows 3.403,
5.11, B 2.74; *in phr.* **ryght(e)** ~ exactly as follows
6.422, 9.285, 11.199; in this way Pr 74, 1.134, 2.44;
and so, consequently 6.123, 11.160, 17.258, 19.273,
21.189; thereupon, and so 2.53, 5.1, 10.1, 22.1

thusgates *av* in the following manner 16.306

thwyten *v* whittle, *ger.* ~**ynge** 8.199

tid *n* time A 2.40

tyd *av* quickly 22.54, *in phr.* **as** ~ straightaway, at once
B 13.319, 16.61

tydy *a* virtuous, upright, ~ **man** 3.474, 20.332, **trewe**
~ **man** / **men** 21.442, B 9.105; profitable, useful †B
3.346; (*comp.*) healthy, sound 12.189

tydynge *n, pl.* ~**s** (message of) warning 21.344

#**tyke** *n* cur, slave 21.37n

tikel *a* loose, lascivious 3.166

til[1] *prep.* (= **to**, *used before vowel*) Pr 167, 229, 5.111,
6.188, 8.98 (2), 13.183, 17.262, 19.123, 20.348, 445,
21.266, **B** 9.84, 10.362, 15.169, 18.223; towards 1.132;
up to 22.134, Z 7.6; until, till 3.307, 6.395, 7.225,
8.180, 274, 313, 10.53 (2), **B** 3.312, 12.245, until it is
B 15.466; *in phrr.* ~ **þat** until (the time when) Pr 212,
6.80, 12.127, 19.191, Z 2.72; **fro morwen** ~ **euen** all
day long 8.180, B 14.15; **vch man** ~ **oþer** every man
to each other 12.131

til[2] *conj.* until Pr 42, 212 *et p.*, B 1.113 *et p.*, **A** 10.60,
12.21, 52, 74, Z 2.147; before 3.132

tyl(e)de *p.t.* 15.266, 270, 17.100 *see* **tylien** *v*; B 12.209 (=
telde) *see* **telden** *v*

tylen *v* reach as far as Z 6.66, †A 6.79; *and see* **tollen** *v*[2]

tylyare (tulyer, tilier) *n* ploughman 17.100, **B** 13.240, 15.367, A 11.184; cultivator Pr 224

tylien (tilion, tulien) *v* (*p.t.* tyl(e)de 15.266, 270) till, plough 9.2, 17.100, 20.108, 21.239, 437, 441, **B** Pr 120, 6.235, A 11.186, *ger.* cultivation B 14.63; grow, cultivate 8.244; (*fig.*) Pr 87, 10.201, 21.262, 318, 335, B 15.107; obtain (food) by cultivation 15.266, 21.437, **B** 6.232, 14.67

tilþe (telþe A, tulthe C) *n* crops, harvest 21.435, B 19.436, A 7.127

tymber *n* timber for building 21.321

tymbren *v* build 3.84, (nest) B 11.360

tyme *n* (*pl.* ~is 1.17 *et p.*, ~ 6.118) time; (profitable / useful) time 3.462, 5.93, 101 (2), 127, 10.187, 12.96, 14.8, B 9.98; use of one's time B 11.377; proper / opportune time 4.20, 7.15, 11.105, 15.106, 21.240, **B** 5.85, 16.138; period (of time) 5.100, 7.131, 8.275, 17.237, **B** 12.249, 13.204; season 6.183; day, age, era 9.313, 11.220, 239, 15.268, 16.354, 21.134, A 11.204, 269; lifetime 21.413; occasion, moment 5.101 (1), 10.230, 17.209, 18.127, 247, 254, 20.423, 426, **B** 5.112, 7.96, 10.466, 11.406, 12.4, 13.68, 14.324, 16.142; point, juncture 10.123; *in cpds.* blowyng ~ B 16.26; **chirie** ~ B 5.159; **flouryng** ~ 18.35, B 16.26; **heruost** ~ 8.121; **Lamasse** ~ 8.313; **lyf** ~ course / days of one's life Pr 50 *etc*, **B** 5.476, 13.142, 15.142, Z 7.77 (*see* **lyf-**); **noon** ~ B 15.283; **pestelence** ~ time of the plague Pr 82, B 10.72; **plener** ~ full time B 16.103; *plenitudo temporis* (**hy**) ~ the moment of the (final) fullness of time 18.127, 139; **rotey** ~ B 11.337; **somur** ~ 16.246, B 14.178; **sondry** ~ at intervals B 15.282; at various times 18.153, B 12.31; **ten hundrit / score** ~s 7.38, 11.128; **wynter** ~(s) 9.78, 12.191, B 14.177; *in phrr.* ~ **comyng aftur** the next life 12.204; ~ **ynowe** soon enough 11.197; ~ **ypassed** while ago 16.369; **alle** ~ at all times, constantly 1.17, 65, 7.211, 17.33, 21.442; **biggen þe** ~ pay interest (on loan for a period) 6.247, B 13.376; **cursid** ~A 10.140; **eleuene** ~s on many occasions 3.226; **eny** ~ at any time 15.161, B 13.164; **fele** ~ many times 6.74, 118, 16.228; **fol** ~ fully time 18.137, **B** 2.96, 5.489*n*; **in a** ~ on one occasion 11.71; **in** ~ at the right time B 9.184; **long** ~ 7.203, 20.5, 65; **mel** ~ 7.132; **mene** ~ meantime 6.281; **mony (a)** ~(s) 3.97, 158, 6.151, 7.48, 9.297, 10.35, 18.259, **B** 11.242, 14.4, A 8.151, ~ **and ofte** 12.241; **ofte** ~(s) 12.241, 18.61, 22.26, B 11.370; **olde** ~ the past B 12.235; **on nyhtes** ~ at night 16.141; **out of** ~ at the wrong time 1.24, 10.291; **som** ~(s) on one (or other) occasion, sometimes 3.104, 120, 6.78, 112, 137, 428, 7.28, 39, 9.149, 12.39, 13.212, 16.334, 343, 18.37, 49, 19.178, **B** 5.376, 12.22, 14.237; at some time 6.115, 8.22, 15.299; at one time 6.207, 15.302, 16.366, 20.330, 22.182, **B** 5.135, 546, 12.293, 15.186, 442, 16.45; ~...~ at one time...at another 6.38, 191, 404, 16.172–3, 21.102–4, ~ **þat** the moment when 21.444; **þat** ~ at that time

3.481, 5.173, 9.294, 322, 10.249, 16.200, 18.104, 148, 205, 20.73, 78, 83, 21.84, **B** 5.365, 13.22, 15.40, 276, A 7.180, **what** ~ at whatever time, whenever 7.145; **when** ~ **is** at the appropriate time 8.10, 80

tynen *v* (*p.p.* (y)tynt 5.93, 20.142) be dispossessed of 21.344, B 1.113; suffer the loss of 10.280, 11.197, B 10.349, A 12.86; lose 20.142; waste 5.93, 14.8

†tynynge *ger.* loss, waste B 9.99

tyn(e)kere *n* tinker [mender of pots and pans] 6.363, **B** Pr 221, 5.547

tynt *p.p.* 20.142 *see* **tynen** *v*

tyraunt *n* unjust lord B 15.419; devilish villain 2.211, 22.60

***titerare** *n* tattler, ~ **in ydel** idle gossip-monger 22.300

tiþe *num. a* tenth, **trauaille þe** ~ **deel** a tenth part of the labour B 15.487

tythe *n* tithe (-payment) 6.298, 304, 8.78, 101, 13.83 (1), 16.258

tithen *v* give as a tithe 13.72; pay tithes 6.305; pay 13.83

title *n* legal claim (to possession) 20.324; 'title' [certificate of presentment to a benefice] 13.103, 105; ? name (of priest), (verbal) guarantee of support 13.113c

tixst (text) *n* (Scriptural) text 3.493, 495, 12.51, 15.135, **B** 2.122, 3.346, 351, 10.269, 11.111, 15.327; authoritative utterance 1.200, 2.129; exact words 19.15

to *av*[1] to B 7.130

to *av*[2] too 1.139, 5.23, 24, 6.166, 8.274, 16.355, 18.199, 22.360, **B** 11.224, 13.72, 14.74, 15.78, 16.148, 17.41 (2), Z 7.245

to *prep.* to Pr 22, 16.108, 20.264, 22.366 *et p.* (*with v. inf.*) Pr 31 *et p.*; in order to Pr 4, 54, 98, 3.33, 49, 6.26, 14.12 *etc*, B 5.377; so as to Pr 32, 4.54, 14.67, A 10.105; (*with inf. as ger.*) ~ **awaken** at awakening B 2.100; ~ **gete** in getting 10.300; ~ **holde** in keeping 3.187; ~ **kepe** for keeping B 6.140; ~ **lese** (even) at the cost of losing 10.194; ~ **leten wel by** for thinking well of 7.267; ~ **leue** for believing 17.124; ~ **preche** by preaching 16.262; ~ **se** at seeing 22.109; ~ **sette** from placing B 7.151; ~ **spille** from wasting B 9.98; ~ **suffre** A 10.118; ~ **wyte** to knowing A 11.259; ~ **worche** for making 2.118; ~ **3yue** in giving B 14.126; (*inf. with implied finite senses*) ~ **dyne** if he dines 16.4, ~ **fonge** if he receives 16.7, ~ **mete** he may meet 16.141, ~ **amenden** (I shall) amend 20.389, ~ **releue** will restore 20.390; ~ **to walke** he will walk B 18.32; **they** ~ **leue / lyue** that they might believe / live 6.48, 21.233; **þei** ~ **haue** and they will have B 2.102; ~ **deure** is to last Z 2.72; ~ **laste** that lasts B 9.45; (*in combin. with* **for**) Pr 7, 187, 1.16, 118, 141, 158, 2.15, 199 *etc*, B 8.93, A 2.65, Z 7.262; (*with infl. inf.*) ~ **done** 3.232, 7.229, 8.117, 210, B 4.28, ~ **gone** 2.21, ~ **lyuene** 9.15, 15.241; (*with understood v. preceding*) (asking) Pr 83, 1.67, 3.216, A 4.60, (enabling) 10.52, (telling) B 12.22, A 2.186; (*with noun (phr.) preceding*) **in hope** ~ Pr 29,

62, *so also* 1.110, 2.196, 241, 3.100, 216, 236, 6.169, 194, 340, 7.22, 9.91, A 12.32, Z 2.158; (*with a. preceding*) Pr 202, 1.171, 2.87, 3.198, 282, 4.28, 5.23, 6.7, 17, 87, A 11.246 *etc*; *in expl. use after various vv.*: (*factitive*) Pr 136, 140, 6.2, A 3.185 (**maken**), 2.221, 10.75, 15.53, 16.226, 22.155, **B** 8.13, 9.90 (**don**), †11.161, B 1.123, A 7.132, 285 (**gare**), (*volitional*) 1.113, (*prohibitive*) 3.69, 14.177, 15.168, (*in absol. phr.*) **treuliche ~ telle** 2.251, *so* 11.277, 12.235, 16.117, 21.70, **B** 9.156, 16.4; (*in phr. qualifying preceding n. / phr.*) 3.206, 243, 251, 260, 269, 284, 349, 374, 461, 4.19, 135, 5.8, 6.49, 8.52, (*qualifying understood prn* him) 3.295, (me) 5.50; (*forming passive inf.*) 13.174, 207, 14.35, 16.106, 370, 18.221, **B** 5.583, 10.475, 12.38, ? 16.192, 219, ? A 10.54, Z 3.159; *in phrasal vv.* Pr 133 (**~ close with heuene** with which to close h.), **~ se ~** to look at 1.55, *so also* 8.273, 21.228; *before nn*: according to B 15.83; after 8.28–9; as (a) 3.146, 269, 5.73, 6.128, 374, 9.199, 11.38, 103, 12.213, **B** 1.82, 7.136, 8.52, 10.47, 12.46; as far as 1.166, 15.284, 16.83, 18.175; as regards 11.45 (2), B 15.457; at 5.36, 6.211 (1,2), 376, 9.35, 18.176, 22.296 (2), **B** 15.300; by 16.198; compared with 6.83, 14.83, 21.19, 22.23, B 13.194; down on B 10.140, A 12.39; for 1.35, 2.35, 175, 3.297, 5.14, 20, 103, 151, 6.271 (2), 7.75, 124, 258, 9.132, 12.82, 189, 16.17, 19.197 (2), 20.471, 22.259, 278, 296 (1), **B** 5.124, 7.78, 8.35, 10.248, 13.205, 14.232, 16.16, 163, 17.32, 40, 76, 77, **A** 7.228, 11.113, Z Pr 99; in 9.125, 318, 17.95; into 3.460, 19.195, 197 (1), **B** 9.66, 18.328; of 11.275, 19.76; on 6.155, B 9.88; (shut) on A 12.36; on to 1.61, 5.14, B 2.26; to (make up) 18.238; to obtain 13.113; (so as) to (produce) A 2.20; to the study of 11.117; towards 2.38, 5.125, 7.261, 286, 9.52, 10.134, 13.147, 14.49, 19.182, 197, 20.398, 22.247, 359, B 9.57, A 10.52, Z 3.166; until 11.196, 12.70, 20.5, 21.218, 22.294, B 16.148; with 3.376, 15.93, **B** 1.62, 3.109, **A** 4.144, 10.11; upon 19.191, B 18.94; up to B 16.151, A 10.145; up towards Pr 133; *in phrr.* **~ þe fulle** fully, satisfactorily 17.57, 20.410, **B** 13.193, 14.178; **~ paye** satisfactorily 14.178; *in comb. with* **ward** (**to...ward**), **~ helleward** towards hell 20.117, **~ heueneward** 16.53, **B** 10.333, 15.457; **~ Ierusalemward** B 17.80; **~ kyrkeward** 6.350, **~ porsward** Pr 101, **~ synneward** 6.179, **~ treuthward** 16.144

to A 3.218, Z 2.38, 215 = **two** *num*

tobersten *v* burst asunder, *p.t.* **tobarst** Z 5.39

to-bollen *p.pl.a* swollen up B 5.83

tobreken *v* (*p.p.* **tobroke(n)**) break down 9.32; tear in pieces 10.85; maim 9.99

tocleuen *v* (*p.t.* **to-cleyef** 20.61) cleave asunder 14.84; split apart 20.61, 112

today *av* today 8.107, 20.404, 21.216

todrawen *v* (*p.t.pl.* **todrowe**) mutilate (*lit.* tear apart) B 10.35

toek *p.t.* 4.166 *et p.*; *see* **taken** *v*

toelde *p.t.* 19.100, 21.276, 344, 22.232 *see* **tellen** *v*

to(e)th (*pl.* **teth** 20.83) *n* tooth, *pl.* B 15.13, **~ ache** toothache 22.82, **~ drawere** puller of teeth 6.369; *in phr.* **maugre his mony ~** in spite of anything he could do 20.83; *and see* **fore ~, wang ~**

tofore, toforn *prep.* in front of B 13.48; before 5.114; in the presence of 7.63, B 13.449; (in times) before B 12.131

toft *n* hillock 1.12, B Pr 12

toged(e)re(s), togidere(s) *av* together, = in one (body / company) 5.140, 6.154, 7.154, 18.112, 273, 21.166, 315, **B** 2.173, 6.182; = in (to) union / contact 1.191, 3.210, 6.218, 226, 16.79, 330, 17.22, 19.115, 131, 170, 199, **A** 2.23, 8.74; = in one whole 10.130, 11.153, B 2.84; = at one (and the same) time 14.147, Z 2.164, 168; successively B 1.121, Z Pr 64; = in concert / co-operation Pr 142, 1.38, 53, 2.194, 3.162, 280, 443, 4.72, 146, 10.27, 13.41, 16.65, 19.172, 175, 187, B Pr 66; = mutually Pr 47, 17.217; = reciprocally Pr 61; = (to / with) each other 4.25, 44, 6.382, 10.283, 13.32, **B** 2.136, 4.195, 9.128, 15.275, 17.48, **A** 2.25, 10.146, 158, 180; along with him / it / them 2.97, 3.174, 451, A 2.107; *in phr.* **leyde his eyen ~** closed his lids upon his eyes 20.59

togrynden *v* (*contr. pr.* **togrynt**) grinds (down) 11.62

tok(e)(n) *p.t.* 3.84 *et p.*; *see* **taken** *v*

tok(e)n *n* sign, **in ~** as a symbol Pr 86; message (of authorisation) 7.244, 13.11, B 10.218, 225, 366; word of introduction 11.105; sign(al) of recognition / greeting B 16.147, 148; agreement, covenant 18.247

tokenen *v* signify, *ger.* **tokenynge, in ~** as a sign / symbol 17.33, B 16.204, portent 5.121

tokkere *n* fuller of cloth A Pr 100

tol *n*[1] tool 11.124; *and see* **eg-toel** *n*

tol *n*[2] toll, payment Pr 98, 13.72

told(e) *p.t.* Pr 229 *et p.*, *p.p.* Pr 111 *et p.*; *see* **tellen** *v*

tollen *v*[1] pay a toll 13.50

tollen *v*[2] stretch, **~ out** †6.220, B 5.210; *and see* **tylen** *v*

toller *n* toll-collector B Pr 221

*tologgen *v* pull about 2.226

tombe *n* grave, tomb 18.144

tomblen *v* fall down flat A 12.91

tom(e) *n* leisure 2.196, A 6.82

tomor(e)we *av* tomorrow 2.41, 46

tonder B 17.246 = **tender** *n*

tonge *n* tongue (*physical organ*) B 15.13; (*of taste*) B 6.265; (*of speech*) 6.109, 331, 425, 7.17, 144, 12.199, 15.160, 16.144, 369, 19.302, 20.148, 21.93, 172, 233, 404, **B** 5.287, 10.165, 11.237, 13.323, A 12.24, 29; (*fig.*) 10.201, 16.144, B Pr 51, **harlotes ~** B 13.416, **neddres ~** B 5.86; speech, utterance 11.282, 13.206, 15.257, B 5.95, **fykel (of) ~** 2.6, 25, 6.72, (*person.*) 2.121, B 2.41; **leel of ~** 7.196; **likerous of ~** B 6.265; **mery ~**

2.167; **pacient of** ~ B 15.201, **pacience of** ~ B 14.99; **resonable of** ~ Pr 176; **talewys of** ~ 3.166; **trewe of** ~ 1.84, 174, 8.48, 10.78, 16.257, B 15.105, (*person*) 3.474, 4.18, **two-** double tongued (*person.*) 22.162; language, **of oure** ~ in our own language 17.293

tonne *n* tun, cask B 15.337

took *p.t.* Pr 117 *et p.*; *see* **taken** *v*

tookene 13.11 = **tok(e)n** *n*

top *n* hair (on the top of the head), **taken by the** ~ = seize with violence 3.176; top of tree [part growing above ground], *in phr.* ~ **and roote** B 16.22

#to-quaschen *v* shatter asunder, *p.t.* 20.63

torche *n* torch 19.169, 178, 260, 20.248

tore *p.p.* 6.203; *see* **teren** *v*

torenden *v* be destroyed (*lit.* torn apart) B 10.114

#to-reuen *v* plunder 3.202

to-riuen *v* (*p.t.* **to-roef**) split asunder 20.62

tornen *v* 17.263, 22.47, **B** 3.42, 347, 13.319, 15.437, 445, 546 = **turnen** *v*

to-roef *p.t.* 20.62 *see* **to-riuen** *v*

tortle *n* turtle-dove 14.161

torw Z 1.59, 7.327 = **thorw** *prep.*

***toshellen** *v* (*p.p.* **to-shullen**) ?peel B 17.192n

toten *v* look, peer 18.53, B 16.22

toth-drawere 6.369 *see* **to(e)th** *n*

to-trayen *v* torment grievously Z 5.113

touchen *v* touch 20.77, 79, 86, 21.172, B 17.150; make contact with 19.124, 146; lay a hand upon 20.198, 305; concern B 11.100; deal with B15.74

touʒ *a* hardy; *comp.* **touore** hardier 12.189

touken *v* tuck [stretch cloth on frame for beating] B 15.454

toun *n* manorial estate **A** 10.138, 11.213, Z 2.54; town Pr 177, 14.91, B 13.304, A 12.40; **to** ~ into the city [of London] B 13.266, [of Jerusalem] B 17.83; *and see* **borw** ~

tounge A 12.24, 29 = **tonge** *n*

touore *comp*; *see* **touʒ** *a*

tour *n* fortress Pr 15, 1.12, A 6.79, 82

tow Z 3.115, 7.238 = **thow** *prn*

toward[1] *a* at hand, about Pr 215

toward(e)[2] *prep.* towards, in the direction of 6.330, 8.190, 15.111, 21.158

towkare Z Pr 88 = **tokkere** *n*

trayen Z 1.13 *see* **bytrayen** *v*

trailen *v* trail, drag, *ger.* B 12.241

traytowr Z 2.169 = **tretour** *n*

#tra(ns)uersen *v* go counter (to), transgress 3.445, 14.209

tras *n* path, way (*fig.*) A 12.91

trauail *n* (hard) work, labour 3.350, 5.127, 9.152, B 6.133, **A** 7.235, 11.186; service B 7.43; effort 3.372, 19.213, **B** 14.153, 15.487; trouble B 11.194; ? journey 9.234n, A 10.145

trauaillen *v*[1] (exert oneself in) labour 3.295, 8.252, 12.97, 13.101, 15.127, 17.254, 21.441, 22.260, **B** Pr 120, 6.139, 9.105, Z 7.234 *ger.* ~ **of hondis** A 7.232, ~ **in preieres** B 6.247

trauaillen *v*[2] journey B 16.10

trauaillour *n* labourer B 13.240

#trauersen 14.209 = **transuersen** *v*

tre(e) *n* tree 13.165, 16.246, 18.75, **B** 11.360, 15.333; [of charity / humanity] 18.9, 29, 68, B 16.4, 8, 10, 22, 61, 63, [of Eden] 20.142 (1), 198, 305, 397, [of Calvary] 20.142 (2), 398

trecherie B 7.77 = **tric(c)herye** *n*

treden *v* (*p.t.* **treden** 13.165) tread / step upon A 10.104; copulate 13.165, 14.161, (with) B 11.355

tremblen *v* tremble 2.251, 12.51, Z 2.215

trental *n* set of thirty requiem masses Z Pr 64

trepget *n* trap A 12.91

treso(u)n *n* breach of faith, deceit Pr 12, 3.87, 20.319, 324, **B** 7.77, 18.289; treachery, betrayal 18.176; treason B 5.49

tresorer *n* paymaster 22.260

treso(u)r *n* treasure, (form of) wealth 1.43, 52, 66, 79, 81, 135, 201, 2.211, 3.159, 9.333, 16.144, 17.211, B 1.135, 208, (*fig.*) 21.218, 226, **B** 12.293, 13.194, **Kynges** ~ 5.181, **Goddes...**~ 10.177, **Cristis** ~ 14.54, B 10.474, ~ **of Treuthe** 10.183, B 7.54

trespas *n* crime, wrongdoing 1.93, Z 2.170

trespassen *v* do wrong, transgress 6.425, 14.209, B 3.293

tretour *n* traitor 20.422; betrayer 19.240; faithless person 21.441; deceiver Z 2.169

treu(e)ly(che) 2.251, 8.20, 9.330, 12.204, 13.101, 16.295 = **trew(e)lyche** *av*

tr(e)uthe (trouþe) *n* fidelity, loyalty 1.192; faithful conduct 8.49; pledged word / promise 2.124 (2), 8.33, 10.274; oath 3.469, 22.118; (*in assev.*) **haue God my** ~ 6.296, 306, **B** 10.45, 13.245, 14.274; faith, trust, sincerity 3.136; righteousness 1.81, 108, 143, 201, 17.141, 18.31, 21.262, 335, 22.53, 56; justice 3.348, 350, 4.170, 8.36, 16.185, 17.45, 21.90, 195, 481, **B** 1. 99, 102, 2.37, 3.241, 243, 11.151, 155, 158, 161, 15.310; just judgement 22.135; integrity 1.99, 102, 3.453, 8.57, 69, 11.17, 27, 12.92, 97, 14.188, 213, 214, 17.211, **B** 1.109, 3.164, 5.461, 11.163, 14.99, 15.470; right(eous) conduct Pr 12, 1.143, 3.144, 308, 5.183, what is right B 13.360; honesty, *in phr.* **with** ~ honestly 8.105, 9.251, 21.231; (*semi-person.*) = man / men of integrity 2.136, 3.176, 191, 14.209, 212, **B** 2.120, 3.243, 10.22; divine righteousness / truth / faithful justice (*person.*) [= God] Pr 15, 1.93 *et p.*, 3.445; **Seynt** ~ 'St' Truth 5.198, 7.176; [= daughter of God] 20.122 *et p.*; something true / truth (of the matter) 4.151, 8.297, 10.245, 11.277, 12.27, 39, 174, 235, **B** 12.130, 15.91; true testimony 20.311, 22.161, B 15.415, *in phr.* **with** ~

truthfully 20.203; true / accurate measure 3.89, 6.224, A 8.41; true estimate 6.385

treuthliche 13.72 = **trew(e)lyche** *av*

treuthward, to *av. phr.* towards / in accordance with righteousness 16.144

trewe[1] *n* truce 8.353, (*excl., with pl. as sg.*) Peace! an end to fighting ! 20.462

trewe[2] *a* reliable, constant 3.381, 16.358, 17.102, 18.247; honest, honourable 2.122, 3.298, 5.127, 8.200, 10.80, 21.238, 442, **B** Pr 120, 12.58, 13.240, A 11.184, 186; ~ **catel** legitimately acquired wealth 19.240; ~ **knyht** 12.77, 14.149, 205; ~ **thyng** 14.8; upright, virtuous 3.354, 444, 456, 4.76, 12.28, B 15.427; ~ **folk** B 7.54, ~ (**...**) **man / men** 3.444, 7.38, **B** 15.419, 487, ~ **tidy man** 21.442, B 9.105, A 3. 222, ~ **wille** B 13.194; *a as n* 3.471, 7.257; true 7.259, 9.212, 11.151, 14.66, 151, 15.135, 239, 274, 17.5, 20.135, B 11.100; truthful, veracious 11.96, 13.87, 17.15, 19.27, 20.431, A 12.18; ~ **bileue** 18.210; ~ **of tonge** 1.84, 174, 8.48, 10.78, 16.257; *cpd.* ~ **tonge** (*person.*) 3.474, 4.18; proper, correct, right 3.405, 487, 19.23; rightful, just 2.129, 14.212 (1), 215, 21.300, ~**accion** 1.94, ~**partie** 1.95, ~ **riȝte** B 10.341; real, genuine Pr 100, 16.39, 17.75, 76, A 12.85, Z 7.260, ~ **charite** 2.37; ~ **feiþ** B 13.211; ~ **loue** 1.135, 18.9; ~ **treuthe** 14.212 (2)

trew(e)ly(che) *av* faithfully B 7.61; honestly, honourably 1.96, 174, 3.84, 8.242, 13.72, 101; steadfastly 16.295; truthfully 2.251, 12.204; exactly 19.15; genuinely, really 18.26, 19.120, 21.178; (*in assev.*) indeed, believe me 8.20, 9.330, B 9.186

triacle *n* healing remedy 1.145, B 5.49

tribulacioun *n* affliction 12.203

tribu(y)t *n* tribute, **vnder** ~ liable to pay tribute 21.37

tric(c)herye *n* violation of faith or 'truth', perfidy Pr 12, 1.192; deceit 20.319, B 7.77

trydest *p.p.* Z 1.75 *see* **trien** *v*

trie *a* choice, excellent **B** 1.137, 15.168, 16.4; *av* ~**liche** choicely B Pr 14

trien *v* select, choose, *p.p. sup.* **trydest** choicest Z 1.75; put to the test, assay, *p.p.* 1.81, 201

triennals B 7.171 = **trionales** *n*

tryfle *n* (trifling) nonsense 14.83, 20.149

trinen *v* lay hand on 20.86

Trinite *n* the Blessed Trinity, God in Trinity 1.133 *et p.*; **in þe** ~ in the name of the Trinity B 14.184; triad 15.103, 111

trionales *n. pl.* masses said for a period of three years 9.320, 330, 333

trist *n* trust, confidence, *in phrr.* **in** ~ **of** (those) trusting in 3.159, **vp(on)** ~ **of** through reliance upon 9.333

tristen *v* trust, have faith / confidence in 1.66, 6.332, 9.330, 13.101, B 13.333

#**troylen** *v* dupe, deceive 20.319

trollilolly, hey *excl.* ho tra-la-la [burden of a song] 8.123c

trollen (**forth**) *v* wander 20.332

tromp(y)en *v* blow a trumpet 15.206, 20.468

trone *n* throne 1.133

tronen *v* enthrone, place on a throne B 1.133

trotten *v* trot B 2.165

trouþe B 10.45, 13.245, 14.274, 15.310, 415, A 11.31 *see* **treuthe** *n*

trowe B 15.96 = **tre(e)** *n*

trowen *v* believe 1.143, 3.20, 6.28, 16.303, 21.178, **B** 15.477, 17.163; think 14.108, 122, A 8.61, (*in (semi)-parenthetic use*) Pr 15, 5.49, 6.202, 298, 16.295, **B** 3.44, 4.41, 9.120, 10.429, 15.164, 301, **A** Pr 34, 5.69, †112, 8.59

truyfle 20.149 = **tryfle** *n*

trussen *v* (pack up and) be off 2.228

trust 9.333, B 3.124 *etc* = **trist** *n*

trusten 9.330, B 13.333 = **tristen** *v*

trusty *a* reliable, trustworthy B 8.82

truþe B 1.99 *etc*; *see* **tr(e)uthe** *n*

tulien *v* 10.201, 20.108, 21.239, 262, 318, 335, 437, 441, B 14.63, 67 *see* **tylien** *v*

tulyer Pr 224 = **tylyare** *n*

tulthe (**telþe, tilþe**) *n* crops 21.435, A 7.127

tunge B 10.165 = **tonge** *n*

tunycle *n* small tunic, jacket B 15.168

turnen *v* turn 5.121, 9.85, 144, 22.54, B 5.108; move about 19.152; come back 20.398; recoil (upon) 20.399; impel A 12.9; be driven 6.167; obstruct (the course of) 3.49; change 5.101, 12.2, 210, 13.18, 19.282, 297, 22.137; transform 15.219, 19.293, 21.109, 453; convert 17.273, **B** 15.437, 445, 16.110; be converted 3.479, 17.254, 20.398

tuto(u)r *n* guardian, keeper 1.52

twe(y)(n)e *num. a* two 5.134, 6.209, 14.116, 18.81, B 13.381, (*post-positive*) †21.347, A 12.83, **hem** ~ the two of them 18.231, B 18.171; a pair (of) 6.363

twel-monthe *n* twelve-month, year 6.80

twelue *num. a* twelve 6.203, 220, 11.32

twenty *num. a* twenty 14.129, ~ **hundred** B 16.10

twies *av* twice 7.29, B 4.23, Z Pr 96, *in num.* ~ **þritty and tene** B 13.270

twynen *v* twist 19.170

twius Z Pr 96 = **twies** *av*

two *num. a* Pr 106, 1.84, 3.332, 381, 5.130, 6.103, 198, 397, 7.1, 222, 8.304, 9.284, 301, 10.8, 78, 80, 11.173, 13.79, 14.104, 15.87, 16.9, 19.13, 76, 20.61, 73, 238, 318, 21.126, 274, **B** 2.55, 3.231, 5.287, 402, 6.282, 325, 9.116, 10.280, 13.128, 176, 247, 317, (*post-positive*) **bothe** ~ both of them; **hem** ~ those two 7.289; **they** ~ those two B 10.153, **vs** ~ the pair of us B 13.107; *in cpd. num.* ~ **and thritty** 20.332; *a as n* 11.37, 13.28, 41, 14.108, 18.87, 21.343, 476; *and see* **twe(y)(n)e** *num.*

Two-Tonge Double-Tongue 22.162

vnlered *a* uneducated Z 3.164

vnlikyng *a* disagreeable 7.23

#**vnlosen** *v* open Pr 162 (B Pr 214); unbend, put forth 19.116; set free 1.196

vnlossum *a* undesirable 10.265

vnlouken *v* (*p.t.* **vnlek** 7.250) unlock, open 7.250, 14.55, 20.193, 359, B 18.263, 315; (*fig.*) split apart 20.266n; spread wide 9.143

vnlouely(ch)(e) *a* unattractive 10.265; unpleasant 14.178; *av* horribly 6.413

vnmaken *v* undo, dissolve B 15.241

vnmeble *n* immovable goods (= lands) 3.421, 10.188

#**vnmesurables** *a. pl.* unfathomable B 15.71

vnnethe *av* scarcely 4.63, 22.190, Z 3.165

vnpensched Z 4.138 = **vnpunisched** *a*

#**vnpiken** *v* pick 6.266 (B 13.368)

vnpynnen *v* unbolt 12.49, 22.331, B 18.263

vnpossible A 11.229 = **impossible** *a*

vnpunisched *a* unpunished 4.137

vnredy *a* improvident 12.218

vnresonable *a* not in accord with reason B 6.151; disordered, unpredictable B 15.355; undisciplined B 15.460

vnrihtfole *a* wrongful 12.17

vnriȝtfulliche *av* wrongfully 21.246

vnrobbed *p.p.a* without being robbed 13.1

vnrosted *p.p.a* uncooked B 5.603

vnsauerly *av* so as to taste unpleasant 15.49

vnsauoury *a* tasteless B 15.432

vnschryuen *p.p.a* unabsolved (of one's sins) Z 8.76

vnseled *p.p.a* not stamped with (an official) mark 16.128

vnsemely *a* hideous 1.55

vnsittyng(e) *a* improper, unbecoming, *in phr.* ~ **soffraunce** 3.207, 4.189

vnskilful *a* unreasonable 6.25, B 13.277

vnsold *p.p.a* unsold 6.214

vnsowen *v* undo the stitching (of) 6.6

vnsperen *v* unbar 20.270, open (*fig.*) 20.88

vnstable *a* unsteady 10.37

vnstedefast *a* inconstant 3.386

vntempred *a* untuned B 9.103

vnþende *a* small, of poor quality B 5.175

vntidy *a* indecent 22.119; not properly made 9.262; (of) poor (quality) 3.87

vntil *prep.* to B Pr 228

vntiled *p.p.a* uncultivated B 15.458

vntyled *p.p.a* without roof-tiles B 14.253

vntyme *n* the wrong time B 9.186

vntrewe *a* false 11.238; invalid Pr 98, ~ **þyng** ill-gotten gains B 15.107

vnwedded *p.p.a* unmarried 22.112

vnwwyse *a as n* those lacking in (spiritual) wisdom 10.91; ~**ly** *av* imprudently 11.224

vnwittiliche *av* foolishly 3.133

vnworþily *av* improperly B 15.243

vnwrast *a* deceitful 20.311

#**vnwriten** *p.p.a* not written down [*sc.* in the 'Book of Life'] 11.209c

vp(pe) *av* up, *in phrasal vv.* Pr 65, 2.131, 188, 6.4, 163, 382, 411, 7.62, 8.114, 12.182, 187, 224, 13.240, 247, 14.22, 130, 17.302, 18.10, 20, 25, 144, 243, 20.52, 281, 21.192, **B** 5.373, 602, 6.111, 214, 7.90, 11.408, 12.120, 15.253, 16.42, 18.52, **A** 2.41, 12.12, 38, Z 6.66; forward 4.45, B Pr 73; down 4.60; out 11.54; *in phr.* ~ **at** up to, as far as A 12.72; **is vppe** will be afoot, stirring B 4.72

vp *prep.* upon, against 1.157; upon pain of 4.128; in 6.35, 9.333, B 20.135; at 20.50; at / with B 11.208

vphaldere, vpholdere *n* dealer in second-hand goods 6.373, 12.220

vp(p)on¹ *prep.* upon 17.234, 19.198, 20.51, **B** 1.162, 2.164, 6.141, 9.153, 10.105, 13.391, 14.79, 16.157; up on 6.106; on 1.12, 64, 150, 170, 2.1, 184, 185, 3.79, 323, 4.20, 5.30, 6.43, 205, 320, 7.60, 8.205, 9.185, 227, 10.64, 13.76, 14.144, 153, †15.212, 18.53, 19.2, 20.74, 21.41, 324, **B** 2.75, 172, 3.312, 4.24, 5.465, 9.100, 10.226, †307, 11.169, 14.31, 16.164, 18.77, 367, **A** 2.130, 5.241, 11.28, 12.117, Z 5.107, 134; on top of 12.232; ~ **molde** anywhere 14.167; on the basis of B 12.292c; in 9.330, 19.24, 94, B 7.183; to 20.51, 89, 22.165, **don** ~ appeal to 1.82, 2.39; towards 2.5, 11.85, 15.122; at 4.167, 6.44, 66, B 4.154, 11.362; about 10.114, 15.25; by, ~ **gesse** haphazardly B 5.415

vpon² *av* at 18.191

vp-so-down *av* upside down 22.54

vpward *av* upwards 5.121; on high 7.155

vs *prn. 2 pers. pl.* us Pr 171 *et p.*; for us 5.88, 15.57, 20.344, **B** 3.48, 13.49, 15.262; to us 11.152, 12.122, **B** 7.75, 13.58, 14.186, 15.262; (*refl.*) ourselves 8.155, 21.359, 22.75, **B** 11.240, 14.81; for ourselves 11.222; ~**selue** ourselves B 7.128

vsage *n* habitual practice B 7.85

vscher *n* attendant 17.112

vsen *v* be accustomed to B 12.131, **be vsed** be the custom 20.421; observe 19.47, 20.339; practise 3.110, 465, 6.231, 239, 9.155, 12.90, 15.198, **B** 18.106, 19.254; pursue 9.103, 11.111, 18.175, **B** 3.240, 313, 15.415, 22.66; engage in B 5.225, A 11.183; (make) use (of) **B** 1.149, 10.131; put to profitable use A 7.23

vserer 16.259 = **vsurer** *n*

vsur(y)e *n* usury [lending at (excessive) interest] 2.91, 6.239, 303, 20.109, 21.353, **B** 2.176, 3.240, **A** 2.63, 8.40; interest B 7.81

vsurer *n* usurer [lender of money at excessive interest] 3.113, 6.306, 338, 16.259, **B** 11.282, 15.85

vuel 6.20 = **euel** *a*

vayne, in, *av. phr.* to no purpose 2.101

vaynglorie *n* empty self-regard 6.35

vayre 17.109 = **fayre** *av*

vale *n* valley 20.411

valewe *n* worth 13.201, A 11.34

vallen 20.411 = **fallen** *v*

van(y)schen *v* vanish, disappear 14.217; cause to waste away 15.8

vanten *v* boast, ~ **vp** ~ in 6.35

variable *a* inconstant 18.69

vaunsen 3.36 = **avaunsen** *v*

vawwarde 22.95 (**vauntwarde** B 20.95) = **faumewarde** *n*

veile *n* watchful one 7.56 (**veyles** Z 5.111)

vele 6.74 = **fele** *a*

velynge *ger.* 20.131 *see* **felen** *v*

vendage B 18.370 = **ventage** *n*

#venemouste *n* poisonousness 20.159

vengeaunce (veniaunce) *n* vengeance 19.271, 273; revenge B 15.261; retribution 20.97, **B** 6.144, 11.378, **taken** ~ inflict retribution Pr 117, 121, 3.409, 20.434, B 6.224; punishment Pr 115, 14.69, **B** 3.260, 9.96, 14.79

vengen *v* avenge 6.74, 94, 19.106

venial *a* pardonable, venial B 14.83, 92

venym *n* poison 17.223, 20.154, 156, A 5.69

veniso(u)n *n* flesh of game-beasts 9.93, **B** Pr 190, 15.462

veniaunce 14.69 = **vengeaunce** *n*

venkusen, venquisshen *v* (*p.t.* **yvenkused**) conquer 20.104

ventage *n* grape-harvest (*fig.*) 20.411

ver 22.23 = **fer** *av*

verilyche *av* truly A 12.28

verious *n* verjuice A 5.69

vernicle *n* vernicle [image of Christ's face on a medal] 7.167n

verray *a* true B 15.268, ~ **charite** even Charity itself 19.273, ~ **God** the true God / God himself 6.437, 21.422; ~ **man** real living human being 21.153,

vers *n* verse B Pr 143; psalm-verse **B** 12.292, 15.82

verset *n* versicle, psalm-text 14.128

versifyen *v* compose verse 17.109

verste 20.159 = **furst(e)** *ord. num.*

vertu(e) *n* divine power 15.8, 20.123; (spiritual) power **B** 14.38, 18.319; (physical) power 15.8; (natural healing) power 20.159; [specific] moral virtue 12.178, 13.201, 21.316, 22.23, 34, 149, B 11.378, Z 1.69; (one of the four) cardinal virtue(s) Pr 131, 21.275, 313, 318, 339, 345, 396, 410, 414, 455, 459, 22.21, 73, 122, 304; (theological) virtue 1.147, 15.279; virtuous way of life 10.77; virtuousness B 2.77

vertuous *a* potent, efficacious Pr 131; excellent, praiseworthy 18.89

vesture *n* clothing 1.23

vycary, vycory *n* representative 14.70; vicar 21.412, 422, 483

vice *n* (moral) vice 6.20, 12.232, 16.371, 21.313, 316, 459, A 10.76

victorie *n* supremacy 3.485, B 3.352

vigilie *n* vigil [eve of feast-day] 7.25, 9.232

viker B 19.484 = **vycary** *n*

vyl(e) *a* despicable 20.97; shameful **B** 10.45, 14.79; destructive 20.156

vilanye *n* outrage 20.97; obscene coarseness 6.432

vine *n* vine 2.28, B 14.31

vynegre *n* vinegar A 5.69

virginite *n* (the state of) virginity 18.89, B 16.203

virres n vir 's **B** 10.320c, 13.52c

visage *n* face B 18.338

vise 21.459 = **vice** *n*

visiten *v* visit 7.21, 16.328, *ger.* inspection [of diocese by bishop] B 2.177

vitailles *n.pl.* provisions (of food) 2.191, 7.49, (*fig.*) 15.187, B 14.38

vitaler *n* provision-merchant 2.61

voiden *v* remove, clear away B 14.94

vois *n* voice 16.169, 20.271, 360, B 15.593

voket *n* advocate 2.61

vorgoer 2.61 = **forgoere** *n*

vowe *n* vow [solemn promise before God] Pr 69, 7.13

vowen *v* vow 6.437, 7.13

vrete *p.t.* 6.74 *see* **freten** *v*[1]

waast *n* waste / uncultivated (common) land B Pr 163

waden *v* go, live 14.125; go about Z 3.157; walk (into) 7.214

waer 9.236, 11.80, 15.78 *see* **war** *a*; 20.298 *see* **waren** *v*

wafre *n* (thin, crisp) cake 15.200, B 13.241, 263, 264, 271

wafrer *n* cake-seller 15.200, **B** 13.227, 14.28, A 6.120

***wafrestere** *n* (female) cake-seller 7.284

wages *n. pl.* salary 13.105; pay, wages 22.260

wagen *v* give as a security 18.284; give a pledge (for) 4.93, 96c; pay wages (to) 22.259, 261, 269

waggen *v* rock, *ger.* rocking 10.34, A 9.28; shake violently 18.45, B 18.61; shake 12.18, 18.109; nudge 21.205

way (wey(ʒ)) *n* road 4.53, 9.31, 13.33, 41, 51, 15.191, 22.187, **B** 6.1, 17.115, (*fig.*) 13.29, **hey** ~ main road 8.2, 9.32, 188, 203, 11.104, 106, B 6.4, A 7.178, Z 7.6, (*fig.*) 13.67, 16.53, **B** 12.37, 15.434; path 7.306, (*fig.*) A 12.64; way Pr 49, 1.199, 2.199, 7.157, 177, 204, 8.4, 11.136, 13.42, 45, 18.290, 19.50, 79, 92, A 7.53; passage Pr 181, 189; distance, **mile** ~ time taken to go a mile 9.296; course of action, progress 3.18; manner, way (of acting) 6.265, 20.298, B 12.69; *in phrr.* **by what** ~ how 1.137; **fer** ~ far and away 16.50; **in / by ...** ~ on the / my / our / her way 15.186, 191, 19.48, 20.117, 21.157, 22.1, A 12.56

wayen 6.210, 224 *see* **wey(ʒ)en** *v*

wayf *n* (*pl.* **wayues**) (piece of) ownerless property Pr 92

wayke *a* weak 5.23

waylen *v* cry out with sorrow 5.108, B 14.332, A 5.254; bewail **B** 5.112, 14.324

wayten *v* keep hostile watch A 7.148; look B 13.343; look intently Pr 16, 9.293, 18.181, stare at 18.274; *ger.* **waytynge(s) of** staring(s) with 2.94, 6.177; plan B 8.98; ~ **after** look for 1.123, 2.78, **B** 14.116, 16.248; look around B 16.169; watch over, look after 6.208, 7.187, B 13.238, 393

wayuen *v* ~ **away** drive away 22.168; ~ **vp** open B 5.602

wayues *pl.*; *see* **wayf** *n*

waken *v* (*p.t.* **wakede** 4.196 *etc*, **woke(n)** 21.156, B 14.69) be awake 19.185, *pr.p.* while awake 13.218; keep guard 21.156; stay awake (in prayer) 22.371; awake, wake up 4.196, 6.418, 18.179, 20.471, 21.1, **B** 5.3, 14.69, 236, *ger.* 9.78, B 15.1; *see* **awaken** *v*

wakere *a* watchful 9.259

waknen *v* wake up 21.484

wal *n* wall 1.153, 16.266, 20.61, 290, B 18.61, A 5.136, (*fig.*) B 5.587

Walch 6.205 *see* **Wal(s)(c)he** *a as n*

walet *n* (money)-bag 10.272

wal(e)wen *v* toss, roll 10.46; heave nauseously A 5.70

walken *v* walk 10.61, 13.246, 15.20, 17.303, 20.117, 120, B 16.114, A 12.68; go about 13.1, 15.2, 16.52, 340, 351, **B** 13.2, 17.113; go forth 20.31; journey, travel 7.175, 10.14, 17.283, B 20.382, A 11.258; travel over 9.110; move about B 9.55; ~ **with** accompany 6.124; live 9.172, 18.251; be rife B 7.77

walkere *n* fuller Pr 223

walkne B 15.361 = **welkene** *n*

wallen¹ *v* (provide with a) wall (*fig.*) 21.328; *ger.* (*fig.*) #**wallynge** wall-work 7.233

wallen² 21.380 = **wellen** *v*

walnote *n* walnut 12.147

Wal(s)(c)he *a as n* Welsh flannel 6.205; Welshman 6.372; ~**man** *n* Welshman 6.308

*****walterot** *n* idle nonsense 20.144*n*

wam Z Pr 132 *etc*; *see* **who** *prn*

wan¹ *p.t.* 6.310, 8.105, 9.251, 11.287, 17.18, 19.234, 242, **B** 4.67, 12.44 *see* **wynnen** *v*

wan² Z 1.30 *etc* = **when** *conj.*

†**wandedes** *n pl.* evil actions Z 5.152n

wandren *v* wander, roam about Pr 21, 6.205, 8.325, **A** 8.79, 10.212, move about B 9.55; *and see* **of-** ~ *v*

wangteeth *n pl.* molars 22.191

wanhope *n* despair (of God's mercy) 2.103, 7.58, 80, (B 13.421), 14.118, 19.293, **B** 5.279, 7.35, 13.407, (*person.*) 7.58, 11.198, 22.160, 166, 168

wanyen *v* wane, decline, *in phr.* **waxen and** ~ 10.44, **B** 7.55, 15.3

wanne *a* pallid 6.418

wannes Z 6.1 = **whennes** *av*

wanten *v* (*impers.*) be wanting, lack 9.106, B 14.173, *ger.* 177

wanto(w)(e)n *a* lascivious 3.142, 7.299; ~**nesse** *n* lasciviousness 3.160, B 12.6; unruliness A 10.67

war *p.t. pl.* Z 8.85 *see* **were(n)**

war *a* aware 11.87, B 2.8, A 3.56, **be** ~ take heed Pr 189, 3.142, 6.148, 9.236, 10.291, 11.80, B 10.269, A 3.56; beware 7.260, be on guard Pr 189, 1.40, 15.78; wary **B** 2.138, 20.163; *see* **ywa(e)r** *a*

waranten *v* declare for certain B 18.46

ward *n* regard, concern (for) **Z** Pr 99, 8.75; guard 20.365; watch, guardianship 5.185*n*; guardianship-case Pr 92*n*

wardeyn *n* guardian 1.51, B 16.187

#**wardemote** *n* meeting of (the citizens of) a (London) ward Pr 92

warden *v* guard 18.42

ware *n* wares, mechandise 2.223, 235, 6.95, 213

wareyne *n* warren [enclosed land for breeding game] B Pr 163

waren *v* (*refl.*) guard oneself 7.58, 10.287, Z 7.323

warien *v* curse 8.336

wariner A 5.159 = **wernare** *n*

warisshen *v* cure B 16.105

warm *a* warm 16.333, B 17.240; hot 19.172, 198, 206; fine, sunny (*comp.*) 20.456; **al** ~ while still alive A 7.170

warnen *v* (give a) warn(ing to) 8.342, 346, B Pr 208, 2.209, 4.69, 12.10; advise A 10.95; inform 5.132, 17.97, **B** 6.131, 15.362, 482, 18.300, A 2.165; command (under penalty) 3.427, 8.162, *ger.* 8.90

warner B 5.309 = **wernare** *n*

warpen *v* (*p.t.* **warp**) utter B 5.86, 363, **A** 4.142, 10.33

warrok(y)en *v* (fasten with a) girth 4.21

warth *p.t.* 5.98, 11.167 *see* **worthen** *v*

was *p.t. sg. of* **ben** *v* was Pr 15 *et p.*; (*with understood impers. subj.*) it was 6.4, 7.159, 11.239, 14.132, †15.52, **B** 14.7, 16.150; there was 1.150, 6.37, 7.298, 10.6, 117, 11.241, 14.159, 167, 20.459, B 10.226, A 2.41; (*with Ø-rel. subj.*) (who) was 6.308, 11.1, 290, 12.76, 22.221, 331, B 16.187; (which) was 15.61, B 12.73; (*with collective n. subj.*) 8.323, 12.49, 15.9, 10; (*with pl. n. subj.*) 3.12, 5.115, 6.393, 14.82, 17.199, 19.13, 21.47, 94, **B** 10.395, 12.45, 15.450, 16.204, 215, **A** 5.80, 11.272; came into being 18.217, 20.168; became 5.108, 6.148; occurred 5.115, B 10.129; appeared 20.238; was shown B 12.81; (*as p.t. auxil. with v. of motion*) had 15.154; *see also* **nas**, **were(n)**

waschen *v* (*p.t. sg., pl.* **wessh(en)** B 16.228, 2.221, 13.28, **wosch(en)** 18.244, 2.230, 15.38, *p.p.* **(y)wasche(n)** 9.268, B 13.460) wash 2.230, 9.80, 268, 18.244, **B** 11.431, 13.315, 14.18, 15.453, (*fig.*) B 15.192, 18.392; wash oneself 9.250, 15.32, 38, B 13.32, (*refl.*) 7.214; clean B 17.70; sweep (away) 10.228

waste *a* uncultivated 9.225; vain, profitless 21.287; *and see* **waast** *n*

wastel *n* cake / loaf of fine flour 6.340

wasten *v* consume 8.139, 10.301, B 6.133, A 5.25 (*or ?* spend); spend 19.248, **wastyng** *ger.* what one spends B 5.25; squander 21.356

wasto(u)r *n* squanderer [one who destroys by consuming without producing] Pr 24, 5.126, 8.27, 139, 158, 170, 208, 344, 21.438, 22.145, B 6.161, A 7.124; (*person.*) 8.149, 162, 164, 171, B 5.24; idle wastrel B 9.120

wat Z Pr 94, 5.43, 6.68, 7.232 = **what** *prn*

watelen *v* construct with wattle (*fig.*) 21.328

water *n* (the element of) water 5.148, 9.56, 10.131, 15.242, 19.195, 20.250; [=body of water], (water of) lake 10.33, 34, 44, 13.167, B 8.36, 18.243, Z 6.71; (water of) stream / river B Pr 9, 15.338, 453, (*fig.*) 7.214; flood 8.344; (drinking) water 21.109, A 7.168, *in phr.* **bred and ~** 6.155; [= tears] 6.2, 326, 7.56, 16.333, 18.147, 21.380; [=urine] 2.234; *in phrr.* **a ~** in the water [river, sea *etc*] 15.19, 20.29, B 16.189, **drop ~** drop of water 6.335, **haly ~** blessed water Z 8.75

watren *v* water (= flow with tears) 8.172

watri *a* watery, rain-bearing 20.456

watschoed 20.1 = **weetshoed** *a*

wauntounesse A 10.67 = **wanto(w)e(n)nesse** *n*

wawe *n* wave 10.45

wax(e) *p.t.* 6.421, 20.4, 133, 22.159, *pl.* ~**e(th)** 10.44, 12.231, 18.42, A 3.273, 6.50, 8.58, 10.126 *see* **waxen** *v*

waxen (wexen) *v* (*p.t.* **wax** Z 2.24, **we(e)x(e)** 3.483, **B** 5.279, 14.76, 15.3, 16.101, 215, 18.4, A 10.33, *pl.* **woxen** B 9.32, 14.60, *p.p.* **waxen** A 3.273, **wexen** 21.124, **woxe(n)** 3.211) grow 2.29, 12.231, 234, 16.253, 21.97, 124, 312, 377, 22.159, A 10.126; increase 22.269, *in phr.* **~ and wanyen** 10.44, B 7.55, A 5.70, [in potency, influence] **B** 10.75, 15.3, A 10.61, **~ an hey** acquire strength 6.124; arise 14.26, 32, 16.227, **B** 11.263, 14.76, A 5.72; be found 1.137, **B** 10.12, 15.459, 16.56; become 3.454, 483, 6.421, 7.77, 17.48, 18.42, 20.4, 133, **B** 4.174, 13.348, 14.323, 16.101, 215; turn into 10.197; fall 12.52, B 5.279; be born A 2.20; be created 15.263, B 9.32

we *1 pl. prn* we Pr 171 *et p.*; (*as subject with prec. subjv. v.*) = let us... Pr 174, 202, 228, 12.118, 121, 122, 13.17, 14.66, 67, 69, 17.111, 18.227, 20.165, 167, 205, 269, 284, 463, 21.360, 22.75, 78, **B** 4.195, 10.437, 11.211, 13.133, 14.81, 15.143, A 12.69; = if we... 17.92, B 13.6; = we would ... 10.189; (*collective*) 3.104, 9.125, 340 *et p.*, 10.54, 19.317, 21.64, **B** 7.126, 10.130, A 11.243; (*in apposition*) **we** ~ Pr 213, 8.6, 17.293, 21.417, **B** 9.87, 15.394; (*indef. generic*) 17.39; (*impers.*) = one 9.242; *in phrr.* **~ (...) alle** all of us 12.119, 132, 187, 18.226, **~ bothe** the two of us 20.168; **~ vchone** each one of us 9.235; *and see* **oure, vs**

web(be) *n*[1] (whole) piece of woven cloth B 5.110 (A 5.92)

webbe *n*[2] weaver 9.204, [female] 6.221

webbestere *n* weaver Pr 223

wed *n* pledge, security 6.243, 13.43, 44, 18.279, 284, 22.13, **B** 5.240, 13.260; wager 3.258; *in phr.* **to wedde** in pledge, as a guarantee 5.73, 20.30

wedden *v* wager 2.36, 4.143; marry 2.123, 124, 3.19, 131, 153, 156, 4.10, 7.299, 9.167, 10.257, 271, 281, 284, 287, 22.160, **B** 9.125, 157, 164, 157, 10.151, 11.72, Z 8.32, *ger.* A 2.102, 10.184; (*fig.*) embrace 16.111; marry, *p.p.a* **wedded** joined in wedlock 2.166, 11.98; married 10.205, 296, 18.71, 22.112, B 9.108

weddewe 14.143 = **wedewe** *n*

weddyng *n* marriage (-ceremony) 2.118, 119, 151, 174

wede *n*[1] weed 8.118, 12.226, 21.314, A 10.126, Z 7.91

wede *n*[2] clothing 22.211; *pl.* clothes 6.177, 13.189, **B** 11.234, 15.226, Z 3.162

weden B 16.17 = **wedyen** *v*

weder *n* weather 6.113, 8.347, 20.456, B 15.355; storm 10.46, 12.191, B 15.362, 482

wederwyse *a* skilled in forecasting the weather 17.94

wedeware *n* widower 10.284, 18.76

wedewe *n* widow 3.160, 420, 4.47, 6.143, 8.12, 10.284, 12.20, 18.71, 76, **B** 9.69, 164, 13.197, 16.214, 216, 218, A 8.32; (consecrated) widow 14.143

wedewhed, wydwehode *n* (the state of) widowhood 18.109, B 16.203

wed(y)en *v* (uproot) weed(s) 8.66, B 16.17, *ger.* 8.186

wedlok (wedlak) *n* (the state of) marriage, matrimony 10.294, 18.88, **B** 9.114, 117, 191, 16.203, 216, 218, A 10.133; marital union B 9.154; *in phrr.* **mariage of ~** the bond of matrimony A 10.207, **out of ~** illegitimately B 9.120

wedore 20.456 = **weder** *n*

weel 4.21 = **wel** *av*

weend *imper.* B 3.266 = **wenden** *v*

weer B 11.116, 16.3 *see* **wer** *n*

weere *p.t. subjv.* (= were) B 15.3, 17.77

weete B 14.171 = **wet(e)** *n*

weet *a* damp, rain-sodden B 14.42

#weetschoed *a* with wet feet 16.14, 20.1

weex *p.t.* **B** 3.331, 5.279, 14.76, 15.3, 16.101, 215, 18.4, 130 *see* **waxen** *v*

wehe(e) *n* (*imit.*) neigh, whinny B 4.23, 7.90

wey[1] 1.137, 6.265, 11.106, 13.29, 33, 41, B 5.555, A 7.53 = **way** *n*

wey[2] 19.67, 20.365 = **w(e)y(e)** *n*[2]

wey[3] *n* whey Z.7.286

weye *n*[1] wey [measure of weight, here = 3 cwt]

w(e)y(e) *n*[2] man 3.225, 6.105, 7.157, 13.13, 157, 14.195 (*with play on* way) 18.229, 279, 19.67, 20.327, 365, 21.166, †230, **B** 5.533, †10.108, 11.382, 12.293, 13.32, 191, 361, 14.156, 17.99, A 6.41, 92, †10.89, 11.67, **Z** 3.115, 5.43; person A 11.224, Z 1.6

wey(3)en, (wayen) *v* (*p.p.* 1.173, 9.271) weigh [in scales] 1.173, 6.210, 224, 242, 9.271, Z 5.100

w(e)y(g)ht *n* (measuring) weight 6.258, 16.128, 19.246

weylawey B 18.228 = **wel-a-way**²

weylen B 14.324, *pr.p.* A 5.254 *see* **waylen** *v*

weke *n* wick (of torch / taper) 19.170, 172, 179, 206

wel¹ Z 7.286 = **welle** *n*

wel(e)² *a* in favour with 3.190; prosperous, happy Z 3.173, *in phrr.* ~ **be** 8.299, ~ **worth** 13.1, 21.433; good (*as n*) 11.274n; *in phrr.* ~ **dedes** 3.69, 15.305, B 3.70, ~ **hope** 7.113; sound, right 11.274n, Z Pr 71; in good order, satisfactory 4.183

wel³ *av* well [morally, = justly, right(eous)ly] (*with* **don, werchen** *etc*) 1.131, 9.321, 10.25, 189(1), 204, 11.215, 226, 14.10, 13, 15.115(1), 16.34, 175, 219, 17.182, 21.481, **B** 1.130, 3.233, 8.56, 9.93, 95, 12.32, **A** 10.75, 88, 11.162, 199, 12.36; kindly 11.116; favourably 7.267, 12.141, B 14.145; faithfully 19.227, **B** 4.181 11.263; carefully 4.52, 9.147, 12.91, 17.116, 21.279, **B** Pr 208, 14.81, 16.47, Z 7.323; properly 4.21, 7.198, 214, 225, 12.237, 13.234, 14.18, 159, 16.321, 17.122, 21.62, 22.231, **B** Pr 152, 5.260, 8.52, 14.278 (2), 14.311; prosperously 5.8, 22.235; profitably B 5.262; deeply B 5.176; easily, readily 13.211, 14.126, 15.46, 16.129, 18.224, 19.242, 21.62, 438, 22.323, **B** 6.46, 8.51, 9.39, 16.218; effectively, successfully 3.48, 12.193, 20.183, 22.305 **B** 5.560, 12.38; thoroughly, completely 2.47, 18.245, **B** 6.195, 13.179, 15.453, **A** 3.75, 5.241, 11.141, 182, *in phr.* ~ **at ese** 15.48, B 16.227; certainly, for sure (*esp. with* **knowen, leuen, seyen, witen** *etc*) Pr 100, 2.142, 3.59, 225, 312, 4.76, 154, 6.326, 8.139, 211, 258, 270, 9.128, 10.137, 202, 242, 11.210, 12.82, 13.81, 14.126, 15.115 (2), 16.235, 281, 17.165, 217, 19.9, 20.224, 342, 21.26, 253, 361, 411, **B** 1.51, 3.217, 337, 4.71, 8.73, 10.154, 13.132, 14.82, 282, 15.263, 461, 553, 18.215, **A** 4.67, 12.99, **Z** 3.171, 5.35; clearly **B** 2.189, 12.20, 153, 15.591; familiarly, intimately 4.32, 15.31, 37, 16.157, 20.252, 22.338, B 13.131; closely B 16.214; satisfactorily 4.96, 7.193, 8.115, 9.289, 21.194, B 14.150, 153; fully 6.108, 161, 8.208, 300, **B** 15.187, 17.73; *as intensive* (*with v*) very much 1.41, **B** 3.54, 13.264, 14.167, (*with a or av*) very 4.53, 6.48, 418, 7.299, 306, 9.67, 236, 244, 11.5, 14.152, 18.111, 22.25, 39, 194, 303, **B** 4.46, 11.35, 194, 14.278(1), **A** 2.56, 105, 3.71, 5.75, 78, 104, 154, 11.157, 12.43, 100, 106; (*with comp. a or av*) much Pr 117, 122, 3.141, 6.200, 10.189 (2), 12.153, 22.62, B 5.113, 140; that much B 13.24, A 7.138; (*av in cpds., with p.pl.*) 10.263, 268, 11.236, 15.64, **B** 10.430, 11.39, 396, (*with v*) **bidde** ~ 7.239, **do** ~ 9.289, **kepe** ~ B 10.165, **se** ~ **wel** *etc* 10.146–8; *in phrr.* ~ **awey** far and away **B** 12.262, 17.43, A 11.218; ~ **neyh** pretty well, almost 15.294; **fareþ** ~ farewell B 13.181; **as ~... as...** both ...and... 6.182, 12.117, 15.14, 16.233, 19.45, 21.438, 22.61, B 15.449

welawey¹ *av* A 11.218 = **wel awey**; *see* **wel** *av*

wel-a-way² 20.237 *see* **welowo** *excl.*

Welche B 5.195 *see* **Wal(s)(c)he** *a as n*

welcome *a* welcome 2.227, 242, 5.50, 7.278, 22.244, 357, B 13.157; *interj.* B 13.32, A 12.62

welcomen *v* welcome 7.96, 9.135, 15.31, 37, 200, 16.170, 20.178, 21.211, 22.60

welden *v* (*contr. pr.* **welt** B 10.85) get control of 12.20, B 10.24; hold A 7.151; possess 11.10, 72, 14.18, 22.12, **B** †9.39, 10.29, 85, 90, Z 7.212

wele¹ *n* wealth, riches 12.238, 15.308; abundance B 19.287; happiness 11.107, 275, 12.211, 20.208, 209, 210, 229, 237; prosperity 21.244, 453, Z 3.173c, 7.281

wele² (? = **wel** *a*) 11.274n, c

welfare *n* good living 21.356

welhope *n* (state of) good hope B 13.454

welkene *n* sky, (vault of) heaven B 15.361; upper air (*aether*) 20.246, B 17.161

well 2.47, 14.126 = **wel** *av*

wel(le) *n* spring of water Z 7.286; (*fig.*) source, origin 1.159, 16.39, 142, 188; well Z 5.70

wellen (wallen) *v* boil Z 7.286; rise up 21.380

welowo *excl. as n* misery 16.77; *excl.* woe! 20.237

welt *contr. pr.* B 10.85 *see* **welden** *v*

welthe *n* happiness, (worldly) well-being Pr 10, 12.158; prosperity 9.116; wealth, riches 9.336, 10.271, 13.13, 16.19, 22.38, B 10.24; valuable possessions B 10.85; goods 1.51; value, worth 4.158, B 9.164

wem *n* stain [of sin] 20.134

wen Z Pr 1, 8.70 *etc* = **when(n)e** *conj.*

wenche *n* girl B 9.163; young woman 12.11, 18.134, 20.116; woman Z 6.88, 101; maidservant, ? daughter 6.414; mistress Pr 52; ~ **of the stuyues** prostitute 21.438, 22.160

wende *p.t.* 6.32, 41 (B 13.280, 292), **B** 5.234, 13.407, **A** 11.219, 224, *2 sg.* **wendest** B 3.192 *see* **wenen** *v*

wenden *v* (*p.t.* **wente** Pr 4 *et p.*, *pl.* **wenten** Pr 49 *etc*, *p.p.* **went** 3.434, 8.211) turn, change 2.247, 3.434, 20.208; turn away 22.284; go (travel, journey) Pr 52, 158, 181, 1.131, 2.174, 218, 3.13, 4.53, 72, 5.104, 6.211, 351, 7.204, 8.4, 57, 62, 94, 186, 211, 278, 10.200, 13.33, 51, 15.32, 162, 16.322, 17.190, 18.290, 19.48, 334, 20.129, 178, 329, 21.129, 193, 334, 358, 22.204, 382, **B** 4.105, 18.299, **A** 10.143, 177, 11.168, 277, 12.51, 89; go about **B** Pr 162, 8.6; go off, depart 8.209, 220, 299, 301, 11.105, 15.151, 18.181, 21.78, 322, ~ **hennes** depart this life 1.173, 6.312; ~ **forth** proceed Pr 4, 49, 10.61, 15.186, 20.1, **B** 15.338, 16.146, A 12.56; walk 20.250, 252; *in phrr.* ~ **(by) the wey** go along the road 13.41, 15.191, 19.92, 22.1, ~ **(my** *etc*) go on (one's) way 11.136, B 10.221

wenen *v* (*p.t.* **wende** B 5.234, A 11.219, (*subjv.* 6.32, 41), *2 sg.* **wendest** B 3.192) think 11.239, 13.160, 14.166, 16.130, *in parenth. phr.* **as I** ~ I (should) think, in my opinion 9.70, 13.160, 20.225, 329, **B** 3.227, 8.69, **A**

5.70; believe 16.304, **B** 13.407, 15.477, 600; suppose 3.454, 6.24, 20.194, 22.32, **B** 3.192, 5.234, A 11.219, 224; hope 6.322, 14.195; *ger.* **wenyng** (mere) surmise 22.33; hope, fantasy B 2.91

wenge *n* wing 14.186, **goose** ~ = thing of no worth B 4.37

went *p.p.* 3.434, 8.211, B 6.204, ~**e(n)** *p.t.* Pr 4, 49 *etc*; *see* **wenden** *v*

wente *n* trick, contrivance 6.263

wepen *v* (*p.t.* **wep** 6.316, A 2.198, Z 5.91, *pl.* **wopen** 9.41, **wepide** A 4.60, **wepte** 2.252, *pl.* **wepten** B 7.37) weep 2.252, 6.316, 9.41, 11.166, 12.84, 16.77, 18.109, 289, 20.94, **B** 1.180, 5.112, 7.121, 11.148, 13.267, ~ **on** beseech (sb.) with tears A 4.60; weep for one's sins 5.108, 16.334, 22.370, **B** 5.185, 11.263, 14.332, A 5.254, *ger.* A 8.108; *in phrr.* ~ **teres** 15.51, B 12.45 ~ **water with eyes** 6.2, 326, 18.147, B 14.324

wep(e)ne (**wypne**) *n* weapon 3.458, 14.50, (*fig.*) 21.219, 227, (*euphem. for*) penis 10.289

weps (**wispe**) *n* wisp, handful 6.401

wepte(n) *p.t.* 2.252 *etc*, B 7.37 *see* **wepen** *v*

wer *n* confusion, perplexity 12.52, B 16.3

wer *p.t. subjv.* Pr 180 *see* **wer(i)en** *v*

werchen *v* (*p.t.* **wro(u)3te** B 1.13, 82 *etc*, *p.p.* **(y)wro3t** B 3.239 *et p.*; *see* **worchen** *v*

wercus *pl.* Z 4.120 *see* **werk** *n*

werd Z 5.43 = **world** *n*

werde *p.t.* A 2.12 *see* **weren** *v*

were(n) *p.t. pl. of* **ben** *v* (*indic.*) were Pr 53 *et p.*, 6.41 *etc*, (*with subj. om.*) **B** 11.225, 15.73; (*with sg. subj.*) 16.346, 18.233, 22.65, †B 5.378, A Pr 81; *p.t.sg.* (*subjv.*) Pr 2, 180 *et p.*, *pl.* 8.136 *etc*; existed Pr 80, 11.206, 12.143, 14.71; should exist 14.166, 18.186, 212; would be 3.171, 6.110, 8.5, B 3.346, A 12.17; should be 2.68, 125, 6.387, B 5.165; might be 1.10, 68, 3.152, 383, 10.200, 12.4 *etc*, **B** 11.246, 14.128, 15.3, 17.77, A 12.80; *in constr.* **as...were** as if (It / he *etc*) were Pr 2, 66, 5.160, 6.156, *etc*, **B** 5.100; *in* (*semi-*)*parenth. phr.* **as hit** ~ as it were, so to speak Pr 11, 2.9, 54, 5.124, 9.114, 210, 12.185, 13.113, 152, 15.176, 16.113, 18.6, 19.253, **B** 12.217, 17.95, 201, as might happen / be the case 6.110, 13.8, 20.116, 200, B 15.205; (*with subj. omitted*) **ne** ~ were it not for **B** 10.45, 18.210, A 11.51

wery *a* tired (out) B Pr 7, 13.205, 15.186; discontented 20.4; ~**nesse** *n* fatigue Pr 7

wer(i)en *v* (*p.p.* **wered** 5.81) wear 3.447, 19.237, **B** 14.329, 15.451, Z 3.162; ~ **out** abolish / exhaust [with the passage of time] 5.81

werk *n* act, deed 1.171, 11.315, 12.141, A 10.65; (= the sexual act) 6.181, 184 (B 13.348), B 9.129, A 10.208; [physical] action 12.128; [moral] action Pr 3, 1.85, 2.206, 4.71, 80, 104, 11.11, 219, 222, 223, **B** 2.130, 3.69, 239, 10.113, 395, 430, 13.295, 14.224, 15.204,

17.102, **A** 10.92, 11.68, 272, Z 3.172; **euel / wikked** ~ sinful act(ion) 6.21, 18.38, 19.296, 21.380, 22.371, B 15.355, **lecherouse** ~ B 2.125; (good) work, (pious / religious) act 6.41, 53, 9.349, 12.83, 14.25, 28, 16.340, 18.12, **B** 10.412, 432, 15.186, 449, **A** 10.130, 12.98; work, labour 5.54, B 12.27; (physical) labour A 7.137; enterprise, undertaking B 9.206; creation 12.75, 18.214, B 1.150; (literary) work / composition A 12.101, 103; workmanship Pr 179; *in phrr.* **a** ~ **to work** 8.197; **Godes** ~ act God approves 10.290, B 10.67; (**worchen**) **in** ~ actually perform 4.143, B 10.254; (**with**) ~ **and / or with word** (by) both action and word(s) 2.94, 6.99, 13.192, **B** 5.85, 366, 9.51, 13.141, 146, 312, 14.14, B 15.116, 198, 477, A 7.211; **Neither þoru3 wordes ne** ~ B 15.210

werk(e)man *n* workman, labourer 5.25, 7.41, 8.116, 186, 336, 342, 11.241, 19.184, **B** 5.277, 6.51, 132, 13.268, 14.137, Z 7.325

werken B Pr 37, A 11.276, 12.97 *see* **worchen** *v*

werkmanschip *n* labour, work B 10.288; action B 9.45; performance 2.96; activity 19.142

wern *p.t.* A 7.180, 10.159, 11.220, 224 = **were(n)** *v* 172, 198

wernard *n* deceiver 2.142, B 3.180

wernare *n* warriner [keeper of game-preserve] 6.362

wernen *v* refuse 22.12

werre *n* war 13.140, 20.236, 459, *in phrr.* ~ **and / or wo** 3.205, 17.204, B 18.414; ~ **and wrake** 17.85, 20.458; **at** ~ in conflict 16.64; **to** ~ to go to war 22.259; battle 11.267, 22.163

werren *v* make war (upon) 17.234

wers *comp.* A 11.218, B 1.26; ~**e** B 5.113, 10.421, A 6.46 *see* **wors(e)** *a, av*

wesch *n* wish, object of desire 6.66

weschen *v* wish, desire 6.401, 10.271, 15.90, 19.330, 22.194, **B** 5.110, 10.468, 12.270, *ger.* desire 2.95

wessh *p.t.* B 16.228, *pl.* ~**en** B 2.221, 13.28 = **wosch(en)** *see* **waschen** *v*

west *n* west 20.116, *a* B 18.113; ~**ward** *av* towards the west Pr 16, 20.121, B 16.169 *and see* **south** ~ (**wynde**)

Westminstre *n as a*, ~ **lawe** the law of the land, the king's justice 10.242

wet(e)[1] *n* wet weather 7.175, B 14.171; rain (water) 19.306

wete[2] Z 7.170 = **whete** *n*

weten 4.100, 18.147, Z 2.2 *see* **witen** *v*

wethe *n* withy, **in a** ~ **wyse** as if with a withy Z 5.160

weth(e)wynde *n* bindweed, ~ **wyse** woodbine-fashion 7.162

wether *n* (castrated) ram 9.267

weuen[1] *v* A 6.92 = **wayuen** *v*

weuen[2] *v* weave B 5.548; *ger.* **fro þe weuyng** from being woven B 15.451

weuere *n* weaver B Pr 220

wex(e) *n* wax Pr 99, 10.272, 19.170, 172, 198

wex(e) *p.t.* 3.483, A 2.20, *pl.* A 10.33 *see* **wexen** *v*[1]

wexen[1] 1.137, 2.29, 7.77, 12.52, 234, 14.32, 15.263, 16.227, 253, 17.48, 21.97, 312, 377, 22.269, **B** 4.174, 10.12, 11.263, 13.348, 14.323, 15.459, **A** 5.72, 61, 11.12 = **waxen** *v*

#**wexen**[2] *v* wax-polish 6.401c

wham *interrog.* 1.43, 13.158, 16.141, 17.89, 20.177, (*rel.*) 1.179, 7.168 = **whom** *prn*

whan(ne) Pr 1, 1.103 *etc*, B 1.25 *et p.*, A 3.96 *et p.*, *in phr.* ~ **þat** B 10.137 *see* **when(ne)** *conj.*

whare *av* 8.166, 10.124, *in phr.* ~ **þat** 11.104; *see* **wher(e)**[2] *av*

whareof 16.171 = **wherof** *av*

what (*interrog.*) *prn* what Pr 217, 1.11 *et p.*, who 10.70, 13.219, **B** 2.18, 10.219, *a* 1.68 *et p.*, which 3.6, 4.53, 10.5, 20.176; what sort of 8.270, 15.251, 20.360; (*excl.*) *a* what great Pr 105, 13.14 *etc*; *prn* what **B** 7.131, 13.184, 18.187; [as call to attention] lo, see! 8.148 (1); hey!, come on! 7.8; (*rel.*) *prn* (= that which) 3.484, 6.47, 8.88, 13.35, *etc*; as to what was 13.175; whatever **B** 3.266, 5.547, 9.58, ~ **þat** whatever 8.148 (2), what A 3.106; ~**... þat** any...who B 3.324; *a* whatever 2.34, 7.145, 9.153, 17.174, 22.67, **B** Pr 207, 9.196, 12.74, A 6.80; whichever 6.247, 301, 19.117, 21.196; *in phrr.* ~ **done** what kind of B 18.300; ~ **euere** *prn* whatever 7.125, B 11.215; ~ **man** = who B 13.25, = whoever 2.36, ~**so** whatever 14.65, B 10.130, A 10.96, ~ **soeuere** *prn* whatever B 10.388; *conj.* whether 17.85, B 13.317, ~ **for** both for 20.113, ~ **thorw** what with 17.85

wheche 7.69 = **whiche** *prn*

wheder[1] *conj.* whether 1.137

wheder[2] A 12.80 = **whoder** *av*

wheiþer *prn* **B** 14.248, 16.96 *see* **whether** *prn*; **B** 1.48, 8.127, 11.83, 117, 188, 14.101 *see* **wher(e)**[3] *conj.*

when A 12.80 = **whennes** *av*

when(ne) *conj.* when 1.45, 81 *et p.*; = whenever 3.169, 8.154, 17.173, A 8.122, ~ **þat** whenever 18.160, when B 10.137; at whatever time A 8.37; after 13.146, 15.24, 16.5, 22.1, 51; if 3.398, 4.52, 5.149, 6.59, 77, 8.37, 16.303, A 12.33

whennes *av* (*interr.*) whence, from where (*prec. by* **of, fro(m)**) 7.169, 18.184, 291, A 12.80

wher(e)[1] 16.88 *see* **whether** *prn*

wher(e)[2] *av and conj.* where Pr 159 *et p.*, **loo** / **se** ~ 2.5, 18.242, 20.170, 341; where (to) Pr 181, 15.151, 16.176; to whichever place 3.175; wherever 15.162, 18.251, 20.298; in the circumstances in which 1.22; from whom 13.169; in whomever B 3.176; to whom(ever) 3.19, 227, 6.343; *in phrr.* ~ **forth** towards whichever direction 16.340, B 17.115, ~ **þat** 7.197, where 10.13, 75, 13.136, wherever 21.129

wher(e)[3] (**whe(i)þer**) *conj.* whether Pr 186, 2.149, 3.296, 9.240, 277, 11.275, 12.22, 53, 14.191, 193, 213, 15.261, 16.97, 18.54, 57, 224, 20.72, 217, 331, 429, 21.353, 22.107, B 10.432, A 1.46, (**wheiþer**) B 1.48 *etc*; (*as particle introducing question*: does...?; is...?) 15.281, 16.337, 17.150, 19.27, B 17.125

wherby *av* (*interrog.*) by what means, how? B 10.435; (*rel.*) by means of which 3.249, 12.187, B 14.41; as a consequence of which 5.34

wher(e)fore *av* (*interrog.*) for what reason 12.36, **B** 11.85, 432, 15.200, *in phr.* ~ **and why** 13.185, 241, (**why and** ~) B 11.301; (*rel.*) by reason of which 15.241; for which reason 1.17, **B** 15.347, 384, 16.134, ~ **and why** 21.84

whereon *av* (*rel.*) on which 19.13

whereso *av, conj.* wherever 6.27, ~ **þat** †6.99, ~ **euere** *av, conj.* wherever B 18.375

wherof *av* (*interrog.*) from what source **B** 12.221, 15.14; to what purpose 12.33, 16.171, (*rel.*) from which 3.60; out of which B 11.263; by means of which 15.241; of which B 19.140

wherwith *av as n* the means by which 6.316, 15.241, B 9.69

whete *n* wheat [grain] 3.42, 4.60, 8.8, 327, Z 7.170, ~ **breed** bread of wheat-flour B 6.137, 7.121; wheat [crop] 12.183, 193, 234, 13.42, B 6.32, A 10.126

whether (**where**) *prn* which of the two 9.277, 16.88, B 16.56, A 12.37

why *av* (*interrog.*) why 3.228, 12.24, 13.193, 195, 15.75, 95, 17.204, 18.84, 20.65, 21.15, **B** 3.260, 9.87, 10.107, 113, 119, 126, 263, 11.76, 12.219, 232, 234, 13.460, 16.24, *in phr.* **wherefore and** ~ 13.185, 241, 21.84; *as n* reason why, **þe** ~ 18.147, *pl.* 14.156, B 10.124, (*ellip.*) 10.248, 13.230, 245, 14.99, 153, 166

whicche *n* clothes-chest 4.111

which(e) (*interrog.*) *a* what (kind of) 4.26, 9.300, 20.127, A 7.124; *prn* which 7.69, 14.108, **B** 10.265, 17.24, 115, A 11.89; (*excl.*) what 11.26; (*rel.*) *a* which 3.196, 9.156, 14.119, **B** 2.108, 13.129, (*with art.*) **þe** ~ 9.137, 15.278, 18.11, 20.339, 22.62, **B** 10.238, 12.86, 13.408, ~ **a** which (kind of) 4.26, A 11.68; *prn* which, that 1.37, 3.365, 7.69, †10.301, 11.288, 19.326, **B** 5.290, 10.133, 323, 435, 11.264, 347, 13.85, 130, 313, 14.83, 16.224, A 10.122, (*with art.*) **þe** ~ 3.496, 5.31, 7.99, 9.107, 137, 140, 10.154, 171, 11.82, 12.152, 13.81, 14.54, 16.27, 112, 17.140, 247, 18.12, 14, 51, 72, 207, 235, 19.8, 87, 20.110 , 223, 21.80, 129, 22.62, **B** 10.475, 11.318, 15.131, 16.148, (= who) 3.191, **B** 6.132, 15.421, 18.134, (= whom) 19.39, B 16.232, (= of whom) 9.98, (*with Ø-antecedent*) those whom 20.449; *in phr.* **þe** ~ **þat** who, which 3.93, 10.184

whider(-out, -ward) **B** 15.13, 16.12, 175, 5.300 *see* **whode(r)-** *av*

whil *n* (space of) time 4.44, B 6.162, *in avl. phrr.* (= for

... time): **eny** ~ 3.204, 4.171, 5.25, B 13.332, **gret** ~ B 4.46, **(a) litel** ~ 1.106, 12.224, 19.47, **longe** ~ 4.44, **þe ~(s)** meanwhile 8.6, 20.167 (*see also* **hand ~, mynte ~, o(u)þer ~, Paternoster ~**); short time, moment Pr 16, 4.16, 21.357, B 3.331

whil(e)(s) *conj.* while, as long as Pr 84, B 2.107, A 7.134 *et p.*, Z 5.73, **þe ~** while Pr 188 *et p.*, **al þe ~** A 7.134, **~ þat** B 1.16, A 12.51

whil er *av* some time ago 10.292

whilen (whilom, whilum) *av* at one time, formerly 9.204, 196, 17.9, 99

whistlen *v* play upon a pipe / whistle B 15.474, *ger.* whistling, piping B 15.463, 473, 478

whistlere *n* whistle / pipe-player = ? 'mouthpiece / spokesman' B 15.482.

whit(e) *a* white Pr 230, 6.103, 20.212, 213, **B** 10.435, 15.408

whiten *v* become white 16.333; **do** ~ have whitewashed B 3.61

whith 3.130 = **wiht(e)** *n*

whitlymen *v* wash with white-lime 16.266

who *prn* (*interrog.*) who 6.419 *etc*, B 3.235 *etc*, (*indef.*) 1.84 *etc*, **as ~** B 9.36, 15.307; *and see* **ho** *prn*

whom (wham) *prn interrog.* (*acc.*) whom 7.168, 20.177, B 18.174; (*dat.*) whom 1.43, 3.221, 6.343, 13.158, 16.141, 17.89, B 1.49; to whom B 15.318; (*rel.*) whom 1.179, 7.168

whos *prn interrog.* (*gen.*) whose 2.17, 1.46 (**hoes**)

whoso Pr 205, 1.57, 11.72, B 1.88 *et p.*, A 12.3 *see* **hoso** *indef. prn*

whode(r) *av* where, whither 18.181, 292, **B** 15.13, 16.175; # ~ **out** forth to where 7.177, from whence, in what place B 16.12; ~ **ward** in what direction 6.353

wy A 6.41, 92, †10.89, 11.67 = **w(e)y(e)** *n²*

wicche *n* sorcerer B 18.46, 69; witch 6.81 (B 13.338), B 18.338; ~ **craft** *n* magic B 13.169; sorcery 20.46, B 16.120

wicke 21.443, A 12.37, **wickede** 3.205, 9.31; *see* **wikke, wikkede** *a*

wid(e) *a* ample, extensive 20.45, B 16.134; far-spreading 9.111, 21.36, 335, B 17.160; capacious 18.270

wyde *av* far abroad 7.175, 10.14, 200, 21.335, 22.382, **B** Pr 4, 14.98; extensively 13.185, A 12.43, *comp.* **wyddore** more extensively 20.400; further 2.213; fully 20.365

wy(d)d(e)we 4.47, 6.143, **B** 9.69, 13.197, 16.214, 216, 218, A 8.32 *see* **wedewe** *n*

wyd(e)w(e)hode 18.88, B 16.203 *see* **wedewhed** *n*

widewhar(e) *av* in distant places 17.271; far and wide 10.61

wye 7.157, 18.229, B 5.533 *etc*, A 6.41 *etc*; *see* **w(e)y(e)** *n²*

wierd 14.32 = **wyrd** *n*

wyf *n* (*dat. sg.* **wyue** 10.145, *pl.* **wyues** 3.160 *et p.*, *gen.*

pl. **wyuen(e)** 5.131) woman B 5.561, A 7.10, Z Pr 48*n*; lady, mistress (of household) **B** 10.223, 224, 15.428; married woman 3.420, B 3.268, A 8.32; wife 2.17, 4.46, 5.132, 6.143, 221, 231, 362, 414, 420, 7.219, 8.55, 10.226, 272, 291, 296, 11.1, 116, 139, 243, 12.158, 13.13, 17.37, 39, 18.245, 19.301, 306, 312, 20.472, 22.193, **B** 5.226, 9.113, 10.223, 229, **A** 10.208, 1.93, 178, (= **Adam's**) 18.230, **Clergies ~** 11.98, **Peres ~** 8.80, 105, 182, **Pilates ~** B 18.300; **to ~, wyue** as a wife 3.146, 368, 4.158 *in phr.* **wedden (a) ~** 2.166, 3.156, 7.299, 11.98, ~ **and wedewes** 3.160, 6.143, 8.12

wight(e) (wiȝt)¹ 1.59, **B** 3.227, 10.168 *etc* = **wiht(e)** *n*

wyght(e)² 16.128 = **w(e)y(g)ht** *n*

wyht(e) (wight(e), wiȝt) *n* creature 1.59, 20.238, B 8.53; person, man 13.219, 220, **B** Pr 208, 3.227, 9.60, 13.193, 15.200, A 12.89; anyone 10.6, 15.167, B 8.69; **eny ~** anyone / body 10.4, 16.218, 21.395, **B** 12.25, 13.123, 324, 16.12, **no ~** no one / body 10.71, 11.273, 16.304, 20.68, 210, 225, 236, **B** 3.227, 13.176, ~ **noon** anyone 22.13, B 5.513, **vch (ech) (a)** everybody 9.116, 13.93, **B** 5.115, 6.246, 10.168, A 10.71; *in av. phrr.* **a litel ~** a little bit 3.130, **no ~** not at all †B 10.274

wyht *a* vigorous 10.147; brave, powerful 15.173; **~li(che)** *av* vigorously 8.18; quickly 18.292, B 10.221, A 2.170; **~ nesse** *n* strength 11.287, **~ of handes** main force 21.247

wyke¹ 19.206 = **weke** *n*

wyke² B 10.96, 13.155 = **woke** *n*

wiket *n* wicket-gate B 5.602

wikke *a* bad, ? wicked 7.117c, 21.443; *as av* wickedly 16.175, A 12.37; *as n* bad, evil 14.164, 166, 21.443

wik(k)ed(e) *a* wicked, evil 1.111, 129, B 4.62, 68, A 11.263, ~ **dede(s)** 1.30, 6.333, 10.240, B 4.68, ~ **folk** B 5.150, ~ **hefdes** 17.85, ~ **hertes** 14.25, ~ **man** 4.65, 14.134, B 16.146, ~ **men** 8.27, 16.275, **B** 5.263, 10.24, ~ **spiritus** Pr 18, ~ **werkes** 18.38, 19.296, 21.380, 22.371, B 15.355, ~ **wille** (= ill-will) 7.41, B 13.321, (= evil will) B 9.206, Z 5.94, *a as n* evil 11.274, A 11.263; evil ones B 1.124, **þe ~** B 8.97; wrong-doers 20.427, 434, 21.199; vicious 7.260, 16.240, 21.356, (*comp.*) 19.104, B 5.150; dishonest B 5.225; bad, pernicious 3.205, 6.162, 19.301, 312, A 10.65; cruel, severe ?7.117, 11.275; harmful 12.238, B 13.324; destructive 18.29, 31, (*comp.*) 20.459, B 5.160; malicious 21.287; harmful B 13.324; difficult 7.306 (B 6.1); in poor condition 9.31

wikkedli(che) *av* wrongfully 6.310, 8.235, 16.274, (*sup.*) **~lokest** most iniquitously B 10.426; sinfully, viciously 1.26, B 5.364, A 11.292; dishonestly 6.210, 19.248, B 5.225; severely 22.303

wikkednesse *n* wicked / evil action(s) 11.209, **B** 8.98, 16.157; iniquity **B** 5.283, 18.415; vicious conduct B 5.178, 185, A 5.207

wil¹ 4.22 *et p.*, (*person.*) (a) 7.233, 12.2, ?Z 4.20c (b) B 8.126 *etc*; *see* **wil(le)** *n*; **wyl** Z 7.281 *see* **wele**¹ *n*

wyl² Z 2.2, 41, 3.162 *see* **willen** *v*

wyl³ Z 4.89, 7.119, 281 = **wel**³ *av*

wilde *a* wild, ~ **bestes** 16.10, 17.28, **B** 7.90, 11.354, 15.299, 459, ~ **foules** 8.30, B 15.302; ~ **brawen** brawn of wild boar B 13.63; ~ **worm(es)** 13.137, 15.293, B 14.42; desolate 9.225, 10.62, 19.54, B 15.459 (1), *a as n* wild creatures 13.169, 15.296; ungovernable B 12.6, A 10.57

wildefowel *n* wild game birds B 10.361

wildernesse *n* wild, uncultivated region 10.62, 17.28, 19.54, **B** Pr 12, 15.273, 459, 17.99

wyle Z 3.28, 33, 5.73, 123, 7.59, ~ þat Z 3.124 *see* **while(s)** *conj.*

wilen B 2.233, 6.58, 13.258, A 2.53 *et p.*; *see* **willen** *v*

wyles *n.pl.* cunning / deceitful tricks 10.136, 13.74, 18.45, 175, 19.242, 246, 22.124, **B** 4.34, 10.109, 15.234, 408, (*person.*) 4.77; stratagems 21.100

wilfulli(che) 4.46, 19.269, 21.373 = **willefolliche** *av*

wily ~ *a* crafty, ~ **man** (*person.*) 4.27, 31

wil(le) *n* desire, wish Pr 174, 3.236, 365, 12.2 (2), 15.90, 17.195, 18.164, 19.289; **B** 5.102, 13.141, 17.179, **grete** ~ 12.85, 15.186, will [of God] 7.142, 11.309, 14.160, 16.27, 18.28, 121, 133, **B** 1.82, 14.125, 15.262, 483, A 5.241; carnal desire 2.96, 6.181, 190, 18.76, B 13.348, **flesches** ~ 20.202, A 9.45; (what one) desire(s) 2.67, 3.29, 152, 8.82, 153, 11.87, 90, 183, 12.140, 13.248, 15.123, 16.101, 17.143, 21.450, 22.203, 332, **B** 3.7, 11.26, 15.486, **A** 2.24, 53, 7.261; (express) wish, command 2.34, 218, 3.246, 325, 12.172, 20.103, **B** 3.265, 5.608, 9.115; will(ing) 6.167; intent, determination 1.109, 2.103, 5.185, 11.87, 13.94, 14.26, 15.277, B 13.194, **kene** ~ 16.81, 22.375, B 12.251; intention 3.71, 6.273, 15.156, 20.435, **B** 8.94, 16.149, A 11.68, *in phr.* **of o(n)** ~ united in purpose 15.277, 16.179, 17.128, 18.190, with a single purpose B 3.238; disposition, attitude (of mind / heart) 12.141, 14.211, 16.204, 19.204, **B** 13.141, 191, 14.14, 15.210, 16.233; (faculty of) will(ing) 16.175, (*person.*) 1.5 *et p.* (*see Index*); wilfulness, self-will 4.22, 23, B 11.45, (*person.*) 6.2, 7.233, 12.2 (1); (final) will (= testament) B 12.257; *in phrr.* **agayne...** ~ against (someone's) will 9.65, 10.219, 20.90, **B** 3.293, 4.48, 9.154; **at (...)** ~ according to one's will / desire Pr 38, 3.19, 240, 374, 6.66, 113, 11.8, 15.261, 22.197, **B** 3.200, 9.58, at one's liking B 10.15, at (one's) command 10.156, **B** 6.206, 18.345, **A** 10.34, 11.267, at (one's) disposal 10.244, 11.68, 12.230, 13.226, 14.175, B 10.446; **by** ~ wilfully B 4.70; **euyl** ~ ill-will / intent 6.87, 18.164, **B** 10.433, 15.127; **fre** ~ 10.51, B 16.223 (= Holy Spirit); **glad** ~ B 8.94; **gode** ~ benign / virtuous intent(ion) 6.336, 7.295, 9.111, 14.24, 19.330, 20.220, **B** 13.193, 14.20; **(ben) in** ~ (be) willing, ready B 10.168, A 12.21, desire **B** 11.278, 12.194; **to...** ~ as one wishes, at one's liking 6.190, 18.176; **wikkede** ~ ill-will 7.41, B 13.321,

evil will B 9.206, Z 5.94; **with (...)** ~ willingly 2.168, 3.217, B 4.101

willefolliche *av* voluntarily 22.49; deliberately 4.46, 19.269, 21.373

willen *v* (*pr.sg. 1,3* **wil(l)e** 2.169, 3.225, A 2.53 *et p.*, **wol(e)** Pr 171 *et p.*, **B** Pr 38 *etc*, 11.196, *2* **willest** B 12.218, **wilt** B 2.45, *assim..* **wiltow** B 3.111, *subj.* **wol(l)e** 8.153, B 13.227, *pl.* **wi(l)l(e)(n)** B 10.248, 13.258, A 8.32, Z 7.140, **wol(e)** 3.18 *etc*, *p.t. sg. 1,3* **wolde** Pr 130 *et p.*, *pl.* **wolde(n)** Pr 38, 3.383, *2 sg.* **wold** 8.299, **woldest** 13.230 *etc*, *assim. form* **woldestow** B 3.49, *p.p.* **wold** B 15.262) [*selected exx. only*] desire, wish 3.123, 21.100, B 5.53, *subjv.* **wolle thow** whether you like 8.153; *p.t.* wanted, desired Pr 130, B 1.29 *etc*, (*with pr. sense*) 8.299, ~ **have** made as if to 6.418, 8.149; be willing 3.8, B 7.35, *p.t.* was willing (to) 8.252, (*neg.*) be unwilling, refuse to 21.399, B Pr 38; intend (to) 3.18, 4.174; be prepared to 3.498, B 13.416; decree 3.419, *p.t.* 8.296; command B 9.125, *p.t.* 1.13; choose to, *p.t.* 22.38; be accustomed to 4.35, 8.335, *p.t.* 6.268; may, can 12.64, B 2.136, *p.t.* might 8.166, would be able (to) 15.167; (*in assev.*) will 20.264; must 18.251, *p.t.* should have to 20.256; demand, require 20.428, 21.397, 472, 22.18, 265, A 10.132, *p.t.* 3.129, (*with pr. sense*) 8.231, 11.65, 20.425; (*elliptical, with inf. to be supplied*) want to (...) 5.81, 14.134, 20.298, *p.t.* wanted to (...) Pr 38, 2.96, 16.182, (*with v. of motion*) intended to go 6.353, 20.176; (*as fut. auxil.*) will, be going to 2.184, 3.51, B 5.640; (*conditional senses*) should, would Pr 210, 4.69, 22.32; should / would like (to) 2.128, 8.220, ~ be willing (to) 1.114, B 10.119; would, wish 5.83; (*subjv.*) if...were willing 3.52, 15.204, 16.254, 17.47; **hoso** ~ if anyone should wish (to) 17.254, let whoever wished 18.155; (*optative*) would [Christ] grant (that) 22.140; *in phrr.* **wiltow...neltow, wolle...ne wolle** like it or not 8.153, 21.467, 22.29, B 6.156

wilnen *v* desire, wish 1.8, 85, 3.131, 146, 4.158, 7.197, 12.20, 82, 84, 13.93, 16.182, 17.190, 269, 19.330, 20.4, 21.68, *pr. p.* 6.32 (B 13.280), 41 (B 13.292), **B** 5.185, 560, 6.258, 10.119, 124, 126, 339, 13.205, **A** 2.30, 10.89, **Z** 1.39, 2.10 ~ **aftur** long for 4.192; **wilneth (-ede) and wolde** desire(d) and wish(ed) 3.383, 13.93, 17.269, 18.260, B 14.173, (*trs*) B 10.353

wymmen *pl.* 2.7, 3.396, 6.190, 8.9, 9.167, 176, 226, 11.110, 215, 13.74, 22.348, Z 7.8 = **wom(m)en**; *see* **woman** *n*

wyn(e) *n* wine 1.30, 31, 6.160, 9.253, 11.110, 15.66, 16.91, 18.262, 19.71, 21.109, 111, B 10.361, ~ **of Oseye... of Gascoyne** Pr 230

wynd(e) *n* wind 3.483, 10.34, 19.334, Z 6.69, **southe- weste** ~ 5.116, *in phr.* ~**es and wederes** 10.46, 12.191; (the element of) air 9.56, 10.131, 15.243, **B** 7.52, 17.161; breath Z 5.34, 40; gas, air [in stomach] A 5.72; (*fig.*) (**wikked**) ~ 18.29, 31, 32, 35, B 16.25

wynden *v* (*p.t.* **wonden** 2.230, *p.p.* **ywounden** B 5.518) wind (yarn) B 5.548; wrap (sb.) around 2.230; *p.p.* wound, twisted B 5.518

wyndow(e) *n* window 3.51, 65, A 3.50; window-glass 3.69

wynge B 4.37 = **wenge** *n*

wynken *v* doze Pr 11, *ger.* 11.167, B 5.3, 363; give a significant glance (at) 4.148, B 4.154

wynlyche *av* with pleasure A 12.46

wynnen *v* (*p.t. sg. 1,3* **wan** 6.310 *etc*, **wonne** Z 7.87, *2* **wonne** 6.255, *pl.* **wonne(n)** Pr 24, Z 8.65, *p.p.* **ywonne** 3.247, 8.235, B 5.263) strive, ? go B 4.67*n*; win (victory) 3.485, 11.287; seize (as spoil) 3.252; get possession of Pr 194, 15.156, (by force) 3.247, 4.192, 7.233, 21.32, B 12.44; acquire 3.498, 6.255, 258, 310, 8.235, 12.6, 237, 16.275, 245, 248, 21.246, **B** 4.35, 5.263, 277, Z 7.87; obtain 4.73, 8.63, 11.68, 222, 15.145, 16.147, 22.15, **B** 5.92, 9.69; make profit(s) 12.229, 16.128, 19.234, 242, 21.353, 22.124, B 13.378; get / earn (by labour) Pr 24, 1.174, 5.126, 6.322, 8.18, 105, 9.251, 13.73, 17.18, 21.231, 236, **B** 6.133, 162, 8.81, 9.109, **A** 3.224, 7.236, 11.185; recover, win back 3.196, 12.111, 20.142, 396, 21.247; entice 6.190, 10.136

wynner(e) *n* earner [one who gets a living by work] Pr 223, A 7.148

wynnyng(e) *ger.* gain 5.98, 6.305, 9.207, 16.259, 17.36, B 5.112; profit 5.137, 6.293, 7.75, 9.26, 29, 12.17, 21.286, 456, Z 3.166

wynsen *v* kick restlessly 4.22

*wynstere *n* (female) winder of thread A 5.129

wynter *n* (*pl.* ~ 6.233 *etc*, *uninfl. gen* 6.203) (the) winter (season) 12.188, 200, 15.293, 16.14, 146, Z 3.157, **a, at** ~ in winter-time 19.193, B 7.129, ~ **(es) nyhtes** 19.185, ~ **tyme** 9.78, 12.191, B 14.177; = year 3.41, 6.203, 233, 7.30, 188, 266, 14.3, 15.266, 270, 271, 17.23, 19.211, 20.136, 309, 329, 22.344, **B** 1.101, 3.192, 11.47, 15.288

wipen *v* wipe dry 2.230, 18.244, (*quasi-refl.*) dry one's hands 9.250, 15.38; rub B 5.262

wypne 3.458 = **wep(e)ne** *n*

wyr *n* wire B 2.11

wyrchen Z Pr 145, 1.23, 3.124, 175, 6.77 = **worchen** *v*

w(y)rd *n* fortune, fate 3.240, 12.211; circumstances (= capabilities) 14.32

wischen 15.90, 19.330 = **weschen** *v*

wyse *n* manner 19.13, B 2.171; habit, guise 7.160, 8.56, Z 5.158; fashion 7.162, 9.154; way 5.51, 7.253, 12.184, 208, 19.265, **none (...)** ~ no way at all 8.328, 10.282, **som manere** ~ one way or another 9.33; (*as suffix*) **on cros** ~ by crucifixion 21.142, **a fuste** ~ in the manner of a fist 19.151

wys(e) *a* wise 1.69, 3.7, 4.44, 11.220, 13.184, 21.166, B 10.8, **A** 11.272, 12.38; *a as n (sg)*, 13.203, 16.227, (*comp.*) one more wise B 11.270, (*pl.*) 10.311, 12.143;

sage Pr 49, 13.27, 14.193, 21.245, 297, B 12.50; prudent 7.94, 10.144, 11.5, 16.20, 22.33, **B** Pr 208, 4.69, 11.281, 14.18, A 10.23, 71; sensible 13.43, 16.20; shrewd, astute 4.83, 9.336, 19.225, **wordliche** ~ experienced (in the affairs of the world) 10.91, A 10.70; (practically) skilled 7.157; learned 8.240, 9.51, 11.98, 224, 13.64, 20.242, 354, 21.84, 22.303, *comp.* **wyser** 6.24, 28, **B** 11.392, 13.293, 15.547; (*comp.*) enlightened, well-informed **B** 9.79, 10.371; *in cpds.* ~ **witted** with wise minds B 10.396, **weder** ~ skilled in weather-lore 17.94

wis(e)do(e)m *n* right (moral) judgement 16.50, 21.453; shrewd practical judgement 16.142, B 10.450, *in phr.* **wit and** ~ 16.50, 188, 22.133, B 12.293, ~ **and wit** 11.14, B 6.51; prudence 2.147, (*person.*) 4.66, 72, 96, B 4.74, 81, 87, A 4.60, (= worldly wisdom) **Waryn** ~ B 4.27, 154, A 4.141; (the) wisdom of God 13.228; a wise thing to do 8.223; knowledge 22.33; (a) wise precept 11.5, 14.82, A 10.111

wys(e)ly(che) *av* with wisdom 11.215; sagaciously 3.7, B 4.46; prudently 10.287; with good judgement 8.235; soundly 15.115; carefully 15.78, (*comp.*) **wisloker** more attentively B 13.343

wisman *n* wise-man (*as name*) 4.27

wispe B 5.345 = **weps** *n*

wissen *v* show 2.199, A 12.40, 46; inform 10.6, 74, 111, 16.155, A 12.31; know (= be informed) A 9.13; show (way) 7.177, 198, B 10.154; direct 11.139; guide 15.20, A 10.92; ? manage, (? advise) 3.18; advise 8.162, *ger.* advice 12.11; teach 1.40, 10.29, 13.203, 14.4, 195, 17.84, 21.64, 247, 10.450, **B** 1.42, 7.128, 10.339, 382, 11.436, 12.72, *ger.* teaching B 15.479; instinct 1.71, 21.234, **B** 5.146, 10.8, 384; show how A 11.275; bid, order **B** 11.382, 15.494

wisshen B 5.110, 10.468, 12.270, *ger.* B 2.91 *see* **weschen** *v*

wissynge(e) *ger.* 12.11, B 15.479 *see* **wissen** *v*

wist *p.p.* 20.209, 217, ~**e** *p.t.* 5.37 *etc*, *pl.* ~**en** 12.128, ~**est**, ~**us** *2 sg.* A 7.196, Z 7.194 *see* **witen** *v*

wit (witte) *n*[1] (*pl.* **wittes** 1.15 *etc*) mind 3.454, 5.185, 6.167, 13.184, 15.75, B 10.131, **fyn** ~ subtlety of mind 11.158; intelligence Pr 38, 3.211, 14.32, 15.20, **B** Pr 37, 8.53, 19.231; intellect 10.9, 11.287, 12.2, 18.28, 190, 21.230, B 10.394; **kynde** ~ native intelligence, natural reason 14.17, 30, 33, 34, 36, 53, 157, 182, 21.317, **B** 12.67, 69, 70, 93, 128, 14.125, (*person.*) Pr 141 *etc*, 1.51, 4.87, 13.238; *pl.* mental powers 1.138, 4.23, 10.121, 11.84, 14.194, 16.214, B 10.6, A 11.87; *in phr.* **at here ~es ende** utterly perplexed 17.105; inner senses 10.172; reason, understanding 6.310, 13.192, 16.188, (*person.*) 7.233, 10.111*n*, **B** 5.364, 11.322, 15.83, 16.187; cleverness 21.453, **B** 13.292, 15.408; astuteness 22.32; (*person*) 4.72, 77, 87, B 4.76; practical know-how 21.240; (sound) understanding, 'right mind', **B** 2.129, 15.3; (faculty of) sense (perception) 18.180, **fyue ~es** five bodily senses 1.15, 15.257, 16.232, 21.217; ingenuity Pr 174, 6.21, 261, 264, 13.157, 21.100, 357; constructive ability **B** 12.223; ingenious contrivance A 11.159, Z 3.166; wisdom, wise judgement 3.211, 8.55, 10.105, 11.212, 13.228, 15.145, 173, 21.118, **B** 9.43, 13.169, 15.130, 19.82; judgement 20.242, **B** 3.7, 10.446, **fre ~** (the power of) moral judgement, 'liberum arbitrium' 10.51c; prudence 2.147, 22.32, **B** 6.51; knowledge 9.56, 11.14, 79, 223, 13.169, A 11.278; knowing Z 3. 175; learning 16.50, 21.234, **B** 12.293; meaning, significance **B** 12.133, 13.155

witted *a* provided with wits / mental powers, **kynde ~** 14.52, 72, **B** 12.158

wyt *n*² blame A 10.75; *see* **wyten** *v*²

witen (weten, wyten) *v*¹ (*infl. inf.* ~**e** B 8.13; *pr. sg.* 1, 3, **wo(e)t** Pr 100, **woot** 4.83, 2 **wost** 3.225, *pl.* **wite(n)** 13.64, B 3.332, **wyteth** 1.121, **wote** B 10.361, 435, *subj.* **wete, wyte** 4.100, 6.343, B Pr 208, *pl.* **wyten** 2.79; *imper. pl.* **witeth** B 2.75; *p.t. 1, 3* **wiste(n)** 6.70, 12.128, *subj.* 6.59, B 14.8, *2* **wistest** A 7.196, *p.p.* **wist** 20.209) [*selected exx.*] know 3.221, 285, 6.326, 343, 9.70, 88, 10.4, 71, 72, 11.275, 12.82, 162, 15.150, 18.147, 275, 20.68, 21.162, **B** 10.119, 124, 126, 133, 11.407, A 7.179, 11.30, 259; (*with neg.*) have no idea 6.343, 16.141, 18.181, 20.225, 236, 22.3, **B** Pr 12, 5.642; *in phrr.* (*parenth.*) **wiltow ~, wol ȝe ~** you may be sure **B** 13.227, 16.25, (*assev.*) **wyte God** God may be sure 7.284, **God woet** God knows [this to be true] 4.37, 75, 83, 5.1, **B** Pr 43, 5.102, 13.385, 14.329, 15.146, **A** 5.154, 11.240, 12.88; **~ þe sothe** know (sth.) for a fact / the truth (of a matter) 1.121, 3.285, 7.244, 284, 9.128, 10.22, 12.79, 162, 14.191, 16.252, 19.9, 20.149, 21.374, **B** 2.122, 6.130, 9.99, 10.431, 11.179, **A** 8.56, 11.30, 194, †12.99; may know B 5.562; might know B 16.12; **~ wel** know for sure 6.326, 8.139, 211, 10.242, 20.342, 21.361, B 14.82, 282, be well / fully aware 8.211, 270, 9.128, 16.235, 21.373, A 4.67; **~ witterly** know for certain 3.296, 9.88, 20.68, 215, B 5.268, **A** 11.259, 12.10; be sure 9.70, 11.274, B 15.263; be aware (of) Pr 100, 2.82, 142, 3.76, 225, 5.181, 6.59, 162, 163, 289, 300, 11.290, 12.36, 13.64, 81, 21.373, **B** Pr 208, 2.78, 3.332, 5.159, 7.69, 76, 10.361, 11.101, 13.324, 14.8, 16.233; understand 5.37, 13.64, 20.168, 210; recognise 17.99, B 10.435, **~ of** acknowledge 10.164; realise 12.128, 13.241; become aware (of) Pr 181, 6.59, B 10.228; find out, discover, learn 4.100, 136, 6.70, 71, 303, 7.197, 8.220, 10.125, 13.218, 230, 16.6, 340, 20.129, 229, 231, 233 (1), B 2.45, A 12.31, Z 2.2; know (by experience), have (direct / practical) knowledge of 15.82, 285, 20.209, 217, 233 (2), 22.319, **B** 8.113, 14.97, Z 3.166; be informed, (*subj.*) let them be informed 2.79, **do to ~e** inform B 8.13

wyten *v*² (*p.t.* **witte** 1.30) (lay the) blame (on) 1.30, 6.113, †B 7.59; blame (for) 20.353, A 5.207

wyten *v*³ preserve B 7.35, A 10.67; protect, defend B 16.25, †A 10.23, 67; (*in oath, subj.*) may ~ protect 7.284; drive away Z 7.59*n*

witene *infl. inf.* B 8.13 *see* **witen** *v*¹

witenesse 19.31 = **wittenesse** *n*

wytful *a* sagacious A 4.19

with *prep.* [*select exx.*] against 12.194, 20.26, 22.168; with Pr 166 *et p.*; (*after prn*) B 1.209, = on the side of 1.94, 108, 2.153, 21.362; in the same way as, like 6.174, **B** 6.137, 181, 7.67; **as ~** in the manner of 19.115; in the case of, in regard to 3.434, 6.184, 8.86, 17.202, 21.301, 22.290, A 10.58; in relation to **B** 13.149, 16.223; in the hands of 11.260, 19.135; among 8.216, 9.95, 196; in the company of 6.116, 235, 14.125, 15.27, 16.335, 18.185, 21.214, B 10.229, A 11.217; accompanied by Pr 45, 2.103, 20.342, B 10.340; together with 2.16, 15.163, 16.175, 330, 17.236, 21.40, 165, 323, **B** 1.111, 8.36, A 11.219; (*quasi-av*) **forth ~** together with 10.233, **B** 17.158; along with 2.89, 9.8, 186, 11.243, 16.300, 20.318, **B** 1.116, 9.37, 10.37, 42, †446, 16.203, A 3.202; to 2.137, 10.138, 15.209, A 10.154; **euene ~** equal to 18.90, **eueneforþ ~** equally with **B** 13.144, 17.135; = having, possessing Pr 51, 6.202, 10.118, 20.273, 22.176, **B** 1.15, 6.237, 9.50; containing 13.55, 15.226, B 5.640, *in phr.* ~ **childe** pregnant 9.176, 22.348; by (means of) Pr 73, 174, 223, 1.67, 2.161, 3.192, 6.246, 288, 8.241, 259, 9.31, 74, 11.100, 299, 16.45, 128, 132, 17.234, 304, 18.150, 19.21, 62, 112, 257, 20.52, 319, 377, 21.144, 236, 248, 466, 22.119, 379, **B** Pr 34, 1.67, 4.75, 9.51, 10.22, 414, 13.129*n*, 15.449, 482 (3), **A** 7.210, 11.186; through Pr 24, 4.149, 7.128, 20.364, 21.296, **B** 2.230, 3.310, 5.366, 488, 9.114, 12.11, 13.146, **A** 7.205, 232, 10.34; by Pr 87, 22.215, **B** 3.2, 102, 16.105, 17.90; from 6.2, B 5.134; in consequence of 6.335, 18.179, A 12.91; at, over 15.65; for B 13.111, 415; on 8.151, 294; of B 7.8; (*in conjv. phr.*) on condition that 6.173, 11.91, 22.250; (*in avl. phrr.*) (**riht**) ~ **þat** at that point / moment, thereupon 4.196, 6.1, 62, 7.55, 13.247, 18.289, 20.69, 94, 471, **B** Pr 146, 3.26, 5.300, ~ **doel** painfully 20.304, ~ **riht** justly 21.353, ~ **treuthe** truly, as true 9.251; ~ **wo** in torment B 2.107; ~ **wrong** wrongfully 19.234, B 1.128; *av* (*with phrasal vv*) **delen ~** 8.77, **fynden ~** B 13.241, **halden ~** 1.94, **meten ~** 4.140; (*preceding obj.*) **close (...) ~** close...with *etc* Pr 133, 6.340, 8.273, 318, 9.75, 76, 157, 11.17, 55, 16.25, 17.121, 19.207, 261, 20.282, 21.228, **B** 2.117, 10.270, 11.398, 12.294, 16.147, (*preceding v*) 9.130, 167, A 10.130

wiþalle *av* completely, ? to be sure B 15.12*n*; moreover, besides 10.132, 144, 17.166, 18.125, **B** 5.3, 15.288, A 12.50

withdrawen *v* (*p.t.* ~**drouh, ~drow** 20.60, 114) draw back 8.351, 20.114, (*refl.*) 19.64; retire 20.60; (*refl.*) cease / refrain from 11.64, 17.245, 22.353, B 9.97

withhalden v (*contr. pr.* ~ **halt**, *p.t.* ~ **helden**) keep back (sth.) from (sb.) 3.306, 7.195; keep (in one's service) 2.238

wythinne[1] *av* (hidden) inside 6.261, 12.249, 16.265, 266; withindoors 7.187 *n*; inwardly, in the soul 6.31, 74

wythinne[2] *prep.* in(side) 10.40; within (the space of) 20.31

withoute(n)[1] *av* on the outside 12.147; outside 7.265; out of doors 7.187; outwardly 6.31, B 10.257

without(e)(n)[2] *prep.* outside 16.365; without 2.128, 3.117, 199, 364, 372, 5.52, 6.121, 7.106, 9.120, 10.217, 11.136, 12.64, 15.272, **B** 2.30, 14.238; without (committing) 10.101, 17.3, 18.133, (recourse to / the action of) 4.181–2, 5.174, 7.3, 9.325, 11.145, 12.87, 14.115, 201, 15.157, 17.8, 129, 19.86, 242, 22.21, **B** 3.227, 7.55, 12.85, 14.63, 15.196, (obtaining) 3.131, (suffering) 11.262, (taking) B 3.243, (the use of) 13.74, 15.83, **B** 9.34, 17.166; in the absence of 2.123, 11.288, 12.88, 94, 14.28, 16.176, 17.130, 18.224, 225, 226, 19.180, **B** 10.451, 15.234, 472, 16.218; free from 3.205, 14.16, 16.20, 138, 153, 19.158, 20.131, 134, **B** 11.214, 14.129, 15.150, 487; lacking 1.181, 183, 9.205, 18.221, 19.181, 215, 20.10, **B** 10.351, 11.82, 15.13, 460; *in phrr.* ~ **chalangynge** undeniably; ~ **doute** undoubtedly 16.32, B 12.32; ~ **drede** have no fear 14.10; ~ **ende** 19.252, B 18.379, = for ever 2.106, 3.359, 10.171, 18.233, 257, 20.235, 21.199; ~ **gyn-nyng** eternal **B** 2.30, 16.187; ~ **gult** guiltlessly 4.75; ~ **nombre** unlimited in number 22.270; ~ **pite** pitilessly B 3.195

withoute[3] *conj.* unless 4.176

withsaet *p.t.* 18.250 *see* **withsit(t)en** v

wiþsiggen v (*p.t.* **wiþseide**) oppose, contradict A 4.142; affirm the contrary of A 11.232; object, put a counter-argument †B 4.91n

withsit(t)en, withsetten v (*p.t.* **withsaet**) oppose, resist Pr 174, 8.202, 10.98, †12.190, 18.250

wytyng *pr. p. a as av* knowingly 21.373

witte 6.113 *see* **wyten** v[3]

wit(te)le(e)s *a* out of one's mind 15.1; mentally deficient 9.111

wit(t)(e)nesse *n* testimony, witness 9.285, 11.215, 14.66, 16.289, B 9.73; **fals** ~ 2.85, 7.226, 16.361, **B** 5.88, 13.359, (*person.*) 2.160, *in phrr.* [giving authority for a statement] the proof is (in) Pr 205*n*, 12.124; **beren** ~ testify, affirm (authoritatively) 7.100, 9.304, 10.213, 12.135, 155, 14.124, 15.222, 18.213, 222, 19.31, 283, 20.240, 21.449, **B** 2.38, 5.144, 7.51, 83, 9.74, 10.88, 246, 279, 340, 11.156, 226, 252, 270, 272, 12.65, 13.135, 14.85, 180, 15.90; **taken to** ~ appeal to as a witness / authority 11.38, 12.135, 14.124, 15.103 (2), 18.222, 20.135, 245, **B** 11.87, 15.488, **taken** ~ **at / of** draw evidence (from) / appeal to (as example) 12.77, 15.103 (1), 158; testimony (by signature) 2.109;

(authoritative) witness, guarantor 6.53, 20.311, B 9.118; (subscribing) witness [to execution of a will] B 12.258*n*

witnessen v bear witness, solemnly affirm 3.123, 426, 7.94, 8.240, 10.240, 11.21, 219, 12.103, 120, 156, 13.203, 14.37, 15.246, 265, 16.238, 240, 17.6, 37, 235, 19.216, 288, 20.356, **B** Pr 195, 1.147, 10.376, 11.39, 396, 13.307, **A** 10.94, 12.25, provide (authoritative) evidence / proof 2.129, 5.87, 12.156, 20.250; give formal evidence, attest 4.87, 20.45, B 4.181; attest by signature B 2.161; be (formally) present as witness B 16.122, A 2.46, (*subjv.*) 'let those witness...(who)' 2.79

witterly(che) *av* clearly, plainly Pr 11, 6.303, 9.88, 20.217, 22.194, A 11.259; certainly 21.361, 22.271; for sure / certain 3.221, 296, 20.68, B 5.268, A 12.10, = you may be sure 15.90, 18.181; truly 1.71, 5.37, 6.273, 20.215, 237

witty *a* wise 2.151, (*comp.*) ~**ore** 5.188, **B** 11.373, 15.130, *a as n* B 10.430; prudent B 11.392, ~ **wordes** sagacious counsel's B 4.21; clever 6.24, 16.20, (*comp.*) 218, *a as n* 11.229, B 12.143, (*person.*) B 4.27, 67, ~ **man** 4.31; expert 9.51, 17.94, 20.354

wyuen B 9.184, **wyuyng** 10.290 *see* **wyf** n

wyuen v take a wife B 9.184, *ger.* ~**yng** marrying 10.290

wyuene *gen. pl.* 5.31 *see* **wyf** n

wo[1] *n* misery, distress Pr 10, 3.205, 9.78, 83, 84, 11.107, 20.210, 219, 233, 22.193, **B** 2.107, 11.398, 14.177, 18.2, 414, A 11.69, *in phr. with* **wele** 12.211, 20.208, 209, 21.244, Z 3.173; suffering, pain 1.164, 4.80, 11.166, 21.68, 199; trouble 4.65, 6.414, 14.68, 125, 17.204, 21.158, **B** 13.208, 263

wo[2] *a* wretched, sorry B 5.3, Z 1. 102n, 4.51

wo[3] *interj.* (of grief / affliction), *in phrr.* ~ **bytyde**, ~ **to** may affliction befall 2.119, 3.156, 18.175, ~ **is** *etc* (+ *dat.*) wretched is / was / will be 3.190, 9.271, 13.215, 14.18, Z 1.102, ~ **worth** evil will befall 10.176

wo Z 7.1 = **who** *prn*

wode *n* wood [collection of trees] 9.196, 225, 13.137, **B** 16.56, 17.103, A 9.54, **by a ~ syde** along the edge of a wood 10.62; [material] 18.24, (fire) wood 16.178, 19.310

wodewe B 9.164, 176 = **wedewe** *n*

Wodnesday *n* Wednesday B 13.155

woen[1] 3.141 = **wone** *n*

woen[2] *n* abundance, *in phr.* **goed** ~ a-plenty, in good measure 22.171

woet *3 sg.pr.* 4.37 *et p.*; *see* **witen** v[1]

woke *n* week 9.253, 12.124, 18.134, **B** 10.96, 13.155, *in phrr.* **of al a** ~ all week 8.269, **þis(e) ~(s)** (the) last week(s) B 5.92, A 11.106

woke(n) *p.t.* 21.156, B 14.69 *see* **waken** v

wok(y)en v moisten, (add) water (to) B 15.338, (*fig.*) 16.333, (= soften) 14.25

wol(e) *3 pr.sg.* Pr 171, 11.196 *et p.*, *pl.* 2.184, B 11.89, **wold** *2 pr.sg.* 8.299, **woldest** 16.205, **wolde(n)** *p.t.* Pr 130, 3.383, *(as pr.)* 3.383 *etc*, *cond.* 7.145 *etc; see* **willen** *v*

#**wold** *n* 'would' [= feeling of conditional desire], *pl. in phr.* ~**es and weschynges** 2.95n

wolf *n* wolf 9.264, 266, *pl.* **wolues** 9.226, *(fig.)* 9.259, 16.269, A 10.212

wolkne B 17.161, 18.237 = **welkene** *n*

wolle *2 pr. subj.* 8.153, *pr.sg.* Z 6.92, *pr.pl.* 8.262, **wollen** 9.86 *see* **willen** *v*

wolle *n* sheep's fleece 9.266, 264; wool 9.271, 11.15, Z 5.100, *(fig.)* A 8.17; wool(len thread) 8.12

wollen(e) *n* woollen cloth 1.18, 13.102, **B** Pr 220, = wool(len thread) A 7.10; *a* woollen 6.221, A 8.43

wollewa(e)rd *a* with wool next to the skin 20.1

wolt *2 p.sg.* 3.146, ~**ow** *contr. interrog.* 3.153 *etc; see* **willen** *v*

wolueliche *a* wolflike, rapacious B 15.116

wolues *pl.* 9.226 *etc; see* **wolf** *n*

wolueskynne *n* wolvish / wolflike nature (~**s** *gen. sg. as a*) B 6.161

wom(m)an *n* (*pl.* **wom(m)en** 1.31, **wymmen** 9.167, *gen. pl.* **wommane** 20.134) woman 2.9, 6.190, 7.107, 11.87, 215, 22.348, **B** 2.19, 3.51, 118, 12.76, 80, 81, 89, A 3.246, 10.23, 208, *as term of address* 3.133; = unmarried woman 3.420; *(generic)* 8.6, 9.83, 176, 20.134, 21.162, 436, B 12.74, *in phr.* **man / men and** ~ 7.205, 17.181, 19.22, **B** 9.186, 12.49, A 10.152; *(spec.)* þe ~ (= Eve) **B** 5.602, 10.108; *pl.* *(meton.)* (intercourse with) women 1.31, 11.110, 13.189; *in phrr.* **commune** ~ prostitute 18.143, 21.370, **B** 5.641, 11.216, **gentil** ~ woman of noble lineage B 11.246, **worthily** ~ honourable woman 8.9; ~ **at þe stuyues** prostitute 13.74; ~ **and childrene** 3.396, 9.226

wombe *n* belly 15.93, *(fig.)* appetite [for material pleasures] Pr 57; stomach 3.83, 5.52, 6.438, 8.172, 226, 269, 9.253, **B** 3.194, 15.291, A 5.70, 72, ~ **cloute** tripe B 13.63; womb 7.238, 18.134, B 15.455

wonden *p.t. pl.* 2.230 *see* **wynden** *v*

wonder *n* miracle 18.149, 21.119; marvel(lous) thing / happening) Pr 4, 11.171, 20.125, 129, B 11.322; extraordinary phenomenon B 15.482; *in phrr.* ~ **ben / thynken** be / seem astonishing 3.228, 13.161, 17.116, B 15.120, 378; **hauen** ~ wonder, marvel 13.158, 184, 16.160, 18.270, **B** 2.18, 3.304, 11.301; *a* exceedingly strange B 14.125; *av* exceedingly 11.220, 13.5, 22.159, **B** 3.302, 14.6, 15.1; ~**fol** *a* astonishing 19.27; marvellous 13.137; ~**ly(che)** *av* marvellously 2.9, 11.167; exceedingly 6.308, 7.278, 11.3; ***~**wise** *av* in a marvellous fashion 1.125

wondren *v* marvel, *(impers.)* **me** ~ 13.153, 15.75; ask oneself in wonder 21.205

wone *n* place Pr 18, abode, dwelling-place 3.141; domain B 3.235; habit, custom 4.22, 16.322, B 15.245

won(y)en *v (p.p.* **(y)woned** 6.143, 17.89, **wont** B 20.371) dwell, live Pr 18, 1.59, 2.79, 234, 242, 5.1, 7.177, 197, 9.83, 196, 11.223, 15.242, 16.65, 17.11, 28, 259, 21.36, 193, 199, 22.39, **B** 2.107, 3.12, 235, 5.174, 10.428, 13.121, 14.97, 15.245, **A** 2.30, 10.144; be accustomed to / in the habit of 6.143, 8.164, 17.89, 22.371, Z 3.157

wonne *p.t. 1 sg.* Z 7.87, *2 sg.* 6.255, *pl.* Pr 24, *p.p.* 8.235 *see* **wynnen** *v*

woord A 11.269 = **word** *n*

woot *pr. sg.* 4.83, 6.273, B Pr 43 *etc* = **woet**; *see* **witen** *v*[1]

wopen *p.t. pl.* 9.41 *see* **wepen** *v*

worchen (werchen, werken, wyrchen) *v (p.t.* **wro(u)hte(n)** 1.164, 8.116, **wroȝte** B 1.82, *p.p.* **(y)wrouhte** 1.131, 2.119, **(y)wroȝt** 3.133, B 3.239) do, perform 8.6, 9.349, 11.90, 10.242, **B** 3.74, 9.176, 12.50, A 1.119, 10.75, ~ **in werke** actually do 4.143, B 10.254, ~ **werk** perform action B 3.239, 10.412, **A** 10.65, 130, 208, 12.103; do (evil, harm) 1.129, **B** 3.80, 4.68, 5.283; carry out (will, command) 3.29, 18.133, B 1.82 (1), **A** 1.75, 12.97; make, construct 13.157, 160, *ger.* **a** ~ **ynge** under construction 3.51; create 8.336, B 1.82 (2); make (textile), (= weave) A 7.10; bring about 4.143, B 9.114; devise 2.118; work, labour Pr 38, 1.124, 5.23, 25, 62, 126, 135, 8.18, 125, 130, 164, 211, 265, 269, 325, 9.176, 19.185, **B** 1.26, 6.211, 240, 9.109, 113, 10.211, A 7.192, labour (at) B 5.24; *(person.)* ~ **when-tyme-is** 8.80, ~ **wel...** 10.147; act, do 2.147, 3.7, 8.55, 90, 11.222, 253, 14.26, 16.218, 219, 17.84, 19.19, **B** 1.147, 2.195, 3.233, 6.56, 7.35, 8.56, 128, 9.43, 12.258, **A** 9.98, 10.95, 11.260; have intercourse 10.291, B 7.90; act (to) 19.138; be active B 10.271; function 16.178; take effect B 10.274

word *n* speech 21.287, Z 5.34, 6.69; = something uttered, (a) speech 6.21, 177, 419, 8.32, 10.123, 11.166, 12.11, 138, 13.189, 14.66, 82, 15.97, 16.142, 18.37, 21.230, **B** Pr 139, 3.36, 4.34, 8.57, 9.129, 10.8, 116, 288, 440, 16.141, 18.289, *pl.* (= what sb. says) Pr 70, 198, 1.41, 4.154, 18.270, 289, 19.27, 20.152; = verdict Z Pr 71; *(with neg.)* anything A 4.142, Z 4.123; speech [as contrasted with thought or action] B 9.36, *in phrr. with* **werk(es)** action(s) and / or word(s) 2.94, 6.99, 11.219, B 5.85, 9.45, 51, 10.254, 366, 13.141, 146, 312, 14.14, 15.116, 198, 210, 477, A 11.269, *with* **wit** 15.145, 21.122, B 9.43; command B 6.56, *esp.* God's command(ent)(s) 1.13, **B** 1.147, 9.32, **Goddes (Cristes)** ~**(es)** (divine teaching in) the Bible 1.69, 87, 6.84, 7.87, 94, 10.89, 11.235, 238, 15.274, 21.389, **B** 10.271, 274, 11.175, 225, **A** 10.94, 11.243, 12.97, Z 5.36, 40; promise, undertaking 20.311, 431, B 18.282; prophecy 21.80; word, *esp.* written word(s) [of a text] 1.194, 3.492, 9.281, 19.13, B 10.198, 384; text **B** 6.237, 13.68; *in phrr.* ~**es**

of grace gracious / grace-bringing words 5.98*n*, ~ **of murthe** 7.77; **goed** ~ friendly word 19.330, **crabbed** ~**es** 14.100, **B** 10.106; **false** ~ 6.258, **felle** ~ 3.492, **foule** ~ 7.114, 10.276, **B** 10.40, **harlotes** ~ 22.144, **kene** ~ 6.65, **paynted** ~ 21.230, **pitous** ~ A 7.115, **profitable** B 6.274; **propre** ~ 9.301, **rousty** ~ 8.75, **selcouthe** ~ 12.47, **two** ~ 19.13, **wyse** ~ 4.44, **B** 10.8, 12.50

worden *v* speak, talk 13.245, 15.150, 19.48, **B** 4.46, 10.427, *ger.* (verbal) exhortation 8.90; say A 10.96

woryen *v* seize by the throat 9.226, 266

world *n* human existence, **this** ~ this present life 1.8, 20.4, 134, 21.68, **B** 5.283, 9.108, A 11.260, Z 3.124, ~**es ende** the end of time 15.284, 18.175; business of life, affairs of the world 19.226, 20.4; the conditions of life (in the world) Pr 21, 12.172, 21.231; life 8.158; experience (of life) 9.88, B 10.273; matters, 'things' 3.434; secular life 9.251; worldly life 6.333, the World [as enemy of the soul, *(semi-)person.*] 1.37, 3.70, 10.44, 48, 11.63, 82, 18.31, **B** 7.126, 16.48, A 10.144; resources of this world 11.68, 12.230, 21.357; = the earth, world 10.200, 248, 18.251, 21.36, 335, 22.382, B 18.61, Z 6.71, **in the** ~ abroad Pr 4, the (created) universe 7.122, 8.239, 18.214, 19.113, 20.195, 22.49, **B** 10.226, 11.322, 17.160, Z 5.40, 43; everything 20.213; the known world B 15.437; the inhabitants of the earth, **al þe** ~ everyone Pr 100, 104, 12.36, B 11.101; (human) society 8.27, 10.205, 21.220, 430, **B** 6.132, 173, 9.109, A 10.133; *as intensif. phr.* **of / in the** ~ alive / in existence / anywhere on earth Pr 10, 3.6, 211, 4.136, 6.414, 10.6, 15.167, 173, 19.104, 20.242, 21.82, B 10.426, **A** 10.71, 11.269; anywhere 20.459, **B** 5.277, 8.69, 13.174, 208, A 11.272; in any way B 5.506; = any at all B 17.99; *in phrr.* **the welthe of this** ~ Pr 10, 9.336, 12.158, B 10.24

wor(l)(d)ly(che) *a* of (human) existence (on earth), human 3.368; earthly, material 12.238, 21.286, 293, 22.211; in this world 10.97

world-ryche *a* possessed of (worldly) wealth 16.16

worm *n* serpent B 10.107 (A 11.66); reptile, **wilde** ~ 13.137, 15.293; (earth) worm 15.242; caterpillar *(fig.)* B 16.34

wors(e) *a (comp.)* more wicked B 9.91; more unpleasant 3.141, 16.14, 66; harder B 17.43; more reprehensible A 11.218; more unfortunate Pr 104; *a as n* a greater evil 3.137, 11.264, B 10.421; something more worthless still 17.73; the less good (bargain) 6.381, 384; **þe** ~ the worse off, the less favoured 10.241; in poorer condition B 1.26, the worse (for it) B 16.157; *av (comp.)* more wickedly 3.137, B 5.113; **þe** ~ the more unluckily 10.237, 16.68; the less (well) 3.220; worse, less agreeably 11.75

wors(c)hip(e) *n* honour, dignity 1.8, 5.75; (credit of a) good name 6.142; respect / honour shown to sb. / sth.

3.486, 498, 14.138, B 12.119; veneration 18.263, 19.263, B 16.244

wors(c)hipen *v* worship, adore 18.262, 21.211; reverence Pr 119, 1.16, 21.443; revere 17.212; honour 8.110, **B** 1.48, 15.483; treat with honour / respect 3.13, 9.135; respectfully salute B 10.224

worst *2 sg. pr.* 21.409 *see* **worthen** *v*

worste *a (sup.)* most wicked 19.265, *a as n* (goods of) poorest quality 6.261 (B 13.363); most grievous state of affairs 3.477; *av* most wickedly 11.272; least, ~ **to louye** the least to be loved B 10.336

worst(e) *av* most wickedly 11.272; least, ~ **to louye** the least to be loved B 10.336

worsted *n* fabric of well-twisted yarn [made from long-staple wool] Z 5.100

worstow *contr. pr.* B 5.613, 19.409 = **worst thow**; *see* **worthen** *v*

wort *n* cabbage 8.331, *(fig.)* B 5.160

worth[1] *n* value, **at** ~**e** at face value 14.66; the equivalent of (*as suffix in cpd.*) *see* **ferthing** ~, **pene** ~

worth(e)[2] *a* of the value (of) Pr 76, 6.244, *(contemptuous)* 8.263, 11.14, **B** 4.170; worth, of value 10.311, 11.79, 13.94, 16.6, B 13.382

worth[3] *3 pr. sg.* *(with fut. sense)* 1.183 *et p.*, ~**e** *(subj.)* 21.433, A 5.241, *pl.* 12.208 *see* **worthen** *v*

worthen *v (p.t.* **warth** 5.98, 11.167) become 11.22, 88, 15.149; will become 12.208; **worst** (you) will be 21.409; **worth, worþ** will be 1.183 *et p.*, 7.264, B 3.314; fall 11.167; befall 5.98, *in phrr.* **wo** ~ ill will befall 10.176, **wel** ~**e** *(subjv.)* may good fortune fall to 13.1, 21.433; ~ **vp** get up / mount [for sexual intercourse] B 7.90

worthy *a* excellent 10.311, 12.193, *(comp.)* 5.188, 13.27, ~**okest** *sup.* Z 5.36; *a as n* 17.201, 18.88, *(sup.)* Z 5.36; valuable B 14.89; entitled to honour 7.113, 15.39; honourable 18.71, 21.24; of sufficient worth B 14.329; of sufficient merit B 18.329; ~**ier** *comp. a as av* in a more honourable place B 6.47

worthily *a* noble 8.9; *av* splendidly B 2.19, Z 2.12

wosch(en) *p.t. sg. / pl.* 18.244 / 2.230, 15.32, 38 *see* **waschen** *v*

wose *n* slime, wet mud 12.231

wost[1] *2 sg. pr.* 3.225, 10.71 *see* **witen** *v*[1]

wost[2] *2 sg. p.t. contr.* 22.188 = **woldest**; *see* **willen** *v*

wot *1,3 sg. pr.* Pr 100 *etc*, A 5.154, 12.1, 88, **Z** 3.147, 166, 173, 175, 5.35; **wote** *pl.* B 10.361, 435 *see* **witen** *v*[1]

wouȝ A 5.136 = **wowe** *n*

wouke B 5.92, A 11.106 = **woke** *n*

wound(e) *n* wound 4.181, 19.67, 71, 85, 20.90, 101, B 17.76, **fyue** ~ **is** [of Christ] A 11.215; *(fig.)* 5.177, B 14.96

wounden[1] *p.t.pl.* B 2.221 = **wonden** *see* **wynden** *v*

wounden[2] *v* (inflict a) wound (on) 19.82, **B** 16.105, 17.54, 18.88; *(fig.)* 22.303, 306, 358,

woware *n* wooer, suitor 12.19

wowe *n* wall 3.65, A 5.136

wowen *v* solicit B 4.74

woxe(n) *p.p.* 3.211, **B** 10.75, 19.124, *p.t.pl.* **B** 14.60, 16.56 *see* **waxen** *v*

wrake *n* destruction, *in phr.* **werre and** ~ 17.85, 20.458

wrang *p.t.* 2.252 *see* **wryng(y)en** *v*

*****wranglynge** *n* noisy quarrelling 4.35

wrastlen *v* wrestle 16.66, 79

wrat(t)h(e) *n* violent anger 4.35, 14.67, 15.255, *spec.* the deadly sin of anger 6.121, 167, 7.16, 11.110, Z 5.94, **B** 4.70, 5.83, 429, 13.321, A 5.79, (*person.*) 6.66, 103, 105, 124, 126, 139, 148, 16.66; resentment 11.166, B 15.171; exasperation A 7.109; wrathful indignation 21.306, B 5.401; act of furious rage Z 4.120

wrathen *v* (*p.t.* **wrathe** 6.148, **-ed** 1.26) get angry (with) 6.148n, B 9.129, (*refl.*) 3.228, 8.149, (*person.*) ~ **þe (nouȝt)** (Don't) get angry 7.260 / A 6.98, (*impers. with Ø-subject*) Pr 189; anger 1.26, 2.118, B 10.288

wrec(c)he *n* wretch Z 7.197, **so muche** ~ so very miserable a soul 19.328; vile creature 2.41, 21.406, **B** 9.120, 15.600, **A** 4.136, 12.21, 24, ~ **of this world** heedless worldling 11.63; scoundrel 2.206, 8.252, 10.220, Z Pr 73; *a* miserable 13.94

wrecchede *a* miserable, miserly B 15.142; wretched, unhappy A 10.144; vile 1.37

wrec(c)hednesse *n* viciousness 6.333, 12.2, 20.353

wreken *v* (*p.p.* **wreke** 20.432, 22.204, Z 2.173, **wroken** 9.259, B 2.195) ? force, **ar wroken into** have forced their way into 9.259n; give vent to, (*refl.*) vent / satisfy oneself B 9.183; be avenged (upon) 20.432, 22.204, (*refl.*) avenge oneself A 5.67

wreth 21.306 = **wrat(t)he** *n*

wryen *v* twist aside, *p.p.* **ywrye** 16.74

wry(g)ht(e) *n* craftsman, carpenter 11.241, 244, 13.160, 19.138, Z 6.77, (*fig.*) 11.253

wryng(y)en *v* (*p.t.* **wronge** 8.172, **wrang** 2.252) wring (*fig.*) B 14.18; (*ellip.*) wring one's hands 2.252; clench and unclench B 5.84; squeeze 8.172; twist, pervert, ~ **lawe** (*person.*) 4.31

writ *n* writing, **holy** ~ authoritative religious tradition 1.125 *etc*, Holy Scripture, the Bible Pr 205 *etc* (*see* **holy** ~); legal document A 2.46, [= the Mosaic law] 19.19, B 17.3

writen *v* (*p.t. sg.* **wro(e)t** 5.139, 14.37, **wroot** B 11.168, *pl.* **writen** B 10.339, *p.p.* **(y)writen** 1.195, 19.13) write 14.40, **B** 9.39, 13.248, *ger.* written words B 12.82, A 8.43; inscribe, incise 19.13, 16, B 15.581, A 10.111, (have) inscribe(d) 3.69, 16.40, *ger.* inscription 3.73; act as a scribe 5.68; write down, record 1.194, 11.116, 122, 14.37, 38, 47, *ger.* 21.465; **B** 10.454, 11.168, 225, 12.258, A 10.109, **don / garen** ~ cause to be recorded 5.146, 8.94, 11.122, B 5.241, ~ **in noumbre** enrol formally 22.259; set down / state in writing 5.139, 8.240, 16.155, **B** 11.392,

13.71, 15.488, A 12.101, *ger. pl.* writings 20.356; compose (poem) 21.1, 484, (book) B 10.339, 427

writhen *v* (*p.t.* **wroþ**, *p.p.* **(y)writhe(n)**) twist 7.162; clench 19.142, A 5.67

writyng *ger. see* **writen** *v*

wroche Z Pr 73 *see* **wrec(c)he** *n*

wroet *p.t.* 14.37 *etc*; *see* **writen** *v*

wroeth 17.3, 4 *see* **wro(o)th** *a*

wroȝt *p.p.* 3.133, **B** 5.366, 7.97, 14.137, **wrouȝthe** A 12.101 = **wrouht** *p.p.*; *see* **worchen** *v*

wroghte, wroȝte *p.t.* 1.26, **B** 1.82, 9.51, 154, 10.34, *subjv.* B 6.246, 248, *pl.* †**wroȝten** B 14.196, **wroghton** *subjv. pl.* 1.13 = **wrouhte(n)**; *see* **worchen** *v*

wroke(n) *p.p.* 9.259, **B** 2.195, 18.391, 20.204 *see* **wreken** *v*

wrong[1] *n* wrong, injustice [esp. in legal sense], **with** ~ unjustly, wrongfully 19.234, 21.353, B 1.128, (*person.*) 1.59 *et p.*; fault, injury 3.221; evil A 10.75; wicked practice 13.74; mischief B 10.19

wrong[2] *av* wickedly A 11.260; ~**ly** unjustly 3.92

wrong(e)[3] *p.t.* 8.172, B 2.237 *see* **wryng(y)en** *v*

wro(o)t *p.t.* 5.139, 11.116, 21.1, **B** 11.168, 392, 15.581, A 10.109 *see* **writen** *v*

wro(o)th *a* angry 11.3, 17.3, 4, B 4.174; (*comp.*) ~**er** Pr 117; stirred to anger A 10.161; annoyed 7.77, 13.43; aggrieved B 15.488; furious 3.483

wroþ *p.t.* A 5.67 *see* **writhen** *v*

wrothe 6.105, 11.110 = **wrat(t)he** *n*

wroþerhele *n* evil fortune, *in phr.* **to** ~ for (a life of) misfortune 15.301, **to** ~ **manye** to the harm of many A 2.20

wroþliche *av* angrily A 5.67

wrouht(e), wrouȝt *p.p.* 2.119, 15.301, 20.353, 22.308, A 10.34, 12.10; *p.t.* 1.164 *etc*, **B** 1.150, 11.168, 396, **A** 10.147, 11.270, 12.101, ~**en** *pl.* 8.116, 11.272, *subjv.* 11.224; *see* **worchen** *v*

wurchen 5.25= **worchen** *v*

ȝa A 3.101, 192, 5.154 = **ȝe**[1] *av*

ȝaf, yaf *p.t.* 1.15, 10.180, B 1.107 *et p.*; *see* **ȝeuen** *v*

yald *p.t.* B 12.192 *see* **ȝelden** *v*

yarken *v* prepare B 7.78

†**yarn** *p.t.* **B** 5.440, 11.60 *see* **ȝernen** *v*[1]

ȝate (yate) *n* gate Pr 132, 7.241 (*fig.*), 11.42, 20.270, 284, 362, 365, 21.168, 22.299, 302, 330, 349, 377, Z 5.39

ȝe[1] *av* yes 3.147, 5.104, 7.199, 8.238, 11.155, 314, 13.246, 15.249, 16.137, 18.58, 81, **B** 5.250, 6.37, Z 3.143; oh yes 11.195, 21.399, 22.189

ȝe[2] (**ye**) *pers. prn.* 2 *pl.* you Pr 74, 11.70 *et p.*; *as polite sg.* 1.136, 3.57, 8.36 *et p.*, 11.91, 12.19 *et p.*, 13.242, 15.117, 19.230, 21.15 *et p.*, 22.323, 366, **B** 2.38, 3.344 *et p.*, 4.187, 6.124 *et p.*, 10.373, 388, 13.184, 15.22

ȝedden *v* sing A 1.138

ȝede(n) *p.t. pl.* Pr 41, 6.181 *et p.*, B 1.73; *see* **go(e)n** *v*

yeep B 11.18 = **ȝep** *a*

yeer B Pr 193 *etc*; *see* **ȝer** *n*

ȝeepliche 16.329 *see* **ȝep** *a* ~

ȝef¹ 7.259 = **ȝif**; *see* **yf** *conj.*

ȝef² *imper.* 12.166, 167, 15.146 *see* **ȝeuen** *v*

ȝefte (ȝift(e), gyft(e)) *n* giving 21.254, **of þe Popes** ~ in the gift of the Pope B 13.246; gift, present 2.212, 3.24, 113, 266, 315, 338, 4.138, 7.268, 9.133, 13.60, 15.210, **B** 10.42, 11.193, 13.185; cash-offering 8.39, 9.48, B 5.53; retainer 3.269; **to** ~ as a present 11.103; (*euphem.*) bribe 2.163, 3.117, 126, 161, 229, 450, 485, B 7.40, A 3.229; (spiritual) gift (from God) 11.288, 14.33, **B** 12.63, 14.298

ȝelden *v* (*p.t.* **ȝeld(e)** 14.132, **yald** B 12.192, *contr. pr.* **ȝelde** 20.103, **ȝilt** B 18.100) pay, requite 8.133; render 9.339; pay back, restore 6.342, 8.41, B 6.43, **to** ~ so as to (have to) pay back 16.370, ~ **aȝeyn** 6.309 (B 5.456); give back 21.394, B 7.78, 81; bring forth 17.88; surrender 14.132, 153, 20.103, *pr.p.* B 2.105; acknowledge, admit 6.424

ȝeman (ȝoman B) *n* attendant, *pl.* 3.269

ȝeme *n* notice, heed 3.485, B 10.197; *and see* **gome** *n*²

ȝemen *v* care for 10.308; govern B 8.52, A 10.72

yemere *n* guardian B 13.171

ȝende (ȝent) *av* (from) over there 20.261; over there 15.132

ȝep (yeep) *a* lusty, vigorous 10.289, 11.179; **~liche** *av* eagerly 16.329

ȝer (yeer) *n* (*pl.* **ȝer** Pr 203, **ȝeres** 8.345) year 11.179, **~s** year's 22.287, = years' remission 9.22; *in phrr.* **dere ~s** 10.199; **fele** ~ many years (ago) 16.354; **(a) fewe ~s** Pr 63, 8.345, A 12.58; **fyue** ~ an indefinite number of years B 6.322; **half** ~ half a year 2.238; **many ....~(es)** 5.35, 6.86, 9.22, 11.260, 15.3, 16.286, 17.26, B 5.119; **one ~es ende** the end of a year **B** 2.105, 6.43; **seuene ~** = a very long time Pr 203, 4.82, 6.108, 214, 7.64, 10.73, B 5.73; **ten ~** 7.29, **t(w)o ~** B 5.415, Z Pr 64

yerd *n*¹ yard, **kyrke ~** church graveyard Z 7.277

ȝerd *n*² (*pl.* **ȝerde(s)**) rod 4.112, B 12.14, A 10.85; yard 6.220

yeresyeue *n* New Year's gift **B** 3.100, 10.47, 13.185, (*fig.*) B 8.52

ȝerne *av* quickly 22.159, B 4.74, **as** ~ as soon, in a trice 7.36; eagerly 4.53, 8.116, 320; earnestly 22.287

ȝernen *v*¹ (*p.t.* **ȝorn** 12.12, †**yarn** B 5.440) run 3.269, 16.329

ȝernen *v*² long for, desire 1.33, B 13.185

yet, ȝet B Pr 185 *et p.*, A 1.127 *see* **ȝut** *av, conj.*

ȝeten *v* form, mould, *p.p.* **yȝoten** 1.149

ȝeuen (ȝyuen, gyuen) *v* (*p.t.* **ȝaf** *sg. and pl.* 1.15 *etc*, **yaf** B 1.107, **gaf** 2.322, *pl.* **ȝeuen** 22.301, **yeuen** Z 8.43, **geuen** 6.374, *pr. subjv.* B 3.166, *p.t. subjv.* **yeue** **B** 4.170, 12.197, 18.384, **ȝoue** 20.425, *p.p.* **yeuen** B 2.31, **gyue** 2.126, **ȝef** *imper.* 12.166, 15.146) give Pr 74, 2.126, 3.212, 287, 289, 292, 411, 485, 498, 6.270,

7.84, 8.204, 177, 254, 10.180, 11.27, 282, 13.82, 14.89, 137, 15.146, 16.150, 17.67, 21.104, 125, 226, 230, 22.58, 291, **B** 1.107, 5.106, 6.241, 7.69, 8.52, 9.46, 91, 10.47, 11.195, 12.17, 13.171, 14.126, 151, 15.436; render 6.347, 439; give (in payment) 3.265, 271, **B** 4.170, 14.250, A 8.43; give (in marriage) B 9.163; grant (to) 3.315, 9.348, 10.60, 304, 11.27, 14.56, 194, 197, 20.425, 21.54, 60, 184, **B** 1.107, 7.198, **A** 8.236, 10.129, 12.111; endow with 1.15, 9.116, 11.282, 15.18, 20; hand out 2.232; distribute (as) alms 8.133, 9.68, 10.308, 12.166, 22.291, **B** 7.78, 81, 15.318, 323, 330, 336, A 11.243; marry 10.259; put 7.53; deliver 8.187, 22.301; ~ **forth** hand over 12.167, ~ **fro** give away, (alienate) from 5.163; ~ **of** care for 4.37, 22.155, A 8.179; *in phrr.* ~ **never tale** take no account whatever 21.457; ~ **sorwe** punish with misfortune 2.126, 19.309, B 2.121

ȝif 6.343 *et p.*, **ȝyf** 7.36, **yif** B 5.424 = **yf**² *conj.*

ȝift(e) 8.39, 9.133, B 2.201 *et p. see* **ȝeft(e)** *n*

ȝilt *contr. pr.* B 18.100 *see* **ȝelden** *v*

ȝis B 5.634 = **ȝus** *av*

ȝit B 15.603, 16.3, 216, 17.43 = **ȝut** *av, conj.*

ȝiuen A 4.91 *et p.* = **ȝeuen** *v*

ȝoke *n* yoke, pair (of oxen) 7.294

ȝone (yond) *dem. a* yonder, that...over there 20.147, 193

ȝong(e) *a* young Pr 215, 5.35, 137, 10.289, *a as n* 308, 11.179, **B** 9.163, 12.6, A 10.58, 67

ȝorn *p.t.* 12.12 *see* **ȝernen** *v*¹

ȝour(e) *poss. a.* 2 *p. pl.* your Pr 74 *et p.*; *as polite sg.* 1.41, 3.56 *et p.*, 162, 182, 4.178, 189, 8.131 *et p.*, 20.92, 21.400, 22.203; *as poss. prn.* yours B 13.11, of you 21.474

ȝoue *p.t. subjv.* 20.425 *see* **ȝeuen** *v*

ȝow(e) (ȝou 1.2, **yow** B Pr 200, Z 2.1) 2 *p.pl. prn. (as dir. or indir. obj.)* you Pr 101 *et p.*; (to) you Pr 9 *etc,* B 10.269; for you 3.32 *etc*; upon you 20.90; (*refl.*) yourselves 5.167, 7.214, 8.125, 9.337, 10.227, 283, 21.258, 22.246, A 1.169; *as polite sg.* 3.56, 5.82, 7.296, 8.35, 131, 266, 20.90, 22.365, **B** 1.60, 3.347, 4.192, 16.1, 53, (*refl.*) 7.243, B 6.24

yowsuluen (yowsylue 5.141, **yowselue** B 10.272, **yow-self** B 16.122) *emph.* 2 *p.pl.prn.* yourselves, *appositive* 5.141, B 16.122; (*refl.*) Pr 216 *etc*, B 10.283; you yourselves B 16.123 (*subj.*), B 10.272 (*obj.*)

ȝowthe *n* (the period of one's) youth 1.139, 6.240, 7.53, 12.12, 16.329, 22.155, B 7.92, **A** 3.89, 12.60

ȝus (ȝis) *av* (*emph. form of* **ye**¹ *in answer to question implying negative*) yes 6.91, 235, 7.286, 19.281

ȝut (yut Z 8.90, **yet** B 2.1 *et p.*, **ȝit** B 15.603, A 7.268) *av and conj.* further, besides Pr 219, 3.77, 229, 4.55, 62, 74, 131, 6.95, 156, 8.307, 16.135, 19.91, 94, 209, 234; furthermore 13.5; then again 13.51; moreover 3.43, 209, 6.36, 292, 8.257, 17.3, 19.245, 20.43, 264, A 11.293; nevertheless, for all that Pr 199, 1.164, 2.151,

3.138, 5.94, 6.230, 317, 440, 7.31, 8.266, 9.105, 10.38, 108, 13.60, 17.75, 133, 298, 307, 19.233, 246, 20.101, 435; yet, still 6.51, 327, 332, 9.134, 10.191, 17.48, 19.179, B 16.3, A 4.21; even now, still 17.182, 19.114, 20.408, B 15.603; ?hereafter, at length 3.451; *in phrr*:

bet ~ still better 10.189; **neuere** ~ never yet B 16.216; ~ **lasse** still / even less 4.156, ~ **leeste** (and) least of all 3.209; ~ **mo(re)** still / even more 9.132, 10.82, 12.241, 16.132, 19.264; ~ **worse, worse ȝit** still / even worse 16.14, B 17.43; *as a* ~ **a** one more 8.35, Z 8.90

Latin and French Words and Phrases

Separable material appended to text-lines appears in the *Index of Quotations,* as do longer words and phrases enclosed in text-lines when they retain the appearance of citations to be recognised as such. This section includes words and a few phrases that clearly form part of the lexical repertoire; some, of indeterminate status in the contemporary language, appear both here and in the main Glossary. As with the latter, items are keyed to the **C** Version but those not occurring there are cited from **B**, **A** or **Z** as appropriate.

LATIN

Actiua active 18.80

Actiua Vita Active Life 15.195, 276, 16.116, 18.83, B 14.28

Amor Love 16.194

Anima soul (a) 10.134 *et p.*; (b) 16.181

Animus Will 16.182

A pena et a culpa from punishment and guilt 9.3, 23, 186

Ad pristinum statum ire to return to the first state 5.171, B 10.319

Archa Dei the Ark of God Pr 108, 112, 14.58, B 10.282

Archa Noe Noah's Ark 11.247

Audiatis alteram partem (provided that) you hear the other party 4.188

Auees Hail Marys 16.321

Benedicite Bless me (Father) 7.6

capias...carceratis take (Mede) and keep her safe, but not with those in prison 4.165

caristia dearth B 14.72

Caritas charity 14.14, 18.14, 32; *Caritatis* of charity B 2.35

Caro Flesh **B** 9.49, 17.108

caute prudently Z 5.143

clamat cotidie cries out daily 21.419

Concupiscencia carnis Lust of the Flesh 11.174 *et p.*

consummatus Deus fully and truly God 20.23

Contemplatiua Vita Contemplative Life 18.83

contra 'I dispute that' 10.20, 14.202, B 10.343

#contumax guilty of contumacy 13.84

Cor-hominis the heart of man 18.4

Cordis contricio... contrition of heart, confession of mouth, satisfaction through works 16.315

Credere in ecclesia to believe in the Church 3.356

*culorum conclusion 3.432, 11.249

cura animarum care of souls B 14.286

Dia perseverans a long-lasting (potion of) perseverance 15.57

*dido old tale 15.172

Dirige (opening antiphon of) Office of the Dead 3.463, 5.46

Disce, doce, dilige (Deum / inimicos) learn, teach, love (God / your enemies) 15.142 (B 13.137)

dominus lord(ship) B 10.330; ~ *virtutum* lord of hosts B 18.319a

dos ecclesie the endowment of the Church 17.215, 223

episcopus bishop 16.203

ergo therefore 10.28, 15.264, 16.126, 20.388, 21.19

Ergo saluabitur therefore he will be saved 14.204

Esto sobrius be sober 6.168

Ex vi transicionis from the power of transitivity B 13.152

Filius Son (of God) 18.121, 194, 19.192; ~ *Dei* son of God *2.31,* ~ *Marie* son of Mary 21.118

fornicatores fornicators 2.191

gaʒophilacium the Treasury B 13.198

Gigas Giant (*as name*) B 18.252

Hic et hec homo this and this (male / female) human being 3.404

humana natura human nature 20.22

Id est, Vetus Testamentum et Nouum That is (to say), the Old Testament and the New 21.274 *a*

ignorancia non excusat ignorance [of church law] does not excuse [bishops] 13.128 (B 11.316–17)

Ymago-Dei the image of God 18.7

In Dei nomine, Amen in the name of God, Amen 8.95

in deitate Patris in the divine nature [Christ has] of the Father 20.25

in die iudicii on the day of Judgement 15.120

in extremis in extreme circumstances, at the point of death B 10.346

in fautores suos on their supporters B 15.215

in genere in / according to the nature B 14.182

in Inferno in hell B 17.109

in Limbo Inferni in the Verge of Hell 18.116

in magestate Dei within the Divine Majesty 18.118

infamis of ill-repute B 5.166

ingrati ungrateful B 14.169

ingratus unkind 19.220

Ite, missa est go, Mass is ended B 5.413

iustus...vix the just man...on judgement day will be not saved witout the help of 'scarcely'

Latro Robber 6.329

laudabimus eum we will praise him 15.283

Lauacrum-lex-Dei a bath, the law of God 19.73

Legende [*legenda*] *Sanctorum* the *Lives of the Saints* [of Jacobus de Voragine] 17.157, **B** 11.60, 219, 15.269

Lex Christi the law of Christ B 17.72

Libera Voluntas Dei the Free Will of God 18.118

Liberum Arbitrium Free Choice / Judgement 16.156, 18.1 *et p.*, B 16.16 *et p.*

Liberum-Dei-arbitrium the Free Choice of God 20.20

licitum lawful, permissible B 11.96

Magi wise men 21. 85

mea culpa through my fault 6.64

Memoria memory, recollection 16.184

Mens mind, thought 16.183

mercedem payment, a fee Z 8.61

Metropolitanus metropolitan, archbishop 16.202, (fig.) 17.267

Modicum a little, scarcity B 18.215

Multi many 12.48

Nominatiuo, Pater... namely, Father, Son and Holy Spirit 3.405*a*

Non de solo not from the soil 5.68

Non saluabitur will not be saved 15.24

Nullum malum... No evil...unpunished...no good unrewarded 4.140–1

Osanna Hosanna ('Save'!) 20.7

Parce [*mihi Domine*] Spare [me O Lord] 21.296, B 18.393

Pastor pastor, shepherd 16.203

Pateat... Let it be manifest...through the passion of the Lord B 14.190*a*

Pater [God the] Father 18.193; *Pater Abbas* Father Abbot 6.153

Paternoster n Our Father [the Lord's Prayer] 5.46, 87, 107, 6.283, 399, 7.10, 11.299, 15.250, 16.321, 21.397, **B** 10.468, 13.237, 14.197

Pauci few

Pax vobis Peace [be with you] 17.238, 21.169

pecuniosus moneyed, rich 12.10

Penitencia (sacramental) penance B 5.475

Per confessionem...occiduntur through confession sins are destroyed B 14.91

Per primicias et decimas by first fruits and tithes 17.219*a*

per secula seculorum for ever and ever 20.467

Petrus, id est, Christus Peter, that is, Christ B 15.212

Placebo [the antiphon] I will please the Lord 3.463, 5.46, B 15.125

plenitudo temporis (*tyme*) the (time of the) fullness of time 18.127, 139

Pontifex pontiff B 15.42

Post-mortem after death 15.50

Potencia Dei Patris the power of God the Father 18.34

pre manibus beforehand 3.299, 9.45

prescite foreknown 11.208

Presul prelate 16.202

preuaricatores legis those who pervert the law 10.95

primus heremita the first hermit 17.13

Principes rulers 20.272

pro Dei pietate for the love of God B 7.45

pseudo-propheta false prophet 17.309

quadriduanus for four days 17.303, 18.145

quasi dormit is asleep, as it were 9.257

quasi modo geniti as if born 12.112

Qui cum Patre et Filio who with the Father and the Son 5.199

Qui turpiloquium loquitur He who utters foul words Pr 40

Quis est ille who is he? 15.284

Quis est iste who is this? B 18.315*a*

quodlibet general problem [in philosophy or theology] B 15.381

†*Quodque mnam* every pound Z 5.124n

Racio Reason 16.186

Ramis palmarum [the feast of] Palm branches (Palm Sunday)

Recordare remember [?= sing psalms / meditate] B 4.120

rectores rectors [of churches] 2.184

Redde quod debes Pay what you owe 21.188, 260, 393, 22.309

Reddere means of repayment 6.321; *Reddite* repay 6.315; *reddit quod debet* pays what he owes 21.194

Redemptor Redeemer 12.116

Regum (the Book) of Kings 3.412

resureccio mortuorum the resurrection of the dead 20.412

Rex Glorie... the King of Glory B 18.318

Sanctorum of the Saints (*see* *Legende~*)

Sapiencia Dei Patris the Wisdom of God the Father 18.40

Sapiense the Wisdom writings (of the Bible) 3.494, *spec.* Proverbs 3.484

sapienter wisely 13.125

satisfaccio satisfaction 16.31

Sensus (sense)-perception, understanding through the senses 16.187

seruus nequam a wicked servant B 6.238

si if (*signifying a condition*) = 'unless, provided that (not)'

simile likeness, comparison 18.228, 19.161

sine restitucione without making restitution [*sc.* of ill-gotten gains] 6.257

solus Deus one sole God 18.191

913

Spes Hope 19.1 *et p.*

Spiritus (disembodied) spirit 16.196

Spiritus Fortitudinis the spirit [= virtue] of fortitude 21.290, 467, 22.24, 25; ~ ***Intellectus*** the spirit of understanding 21.466; ~ ***Iusticie*** the spirit of justice 21.299 *et p.*, 22.24; ~ ***Prudencie*** the spirit of prudence 21.277, 458, 22.31; ~ ***Temperancie*** the spirit of temperance 21.282, 22.8 *et p.*

Spiritus Sanctus the Holy Spirit (of God) 18.51, 121, B 17.209, ~ ***Paraclitus*** Comforter 21.202, 207

stella comata star trailing fire (*lit.* 'long-haired star'), = comet 20.247

supersedeas (name of) a writ staying or ending a legal proceeding 2.187, 4.190, 9.263

transgressores wrongdoers, law-breakers 1.92

turpiloquio (with) foul speech 7.116 (B 13.447)

Verbi gratia by way of example B 15.267

Vigilare to keep watch 9.258

Vigilate keep watch 7.56

FRENCH

Beau fitz fair son 9.311

Beaute sanz bounte beauty without goodness 17.163

bele fine 16.268

bele paroles fine words 16.268

chaud...pluchaut hot...piping hot 8.334

Dew vous saue, Dame Emme God keep you, Lady Emma Pr 226

douce vie luxurious living 15.303

pur charite for charity's sake 8.169, 266, 10.11, 15.33, A 7.182

semyuief half-alive 19.57

treys encountre treys three against three 18.239

Supplementary Index

This list includes words (mainly variants recorded in the Apparatus and some major rejected conjectures) that are discussed in the **Textual Notes** but not listed in the **Indexical Glossary**.

abanen B 6.216
auarouser 1.186

battys A 12.70
becauȝte 14.62
bishiten 9.264
bisshopid 17.268
bonchef 3. 33
†bouste B 13.162

chiteryng B 12.251
conterfetyþ A 11.19
corsement 6.65

deyntifliche 8.323
delfulliche 3.415
desalowe 3.319
†douth A 9.60
duite 5.10

falste 3.176
feyntles A 2.94
feyntliche A 2.130
fial 8.216
flite Pr 43
flonke 6.334
forbete 20.34
fraiel B 13.104

gylefully Pr 36
gylously Pr 36
gypsers B 20. 219

hagge B 5.188

yhonted 2.228
inproued A 8.153

†iauelot B 18.82
iotten A 2.144.
ioynide 1.180

lakeryng 6.393
leix 10.275
lighteth A 5.93

macchen Pr 61
maken Pr 61
manliche 8.51, 9.335

marre 3.140
maundee B 16.140
†*memoria* 22.367
mente 3.10
mercede 21.76
mynchons A 9.206
myre 3.380

ondyng 15.248

ploughfoot 8.64
poudren Pr 161
pounden Pr 161
pounen Pr 161
poraille Pr 80
pryckide A 5.126
prochide A 5.126
purid A 4.82

questemongere B 19.373

recetteþ 3.499
ryot Pr 216
rorede 7.7

schawes 10.160
*schyȝen 5.107
schregges Pr 2
*shien 7.300
shrobbis Pr 2
sywestre 6.361
spryg 5.138
sweyued Pr 7

tawny B 5.193
teldit A 2. 42
tripe 9.262
trollyþ 5.150

†þerf 6.135

vnconnabelyche 3.262
vnlese Pr 162
†unnit 5.10

†wenes B 2.91
*withes 4.23
wonte 15.242
writhen 9.259

Index of Proper Names

Morales (the *Moralia in Job* of Pope St Gregory the Great) B 10.293

Munde þe miller 2.113, B 10.44

Nabugodonasor (Nebuchadnezzar) 9.306

Nasareth 17.189, 21.137

Nede 13.240, 22.4, 51, 232

Neptalym (Naphtali) 17.189, 261

Nyneue (Nineveh) 17.189, 261

Noe 10.179, 223, 11.239, 242, 254, **B** 9.131, 10.406

Normandie B 3.189, **Normawndye** Z 3.148

Nor(th)folk, B 5.235, **Z** 3.148, 5.98

Offini (Ophni) Pr 107, 123, **Offyn** B 10.281

Omnia-probate (Try everything) A 12.50, 56

Oseye (Alsace) Pr 230

Oȝias (Hosea) B 15.576

Pacience 7.273, 15.33 *et p.*,95 *et p.*, 154 *et p.*, 234 *et p.*, 16.114, 161, B 13.355

Pampilon (Pamplona) 19.219

Paradys 16.223, 20.378

Pasche (Easter) 18.167

Paul the Apostle *see* **Pou(e)le, St**

Paul *primus heremita* (the first Hermit) 17.13

Paulines (the Pauline friars) 2.110c

Pees (King's Peace) 4.45 *et p.*, (Truth's porter) 7.273, (Daughter of God) 20.170 *et p.*, 451 *et p.*, (Porter of Unity 22.299, 331 *et p.*

Penetrans-domos, **Sire** Sir-Piercer-of-Homes 22.341

Penitencia B 5.475

Peres, Syre ~ of Prydie 6.366

Peres þe Pardoner 2.110

Per(e)s (the Plouhman) 7.199 *et p.*, 8.7 *et p.*, 9.1 *et p.*, 282, 299, 300, 15.34, 132, 139, 151, 154, 196, 214, 16.338, 20.8 *et p.*, 21.6 *et p.*,184 *et p.* 22.77, 309, 321, 383, 386, B 16.17 *et p.,* 13.130, 238, 15.196, 212, 16.17, 18.20, 21, 103, 168, 171, **A** 8.152, 12.102

Perkyn (familiar diminutive of **Peres Plouhman**) 8.1, 56, 112 *et p.*, 9.292, B 7.131, Z 8.90

Pernel, St A 7.259 *see* **Purnele**

Peter, St, the Apostle Pr 128, 136, 9.112, 15.226, 16.167, 17.19, 224, 20.251, 21.163 *et p.*, **B** 10.344, 442, 15.265, A 11.233, Z 5.92; (church) B 7.173; (in oaths) 7.181, 8.1, **B** 7.131, 11.87, Z 7.26

Pilat(us) (Pontius Pilate) 20.35, 39, 82, B 10.34, A 12.26

Plato 11.120, 308, 12.175, 14.189, 22.275

Pocalips (*Apocalypse*) 15.100

Pope 2.23, 244, 3.183, 5.192, 15.174, 17.233

Porfirie (Porphyry) 12.175, 14.189

Potencia-Dei-Patris (Power of God the Father) 18.34, B 16.30

Pou(e)l(e), St (St. Paul the Apostle) Pr 39, 9.112, 10.89, 11.269, 15.73, 76, 16.167, 289, 17.17, 19.224, 319, **B** 10.344, 12.29, 15.156, 265, **A** 7.3, 10.109, 12.22, Z 5.92; (*in oaths*) 8.297, **B** 5.639, 6.24, 11.87, A 7.3

Poules (St. Paul's Church) 11.56, 15.71, B 10.46

Pouerte 13.1

Prydie, Sire Peres of 6.366

Princeps huius mundi (Prince of this world) 10.135, A 10.62

Prucelond B 13.393 = **Pruys-lond**

Pruyde 6.14, 16.47 *et p.*, 210, 330, 21.224, 229, 337, 384, 22.70 *et p.*, 353 *et p.*; **~ of Parfit Lyuynge** 11.176, 194

Pruyslond (Prussia), 6.279 (B 13.393)

Purnele (St Petronilla) Z 7.279, [as type name (a) for proud woman 4.111, 5.128, 6.3 (b) for a nun 6.135 (c) for a priest's concubine 6.366, 17.72]

Quod-bonum-est-tenete Hold what is good [*allegorical place*] A 12.52, 57

Racio (Reason) 17.86

#**Ragamoffyn** 20.281

Raynald þe Reue 2.112

Randolf, Erle of Chestre 7.11

Rechelesnesse 11.199, 276, 286, 12.4, 13.129

Reignald B 4.49

Repentaunce 6.1 *et p.*, 7.8, 55, 119

Resoun 1.50, 3.437, 4.5 *et p.*, 5.6 *et p.*, 6.12, 12.67, 13.34, 143, 180 *et p.*, 15.27 *et p.*, 53, 152, 16.186, **B** 12.218, 15.11, A 4.142, 144, Z 4.126, 158

Reule (La Reôle, Guienne) Pr 231

Reuthe 21.83

Reuel 22.181

Richard, King A 12.113

Rycher, St (St Richard of Chichester) Z 4.152

Rychesse 11.108

Rihtfulnesse 21.83

Rihtwisnesse 20.167 *et p.*, 466, 21.88

Ryn (Rhine) B Pr 230

Robardus (vagabonds) Pr 45

Robert Renaboute B 6.148

Robert the ruyflare (robbere B) 6.315, 321 (B 5.462)

Robyn Hode 7.11; **~ þe Ribauder** 8.75; **~ the Ropere** 6.386

Rochele (La Rochelle) Pr 231

Rochemador (Rocamadour) B 12.36

Romaynes (Romans) 17.282

Rome Pr 48, 2.243, 4.123, 125, 5.197, 6.246, 7.166, 8.1, 9.323, 16.38, 17.222, 19.219, 21.426, B 12.36, Z Pr 57; (ancient) **B** 11.153, 162

Rosamounde B 12.47

Rose (a widow) 4.47; **~ þe Regrater** 6.232; **~þe Disshere** 6.371

Ruth 3.412

Rutlande B 2.111

Index of Quotations

Quotations are in abbreviated form; references to versions other than **C** are given only if the quotation is not in parallel position. For translations and full details of sources given in brief see the **Commentary**.

A LATIN

A regibus et principibus (after Ecclus 38:2) B 7.43*a*, A 8.46*a*, Z 7.271

Absit nobis gloriari (Gal 6:14) 17.198*a*

Absque solicitudine felicitas (Vincent of Beauvais) 16.153*a*

Ad pristinum statum ire 5.171, B 10.319

Ad vesperum demorabitur fletus (Ps 29:6) 20.183*a*

Aduenit ignis diuinus (after Acts 2:3) 14.208*a*

Agite penitenciam (Job 21:2, Ezech 18:30) 15.56

Alter alterius onera portate (Gal 6:2) 8.231*a*, 13.77*a*, B 11.210*a*

Amen, Amen...mercedem suam recipiunt (Mt 6:5) 3.311, A 3.64*a*

Amen dico vobis, nescio vos (Mt 25:12) 19.216*a*, **B** 5.55, 9.66*a*

Amen dico vobis, quia hec vidua paupercula (Lk 21:3) 13.97*a*

Amice, ascende superius (Lk 14:10) 8.44*a*

Anima pro diuersis accionibus (Isidore of Seville, *Etymologiae* xi, i 13) 16.199*a*

Animam autem aufert accipiencium (Prov 22:9) 3.496*a*

Aperis tu manum tuam (Ps 144:16) 15.265*a*, 16.318

Appare quod es (Pseudo-Chrysostom) B 10.255*a*

Argentum et aurum non est michi (Acts 3:6) 15.226*a*

Ars vt artem falleret (Fortunatus' *Pange lingua*, *OBMLV*, no. 54, l. 8) 20.164*a*

Attollite portas (Ps 23:9) 20.270*a*

Audiui archana verba (II Cor 12:4) 20.438*a*, A 12.22*a*

Aue, raby (Mt 26:49) 18.169, 20.50

Beacius est dare (Acts 20:35) 14.16*a*

Beati omnes (Ps 127:1) **B** 5.419, 6.249

Beati pauperes (Mt 5:3) B 14.215*a*

Beati qui non viderunt et crediderunt (Jn 20:29) 21.182*a*

Beati quorum remisse sunt iniquitates (Ps 31:1) 7.152, 14.117*a*

Beati quorum tecta sunt peccata (Ps 31:1) **B** 12.177*a*, 13.53*a*, 14.93

Beatus est diues (Ecclus 31:8) 16.357*a*

Beatus est qui scripturas legit (St Bernard) 16.220

Beatus vir (Ps 1 *or* Ps 111) **B** 5.419, 10.320, 13.52

Benedictus qui venit (Mt 21:9) 20.15*a*

Bona arbor (Mt 7:17) 2.29*a*, 10.246*b*

Bonum est vt unusquisque uxorem suam habeat (I Cor 7:1–2) 10.297

Bonus pastor animam suam ponit (Jn 10:11) 17.193, 291*a*

Breuis oracio penetrat celum (after Ecclus 35:21) 11.300*a*

Brutorum animalium natura... (after Job 6:5) 17.53

Canes non valentes latrare (Is 56:100) B 10.287*a*

Cantabit paupertas coram latrone viator (Juvenal, *Sat.* x, 22) B 14.304*a*

Captiuam duxit captiuitatem (Eph 4:8) 7.130*a*

Caritas expellit omnem timorem (I Jn 4:18) 15.166*a*

Caritas nichil timet (I Jn 4:18) B 13.164*a*

Caritas omnia suffert (I Cor 13:70) 17.5*a*

Celi enarrant gloriam Dei (Ps 18:1) 18.214*a*

Christus resurgens (Rom 6:9) 21.160

Clarior est solito post maxima (Alan of Lille) 20.453–4

Claudi ambulant (Mt 11:5, Lk 7:22) 18.142*a*

Clemencia non constringit (legal maxim) 5.60*a*

Concepit in dolore (Ps 7:15) 10.213*a*

Conflabunt gladios suos (Is 2:4) 3.460*a*

Confundantur omnes qui adorant sculptilia (Ps 96:7) B 15.81*a*

Consencientes et agentes (maxim of canon law) 7.86*a*, B 13.427*a*

Consummatum est (Jn 19:30) 20.57

Contricio et infelicitas (Ps 13:3) 4.36*a*

Contriuit Dominus baculum impiorum (Is 14:4–6) 5.177*a*, B 10.328

Conuertimini ad me (Is 45:22) B 14.180*a*

Cor contritum et humiliatum (Ps 50:19) 15.63, 16.334*a*

Cordis contricio... (penitential formula) 16.31*a*

Credo in Deum patrem (Apostles' Creed) 16.320, 17.316, B 10.467

Credo in Spiritum Sanctum (Apostles' Creed) 3.480

Crucifige (Jn 19:15) 20.38, 46

Cui des, videto (*Distichs of Cato*) 9.69

Cuius maledictione os plenum est (Ps 9B(10):7) 6.76*a*, 10.331*a*

Culpat caro, purgat caro ('Aeterne rex altissime', stanza 4) 20.450*a*

Cum ceciderit iustus non collidetur (Ps 36:24) B 16.25*a*

Cum facitis conuiuia (Lk 14: 12) 12.104*a*

Cum recte viuas (*DC*) A 10.98

Cum sanctus sanctorum veniat (after Dan 9:24, 26) B 15.599

Cum sancto, sanctus eris (Ps 17:26) 21.425, B 5.278

Cum veniat sanctus sanctorum (after Dan 9:24) 20.112*a*

Dabo tibi secundum peticionem tuam (Ps 36:4) 15.275

Dare histrionibus (? St Jerome) 7.118*a*

Date, et dabitur vobis (Lk 6:38) 1.195, B 12.54*a*

De delicijs ad delicias (St Jerome) B 14.144*a*

De peccato propiciato (Ecclus 5:5) 14.146*a*

De re que te non molestat noli certare (Ecclus 11:9) 13.197

Deleantur de libro viuencium (Ps 68:29) 8.77

Non de solo...pabulo (cf. Mt 4:4) 5.86–7

Non dimittitur peccatum (see *Numquam dimittitur peccatum*)

Non eligas cui miserearis (Jerome) B 7.75*a–b*

Non est sanis opus medicus (Mt 9:12) B 16.110*a*

Non est timor Dei (Ps 13:3) B 4.37*a*

Non excusat episcopos B 11.316

Non habitabit in medio domus mee (Ps 100:7–8) 7.92*a*, B 13.433*a*

Non inflatur (I Cor 13:4–5) 16.289*a*

Non in solo pane (Mt 4:14) 15.246*a* (and see *Non de solo*)

Non intres in iudicium (Ps 142:2) 20.442*a*

Non leuabit gens (Is 2:4) 3.476*a*

Non licet nobis legem voluntati (maxim, source unknown) 9.212*a*

Non mecaberis (Ex 20:14) B 10.366

Non morabitur opus (Lev 19:13) 3.307*a*

Non occides (Ex 20:13) 1.449*a*

Non oderis fratres (Lev 19:17) 12.35

Non omnis qui dicit Domine (Mt 7:21) 19.230*a*

Non plus sapere (Rom 12:3) 16.227, B 10.118*a*

Non reddas malum (Prov 20:20) 5.58*a*

Non saluabitur 15.23 see *Vix saluabitur*

Non veni solvere legem (Mt 5:17) 20.395*a*

Non veni vocare iustos (Lk 5:32) 7.138*a*

Non visurum se mortem (Lk 2:26) 20.259*a*

Nullum malum inpunitum (Pope Innocent III) 4.140–1, 20.433

Numquam colligunt de spinas (Mt 7:16) 10.247*a*

Numquam, dicit Iob, rugiet onager (Job 6:5) 17.52*a*

Numquam dimittur peccatum (St Augustine,) 6.257*a*, 19.288*a*, B 5.272*a*

Nunc princeps huius mundi (see *Princeps huius mundi*) 20.349*a*

O felix culpa (*Exultet* Prose from Liturgy of Easter Saturday) 7.125*a*

O Mors ero mors tua (Osee 13:14) 20.34*a*, B 17.112*a*

O stulte (Lk 12:20) 12.217*a*

O vos omnes sicientes (Is 55:1) 12.58*a*

Ociositas et habundancia panis (*after* Peter Cantor) B 14.76*a*

Odisti omnes qui operantur iniquitatem (Ps 5:7) 20.356*a*

Omnia celestia terrestria flectantur (Phil 2: 10) 21.80*a*

Omnia probate (I Thess 5:21) 3.489, 20.233*a*, A 12.50, 56

Omnia que dicunt, facite (Mt 23:3) 8.90*a*

Omnia traham ad me ipsum (Jn 12:32) 19.127*a*

Omnia sunt tua ad defendendum 21.482*a* (legal saying)

Omnis iniquitas quoad misericordiam Dei (after Augustine) 6.337*a*

Opera illorum sequuntur illos (Rev 14:13) 16.54*a*

Operibus credite (Jn 10:38) 16.340*a*

Oris confessio, Operis satisfaccio 16.30, 31*a*, B 14.17*a* see *Cordis contricio*

Pacientes vincunt (from *Testament of Job*) 15.139, 158*a*, 256, **B** 13.135*a*, 15.267, 597*a*

Panem nostrum cotidianum (Mt 6:11) 16.372*a*

Parce michi Domine (Job 7:16) 21.296

Parum lauda (attrib. to Seneca) 12.41*a*

Pastores loquebantur ad inuicem (Lk 2:15) 14.86*a*

Pauper ego ludo (Alexander of Ville-Dieu) 12.155*a*

Pauper non habet diuersorium B 12.147*a* see *Set non erat ei locus*

Paupertas est absque sollicitudine semita 16.141*a* (see next)

Paupertas est odibile bonum (Vincent of Beauvais) 16.115

Paupertatis onus (*DC*) 8.337*a*

Peccatoribus dare (Peter Cantor, after Jerome) B 15.342*a*

Pena pecuniaria non sufficit ... (Canon law maxim) 12.10*a*

Penetrans-domos (II Tim 3 6) 22.341

Penitet me fecisse hominem (Gen 6:7) 10.224

Per confessionem...peccata occiduntur (penitential maxim) B 14.91

Per Euam cunctis (Lauds of BVM) 7.249*a*

Periculum est in falsis fratribus (II Cor 11:26) 15.76*a* (see also *Vnusquisque a fratre*)

Perniciosus dispensator (perhaps after Peter Cantor) B 9.92*a*

Petite et accipietis (Mt 7:73) B 15.427*a*

Philosophus esses si tacuisses (John Bromyard, after Boethius) 13.225*a*

Piger propter frigus (Prov 20:4) 8.246*a*

Pilatus...sedens pro tribunali (Mt 27:19) 20.35

Ponam pedem meum in aquilone (Augustine, after Is 14:13–14) 1.110*a*, 16.211*b*

Populus qui ambulabat in tenebris (Is 9:2) 7.133*a*, 20.366

Porro non indiget monachus (cf. I Tim 6:8) B 15.342*a*

Possessio sine calumpnia 16.126a (Vincent of Beauvais)

Precepta Regis (Roman law maxim) B Pr 145

Princeps huius mundi (Jn 16:11) 10.135, 20.349*a*, A 10.62

Pro hac orabit ad te (Ps 31:6) 15.61

Proditor est prelatus (after Peter Cantor) B 9.92*a*

Propter Deum subiecti estote (I Pet 2:13) B 11.382*a*

Psallite deo nostro (Ps 46:7–8) 13.123*a*

Qualis pater, talis filius (proverbial) B 2.27*a*

Quam olim Abrahe promisisti (from the *Magnificat*, based on Lk 1:55) B 16.242*a*

Quando misi vos sine pane (after Lk 22:35) 9.120*a*

Quandocumque ingemuerit peccator (pseudo-Ezekiel; cf. Jer 31:34b) 7.147*a*

Quare impij viuunt (Job 21:7) B 10.25*a*

Quare non dedisti pecuniam (Lk 19:23) B 7.81*a*

Quare placuit (cf. Ps 134:6, 113b: 3, Job 23:13) 14.155*a*

Quare via impiorum prosperatur (Job 21:7, Jer 12:1) A 11.23*a*

Sunt iusti atque sapientes (Eccl 9:1) 11.275*a*
Super cathedram Moysi (Mt 23:2) 8.86*a*, 11.238*a*, A 11.223
Super egros manus (Mk 16:18) 15.223*a*
Super innocentem munera (Ps 14:5) B 7.41*a*

Talis pater, talis filia 2.27*a* (see *Qualis pater, talis filius*)
Tanquam nichil habentes (II Cor 6: 10) 13.4*a*
Te Deum laudamus (hymn for Sunday Matins) 20.468
Ter cesus sum (II Cor 11:25) B 13.67*a*
Tezaurisat et ignorat (Ps 38:7) 12.217*a*
Tibi soli peccaui (Ps 50:6) 20.420*a*
Tolle, tolle (Jn 19:15) 20.47
Tres vidit et unum adorauit (antiphon for Quinquagesima Sunday) 18.242*a*
Trinitas unus Deus (cf. Athanasian Creed) 3.405
Tristicia vestra vertetur in gaudium (Jn 16:20) 12.209
Tu dicis (Mt 26:25) B 16.145
Tu fabricator omnium (Compline Hymn 'Jesu salvator saeculi') 19.134*a*

Vbi tezaurus tuus (Mt 6:21) 6.285*a*, B 13.399*a*
Vnusquisque a fratre (source unknown) B 13.73*a* (see also *Periculum est*)
Vnusquisque onus suum portabit (Gal 6:5) B 10.114*a*
Vt quid diligitis vanitatem (Ps 4:3) B 15.81*b*
Vxorem duxi (Lk 14:20) 7.303*a*, B 14.3*a*

Ve homini (Mt 18:7) 18.175*a*
Ve soli (Eccles 4:10) 20.316*a*
Ve terre vbi puer est rex (Eccl 10:16) Pr 206
Ve vobis qui potentes estis (Is 5:22) 15.66*a*

Ve vobis qui ridetis (Lk 6:25) 7.83*a*, B 13.424*a*
Velud sompnium surgencium (Ps 72:20) 15.310*b*
Veni Creator Spiritus (Pentecost Hymn at Terce) 21.211
Verbum caro factum est (Jn 1:14) 3.355, 7.140*a*
Vere filius Dei erat iste (Mt 27:54) 20.70*a*
Via et veritas (Jn 14:6) 10.258
Videatis qui peccat in Spiritum Sanctum (Mt 12:32) B 16.47*a*
Videte ne furtum sit (Tob 2:21) 17.40*a*
Vidi preuaricantes et tabescebam (Ps 118:158) A 12.19*a*
Vidit deus (see *Et vidit Deus*)
Villam emi (Lk 14:18) 7.291
Vindica sanguinem iustorum (cf. Apoc 6: 10) 19.272*a*
Virga tua et baculus tuus (Ps 22:4) B 12.13*a*, A 10.87
Virtus in infirmitate perficitur (II Cor 12: 9) 19.319*a*
Vix saluabitur iustus (I Pet 4: 18) 14.204, 15.23
Volucres celi Deus pascit (Mt 6:26) B 14.34*a*
Vos estis sal terre (Mt 5: 13) B 15.428*a*
Vos qui peccata hominum comeditis (? Osee 4: 8) 15.51*a*
Vultus huius seculi (source unknown) 14.32*a*

B FRENCH

Beaute sanz bounte...[kynde] *sanz cortesie* (proverbial) 17.163–4
Bele vertue est suffraunce (proverbial) 13.204–5

C LATIN / FRENCH

Quant oportet *vient* (proverbial) B 10.438

F. APPENDICES

Appendix I

THE LANGUAGE AND METRE OF *PIERS PLOWMAN*

This Appendix on Langland's dialect and verse-practice provides supporting data for the arguments in the *Introduction* IV §§ 37–49 concerning aspects of both that are potentially significant for establishing authenticity, from the level of the individual reading up to that of an entire version. Because the norms illustrated below are of a 'critically empirical' type, they are open to being tested against the entire corpus of alliterative verse. It is proposed here that the combination of certain linguistic and metrical features suffices to establish (i) that Langland's original language was that of SW Worcs, (ii) that the features isolated as 'characteristically Langlandian' became for the most part more intensely concentrated as composition and revision proceeded, and (iii) that he wrote the four versions **ZABC** in that order. All core-text line-references are to the 'senior' version (e.g. **C** for **BC**, **B** for **AB** references).

A. METRICAL AND LINGUISTIC ASPECTS

§ 1. Linguistic and metrical considerations[1] are closely related. From the textually secure core-text lines and unique lines that meet their norms Langland's original language can be reconstructed by reference to surviving manuscript copies and the evidence of his alliterative practices (Samuels 1985, 1988). The second is the more important testimony, since it goes beyond the scribe's 'language' (which refracts the exemplar's through his own) to the author's original dialect. This is the language of the SW Midlands, more specifically of SW Worcestershire, and accords with the internal references to Malvern at Pr 6 and 9.295. That the poem's main geographical location (where indicated) is London fits with the probable place of origin of most **B** and **C** copies; and the SW Worcs character of XYHIU, the best representatives of **C-x**, is ascribable to their London scribes' faithful retention of regional features deriving from the original (see p. 208n12 above). In the **B** tradition, relict forms in mss L and R, the two that best represent respectively the sub-archetypes β and α, likewise point to the presence of SWM features in their common original Bx (see B Pr 190) that probably go back to the author. These are: the spelling *oe* for |o:|, as in *goed*, *doem*; the form *heo* for 'she'; *a* for 'he' or 'she'; *noyther* 'neither'; *no* 'nor'; *ar* 'ere'; *ʒut* 'yet', and the Western spellings *u* or *uy* for |y:| (*buggen*, *puyr*). Western *heo* appears (as a stave-word) at 11.113 and B 3.29, *a* at 11.114, and pl. *hy* at B Pr 66.

§ 2. The notable features of **L**'s metrical practice from the point of view of dialect are (i) de-aspiration of historic initial *h* to alliterate with vowels and (ii) the alliteration of |f| with |v| (including *v* in Latin words). The last feature could indicate 'metrical allophony' (like that of |s| with |ʃ|) or deliberate 'cognation' (as of |k| ~ |g|, |t| ~ |d|, |p| ~ |b|). But *f / v* are more likely to show phonological identity (voicing of *f*) since the alliterative features *combined* with the two morphological features illustrated confirm the writer's presumptive home region as that indicated by internal references.[2] With delimitations by *heo*[3] from the east, by *aren* from the south, by *f*-voicing from the north and by de-aspiration from the west, this region is SW Worcs, including Malvern (Samuels 1985:234–7, 242ff). In the following list (m) = 'macaronic'.

(a) *f / v:*
Twenty examples from the core-text: **ZABC** II 191 (m). III 36. V 191 (m). VI 437. VII 56. **ABC** Pr 69. **ZAB** I 23 (*f / v / þ*). **BC** VII 21. 25. 49. 103 (*f / þ*). XVI 221(m). XVII 109. XIX 271. XX 123. 154. 159. XXI 153. 422. 483. Fifteen examples from the four versions severally: **C** V 49. 58. IX 93. 232. 258 (m). XV 8. **B** Pr 190. II 61. 77. III 271 (*f / þ*). 334 (*v / þ*). V 410 (*f / v / þ*). XVIII 337 (*f / þ*). **A** X 70 (*f / þ*). XII 45 (*f / þ*).

(b) *Vowel with historic organic* h
ZABC I 17. 46 (**Z** *spells with* w). 72. VI 5. **ZAB** I 197. **AB** III 72. **BC** III 458.

Other 'broader' dialect features of this area appear in the **Z** portion of Bodley 851, such as forms showing intrusion as well as omission of inorganic / historic *h* in words like *ast* 'hast', and de-voicing of terminal *-d* (as in *ant* 'and'). The spellings *wyt* 'with' and *hasket* 'asketh' illustrate development of spirantal |θ| in inflexional morphemes to an aspirated stop. One consequence of this is falling together with the de-voiced preterite morpheme *-ed* to produce the occasional tense-ambiguous 3rd person ending *-et* (for either *-eth* or *-ed*: see on B Pr 140 at III *B* § 67 above).

B. LEXICAL ASPECTS

§ 3. i (a) Some 90-odd particular words are found only in the texts of *Piers Plowman*. Although it is uncertain which if any Langland introduced (possible examples are marked †), and lexical evidence of unique usage is of necessity mainly negative, study of them in the context of revision can be helpful.[4] The roughly 50 core-text items (here ordered by 'versional seniority' without further differentiation) may be considered 'weakly criterial' for the authenticity of single versions in which they occur at least once. Parallel uses will be found in *IG*.

Core-text
abosten 8.152. [aythe 21.274]. alery 8.129. batauntliche 16.55. cauken 13.170. clyketen 7.265. clokken 3.37. coten 3.179. diademen B 3.288. diapenidion B 5.122. dido B 13.173. dremeles 15.17. fauntelte 11.314. fendekyn 20.415. fibicches B 10.213. fobbe 2.193. fobbere B 2.183. forager 22.85. forglotten 11.66. forwanyen Z 5.62. handydandy 68. ycheuelen 6.200. iutte B 10.461. kaurymaury B 5.78. †mangen 8.271 (*see* A 12.72). †mercede 3.290. myswynnen 15.48. †*mnam* B 6.238. nype 20.166. ofwandred Pr 7. ouer-plentee 12.236. ouerskippere 13.122. parentrelynarie 13.118. prouendren 3.186. rybauder 8.75. romere 4.120. schingled 10.235. so(uþ)den 2.187. sprakliche 20.10. tasch 19.212. taxour 8.37. titerare 22.300. tologgen 2.226. vngraue 4.127. wafrestere 7.284. †walterot 20.144. wonderwyse 1.125. wranglynge 4.35 (49)

Versions separately
C begyneld 9.154. byglosen 20.380. bytulye 8.242. clerkysh 6.42. deuoutours 2.184. dompynge 13.168. filial 8.216. gnedy 15.87. ?heggen 5.19. iacen 19.52. ouer-soppen 6.428. †rect 3.333. redyng-kyng 2.112. reule 9.79. roteyen 13.146. saunbure 2.178. *simile* 18.228 (?semi-Latin). termison 3.405. (18)
B ballok-knyf 15.124. befloberen 13.401. bymolen 14.4. clausemele 5.420. decourren 14.194. deuoutrye 2.176. envenyme 2.14. flobren 14.15. forgrynden 10.79. foresleue 5.80. mysfeet 11.374. mysstanden 11.380. mol(en) 13.315, 275. oriental 2.14. rotey 11.337. †speke 15.275. †spelonke 15.275. to-shellen 17.192. (18)
A baudekyn 3.40. belouren 8.107. cateles 10.68. pilewhey 5.134. poperen 11.213. wynstere 5.129. (6)
Z feym 7.326. stuty Z 4.124. (2)

i (b) Some 30 *Compound Words* (excluding longer allegorical phrase-names) also occur:
Core-text amende-ʒou 7.243. dobest; dobet 10.76. do-euel 10.17. dowel 9.289. go-wel 10.148. here-beynge 14.141. here-wel 10.146. lach-draweres 8.287, 9.192. land-tilynge 8.140. nyghtcomere 19.144. pykeharneys 22.263. Rome-rennare 4.125. sle-nat 7.224. spille-loue 21.342. swere-nat 7.216. tale-tellare 22.300. worch-wel 10.147. world-ryche 16.16. wryng-lawe 4.31.
C corse-men 6.65. ers-wynnynge 6.305. queynte-comune 4.161. spille-tyme 5.28.
B bely-ioye 7.119. brewecheste 16.43. God-man 12.115. hand-fedde 15.471. hennes-goyng 14.165. londlepere 15.213.

ii Some 150-odd words are first recorded in *PP* and some may have been introduced by Langland (88 in the core-text and 66 in the versions separately, with progressive intensification from **B** → **C**). Here the citation is given in order of date of version (the *IG* entry is in 'seniority' order). Items occurring in the core-text, which in the present case is extended to signify not parallel-lines but *repeated word-appearances*, are weakly criterial for authenticity (those in **Z** and one canonical version are in italics).

Core-text
anyenten B 17.287. avengen B 13.330. baselard A 11.214. baude A 3.45. beaupere 18.230. bedbourd A 10.203. beggerie B 7.86. betilbrowed A 5.109. bislaberen B 5.386. braggen B 13.281. braulen B 15.238. brawlere B 16.43. breedles B 14.160. brocage B 2.88. bummen A 5.137. cleramatyn Z 7.308. clomsen B 14.51. coket Z 7.308. collateral B 14.298. copen Z 2.211. countreplede B 12.98. crem A 7.266. crymylen B 15.229. *crod* Z 7.286. curato(u)r Z 1.118. cure B Pr 88. defyen B 20.66. despeyr Z 5.144. desperacion 17.309. dya B 20.174. dowen B 15.556. dregges B 19.403. enbawmen B 17.71. enblaunchen B 15.115. entisen B 13.322. eueneforþ B 13.144. euidence 8.268. fauorable Z 3.90. festren B 17.93.

fleckede B 11.329. *forslewthen* Z 7.64. frenesie B 20.85. gendre B 16.222. glosere B 19.222. goky B 11.306. huxterie (hokkerye) A 5.141. houpen Z 7.154. hungirly A 5.108. indulgence B 7.56. iogelen B 13.233. iurdan B 13.84. lauendrye B 15.187. lollere B 15.213. macche 17.214. megre B 5.127. mercyen Z 3.20. motyf B 10.115. moustre B 13.362. necessarie B 20.214. nounpower B 17.312. ouertilden B 20.54. payn ('bread') B 6.150. parlen B 18.270. parroken B 15.286. penauncelees B 10.463. permutacioun A 3.237. permuten B 13.111. petit Z 8.60. pyuysche Z 7.139. poete B 10.338. portatif B 1.157. posen B 19.275. poundmele Z 2.203. radegunde B 20.83. regratour A 3.79. relyen B 20.148. riflen B 5.234. salarie B 14.142. Sapience ('Wisdom Books') Z. 8.46. †semiuief B 17.56. smolder B 17.323. thromblen A 5.200. tike B 19.37. trauersen B 12.284. vnlosen A Pr 87. vnwriten A 11.263. venymouste B 18.156. wardmote B Pr 94. (88)

Versions separately

Z bewsoun 3.158. clumse 7.54. mytygacion 5.141. morgagen 3.96. sowsen 2.100. stemen 6.75. (6)

A axesse 5.203. begynnere 10.53. cheuisshen 10.73. moneylees 8.129. perimansie A 11.161. tercian 12.85. (6)

B baddenesse 12.48. bidroppen 13.321. ewage 2.14. †festu 10.277. fullen 15.452. kaylewey 16.69. meteȝuere 15.147. pallen 16.51. peren 15.417. poesie B 18.410. vnmesurable 15.71. (11)

C angryliche 16.113. antecedent 3.353. arbitrere 6.381. bytrauaylen 8.242. bollare 9.194. cheken 20.285. coken 15.60. compacience 15.89. contrerollor 11.302. coterel 9.97. decretistre 15.86. dentiesliche 8.323. desauowen 3.319. drosenes 8.193. encloyen 20.294. enspiren 16.242. enterely 10.190. fallas 11.20. fisken 9.153. hastite 17.118. indepartable 18.27. insolible 16.229. kelen 21.281. lykyngliche 19.243. loupe 20.286. nyppen 6.104. outrydere 4.116. ouermore 9.157. papelote 9.75. †peccunie 3.389. predestinaeten 11.207. prescite 11.208. pue 6.144. samrede 8.310. seneschal Pr.93. sylen 20.341. spiek 12.182. strikare 9.159. to-quaschen 20.63. to-reuen 3.202. troylen 20.319. vnder-shoren 18.47. wold 2.95 (43)

C. METRICAL ASPECTS

Selected examples of two *structural* and four *textural* features potentially criterial for authenticity are illustrated below. Their presence in the core-text (here taken to include XXI–XXII / XIX–XX) points to unity of authorship of the four versions; their rise in density over the course of revision supports the sequence Z > A > B > C. Of the two longer versions, which alone admit of extended comparison, C shows a marked increase in the abundance of all these features over B.

STRUCTURAL

§ 4. i. The *muted stave*, which enlarges the metrical possibilities by deferring natural sentence-stress to a following lexical word, can occur in positions 2 and 3 in the a-half and in position 1 in the b-half. Mute staves are not themselves criterial, but muting of the key-stave (usually a non-lexical word), when followed by a secondary stave-sound in both lifts of the b-half, makes possible Langland's 'transitional' or 'T'-type line (which is illustrated at IV §§ 41–2), and this is apparently unique. 'Compensated' mute staves form a small group of some two dozen (10 in the core-text, 16 in the versions) that may also be potentially criterial (see below). 'Normal' key-stave muting in Type I does not generate a separate line-type, and so might perhaps be better interpreted as a syntactically-determined 'variation' than as a metrical 'variant'. But in that it retains half of a full stave (the alliteration), while relinquishing the other half (stress) to a following (blank) lift, it cannot simply be called 'non-structural', and is far more than merely 'textural'. Like its much rarer mirror-image, the full-stave grammatical lexeme, it extends the alliterative writer's capacity to 'versify fair'. In the list below, examples involving prefixes in (mainly Romance-derived) words with variable stress (such as *receyue* B 17.178) are largely omitted as uncertain, except for those always stressed on the same syllable (like *entisen*). Those from revised lines are marked '±'; ambiguous cases (which are not counted in the totals) '?'; macaronics 'm'; and lines with a 'compensatory' stave in final position 'c'. *Italics* are used where muting occurs in the (roughly two dozen) lexical words used as mute staves: nouns, adjectives, verbs and adverbs (but excluding titles, modal verbs, the verbs *be*, *have* and auxiliary *do*, and conjunctive adverbs). Emended lines are given in brackets. There are some 410 mute key-staves in all (i.e. about 2.15% of the entire total of key-staves), with 195 in the core-text and 215 in the versions severally (an increase of 18 from B to C).

Core-text
29 in ZABC (keyed to C): Pr 24. I 54. II 141. 209. III 36. 164. 226? IV 21. 57. 93. 141 (m). V 119. 131. VI 322. 437ᶜ. 439. VII *56*. 167. 201. VIII 54. 105. *171*. 180. 218. 238. 270. 328. IX 1. 30. 41.
10 in ABC (keyed to C): III 51. VI 93ᶜ. 210. 394. X 30. 74. 120. XI 1. 90. 136. 205?

10 in **ZAB** (keyed to **B**): **I** 23. 131$^{\pm}$. 146. **II** *120*. **IV** 28. *194.* **V** 25. **VI** 88. 166^{C}. *174.*

7 in **AB** (keyed to **B**): **Pr** 62. **I** 146. **III** *221*. 227. **V** 109. 325. **X** 107.

4 in **ZA** (keyed to **A**): **II** 30. 71. **IV** 67. **VIII** 17.

135 in **BC** (keyed to **C**): **Pr** 85. 180. **II** 36$^{\pm}$. 66$^{\pm}$. 82. 95. **III** 76. 434. **IV** *160*. **V** 171 (m). **VI** 37. 79. 125. 184. 205? 265. 284 (? or IIa). 342. **VII** 4. 20$^{\pm}$. 25. *45*. [54]. 86. 90. 99. ?102. *286* (cf. A VI.122). **VIII** 9. **X** 309^{C}. **XI** *56*. *65*. 192. ?239. 244. **XII** 54. 77. 113. 124. 145. **XIII** 113. 124. 136. 212. 226. **XIV** *59*. 76. 105. 106. 111. 146. 150. **XV** 17. 56 (m). 69. *103*. 106. 195 (m). 205^{C}. 230. 265. 296. 301. **XVI** 7. 10 (?or IIa). 64. 128. 129. 155. 169. 203 (m). 206. 207. 216. 274. 350. **XVII** 105. 113. 195. 269. 320 (m). **XVIII** 34 (m)^{C}. 40 (m). 116 (m). 133. 134^{C}. 289. 291. **XIX** 144. 160. 170. 229. 249. 260. 261^{C}. 262. 264. 269. 271. 272. 273. 299 (? or IIa). **XX** 22 (m). 114, 115 (m). 136. 199. 200. 215. 219. 238. 248. 264. 301. ?431. 437. 458. 467 (m). **XXI** 24. *30*. 66. 82. *104*. 145. 167. 190. 193. 211. (m). 218. 227. 239. 329^{C}. 334. 373. 397. **XXII** 7. 94. 96. 128. 136^{C} (?or IIa). *143*. 241. 252. 267. 291. 333. 368.

Versions Separately

C (105) **I** 18. 149. **II** 90. 91. 124. **III** 88. 108? 131. *144*. 236. 245. 292. 300. *411*. **IV** 26. *47*. 52. 53. 121. 154. **V** 19. 27 (possibly IIa). 32. 70^{C}. 71. 101^{C}. 198^{C}. **VI** 16. 35. 48. 59. 100. 105. 115 (?or IIa). 169. 193. 257 (m). 300. 303. **VIII** 57. 69. **IX** 17. 31. 32. 38^{C}. 89. 115. 128. 132. 135. 180. 196 (or IIa). 250. 258. 262. **X** 41^{C}. 95 (m). 181. 183. 208. 259 (or IIa). **XI** 13. 151. 238. 282. **XII** 6. 22. 31. 188. 208. 234. **XIII** 33. 83. **XIV** 180. **XV** 25. 81. 114^{C}. 135^{C}. 141. 237. 264. **XVI** 20. 34^{C}. 153. 180 (m). **XVII** 2. 3. 29. 32. 58. 146. 194. **XVIII** 2. 17. 25. 70. 75 (or IIa). 141. *179*. 190. 260. **XIX** 27. 54. 82. 107. 234. 247. **XX** 109. 161. 356. 436.

B (89) **Pr** 180. [206]. **I** 131 (?IIa). 132. **II** 107 (? or IIa). **III** 235. 243^{C}. 254. **IV** 34. 120 (m). **V** 86. 150. 280. *366*. [378]. 624. 639. **VI** 47. 58. **VII** 55. 81. 126^{C}. **IX** 36. 114. **X** 151. 218. 251. 269^{C}. 277^{C}. 345. 351 (?or IIIa). 388. 395. 428^{C}. 447. *454*. **XI** 65. 66. ?74. 77. *94*. 168. *309*^{C}. *313*. 354. 387. **XII** *64*. 90. 91. 171. 235. 289. **XIII** [63]. 65. 193. 198 (m). 211. 230^{C}. 268. 271. 296. [300]. 349. **XIV** 15. 25. 26. 27. 38. 85. 124. 319. **XV** 35. 70. [126]^{C}. 140. 283. 288. 322. 405. 449^{C}. 532. **XVI** 120. 138. 147. 162. 170. 187. 200. 203. 207. 216. **XVII** [38]. 54. 77^{C}. 98 (?or IIa). 160.

A (9) **III** ?51. 87. 243. **IX** 63. **X** 34. 57. **XI** 221. 244. **XII** 56–7 (m).

Z (12) **Pr** 17. 145. **II** 2. 97. **III** 30. **IV** 159. **VII** 152. 163. 231. 260. 261. 266.

ii The *Transitional* or 'T'-type line arises in circumstances where the key-stave is mute and the immediately following lift compensates with a new stave sound that is repeated in the last lift, giving the scansion *aa / [a]bb* (see Schmidt 1987^2:38–9). As this feature is apparently not found outside Langland, it may be regarded as criterial (*Introduction* IV §§ 42, 48).

TEXTURAL

§ 5. i The 'textural' features of rhyme, pararhyme, running and translinear alliteration are illustrated in all versions. When compared extensively in **B** and **C**, which are of similar length, they too show a steady increase in density from **B** > **C**.

ii *Rhyme* is in alliterative verse (which Langland called *ryme* at IX 82) a decorative element (*ornatus*), and is common as a device for rhetorical heightening. There are over 90 examples, 44 in the core-text and about another 49 in the versions severally (increasing from 18 in **B** to 35 in **C**).[5] Rhyme approaches being criterial especially under (b), where the **A** and **Z** examples are both on *tolde*.

(a) *End-rhyme*: **ABC** VIII 343/4. **ZAB** I 198/9. V 57/8. **BC** IV 65/6. XI 183/4. XIII 156/7. XV 122/3. XX 388/9. XXI 150/1. **C** II 246/7. III 351/2. VII 209/10. IX 92/3. XI 110/111, 167/8. XVIII 144/5. XX 287/8. **B** II 100/01. XI 344/5. XIII 199/200. 272/3. XVII 336/7. XVIII 61/2, 368/9. **A** III 245/6. **Z** II 17/18. ?VI 80/1. VII 258/9. 262/3. 324/5

(b) *Identical end-rhyme*: **ABC** VII 234/5. **BC** XVI 265/6. XXII 25/6. 49/50. XXII 269/70. 359/60. **AB** I 146/7. **C** II 75–6. 133/4. III 470/1. VI 304/5. XI 297/8. XIV 61/2. XV 126/7. 210/11. XVI 316/7. XVII 39/40. 150/1. XVIII 88/9 (phrasal). 237/8. **B** Pr 127/8. VII 36/7. X 302/3. XII 288/9. **A** V 9/10. **Z** IV 49/50.

(c) *Internal*: **ZABC** I 161. II 209. VIII 42. 291. 330. **ABC** III 280. VIII 344. **ZAB** VI 15. **BC** XII 85. XIII 165. XIV 84. XVII 222. XX 173. XXI 269. XXII 15, 55, 322, 373. **AB** VI 253. **ZA** VII 2. 176. **C** III 274. 281. V 16a/17a. 209/10 (running). VI 193. 289. VII 208. X 61/2/3 (running). 303. XII 78. 188. XIII 89/90 (running). XVI 33. **B** I 33. 115. III 244–5 (running). 265. XI 363 (double). XII 257. XIV 185. XVI 116. **A** V 52. 129/30 (running). VII 6. X 147. XI 185. 245. **Z** IV 131. ('*Leonine*'type): **BC** XVIII 292. XIX 56. XX 199. 225. 258. XXI 325. XXII 190. **C** III 277. VI 100 (cf. *WW* 43).

(d) '*Trailing*' (unusual type rhyming translinearly): **ZABC** IV 108/9. **C** X 228/9. XVI 272/3.

§ 6. iii *Pararhyme*, lexical within the half-line and morphemic after the caesura, is to be expected as perhaps an accidental feature of alliterative style (e.g. in formulaic lines like X 210 / XI 293). But the 140 whole-word cross-caesural pararhymes on full staves are frequent enough in the core-text (73) and in the versions severally (68) to qualify as potentially criterial.[6] This is particularly true of the dozen examples of clashed stresses at the caesura, including one from **Z**, which are starred, and the further dozen examples showing cross-linear or running pararhyme listed separately[7]. The increase from 23 in **B** to 32 in **C** may be noted.

Core-text

ZABC I 87. II 196. 228. III 23. 29. 166.* IV 89. 178. V 133. VII 186. IX 64 (with contracted C form). **ABC** I 49. III 126. VII 220. 288. X 64. 151. XI 128. **ZAB** II 210. IV 30. V 33. 380. VI 129. VII 62. **BC** Pr 169. 187. 218. IV 133. V 142. VI 55. VII 38. 135. 183. XII 44.* 82. XIII 105. 181. 207. 239. XIV 119. XV 165. 229. 244. XVI 72. 103. 137. 316. XVIII 177. XIX 87. 209. XX 169. 171. 200. 206. 233. 237. 301. 438.* XXI 418. 483. **AB** I.144.* III 278.* V 6. 93. VI 297. VIII 94. IX 50. 137. 178. **ZA** II 22. IV 96. VII 131. 261. *Cross-linear pararhyme*: **ABC** I 171/2. X 46/7. **BC** XII 44/5. XVI 348/9. XVII 200/01. XX 169.

Versions Separately

C Pr 8. I 46.* III 95. 281. 301.* 395. IV 37. 49. VI 23. 178. IX 110.* X 39. 210. XI 152. 293. XII 168. XIII 65. 82. 150. 167. XIV 8. 9. 12. XVII 41. 139. XVIII 160. 198. XIX 76. 102. XX 63.* 98. 318. **B** V 257. 487. VII 76. X 407. 437. XI 162. 176. 321. 358. 398. XIII 344. 365.* XIV 47. 186. XV 204. 353. XVI 8. 59. 156.* 233. XVII 76. 94.* XVIII 31. **A** IV 143. IX 96. X 78. 109. 142.177. XI 115. 185. XII 6. 23. **Z** Pr 36.* II 60. III 175. *Cross-linear pararhyme*: **C** IV 27/8. 162/3. V 51/2. VII 208/9. X 22/3. XVII 158/9. **B** XI 99/100. XIII 267/8. XVII 71/2.

§ 7. iv. *Running alliteration*[7] is not a strictly criterial metrical feature, as it is found in other alliterative poems; but it is worth describing here as a marked rhetorical element in **L**'s style. The symbol '-' in core-text entries means that one line is missing or another intervenes (but single intervening *Latin* lines are ignored in counting); '+' that an extra same-stave line appears in the // of the keyed item; '>' = consecutive running alliteration in the immediate version-category (when no number follows '>', the entry denoted is in another category). The number of instances in each category is in brackets at the end of each group. There are 356 examples in the core-text and 345 examples in the versions separately. These cover respectively totals of 800 and 727 lines, or about 8% of the entire text. Again there is an increase from about 130 instances in **B** to 180 in **C**.

Core-text

(a) *2-line runs*

ZABC Pr 41–2. 225–6. I 41–2. 47–8. 68–9. 88–90 (-Z: *inserted unique line*). 171–2 (-Z). II 71–2. 118–19. 125–6. 177–8. 193–4. 202–4. 219–20. 225–6. III 6–7. 18–9. 152–3. 178–9. 214–15. 218–19. 229–30. 258–9. IV 1–2 > 3–4. 78–9. 88–9. 133–4. 144–5 > 146–7 (+1 **B**). 179–80. V 117–18. 134–5 (-A; see *TN*). 140–1. VI 437–8 > 439–40. VII 56–7. 67–8. 182–3 > 184–6 (+C). 197–8 >199–200. 218–19. 222–3. VIII 2–3. 15–16 (+ZA). 31–2. 58–9. 100–01. 106–7. 111–12. 118–19. 142–3. 179–80. 269–70. 273–4. IX 1–2. 11–12. 168–9. 171–2. (60)
ABC Pr 60–1. 163–4. III 37–8. 120–1. 149–51. 428–9. V 117–18. VI 92–3. 210–11. 228–9. 370–1. VIII 294–5. IX 185–6. 350–1. X 30–1. 61–2. 64–5. 75–6. 81–2. 102–3. 138–9. 302–3. XI 15–16. 49–50. 124–5. 222–4 (+ A). 299–300 (+ **B**). (27)
ZAB I 107–8. [111–12]. II 107–8. 135–6. V 5–6. 24–5. 476–7. VI 128–9. 218–19. 322–3. VII 42–3. 89–90. (11)
ZA IV 141–2. V 12–13. VII 131–2. 177–8. (4)
AB I 193–4 > 195–6. III 81–2. 220–1. 246–7 (+ A). V 78–9. 81–2. 84–6 (+ **B**). 104–5. 225–6. VI 245–6. VII 124–5. 127–8 > (A). X 108–9. 115–16. 129–30. 163–4. 346–7. 363–4 >. (19)
BC Pr 93–4. 135–6. 138–9. 167–8. I 147–8. II 13–14 (+ **B**). 42–3. 51–2. 67–8. 82–3 (+ **B**). III 57–8. 61–2. 71–2. 195–6. 487–8. IV 21–2. 65–6. 71–2. VI 70–1. 236–7. 245–6. 248–9. 264–5. 296–7. 396–7. VII 7–8. 18–19. 47–8. 115–16. 128–9. 137–8. VIII 351–2. X 184–5. 289–90. XI 55–6. 76–8. 148–9 (+ **B**). 166–7. 177–8. 185–6 (+ **B**). 249–50. XII 7–8 (+ **B**). 23–4 (+ **B**). 44–5. 49–50. 56–7. 75–6. 79–80. 114–5. 132–3. XIII 119–20. 157–8. 161–2. 213–14. 221–2. 242–3. XIV 23–4>. 35–6. 47–8. 61–2. 114–15. 117–18. 137–8. 159–60. 170–1. 191–2. 207–8. XV 3–4. 11–13>. 33–4. 112–13. 159–60. 239–40 > 241–2. 266–7. [284–5]. 296–7. XVI 4–5>. 45–6. 51–2. 61–2. 88–9. 100–01 > 102–3. 106–7. 125–6. 200–01. 207–8. 212–13. 216–17. 232–3. 251–2. 274–5. 315–16. 344–5. 353–4. 358–60. XVII 200–01. 232–3. 304–5. XVIII 133–4 >. 152–3. 277–8. 285–6. XIX 5–6. 10–11. 32–3. 56–7. 99–100. 117–18. 133–4. 152–3. 161–2. 188–9. 210–11. 255–6. 277–8. 304–5. 326–7. 332–3. XX 29–30. 69–70. 74–5. 116–17. 130–1. 160–1. 227–8. 236–7. 247–8.

276–7. 295–6 (+**B**). 299–300. 322–3. 374–5. 397–8 > 399–400 (+**B**). 418–19. 437–8. 448–9. 458–9. **XXI** 19–20. 46–7. 62–3. 111–12. 126–7. 133–4. 179–80. 185–6. 195–6. 200–01. 237–8. 341–2. 356–7. 363–4. 411–12. 419–20. 429–30. 441–2. 446–7. **XXII** 9–10. 32–3. 42–3 > 44–5. 50–1. 67–8. 129–30. 140–1. 144–5. 150–1. 171–2. 185–6. 193–4. 203–4. 206–7. 218–19. 226–7. 236–7 > 238–9. 242–3. 245–6. 301–2. 304–5. 315–16. 320–1. 329–30. 373–4 >. (185)

(b) *3-line runs*

ZABC I 186–8 (2 in **ZAB**). **II** 202–4. **III** 149–51.

ABC III 310–12 (-**B**). **VI** 418. **IX** 4–6. 295–7. 324–5. **X** 150–2 (+ **A**). **XI** 132–4. 222–4 (+**A**).

ZAB II 168–70.

ZA II 48–50.

AB VIII 21–3. 33–4. **IX** 55–7 (-**A**).

BC Pr 132–4. 199–201. **II** 94–6. **VI** 36–8 (-**B**). 280–2. **VII** 1–3. **IX** 278–80 (-**B**). **X** 66–8 (-**B**). **XI** 76–8 (-**B**). 132–4 (+**B**). **XII** 65–7. **XIV** 52–4. **XV** 11–13 (-**B**). 47–9. 88–9. **XVI** 137–9. 164–6 (+**B**). 192–4 (-**B**). 358–60. **XVII** 217–19. **XIX** 158–60. **XX** 162–4. 208–10. 236–8. 239–41. 347–9. 359–61. 368–70 (-**B**). 420–2 (-**B**). 443–5. **XXI** 41–3. 415–17. 468–70. **XXII** 72–4. 120–22. 212–14. 361–3. 375–7. (54)

(c) *4-line runs*

ZABC Pr 79–82. **ZAB IV** 67–70. **AB X** 186–9 (-**A**).

BC Pr 141–4. **XXI** 12–15. (5)

(d) *5-line runs*

BC XXI 26–30. 347–51. (2)

Versions Separately

(a) *2-line runs*

C Pr 88–9. 102–3. 138–9. 147–8. 212–13. **I** 97–8. 107–8. > 109–10. 118–19. 203–4. **II** 13–14. 39–40. 48–9. 75–6. 122–3. 130–1. 133–4. 185–6. **III** 141–2. 243–4. 247–8. 289–90. 297–8. 300–01. 338–9. 348–9. 363–4. 371–2. 395–6 > 397–8. **IV** 21–2. 32–3. 52–3. 55–6. 98–9. **V** 3–4. 47–8. 109–10. 162–3. **VI** 16–17. 44–5. 64–5. 119–20. 170–1. 187–8. 194–5. 313–14. 340–1. 432–3. **VII** 33–4. 73–4. 173–4. 254–5. **VIII** 22–4. 46–7. 247–8. **IX** 18–19. 42–3. 58–9. 81–2. 103–4. 120–1. 140–1. 155–6. 187–8 (*see* **ABC** 185–6). 197–8. 225–6. 250–1. 256–7. 278–80. **X** 25–6. 41–2. 99–100. 102–3. 173–4. 178–9. 208–9. 251–2. 254–5. **XI** 30–1. 70–1. 73–4. 93–4. 100–01. 144–5. 207–8. 219–20. 233–4. 262–3. **XII** 169–70. 181–2. 213–14. 221–2. 239–40. **XIII** 52–3. 93–4. 96–7. 98–9 > 99–100. 170–1. 173–4. 182–3. > 184–5. 195–6. 208–9. **XIV** > 25–6. 72–3. 176–7. **XV** 8–9 >14–15. 139–40. 174–5 > 176–7. 183–4. 249–50. 280–1. **XVI** 176–7. 247–8. 280–1. 305–6. **XVII** 3–4. 42–3. 58–9. 63–4. 84–5. 126–7. 130–1. 143–4. 150–1. 157–8. 183–4. 288–9. **XVIII** 15–16. 54–5. 94–5. 183–4. 200–01. 224–5. 231–2. 249–50. **XIX** 94–5. 147–8. 275–6. **XX** 171–2. 189–90. 306–7. 316–17. 334–5. 338–9. 351–2. 404–5. (151)

B Pr 122–3. 143–4. 159–60. **II** 29–30 > 31–2. 56–7. **IV** 22–3. **V** 128–9. 137–8. 270–1. 490–1. **VI** 149–50. 161–2. 193–4. 325–6. **VII** 71–2. 79–80. **IX** 46–7. 108–9 > 110–11. 113–14. **X** 43–4. 95–6. 320–1. 354–5. 395–6. 435–6. 466–7. **XI** 77–8. 160–1. 178–9. 192–3. 195–6. 215–16. 356–7. 390–1. 419–20. **XII** 15–16. 35–6. 43–4. 77–8. 92–3. 96–7. 228–9. 246–7. **XIII** 16–17. 19–20. 55–6. 85–6. 115–16. 133–4. 142–3. 165–6. 172–3. 216–17. 246–7. 264–5. 287–8. 399–400. 415–16. **XIV** 11–12. 16–17. 35–6. 47–8. 136–7. 179–80. **XV** 22–3. 121–2. 145–6. 150–1. 164–5. 178–9. 197–8. 224–5. 257–8. 260–1. 266–7. 271–2. 297–8. 308–9. 332–3. 346–7. 353–4 > 355–6. 383–4. 388–9. 390–1. 393–4. 432–3. 465–6. 482–3. **XVI** 23–4. 37–8. 46–7. 64–5. 101–2. 141–3. 179–80. 234–5. 241–2. 245–6. **XVII** 44–5. 105–6. 119–20. 134–5. 137–8. 160–1. **XVIII** 253–4. 282–3. 305–6. 328–9. 342–3. (112)

A II 51–2. **V** 149–50. **X** 55–6. 102–3. 105–6. 123–4. 155–6. 163–4. **XI** 63–4. 229–30. 259–60. 268–9 > 270–1. **XII** 58–9. 70–1. (15)

Z I 64–5.–**II** 16–17. 41–2. 163–4. 169–70. **III** 95–6. 153–4. 163–4. **IV** 156–7. **V** 74–5. **VII** 262–3. 272–3. **VIII** 68–9. (13)

(b) *3-line runs*

C III 243–5. 315–17. **VI** 36–8. 106–8. 305–7. **IX** 93–5. 160–2. **X** 158–60. **XI** 140–2. **XII** 27–9. **XIII** 1–3. 218–20 >· **XIV** 40–2. **XV** 27–9. 230–2. 234–6. **XVI** 366–8. **XVIII** 216–18. **XX** 326–8. (19).

B Pr 203–5. **V** 252–4. **VI** 195–7. **IX** 95–7. **X** 365–7. 426–8. **XII** 81–3. 85–6. 126–8. **XIII** 22–4. **XV** 4–6. 462–4. (12).

A X 94–6. 141–3. **XII** 66–8. (3)

Z III 158–60. **V** 34–6. (2)

(c) *4-line runs*

C V 60–3. **XVIII** 191–4. **XIX** 42–5. (3)

B XVI 205–8. (1)

A X 24~7. **XI** 275~8. (2)
Z IV 129~32. (1)
d) *5-line runs*
C V 41~5. 177~81. 183~4. 193~4. **XVII** 153~9. **XVIII** 63~7. 216~20. **XIX** 130~4 (8)
B XIV 191~5. (1)
(e) *6-line runs*
B XI 218~23. (1)

§ 8. v. *Translinear Alliteration*[8] (~) occurs when the last lift of a line (blank except when within a Type Ib), which may be called the 'trigger-stave', alliterates with the first lift of the next line, the 'target-stave'. There are nearly 600 instances, some 285 in the core-text and 305 in the versions severally, including over 30 in which the translineation continues for a second and half a dozen where it continues for a third line (this represents, counting two lines for each translineation, about 6% of the entire text). A very striking variety of this difficult alliterative *ornatus* is the 'homolexical translinear' in which the trigger and target staves are the same word (marked here by '*sw*').[9] By contrast with the other *ornatūs* discussed, there is no increase in use of translineation from **B → C**. In the following list '>' = consecutive translineation; linked consecutive translineations are starred; translineations joined directly to running alliteration are underlined. As in § 7 above, intervening Latin lines are ignored, and totals of translinears in group-categories are given in brackets. The probable number is undercounted, since it omits lines where all alliterations are on metrical allophones.

Core-text
ZABC I 3~4. 15~16. 90~1. **II** 23~4. 114~15. 137~8. 159~60. 172~3. **206~7~8~9. III** 2~3 *sw*. 36~7. 184~5. 220~1. 231~2. **IV** 27~8. **V** 114~15 (-B). 119~20 > 121~2. **VI** 16~17. **VII** 60~1. 63~4. 162~3 > 164~5. 180~1. 199~200. 224~5. 228~9. *264~5~6. **VIII** 30~1. 103~4. 119~20. 156~7. *161~2~3. 167~8. 227~8. 293~4. 312~13. 318~19. 325~6. **IX** 62~3 *sw*. (40)
ZAB I 27~8. 50~1. 90~1. **III** 23~4. 105~6. 189~90. **IV** [43~4] *sw*. 51~2. 187 *sw*. **V** 72~3. **VI** 131~2. 219~20. *241~2~3 (-ZA). [285~6]. **VII** 4~5. 10~11. 22~3. 100~01. (16)
ABC Pr 67~8. 71~2. 78~9. 159~60. **III** 115~16. 121~2. 267~8. 438~9. **IV** 4~5. **VI** 388~9. 399~400. **VIII** 180~1. **IX** 328~9. **X** 8~9. 21~1. 33~4. 35~6 *sw*. *45~6~7. 85~6. **XI** 32~3. 85~6. 134~5. (22)
ZA I 31~2. **II** 32~3. **VII** 128~9. 239~40. 287~8. (5)
AB II 209~10. **III** 44~5. 69~70. 219~20. 255~6. 278~9. **V** 108~9. 461~2. **VI** 54~5. 99~100. 276~7. 461~2. **VII** 285~6. **VIII** 46~7. 51~2. 97~8. **X** 66~7. 95~6. 125~6. 132~3. 140~1. *228~9~30. *272~3~[4]. 350~1. 362~3. (25)
BC Pr 92~3. 161~2. 168~9. 181~2. **I** 130~1. **III** 426~7. 471~2. **VI** 86~7. 161~2. 178~9. 416~17. **VII** 18~19. 47~8. 104~5. *122~3~4. 134~5 > 136~7. **VIII** *45~6~7 (-B). **IX** 297~8. 318~19. **X** 15~16. **XI** 14~15. 59~60. 64~5. 164~5. 243~4. 284~5 *sw*. **XII** 19~20. 45~6. 57~8. 82~3. *146~7~8. 164~5. **XIII** 117~18. 125~6. 137~8. 144~5. 165~6. 199~200. 212~13. 220~1. 223~4. 233~4. **XIV** 64~5. 115~16. 141~2. 152~3. 194~5. 209~10. **XV** 70~1. 75~6. 106~7. 168~9. 209~10. 229~30. 262~3. **XVI** 15~16. 42~3. 47~8 *sw*. 96~7. 131~2. 166~7. 169~70. 196~7. 206~7. 208~9. 254~5. 308~9. 322~3. 348~9. **XVII** 199~200. *225~6~7. 299~300. **XVIII** 37~8. 40~1. 114~15. 124~5. 275~6. **XIX** 15~16. 32~3. 51~2. 63~4. 98~9. *150~51~52 (-B). 167~8. 177~8. 184~5. 187~8. 202~3. 209~10. 254~5 *sw*. 260~1. **279~80~81~82. 294~5. 321~2. 324~5. **XX** 7~8. 14~15. 18~19. 21~2. 27~8. 33~4. 119~20. 129~30. 146~7. 164~5. 167~8. 221~2. 243~4. 254~5. 268~9. 279~80. 302~3. 403~4 *sw*. 413~14. 436~7. **XXI** 25~6. 57~8. 59~60. 65~6. 77~8. *85~6~7. 92~3 *sw*. 130~1. 138~9. 141~2. 154~5. 159~60. 180~1. 187~8. 191~2. 213~14. 232~3. 241~2. 248~9. 284~5. 289~90. 334~5. 365~6. 369~70. 390~1 > 392~3. 417~18. 429~30. 440~1. ?445~46~47. **XXII** 5~6. 14~15. 36~7. 49~50. 53~4. 90~1. 96~7. 106~7. 110~11. 131~2. 160~1. 168~9. 179~80. **187~88~89*sw*. ~90. 200~01. 204~05. 214~15. 225~6. 234~5. 244~5. 249~50. 255~6. 274~5. 300~01. 310~11. 331~2. 364~5. 370~1. 373~4. (175)

Versions Separately
C I 70~1. **II** 182~3. **III** 10~11. 43~4. 53~4. 74~5. 77~8. 239~40. 248~9. 290~1. 306~7. *320~1 > 321~2. 358~9. 362~3. 370~1. 373~4. 376~7. **IV** 50~1. **V** *1~2~3. 27~8. 47~8. 59~60. 77~8. 90~1. 114~15. 158~9. **VI** 13~14 *sw*. *17~18~19. 62~3 *sw*. 65~6. 75~6. 91~2. 111~12. *116~17~18. 124~5. 142~3. 188~9. 244~5 *sw*. 258~9. **VII** 22~3. 208~9. 244~5. **VIII** *221~2~3. 275~6. **IX** 44~5. 79~80. 90~1. 110~11. 196~7. 203~4. **X** 22~3. 95~6. 178~9. 241~2 > 243~4. 261~2. 265~6. 269~70. **XI** 82~3. 94~5. *146~7~8. 154~5. 226~7 (homophonic pun). 274~5. 298~9. 301~02. **XII** 26~7. 92~3. 96~7. 109~10. 117~18. 151~2. 163~4. *180~81~82. 229~30. **XIII** 16~17 (m). 33~4. 38~9. 64~5. 66~7. 73~4. 79~80. *89~90~91. 185~6. 216~17. 231~2. **XIV** 3~4. 26~7. 198~9 *sw*. **XV** 19~20. 43~4. 149~50. 160~1. **167~68~69 >170~1. 179~80. 222~3. 259~60. **XVI** 243~4 *sw*. 262~3. **XVII** 1~2. 123~4. 142~3. 159~60. 165~6. 169~70. 173~4 *sw*.

243~4. 274~5. 299~300. **XVIII** 2~3. *9~10~11 *sw.* *39~40~41. 48~9. 81~2. *91~2~3. *96~7~8. 153~4. 216~17. 94~5. 108~9. **XX** 7~8. 109~10. 281~2. 316~17. *319~20~21. 354~5. 357~8. 405~6. (130)

B Pr 89~90. 127~8. *210~11~12. 221~2. **I** 121~2 ~[3]. 150~1. 154~5. **II** 26~7. 32~3 >34~5. 36~7. 65~6. **III** 238~9. <u>255~6</u>. 297~8 *sw.* **IV** 171~2. 187~8 *sw.* **V** 59~60. 89~90. 141~2 *sw.* > 143~4. 161~2. <u>248~9</u>. 254~5. <u>280~1</u> > 282~3. 413~14. 486~7. **VII** 74~5. 122~3. **VIII** <u>61~2</u>. <u>66~7</u>. **IX** 57~8. 89~90. 113~14. **X** 23~4. 38~9~40. 93~4. 204~5. 321~2. 341~2. 370~1. 394~5. 430~1. 467~8. **XI** 49~50. <u>76~7</u>. 99~100. 165~6. 169~70. 262~3 > 264~5. 274~5. 277~8. 280~1. 284~5. 299~300. 319~20. **XII** 33~4. 97~8. 165~6 *sw.* 168~9 *sw.* 192~3. 235~6. 255~6. 259~60. **XIII** 86~7. 109~10. 123~4. 128~9 *sw.* 134~5. 143~4. 150~1. 186~7. 273~4 > 275~ 6~7. 284~5. 407~8. **XIV** 32~3. 43~4. 48~9. 77~8. <u>92~3</u>. 98~9. 148~9. 189~90. 195~6. 237~8. <u>266~7</u>. 274~5 *sw.* 304~5. 314~15. *322~3*sw*~4. 327~8. **XV** 7~8 > **9~10~11~12. *66~7~8. 131~2. 146~7. 148~9 *sw.* <u>163~4</u>. 184~5. *213~14~15. 219~20. 328~9. 341~2 > 343~4 *sw.* 347~8. 360~1. 392~3. 397~8. 402~3. 461~2. 581~2. **XVI** 12~13 *sw.* 50~1. *58~9~60. 70~1. 104~5. 109~10. <u>140~1</u>. 185~6. 200~01. 204~5. 219~20~21. **XVII** 34~5. 64~5. 71~2. 105~6. 136~7.157~8. 161~2. 172~3. 307~8. **XVIII** 95~6. 183~4. 280~1. 287~8. 299~300. 339~40. [343~4]. 356~7. (140)

A II 37~8. 47~8. 60~1. 65~6. **III** *57~8~9. 148~9. 252~3. **IV** 17~18. **IX** 94~5. **X** 15~16. 52~3 *sw.* *70~1~2. *82~3~4. 118~19. 140~1. 143~4. 207~8. **XI** 101~2. 106~7. 145~6. 188~9. 248~9. <u>258~9</u>. **XII** 10~11. <u>69~70</u>. (25)

Z I 18~19. **III** 149~50. **IV** 125~6 *sw.* **V** 44~5. 95~6. **VI** 73~4. **VII** 53~4. 107~8. **VIII** 89~90. (9)

§ 9. vi. *Monolexical b-verses*, in which a single or compound word contains the half-line's two lifts with no intervening dip, have been proposed as criterial at *Intro.* IV § 38 and the dozen examples are now listed here. Whereas common rhythmical patterns in the b-half are / xx / x (Pr 1) and (x) / x / x (Pr 6), this type scans xx // x (as at Pr 10), corresponding to OE Type C, but with an extra syllable to provide the strong dip required by Duggan's Metrical Rule V (1990:159), which **L** apparently observes. This rhythmical variety is instanced in compound-lift b-verses like *or eny blóed shédynge* at XV 157, which is paralleled in the commoner monolexical half-line with intervening dip, as in *as for his kýnneswómman* II 146, *and in cóueytíse* III 201, *þat ben cátecúmelynges* B XI 77, *aren ful wóluelíche* B XV 116. But it finds its most distinctive form in the dozen 'zero-dip' monolexicals and its true counterpart in the very rare monolexicals sometimes found in the a-half, as in *cónféssioun* XXI 351; *liflóde* B XIX 240 (revised // C); and possibly *pálmére* VII 179 // (unless *l* is syllabicised). Instanced in both core-text and all versions severally, it is a strongly criterial feature.

Core-text AC?ZB *sepúlcre* VII 170. **BC** *bíhéstes* XX 320. *desérued* IV 172. *déuýsed* XXI 331. *émcrístene* 19.228. *cóntrícioun* XXI 350. *?Iústicie* XXI 400.
Versions Separately B *vitáilles* V 437. *decéites* XII 130. **A** *begýnnére* X 53. **Z** *déstréres* II 146

§ 10. vii. *Wrenched Stresses* resemble the monolexicals, which distort stress by promoting the word's unstressed syllable to full-stress status, sometimes with retraction of the common stress-position. True wrenching of stress for metrical reasons must be carefully distinguished from 'normal' variation of stress in words with an unfixed stress-pattern (*réligious*; *dobét*). Examples are very conservatively estimated here, and they are only doubtfully criterial.

Core-text
ZABC VII 187 *?withinne.* VIII 95 *nomíne.* IX 47 *innócent.* **ABC** VIII 79 *áscaped.*
AB V 108 *áwey.* **BC** XII 38 *neuéremore.* XVIII 37 *norischéth.* XIX 270 *innócence.*
C III 396 *wymmén.* XV 37, XVI 170 *welcómede.* XVII 288 *enemýes.* XIX 242 *wíthoute.*

By way of summary, it may be said that (together with those features described at *Intro.* IV § 48 above), T-type lines, 'compensated' mute staves, identical end-rhymes, cross-caesural clashed pararhymes, homolexical translineation and monolexical half-lines are textually criterial metrical features, whose presence in **Z** and A XII must be judged a powerful indicator of authenticity.

NOTES

1 The principles of Langland's metre, which are most reliably drawn from an analysis of the core-text, have been exemplified in *Introduction* IV, where a selection of the variant-types in the versions severally (§ 42) are listed, as well as all core-lines of authentic variant-type (§ 41) according to their core-text grouping (the remaining lines of the core-text, given entire in §§ 9–12, are of normative type). For further discussion see Schmidt 1987²:21–80, M. Smith 2008, 2009.

2 It is certain that *f* and *v* are true dialectal allophones (I 23, VII 25, 49), as are the pairs |f| and |θ| = *th, þ* in lexical words, |v| and |ð| = non-lexical *th, þ* (see B III 271, XVIII 337; B III 334). But it is uncertain whether the poet's idiolect levelled *f, v* and lexical *þ* to |v| or whether the one certain case is an instance of cognative alliteration (B V 410).

3 In stave-position at ZAB III 29, BC XX 173, B IX 55.

4 Discussion of a number of these words appears in the *Commentary* ad loc.

5 For discussion of rhymes see *Commentary* ad loc on most of these examples.

6 The proposal has a 'critically empirical' character as it is open to falsification as criterial if such clashed pararhyme is instanced in other writers.

7 See Schmidt 1987[2]: 55–8.

8 See Schmidt 1987[2]: 52–5.

9 This kind of 'translinear trigger-target identity', which again meets the requirements of strict falsifiability, is a powerful criterion for assaying authenticity in disputed passages of the canonical texts, in Z, and in *WPal*. (See *Intro.* IV § 48).

Appendix II

THE RUBRICS

Treatment of the manuscript **rubrics** in this edition has attempted to be critical instead of merely reproducing the lay-out of the copy-text, as is customary in standard editions of Chaucer and Gower, where the likelihood of their authorial origin may be no higher. At the head of each passus of text in Volume I has been placed an Englished equivalent of the numbered 'sequential' rubrics (*Passus primus* etc). The sectional or 'thematic' rubrics (*Incipit Dowel*, etc) have accordingly been consigned to the Apparatus, along with the original Latin passus-headings. This difference of treatment reflects a judgement that the sequential rubrics, whether **L**'s or a scribe's, accurately correspond to the work's internal arrangement in each of its versions. The thematic rubrics, however, could result from inferences by the archetypal scribes from their reading of the poem (this seems the case with both types of rubric below the archetypal level). There is a greater antecedent probability of authorial origin[1] for the major rubrics at beginning and end of each passus than for *ordinatio* features internal to the passus, which are clearly non-archetypal. These include the Latin headings in Skeat's C-Text (ms P) for the Deadly Sins (p. 95 etc), for Poverty (p. 287), or for Charity (p. 299, from ms M).

Z-Text

Z has no passus-heading for the Prologue but has them from I–VIII (*passus primus* >> *passus octauus*). After VIII 92 the text continues as an **A** Version in hand Q and has at the end of VIII a scribal rhyming couplet 'And þat it so mote be to God preye we alle, / To vs and to alle cristin God leue it so beffalle. Amen' and then the unique EXPLICIT VITA ET VISIO PETRI PLOWMAN, which has no parallel at any level in any of the other versions. This rubric conflates the notions of the 'Vision' of Piers Plowman and that of the 'Life' of Dowel, &c found in the A-Text; and it may be explained as reflecting the scribe's knowledge of this version and his awareness that **Z** does not deal with Dowel.

A-Text

The archetypal text (Ax) seems to have had no initial rubric; but ms R (Rawlinson Poetry 137), the most complete copy of this version (and the only one with Passus XII entire) has a heading for the Prologue: 'Hic incipit liber qui uocatur pers plowman. prologus'. MS Digby 145 (K) calls the Prologue 'Primus passus'; but the remaining mss, like those of **B** and **C**, have nothing. So it may be that this is a scribal insertion and that, while the first numbered section (in all versions) was 'Passus One', the Prologue in **L**'s own copy distinguished itself as such by having a 'zero' section-heading (contrast Chaucer's *CT* and Gower's *CA*, which have 'Prologe / Prologus' before the first section).

From Passus I–VIII, the A-Text has a numbered sequence, varyingly attested by the r^j copies though not by all the **m**-witnesses till Passus III, but still quite possibly archetypal. It runs 'Passus primus de visione' >> 'Passus octauus de visione', the last ending with a long colophon 'Explicit hic visio willelmi de Petro de Plou3man Eciam incipit vita de do wel do bet & do best secundum wit & resoun'. Four copies from both families (DVW; A) omit the first part (the explicit) and WM have 'prologus' for 'vita'. A version of this colophon, replacing 'incipit' with 'sequitur' is copied in a later hand at the end of B VII in ms C² (CUL Ll. 4.14), probably from an A-copy (the C-Text colophon has 'visio eiusdem' for 'vita' and the B-Text nothing). Ax therefore seems to have had no through-numbered passus-headings for IX–XII. The rubric in the one A-copy that does, N (NLW 733B), reads 'Passus nonus de visione et vltimus & hic desinit', an obvious scribal addition due to the fact that the exemplar was defective and the text ceases here. A X is headed 'Passus primus de dowel &c' in **r** and two **m** copies (AW), A XI 'Passus secundus de dowel &c' (*om* DVJM), and A XII 'Passus tercius de dowel' in RUJ. These would seem to have been the passus headings in the sub-archetype **r** and possibly also in **m** (no **m**-copy of XII is extant). It is likely therefore that the Ax text of Pr–XI had a zero Prologue heading; through-numbered passus-headings from I–VIII; an explicit / incipit colophon at the end of VIII; a zero-heading for A IX, which could have been accounted as the Prologue to Dowel (rather as with the main Prologue in Bx); and 'thematic' headings 'primus' and 'secundus' for A X and XI. Passus XII, derived from a separate exemplar and preserved in **r** copies only (see *Intro*. III, *A Version* §§ 1, 67–8) may not have existed in **m**. But its rubrics must go back to the unique common source of <{RU} J>, which could have been annexed to **r** after the ancestor of Pr–XI (Ax) was generated.

B-Text

The archetypal B-Text (Bx) resembles Ax in having a zero Prologue-rubric. This was erroneously supplied as 'liber primus' in the late copy G (CUL Gg. 4.31) following a heading 'Hic incipit petrus plowman' that it shares with the unrelated F (CCCO 201). Both are evidently scribal insertions by the copyists of those manuscripts or their exemplars. Where Bx differs from Ax is that instead of introducing a new sequence-numbering after the end of B VII = A VIII (where G and F have wrong numeration and there was evidently no archetypal explicit), it through-numbers the entire sequence and intermittently employs a second, parallel 'thematic' numbering of the passūs from VIII on as 'primus de dowel' >> 'primus de dobest' at XX. That at least the initial part of these 'thematic' rubrics was in Bx seems confirmed by the substantial agreement of β and R (representing α; F must be set aside as evidence for Bx, since its numbering is totally idiosyncratic). R's longer form 'de visione petri plowhman incipit dowel dobet et dobest' after the shared 'Passus viij^us' may indeed preserve the archeypal text; but as it is very close to the Ax colophon, it may have been taken from an A-copy (there is clear evidence of such consultation in α at III 51–62, on which see *TN*).[2] The sporadic persistence of the 'dual system' of numbering right to the end allows the partial emergence of a structural pattern of interest for interpretation when the (possibly) original rubrical divisions are correlated with the incontestably authorial division into dreams (in what follows, the inner dreams in Visions 3 and 5 [Passus XI and XVI] are ignored, and the total reckoned as eight). The following vision / passus correlation appears:

VISION 1 (Prologue–IV) **VISION 2** (Passūs V–VII) **VISION 3** (Passūs VIII–XII) VIII 'Passus Eight of the Vision and the First of Dowel' β; 'Passus VIII of the Vision of Piers Ploughman. [Here] begins Dowel, Dobet and Dobest' α. IX Dobet One: supported only by w and, since LMRF omit, the likely reading of neither β nor α (HmB's 'Dowel Two' must be a scribal guess). X Dowel Two: supported by LM, this may = β, but while R (? = α) and C have only 'as above', this may imply what wLM spell out (HmB have it as 'Three'). XI: here β read 'of the vision' (R adds 'as above') but Bx clearly had no 'Dowel' heading (HmB insert it as 'Four' of Dowel). XII: again there is no mention of Dowel except in HmB (which have it as Dowel Five). R adds 'of the vision as above' in its usual style but, having mis-numbered XII as XI, from this point on numbers the remaining passūs incorrectly. If β and α each preserve part of their source, it may be that Bx read something like *Passus XIIus de visione ut supra* 'Passus XII of the Vision as above' ('vision' here signifying not the dream-unit of modern critical analysis but the general title for the poem as a whole). HmB's identification of XII as Dowel Five may be judged 'thematically' correct; but since this pair proceed to count the following passūs as 'six' >> of Dowel, their thematic numbering is less likely to be archetypal than a scribal inference from the fact that 'Dowel One' clearly began at Passus VIII. **VISION 4** (Passūs XIII–XIV) These are correctly numbered in β, which has no thematic rubrics. R (? = α) has them as XII and XIII and adds its usual 'of the vision as above'. HmB make them Six and Seven of Dowel. As with XII above, since β is correct and R's 'vt supra' a tacit pointer to the thematic rubric, it may be again that Bx read 'Passus XIII /XIV of the Vision as above'. **VISION 5** (Passūs XV–XVII) XV is misnumbered as XIV in R, but the β mss have the very full rubric 'Passus XV &c; Dowel ends and Dobet begins', B reading 'the first of Dobet begins', M omitting the thematic portion and G having only a thematic rubric 'the first Passus of Dobet'. It seems possible that wgL may here represent β accurately, since the expressions 'finit' and 'incipit' may denote that Passus XV (the Anima passus) is meant to be the 'prologue' or introduction to Dobet proper (which deals with the life and passion of Christ). Rubrical evidence for this is found at the beginning of XVI and later of XIX, where wL have both the number ('Passus XVI'; 'Passus XIX') and after it 'and the first of Dobet' / 'Dobest' (where 'primus' refers back to 'passus'). These thematic rubrics are omitted by both M and by YOC²C, but their inclusion in B (despite the latter's wrong main-sequence numbering, shared by Hm) and also in the wholly independent L support their claim to be the reading of the family original. In XVII exactly the same situation recurs, the Passus being numbered sequentially 'XVII' and thematically 'and the second of Dobet'. **VISION 6** At this point there occurs a disjunction between Vision-structure and thematic sectioning. For whereas Passus XVIII contains the sixth dream in its entirety, it also receives the thematic rubric 'and the third of Dobet'. Once again, it is mis-numbered by B and omitted by the same copies, now by Hm as well. But this fact should not be seen as damaging the claim of WCrLB to represent β (and so potentially Bx), since it more probably reflects loss from Hm than addition to W and Cr severally. **VISION 7** Passus XIX observes the pattern of XVI as noted above, following the number ('Passus XIX') by 'Dobet ends and Dobest begins'. Omissions and variants are as at XVI above, Hm however calling XIX 'the first Passus of Dobet'. But if WCrL here preserve their family original, it seems likely that β intended its rubric to signify that this passus (again incorporating a complete dream) is in effect the 'prologue' of Dobest, which deals with the spreading of Christianity after the Ascension. Rubrical support for this claim appears at the opening of the final passus. **VISION 8** Passus XX repeats the rubrical pattern of XIX, following 'Passus XX' with 'and the first [passus *understood*] of Dobest' (W's addition 'of the vision' after the number is not shared by any other witness and looks like an addition by the scribe of this copy, while Hm's thematic rubric 'the second and last passus of Dobest' is due to its having numbered incorrectly to this point. There is no reliable evidence for establishing what the α rubric might have read, for R is defective from the end of XVIII to after the beginning of XX; but it is present at the end to supply its own distinctive reading.[3] The final colophon has an interesting form in wLM with no other-version parallel: 'Here ends the Dialogue of Piers Plowman'. Hm's replacement of 'dialogue' by 'vision' recalls the colophon of **Z** (which has been argued above to be scribal) and is very unlikely to represent β. R's form 'Passus Two of Dobest' (with a preceding 'explicit' understood) may imply that α earlier read 'Passus One of Dobest' at the beginning of XIX; but failing recovery of R's lost leaves, it may not be affirmed that α's rubric did not share the 'implied prologue' form of β.

The **Bx** rubrics, then, cannot be reconstructed with certainty because of the defective and sometimes corrupt evidence for α which, however, does not seriously contradict what can be (more or less reliably) recovered for β. Accordingly, a tentative outline of them, drawing on both family traditions, may be offered:

[Prologue].
Passus I–VII of the Vision [of Piers Ploughman]
Passus VIII of the Vision [of Piers Ploughman]
and the first of Dowel / Here *begins* Dowel,
Dobet and Dobest
Passus IX of the Vision as above
Passus X of the Vision [and the second of Dowel as above]
Passus XI of the Vision [as above]
Passus XII [of the Vision as above]
Passus XIII of the Vision [as above]
Passus XIV [of the Vision as above]

Passus XV [of the Vision as above]. Dowel
ends and Dobet *begins*.
Passus XVI [of the Vision as above] and
the first of Dobet
Passus XVII [of the Vision as above] and
the second of Dobet
Passus XVIII [of the Vision as above] and
the third of Dobet
Passus XIX [of the Vision]. Dobet *ends*
and Dobest *begins*
Passus XX [of the Vision] and the first
[passus] of Dobest

It seems from this outline that Bx's text will have consisted of i: a 'Prologue to the Poem' + the 'Vision of Piers Plowman' (Passūs I–VII) = Visions 1 and 2. ii: a 'Prologue to Dowel, Dobet and Dobest' (Passus VIII) + six passūs of Dowel (IX–XIV) = Visions 3 and 4. iii: a 'Prologue to Dobet' (XV) + three passūs of Dobet (XVI–XVIII) = Visions 5 and 6. iv: a 'Prologue to Dobest' (XIX) + Dobest (XX) = Visions 7 and 8.

Thus Bx may be inferred to have contained *four* 'Prologues': the 'general prologue' of the Field of Folk introducing the whole poem; a prologue preparing the 'interior quest for Dowel' through the encounter with the Friars and Thought (VIII); one introducing the 'scriptural quest for Christ' through the long disquisition of Anima (XV); and one announcing the 'historical quest for Christ through the Church' (XIX). The effect of Bx's 'Prologues' (if that is what they were) is to divide the poem into four distinct sections, containing two Visions each but a varying number of passūs (eight; seven; four; two). However, the most visible division remains that between 'Prologue 1'–Passus VII (the 'Visio' of traditional critical discussion) and the rest of the poem (the so-called 'Vita'). Somewhat less prominent is another division, that between 'Pr 1'–VII (where the Dreamer is a spectator of the social world), 'Pr 2'–XIV, where he plays an important part in the action (largely as disputant); and 'Pr 3'–XX, where he is half-spectator and half-participant. This latter division involves aggregating the last two sections into one, to produce a vision-pattern of 2+2+4 and a passus-pattern of 8+7+6. Both these patterns possess some interest, but there is no proof that they are authorial in origin and were designed to play a structural rôle in communicating the poem's meaning. **L** in none of the four versions refers to any division of his work (whether by vision, passus, or theme) in the way that Chaucer, say, refers to his 'books' in both *Troilus* (II 10) and *The House of Fame* (III 1093).[4] On the other hand, it is clear that, even as tentatively reconstructed here, Bx's 'thematic rubrics' do not run counter to the sense of the poem or undermine its cohesion. So there seems insufficient reason to conclude that they cannot be of authorial origin (as the passus-divisions seem likely to be) and very little reason to dismiss them as too insignificant to warrant recording.

C-Text

The archetypal rubrics of the C-Text are easier to establish than those of the B-Text, since this version has nearly twice as many witnesses and its two main textual traditions are well attested throughout the work. The most striking feature of the 'sequential' rubrics, well-known since the appearance of Pearsall's edition, is that the **x** tradition appears to have a Prologue (untitled) and 22 Passūs, whereas the **p** tradition calls this Prologue Passus I and has accordingly 23 passūs. Like **Z**, Ax and Bx (discussed above), Cx would seem to have had a zero-rubric for its Prologue, whence the two sub-archetypes have numbered their sequence in two different ways, **x** treating the passus coming after the 'Prologue' as *primus* and **p** treating it as *secundus*. The **x** tradition is likely to be nearer to the authorial intention, since the other versions all zero-number their opening 'Prologues' and count as Passus I what is the equivalent passus in **x**. The sequential rubrics of **p** can therefore be mostly set aside as of no account and those of **x** taken to represent Cx. It is equally probable that the poem had no overall title in the archetypes, and that the title-rubric 'Here begins the Vision of William concerning Piers Ploughman' in ms P's immediate group must be a scribal addition. It is however quite unobjectionable and answers closely to the Passus I rubric in **x**, which effectively serves as a title: 'Passus I of the Vision [of] Piers Ploughman'.

The major structural divisions in Cx occur at closely similar points to those in Bx, and a similar outline may be reconstructed, with certain key differences consequent on the disposition of the material into a new pattern of visions.

VISION 1 Pr–IV **VISION 2** Passūs V–IX **VISION 3** Passūs X–XIV. The rubric serving to end IX and begin X reads '[Here] ends the Vision of William W concerning Piers the Ploughman and here begins the Vision of the same William concerning Dowel' (**p** omits the unexplained 'W' and the second William). This rubric, though mentioning only Dowel, basically resembles that in Ax (a corresponding rubric is lacking in Bx), and has the effect of treating Passus X as a Prologue, since Passus XI is described as 'the first passus of the Vision of Dowel' (**p** treats this 'Prologue' as Dowel One and numbers XI as Dowel Two). Most significantly Cx, like Ax but unlike Bx, ceases through-numbering at this point and continues with thematic numbering, so that the passus-headings in the printed text are all editorial hereafter. The thematic rubrics cut across the vision-structure: thus 'Dowel' (XI–XVII) runs across from Vision 3 to Vision 4 in a manner more confusing than at B XIII–XIV, which can be accommodated within an understood thematic rubric of 'Dowel': 'Passus one of the Vision of Dowel'. **VISION 4** Passūs XV–XVIII 178 **VISION 5** Passūs XVIII 179–XIX **VISION 6** Passus XX **VISION 7** Passus XXI **VISION 8** Passus XXII.

A tentative schema of **Cx**'s rubrics, drawing mainly on the **x** tradition, may be offered:

[Prologue]	Passus I of the Vision of Dowel [XI]
Passus I of the Vision [of Piers Ploughman]	Passus II of Dowel [XII]
Passus II of the Vision as before	Passus III of Dowel [XIII]
Passus III of the Vision as before	Passus IV of Dowel as before [XIV]
Passus IV of the Vision as before	Passus V of the Vision as above [XV]
Passus V of the Vision as before	Passus VI of Dowel [XVI]
Passus VI of the Vision	Passus VII of Dowel and *ends* [XVII]
Passus VII of the Vision	Passus I of Dobet [XVIII]
Passus VIII [of the Vision] as before	Passus II of Dobet [XIX]
Passus IX [of the Vision] as before	Passus III of Dobet [XX]
[Passus X] Here *ends* the Vision of William [W] concerning	Dobet *ends* and Dobest *begins* [XXI]
Piers the Ploughman and here *begins* the Vision of the same	Passus II of Dobest [XXII]
[William] concerning Dowel	

This outline suggests that Cx consisted of i: a Prologue + Passūs I–IX (the Vision). ii: a 'Prologue' to Dowel (X) + six passūs of Dowel (XI–XVI). iii: a 'Prologue' to Dobet, called in the **x** rubric Passus Seven of Dowel and in the **p** rubric Passus One of Dobet (XVII), + three passūs of Dobet, called by **x** 'Passus I, II and III of Dobet' (XVIII–XX). iv: a Prologue to Dobest (XXI), so understood by **x** (as by *B*-β) but called 'Passus One' by **p**, + one passus of Dobest (XXII), called 'Passus Two of Dobest' by both **x** and **p**. The near-agreement of both **C** families in XXI–XXII suggests that the nomenclature here is that of Cx; but though Cx and Bx in these passūs go back to the same ultimate ancestor (B-Ø), their immediate source was not the same copy (see *Intro.* III, *B Version* §§ 72–4). This may account for the small differences in the rubrics of these last passūs, which are otherwise not altered in the way that previous passūs have been up to and including C XX. It therefore seems reasonable to conclude that the main structural outline of the C-Text as reflected in its archetypal rubrics does not differ greatly from that of its predecessor, and that much of what was said about the latter may be thought to apply here too (see above under B-Text). This last consideration strengthens the antecedent probability that the rubrics reflect authorial directions; but as it is not possible to be certain about the details, and all use of the 'thematic' rubrics for literary interpretation must remain circumspect, they have been given no prominence in the edited text.

NOTES

1 This is not to deny that specific sequential and display features, even if of archetypal origin, may belong to 'the publication process' rather than 'the author himself' (Adams 1994:55). For arguments in support of the Langlandian origin of the rubrics, see Burrow 2008.

2 Adams (ibid. 58) shows that the rubric was added later over a partially deleted 'enumerative' rubric in a different hand.

3 Adams (ibid. 58) contends that this rubric ('in form an *incipit*') was imported from a **C** copy of **x**-type where an identical rubric occurs (see Text Vol I, p. 721 and below under **C** rubrics).

4 In the case of Chaucer's *Troilus*, the archetype may have been corrected by Chaucer himself. The first and fifth Books have no formal Prohemium like Books two, three and four; but in the standard text based on CCCC 61 each has an explicit (and all except the first an incipit) that occurs in the only appropriate place it can, while the fifth ends with an *Explicit liber Troili et Criseydis* that provides a definitive ending to the entire work.

Appendix III

LANGLAND'S 'REPERTORY' OF LINES AND HALF-LINES[1]

Some 65 lines and some 250 half-lines appear more than once at different (non-parallel) places in the four versions. In the lists below, the total numbers are given in brackets for each version, and they amount to about 0.1 and 1% respectively (multiple re-uses are treated as a single repetition). **Z** / **A** (half-)lines repeated in **C** but nowhere in **B** and likewise **Z** lines repeated in **B** but not in **A** are highlighted by underlining because of their bearing on the linear postulate of revision. Each entry is given at its earliest appearance in a version in the referencing sequence **ZABC** followed by later ones in passus-order. Items that recur only in a parallel line are excluded, but *further* appearances are recorded even if they are in a line with a parallel ('//' denotes that the item occurs in one or more later versions at the same point). Half-line repetitions are in the a-verse unless stated otherwise. The colon after a line-reference signifies that the (half-)line recurs at the place indicated after the colon, whether this is in the same version or another; the symbol '±' = 'small difference in wording'.

Z-Text

Lines

I 66b//:C 1.131b. 76:A 9.48//. **II** 40:119$^{\pm}$. 117:167$^{\pm}$. 157//:C 17.249. <u>188:B 2.207</u>$^{\pm}$. **VI** 1//:B 16.274//$^{\pm}$. **VII** 27//:C Pr 36, 5.57. <u>230:B 9.72, 15,89</u>. 272–3:8.48–9$^{\pm}$, A 8.47–8. (10)

Half-Lines

Pr 53:C 9.13. **I** 40:A 10.137, **B** 9.111, 20.101, 257. **II** 10:6.29, A 11.80. 54:4.12//, **B** 10.234b, 274b, 15.394, 410//, 19.114//, 22.102//, 247//, **C** Pr 88b, 3.169b, 9.230b, 14.55b, 15.14, 17.182b. 68//:3.141//. (86:169$^{\pm}$; summarising line). 116//:120//. 121//:127//. 121b//:B 20.197b//. 164b:168b. 175//:C 14.167. 178//:4.74//. 180//:C 3.113b. <u>189:C 3.78</u>$^{\pm}$. 208//:C 9.136. **III** 78b//:C 12.198b. 82//:C 9.138. 93b//:C13.90b. 118b//:B 15.120b, **C** 13.161b, 17.116b. <u>150:C 5.51,6.56. 153:C 8.185</u>$^{\pm}$. 167:A 7.208//, **B** 10.268, 278, 11.177, 17.349//, 20.112//, **C** 3.396, 13.70. **IV** 84//:7.299//. 98//:7.17//, B 10.146//. 138b//:7.80//, 153//, B 6.117. 155b//:A 10.188b//. **V** 6//:A 6.116//. 49b//:C 5.22. 136:**B** 11.136//, 12.111//, 13.386//, 16.242//. 152//:B 14.332$^{\pm}$, C 5.108. **VI** 9//:C 2.199. 67//:7.295//$^{\pm}$. **VII** 52//:A 6.4//. 69//:8.86$^{\pm}$, C 6.193. 113//:C 5.8, 9.103. 155//:C 8.158. 175//:8.88//. 200//:B 4.104b. **VIII** 4b//:A 12.39, B 18.184, C 3.249b. 25//:C 9.138$^{\pm}$. 68//:C 9.160. (40)

A-Text

Lines

Pr 62//:12.58$^{\pm}$. **I** 119:12.97$^{\pm}$. **X** <u>28:C 19.134</u>. **XI** <u>306:C 3.395</u>$^{\pm}$. (4)

Half-Lines

Pr 80//:C 16.250. **II** 1:12.47. 78b:(B)C 2.156b. **III** 55b//:10.13b. 75b//:C 13.28b. 82//:C 8.243. 180//:C 13.56. 236b//:B 18.215b//. **V** 5b:12.67b. 116b//:B 13.393b//. 233b:7.92b. **VI** 114b//:C 9.129$^{\pm}$, 322. **VII** 294//:B 15.431. **VIII** 183:10.130. 180:B 11.224. 183:10.130. **IX** 61//:C 19.55$^{\pm}$. 72b//:C 10.80b. **X** 105b:110b. 131:B 19.120//$^{\pm}$. <u>125:C 13.23, 16.242</u>. <u>143:C 12.208</u>$^{\pm}$. **XI** 204//:B 19.272//. 218:B 17.43. **XII** 10:B 5.268, 18.66//, **C** 3.296, 9.88. 24:B 5.402//$^{\pm}$. 58:C Pr 63. (27)

B-Text

Lines

Pr 18:2.56. **I** 135:207. 188:194. **V** 95:13.328. 460:6.100$^{\pm}$. 486:C 18.135. 525:16.174$^{\pm}$. **VI** 197//:C 8.197$^{\pm}$. **IX** 28:10.235. **X** 120:127. 247:12.215. **XI** 280:287$^{\pm}$. **XII** 45:55$^{\pm}$. **XIII** 141:14.14$^{\pm}$. **XV** 273:C 17.28. 335:339$^{\pm}$. 395:498. **XVI** 1:53. 125:19.126$^{\pm}$. 212:17.144$^{\pm}$. **XVII** 27:C 19.98. 215:249. 349//:19.185//. **XVIII** 280:332$^{\pm}$. (24)

Half-lines

Pr 19b:19.231b. 164:8.26. **I** 28b:14.78b. 39b:5.445b. 76b:15.447b. 166b:10.105b. **II** 42b:20.379b. 50b//:5.511b//. 83b//:7.184b//. 122b:6.130b, 9.99b. 129:3.180. 148b:20.197b. **III** 100:13.185. 117:20.280. 182:250$^{\pm}$. 183b:15.120b. 193:C 13.56. 251:18.404. 332b:11.143b. **IV** 32:13.27, C 15.37. 34:10.109$^{\pm}$. 64:75. **V** 36:12.11. 61b:14.324, 16.116. 88:15.238. 95:13.328. 150b:C 6.83b. 120//:16.136//. 200:225. 273b//:C 6.306b. 287:C 1.84. 346//:17.56//. 410//:9.232. 480//:C 16.261. 481//:C 6.61. 486//:C 11.145. **VI** 68b//:C 8.69b. 143:10.49. 191:7.100. 193//:C 8.178. 309:15.431. **VII** 12//:13.428, C 10.207, 11.150. 57b:C16.159b. 126:14.34. 165:167.$^{\pm}$ **VIII** 63:C 19.54. **IX** 74b:11.272b. 97b:11.31b//, 13.369,$^{\pm}$ 18.97, C I 32, 9.222, 17.29. 103:15.418. 114:117 .174//:C 10.260, 282, 12.243. **X** 23:C 13.14. 63:C 11.65, 15.117$^{\pm}$. 121b:C 9.104b. 237b:16.266b. 338:16.251. **XI** 31//:C 11.192$^{\pm}$. 35//:C 11.311. 97:C 9.146, 19.116. 143:154. 151b:161b. 204:12.73. 252b:C 12.135b. 255b//:C 13.2b. 330:370. 340b//:C 13.151b. 387//:C 14.159. 423:C 6.68$^{\pm}$. **XII** 77:14.147. 116b//:C 14.62b. 203//:C 18.97. 218:14.111. 244:260. 278b//:C 15.22b, 120b (*Latin*). 286b:17.238b. 293:15.30, C 16.50$^{\pm}$. **XIII** 78:C 15.85$^{\pm}$. 109b//:C 16.294b, 17.112b. 142:15.142, C Pr 50b, 1.75, 2.32, 6.436, 10.169, 11.256, 15.198, 17.36, 18.200, 19.110. 144b:17.135b. 209b:C 3.234b. 302:15.204. 349//:C 9.94$^{\pm}$. 354:C 7.75. 422//:15.321, C 12.221. 426b//:C 7.9b. **XIV** 32:18.30. 46:16.200$^{\pm}$. 82b:282b. 104b:C 18.175b. 147:C 19.208. 182:C 13.57. 197b//:C 4.123b, 9.323b. 220//:C 13.2b. **XV** 15.129//:C 19.248. 129b:C 2.91b. 259:271b, C 6.114. 420b:C 4.117b. 429:486, C 17.230. 532//:C 9.82. **XVI** 1:53. 91b:18.115b. 177//:18.16//. 185b:188b. 199//:C 19.8. 251:256//. **XVII** 19:C 2.7b. 27b//:C 18.188b,19.98b. 39:155. 39b:155b, 186b. 144//:C 18.26. 185b//:C 18.6. 188b//:C 6.256b. **XVIII** 157b//:C 4.191. 203//:C 12.211. 210:224. 229//:C 13.219. 240b//:C 14.85b. 278b//:C 20.318b. 414:C 3.205. 421b:C 5.99b. **XIX** 36//:336//. 45b//:89b//, 176b//. 46//:20.81b//. 158b//:C 18.239b. 380//:C 13.81. 419//:C 4.115. **XX** 52:C Pr 9, 10.67. (131)

C-Text

Lines

Pr 36:5.57$^{\pm}$. 108:112$^{\pm}$. 138:8.53$^{\pm}$. 195:19.213$^{\pm}$. 222:3.80. **II** 161:167$^{\pm}$. **III** 339:9.50$^{\pm}$. **V** 29:16.336$^{\pm}$. **VII** 190:8.200$^{\pm}$. **VIII** 178:192$^{\pm}$. **IX** 21:21.197$^{\pm}$. 51:20.354$^{\pm}$. 107:137. **XI** 12:16.102$^{\pm}$. 156:14.155. 162:13.130$^{\pm}$. **XII** 150:16.326$^{\pm}$. 175:14.189$^{\pm}$. **XV** 31:37$^{\pm}$. 32:38$^{\pm}$. **XVI** 372:17.8$^{\pm}$. **XVII** 135:19.42$^{\pm}$. 303:18.145$^{\pm}$ (*cf.* B 16.114). **XVIII** 135:20.221. 188:19.98$^{\pm}$. **XX** 196:303. (= 26).

Half-Lines

Pr 15b:1.12b. 20:8.17. 20b:219b. 49:15.186, 191$^{\pm}$. 83:6.121. **I** 25b:10.178b. 110b:5.99b$^{\pm}$. 121b:3.285b,12.162b. **II** 81:11.13,18.13. 148b:9.49b. **III** 103:11.62. 245b:17.70b$^{\pm}$. 288:11.256. 329:12.195. 356b:397b. 421:10.188. 432:11.249$^{\pm}$. 432b:13.233b. 448b:9.45b. 463b:5.46b. 487b:9.212b. **IV** 139b:173b, 11.189b. 175:14.188. **V** 22:18.58. 26b:13.110a^{2}. 31:9.140. 40:11.277, 16.287. 42b:45b. 44:16.286$^{\pm}$. **VI** 76:16.238. 119b:16.243b. **VIII** 58b:11.124, 15.133b. **IX** 19b:59b. 192b:240b. **X** 53:12.71. 191b:193b. 198:17.244, 317. **XI** 145:18.135. 279:12.206. 286b:19.161b. **XII** 26b:15.10b$^{\pm}$. 175b:14.189. 195:227, 235. 210:13.18$^{\pm}$. 238b:243b. **XIII** 28:18.87b. 220:15.112$^{\pm}$. **XVII** 8:27. 51:20.151. 134:19.113. 169b:19.236b. **XIX** 113b:20.195. 236b:20.333b. 237:243. **XXI** (54)

1 For discussion see *Intro*. V §30.

Typeset in 10.5/12.5 New Times Roman
Cover designed by Linda K. Judy
Composed by Tom Krol
Manufactured by Cushing-Malloy, Inc.

Medieval Institute Publications
College of Arts and Sciences
Western Michigan University
1903 W. Michigan Avenue
Kalamazoo, MI 49008-5432
http:/ /www.wmich.edu/medieval/mip

 WESTERN MICHIGAN UNIVERSITY